8

Development Office in Sachs Hall ask Entickets

MAC 2265

2985

8 pm
2pm

714
207
326

MARKETING RESEARCH

AN APPLIED APPROACH

McGraw-Hill Series in Marketing

MARKETING RESEARCH

AN APPLIED APPROACH

FIFTH EDITION

Thomas C. Kinnear
Professor of Marketing
School of Business Administration
The University of Michigan

James R. Taylor
Professor of Marketing
School of Business Administration
The University of Michigan

McGRAW-HILL, INC.

New York   St. Louis   San Francisco   Auckland   Bogotá   Caracas
Lisbon   London   Madrid   Mexico City   Milan   Montreal
New Delhi   San Juan   Singapore   Sydney   Tokyo   Toronto

This book was set in Optima by Ruttle, Shaw & Wetherill, Inc.
The editors were Karen Westover and Larry Goldberg;
the production supervisor was Louise Karam.
The cover was designed by Amy Becker.
The photo editor was Anne Manning.
R. R. Donnelley & Sons Company was printer and binder.

MARKETING RESEARCH
An Applied Approach

This book is printed on acid free paper.

2 3 4 5 6 7 8 9 0   DOC   DOC   9 0 9 8 7 6

P/N 034799-9
PART OF
ISBN 0-07-912252-3

PHOTO CREDITS *CHAPTER 1:* p. 7, Courtesy Black & Decker. p. 9, Courtesy Biosite Diagnostics. p. 20, Courtesy General Motors. *CHAPTER 2:* p. 29, Courtesy Marriott Hotels. p. 46, Courtesy Amoco. p. 52, Courtesy Simmons. *CHAPTER 3:* p. 65, Courtesy Microsoft. *CHAPTER 4:* p. 87, Pickerell/The Image Works. *CHAPTER 5:* p. 125, John Abbott. p. 128, Beryl Goldberg. *CHAPTER 6:* p. 173, John Abbott. p. 215, Courtesy Nestle. *CHAPTER 7:* p. 219, Courtesy General Motors. *CHAPTER 8:* pp. 241, 257, James R. Holland/Stock, Boston. *CHAPTER 9:* p. 263, Beryl Goldberg. p. 295, U.S. Navy. p. 298, Courtesy Swatch. *CHAPTER 10:* p. 303, Tim Davis/Photo Researchers. p. 311, Courtesy Macro•AHF. *CHAPTER 11:* p. 325, AP/Wide World. *CHAPTER 12:* p. 351, Courtesy Macro•AHF. p. 383, Courtesy General Motors. *CHAPTER 13:* p. 405, B. Daemmrich/The Image Works. p. 418, AP/Wide World Photos. *CHAPTER 14:* p. 423, Courtesy Exxon, photo by Gary Lok. *CHAPTER 15:* p. 459, Courtesy AT&T. p. 475, Courtesy Macro•AHF. *CHAPTER 16:* p. 499, R. Sidney/The Image Works. p. 506, Courtesy Macro•AHF. p. 507, Barbara Rios/Photo Researchers. *CHAPTER 17:* p. 543, Courtesy Macro•AHF. *CHAPTER 18:* p. 565, Ogust/The Image Works. *CHAPTER 19:* p. 587, Reprinted with the permission of The Ritz-Carlton Hotel Company, L.L.C. Ritz-Carlton is a federally registered trademark. *CHAPTER 20:* p. 623, Courtesy Bank of America, Marine Midland Bank, and Western Federal Savings Bank. *CHAPTER 21:* p. 643, Jim Pickerell/The Image Works. *CHAPTER 22:* p. 683, Pickerell/The Image Works. *CHAPTER 23:* p. 725, Courtesy Compuserve. p. 743, Owen Franken/Stock, Boston. *CHAPTER 24:* p. 747, Albert Normandin/The Image Bank. p. 758, Courtesy Marketsource. p. 775, M. Siluk/The Image Works. *CHAPTER 25:* p. 781, Suzanne Arms/The Image Works. p. 800, Courtesy Nielsen Media Research. *CHAPTER 26:* p. 805, Art Stein/Photo Researchers. p. 810, David Wells/The Image Works.

Library of Congress Cataloging-in-Publication Data

Kinnear, Thomas C., (date).
   Marketing research: an applied approach / Thomas C. Kinnear,
James R. Taylor. — 5th ed.
     p.   cm. — (McGraw-Hill series in marketing)
   Includes bibliographical references and index.
   ISBN 0-07-912252-3 (set)
   1. Marketing research.   2. Marketing—Management.   I. Taylor,
James R. (James Ronald), (date).   II. Title.   III. Series.
HF5415.2.K53   1996   95-22571
658.8'3—dc20

INTERNATIONAL EDITION

ABOUT THE AUTHORS

THOMAS C. KINNEAR is Professor of Marketing at the School of Business Administration, The University of Michigan. He is also Interim Vice President for Development at Michigan. He holds an undergraduate honors degree from Queen's University, Kingston, Ontario; an M.B.A. from Harvard University; and a Ph.D. in Business Administration from The University of Michigan.

He previously held a faculty appointment at the University of Western Ontario and visiting appointments at Harvard University, Stanford University, and the European Management Institute (INSEAD) at Fontainebleau, France. His teaching and research interests are in the areas of marketing planning and marketing research. His research activity has resulted in publications in numerous scholarly journals, including the *Journal of Marketing, Journal of Marketing Research, the Journal of Consumer Research, the Journal of Public Policy and Marketing,* and *the Journal of Business Research.* He is former editor of the *Journal of Marketing.*

He is coauthor of *Principles of Marketing* (4th edition, Scott Foresman, 1995), *Marketing Research: An Applied Approach* (5th edition, McGraw-Hill, 1996), *Promotional Strategy* (8th edition, Irwin, 1994), and *Cases in Marketing Management* (6th edition, Irwin, 1994).

Professor Kinnear has worked in the field of marketing management and marketing research consulting. His major consulting relationships are in the telecommunications, automotive, petroleum, heating and air conditioning, and beverage industries. His clients have included Aetna, AT&T, Chrysler, General Motors, General Electric, Kodak, Machine Vision International, and Steelcase. He is an associate of Gemini Consultants. He has served as a director of the American Marketing Association and the Association for Consumer Research, and he currently serves as a member of the board of directors in several companies.

JAMES R. TAYLOR is Professor of Marketing at the School of Business Administration, The University of Michigan. He received his M.B.A. and Ph.D. in Business Administration from the University of Minnesota, with a specialization in marketing, psychology, and statistics. His dissertation, "An Empirical Evaluation of Coombs' Unfolding Theory," won the American Marketing Association Dissertation Award. During his academic career, he has been area chair for marketing, the chair of 15 Ph.D. dissertation committees, and a member of 16 additional dissertation committees.

Dr. Taylor has published over 40 articles in academic journals, including the *Journal of Marketing, Journal of Marketing Research,* and the *Journal of Consumer Research.* He has authored 10 books and monographs

Dr. Taylor's current teaching interests are in the areas of strategic marketing planning, market segmentation, marketing research, and marketing management. His research interests is in the area of studying the marketing management decision-making process and the role of market segmentation and positioning in the strategic planning process.

His professional activities include membership in the American Marketing Association and the Association for Consumer Research. He has been Vice President of the Detroit Chapter of the American Marketing Association and Executive Secretary of the Association for Consumer Research, and he has served on the editorial boards of the *Journal of Marketing, the Journal of Marketing Research,* and the *Journal of Consumer Research.*

Dr. Taylor's business experience includes 7 years with General Mills, Inc., in marketing and new product development. In addition, he has been project director on several projects for Booz Allen & Hamilton. His consulting focuses on the formulation and implementation of strategic marketing plans and market segmentation studies. During his career, Dr. Taylor has served as consultant in a number of organizations in business and government, including General Electric, Ford, DuPont, GTE, Thetford, SCM, General Foods, Proctor & Gamble, Lorillard, AT&T, Owens-Illinois, Whirlpool, Heublein, IBM, Hewlett Packard, Kaiser Aluminum, and the state of Michigan. He actively participates in company management education programs in addition to those sponsored by the Michigan School of Business Administration. Courses he is currently teaching include Strategic Marketing Management, Marketing Research, Market Segmentation, and Business-to-Business Marketing Strategies.

CONTENTS

PREFACE

The quality of marketing decisions depends to a great extent on the information available to the marketing decision maker. It is the function of marketing research to provide information for this decision making. A marketing manager who does not know how to use or evaluate marketing research is much like a general manager who does not understand the income statement for the company. Both individuals are severely limited in their ability to perform their jobs effectively.

OBJECTIVES

The main purpose of this book is to provide the prospective marketing manager with an understanding of marketing research. The book may also serve as a first text for people with career objectives in the field of marketing research. The book is designed for use in either a junior or senior undergraduate course in marketing research or in a first graduate course in marketing research.

UNIQUE FEATURES

There are certain attributes of this book that define its competitive positioning. These are:

1 It is designed to be easily read and understood. Great care has been taken to explain the basic technical issues in a step-by-step fashion.

2 It presents marketing research as a managerially and decision-making-oriented subject.

3 It presents marketing research in a pragmatic, "here's how to do it" fashion.

4 Advanced quantitative procedures are not dealt with in detail. It is not a text on quantitative techniques in marketing research.

5 It contains 35 real cases that are designed to allow students to apply material presented in the chapters. Of these cases, 14 are new to this edition.

6 Three marketing research databases on a PC disk are provided to accompany the book; they contain real results from actual marketing research studies. Students' ability to analyze and interpret marketing research data is reinforced by doing these tasks. These databases are all keyed to the major PC-based analysis packages: SPSS-PC, SAS-PC, SYSTAT-PC, and MYSTAT-PC.

7 The book contains one whole chapter that presents an actual research project from beginning stages to completion. Managerial interactions are described, along with study objectives and some results.

8 It contains "application" chapters in the major areas of demand measurement and forecasting, product research and test marketing, advertising research, and distribution and pricing research.

9 It has been designed for flexibility of use; the more complex chapters and appendixes may be skipped without disrupting the flow of the book.

10 It contains a glossary of important marketing research terms.

11 Each chapter concludes with a point-by-point summary.

12 Each chapter has questions and/or problems for student discussion, plus a minicase.

13 The book contains many extended real-world illustrations labeled Marketing Research in Action. These illustrations add life to the chapter materials and present the real world of marketing research to the reader.

14 A major new thrust on this edition is the addition of substantial insights and examples on international marketing research. Major new illustrations entitled Global Marketing Research Dynamics appear throughout the text.

15 Throughout the book, exclusive results of a survey of marketing research practice are presented to indicate to the reader the extent to which various marketing research procedures are actually used by practitioners.

The use of the term "applied" in the subtitle of this text signals three important aspects of the book:

1 It is highly concerned with the managerial use of marketing research and with the role of managers and researchers in this process.

2 It deals with the technical aspects of marketing research in a manner that allows the reader to apply these procedures to real applications.

3 It presents materials on major application areas with marketing research such as demand measurement and forecasting, product research and test marketing, pricing research, distribution research, and advertising research, plus extensive applications in the Marketing Research in Action illustrations and the Global Marketing Research Dynamics illustrations.

ORGANIZATION OF THE BOOK

This book is organized around the steps one would actually take in conducting a marketing research project. Part 1 presents an introduction to marketing research as it relates to marketing decision making. Chapter 1 defines marketing research and positions it within marketing management. Chapter 2 describes many aspects of the business of marketing research, including types of institutions, jobs, use of outside suppliers, and ethics. Chapter 3 presents both an overview of the steps involved in doing marketing research—the marketing research process—and a detailed example of a real marketing research project that illustrates this process. It also presents a description of the errors that can occur in marketing research. Chapter 4 discusses when marketing research should be undertaken and includes a discussion of problem definition and a discussion of the cost and value of marketing research information.

Part 2 consists of two chapters on research design and data sources. Chapter 5 discusses issues related to the appropriateness of alternative research designs and the appropriateness of data sources as they relate to these designs. The appendix to the chapter provides an extensive listing of syndicated sources of marketing data. Chapter 6 presents a detailed review of available secondary data, including census and library data. The appendix to the chapter provides an extensive listing of library sources of marketing data.

Part 3 examines issues related to the development of data collection procedures in marketing research. Chapter 7 discusses how numbers can be assigned to the types of variables researchers attempt to measure in marketing data. This is a necessary step in the quantitative analysis of marketing data. Chapter 8 covers in detail an area of measurement that is extremely important in marketing research: attitude measurement. Different scaling techniques are examined. Chapter 9 discusses the use of experimental procedures in marketing research by outlining the preconditions that enable researchers to infer causality in marketing situations. Chapter 10 presents an in-depth discussion of data collection procedures designed to support exploratory research. These procedures include focus groups and depth interviews. Similarly, Chapter 11 discusses data collection procedures designed to support conclusive research. Procedures presented here include mail, phone, and in-person interviews, plus observation methods. Chapter 12 discusses ways to design effective data collection forms, including questionnaires.

Part 4 describes how to find appropriate respondents and how to collect data from them. It does this by examining sampling procedures in marketing research and by examining the field operations involved in the collection of data from respondents. Chapter 13 presents an overview of sampling issues in marketing research and a discussion of nonprobability sampling procedures. Chapter 14 discusses the most straightforward type of probability sampling: simple random sampling. This is done from an applied point of view in which it is assumed that the reader understands certain basics of statistical sampling theory. For the reader who does not know or remember the appropriate statistical theory, the appendix to the chapter provides this background. Also, various aspects of determining sample size are presented. In Chapter 15 more complex and more useful sampling procedures are discussed, including stratified sampling and cluster sampling. An appendix to the chapter describes the appropriate statistical concepts for those who need a review. The section concludes with a presentation of field operations procedures in Chapter 16. This involves the planning and controlling of the selection of respondents and the control of actual interviews in the field.

Part 5 presents a discussion of the issues related to the analysis of marketing research data once the data have been collected and discusses issues of the presentation of the information derived from these data to appropriate audiences within and outside the organization. Chapter 17 describes how data on data collection instruments can be converted into computer-readable form. Chapter 18 presents data analysis techniques of the simplest type—those used for analyzing only one variable at a time. Data analysis involving two variables at a time is discussed in Chapter 19. The emphasis is on the pragmatics of data analysis. More advanced topics in the analysis of data are presented in Chapters 20 and 21. These topics are not examined in the detail in which other material in the book is presented, however. Our objective is to acquaint readers with this material so that they will be familiar with the terms and concepts and will have some understanding of how these procedures might be used. Chapters 20 and 21 offer an overview of data analysis procedures that analyze more than two variables at a time. Specifically, Chapter 20 discusses factor analysis, cluster analysis, and multidimensional scaling, while Chapter 21 examines such procedures as multiple regression, discriminant analysis, analysis of variance, conjoint measurement, and AID. Chapter 22 covers the reporting of research findings both orally and in written form.

Part 6 presents selected important applications areas within marketing research. We have presented numerous real-world applications of concepts throughout the text. Part 6 adds depth to these illustrations. Chapter 23 discusses demand measurement and forecasting terminology and procedures. The emphasis is on the conceptual foundation of various procedures, not on their mathematical complexities. Chapter 24 examines various marketing research procedures used in product development and presents a detailed look at the field-testing tool of test marketing and its laboratory-based alternative, simulated test marketing. Chapter 25 discusses the marketing research procedures and issues that arise in the measurement of media audiences and the copy testing of advertising messages. Chapter 26 discusses marketing research applications and procedures in distribution and pricing research.

CASES

Throughout the book, the thrust is pragmatic in terms of showing what it is like to actually do a marketing research project in the context of providing the decision maker with relevant information. This approach is aided by 35 real cases. These cases allow the student to actually do the things presented in the chapters.

ALTERNATIVE USAGE PATTERNS

The book is designed for flexibility of use. We have opted for a large number of relatively short chapters and appendixes to accomplish this. More complex material can easily be skipped without disrupting the flow of the book. We have employed this approach in order to use this text at the undergraduate and graduate levels. Some possible usage patterns might be:

1 A course designed to provide a managerial overview with little quantitative material (Chapters 1–13, 17–19, 22–26).

2 A course designed to provide both a managerial overview and a good understanding of the basic quantitative concepts (Chapters 1–19, 22–25).

3 A course designed to provide a managerial overview and a more detailed understanding of quantitative material (Chapters 1–26).

ACKNOWLEDGMENTS

We owe special thanks to many people involved in preparing this manuscript. Our McGraw-Hill editors, Bonnie Binkert and Karen Westover, provided innovative ideas and support. Helpful review comments were provided by a number of colleagues (listed below).

Reviewers

David Andrus, *Kansas State University*
John Brooks, *Houston Baptist University*
Gerald Cavallo, *Fairfield University*
Andrew Forman, *Hofstra University*
Ray Hubbard, *Drake University*
Jerry Katrichis, *Temple University*
Jim Leigh, *Texas A&M University*
Kalyan Raman, *University of Michigan*
Edward Rigdon, *Georgia State University*
Daniel Seiden, *DePaul University*
David Urban, *Virginia Commonwealth University*
Charles Vitaska, *Metropolitan State College*

Survey Respondents

Bill Carner, *St. Edwards University*
Caroline Considine, *Simmons College*
Jim Gould, *Pace University*
Berhe Habte-Giorgis, *Glassboro College*
Jerry Katrichis, *Temple University*
Sreedhar Kavil, *St. John's University*
C.S. Kohli, *California State University, Fullerton*
William LaFief, *University of Evansville*
Kay Lawrimore, *Francis Marion University*
James Leigh, *Texas A&M University*
Christopher McCarthy, *University of Florida*
Deborah Marlino, *Simmons College*
Charles Patton, *University of Texas*
Mannie Plotkin, *DePaul University*
Kaylan Raman, *University of Florida*

Edward Rigdon, *Georgia State University*
David Urban, *Virginia Commonwealth University*
Don Wallace, *St. Martin's College*
Joe Welch, *University of North Texas*
Michael Zenor, *University of Texas, Austin*

In addition, we wish to thank Amy Cox, Sheryl Petras, Linda Powell, Elizabeth Thompson, and Paul Verner for their case and Marketing Research in Action research and writing, Laura Richardson and Kapil Raina for their excellent contributions to the instructor's manual, and Michael McCreight for his outstanding effort in preparing the databases for computer analysis and in proofreading the text.

We are grateful to the Literary Executor of the late Sir Ronald A. Fisher, F.R.S.; to Dr. Frank Yates, F.R.S.; and to Longman Group Ltd., London, for permission to reprint Table III from their book *Statistical Tables for Biological, Agricultural and Medical Research* (6th ed., 1974).

Finally, we wish to thank Larry Goldberg for his hard work and support throughout the editing, design, and production of this book.

Thomas C. Kinnear

James R. Taylor

MARKETING RESEARCH
AN APPLIED APPROACH

PART ONE

INTRODUCTION TO MARKETING RESEARCH IN MARKETING DECISION MAKING

CHAPTER 1

THE MARKETING RESEARCH ROLE IN MARKETING MANAGEMENT

MARKETING RESEARCH IN ACTION

MARKETING RESEARCH GUIDES KELLOGG'S/NBC

In one of the biggest promotional deals ever between a television network and an advertiser, NBC and Kellogg's used marketing research to match cereals with the stars and shows most likely to share a target market.

These two industry giants employed multiple marketing research techniques in formulating the joint strategy for their "Breakfast Around the World" megapromotion. They formulated audience profiles for various shows by using factors such as the show's ratings, audience, demographics, and Q scores (audience appeal scores) of its stars. Consumer profiles for various cereals were developed using purchasing and consumption patterns. The two sets of profiles were matched to determine the best pairings.

For example, NBC teamed its popular *Seinfeld* cast with Kellogg's Low Fat Granola. Low Fat Granola is a new Kellogg's product and its hottest seller. According to Alan Cohen, senior vice president—marketing at NBC-TV, "It just makes sense to put it with our hot show. The demographics work too. It's an adult show. Low Fat Granola is an adult cereal."

Five other NBC shows were featured on specially designed cereal boxes. Kellogg's two biggest brands, Corn Flakes and Raisin Bran, were paired with *Blossom* and *The Fresh Prince of Bel Air*. According to Cohen, these two shows are "All-American, family type shows which match the image of these two cereals. Marketing research also determined that the purchase of Corn Flakes and Raisin Bran is often stimulated by teens. This group is also the primary audience for these two shows. Teens are also the target market for both *Saved by the Bell: The New Class* and its partner Rice Krispies, a cereal which has traditionally high teen appeal.

Adults were the dual targets of the other two cereal/television pairings. *Wings,* an adult comedy, was paired with Bran Flakes. And when research showed that many adults consume Crispix as a late-night snack, the two companies decided to pair it with *The Tonight Show.*

The two companies also developed premium offers to appeal to the corresponding audience and consumer groups. The star of *Seinfeld* is characterized as a cereal lover, so Kellogg's offered a "Have Breakfast with Seinfeld" cereal bowl with proof of purchase and a minimal fee. Other premiums included a *Blossom* telephone, a *Fresh Prince* jersey, and a *Tonight Show* T-shirt designed by Jay Leno himself.

NBC's Cohen emphasized the importance of developing pairings that made sense to both the consumers and the advertisers. "What's important about this was that before there was strategy, there was research. We developed an understanding of their purchasers, and they developed an understanding of our shows from an audience and consumer perspective." The dual promotion also offered NBC an opportunity to break out of its traditional image as a media company that skews to youth. By working with Kellogg's the network was able to show other advertisers that it could be a promotional partner, while simultaneously pushing the family and adult entertainment bent of its new lineup. According to Cohen, "We want to show advertisers we're more than just a media company. We want to be a marketing company." And "If you want to be known as all-family, Kellogg is the right company." Marketing research allowed NBC to effectively accomplish all these goals.

Source: Cyndee Miller, "Research Guides NBC, Kellogg in Matching Granola with 'Seinfeld,'" *Advertising Age,* p. 18, September 13, 1993.

This NBC-Kellogg Marketing Research in Action illustrates the effective use of both marketing research and marketing management judgment in the successful planning and implementation of an important joint consumer promotion. It shows: (1) the use of television audience survey research and diary panels to determine a show's audience size and demographic composition; (2) the use of consumer data on the usage demographics and life-style of users of different brands of cereal; and (3) the ratings of celebrities by consumers in terms of their likability, believability, image, etc. These are but a few of the different methodologies that can be utilized in marketing research. In addition, other decision areas in marketing beyond consumer promotions can benefit from effective marketing research.

This book is designed to introduce the reader to the important topic of marketing research in terms of both how it should be practiced and how it is actually applied in the real world of business. All the marketing research terms in the NBC-Kellogg profile and their relevance will be explained in detail, along with many other terms and methods, throughout this book.

The usefulness of marketing research to NBC and Kellogg is clearly illustrated in the above example. The importance of marketing research has grown over the last three decades. The advent of a focus on the quality of products and services by organizations has increased the emphasis on marketing research in identifying consumer needs and in measuring consumer satisfaction. In addition, the increasingly global nature of markets and competition has expanded the need to do marketing research in nondomestic environments. However, organizations vary substantially in terms of the role and responsibility they assign to marketing research. Some, for example, view research as mainly an ad hoc data gathering and analysis function, while others broadly define the role and responsibility of research and view the marketing research department as an information center for decision making. The latter view of research is what we refer to as a *marketing research system.*

The concept of a marketing research system implies a deeply involved role for research in the marketing management process. This includes the active participation of research in the decision-making process, with particular emphasis on the provision of meaningful information for the planning and control functions. The purpose of this information input is to narrow decision-making error and broaden the decision-making perspective. Better decisions should result from better information inputs.

MARKETING RESEARCH DEFINED

What is marketing research? There are many excellent definitions. For example, the American Marketing Association (AMA) has defined marketing research as follows:

> Marketing research is the function which links the consumer, customer, and public to the marketer through information—information used to identify and define marketing opportunities and problems; generate, refine, and evaluate marketing actions; monitor marketing performance; and improve understanding of marketing as a process.
>
> Marketing research specifies the information required to address these issues; designs the method for collecting information; manages and implements the data collection process; analyzes the results; and communicates the findings and their implications.[1]

This is a rich and useful definition, as it outlines many of the uses of marketing research and summarizes the process of actually doing a marketing research project. However, for the purposes of this book we prefer a shorter definition. Our definition focuses on the essence of what proper marketing research is, and leaves

---

[1]Peter D. Bennett (ed.), *Dictionary of Marketing Terms* (Chicago: American Marketing Association, 1988), p. 117.

the detailed uses of marketing research and the actual process of doing it to be discussed later in the book. For our purposes, there are four terms that need to be included in such a definition. These are (1) systematic, (2) objective, (3) information, and (4) decision making. Thus,

Marketing research is the systematic and objective approach to the development and provision of information for the marketing management decision-making process.

A few comments are in order regarding this definition. *Systematic* refers to the requirement that the research project should be well organized and planned: the strategic and tactical aspects of the research design must be detailed in advance, and the nature of the data to be gathered and the mode of analysis to be employed must be anticipated. *Objective* implies that marketing research strives to be unbiased and unemotional in performing its responsibilities. One often hears that marketing research is "the application of the scientific method to marketing." The hallmark of the scientific method is the objective gathering, analysis, and interpretation of data. While one may learn of a scientist who violates the rule of objectivity, this is rare and often results in sanctions by the scientific community. Marketing research may operate in settings different from those of the physical, social, and medical sciences, but it shares their common standard of objectivity.

The remaining two elements of this definition are *information* and the *decision-making process*. It is important to recognize that these are the two elements that differentiate marketing research from research in other fields. The primary purpose of marketing research is to provide information, not data, for the management decision-making process.

Recently, there has been some debate among practitioners about whether we should be defining "market" research instead of "marketing" research.[2] In this book we do not limit our interest to information about the market or consumers only. We discuss issues related to providing information for marketing decision making from all sources: the market, competitors, distribution structure, social and technological environment, and so forth. Thus, we are clear that our interest is in marketing research, not just market research.

EXAMPLES OF MARKETING RESEARCH

The importance of marketing research to the success of marketing actions can be seen in the following examples.

Black & Decker[3]

In the 1990s, Black & Decker (B&D) has had great success bringing new products to market by extensively studying consumers known as the do-it-yourselfers

---

[2]For example, see William D. Neal, " 'Marketing' or 'Market' Research?" *The Research Report*, p. 1, Summer 1989; and Paul Gerhold, "Defining Marketing (or Is It Market?) Research," *Marketing Research*, vol. 5, no. 4, pp. 6–7, Fall 1993.

[3]Adapted and edited from Susan Caminiti, "A Star Is Born," *Fortune*, pp. 44–47, November 29, 1993.

The Quantum tools team from Black & Decker.

(DIYers). These consumers, as the descriptive name implies, are directly involved in their own construction, remodeling, and other work. This example describes some of the marketing research and management activity that Black & Decker utilized to bring its Quantum line of tools to the market.

While Black & Decker was developing its high-end DeWalt line, a pricey line of tools aimed at professional craftsmen and contractors, they discovered a gap in the midpriced tool market. According to Joseph Galli, chief of the U.S. power tool division, "We were finding in our research that a lot of nonprofessional consumers were really price-sensitive when it came to power tools. Sure, we knew some serious DIYers were going to pay up and buy DeWalt. But others would just go elsewhere, and we're not a company that likes to leave business on the table for our competitors." Black & Decker confirmed its research findings by talking to retailers like Home Depot, Lowe's, Hechinger, and Wal-Mart. The feedback was consistent with the response of a buyer from one of the large chains: "We told them, 'Look, we're giving business away to your rivals 'cause you don't have what these customers want.' "

To gather consumer intelligence on the DIYers, Black & Decker hired Fieldwork Atlanta, an independent research firm, for a tightly specified assignment: Find 50 homeowners, ages 25 to 54, who own more than six power tools. The list was compiled in less than 2 weeks and included an airline pilot, a bank manager, a vet (one of only two bachelors on the list), and a teacher. B&D followed these people from June to September 1991, questioning them about the tools they used and why they chose particular brands. The company's researchers watched how these homeowners used their tools, and asked why they liked or disliked certain ones, how the tools felt in their hands, and how they cleaned up their work spaces. They followed the DIYers on shopping trips, recording what they bought and how much they spent. Black & Decker supplemented this research by interviewing hundreds of B&D customers who had mailed in warranty cards.

The Quantum team reviewed feedback from the DIYers and set out to produce what they wanted. For example, DIYers wanted a cordless drill that did not run out of power before they finished the job. Team Quantum created a more powerful drill with a detachable battery pack that recharges in an hour rather than overnight. DIYers hated cleaning up sawdust after cutting or sanding wood. B&D engineers developed a sander and a circular saw equipped with a bag that acts like a minivacuum, sucking up sawdust before it disperses. DIYers also expressed safety concerns over saw blades that keep spinning for 10 or 12 seconds after they switch the saw off. Engineers built an auto braking system (ABS) into the saws which stops the blades within 2 seconds of turning off the saw. In response to a need for occasional expert advice, Black & Decker established Power-Source, a service that provides free maintenance checks on all tools and a toll-free hotline to answer home repair questions from 7 A.M. to 10 P.M. 7 days a week. Archibald reiterates, "The whole point behind this product line was to have it driven by what consumers really want."

"Quantum" was retained as the name of the line because customers liked it best, saying that it was a name they could pronounce and it sounded a step above other things. B&D wasn't sure whether to identify "Black & Decker" on the tools or the packaging. Research showed that DIYers had a lot of respect for the Black & Decker name, and surveys by Landor Associates, a consulting firm, showed that Black & Decker was the seventh most powerful brand in the United States. Power tool division chief Galli explained, "Since we were positioning Quantum as a step-up product for consumers, it made a lot of sense to have it carry the Black & Decker name too."

Black & Decker got the Quantum line on the market and into people's hands, and their hard work paid off. Quantum produced about $40 million in sales by the end of 1994. "Black & Decker has become very good at taking market share away from rival companies. They just know their customer."

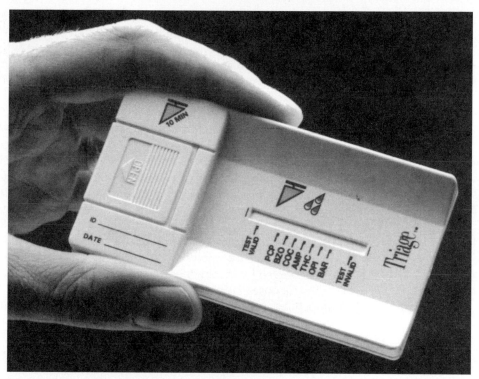

Triage—a device from Biosite Diagnostics that tests for drugs.

Biosite Diagnostics, Inc.[4]

Despite the seemingly large up-front cost, start-up companies struggling to get off their feet can gain long-term benefits from an investment in marketing research. Biosite Diagnostics is a prime example.

Biosite Diagnostics, Inc., is a biotechnology start-up company based in San Diego, California. The company was founded by entrepreneurs who developed a diagnostic technology they thought could speed up diagnostic testing and lower costs. This technology combined multiple antibodies to test for a variety of diseases and substances from the same sample. Biosite's first product, Triage, is a small disposable system that can test a single urine sample for the presence of up to seven drugs, including cocaine, heroin, and amphetamines. Besides the advantage of being able to conduct multiple tests from a single sample, Triage also produces results in an exceptionally fast period of 10 minutes.

Biosite decided to focus on emergency room drug testing. This $300 million

[4]Adapted and edited from Udayan Gupta, "Costly Market Research Pays Off for Biotech Start-Up," *Wall Street Journal*, p. B1, August 2, 1993.

market was considered relatively small, and two major competitors were already established in the field. Potential investors were afraid to commit funds without proof that the technology would work in this market and would offer a competitive advantage. According to venture capitalist Fred Dotzler of Medicus Venture Partners, a Menlo Park, California, venture capitalist firm, "We liked the management and we liked the technology. We needed confirmation that the market was large enough."

In order to confirm the existence of a market, both for their investors and for the company itself, Biosite invested $150,000 to hire Migliara/Kaplan Associates, a marketing research firm based in Towson, Maryland. Migliara/Kaplan surveyed about 400 physicians, laboratory technicians, and other potential users of diagnostic tests, then conducted interviews with about 100 potential users of Triage. The survey results affected both short- and long-term planning for the company. Physicians emphasized that quick drug analysis is vital, since the presence of drugs or alcohol can affect which treatment is suitable for many emergency room patients. Drug analysis tests currently on the market are reliable, but they are conducted by laboratories and usually take several hours to produce results. These responses confirmed the existence of a market for Triage, as well as its competitive advantage over the tests currently on the market. The results, summarized in a 20-minute film, were a key factor in attracting over $13 million in venture capital.

But the advantages of Biosite's marketing research investment did not stop there. The results also showed that while emergency room doctors were the users of the drug test information, it was usually the lab technicians who made the decision on which drug test to use. Charles Patrick, Biosite's vice president of sales and marketing, asserted that this finding "made us recognize that we need a two-pronged approach" involving marketing to both doctors and lab technicians. The studies also showed that the target market consisted of about 6000 emergency rooms, and that it would be more cost-effective for Biosite to find partners and distributors to sell its product than to establish a full-time sales force. This would also allow the company to concentrate on its competitive strengths, development and manufacturing. In early 1992, Biosite signed a contract with Curtin Matheson Scientific, Inc., to sell the product in the United States through Curtin Matheson's 250 salespeople. The company entered into a similar agreement with Germany's E. Merck & Co. to sell the product in Europe. According to Biosite executives, the extensive marketing research also helped move Triage through the FDA approval process. While the average FDA approval of diagnostic products takes about 6 months, Triage was approved in less than 30 days.

Triage was successfully launched in 1992. It obtained revenues of just over $3 million in its first year, and about $8 million in 1993. Marketing research helped Biosite prove the existence of a market for its product and to focus on a manageable market niche. It also helped Biosite attract investors, avoid unnecessary cost and product delays, redefine its potential market, and reshape its business strategy.

The Jacksonville Symphony Orchestra[5]

In an attempt to expand its traditionally narrow market segment, the Jacksonville Symphony Orchestra adopted a "packaged goods mentality" and dedicated itself to a sophisticated marketing research program. The symphony enlisted the aid of West & Co. Marketing & Advertising of Jacksonville, Florida; Sun Research of Norwalk, Connecticut; and Message Factors, Inc., an Atlanta-based marketing research company. These companies employed both qualitative and quantitative methods. The qualitative phase used focus groups consisting of current subscribers, former subscribers, and qualified prospects to learn about attitudes and life-style activities. According to Ben West of West & Co.: "Our research measures life-style marketing issues, explores entertainment alternatives, and gives us some clues to what future audiences will want and expect of the Jacksonville Symphony Orchestra." The quantitative phase, which was designed to numerically measure the key issues identified in the qualitative stage, involved telephone interviews with over 500 people. Interviewers' questions concerned programming and location of events, and the appearances of guest artists. Russell Boyd, managing director for Message Factors, Inc., felt the telephone survey indicated why people subscribe to the symphony, why they fail to renew their subscriptions, and what methods would help the symphony boost ticket sales.

West & Co. then used this information to reposition the symphony. The company employed additional marketing techniques, such as direct mail, telemarketing, billboards, and public service announcements, to further change the symphony's image. West asserted, "We want to portray some of the romance and sensuality of the symphony as well as the emotional quality of classical music." The symphony scheduled five different series for the coming season. One of three concert halls will be used for each series, allowing the company to coordinate the different types of music with the size and intimacy of each hall. Several celebrity guests, including Luciano Pavarotti, were scheduled to appear.

These marketing research-directed changes led to subscription sales of 72,000 in the next year, a total nearly doubling the previous year's total.

We see in these examples and in the NBC-Kellogg profile the power of marketing research to aid marketing decision makers in consumer package goods businesses (Kellogg), consumers durables businesses (Black & Decker), media businesses (NBC), industrial goods and high-technology businesses (Biosite Diagnostics), and nonprofit organizations (Jacksonville Symphony). Every business, social cause, nonprofit organization, and government agency can benefit from the effective use of marketing research. The details of the specific techniques mentioned will become clear as we progress through the book. We now turn our attention to how marketing research fits into the practice of marketing management.

[5]"Symphony Strikes Note for Research to Launch a New Season," *Marketing News,* p. 12, August 29, 1988.

THE MARKETING SYSTEM

It is tempting to turn immediately to a discussion of contemporary research techniques and methodology. But this would be hasty; several introductory concepts and issues must be discussed first. In particular, we must address the following questions:

1 What is the character of marketing activity?
2 What is the task of marketing management?
3 What type of information is needed by marketing management?
4 What are the sources of information for marketing decision making?
5 What is the role of marketing research in the marketing system?

To facilitate our understanding of the nature and role of marketing research, we must first characterize the marketing system of which it is a part. Figure 1-1 presents a diagrammatic model of this system. This conceptual scheme depicts the marketing system from the perspective of the selling organization. The model specifies one or more performance measures for the organization, identifies relevant variables in the process, and classifies the variables as independent or dependent.

Marketing Mix

By *variable* we mean a property that takes on different values at different times. For example, an organization may vary its advertising budget or change its selling price. An *independent variable* is the presumed cause of the dependent variable, which is the presumed effect. The independent variables are classified as to whether they can be manipulated or controlled by the selling organization. Those variables that can be controlled are identified as the marketing mix components of *product, price, place,* and *promotion.* Different levels of these variables can be combined to form alternative marketing programs or courses of action.

Situational Factors

The situational variables represent independent variables that are not under the control of the marketing organization. These variables make up the state of nature which the selling organization must adapt to in formulating and implementing a marketing program. The state of nature consists of factors such as the availability of energy, competitive actions, economic climate, market trends, and government regulation.

Behavioral Response

Both sets of independent variables—marketing mix and situational factors—combine to influence a behavioral response such as purchase, buying intentions, preference, and attitudes. This behavioral response is the dependent variable, or the presumed effect. A complicating factor is that the behavioral response is

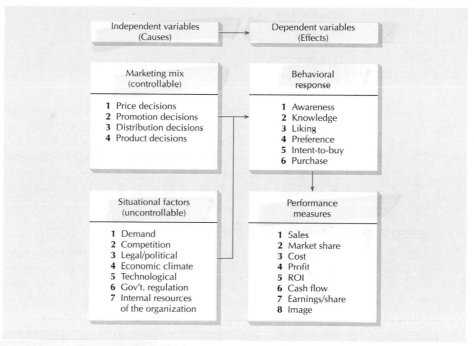

FIGURE 1-1   Model of the marketing system.

influenced by the consequences of past behavior in addition to the immediate influence of the independent variables. Consequently, developing an effective marketing program is a challenging and complicated process involving a dynamic set of variables and a behavioral response which changes as a result of learning. This situation requires skilled managers who can give proper perspective to past experience and effectively use marketing research information in their decision making.

Formally identifying the functional relationships among the independent and dependent variables is obviously a difficult assignment. Regardless of how difficult, it is important to recognize that the nature of these relationships is *implicit* to the manager's choice of alternative courses of action. In attempting to use marketing research to formalize these relationships, the manager must consider the cost of gathering the information relative to the level of confidence gained in selecting the optimum course of action. In practice, management experience and judgment, combined with information from the marketing research system, form the basis for management decision making.

It should be clearly understood that managers can and do make decisions without using marketing research. These decisions may be very sound if the manager's experience is relevant and his or her judgment is good. The idea is to make an effective decision, not to spend money on marketing research that will not be used to aid a decision. It is when the decision maker needs additional information to decrease the uncertainty associated with a decision that marketing research is used.

Performance Measures

The behavior responses form the basis for the organization's monetary and non-monetary performance measures. Monetary measures are sales, market share, profit, internal rate of return, return on investment (ROI), and so on. Nonmonetary measures are the organization's image, consumer attitudes toward the organization, and so on. Developing valid performance measures is central to the effective management of the marketing system. Marketing research plays an important role in supplying the tools and data sources for performance measurement.

THE MARKETING MANAGEMENT PROCESS

What do marketing managers do? One of their key roles is to make decisions about marketing mix elements. This involves them in the decision-making process. Fundamental to the decision-making process is information. Marketing managers rely on two information inputs, namely their own experience and judgment and the more formalized information available from the marketing research system. Let's discuss the components of the marketing management process in more detail.

The Decision-Making Process

A characteristic of fundamental importance to the marketing management process is decision making. The decision-making process permeates the management process, and the two terms are often considered synonymous.

The organization's well-being is dependent on the wisdom of the decisions made by its managers. The vast majority of decisions made by managers are *programmed* and involve recurring situations which have been dealt with previously. We will refer to these as *routine decision situations,* since they contain practically no uncertainty and have a low potential for surprise. Managers rely heavily, if not exclusively, on their experience and judgment in making such decisions.

A second type of decision involves situations in which past experience and judgment are less relevant. These are called *nonroutine decision situations.* Here, the problem is new or the situation is unique in some way so that the manager's normal decision-making approach does not fit neatly into the new setting. Confronted with this nonroutine decision situation, the manager would follow a more formal approach which we will call the decision-making process.

The decision-making process may be thought of as involving a series of steps (see Figure 1-2). *The first step is the recognition that a unique marketing problem exists or that an opportunity is present.* Marketing problems and opportunities result from the dynamic nature of the situational factors and/or the implementation of the marketing program. Performance measures often signal the presence of

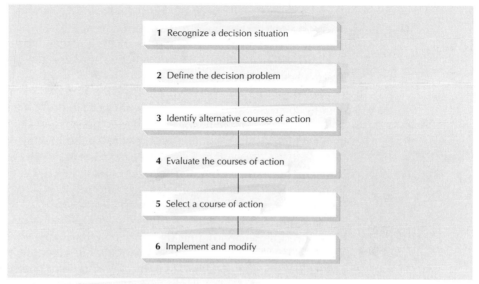

FIGURE 1-2   Steps in the decision-making process.

problems, while the monitoring of the situational factors can signal the presence of both problems and opportunities. For example, a manager may be informed that a product's market share has declined, that a competitor will be introducing a new product, that primary demand for a product has risen faster than anticipated, or that government action has negatively influenced the sale of a competitor's product. Consequently, managers will make decisions to solve problems or to capitalize on opportunities.

The second step in the decision-making process is the definition of the decision problem. The manager needs to define and clarify the main issues and causal factors operating in the decision situation. It is not always easy to identify what fundamental variables are causing trouble and what needs correcting. Marketing research personnel and techniques play an important role here. By involving the research function in this early phase of the decision-making process, the marketing manager can benefit from more effective formulation of problems and opportunities, while at the same time assuring more effective use of marketing research in later stages of the decision process.

The third step in the decision process is the identification of alternative courses of action. In marketing, a course of action involves the specification of some combination of the marketing mix variables. "Doing nothing new" or "maintaining the status quo" is just as much a course of action as is changing marketing activities.

The effectiveness of management decision making is constrained by the quality of the alternatives considered. Consequently, it is critical that the "best" alternative be identified. The process of identifying courses of action is a *creative process* similar to the first stage of the decision-making process. The manager and the marketing researcher have to search for new ideas, which come from creative thinking and imagination. Various marketing research approaches are available that can stimulate the manager's creative process and broaden the domain of alternatives identified.

The fourth and fifth steps in the decision process are the evaluation of alternatives and the selection of a course of action. In order for a decision to be made, at least two courses of action must be identified, and there must be uncertainty about which course of action will maximize the attainment of management objectives. If the decision maker is faced with a situation in which there is only one realistic course of action, and that is to "do nothing," then there is no decision involved, even though the problem or opportunity confronting management may have significant consequences for the organization.

Marketing research is a valuable tool in the evaluation of alternative courses of action. Often, nonroutine decision situations involve substantial uncertainty and risk. The manager is interested in marketing research information as a way to reduce the uncertainty inherent in the selection of a course of action.

The final step in the decision-making process is the implementation of the selected course of action. Again, marketing research supplies the means for monitoring the effectiveness of the action selected and the situational variables that influence the program's performance.

Decision making involving nonroutine decision situations can never be as well done as managers would like. This is partly because of the uncertainty regarding the future state of the situational factors, partly because of limitations on the ability to gather clear and precise information regarding the outcomes of the alternatives considered, and partly because decision making is a human process. The long time span between making decisions and receiving definite feedback plus the uncertainty regarding the nature of cause-and-effect relations in the marketing system contribute substantially to this situation.

Figure 1-3 links the informational inputs of management experience and marketing research, the decision-making process, and the marketing system. Managers make decisions about the marketing system based upon their information about this system. Basically, they plan their future actions and control the performance of these implemented plans by comparing actual performance against objectives.

It is useful to make a distinction between the terms "information" and "data." *Data* are observations and evidence regarding some aspect of the marketing system. *Information* refers to data which reduce uncertainty in a decision situation. This definition makes the uses of the term "information" dependent upon the manager and the decision-making situation. An example will clarify this distinction. A ship's captain is confronted with the problem of piloting the ship into a treacherous harbor at night. To aid the decision-making process, the captain is radioed the following data: (1) channel depth, (2) wind speed and direction, (3) the score of the local baseball game, (4) tide speed and direction. Given the captain's problem, which data could be labeled information? Most readers, it is

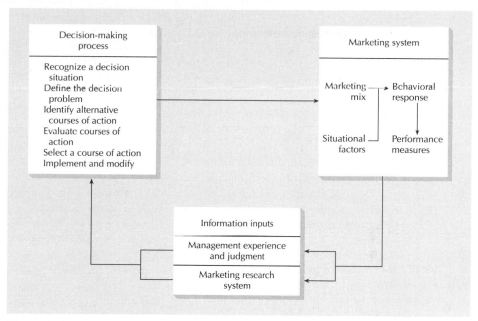

FIGURE 1-3   The marketing management process.

hoped, will find this distinction fairly easy, but given a typical marketing decision-making situation, distinguishing between data and information becomes substantially more challenging.

Information Needs

There are certain essential groups of information required by the marketing manager for planning and control purposes. Exhibit 1-1 illustrates this type of information. While this listing is not intended to be complete, it does indicate that information is needed regarding the controllable and uncontrollable variables in the marketing system plus the measurement of their influence on the behavioral response.

Marketing research plays a central role in supplying information for the planning and control functions. It is in response to the need for formal planning and control that research is able to develop a systematic approach to the information needs of management. The activities of research can be built to a large extent around the needs of the planning process. The responsibility of research is not only to have such information on hand but also to organize and present it in a manner that contributes to the organization's planning and control activities. With a continually updated library of information available to facilitate decision making, the manager should be able to do an effective job of (1) developing the objectives,

EXHIBIT 1-1

TYPES OF INFORMATION NEEDED FOR PLANNING AND CONTROL

I Situational analysis
  A Demand analysis
    1 Buyers' behavior and characteristics:
      a What do they buy?
      b Who buys?
      c Where do they buy?
      d Why do they buy?
      e How do they buy?
      f When do they buy?
      g How much do they buy?
      h How will buyers' behavior and characteristics change in the future?
      i Are customers satisfied? At what level?
      j Are customers retained? At what level?
    2 Market characteristics:
      a Market size potential
      b Segments
      c Selective demand
      d Future market trends
  B Competition
    1 Who are competitors?
    2 Competitor characteristics:
      a Marketing programs
      b Competitive behavior
      c Resources
    3 Major strengths and weaknesses
    4 Future competitive environment
  C General environment
    1 Economic conditions and trends
    2 Government regulation and trends
    3 Pollution, safety, consumerism concerns
    4 Technological trends
    5 Political climate
  D Internal environment
    1 Marketing resources/skills
    2 Production resources/skills
    3 Financial resources/skills
    4 Technological resources/skills
    5 Future trends in internal environment
II Marketing mix
  A Product
    1 What product attributes/benefits are important?
    2 How should the product be differentiated?
    3 What segments will be attracted?
    4 How important are service, warranty, and so on?
    5 Is there a need for product variation/product line?
    6 How important is packaging?
    7 How is the product perceived relative to competitive offerings?
  B Place
    1 What types of distributors should handle the product?
    2 What are the channel attitudes and motivations for handling the product?
    3 What intensity of wholesale/retail coverage is needed?
    4 What margins are appropriate?
    5 What forms of physical distribution are needed?
  C Price
    1 What is the elasticity of demand?
    2 What pricing policies are appropriate?
    3 How should the product line be priced?
    4 How do we establish price variations for a product?
    5 How should we react to a competitive price threat?
    6 How important is price to the buyer?
  D Promotion
    1 What is the optimal promotional budget?
    2 How important are sales promotion, advertising, and personal selling in stimulating demand?
    3 What is the proper promotion mix?
    4 How do you measure the effectiveness of the promotion tools?
    5 What copy is most effective?
    6 What media are most effective?
III Performance measures
    1 What are current sales by product line?
    2 What are current market shares by product line?
    3 What are current sales/market share by customer types, sales region, and so on?
    4 What is our product/company image among customers, distributors, and the public?
    5 What is the awareness level of our promotion?
    6 What is the recall level of our brand name?
    7 What percentage distributorship do we have in large retailers? Medium? Small? By geography? Customer type?
    8 What percentage of the channel is selling below suggested retail price? What is the average retail price of our product?
    9 What percentage of customers are satisfied?
    10 What percentage of current customers are likely to repeat?

(2) allocating marketing resources, and (3) auditing performance. The balance of the research activities will arise ad hoc as problems and opportunities develop in the course of implementing the marketing plan.

The marketing manager utilizes the structure of the marketing system shown in Figure 1-1 and the types of question presented in Exhibit 1-1 to develop a *marketing plan.* In this context, the marketing manager's task is to plan and implement a marketing program that accomplishes the desired level of performance measures (dependent variables), through the utilization of the marketing mix (controllable independent variables). Thus, the marketing manager utilizes the information derived from marketing research to *understand* the current situation, to *predict* the future, and to improve *control* over the outcomes of the marketing plan.

THE MARKETING RESEARCHER AS HERO

In the context of the need to make effective marketing decisions in the face of uncertainty, the potential for marketing research to provide both strategic and tactical insight is tremendous. As a result, a marketing researcher with capabilities to provide managerial insights from technically competent marketing research is an almost invaluable person. Companies where such people are highly valued include Procter & Gamble (P&G), Lexus, Revlon, Leo Burnett, and Marriott. One such example is presented in some detail in the Marketing Research in Action about Vince Barabba of General Motors (GM). The marketing research function headed by Barabba has become critical in General Motors' attempt to turn around its declining market share, its image, and its profitability.

MARKETING RESEARCH IN ACTION

MARKETING RESEARCH HELPS DRIVE GENERAL MOTORS TURNAROUND

The increasingly active role of marketing research at General Motors corresponds to the company's recent turnaround. Long treated as an ivory tower by the engineering and design departments, past GM research departments conducted thousands of surveys, hoarded reams of information and reports, and didn't get involved in the car production process until it was time to figure out who might buy a new model. According to current marketing research chief Vince Barabba, car creators were so protective that "they wouldn't even let you in the building" before a car was finished.

GM's market share started to slide in the late 1980s. Barabba recalls, "There was a sense that things needed to be improved. But this was GM, which said, 'Yes, we'll tell you what you need to know, when you need to know it, and it will look like this.'" Robert O'Connell, former chief financial officer (CFO) of GM, is credited with the insight and willingness to hire an outsider who was not entrenched in the General Motors philosophy of proprietary information. He "was the person who had the insight to say, 'We really need someone here to help us use our information.'"

The car company hired Vince Barabba, former director of market intelligence for marketing giants Eastman Kodak and Xerox, and advocate of the philosophy that information should be available for anybody who wants to use it. Upper management

The Oldsmobile Aurora.

continued to resist change. GM's $15 billion in North American losses starting in 1990 and the replacement of the upper management team forced the company to acknowledge the need to incorporate consumers' opinions from the start. Backed by current Chairman John Smale and Chief Executive Officer (CEO) Jack Smith, marketing researchers now work with designing, engineering, and manufacturing experts from the inception of a car concept, long before the first sketch is drawn and the first parts are ordered. The four groups have developed a four-step process to determine who will buy a car, how much the car will cost to develop, what features the car should have, and the price the car should command.

GM's new "value pricing" is an example of this new proactive philosophy. Under this program, GM is selling a series of special-edition cars and trucks equipped with popular options such as air conditioning and antilock brakes. The company and its dealers are accepting lower profits so that cars can be priced hundreds and sometimes thousands of dollars lower than consumers would pay if extras were priced individually. Barabba explained, "The whole company's got to come together for value pricing to work." Using information collected by the marketing research staff, manufacturing assembled cars with the options customers requested at prices they were willing to pay. Marketing and advertising used research information to figure out who would buy the cars, as well as ways to reach the customers. Research also persuaded dealers to sell cars at lower individual profit margins based on projections of higher overall sales volume.

The result has been a halt to GM's 6-year market-share slide. Acceptance of this new information-driven philosophy is further characterized by the move of the marketing research department from GM's Detroit headquarters to GM's Design Center.

Source: Adapted from Micheline Maynard, "Barabba Helps GM Tune In," *USA Today,* p. 5B, August 25, 1993.

THE GLOBALIZATION OF MARKETING RESEARCH

As businesses become more global in the markets that they serve, marketing research is becoming even more useful to marketing managers. This is because managers with useful experience and insights in one country or region lack these same dimensions as they enter unfamiliar and foreign contexts. One study found that insufficient marketing research was a critical factor in determining the failure of global marketing activity. In this study, two-thirds of the global programs that did not undertake formal marketing research programs before launch failed to meet expectations, while two-thirds of those that utilized marketing research attained their expectations.[6]

Unfortunately, this lesson has been learned the hard way by many managers who have taken the short cut of not using marketing research in their international operations. The Global Marketing Research Dynamics illustrates this problem with real examples of global blunders that likely would have been avoided with competent marketing research.

GLOBAL MARKETING RESEARCH DYNAMICS

BLUNDERING INTERNATIONALLY WITHOUT MARKETING RESEARCH

Listed below are examples of international marketing failures in which the absence of marketing research played a significant role in the failure.

• A large U.S.-based carbonated soft-drink firm set up large bottling facilities in Indonesia in an attempt to make large sales to the 176 million people of Indonesia. The judgment of management proved wrong as the sales of the product fell substantially below expectations. Later marketing research revealed the reasons. First, demographic data revealed that there was little disposable income to support the purchase of the product. Second, the consumption of the product was mainly by tourists and expatriates in the major cities. Third, most Indonesians preferred noncarbonated, coconut-based drinks.

• Vic Tanny's franchised health club tried to implement its U.S.-based marketing strategy in Singapore. Its U.S.-style facilities and exercise equipment drew few customers. Again, basically only expatriates were served. Later marketing research revealed that to be successful the club would need to appeal to Singapore residents' preference for Western-style competitive sports, Chinese calisthenics, and traditional Asian exercise.

• Lego A/S, the Danish toy company, implemented a Western-style consumer promotion in Japan. This promotion consisted of bonus packs of legos and gift promotions, and had caused sales increases in the United States and Europe when implemented there. It seemed to have no impact in the Japanese market. Subsequent marketing research revealed that Japanese consumers considered the promotion to be wasteful, expensive, and not very appealing.

Sources: Charles F. Valentine, ''Blunders Abroad,'' *Nation's Business,* pp. 54, 56, March 1989; Kamran Kashani, ''Beware the Pitfalls of Global Marketing,'' *Harvard Business Review,* pp. 91–98, September–October 1989.

[6]Kamran Kashani, ''Beware the Pitfalls of Global Marketing,'' *Harvard Business Review,* pp. 91–98, September–October 1989.

SPECIAL ASPECTS OF GLOBAL MARKETING RESEARCH

The effective implementation of a program of marketing research requires great understanding of and skills in techniques, methods, and marketing management concerns, in the domestic context. This book is designed to provide the reader with the necessary basic knowledge and skills. In addition, we are concerned with the same issues in the context of global marketing. Effective marketing research in the international environment raises additional concerns that are discussed throughout this book. We will just note them here and discuss them in detail in the appropriate sections of the book. They include:[7]

• The marketing researcher must often deal with multiple languages and cultural dimensions that complicate data collection and interpretation.
• There is often a lack of secondary data (data already collected and published in some form) for the marketing researchers to utilize.
• In addition, these secondary data are often of questionable quality relative to the standards of U.S. data.
• The institutional structure of marketing research companies that provide syndicated data, select samples, do interviews, and so forth is often underdeveloped or absent.
• In some countries, either cultural dynamics or concern about government spying on citizens negatively impacts the willingness of consumers or distributors to participate in marketing research data collection, or may bias the nature of the responses obtained.
• The logistical dimensions of implementing marketing research internationally are complex, and the costs can be high.

We will take these special concerns into account throughout this book, in sections related to global marketing research.

WHAT ORGANIZATIONS DO

What types of information do organizations collect for decision making? Who collects the information? Table 1-1 presents the findings of a survey conducted for the AMA to answer these questions.[8]

Companies collect information on all aspects of the marketing system, that is, situation variables, marketing mix variables, and performance measures. For example, related to situation variables, over 90 percent of companies do industry and market characteristic studies, and about 80 percent do many different kinds of buying behavior studies. In terms of performance measurement, about 85 percent of companies do market-share analysis studies and almost 90 percent do satisfaction research. Much of the rest of Table 1-1 shows the breadth of studies

---

[7]For additional background on these global concerns see, for example, Susan P. Douglas and C. Samuel Craig, *International Marketing Research* (Englewood Cliffs, NJ: Prentice-Hall, Inc., 1983).
[8]Thomas C. Kinnear and Ann R. Root, *Survey of Marketing Research 1994* (Chicago: American Marketing Association, 1995). This survey is the eighth in a series begun in 1947.

done in the marketing mix components of product, distribution, promotion, and price. Part 6 of this book concerns applications in marketing research. That section discusses the details of research done in practice for the types of applications presented in Table 1-1.

The vast majority of these studies were conducted by the companies' own marketing research departments. However, a significant amount of work in marketing research, especially in demand analysis, product testing, promotion, and consumer studies, is done by outside firms. The industry structure that exists to do this work is discussed in Chapter 2.

OVERVIEW OF THE BOOK

This textbook provides an introduction to the world of marketing research in terms of its methods and techniques, and also its managerial applications. The emphasis is on the practicalities involved in actually utilizing marketing research within the organization.

Part One presents an introduction to marketing research in marketing decision making by managers. This includes the role of marketing research in marketing management, which we have just completed in Chapter 1. Included in Chapter 2 is a description of the marketing research business as it is practiced: institutions, supplier relationships, ethical aspects, and job dynamics. Chapter 3 describes the marketing research process, and Chapter 4 presents the considerations that drive the decision to undertake marketing research.

Part Two deals with research design and data sources (Chapter 5) and the issues involving secondary data (Chapter 6). Part Three discusses data collection procedures in marketing research: the measurement process (Chapter 7), techniques of attitude measurement (Chapter 8), experimentation in marketing research (Chapter 9), different procedures for actually collecting the data in the context of exploratory research (Chapter 10) and for conclusive research (Chapter 11), and the designing of questionnaires and other data collection forms (Chapter 12).

Part Four presents the theory and practical dimensions of sampling in marketing research (Chapters 13, 14, and 15). In addition, Chapter 16 discusses the actual collection of data from respondents in the field. Part Five follows with a discussion of what we need to do with the data once they are collected. Processing the data is discussed in Chapter 17, and various data analysis procedures are presented in Chapters 18 through 21. The issues in the presentation of research results are discussed in Chapter 22.

We conclude the book, in Part Six, by presenting details of applications areas in marketing research. Chapter 23 discusses demand measurement and forecasting; Chapter 24 discusses product research and test marketing; Chapter 25 deals with advertising research; and Chapter 26 presents the dynamics of marketing research in distribution and pricing decisions. Applications are not limited to Part Six of the book. We have included applications in all chapters of the book to continuously draw whatever topic is being discussed back to the real world of marketing management decision making.

TABLE 1-1   TYPES OF RESEARCH ACTIVITY CONDUCTED BY COMPANIES

	Research frequency			Data developed by			Data analyzed by		
	Not done	Some-times done	Freq. done	Corp. mktg. res. dept.	Other corp. dept.	Outside firm	Corp. mktg. res. dept.	Other corp. dept.	Outside firm
A Business/Economic and Corporate Research									
1 Industry/market data and trends	8	38	54	64	95	28	82	11	7
2 Acquisition/diversification studies	50	38	12	54	30	18	60	31	10
3 Market-share data	15	33	52	61	11	29	82	12	8
4 Internal employee data (morale, communication, etc.)	28	56	16	54	27	29	58	27	16
B Pricing									
1 Cost data	43	26	31	36	57	9	42	57	5
2 Profit data	44	22	34	27	66	8	32	67	1
3 Price elasticity data	44	40	16	51	34	16	61	32	9
4 Demand analysis									
a Market potential	28	36	36	66	21	14	78	20	9
b Sales potential	22	40	38	71	16	15	78	17	7
c Sales forecasts	25	41	34	65	25	13	70	26	7
5 Competitive pricing data	29	39	32	58	31	12	65	32	5
C Product									
1 Concept testing	22	38	40	68	6	27	84	6	11
2 Brand-name testing	45	36	19	62	4	37	81	2	19
3 Test market data	45	37	18	58	11	31	80	8	14
4 Product testing of existing products	37	37	26	65	10	25	82	9	11
5 Packaging design testing	52	36	13	61	10	34	78	9	14
6 Competitive product testing	46	36	18	55	20	25	72	16	12

D Distribution

1 Plant/warehouse location data	75	20	5	45	48	10	47	51	5
2 Channel performance data	61	26	14	54	31	18	61	35	4
3 Channel coverage data	69	20	11	53	31	19	63	34	5
4 Export and international data	68	23	8	39	40	22	50	44	8

E Promotion

1 Motivation research	44	39	17	61	6	38	79	8	22
2 Media research	30	40	30	55	8	41	68	13	28
3 Copy research	32	42	26	54	8	39	72	9	21
4 Advertising effectiveness testing									
a Prior to marketplace airing	33	36	31	56	7	39	75	5	23
b During marketplace airing	34	37	29	55	8	36	75	8	19
5 Competitive advertising testing	57	28	15	55	7	39	79	7	15
6 Public image testing	35	40	25	61	8	31	75	10	16
7 Sales-force compensation data	66	25	9	39	47	14	40	52	8
8 Sales-force quota data	72	18	10	37	58	6	38	59	4
9 Sales-force territory structure data	68	24	8	43	53	6	46	52	4
10 Studies of premiums, coupons, deals, etc.	53	37	10	65	13	23	79	13	15

F Buying Behavior

1 Brand preference	22	42	36	63	3	34	81	4	15
2 Brand attitudes	24	37	39	63	3	42	83	4	13
3 Product satisfaction	13	35	52	65	4	32	81	5	13
4 Purchase behavior	20	36	44	64	4	34	85	4	11
5 Purchase intentions	21	36	43	63	4	34	85	4	11
6 Brand awareness	20	37	43	62	2	37	83	3	14
7 Segmentation data	16	44	40	62	5	34	82	5	14

Source: Adapted from Thomas C. Kinnear and Ann R. Root, *Survey of Marketing Research* (Chicago: American Marketing Association, 1995).

SUMMARY

1 The need for marketing research parallels acceptance of the marketing concept. Organizations of all types are integrating and directing their activities to meet the needs of the marketplace. The growing acceptance of the marketing concept has increased the need for a formal process of acquiring information, namely, marketing research.

2 Marketing research can supply information regarding many aspects of the marketing system. This domain ranges from monitoring and describing situational factors to evaluating marketing programs and measuring the performance of these programs.

3 The primary purpose of marketing research is to provide information for decision making. Marketing research information can be useful in all stages of the decision-making process. This ranges from information to aid in recognizing that a decision situation is present to information that will guide the selection of a course of action.

4 Marketing management's increased emphasis on the planning and control functions has influenced the nature of marketing research activity. A more systematic and continuous flow of information is required. The activities of marketing research must be designed in accord with the requirements of the planning and control process. Marketing research is required to have available a continually updated library of information to facilitate the decision-making process.

5 Most marketing decisions involve limited marketing research input. These decisions are repetitive in nature, and the manager's experience and judgment provide adequate information for sound decisions. Marketing information is typically the main input to nonrepetitive decision situations.

6 The concept of a marketing research system implies a broadly defined role for marketing research in the marketing management process. Here, marketing research is viewed by management as an information center for decision making as opposed to an activity that merely gathers and analyzes data.

7 Marketing research is defined as the systematic and objective approach to the development and provision of information for the marketing management decision-making process. This definition emphasizes the applied-research focus of this book. Information based on management experience and judgment differs from marketing research information in terms of objectivity and of how systematically the data were collected and processed.

8 Marketing research is becoming even more useful to marketing managers as businesses become more global in the markets that they serve. This is because managers with useful experience and insights in one country or region lack these same dimensions as they enter unfamiliar and foreign contexts.

DISCUSSION QUESTIONS

1 What effect has the increasing adoption of the marketing concept by organizations had on marketing research?
2 Present the four essential components of the marketing system and examples of each.

3 In what aspects of the marketing system is marketing research of limited applicability?

4 Outline the steps in the marketing decision-making process for marketing managers considering introducing a new formulation of a laundry detergent.

5 What factors determine the relative importance of managerial experience versus marketing research in a given situation?

6 A marketing manager responsible for CD-ROM-based video games (CD-ROM stands for compact disk-read only memory) for personal computers (PCs) has received a copy of 10 new books on this industry and 5 new industry reports prepared by industry consultants. These items total over 3000 pages. "All this data will be great help with the new games we are planning," noted the analyst who delivered the documents. Comment on this quote, and describe how the manager should proceed.

7 One of the key marketing trends of the 1990s is that organizations are trying to become more market-driven. What role should marketing research play in the process? Some legendary businesspeople, such as Charles Revson of Revlon, have had great success without using marketing research in any systematic way. How is this possible?

8 How might the following organizations effectively utilize marketing research?
   a Wal-Mart
   b Diet Pepsi
   c National Museum of Art
   d American Airlines
   e Dell Computer
   f Your favorite restaurant
   g Sysco Food Services—a food wholesaler

9 **MINICASE**

Swatch watch's management (a Swiss company) was considering simultaneously launching a new line of women's watches in the United States, Canada, the United Kingdom, France, Germany, Italy, Spain, Switzerland, Japan, Hong Kong, and Korea. How might marketing research be useful to the planning of all marketing aspects of this launch: product design, advertising, consumer and trade promotion, and price points?

CHAPTER 2

THE MARKETING
RESEARCH BUSINESS

Residence Inn

Marriott Marquis

MARKETING RESEARCH IN ACTION

THE MARKETING RESEARCH FUNCTION AT MARRIOTT CORPORATION

Marriott Corporation is a leader in the services sector. The company has three major commitments: (1) to providing superior service, (2) to being the employer of choice, and (3) to continuing growth. Marriott pursues these commitments by listening to customers, investing in employees, and growing through both expansion of its current businesses and the addition of new businesses that are strategically aligned with its corporate strengths. Marriott's marketing research department plays an integral part in achieving each of these goals.

While Marriott structures many of its major functions (finance, marketing, operations, etc.) within autonomous strategic business units (SBUs), marketing research is set up as a corporate-level function. This enables marketing research to provide support to each SBU as needed, and it facilitates the transfer of relevant knowledge between different SBUs. The department is made up of over 30 research professionals and is referred to as Corporate Marketing Services (CMS).

CMS is headed by the vice president of Corporate Marketing Services, who reports to the senior vice president for strategic and business development, who reports directly to Chairman J. Willard Marriott, Jr. Ten research directors report directly to the vice president of CMS. Each director provides research to a specific business or set of businesses, and each has a vertical "reporting relationship" with the senior managers of these businesses. In businesses with extensive research needs, directors have one or more additional researchers reporting to them. These researchers also work exclusively with the same businesses. This structure allows the research directors to maintain an ongoing relationship with the business and its key clients, enabling each of them to better act as a consultant to that particular SBU and to proactively recommend necessary research, as well as advising the business on actions supported by research findings.

The marketing research has its own formal mission statement.

Department Mission Statement

Corporate Marketing Services' mission is to improve the quality of business decisions at Marriott through:

1 Building a knowledge base on customers, competitors, and markets for our major businesses, and transferring that knowledge between strategic business units and among key managers.

2 Conducting primary marketing research for strategic business units to ensure that projects meet their objectives, are cost-effective, and avoid duplication of other work.

3 Providing quality control and oversight on all marketing research conducted for Marriott or its subsidiary companies.

4 Consulting with corporate and strategic business unit management on marketing strategy and tactics.

Implications drawn from this mission statement include: the need for a systemic understanding of customers, competitors, and markets; the need to distinguish relevant information; the importance of cross-functional knowledge; the need to ensure quality in research; and the need to ensure that research is interpreted properly and that recommended actions are consistent with research implications.

The marketing research function has grown along with the Marriott Corporation. While the corporation has grown at a rate of approximately 20 percent over the past 5 years, Marriott's marketing research volume has increased over 25 percent. Marriott allocated over $10 million to CMS in 1988, funding over 200 separate research projects. Yet these research expenditures represent only one-tenth of 1 percent of annual sales. Research is conducted for long-term strategic purposes and short-run tactical needs. Typical topics covered include: (1) market segmentation and sizing, (2) concept development and product testing, (3) price sensitivity assessment, (4) advertising and promotions testing, (5) market tracking, and (6) customer satisfaction. Standard qualitative and quantitative methods are often used: telephone interviews, mail surveys, in-person interviews, focus groups, central-location tests, and customer intercepts.

The actual research process follows a basic series of steps. The first step requires precisely defining the research needs for a particular project and attaining project approval. The second step is a detailed design of the study. The third step involves delivering the study findings, whether by writing a brief summary or making a formal presentation. The last step is the consultative phase, in which the director works with the client to assess the implications of the research and to determine alternative courses of action that are consistent with the findings.

The company must continue to identify new business opportunities if it is to achieve this goal. Three additional areas of concern are also targeted for the future: customer satisfaction, corporate synergies, and employees as a new market. Marriott's marketing research staff is expected to play a major role in achieving these goals.

Source: "Listening to Customers: The Market Research Function at Marriott Corporation," *Marketing Research,* pp. 5–14, March 1989.

In Chapter 1, we discussed the nature and role of marketing research as it relates to marketing decision making. Now our objective is to add life to the topic of marketing research by presenting a description of a very exciting business, the marketing research business; unfortunately, no words on paper can do justice to its dynamic nature.

This chapter will first present a brief history of marketing research and then describe the amount of money that is spent on marketing research and the types of institutions that use and perform such research. In this context, we shall discuss how companies organize the marketing research function, the types of job opportunities that are available, and the procedures by which the users of marketing research select those who will actually perform it. With a good understanding of the practice of marketing research in hand, we will then address the ethical constraints that affect this field. The importance of marketing research in the organization and as a business is clearly presented in the Marriott Marketing Research in Action at the beginning of this chapter.

HISTORY OF MARKETING RESEARCH

To put the nature of marketing research in perspective, let's review the history of the field. The development of marketing research during the early part of the twentieth century parallels the rise of the marketing concept. Over this period, the management philosophy guiding organizations gradually changed to the consumer orientation of today. During the period 1900–1930, management concern was focused primarily on the problems and opportunities associated with production; between 1930 and the late 1940s, this orientation shifted to the problems and opportunities associated with distribution; since the late 1940s, increased attention has been focused on consumer needs and desires. The nature and role of marketing activity in these organizations reflects this shift in management philosophy.

Pioneers and Institutions[1]

While numerous people and institutions were involved in the occasional use of marketing research prior to 1910, the period 1910–1920 is recognized as the formal beginning of marketing research. In 1911, J. George Frederick established a research firm called The Business Bourse. Charles Coolidge Parlin was appointed manager of the Commercial Research Division of the Curtis Publishing Company that same year. The use of the name "commercial research" had special significance, since most businesspeople considered the term "research" too eloquent for a business service. Parlin managed one of the leading research organizations of this period.

The success of Parlin's work inspired several industrial firms and advertising media to establish research divisions. In 1915, the United States Rubber Company hired Dr. Paul H. Nystrom to manage its newly established Department of Commercial Research. In 1917, Swift and Company hired Dr. Louis D. H. Weld from Yale University to become manager of its Commercial Research Department.

In 1919, Professor C. S. Duncan of the University of Chicago published *Commercial Research: An Outline of Working Principles.* This was considered to be the first major book on commercial research. In 1921, Percival White's *Market Analysis* was published. This was the first research book to gain a large readership, and it went through several editions. *Market Research and Analysis* by Lyndon O. Brown was published in 1937. This became one of the most popular college textbooks of the period, reflecting the growing interest in marketing research on the college campus. After 1940, numerous research textbooks were published, and the number of business schools offering research courses rapidly expanded.

Following World War II, the growth of marketing research activity dramatically increased, paralleling the growing acceptance of the marketing concept. By 1948, over 200 marketing research organizations had been formed in the United States. Expenditures on marketing research activities were estimated to be $50 million a year in 1947. Over the next four decades this expenditure level increased more than twentyfold.

The growing acceptance of the marketing concept brought a change in emphasis from "market research." Market research implied that the focus of research was on the analysis of markets. The shift to marketing research broadened the nature and role of research, with the emphasis on contact between researchers and the marketing management process.

Methodological Development

Advances in marketing research methodology parallel the development of research methodology in the social sciences, of which marketing is a part. The methodological advances made by psychologists, economists, sociologists, polit-

---

[1]For a recent discussion of the history of marketing research, see Christine Wright-Isak and David Prensky, "Early Marketing Research: Science and Application," *Marketing Research,* vol. 5, no. 4, pp. 16–23, 1993.

ical scientists, statisticians, and so on had a pronounced influence on marketing research methodology, and consequently its history is interwoven with the historical development of the social sciences.

Marketing research made major methodological advances from 1910 to 1920. Questionnaire studies or surveys became popular modes of data collection. With the growth of survey research came improvements in questionnaire design and question construction, along with an awareness of biases resulting from the questioning and the interviewing process. Several social scientists who entered the field were interested in working on these applied methodological problems. This established a methodological communication link between marketing and the other social sciences that exists to this day.

During the 1930s, sampling became a serious methodological issue. As statistical training developed beyond descriptive statistics (calculation of means, variances, simple correlation, and construction of index numbers) to an emphasis on inferential statistics, nonprobability sampling procedures came under heavy attack. Modern probability sampling approaches slowly gained acceptance during this period.

Methodological innovation occurred at a fairly steady pace from 1950 through the early 1960s. At this time, a major development occurred: the commercialization of the large-scale digital computer. The computer rapidly increased the pace of methodological innovation, especially in the area of quantitative marketing research.

The 1990s find technological advances in computer and related areas having a major impact on many aspects of the marketing research profession. These include checkout scanners in supermarkets which provide panel data, computer-assisted telephone interviewing, data analysis by microcomputer and remote terminals, and the potential for interviewing through two-way cable television systems. All of these advances are amplified later in this book.

THE PRACTICE OF MARKETING RESEARCH

Dollar Expenditures

It is difficult to obtain accurate estimates of dollar expenditures for marketing research activity. Most of the studies of this issue survey only large users of marketing research or large marketing research suppliers. Thus, the marketing research activity of thousands of smaller users and smaller suppliers does not form part of the estimates. One well-respected estimate that utilizes the billings of the largest marketing research suppliers noted the top 50 marketing research firms billings as $3.7 billion worldwide and as $2.4 billion in the United States. The top 161 marketing research firms are estimated to have worldwide billings of approximately $4.05 billion.[2] Table 2-1 notes which these firms are and their billing levels by region. Considering all the money that was spent on marketing

---

[2]Jack Honomichl, "The Honomichl 50," *Marketing News,* p. H4, June 6, 1994.

TABLE 2-1 1993 U.S. AND NON-U.S. REVENUE OF THE 50 LEADING MARKETING RESEARCH COMPANIES, AND TOTAL REVENUE FOR THE TOP 161 MARKETING RESEARCH COMPANIES

Rank 1993	Rank 1992	Organization	Headquarters	Total research revenues* (millions)	Percent change from 1992†	Percent from outside U.S.	Revenues from outside U.S. (millions)
1†	1/2	D&B Marketing Information Services	Cham, Switzerland	$1,868.3	−1.2%	61.0%†‡	$1,139.7†‡
2	3	Information Resources Inc.	Chicago, IL	334.5	21.1	15.0	50.2
3	4	The Arbitron Co.	New York, NY	172.0	−3.4		
4	6	Walsh International/PMSI	Phoenix, AZ	115.4	32.1	34.4	39.7
5	5	Westat Inc.	Rockville, MD	113.1	−0.5		
6	7	Maritz Marketing Research Inc.	St. Louis, MO	74.4	6.7		
7	8	The NPD Group	Port Washington, NY	66.0	15.6	23.8	15.7
8	10	NFO Research Inc.	Greenwich, CT	51.9	10.2		
9	11	Elrick & Lavidge Inc.	Atlanta, GA	47.1	0.6		
10	12	Market Facts Inc.	Arlington Heights, IL	45.6	12.0		
11	9	The M/A/R/C Group	Las Colinas, TX	44.7	−17.1		
12	13	Walker Group	Indianapolis, IN	38.1	−3.0	1.9	.7
13	19	Abt Associates Inc.	Cambridge, MA	36.4	33.8		
14	14	MRB Group	London, England	35.0	2.8		
15	18	The National Research Group Inc.	Los Angeles, CA	34.5	25.5	15.0	5.2
16	15	NOP Information Group	Livingston, NJ	33.0	3.4		
17	16	Intersearch Corp.	Horsham, PA	32.2	7.0		
18	17	The BASES Group	Covington, KY	31.0	10.7	5.0	1.6
19	20	Millward Brown Inc.	Naperville, IL	29.0	15.1		
20	—	Opinion Research Corp.	Princeton, NJ	26.6	−8.6	27.9	7.4
21	21	Burke Marketing Research	Cincinnati, OH	26.1	7.0	2.9	0.8
22	25	Roper Starch Worldwide Inc.	Mamaroneck, NY	24.9	9.2	4.0	0.9
23	26	J.D. Power & Associates	Agoura Hills, CA	24.5	17.1		
24	28	Creative & Response Research Svcs.	Chicago, IL	23.8	28.1		
25	24	Research International USA	New York, NY	22.7	−.1	30.4	6.9
26	22	Louis Harris and Associates Inc.	New York, NY	22.0	−8.7	68.2†‡	15.0‡
27	23	Chilton Research Services	Radnor, PA	22.0	−7.6		
28	30	Mercer Mgt. Consulting/Decision Research	Lexington, MA	20.7	18.3		

29	27	Yankelovich Partners	Westport, CT	20.1	1.0	8.0	1.6
30	29	ASI Market Research	Stamford, CT	17.5	2.4	7.5	1.2
31	32	M.O.R.-PACE	Farmington Hills, MI	16.7	11.1		
32	34	The Wirthlin Group	McLean, VA	16.2	19.1	6.6	1.0
33	36	Lieberman Research West Inc.	Los Angeles, CA	15.2	15.2		
34	31	Custom Research Inc.	Minneapolis, MN	15.0	–7.7		
35	33	Data Development Corp.	New York, NY	14.8	NC	20.0	2.7
36	37	Total Research Corp.	Princeton, NJ	13.5	13.4		
37	44	Response Analysis Corp.	Princeton, NJ	13.4	30.5		
38	41	Market Strategies Inc.	Southfield, MI	13.0	14.2	1.0	0.1
39	35	National Analysts Inc.	Philadelphia, PA	12.8	13.3		
40	38	ICR Survey Research Group	Media, PA	12.6	15.2		
41	43	Research Data Analysis Inc.	Bloomfield Hills, MI	12.0	16.5		
42	40	Strategic Research & Consulting	Maumee, OH	10.5	NC		
43	45	Conway/Milliken & Assocs.	Chicago, IL	10.2	–8.6		
44	42	Guideline Research Corp.	New York, NY	10.0	–3.8		
45	46	Market Decisions	Cincinnati, OH	10.0	12.4		
46	39	MSW-McCollum Spielman Worldwide	Great Neck, NY	9.8	–7.5	5.0	0.5
47	49	Newman-Stein Inc.	New York, NY	8.9	20.3		
48	—	BAI (Behavioral Analysis Inc.)	Tarrytown, NY	8.7	23.7	25.1	2.2
49	50	Gordon S. Black Corp.	Rochester, NY	8.4	13.7		
50	—	CLT Research Associates Inc.	New York, NY	7.9	23.2		
		Subtotal, Top 50		$3,692.7	3.5%	35.0%	
		All other (111 CASRO member companies not included in Top 50)§		357.8	4.8		$1,293.1
		Total (161 organizations)		$4,050.5	3.6%		

* Total revenues that include non-research activities for some companies are significantly higher This information is given in the individual company profiles in the main article.

† Rate of growth from year to year has been adjusted so as not to include revenue gains from acquisition. See company profiles for explanation.

‡ Estimate.

§ Total revenues of 111 survey research firms—beyond those listed in Top 50—that provide financial information, on a confidential basis, to the Council of American Survey Research Organizations (CASRO).

¶ Reflects the acquisition of A. C. Nielsen by Dun & Bradstreet.

Source: Jack Honomichl, "The Honomichl 50," *Marketing News*, p. H4, June 6, 1994.

research where outside marketing research suppliers were not used, and the marketing research done by thousands of marketing research suppliers not in the top 50, then annual expenditures on marketing research in the United States are estimated to be approximately $2.8 billion. This is at best an imprecise estimate, but one that gives us a feel for the scope of the industry in dollar terms.

These dollar expenditures are small relative to the scope of U.S. and worldwide gross domestic product (GDP). However, what must be clearly understood is that these expenditures on marketing research have significant impact on literally hundreds of billions of dollars of spending on marketing activity. The success of expenditures on product development and commercialization, advertising, consumer and trade promotion, distribution, and sales force are meaningfully impacted by marketing research.

Estimates are also available for expenditures on marketing research in many other countries. These expenditures are presented in the Global Marketing Research Dynamics.

Marketing research is a big, global, and growing business that offers interesting employment opportunities. We now turn our attention to where the employment opportunities are by examining the institutional structure of the industry.

GLOBAL MARKETING RESEARCH DYNAMICS

EXPENDITURES ON MARKETING RESEARCH BY REGION
(in millions of $)

European Economic Community (EEC) (12 countries)	$2,500
Other European countries	250
Japan	370
United States and Canada	2,800
All other countries	650
Total world	$6,570

Source: ESOMAR Annual Market Study, various years, plus estimates by the authors.

Institutional Structure

The institutional structure of the marketing research business is complex, with many thousands of different types of organizations being part of the industry. To simplify our discussion we will position each of these organizations in one of three categories. These categories are (1) users, (2) users/doers, and (3) doers. Figure 2-1 presents a graphic representation of this structure. Different types of organizations are listed under each of the three categories. The arrows indicate the direction of the flow of marketing research services. As one would expect, services flow from doers to users. In actuality, the industry is more complex than this representation. To show it in all its complexity would reduce any graphic display to chaos.

Users In Figure 2-1 certain organizations are placed in two categories, namely, users and users/doers. These organizations are manufacturers, wholesalers, retailers, service organizations, trade associations, and government agencies. All these organizations use marketing research data for the purpose of making marketing decisions of various kinds: product planning and evaluation, distribution planning and evaluation, promotional activity development and assessment, and pricing. However, some do not do any of their own research. These are the organizations designated as users only. Others do some of their own research, while making use of outsiders for the rest. Thus, the graphic representation shows these organizations in both categories.

Users/Doers Certain other institutions are almost always users/doers. Foremost among these are advertising agencies, which undertake research studies for their own planning purposes but also do a great deal of research on behalf of clients. The latter research is usually specially funded by client organizations if large, and often absorbed by the agency for their standard 15 percent of media billings if small. Most agencies have their own research departments, but they also make use of outside suppliers for some studies.

Advertising media are also users/doers. It is important to them to be able to provide accurate information about the size and composition of their audiences,

FIGURE 2-1   The institutional structure of the marketing research business.

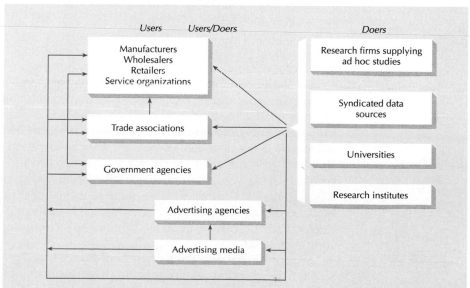

since their advertising revenues per insertion depend on this. This information is communicated to advertising agencies and the clients of agencies. Most media have good reputations for doing competent research in this regard and for providing accurate information. However, the media often make use of outside research suppliers in order to add even more credibility to their audience estimates.

Doers   Doer institutions undertake marketing research solely to provide information for the use of other institutions. Marketing research firms supplying ad hoc studies are one type of doer. We need to distinguish between full-service and limited service research suppliers. Full-service suppliers will undertake complete research studies for client organizations. That is, they will do problem definition work, questionnaire design, sampling, interviewing, coding, editing, and data analysis and interpretation, and they are prepared to provide all these services for the full range of marketing decision problems. Limited-service suppliers do only some of these activities. There are firms that do only field interviewing or data analysis, for example, or firms that specialize in, say, advertising research or product testing. Limited-service firms often concentrate on one geographic region of the country. This is especially true in interviewing work. These local interviewing firms make themselves available to users/doers and doers. The cost and trouble of maintaining a national interviewing force is too much for most users/doers and doers, and so local firms have set up arrangements with other firms to be able to put together a national interviewing system as needed. (It would not be uncommon for two studies performed through two different doers to end up using the same field interviewers.)

Marketing research supply firms can range from large multinational organizations all the way down to one-person businesses operating out of a basement office. The common denominator is that they all have a client or clients who will pay for the services they provide.

It is important to note the difference between ad hoc studies and syndicated studies. All ad hoc studies are designed to solve *client-specific problems*; syndicated data sources provide information that is *not client-specific*. Syndicated data sources collect certain types of data and then sell these data on a subscription basis to any organization that will buy them. Common types of syndicated data measure retail sales, wholesale product shipments, consumer panels, advertising media audiences, advertising effectiveness, and consumer attitudes. Significant companies in this field include A. C. Nielsen, Information Resources, Inc., Audits and Surveys, and Daniel Starch and Staff. A detailed description of the types of syndicated data available and some of the better-known organizations providing it is presented in Chapter 5. We should recognize that many of the firms doing syndicated studies are also in the ad hoc study business. The big users of syndicated data are consumer products companies, advertising agencies, and the advertising media.

Universities, through their division of business research, are also doers. Research may be undertaken for specific client organizations, but usually it is made public because of university regulations. Government agencies are the biggest users of this group of doers. Commercial firms rarely use universities. Individual professors doing marketing research work on a consulting basis would be included as suppliers of ad hoc studies.

Research institutes can be located within a university structure or independent of the arrangement. They can be providers of both ad hoc and syndicated information. Their ad hoc clients are usually government agencies. An example of such a syndicated service would be the "Index of Consumer Sentiment" published by the Survey Research Center of the University of Michigan.

Career Aspects

A discussion of institutions can hide the fact that it is people pursuing individual careers who actually do the work of marketing research. This section presents an overview of some of the careers available in marketing research. In corporations and suppliers, there are basically four types of jobs: (1) research director, (2) analyst, (3) technical specialist, and (4) clerical worker.

Research Directors   These individuals are responsible for all activities of the other people in a department. For research directors in large companies, the majority hold at least a bachelor's degree, a significant number hold a master's degree, and a few hold a doctoral degree. Most became research directors after holding positions in marketing research or other marketing staff jobs. Their role was seen to be largely advisory to top management, but with some policy-making aspects. The average marketing research director in a large company earns between $80,000 and $120,000. Many firms now have a vice president of marketing research, who earns from $125,000 to over $250,000 (see Figure 2-2).

Analysts   These individuals do the bulk of the designing and supervision of actual marketing research studies. They are sometimes referred to as *research generalists* because they act as intermediaries between marketing managers and technical people. Table 2-2 lists the responsibilities of the research generalist.

There are different grades of analysts. Senior analysts in large organizations usually supervise other analysts who do the majority of project work. In turn, these more junior analysts may have apprentice analysts assisting them. The position of analyst can be an entry-level job for someone pursuing either a B.B.A. or an M.B.A. Most large organizations pay competitive salaries to attract new graduates. In the long run, a successful career in marketing research usually pays less than a successful line career in marketing. However, many find the nature of marketing research work worth the sacrifice.

Most managers want their new analysts to have a master's degree or a bachelor's degree. Most want an interdisciplinary degree, with a major in marketing, statistics, economics, general business, or psychology. Most managers will hire analysts right out of school. The characteristics they most desire are brightness/intelligence, analytic ability, imagination/creativity, interpersonal skills, curiosity, writing proficiency, and drive/ambition. A competent analyst is a person of many

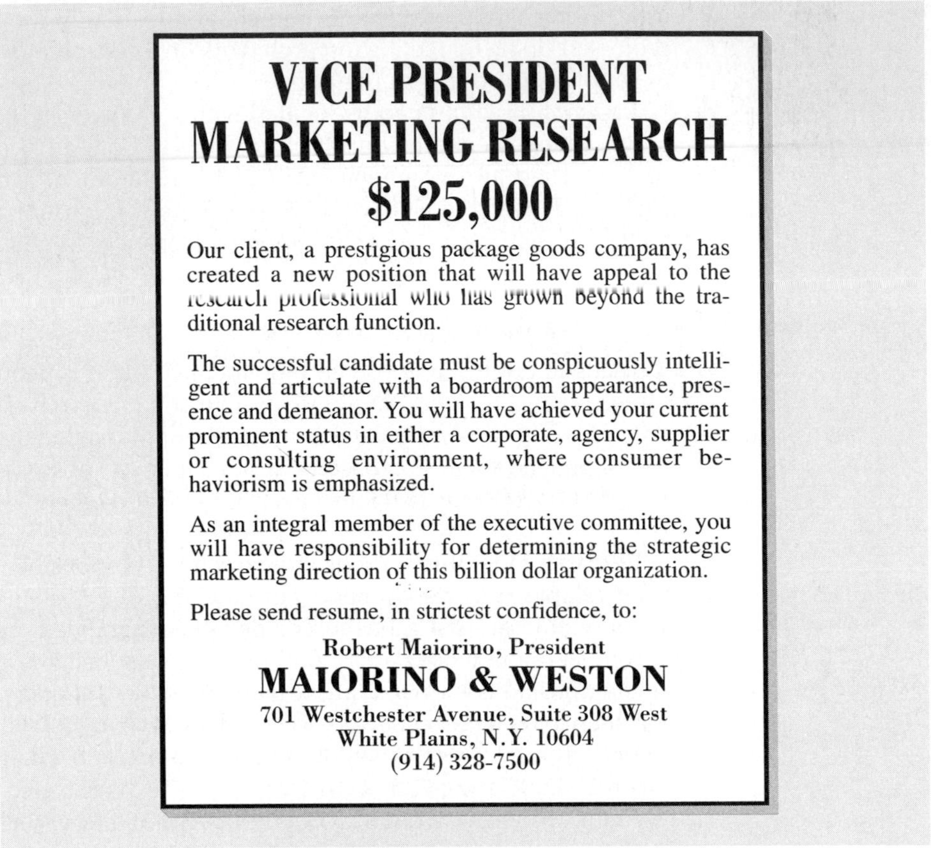

VICE PRESIDENT
MARKETING RESEARCH
$125,000

Our client, a prestigious package goods company, has created a new position that will have appeal to the research professional who has grown beyond the traditional research function.

The successful candidate must be conspicuously intelligent and articulate with a boardroom appearance, presence and demeanor. You will have achieved your current prominent status in either a corporate, agency, supplier or consulting environment, where consumer behaviorism is emphasized.

As an integral member of the executive committee, you will have responsibility for determining the strategic marketing direction of this billion dollar organization.

Please send resume, in strictest confidence, to:

Robert Maiorino, President
MAIORINO & WESTON
701 Westchester Avenue, Suite 308 West
White Plains, N.Y. 10604
(914) 328-7500

FIGURE 2-2   An example of an upper-end marketing research job.

analytical and interpersonal skills with a solid understanding of both marketing and marketing research. (A more detailed look at three different analysts is presented below.)

Technical Specialists   These individuals are available to solve very narrow aspects of marketing research problems. They include, for example, experts in questionnaire design, sampling, data analysis, and computers. Analysts make use of their knowledge when needed.

Clerical Workers   These individuals perform functions as directed by analysts. For example, they type reports, pull sample elements as directed, and prepare computer runs.

Table 2-3 presents a more detailed description of the jobs that one would expect to find in a sophisticated marketing research organization, as well as the

TABLE 2-2   RESPONSIBILITIES OF THE RESEARCH GENERALIST

1 Develop knowledge and judgment about various businesses.
2 Understand the research process and language.
3 Define problems and identify opportunities.
4 Identify management alternatives.
5 Marshall evidence to evaluate alternatives.
6 Propose profit-oriented research to close information gaps.
7 Balance decision risks and research costs to achieve high-payoff research projects.
8 Provide an element of entrepreneurial spirit in the planning of research.
9 Bring an element of creativity and insight to research findings and their implications for decision making.
10 Provide perspective on the long-range research needs for a business.
11 Be an educator, a liaison person, a communicator, and a counselor.

associated compensation averages from a 1994 study. In general, people in larger companies and in consumer goods companies tend to be paid the most, and at rates substantially above the averages.

A Week in the Life of . . .

After this brief overview of the available jobs, let us now focus on the analyst's job by outlining the activities undertaken by analysts in three different types of organizations. Excerpts from their daybooks are given below.

Sandra Jenkins, Consumer Products Analyst   The following is a typical week for Ms. Jenkins, who works for a large consumer products company.

Monday A.M.	Made oral presentation to the vice president of marketing on just-completed product test for new brand.
P.M.	Completed work on a questionnaire for advertising evaluation study; in evening, attended group interview done by supplier.
Tuesday	Flew to Denver to supervise the setup of a test market.
Wednesday A.M.	Met with brand manager to discuss problem definition for new study on her brand.
P.M.	Discussed the brand problem with research director and brand manager.
Thursday A.M.	Met with contact analyst from research supplier who is handling field work on pricing study; discussed design issues and timing.
P.M.	Wrote part of report on product test study.
Friday A.M.	Received solicitation from a new research supplier seeking our business.
P.M.	Briefed computer people on data analysis runs to be made on image and distribution penetration study involving 2000 respondents. Did some sample run and demonstration graphics on my personal computer.

William Brunner, Industrial Products Analyst   The following is a typical week for Mr. Brunner, who works for a large industrial products company.

TABLE 2-3   GENERAL DESCRIPTION OF MARKETING RESEARCH JOBS AT 11 DIFFERENT LEVELS

	Compensation average
1 **Research Director/Vice President of Marketing Research.** This is the senior position in research. The director is responsible for the entire research program of the company. Accepts assignments from superiors or from clients, or may on own initiative develop and propose research undertakings to company executives. Employs personnel and executes general supervision of research department. Presents research findings to clients or to company executives.	$80,800
2 **Assistant Director of Research.** This position usually represents a defined "second in command," a senior staff member having responsibilities above those of other staff members.	67,500
3 **Statistician/Data Processing Specialist.** Duties are usually those of an expert consultant on theory and application of statistical technique to specific research problems. Usually responsible for experimental design and data processing.	50,380
4 **Senior Analyst.** Usually found in larger research departments. Participates with superior in initial planning of research projects, and directs execution of projects assigned. Operates with minimum supervision. Prepares, or works with analysts in preparing, questionnaires. Selects research techniques, makes analyses, and writes final report. Has budgetary control over projects and primary responsibility for meeting time schedules.	45,770
5 **Analyst.** The analyst usually handles the bulk of the work required for execution of research projects. Often works under senior analyst supervision. The analyst assists in questionnaire preparation, pretests questionnaires, and makes preliminary analyses of results. Most of the library research or work with company data is handled by the analyst.	36,740
6 **Junior Analyst.** Working under rather close supervision, junior analysts handle routine assignments. Editing and coding of questionnaires, statistical calculations above the clerical level, and simpler forms of library research are among their duties. A large portion of the junior analyst's time is spent on tasks assigned by superiors.	23,120
7 **Librarian.** The librarian builds and maintains a library of reference sources adequate to the needs of the research department.	35,000
8 **Clerical Supervisor.** In larger departments, the central handling and processing of statistical data are the responsibilities of one or more clerical supervisors. Duties include work scheduling and responsibility for accuracy.	31,300
9 **Field Work Director.** Usually only larger departments have a field work director who fires, trains, and supervises field interviewers.	25,430
10 **Full-Time Interviewer.** The interviewer conducts personal interviews and works under direct supervision of the field work director. Few companies employ full-time interviewers.	16,100
11 **Tabulating and Clerical Help.** The routine, day-to-day work of the department is performed by these individuals.	22,930

Source: Thomas C. Kinnear and Ann R. Root, *Survey of Marketing Research* (Chicago: American Marketing Association, 1995).

Monday A.M.	Returned from Boston after completing a set of interviews with engineers about the potential for a new electrical component we have developed; interviewed a total of 20 engineers in 6 industries.
	P.M.	Began writing report on the project.
Tuesday A.M.	Met with director of sales to design study on sales force turnover.
	P.M.	Gave oral report to top management on corporate image advertising results.

Wednesday A.M.	Met with Department of Commerce people to find if they had industry data on the potential for one of our products.
P.M.	Worked with data provided to try to make an estimate.
Thursday	Flew to Chicago to talk to trade association people about their database and our problems.
Friday A.M.	Began designing a new questionnaire for second round of corporate image advertising.
P.M.	Explained the type of work I do to a new analyst.

Dan Razinski, Supplier Analyst   The following is a typical week for Mr. Razinski, who works for a full-service research supplier.

Monday	Met with client to give findings on branding study; handed in written report, gave oral presentation.
Tuesday A.M.	Prepared bid for field work portion of national study by large petroleum company.
P.M.	Made call on new director of research at large company; explained why we should be one of their suppliers.
Wednesday	Worked on study design for product taste test as directed by client.
Thursday A.M.	Briefed interviewers on media habits questionnaire, made sure their task was clear.
P.M.	Flew to Los Angeles for Friday presentation.
Friday	Made oral presentation to client on study; discussed possible follow-up work.

These three analysts have much in common. They all give oral and written reports, define problems in concert with management, design studies, and execute parts of studies and delegate parts to other people.

Note that the industrial products analyst and the consumer products analyst perform similar functions, except that the sample sizes used for industrial products are smaller and more time is spent searching out secondary data and doing interviewing.

Consumer and Industrial Marketing Research

We need to stress further some of the differences between marketing research in consumer organizations and marketing research in industrial product organizations. Table 2-4 presents a summary of the major differences that relate to the areas of size of populations dealt with, respondent accessibility, respondent cooperation, sample sizes used, respondent definition, interviewers, and study costs. As Table 2-4 indicates, there are many differences arising from the nature of the products and markets for the two types of organizations.

Despite these differences, the underlying methods and skills are the same for both consumer and industrial marketing research. Both are concerned with problem definition, research design, use of secondary data, sampling, measurement, field work, data processing and analysis, and presentation of results. One practicing researcher with experience in both areas of marketing research has noted:

TABLE 2-4   CONSUMER VERSUS INDUSTRIAL MARKETING RESEARCH; WHAT ARE THE DIFFERENCES?

	Consumer	Industrial
Universe/ population	Large. Dependent on category under investigation but usually unlimited. Consists of 110 million U.S. households and 250 million persons.	Small. Fairly limited in total population and even more so if within a defined industry or Standard Industrial Classification (SIC) category.
Respondent accessibility	Fairly easy. Can interview at home, on the telephone, or using mail techniques.	Difficult. Usually only during working hours at plant, office, or on the road. Respondent is usually preoccupied with other priorities.
Respondent cooperation	Over the years has become more and more difficult to obtain; yet millions of consumers have never been interviewed.	A major concern. Due to the small population, the industrial respondent is being overresearched. The purchaser and decision makers in an industrial firm are the buyers of a variety of products and services from office supplies to heavy equipment.
Sample size	Can usually be drawn as large as required for statistical confidence since the population is in the hundreds of millions.	Usually much smaller than consumer sample, yet the statistical confidence is equal due to the relationship of the sample to the total population.
Respondent definitions	Usually fairly simple. Those aware of a category or brand, users of a category or brand, demographic criteria, etc. The ultimate purchaser is also a user for most consumer products and services.	Somewhat more difficult. The user and the purchasing decision maker in most cases are not the same. Factory workers who use heavy equipment, secretaries who use typewriters, etc., are the users and, no doubt, are best able to evaluate these products and services. However, they tend not to be the ultimate purchasers and in many cases do not have any influence on the decision-making process.
Interviewers	Can usually be easily trained. They are also consumers and tend to be somewhat familiar with the area under investigation for most categories.	Difficult to find good executive interviewers. At least a working knowledge of the product class or subject being surveyed is essential. More than just a working knowledge is preferable.
Study costs	Key dictators of cost are sample size and incidence. Lower-incidence usage categories (for example, users of soft-moist dog food, powdered breakfast beverages) or demographic or behavioral screening criteria (attend a movie at least once a month, over 65 years of age, and do not have direct deposit of social security payments, etc.) can raise costs considerably.	Relative to consumer research, the critical element resulting in significantly higher per-interview costs are: the lower incidence levels, the difficulties in locating the "right" respondent (that is, the purchase decision maker), and securing cooperation (time and concentration of effort) for the interview itself.

Many marketers and marketing researchers perceive consumer and industrial marketing research as two entirely different fields of endeavor. Having worked in both environments, I see more and more important similarities than differences.

Of course, the markets and respondents are different, but the skillful marketing researcher can apply her or his art to an infinite variety of markets, products, and services in both the consumer and industrial environments. The theory and basic skills required are the same.

Whether it's a consumer or industrial marketing research study:

- The overall administration, design, execution, and analysis of research tend to follow the same basic rules and procedures;
- The research study design should address the problem and the information needed in a valid and reliable manner;
- The data processing procedures—coding, editing, and weighting—are consistent;
- The analysis of data requires the same type of skill and knowledge;
- The marketing researcher in a business environment is a problem solver and marketing consultant; and
- The researcher's "tools of the trade" are the application of valid and reliable research techniques to uncover information that aids in problem solution and helps make a better business or marketing decision.[3]

The service sector is also now learning to effectively utilize marketing research, as the Marriott example illustrates.

As can be seen, analysts work in an organizational context. The next section discusses the organization of the marketing research function in corporations.

IMPLEMENTING MARKETING RESEARCH INTERNATIONALLY

Although the skills and methods needed remain constant whatever the context or location of the implementation of marketing research, there are many cultural and institutional differences that are important to consider in working with marketing research in different parts of the world. Some of these are noted in the Global Marketing Research Dynamics. The key conclusion about this is that marketing researchers must learn the appropriate cultural and social dimensions related to the implementation of marketing research in whatever part of the world they are working. This requires in-depth study beyond what we can report here.

GLOBAL MARKETING RESEARCH DYNAMICS

UNDERSTANDING THE DIFFERENT PARTS OF THE WORLD FOR MORE EFFECTIVE MARKETING RESEARCH

Each part of the world has unique characteristics in relation to marketing research. Understanding these differences is imperative for effective collection and utilization of marketing research. Describing each region of the world's marketing research dynamics would require a complete book by itself. The following examples illustrate some of these dimensions for just a few regions.

[3]Marvin Katz, "Use Same Theory, Skills for Consumer, Industrial Research," *Marketing News,* p. 16, January 12, 1979. Used with permission.

An Amoco Oil natural gas plant in Egypt.

The Middle East

In an oil company such as Amoco Oil, marketing research must operate effectively in both Western and Middle Eastern cultures. Marketing research in the Western world tends to be strict and highly structured. It can be summarized by five basic responsibilities: (1) score keeping on products, services and customers, (2) evaluating strengths and weaknesses, (3) anticipating problems and opportunities, (4) stimulating and encouraging ideas, and (5) information gathering and retrieving.

In stark contrast, the Middle Eastern culture is more freewheeling, resembling a bazaar that emphasizes one-on-one interactions. Charm and personal relationships are almost more important than the product. Marketing research in the Middle East must take into account the needs and wants of many different factions, including customers, suppliers, government officials, and internal buyers who are the actual "clients" of the marketing research staff. In order to be effective and to sell ideas and recommendations, marketing researchers must first research the clients. They must thoroughly understand the clients' needs and wants. In the Middle East, marketing the staff themselves to the clients is as important as marketing the clients' products and services to their target groups.

Asia

Western marketing researchers have many perceptual biases about the Asian market. They must overcome these myths in order to increase the effectiveness of their research. Asia is not a homogeneous continent. The presence of the English language does not indicate prevalence of Westernized consumption patterns. There is not significant marketing cross-fertilization among Asian countries. And marketing expertise has developed at different rates and in different ways than in the United States.

Aside from these biases, four basic problems usually affect market research in

Asia: (1) Attitudes toward research vary from country to country in Asia, as do reactions to pricing, distribution, and promotion strategies. Asians generally respond differently to being interviewed than Americans do. Low literacy rates in some countries lower the effectiveness of written questionnaires. Pricing studies may be skewed by the fact that many Asians equate high prices with high quality. (2) Research capabilities and techniques are inconsistent across Asian countries. Japan, Hong Kong, Singapore, and the Philippines have fairly advanced Western-style techniques. The governments in some countries, such as Japan and Taiwan, collect and release enough significant census data to build better samples than is possible in most Western countries. Other countries are years behind. In many Asian countries, including both those with sophisticated and those with unsophisticated research techniques, actual market conditions are often not available through official channels, requiring that regional marketing managers be on site to know the actual markets and what methods and actions will work best under the prevailing conditions. (3) Databases collected in various Asian countries are often not comparable. Censuses are conducted in different years and use different criteria, as well as different tabulating breaks. Governments gather information based on their own needs, with little regard to the needs or interests of their neighboring countries or outside agencies. (4) Asia is undergoing higher rates of change than most of Europe and North America. Changes in discretionary income, laws, and regulations have great effect on the various countries' consumption patterns. The higher the rate of change, the more difficult it is to forecast the future.

Source: Edited from Sabra E. Brock, ''Marketing Research in Asia: Problems, Opportunities, and Lessons,'' *Marketing Research,* pp. 44–51, September 1989; Abdul C. Azhari and Joseph M. Kamen, ''Marketing Research at Amoco Oil: The Culture, the Principles, and the Contributions,'' *Marketing Research,* pp. 3–10, June 1989.

ORGANIZATION FOR MARKETING RESEARCH

This section considers the question ''Where should the marketing research function be positioned within an organizational structure?'' Unfortunately, there is no easy or technically right way to answer this question, for two reasons. First, every organization will differ in the relative importance attached to marketing research and the scale and complexity of research methods employed. Therefore, the marketing research department should be custom-tailored to fit the firm's informational requirements. Second, within each firm the organization of the research department is inevitably going to demonstrate dynamism. Despite these limitations, it is possible to give a company and its officers some guidelines as to where the research department should be located within its organization. This discussion applies most directly to large organizations. More will be said about smaller research operations later.

Centralized Organization

The first structural option to be considered is that of completely centralizing the research function of a company by locating it at corporate headquarters. In such

TABLE 2-5 CENTRALIZED ORGANIZATION

Advantages
1 Effective coordination and control of the research activity is possible.
2 Encouragement of economical and flexible use of facilities and personnel occurs.
3 Increased usefulness and objectivity of research results to corporate executives develops.
4 Greater prestige to marketing research occurs.
5 Better likelihood of attracting top-notch researchers is possible.
6 Cross-fertilization of ideas occurs.
7 Greater likelihood of obtaining an adequate budget is possible.

Disadvantages
1 Isolates researchers from day-to-day activities and problems.
2 Corporate problems receive all the time and attention, at the expense of the divisions.
3 Separates researchers from the action programs based on the research; takes no responsibility for their implemented recommendations.

a case, all research is under the control of the vice president in charge of marketing. Table 2-5 shows the advantages and disadvantages of this structure.

Decentralized Organization

The second option open to a divisionalized firm wishing to position its marketing research function is to completely decentralize the department along divisional lines. In this system, the marketing researcher is responsible to the division manager and not to a top corporate executive. Divisions of companies may be organized by products, by customers, or by geographic regions. The divisional assignment of research personnel exactly parallels the type of divisional basis used by the company. Thus, research people are expected to become expert in the research problems of particular products, customer markets, or geographic regions. In many cases, decentralization's advantages and disadvantages are inverse arguments of our previous discussion on centralization. Still, there are a few pros and cons that should be highlighted. Table 2-6 lists these advantages and disadvantages.

Integrated Organization

A viable alternative form to the extremes of centralization and decentralization has proved to be the "integrated" organization structure. This increasingly popular research structure makes use of a central staff (which includes a highly qualified marketing research function) available as needed to counsel with and reinforce individual research departments within each division. This central staff is responsible to a top-level corporate executive, usually the vice president in charge of marketing. Divisional work is conducted by division research staffs directly re-

TABLE 2-6   DECENTRALIZED ORGANIZATION

Advantages
1 Researchers are close to the action of marketing problems and implementation of their recommendations.
2 More specialization is available on product, customers, or markets.
3 More attention will be paid by divisional managers to marketing research.
4 Breakdown of the corporate/divisional barriers can occur.

Disadvantages
1 Tendency to bias results in favor of the marketing group for which the researcher works.
2 Inadequate research controls, standards, and procedures.
3 Difficulty in finding qualified people.
4 High cost.
5 Duplication of effort.
6 Central management needs not attended to.

sponsible to division managers. Their research projects deal with divisional marketing problems. The thought behind this matrix organization is that it combines the best features of centralization and decentralization into one effective system. Unfortunately, there are also pluses and minuses to this type of research structure.

All the advantages of the hybrid relationship can be summed up as "more coordinated and effective research." Both levels of the research function contribute to this process. The central research staff arranges for the exchange of pertinent marketing data to the various divisions, acts as a central purchasing agent for all services common to the needs of the research teams, and carries out research projects with companywide implications. In addition, the central corporate staff sets and explains company research standards, undertakes projects for departments too small to have their own research staffs, and assists divisional research staffs when they become overloaded with research requests. By having additional research teams located at the divisional level, a company achieves its goal of making the research function part of the firm's marketing team. This allows researchers to become experts in their fields and places their information-gathering techniques closer to the consumer of research.

The main disadvantage to the integrated system is the potential occurrence of control conflicts over the research staffs and their projects. Control conflicts can result when the lines of authority in a company are not clearly delineated. Theoretically, the central research staff is organized solely as a helping, advisory branch. But all too often, divisional researchers look to corporate staffers as their ultimate bosses instead of to their divisional heads. Any other disadvantages inherent in the integrated system resemble the disadvantages attributed to decentralized research departments—such as high cost, duplication of efforts, and lack of an adequate number of competent specialists. Nonetheless, the control-conflict problem is by far the most serious obstacle to implementing the integrated marketing research system.

Choosing a Structure

Now that the main alternatives to organizing the marketing research function have been outlined, the question becomes: "How is one to choose the structure that is 'best' for one's particular firm?" There are no simple answers, no handy "cookbook" ways to determine the optimum choice. There are, however, a number of criteria which can be followed to help narrow the selection alternatives. In the final analysis, there is no completely right or wrong organizational structure for marketing research in a firm.

The first criterion, and perhaps the most important, is this: the marketing research function should be placed where the marketing decisions are made. The researcher's task is to provide information to marketers to help them in their decision-making process. At whatever level decision making is performed, the research function should be there to help. For example, if a firm makes one or two industrial products for a few customers, a research staff located at the corporate level might suffice. However, if the firm is like General Foods, which produces myriad products for a host of different customers, it would be better to decentralize or integrate the research function. This would allow all market information to be closer to the person who uses it. In essence, the research function should reside where the marketing decision-making power resides. Figure 2-3 shows General Foods' integrative structure.

The second criterion to consider when organizing the research department is: researchers should be free from undue influence or manipulation by those areas or people for whom they conduct research projects. A third criterion is: the marketing research function should be organized so that the firm can satisfy the demand for research projects quickly and efficiently. If the firm's divisions exhibit a steady volume of requests for research projects, it would be advisable to decentralize the research function. On the other hand, if the demand for research within a firm is sparse or fluctuates widely, it may be more expedient to centralize all research activities in a corporate office. The final criterion is a matter of practicality that many times is overlooked: the research department should report to an executive who has a genuine interest in marketing research, understands how it operates, knows its potentials, and possesses sufficient authority to ensure that the actions called for by the research are undertaken.

The effective functioning of a central marketing research department is illustrated in the Digital Equipment Corporation (DEC) Marketing Research in Action. At the time when this description of DEC's marketing research department was written, DEC was attempting to become more attuned to its market and to the competitive dynamics of its computer competitors. This was in response to declining market share, a shift in the market away from its traditional products, and the advent of new competitors, especially in the desktop computer arena.

UTILIZING RESEARCH SUPPLIERS

One situation that confronts all marketing research directors and a great many analysts is the utilization of research suppliers. These suppliers may be involved

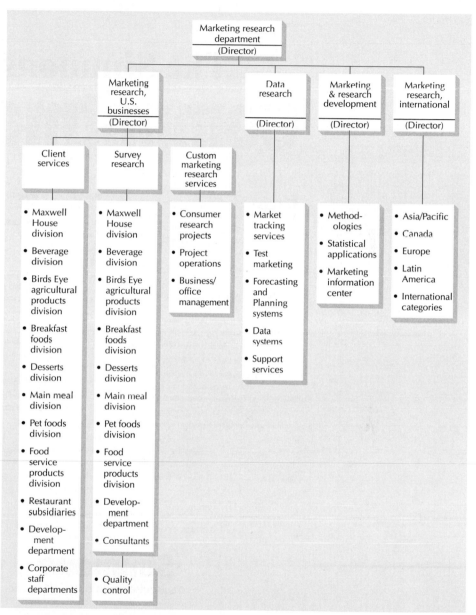

FIGURE 2-3   General Foods' marketing research organization. (*Source:* "Marketing Research: Career Opportunities at General Foods," General Foods Corporation, White Plains, NY.)

An ad for a marketing research supplier.

with a few aspects of a research study, or they may be given total responsibility for all aspects of a study.

The primary advantages of using research suppliers include: (1) the cost may be less than that of hiring additional personnel and paying the other costs of an internal project; (2) the supplier costs to the user are a variable cost, whereas internal personnel constitute a fixed expense—that is, if the workload varies in the department, outside suppliers can be used at peak times only; (3) suppliers offer special skills not available internally; (4) the users of outside services retain great flexibility, as they can pick the best supplier available for a specific type of problem; (5) outside suppliers have greater objectivity and are usually not involved in the politics of specific problems; (6) the sponsoring company can remain anonymous.

We must also recognize some disadvantages in the use of research suppliers. These are: (1) the outside service firm may not be completely familiar with the objectives and problems of the company and/or industry; (2) there is a risk, especially in the first purchase from a supplier, that the research will not be done well or on time; (3) there is a greater risk that results of studies or company activities will become known to competitors; (4) the costs can be higher, as suppliers must earn a profit that allows for slack periods and for studies that lose money.

Selecting a Supplier

Just how does one go about selecting a specific supplier for a project? First of all, a list of possible firms must be drawn up. Learning about and evaluating suppliers are subjects in which word-of-mouth influences are high. Buyers seek recommendations from associates within their company, from other researchers outside their company, and from advertising agencies, trade associations, and even university professors. Impersonal sources such as trade publications, professional directories,[4] journals, and promotional material of suppliers may also provide prospective supply firms.

MARKETING RESEARCH IN ACTION

AT DIGITAL EQUIPMENT, CENTRAL MARKETING RESEARCH HELPS WITH THE TURNAROUND

Digital Equipment Corporation (DEC) has fallen on hard times in the marketplace recently, which has resulted in poor financial performance. Thus, DEC is completing a difficult transition from a product-focused to a market-driven strategy. In this transition, DEC's Corporate Marketing Services (CMS) has served as a catalyst for and

[4]For example, see *International Directory of Marketing Research Houses and Services* (New York: Marketing Review, New York Chapter of the American Marketing Association); Ernest S. Bradford, *Bradford's Directory of Marketing Research Agencies and Management Consultants* (Fairfax, VA); and *A Geographic Listing of Marketing Consultants and Research Agencies* (Chicago: American Marketing Association).

coordinator of the company's voice of the market activities. CMS, in its role as the focal point, functions as the voice of the market.

Challenges of Computer Industry Marketing Research

The computer industry offers unique challenges for marketing research. Technology has its own logical development, almost independent of market considerations. Traditionally, there has been no direct connection between articulated and known customer needs and new-product technologies, making the market for high-technology products highly unpredictable. The vast size of the computer market, from the number and types of computers in existence to the varied functions they perform in diverse business organizations, contributes to that ambiguity on both the consumer and the producer sides of the market. Computer technology also changes very rapidly.

CMS acts as a communication center in this complex environment. Understanding the technological capabilities and potential of the computer industry, CMS staff investigate the problems, solutions, needs, and opportunities that exist on the consumer side of the market and translate this data into information that can be used by Digital to drive technology in market-defined directions. As part of this process, CMS offers fee-based primary and secondary research services for client managers throughout Digital. CMS staff work with these clients to understand their businesses, allowing CMS to better define research objectives and subsequently to develop more effective analyses and recommendations. Both CMS and its internal clients benefit from this open relationship, a situation that is not possible with external firms in an industry where confidentiality is a major key to competitive success.

CMS's primary research activities include the following: (1) Telephone surveys of customers questioning the direction of specific products and related customer needs. (2) Large mail surveys to study customers' long-range purchasing plans and requirements. (3) Two-way seminars with selected customers to solicit feedback on Digital's long-range product plans. (4) Focus groups (composed of customers, suppliers, and business partners) for product and marketing business units.

Vast amounts of secondary data are also available, including both raw data sources and external marketing research firms. This information covers all segments of the computer industry and includes detailed descriptions of the installed computer base worldwide, estimates of market share, predictions for market growth, product comparisons, computer vendor analyses, and technology trend forecasting. This body of information is immense, very general, and often developed from definitions and methodologies that vary among the different firms. CMS converts this mountain of data into user-friendly information through various quality management functions. The staff members coordinate cross-company data acquisition. They evaluate and disseminate information about the quality of external marketing research sources. They survey the internal business units to find out about their specific marketing research needs. And they educate the external market research firms about Digital's marketing research needs. CMS also designs, develops, and maintains corporate databases that provide news, information, and analysis on Digital's markets, accounts, competitors, and targeted industries.

Source: Adapted from Peter Jancourtz and Gil Press, ''Digital Hears the Voice of the Market,'' *Marketing Research: A Magazine of Management & Applications,* pp. 28–33, December 1992.

The evaluation of prospective suppliers usually involves direct contacts with the firms, discussions with other people for whom they have done work, and the examination of some piece of research they have done. These information sources are used to collect information about the criteria that will be used to make the actual choice. These criteria may include (1) the capabilities of individuals who will be assigned to the project, (2) the degree of specialization needed and provided, (3) technical competence, (4) orientation toward marketing management, (5) education of staff, (6) personal characteristics of key personnel, (7) facilities (field work, data processing, analysis), (8) creativity, (9) ethics, (10) communication skills, (11) ability to perform on time, (12) location close to buyer to allow for better communication, (13) stability, and (14) cost of the project.

The list of firms may be reduced using these criteria, and then the remaining firms may be asked to submit proposals. Proposals are usually provided to prospective clients without charge. The average cost to the supplier of preparing a proposal is $5000 to $8000, with the high end being about $30,000 for a large project. The quality of the proposal constitutes another criterion on which firms would be evaluated.

Sometimes competitive bids for a project are asked for, but this approach is not now a significant way of selecting a supplier. Only between 15 and 20 percent of business involves competitive bidding. The rest comes through negotiations. Furthermore, the majority of suppliers of ad hoc studies refuse to bid competitively, and firms that do bid usually face only one or two other firms in the competition. Most perceive that price is ranked low on a list of important factors for firms choosing a supplier. Quality of work, understanding of the problem, reputation, integrity, experience, referrals, personality of key people, skill of individuals assigned to projects, specialization, and personal contact all ranked higher in perceived importance.

As in all buying decisions, customers will find some brands they prefer over others. Thus, most experienced buyers of research develop a short list of suppliers with whom they deal on a regular basis. It is often difficult for a new firm to get on the approved list.

Ground Rules for Buyer-Supplier Relationships

In the interaction between the buyers of research and the suppliers, certain ground rules should apply. The supplier should be able to expect certain things from the buyer. These include:

1 A statement of the general background of the management problem at hand
2 A statement of the management problem
3 A statement of the research problem and objectives, and the use to which the research result will be put
4 A chance to discuss these problem statements and background
5 A range of budget available for the project
6 The desired timing
7 An assurance that the supplier will be approached only when there is a reasonable expectation that the buyer will select it

The supplier also must be able to satisfy certain requirements of the buyer. In general, the supplier must provide information on the list of criteria the buyer is using in making the selection.

Most clients desiring marketing research require that all interested research firms submit a proposal for research. Because this proposal is vital in securing a marketing research contract, we will spend some time discussing how a good proposal is put together.

The topics listed below create guidelines around which to write a research proposal. The number of topics covered in the proposal will depend upon the size of the project. Obviously, the proposal for a million-dollar research project will cover more topics and go into much greater depth than the proposal for a $5000 project. You must use common sense to determine which topics to include in any specific proposal.

Topics to Consider

1 *Problem.* The problem (or opportunity) must be clearly defined. Does it affect only one area of the firm or agency, or is it companywide? What are the underlying causes of the decision situation?

2 *Objectives.* What are the decision objectives? What does management expect to gain from research? Objectives should be stated clearly and concisely.

3 *Alternatives.* What are the alternative courses of action?

4 *Information needs.* What information is needed? How will it be gathered? State your initial plan and organization, search of literature, interviews, questionnaires, experiments, and so forth.

5 *Personnel qualifications.* Cite your experience and success with problems of a similar nature. Include dates and references (with permission, of course) so your statements can be verified. Also, give job descriptions, names, and one-page résumés of key personnel who will be working on the project.

6 *Evaluation.* State how the data will be handled and stored. Tell whether or not the project can be duplicated in other branches of the company or other areas of the country. Show how you will evaluate the project while it is under way, and how you will determine whether to continue, change, or terminate it. What criteria will be used to recommend the best alternative? What is the likelihood of success? Be realistic—don't promise more than you can deliver.

7 *Budget.* Do not overbudget: a padded budget is quickly rejected. Show clients where their money will go—list the salaries, equipment and supplies, travel requirements, miscellaneous expenses and indirect costs, and allowances for the unexpected. Provide justification for each budget item.

8 *An accurate timetable.* After the appropriate topics have been covered in rough-draft form, assemble these answers in a logical, coherent format, such as the one presented below.

1 Prefatory parts

Letter of transmittal (a short note accompanying the proposal which explains or justifies documents being transmitted)

Title page
Table of contents
List of tables (if any)
List of figures (if any)
2 Body of proposal
Introduction
   Problem
   Need
   Background
Objectives/purpose
Procedures
   Methods and sources
   Plan of attack
   Sequence of activities
   Equipment and facilities available
   Personnel qualifications
Evaluation
Budget
3 Supplementary parts
Agency forms
   Budget justification (if any)
   References
Tables or figures (if any)

Getting the highest quality from outside marketing research suppliers is of great concern to marketing research directors and analysts. It is necessary to maintain control of all aspects of the suppliers' work. Some practitioners suggest the approach presented in Table 2-7.

We can see that marketing research involves complex relationships among buyers and suppliers. Furthermore, in the process of collecting marketing research information, researchers are dealing with providers of the required information, who may be respondents to a survey, subjects in an experiment, and so on. In all relationships among buyers, suppliers, and providers, the chance for unethical behavior exists. Thus, a very relevant part of the domain of any practitioner of

---

TABLE 2-7   HOW TO IMPROVE OUTSIDE RESEARCH QUALITY

1 Increase your involvement—at the decision-making level—especially at the beginning stages of the research.
2 Use suppliers with qualified personnel.
3 Review the supplier's data validation procedures.
4 Maintain continual evaluation and individual assessment of your suppliers.
5 Use more than one supplier.
6 Get several proposals for each project.
7 Ask the supplier's views on the research findings' implications.
8 Get involved in the specifications of the tabulation (data analysis).
9 Consult with outside agencies about the reputation of the outside agencies under consideration.

EXHIBIT 2-1

AMERICAN MARKETING ASSOCIATION'S MARKETING RESEARCH CODE OF ETHICS

For Research Users, Practitioners, and Interviewers

1 No individual or organization will undertake any activity which is directly or indirectly represented to be marketing research, but which has as its real purpose the attempted sale of merchandise or services to some or all of the respondents interviewed in the course of the research.

2 If a respondent has been led to believe, directly or indirectly, that he is participating in a marketing research survey and that his anonymity will be protected, his name shall not be made known to anyone outside the research organization or research department, or used for other than research purposes.

For Research Practitioners

1 There will be no intentional or deliberate misrepresentation of research methods or results. An adequate description of methods employed will be made available upon request to the sponsor of the research. Evidence that field work has been completed according to specifications will, upon request, be made available to buyers of research.

2 The identity of the survey sponsor and/or the ultimate client for whom a survey is being done will be held in confidence at all times, unless this identity is to be revealed as part of the research design. Research information shall be held in confidence by the research organization or department and not used for personal gain or made available to any outside party unless the client specifically authorizes such release.

3 A research organization shall not undertake marketing studies for competitive clients when such studies would jeopardize the confidential nature of client-agency relationships.

For Users of Marketing Research

1 A user of research shall not knowingly disseminate conclusions from a given research project or service that are inconsistent with or not warranted by the data.

2 To the extent that there is involved in a research project a unique design involving techniques, approaches, or concepts not commonly available to research practitioners, the prospective user of research shall not solicit such a design from one practitioner and deliver it to another for execution without the approval of the design originator.

For Field Interviewers

1 Research assignments and materials received, as well as information obtained from respondents, shall be held in confidence by the interviewer and revealed to no one except the research organization conducting the marketing study.

2 No information gained through a marketing research activity shall be used, directly or indirectly, for the personal gain or advantage of the interviewer.

3 Interviews shall be conducted in strict accordance with specifications and instructions received.

4 An interviewer shall not carry out two or more interviewing assignments simultaneously unless authorized by all contractors or employees concerned.

Members of the American Marketing Association will be expected to conduct themselves in accordance with the provisions of this code in all of their marketing research activities.

---

marketing research is to be aware of the ethics of the field. This is the topic to which we now direct our attention.

ETHICS

Ethics as related to marketing research deal with the judgment that (1) certain types of activities are inappropriate, and (2) certain types of activities must be undertaken. An example of the former would be the prohibition against using marketing research as a trick to sell products. An example of the latter would be to present to a client the details of how a sample was selected. Ethical issues arise in both the relationship between users and doers of research and the relationship between doers and providers (respondents) of research data.

Codes of Ethics

Because of actual and potential abuses in these areas, a number of codes of ethics have been developed to guide researchers. Exhibit 2-1 presents Marketing Research Code of Ethics of the American Marketing Association (AMA).

This code deals with user-doer and doer-provider relationships. Some people feel that the code does not go far enough, as it deals mostly with prohibition. The Market Research Council developed a code of ethics that deals with things that ought to be done in marketing research. Shown in Exhibit 2-2, the code gives details on what should be included in a marketing research report. Both of these codes focus on ethical issues between users and doers and deal with some issues between respondents and doers-users as well.

The ethical dimensions of marketing research will confront anyone who works in marketing research or even in marketing management. What would you do if (1) a study design error came to your attention after a report was written, (2) a study design required that respondents be misled as to the actual purpose of a study, or (3) a manager deliberately withheld details of a study in order to make his or her pet project look better? These and other similar situations are tough to deal with, since questions of ethical standards, not law, are involved.

EXHIBIT 2-2

MARKET RESEARCH COUNCIL'S CODE OF ETHICS

The Respondent's Right to Privacy

The goodwill and cooperation of the public are necessary to successful public opinion and market research. Actions by researchers which tend to dilute or dissipate these resources do a disservice both to the research profession and to the public.

By its very nature, research must in some measure invade the privacy of respondents. The ringing of a respondent's doorbell or his telephone is an intrusion. If he agrees to participate in a study, his private world of attitudes, knowledge, and behavior is further invaded.

Researchers should recognize that the public has no obligation to cooperate in a study. Overly long interviews and subject matter which causes discomfort or apprehension serve to reduce respondent cooperation.

When such interviews cannot be avoided, efforts should be made to explain the reasons to the respondent and to mitigate his anxieties to the extent possible.

One of the greatest invasions of the privacy of respondents is through the use of research techniques such as hidden microphones and cameras. When such a technique has been used, a respondent should be told and, if the respondent requests it, any portion of the interview that serves to identify the respondent should be deleted.

Even after the respondent has been interviewed, his privacy is endangered while his interview is being coded, processed, and analyzed. Research agencies have the same responsibility as other professional groups to take all reasonable steps to insure that employees with access to these data observe the canons of good taste and discretion in handling this information.

Since public opinion and market researchers must

infringe on the privacy of the public at several stages of the research process, it is unlikely that any set of rules or code of ethics can prevent abuses by unscrupulous or careless researchers, even though such abuses are inexcusable. The best hope of maintaining an attitude of goodwill and cooperation among the public will depend on researchers':

1 Being constantly mindful of the problem
2 Keeping in mind the recommendations above
3 Doing everything in their power to inform the public of the benefits of market and opinion research

Maintaining Respondent Anonymity

Good and accurate research requires obtaining honest and frank expressions of opinions and beliefs. Respondents are more likely (a) to participate in a survey and (b) to speak honestly and frankly if they believe that they will remain anonymous and will not be called to account for their expressed opinions or stated behavior. For this reason, every researcher should do everything in his power to protect the anonymity of the people he interviews unless he obtains their permission to reveal their names.

This does not preclude follow-up contacts for further research or for verification purposes. However, if there seems to be a reasonable possibility that there will be contacts for any other purposes, it is incumbent on the researcher to warn the respondent of this possibility.

The researcher should be willing to make reasonable efforts to provide evidence on the authenticity of the interviews he has made, providing this does not subject the respondent to harassment.

Disclosure or Release of Survey Results

Implicit in the nature of surveys is the fact that they purport to reflect the opinions or behavior of the population under study. It is the obligation of the researcher to present survey results in such a manner that they do not give a distorted or biased picture of his findings. The client also has this same obligation in reporting survey findings. When others report his findings, the researcher has an additional responsibility to make all reasonable effort to see that they, likewise, present the results impartially.

It is not incumbent on the researcher to insist on an "all-or-nothing" policy in the release of his findings. Only part of the results may be released provided this part does not give a distorted picture of the subject matter it covers.

If the client misuses, misstates, or distorts a survey finding, the researcher should release such other findings and information about how the data were obtained as will put it in proper perspective. Client-researcher agreement prior to release would minimize misunderstandings in this respect.

Any release of findings should include appropriate information about objectives, sample, research techniques, the name of the research organization, etc., that will be helpful in evaluating the results.

Buyer-Seller Relationships

A successful marketing research study is a joint operation involving a research company and its client. It requires mutual respect and confidence between the two parties and imposes certain obligations on each of them.

The buyer of research services has the right to make sure that the work he has contracted for meets all the specifications. He has the right to examine all operations of the research company to see that they are being carried out in the manner agreed upon. However, in doing so he should respect the research company's obligations to the public in matters of anonymity and invasion of respondents' privacy.

The buyer should recognize that the research company is a professional organization engaged in collecting marketing and/or opinion data. The buyer should not, therefore, ask or expect the research company to violate any of the suggested rules of procedure covered elsewhere in this statement. The buyer should not publicly identify the research agency in any release of findings, implying the endorsement of the research agency without prior agreement from the agency.

It is understood that in seeking a research agency the buyer may request proposals from more than one research company. However, generating ideas and planning research designs to solve specific problems are an important part of the services a research agency offers. The buyer, therefore, should not (1) lift ideas from one proposal and give them to another research agency or (2) ask for a proposal from a company which he knows has little or no chance of obtaining his business, unless he so informs them in advance. Soliciting bids for the purpose of obtaining free ideas which will be turned over to another bidder, or for purely technical compliance with a company's policy of obtaining competitive bids, does a disservice to the research firms involved, reflects on the integrity of the client company, and generally lessens the professional level of the research profession.

Kickbacks, rebates, and other "inducements" similarly destroy the professional character of research and should not be solicited, offered, or agreed to.

The research agency has the obligation to express, as they become apparent, any reservations about the usefulness of the proposed research in solving the client's problem. The agency also has the obligation, of course, to do the study contracted for in the manner agreed on. No additional questions designed for another purpose should be included in interviews done for a client without the client's knowledge and consent.

Unless otherwise agreed on by the seller and the buyer, the study report and the compiled tabulated data on which it is based are the property of the buyer. No by-product information should be sold to another buyer unless express permission is obtained from the original buyer.

In the course of conducting research, the researcher may become privy to confidential information relating to the client company. The researcher should not reveal any of this material to any outsider at any time.

Information to Be Included in the Research Firm's Report

Every research project differs from all others. So will every research report. All reports should nonetheless contain specific references to the following items:

1 The objectives of the study (including statement of hypotheses)
2 The name of the organization for which the study [was] made and the name of the organization that conducted it
3 Dates the survey was in the field and date of submission of final report

4 A copy of the full interview questionnaire, including all cards and visual aids used in the interview; alternatively, exact question wording, sequence of questions, etc.
5 Description of the universe(s) studied
6 Description of the number and types of people studied:
  a Number of people (or other units)
  b Means of their selection
  c If sample, method of sample selection
  d Adequacy of sample representatives and size
  e Percentage of original sample contacted (number and type of callbacks)
  f Range of tolerance
  g Number of cases for category breakouts
  h Weighting and estimating procedures used

Where trend data are being reported and the methodology or question wording has been changed, these changes should be so noted.

On request—clients and other parties with legitimate interests may request and should expect to receive from the research firm the following:

  a Statistical and/or field methods of interview verification (and percentage of interviews verified)
  b Available data re validation of interview techniques
  c Interviewing instructions
  d Explanation of scoring or index number devices

Source: Paper developed by The Market Research Council's Ethics Committee. Reprinted with permission from Leo Bogart.

SUMMARY

1 The history of marketing research parallels the rise of the marketing concept. Early practitioners were concerned with gathering information on markets and developing the applied aspects of survey research. The gradual shift to a focus on marketing research broadened the nature and role of research activities. The emphasis was on gathering information for marketing management decision making. Methodological development in marketing research parallels the development of research methodology in the social sciences. Early methodological development focused on data collection and sampling issues. More contemporary methodological advances relate to computer-based technologies for data analysis and interviewing.

2 Marketing research is a big and dynamic business.

3 Institutions in the marketing research business can be classified as users, users-doers, or doers.

4 Doers supply both ad hoc studies and syndicated data, on a full- or limited-service basis.

5 Careers are available as research directors, analysts, technical specialists, or clerical workers.

6 A firm may organize the marketing research function so that it is centralized, decentralized, or integrated.

7 There are many differences between consumer and industrial marketing research in the areas of population, respondent accessibility, respondent cooperation, sample size, respondent definitions, interviews, and study costs.

8 The fundamental marketing research process and required skills are the same for both consumer and industrial marketing research.

9 The effective use of outside marketing research suppliers is important.

10 Ethical issues arise in user-doer and doer-provider relationships. Various codes of ethics have been developed to direct researchers.

DISCUSSION QUESTIONS

1 What is the institutional structure of the marketing research business?

2 What type of person would make a good research analyst?

3 How can the marketing research function be organized?

4 What are the advantages and disadvantages of each organizational alternative?

5 On what basis should an organizational structure be selected?

6 How should a research supplier be selected?

7 What should buyers and suppliers of research expect from each other?

8 Should legal action be taken to regulate marketing research activity? If so, state specifics.

9 For the Marketing Research in Action at the beginning of this chapter, evaluate Marriott's use of a centralized marketing research function.

10 What type of marketing research organization would the following organizations logically have?

  a A large multidivision package goods company such as Procter & Gamble

  b A local pizza company with 15 locations

  c The university or college that you attend or attended

  d A large multidivision chemical company such as Monsanto Chemical

  e An industrial supply house that provides over 2000 items to industrial buyers

11 What role does central marketing research services play in marketing planning at Digital Equipment Corporation? (See Marketing Research in Action.) What might limit the effectiveness of this group?

12 How might the life of a marketing researcher change as he or she moved from an assignment in the United States, to one in the Middle East, and then to one in Asia? Be as specific as possible. (See Global Marketing Research Dynamics.)

13 MINICASE

Pacific Gas and Electric (PG&E) is one of the largest public utilities in the United States. As part of its activities, it both generates and transmits electric power to much of

California and the southwest. This power is marketed to industrial, commercial, and residential users. For most of its history, this has been done with PG&E holding a monopoly with its customers. The deregulation of the electric power industry will result in reasonably open competition for customers in all sectors by the late 1990s. How should PG&E structure a marketing research department to allow PG&F to effectively compete for customers? What activities should this department perform? What type of person should head this department? To whom should the head of this department report?

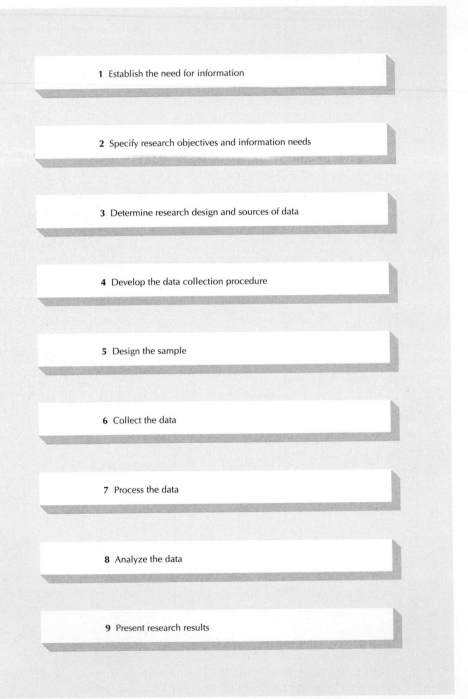

FIGURE 3-1 Steps in the research process.

CHAPTER 3

THE MARKETING RESEARCH PROCESS: CONCEPT AND EXAMPLE

This chapter is designed to (1) overview the stages of the marketing research process, (2) serve the frequently expressed desire of students to see what a marketing research project looks like, and (3) introduce the concept of errors in marketing research. The research project presented here is not intended to illustrate good or effective marketing research. The focus is on the stages of the research process and the types of research that can be utilized.

This chapter is also intended to serve as a unifying reference for the student reading subsequent chapters dealing with specialized aspects of the research process. At several points in the chapter, you may encounter terms and techniques which are new. In such cases, we have tried to identify the chapters where these are explained in detail. The intent is not to have you turn to these chapters for explanation but rather to develop an understanding of the sequencing and role of future topics as they relate to the marketing research process. When studying subsequent chapters dealing with specialized aspects of the research process, you may find that reference to this chapter will help to bring perspective to the area being studied.

THE RESEARCH PROCESS

The formal marketing research project can be viewed as a series of steps called the *research process.* Figure 3-1 illustrates the nine steps in this process. To effectively conduct a research project it is essential to anticipate all the steps and recognize their interdependence. These nine steps represent the framework for the chapters in the book. We will touch briefly on each of these steps in order to emphasize their sequencing and interdependence.

1   Need for Information

Establishing the need for marketing research information is, of course, the first step in the research process. Rarely does the manager's initial request for help adequately establish the need for research information. The researcher must thoroughly understand why the information is needed. The manager is responsible for explaining the situation surrounding the request for help and establishing that research information will facilitate the decision-making process. If the research project is to provide pertinent information for the decision making, the need for research information must be precisely defined. Chapter 4 will discuss this area in more detail along with issues related to the management-research interface.

Managers often react to hunches and symptoms rather than to clearly identified decision situations. Consequently, establishing the need for research information is a critical and difficult phase of the research process. Too often the importance of this initial step is overlooked in the excitement of undertaking a research project. This results in research findings that are not decision-oriented.

2   Research Objectives and Information Needs

Once the need for research information has been clearly established, the researcher must specify the objectives of the proposed research and develop a specific list of information needs. Research objectives answer the question "Why is this project being conducted?" Typically, research objectives are put in writing before the project is undertaken. Information needs answer the question, "What specific information is needed to attain the objectives?" In practice, information needs may be thought of as a detailed listing of research objectives.

3   Research Design and Data Sources

Once the study objectives have been determined and the information needs listed, the next step is to design the formal research project and identify the appropriate sources of data for the study. A research design is the basic plan that guides the data collection and analysis phases of the research project. It is the framework that specifies the type of information to be collected, the sources of data, and the data collection procedures and analysis.

Data sources can be internal or external to the organization. Internal sources include previous research studies and company records. External sources include commercial research reports, trade magazine or industry reports, and government reports. If data are found which fit the information needs, the researcher must examine the research design to determine their accuracy. The reputation of the organization that collected and analyzed the data is often a guide to reliability.

If the data are not available from internal or external sources, the next step is to collect new data by means of mail, telephone, and personal interviews; observation; experimentation; or simulation. The remaining steps in the research process relate to data collected through these sources.

4   Data Collection Procedure

In developing the data collection procedure, the researcher must establish an effective link between the information needs and the questions to be asked or the observations to be recorded. The success of the study is dependent upon the researcher's skill and creativity in establishing this link. The responsibility for this task rests mainly with the researcher.

5   Sample Design

The first issue in designing the sample concerns who or what is to be included in the sample. This means that a clear definition is needed of the population from which the sample is to be drawn. The next issue concerns the methods used to select the sample. These methods can be classified as to whether they involve a probability or a nonprobability procedure. The third issue involves the size of the sample.

6   Data Collection

The process of collecting data is critical since it typically involves a large proportion of the research budget and a large proportion of the total error in the research results. Consequently, the selection, training, and control of interviewers is essential to effective marketing research studies.

7   Data Processing

Once data have been recorded, the processing of the data begins. This includes the functions of editing and coding. Editing involves reviewing the data forms as to legibility, consistency, and completeness. Coding involves establishing categories for responses or groups of responses so that numerals can be used to represent the categories. The data are then ready for computer analysis.

8   Data Analysis

It is important that the data analysis be consistent with the requirements of the information needs identified in step 2. It is usually done using appropriate data analysis software packages.

9   Presentation of Results

The research results are typically communicated to the manager through a written report and an oral presentation. It is imperative that the research finding be presented in a simple format and addressed to the information needs of the decision situation. No matter what the proficiency with which all previous steps have been dispatched, the project will be no more successful than the research report.

EXAMPLE OF MARKETING RESEARCH

The research project described here was conducted for the Rigid Container Division of the Society of the Plastic Industry (SPI) by a leading marketing research firm. The Rigid Container Division of SPI represents the majority of U.S. manufacturers of rigid plastic containers. Many of these companies are small manufacturing units with limited marketing and marketing research capabilities. A six-member executive board administers the activities of the Rigid Container Division. The marketing research described here focuses on the part of the study that was domestic United States in content. There was an international component to the study, as SPI had a great deal of interest in global opportunities. The international component of the marketing research is briefly outlined at the end of this example.

Problem Recognition and Definition

In the last 20 years, the plastic packaging industry has experienced dynamic growth, making significant penetration into the markets of more conventional packaging materials such as paper, paperboard, glass, and metal. Sales of plastic packaging totaled around $9 billion in 1993, up from approximately $2 billion in 1970. Plastic containers represent about 10 percent of the industry volume.

Several SPI research studies indicated that rigid plastic containers offer important advantages over other container materials. The consumer advantages include their light weight, resistance to breakage, toughness, resealability, and potential for reuse. Plastic containers are attractive to producers in that they are often less expensive than other containers. They store easily because they can be "nested," a feature that reduces shipping costs and warehouse space. In addition, they can be printed with an unlimited variety of colors and designs.

Much of the growth in plastic container sales had stemmed from the initiative of food manufacturers in seeking new packaging concepts for new products being developed. An example of this situation was the development of soft margarine. The manufacturer had requested the development of a reusable container specifically designed for this new product. Similar situations could be cited for other plastic containers for dairy products. An example of a plastic container replacing the traditional package is found with cottage cheese. Here, the advantages of the plastic container were reflected in the consumer's preference for brands of cottage cheese packaged in plastic rather than paper containers. Today, plastic is the dominant packaging form for soft margarine and cottage cheese.

The future outlook for further penetration of the packaging business was optimistic, but expectations were for a much slower growth rate than had been experienced in the previous decade. There were several constraints on future growth:

1 Growing uncertainty regarding the cost of raw materials and the competitive influence this would have on container selection.

2 Future competitive moves from glass, metal, and paper manufacturers. Many of these firms were large and had extensive research and development (R&D) and marketing capabilities.

3 Debate over environmental and safety issues regarding packaging containers. The nonbiodegradable property of plastic was a matter of concern, and the SPI commissioned a leading marketing research firm to analyze the issues in this area. A report entitled "Resource and Environmental Profile Analysis of Plastic and Nonplastic Containers" was prepared.

4 Growing concern among SPI members that possibly the high potential markets for plastic containers had been saturated (for example, soft margarine and cottage cheese).

The rapid growth of plastic container sales over the last decade resulted in the modernization and expansion of production facilities to meet this demand. As a result, manufacturing capacity was currently in excess of demand for the majority of SPI members. It was the concern of these members that new markets for plastic products should be identified and programs developed to capture the market potential. Such action would help solve the excess-capacity problem and would continue the trend of plastic penetration of the container industry. Consequently, the executive board of the Rigid Container Division of SPI concluded that a marketing research study was needed to identify and evaluate the market opportunities for rigid plastic containers.

A leading marketing research firm in Chicago was recommended by the SPI New York office as highly qualified to conduct the study. A preliminary meeting was then arranged. The SPI representatives included a staff member from the New York office and three members representing the Rigid Container Division executive board. The three board members were managers of plastic container manufacturing operations. The purpose of the meeting was to explain why marketing research information was needed. This was to be accomplished by a series of presentations which characterized the plastic container industry and the past, current, and future situation that faced the industry. The previous discussion on problem recognition and definition summarizes the focus of this initial meeting with the marketing research firm. At the end of this meeting, the research firm requested one week to review the problem situation and formulate specific questions.

At the second meeting, the research firm requested a formal statement of objectives and potential courses of action available for reaching the objectives. A lengthy discussion was required before the SPI members committed themselves to specific statements in this regard. They indicated that these two matters had been discussed previously but only in general terms. The SPI members finally agreed to the following statement:

I SPI objective: To increase the market penetration of plastic containers to 30 percent by 1998.

II Courses of action:

A Develop and implement a marketing program to maintain or improve the acceptance of plastic containers in markets where plastic now dominates.

B Develop and implement a marketing program to expand the acceptance of plastic containers in markets where plastic has a low or moderate penetration.

C Develop and implement a marketing program to enter new markets currently dominated by paper, paperboard, glass, or metal.

D Develop and implement a marketing program to work actively with manufacturers of new products.

The discussion turned to the type of information needed to select and implement one or more of the alternatives identified. Again, a lengthy discussion followed, reflecting the complexity of the problem (see Chapter 4).

The Problem Setting in Perspective

The marketing alternatives of concern to the Rigid Container Division involved broad and extensive information requirements. A program of research for developing a marketing plan was required. This implied the use of multiple data sources and specialized research projects.

One research approach involved studying the reactions of individuals and organizations that influenced the market acceptance of plastic containers. The ultimate consumers can be an influential group in this acceptance process. Consumers may have preferences for packaging characteristics that favor plastic over other packaging materials. The retailer and wholesaler may find packaging characteristics important in the selection of products to handle. Characteristics such as stacking ability, display appeal, and potential for breakage may influence their selection. Manufacturers who must decide on a packaging container for their product may consider many areas in making a decision. The preferences and reactions of consumers, retailers, and wholesalers may be important considerations. Container costs and related investment would be important. Manufacturing considerations, degree of product protection, promotional features, and ecological issues could all enter into the decision. Several research projects would be required to study this complex chain of influence for each market under consideration.

Another area of investigation concerned an analysis of current markets. The task here would be to quantify markets on characteristics such as size, trends in size, current mix of packaging forms, and fit of packaging requirements with existing plastic container manufacturing processes. This research approach involves the use of published data sources such as research reports, trade association data, and trade periodicals.

Additional studies could be required, depending on the breadth of the sponsor's information needs. These might include profitability analysis of current lines of plastic containers, customer analysis, competitive analysis, and environmental analysis.

The information needs of this project were extensive and required a variety of research approaches and studies. These could range from small exploratory studies with consumers, retailers, wholesalers, and manufacturers to more formal studies using observation, interrogation, and experimentation. In addition, studies using published data sources internal and external to the sponsoring organizations could be required.

THE STUDY PROPOSAL

After several weeks of preparation, a research proposal was developed and sent to each of the executive board members for review. At a subsequent meeting with the research firm and after several changes, the proposal was approved. Following is a summary of the finalized proposal, which contains two sections: (1) packaging markets and (2) consumer acceptance.

Study of Packaging Markets

Rationale for the Study   The purpose of this study is to identify and characterize packaging markets and to screen these markets as to their potential for penetration by plastic containers. The high-potential markets identified through this study will be further screened in the study of consumer acceptance.

Research Objectives

1 To compare current and potential packaging markets with regard to dimensions indicative of market potential.

2 To categorize packaging markets as to the degree of plastic container penetration.

3 To evaluate the high-potential markets in terms of the compatibility of packaging requirements with existing production and material capabilities.

Information Needs

1 To rank container markets by number of containers used per year. To illustrate trends over the past 5 years.

2 To classify markets as to the most likely plastic manufacturing process (thermoforming, injection molding, spin welding, or blow molding).

3 To classify markets by proportion of containers that are paper, paperboard, glass, metal, and plastic. To illustrate trends over the past 5 years.

4 To rank container markets by retail price of the product. To illustrate trends over the past 5 years.

5 To rank container markets by proportion of retail price represented by packaging costs. To illustrate trends over the past 5 years.

6 To rank container markets by magnitude of packaging cost increase or decrease resulting from a change to a plastic container.

7 To classify markets as to the degree of fit with existing production and material capabilities—high, medium, or low fit.

8 To calculate the plastic container manufacturer's break-even volume for each market. To determine the proportion of market penetration required to break even for each market. To rank the markets or proportion of market penetration required to break even.

Data Sources   The data used to meet the information needs will include internal and external reports, publications, and records. (See Chapter 5.) Data that are not available in published form will be gathered by interviews with knowledgeable people in the industry.

The following published sources have been identified:

1 SPI, "The Plastic Industry in the Year 2000."
2 Harvard Business School, "The Packaging Revolution" from *A Note on the Metal Container Industry.*
3 "New Container Push Accents Packaging," *Industrial Marketing,* December 1991.
4 "Packaging Seen as Effective Marketing Tool," *Advertising Age,* September 1990.
5 *Standard and Poor's Industry Surveys—Containers.*
6 1992 *Census of Manufacturers:*
  a Food Sales—SIC 20.
  b Plastic Sales—SIC 30794.
7 *Standard and Poor's Industry Surveys—Retailing Food.*
8 *Modern Plastics.*
9 *Modern Plastics Encyclopedia.*
10 *Plastics Journal.*
11 *Society of Petroleum Engineering Journal.*
12 *Modern Packaging.*
13 *Modern Packaging Encyclopedia.*
14 Midwest Research Institute, *Resource and Environmental Profile Analysis of Plastic and Non-Plastic Containers.*
15 United Nations Report, *World Demand for Plastic,* 1993.

Study of Consumer Acceptance

Rationale for the Study   It was the opinion of the research firm that demonstrating consumer acceptance or preference would be the critical factor in influencing a manufacturer to use a plastic container, in the absence of an unfavorable cost differential or excessive distribution problems. Consumer preference for a plastic container over existing packaging would provide strong evidence for a potential sales increase resulting from a change to a plastic container. In addition, understanding the underlying characteristics of the plastic container which cause this preference would be useful in developing a promotional program directed to manufacturers. The same information would be useful to manufacturers in developing a promotional program for trade and consumer acceptance.

Research Objectives

1 To determine which container markets have the greatest consumer acceptance of plastic containers.

2 To determine the characteristics of plastic containers that represent advantages compared with paper, paperboard, glass, and metal containers.

Information Needs

1 To identify the characteristics or attributes that differentiate alternative packaging materials.

2 To determine the importance of packaging attributes in container markets.

3 To determine consumer preference for alternative packaging materials in container markets.

4 To identify the characteristics of packaging containers that influence consumer preference.

5 To determine which attributes of plastic containers represent important selling points.

6 To determine the characteristics of the ideal packaging container.

7 To determine the likes and dislikes of consumers regarding current packaging containers.

8 To determine what suggestions consumers have for packaging improvement in container markets.

9 To determine which markets have the most inadequate packaging and whether plastic containers represent an improvement.

10 To determine consumer attitudes toward ecological aspects of packaging materials, specifically plastic.

11 To determine consumers' perceptions regarding the cost of alternative packaging materials. Do some containers have a "high-price/high-quality" image?

12 To determine the nature of the trade-offs consumers will make in selecting a brand or package. How large a price increase will be accepted for a superior packaging form? How much will a lower price offset packaging deficiencies?

13 To determine the characteristics (demographic, life cycle, usage rates) of consumers who are most receptive to plastic containers.

Data Sources   Acquiring data to meet the information needs will involve the interrogation of consumers. The first phase will include a series of focus group interviews (see Chapter 10). The purpose is to explore consumer attitudes, feelings, and motives concerning the information-need areas such as attributes of packaging, pros and cons of packaging, and ecological issues. Based on these findings, specific questions can be developed for more systematic data collection. The second phase will involve a survey of consumers using a questionnaire administered by personal interview (see Chapter 11). The main conclusions of the study will be based on the results of this survey.

THE RESEARCH PROJECT

Results of the Study of Packaging Markets

The starting point for this phase of the research project was an extensive list of packaging markets that, at least superficially, seemed to hold good potential for rigid plastic containers. The list was furnished by the SPI, where it had been developed through continuous monitoring and contact with the packaging industry. The list was further screened by the SPI to include only those markets where rigid plastic containers were judged to be feasible from the standpoint of both technology and cost.

The next step was to trim from the list those markets with obviously undesirable demand characteristics based on research using secondary data sources (see Chapter 6). While length prohibits presenting these detailed findings, the markets that survived this process appear in Exhibit 3-1, where they are classified according to the current penetration of plastic containers. A major plastics market, for example, is one in which there is already high penetration.

By now, it may have occurred to the discerning reader that there are at least two types of markets with high potential for rigid plastic containers. One is rapidly growing markets where plastic already has significant penetration, while the other is large or growing markets where the penetration of plastic could be significantly improved. On the other hand, high-penetration markets with stable or declining primary demand afford little opportunity and therefore do not appear on the list.

The study of packaging markets can be viewed as exploratory research (see Chapter 4) for the purpose of identifying specific alternative courses of action to reach the SPI objectives previously discussed. In this case, "alternative courses of action" can be construed as different container markets at which the members' efforts might be directed. The study of consumer acceptance, to which we now

---

EXHIBIT 3-1

POTENTIAL MARKETS FOR RIGID PLASTIC CONTAINERS

Major Plastics Markets

Cultured dairy (cottage cheese, yogurt, etc.)
Butter and margarine
Portion packs (e.g., meat cold cuts)
Pantyhose

Minor Plastics Markets

Shortening   Cosmetic creams and gels
Ice cream   Auto oil and grease
Spreads and dips   Food sauces
Frozen juice   Meat trays

Nonplastics Markets

Jelly and preserves   Pet foods
Salad dressing   Auto parts and kits
Baby food   Cheese
Coffee   Household cleaners, wax, car care
Drink powders (e.g., Kool-Aid)

---

turn, concerns not only the identification and evaluation of these specific container market alternatives but the selection of a course of action as well. This study involves both exploratory and conclusive research.

Results of the Study of Consumer Acceptance

Group Studies   This stage of the project involved a series of group discussion sessions to explore consumer attitudes on the advantages and disadvantages of different types of containers. The sort of information derived from these sessions was qualitative in nature and served to guide the quantitative research conducted later. Use of group sessions is a fairly well-established technique in the marketing research business for probing a topic that is not yet well defined. Chapter 10 will discuss the area of qualitative research in detail.

Design and Procedure   Anywhere from 8 to 12 paid participants attended each of the sessions, which were held at a special facility for group sessions run by the research firm. The sessions took place in a family-living-room environment made as comfortable as possible to help put the participants at ease. The sessions were videotape-recorded for later analysis, but an effort was made to keep the equipment as unobtrusive as possible, again to minimize anxiety.

In order to ensure that the sessions were of reasonable length ($1\frac{1}{2}$ hours is usually optimal), it was necessary to restrict the number of uses of plastic containers discussed in depth in any one session. A master plan was devised whereby each use was discussed in more than one session but usually in the context of a different set of other possible uses. Of course, when uses such as baby food and pet food containers were discussed, it was necessary to have panel members who were all purchasers of these products. To assure this, a screening process was employed which we will now examine.

Sample Selection   Each session was conducted with a panel of consumers who were largely homogeneous in terms of their position in the family life cycle. While pros and cons exist for this sort of design, recruiting along life-cycle lines helped in the identification of the most probable users of certain sets of products. To facilitate the selection process, a screening questionnaire was constructed to determine marital status, number and ages of any children living at home, occupational status of the adult family members, and usage rates of those products previously defined as markets for plastic containers. Using this questionnaire, interviewers then selected a convenient sample at a nearby shopping center (see Chapter 13). Those who agreed to participate were given a time and place at which to appear.

Moderator and Guide Questions   The group discussions were led by trained moderators whose function was to channel the conversation along particular lines. They in turn were directed by a "moderator's guide," which specified the minimum set of topics that the group was to cover and how the topics were to be broached. A few sample questions from the guide appear in Exhibit 3-2.

The job of moderating a group session tends to be a very sensitive task. To be most useful, the conversation needs to be lively and uninhibited but should not be dominated by a few panel members and should not stray too far from the

EXHIBIT 3-2

EXAMPLES OF QUESTIONS FROM THE MODERATOR'S GUIDE

When was the last time you found yourself extremely dissatisfied with the container used for a product you had purchased?

Certain types of containers are best suited for certain types of products. Describe for me the kind of product you would expect to find in a glass jar. How about a metal can? Paper or cardboard? Plastic?

In general, what do you consider to be the advantages and disadvantages of glass, metal, paper, and plastic containers?

Let's discuss the kinds of experiences you have had with the containers used for ice cream, jelly, coffee, meat.

Do you think it usually costs more to package a product in plastic rather than glass? Metal? Paper?

Assume that the brand of ice cream you buy was available in the standard paper carton, a plastic container, or a sturdy cardboard container (the cylindrical kind with the separate top). If the price were the same for the three versions, which would you buy? What sort of person can you visualize buying the other two versions?

---

assigned topics. The moderators applied various techniques to help achieve this result. One such technique was to identify panel members holding widely divergent points of view and then guide them into a debate. Another was to call on shy or retiring members directly for their opinions.

Analysis   After all the sessions were completed, the tapes were replayed and transcribed, and summary reports were written based on what they contained. Given that the data were qualitative, no statistics were formally presented, such as what percentage said this or that. Instead, the format was to categorize and list comments in such a way as to define the domain of the problem without trying to determine the relative importance of its various aspects. As an aid to the analysis, the individual tapes were edited into a summary tape that included only the most meaningful dialogue from each session. In the research business, such tapes are often used for management presentations.

Results   At the general level, what emerged from these sessions was as follows:

1 A better understanding of how consumers think about containers, the terms they use, and the attributes and characteristics they consider relevant

2 A more thorough list of the advantages and disadvantages associated with different types, depending on how they are used

3 Some new ideas on the kinds of products that might be contained in rigid plastic

To help make this discussion more concrete, we might consider the results obtained for one packaging market in particular, namely, ice cream. It represents a market with minor plastic penetration and would therefore seem to offer good potential for the future. Most ice cream is now contained in paper cartons, which, according to the panel members, have these deficiencies:

1 When the ice cream melts, they leak.
2 They are flimsy and tear easily.
3 Children don't know which end is the top, and they open both.
4 They are susceptible to freezer burn.
5 They tend to absorb moisture.

In comparison, the participants tended to view plastic containers mainly in positive terms, such as the following:

1 They are reusable.
2 They are resealable.
3 They are strong.
4 They are less messy, because they don't leak.
5 They prevent freezer burn.
6 Sherbet comes like this, and experiences with it have been good.
7 Plastic has a higher price/quality image.
8 They are easy to use and have a wide mouth.
9 There is an incentive value in seeing the ice cream.

In spite of these positive findings from the qualitative research there was not sufficient evidence to say that ice cream in rigid plastic containers would definitely have consumer acceptance. For one thing, the sample was small and not representative. There were no statistics projectable to the general population as to the level of acceptance. Also, it was possible that all nine positive aspects on the list could be easily outweighed by a single important disadvantage not uncovered for some reason. Finally, some other use might exist where the acceptance of plastic would be much more certain. For these reasons and others, the conclusive research discussed in the next section was undertaken.

Survey of Consumers   In contrast to the focus group sessions discussed above, the methodology of the survey of consumers was more heavily influenced by an existing body of scientific knowledge. This body of knowledge specifies the manner in which surveys should be conducted and analyzed so as to minimize the amount of error in the results. This survey employed some error-reducing techniques that are not always used in marketing research because the benefits of the reduction in uncertainty do not, in every case, justify the increased cost.

As is the case with most well-developed areas of science, survey research has its own terminology, some of which may be confusing to the uninitiated. Various technical terms are introduced in the rest of this chapter without elaboration or apology, because considerable effort will be expended in defining them in detail in the remainder of the book.

The survey of consumers followed a fairly standard series of steps for doing this type of research. The processes that will be discussed are, in the order of their occurrence: questionnaire design and pretesting; sample selection and field work; editing, coding, and data processing; and analysis and reporting.

Questionnaire Design and Pretesting   Some say that questionnaire design is as much an art as it is a science. While this may be true, there is much more to designing a questionnaire than its literary aspects (see Chapter 12). Perhaps one scientific principle in the design of a questionnaire is that the questions should proceed from the general to the specific. For example, in this study respondents were asked to recall some products they had seen contained in plastic. It made sense that this question should occur before one that specifically mentioned product names. A few other refinements incorporated in the questionnaire were alternate question wordings to avoid an acquiescence bias, the rotation of item lists to avoid an order bias (for example, the list of attributes and the list of container uses), and precoding of the response categories for machine processing. Some of the questions used in this study have been paraphrased in Exhibit 3-3.

The questionnaire was pretested on a convenience sample of about 75 consumers to make sure that the proper flow existed and that the questions were understandable to ordinary individuals. The pretesting also provided the opportunity to analyze the items for redundancy. This was accomplished by taking the data for the total sample and subjecting them to a technique known as factor analysis (see Chapter 20). The procedure revealed that several of the attributes actually measured the same underlying characteristic, so it was possible to eliminate a few of the items.

Sample Selection and Field Work   It was determined that the interviews could be successfully conducted over the telephone. Telephone numbers were selected using the method of random-digit dialing (see Chapter 15). Under this procedure, three-digit exchange codes supplied by the telephone company are combined with four-digit random numbers to give every operating telephone in the country an equal probability of selection. An advantage of random-digit dialing is that there is no bias against newly listed or unlisted numbers, as occurs when samples

---

EXHIBIT 3-3

EXAMPLE OF QUESTIONS ON THE QUESTIONNAIRE

  1 Of the packages you currently purchase, which do you feel could be improved? Why?
  2 What products do you currently purchase that come packaged in a plastic container?
  3 What are the advantages of a plastic container?
  4 What are the disadvantages of a plastic container?
  5 Would you please evaluate (packaging container) in regard to the degree it possesses the characteristic of (attribute)? (rating scale)
  6 How important is the packaging characteristic of (attribute) for a (packaging container)? (rating scale)
  7 (Interviewer checks "male" or "female.")
  8 What is your marital status?
  9 How many people are there in your household?
  10 How many children do you have at home?
  11 What are their ages?
  12 What is the highest grade of school or college that you have completed?

are selected from telephone directories. However, households without telephones are excluded from the target population, and there is some inefficiency in connections made to business numbers. In addition, households with two or more phone listings have a higher probability of being included in the sample. The interviews were conducted at various times of the day over Wide Area Telecommunications Service (WATS) lines. A number of callbacks were made when there was no answer or the line was busy. In all, about 500 interviews were completed over the course of several weeks.

Editing, Coding, and Data Processing   At this stage, completed interviews were edited to make sure that they were legible, complete, consistent, and accurate and that all the instructions had been properly followed (see Chapter 17). In some cases where data were missing, estimates were made of what the responses would have been based on other information in the questionnaire. This was necessary only in a few critical places in the questionnaire. Open-ended questions were then coded to make the data machine-readable. As the coding process was getting under way, a "round robin" was used whereby several individuals coded the same questionnaire. This revealed a few ambiguities in the codebook.

As soon as the completed interviews were edited and coded, they were key-punched onto computer cards and verified 100 percent. The research firm had available standard computer programs to process the survey data.

Analysis and Reporting   The objectives of this chapter, together with space limitations, restrict the presentation of the results of the study and the course of action selected and implemented by SPI. Consequently, the following discussion is designed to illustrate the data analysis and to discuss a few of the research findings.

The first step in the analysis process was to obtain a description of the sample in terms of demographic characteristics. The sample demographics were then compared with U.S. census data to determine whether the sample was representative of the population. Except for minor sampling variations, the sample and population distributions were very similar.

In like fashion, descriptive statistics were obtained on the response to every item in the questionnaire (see Chapter 18). These statistics included measures of central tendency and dispersion. Among the benefits of doing this was the identification of a number of "wild codes" that needed to be corrected. Some of these univariate statistics were used to make interval estimates of the proportion of consumers in the general population who felt a particular way on a certain issue. For example, it was of interest to the SPI to know that, at the 95 percent confidence level, somewhere between 43 and 51 percent of the population would prefer that their ice cream come in a rigid plastic container. These statistics were especially valuable when compared with similar figures for other products.

There were other cases, however, where a simple univariate analysis was not revealing enough and a cross tabulation or bivariate analysis seemed necessary (see Chapter 19). For instance, 25 percent of the respondents said they would switch brands of ice cream to obtain a plastic container. However, a cross tabulation revealed that the result varied, depending on the level of educational attainment, as evidenced in Table 3-1. Only 17 percent of those who had graduated

TABLE 3-1 INTENTION TO SWITCH BRANDS BY LEVEL OF EDUCATIONAL ATTAINMENT

	Total, %	Did not graduate, %	Graduated from high school, %
Would switch	25	37	17
Would not	75	63	83
Total	100	100	100

from high school said they would switch brands to get plastic, compared with 37 percent of those who had not graduated. Was it safe to conclude, then, that educational attainment was a causal factor affecting the intention to switch brands? The fallacy of this conclusion is evident in Table 3-2. Note that regardless of the level of educational attainment, only 20 percent of those who were aware that plastic is nonbiodegradable said they would switch brands, compared with 43 percent of those who were not aware. The influence of education was that more people with a high school education were aware that plastic is nonbiodegradable (50 percent compared with 25 percent).

Many other two-way relationships were studied, and in addition some more complex multivariate analysis was performed (see Chapters 20 and 21). These results were not reported here, but they were useful to management in decision making.

SPI GLOBAL MARKETING RESEARCH

The marketing research process described in detail for SPI's U.S. market in this chapter was repeated in numerous other countries, including Canada, Mexico, the United Kingdom, France, Germany, Japan, and Australia. In each country secondary data were analyzed, focus group interviews were held, and survey research was implemented. Some general insights that were common across countries were found, as were some very specific country differences. The details of the process and the country-by-country results would take too much space to present here. However, some unique country findings are presented in the Global Marketing Research Dynamics.

TABLE 3-2 INTENTION TO SWITCH BRANDS BY LEVEL OF EDUCATIONAL ATTAINMENT AND BIO-AWARENESS

	Did not graduate from high school			Graduated from high school		
	Total, %	Aware, %	Not aware, %	Total, %	Aware, %	Not aware, %
Would switch	37	20	43	17	20	43
Would not	63	80	57	83	80	57
Total	100	100	100	100	100	100

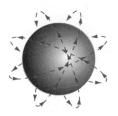

GLOBAL MARKETING RESEARCH DYNAMICS

SPI MARKETING RESEARCH: SELECTED COUNTRY-SPECIFIC DIFFERENCES

• In France, the lack of refrigeration space in the typical small French kitchen combined with the French custom of shopping for food almost daily reduced the need for reusing plastic containers for leftover food.

• In Canada, environmental laws associated with reducing the amount of plastic in landfills would seriously limit the market potential for almost all rigid plastic packaging.

• The strong presence in Japan of import restrictions on processed plastic products from abroad would limit the ability of U.S.-based producers to export rigid plastic containers to Japan.

• German consumers placed the highest value of any country group on the solid structure of plastic containers and on the reusability feature of the containers.

ERRORS IN MARKETING RESEARCH

While the results of the previous study may appear accurate, managers and researchers need to recognize that every marketing research study contains errors. These errors can result in serious misinformation being communicated to managers. Consequently, a professionally designed and managed research study must recognize the potential sources of error and manage the size of those errors consistently with the accuracy required by the manager's decision situation.

Every step in the marketing research process can produce serious errors. The control of these errors is of critical concern in marketing research. Much of the rest of this book is concerned with understanding and controlling these errors. In this section we note that basically there are two types of errors: sampling errors and nonsampling errors. The Marketing Research in Action on Hertz versus Avis illustrates the critical nature of error control in marketing research.

MARKETING RESEARCH IN ACTION

HERTZ VERSUS AVIS AND AVIS'S MARKETING RESEARCH SUPPLIER

Avis, famous for its "We're number two so we try harder" campaign, may not have tried hard enough in obtaining and verifying its marketing research results, alleges Thomas Werbe, Hertz Corporation's vice president of marketing research and planning. Werbe's claims were initiated by an Avis press conference, during which Avis announced a gain in market shares relative to Hertz. Avis said this gain was reflected in a recently conducted poll. But, according to Werbe, Avis's survey was timed to yield optimum results. People were interviewed after receiving a free promotional gift from Avis, which materially altered the results of the survey. The poll was conducted for Avis by Garth-Mariorana-Connelly (GMC), a subsidiary of the political campaign management company, Garth Organization, Ltd.

Werbe's assertions implied that GMC's research was tailored and in its own self-interest. He called GMC's sampling procedures "so lax, so sloppy, that they have [even] been interviewing Hertz managers." Werbe went on to say that the Hertz manager at Chicago's O'Hare airport was approached and interviewed in one of the surveys.

David Garth, the head of GMC, vehemently denied the Werbe-Hertz allegations. He said, "We don't tailor our polls. If anything, we go the other way; we are twice as tough on our client . . . as their opponents are."

Mr. Garth compared his polling strategy to the political strategy his corporation used in political surveys. "It's the exact same thing you do in a political campaign," he said. "You want to look at the candidate [Avis], you want to look at the person you are running against [Hertz] and the people who are his or her supporters." Mr. Mariorana, a partner in GMC, called Werbe's claims "hysterical, assumptive, and inaccurate."

This type of allegation of incompetence in field work has the potential to damage both the research firm's and the client's reputations. Furthermore, poor research techniques open the door to a host of potentially injurious lawsuits from the competition, making the costs of the research far outweigh any potential benefits.

Sampling Errors

Most marketing research studies utilize samples of people, products, or stores. Based upon these sample results, the researcher and the manager make conclusions about the whole population from which the sample was selected. For example, the attitudes of all Chevrolet owners could be inferred from a sample of a thousand owners. Because the sample is used to estimate the population, differences exist between the sample value and the true underlying population value. This difference, called *sampling error,* is discussed in Chapters 14 and 15.

Nonsampling Errors

Nonsampling errors are all the errors that may occur in the marketing research process except the sampling error. This concept simply includes all the aspects of the research process where mistakes and deliberate deceptions can occur. Unfortunately, these mistakes and deceptions occur with great frequency in the marketing research process. We must therefore be aware of (1) what nonsampling errors may occur, (2) what effect these errors may have on our results, and (3) what steps we can take to reduce these errors. This chapter deals with the first two issues, identification of nonsampling errors and possible effects of these errors. The details of how to reduce nonsampling errors will be left to the remaining chapters of the book, since most of them focus on that topic. The chapters that deal with the reduction of nonsampling errors will be identified with the specific error in the list of errors described below.

The Effect of Nonsampling Errors

Sampling error has two properties that make it useful to the researcher: (1) it is measurable and (2) it decreases as the sample size increases. Unfortunately, nonsampling errors are not easily measurable, and they do not decrease with sample size. In fact, in all likelihood, nonsampling errors increase as sample size increases. What nonsampling errors do is put a bias in our results of unknown direction and magnitude. One practicing researcher put forth the following view of the effect of nonsampling errors:

> Over the years I have used a simple rule of thumb that the true mean square error of field studies is at least twice the size of reported theoretical sampling error, though there is evidence to suggest that it is larger in many commercial surveys.[1]

Indeed, nonsampling error can render the results of a study useless. Examples of different types of these errors follow.

Types of Nonsampling Errors

Faulty Problem Definition   A product manager requests a study to test a media mix. If the true problem is pricing strategy, then any research that is conducted, no matter how technically correct, will not be helpful to the manager. This issue is discussed in detail in Chapter 4.

Defective Population Definition   The study population must be defined to fit the study objectives. Consider the case of the manager of one of the restaurants in a major metropolitan airport. She would like to know what sort of image the restaurant has among those who have some likelihood of eating in the airport. The population is defined as people over 18 years old, getting off planes in the week of September 12 to 19. If the sample is selected from this population, one might get misleading results. It does not include significant numbers of potential customers, that is, people who are visiting the airport but who are not landing on planes, and people who are just taking off. Also, the sample includes people who have no chance of eating at the restaurant, that is, people who change planes without going into the main terminal where the restaurants are located. Conclusions from the study are questionable.

Frame Nonrepresentative of the Population   The sampling frame must match the defined population. Consider the case of an investment company that uses the telephone book (the frame) to select a sample of "potential stock buyers." This frame would not cover the defined population well, as a significant number of high-income people have unlisted phone numbers. These high-income people are the prime potential stock buyers. Again, conclusions are suspect.

Nonresponse Errors   Errors occur because people in the selected sample either refuse to be a part of the sample or are not at home during the sampling period. A sample is a representative sample as selected. If some of the selected elements

---

[1]Benjamin Lipstein, "In Defense of Small Samples," *Journal of Advertising Research,* vol. 15, p. 39, February 1975. See also Gary Lilien, Rex Brown, and Kate Searls, "How Errors Add Up," *Marketing News,* pp. 20–21, January 7, 1991.

do not form part of the realized sample, it is not a truly representative sample. The resulting error is called *nonresponse error.*

As an example of this problem, consider the case of a resort developer who attempts to interview people during the day. The study yields some refusals and a lot of "not at homes." We must wonder whether the refusals as a group hold different attitudes about the development from those who respond. Also, by interviewing only in the day, the developer missed all families in which both the spouses work. This group may be a prime prospect.

Frame problems and nonresponse errors are discussed in Chapter 16. The remaining nonsampling errors, which follow, are related to areas of the research process other than sampling.

Measurement Error   Measurement is the process of assigning numbers to observed phenomena. A researcher may try to develop a scale of interest in a new product, but the scaling may be done improperly. This complex area is discussed in detail in Chapters 7 and 8.

Improper Causal Inferences   A producer of heavy equipment changes the compensation scheme of its sales force, and the following year sales double. Management infers that the new compensation plan caused the sales increase. It is also possible that other factors could have caused it—for example, the economy could have improved, the product could have improved, or the salespersons could have become more experienced. Management has observed an association between sales and compensation and has inferred the cause. The search for causes is discussed in Chapter 9.

Poor Questionnaire Design   In a survey of his constituents, a member of Congress asked, "Should the Congress challenge the do-nothing administration and take action on unemployment?" This is hardly the way to find the true feelings of members of Congress on a complex issue. What good is measuring sampling error here? Most questionnaire design problems are more complex than this, relating to question sequence, length, word usage, and so on, and the topic is discussed fully in Chapter 12.

SUMMARY

1 The purpose of this chapter was to present the stages of the research process and illustrate this process through an example of a marketing research project. Finally, the chapter emphasized the sources of error in projects of this nature.

2 The research process is composed of nine steps, starting with the establishment of the need for information and ending with the presentation of the research results. To effectively conduct a research project, it is essential to anticipate the nine steps and to recognize their interdependence. What is done in one step can greatly influence the other steps.

3 The first phase of the project in our example involved the recognition by the

Rigid Container Division's executive board that a problem existed. The problem was defined as the need to identify and evaluate the market opportunities for rigid plastic containers.

4 The next phase involved specifying the objective of the executive board and identifying potential courses of action to accomplish the objective.

5 The project next turned to identifying the type of information needed to select and implement one or more of the alternatives identified.

6 The information requirements suggested that a series of projects were required. Research objectives and specific information needs were specified for a study of packaging markets and a study of consumer acceptance. The study of packaging markets was an exploratory research study using secondary data sources to identify specific alternative courses of action. The study of consumer acceptance was mainly concerned with conclusive research directed at the selection of a course of action. This study involved a national probability sample of households, with interviews conducted over the telephone.

7 The results of the telephone survey were analyzed by means of univariate and bivariate analysis. Illustrative results were presented for the ice cream container market.

8 The presentation of the research project was not intended to illustrate how a research report should be organized and written. Chapter 22 discusses this in detail.

9 The researcher should be concerned with total error, which is the sum of sampling and nonsampling errors.

DISCUSSION QUESTIONS

1 Specify the sequence of steps in the research process.

2 Why is it essential that a researcher anticipate all the steps of the research process?

3 How did the marketing research firm ascertain the information needs of SPI?

4 What type of research did the study of packaging markets involve? Why?

5 What type of research did the study of consumer acceptance involve? Why?

6 Evaluate the manner in which the group phase of the study of consumer acceptance was carried out.

7 What is a nonsampling error?

8 What are the properties of nonsampling errors?

9 Define and then give an example of each type of nonsampling error listed in this chapter.

10 A major marketing research firm once declared one of its survey-based services to be "free from all error, except sampling error." Do you think this could be a true statement?

11 MINICASE

The Wool Producers Board of New Zealand wants to stimulate the primary demand for wool in the world. What marketing research could the board do to facilitate the development of such a primary demand stimulation campaign? Describe a program of marketing research in detail. Explain how potential errors in marketing research will be controlled in this program.

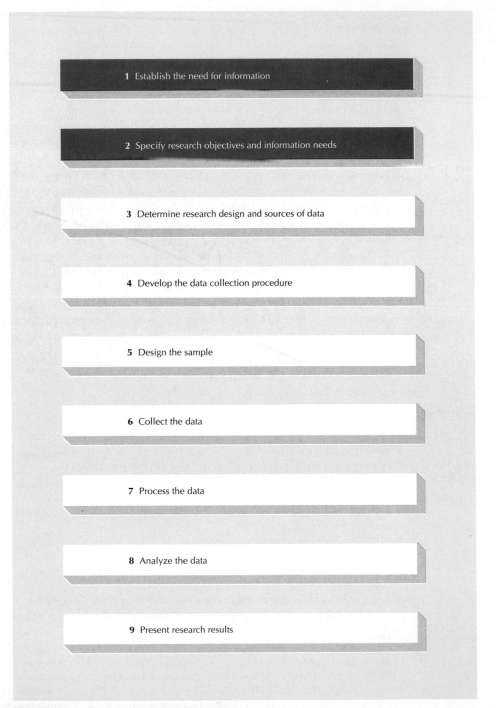

FIGURE 4-1   Steps in the research process.

CHAPTER 4

THE DECISION TO UNDERTAKE RESEARCH

MARKETING RESEARCH IN ACTION

MARKETING RESEARCH VICE PRESIDENT DISTURBED BY MISUSE OF STUDIES

Melissa Molloy had been vice president of marketing research for a major consumer food company based in Minneapolis for just over a year. During her tenure as vice president, she believed, great progress had been made in the effective use of marketing research by marketing managers. She noted: "We have worked very hard in the research department to be part of the marketing planning process with the brand groups and the division managers."

In order to assess the impact of marketing research on the marketing organization, Melissa had to obtain the services of an outside consulting firm to survey the attitudes of marketing managers within the company. This firm specialized in employee attitude studies, and it had a strong reputation for providing valid results on employee attitudes. The report of the consultants contained many positive remarks concerning how marketing research personnel were perceived by the managers. However, Melissa was very disturbed by some of the results of the study. Four of the question areas were of prime concern to her. These questions and the percentage of managers either agreeing or strongly agreeing with the question statement were as shown below.

Question	Percent in agreement
Managers often request marketing research in order to have power and knowledge over other managers.	45
Managers often request marketing research in order to support a decision that has already been made.	53
Managers often request marketing research reports in order to appease their superiors.	30
Managers often request marketing research studies because it is a policy requirement.	37

Melissa wanted marketing managers to use marketing research as an aid to real decision making, not for the politics of office power, nor just to pay lip service to some policy requirement, nor to keep superiors off their backs. She was most disturbed to see that over half of the managers were sanctioning studies related to decisions that had already been made. She said: "Clearly, we've won some battles here in the effective use of marketing research, but I'm afraid that the war is still in doubt. We need an approach in this marketing department to assure that these types of abuses of marketing research do not continue."

This company is struggling with what all organizations must deal with in the use of marketing research. Studies need to be undertaken and used to support marketing decision making, and not done for political, power, or ceremonial reasons. Thus, the decision to undertake marketing research is a critical one, full of many potential traps, as noted in the responses to the questions above.

Source: Internal Report, Michigan Marketing Associates, Ann Arbor.

This chapter discusses the important topic of the decision to undertake marketing research. Indeed, if this aspect of the marketing research process is not done well, then all the other steps in the process will be wasted.

It has been stated that there are three basic components in any marketing research undertaking: (1) making certain that the right questions are being asked, (2) using appropriate research techniques and controls, and (3) presenting research findings in a clear, comprehensible format that leads to management action.

The purpose of this chapter is to highlight the first component, namely, making certain that the right questions are being asked. Subsequent chapters will deal with the remaining two components.

There is probably no activity more critical to the success of the research project than the analysis leading to the decision to undertake research. Frequently, this analysis is poorly executed or superficially passed over in the excitement of doing a research study. The consequences are inadequate information for decision making, wasted research funds, and management dissatisfaction with the marketing research system.

The decision-making process and the management process are often considered to be synonymous. An organization's well-being is dependent on the wisdom of the decisions made by its managers. When confronted with decision situations where the setting is unique, the manager turns to a formal approach to decision making called the decision-making process.

PRELIMINARY STEPS IN THE DECISION-MAKING PROCESS

According to some sources, the analysis that was done leading to the decision to build the aircraft carrier *Enterprise* resulted in reports that weighed more than the ship itself. While this is obviously an exaggeration, it does emphasize the importance of adequate planning and analysis preceding the decision to undertake an important project such as research. The quality of this preparatory activity largely determines the success of the research project.

In marketing research, this preparatory activity should establish an effective link between the early stages of the decision process and the research process. Figure 4-2 illustrates the nature of this link. The relevance of the research findings to the information requirements of management is established at this crucial stage.

This section will cover the issues involved in the first three stages of the deci-

FIGURE 4-2   Links between the decision process and the research process.

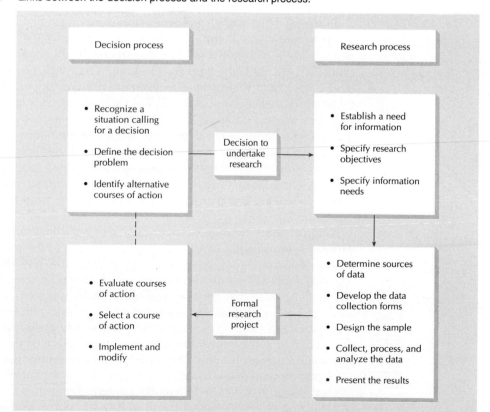

sion-making process: (1) recognition of a decision situation, (2) definition of the decision problem, and (3) identification of alternative courses of action. The next section will focus on the remaining steps: (4) evaluating courses of action, (5) selecting a course of action, and (6) implementing and modifying the action. The discussion will emphasize the requirements for each of the stages and the role of research in each stage.

Recognition of a Decision Situation

Figure 1 3 presents the preliminary steps in the decision-making process and illustrates how the marketing system triggers the recognition of a situation calling for a decision. Here, the behavioral response and performance measures signal symptoms, while the marketing mix and situational factors produce the underlying problems and opportunities. The decision maker's task is to respond to symptoms and analyze the underlying problems and opportunities to determine whether a situation is present that calls for a decision. If the answer is affirmative, the decision maker proceeds to the second and third stages of the decision process—developing a clear statement of the decision problem and identifying alternative courses of action.

Problems   The word "problem" carries a connotation of trouble; something is wrong and needs attention. The existence of a problem is detected when objectives are established and a measurement of performance indicates that the objectives are not being met. For example, a product's share of market could be below forecasted share. The effectiveness of a new advertising campaign could be below desired awareness levels. The expenses associated with the introduction of a new product could be over budget. Consequently, a problem results when actual performance does not match expected performance.

When we use the word *problem,* we refer to those independent variables that cause the organization's performance measures to not meet objectives. Problems can result from an ineffective marketing program (product, price, distribution, and promotion), from changes in the situational factors, or from a combination of both.

Opportunities   Managers make decisions regarding opportunities as well as problems. In using the word *opportunity,* we refer to the presence of a situation where performance can be improved by undertaking new activities. An opportunity may result in the establishment of even higher objectives. Opportunities differ from problems in that the manager may not be required to do anything about them. In fact, opportunities may not even be recognized. Most opportunities do not force themselves on managers in the same way that problems do, since most firms have formal methods for detecting the presence of problems via their performance measures but less formal methods for monitoring the opportunities.

As an example of an opportunity, note that it was changes in consumer tastes toward snack products with less fat content that created an opportunity. The introduction of the Snackwell brand of low-fat cookies was a successful actuali-

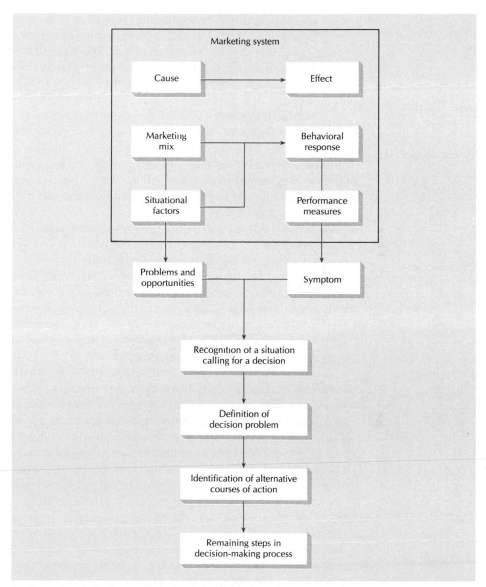

FIGURE 4-3   Preliminary steps in the decision-making process.

zation of this opportunity. The opportunity would have existed even if the firm had not made an effort to actualize it. Most of Snackwell's competitors were very slow to market similar products.

Symptoms   A symptom is a condition that signals the presence of a problem or an opportunity. Performance measures act as this signal for marketing management. It is important to recognize that symptoms are not the same as problems and opportunities. For example, a decline in sales volume from forecasted levels is not a problem; it is the symptom of a problem yet to be identified. A symptom can be viewed as the result of a problem or an opportunity.

For example, the statement "Sales and profits are down" notes symptoms that all is not well in a firm. However, these symptoms give no clue to the cause of the symptoms. The root causes of the observed symptoms are what we call *problems.* For example, the introduction of a better product by a competitor may be the real cause of the decline in sales and profits. This new product is the problem. One task of marketing research is to provide measures of a symptom such as a decline in customer satisfaction, while another task is to help identify root cause. For example, the customer satisfaction may be down because of poor training of customer representatives.

Symptoms occupy a critical position in the process of recognizing that a situation exists calling for a management decision. Once the existence of a problem or opportunity has been recognized, the main issues and causal factors need to be identified. Effective decision making is dependent upon a clear statement regarding the basic problem or opportunity. This statement is often developed only after a thorough investigation of the marketing program and/or the situational factors. Rarely can the problem or opportunity be adequately identified solely on the knowledge that a symptom is present. Decisions are made to solve problems and/or to take advantage of opportunities, not to treat symptoms.

Symptoms often trigger the analysis process designed to identify and define the problems or opportunities. During this process, one may find that the initial variables identified as causing the symptom are the result of even more fundamental variables. An intensive investigation may uncover a complicated sequence of influences which interact to produce the symptom. Once this analysis is completed, the manager can formulate the decision problem and determine the course of action which, it is hoped, will attack the problem and/or exploit the opportunity.

Definition of the Decision Problem

Once the manager recognizes that a situation exists which calls for a decision, the next step is to clearly define the decision problem. A clearly defined decision problem has two components: (1) a thorough understanding of the objectives surrounding the decision situation and (2) a statement of the problems and opportunities present in the decision situation.

The decision maker has two approaches to defining the decision problem. They can be used in combination, or a single approach can be employed. The first approach is to formulate the decision problem based on the analysis of existing information. This approach relies upon the manager's experience and judgment plus skills in analyzing existing data regarding the decision situation. The second approach is to use exploratory research to aid in defining the decision problem. If the latter route is selected, there will be a process of interaction between hypotheses previously formulated based on existing information and hypotheses developed from the exploratory research findings. At some point in this interactive process, the decision maker must clearly define the decision problem and proceed to the remaining steps of the decision-making process.

The remainder of this section will discuss the issues involved in the process of defining the decision problem. First, it is important to understand clearly what is meant by a decision problem. Second, the role and responsibility of the decision maker in guiding the definition of the decision problem are emphasized. Next, the two components of the decision problem are reviewed: (1) objectives and (2) statement of problems and opportunities.

What Is a Decision Problem?   A decision problem exists whenever management has an objective to accomplish and is confronted with a situation involving two or more courses of action to reach the objective. In addition, uncertainty must exist regarding the best course of action. If a manager is certain as to the best course of action, there is no decision problem. If there is only one course of action available, and that is to "do nothing," there is no decision problem.

Decision problems can exist for situations involving both problems and opportunities. Uncertainty can exist regarding the best course of action to solve a problem as well as how to take advantage of an opportunity. Consequently, a decision problem is present in situations regarding problems and opportunities whenever the manager faces a choice among alternative courses of action in which uncertainty exists about the outcome of the decision.

Role of the Decision Maker   The decision maker plays a central role in the definition of the decision problem. After recognizing that a potential decision problem exists, the decision maker has the responsibility to ensure that the decision objectives are specified and the problems and opportunities are clearly identified.

Decision Objective   The decision-making process typically has two sources for objectives. The primary sources for objectives is the organization. For example, an organization may have an objective to increase earnings per share by 10 percent next year. The second source involves the personal objectives of the decision maker (or the decision makers) and those who influence that individual. For example, a marketing manager may have the personal objective of becoming the vice president of marketing or of acquiring more prestige among his or her peers.

In order to understand the motivation for a decision, we must be sensitive to the roles played by both organizational and personal objectives. When both sets of objectives coincide, the decision-making process flows more smoothly than when there is conflict between them. The question of how to resolve this conflict in favor of organizational objectives is obviously a complex one, but one approach is to have organizational objectives stated explicitly to others in the organization. In addition, the development of explicit decision criteria for the selection among alternative courses of action often ensures that organizational objectives will predominate in the decision. More will be said on this issue shortly.

In many decision situations the "decision maker" may not be a single individual. Decision making in organizations can involve two or more people who must make decisions as a group. Other situations involve one predominant decision maker who is strongly influenced by other individuals who are part of the decision-making process. In such situations, not only is there potential conflict between organizational and personal objectives, but also there is conflict among the personal objectives of the individuals involved in the decision process.

It is a serious mistake to assume that the decision maker clearly knows what the organizational objectives are and that formulating an explicit statement of these objectives will be viewed with favor. An explicit statement of organizational objectives can force the decision maker to suppress personal objectives. In addition, some individuals may feel that making certain aspects of the decision process explicit can threaten their status and position as decision makers.

Statement of Problems and Opportunities   The process of identifying problems and opportunities is called *situational analysis.* Its purpose is to analyze the past and future situations facing an organization to uncover those variables that cause poor performance or represent opportunities for future growth. Specifically, this means that a diagnosis and a prognosis must be made of the marketing program and situational variables in the marketing system.

The situational analysis is a creative process in which an attempt is made to isolate and understand the causal variables influencing the marketing system. During this investigation, one must be sensitive to the fact that symptoms are not the same thing as problems and opportunities.

In conducting a situational analysis, diversity of information sources may be needed to develop insight and hypotheses regarding the causal factors. Flexibility in thinking and the use of multiple information sources are often critical to a successful situational analysis.

Alternative Courses of Action

Given a clear statement of the decision problem, the next stage of the decision process is to identify alternative courses of action. (Remember that a decision problem exists only when there are two or more actions to be taken and uncertainty as to which is the best one to take.)

A *course of action* specifies how the organization's resources are to be deployed in a given time period. Maintaining the status quo or "doing nothing new" is a course of action just as much as is designating a change in the status quo.

The development of alternative courses of action is crucial in the formulation of the decision problem. The management decision can be no better than the best alternative under evaluation. Identifying mediocre courses of action is often an easy task. Implementation of a mediocre action may partially solve a problem or take advantage of an opportunity to some degree. The real management challenge is to identify the best course of action that will result in high performance and give the organization a competitive edge.

Creativity is needed to identify innovative and highly effective courses of action. Various approaches are available that can stimulate the manager's creative process and broaden the domain of alternatives identified. Exploratory research can be especially helpful in identifying innovative courses of action.

Remaining Steps in the Decision Process

Once the alternative courses of action have been identified, the next step is one of evaluation. At this point, the manager is faced with the question "What information is needed to properly choose among the courses of action?" This may be answered with the help of information inputs from the manager's experience and judgment plus information currently available through the marketing research system. Alternatively, the manager may decide that new information is needed and request that a formal marketing research study be conducted. The decision to use research implies that the desired information can be obtained and that the cost and time delay associated with collecting it are more than offset by its potential value. The value or benefit of research is typically commensurate with the ability of research information to reduce the management uncertainty regarding the selection of a course of action. Once this information has been obtained and presented in a meaningful format, the manager can proceed to the final stage of the decision-making process, namely, the selection of a course of action and the development of a plan for implementation.

A research study designed to evaluate alternative courses of action is called conclusive research. Let us turn now to a discussion of how to get the formal research project under way.

PRELIMINARY CONSIDERATIONS FOR CONDUCTING CONCLUSIVE RESEARCH

Conclusive research provides information that helps the decision maker evaluate and select a course of action. The formal research project contains a series of steps called the research process. The nine steps in this process were outlined in Chapter 3 and may be reviewed by referring to Figure 3-1. Our discussion here will focus on the initial three stages of the research process: (1) establishing the need for information, (2) determining research objectives, and (3) specifying information needs. During our discussion of these initial research stages, the role of the researcher in establishing an effective link with the early stages of the decision-making process will be emphasized.

Establish the Need for Information

Establishing the need for marketing research information is a critical step in the research process. The wisdom of this initial step largely determines the success or failure of the research project.

Role of the Researcher   Rarely does the manager's initial request for help adequately establish the need for research information. Consequently, the researcher has an important role to play in making sure that information is in fact needed and that the research study will provide useful information for decision making. The following questions should be thoroughly addressed by the resarcher at this initial stage:

1 Who is the decision maker?
2 What are his or her objectives?
3 Has a clear and concise statement of problems and/or opportunities been developed?
4 What courses of action are to be evaluated?

Decision Maker   The researcher must distinguish between the decision maker and those who represent the decision maker. Often the person who first requests assistance from the marketing research system is not the decision maker. This individual may or may not know how the decision maker views the specifics of the decision situation. Valuable time and effort can be saved if the researcher insists on meeting directly with the individual who has major responsibility for making the decision.

A meeting with the decision maker may be difficult in practice. Many organizations have complicated formal and informal command structures; also, the organizational status of the researcher or the research department may make it difficult to reach the ultimate decision maker in the early stages of the research process. Finally, in many decision situations a number of individuals may influence the decision or act together as the decision maker. Meeting with them as a group or individually may be difficult, and the coordination of a clear statement regarding the decision situation may be even more so. Despite these potential problems, it is essential that the researcher understand the problem situation from the perspective of the decision maker.

Objectives of the Decision Maker   Decisions are made to accomplish objectives. The success of a research study is dependent on a clear understanding of the decision objectives. A major task of the marketing researcher is to skillfully identify the organizational objectives and be sensitive to the personal objectives lurking in the background of the decision process. A successful researcher may be one who can design research to serve the needs of the organization effectively while at the same time enhancing the personal objectives of the decision maker.

The identification of objectives can be a difficult assignment in practice. Despite a popular misconception to the contrary, objectives are seldom given to the researcher. The decision maker seldom formulates objectives accurately. He or she is likely to state his or her objectives in the form of platitudes that have no operational significance. Consequently, objectives usually have to be extracted by the researcher. In so doing the researcher may well be performing his or her most useful service to the decision maker.

Direct questioning of the decision maker seldom reveals all the relevant objectives. One effective technique for uncovering these objectives consists of confronting the decision maker with each of the possible solutions to a problem and asking whether he or she would follow that course of action. Where the answer is "no," further probing will usually reveal objectives that are not served by the course of action.

Effective Statement of Problems and Opportunities There is probably no activity more critical to the success of the formal research process than a clear and concise statement of problems and/or opportunities. Far too often this task is the most neglected phase in initiating the research project. Improper definition of the problem or opportunity can easily lead astray all subsequent efforts to provide useful information for decision making.

The researcher must be sensitive to managers who are reacting to symptoms or vague feelings regarding a possible problem and/or opportunity. The researcher's task is to ask probing questions of the manager to determine the existing degree of knowledge regarding the underlying causes of the decision situation. As discussed previously, exploratory research may be needed to facilitate the development of the statement of problems and opportunities.

Courses of Action The researcher must be satisfied that the relevant courses of action have been identified and approved by management. Nothing can destroy an otherwise successful research study more readily than finding that a key alternative was not evaluated.

Given a clear understanding of the courses of action relevant to the decision situation, the researcher can turn to the task of establishing the research objectives and identifying the scientific information needs for evaluating the courses of action.

Determine Research Objectives

Research objectives answer the question "What is the purpose of the research project?" For example, the research study discussed in Chapter 3 had the following objectives:

1 To determine which container markets have the greatest consumer acceptance of plastic containers

2 To determine the characteristics of plastic containers that represent advantages compared with paper, paperboard, glass, and metal containers

The research objectives should be put in writing and communicated to the decision maker; they explain why the project is being conducted, and it is important that the researcher and decision maker be in agreement.

Research objectives can be stated so broadly that they fail to communicate the specifics of why the study is being conducted. For example, the following lacks the precise detail of the research objective given previously: *To study consumer reactions to containers.*

A broad statement like this does not indicate what type of container is to be studied, what is to be measured, and how the information might be used. While the degree of detail in the research objectives is dependent upon the nature of the decision situation, generally the more specific the statement of objectives, the lower the risk that management will misperceive the purpose of the study.

In some respects, the more detailed the statement of research objectives, the more it coincides with the listing of information needs. Figure 4-4 highlights the pyramiding aspect of research objectives, information needs, and questions on the data collection forms.

Specify Information Needs

After the research objectives have been specified, the next question concerns "What specific information is needed by the decision maker?" A listing of specific information needs is designed to answer this question.

Research objectives that are specified in great detail often coincide with a more general listing of information needs. In the same manner, a more detailed listing of information needs coincides with the specific questions developed for the questionnaire. Consequently, research objectives serve to guide the research project by giving direction to the specific information to be gathered and the specific questions to be developed for the questionnaire.

From another perspective, we can say that each question on the questionnaire should have a direct correspondence to an information need, and each information need should have a direct correspondence to a research objective. If such a correspondence is not established, unneeded data will be collected.

The decision maker should be actively involved in formulating the research objectives and in specifying the information needs, because only the decision maker has a clear perspective on the character and specificity of the information needed to reduce the uncertainty surrounding the decision situation. Failure to involve the decision maker in this regard can severely hamper the success of the research project.

(An example of specifying research objectives and listing information needs was presented in Chapter 3; a review of this chapter should provide a concrete illustration of the points discussed here.)

In developing the list of information needs, both the manager and the researcher should ask, for each item, "Can this information be obtained?" The skills and judgment of the researcher come to the fore at this point.

The data collection process imposes many limitations on the types of information that can be collected. In surveys, buyers or distributors may refuse to

FIGURE 4-4   Pyramid of research objectives and information needs.

disclose certain types of information, or they may not have the knowledge to answer the questions accurately. Consequently, many excellent information needs may be developed, but if it is not possible to collect the information, time and effort will be wasted in the research process. The manager and researcher need to work closely in this regard to assure a correspondence between the information required and the ability of the marketing research system to gather it.

Visualize the Research Findings

Assuming that the information can be gathered, it is important that the potential research findings be visualized and the question asked, "Of what use are these data to the decision situation?" Many managers and researchers find that mocking up the potential research findings is a valuable way to ensure that the data to be collected will fit the information needs specified by the decision maker. Often, the decision maker can identify gaps in the original list of needs which can be easily corrected at this preliminary stage of the research project.

The concept of mocking up the potential research findings means that each stage of the research process must be anticipated. For example, in survey research specific questions must first be developed for the questionnaire. Next, the data processing and analysis must be established; then the resulting data can be visualized. At this point, the decision maker would be presented with a mock-up of the data in the form of various tables or graphs containing potential research findings. In essence, the research presentation or report is simulated prior to conducting the project.

The actual data presented may represent a range of optimistic, most likely, and pessimistic results. From this mock-up of findings, the manager and researcher may be able to determine whether the data intended to be collected will serve to reduce the uncertainty surrounding the decision situation. If not, the wisdom of collecting the data should be challenged.

Often, the manager can more clearly specify how the data should be analyzed and presented after seeing a mock-up of the potential findings. Additional cross tabulations may be requested, and several multivariate analysis approaches may be required. Often, certain data analysis approaches require that the questionnaire be developed in a certain format, that specific questions be asked, or that the data be tabulated in a certain manner. If these issues are not addressed prior to executing the project, it may be that added costs and delays are incurred at later stages or that the data cannot be obtained. Consequently, the directions received from the manager before beginning the project can be invaluable to its success.

Develop Decision Criteria

Once the research findings have been visualized and the decision maker and researcher are confident that the information needs are complete and the data analysis appropriate, the issue of *decision criteria* should be addressed. Decision criteria are concerned with the rules for selecting among courses of action given various data outcomes.

Developing decision criteria often means setting up a series of "if then" statements. For example:

1 If the research finds a 5 percent potential market share or larger for our new product, then we will proceed to test-market.

2 If the research finds a 3 to 5 percent potential market share, then we will reformulate the new product.

3 If the research finds less than a 3 percent potential market share, then we will abandon the project.

It is important that decision criteria be developed before the decision maker and the researcher experience the actual results. Having clear decision rules prior to the research results ensures that organizational objectives take priority over personal objectives and that they assist the data analysis and reporting stages. In addition, decision rules maintain a balance between the weight assigned to information existing prior to the research and the research findings. The absence of decision criteria can result in assignment of an inappropriate weight to the research findings, depending upon the research outcome and the reaction of management to experiencing the outcome for the first time.

Determine the Cost and Value of the Research

The evaluation of most activities in an organization is approached on a cost-benefit basis. While it is fairly easy to quantify the costs directly associated with a research project, it is very difficult to quantify the benefits. Benefits are often subjective in nature. Consequently, the evaluation of research is inherently subjective.

Given the cost of research, it is possible to determine the number of units of a product that need to be sold to break even on the cost of the research project. Table 4-1 illustrates this type of thinking for two market sizes and two contribution levels. For example, if the research project costs $10,000 and the contribution

TABLE 4-1   RESEARCH VALUE AS FUNCTION OF CONTRIBUTION MARGIN AND MARKET SIZE

Market size	Contribution margin	
	Small	Large
Small	Unlikely research can be supported, e.g., hobby glue (Elmers), nail clippers (Trim), screwdriver (Stanley)	Can support some small research, e.g., specialty tape (3M), specialty drugs (Upjohn), executive aircraft (Lear)
Large	Can support large amount of research, e.g., razor blades (Gillette), soap powder (Tide), soft drinks (Coca-Cola)	Easy to support large amount of research, e.g., automobiles (Ford), appliances (Hotpoint), long-distance calls (AT&T)

margin is $0.10 per unit (selling price = $1; variable cost = $0.90), the breakeven point is 100,000 units. However, if the contribution margin is $0.90 per unit (selling price = $1; variable cost $0.10), the breakeven point is reduced to 11,111 units. Given a large market size (e.g., 1 million units), the breakeven points represent a small share of market (i.e., 1 percent and 0.1 percent). Assuming a smaller market size (e.g., 10,000 units), the breakeven points are substantially higher (i.e., 100 percent and 10 percent).

Extending this thinking to real products, the contribution margin of $100 per automobile in a market of 500,000 units is a total contribution of $50 million. This level of contribution can easily support a research project of $10,000. However, the contribution margin of $0.20 per screwdriver in a market of 100,000 units is $20,000. Spending half of this contribution on a $10,000 research project is obviously difficult to justify.

In general, these calculations suggest that it is easier to justify the cost of research as the market size increases and as the ratio of variable cost to selling price decreases. Therefore, the benefits resulting from a $10,000 research project designed to evaluate alternative advertising campaigns to stimulate demand for long-distance phone calls may be easier to justify than a similar study dealing with a new hobby kit glue. While this type of calculation does not determine the actual benefit derived from such a study, it does indicate the level of benefit needed to cover the cost of research.

There is an additional concept that relates directly to the manager's evaluation of the benefits of marketing research. This concept is the degree of certainty that the manager holds about particular outcomes of the organization's courses of action. For example, a manager might say, "I am 95 percent sure that this advertising theme will be a success." This manager should be much less likely to undertake research on the new advertising theme than a manager who says, "I am about 50 percent sure that this advertising theme will be a success." The purpose of marketing research is to reduce the uncertainty about the outcomes of alternative courses of action. Thus, the value of research to a manager increases as the degree of certainty decreases. Again, it is a subjective evaluation by the manager.

In summary, the value of research to a manager increases as (1) the market size increases, (2) the ratio of variable cost to selling price decreases, and (3) the degree of certainty held about outcomes of actions decreases.

Control the Use of the Research

The success of the research project depends heavily upon the ability of the managers and researchers to work together effectively. For most managers, decision making is a highly personalized process which is influenced by the individual's management style and the specifics of the decision situation. The researcher must be sensitive to this situation in developing an effective working relationship with the decision maker. The success of the research project rests upon the quality of this marriage. There are several ways to ensure that research is being used effectively in the decision-making process.

Organizational Design   The various organizational designs discussed in Chapter 2 can serve to control the effectiveness of contacts between decision makers and researchers. One design is to assign management responsibility for the initial and final stages of the research process; here the responsibility for the effectiveness of the research rests predominantly in the management camp. The researcher's responsibility is that of adviser regarding the initial and final stages, with primary responsibility for the middle stages of data collection and processing. Typically, the researcher has the right to refuse to conduct a study which he or she views as inappropriate.

An alternative organizational design involves keeping the responsibility for the research process within the research camp while giving the researcher a more powerful organizational role in dealing with management. For example, the researcher may be required to participate in the majority of management meetings regardless of whether the use of research is an issue. Here, the researcher is viewed as part of the management team and is assigned responsibility for identifying decision situations in which research is appropriate.

A compromise between these two organizational designs involves the creation of the position of research generalist, someone who serves as an intermediary between the research and management camps. The generalist's main responsibility is to promote effective contacts between decision makers and researchers. The research generalist concept was discussed in Chapter 2.

Research Request Forms   Most organizations require that the decision to undertake research be in writing and approved by upper management and the director of marketing research. This formal request typically involves a standard form which is completed by the decision maker and/or the marketing researcher. Exhibit 4-1 illustrates the type of information requested on such a form.

The purpose of the research request form is to ensure that all the areas identified on the form have been covered by the decision makers and researchers. There is a degree of commitment associated with things in writing that rarely exists with informal agreements.

Additional forms may be used in some companies for the remaining steps in the research process—for example, project budget estimate forms, project control forms, and project evaluation forms.

Present the Proposal for Research

For projects conducted predominantly within the organization, the research request form usually serves as the research proposal. In practice, most research projects have some phase of the study conducted by outside contractors. Typically, this involves the field interviewing phase. A growing number of organizations are expanding their reliance on outside contractors and using them to conduct more phases of the research process. In some situations, an organization may rely entirely on an outside contractor to conduct the research study. Here, several outside contractors could be asked to submit a proposal for research.

EXHIBIT 4-1

RESEARCH REQUEST FORM

Title: _____   Date prepared: _____

Requested by: _____   Start of project: _____

Approved by: _____   Report due: _____

Date approved: _____   Budget: _____

Project number: _____   Supplier: _____

1 *Background.* What led to the recognition that research was needed?
2 *Objectives.* What are the decision objectives?
3 *Problem/opportunity.* What are the underlying causes of the decision situation?
4 *Decision alternatives.* What are the alternative courses of action?
5 *Research objectives.* What is the purpose of the research?
6 *Information needs.* What type of information is needed?
7 *Example of questions.* What kind of questions should be asked?
8 *Decision criteria.* What criteria should be used to select the best alternative?
9 *Value of research.* Why is the research useful?

SANCTIONING INTERNATIONAL MARKETING RESEARCH

The approach to the sanctioning of marketing research outlined in this chapter is totally applicable to both the domestic and the international context. However, there are some special issues that are unique to the international arena.

First, the level of uncertainty held by a manager *should* be higher in the international than in the domestic context. This is because the manager's experience and insights are often less developed for the international situation. Unfortunately, some marketing managers believe that domestic-based research findings and experience apply directly to the international situation. Thus they actually perceive less uncertainty than they perceived in the domestic context prior to the completion of the domestic research. The successful application of a marketing research-based marketing strategy domestically gives some managers the mistaken belief that they now really understand the marketing of their product or service in all parts of the world. The domestic research and program success has reduced their uncertainty about the rest of the world.

The dire consequences of this lowered uncertainty level are well illustrated in Chapter 1 in the description of the attempts at international marketing by a soft-drink company, Vic Tanny's, and Lego A/S. If you believe that domestic research results apply to an international situation, then you will have little uncertainty about the results that would occur in that foreign environment. Thus your perception of the value of marketing research will decline.

Second, the cost of doing marketing research is often much higher internationally than in the United States. Samples are harder to select, interviewing is more complicated, the infrastructure of marketing research firms is often less competent or less available, and communications facilities are not as well developed. Third, the markets are often not as large as the domestic U.S. market. Thus, the potential revenue and profit outcomes are less than in the U.S. market.

We can now see why the sanctioning of international marketing research is often restricted relative to that of domestic marketing research: the managers' perceived uncertainty may be less (often erroneously), the cost of the marketing research is often higher, and the positive profit consequences of the decision are often lower. These factors all act to reduce the perceived value of the marketing research to the manager.

To improve managers' perceptions of the value of marketing research, several steps can be taken. First, there is a great need to educate managers to the level of uncertainty that they actually should hold in foreign environments. Second, a research study can be designed in which several countries are combined on the basis of relevant similar characteristics, such as geography and economic conditions. This will increase the market size and the potential profit outcome of the marketing decisions. Obviously, great care must be taken not to combine so many countries that really meaningful marketing differences are lost.

There are some general differences in international marketing research, and there is a pattern of different types of marketing research needs of firms at different levels of global development in their marketing strategy. These issues are noted in the Global Marketing Research Dynamics.

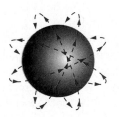

GLOBAL MARKETING RESEARCH DYNAMICS

SANCTIONING INTERNATIONAL MARKETING RESEARCH

Compared to domestic marketing research, international marketing research is found to be generally less formal and less quantitative. Managers seem to rely more on their subjective assessments than on systematic, objective analyses in assessing foreign market potentials and in evaluating foreign distributors. Reasons for this more casual and subjective approach include the difficulty involved in gathering relevant and reliable information, as well as time and budgetary constraints.

The nature and complexity of international marketing research is also found to be a function of a company's international involvement and the risks it encounters. When the amount at stake is not substantial, managers often prefer to make decisions on the basis of limited research, aided by "judgment calls." The stage of a company's internationalization is another determinant of the nature and complexity of research. Many multinational companies with high degrees of internationalization have developed fairly formalized and sophisticated procedures for international marketing research. They have also accumulated large bases of relevant information and expertise concerning foreign markets.

Different stages of international involvement also require different levels of information regarding foreign marketing operations. Four basic levels of internationalization can be identified, as follows: (1) reactive/opportunistic, (2) experimental, (3) active, and (4) committed. Exhibit 1 outlines the dominant research issues for companies at each level.

EXHIBIT 1

**DOMINANT RESEARCH THEMES FOR COMPANIES AT
DIFFERENT STAGES OF INTERNATIONALIZATION**

1 Reactive/Opportunistic Exporting

How to determine profitability of exporting
   How to respond to overseas inquiries and orders
   How to check creditworthiness
   How to obtain export financing
   How to arrange for export packing, documentation, and shipping

2 Experimental/Active Exporting

How to locate potential customers
   How to assess sales opportunities in specific markets
   How to select overseas distributors and support them
   How to adapt products for foreign customers
   How to prepare promotional materials and exhibit products
   How to handle internal organization for exporting

3 Complex/Committed International Business

How to develop long-term opportunities
   How to prioritize markets
   How to choose from available entry alternatives
   How to prepare and implement marketing plans
   How to monitor performance of foreign subsidiaries and distributors

The *reactive/opportunistic exporters* are companies "getting their feet wet" in exporting. Their main research issue is *how to export*, and they concentrate their efforts on the mechanics of exporting, such as documentation, shipping, and payments. They are reluctant to commit significant resources or to aggressively seek export market opportunities.

The *experimenting exporters* are more committed to international marketing, but their exporting activities are still marginal. Their main research issue is *proficiency in exporting*, and they concentrate on identifying specific sales leads and foreign distributors/agents. They must build in-house expertise and experience to advance.

The *active exporters* are experienced exporters who have built a substantial volume of foreign sales, usually more than 20 percent of total sales. Their main research issue is *generating a constant stream of international marketing opportunities*.

The *committed exporters* have the highest level of international involvement and include many multinational companies. Their main research issues are the *strategic concerns of exporting*. There is a constant flow of information between the headquarters research staff and their counterparts in foreign markets, and coordination of research activities among all units of the company is a major concern.

Source: Adapted from S. Tamer Cavusgil, "Qualitative Insights into Company Experiences in International Marketing Research," *The Journal of Business and Industrial Marketing,* pp. 41–54, Summer 1987.

THE MANAGEMENT-RESEARCH RELATIONSHIP

The effectiveness of the research system is dependent upon researchers' relationship with marketing managers. Many factors influence the success of this interpersonal contact, such as differences between some managers and researchers in job responsibilities, career objectives, and educational backgrounds.

The research system requires the skills and knowledge of specialized people. A research department may have individuals specializing in various steps of the research process—for example, questionnaire design, field supervision, data processing, data analysis, and report preparation. Specialization involving the marketing mix decision areas is common; individuals or groups may specialize in advertising research, distribution research, product development research, and so on. People trained in statistics, mathematics, psychology, computer science, and economics often qualify for these specialized positions. Frequently, these individuals have limited training and perspective regarding the role of applied research in the management decision-making process.

A research specialist who is not management-oriented will often accept a request for research help without clearly establishing the need for research. This person may fail to ask perceptive questions regarding the decision situation and may be uncritical of whether research will facilitate the decision-making process. In addition, many specialists are more concerned with the technical sophistication of the research design and methodology than with the information needs of management. This focus leads many researchers to look for decision situations where they can apply the latest research techniques. Many managers view researchers as more concerned with finding an application for their techniques than with supplying information for decision making. This emphasis on technique results in use of technical jargon and standardized ways of presenting research findings, which tends to inhibit the management research communication process, especially in the reporting of research results.

In reporting research findings, some researchers fail to recognize that their role is advisory; they are not being asked to make the decision for management. The researcher can play a very active and supportive role in the decision-making process, but the responsibility for making the decision rests with management. The researcher may become frustrated by the constraints of this advisory role and develop the feeling that "I can make better decisions than management."

Why shouldn't the researcher participate in making the decision? First, the objectivity of the research process could be influenced. The researcher's personal biases and vested interests associated with various decision outcomes could decrease the objectivity of the research design and the analysis of the findings. Second, the researcher would weigh the research findings heavily in selecting a course of action. In contrast, the manager can evaluate and weigh the significance of the research findings in the context of experience and knowledge plus the broader policy considerations associated with the decision.

While many researchers are not sufficiently management-oriented, many managers are not sufficiently research-oriented. Far too many managers have no training in marketing research and a limited perspective on the nature and role of research in the decision-making process. This inhibits their active involvement in the stages of the research project. This lack of participation can diminish the usefulness of the research findings. If the manager does not view research as a natural aspect of the decision-making process, the researcher is forced to solicit research studies from the manager. This results in myopic and fragmented studies which rarely make a significant contribution to the decision-making process. The effectiveness of marketing research is dependent on the skills and perspective of the manager in using the research function in decision making.

Some managers operate as if the researcher were clairvoyant regarding the nature of the decision situation, the courses of action that appear reasonable, the objective to be accomplished, and the information needed to reduce the decision uncertainty. Few managers explain these areas lucidly to the researcher. In some cases the manager may be unwilling or unable to communicate this type of information. Consequently, many research projects are not decision-oriented because of the manager's poor communication skills.

The manager may view research as a way to satisfy needs other than those related to decision making, resulting in a phenomenon that has been called pseudo-research. Some typical "other needs" are listed below.

1 The manager can use marketing research as a way to gain visibility and power in the organization.

2 Marketing research can be used to justify decisions already made. If the research results contradict the decision, the manager can declare the research invalid or simply ignore it altogether.

3 Marketing research can be conducted to establish a scapegoat for marketing decisions that do not accomplish objectives. If the decision is successful, the manager can take full credit; if it is not successful, marketing research is to blame.

4 Marketing research can be used as a promotion tool for service organizations like advertising agencies and media to attract new business and impress current clients.

5 Marketing research can serve to soothe an anxious manager with the knowledge that "something is being done."

6 Managers may support marketing research studies and new research methodology because they believe it is the "faddish thing to do" or the current trend in management practice.

Several barriers to the effective management utilization of marketing research have been identified, including:

1 Some managers view research as a threat to their personal status as decision makers. They fear that marketing research information may conflict with or invalidate the "knowledge" gained from experience and judgment. These managers may believe that this "knowledge" is what justifies their status and position.

2 The absence of systematic planning procedures in many organizations contributes to the lack of common organizational objectives for managers. In the absence of clear organizational objectives, the managers will substitute their own objectives, which can result in conflict among managers. Research may be seen as a way to support one's view in this internal struggle for power. Managers who believe that marketing research will enhance their position will favor it, while others will oppose it.

3 Some managers are unable to effectively work with, understand, and use the knowledge and skills of research specialists. The interdisciplinary training of specialists makes communication difficult.

4 The isolation of marketing research personnel from the managers can be a problem. The effective use of marketing research assumes that research personnel will have a close and continuous relationship with the managers. Often marketing research departments are handicapped in this regard by low organizational status. The weakness of this organizational arrangement is that it depends on the initiative of the manager for effective use of marketing research. Too often managers are unfamiliar with the nature and role of research and are unable to identify problems well enough to ask for the help they need. Those research departments that operate on management request tend to be occupied with routine, short-range operating problems.

Listed below are some industry-based words of advice with respect to the manager-research interface.

1 Researchers love a surprise. Managers do not like surprises; when they are surprised, they tend to reject the research.

2 Researchers like to explore. Managers prefer to confirm. Researchers should be sensitive to managerial "comfort zones."

3 Technical quality does not speak for itself. Working together influences perceptions of technical quality and creates trust in the research results.

4 Political acceptability of research results is perceived by researchers as a major consideration for use. An effective working relationship between researcher and manager can enhance political acceptability.

5 Manager-researcher interaction, of all variables studied, has the highest total influence on research use. Open and frequent communication between researchers and managers is vital to marketing research effectiveness.

6 Good horizontal relationships (teaming of researchers with product managers) are more important than vertical relationships (e.g., reporting to the senior marketing executive).

7 Involvement in the strategic planning process separates more effective marketing research departments from less effective ones. But most research is tactical, and researchers feel excluded from strategy formulation.

8 Managers expect research to come up with innovative solutions or courses of action. Research is not perceived as doing so. More involvement in strategy formulations might help.

9 Smooth planning and delivery of marketing research services have a strong influence on management satisfaction. On the other hand, researchers perceive managers as making sudden changes in data needs, priorities, or deadlines.

TABLE 4-2   PROBABLE AREAS OF TOP MANAGEMENT-MARKETING RESEARCH CONFLICT

Top management position	Area	Marketing research position
Marketing research (MR) lacks sense of accountability. Sole MR function is as an information provider	Research responsibility	Responsibility should be explicitly defined and consistently followed. MR desires decision-making involvement with top management (TM).
Researchers are generally poor communicators. They lack enthusiasm, sales expertise, and imagination.	Research personnel	TM is anti-intellectual. Researchers should be hired, judged, and compensated on research capabilities.
Research costs too much. Since MR contribution is difficult to measure, budget cuts are relatively defensible.	Budget	"You get what you pay for." There needs to be a continuing, long-range TM commitment.
Assignments tend to be overengineered. They are not executed with a proper sense of urgency. MR exhibits ritualized, staid approach.	Assignments	There are too many nonresearchable requests. There are too many "fire-fighting" requests. Insufficient time and money are allocated.
MR is best equipped to do this. General direction is sufficient. MR must appreciate and respond. Circumstances change.	Problem definition	TM is generally unsympathetic to this widespread problem. MR is not given all the relevant facts. Problems change after research is under way.
Reports are characterized as dull, with too much "researchese" and too many qualifiers. Reporting is not decision-oriented. Too often, reports come after the fact.	Research reporting	TM treats reports superficially. Good research demands thorough reporting and documentation. Insufficient lead time is given.
TM is free to use research as it pleases. MR shouldn't question. Changes in need and timing of research are sometimes unavoidable. MR is deceived by not knowing all the facts.	Use of research	TM uses research to support a predetermined position—represents misuse. Research isn't used after it has been requested and conducted; it's wasteful. TM uses research to confirm or excuse past actions.

The previous discussion has emphasized many of the factors that can influence the effectiveness of the management-research relationship. The most basic causes of conflict have been identified as research responsibility, research personnel, budget, assignments, problem definition, research reporting, and the use of research. Table 4-2 presents the typical positions of top management and marketing research staff on these areas of conflict.

What can be done to minimize this organizational conflict? The research system requires the skills and knowledge of specialists. It also must be sensitive to the needs of management and communicate in management language. Those specialists who find it difficult to communicate with management must be restricted to an analytic role within the research system. The specialist's work can be guided by the use of people who have been referred to as "research generalists." (See Chapter 2.)

SUMMARY

1 The analysis underlying the decision to undertake research largely determines the success of the research project. Failure to establish an effective link between the decision process and the research process can result in inadequate research findings and management dissatisfaction with the marketing research system.

2 Marketing research can be classified according to the way it interacts with the decision-making process. Exploratory research is designed to facilitate recognition of a decision situation and to aid in identifying alternative courses of action. Conclusive research is concerned with providing information to evaluate and select a course of action. Performance-monitoring research serves to control the marketing program in accordance with objectives by providing feedback regarding performance. Effective management is dependent upon an effective control system that can signal the existence of problems and/or opportunities.

3 The decision process begins with the recognition that a unique marketing problem exists or that an opportunity is present. Problems are detected when objectives are established and a measure of performance indicates that the objectives are not being met. Opportunities are present in situations where performance can be improved by undertaking new activities. A symptom is a condition that signals the presence of a problem or opportunity. It often triggers the analysis process designed to identify and define problems and opportunities.

4 A decision problem is present in situations where the manager faces a choice among alternative courses of action in which uncertainty exists regarding the outcome of the decision. Implicit in any decision problem is a clear statement of objectives plus the identification of problems and/or opportunities.

5 A situational analysis is the process which leads to the identification of problems and opportunities. This involves a diagnosis and prognosis of the marketing program and situational variables in the marketing system.

6 Once the decision problem has been formulated, the next step is to identify alternative courses of action. A course of action is the specification of how the organization's resources are to be developed in a given period. Creativity is needed to identify innovative and highly effective courses of action. Exploratory research can be very useful in this regard.

7 Once the alternatives have been established, the manager may turn to the use of conclusive research. Conclusive research provides information for the evaluation of courses of action.

8 The first step in the conclusive research process is to establish the need for information. The researcher plays a vital role in this process. The decision maker must be clearly identified and the objectives of the decision situation established. A clear statement of problems and/or opportunities must be developed and the alternative courses of action identified. Based on this information, the researcher can formulate the research objectives.

9 Research objectives establish the purpose of the study. They should be in writing and should be clearly communicated to the decision maker.

10 The specific types of information needed by the decision maker should be identified in writing. The researcher must determine whether it is indeed possible to obtain the type of information requested.

11 The potential research findings should be visualized prior to conducting the study. Preparing a mock-up of the results is a valuable way to ensure that the data to be collected meet the information needs of the decision situation.

12 Decision criteria for selecting among courses of action given various data outcomes should be established prior to conducting the study.

13 The cost of obtaining the information should be weighed against the benefits which result from a reduction in the decision uncertainty. This type of evaluation is inherently subjective.

14 Various organizational designs can facilitate the establishment of an effective link between the decision process and the research process. Requiring research request forms to be completed prior to undertaking research also strengthens the effectiveness of this link.

15 For research projects conducted within an organization, the research request form serves as the proposal for research. When outside contractors bid on the research project, more elaborate research proposals are required. It is important that clear decision criteria be established for the evaluation of the proposals submitted.

16 Many factors influence the effectiveness of the management-research relationship. An effective research system is one which is respected by management and focuses on the needs of management. Many sources of conflict can be reduced by proper training of both research and management regarding the role of research in the decision-making process. The creation of the position "research generalist" has substantially increased the effectiveness of the management-research relationship.

DISCUSSION QUESTIONS

1 Why is the analysis preceding the decision to undertake research so crucial to the success of the project?

2 Discuss the types of marketing research appropriate for various stages of the decision-making process.

3 Distinguish among problems, opportunities, and symptoms.

4 What are the essential elements of a decision problem?

5 What are the implications for the marketing researcher of a decision situation characterized by primary (organizational) and secondary (personal) objectives?

6 What are the purpose and the nature of a situational analysis?

7 What is the basic criterion in deciding whether or not to conduct a research project?

8 What are the responsibilities of the researcher in establishing the need for marketing research information?

9 What characteristics should research objectives possess?

10 Should the decision maker be involved in formulating research objectives and listing information needs? Why or why not?

11 Of what use is a mock-up of potential research findings?

12 What are decision criteria? When should they be developed?

13 Why is the evaluation (a priori) of marketing research inherently subjective?

14 How might an organization ensure that marketing research is being used effectively in the decision-making process?

15 What are some of the factors which impinge upon the management-research relationship?

16 What actions should Melissa Molloy (see the Marketing Research in Action at the beginning of this chapter) take related to her perceived misuse of marketing research results?

17 It is reported that General Motors expended over $500,000 on marketing research for the 1995 Oldsmobile Aurora. Why would this much expenditure be justified?

18 **MINICASE**

Procter & Gamble is considering the simultaneous launch of a liquid detergent in 10 European countries. This product is based on a successful product introduction in the United States. What marketing research program would you recommend that P&G undertake?

CASES FOR PART ONE

CASE 1-1   National Markets—Nutritional Labeling*

Jose Martinez was the president of Midwest Marketing Research Associates (MMRA). He was in the process of preparing a marketing research proposal for National Markets, the largest supermarket chain in the midwestern United States. National's market share had been declining steadily for the past year and a half, and the marketing department was determined to turn things around. The senior members in the department had formulated a plan, but they needed marketing research data in order to verify the plan's validity to other National departments. MMRA was one of three major marketing research firms vying for this research project. The completed research proposal was due in 2 weeks.

Martinez had had a meeting with National's marketing department earlier in the month to roughly define the purpose of the project. Michelle Stead, vice president in charge of marketing at National, hadn't outlined the specific information needs; rather, she had gone over the problems that were facing National. She had indicated to Martinez that it would be up to him to formulate research objectives based on his perception of the information needs.

Stead told him that National's sales had been increasing at a slower pace than its competitors' and that National wanted to reverse this trend through "goodwill gestures" aimed at consumers. The tentative plan was to provide shoppers with detailed nutritional information about the packaged foods sold in National stores. But National executives weren't sure exactly how the information should be presented to consumers, how the consumers would react to it, or even whether they

*Source: Coauthored by Sheryl Petras.

would use the information. Because of these concerns, initiation of the program had been delayed until consumers' attitudes could be researched.

Bart Russell, National's district manager for Illinois and Indiana, foresaw several potential problems with the proposed "solution." First of all, he related to Martinez, stores would be reluctant to post information that might cut their profits. Since many of the high-margin items were also the least nutritious, consumers might avoid the nonnutritious—but highly profitable—foods if nutritional information were available. Second, the cost to provide this information would be high unless the stores were subsidized by the National main office. The majority of National's stores could not afford to offer additional services to shoppers without boosting prices. But, said Russell, store managers would furnish nutritional information readily if they were shown that the cost of providing this information would be offset by the benefits gained if more people began shopping at National. The marketing department hoped that presenting favorable marketing research results to the store managers would make them more willing to accept the idea of forgoing some short-term profits for long-range benefits.

The nutritional information had already been gathered by National, so the only cost to the individual stores would come from disseminating these data to consumers. The information had, for the most part, been obtained from outside sources. For 85 percent of all products, the required nutritional information had been collected from the manufacturers—either directly from the food labels or in response to a written request. For another 9 percent of the products, National managers had weighed

113

the contents of the packages and combined that data with information from the manufacturers, or from the U.S. Department of Agriculture, to determine the nutrient content of the foods. For the remaining 6 percent, National could not acquire nutritional information. Most of these foods were "mixed" foods with low sales volume, like frozen mixed vegetables, or multipacks of single-serving breakfast cereals.

National executives from other (nonmarketing) departments had indicated a willingness to help stores implement the program, but only if marketing research showed that:

1 Shoppers would actually benefit from the information.

2 They would make use of the information.

Even if sales did not increase right away, National top management felt that providing this extra service to consumers would benefit National in the long run by increasing customer loyalty.

Because this project was such a major undertaking, Martinez spent a great deal of time conversing with Stead, as she would be very influential in choosing which company got the research grant. Martinez wanted to be absolutely certain that he had enough information to identify the problem

areas National was most concerned with so that he could define the research objectives correctly. Stead had not set an upper limit on the project's budget, but Martinez wanted to keep it at a reasonable level so as to remain competitive. In the end, though, he knew that the quality of his research proposal would determine whether or not MMRA would be awarded the project.

CASE QUESTIONS

1 Develop a statement of research objectives. Think about: Why the request for information was made. Who the decision makers are. The goals or objectives of the decision makers. The decision-making environment.

2 What are the key information needs? List the five you feel are most important, and be prepared to defend your reasons for listing each.

3 One possible research design would be to interview (in person, by telephone, or through the mail) supermarket shoppers. What are other possible designs?

4 Make a detailed outline of the research proposal you would submit if you were Jose Martinez. (Think about the information that National will be looking for in a research proposal.)

5 Prepare a research proposal. Use the outline you developed in Question 4.

CASE 1-2   Weston Food Company

The following five episodes deal with the relationship between research and management. In each episode, ask yourself: What is going on? Is the research management connection effective? Why or why not? How could the situation be improved? What generalizations can be made about how to establish an effective research/management relationship in an organization?

EPISODE A

Tom Murphy, director of research for the Weston Food Company, has been striving to establish a cordial relationship with the advertising department for several months. He feels that the research

department can supply very useful information regarding the advertising programs of the Weston Food Company.

In response to these efforts, Samantha Jones, the advertising manager, called Murphy, asking for help in developing a new advertising program. "We need to know customers' perceptions, attitudes, and preferences toward our new line of diet products."

Murphy personally directs an extensive research study on the diet product line. Seven weeks later, a thorough report and presentation on current users' attitudes, perceptions, and preference patterns is presented to Jones and her staff. After the presentation, Jones's reaction is: "Certainly a lot of interesting data that we weren't aware of; but how does this help us design a new advertising campaign to switch buyers from competitive diet lines to ours and entice potential dieters to try our line?"

EPISODE B

Jane Phelps, product manager for Weston's "Magic" scouring pads, calls upon Tom Murphy, director of research, to discuss a problem she has. "Good to see you again, Tom. As you know, sales volume on 'Magic' has not reached the targeted market share. We are seven points off target. I feel it is time to do some research on this problem. It's obvious to me that the culprit is our package design. We just don't catch the eye of the consumer like SOS does. Also, the package does a poor job in conveying the product concept and our point of difference from SOS."

Murphy concurs with Jane Phelps that the packaging is poorly done and that the research department could provide useful information concerning the selection of a new package design.

He goes on to say, "This type of problem lends itself to controlled experimentation very well. As you know, Barbara Kindle is an expert on experimental design and would be delighted to develop a research proposal that would get right at this problem."

Phelps reacts: Sounds excellent to me. Can you have a proposal put together by Thursday?

Murphy replies: I'll have to check with Barbara first; but let's plan on a Thursday afternoon meeting in conference room C.

Phelps: That's great. I know I can always count on the cooperation of the research department.

EPISODE C

Tom Murphy, director of research, cautious about vaguely stated research study objectives, has been impressing on a senior staff member, Sid Alsen, the need for clearly written research proposals including management objectives, information requirements, and anticipated uses of expected results.

During their conversation, Murphy receives a call from the marketing department asking for a research staff member to participate in a planning meeting where research needs will be discussed. Tom tells Sid about the call and suggests that he attend the meeting. Before leaving, Alsen is advised: "Be sure to develop a careful specification of how the information required will be used."

Later in the afternoon, Sid returns from the meeting thoroughly defeated. "They told me it wasn't any of my damn business what they were going to do with the information. We are just supposed to get it and they will decide what to do with it."

EPISODE D

Ellen Tod, senior research analyst, reviews the marketing plan for the instant potato line and reports to her manager, Tom Murphy: "If they had paid any attention to my research report they wouldn't be doing these things. They must be stupid up there; why, I could run that program better!"

Murphy later receives a call from the planning manager, telling him: "If that analyst [Ellen Tod] can't just report the facts and stop trying to make us look stupid, we would rather do without!"

EPISODE E

The following dialog takes place between a product manager, Jim Phiel, and Ellen Tod, senior research analyst.

Tod: I understand you are interested in a consumer test on product C-11.

Phiel: Yes, we definitely need to get some good market feedback.

Tod: What will you do if the results are favorable?

Phiel: National introduction, of course. This product has a great future.

Tod: What if the results are negative?

Phiel: Don't worry about that. I know C-11 will be accepted with enthusiasm.

Tod: But what happens if your expectations are wrong?

Phiel: Look, if you design a good test, we won't have any problems. There are a lot of hopes riding on the success of this product, and we need some good information behind it.

CASE 1-3   Field Modular Office Furniture*

INTRODUCTION: AUGUST 1993

Jane Donne, product manager for Field modular office furniture, one product line of the office furniture division of Stone Corporation, was discussing ways to expand sales with one of the summer interns. The Field line was currently focused on panel technology for office buildings, but Jane was looking for new markets. The new product intern, Cindy Cole, was an M.B.A. from the University of Michigan.

Jane had long felt that sales of panel technology and modular furniture in office buildings were approaching saturation point. Modular furniture and panels allow construction of cubicles and the division of open spaces, and are easily reconfigured for design changes. Field needed to expand into other markets. Cindy's assignment for the summer had been to conduct preliminary research and identify promising areas for further research. The presentation of her ideas had gone well, and Jane had invited Cindy to her office to discuss the action plan.

"Cindy, this is a great report. I think you've done an excellent job in identifying areas where Field may have an advantage. I was especially interested in this section on day-care centers . . . no, that's not the official name . . . early childhood institutions (ECIs). With the increase in working mothers and working hours, their enrollments must be skyrocketing. I know our corporate center is furnished with the panels, but no one realized that other places might be interested. What do you propose we do to follow up on your report?"

Cindy smiled. "Actually, Jane, I wanted to discuss that with you. You'll note that I listed ECIs as one of my 'hot' prospects. That status comes from their growth, which is very healthy. My research was based on secondary sources, of course, including your department's 'idea' file. What we need now is some primary research in this market. You need to get someone to actually talk to the people running the ECIs and learn what they look for in furnishings, what their budgets are like and how they respond to the concept."

"In other words, marketing research. I wish you were going to be here to continue on this project. It would really be a blessing for me not to have to supervise another research project. The research department is great technically, but they're corporate. It's not always easy to get them to see the divisional point of view. And you know so much about it by now."

"Jane, if you're serious, I have a suggestion. My marketing research professor just called me to ask if there was any possibility of Field or Stone sponsoring a project for his class in the fall. As I told you in my interviews, at Michigan the class is taught through the use of one comprehensive project, from design to final report. The student team writes a proposal, prepares a study design, conducts the research and writes a report. Since we have such a clear-cut problem, this project would be ideal for the class. I could serve as your liaison to the class team, advise you on the progress of the project and prepare recommendations at the end, based on my knowledge of Field and the research findings. What do you think?"

"It sounds like a great idea. Why don't you write a memo detailing your involvement and have your professor send me a letter explaining the arrangements?"

Source: Coauthored by Amy Cox. All names have been altered.

Initial Steps: September 6, 1993

"Cindy, this is Professor Jenkins. There is a small problem with the Stone research project."

Enrollment in Professor Jenkins' marketing research class had been higher than anticipated. He was running out of corporate research projects, and was now preparing one to be done under his own auspices on the cultural background on food choice at fast-food restaurants. Two student groups had requested to work on the Stone project, and neither one seemed thrilled about fast food. He had a solution to the impasse, but it required Stone's cooperation. His proposal was as follows.

Each group was to submit a well-written, comprehensive proposal to its company for review. The proposal, prepared after several exploratory meetings, was to include the research goals, information needs, and preliminary research design, including details of methodology.

Professor Jenkins' idea was to have Cindy and her manager brief each group separately. Each group would prepare a proposal. Both would be submitted to Field, and Field would select the one it preferred. The other group would then conduct the professor's fast-food study. After consulting Jane, Cindy gave Professor Jenkins the go-ahead and provided the following information to the groups.

Company Background Field modular office furniture and panel technology was one product line of the Sword Group, which was a fully owned subsidiary of the Stone Corporation. Field's product was a high-quality panel system of modular furniture for office buildings. The line was currently selling well, through a sales force of 30 representatives and 120 dealers.

Sword Group manufactured office furniture of all types, including metal work stations. Sword Group's sales in 1993 were $30 million. The current employment level was 400.

Stone Corporation functioned as a holding company, having diversified into home and office furniture in the early 1980s. Other areas of involvement were automobile products and building supplies. Stone Corporation's total sales in 1993 were $1.4 billion.

ECI Preliminary Information Early childhood institutions included day-care centers, preschools, and kindergartens. One industry source estimated that there were 150,000 ECIs in the United States. This included for-profit (both franchise and independent organizations) and nonprofit institutions, as well as those sponsored by organizations such as military bases, hospitals, and corporations. Approximately 60 percent of the institutions were run on a for-profit basis.

It was estimated that, in 1995, 15 million children of preschool age would have mothers in the work force. In 1985, approximately 23 percent of these children were in ECIs. The real growth rate of the market was estimated at 5 percent per year.

Field Goals: September 13, 1993

Cindy's research, based on several previous studies and notes in the "idea" file, suggested that Field might have a line extension opportunity which would enable it to serve the child-care market, which appeared to be growing quickly.

Field's overall goal for the research project was clear. They wanted to determine:

• Whether it was worthwhile to develop a product line for ECIs.
• If so, how to design products that would have an advantage in this market.
• If so, how and to whom the products should be marketed.

With this background, and operating on a tight deadline, the student groups went to work.

Submission of Proposals: September 27, 1993

Two weeks later, Cindy and Jane met to hear the groups' presentations of the following proposals.

PROPOSAL OF GROUP 1

RESEARCH OBJECTIVES

To enable the Sword Group to determine whether market pricing and budgetary considerations would support introduction of a high-quality room partition into the day-care market.

Primary research will be conducted to determine price points, interior furnishing budgets, purchase frequency, and desirable product attributes.

Secondary research will be conducted to collect complementary information on the structure of the market, the purchase decision process for interior furnishings, spatial design of centers, competitor identification, and distribution methods.

PRIMARY RESEARCH DESIGN

Focus Groups

Two focus groups will be held, in Ann Arbor and Dearborn, Michigan. Participants will be recruited from the administrative level of local day-care centers. Efforts will be made to recruit participants representing a wide variety of centers: corporate- and church-sponsored as well as independent and franchise centers. Participants will be informed of the topics in advance, and offered a $35 incentive. Each session will last approximately 2 hours and will be videotaped for client review.

The focus groups will probe a center's current use of space and physical layout, desirable attributes in furniture, and budgeting and purchasing decisions. The Field product line concept will then be expanded. Participants will be shown several drawings of the panels in question. General feedback about the concept will be requested, as will specific benefits, drawbacks, and suggestions. Pricing issues will also be discussed, in the context of what the participants would be willing to pay for such a product.

Survey

The focus group findings will then be incorporated into a survey, which will be administered over the telephone to day-care directors. Respondents will be drawn from a national list in *Child Care Information Exchange,* a publication targeted at day-care administrators. A sample frame of 100 has been selected. The survey will include a broad array of questions, exploring such areas as:

- The purchase decision process
- Competitors
- Desired attributes in furniture
- Current methods of space division
- Pricing
- Demographics

The survey will also test the Field product concept, by describing the panel and its uses and asking for an evaluation of the concept, likelihood of use, and willingness to pay.

Detailed statistical analysis will be performed on the results, including cluster analysis.

PROPOSAL OF GROUP 2

RESEARCH OBJECTIVES

- Determine the extent of demand for equipment such as furniture among early childhood institutions [ECIs].
- Identify the nature of demand for such products, including product attributes, price, distribution channels, and information sources.
- Suggest which market segments are the most viable for Sword/Field day-care equipment.

RESEARCH DESIGN

Preliminary Research

Secondary sources will be used to determine market size, growth, and interior environment needs. These data will then be used as initial input for the primary research.

Primary Research

A two-step primary research approach will be used.

Interviews   The first exploratory stage of research will be achieved by conducting in-depth, one-on-one interviews with local ECI directors. The group will conduct eight interviews. An outline of suggested topics will be followed for each interview, in order to guarantee consistency. The interview will conclude with the display of a drawing of the product to the director, to solicit their feedback. The group members feel that in-depth interviews at the center will allow them to better understand the functioning of the ECIs.

Survey   The data from the interviews will then be used as input for a mail survey. The goal of the written survey is to develop profiles of different segments of the ECI market, through the use of cluster analysis.

The survey will be mailed to 1000 ECIs throughout the United States. The list used for the survey will be purchased from a mailing list broker whose database includes 152,038 ECIs, excluding family-run or in-home institutions.

The survey is currently expected to cover issues such as:

- Distribution
- Physical layout
- Furniture purchase process
- Type of center operated

The group also plans to include a question on the amount spent by the ECIs on adult office furniture, in order to determine whether this could be a new market for Field's traditional panel technology.

Statistical analysis will be performed, including cross-tabulations, cluster analysis, and regression analysis.

QUALIFICATIONS OF THE RESEARCH GROUP

Pierre Duchesne

Mr. Duchesne is currently earning his M.B.A. at the University of Michigan. His areas of emphasis are marketing and international business. Prior to returning to school for this semester, he was a credit analyst at Credit Suisse.

Teresa Tompkins

Ms. Tompkins has over 10 years of experience in industrial marketing communications. The last seven years of her career have been spent with Mustard & Swerther, Inc., a business-to-business advertising agency in the Detroit area. She is currently the agency's marketing specialist and senior account executive. She is just completing the M.B.A. program at the University of Michigan.

Jonathan Williams

Mr. Williams is currently earning his M.B.A. at the University of Michigan. His area of emphasis is international finance. He is currently a loan officer with Formidable Bank.

CONCLUSION

Cindy and Jane adjourned to a local coffeehouse after thanking the groups for the presentation. There they drank cappucino and reread the proposals.

Jane looked across the marble table. "Well, Cindy, which proposal do you suggest we go with? And why?"

CASE 1-4   United Way of America*

Understanding the dynamics of the marketplace, as well as the needs and wants of customers, and responding to them appropriately is the hallmark of the United Way of America philosophy. To remain successful, the United Way organizations are using a management approach that integrates strategic management and marketing. This approach relies heavily on marketing research data. Today, two-thirds of the 2300 local United Ways are con-

*Source: This case is adapted from George W. Wilkinson, "Getting and Using Information the United Way," *Marketing Research*, pp. 5–12, September 1989. Dr. Wilkinson is vice president of Strategic Institute, United Way of America.

tinually developing and refining this marketing research-based approach.

UNITED WAY OF AMERICA

United Way of America is a nonprofit membership organization for 2300 autonomous local United Way organizations across America. Headquartered in Alexandria, Virginia, it serves as the national service and training center for its members, liaison to national organizations and the federal government, and secretariat for United Way International affiliates in 22 foreign countries. United Way of America raises billions of dollars through its annual campaign. These funds are distributed to more than 37,000 local and national nonprofit organizations providing health and human service programs. Surveys indicate that United Way has almost 11 million volunteers, making it the largest charitable movement in the country.

UNITED WAY OF AMERICA'S CUSTOMERS AND MARKETS

United Way of America serves a large and diverse customer base in many different markets. Because United Way is a membership organization that collects dues, local United Way organizations can easily be identified as its prime customers. Other customers include national agencies such as American Red Cross and Girl Scouts of America, national media, national labor organizations, national and international corporations, national associations, and the federal government.

United Way's markets include individual and corporate donors, volunteers, and people in need. The organization interacts through its customers to affect these markets, including the contributions by its *donors,* the quality and amount of time given by *volunteers,* and the amelioration of the health and human service problems of *people in need.*

INFORMATION FOCUS/USES

With its broad base of customers and markets, United Way of America has diverse information needs. The most general information collection conducted is classified as *environmental analysis* and includes social, economic, political, technological, and philanthropic forces of change in the United States. A volunteer committee monitors over 150 publications, analyzes their contents, and arranges relevant data for distribution to customers. The information is distributed through several United Way publications, the Soundings electronic database on the Human Care Network, and slide and video presentations which are sold to the public to offset the operational cost of gathering the data. United Way of America uses this information to identify threats and opportunities for the organization and its customers as a result of changes in the marketplace. This often triggers national studies on critical issues such as illiteracy, for-profit/non-profit competition, and health care. United Way of America's Strategic Planning Committee studies these issues and recommends actions for both local United Ways and United Way of America.

Most formal data collection is conducted by United Way of America's Research Division. This group concentrates on *attitudinal* and *statistical* data. *Comparative cities databases* are available with both zip code and county-level data and are sold as software packages by United Way of America. One package provides social and economic information, while the second is organized by employment according to SIC code to show number of employees and total payroll. This allows local United Ways to analyze key characteristics and to locate similar United Ways with which to share information. Several standard surveys are conducted regularly to obtain *performance data on local United Ways,* such as who gives to the annual campaign fund, where the funds are distributed, and costs and income sources for United Way operations. The organization compiles these data and makes them available to members in its *Profile* series of reports, on individualized Leader boards, and through the Human Care Network, the electronic system linking United Way of America to over 300 local United Ways for mail and data sharing. *Corporate information* on the top 1000 companies is collected and maintained. These data are purchased and "scanned" from business publications. They include profitability, changes in executive management, and mergers and acquisitions, and are available through both newsletters and the Human Care Network. *National polls and focus groups* track attitudes and perceptions of donors and volunteers toward charity and United Way. These include purchasing sections of the Gallup omnibus polls and using national marketing research firms to conduct segmentation studies, point-of-sale (POS) research, and focus groups on why people volunteer and give to United Way, as well as to test the impact of the organization's advertising. United Way's *Information Center* is a collection of materials produced by local United Ways including annual reports, issue studies, community assessments of need, special project reports, and advertising and communication materials.

United Way of America also uses informal data collection methods to "listen" to its prime customers, the local United Ways. These methods include the following:

- *Participant evaluations* of training sessions to judge context, methodology, and competence
- Divisional or departmental *surveys* to test reactions to new product/service ideas or issues
- *Mail* to the president and divisional vice presidents
- *Dues payments* and *purchases* of products
- *On-site visits* by national staff to local United Ways
- *Special individualized liaison efforts* for each of the 25 largest local United Ways
- A *National Professional Advisory Council and Advisory Committee (NPAC)* of over 500 local United Way professionals which tailors United Way programs to fit the needs of both the entire system and its 2300 individual organizations
- A *satisfaction survey* of United Way of America regarding responsiveness of the organization

and reaction to a variety of products and services offered

DECENTRALIZED MANAGEMENT

Marketing research is a very decentralized function at United Way of America, where "Listening and responding to our customers is everyone's primary job." The Marketing Group, its Research Division, and the Strategic Studies Institute manage the majority of the data collection. Senior executives meet weekly to review information needs and findings and to authorize new ventures. United Way of America dedicates 15 percent of its staff and over $3 million in resources to marketing research.

United Way of America views information as its main service. Members provide information to the national organization, and general and specialized reports such as the Profile Series and Leader boards are provided to the customers in return. The data are also used in training programs, presentations, support for specialized research, and consultation programs, as well as for the creation and maintenance of an electronic database on the Human Care Network that can be manipulated by the customer. The data are further used to support activities of the United Way system as an information source for interface with national corporations' giving programs and legislative initiatives within the federal government.

CASE QUESTIONS

1 What marketing management problems and opportunities form the basis for United Way of America's need for marketing research?
2 What research objectives might United Way have for the marketing research that it implements?
3 What information needs might United Way have for the marketing research that it implements?
4 Evaluate the research designs that United Way utilizes.
5 Evaluate the appropriateness of each of the data sources that United Way utilizes.

CASE 1-5 Ethical Dimensions in Marketing Research*

The following situations and questions have occurred many times in the real world of marketing research. Each raises ethical concerns about the practice of marketing research. For each situation or question, identify what you believe to be the ethical issue and indicate what you would do.

1 A research buyer asks for competitive proposals from a number of research suppliers. The buyer takes ideas from a number of these proposals without offering payment for the ideas and then awards the contract to one of the research suppliers to conduct the study using all the ideas.

2 A research organization uses questions developed for one client in designing a questionnaire for another client.

3 Without obtaining the approval of the client, a simple set of questions for that client is added to another client's questionnaire.

4 A major error is discovered by a research supplier in a study that has been completed and submitted to the client.

5 A research firm is asked to conduct a study by a firm that is in direct competition with one of the research firm's clients.

6 A research firm accepts an assignment with the knowledge that it cannot complete the project in the designated time.

7 A research firm wonders what the ethical issues, if any, are in using entertainment and gifts to help in soliciting business.

8 The director of marketing research presents to senior management the results of a study conducted by a member of the marketing research staff. No mention of this staff member is made during the presentation. In a footnote in the written report, the staff member is given credit for the contribution.

9 A consultant is asked by a highly conservative publication to conduct a readership survey. Although the consultant is well qualified to do the research, the magazine's philosophy is quite inconsistent with her own. She is having difficulty resolving this professional/moral dilemma.

10 A project director has proposed using ultraviolet ink on a questionnaire in a mail survey. The letter with the survey promises that the respondent will not be identified, but the director thinks that the ink identification is needed to save money in the mailing of a follow-up questionnaire to those who do not respond to the first mailing. Without the ink marking, the follow-up questionnaire will have to be mailed to all subjects in the sample, including those who responded to the first mailing.

11 An interviewer tells a respondent that an interview will last only 15 minutes, fully knowing that it takes a half hour. Experience has shown that many respondents who will grant a 15-minute interview would refuse a 30-minute interview. However, once subjects agree to participate, they usually complete the interview process—even if it runs longer than the originally cited time. Thus, nonresponse error can be reduced and data accuracy increased.

12 As part of a study on family buying processes, a family is videotaped as it examines automobiles in a dealer showroom. Also, conversations within the family are recorded by a ''shopper''/researcher. The family is not aware that it is being monitored.

13 A family places its trash in a public alley for pickup. Without asking permission, a researcher sorts through the garbage as part of a brand-preference survey.

*Source: This case was developed using a number of sources, including *Marketing Educator,* vol. 3, no. 1, Winter 1984; Richard Crosby, "Uniform Ethical Cost Is Impractical due to Shifting Marketing Research Circumstances," *Marketing News,* p. 16, September 19, 1981; C. Merle Crawford, "Attitudes of Marketing Executives toward Ethics in Marketing Research," *Journal of Marketing,* pp. 46–52, April 1970; plus suggestions by Philip Hendrix.

PART TWO

DETERMINE RESEARCH DESIGN AND DATA SOURCES

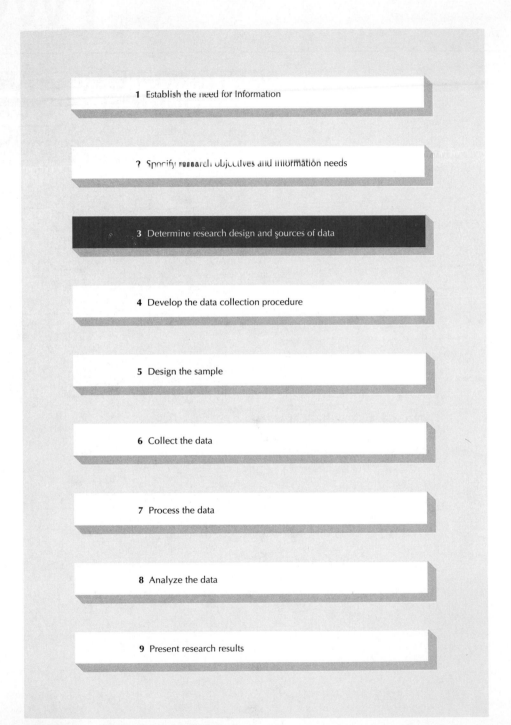

1 Establish the need for Information

2 Specify research objectives and information needs

3 Determine research design and sources of data

4 Develop the data collection procedure

5 Design the sample

6 Collect the data

7 Process the data

8 Analyze the data

9 Present research results

FIGURE 5-1   Steps in the research process.

CHAPTER 5

RESEARCH DESIGN AND DATA SOURCES

MARKETING RESEARCH IN ACTION

MULTIPLE DATA SOURCES USED TO PROFILE SUPERMARKET SHOPPERS

Supermarket shoppers are becoming a far more varied lot. Drawing on a research design using focus groups, surveys, trade journal reports, and retailer experience, consulting firm Booz, Allen & Hamilton concludes that changes in cooking and eating habits in recent years have created six distinct types of supermarket customers, each with different food-shopping needs and attitudes.

Slightly more than a fourth are avid shoppers, the traditional supermarket customers who cook practically all family meals, shop frequently, and search for bargains.

About 20 percent are kitchen strangers—childless men and women who find cooking an inconvenience and rely instead on take-out food and restaurants. Close behind come the constrained shoppers—low-income families and individuals who buy little but basic food needs—and the hurried shoppers, busy people who mostly eat at home but look for shopping and cooking shortcuts.

The last two groups are unfettered shoppers, 13 percent, chiefly older working people whose children have flown the nest, leaving them with more disposable income to spend on food, and the kitchen birds, 6 percent, mainly very old people who are light eaters.

The study, done for the Coca-Cola Retailing Research Council, predicts that over the coming decade, there will be a 7 percent drop in the number of avid shopper households, while the unfettered shopper and kitchen stranger households will both increase by well over 50 percent. The other three categories will show smaller increases.

Source: Wall Street Journal, June 13, 1989.

This research study demonstrates the importance of using several sources of data in a research design. This chapter will discuss the nature of research design and potential sources of data.

The previous chapter discussed the importance of the planning and analysis leading to the decision to undertake a formal research project. It was stressed that the decision problem must be clearly stated and the alternative courses of action specified. The role research can play in both formulating the problem and stimulating the creative process involved in identifying alternative courses of action was emphasized, along with the importance of clearly stated research objectives and detailed information needs. The success of the formal research project is highly dependent upon how skillfully these preliminary issues are addressed.

Once the initial phase of the research process has been adequately performed, the researcher can turn to designing the formal research project and identifying the appropriate sources of data for the study. The primary task of the formal research project is to supply the decision maker with conclusive research information that will increase the level of confidence regarding the best course of action to accomplish objectives.

In this chapter, we first discuss three types of research design and their relationship to the stages of the manager's decision-making process. Next, we discuss the nature and role of research design in the research process. This includes a detailed discussion of the basic sources of marketing data: (1) interrogation of respondents, (2) observation, (3) study of analogous situations, (4) experimentation, and (5) secondary data. We conclude the chapter with a discussion of marketing decision support systems.

TYPES OF RESEARCH

Marketing research can be classified as (1) exploratory research, (2) conclusive research, and (3) performance-monitoring (routine feedback) research. The stage in the decision-making process for which the research information is needed determines the type of research required. Figure 5-2 illustrates this interdependence, while Exhibit 5-1 presents a real-world example of using different types of research in the decision-making process involving a cereal product.

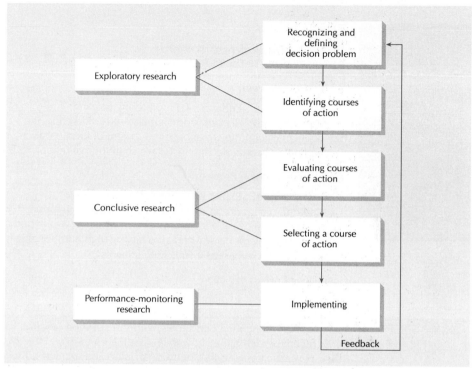

FIGURE 5-2   Types of research.

Exploratory Research

Exploratory research is appropriate for the early stages of the decision-making process. This research is usually designed to obtain a preliminary investigation of the situation with a minimum expenditure of cost and time. The research design is characterized by flexibility in order to be sensitive to the unexpected and to discover insights not previously recognized. Wide-ranging and versatile approaches are employed. These include secondary data sources, observation, interviews with experts, group interviews with knowledgeable persons, and case histories.

Exploratory research is appropriate in situations of problem recognition and definition. Once the problem has been clearly defined, exploratory research can be useful in identifying alternative courses of action. Here, the manager seeks clues to innovative marketing approaches. The objective is to broaden the domain of alternatives identified, with the hope of including the "best" alternative in the set of alternatives to be evaluated.

Conclusive Research

Conclusive research provides information which helps the manager evaluate and select a course of action. The research design is characterized by formal research

EXHIBIT 5-1

USING DIFFERENT TYPES OF RESEARCH—
REPOSITIONING TOTAL CEREAL

Problem Recognition

Research type: Performance-monitoring research.

Method: SAMI Reports (from Selling Areas Marketing, Inc., a marketing research supply company) audit the warehouse movement of food products.

Finding: Gradual decline in Total's share of market during the mid-1970s.

Definition of Decision Problem

Research type: Exploratory research.

Method: Focus group interviews with current and former Total users.

Finding: The cause of declining share of market was hypothesized as consumers misperceiving granola or natural cereal as having high nutritional value in comparison to Total and therefore viewing it as a substitute for Total.

Identifying Courses of Action

Research type: Exploratory research.

Method: Focus group interviews with adult cereal buyers.

Finding: Presenting consumers with the nutrition labeling information (percentage of U.S. recommended daily allowance) existing on the Total and granola containers lowered their perception of granola's nutritional value and increased their preference for Total.

Evaluating Courses of Action

Research type: Conclusive research.

Method: Advertising copy testing using experimental design.

Finding: Several copy approaches were tested. One approach compared the amount of granola cereal one must eat (25 ounces) to get the same nutrient value as a bowl of Total. An alternate approach compared Total's percent of recommended daily allowance of vitamins and iron to that of granola cereal (100 percent versus 6 percent). The first approach tested higher and was selected for the national advertising campaign. The second approach was used later in the campaign.

Implementation and Control

Research type: Performance-monitoring research.

Method: SAMI Reports.

Finding: There was a substantial increase in Total's share of the market over the next several years and a serious decline in granola's market penetration.

Source: Based upon a presentation by General Mills, Inc., at the School of Business Administration, the University of Michigan.

procedures. This involves clearly defined research objectives and information needs. Often a detailed questionnaire is drawn up, along with a formal sampling plan. It should be clear how the information to be collected relates to the alternatives under evaluation. Possible research approaches include surveys, experiments, observations, and simulation.

Performance-Monitoring Research

Once a course of action is selected and the marketing program is implemented, performance-monitoring research is needed to answer the question "What is happening?" Performance monitoring is the essential element needed to control marketing programs in accordance with plans. Deviation from the plan can result from improper execution of the marketing program and/or unanticipated changes in the situational factors. Consequently, effective performance monitoring involves monitoring both the marketing mix variables and the situational variables in addition to traditional performance measures such as sales, share of market, profit, and return on investment.

RESEARCH DESIGN

A research design is the basic plan that guides the data collection and analysis phases of the research project. It is the framework that specifies the type of information to be collected, the sources of data, and the data collection procedure. A good design will make sure that the information gathered is consistent with the study objectives and that the data are collected by accurate and economical procedures. There is no standard or idealized research design to guide the researcher, since many different designs may accomplish the same objective.

The objective of the research project logically determines the characteristics desired in the research design. Research objectives are dependent upon the stages of the decision-making process for which information is needed. Three types of research have been identified in this regard: exploratory, conclusive, and performance-monitoring research.

Research designs are typically classified according to the nature of the research objectives or types of research. While this classification is far from perfect, it will organize our discussion of research design. It is important to remember that research designs can serve many research objectives and types of research. The following classification reflects a judgment about the research objectives more predominantly associated with a design; it does not imply exclusive association. (See Figure 5-3.)

Exploratory Research

Exploratory research is appropriate when the research objectives include (1) identifying problems or opportunities, (2) developing a more precise formulation of a vaguely identified problem or opportunity, (3) gaining perspective regarding the

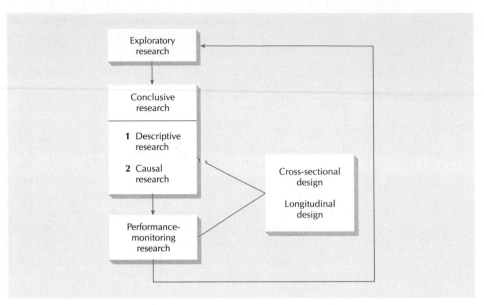

FIGURE 5-3   Research design.

breadth of variables operating in a situation, (4) establishing priorities regarding the potential significance of various problems or opportunities, (5) gaining management and researcher perspective concerning the character of the problem situation, (6) identifying and formulating alternative courses of action, and (7) gathering information on the problems associated with doing conclusive research.

Exploratory research is often the initial step in a series of studies designed to supply information for decision making. The purpose of this research is to formulate hypotheses regarding potential problems and/or opportunities present in the decision situation. We use the term *hypothesis* to refer to a conjectural statement about the relationship between two or more variables. This statement should carry clear implications for measuring the variables and testing the stated relationship. For example, exploratory research would be appropriate in a situation where management responds to the symptom of declining share of market by asking, "What is the problem?" The task of exploratory research would be to identify tentative hypotheses concerning the cause of this decline. Potential hypotheses may be narrowed by further research to the point where a statement of problems and opportunities can be developed. This statement represents the formal hypotheses regarding the causes of the decision situation. These hypotheses can be tested at a later stage of the decision process with conclusive research methods.

Examples of hypotheses developed from exploratory research are as follows:

1 An advertising theme emphasizing the "nutrition value" of food product X will increase brand awareness more than a theme emphasizing "good flavor."

2 A change in the ingredients of product X from artificial chocolate to real chocolate will increase the preference for product X compared with its competition.

3 A 10 percent cut in the retail price of product X will result in a 1 percent market share gain within 6 months.

The formulation of hypotheses rarely comes to the mind of the manager or researcher through the application of fixed and rigid procedures. Of all the stages of the decision-making process, identification of problems and opportunities eludes formal description. While the ability to formulate the decision problem must be relegated in part to the realm of inspiration, it is also true that various procedures can assist this creative process. These procedures are (1) searching secondary sources, (2) interviewing knowledgeable persons, and (3) compiling case histories.

Conclusive Research

Conclusive research is designed to provide information for the evaluation of alternative courses of action. It can be subclassified into descriptive research and causal research.

Descriptive Research   The vast majority of marketing research studies involve descriptive research. Figure 5-4 indicates that about 84 percent of businesses use a descriptive research design in their marketing research. Most studies of this nature rely heavily on interrogation of respondents and data available from secondary data sources. Descriptive research is appropriate when the research objectives include (1) portraying the characteristics of marketing phenomena and determining the frequency of occurrence, (2) determining the degree to which marketing variables are associated, and (3) making predictions regarding the occurrence of marketing phenomena.

A significant share of research falls under the first of these objectives, portraying

FIGURE 5-4   Use in practice of descriptive design. (*Source:* Thomas C. Kinnear and Ann R. Root, *A Study of the Marketing Research Business,* unpublished study, 1994. Copyright 1994, Thomas C. Kinnear. Not to be reproduced.)

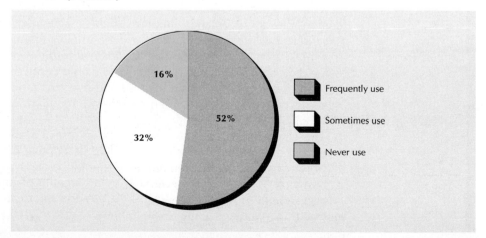

the characteristics of marketing phenomena and determining the frequency of occurrence. Consumer profile studies are conducted by firms like General Motors and Procter & Gamble to describe the characteristics of the users of a product or service. Such profiles can use demographic, socioeconomic, geographic, and psychographic characteristics, as well as consumption rates. Descriptive studies determine buyer perceptions of product characteristics and audience profiles for media such as television and magazines. Market potential studies describe the size of the market, the buying power of consumers, the availability of distributors, and buyer profiles for a product; product usage studies describe consumption patterns; market-share studies determine the proportion of total sales received by both a company and its competitors; sales analysis studies describe sales patterns by geographic region, type, size of account, and product line characteristics; distribution research determines the number and location of distributors; pricing research describes the range and frequency of prices charged for both a company's products and those of its competitors. These examples of descriptive research represent only a sampling of the numerous studies conducted in this area.

Descriptive research often involves determining the degree to which marketing variables are associated. For example, a company may study the degree of association between sales of a product and such buyer characteristics as income and age.

Descriptive information can be used to make predictions about the occurrence of marketing phenomena. While data regarding the presence of an association among variables can be used for predictive purposes, these data are not adequate to establish a causal relationship. However, it is not always necessary to understand causal relations in order to make accurate predictive statements. A company may establish an association between the sales of a product and the months of the year, and a sales forecast based on this association may have a high probability of success regarding future sales volume even though the causal relationship has not been established. The concept is to identify variables which are associated with the variable to be predicted and are measurable at the time the prediction is required.

While descriptive research may characterize marketing phenomena and demonstrate an association among variables, statements regarding cause-and-effect relationships are not possible with descriptive research. The decision maker may make predictions that certain actions will result in certain performance outcomes based on the evidence provided from a descriptive study, but this evidence in itself does not demonstrate a cause-and-effect relationship. (Where such evidence is needed, causal research designs are required, which will be discussed shortly.)

The character and purpose of descriptive research are substantially different from that of exploratory research. Effective descriptive research is marked by a clear statement of the decision problem, specific research objectives, and detailed information needs. It is characterized by a carefully planned and structured research design. Since the purpose is to provide information regarding specific questions or hypotheses, the research must be designed to ensure accuracy of the findings. By *accuracy* we mean a design that minimizes systematic error and maximizes the reliability of the evidence collected. *Systematic error* refers to a constant bias in the measurement process, while *reliability* refers to the extent to which the measurement process is free from random errors. For a detailed discussion of systematic error and reliability in connection with the measurement process, see Chapter 7.

Cross-Sectional Design   Descriptive research typically makes use of a cross-sectional research design, that is, taking a sample of population elements at one point in time. Frequently this is called the *survey research design*. This is the most popular type of research design and the one with which people are most familiar. The survey design is useful in describing the characteristics of consumers and determining the frequency of marketing phenomena, although it is often expensive and requires skillful and competent research personnel to conduct it effectively.

Decision Maker's Implicit Causal Model   The evidence provided by descriptive research can be very useful when combined with the decision maker's implicit model of how the marketing system functions in regard to the specific area under investigation. This causal model is typically based on the experience and judgment of the decision maker and represents key assumptions regarding the cause-and-effect relationships present in the marketing system. A descriptive study can provide evidence regarding specific questions or hypotheses relating to the current state of the variables present in this causal model. Given this descriptive evidence, the decision maker can draw conclusions about the effects of various courses of action and reach a decision about which course of action will best accomplish objectives. Consequently, descriptive research in itself may not provide evidence directly related to the selection of a course of action. It is when descriptive evidence is incorporated into the decision maker's personal model of the marketing system that it contributes directly to the decision-making process.

To illustrate, a marketing manager wishes to test the hypothesis that the reason for the decline in share of market for the firm's aspirin-free analgesic product is due to the consumer's misperception that the product contains aspirin. This hypothesis was developed from several exploratory group interviews with former users of the firm's product. Descriptive research was conducted to test this hypothesis, and an extensive survey of several hundred former and potential consumers supported it. The marketing manager combined this descriptive evidence with a personal causal model of how the analgesic market functions to reach a decision on a course of action. The decision was to develop an advertising campaign stressing the product's absence of aspirin and the benefits associated with a nonaspirin product. The strategy was to correct the market misperception about the presence of aspirin in the product and to reposition the product in the growing aspirin-free segment of the analgesic market. The result was a substantial increase in the product's share of market.

As this example points out, descriptive research presupposes that a sound causal model of the marketing system exists in the mind of the decision maker. The lower the decision maker's confidence in the wisdom of the causal model, the lower the value of descriptive research in the decision-making process. For example, descriptive research for the positioning of a brand is of little value if the decision maker does not know how brand positioning relates to the success of the brand.

Descriptive research is easy to conduct when the decision maker gives the researcher free rein to collect what are believed to be interesting facts. Too often, research objectives are vague, specific research questions or hypotheses have not been formulated, and limited thought has been given to how the evidence can be used in the decision-making process. The results are that the majority of the data turn out to be useless and management has wasted both funds and time. In this situation, possibly an exploratory research study would provide better information, faster and at a lower cost, than a fact finding descriptive study. Since descriptive studies often cost several thousand dollars, the collection of interesting but useless facts can be very costly.

Descriptive research designs can utilize one or more of the following sources of data: (1) interrogation of respondents, (2) secondary data, and (3) simulation.

Causal Research   The decision-making process calls for assumptions regarding the cause-and-effect relationships present in the marketing system, and causal research is designed to gather evidence regarding these relationships. It requires a planned and structured design that will not only minimize systematic error and maximize reliability, but will also permit reasonably unambiguous conclusions regarding causality.

Causal research is appropriate given the following research objectives: (1) to understand which variables are the cause of what is being predicted (the effect)—here the focus is on understanding the reasons things happen; and (2) to understand the nature of the functional relationship between the causal factors and the effect to be predicted.

Marketing executives continually think and make decisions based on an implicit causal model of the marketing system. If prices are reduced on a product or the promotion budget is increased, and subsequent unit sales of the product show an upward surge, this effect could be assumed to be caused by the changes in price level and/or the promotion budget. However, can we confidently say that the change in unit sales was caused by the change in price and promotion levels? Certainly not with a high degree of confidence. Many other variables could be the cause. Consequently, causal research must be designed such that the evidence regarding causality is clear. Research designs vary substantially in the degree of ambiguity present in the evidence regarding causality.

The main sources of data for causal research are (1) interrogating respondents through surveys and (2) conducting experiments.

While surveys can determine the degree of association among variables and test hypotheses, they cannot distinguish causality as well as experiments. A skillfully designed experiment can ensure that the evidence regarding causality is reasonably unambiguous in interpretation.

Because of the complexity of the research designs appropriate for experimental research, a separate section of this book has been devoted to their explanation. Chapter 9 discusses the principles of experimentation and alternative research designs.

Performance-Monitoring Research

Performance-monitoring research provides information regarding the monitoring of the marketing system. It is an essential element in the control of marketing programs in accordance with plans. The purpose of this research is to signal the presence of potential problems or opportunities.

The objectives of performance-monitoring research are to monitor and report changes (1) in performance measures, such as sales and market share, to determine whether plans are accomplishing desired objectives; (2) in subobjectives, such as awareness and knowledge levels, distribution penetration, and price levels, to determine whether the marketing program is being implemented according to plans; and (3) in the situational variables, such as competitive activity, economic conditions, and demand trends, to determine whether the situational climate is as anticipated when plans were formulated.

The data sources appropriate for performance-monitoring research include (1) interrogation of respondents, (2) secondary data, and (3) observation.

Performance-monitoring research can involve a special (ad hoc) study or a continuous research program.

Ad hoc performance monitoring consists of research programs designed to monitor new or special marketing programs of the organization or competitor. Typical here is the monitoring of a test market for a new product. Recent years have shown growing interest in monitoring such situational variables as government regulation, availability of resources, changing life-styles of buyers, concerns of consumer groups, and so forth. The previously discussed cross-sectional research design is appropriate in this situation. This typically involves survey research.

Continuous performance measures are, in general, formal systems designed to monitor the dependent variables in the marketing system. In recent years, increased effort has been directed to monitoring the independent variables as well. The most common performance measures involve product movement data such as units sold, sales volume, and market share. Many organizations, such as General Foods and Westinghouse, have formal systems to monitor the performance of the distribution system, sales force, and promotional programs. Most firms have the sales force submit to management, on a routine basis, formal reports concerning market and competitive conditions.

Longitudinal Design   Continuous performance monitoring typically requires a *longitudinal research design,* that is, one in which a fixed sample of population elements is measured repeatedly. Figure 5-5 indicates that about 62 percent of businesses use a longitudinal design in their marketing research. The term "panel" is often used synonymously with "longitudinal design." Two types of panels exist: the traditional panel and the omnibus panel. The *traditional panel* is a fixed sample where the same variables are repeatedly measured. For example, Information Resources' BehaviorScan continuously tracks 21,000 households in seven carefully selected markets. BehaviorScan constantly measures purchases by capturing sales data through store checkout scanners.

The *omnibus panel* is a fixed sample of respondents which is measured re-

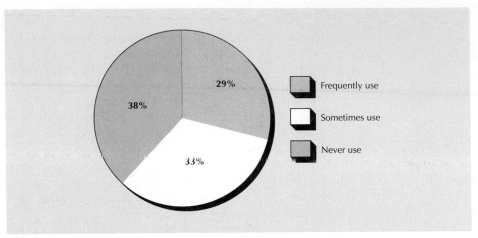

FIGURE 5-5   Use in practice of longitudinal. (*Source:* Thomas C. Kinnear and Ann R. Root, *A Study of the Marketing Research Business,* unpublished study, 1994. Copyright 1994, Thomas C. Kinnear. Not to be reproduced.)

peatedly, but the variables measured are different each time. For example, a food company maintains a panel of households, members of which are asked to evaluate different food products at different times.

The motivation for obtaining longitudinal data is the decision makers' need to measure the effect of marketing variables over time for the same buying units. The following examples illustrate situations where panel data are useful.

1 *Measuring the effect of a soft-drink offer.* The "steady state" purchasing pattern is established for a sample of households by monitoring purchases using grocery store scanner data. A special soft-drink promotion is introduced to the family through split-cable television or special inserts in magazines and newspapers every week for 4 weeks. The researchers continue to monitor purchase patterns to measure the short- and long-term effects of the promotional deal.

2 *Tracking brand purchases of frozen food.* Detailed data are collected every week for several years regarding family purchases of frozen food. Estimates are derived regarding the extent to which purchasers remain loyal to different brands and how market shares shift over time among different groups of consumers.

3 *Monitoring the acceptance of a new toy line.* Information is obtained every month on the toy purchases of families with children. Such information allows marketers to determine the types of families that are buying new toys and how soon after market introduction they make their purchases.

Most companies use the data for monitoring trends, making demographic profiles, conducting brand-switching analyses, examining new tryer–repeat buyer patterns, checking combination purchases, predicting product success in test markets, and evaluating special promotions. This diverse list of uses illustrates that panel studies come in many different forms and varying time intervals and involve different data collection methods. Panels need not be limited to individuals or to individual households but can consist of stores, business firms, or some other type of entity.

A major advantage of longitudinal data over cross-sectional data is their ability to reflect the true extent of change taking place in a population. This is possible due to the repeated measurement of a topic with the same sample of respondents. Cross-sectional data can be very misleading, since surveys at two points in time with different respondents in the sample can show no change when in fact very dramatic changes are taking place in the population.

Table 5-1 shows how cross-sectional reported purchases of brands A and B remain the same in time periods 1 and 2 but show dramatic differences when longitudinal purchases are reported. In the cross-sectional surveys the purchase of brands A and B both represent 20 percent of purchases in each time period. In the longitudinal data we see that the total purchases within a time period reflects the cross-sectional data in that 20 percent of purchases are brands A and B. However, substantial variation exists when we observe the repeat purchase patterns. In particular, none of the individuals who purchase brand B in time period 1 repeat their purchase in time period 2. Conversely, all individuals who purchase brand A in time period 1 repurchase brand A in time period 2. These dramatic differences in the repurchase patterns for brands A and B are not reflected in the cross-sectional data and have significant implications for the marketing strategies of the two brands.

Various data analysis approaches have been developed to analyze this type of data set. These approaches allow the study of changes in attitudes, knowledge, and behavior for the same respondents or households at different points in time. Such changes (or lack of change) can be related to changes in marketing program variables (price, promotion, distribution, and product) as well as to changes in situational variables (e.g., competition and economic conditions).

Another advantage of the panel design relates to the amount of information which can be collected. Since panel members are often compensated for their participation, they are more cooperative regarding longer and more demanding interviews. Consequently, panels are able to gather extensive background data on the respondents in addition to more detailed data regarding the primary variables of interest.

Panel data are generally more accurate than cross-sectional surveys. Surveys require the respondent to recall past purchases that can be biased by forgetfulness and misassociation. Bias is reduced in the panel design because there is continuous recording of purchases either in a diary or through captured scanner data. Historically, panel members have been paid to maintain accurate records. Even small payments tend to produce very accurate records, and variations in workloads among panel members have little effect on accuracy.

The cost of panel data can be lower than the cost of comparable data collected through a survey. The fixed costs associated with developing and maintaining a panel can be spread over the many clients who use it, while a comparable survey requires that the incurred fixed cost be charged directly to a single client.

TABLE 5-1   CROSS-SECTIONAL DATA MAY NOT REFLECT LONGITUDINAL DATA

	Cross-sectional data	
	Period 1 survey	Period 2 survey
Brand A		
Purchase	100	100
No purchase	400	400
Total	500	500
Brand B		
Purchase	100	100
No purchase	400	400
Total	500	500

	Longitudinal data		
	Period 1 panel reporting		
	Brand A		
Period 2 panel reporting	Purchase	No purchase	Total
Brand A			
Purchase	100	0	100
No purchase	0	400	400
Total	100	400	500
	Brand B		
	Purchase	No purchase	Total
Brand B			
Purchase	0	100	100
No purchase	100	300	400
Total	100	400	500

Source: Adapted from Seymour Sudman and Robert Ferber, *Consumer Panels* (Chicago, Ill.: American Marketing Association, 1979), p. 5.

The main disadvantages of panels stem from the fact that they are not representative. The two major problems are (1) unrepresentative sampling and (2) response bias.

The unrepresentative sampling problem arises from the need to have panel members serve for a long period. As an inducement to serve, they are offered gifts and money. It is argued that individuals who are mobile, employed, and uninterested in panel activities, gifts, or money, and individuals who are unable to perform the tasks required will not serve on the panel. Despite attempts to match the sample on selected population characteristics such as age, education, occupation, and so on, it is feared that the sample may be unrepresentative of the particular variable being measured.

Another issue relates to the mortality rates of existing panel members and the representativeness of the new members chosen to replace them. Mortality rates (resulting from members moving, losing interest, and dying) can range as high as 20 percent per year for panels operating over a long period of time.

Despite these potential biases in representativeness of the sample, the available research evidence suggests that this problem is not a serious issue for professionally administered panels.

The response bias issue is not serious for well-managed panels. The response biases that need to be controlled result from the panel members believing they are "experts," wanting to look good or give the "right" answer, becoming biased from boredom and fatigue, and not routinely completing diary entries.

Research evidence does suggest that new panel members are often biased in their initial responses. New members tend to increase the behavior being measured, for example, television viewing and food purchasing. Professionally managed panels minimize this type of bias by initially excluding the data of new members from panel results. After the novelty of being on the panel declines, the accuracy of the data increases.

DATA SOURCES

There are four basic sources of marketing data. These are (1) respondents, (2) analogous situations, (3) experimentation, and (4) secondary data.

Respondents

Respondents are a major source of marketing data. There are two principal methods of obtaining data from respondents—communication and observation. Communication requires the respondent to actively provide data through verbal response, while observation requires the recording of the respondent's passive behavior.

Communication with Respondents   The most common source of marketing data is communication with respondents. It is logical to acquire data from people by asking questions. In our daily activities we gather information by asking questions of persons whom we consider knowledgeable. Marketing research is just a more formal and scientific way of gathering such information.

When the information needs of a study require data about respondents' attitudes, perceptions, motivations, knowledge, and intended behavior, asking questions is essential. The respondents can be consumers, industrial buyers, wholesalers, retailers, or any knowledgeable persons who can provide data useful to a decision situation. Effective communication with respondents requires special training and skill if the data are to be useful. Misleading data can result when the questions are biased or require respondents to provide data which they do not possess or choose not to disclose.

The research design can range from questioning a few knowledgeable individuals (exploratory research) to surveying hundreds of respondents (conclusive research). *Exploratory research* usually consists of questioning knowledgeable respondents individually or in small groups (i.e., five to six people). *Focus group interviews* provide free-flowing unstructured situations designed to stimulate ideas and insights into a problem situation through group interaction. This typically means asking deeply probing questions over a long time span (i.e., 1 or 2 hours). *In-depth interviews* use extensive questioning of respondents individually to explore the reasons underlying attitudes and behavior. The focus is on developing hypotheses and insight regarding the "why" of past and future behavior. In contrast, *conclusive research* is designed to explain what is happening and the frequency of occurrence; it is normally conducted by asking a large sample of respondents a few simple questions in a brief time span (i.e., 10 to 20 minutes). Formal and structured research procedures designed to control bias in the data are employed.

The data collection methods used in communicating with respondents include personal interviews, telephone interviews, and mail questionnaires. The questions are asked of the respondent and answered verbally with the personal and telephone interview, in writing with the mail questionnaire. The popularity of the telephone interview has increased significantly in recent years.

Observation of Respondents Observation is the process of recognizing and recording relevant objects and events. It is an important and commonplace activity in our daily routines. Similarly, in marketing, valuable information pertaining to a decision situation can be obtained by observing either present behavior or the results of past behavior.

Observational methods allow the recording of behavior when it occurs, thus eliminating errors associated with the recall of behavior. This is often less costly and/or more accurate than asking the respondent to recall the same behavior at another point in time. While observation can accurately record what people do and how it is done, it cannot be used to determine the motivations, attitudes, and knowledge that underlie the behavior.

The many issues involved in obtaining data from respondents through communication and observation are discussed in Chapters 10, 11, 12, and 16.

Analogous Situations

A logical way to study a decision situation is to examine analogous or similar situations. Analogous situations include the study of case histories and simulations.

Case Histories The case history approach is an old and established method in the behavioral sciences and has been used successfully in marketing research for decades.[1] The design involves the intense investigation of situations which are relevant to the problem situation. The concept is to select several target cases where an intensive analysis will (1) identify relevant variables, (2) indicate the nature of the relationship among variables, and (3) identify the nature of the problem and/or opportunity present in the original decision situation. For example, the research might investigate selected retail stores, sales territories, markets, salespeople, or industrial buyers. The purpose is to obtain a comprehensive description of the cases and to formulate a better understanding of the variables operating.

The case history method is especially useful in situations in which a complicated series of variables interact to produce the problem or opportunity. Cases that can be studied are those reflecting (1) contrasting performance levels, for example, good and poor markets; (2) rapid changes in performance, for example, entry of a competitor into a market; and (3) the order in which events occurred, for example, sales regions that are in various stages of transition from indirect to direct selling efforts.

Data can be obtained through the search of records and reports, observation of key variables, and interrogation of knowledgeable persons. The research style is one of flexibility in the analysis to take advantage of the unexpected and develop insights into the problem situation.

Simulation   The creation of an analogy or likeness of a real-world phenomenon is known as *simulation*. It is an incomplete representation of reality that tries to duplicate the essence of the phenomenon without actually attaining reality itself. Common examples of simulation are model airplanes, road maps, and planetariums.

What is a *marketing simulation?* It can be defined as an incomplete representation of the marketing system or some aspect of this system. It is a relatively new source of data and is largely computer-based. Simulation can be used to gain insight into the dynamics of the marketing system by manipulation of the independent variables (marketing mix and situational factors) and observation of their influence on the dependent variable(s). A marketing simulation requires data inputs regarding the characteristics of the phenomenon to be represented and the relationships present.

The development of a marketing simulation requires that the builder conceptualize and document the structural components of the system and establish probabilities to represent the behavior of the components. The components or units of

---

[1]This method of investigation has been widely used in the behavioral sciences and marketing research under the label "case study." The term "case history" is used here to differentiate the research-oriented case study from the classroom case study most familiar to students. The classroom case study is a pedagogical device designed to put the student in a situation similar to that encountered by a management group. The student's task is to analyze the situation and logically proceed through the decision-making process, ending with a recommendation for action. Research case histories or case studies are typically more myopic than classroom case studies and are intended to aid the decision-making process by providing ideas and insight into a decision situation. The classroom case study may include one or more case histories as part of the background information in the case.

the marketing simulation represent objects in the marketing system. Depending on the marketing phenomenon under study, the units can be buyers, households, retailers, and so on. The variables in the system establish how the units behave. Variables can be price levels, advertising expenditures, product quality, deals, competitive strategy, and so on. Probabilities are assigned to the units corresponding to their response to the variables. The objective is to make the simulation units imitate the behavior of the marketing system units which they represent. The behavior of these units results in the numerical output, or data, from the simulation. For example, the numerical output could be share of market, sales, or profitability. The parameters of the simulation represent the constraints that can be changed only at the direction of the user. These might be level of advertising, price elasticity, proportion of children in the market, competitive advertising levels, and so on. Parameters allow the user to experiment with the simulation, explore alternative marketing strategies, and determine the influence of changes in situational factors.

What are the advantages of simulation compared with other data sources? It can be less expensive than conducting a survey of respondents or test marketing, and the time required to collect and analyze the data may be less. Simulation can be conducted with complete secrecy within an organization; other data sources may not assure this degree of security. Simulation allows the evaluation of alternative marketing strategies and provides "proof" regarding the superiority of one strategy over another. In addition, the consequences of changes in the marketing system can be evaluated without the risk of making changes in the real system. This allows the evaluation of multiple strategies and encourages creativity in that radical strategy changes can be evaluated. Simulation can be useful in determining the sensitivity of a strategy option to departures in the initial assumptions. This is called *sensitivity analysis.* Finally, simulation can be used as a training device for members of the organization. Individuals not directly involved in marketing activities may develop an appreciation of how the marketing system operates and how it affects decisions in their areas, for example, R&D or manufacturing.

The limitations of simulation are the difficulty of developing a valid simulation model and the time and cost of updating the model as conditions change. In situations where the organization has limited background and experience regarding the marketing phenomenon under investigation (e.g., new markets), simulation may not be a feasible data source.

Experimentation

Experimentation is a relatively new source of marketing data. The data from an experiment are organized in such a way that relatively unambiguous statements can be made regarding cause-and-effect relationships.

An experiment is conducted when one or more independent variables are consciously manipulated or controlled and their effect on the dependent variable (or variables) is measured. The objective of an experiment is to measure the effect of the independent variables on a dependent variable, while controlling for other variables that might confuse one's ability to make valid causal inferences. Various experimental designs have been developed to reduce or eliminate the possible influence of extraneous variables on the dependent variable. Chapter 9 deals exclusively with the concept of experimentation and the research designs used in this area.

Secondary Data

There are two general types of marketing data—primary and secondary. *Primary data* are collected specifically for the research needs at hand. *Secondary data* are already published data collected for purposes other than the specific research needs at hand. Consequently, this distinction is defined by the purpose for which the data were collected.

Secondary data can be classified as coming from *internal sources* or *external sources,* the former being available within the organization and the latter originating outside it. External data come from an array of sources such as government publications, trade association data, books, bulletins, reports, and periodicals. Data from these sources are available at minimal cost or free in libraries. Chapter 6 deals specifically with the data sources available in a library. External data sources not available in a library are usually standardized data which are expensive to acquire. We refer to these data sources as *syndicated sources.* Such sources are predominantly profit-making organizations that provide standardized data to an array of clients. The remainder of this section will discuss internal data sources and syndicated external data sources.

Internal Data   As stated already, internal data originate within the organization for which the research is conducted. Internal data collected for purposes other than the research being conducted are *internal secondary data.*

All organizations collect internal data as part of their normal operations. Sales and cost data are recorded, sales reports submitted, advertising and promotion activities recorded, and research and development and manufacturing reports made; these are but a few of the data sources available for research purposes within a modern organization. Figure 5-6 indicates that about 88 percent of businesses use internal company records for marketing purposes.

Sales and cost data collected for accounting purposes represent particularly promising sources for many research projects. For example, if the research objectives of a project are to evaluate previous marketing activity or to determine the organization's competitive position, sales and cost data can be very helpful.

Many organizations do not collect and maintain sales and cost data in sufficient detail to be used for many research purposes. Sales records should allow for classification by type of customer, payment procedure (cash or credit), product line, sales territory, time period, and so on. By simple analysis of this type of data the researcher can determine the level and trend in sales, costs, and profitability by customer, territory, and product. More sophisticated analysis could attempt to measure the effect of changes in the marketing program and/or situational variables on sales, costs, and profitability.

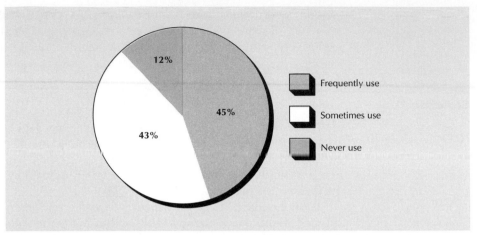

FIGURE 5-6   Use in practice of internal company records. (*Source:* Thomas C. Kinnear and Ann R. Root, *A Study of the Marketing Research Business,* unpublished study, 1994. Copyright 1994, Thomas C. Kinnear. Not to be reproduced.)

The advantages of internal secondary data are their low cost and their availability. Unfortunately, many organizations fail to recognize that they have or could have useful internal data available at low cost. These organizations could benefit from specially designed programs to organize and maintain secondary internal data for marketing research purposes.

External Data—Syndicated   The growing demand for marketing data has produced a number of companies that collect and sell standardized data designed to serve information needs shared by a number of organizations; the most common are information needs associated with performance-monitoring research. Figure 5-7 indicates that about 83 percent of businesses use syndicated data in their marketing research.

Syndicated data sources can be classified as (1) consumer data, (2) retail data, (3) wholesale data, (4) industrial data, (5) advertising evaluation data, and (6) media and audience data. The following section presents an overview of the main types of data available in each of these classifications. A more comprehensive listing and discussion of syndicated data sources is provided in the appendix.

Consumer Data   Several services collect data from consumers regarding purchases and the circumstances surrounding the purchases. The National Purchase Diary (NPD) Group, Inc., maintains the NPD panel, comprising over 30,000 households who keep diaries of purchases in several consumer good categories from food to automotive supplies. The Marketing Research Corporation of America (MRCA) maintains a diary panel that records details regarding the purchase of groceries and personal-care items. Panel services of this type provide data on sales by brand, type, flavor, or variety purchased; the quantities bought; the price paid; the store patronized; the brand switched; demographic and socioeconomic characteristics of the purchase; and so on.

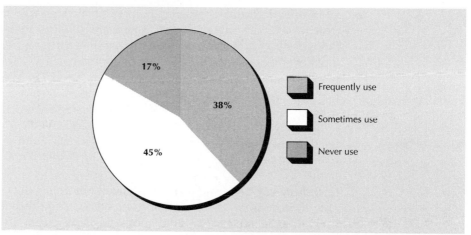

FIGURE 5-7   Use in practice of syndicated data. (*Source:* Thomas C. Kinnear and Ann R. Root, *A Study of the Marketing Research Business*, unpublished study, 1994. Copyright 1994, Thomas C. Kinnear. Not to be reproduced.)

Various services survey large groups of consumers regarding purchases and the buying situation. The National Menu Census conducted by MRCA provides data regarding food consumption in the home. Data are provided on the menu at each meal, snack items, carry-out items, and so on. Mediamark, Inc. prepares an annual survey of 450 products that includes overall usage and a breakdown of usage by demographic category, as well as information on light, medium, and heavy users.

Numerous other surveys are designed to measure other attitudes and opinions that may be relevant to marketing. The Roper Organization conducts surveys with a scientific sample of 2000 adults 10 times per year on a wide variety of social and political topics as well as on opinions of various consumer products and services. Yankelovich Partners conducts a yearly survey of 2500 households that includes data on approximately 50 social trends designed to measure the country's mood and outlook for the future. The Survey Research Center at the University of Michigan monitors consumer consumption patterns, attitudes, and intentions on financial issues and the purchase of durable goods. Other services monitor consumers' attitudes regarding the food shopping process and their awareness levels of various brands or advertisements.

Retail Data   Numerous services rely on retailing establishments for their data. The data collected focus on the products or services sold through the outlets and/or the characteristics of the outlets themselves. Two of the better-known services are A. C. Nielsen's Retail Index and Audits and Surveys' National Total-Market Audit. The Nielsen Retail Index involves a store audit of supermarkets, drugstores, and mass merchandisers taken every 2 months. The data reported to a client include total sales by product class, sales by brand, and sales of competing brands. Audits and Surveys' National Total-Market Audit provides bimonthly reports which contain data similar to the Nielsen Retail Index. Many of the product categories included in the audit are different from the Nielsen service.

Wholesale Data A growing number of services rely on warehouse shipment data to estimate sales at retail. These are services to manufacturers who sell through retail stores. Clients who buy these reports can receive monthly data on the movement of each brand in each product category. These data estimate sales of a brand and competitive brands in markets. Such data allow the client to analyze trends in sales or package size and the impact of promotions and competitive actions. The Nielsen Retail Index and wholesale services are competitive services in that they provide similar data for similar product categories. Wholesale reports become available more quickly than Nielsen data, but the latter represent actual retail purchases, whereas wholesale data represent retail orders from the warehouse.

Industrial Data There are substantially more syndicated data services available to consumer goods manufacturers than to industrial goods suppliers. The services available for industrial goods are fairly recent and still evolving; an example is Dun & Bradstreet's "Market Identifiers," which provides data on companies rated by Dun & Bradstreet (D&B). The data can be used to construct sales prospect lists, identify sales territories, establish sales potentials, and so on. Other industrial services include McGraw-Hill's Dodge Reports and Polk Co.'s Motor Statistics.

Advertising Evaluation Data Billions of advertising dollars are spent each year on media such as magazines and television with the expectation that these expenditures will result in sales. Consequently, advertisers are interested in data that measure the effectiveness of these expenditures. Our discussion will focus on services that evaluate advertisements in broadcast and print media.

Several services evaluate advertising in print media. Two of the well-known syndicated readership services are the Starch Message Reports and the Gallup and Robinson (G&R) Magazine Impact Studies.

Starch reports measure an advertisement's effectiveness by classifying magazine readership into three groups: (1) those who remember seeing a particular advertisement ("Noted"), (2) those who associated the sponsor's name with the advertisement ("Seen-Associated"), and (3) those who read half or more of its copy ("Read Most"). This evaluation is provided for most consumer magazines and selected business and industrial publications. Starch is the most widely used syndicated readership service.

G&R is Starch's major competitor. It uses a more rigorous method in gathering data from magazine readers. G&R first asks the reader to recall and describe advertisements from the closed issue of the magazine, whereas Starch shows the reader the advertisements by turning through the magazine. G&R measures three levels of advertising effectiveness: (1) "Proved Name Registration" (PNR) score, which gives the percentage of readers who remembered the ad and proved its recall by describing the ad; (2) "Idea Playback Profile," a measure of sales message recall; and (3) "Favorable Buying Attitude" score, which measures message persuasiveness. Both Starch and G&B allow the assessment of individual advertisement effectiveness and the tracking of successive campaigns over time.

The services that evaluate television commercials use two basic approaches—the recruited audience method and the normal viewing environment method.

With the recruited audience method, respondents are recruited and brought to a viewing center (a theater or mobile viewing laboratory) for purposes of pretesting television commercials. Data are gathered regarding the viewers' attitudes, knowledge, preference, and selection of products. Services which use this approach include Gallup and Robinson's In-View and Burgoyne, Inc.'s PACE (Persuasion and Communication Effectiveness).

With the second approach, the normal viewing environment method, commercials are evaluated in the home. New commercials are pretested by substituting the test commercial for a regular commercial on established programming. This can be done at the network level or in local markets. A sample of viewers is then interviewed to determine the new advertisement's effectiveness. The services which use this approach are AdTel, Ltd.; Advertising Research System (ARS) Division, Research Systems, Inc.; Audience Studies/Communication Lab., Inc.; and Television Testing Company.

Media and Audience Data   The task of a media planner is to identify media that have audience characteristics similar to those of the target market to be reached. The types of data used in matching markets and media typically include demographics, psychographics, and product usage rates. A number of syndicated audience measurement services provide this type of data. The A. C. Nielsen Company and the American Research Bureau provide audience data for television programs. Other services specialize in providing audience measurement data for a particular medium.

The Simmons Market Research Bureau, on the other hand, offers a multimedia service that allows the media planner to compare audience characteristics over an array of media. Simmons describes the audiences of magazines and newspapers and their supplements as well as all network television programs. Audience data are provided on demographic characteristics and usage of products and services.

Media planners need data regarding the advertising effects of competitors. It is important to know how much competitors are spending, where they are spending their advertising dollars, and in what media mix. Several syndicated services provide this type of data.

Perhaps the best-known competitive data service is Leading National Advertisers (LNA). This service monitors over 150,000 ads each year in 86 consumer magazines and 3 national newspaper supplements. Data regarding other media are supplied by services such as A. C. Nielsen and the Advertising Checking Bureau (ACB).

TECHNOLOGY CHANGES

As technology improves, all the data types mentioned are increasingly gathered by electronic methods; image scanners in grocery stores capture more exact purchase data, split-cable TV targets new advertising, and A. C. Nielsen's "people meters" more accurately measure television viewership.

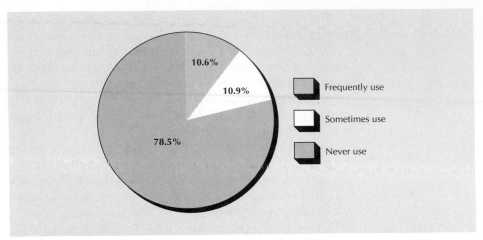

FIGURE 5-8   Use in practice of scanner data. (*Source:* Thomas C. Kinnear and Ann R. Root, *A Study of the Marketing Research Business,* unpublished study, 1994. Copyright 1994, Thomas C. Kinnear. Not to be reproduced.)

Figure 5-8 indicates that about 22 percent of businesses use scanner data in their marketing research. The computerized checkout scanner has led to several important changes in marketing research. Scanner data are recorded by passing merchandise over a laser scanner that optically reads the bar code description printed on the merchandise. The bar code is then linked with price and product information. The obvious advantage of the system has also changed marketing research.

The panel of consumers who manually maintain a diary of purchase is quickly being replaced by panels whose purchases are recorded and compiled by check-out scanners. Panel members simply present an ID card when checking out at the store, and each item of the panel member's purchases is quickly captured and compiled by a computer.

One study performed by J. Walter Thompson Inc. lists eight significant changes spurred by the proliferation of scanner data.[2]

1 Significantly better data in certain areas, such as volume/share tracking, promotion tracking, and consumer purchase dynamics.

2 A necessity for analysis packages, including data, software, and hardware, to be provided by scanning services, because of the huge amount of data these systems generate.

3 A shortening of reaction time by advertisers to their competitors, since store-specific data will be available on a weekly basis.

[2]Adapted from *Marketing Information in Transition: Scanner Services and Single Source Systems* (New York: J. Walter Thompson Inc.), p. 10.

4 The possibility of new insights into stimuli/response functions, and the opportunity to perform new studies on purchase dynamics and the impact of marketplace influences on product purchase.

5 The availability of timely data, which may lead to more preemptive and reactive marketing strategies.

6 The ability to quickly determine short-term effects of pricing differentials and trade dealing, which may lead businesses to favor promotions over advertising.

7 Since scanner data systems tell what is happening rather than why it is happening, marketers must learn about consumer attitudes by placing greater emphasis on conventional awareness tracking.

8 There is a critical shortage of trained professionals who can analyze and interpret data. The entire research industry will need to develop and train people to utilize the data provided by scanner systems.

The scanner system also provides more accurate data than a traditional diary panel or store audit. First, the data are available more quickly. Second, there is less selection bias and less price sensitivity bias. Because the scanner method requires little effort, the panel members are much less conscious of their roles as members of the panel. Third, scanner data eliminate recall bias. Because information is captured instantly, the data are generally more complete and more accurate. Finally, in-store data, such as different pricing or promotional offers, are built into the data.

The shift toward scanner data has done more than change the physical collection of data. Scanner data have changed the way the data are interpreted. The extensive detail afforded by the computer data allows marketers to review data on a regional, city, or even store-by-store basis. The scanner also provides more detailed product data. Purchases can be analyzed in more narrow product categories than with diary panels.

The system has also given stores much more detailed information on their sales, which makes it easier for them to make business decisions. The Safeway store chain tests different promotional concepts and measures the results using detailed scanner data. For example, one test showed that sales of candy bars nearly doubled when the products were displayed near the checkout counter. Another determined that sauce mixes sold much better when displayed near their companion products, for example, when spaghetti sauce was sold near the spaghetti.

The immediacy of the scanner process has helped Procter & Gamble (P&G) develop a system that generates coupons right at the checkout counter. Consumers who purchase a rival brand are given a computer-generated coupon for a discount on the comparable P&G product for their next purchase.

With BehaviorScan, diary panel households receive all their at-home television programming through the local cable company. This allows researchers to split the panel by feeding an experimental commercial to one segment of the test group and the standard commercial to a control group. The effects of the ad are tested by tracking the purchases of the test group with detailed scanner data.

SINGLE SOURCING

Single sourcing is a syndicated marketing research concept that has gained credibility as technology has allowed the gathering of more and more resources and data under one roof. A *single source* is a marketing research provider having a single, comprehensive, and integrated database that essentially contains everything the client needs to conduct its marketing research program. Typically, the services provided are sales tracking and household purchasing behavior. Scanner technology,[3] passive people meters for media measurement, split-cable advertising, and customer databases are examples of the technologies that suppliers are putting together to form their databases. For example, the same family could have its product consumption, media consumption, and demographic characteristics monitored to provide integrated data.

One of the goals of single-source information is to achieve real-time decisions, that is, to respond to market opportunities as they appear. The quicker a supplier can provide the data to identify the opportunity, and the more comprehensive and integrated the data, the greater the decision-making value to the client.[4] Cause-and-effect relationships will become easier to identify, including through experimentation.

The marketing researcher, however, must not lose sight of the fact that while these technologies can capture consumer activities and transactions, interpretation of the huge amounts of data will still be a key to success in the marketplace. The information will also become more available on a decentralized basis rather than only through a centralized marketing research location. User-friendly computer application systems and decision-based systems have been and continue to be in development as the industry learns how to access and use the information explosion. Custom marketing research will still continue to play a role alongside single-source systems.[5]

INTERNATIONAL RESEARCH DESIGN AND DATA SOURCES

All the types of research designs described above are applicable to both domestic and international situations. Though the fundamentals of marketing research apply universally, there are differences in the implementation of research designs required by the variations in available technology, research institutions, and culture across countries. These differences will be discussed in some detail in the appropriate later chapters.

There are a great many differences in the data sources available to marketing researchers across countries. Some generalizations about these differences are presented in the Global Marketing Research Dynamics.

[3]Laurence N. Gold, "The Coming of Age of Scanner Data," *Marketing Research: A Magazine of Management & Applications,* vol. 5, no. 1, pp. 20–24, March 1993.

[4]Blair Peters, "The 'Brave New World' of Single Source Information," *Marketing Research: A Magazine of Management & Applications,* vol. 2, no. 4, pp. 13–21, December 1990.

[5]Verne B. Churchill, "The Role of Ad Hoc Survey Research in a Single Source World," *Marketing Research: A Magazine of Management & Applications,* vol. 2, no. 4, pp. 22–26, December 1990.

GLOBAL MARKETING RESEARCH DYNAMICS

INTERNATIONAL DATA SOURCES

International marketing research data can be obtained from a variety of sources, including the U.S. Department of Commerce (U.S. DOC) and other governmental agencies; international organizations such as the Organization for Economic Cooperation and Development (OECD), the Food and Agriculture Organization (FAO) of the United Nations (U.N.), United Nations Commission on Trade and Development (UNCTAD), and the General Agreement on Tariffs and Trade (GATT); service organizations such as banks, export trading companies, trade associations, and world trade clubs; as well as numerous private research organizations and their respective publications. Vast quantities of data are available, and managers must sort out the relevant, timely, useful, and consistent information for their particular company. They must filter and interpret the information by developing a sense of familiarity and history with a source of information, using the data to identify trends, but using caution when interpreting statistics, especially those prepared by the developing countries. Selection of the most effective sources of international marketing research data varies by company, with the key determinants being the company's size and stage of internationalization.

The U.S. DOC offers various assistance programs, including business counseling, new product information service, agent/distributor service, trade opportunities programs, catalog exhibitions, and trade missions. Research suggests that U.S. DOC information and assistance are most effective for smaller firms and firms that are new to exporting. For example, the Weiler Company, a small producer of industrial meat grinders and other specialty equipment, is relatively new to exporting. In the early stages of internationalization, Weiler managers discussed their foreign marketing plans with the international trade experts at the local DOC district office. A global market survey on the food processing industry helped them target countries with attractive market opportunities. The Agent/Distributor Service was useful in identifying prospective distributors within individual markets. Trade fairs proved to be a relatively inexpensive way of gaining exposure for Weiler's products, as is often the case for smaller companies.

In contrast, the larger and more internationally involved firms, especially multinational corporations, often have sophisticated internal databases. These firms rely more heavily on private sector suppliers such as *Business International*, Dun & Bradstreet, *Predicasts*, and the international departments of major banks. For example, S. C. Johnson uses A. C. Nielsen data collected in each foreign market. Syndicated research data gathered from each market appears to suit the company's needs. Secondary sources of information, such as *Business International* publications or government statistics, are more helpful in providing general information such as economic indicators, political stability, and the exchange rate fluctuations.

A summary of data sources for specific stages of foreign market opportunity analysis is presented in Exhibit 1.

Source: Adapted from S. Tamer Cavusgil, "Qualitative Insights into Company Experiences in International Marketing Research," *The Journal of Business and Industrial Marketing,* pp. 41–54, Summer 1987.

EXHIBIT 1

SPECIFIC TECHNIQUES FOR FOREIGN MARKET OPPORTUNITY ANALYSIS

Preliminary Screening for Attractive Country Markets

- Scrutiny of news media and trade publications
- Examination of favorable and unfavorable aspects of country markets
- Analysis of secondary statistics
- Participation in overseas trade fairs and shows
- Promotions and/or inquiries directed to prospective distributors or end users
- Country clustering (e.g., by demographic characteristics)

Industry Market Potential Assessment

- Trend Analysis—domestic production plus imports minus exports
- Regressions and econometric forecasting
- Analysis of key indicators of demand
- Following major contractors around the world
- Estimation by analogy
- Other top-down estimates (multiple-factor indexes, chain-ratio analysis, income elasticity measures, input-output analysis, etc.)

Company Sales Potential and Profitability Analysis

- Surveys of end users and distributors
- Trade audits
- Competitive intelligence gathering
- Customized market research

MARKETING DECISION SUPPORT SYSTEMS

Throughout history, a common problem for marketers has been a lack of information about their customers. The constant challenge has been to obtain more information. The proliferation of supermarket optical scanner data and rapid changes in personal computer technology have changed the nature of the information problem for marketing companies. Now, executives must intelligently use the enormous amount of information available.

A *marketing decision support system* (MDSS) is defined as an integrated system of data, statistical analysis, modeling, and display formats using computer hardware and software to provide information for the marketing decision-making process. Figure 5-9 indicates that about 17 percent of businesses use an MDSS in their marketing department, and Figure 5-10 presents the MDSS concept.

THE NATURE OF AN MDSS

In today's increasingly fast-moving and competitive business environment, it is no longer good enough to know what happened to sales last month. The marketer

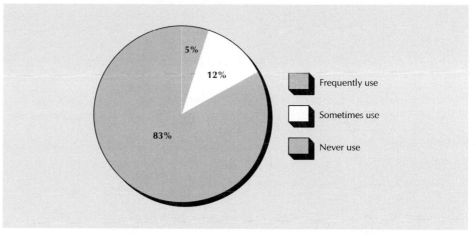

FIGURE 5-9   Use in practice of marketing decision support system. (*Source:* Thomas C. Kinnear and Ann R. Root, *A Study of the Marketing Research Business,* unpublished study, 1994. Copyright 1994, Thomas C. Kinnear. Not to be reproduced.)

must know why sales changed as they did and, more important, what will happen to sales next month if part of the marketing mix is changed. Here are examples of questions that an MDSS is designed to help answer quickly and easily:

- What is the change in the cost per unit if we drop one optional feature and add a new one?
- What are the sales for product X each month? For the year to date? How would that change if we offered wholesalers new incentives?
- How do our year-to-date expenditures on magazine advertising compare to our budget? What would happen to sales and profits if we put more money into magazine advertising?

To answer difficult managerial questions like these, an MDSS must have the following features:

1 The system must be interactive. The system must provide the manager with easy-to-follow instructions and give results on the spot. The manager must control the process and must not need to wait for the results.

2 The system must be flexible. The manager can sort, average, total, or otherwise manipulate the data. The manager's needs are hard to predict; a particular problem may mean looking at the data in a totally unique way.

3 The system must be discovery-oriented. The manager can search for trends, identify problems, and ask new questions on the basis of information provided.

4 The system must minimize the frustration quotient. Novice users who are not particularly computer-knowledgeable should be able to work the basic system easily and eventually learn the more intricate parts of the system through continued use and experimentation.

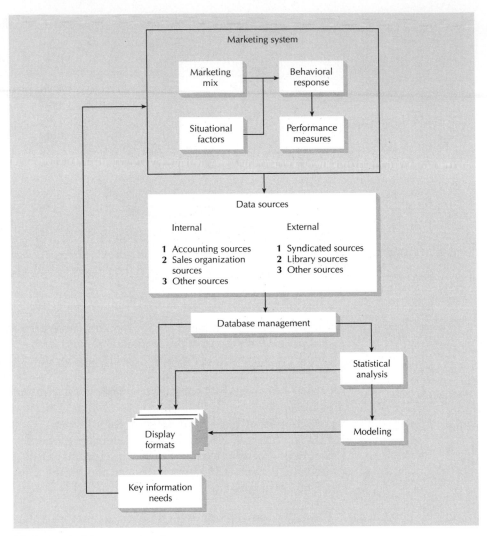

FIGURE 5-10   Marketing decision support system.

MDSS Components

Marketing decision support systems should have five components: (1) data sources, (2) database management, (3) display, (4) statistical analysis, and (5) modeling.

Data sources represent the backbone of an MDSS. Before developing an MDSS, an organization must review and overhaul its relevant data sources, identifying and organizing them into systematic structures.

An organization's accounting system and sales organization are important internal data sources for a marketing information system. Syndicated services and library sources represent key external data sources.

The organization's accounting system is a critical data source for marketing decision makers. This system contains data regarding sales, inventory levels, cost allocations, accounts receivable, and so on. Such information is important in monitoring the performance of marketing programs and signaling problems and opportunities.

The organization's sales organization is an excellent source of data. Sales personnel can provide data regarding many aspects of the marketing system.

MDSS Current Status

The growing acceptance of the computer in the business community and its significant achievements in data processing and analysis created a movement that advocated an idealized MDSS concept—a total system that encompasses a significant proportion of the information requirements of the decision maker. This excitement was soon dampened by the practical difficulties of implementing such a concept. In fact, only 17 percent of companies used an MDSS in 1994.

Part of the problem with the idealized MDSS concept relates to the failure of its proponents to recognize that the information needs of decision makers are varied; often complicated; and specific to the skills, knowledge, experience, and personalities of the decision makers. No simple combination of data inputs and information outputs is going to meet a significant proportion of a given decision maker's requirements for information. This becomes more of a problem the higher the decision maker is in the organization.

While significant progress is being made in the development of MDSSs, many hurdles must be overcome before the final goal is reached. Presently, we appear to be at a more intermediate stage, previously defined as the marketing research system (see Chapter 1). The marketing research system includes many of the diverse data sources found in an MDSS, but it does not have the degree of structure and interactive people-machine concepts found in the complete MDSS concept. The objective of a marketing research system is to create an information center for marketing decision making through use of a combination of research approaches and philosophies that fit the special needs of the organization and the individual decision makers.

SUMMARY

1 A research design is the basic plan that guides the data collection and analysis phases of the research project. An effective design assures that the information gathered is consistent with the research objectives and that the data collection and analysis phases involve accurate and economical procedures.

2 The research design for exploratory research is best characterized by its lack of structure and its flexibility. The data collection and analysis strategy is one of diversity and searching in new directions until new ideas or better ideas can no longer be discovered. It facilitates the development of hypotheses regarding potential problems and/or opportunities.

3 Conclusive research provides information for the evaluation of alternative courses of action. It can be subclassified into descriptive and causal research.

4 Descriptive research characterizes marketing phenomena, determines the association among variables, and predicts future marketing phenomena. It is characterized by a carefully planned and structured research design. A cross-sectional design or survey research design is typically used in descriptive research projects. This design involves taking a sample of population elements at one point in time. The evidence provided by descriptive research can be very useful in evaluating courses of action when combined with the decision maker's implicit model of how the marketing system functions.

5 Causal research is designed to gather evidence regarding cause-and-effect relationships. The appropriate research designs vary substantially in complexity and in the degree of ambiguity present in the evidence regarding causality. With causal research, the research design may directly evaluate the alternative courses of action under consideration.

6 Performance-monitoring research provides evidence regarding the monitoring of the marketing system. It can involve either an ad hoc study or a continuous program of research. Continuous performance monitoring typically requires a longitudinal research design which is often called a panel design. In this sort of design, a fixed sample of population elements is measured repeatedly. In a traditional panel, the same variables are measured every time, as opposed to an omnibus panel where different variables are measured each time. In both types of panels, the sample of respondents remains fixed.

7 The basic sources of marketing data are (a) respondents, (b) analogous situations, (c) experiments, and (d) secondary data.

8 There are two main types of data from respondents—those obtained by communication and those obtained by observation. Communication requires the respondent to actively provide data through verbal responses, while observation involves the recording of the respondent's behavior.

9 The study of analogous situations includes the study of case histories and simulations. With the case history approach, there is an intensive investigation of situations that are relevant to a particular problem setting. With simulation, an analog or likeness of a real-world phenomenon is created. Simulation models can be classified as descriptive, predictive, and prescriptive.

10 Experimentation calls for the organization of data in such a way as to permit relatively unambiguous statements regarding cause-and-effect relationships.

11 Secondary data are collected for purposes other than the specific research needs at hand. Internal secondary data are those available within the organization, whereas external secondary data are provided by sources outside the organization. The latter can be classified as either library sources or syndicated sources.

12 External syndicated data sources are predominantly profit-making organizations that provide standardized data. Such data can be classified as (a) consumer data, (b) retail data, (c) wholesale data, (d) industry data, (e) advertising evaluation data, (f) media and audience data, or (g) scanner data.

13 A *marketing decision support system* is defined as an integrated system of data, statistical, modeling, and display formats using computer hardware and software technology to provide information for the marketing decision-making process. An organization's accounting system and sales organization are important internal data sources, while syndicated services and library sources are key external data sources for an MDSS. The five components of an MDSS are: (a) data sources, (b) database management, (c) display, (d) statistical analysis, and (e) modeling. The output of an MDSS should have the attributes of timeliness, flexibility, inclusiveness, accuracy, and convenience. The current status of the MDSS is marked by growing acceptance of the staged evolution of more customized decision support systems but limited acceptance of the idealized MDSS concept.

DISCUSSION QUESTIONS

1 Discuss the nature and role of research design in marketing research.

2 What type of research design is associated with exploratory research?

3 Why is exploratory research often utilized in the initial steps of the decision process?

4 What is descriptive research?

5 How does the research design in descriptive research differ from that in exploratory research?

6 How does the cross-sectional design differ from the longitudinal design?

7 What role does an implicit causal model play in descriptive research?

8 What are the objectives of performance-monitoring research?

9 What advantages does the longitudinal design offer relative to the cross-sectional design?

10 What problems are associated with longitudinal designs?

11 Discuss the four basic sources of marketing data.

12 What is the primary distinction between qualitative and quantitative research?

13 What are the benefits and limitations of simulation?

14 What is meant by a "syndicated source"?

15 What types of data are available from syndicated data sources?

16 Describe and evaluate the concept of single sourcing.

17 What is the role of a marketing information system within an organization?

18 What attributes should MDSS output possess?

19 What could cause MDSS to be more utilized by marketing managers in the future?

20 MINICASE

The marketing department of a major U.S. fast-food retailer has hired you to develop a set of research designs and data sources to assist the company with performance monitoring, and with problem and opportunity identification. What research designs and data sources would you recommend? How would your recommendation change if the company expanded into the Korean and Hong Kong markets?

APPENDIX   Syndicated Sources of Marketing Data

The purpose of this appendix is to catalog the leading syndicated sources of marketing data. For each service, the name of the sponsoring organization, the name of the service, and a brief abstract are presented. Because of the evolving nature of syndicated services and the rapid entry and withdrawal of services, omissions and inaccuracies are unavoidable. More detailed and contemporary information regarding a particular service can be obtained by contacting the organization directly. For information on how to contact these data services, consult such publications as the American Marketing Association's *International Directory of Marketing Research Houses and Services,* which is called the *Greenbook* (AMA—New York Chapter, 420 Lexington Avenue, New York, NY 10017), or *Bradford's Directory of Marketing Research Agencies and Management Consultants in the U.S. and the World* (P.O. Box 276, Dept. A, Fairfax, VA 22030). The data services listed here are classified under the following headings:

A Consumer Data: Purchase and Consumption Patterns

B Consumer Data: Attitudes, Opinions, and Behavior Patterns

   C Retail Data

   D Wholesale Data

   E Industrial Data

   F Advertising Evaluation Data: Broadcast Media

   G Advertising Evaluation Data: Print Media

   H Media and Audience Data: Media-Market Fit

   I Media and Audience Data: Competitive Efforts

   J Online Databases

   K Demographic Data

A.   CONSUMER DATA: PURCHASE AND CONSUMPTION PATTERNS

A.1   Market Research Corporation of America (MRCA) Information Services, Inc.

Service: Menu Census

A comprehensive food usage information service with over 30 years of comparative data on food and beverage preparation and consumption behavior. Consumption of all foods (except salt, pepper, and tap water, but including ingredients, cooking agents, and even method of preparation) is tracked at home on a continuous basis by a nationally representative panel of 2000 households (containing over 5500 members). Food consumption and preparation information is accessible by eating occasion, food item, and individual (both demographic and psychographic). Available on an interactive PC-based system.

Service: National Consumer Panel (NCP)

Tracks packaged goods purchasing behavior of a nationally representative sample of the American population. The weekly, diary-based NCP service features full product description information, reporting from all outlet types, and powerful online analytic capabilities to help packaged goods marketers understand who their customers are, what and where the customers purchase, and what the customers pay, and what this information means to the marketers' businesses. The ongoing panel participation lets NCP look at long-term purchasing trends and identify the factors that influence purchasing behavior. The NCP tracks purchasing of food, personal care, over-the-counter (OTC) medicine, and household cleaning products on a continuous basis.

Service: Nutritional Marketing Service

Brings together five proprietary databases to create profiles of target consumers. Data include not only what people actually eat but their attitudes toward a range of nutritional and lifestyle issues. Food consumption may be further projected to actual nutritional intake. Projects may be custom-designed or follow syndicated formats.

Service: Healthcare Usage Service

Tracks actual usage of OTC health-care remedies in a representative panel of 6000 households (500 per month). Panelists complete a personal daily diary indicating product details as well as symptoms and causes. Combinations of medications may be observed over the complete time span of the illness. Actual compliance is identified, and many diagnostic measures are possible. Available on an interactive PC-based system.

Service: Soft Goods Information Service

Measures purchasing behavior of a 12,000-household nationally representative sample panel. The monthly, diary-based service reports on all apparel, home furnishings, and footwear from all outlets, helping manufacturers, mills, fabric merchants and associations, and retailers understand who their customers are, what and where the customers purchase, what the customers pay, and what this information means to their businesses. The ongoing nature of the panel enables evaluation of long-term trends and identification of the factors influencing purchase behavior. Available on an interactive PC-based system.

Service: CAUS Apparel Usage Service

Tracks actual wearing of apparel for all family members in a panel of 2500 households over the course of a year. Panelists complete a daily diary indicating all clothes worn and each specific occasion and time. This diagnostic service enables evaluation of trends, identification of new developments, and better understanding of a client's business. Available on an interactive PC-based system.

Service: Communication Awareness Service

An overlay to the MRCA NCP, the Communication Awareness Service allows tracking of brand and advertising awareness and actual product purchases in the same households. Important ratios, such as awareness-to-trial and repeat-to-trial, may be gauged. A broad array of awareness stimuli is tracked, in addition to the usual mass media. Copy point recall is also possible. Twenty-five hundred households from the NCP panel are telephoned in the course of a year, at the rate of 50 per week. A series of categories is tracked within the same phone call.

A.2   The NPD Group, Inc.

Service: Consumer Market Research

The NPD Group, Inc., is a diversified marketing information company specializing in data collection and analysis techniques. Custom services include household tracking index panel (HTI) consumer mail studies, monthly Insta-Vue cooperative mailings, and empirically derived and analytical system for the packaged goods industry. Through its National Purchase Diary (NPD) panel, this syndicated service division tracks consumer purchase behavior, distribution, and sales for a variety of nonpackaged goods industries (including apparel and textiles, toys and games, petroleum products, sporting goods, consumer electronics, and cameras). It also measures food consumption, away-from-home eating, and product tracking for the food service industry.

A.3   Information Resources, Inc.

Service: BehaviorScan

Provides multiple-market test-marketing capabilities in a highly controlled environment. A split-cable TV system is used to vary advertising stimuli in 18,000 sample households. The sample's purchases are then identified as to price, brand, flavor, and so on, through checkout scanner data. The system allows advertisers to analyze the results of the various promotional strategies in terms of in-store purchases. This service is also widely used to test new products.

A.4   Mediamark Research Inc.

Service: Mediamark Research

A syndicated media/product purchase service based on (1) in-home interviews with 20,000 adults each year regarding their exposures to advertising media and (2) a leave-behind questionnaire.

Services: Respondent Data Bases
Product Volumes
Data Retrieval
Analysis Software

Provide data on volume of usage and demographics of users, and assigns users to light, medium, and heavy categories. Data are provided for 450 product categories and 5700 individual brands. The survey is done annually with a sample of 20,000.

A.5   Market Facts, Inc.

Service: Consumer Mail Panel

A controlled panel facility that covers over 400,000 households. Data Gage and TELENATION are shared cost/omnibus services. Marketest 2000 is a sales volume estimation model, and the Conversion Model is a strategic segmentation procedure that focuses on commitment of brand users and "availability" of nonusers.

A.6   NFO Research, Inc.

Service: NFO Panel

Provides access to a 425,000-household panel. Subpanels include the Hispanic Panel, the Mover Panel, the Baby Panel, the 50 Plus Panel, and the Chronic Ailment Panel.

Service: NFO Syndicated Services

Provides ongoing monitoring of beverage consumption through diary reporting, travel for pleasure on a national and a state level, and carpet purchase studies.

A.7   Survey Sampling, Inc.® (SSI)

Service: SSI

Maintains databases that allow construction of samples for business-to-business consumer, telephone, mail, and door-to-door research.

B.   CONSUMER DATA: ATTITUDES, OPINIONS, AND BEHAVIOR PATTERNS

B.1   Spar/Burgoyne Information Services Inc.

Service: In-Store Consumer Surveys

In testing merchandising alternatives, zeros in on the people who are actually buying a client's products in order to measure on-the-spot reactions to marketing and production innovations. These are far more revealing than either random interviews by phone or door-to-door calls.

B.2   The Gallup Organization, Inc.

Service: The Gallup Omnibus

A survey conducted at 3-week intervals. The data involve attitudes and opinions on a variety of contemporary topics. Trends are analyzed on the basis of questions that are repeated on each survey. The data can be cross-classified with demographic and socioeconomic characteristics. The sample size is 1500 adults. In addition, other omnibus services are available, including the Hispanic Consumer Omnibus and the College Student Omnibus.

B.3   Louis Harris and Associates, Inc.

Service: Harris Poll

A reprint of the column written once or twice a week by Humphrey Taylor and syndicated through the Creators Syndicate. Surveys are conducted nationwide, approximately monthly, on a wide variety of public affairs issues. The survey deals with political, social, economic, and

consumer issues, as well as sports entertainment and popular cultures. The sample size is usually 1250 adults.

B.4   The Roper Organization, Inc.

Service: The Roper Reports

A survey that is conducted 10 times a year, to monitor public opinion and consumer behavior on a broad range of existing and emerging social, political, and economic subjects and issues, as well as interests in and attitudes toward various services, products, and life-styles. The sample size is 2000 men and women, ages 18 and up. Personal interviews are conducted in the home.

Service: Roper College Tracks

A survey that is conducted six times a year, to monitor attitudes, values, consumer activity, and media behavior of college students, as well as their interests in areas of financial services, automobiles, consumer electronics, and computers. The sample size is 4000 personal interviews per year.

Service: Roper Youth Report

An annual survey on attitudes, values, and opinions of youths from 8 to 17 years old in the United States.

Service: Roper High School Report

In-home interviews with 500 high school students (from tenth grade through twelfth grade), to monitor attitudes, life-styles, purchase activities, and media habits.

B.5   Survey Research Center, University of Michigan

Service: Survey of Consumer Finances

From 1946 to 1970, the Survey Research Center, with the support of the Federal Reserve Board, conducted the annual Survey of Consumer Finances. These surveys were updated and enlarged in 1977, 1983, and 1986. They provide cross-sectional and trend data on the distribution of assets, debts, durable goods, and financial transactions among American families. Each survey includes approximately 2500 personal interviews. The reporting frequency is irregular.

Service: Survey of Consumer Attitudes

Provides data regarding consumer consumption patterns, attitudes, and intentions as related to personal finances, business conditions, and market conditions for housing, automobiles, and durables as well as topics of particular timeliness and interest. The Index of Consumer Sentiment, an overall measure of consumer attitudes toward the economy, is developed from these data. Five hundred households are interviewed by telephone each month. Monthly reports and data books are available on a subscription basis.

B.6   Yankelovic Partners

Service: The Yankelovic MONITOR®

A survey that has been conducted annually since 1971. The data include statistics on over 50 social trends and issues that measure the country's mood and outlook on life and influence marketplace decisions. Annual changes in these trends are analyzed by demographic and socioeconomic segments, among others. The sample of 2500 individuals is representative of the American population over 15 years of age. The data are collected by personal interview. Implications relative to the marketing of consumer products and services are discussed. This syndicated study is available by annual subscription, which includes custom analyses of the data.

Service: LITMUS

A stochastic model designed to aid marketing managers in developing more profitable new-product introductions. The LITMUS model uses category data, market response data, and the company's own marketing plan to compute monthly projections of awareness, penetration, and volume for new products. The model also provides a sensitivity analysis for each ingredient in the marketing mix—an analysis of the impact of each input on the market projection outputs. LITMUS provides insight into actions that should (and shouldn't) be taken in introducing new products.

B.7   Opinion Research Corporation

Service: Public Opinion Index

A continuing program of attitude research to help companies deal with the problems and opportunities of fast-moving social, economic, and political trends affecting business now and in the future. The index regularly tracks, analyzes, and interrelates changes in opinion among members of the general public and many target groups, including members of Congress, federal regulatory officials, union leaders, corporate social activities,

and the Washington press corps. Reports are issued monthly.

Service: Caravan Surveys

Three services are offered: (1) a weekly telephone survey with a probability sample of 1000 adults nationwide; (2) a quarterly telephone survey with 50 top- and middle-management executives in the 1500 largest industrial and service companies, including an annual familiarity/favorability/image measurement of 40 major companies; and (3) a quarterly telephone survey of 300 executives from a cross section of major companies in France, Germany, and England.

B.8   Claritas Corp./NPDC Inc.

Service: Potential Rating Index for Zip Markets (PRIZM®)

Classifies every American neighborhood into one of 40 life-style segments. Using census data, consumer purchase data, and computer modeling, PRIZM attempts to explain, predict, and target consumer behavior by targeting areas as small as one or more of the nation's 22 million zip + 4 areas.

Service: P$YCLE®

Analyzes current data from Claritas/NPDC's Market Audit Survey of 90,000 households to produce the six most powerful predictors of consumer usage of financial products. Using these predictors, the service segments the market into 8 primary segments and 27 subsegments. The segments are used by financial institutions to determine targets for their financial services.

Service: Compass

A desktop computer software application package which is a marketing system that integrates, analyzes, and maps information drawn from company databases, the client's customers' databases, and third-party databases. It links demographics and geography using life-style clusters down to zip + 4 levels.

B.9   Bruskin/Goldring Research Inc.

Service: Omnibus Interviewing—OmniTel and Integrated Survey Information Systems (ISIS)

OmniTel and ISIS provide continuous interviewing of nationally representative consumers based on random-digit dialing. Results are available within 72 hours at a cost significantly below that of a dedicated survey, though this interviewing produces the same results as dedicated surveys. Interviewing is conducted weekly.

B.10   J. D. Power & Associate

Services: Marketing Information and Consulting

Provides information on product quality and customer satisfaction in several industries, most notably in the automotive industry. Offers annual syndicated studies of car and light truck owners as well as the computer and airline sectors.

B.11   Overlooked Opinions, Inc.

Service: The Gay Market—Wellness Matters

Provides information on the physical and mental health-care needs and concerns of gay men and lesbian women, including everything from aging and HIV issues to cosmetic surgery and eating disorders. Wellness Matters also includes detailed assessments of mental health issues faced over the past 12 months and physical treatment obtained over the past 12 months. Updated annually.

C.   RETAIL DATA

C.1   Audits and Surveys, Inc.

Service: Retail Census of Brand Distribution

A study of products and brands, based on personal interviews and inspections conducted in some 40,000 retail outlets. The data focus on the number and types of outlets in the United States carrying various product categories and the specific brands in stock. The data are analyzed by city size, geographic region, type of outlet, and annual store volume, as well as according to whether the outlet is part of a chain or is independent. The kinds of product categories studied include automotive supplies; electrical appliances; household products; food, health, and beauty aids; photographic supplies; tobacco; and writing instruments. The reporting frequency is annual, and the study results are projectable to all U.S. retail outlets.

Service: National Total Market Audit

Provides bimonthly retail sales, retail distribution, and retailer inventory for product categories such as automotive supplies; electrical products; food; tobacco, photographic, health, beauty, and household products; and writing instruments. The service provides data on market size and market shares; sales by outlet type, region, and size of city; inventory levels; and percentage of distribution and out-of-stock situations. Retail stores are the sampling units. The study results are projectable to all U.S. retail outlets carrying the specific product category.

Service: National Restaurant Market Index

Provides data on the commercial restaurant market. Trained enumerators personally call on a national probability sample of 6000 restaurants, projectable to all commercial restaurants in the United States. The clients are institutional food product distributors, and the service provides data by product category on brand usage, package sizes, and product types. The data are reported separately for five restaurant types, nine geographic regions, and six city sizes or client sales regions. The reporting frequency is annual.

Service: Selling-Areas Distribution Index

A service designed to provide companies using SAMI (warehouse withdrawals to food stores; see section D, Wholesale Data) with measurement of in-store conditions important in evaluating warehouse movement data. For example, the service reports on the number of facings, the shelf price, and promotional activity. Fifty-four marketing areas are defined, providing in-store observation data for the food trade; for drug, discount, and variety stores; for hardware/home centers; and for retail automotive parts stores.

Service: Aftermarket Sales Index

Measures sales volume of specific product categories in the retail automotive chain store market, providing continuous bimonthly measures of retail (consumer) sales, on a stock keeping unit (SKU) by-SKU basis. The service is designed to enable aftermarket product manufacturers to continuously monitor their own and competitors' sales volumes and market share trends so as to plan better marketing strategies for the retail automotive aftermarket.

The database consists of retail sales volume derived from point-of-sale (POS) systems from major aftermarket chain retailers that operate stores throughout all regions of the country. Statistical projections of the database yield reports that reflect sales activity for the universe of aftermarket chains in the United States.

C.2 SPAR/BURGOYNE Information Services, Inc.

Service: In-Store Observation Systems

Combines an in-store observation and reporting service with panels composed of stores with over $40,000 in weekly volume. The panel data are available by area and store type to tie in with the audit data. The observed measurements include shelf position, out-of-stock merchandise, average price, shelf facings, package type, point-of-purchase (POP), age, displays of stock, and condition of product. Reporting frequency is monthly.

C.3 The Ehrhart-Babic Group

Service: National Retail Tracking Index, Inc.

Provides syndicated in-store distribution and other observational data in six classes of retail trade covering over 10,000 stores nationwide.

Service: National Alcohol Beverage Index

Provides syndicated observational surveys of retail conditions in 2900 off-premise outlets in 68 markets and in 3100 on-premise accounts in 40 top markets.

Service: Ehrhart-Babic Associates, Inc.

Provides custom in-store research in all types of retail outlets. Services include trended and projectable sales audits, controlled store tests, minimarket, product purchases, and new-product-introduction performance data.

C.4 Information Resources, Inc.

Service: BehaviorScan

Provides multiple-market test marketing capabilities in a highly controlled environment. A split-cable TV system is used to vary advertising stimuli in 18,000 sample households. The sample's purchases are then identified as to price, brand, flavor, and so on, through checkout scanner data. The system allows advertisers to analyze the results of the various promotional strategies in terms of in-store purchases. The service is also widely used to test new products.

Service: InfoScan

A national- and local-market single-source tracking service. InfoScan incorporates data from 2700 scanner-equipped supermarkets, 500 drugstores, 250 mass merchandisers, and a nationwide panel of 60,000 households to provide information on sales, brand share, and promotional activities, as well as consumer shopping behavior. This information is delivered via a powerful, easy-to-use decision support system.

C.5 Dun & Bradstreet/A. C. Nielsen Company

Service: ERIM

Measures consumer buying habits and effectiveness of commercials by comparing store purchases with advertising beamed to cable and noncable TV participants' homes. The information is collected by entering a participant's card in a store's cash register each time a purchase is made. Competes directly with Information Resources' BehaviorScan.

Service: National Scan Track

Provides clients with a sample projection to the national scanner universe of supermarkets doing $4 million or more in retail sales. Scanner data are combined with regular staff visits to supermarkets to monitor displays and other in-store promotions. Weekly reports are available.

Service: Nielsen Retail Index

Involves a store audit of 1300 supermarkets, 700 drugstores, and 150 mass merchandisers taken every 2 months. The types of data provided include share of market, prices, displays, inventory, and promotional efforts. Available for grocery, drug, pharmaceutical, confectionery, liquor, appliance, perfume, and photographic products.

Services: SALESCAN
            TELE-SCAN

Designed to analyze sales movement information from grocery and drug chains for manufacturers, advertising agencies, and retailers. SALESCAN is a proprietary set of PC software designed to integrate scanner data with in-store causal information, such as feature ads, reduced prices, displays, and margins.

C.6   Overlooked Opinions, Inc.

Service: The Gay Market Automotive Report

Provides detailed purchasing behavior and brand preferences for the gay and lesbian automotive market. Current ownership and anticipated purchases are revealed, as well as motivational factors that influence purchasing behavior. Updated annually.

C.7   Spectra Marketing Systems, Inc.

Service: Spectra

Provides Spectra Advantage®, a PC database covering retail packaged goods sales; and Supermarkets Plus™, a supermarket and discount store information database covering 126,000 U.S. stores.

D.   WHOLESALE DATA

D.1   Dun & Bradstreet/A. C. Nielsen Company

Service: Nielsen Early Intelligence Service

Collects data from warehouses concerning movement of new products through 150 food chains and independent warehouses. The reporting frequency is bimonthly.

E.   INDUSTRIAL DATA

E.1   McGraw-Hill Information Systems Company

Service: Dodge Reports: Dodge Construction
       Potential

Collects data from 165,000 building material manufacturers and distributors, and from governmental and educational institutions. The data, useful in the marketing of building products, cover public and private contract totals by type and number of projects, square feet, and dollar value. Possible geographic classifications include counties, metropolitan areas, states, and individual sales territories. The reporting frequency is monthly.

E.2   McGraw-Hill Publications Company, Department of Economics

Service: Annual Survey of U.S. Business' Plans for
       New Plants and Equipment

Surveys about 900 industrial or commercial companies regarding planned capital investments. Thirty major industries are reported for the coming 4-year period. The data are collected by mail questionnaire, and the reporting frequency is annual.

E.3   R. L. Polk and Co.

Service: Statistical Services Division

Provides statistical information on first-time title and registration of new vehicles, the total registered vehicle population, vehicle purchasing habits of consumers, and life-style characteristics. Statistics are compiled for cars, trucks, commercial trailers, and motorcycles. Information is tabulated by zip code, postal code, community, county, state or province, and nation (for the United States and Canada). Detail by census tract is provided for all major markets in North America. The National Vehicle Population Profile (NVPP) catalogs individual vehicles by make, series, body style, engine size, year, and model.

The information is provided in hard copy reports and is also available to clients online via DIALPOLK, Trucking Industry Profile (TIP), Decision Point, and other services.

Service: Geographic Data Technology, Inc.

Creates and markets computer-readable maps for the special analysis and geographic information systems market. Map products are derived from 1990 Census files and cover the entire United States at the street level. The company also produces GeoDistrict, a computer system used for political redistricting.

Service: National Demographics & Lifestyles Inc.

Compiles databases profiling lifestyles and demographic characteristics of consumers based on responses to questionnaires inserted in consumer goods. From that same information, The Lifestyle Selector is a consumer database compiled of 28 million names from which mailers make precision-targeted mailings. The company also copublishes the *Lifestyle Market Analyst,* a marketing sourcebook containing demographic and life-style profiles of 212 metropolitan areas. The company operates a data entry plant in Barbados and holds an interest in NDL International Ltd., a leading London-based company serving about 80 questionnaire clients. Its consumer database contains life-style and demographic information on over 2.5 million households.

E.4   American Business Information, Inc.

Service: Business-to-Business Marketing Databases Covering the United States and Canada

Marketing databases compiled and maintained to provide the most current information available on approximately 9.5 million U.S. businesses and 1.4 million Canadian businesses. Each database is updated continuously throughout the year using yellow page directories as the primary source. Additional sources are used to supplement the respective databases. Information is available in a variety of formats: mailing labels, diskettes, magnetic tape, online services, directories by state and SIC codes, big-business directories, manufacturers directories, and CD-ROM, to name a few.

E.5   Compusearch

Service: StoreBase

Provides a database of 10,000 Canadian stores in the packaged goods and food retailing industries.

E.6   Infratest Burke

Service: FAKT

Provides an information database for European and international business sectors. Tables and synopses are included.

E.7   Frost and Sullivan/Market Intelligence

Service: Market Research Studies

Offers syndicated marketing research studies to a wide variety of clients. As a leading publisher of marketing research reports, it publishes 250 industry analyses a year covering data communications, telecommunications, industrial electronics, process control, consumer areas, chemical areas, computers and software, medical electronics, biotechnology, and health care.

E.8   M.O.R.–PACE

Service: F.A.C.T.

A database management and information retrieval system that concentrates on consumer and industrial marketing research, media audience studies, social and public policy research, health care, public utilities, and transportation studies.

F.   ADVERTISING EVALUATION DATA: BROADCAST MEDIA

F.1   AdTel, Ltd (Division of SAMI Burke International Research Corp.)

Service: AdTel

Measures sales responses over a period of time to compare results of different television commercials and consumer promotions. A split-cable TV system and two balanced consumer purchase diary panels of 1000 households each are used as control groups for variables other than those being tested. The scanner panel members' purchases are recorded. The impact of a particular television commercial on sales can be determined by comparing panel sales results. In addition, AdTel can track buying habits of both test and control groups with supermarket scanner systems.

F.2   Research Systems Corporation

Service: Advertising Research System (ARS)

A copy-testing service that assesses the impact of television advertising on consumer behavior by simulating the advertising process. From 400 to 600 randomly selected respondents preview pilot programs and commercials via closed-circuit television monitors. Pretest and posttest behavioral measures of brand preferences are taken at the beginning and end of each preview. Three days later, respondents are telephoned to determine delayed recall. The reliability of persuasion and recall measures is established by randomly retesting commercials within 1 to 3 weeks. The validity of these measures is established by comparisons with actual consumer behavior studies using controlled test markets and national scanner data.

Service: Comprehensive Advertising Tracing System (CATS)

Provides continuous tracking of weight and ad quality for all major brands in a category. Combines commercial gross rating points (GRPs) with ARS persuasion rating points (PRPs) to provide a complete look at how advertising performs in comparison to the competition and other marketing elements such as promotion and pride.

Service: Outlook Advertising Management Software

An empirically derived model that predicts commercial wearout (sales effectiveness using ARS PRPs and GRPs. The model allows optimization of advertising "selling power" for planned media expenditures. The model has had 100+ verifications ($r = .87$).

F.3   Gallup and Robinson, Inc.

Service: In-View

Tests rough or finished commercials. The sample, drawn from three markets (in Pittsburgh, Louisville, and San Diego), is composed of 150 men and/or 150 women, aged 18 to 65. The sample members are recruited in advance to watch the normal program broadcast and are then interviewed 24 hours after exposure to measure recall, idea communication, and persuasiveness.

Service: InTeleTest

Tests rough or finished commercials. The sample includes 150 to 200 men and/or women who are recruited in person. They are asked to view a 1-hour TV pilot program on a videocassette recorder (VCR) tape in which one or more test commercials are embedded, along with other commercials. A telephone interview follows the next day, to obtain measurement of (1) the percentage of viewers who remember the commercial, (2) sales message recall, and (3) message persuasion. The study concludes with reexposure of the commercial and additional diagnostic and evaluative questioning via a self-administered questionnaire.

F.4   Millward Brown, Inc.

Service: Advance Tracking Program (ATP)

Evaluates and models the effects of advertising expenditures, using continuous survey data. LINK is a pretesting system that provides diagnostic data for use in optimizing advertising communication.

G.   ADVERTISING EVALUATION DATA: PRINT MEDIA

G.1   Chilton Company

Service: Chilton Ad-Chart Services

Evaluates the effectiveness of advertisements in magazines. The sample for each publication includes about 100 subscribers. A personal or telephone interview is used to determine the degree to which each subscriber noticed and/or was informed by the advertising or editorial content of the publication. The data are arranged by product category and by purchase influence group.

Over 60 issues are studied annually. This service conducts Ad-Analysis studies for tutorial "how-to"-type publications, with readership scores for "noticed," "started to read," "read half or more," and "informative." Ad-Action studies conducted for tabloid publications also determine what actions readers may have taken as a result of reading the ad. Ad-Access is a quick, convenient, up-to-date, online, 5-year database of Ad-Analysis and Ad-Action results. International readership and mail subscriber studies are also offered.

G.2   Gallup and Robinson, Inc.

Service: Magazine Impact Research Services (MIRS)

Evaluates the effectiveness of advertisements in magazines, including "tip-in" pretests. The sample includes 150 readers of the magazine type (news, women's, etc.). The study method used is a personal placement of the publication (in 10 MSAs) and a telephone interview the following day. Three levels of effectiveness are measured: (1) percentage of readers who remembered the ad, (2) sales message recall, and (3) message persuasiveness. The ad may be reexposed to any or all of the sample to obtain additional evaluative and diagnostic information.

Service: Rapid Ad Measurement (RAM)

Tests magazine ads twice a month, with either *People* or *Time* magazine as the vehicle. The sample is composed of 150 men and/or 150 women from 10 major markets. Evaluative measures same as MIRS.

G.3   Harvey Research Organization, Inc.

Service: The Harvey Communication Measurement Service

Evaluates the effectiveness of advertisements in magazines. A sample of 100 readers is interviewed to determine the effectiveness of the advertising and editorial content of the publication. Open-ended questions are used to probe for ideas and impressions about the advertising. Another service of Harvey, Ad-Q Studies, uses a mailed questionnaire to perform the same function.

G.4   Dun & Bradstreet/A. C. Nielsen

Service: Grocery Ad Book

Provides a visual overview of the advertising of major grocery chains across the nation in the top 50 markets.

The country is divided into four regions. Copies of the actual advertising are included, along with each advertiser's share of retail food volume in its metropolitan area. The service is available weekly, biweekly, or monthly.

G.5   Readex, Inc.

Service: Mail Survey Research

Specializes in conducting surveys by mail for communicators and marketers. Services are offered to magazine publishers, associations, and corporations.

In the magazine industry, the company conducts custom-designed reader profile surveys as well as readership surveys of advertising and editorial content. For associations, the company offers member need assessment surveys, industry demographics, and financial studies. Finally, in the corporate world, Readex typically works for the corporate communicator who publishes a customer magazine, an employee newsletter, or an annual report. On the corporate marketing side, the firm conducts survey research of various types for which the mail technique is appropriate.

G.6   Roper Starch Worldwide, Inc.

Service: Starch Ad/Editorial Readership Reports

Evaluates the effectiveness of advertisements and editorials in general magazines, business publications, and newspapers.

Service: Starch Ad Readership Service

Conducts in-person ad readership reports for consumer and business-to-business publications. Over 30,000 ads are studied each year in over 500 magazine issues.

Service: Starch Plus

Conducts detailed ad readership studies according to demographic and product usage categories. Provides product category reports (automotive, food, liquor, etc.).

Service: Adnorm Reports

Details ad readership scores by size, color, and product categories for the major consumer and general business publications. Each report is over 200 pages long.

Service: Tested Copy

A monthly newsletter offering guidance on advertising effectiveness.

G.7   Overlooked Opinions, Inc.

Service: The Gay Market—Reader

Provides information needed for media planning and ad placement choices in a wide variety of publications, from general readership periodicals to specialty titles. Reader is available in two editions, Executive and Standard. The Executive Edition provides penetration scores and rankings for the 700 mainstream periodicals most popular with gay men and lesbians, in addition to detailed demographic and behavioral data from the top 100 publications. The Standard Edition provides penetrations and rankings for the leading 100 publications, as well as detailed demographics from any 10 of the top 100 provided in this report. Updated annually.

H.   MEDIA AND AUDIENCE DATA: MEDIA-MARKET FIT

H.1   The Arbitron Ratings Company

Services: Arbitron Radio Local Market Reports
Condensed Radio Market Reports
County Coverage (Radio)
Arbitrends Monthly Microcomputer Delivered Audience Estimates (Radio)

Measures listening audiences in 263 radio markets nationwide. The information is collected in diaries and reported in terms of sex and age demographic characteristics. Sample sizes range from 450 to 8000. All radio markets are measured from 12 weeks up to 48 weeks each year.

H.2   Audit Bureau of Circulation (ABC)

Service: ABC Audit Reports

Semiannual publisher's statements from member newspapers, business publications, consumer magazines, and farm publications are verified or corrected through annual field audits and the resulting ABC Audit Reports. Services also include: Circulation Data Bank, Supplementary Data Reports, quarterly FAS-FAX reports, annual Magazine Trend Reports, semiannual Blue Books, and Coupon Distribution Verification Services. Reports are available in both hard copy and electronic format (diskettes and CD-ROM).

H.3 Dun & Bradstreet/A. C. Nielsen Company

Service: Nielsen Television Index

Provides estimates of the size and nature of the audience for individual television programs. The data are collected by an audiometer device attached to the television receiver. Data are available on the program's audience size and characteristics, viewing habits, switching, and so on. The sample size is over 1000 TV households. The frequency of reporting is both weekly and semiannual. Another service available is the Nielsen Station Index, which measures television station audiences in over 200 local markets and provides season-to-season data on viewing by time period and program.

H.4 Marketing Evaluations, Inc.

Service: Q Evaluations

Performs annual surveys to measure the familiarity and popularity of over 1500 personalities and 385 cartoon characters. Also measures numerous television programs and consumer products. Used for selecting spokespeople and casting for series, specials, hosts, and guest stars.

H.5 Simmons Market Research Bureau, Inc.

Service: Study of Media and Markets (SMM)

Reports on media exposure and product-usage behavior. The data include readership and exposure to magazines, newspapers, television, radio, cable television, the yellow pages, and outdoor billboards. The data are cross-referenced with product-usage, demographic, and socioeconomic characteristics. The national probability sample includes 19,000 adult males and females. The data are collected through a series of interactions with the respondents; personal interviews, a self-administered questionnaire, and a personal viewing diary are used. All data are available also on the bases of the Vals Lifestyle and ClusterPlus and PRIZM geo-demographic segmentation systems.

Service: Simmons Teen-Age Research Study

Similar to the study of media and markets in terms of data availability and survey procedures. This service utilizes a national probability sample of 2000 teenagers. Reporting frequency is every other year.

Service: Simmons Kids Study

Collects media, consumer, and personal information on children ages 6 to 14.

Service: National Study of Local Newspaper Ratings

Reports on readership of major daily and Sunday newspapers in each of the top 50 markets. Data, cross-referenced with demographic and product-usage characteristics, are collected through two telephone interviews with each of approximately 60,000 adults, representing random-digit dialing samples. Reporting frequency is every other year.

H.6 Lee Slurzberg Research, Inc. (LSR)

Service: LSR National Hispanic Omnibus

Conducts 1000 personal, in-home interviews with a national probability sample of Hispanics. Fifty primary sampling points are used, and all interviews are conducted by trained bilingual interviewers. Note: This service was started in 1975 and is not syndicated. Back data are not available.

H.7 Mediamark Research Inc.

Service: Mediamark Report and Database

Reports on the Survey of American Consumers, covering media audiences, their demographics, and product/service usage. Mediamark executes an ongoing survey of the U.S. population. The annual sample of 20,000 adults is conducted in two waves, and reports are published every 6 months (April and October), using a 12-month moving average. All basic media usage information (except TV program viewing) is collected in the personal interview. Product usage and TV program viewing data are collected in a personally placed and picked up self-administered questionnaire.

H.8 The Traffic Audit Bureau for Media Measurement

Service: Traffic Audit Bureau (TAB)

An outdoor media industry service that is a national circulation authority for out-of-home advertising. TAB verifies via audit the circulation figures for Bulletins, 30-Sheet and 8-Sheet Posters, Bus Shelters, and Ski Area Displays. There are 350 company members, covering advertising structures in over 1000 markets nationally.

I.   MEDIA AND AUDIENCE DATA: COMPETITIVE EFFORTS

I.1   The Advertising Checking Bureau, Inc.

Service: Magazine Checking: Newspaper Advertising Research

Provides advertising research information specifically designed to meet the client's research requirements. Information is provided on lineage and cost of advertising for the client's brand and competitive brands, national and retail advertising reports, pricing reports, and so on. Data are provided via tearsheets, manual and computer reports, data tapes, scrapbooks, and other methods. Reporting frequency is determined by the client.

I.2   The Arbitron Company

Service: The Arbitron Commercial Monitoring Service

Monitors television, cable TV and radio networks, spot television on 351 stations in 75 major markets, and over 260 programs in national syndication. Data are presented by brand, parent company, and product category. The data are used by advertisers and agencies for proof of performance and are also the industry sources for competitive expenditures for the four media categories monitored. Also available is Brand TraQ, a PC-based application that produces analysis for 21 demographic groups for network television and 16 major markets.

I.3   Leading National Advertisers

Service: Multi Media Service

Provides summaries of brand and company expenditures in 10 major media: magazines, newspaper supplements, network TV, network radio, spot radio, syndicated TV, cable TV, newspapers, national newspapers, and outdoor advertising. Data are presented in three easy-to-read reports: (1) Ad $ Summary, with brands listed alphabetically, showing total advertising expenditures and media used; (2) Company Brand, with brands listed within parent company; and (3) Class Brand, with brands listed within each of the 375 product classes, showing advertising dollars spent in each of the 10 media by brand, company, or class.

Service: PIB Magazine Analysis Service

A detailed monthly analysis of brand expenditures in about 190 consumer magazines and 4 national news-

paper supplements. This service shows magazines used, size of ad, coloration, and cost of ad. Special sizes and types of advertisements are denoted, such as digest-sized units, partial run, and geographic split run. The Regional Advertising Service provides the same type of data for 98 percent of the regional demographic advertising. Quarterly and year-end summaries are included.

Service: Outdoor Advertising Expenditures

A quarterly report of brand expenditures in outdoor (billboard) advertising. Showing poster, paint, and markets used by each brand, it covers markets of over 100,000 population.

Service: Business to Business (MMS-ROME)

Audits about 700 industrial and professional magazines to determine the advertising space and investment of over 90,000 advertisers. The report frequency is quarterly. Data are available on PC diskettes and in customized reports.

I.4   Media Records, Inc.

Service: Quarterly Blue Book
        Green Book
        Other Special Reports

Measures newspaper advertising space and reports in inches and expenditures by advertiser. Provides standardized competitive data used extensively by media planners and researchers on national advertising coverage over 200 daily and Sunday newspapers. Publishes an annual summary of newspaper advertising expenditures by classification and advertisers. Other publications on retail and financial advertisers, published at different frequencies, are also available.

I.5   NFO Research, Inc.

Service: National Yellow Pages Monitor (NYPM)

Provides a rating system for yellow pages audience measurement.

J.   ONLINE DATABASES

J.1   Dialog

Service: Dialog

Provides online database access to business, industry, financial, science, law, and social science information.

Data include the complete texts of articles from more than 2500 journals, magazines, newsletters, and wire services.

J.2   Dow Jones and Company, Inc.

Service: Dow Jones News/Retrieval

An electronic library of 1750 business and financial information sources covering millions of companies around the world. Provides exclusive access to five real-time Dow Jones news wires.

J.3   Information Access Company

Service: Predicast Databases

Information Access Company provides 24 online business and periodical databases, including articles from 1750 publications covering business and industry, computers and technology, law, health, marketing, management, popular culture, academia, and current events. It also offers a complete range of CD-ROM databases on the InfoTrac system, including F&S INDEX plus TEXT, which provides significant international coverage of companies, industries, products, and technologies.

J.4   NewsNet, Inc.

Service: On-Line Database Company

Provides direct access to more than 650 newsletters, trade journals, and industry magazines; 26 news wires; and five gateway services: Dun & Bradstreet (D&B), TRW Business Profiles, American Business Information, Inc. (ABI), Investment ANALY$T, and The Official Airline Guides. NewsNet also features an electronic clipping service, NewsFlash, that collects data even when the client is off the system. Sources cover over 35 industries, including publishing, aerospace, medicine, electronics, finance, government, international affairs, telecommunications, education, travel, manufacturing, and environment. Information is delivered in full text, for both current and back issues, and in many cases is available online before it's available in print.

K.   DEMOGRAPHIC DATA

K.1   CACI Marketing Systems

Service: Full-Service Demographic Information

Provides demographic and business data. Includes current-year updates, 5-year forecasts, and 1990 and 1980 census information. The data are available in reports and sourcebooks, as well as on diskettes, CD-ROM, and magnetic tape. Also provided are custom maps that portray multiple demographic or business characteristics for census, postal, and media geographics.

K.2   Compusearch

Service: Lifestyles and Wealth Styles

Provides a Canadian geo-demographic cluster system that allows market segmentation.

K.3   Donnelley Marketing Information Services (DMIS)

Service: DMIS

Provides geo-demographic information including current-year estimates and 5-year projections for population, age, and income, along with access to information including life-styles, retail sales, business, automotive, health-care, and household-level databases. CONQUEST® is a PC-based geo-demographic system that provides access to demographic, economic, and geographic databases. Demographica On-Call™ provides custom demographic and business reports, full-color maps, and specialized industry directories.

K.4   Overlooked Opinions, Inc.

Service: The Gay Market-Finder: Population Estimates and Lifestyle and Demographics

Provides gay market population and density estimates by census division and region, 5-digit zip code, MSA, state, county, gay market area (GMA), and primary gay market area (PGMA). For a quick visual inspection, density maps are provided by state and 3-digit zip code. This report also provides detailed demographic and behavioral information for the gay market nationally, by census division and region, and for each of the PGMAs as defined by Overlooked Opinions, Inc. Updated annually.

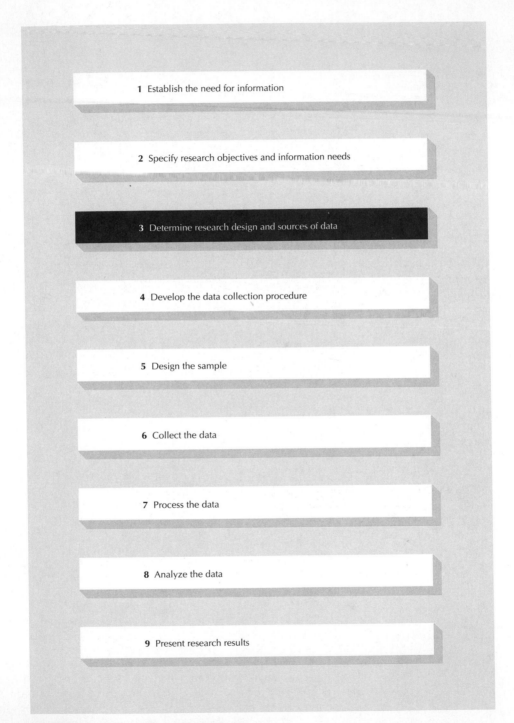

1 Establish the need for information

2 Specify research objectives and information needs

3 Determine research design and sources of data

4 Develop the data collection procedure

5 Design the sample

6 Collect the data

7 Process the data

8 Analyze the data

9 Present research results

FIGURE 6-1 Steps in the research process.

CHAPTER 6

SECONDARY DATA

MARKETING RESEARCH IN ACTION

THE ZIP + 4 POSTAL CODE: A MARKETING RESEARCH TOOL FOR CONSUMER TARGETING

The zip + 4 postal code has become an important marketing research tool.

Geo-coded zip + 4 files can be created by matching zip + 4 postal codes with their geographic coordinates (longitude and latitude). Traditional geographic delineations such as 5-digit zip codes and county lines can define only preestablished boundaries, limiting their usefulness. The zip + 4 code supplies high and low coordinates that bring researchers to within 250 feet or less of the actual address. Like most geographic information systems (GISs) or mapping applications, geo-coded zip + 4 files allow users to create customized boundaries, so that they can target individual streets, neighborhoods, or specific geographic areas.

For example, a company may want to compare purchases in several adjacent urban neighborhoods composed of different minority groups. Purchase and payment data from retail purchasers can be summarized according to the user-defined neighborhood boundaries that they occupy. Since purchase data can also be brought to within 250 feet of the actual location, researchers can calculate the distance customers travel to the business.

Geo-coding by zip + 4 allows companies of all sizes to code enormous volumes of customer files and project them onto computer-generated maps. Prior to development of the zip + 4 postal codes, geo-coding of an address could be done by converting the address through the mapping application, a potentially slow process, or it could be processed by a third party at considerable expense and delay. Zip + 4 allows in-house management information systems (MIS) departments to achieve a hit rate of 90 percent or better, as well as save time and money. The geo-coded files can be used by any department within the company that has a GIS, allowing departments such as sales and billing to use the data to analyze their experiences in target areas on a regular basis.

The primary business of direct marketing list brokers is the multiple sale of selected datasets for mailing purposes. While these brokers have traditionally sold their lists for single use only, not for inclusion in databases, most brokers also append zip + 4 information to their fields. If this information can be packaged in a way that protects the broker's interests, it will be a potentially rich new data source for marketers.

For example, a company might purchase a list of a specific area's new residents who possess common characteristics. The company could merge the list with its corresponding zip + 4 geo-coded file, allowing it to map the list. The resulting map could help the company effectively realign its sales staff and territories to meet new opportunities. Lists could also be compiled and sold according to SIC code, number of employees, sales volume, and so forth, and then geo-coded to create route maps for sales staffs. This would improve call efficiency and help target the best prospects within a given area.

Many zip + 4 geo-coded files also contain census tract, block group, and mail carrier route identifiers. Census statistics can be appended to a customer record as easily as geographic coordinates, creating a wider range of related research data. These statistics are available for purchase from the Bureau of the Census or from outside vendors on CD-ROM disks. Sophisticated GIS analysis is becoming an increasingly important marketing tool. Marketing researchers can purchase and run advanced mapping software and data on a personal computer. As the costs of software and data continue to drop, this new technology is likely to penetrate the market and increase the use and effectiveness of GIS marketing research.

Source: Sumner R. Andrews, Jr., "Zip + 4 Postal Code Evolves into an Important Marketing Research Tool," *Marketing News,* p. 9, April 1992.

Once research objectives and information needs have been specified, the researcher turns to the task of formulating the research design and determining the appropriate sources of marketing data. The previous chapter discussed the research design options available to the researcher and presented an overview of the basic sources of marketing data. This chapter continues the discussion by focusing on secondary data and their role in the research process.[1]

[1]The authors wish to acknowledge the valuable assistance of Nancy S. Karp, Librarian, School of Business Administration, The University of Michigan, in preparing this chapter.

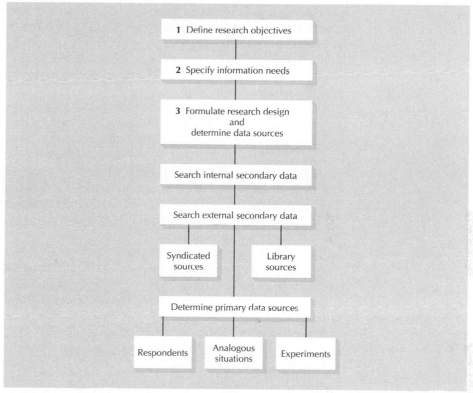

FIGURE 6-2   Initial steps in the research process.

ROLE OF SECONDARY DATA

Figure 6-2 presents the initial steps in the research process, with an emphasis on the types of data sources available at the data collection stage. All too frequently, the beginning researcher assumes that surveying respondents is the only way to collect data for a research project. Actually, survey research should be used only if the data cannot be collected with more efficient data sources. Consequently, the first step in the data collection stage is to determine whether the data have already been collected.

The data sources available to the marketing researcher can be classified as primary or secondary. *Secondary data* are already published data collected for purposes other than the specific research needs at hand. A study of marketing research practices in business indicates that about 90 percent of businesses use secondary data in their activities.[2] Such data can be classified as internal or

[2]Thomas C. Kinnear and Ann R. Root, "A Study of the Marketing Research Business," unpublished study, 1994. Copyright 1994, Thomas C. Kinnear.

external. *Internal secondary data* are available within the organization (e.g., accounting records and sales reports), whereas *external secondary data* are provided by sources outside the organization (e.g., reports, periodicals, and books). *Primary data* are collected specifically for purposes of the research needs at hand. For example, if a retailer collects data from shoppers regarding store image, the resulting data are primary.

As Figure 6-2 shows, internal secondary data sources should be searched thoroughly before turning to external sources. External secondary data are available from two main sources: (1) syndicated sources and (2) library sources. Syndicated sources, discussed in Chapter 5, are services that collect standardized data to serve the needs of an array of clients. These data are often expensive, and their availability may be restricted to certain clients. Library sources, the focus of this chapter, include a wide range of publicly circulated publications.

Once the search of secondary data is completed, the researcher typically will find that primary data must be collected to supplement the secondary data. Rarely will secondary data fulfill the data requirements of a research project. The remaining chapters in this book concentrate on the data collection, analysis, and reporting phases of the research process involving primary data.

It is important that the marketing researcher be familiar with the advantages and disadvantages of secondary data as well as the sources of such data, and these topics will occupy the remainder of this chapter.

Advantages of Secondary Data

The central advantage of secondary data is savings in cost and time in comparison with primary data. Consider the research objective of estimating the market potential for a product. If secondary data are available, the researcher may be able to visit a library, identify the appropriate source, and collect the desired data relating to market potential. This may take a day of the researcher's time and involve minimal cost. Contrast this situation with collecting similar data via a survey. Several weeks or months may be required to design and pretest a questionnaire, train the interviewers, devise a sampling plan, and collect and process the data. In addition, the cost of such a project could involve thousands of dollars. Consequently, it is important to search secondary data sources before proceeding to primary sources. While it is rare that secondary data completely fulfill the data requirements of a research project, typically they can (1) aid in the formulation of the decision problem, (2) suggest methods and types of data for meeting the information needs, and (3) serve as a source of comparative data by which primary data can be interpreted and evaluated.

Another advantage of secondary data is that they may be so wide-ranging and/or so sophisticated that collecting them would be beyond the means of the typical organization. For example, this would be true of the data available from the Bureau of the Census.

Disadvantages of Secondary Data

The major disadvantages of secondary data relate to (1) the extent that the data fit the information needs of the project, (2) the accuracy of the data, and (3) the timeliness of the data.

Data Fit Problem   As discussed previously, since secondary data are collected for purposes other than those of the research project at hand, they will rarely completely serve the information needs of the project. The degree of fit can range from completely inadequate to very close. This degree of fit is influenced by two factors: (1) units of measurement and (2) definition of classes.

It is common for a researcher to discover that the secondary data are expressed in units different from those required by the project. For example, a project may require data regarding household income. The researcher may find that income is measured by individual, family, spending unit, or tax return rather than by household. Extreme caution should be exercised in estimating the desired data from measurements in other units.

Another problem relates to the class boundaries used to summarize the data. Assuming the unit of measurement is correct, a researcher could find that data on household income are cited with $7000 boundaries ($0 6999, $7000–13,999, and so on), when the project's information needs require $5000 boundaries.

Accuracy Problem   The researcher must determine whether the secondary data are accurate enough for the purposes of the research project at hand. A serious limitation of secondary data is the difficulty of evaluating their accuracy. There are a number of sources of error in the sampling, data collection, analysis, and reporting stages of the research process that influence the accuracy of the data. These sources of error can be more easily evaluated when the researcher directly participates in the research process, as is the situation with primary research. The lack of participation in the research process in no way reduces the responsibility of the researcher to evaluate the accuracy of the data used. The following criteria can be used in the difficult task of assessing the accuracy of secondary data: (1) source, (2) purpose of the publication, and (3) evidence concerning quality.

The source of data is very important in evaluating their accuracy. Secondary data may be secured from an original source or an acquired source. An *original source* is the source that originated the data, while an *acquired source* is the source that procured the data from the original source. The *Statistical Abstract of the United States* is an example of an acquired source. All the data in the *Statistical Abstract* are taken from other government and trade sources. A fundamental rule in using secondary data is to secure data directly from the original source rather than using acquired sources. The reasons for this rule are two. First, the original source is in most cases the only place where the details of the data collection and analysis process are described. Knowledge of the research process is essential in evaluating the accuracy of the data. Second, the original source is generally more detailed and more accurate than the acquired source. Errors in transcription and failure to reproduce footnotes and other textual comments can seriously influence the accuracy of the data.

Evaluation of the purpose of a publication is the second criterion for determining the accuracy of secondary data. The researcher needs to be sensitive to the purpose of the publication and cautious in evaluating the data, to detect those who would misrepresent and distort statistics to support a position or belief.

The third criterion for evaluating the accuracy of secondary data is to assess the general evidence regarding the quality of the data. If the primary source does not disclose details of the research design, be very cautious. This frequently suggests that the supply organization has something to conceal. When the details of the research design are disclosed, the researcher should evaluate areas such as (1) sampling plan, (2) data collection procedure, (3) quality of field training, (4) questionnaire technique, and (5) data analysis procedures. A section discussing the limitations of the research design and data should be included. When limited information is available regarding the research design, the researcher can still evaluate the quality of the reporting of the data. Important here are items such as the labeling of tables and figures, the internal consistency of the data, and whether the data support the conclusions drawn in the report.

Timeliness Problem Secondary data present a set of facts about the world at the particular point in time that the data were collected. Between data collection and the use of the data by a marketing researcher, a significant amount of time may pass. This is because the data need to be analyzed and then published in a source available to the researcher. It is common for a marketing researcher to be utilizing secondary data that is 2 to 5 years old. There is danger in this, as all data are perishable with the passage of time. Therefore, the data may not be relevant to the time that the marketer is researching.

LIBRARY SOURCES OF SECONDARY DATA

Library sources of marketing data include an array of publicly circulated material—for example, government documents, periodicals, books, research reports, and trade association publications. What types of research objectives and information needs might call for secondary data? Some examples would be: (1) to estimate the total market potential for corrugated and solid fiber boxes in a given area; (2) to develop a method for establishing sales quotas for television sets by states; (3) to establish national, state, and county sales quotas and a method for estimating the potential market for battery replacements for automobiles; (4) to determine the market potential for industrial lubricants in Cook County, Illinois; (5) to predict the potential market for paper and allied products to merchant wholesalers and the retail trades to 1995; (6) to estimate the market for clothes-washing machines and dryers, dishwashers, and television sets in the Fort Wayne, Indiana, metropolitan statistical area (MSA), which consists of Allen County; (7) to select a county in the Syracuse, New York, MSA in which to locate new supermarkets (the area is composed of Madison, Onondaga, and Oswego counties); or (8) to disperse an advertising budget in proportion to the potential markets, by states, in the South Atlantic region.

Secondary data can be used to meet the information needs represented by the above research objectives. The following types of secondary data would be appropriate: (1) employment data, (2) population data, (3) radio and television sales, (4) number of households with television, (5) family median income, (6) aggregate income of the population, (7) occupied housing units, (8) automobile registration, (9) housing units without automobiles, (10) grocery store sales, (11) value of box shipments by end use, and (12) employment by industry group. These data are available from library sources.

Government Data Sources

The largest single source of statistical data is the U.S. government. For years, marketing researchers have relied on this source of data for developing market potential and sales forecasts; determining sales territories and sales quotas; and locating retail, wholesale, and manufacturing establishments. As the breadth and depth of government data have increased over the years, the relevance of this source of data to marketing information needs has increased dramatically. Consequently, effective marketing research requires a thorough knowledge of government data.

Census Data

Within the federal government, the Bureau of the Census is the leading source of data relevant to marketing. Its vast resources and years of experience combine to give census data a high reputation for quality. The data are generally detailed enough for most marketing information needs. They are reasonably priced and accessible in printed form or on computer tape, disk, or CD-ROM. Unpublished data contained on the census computer tapes can be purchased on microfiche, tape, disk, or CD-ROM. The bureau will do individualized computer runs for a small fee.

The Bureau of the Census collects and publishes many types of data, including Census of Population, Census of Housing, Census of Manufacturing, Census of Retail Trade, Census of Wholesale Trade, Census of Transportation, Census of Agriculture, and Census of Business. Other publications that make use of bureau information or that are originated by the bureau are described in the appendix to this chapter.

The available census data on population and housing are summarized in Table 6-1. Note that some census items are collected through the use of samples. Many census data can be very useful to marketers; examples are demographic profiles, housing patterns, and appliance ownership.

The census data are available at many levels, ranging all the way from the nation as a whole down to city blocks. Figure 6-3 shows the hierarchical relation-

Text continued on p. 183.

TABLE 6-1   SUBJECTS IN THE 1990 CENSUS CLASSIFIED AS COMPLETE-COUNT OR SAMPLE ITEMS

Population	Housing

Items collected at every household ("complete-count items")

Population	Housing
Household type	Number of units at address
Sex	Complete plumbing facilities
Race	Number of rooms
Age	Tenure (whether the unit is owned or rented)
Marital status	Condominium identification*
Spanish/Hispanic origin or descent	Value of home (for owner-occupied units and condominiums)
	Rent (for renter-occupied units)
	Vacant, for rent, for sale, and so forth; and period of vacancy

Additional items collected at sample households[†]

Population	Housing
School enrollment	Type of unit
Educational attainment	Stories in building and presence of elevator
State or foreign country of birth	Year built
Citizenship and year of immigration	Year moved into this house*
Current language and English proficiency	Acreage and crop sales
Ancestry	Source of water
Place of residence 5 years ago	Sewage disposal
Activity 5 years ago	Heating equipment
Veteran status and period of service	Fuels used for house heating, water heating, and cooking
Presence of disability or handicap	Presence of solar heat
Children ever born	Costs of utilities and fuels
Marital history	Complete kitchen facilities
Employment status last week	Number of bedrooms
Hours worked last week	Number of bathrooms
Place of work	Telephone
Travel time to work	Number of automobiles
Means of transportation to work	Number of light trucks and vans
Persons in carpool	Homeowner shelter costs for mortgage, real estate taxes, and hazard insurance
Year last worked	
Industry	
Occupation	
Class of worker	
Work in 1989 and weeks looking for work in 1989	
Amount of income by source and total income in 1989	

Derived variables (illustrative examples)

Population	Housing
Families	Persons per room ("crowding")
Family type and size	Household size
Poverty status	Plumbing facilities
Population density	Institutions and other group quarters
Size of place	Gross rent
	Farm residence

*Changed relative to 1980.

[†]For most areas of the country in 1990, one out of every six housing units or households received the sample form. Areas estimated to contain 2500 or fewer persons in 1980 had a 3-out-of-every-6 sampling rate, which is required in order to obtain reliable statistics needed for participation in certain federal programs.

Source: The 1990 Census Questionnaire (American Demographics, 1989).

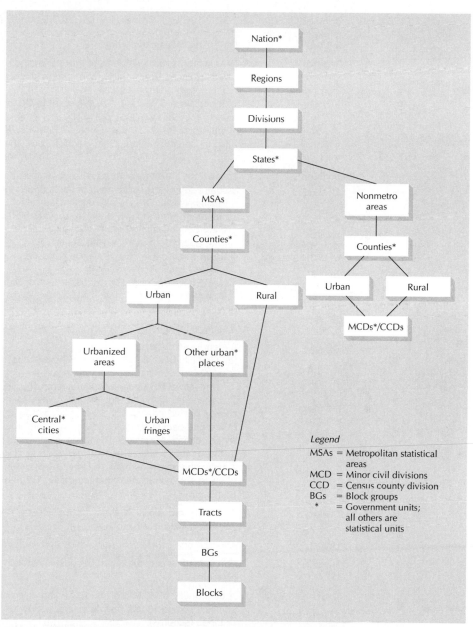

FIGURE 6-3   Bureau of the Census geographic units and their hierarchical relationships.

TABLE 6-2   DEFINITIONS OF GEOGRAPHIC UNITS USED BY THE BUREAU OF THE CENSUS

Nation	The United States as a whole.
Region	The United States is divided into four regions, as follows: West: Wash., Oreg., Calif., Mont., Idaho, Nev., Utah, Ariz., N. Mex., Colo., Wyo., Alaska, Hawaii South: Tex., Okla., Ark., La., Miss., Ala., Ga., Fla., S.C., N.C., Tenn., Ky., W. Va., Va., Md., Del., D.C. Northeast: Pa., N.J., N.Y., Conn., R.I., Mass., Vt., N.H., Maine North Central: Ill., Ind., Ohio, Mich., Wisc., Minn., Iowa, Mo., Kan., Nebr., S.D., N.D.
Division	The regions are divided into a total of nine geographic divisions, each of which is composed of a specific group of contiguous states, as follows: Pacific: Wash., Oreg., Calif., Alaska, Hawaii Mountain: Mont., Idaho, Utah, Nev., Ariz., N. Mex., Colo., Wyo. West South Central: Tex., Okla., Ark., La. East South Central: Miss., Ala., Tenn., Ky. South Atlantic: Fla., Ga., S.C., N.C., W. Va., Va., Md., Del., D.C. Middle Atlantic: Pa., N.J., N.Y. New England: Conn., R.I., Mass., Vt., N.H., Maine East North Central: Ill., Ind., Ohio, Mich., Wisc. West North Central: Minn., Iowa, Mo., Kan., Nebr., S.D., N.D.
State	A state of the union.
MSA	A metropolitan statistical area is: (a) One city with 50,000 or more inhabitants, or (b) A Census Bureau–defined urbanized area of at least 50,000 inhabitants *and* a total MSA population of at least 100,000 (75,000 in New England). The standards provide that the MSA include as "central county(ies)" the county in which the central city is located, and adjacent counties, if any, with at least 50 percent of their population in the urbanized area. Additional "outlying counties" are included if they meet specified requirements of commuting to the central counties and of metropolitan character (such as population density and percent urban). In New England the MSAs are defined in terms of cities and towns rather than counties. There are 261 MSAs in the United States.
County	A primary division of a state, as defined by state law (called a *parish* in Louisiana; there are none in Alaska).
Urban	The part of a county containing cities and towns of 2500 population or more.
Rural	The complement of the urban population, containing farm and nonfarm components.
Urbanized area	A central city of 50,000 or more, or twin cities of 50,000 or more, with the smallest having 15,000 people or more, plus the surrounding urban buildup or fringe (suburbs).
Other urban places	An urban area not qualifying as an urbanized area; i.e., a place of over 2500 but less than 50,000.
Central city	The area designated by the title of an urbanized area; e.g., Boston does not include Cambridge, etc.
Urban fringe	A suburb of a central city.

TABLE 6-2 (*continued*)

MCD	A minor civil division is a component part of a county. MCDs represent political or administrative subdivisions called *townships, districts, precincts,* etc.
CCD	Census county divisions were formed by the Bureau of the Census in 21 states for the purpose of dividing counties into statistical areas; they are used instead of townships, etc.
Tract	One of the small areas into which large cities and their adjacent areas have been divided for statistical purposes.
BG	A block group is a subdivision of a tract made up of a number of city blocks.
Block	The smallest area for which data are available; it is usually a well-defined rectangular piece of land bounded by streets or roads.
Nonmetro area	A part of a state not included in an MSA.
Unincorporated place	A concentration of population of at least 1000 which is not legally a city.

ships among the geographic units used by the Bureau of the Census. Most census data are published only down to the "tract" level. Some of the levels are governmental units—states, counties, and so on—while others are just statistical units used by the Bureau of the Census—divisions, MSAs, and so forth. Table 6-2 presents definitions of the geographic units shown in Figure 6-3.

MARKETING RESEARCH IN ACTION

GOODLIFE MAGAZINE

Sophisticated computer modeling played a key role in the successful introduction of *Goodlife,* a monthly magazine direct-mailed to 1 million affluent U.S. households. The model, called the Goodlife Index (GLI), was developed by Demographic Research Co., Inc., Santa Monica, Calif. According to E. Wayne Hansen, senior technical representative at Demographic Research, "Because the credibility of a controlled-circulation magazine rests entirely on its ability to efficiently reach its audience, the methodology and development of the mailing lists were carefully designed and evaluated." The magazine's publisher, Printcast Publishing Network, Toronto, used the GLI to choose which households—50,000 from each of 20 major MSAs—would qualify as *Goodlife* recipients.

The consumers targeted to receive *Goodlife* were aged 40 to 50, with incomes of $60,000+. They were in professional or top management positions and held at least an undergraduate degree. "They must not only have money, they must also have style and taste," said Hansen. Thus, the GLI was a weighted, multivariate index combining measures of income, occupation, life-cycle stage, home value, and education.

Within each MSA it was assumed that smaller areas were more homogeneous than larger areas, so analysis was based upon the smallest unit for which census data was available—the block. For each MSA, data from the Current Population Survey, the Annual Housing Survey, and the Survey of Consumer Expenditures were entered into the GLI model. A GLI score was generated, and the neighborhoods with the highest scores were checked further for potential *Goodlife* recipients. Then, within the selected blocks, individual addresses were selected. Because census data are not available at the household level, *Goodlife* households were chosen on the basis of other "desirable characteristics . . . to maximize the likelihood that every selected address met the criteria needed for receiving *Goodlife*," said Hansen.

Finally, computer maps which highlighted the *Goodlife* neighborhoods were produced, enabling Printcast to attract lucrative advertising. These maps accurately demonstrated to the advertisers that *Goodlife* provided an effective advertising vehicle because it was, in fact, reaching only the specific market advertisers wanted to reach.

Figure 6-4 further illustrates the types of geographic units used. It presents the geographic subdivision of an MSA all the way down to a city block. Clearly, many detailed data of relevance to marketers are available in the census reports.

Census data are not without defects. Like all secondary data, they have the limitation of not being collected for the specific information needs of a marketing research project. Some definitions have been changed from census to census. Even within a census, definitions can have different meanings. For the researcher who is not familiar with the details of census data, it can be very useful to seek the advice of a professional in this area regarding the specifics of how the data are to be used. Numerous publications, workshops, and conferences sponsored by the U.S. Department of Commerce and the Bureau of the Census are designed to aid the user of census data.

In addition, the accuracy of the 1990 census has been questioned because of potential undercounts of minority groups, especially in urban areas. This situation underscores the necessity of approaching all data sources cautiously.

Standard Industrial Classification   Many sources of marketing data are classified according to the Standard Industrial Classification code, or SIC code. This system of classification was developed by the federal government in connection with its Census of Manufacturers. The classification system is based on the products produced or operations performed. The SIC code classifies all manufacturing into 20 major industry groups, each having a two-digit code (e.g., SIC 25 is Furniture and Fixtures). Each major industry group is further classified into approximately 150 industry groups which are identified with a three-digit code (e.g., SIC 252 is Office Furniture). Each industry group is further classified into approximately 450 product categories designated by a four-digit code (e.g., SIC 2522 is Metal Office Furniture). This kind of hierarchical system is also used to classify other areas of the economy. For detailed information on how to use the SIC code, see the *Standard Industrial Classification Manual* and Chapter 23 of this book.

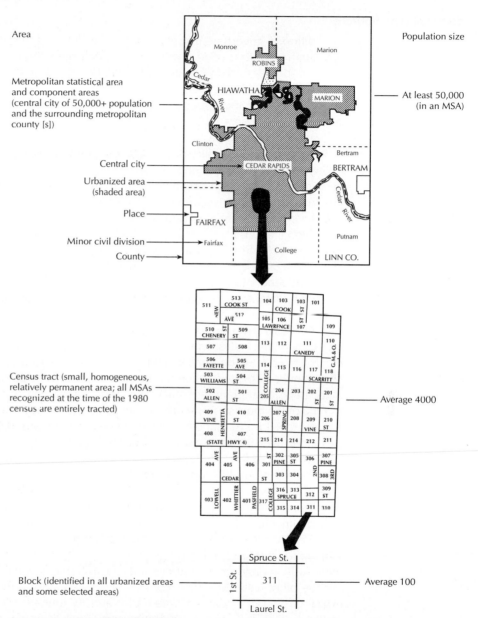

FIGURE 6-4   Geographic subdivisions of an MSA.

Additional Data Sources

In addition to government sources, a large number of other publications contain data applicable to a wide number of research objectives. The task of identifying relevant sources of data can be a difficult one for researchers who are not familiar with the area under investigation. Fortunately, there are many published guides and indexes (see the appendix to this chapter) to assist them in this pursuit. In addition, researchers will find that a competent reference librarian can identify relevant sources of data.

In evaluating the quality of the data identified, the researcher must be sensitive to the origin of the data and the research design. At times, this may be difficult to determine. Library data originate from an array of sources such as federal, state, and local governments; colleges and universities; trade associations; chambers of commerce; commercial organizations; foundations; and publishing companies. Some publications mainly present the results of original research, some summarize the research findings of others, and some mainly present interpretations and conclusions regarding the research findings of others.

The appendix to this chapter gives a listing of the main guides and indexes to marketing data, as well as the more predominant sources of marketing data.

One development in the provision of demographic data to marketers is the growth of private companies that market census-related products. These companies provide the fastest way to get census data tailored to one's needs. In addition, they offer updates on census data at the tract level and above, between census years, and they provide clients with a range of services designed to assist in using demographics in planning, marketing, and forecasting.

One of the most sophisticated systems that uses census data is PRIZM (Potential Rating Index for Zip Markets) developed by Claritas Corp. PRIZM uses census data combined with national surveys, hundreds of individual interviews, other marketing data, and the U.S. Postal Service's Zip + 4 Code System to group America's population into 40 life-style clusters.

PRIZM claims to consistently predict consumer behavior based on neighborhoods as defined by the consumer's zip + 4 code. PRIZM puts people into colorfully nicknamed clusters that can predict everything from what kind of car they will drive to what kind of frozen food they prefer. For example, the people belonging to the cluster named "gray power" consist mostly of retirees. This group likes Cadillacs and frozen entrees and detests Subarus and cake mixes. The cluster of blue-blood estates, which consists of very wealthy people, likes Jaguars and frozen pastry but disdains Monte Carlos and TV dinners. PRIZM has been refined so that the PRIZM clusters can be integrated with a marketer's existing customer file or other segmenting data such as psychographic data, making for a highly refined targeting system.

INTERNATIONAL SECONDARY DATA SOURCES

Virtually every country in the world has available secondary data from both government and private sources. In addition, international organizations such as the United Nations and the World Bank have secondary data available.

Great care must be taken in utilizing international secondary data. The data are often not comparable across countries, as the definitions used for variables are often different and the time frames in which the data are collected may be different. In addition, the accuracy of the data from some countries is suspect because of lack of careful procedures, or even because of outright government falsification of the data for political reasons. Even with these constraints in mind, a specific country's census data and other secondary data about this country can be highly relevant to the marketer. The Global Marketing Research Dynamics lists some commonly used international, noncensus, secondary data sources.

GLOBAL MARKETING RESEARCH DYNAMICS

SOME SOURCES OF INTERNATIONAL SECONDARY DATA

You can learn a great deal about a foreign competitor without ever leaving your office. Although armchair research techniques are no substitute for a trip to the country in question, they can yield valuable strategic and tactical information about your international competitors without costing a lot of money. Special foreign newspaper subscription services will locate and ship foreign publications, acting as a literature shopping service. Two of the most prevalent are Overseas Courier Service, a source of Japanese periodicals, and German News Company, a European periodicals service.

In addition to newspapers and magazines, there are numerous other published research sources and techniques for conducting secondary research on foreign competitors. These include:

- *Corporate information databases.* Dozens of foreign-produced databases have come online in the United States within the past 2 years.
- *Telex, facsimile, and long-distance telephone calls.* Direct contact generates fast and accurate information. Foreign telephone books can be purchased from your local telephone company business agent for as little as $25 per volume.
- *Foreign brokerage houses.* These firms specialize in their parts of the world and produce analytical reports on companies in their home countries.
- *International chambers of commerce.* Foreign chambers of commerce often act as public relations offices for their mother countries, dispensing large quantities of company data.
- *The Library of Congress.* The section head for the country in question regularly tracks new sources of information, including those that are privately published, government-produced, or issued on a database. By calling the Library of Congress at (202) 287-5000 you can receive lists of all these sources, as well as reports on your area of interest.
- *Foreign trade organizations.* Organizations such as the Japanese External Trade Organization (JETRO) are hired by both foreign corporations and their governments to promote their industries in the United States. Many have offices in major U.S. cities and publish books, directories, and lists of companies with offices in the United States.

The list of foreign intelligence-gathering sources and techniques is extensive. Each source underscores the volume and quality of foreign intelligence one can obtain without ever leaving one's desk. Additional sources include:

- *MarketSearch, the International Directory of Published Market Research.* This annual directory provides more than 18,000 multiclient study references throughout the world. Subdivided by British SIC classifications.
- *FINDEX, the Directory of Market Research Reports, Studies and Surveys.* This directory includes company and industry research from Wall Street as well as a variety of multiclient studies published by research firms throughout the world.
- *Marketing Surveys Index (MSI).* This index includes virtually all international multiclient studies and is usually the most current index available because it is updated ten times per year by supplements.

It is also useful to check some general reference guides. These include:

- *Regional Directories.* These directories are available for Europe and the Far East.
- *Croner's A-Z of Business Information Sources.* This directory includes categories for company, product, and market information divided for both consumer and industrial/commercial markets.
- *Consumer Japan.* This publication covers major consumer markets in Japan with specific information on markets, products, and key commercial organizations.
- *Consumer Europe.* This publication covers over 500 products bought by consumers in 17 Western European countries, including market data, trends, and forecasts.

Country directories such as *Ireland 1994* and publications of industrial development organizations such as the Scottish Development Agency are also useful. Marketing information is also frequently available in published form, such as the *European Directory of Trade and Business Journals;* the *European Directory of Trade and Business Associations;* the *European Directory of Consumer Goods Manufacturers;* the *European Directory of Retailers and Wholesalers;* the *European Consumer Electronics Directory;* the *European Electrical Appliances Directory;* the *European Drinks Marketing Directory;* and a variety of similar publications that cover food, household chemicals, cosmetics, toiletries, and other product categories.

Following are the main sources of European marketing statistics.

- *International Marketing Data and Statistics 1994*
- *European Marketing Data and Statistics 1994*
- *The International Directory of Marketing Information Sources*
- *The European Directory of Non-Official Statistical Sources*
- *The European Directory of Marketing Information Sources*
- *The Worldwide Government Directory*

For updated information on potential domestic competitors, you can check sources such as local newspapers, *The Corporate Directory,* the *Dun & Bradstreet Million Dollar Directory, Standard & Poors' Register,* the *International Dun & Bradstreet Million Dollar Directory, Value Line Selection and Opinion, The National Directory,* and reports filed with the SEC. For international references, you can use the *Kompass Directories, The International Corporate 1000, The City Directory, Europe's 15,000 Largest Companies, The London Business Pages,* and *The Canadian Trade Index.* You can also check *The City Directory* for London-based financial information sources, and *ARK,* which covers 14 major industries in Europe and provides information on over 2000 public companies throughout western Europe.

One good place to find outside firms to conduct secondary research is *Burwell's Directory of Fee-Based Information Services.* This directory describes hundreds of information brokers throughout the world and is subdivided by country, state, company, subject, and service. Secondary research can also be facilitated by online research services such as Dialog, Nexis, Bibliographical Retrieval Services (BRS), Chemical Abstract Service (CAS), CompuServe, Lexis, and Regulatory Information Service (RIS). The key is knowing which of the hundreds of databases to check for appropriate questions, keywords, and subjects. Other online references include the following:

- *Business-Line Management, Marketing and Administration.* This reference lists over 200 online services worldwide for product, market research and customer analysis.
- *Business-Line Finance.* This resource lists over 300 financial databases worldwide.
- *Business-Line Company Information.* This reference lists over 300 databases for company financial information, key personnel, products and services, subsidiaries, and other database categories.

Source: Part 1 is adapted from Leonard M. Fuld, "How to Gather Foreign Intelligence without Leaving Home," *Marketing News,* pp. 24 and 47, January 4, 1988; Part 2 is adapted from Ian McFarlane, "Do-It-Yourself Marketing Research," *Management Review,* pp. 34–37, May 1991.

SUMMARY

1 Sources of marketing data can be classified as primary or secondary. *Secondary data* are defined as data collected for purposes other than the specific research needs at hand. *Primary data* are defined as data collected specifically for purposes of the research needs at hand.

2 Secondary data can be subclassified as internal or external. *Internal secondary data* are those available within the organization, while *external secondary data* are those provided by sources outside the organization.

3 External secondary data are available from syndicated sources and library sources. *Syndicated sources* refer to data services that collect standardized data to serve the needs of many clients. *Library sources* include an array of publicly circulated publications.

4 The first phase of the data collection stage of the research process involves a search of internal and external secondary data sources. Primary data sources should be employed after it is determined that the data are not available from secondary data sources. Rarely will secondary data completely meet the data requirements of a research project.

TABLE 6-3   POPULATION GROWTH FOR WASHINGTON, DC, MSA

Political unit	1990	1995 (est.)
District of Columbia	637,651	626,000
Maryland (total)	1,316,875	1,435,600
Montgomery Co.	579,053	665,200
Prince Georges Co.	665,071	681,400
Charles Co.	72,751	89,000
Virginia (total)	1,105,714	1,276,000
Arlington Co.	152,599	158,700
Alexandria City	103,217	107,800
Falls Church City	9,515	9,700
Fairfax City	19,390	19,900
Fairfax Co.	596,901	710,500
Loudoun Co.	57,427	66,800
Prince William Co.	144,703	175,400
Manassas Park City	6,524	7,100
Manassas City	15,438	20,100
Total	3,060,240	3,337,600

Source: U.S. Department of Commerce, Bureau of the Census.

5 The advantages of secondary data are their lower cost and fast retrieval compared with primary data. In addition, collection of the data using primary data research methods may be beyond the means of the organization.

6 The disadvantages of secondary data are related to the accuracy of the data and the degree of fit between the data and the information needs of the project. The accuracy of secondary data can be evaluated in terms of (a) the source, (b) the purpose of the publication, and (c) evidence regarding quality.

DISCUSSION QUESTIONS

1 What is the role of secondary data in the research process?
2 What are the disadvantages of secondary data relative to primary data?
3 Discuss the shortcomings of secondary data.
4 Suggest some examples of census data useful to marketers.
5 Indicate the main components of the hierarchy of geographic units in descending order of level of aggregation.
6 Using the most recent edition of *General Social and Economic Characteristics* published by the Bureau of the Census for your state, compare the United States, your state, and your county. Include analyses of total population, general level of education, income, and employment in each population unit. Write a short paragraph describing how your county compares with your state and the nation.
7 Using the U.S. Bureau of the Census's most recent edition of *Census Tracts,* report for the MSA of your choice. Compare the totals for the MSA to two tracts within the MSA.

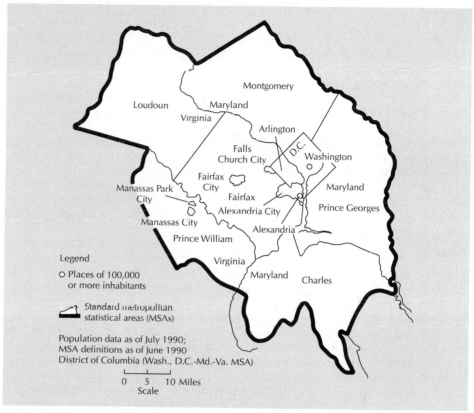

FIGURE 6-5   The Washington, DC, MSA.

Select and compare two tracts that will provide significant contracts in areas that interest you, such as racial makeup, age population, industries employing residents, or education level or income of population. Write a short paragraph comparing the two tracts and the MSA for each area you studied.

8 a What types of geographic areas are shown in Table 6-3 and Figure 6-5?

b Using the data in Table 6-3, analyze the changes in the population. Which areas experienced the greatest growth or decline? Do the areas of growth and decline share any significant characteristics?

9 MINICASE

You have been hired by an electronics automobile parts marketer to research the market in Europe for its products. The company has tentatively targeted SAAB and Volvo in Sweden, Fiat in Italy, Renault in France, and Audi in Germany as its prime prospects. Outline an approach to the use of secondary data to help assist the marketers in the assessment of these markets.

APPENDIX   Library Sources of Marketing Data

The purpose of this appendix is to catalog the predominant library sources of marketing data and to identify the main guides and indexes to marketing data. For each listing, the name of the publication, the publisher, and a brief description are presented. Because of the ever-changing nature of library data sources, omissions and inaccuracies are unavoidable. More contemporary information regarding a particular data source as well as information on additional sources can be obtained from a reference librarian. Where so noted, the U.S. Government Printing Office, not the producing agency, is the publisher (and sales agency) for government publications.

COMPUTERIZED INFORMATION SOURCES

A substantial portion of the information contained in the following sources can also be accessed through online CD-ROM, diskette, and magnetic tape databases. The amount of business information available in these formats has grown substantially in recent years. Many libraries of all types now offer these resources. National and international communication networks such as Internet offer access to business information.

A variety of information of interest to business is available. A list of articles and other materials on a specific topic can be retrieved. Also available are financial and other information about companies, and business and economic statistical data. Some databases contain references to publications, while others contain the actual information. Often the full texts of articles are available. Using these systems offers many advantages over searching through printed sources. These advantages include (1) faster access to needed material, (2) listings of company addresses and other information that may not be cited in printed sources, (3) availability of information on specific terms or jargon words that do not appear as subject headings in printed sources, and (4) access to material that may be too recent to appear in printed sources. This last advantage applies mainly to online databases. Because of the frequency with which CD databases are issued (at present, on schedules ranging from monthly to annually), the information is often not as current as that in online systems or even in some printed sources. Because of the often limited time periods covered, the journals indexed, and other factors, a computer search in any one format rarely retrieves an exhaustive list of references on a topic; therefore, it is often useful to supplement a computer search with a search of printed sources.

Many databases are offered through vendors; others are products of separate companies. Two leading vendors offering access to online business-related databases are Dialog Information Services (Palo Alto, California) and BRS Online Products (McLean, Virginia). University Microfilms International (Ann Arbor, Michigan), Disclosure (Bethesda, Maryland), Lotus (Cambridge, Massachusetts), and Information Access Corporation (Foster City, California) are major vendors offering business-related CD products. The advantage to using a vendor is that search techniques are generally similar for all its databases. Vendors usually have customer service departments that offer the user good search support. The Dow Jones News/Retrieval database, a product of a separate company (Dow Jones & Co., Princeton, New Jersey), focuses on current company and industry information. CD-ROM systems are designed specifically for ease of use. Perusal of available CD-ROM user manuals and on-screen information usually is adequate to allow effective searching. Search techniques for online databases are generally more sophisticated; it is often useful for the searcher to take one of the search courses usually offered by database vendors to learn to search files that are not menu-driven.

Costs of the various databases vary widely. The user of online databases usually pays an hourly connect-time fee plus, in many cases, a citation fee. These costs vary with the database used. People who purchase a CD-ROM database, on the other hand, pay one price that allows for unlimited searching. There is no per-hour cost. The cost of a CD-ROM database can be substantial; the investment should be weighed against the volume of anticipated use. Many CD-ROM database vendors provide a disk drive with the subscription; in other cases, the user must purchase this piece of equipment separately.

Among the useful sources of current information available on databases in all formats is the *Gale Directory of Databases* (2 volumes), updated every 6 months (Gale Research, Inc., Detroit). *The Directory of Periodicals Online*, published annually (Federal Document Retrieval, Inc., Washington, DC), includes journals and newspapers and lists the database or databases in which each appears.

Many of the reference sources and journals listed below can also be accessed by searching a corresponding database; these titles are marked with an asterisk. For further information, refer to the resources listed above or to the publication itself. Included in the following are a few of the major business CD-ROM databases.

GUIDES TO BUSINESS LITERATURE SOURCES

Business Information: How to Find It, How to Use It, 2d ed., Michael R. Lavin, ed. (Phoenix, AZ: Oryx Press, 1992). Combines basic concepts of how to use business information sources with detailed descriptions of hundreds of business publications. Includes sections on how to research a company, how to use statistical information, and how to do research on a particular discipline such as consumer research or labor law.

Business Library Review (New York: Gordon and Breach Science Publishers). Offers reviews of publications, computer software, film, and video on a variety of business topics, including marketing. Includes comparisons of several works on a particular topic. Published three or four times a year.

Business Organizations, Agencies and Publications Directory, 7th ed. Catherine M. Ehr and Kenneth Estell, eds. (Detroit: Gale Research, Inc., 1993). The focus is on business-related U.S. and international organizations and agencies: professional societies, trade associations, government agencies, research centers, and educational institutions. Includes a brief description of each organization's activities.

Dissertation Abstracts International* (Ann Arbor, MI: University Microfilms International, since 1952). Publishes title, keyword, and author indexes. The "Humanities and Social Science" section includes subsections on such topics as marketing, business administration, and banking. This source abstracts doctoral dissertations from almost 500 institutions worldwide. Monthly.

Encyclopedia of Business Information Sources, 9th ed. (Detroit: Gale Research, Inc., 1993–1994). Lists periodicals, statistics sources, directories, bibliographies, general works, CD databases, and other sources. Arranged by subject.

Handbook of Business Information: A Guide for Librarians, Students and Researchers (Englewood, CO: Libraries Unlimited, Inc., 1988). Gives descriptive information on a large number of key business publications. The first section covers general titles according to format, such as guides, directories, government documents, and loose-leaf services. The second section focuses on specific fields of business, including marketing. Background discussions on each discipline are included.

University Research in Business and Economics (Morgantown, WV: Bureau of Business Research, College of Business and Economics, West Virginia University, for the Association for University Business and Economics Research). Books, working papers, periodical articles, monographs, and other publications are indexed by author, subject, and institution. Annual; published late.

Washington Researchers (Washington, DC). The Washington Researchers group publishes a variety of guides to locating information about companies, industries, and other topics. Both standard and little-known resources are included. Among currently available titles are *How to Find Information about Companies; Who Knows about Industries and Markets; Business Researcher's Handbook: The Comprehensive Guide for Business Professionals;* and *How to Find Information about Private Companies.*

GUIDES TO MARKETING SOURCES

American Marketing Association Bibliography Series (Chicago: The American Marketing Association). A series of annotated bibliographies with emphasis on books and periodicals. Each covers a particular topic in some depth. Issued periodically.

Communication Abstracts (Newbury Park, CA: Sage Publications, Inc.). Indexes and abstracts major communication-related articles, reports, and books. In addition to advertising and marketing, covers such topics as mass communication, small-group communication, the media, and public opinion. Bimonthly.

Findex, the Directory of Market Research Reports, Studies and Surveys* (New York: FIND/SVP). A guide to published, commercially available market and business research reports. The latest edition includes over 14,500 reports from about 540 domestic and foreign research publishers. An increasing number of reports listed are moderately priced. Annual, with a midyear supplement.

Journal of Marketing* (Chicago: American Marketing Association). Includes a "Marketing Literature Review" section in each issue. Contains an annotated bibliography of articles published within the last year in major business, economic, and social science periodicals, and also a brief book review section. Quarterly.

Marketing Information, 2d ed., Jac L. Goldstucker, ed. (Atlanta: Business Publishing Division, Georgia State University, 1987). A guide to information in the marketing field. Material is organized under 22 subject areas. Books, periodicals, and other information sources are presented for each category. Lists marketing associations and organizations by subject and location, and details other sources, such as libraries, government agencies, and private research and consulting companies.

INDEXES: GENERAL BUT USEFUL

New York Times Index (New York: The New York Times). Detailed subject index includes very brief summaries of articles. Published since 1913. Semimonthly, with quarterly and annual cumulations.

PAIS International in Print. [New York: Public Affairs Information Service (PAIS)]. A subject index to books, pamphlets, government documents, periodical articles, and other publications dealing with economic and social conditions and public affairs. Includes publications issued worldwide, most in English. Published since 1915. Monthly, with periodic cumulations.

Readers' Guide to Periodical Literature* (New York: H.W. Wilson). Contains a subject index and an author index of over 240 general U.S. periodicals. Published since 1900. Seventeen issues per year plus an annual compilation.

Social Sciences Citation Index* (Philadelphia: Institute for Scientific Information). Indexes all articles in about 1400 social science periodicals and selected articles in about 3300 periodicals of other disciplines. Subjects covered include marketing, economics, and management. Provides a citation index, an author (source) index, and a subject index. Published since 1969. Three times yearly, with annual cumulations.

INDEXES: BUSINESS

ABI/Inform Ondisc (Ann Arbor, MI: University Microfilms International). A CD index that includes references and abstracts to articles on companies, industries, and other business topics in 1000 business and management journals. Monthly.

Business Periodicals Index* (New York: H.W. Wilson). An important subject index to selected periodicals in all major fields of business. Covers almost 350 English-language periodicals, primarily in the United States. Published since 1959. Monthly (except for August), with cumulations quarterly and annually.

Predicasts F & S Index, United States* (Cleveland: Predicasts, Inc.). Indexes U.S. industry, product, and company information from over 750 business and financial publications. There are two sections, covering industry/product and company. Weekly, with quarterly and annual cumulations.

Similar publications, *Predicasts, Inc. F & S International** and *Predicasts F & S Europe,** deal with international business articles. *Predicasts F & S Index of Corporate Change* (quarterly plus annual cumulations) indexes information by company name, industry, and type of event.

Wall Street Journal Index (Princeton, NJ: Dow Jones Books). Subject index to the eastern edition of *The Wall Street Journal.* There are two sections: general news and corporate news. Includes an index to *Barron's.* Published since 1957. Monthly, with annual compilations.

Business Index (Belmont, CA: Information Access Corporation). Comprehensive subject coverage of over 300 periodicals and major newspapers, primarily from the United States. Also available in CD and online formats. Published since 1979. Microfilm index, cumulated and updated monthly.

GUIDES TO STATISTICAL SOURCES

American Statistics Index: A Comprehensive Guide and Index to the Statistical Publications of the U.S. Government* (Washington, DC: Congressional Information Service). An excellent guide to the statistical publications of federal government agencies, Congress, and other organizations. A typical abstract includes a complete description of the data given. Material is indexed according to subject, author, title, report number, and demographic or other category. Published since 1973. Monthly, with cumulations.

Two similar publications are *Statistical Reference Index: A Selective Guide to American Statistical*

Publications from Private Organizations and State Government Sources and Index to International Statistics: A Guide to the Statistical Publications of International Intergovernmental Organizations. Both are issued monthly, with cumulations.

Census Catalog and Guide, Bureau of the Census, Department of Commerce (Washington, DC: U.S. Government Printing Office). A comprehensive annotated guide to U.S. Census Bureau publications, including data files and special tabulations. Publications cover agriculture, foreign trade, governments, population, and the economic censuses, as well as retail trade, wholesale trade, service industries, construction industries, manufacturers, mineral industries, and transportation. Also listed are materials available in nonprint formats (such as CD), as well as special tabulations. Annual; updated by a monthly Bureau of the Census publication, Census and You.

Guide to Foreign Trade Statistics, Bureau of the Census (Washington, DC: U.S. Government Printing Office). A guide to primarily monthly and annual foreign trade statistics. Includes descriptions of Bureau of the Census publications dealing with foreign trade, and sample tables. Issued periodically.

Statistics Sources, 17th ed., Jacqueline O'Brien and Steve Wasserman, eds. (Detroit: Gale Research, Inc., 1994). A subject guide to business, industrial, financial, social, and other topics. Detailed subheadings are used under each subject.

GENERAL SOURCES OF STATISTICS

Economic Indicators, Council of Economic Advisers (Washington, DC: U.S. Government Printing Office). Presents current statistical series considered to be key indicators of general business conditions. These include GNP and personal consumption expenditures. Researchers find this document useful in developing and updating industry and company forecasts. Monthly.

Economic Report of the President (Washington, DC: U.S. Government Printing Office). This publication documents the President's annual address to Congress regarding the economic condition of the United States. The annual report of the Council of Economic Advisers is included; it reviews economic policy and outlook. Included are statistical series from other documents published by the government dealing with numerous economic indicators. Annual.

Federal Reserve Bulletin* (Washington, DC: Federal Reserve System Board of Governors). Contains current financial data on banking activity, savings, interest rates, credit, and domestic nonfinancial statistics. An index of industrial production and some statistics on international trade and finance are also supplied. Monthly.

International Marketing Data and Statistics (London: Euromonitor). Includes current and historical statistical data on countries in Asia, Africa, Oceania, and the Americas. Topics covered include demographic trends and forecasts, economic indicators, trade, consumer expenditures and markets, retailing, and advertising. Annual.

A comparison volume by the same publisher, European Marketing Data and Statistics, covers essentially the same topics. Annual.

Monthly Labor Review,* Bureau of Labor Statistics (Washington, DC: U.S. Government Printing Office). Presents current data and related articles on employment, earnings, wholesale and retail prices, and so on. Monthly.

For more detailed data, see Employment and Earnings, CPI Detailed Report, and Producer Price Indexes, all produced by the Bureau of Labor Statistics.

Predicast Forecasts* (Cleveland: Predicasts, Inc.). Gives short- and long-range projection data for U.S. economic indicators, products, and industries. Also serves as a guide to statistics; for further reference, the source of the data (trade journal, newspaper, government report, or other publication) is given with each entry. Other Predicast publications include separate digest, index, statistical, and research events. Quarterly, with annual cumulations.

Statistical Abstract of the United States, Bureau of the Census (Washington, DC: U.S. Government Printing Office). This valuable publication is a basic reference for individuals searching for secondary data. Includes over 1400 tables, presenting social, economic, political, and demographic data. The tables serve as an abstract and reference for data available in other published sources. For many researchers, this publication is the initial reference in their search for external secondary data. Includes "Guide to State Statistical Abstracts" and "Guide to Foreign Statistical Abstracts." Sources listed contain statistical tables on a variety of subjects for states, countries, cities, and selected foreign countries. Annual.

Statistical Service (New York: Standard & Poor's Corporation). Presents current and historic statistical data covering banking and finance, production and labor, price indexes, income and trade, transportation and communication, and some major industries. Basic material plus monthly supplements.

Survey of Current Business,* Bureau of Economic Analysis, Department of Commerce (Washington, DC: U.S. Government Printing Office). This important publication provides some 2600 current statistical series covering areas such as indicators of general business conditions, domestic trade, industry statistics, personal consumption expenditures, and earnings and employment by industry. Monthly.

A historical record of the *Survey of Current Business* is provided in a biennial supplement, *Business Statistics, Bureau of Economic Analysis.*

World Almanac and Book of Facts (New York: Pharos Books). A handbook of statistics and factual information on a wide variety of subjects—for example, industry, finance, and religion. Annual.

Worldcasts (Cleveland: Predicasts, Inc.). Includes two series: four "World Regional Casts" and four "World Product Casts." Provides data from nearly 1000 foreign and domestic journals, bank letters, special studies, and other publications. The available information includes product, country, economic indicator, base-period data, short- and long-range forecasts, and a key to indicate the source of each article. Summary coverage of 150 countries ranges from detailed product information to general economic information. Product summary volumes contain aggregate data for all major countries. One volume for each series is published quarterly.

MARKET GUIDES AND DATA

Country and City (Lassham, MD: Bernan Press). Contains federal government data pertaining to states, countries, and cities. Statistics are provided on population, income, education, employment, housing, retail and wholesale sales, and so on. The data are compiled from numerous government and private agency publications, with a heavy emphasis on Bureau of the Census titles. An extra is the annual *Metropolitan City and Country Data Book.*

A related publication, *State and Metropolitan Area Databook,* Bureau of the Census (Washington, DC: U.S. Government Printing Office, 1991), focuses on MSAs and other metropolitan areas.

Market Guide (New York: Editor and Publisher Magazine). Contains data for 1500 U.S. and Canadian newspaper markets. Data include principal industries, population, transportation facilities, households, banks, and retail outlets. Includes estimates based on government data. Annual.

Market Share Reporter (Detroit: Gale Research, Inc.). Provides market-share statistics on companies, services, and products. Information is taken from periodical articles and brokerage house reports. Each table includes the source of the data or the periodical reference. Statistics tend to cover the last few years or so. Annual.

Market for the U.S. for Business Planners (Detroit: Omnigraphics, Inc., 1992). Current and historical profiles of 183 U.S. urban areas. Covers such topics as income history by industry, market profiles, and analytical commentary. Projections for the years 1995 and 2000.

Rand McNally Commercial Atlas and Marketing Guide (Chicago: Rand McNally Company). Contains detailed statistics for countries, cities, MSAs, and principal business centers. Covers trade, manufacturing, transportation, population, and related data. Each state section includes maps and some business data for countries and cities. Includes estimates based on government data. Annual.

Registration Data. A wide variety of registration data is collected by government. Typically, this information is difficult and inconvenient to locate and acquire. Examples are automobile and boat registrations; licenses for business activities; data on births, deaths, and marriages; income tax returns; and school enrollments.

Sales and Marketing Management* (New York: Sales and Marketing Management). The "Survey of Buying Power" issue (August, annual) contains data on population, effective buying income, and retail sales for U.S. markets, as well as comparable data for Canada. Includes estimates based on government data. Provides tables ranking metropolitan areas and other markets according to population, income, and sales. The "Survey of Metro Markets" issue (October, annual) gives population, income, and retail sales data for TV markets, and projects data for U.S. and Canadian markets. The separate *Data Service* volume (February, annual) provides additional data. *Sales and Marketing Management* also publishes the "Sales Manager's Budget Planner" issue.

Sourcebook of Zip Code Demographics (Fairfax, VA: CACI, Inc.). Zip codes are arranged first by state, then numerically within each state. Gives total population, population profile, housing profile, and income and employment statistics for each zip code. Also provides the Market Potential Index, which measures the propensity of the residences of a particular zip code to purchase goods in one of 13 categories of goods and services. A special 1990 census edition provides expanded information. Issued periodically.

The same publisher also issues *Sourcebook of Country Demographics* (published periodically) and *Sourcebook of City Demographics* (latest ed. 1990). While the country publication is similar to the zip code publication in scope, the city volume contains primarily income and population data in one-page city summaries.

CONSUMER DATA

American Demographics (Ithaca, NY: American Demographics, Inc.). Features stories about consumer behavior and population trends in the United States that have implications for marketers, as well as how-to and technical articles for the marketing researcher. Monthly.

Census of Housing, Bureau of the Census (Washington, DC: U.S. Government Printing Office). Taken in conjunction with the *Census of Population.* Enumerates types and sizes of structures, the years in which they were built, occupancy, equipment (such as clothes washer, stoves, and air conditioners), average value, monthly rent, number of persons per room, ethnic category of occupants, and so on. The 1990 *Census of Housing* includes a "General Housing Characteristics" series for places with a population of 1000 or more, a "Detailed Housing Characteristics" series for places of 2500 population or more, and a "General Housing Characteristics" report for metropolitan areas providing considerable detail and cross classification of housing subjects. These data have been found to be very useful for marketing research purposes.

Interim information regarding the percentage distribution of rental and homeowner vacancies, general housing characteristics, urban and rural housing data, and other characteristics is furnished by the bureau's *Current Housing Report* series and *American Housing Survey.* Annual.

Census of Population, Bureau of the Census (Washington, DC: U.S. Government Printing Office). Presents population counts by states, counties, MSAs, urbanized areas, county subdivisions, and other areas. The 1990 *Census of Population* identifies the population by age, sex, race, national origin, marital status, citizenship, family composition, employment status, income, and other demographic characteristics. Taken every 10 years, in the years ending with a zero.

Various interim reports are prepared by the Bureau of the Census. The *Current Population Report* series is a continual updating of population figures. U.S. aggregate data are presented on family characteristics, mobility, income, education, population estimates and projections, and other subjects. Issued either monthly, quarterly, or annually.

Census of Population and Housing, Bureau of the Census (Washington, DC: U.S. Government Printing Office). Taken in conjunction with the *Census of Population.* Covers summary population and housing characteristics and housing unit counts. Also covers population and housing characteristics for census tracts, block numbering areas, and congressional districts.

The Lifestyle Zip Code Analyst (Wilmette, IL: Standard Rate & Data Service). For over 15,000 zip codes, covers such demographic categories as population, income, age, and household type. Life-style profiles for each zip code focus on over 50 interests and activities. Annual.

A related title from the same publisher, *The Lifestyle Market Analyst,* provides similar data for 210 DMAs (designated market areas) plus related counties. Annual.

BUSINESS AND INDUSTRY DATA

Agricultural Statistics, Department of Agriculture (Washington, DC: U.S. Government Printing Office). Presents statistics on prices, production, costs, consumption, and so on, for various agricultural products. Annual.

Census of Construction Industries, Bureau of the Census (Washington, DC: U.S. Government Printing Office). Data, arranged according to SIC code, include number of establishments, receipts, employment, and payments for materials. Area statistics reports cover states. Taken every 5 years, in the years ending with 2 and 7.

Interim data on housing starts, housing completions, new housing authorized, and other topics are published in the *Current Construction Reports* series and in *Construction Review,* Bureau of Industrial Economics. Monthly.

Census of Manufacturers, Bureau of the Census (Washington, DC: U.S. Government Printing Office). An enumeration of establishments engaged in manufacturing activities. Manufacturing establishments are categorized under approximately 450 industries. Statistics are provided on number and size of establishments, capital expenditures, quantity of output, inventories, employment, payroll, and consumption of fuel, materials, and energy. Additional reports cover special subjects, such as concentration ratios and plant and equipment expenditures. Separate state reports provide a geographic approach to the data. Taken every 5 years, in the years ending with 2 and 7.

Interim reports include the *Annual Survey of Manufacturers,* which updates in part the *Census of Manufacturers,* and the *Current Industrial Reports,* which contain monthly, quarterly, and annual reports on production, inventories, and orders for commodities. In all three publications, data are arranged by SIC code.

Census of Mineral Industries, Bureau of the Census (Washington, DC: U.S. Government Printing Office). An enumeration of establishments primarily engaged in the extraction of minerals. Statistics are available on some 42 mineral industries regarding such things as number of companies, production, number of employees, capital expenditures, water use, power equipment, and value of shipments. There are also area statistics, covering states, counties, and other areas. Data are arranged by SIC code. Taken every 5 years, in the years ending with 2 and 7.

Minerals Yearbook provides annual data that supplement the *Census of Mineral Industries.*

Census of Retail Trade, Bureau of the Census (Washington, DC: U.S. Government Printing Office). Contains information on about 100 kind-of-business classifications. Statistics are available on number of establishments, total sales, sales by merchandise lines, size of firm, employment and payroll for states, MSAs, counties, and cities of 2500 or more. Data are arranged by SIC code. Taken every 5 years, in the years ending with 2 and 7.

Interim publications include *Monthly Retail Trade.*

Census of Service Industries, Bureau of the Census (Washington, DC: U.S. Government Printing Office). Provides data, arranged by SIC code, on more than 200 kind-of-business classifications. Statistics are available on the number of establishments, receipts, and payroll for states, MSAs, counties, and cities for service organizations such as hotels, barber shops, and laundries. The census does not include the finance, insurance, and real estate industries. Some data relating to health, educational, legal, and other services are included. Data are not available on the professions (with the exception of legal services). Taken every 5 years, in the years ending with 2 and 7.

An interim annual publication is *Service Annual Survey.*

Census of Transportation, Bureau of the Census (Washington, DC: U.S. Government Printing Office). Provides a summary of establishment-based statistics for selected transportation industries. Also includes the results of a truck inventory and use survey. Authorized every 5 years, in the years ending with 2 and 7.

Census of Wholesale Trade, Bureau of the Census (Washington, DC: U.S. Government Printing Office). This publication presents data on about 118 kind-of-business classifications. Statistics are available on the number of establishments, sales, personnel, and payroll for states, MSAs, counties, and cities. Data are arranged by SIC code. Taken every 5 years, in the years ending with 2 and 7.

Interim publications include *Monthly Wholesale Trade: Sales and Inventories* and *Wholesale Trade* (annual summary).

Commodity Yearbook, Commodity Research Bureau (New York: Commodity Research Bureau). Contains data on production, prices, consumption, and import and export flow for approximately 100 individual commodities. Annual. A supplement is issued three times yearly. Commonly called *CRB Commodity Yearbook.*

County Business Patterns, Bureau of the Census (Washington, DC: U.S. Government Printing Office). Presents a county breakdown of business by type, employment, and payroll. The data can be used to develop industrial market potential studies. There is a separate report for each state as well as one for the United States. Data are arranged by SIC code. Annual.

Enterprise Statistics, Bureau of the Census (Washington, DC: U.S. Government Printing Office). Presents statistics based on data collected in the Bureau of the Census economic census program. Regroups census data records of establishments under common ownership or control to show various economic characteristics of owning or controlling companies. Issued every 5 years, in years ending with 2 and 7.

Dealerscope Merchandising, * Statistical Surveys and Report (Philadelphia: North American Publishing Co.). The March issue reports on consumer goods; the April issue reports on major appliances. Presents tables and charts (some with 5-year figures) covering shipments, sales, and product saturation.

Manufacturing USA: Industry Analyses, Statistics and Leading Companies, 2d ed. (Detroit: Gale Research, Inc., 1992). Covers 459 manufacturing industries for such areas as leading companies, materials consumer, industry data by state, employment, compensation, production, and establishment statistics.

Service Industries USA: Industry Analyses, Statistics and Leading Organizations, 1st ed. (Detroit: Gale Research, Inc., 1992). Provides income information for about 150 service industries. Part I, arranged by industry category, gives employment, payroll, and revenue data; a list of leading companies; and industry data by state. Part II, arranged by city and metropolitan area, gives employment, payroll, and receipt date for service industries within each geographic location.

Standard & Poor's Industry Surveys (New York: Standard & Poor's Corporation). Covers 69 major domestic industries, arranged into 36 major industry groups. Text and summary statistics in a basic (annual) and current (three times yearly) analysis for each group. Discussion of current situation, recent trends, and outlook. The basic analysis includes financial data allowing comparison of major companies within an industry. Updated regularly.

Standard Industrial Classification Manual (1987 latest), Office of Management and Budget (Springfield, VA: National Technical Information Service). Presents a numerical classification of business establishments according to the product or service involved. Covers all areas of the economy. Widely used by both governmental and private organizations to collect and tabulate data. Commonly known as the SIC code.

Statistics of Income, Internal Revenue Service (Washington, DC: U.S. Government Printing Office). Presents data collected from corporate, proprietorship, and partnership income tax returns, as well as the returns of individuals. The corporate report presents balance sheet and income statement data broken down by industry type, asset size, and so forth. Annual.

These publications are preceded by a series of preliminary summary reports.

U.S. Industrial Outlook, International Trade Administration, U.S. Department of Commerce (Washington, DC: U.S. Government Printing Office). Presents a detailed analysis of about 350 manufacturing and nonmanufacturing industries. For each, information is given on recent developments and outlook. Researchers find this publication useful for forecasting and market planning. Annual.

COMPANY DATA AND FACTS: CONSULTANTS, ASSOCIATES, MARKET RESEARCH FIRMS

Bradford's Directory of Marketing Research Agencies and Management Consultants in the U.S. and the World (Fairfax, VA). Listings arranged geographically—by state and city, and by foreign country. There is heavy emphasis on U.S. listings. Each entry gives the address and, usually, the chief officer's name. A separate list classifies agencies according to the specific service offered. Includes a personnel index. Biennial.

Consultants and Consulting Organizations Directory, * 13th ed., Janice McLean, ed. (Detroit: Gale Research, Inc., 1993). Lists about 18,000 firms and individuals, mostly U.S., some Canadian. Each entry briefly describes services and field of interest. Includes an index of firms arranged by subject area and state. Updated by supplements.

Direct Marketing Market Place (New Providence, NJ: National Register Publishing, 1993). Organizations are grouped under these categories: direct marketers; service firms, and suppliers; creative services and firms; and courses and events. Entries list company or organization, address, key personnel, and a brief description of activities. Some listings include gross sales and billings, number of employees.

Dun's Consultants Directory (Parsippany, NJ: Dun's Marketing Services, Inc.). Lists more than 25,000 consulting firms alphabetically, geographically, and by specialty among the firms. Included are those specializing in finance, business management, marketing, engineering design, and data processing. Each entry includes sales volume, number of employees, principal officers, and the year in which the business was started or last changed ownership. Annual.

*Encyclopedia of Associations** (Detroit: Gale Research, Inc.). Volume 1, *National Organizations of the United States,* lists active trade, business, professional, and other national organizations; each entry briefly describes the organization's activities and lists available publications. Inactive, defunct, and "missing" organizations are identified as such in the index. Issued periodically, annually since 1975.

The series includes volume 2, *Geographic and Executive Indexes,* and volume 3, a supplement. Other titles in the series include *International Organizations* and *Regional, State and Local Organizations,* a five-volume guide to 50,000 nonprofit organizations with a state, city, or regional focus.

A related publication is *National Trade and Professional Associations of the United States and Canada and Labor Unions* (Washington, DC: Columbia Books, Inc.), which lists associations and publications of associations and has a key-word index (annual).

European Business Services Directory, 1st ed., Michael B. Huellmantel, ed. (Detroit: Gale Research, Inc., 1993). Lists over 20,000 business service firms in more than 30 countries. Emphasis on firms that provide services to other countries. Companies are listed geographically within service topics. Coverage includes such areas as advertising and marketing, finance, consulting, and business and management consulting. Each company listing includes an address and a brief description of services offered.

Green Book: International Directory of Marketing Research Houses and Services (New York: American Marketing Association). An alphabetical listing of marketing research houses in the United States and some foreign countries. Each entry describes available services. Firms are also listed by geographic location. Annual.

International Directory of the American Marketing Association and the Marketing Yellow Pages (Chicago: American Marketing Association). The directory portion lists each AMA member's title, business and home addresses, and professional interests. The yellow pages section includes the names and addresses of marketing research services, consultants, software firms, and marketing communication companies. Annual.

The Directory of Management Consultants (Fitzwilliam, NH: Kennedy Publications). Provides descriptive information on over 1500 primarily U.S. firms; along with limited Canadian and Mexican coverage. Each listing describes activities; lists services; and includes revenues, area served, year founded, and contact person. Listings are indexed by service, industries served, and state or city. Biannual.

COMPANY DATA AND FACTS: DIRECTORIES

Directories in Print, 10th ed. (Detroit: Gale Research, Inc., 1993). Lists over 14,000 directory information sources arranged under 16 subject areas. Each listing includes name, mailing address, description of directory (including number of entries in directory), frequency of publication, and price. Indexed by title and keyword.

*Directory of Corporate Affiliations** (New Providence, NJ: National Register Publishing Co., Inc.). Section 2 lists parent companies; each entry includes divisions, subsidiaries, and affiliates. Section 1 is an alphabetical listing of all entries in section 2, to aid in identifying parent companies of subsidiaries. A geographical index lists all parents and subsidiaries by state and city. Annual.

A related publication from the same publisher, *International Directory of Corporate Affiliations,* lists foreign parent companies with their U.S. subsidiaries, and U.S. parent companies and their foreign holdings. Annual.

Dun's Directory of Service Companies (Parsippany, NJ: Dun's Marketing Services, Inc.). Provides brief information on 50,000 service businesses, including sales volume, number of employees, and primary areas of operation. Organized alphabetically, geographically, and by SIC code. Annual.

*Million Dollar Directory** (Parsippany, NJ: Dun & Bradstreet). Volumes 1 to 3 collectively list over 160,000 U.S. businesses with an indicated net worth of over $500,000. Each entry identifies officers, products, applicable codes, sales, and number of employees. Volume 4, a cross-reference volume, lists businesses geographically and by industry classification. Volume 5 lists the "top 50,000 companies." Annual.

Moody's Manuals (New York: Moody's Investors Service, Inc.). Eight manuals: *Industrial, OTC Industrial, OTC Unlisted, Municipal and Government, Public Utility, Transportation, International,* and *Banks and Finance.* A typical listing includes location of agency or company, brief history, description of operation, officers, subsidiaries, detailed current and historic financial data, and securities information. The *Banks and Finance* volume also covers insurance companies and real estate and investment companies. Annual, plus weekly or twice-weekly news issues.

Principal International Businesses: The World Industry Directory (Parsippany, NJ: Dun & Bradstreet Information Services). Information on 55,000 companies in 143 countries. A typical listing provides address, sales, number of employees, year started, nature of the business, and principal officers. Annual.

Sheldon's Retail Directory of the United States and Canada and *Phelon's Resident Buyers and Merchandise Brokers* (Fairview, NJ: Phelon, Sheldon & Marsar, Inc.). A directory of the largest chain and independent department and specialty stores, arranged by U.S. state and city, and by Canadian province and city. Also lists merchandise managers and buyers. Annual.

Standard & Poor's Register of Corporations, Directors, and Executives* (New York: Standard & Poor's Corporation). Volume 1 covers about 55,000 U.S., Canadian, and major international corporations, with the same information as in Dun's directories. There is a very heavy emphasis on U.S. firms. The biographical volume provides brief information on 70,000 executives and directors. Companies are also arranged in the index volume by state and major city, and by SIC code number. Annual.

State Manufacturing and Service Directories. Directories are published for every state. A typical listing is arranged by geographical location and includes company addresses, officers, products, and related data. Companies are also usually listed under the SIC codes.

Thomas Register of American Manufacturers and *Thomas Register Catalog File** (New York: Thomas Publishing Co.). This multivolume source lists companies by specific product or service. A separate alphabetical listing of manufacturers aids in locating small companies. There is also a brand name/trademark index. Annual.

Ward's Business Directory of U.S. Private and Public Companies (Detroit: Gale Research, Inc.). Contains brief profiles of over 135,000 private and public U.S. companies. Also ranks companies by sales within SIC codes. Often sales or assets statistics are the only financial data available for private firms. A good source of this information. Annual.

COMPANY DATA AND FACTS: FINANCIAL

Compact Disclosure (Bethesda, MD: Disclosure Inc.). A CD database containing financial, textual, and descriptive information on 12,000 public U.S. companies. Information is taken from corporate annual reports and Securities and Exchange Commission (SEC) documents. Monthly.

Other Disclosure Inc. CD products, *Worldscope/Global* and *Worldscope/Europe,* contain financial information on thousands of international companies.

Company Reports. Company annual reports are useful sources of information. Business libraries and large public libraries with sizable business collections generally collect some of these reports, or they can be requested directly from the company. Among reports filed with the SEC, the annual 10-K report is the most detailed. Individual SEC reports may be ordered from companies such as Disclosure Inc.

Corporate Records (New York: Standard & Poor's Corporation). A source of the latest financial statistics on companies. Contains brief background information and news items relating to a company's operation. Updates material in Moody's Manuals and corporate annual reports. A good source of quarterly financial data. Updated quarterly.

Fortune Double 500 Director (New York: Time, Inc.). Published annually in *Fortune* magazine (usually between May and August). Provides information on sales, assets, profits, and so on, on the 500 largest U.S. industrial corporations, and ranks them by sales. In a separate "Service 500" section, ranks the 100 largest diversified service and commercial banking companies, and the 50 largest diversified financial, savings institutions, life insurance, retailing, utility, and transportation companies. Also ranks non-U.S. firms, non-U.S. banks, and worldwide firms.

Standard & Poor's Stock Reports (New York: Standard & Poor's Corporation). Contains two-page summaries on 4700 of the stocks of most interest to investors. Information for each company covers important developments, outlook, financial and dividend data, and a description of the business. Reports are updated every 3 months and are arranged in three subsets: The American Stock Exchange (AMEX), the New York Stock Exchange (NYSE), and the over-the-counter (OTC) stock exchange.

Moody's Industry Review (New York: Moody's Investors Service, Inc.). Provides extensive financial information and operating data on 4000 companies in 137 industry groups. Companies in every industry are ranked by revenues, net income, profitability, operating margin, return on capital, price-earnings ratio, and Moody's 7-year and 12-month price scores. Operating data of particular significance to a particular industry are also included (e.g., passenger miles in the airline industry). Each review is updated semiannually.

ADVERTISING AND PROMOTION DATA

LNA/MediaWatch Multi-Media Service (New York: Competitive Media Reporting). A series of quarterly reports that provide advertising expenditure statistics in six major media. The "AD $ Summary Report" has statistics arranged by specific brand. Data in other reports are arranged by company and product class.

Advertising Age (Chicago: Crain Communication, Inc.). Selected special issues include "U.S. Advertising Agency Profiles" and "Foreign Agency Income Reports" (April, annual). Covers large U.S. and foreign agencies. Each agency profile lists billing figures, accounts won and lost, billings breakdown by media, and gross income. Same data are given for foreign agencies, when data are available. Agencies are arranged by country.

"100 Leading Advertisers" (September, annual) gives, for each agency, data on advertising expenditures, sales and profits, rank of leading product line and brands, market share, sales, and advertising personnel. Also publishes "100 Leading Media Companies" (August, annual).

Broadcasting (Washington, DC: Broadcasting, Inc.). The "Broadcasting and Cable Yearbook" issue (published each spring) is a directory of U.S. and Canadian television and radio stations. Also included are market data and additional industry-related information. A cable section includes information on cable system in the United States and Canada.

A related publication is *Television and Cable Factbook* (Washington, DC: Television Digest, Inc.). Annual.

The *TV Stations* volume gives expanded information on TV stations, including market data. The *Cable Systems* volume covers such areas as cable systems and TV household data. The *Services* volume covers such areas as equipment and supplies, and associations and organizations. Each issued annually.

Journal of Advertising Research* (New York: Advertising Research Foundation). This publication presents research studies, literature reviews, and listings. Bimonthly.

Standard Directory of Advertisers (New Providence, NJ: National Register Publishing). Lists U.S. companies doing national or regional advertising. Data include company personnel, name of advertising agency, advertising budget figures, and types of media used. Also included are separate geographic and trade name indexes. Annual, plus supplements.

Standard Directory of Advertising Agencies (New Providence, NJ: National Register Publishing). Lists agency officers, accounts, and approximate annual billings of about 5000 U.S. and foreign agencies. Issued three times yearly, plus supplements.

Standard Directory of International Advertisers and Agencies (New Providence, NJ: National Register Publishing). Covers 2000 foreign advertisers and 2000 foreign advertising agencies. Advertiser information includes approximate advertising expenditures, media used, and ad agency. Agency data covers billings information, key personnel, and clients. Annual.

Standard Rate and Data Service, Inc. (SRDS) (Wilmette, IL: SRDS). Various titles, many issued monthly. Provides current advertising rates and related data for U.S. radio and TV stations, consumer magazines, business publications, newspapers, and other media. Some market data included in the ratio, TV, and newspaper volumes. The SRDS is considered the standard source of cost estimation for media planning.

Survey of World Advertising Expenditures (Mamaroneck, NY: Starch INRA Hooper). Provides estimates of expenditures in various media categories, arranged by country. Annual.

CASES FOR PART TWO

CASE 2-1   AGT, Inc.*

AGT, Inc., is a marketing research company, located in the city of Karachi, Pakistan. Jeff Sons Trading Company (JST) has approached it to look at the potential market for an amusement park in Karachi. As the city is crowded and real estate costs are high, it will be difficult to find a large enough piece of land to locate such a facility. Even if there is some land available, it will be expensive and that will have a detrimental effect on the overall costs of the project. JST wants to know the potential of this type of investment. Its managers have asked AGT to determine whether a need for an amusement park exists and, if so, what is the public's attitude toward that type of recreational facility. If a need is found and support is sufficient, then they want to know what type of amusement park is required by the potential customers. JST will make its investment decision based on the results of this study.

BACKGROUND

Pakistan qualifies as a less developed country (LDC). It is a typical developing country of the Third World faced with the usual problems of rapidly increasing population, sizable government deficit, and heavy dependence on foreign aid. The economy of Pakistan has grown rapidly in the last decade, with GDP expanding at 6.7 percent annually, more than twice the rate of population growth. Like any other LDC, it has dualism in its economic system. For example, the cities have all the facilities of modern times, whereas the smaller towns have some or none. Such is also true for income distribution patterns. Real per capita GDP is rupees (Rs) 10,000, or $400, annually. There is a small wealthy class (1 to 3 percent) of the population and a middle class consisting of another 20 percent, while the remainder of the population is poor. Half the population lives below the poverty line. Most of the middle class is an urban working class. Only 24 percent of the population is literate.

Karachi, the largest city, with a very dense population of over 6 million, has been chosen for the first large-scale amusement park in Pakistan. The recreational facilities in Karachi are very small, including a poorly maintained zoo, and people with families avoid visiting most facilities due to the crowds. There are other small parks besides the zoo, but not enough to cater to such a large population. The main place people go for recreation is the beach. The beaches are not well developed and are regularly polluted by oil slicks from the nearby port. There seems to be a growing need for recreational activity for people who have leisure time. Many of the people in the higher social classes take vacations with their families and spend money on recreational activities abroad. To see whether there is a true need for an amusement park, JST proposes to conduct a marketing research study of its feasibility. Potential problems facing the project include:

- The communication system is very poor.
- Only a small percentage of the people own their own transportation.
- Public and private systems of transportation are not efficient.
- Law and order is a problem, described as similar to that of Los Angeles.

*Source: Copyright by William J. Carner, Ph.D., 1993. All rights reserved. Used with permission.

RESEARCH OBJECTIVES

As it considered making an investment decision, JST outlined the research objectives necessary to design a marketing strategy that would accomplish the desired return-on-investment (ROI) goals. These objectives are as follows:

1 Identify the potential demand for this project.
2 Identify the primary target market and what they expect in an amusement area.

INFORMATION NEEDS

To fulfill our objectives, JST will need the information listed below.

Market

1 Is there a need for this project in this market?
2 How large is the potential market?
3 Is this market sufficient to be profitable?

Consumer

1 Are the potential customers satisfied with the existing facilities in the city?
2 Will these potential consumers utilize an amusement park?
3 Which segment of population is most interested in type of facility?
4 Is the population ready to support this type of project?
5 What media could be used to get the message across successfully to the potential customers?

Location

1 Where should this project be built to attract the most visitors?
2 How will the consumers' existing attitudes about location influence the viability and cost of this project?
3 Will the company have to arrange for transportation to and from the facility, if the location is outside the city area?
4 Is security a factor in the location of the facility?

Recreation Facilities

1 What type of attractions should the company provide at the park to attract customers?
2 Should there be an overnight facility within the park?
3 Should the facility be available only to certain segments of population or open to all?

With the objectives outlined above in mind, AGT, Inc., presented the following proposal.

PROPOSAL

The city of Karachi's population has its different economic clusters scattered haphazardly throughout the city. To conduct the marketing research in this type of city and get accurate results will be very difficult. We recommend an extensive study to make sure we have an adequate sampling of the opinion of the target market. Given the parameters above, we recommend that the target market be defined as described below.

DESIRED RESPONDENT CHARACTERISTICS

- Upper class—1 percent (about 60,000)
- Middle class—15 to 20 percent (about 900,000 to 1,200,000)
- Male and female
- Age—15 to 50 years old (for survey; market includes all age groups)
- Income level—Rs 25,000 and above per year (Rs 2000 per month)
- Household size—family with children
- Involved in entertainment activities
- Involved in recreational activities
- Actively participates in social activities
- Members of different clubs
- Involved in outdoor activities

To obtain accurate information regarding respondents' characteristics, we have to approach the market very carefully because of the prevailing circumstances and existing cultural practices (the country is 97 percent Muslim). The people have little or no knowledge about market surveys. Getting their cooperation, even without the cultural barriers, through a phone or mail survey would be very difficult. In the following paragraphs we will be discussing negative and positive points of all types of surveys and the selection of the appropriate form for our study.

The first, and possibly the best, method for conducting the survey under these circumstances might be through the mail, which would not only be cheap but could also cover all the clusters of population easily. However, we could not rely totally on mail survey, as the mail system in Pakistan is unreliable and inefficient. We could go through courier services or registered mail, but this would skyrocket the cost. It would not be wise to conduct a mail survey only.

Another option would be to conduct a survey by telephone. In the city of 6 million, there are about 200,000 working telephones (1 telephone per 152 persons). Most of the telephones are in businesses or government offices. It is not that the people cannot afford a telephone, but that they cannot get one because of short supply. Another problem with a telephone survey is cultural; it is not considered polite to call someone and start asking questions. This would be even more of a problem if a male survey member were to reach a female household member. People are not familiar with marketing surveys and would not be willing to volunteer the information we require on the telephone. The positive aspect of a telephone survey would be that most of the upper-class women do not work and can be reached easily. However, we would have to use an exclusively female survey staff. Overall, the chances of getting cooperation through a telephone survey would be very low.

A mall/bazaar intercept could also be used. Again, however, we would face some cultural problems. It's not considered ethical for a male to approach a female in the mall. The only people willing to talk in public would be likely to be the males, and thus we would not get female opinion.

To gather respondent data by survey in a country such as Pakistan, we will have to tailor our existing data collecting methods to make them fit the circumstances and cultural practices of the marketplace. As a company based in Pakistan with experience in living with these cultural practices, we propose the following design for the study and the questionnaire.

DESIGN OF THE STUDY

Our study's design will be such that it will have mixture of three different types of the surveys. Each survey will focus on a different method. The following are the types of surveys we recommend, tailored to fit the prevailing circumstances:

1   Mail Survey

We plan to modify this type of survey to fit existing circumstances and to be more efficient. The changes made are to counter the inefficient postal system and to generate better percentage of response. We plan to deliver the surveys to the respondent through the newspaper deliverers. We know that average circulations of the various newspapers are 50,000 to 200,000 per day. The two dailies chosen have the largest circulation in the city.

A questionnaire will be placed in each newspaper and delivered to the respondent. This will assure that the questionnaire has reached its destination. This questionnaire will introduce us to the respondent and ask for his or her cooperation. We will include return postage and the firm's address. This will give the respondents some confidence that they are not volunteering information to someone unknown. A small promotional gift will be promised on returning the completed survey. Since respondents who will claim the gift will give us their addresses, this will help us maintain a list of respondents for future surveys. Delivery through newspapermen will also allow us to easily focus on specific clusters.

We expect some loss in return mail because there is no acceptable way to get the questionnaires back except through the government postal system. We plan to deliver 5000 questionnaires to the respondents to counter the loss in return mail. The cost of this survey will be less than if we mailed the questionnaires. As this will be the first exposure for many respondents which allows them to give their views about a nonexisting product, we do not have any return percentage on which to base our survey response expectations. In fact, this may well be the base for future studies.

2   Door-to-Door Interviews

We will have to tailor the mall/bazaar intercept, as we did the mail survey, to get the highest possible response percentage. Instead of intercepting at malls, it will be better to send surveyors from door to door. This can generate a better percentage of responses and we can be sure who the respondent is. To conduct this survey we will solicit the cooperation of the local business schools. By using these young students we stand a better chance of generating a higher response. Also, we plan to hire some additional personnel, mostly females, and train them to conduct this survey.

3 Additional Mail Survey

We are planning to conduct this part of the survey to identify different groups of people already involved in similar types of activity. There are 8 to 10 exclusive clubs in the city of Karachi. A few of them focus solely on some outdoor activity such as yachting, boating, or golf. Their membership numbers vary from 3000 to 5000. High membership cost and monthly fees have restricted these clubs to the upper-middle class and the wealthy. We can safely say that the people using these clubs belong to the ninetieth percentile of income level. We propose to visit these clubs and personally ask for the members' cooperation. We also plan to get the member list and have the questionnaire delivered to the members. They will be asked to return the completed questionnaire to the club office or to mail it in the postage-paid reply envelope. We believe that this group will cooperate and give us quality feedback.

The second delivered survey will be to local schools. With the school's cooperation, we will ask that this questionnaire be delivered by their pupils to the parents. The cover letter will request that the parents fill out the questionnaire and return it to school. This will provide a good sample of people who want outdoor activities for their children. We hope to generate a substantial response through this method.

QUESTIONNAIRE DESIGN

The type of questions asked should help our client make the decision of whether to invest in the project. Through the survey questionnaires we should answer the general questions "Is the population ready for this project? And are they willing to support it?" The questionnaire will be a mixture of open-ended and close-ended items. It will attempt to answer the following specific questions:

- Is there a market for this type of project?
- Is the market substantial?

- Is the market profitable?
- Will this project fill a real need?
- Will this project be only a momentary fad?
- Is the market evenly distributed in all segments/clusters, or is there a high demand in some segments?
- Is the population geared toward and willing to spend money on this type of entertainment facility? If so, how much?
- What is the best location for this project?
- Are people willing to travel some distance to reach this type of facility? Or would they want it within city limits?
- What types of entertainment or rides would people want to see in an amusement park?
- Through what type of media or promotion can the prospective customers best be reached?

INTRODUCTION OF THE FIRM

Hello, we are AGT, Inc. We are a marketing research company located in Karachi. As a public service, we are conducting a marketing study about the possibility of setting up an amusement park in your city, Karachi. This would provide healthy entertainment to the younger generation. The answers you give to the following questions will help us determine whether or not to introduce this idea, and what features, rides, and other entertainment facilities to include in the park. It will also help us to provide you with better service and take care of your needs.

We are highly thankful to all the companies that are sponsoring this survey. It proves their commitment toward building up this society and investing in the future. We appreciate your time. Thank you.

Please note:

- This survey is purely for finding out attitudes.
- We do not need to know your identity.
- All information volunteered will be kept strictly confidential.
- A recreational facility can be defined as an outdoor developed facility.
- Please do not confuse "clubs" with recreational facilities.

AGT Marketing Researchers
Room #26, 4th Floor, Sasi Arcade
Clifton, Karachi 75600
Phone: (021) 533422   Fax: 532246

P.S.   If delivered in *school:* Please bring it back to school the next day.

If delivered at the *club or hotel:* Please drop it at the front desk.

Or: Please *mail* it in enclosed envelope. No stamp necessary, thank you.

QUESTIONNAIRE

Please check the appropriate boxes. Thank you.

1 Are there adequate recreational facilities in the city?

Yes □   No □

2 How satisfied are you with the present recreational facilities? (Please rate from 0 to 10.)

0 1 2 3 4 5 6 7 8 9 10
Poor   Excellent

3 How often do you visit the present recreational facilities? (Please check one box.)

Weekly   □
Fortnightly   □
Monthly   □
Once in two months   □
Yearly   □
More (indicate number)   □ _____
Not at all   □

4 Do you visit recreational areas with your family?

Yes □   No □

If no, why not?

Security   □
Distance   □
Expense   □
Crowd (not family type)   □
Poor service   □
Other (please specify) _____
_____
_____

a Do you stay overnight?

Yes □   No □

b If yes, how long? _____
(Please indicate number of days.)

c If no, would you have stayed if the right circumstances or facilities had been provided?

Yes □   No □

5 a Have you ever visited an amusement park?

Here in Pakistan □
Abroad   □

Yes □   (Please go to Question 5b.)
No □   (Please go to Question 5c.)

b If yes, when did you last visit an amusement park?

Last month   □
Within the last six months   □
Within a year   □
More (specify number)   □

Where? _____

c If no, why not?

Security   □
Distance   □
Expense   □
Crowd (not family type)   □
Poor service   □
Other (please specify) _____

6 a What did you enjoy the most in that park?

Roller coasters   □
Water slides   □
Children's play areas   □
Shows   □
Games   □
Simulators   □
Other _____

b How much did you spend in that park (approximately)?

Rs 50 or less   □
51–100   □
101–150   □
151–200   □
More than 200   □

c How would you rate the value received? (Please rate from 0 to 10.)

0 1 2 3 4 5 6 7 8 9 10
Poor   Excellent

7 Would you utilize an amusement park if one were built locally?

Yes □   No □

8 What would you like to see in an amusement park? (Please give us your six best choices.)

a _____

b _____

c _____

d _____

e _____

f _____

9 Where would you like it to be located?

Within city area   □
Beach area   □
Suburbs   □
Outskirts of city   □
Indifferent   □

10 How many kilometers would you be willing to travel to the park?

Under 10 k   □
11–20   □
21–35   □
35–55   □
55–65   □
More than 65   □

11 How often do you take vacations for recreation purposes?

Never   □
Once a year   □
Twice a year   □
More often (please specify) _____

Please tell us about yourself:

12 Please indicate your age.

Under 15 years □
16–21   □
22–29   □
30–49   □
50–60   □
Over 60   □

13 Please indicate your gender.

Male □   Female □

14 Are you married?

Yes □   No □

15 How many children do you have?

Please indicate number: _____

16 Please indicate your total family income (yearly).

Under Rs 12,000 □
12,000–14,999   □
15,000–19,999   □
20,000–24,999   □
25,000–39,999   □
40,000–59,999   □
60,000–79,999   □
Over 80,000   □

17 Do you own a car?

Yes □   No □

18 Any other comments? (If you need more space, please attach an additional sheet.)

_____

_____

_____

_____

_____

_____

_____

Thank you. We appreciate your time.

Important: If you *want* us to contact you again in later stages of this project or if you will be interested in its results, give us your name and address. We will be glad to keep you informed. Thank you.

_____

_____

_____

_____

_____

CASE QUESTIONS

1 What marketing management problems and opportunities form the basis for JST's need for marketing research?

2 Evaluate the research objectives of JST for the marketing research that it plans to implement.

3 Evaluate the information needs of JST for the marketing research that it plans to implement.

4 Evaluate the research designs that AGT proposes for JST.

5 Evaluate the appropriateness of each of the data sources that AGT proposes for JST.

CASE 2-2   Twin Pines Golf and Country Club (A)

In mid-May, the Capital Planning Committee of the Twin Pines Golf and Country Club met to discuss a research report that they had just received. This report gave the results of a survey of the club members on the issue of which projects the club should begin this fiscal year. Members of the committee intended to use the report as a basis for selecting among alternative capital projects. A biographical description of the committee members is given in Appendix 1.

APPENDIX 1   BIOGRAPHICAL DESCRIPTIONS OF CAPITAL PLANNING COMMITTEE MEMBERS

	Age	Family	Occupation	Club activities
John B. Watts (Chairman)	62	Married, 2 sons, ages 29 and 27	President, Exeter Tool Company	Golf
Dr. L. Gary Johnston	45	Married, 1 daughter, age 20; 2 sons, ages 17 and 12	Dentist	Golf, tennis
Joseph R. Taylor	35	Married, 1 son, age 7	Lawyer	Golf
Robert H. Robertson*	59	Married, 3 daughters, ages 32, 30, and 27	President, Robertson Advertising	Golf
Dr. Malcolm R. Richardson	42	Unmarried	Internal medicine specialist	Golf, tennis
Kenneth L. Wecker*	69	Widower, 2 daughters, ages 42 and 38	Retired, president of Alpha Associates, Management Consultants	Golf
Dr. W. Lloyd Hains	53	Married, no children	General practitioner	Golf
Bruce A. Frederick*	46	Married, 1 son, age 16	Sales manager, Beta Electronics	Golf

*Member research subcommittee.

TABLE 1   PROJECTS AND COSTS

	Capital cost	Operating cost per year
An additional nine golf holes, complete with automatic watering systems on existing lands	$1,400,000	$220,000
Swimming pool and clubhouse with lockers	380,000	80,000
Tennis clubhouse, court lighting, and bubble cover for winter.	220,000	40,000
Three new tennis courts	130,000	30,000
Purchase of 150 acres of land adjacent to club as a buffer against city expansion or for club expansion	1,300,000	67,000

BACKGROUND

Twin Pines Golf and Country Club was a private club situated in the southwestern corner of Hinsdale, Illinois, a suburb of Chicago. The club was founded in 1956 with an 18-hole golf course and a dining room. In 1966, an additional 9 holes were built, and in 1989 three outdoor tennis courts were added to the club.

The Capital Planning Committee was a permanent committee of the Twin Pines Club. Its task in recent years involved the overseeing of the maintenance of current facilities. However, in this particular year the board of directors of the club had given an additional task to the committee: making recommendations on new capital facilities. In a letter to the committee, the president of the club stated, "We must be prepared to add new facilities to serve the current and future interests of our members and to attract new members. It is your task to make recommendations in this matter."

In response to this request, the Capital Planning Committee held a series of meetings to discuss possible projects requiring capital expenditures during the next few years. They identified five potential projects and the associated capital costs and operating costs per year. These projects and their costs were as shown in Table 1.

The committee decided to obtain the opinion of the membership on the five projects before reaching a decision. In December, a research subcommittee was formed to obtain the views of the membership. It was the expressed intention of the whole committee to recommend the capital project or projects that the membership desired.

APPENDIX 2   QUESTIONNAIRE

1 Class of membership

Please indicate your membership class:

Senior	( )
Senior female	( )
Intermediate male	( )
Intermediate female	( )

2 Junior members living at home

Ages of sons	( )	( )	( )	( )	( )
Ages of daughters	( )	( )	( )	( )	( )

3 Proposed capital projects

Your Capital Planning Committee is presently evaluating a number of possible projects. As part of this evaluation we would like your opinion on the projects listed below.

	Capital cost	Operating cost per year
Nine-hole golf course with automatic watering system	$400,000	$45,000
Swimming pool and clubhouse with lockers	80,000	30,000
Tennis clubhouse, court lighting, and bubble cover for winter	120,000	20,000
Three new tennis courts	30,000	10,000
Purchase of land (150 acres) adjacent to the 16th and 17th holes	300,000	27,000

a What is *your* interest in these projects?

	High	Medium	Low
Additional 9 holes	( )	( )	( )
Swimming pool	( )	( )	( )
Tennis clubhouse and lights	( )	( )	( )
Three tennis courts	( )	( )	( )
Land	( )	( )	( )

b What priority should the club attach to each of these projects?

	High	Medium	Low
Additional 9 holes	( )	( )	( )
Swimming pool	( )	( )	( )
Tennis clubhouse and lights	( )	( )	( )
Three tennis courts	( )	( )	( )
Land	( )	( )	( )

4 Financing

Your committee has expressed above the capital and operating costs for each project. Below, we have stated these costs in terms of the effect these projects will have on the fees of senior members. Would you be in favor of proceeding with the following projects?

	To finance construction over 10 years	Operating costs	Total	In favor	
				Yes	No
Additional 9 holes	$29	$33	$62	( )	( )
Swimming pool	6	22	28	( )	( )
Tennis clubhouse and lights	9	15	24	( )	( )
Three tennis courts	2	7	9	( )	( )
Land	22	20	42	( )	( )

The Study

The research subcommittee developed a questionnaire (see Appendix 2) designed to measure the preferences of the membership in relation to the five projects. In March, this questionnaire was mailed to all senior and intermediate members of the club. Table 2 shows the number of questionnaires mailed to each class of membership and the associated return rate. The report prepared by the research subcommittee consisted of a set of tables giving what the committee members thought were the main findings of the survey. These are presented as Tables 3 to 5.

May 15 Meeting

All members of the Capital Planning Committee were present for the meeting held in the Twin Pines boardroom on May 15. John Watts, the committee chairperson, opened the meeting by thanking the research subcommittee for their efforts. He also noted that the board of directors of the club had asked him to be prepared to make a recommendation concerning capital expenditures at the next board meeting. This meeting was to be held on May 21. Because of this time pressure, it would be necessary for the Capital Planning Committee to reach a decision at the May 15 meeting.

CASE QUESTIONS

1 What action should the committee take?
2 Why?

TABLE 2   QUESTIONNAIRE RETURNS BY CLASS OF MEMBERSHIP

	Number mailed	Number returned	Percent returned
Senior male (club shareholders)	710	540	76
Senior female	650	402	62
Intermediate male (ages 21–26)	250	110	44
Intermediate female (ages 21–26)	75	32	43
Total	1685	1084	64

TABLE 3   PROJECT PREFERENCE GIVEN KNOWLEDGE OF THE EFFECT ON ANNUAL FEES
(Question 4 in the Questionnaire)

Response	Projects					Total responses
	Golf	Swimming pool	Tennis clubhouse	Tennis courts	Land	
Yes	32.5%	37.1%	32.9%	27.4%	23.7%	
	(352)	(402)	(357)	(297)	(257)	1665
No	50.6%	59.6%	51.1%	53.6%	60.4%	
	(549)	(646)	(554)	(581)	(655)	2985
No opinion	16.9%	3.3%	16.0%	19.0%	15.9%	
	(183)	(36)	(173)	(206)	(172)	770
Total respondents	1084	1084	1084	1084	1084	5420

TABLE 4   PROJECT PREFERENCE BY TYPE OF MEMBERSHIP
(Yes to Question 4 and Categories of Question 1)

Membership type*	Projects					Total responses
	Golf	Swimming pool	Tennis clubhouse	Tennis courts	Land	
Senior male	30.2%†	25.9%	27.6%	23.5%	27.2%	
	(163)	(140)	(149)	(127)	(147)	726
Senior female	36.4%	38.8%	28.1%	28.7%	19.7%	
	(146)	(156)	(113)	(115)	(79)	609
Intermediate male	31.2%	73.6%	67.3%	38.2%	21.4%	
	(34)	(81)	(74)	(42)	(24)	255
Intermediate female	29.7%	78.1%	65.6%	40.1%	20.7%	
	(9)	(25)	(21)	(13)	(7)	75
Total responses	352	402	357	297	257	1665

*Total response per membership type adds up to more than 100% of the respondents because of multiple responses. Total number of respondents = 1084.

†That is, 30.2% of senior male members are in favor of the golf project.

TABLE 5   PRIORITY CLUB SHOULD ATTACH TO PROJECTS
(Responses to Question 3b)

	High	Medium	Low	No opinion
Additional nine holes	24.7	21.0	45.1	9.2
Swimming pool	28.5	18.7	45.9	6.9
Tennis clubhouse and lights	16.4	16.9	51.2	15.5
Three tennis courts	17.6	15.9	52.0	14.5
Land	19.7	21.4	46.0	12.9

Note: All numbers are percentages by rows. Total number of respondents = 1084.

CASE 2-3   Automotive Supply, Inc.*

Automotive Supply, Inc. (ASI), is a large wholesaler located in Tulsa, Oklahoma. It supplies auto parts to service stations, department stores, discount houses, and retail parts outlets in and around the Tulsa area. Bill Douglass, president of Automotive, was concerned about his company's declining sales. Between 1991 and 1995, revenues dropped from $8 million to $5 million, and he feared the business would go under unless something was done to improve its sales picture. "It's those foreign

*Source: Coauthored by Sheryl Petras.

imports," lamented Douglass, "they're ruining my parts business." ASI only sold parts for domestic cars, and Douglass did not want to enter the foreign parts market.

In an effort to improve profits, Douglass had asked the Rightway Research firm to submit a proposal for marketing research that would help in formulating a long-range growth strategy for Automotive. Limited funds forced Douglass to set a low budget for the research project. Douglass had received Rightway's proposal and was in the process of evaluating it. The proposal is shown below.

RIGHTWAY RESEARCH

The influx of foreign cars into the American auto market has had an adverse effect on all suppliers of domestic parts. Success in this market is dependent on two things: accurate automobile demand forecasts and a sufficient inventory to meet retailers' needs. Lack of either can result in disaster. Automotive's research objective is thus:

To obtain the data which would enable Automotive to (1) accurately forecast demand for autos, and (2) make proper inventory decisions.

A list of the information needs and sources of information to meet those needs follows.

As you can see, most of the information needed is readily available in federal, state, and county publications; trade journals; manufacturers' publications; and syndicated sources. These data can be obtained at low or moderate cost. The above list is by no means complete; rather it represents the minimum sources that Automotive should be aware of and carefully monitor.

CASE QUESTIONS

1 Evaluate the stated research objective and the information needs presented in the proposal.
2 Are the data sources appropriate to the information needs and research objectives? Why or why not?
3 Evaluate the data collection framework.
4 What other possible research design and data sources could be used?

Information needs	Source(s)
Auto industry	
Total demand	*Wards Automotive Reports*
Demand by make and model	
Proportion of new versus used sales	*Motor Statistics* (R.L. Polk & Co.)
Diesel car sales	City, county, and state planning commission reports
Projected gasoline prices	
Availability of parts from manufacturers	Manufacturers
Government regulations	
Population	
Growth	*Statistical Abstracts of the United States*
Age and sex composition	
Economic	
Number of dual-career households	Local employment bureau
Employment, payroll, and sales of the major industries in the market area	*Statistical Abstracts of the United States*
Labor market	
GNP for market area	
Availability of money for loans; status of interest rates	
Current government position on imports—quotas versus free trade	

CASE 2-4   Nestle*

As the power of traditional brand advertising wanes and price competition spurred by economy-priced store brands heats up, several packaged goods companies are taking a radically new value-added approach to marketing. This approach concentrates on establishing consistent dialog with interested consumers, as opposed to the traditional monolog with the mass market. Nestle offers a prime example of this new packaged goods marketing strategy.

Nestle is pouring its creative energies into building credibility around its products and its company, rejecting the traditional and often suicidal approach of mass advertising and mass discounts in favor of relationship-based marketing strategies. Sopad-Nestle, Nestle's Paris-based baby food di-

*Source: Based on Stan Rapp and Thomas L. Collins, *Beyond Maximarketing: The New Power of Caring and Sharing* (New York: McGraw-Hill Inc., as reprinted in *Advertising Age*, pp. 16, S7, and S10, October 25, 1993).

A *Le Relais Bébé* rest stop.

vision, has successfully implemented this new creative strategy. The French baby food market has long been dominated by the Bledina brand. Sopad-Nestle used interactive marketing to gain significant market share, passing Gerber and moving into a close second behind Bledina.

Traditionally, brand building for packaged goods has been a process with three parameters, as follows:

1 The height of the impressions on consumers—the sheer extent of the advertising bombardment achieved by the purchase of advertising time and space in the various media

2 The depth of the brand awareness achieved, based on the power of the image or sales argument in the advertising

3 The width of the distribution and the muscle available to push the brand to a prominent place on the shelf at the point of sale

Sopad-Nestle added a fourth dimension by using individualized marketing and moving into the lives and activities of prospects and customers as a genuinely helpful, caring, trusted companion. This strategy was nurtured by Fabienne Petit, marketing director for Sopad-Nestle, with a guiding passion to make life better for parents of babies. Here is how Nestle implemented this approach.

In France, almost everyone takes off for a long vacation in the summer, and the majority of these

people drive to their destinations. For families traveling with a baby in diapers, going anywhere by car creates a significant amount of inconvenience. Concentrating on their target customers, Sopad-Nestle developed a way to dramatically improve the quality of life for any parent and baby on the road.

Through a program called *Le Relais Bébé*, Nestle provides rest-stop structures alongside the highway where parents can feed and change their babies. In eight locations along the main travel routes, a sparkling clean *Le Relais Bébé* awaits and welcomes the family. Each summer, 64 hostesses at these rest stops welcome 120,000 baby visits and dispense samples of baby food. They also offer free disposable diapers, a changing table, and high chairs for feeding their babies.

According to Marketing Director Petit, "*Le Relais Bébé* has important benefits for Nestle. For one thing, it is a genuine showcase of brand image. Nestle is the only mass-marketing brand to have such a presence on the highways. But it is above all the quality of contact of more than 20 minutes with the mothers that distinguishes this operation. At the key moment of the baby's meal, Nestle through its hostesses finds itself in direct contact with the mothers in a consumer/brand relationship that is quite unusual."

Nestle interacts directly with consumers in many other ways as well. For example, in all media advertising, direct mail, and packaging, parents are invited to call the toll-free number for its free baby-nutrition counseling service, *Allo Nestle Diététique*.

Another key aspect of interactive marketing is the establishment of quality databases, a process which has become increasingly cost-effective as hardware and software technology has improved while their respective prices have dropped. Nestle maintains and constantly updates a database of 220,000 new mothers with names and addresses extracted from maternity records. The first mailing contains a reply card on which the new mother can fill in baby's name and indicate interest in receiving further mailings. This ensures that future mailings target interested consumers and thereby increase their effectiveness. This file is then used to send six direct-mail packages, personalized with the first name of the baby, at key stages of development in the baby's life. Packages are sent at ages 3 months, 6 months, 9 months, 1 year, 18 months, and 2 years. Each package is bulging with "goodies," such as samples of baby food, promotional coupons, cutouts of the Nestle teddy bear, and information cards with tips from pediatricians on what to expect at each stage of the baby's development.

There is also a special Mother's Day mailing that sends a rose for mama from a local florist as a gift from baby and a loving postcard with a "handwritten" greeting from baby to mama (courtesy of Nestle).

Petit defines four key elements in the brand's success, as follows:

1 The tone of the mailings, which is affectionate and personal.

2 The progressive evolution of the message, so that as the baby grows, Nestle is there at the right time with the right products and the right message.

3 The helpful, informative content of every communication in prioritizing "getting help" ahead of selling Nestle products, putting the consumers' needs ahead of the sellers'.

4 The companionship and consistent direct contact that Nestle provides at critical stages of the baby's development.

A recent market research survey of 1000 mothers showed a 97 percent approval rating for Nestle's direct-mail campaign and a 94 percent approval rating for *Le Relais Bébé*. Sopad-Nestle now holds 43 percent of the market, reflecting a gain of over 23 share points in less than 7 years. During that same time period, market leader Bledina outspent Nestle 7 to 1 in advertising and lost market share. As Nestle executive Peter Brabeck asserted, "You can triple advertising spending, but if you can't establish a credible communication link with consumers, they won't act."

Recognizing that repeat business represents a much greater share of the market than trial business, Sopad-Nestle identified and targeted the heavy users of its products—parents with babies. The company opened an information exchange with its primary consumers, treating them as special customers, listening to and anticipating their needs, and rewarding their brand loyalty with extra value instead of employing mass advertising and discounts. Nestle's approach in the French baby food market utilizes the value-added approach as a strategy for packaged goods marketing.

CASE QUESTIONS

1 What marketing management problems have led Nestle to establish these types of databases?

2 What types of marketing management questions may these types of databases help provide answers for?

3 What are the technical requirements and costs associated with the development of these types of databases?

4 How should a marketing decision support system (an MDSS) interface with these types of databases?

5 Are there any ethical questions raised by Nestle's having this database? If yes, what are they?

DEVELOP THE DATA COLLECTION PROCEDURE

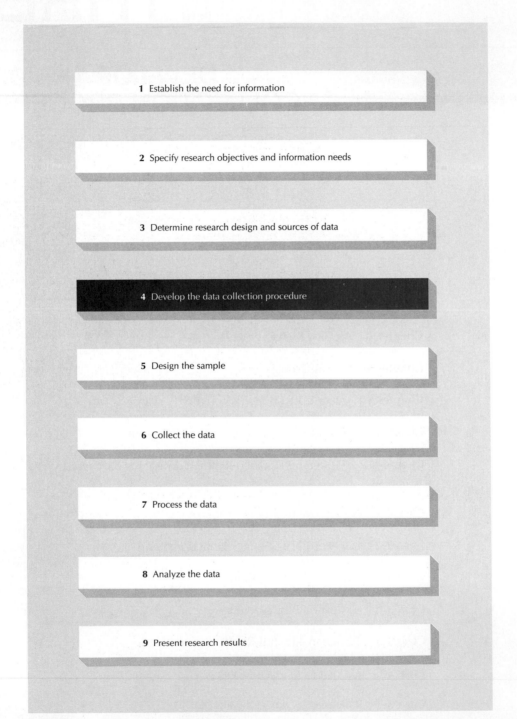

FIGURE 7-1   Steps in the research process.

THE MEASUREMENT PROCESS

MARKETING RESEARCH IN ACTION

J. D. POWER'S CUSTOMER SATISFACTION INDEX IMPACTS AUTOMOBILE INDUSTRY

Ford Motor Co. was notably upset by Chrysler Corporation ads implying that buyers rank Chrysler first among U.S. automakers. Ford asserted that such claims were false, but it allocated some of the blame to the automobile marketing research firm of J. D. Power & Associates. Power & Associates approved the ads based on one of their customer satisfaction surveys. The survey did, indeed, rank Chrysler first in the domestic market, but the ranking was based more on dealer service than on actual car quality, a fact that failed to come out in the ads.

Chrysler's use of the J. D. Power name in its ads fueled Ford's anger. Many equate the Power name to the automobile version of the *Good Housekeeping* Seal of Approval. Power's marketing research company and its Customer Satisfaction Index exert a major influence over customer buying patterns. Mary Treisbach, Subaru's U.S. marketing/research manager, agreed: "Buyers know J. D. Power—his customer satisfaction index has crept into parlance." This ultimately affects all competitors in the $150 billion U.S. automotive industry.

Those who are ill-affected are far from happy. And some may have good reason. Most of Power's studies are based on questionnaires sent to car owners. Some automakers feel that these questionnaires are superficial. Thomas J. Wagner, Ford division general manager, complained that many of Power's opinion samples are not extensive enough to support the broad conclusions he draws. Speaking anonymously, one former employee said that the company's research fails to meet purist standards: "From a methodological standpoint, there are many automotive manufacturers with better resources than Dave's [J. D.'s]." Internal researchers often referred to "Dave's OK research," thus implying questionable research methods. Their major criticism of the Power methods include: samples are too small, questions may be worded in a way that may influence results, there may be measurement error in terms of whether the construct of satisfaction is really measured, and there is a lack of variance in the time of year that the data are collected.

Power admits that his methods used to be sloppy, but he claims to have improved. Many of his clients agree, and they dismiss his critics as "jealous snipers" who don't understand an enterprising entrepreneur conducting business in a slightly different way. Nonetheless, these types of allegations of incompetencies in sampling, measurement, and field work have the potential to damage both the research firm's and the client's reputation.

Measurement issues form the basis of interest in this chapter. Just how do we know whether we have a reliable and valid measure of a construct like consumer satisfaction? The process of measurement is a commonplace occurrence for college students. Entrance examinations are measuring devices designed to assess the student's potential for college-level work. Once in college, the student is confronted with an array of examinations to measure achievement in courses such as marketing research. Measurement is involved when students in a class are counted, classified as male or female, or judged as to which are most attractive in appearance or personality. These are only a few examples of the use of measurement in our daily activities. Typically, the measurement process is taken for granted. Rarely do we stop to think about the differences in the type of measurements taken and the accuracy of the conclusions drawn. This chapter is designed to stimulate your thinking in this regard.

MEASUREMENT IN MARKETING

The process of measurement is a fundamental aspect of marketing research. It is often stated that the best way to really understand a thing is to try to measure it. For this reason, if for no other, the topic of measurement is of growing concern to those in the field of marketing.

Decision makers are interested in measuring many aspects of the marketing system; for example, they may want to measure the market potential for a new product; to measure group buyers by demographic or psychographic characteristics; to measure buyers' attitudes, perceptions, or preferences toward a new brand; or to determine the effectiveness of a new advertising campaign. Consequently, the measurement of marketing phenomena is essential to the process of providing meaningful information for decision making.

Developing effective measures of marketing phenomena is not an easy task. In Chapter 3, measurement error was cited as being a substantial share of the total error in marketing research information. For many research projects, measurement error can be substantially greater than sampling error. Having a clear understanding of the measurement problem and how to control this error is an important aspect of designing an effective marketing research project.

The marketing manager rarely becomes directly involved in the actual measurement process. The task of selecting and designing measurement techniques is the responsibility of the research specialist. However, the decision maker must often approve the measurement techniques that are recommended and needs to be confident that these techniques are effective in controlling measurement error.

In order to control measurement error effectively, the marketing manager should be concerned with three issues. First, the specification of information needs should recognize the degree of difficulty in obtaining accurate measures. Second, the alternative measurement procedures for obtaining the information should be recognized. Third, the cost of measurement versus the accuracy of measurement should be evaluated. This chapter and many of the remaining chapters deal with these three issues.

The Measurement Process

In marketing research, the measurement process involves using numbers to represent the marketing phenomena under investigation. Stated formally, the *empirical system* includes marketing phenomena, such as buyer reactions to products or advertisements, while the *abstract system* includes the numbers used to represent the marketing phenomena. Figure 7-2 depicts the measurement process as one of developing a correspondence between the empirical system and the abstract system. The former is composed of the physical sciences (the study of physical things) and the social sciences (the study of people). Marketing is one of the social sciences in that it involves human activity directed at satisfying needs and wants through exchange processes.

Definition of Measurement

The previous discussion suggests that measurement is concerned with developing a correspondence between the empirical system (e.g., preference) and the abstract system (e.g., numbers). Therefore, *measurement* may be defined as the assignment of numbers to characteristics of objects or events according to rules. Effective measurement is possible when the relationships existing among the objects or events in the empirical system directly correspond to the rules of the number system. If this correspondence is misrepresented, measurement error has occurred. More will be said about this shortly.

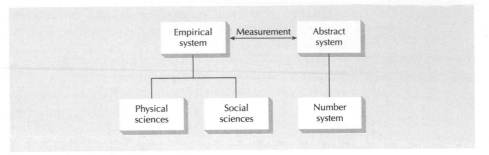

The term "number" in the definition of measurement imposes certain restrictions on the type of numerical manipulations admissible. Numbers are being used as symbols to model the characteristics of interest in the empirical system. The nature of the relationships existing in the empirical system determines the type of numerical manipulations that are valid in the abstract system. There is a great temptation to use all the characteristics of the number system in our data analysis and to disregard the restrictions imposed by the empirical phenomena under study. We now turn to a discussion of the characteristics of the number system, which should provide a better understanding of this issue.

Number System Characteristics

Very early in our educational career we learned four characteristics of the number system 0, 1, 2, 3, 4, 5, 6, 7, 8, and 9. First, each number in the series is unique, and there are 10 numbers. Second, the ordering of the numbers is given by convention, for example, $2 > 1, 1 > 0$. Third, we can define equal differences, for example, $3 - 2 = 7 - 6, 7 - 5 = 3 - 1$. Fourth, we can define equal ratios, for example, $10 \div 5 = 6 \div 3$.

The manipulation of numbers using mathematics or statistics involves one or more of these four characteristics of the number system. There is a great temptation to use more of these characteristics in our data analysis than may actually exist in the empirical system being modeled. The problem is one of focusing clearly on determining how many of these four characteristics are present in the marketing phenomena under investigation, and then restricting our data analysis to using only appropriate characteristics in our manipulation of the numbers. Often, this restriction hampers the sophistication of data analysis that can properly be performed.

Types of Scales

Scales have been classified in terms of the four characteristics of the number system. These scales of measurement are *nominal, ordinal, interval,* and *ratio.* The

TABLE 7-1 CHARACTERISTICS OF MEASUREMENT SCALES

Scale	Number system	Marketing phenomena	Permissible statistics*
Nominal	Unique definition of numerals (0, 1, 2, . . . , 9)	Brands Male-female Store types Sale territories	Percentages Mode Binomial test Chi-square test
Ordinal	Order of numerals (0 < 1 < 2 . . . < 9)	Attitudes Preferences Occupations Social classes	Percentiles Median Rank-order correlation
Interval	Equality of differences (2 − 1 = 7 − 6)	Attitudes Opinions Index numbers	Range Mean Standard deviation Product-moment correlation
Ratio	Equality of ratios ($^2/_4 = ^4/_8$)	Ages Costs Number of customers Sales (units/dollars)	Geometric mean Harmonic mean Coefficient of variation

(handwritten annotations: "Descriptive" bracketing Nominal and Ordinal; "Inferential" bracketing Interval and Ratio; "mode" next to Median row; "median mode" next to Mean row)

*All statistics appropriate for nominal measurement are appropriate for higher scale measurement. The same is true for ordinal- and interval-scale measurements.

characteristics of these scales are summarized in Table 7-1, and the following paragraphs discuss each of these scales and their characteristics in detail.

Nominal Scale A *nominal scale* is one on which numbers serve only as labels to identify or categorize objects or events. A familiar example is the use of numbers to identify football players. Assume that the quarterback for the blue team is number 12, and the quarterback for the green team is number 9. Numbers used in this manner serve only as labels to identify the players. The numbers assume equality with respect to the characteristics of the players. For example, we cannot infer that the quarterback of the blue team is superior in ability to the quarterback of the green team due to the higher number of 12. Therefore, the number 12 does not imply a superior characteristic compared to the number 9; it serves only as a unique label for identification of the player.

Nominal scales are used for the lowest form of measurement, namely classification and identification. Few restrictions are imposed in the assignment of numerals to the objects or events. The rule is simply: do not assign the same number to different objects or events, or different numbers to the same object or event.

A substantial proportion of marketing phenomena require nominal-scale measurement. Such nominal-level identification are needed to measure brands, store types, sales territories, geographic locations, heavy versus light users, working versus nonworking women, and brand awareness versus nonawareness. It is a rare marketing research study that does not involve marketing data of this nature.

Ordinal Scale An *ordinal scale* defines the ordered relationship among objects or events. It involves the number system characteristic of the order of numerals. Ordinal scales measure whether an object or event has more or less of a characteristic than some other object or event. However, this scale does not provide information on how much more or less of the characteristic various objects or events possess.

Let's illustrate ordinal measurement by assuming that a bicycle manufacturer is interested in determining the preference ordering of males among the firm's 10-speed bicycle (A) and two leading competitors (B and C) with regard to the characteristic of speed. A survey was conducted of 200 male potential buyers. The results are reported in Table 7-2.

An ordinal scale can be developed by assigning numerals to the first-, second-, and third-order preference judgments. This involves the assignment of numerals such that the resulting numerical series properly maintains the ordered relationship of the preference judgments. But which set of numbers should be assigned? Obviously, a large number of sets of numbers might be assigned, the only restriction being that the numbers be assigned in such a manner that their order corresponds directly with the ordinal relationships present in the preference judgments. For example, the number 1 can be used to represent the first-order preferences; number 2, for the second-order preferences; and number 3, the third-order preferences. Alternatively, another set of permissible numerals would be the number 1 assigned to the first-order preferences, the number 3 to the second-order preferences, and the number 30 to the third-order preferences. Other numerical sets include 5, 6, and 7; 1, 20, and 100; and so on. All these numerical sets form acceptable ordinal scales, and we cannot argue that one set is better than the others.

A more restrictive rule for the assignment of numerals exists with ordinal measurement than with nominal measurement. An important characteristic of measurement is its power to enable us to establish rules that define the domain of numerical sets that can properly be assigned to the empirical system under investigation.

Ordinal measurement involves the rule that any series of numbers can be assigned that preserves the ordered relationships present in the empirical system.

TABLE 7-2   MALE PREFERENCE ORDERING OF BICYCLES A, B, AND C WITH REGARD TO SPEED
(n = 200)

Preference ordering	Proportion of preferences			Total
	A	B	C	
First	.15	.35	.50	1.00
Second	.50	.25	.25	1.00
Third	.35	.40	.25	1.00
Total	1.00	1.00	1.00	

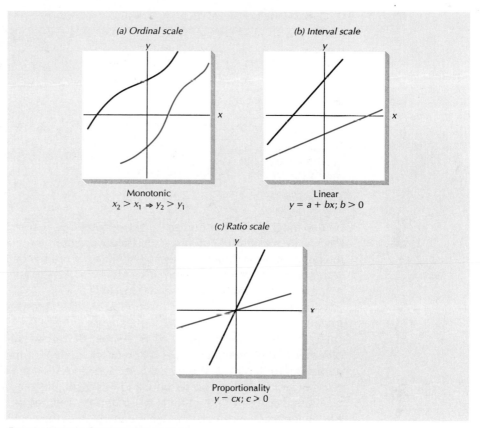

FIGURE 7-3   Permissible transformation by scale type.

This restriction that the numbers be arranged in serial order substantially eliminates many numerical series from consideration. It is equally true, however, that a great deal of freedom remains regarding which numerical set can be used. This domain of freedom can be formally defined as any order-preserving (i.e., monotonic) transformation of the numerical series chosen. Consequently, with an ordinal scale, the only restriction in the assignment of a new series of numbers is that an increasing monotonic transformation be used. Such transformations are illustrated in Figure 7-3(a).

The overall ranking of the three bicycles based on the mode is presented in Table 7-3. The results are presented for both numerical sets, 1 and 2. It is important to note that the preference ordering of the three bicycles is identical for both numerical sets. Here, the overall preference ordering is bicycle C first, A second, and B third. We can generalize these findings to all statistics appropriate for the analysis of ordinal data. Consequently, regardless of which order-preserving numerical set is selected for data analysis, the research findings will not change or

TABLE 7-3   OVERALL RANKING OF BICYCLES A, B, AND C

Descriptive statistic	Ranking		
	1st	2d	3d
Mode (numerical set 1)*	C (1)	A (2)	B (3)
Mode (numerical set 2)†	C (1)	A (3)	B (30)
Mean (numerical set 1)	C (1.75)‡	B (2.05)	A (2.20)
Mean (numerical set 2)	C (8.75)	A (12.15)	B (13.10)

* 1st = 1, 2d = 2, 3d = 3.
† 1st = 1, 2d = 3, 3d = 30.
‡ Mean = (1) (.50) + (2) (.25) + (3) (.25) ÷ 1 = 1.75.

be dependent upon the numerical set selected. More formally, we can state that for any increasing monotonic scale transformation, the conclusions drawn from the data analysis using statistics appropriate for ordinal data *will not change as a result of the assignment of alternative numerical sets.* Some of the statistics appropriate for ordinal data are presented in Table 7-1.

Note that the mean is not an appropriate statistic for ordinal data. What happens if we do calculate the mean? The means for numerical sets 1 and 2 have been calculated to answer this question (see Table 7-3). The result is that the preference ordering of the three bicycles is different for the two numerical assignments. For numerical set 1, bicycle C is first, B is second, and A is last. However, for numerical set 2, bicycle C is first, A is second, and B is third. Bicycles A and B have reversed positions because of the scale transformation. This result is not surprising when we realize that the calculation of a mean involves the equal-interval characteristic of the number system. Since the scale transformation maintained only a monotonic or ranked relationship rather than an equal-interval relationship, the results of our statistical analysis are dependent upon the number series selected. This is a clear example of measurement error occurring in our results.

An important segment of marketing data involves ordinal measurement. Most data collected by the process of interrogating people have ordinal properties. For example, the measurement of attitudes, opinions, preference, and perception frequently involves a "greater than" or "less than" judgment. In addition, many characteristics of buyers or purchasing units can involve a ranked characteristic (e.g., occupation, social class, or image). Consequently, a significant share of marketing research data involve ordinal judgments, and the analysis of these data should be subject to the restrictions discussed previously.

Interval Scale   An interval scale involves the use of numbers to rank objects or events such that the distances between the numerals correspond to the distances between the objects or events on the characteristic being measured. Interval scales possess all the requirements of an ordinal scale plus the "equality of difference" characteristic of the number system. The remaining freedom in assigning numbers is reduced to the arbitrary selection of a unit of measurement (distance) and an origin (zero point). Suppose that we have measured four ordered objects A, B, C, and D and determined that the distance between adjacent objects is equal on some characteristic. In the assignment of numbers to the objects, we must arbitrarily decide how to represent the size of the distance between adjacent objects and where to assign the zero points. For example, the numbers 0, 1, 2, and 3 represent an arbitrary assignment of zero to one object and of a one-unit difference between adjacent objects. An alternative number assignment could be 7, 9, 11, and 13. Both numerical assignments are acceptable, and we cannot say that one is better than the other.

The most common examples of interval scales are the Fahrenheit and Celsius scales used to measure temperature. The freezing point of water is assigned a different numerical value on each scale, 32 on Fahrenheit and 0 on Celsius. The unit of measurement and the origin or zero point have been arbitrarily determined for these scales. Equal differences in the temperature are measured by equal-volume expansion in the mercury used in the thermometer.

The arbitrary assignment of the zero point on an interval scale places restrictions on the statements that can be made regarding comparisons of intervals. For example, you cannot say that 100° Celsius is twice as hot as 50° Celsius. A scale transformation to Fahrenheit demonstrates why. The formula is $C - (F \quad 32)\frac{5}{9}$. Using the formula, the previous Celsius temperatures of 100° and 50° correspond to 212° and 122° on the Fahrenheit scale. Our previous statement that 100° Celsius is twice as warm as 50° does not hold with our new numbers for the Fahrenheit scale. We cannot say that 212° is twice as warm as 122°, because the zero point on each scale is arbitrary. Consequently, comparison of absolute magnitude or ratios is not possible.

The above example with a temperature scale applies to all interval scales. Assume that we have scaled brands A, B, and C on an interval scale regarding buyers' degree of liking of the brands. Brand A receives a 6, the highest liking score; B receives a 3; and C receives a 2. We cannot say that brand A is liked twice as much as brand B. Such a statement assumes that the absolute zero point or the absence of liking has been identified and assigned the value zero on the interval scale. What can we say about these interval-scaled data? First, the liking for brand A is more favorable than that for brand B (order of numerals). Second, the degree of liking between A and B is three times greater than the liking between B and C (equality of differences).

The area of freedom in assigning new numerical sets to an interval scale is more restricted than for an ordinal scale. This new numerical assignment involves a positive linear transformation of the form $y = a + bx$, where b is positive. Here, x is the original scale number and y is the new scale number. Figure 7-3(b) gives examples of two such transformations. Statements comparing intervals are valid with an interval scale because, by taking differences, the nature of the functional relationships is the same regardless of the constants chosen for a and b in the scale transformation formula.

A positive linear scale transformation of an interval scale will not change the research findings when appropriate statistical techniques are used. The majority of such techniques can be used to analyze interval data (see Table 7-1); they include the range, arithmetic mean, standard deviation, product-moment correlation, and so on. Only a few statistical techniques (such as geometric mean, harmonic mean, and coefficient of variation) could lead to misleading results if applied to interval data.

In marketing, it is very common for attitudinal, opinion, and predisposition judgments to be treated as interval data. To be technically correct, these judgments are ordinal. Researchers disagree as to the amount of measurement error present in the results given by ordinal data treated as interval data. The magnitude of this error must be weighed against the data analysis advantages associated with the more sophisticated statistical techniques applicable to analysis of interval data. It is often argued that while the equality-of-interval characteristic may be violated, the degree of violation is typically small, and the results of most statistical techniques are not affected to the point that significant measurement error exists. In the final analysis, it is the responsibility of the researcher to determine (1) how closely the relationships existing in the marketing phenomena under study approximate an interval scale and (2) the appropriateness of treating the data as interval-scaled. Various data collection instruments for developing interval scales will be discussed in Chapter 8.

Ratio Scale   A *ratio scale* has all the properties of an interval scale plus an absolute zero point. With ratio measurement, only one number may be assigned arbitrarily, namely, the unit of measurement or distance. Once this is determined, the remaining numercial assignments are completely determined.

Absolute or natural zero point refers to the assignment of the number zero to the absence of the characteristic being measured. For example, in our discussion of the Fahrenheit and Celsius temperature scales, it was stated that the zero points were arbitrarily assigned on both scales. Consequently, the zero points on these scales do not correspond to the absence of heat and are not absolute zero points. The ratio measurement of temperature is known as the Kelvin scale. Here, the zero point is absolute and represents the absence of heat ($-273.15°C$).

A ratio scale implies that equal ratios among the scale values correspond to equal ratio among the marketing phenomena being measured. The statement that the sales of product A are twice as large as the sales of product B is perfectly legitimate with ratio scale data. The scale transformations for a ratio scale involve a positive proportionate transformation of the form $y = cx; c > 0$. Figure 7-3(c) presents two such transformations.

A great many very important marketing phenomena possess the properties of a ratio scale. These include sales, market share, costs, ages, and number of customers. In each case a natural or absolute zero exists.

The entire range of statistical techniques can be applied to the analysis of ratio-scaled data. However, the significance of the data analysis techniques gained by having a ratio scale is not great compared with those available for the analysis of interval-scaled data.

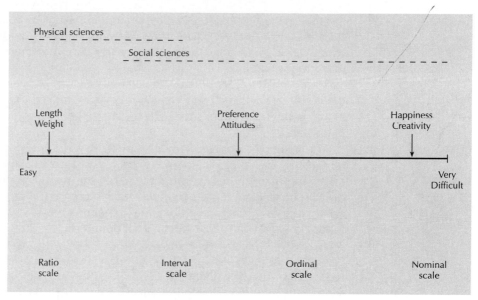

FIGURE 7-4   Difficulty of the measurement process.

DIFFICULTY OF MEASUREMENT

When we discuss the measurement process, most people think in terms of their own experiences with weight, height, and distance, "Since I've been jogging 2 miles each day, my weight has dropped by 5 pounds." The measurement of weight, length, and height is typically an easy task involving the use of a ratio scale. The natural zero point and equality of differences are obvious. This type of measurement situation is more characteristic of the physical sciences than of the social sciences, of which marketing is one. Consequently, the measurement task in marketing is typically more difficult and involves lower scales of measurement than those found in the physical sciences. Figure 7-4 illustrates this type of comparison.

Why is measurement so difficult in marketing? A key problem area relates to the domain of the phenomena studied, namely, the behavior of people. The typical measurement device is interrogating people regarding their behavior. The use of a questionnaire is a relatively crude technique which is subject to substantial measurement error.

The measurement task in marketing is complicated by the many concepts or constructs that pervade marketing thought. These concepts or constructs must be precisely defined and measured in a marketing research project if useful information is to be provided for management decision making.

The terms "concept" and "construct" have similar meanings and are used interchangeably in this book. A *construct* is defined as the mental abstraction formed by the perception of a phenomenon. In marketing, we refer to constructs such as sales, product positioning, demand, attitudes, and brand loyalty. Constructs serve to simplify and synthesize the complex phenomena present in the marketing system.

Some constructs are directly related to aspects of physical reality. For example, the constructs of length and weight are closely related to observations regarding heavy or light and tall or short. The measurement of these constructs is commonplace and fairly easy.

In marketing there are many constructs that do not have observable physical references. Examples include constructs such as predisposition, attitude, preference, and image. These constructs exist in the minds of individuals and are not directly observable. Effective marketing research requires that constructs be defined precisely. This can be done in two general ways—by means of (1) a constitutive definition and (2) an operational definition.

A *constitutive definition* defines a construct with other constructs. This approach is similar to that used in a dictionary, where words are used to define other words. A constitutive definition should identify the main features of the construct such that it is clearly differentiated from other constructs. For example, how would you define brand loyalty? Engel and coauthors define it as "the preferential attitudinal and behavioral response toward one or more brands in a product category expressed over a period of time by a consumer."[1] In this definition, constructs such as preferential attitudes, behavior response, and consumer are used to define the construct "brand loyalty."

An *operational definition* specifies how a construct is to be measured. An operational definition is a sort of manual of instructions to the investigator. It says, in effect, "Do such-and-such in so-and-so manner." In short, it defines or gives meaning to a variable by spelling out what the investigator must do to measure it.

A constitutive definition directs the development of an operational definition. Consider our previous constitutive definition of brand loyalty by Engel and coauthors, which clearly rules out the measurement of brand loyalty solely in terms of consecutive purchases of the brand. For example, the pattern of consecutive purchase of brand B (BBBB) could result from convenience, lack of availability of substitutes, indifference, or lower price rather than from an intrinsic preferential attitude toward the brand. Consequently, an operational definition that is consistent with this constitutive definition of brand loyalty must specify how the preferential attitude is to be measured, what type of behavioral response is consistent with this loyalty state, and how the consumer is to be defined.

Marketing has few examples of standardized constitutive and operational definitions of constructs. This has been a serious hindrance to the effectiveness of marketing research projects, largely reflecting the difficulty of the measurement process in this young field of study.

[1] James Engel et al., *Consumer Behavior,* 7th ed. (Fort Worth, TX: Dryden Press, 1993).

CONCEPTS OF VALIDITY AND RELIABILITY

Measurement error is minimized when a direct correspondence exists between the number system and the marketing phenomena being measured; in this case the numbers accurately represent the characteristics being measured and nothing else. Obviously, this is an idealized situation which rarely exists in practice. More typically our measurements possess some degree of error in that the numerical scale does not exactly represent the marketing phenomenon under investigation.

There are many ways to describe and classify potential sources of error. The following discussion outlines several of the more common sources, as follows:

1 *Short-term characteristics of the respondent.* Personal factors such as mood, fatigue, and health.

2 *Situational factors.* Variations in the environment in which the measurements are reached.

3 *Data collection factors.* Variations in how the questions are administered and in the influence of the interviewing method (e.g., phone, personal contact, or mail).

4 *Measuring instrument factors.* The degree of ambiguity and difficulty of the questions and the ability of the respondent to answer them.

5 *Data analysis factors.* Errors made in the coding and tabulation process.

The total error of measurement consists of two components. The first is *systematic error,* which is error that causes a constant bias in the measurements. For example, assume we are measuring the speed of events at a swimming meet using a stopwatch that systematically runs fast. To the disappointment of the swimmers, this will cause an upward bias in the measured swimming speeds for all events.

The second component of the total error of measurement is *random error,* which involves influences that bias the measurements but are not systematic. For example, in our swimming meet several stopwatches could be used to time the race. Assuming the absence of systematic error, you would find that the recorded times fall within a range around the true time. This random error has been discussed previously in the chapters dealing with sampling.

Returning to our swimming meet example, we can think of the stopwatch time or observed measurement O_m as composed of three elements: (1) the true speed or score T_s, (2) systematic error S_e, and (3) random error R_e. Formally we can state the relationship as

$$O_m = T_s + S_c + R_e$$

where O_m = observed measurement
T_s = true score of the characteristic measured
S_e = systematic error
R_e = random error

Validity and Reliability Defined

The *validity of a measure* refers to the extent to which the measurement process is free from both systematic and random error. The *reliability of a measure* refers to the extent to which the measurement process is free from random errors. Reliability is concerned with the consistency, accuracy, and predictability of the research findings. Validity is concerned with the question: Are we measuring what we think we are measuring? Validity is a broader and more difficult issue than reliability.

Assume we are conducting a survey of buyers to estimate the market share for brand X. For purposes of illustration, assume the market share is actually 10 percent. Let us also assume that four potential conditions exist regarding the influence of systematic and random error on our observed measure of market share. Condition (*a*) is no systematic error and low random error; condition (*b*) is high systematic error and low random error; condition (*c*) is no systematic error and high random error; and condition (*d*) is high systematic error and high random error. These four conditions represent extremes, and the more typical situation would lie somewhere in the middle. Figure 7-5 illustrates these four conditions.

The figure also presents the influence of systematic and random error on the distribution of sample means for each of these four conditions. In condition (*a*), the expected value of the distribution of sample means is identical to the true market share of 10 percent. The low random error is reflected in a tight distribution of sample means. Here, repeated samples consistently produce means that are close to the true market share. In this condition, our survey results would be described as both valid and reliable. Condition (*b*) has the same tight distribution of sample means, but the influence of the high systematic error has biased the expected value 3 points above the true share of market. Repeated sampling would produce means which are close to the 13 percent result. In this situation, our survey results would be reliable but not valid.

In condition (*c*), the expected value of the distribution of sample means is identical to the true market share of 10 percent, but the high random error causes the distribution of sample means to be highly dispersed. Here, repeated sampling would find many sample means dramatically different from the true market share. In this condition, our survey results would be described as neither valid nor reliable. Finally, condition (*d*) has the same high random error as condition (*c*), but here the systematic error is also high, causing the expected value of the sampling distribution to be 5 points below the true market share. In this situation, our survey results would again be described as neither valid nor reliable.

To summarize, for a measure to be valid, it must be reliable. Here, systematic error S_e and random error R_e are small or zero. However, if a measure is not reliable, it cannot be valid, and if it is reliable, then it may or may not be valid. Reliability is a necessary but not a sufficient condition for validity. Consequently, the validity of a measure is of main concern since it deals with both systematic and random error. Reliability is a weaker concept since it involves only random error. The ease of measuring reliability compared with validity has given emphasis

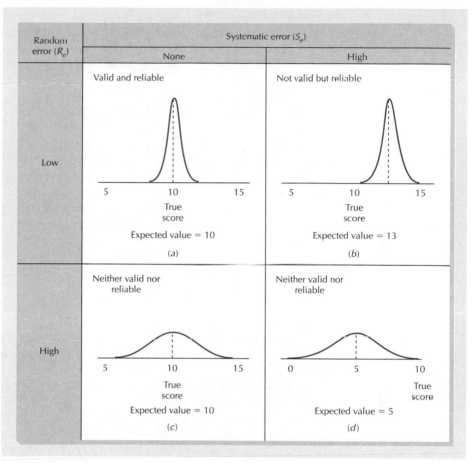

FIGURE 7-5   Reliability and validity.

to the reporting of reliability scores in preference to validity scores in research studies.

Estimation of Validity and Reliability

It is rare to find a decision maker spending the money and taking the time to determine the validity and reliability of research results. The pressures and practical considerations of the typical decision-making situation leave the issue of validity and reliability to those concerned with basic research or academic research projects. Consequently, we will overview only the main methods for estimating validity and reliability.

The major methods of estimating the reliability of measurement are the test-retest, the alternative-forms, and the split-half methods.

Test-Retest Reliability   Test-retest reliability involves repeated measurement of the same person or group using the same scaling device under conditions that are judged to be very similar. The results of these measurements are compared to determine their similarity. This approach assumes that the greater the discrepancy in scores, the greater the random error present in the measurement process and the lower the reliability.

Let's return to our multi-item technique for measuring retail store image, discussed in reference to content validity. Test-retest reliability would involve administering our 20-item measuring technique to a group of store shoppers at two points in time. The results of the two measurements would then be correlated to determine the degree of correspondence. The lower the correlation, the lower the reliability.

There are a number of problems with this approach to measuring reliability. First, it may not be logical or possible to administer the measurement twice to the same subject. Second, the first measurement may change the subject's response to the second measurement. Third, situational factors may change, causing the second measurement to change. These types of problems can bias our measurement of reliability.

Alternative-Forms Reliability   Alternative-forms reliability involves giving the subject two forms which are judged equivalent but are not identical. The results of the two measurements are compared to determine the degree of discrepancy in scores, as in the test-retest approach.

Using this approach to determining reliability would require a second set of 20 items to be developed for our retail image–measuring instrument. The two equivalent forms would be administered to the same subjects and the degree of correspondence determined. The problems associated with the alternative-forms approach are the expense and delay associated with developing a second measuring instrument and the difficulty of making the two instruments equivalent.

Split-Half Reliability   Split-half reliability involves dividing a multi-item measurement device into equivalent groups and correlating the item responses to estimate reliability. This approach is really a version of the alternative-forms technique.

For example, if we believed that the retail image was composed of a single characteristic or dimension (e.g., favorable-unfavorable image dimension), we could use split-half reliability to measure the internal consistency or internal homogeneity of the 20 items forming the retail image–measuring instrument. Here, each item is assumed to measure this single characteristic independently. The approach would be to randomly divide the 20 items into two groups and determine the degree of correspondence. A high correlation coefficient means that the items are measuring the same characteristic.

An easy measure of validity would be to compare the observed measurement with the true measure. However, rarely do we know the true measure, and if we did, there would be no reason to measure it in the first place. Consequently, what we do is to infer the validity of the observed measurement using one or more estimation methods. The major ways to estimate the validity of measurement are (1) construct validity, (2) content validity, (3) concurrent validity, and (4) predictive validity.

Construct Validity   *Construct validity* involves understanding the theoretical rationale underlying the obtained measurements. The approach is to relate the construct of interest to other constructs such that a theoretical framework is developed for the marketing phenomenon being measured. Construct validity increases as the correlation between the construct of interest and the related constructs increases in the predicted manner.

To illustrate construct validity, assume that a sales manager believes there is a relationship among job satisfaction, degree of extrovert personality, and job performance of a sales force. Construct validity could be assessed by developing measures of these three constructs and ascertaining the relationship among the measures for a group of sales personnel. Those who have high job satisfaction and extrovert personalities should exhibit high job performance scores; if they do not, we could question the construct validity of the measures and/or question the validity of the hypothesized relationship. If that relationship is sufficiently confirmed from previous research, the conclusion could be drawn that the measures do not measure what we think they measure.

Construct validity can be evaluated with other approaches. If a construct exists, it should be successfully measured by methods that are different or independent. *Convergent validity* involves the measurement of a construct with independent measurement techniques and the demonstration of a high correlation among the measures. Alternatively, if a construct exists, it should be distinguished from constructs that differ from it. *Discriminant validity* involves demonstrating a lack of correlation among differing constructs.

Content Validity   *Content validity* involves a subjective judgment by an expert as to the appropriateness of the measurement. This is a common method used in marketing research to determine the validity of measurements.

To illustrate content validity, assume we are going to measure the image of retail stores in a grocery chain. Rather than asking a simple question, we will develop a multi-item measuring technique. Assume that 20 items or questions are proposed which, when combined in an index, represent the measure of store image. The content validity of these 20 items would be determined by having an expert or experts assess the representativeness of the items used to measure store image. The content validity could be challenged if items such as store cleanliness, friendly atmosphere, or price competitiveness were excluded from the list of items. Content validity is frequently called *face validity* because of the emphasis on the expert's critical eye in determining the relevance of the measurements to the underlying construct.

Concurrent Validity   *Concurrent validity* involves correlating two different measurements of the same marketing phenomenon which have been administered at the same point in time. It is primarily used to determine the validity of new measuring techniques by correlating them with established techniques.

To illustrate concurrent validity, assume that our previous 20-item measurement technique of store image is valid. Also, assume that an alternative and shorter technique is proposed. Concurrent validation would involve administering both techniques under similar or identical conditions and correlating the two measures of store image. A high correlation would establish the concurrent validity of the new technique. The key issue here is that the validity of the measurement is judged by the existence of another criterion measure taken at the same time. For example, a positive medical test for mononucleosis is highly correlated with the existence of the disease now.

Predictive Validity   *Predictive validity* involves the ability of a measured marketing phenomenon at one point in time to predict another marketing phenomenon at a future point in time. If the correlation among the two measures is high, the initial measure is said to have predictive validity, sometimes also called *pragmatic validity* or *criterion-related validity.* It is to be distinguished from concurrent validity, when the two correlated measures occur at the same point in time.

To illustrate predictive validity, consider the use of the Scholastic Aptitude Test (SAT) to predict college performance. Here, the test measures the student's aptitude for college-level work, and this is used as a predictor of future performance at college. The wide use of this test by colleges attests to its predictive validity.

MEASUREMENT IN INTERNATIONAL MARKETING RESEARCH

All the difficulties of measurement in marketing, the nature of the number system, types of scales, and the issues of reliability and validity apply equally well to both domestic and international marketing research. However, there is one major measurement concern that arises uniquely in international marketing research. This is the issue of the reliability and validity of a measurement construct across countries or cultures.

For example, a global consumer financial services company may want to use demographic and life-style measures across many countries in its marketing research for a new type of mutual fund. Would such measures be reliable and valid across many countries? The evidence to date suggests that measures are highly reliable across countries for hard variables like demographics, but have limited reliability for soft variables such as life-style, product involvement, and attitude scales.[2] In addition, the validity of these types of soft constructs needs to be

[2]For examples of these types of results, see Harry L. Davis, Susan P. Douglas, and Alvin J. Silk, "Measurement Unreliability: A Hidden Threat to Cross-National Marketing Research," *Journal of Marketing,* pp. 98–109, Spring 1981; Ravi Parameswaren and Attila Yaprak, "A Cross-National Comparison of Consumer Research Measures," *Journal of International Business Studies,* pp. 35–49, Spring 1987.

ascertained uniquely in each country. Thus great care must be taken when using these soft measures in the international context.

The Global Marketing Research Dynamics gives some examples of international measurement difficulties.

GLOBAL MARKETING RESEARCH DYNAMICS

MEASUREMENT DIFFICULTIES IN INTERNATIONAL MARKETING RESEARCH

• A set of attitude questions about the need for government regulation of business affairs received very high scores (indicating the desire for high government involvement) from respondents in Poland and Russia. However, when it was made clear to the respondents that government officials and police would not have access to their answers, the desire for government involvement in business affairs declined significantly.

• A major international marketer of industrial machine tools found significantly different reliability measures on attitude measures related to the use of technology in manufacturing. Middle Eastern manufacturers had much lower reliability measures on these measures than did their U.S. counterparts, for whom the measures were originally developed.

• The sales manager of a German company used an aptitude test to screen prospective hires for the company's sales force. This instrument had high measures of predictive validity for the success of its German salespeople. However, when the test was applied elsewhere, it had very low predictive validity results in its French and U.S. subsidiaries.

SUMMARY

1 The process of measurement is a fundamental aspect of marketing research. It involves the use of numbers to represent the marketing phenomena under investigation.

2 Measurement is defined as the assignment of numbers to characteristics of objects or events according to rules. It is the characteristics of the objects or events that are measured, not the items themselves. Measurement error is present when the characteristics of the number system do not represent the relationships present in the marketing phenomena being measured.

3 The four characteristics of the number system—equality of numerals, order of numerals, equality of differences, and equality of ratios—correspond to the four scales of measurement, that is, nominal, ordinal, interval, and ratio. A nominal scale consists of identifying and categorizing, with no implications of "more or less." An ordinal scale involves the determination of more or less but with no indication as to the distance or interval. An interval scale involves the determination of distance, while a ratio scale involves the additional characteristic of an absolute zero point.

4 Each of these four types of measurement is important in marketing research. Significant marketing phenomena exist at each level of measurement. As we move from nominal to ratio measurement, the rules for assigning numerals to the marketing phenomena become increasingly more restrictive. However, as these rules become more restrictive, the range and sophistication of statistical techniques for data analysis increase.

5 The measurement task in marketing is typically more difficult and involves lower scales of measurement than those found in the physical sciences. The problem lies in the measurement of the behavior of people. This often involves measuring concepts or constructs believed to exist in people's minds. The measurement process requires that the construct be operationally defined. Marketing has few examples of standardized operational definitions of constructs.

6 The total error of measurement consists of two components: systematic and random error. The validity of a measurement refers to the extent to which the measurement process is free from both systematic and random error. The reliability of a measure refers to the extent to which the measurement process is free from random error. Measurement can be valid and reliable; not valid, but reliable; or neither valid nor reliable. Reliability is a necessary but not a sufficient condition for validity.

7 The main methods for estimating validity and reliability are (a) construct validity, (b) content validity, (c) concurrent validity, (d) predictive validity, (e) test-retest reliability, (f) alternative-forms reliability, and (g) split-half reliability. Reliability is a weaker concept than validity since it involves only random error. Consequently, reliability is easier to measure than validity and is reported more frequently in research studies.

DISCUSSION QUESTIONS

1 What is measurement?

2 What is the objective of the measurement process?

3 What role does measurement play in marketing?

4 Why is measurement so difficult in marketing?

5 What are the four characteristics of the number system?

6 Distinguish among the four scales of measurement. Give examples of the types of marketing phenomena which each scale might be used to measure.

7 What is measurement error?

8 Distinguish between the validity and the reliability of a measure.

9 Discuss the major ways in which the validity of measurement is assessed.

10 How may the reliability of a measure be evaluated?

11 MINICASE

In its domestic U.S. operations, the Gillette Company makes extensive use of consumer measures about advertisements that it is considering using on television. These measures include: awareness, brand association, recall, and believability. Gillette has standard measures of each of these constructs. While the company is considering a major new marketing entry into Korea, Japan, Singapore, and Indonesia, concern has been raised about the appropriateness of these standard measures.

a How could each of these constructs be measured?

b What scale level would these constructs be?

c What steps could Gillette take to determine the appropriateness of these measures in the new markets? Be specific.

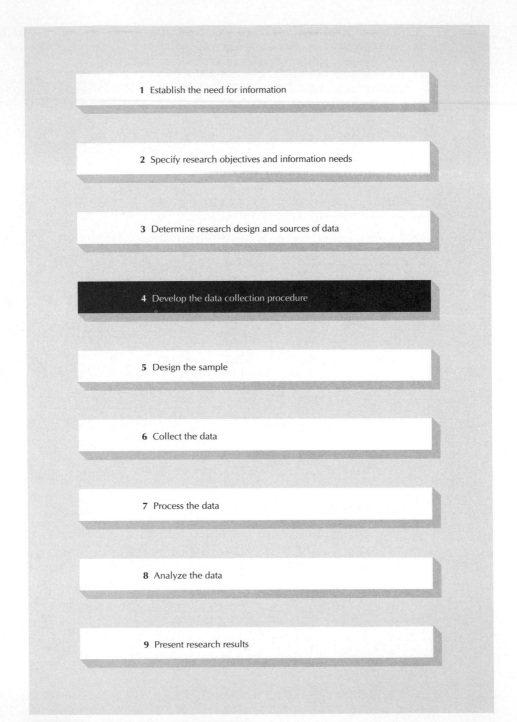

FIGURE 8-1   Steps in the research process.

CHAPTER 8

ATTITUDE MEASUREMENT

MARKETING RESEARCH IN ACTION

WAL-MART THRIVES IN HONG KONG

Wal-Mart has made a successful entry into the Hong Kong market and is now considering entry into the mainland Chinese market. This has been accomplished without opening stores that resemble, in any meaningful way, the classic U.S.-based Wal-Mart or Sam's Club stores. "There was a tremendous need for Wal-Mart to adapt to the unique Hong Kong shopping attitudes and habits," noted one marketing expert.

The outlets that Wal-Mart chose to open are called "Value Clubs." These outlets are targeted at both individual consumers and small businesses. Each is somewhat like a small Sam's Club. Even the location of these stores reflects unique Hong Kong dynamics. They tend to be located in malls, amid high-rise apartment buildings. In addition, Wal-Mart offers small sizes of packages and smaller lots than in the United States.

Just what attitudes of Hong Kong residents and business managers make this different format a successful one? Listed below are some of the attitude findings of a study of Hong Kong residents and business managers.

1 They are extremely price-sensitive, and they view shopping almost as a game to find the lowest price.

2 They view store location as critical, and view traveling long distances to shop as wasteful and difficult.

3 Even a trip of a few miles is viewed as long due to the inconvenience of cars and the subway in the crowded environment of Hong Kong.

4 Hong Kong residents view their apartments as small and not able to store much inventory of goods. For example, they have no desire to store five or six bottles of shampoo just to get a bargain.

By understanding and adapting to these attitudes Wal-Mart has created real value for its Hong Kong consumers and a success story for itself. Thus, Wal-Mart's locations are located near where the consumers live. They are small stores, reflecting the size of the population within walking or biking distance from each store, and they carry small sizes of products that are sold in small lot sizes.

Source: Based on Neil Herndon, "Wal-Mart Goes to Hong Kong, Looks at China," *Advertising Age,* p. 2, November 21, 1994.

The marketing manager for a leading hair shampoo aimed at the female market is listening to an exploratory research group discussion on women's reactions to the product. The following statements are typical of this discussion:

"I like the plastic bottle."

"It has lots of suds."

"I don't like the rose smell."

"This is a high-priced product."

"I don't buy it anymore."

"I always purchase that product."

After listening to this discussion for more than an hour, the marketing research manager is asked to comment on what this discussion means and why it is important. How would you respond? It would be important to characterize clearly the meaning of the attitudes expressed by the discusson group, to establish why these attitudes are important to the successful marketing of the product, and to point out how the significance of these attitudes can be established by formally measuring the attitudes in the context of a conclusive research study.

The objective of this chapter is to address the above issues by building on our discussion of the measurement process in the previous chapter. In the first section the importance of attitudes in marketing will be discussed. The second section provides a detailed discussion of the nature of attitudes, and the final section discusses the many approaches used to measure attitudes.

IMPORTANCE OF ATTITUDES IN MARKETING

The measurement of attitudes is central to many marketing situations. The strategy of market segmentation is often based on attitudinal data. Determining the attitudes of different market segments toward a product can be essential to developing a "positioning" strategy. Attitude measurement is often the basis for evaluating the effectiveness of an advertising campaign. In addition, the assumed relationship between attitudes and behavior helps in the prediction of product acceptance and in the development of marketing programs.

NATURE OF ATTITUDES

An *attitude* is an individual's enduring perceptual, knowledge-based, evaluative, and action-oriented processes with respect to an object or phenomenon.

Components of Attitude

Attitudes are generally considered to have three main components: (1) a *cognitive* component—a person's beliefs about the object of concern, such as its speed or durability; (2) an *affective* component—a person's feelings about the object, such as "good" or "bad"; and (3) a *behavioral* component—a person's readiness to respond behaviorally to the object.

Link between Attitude and Behavior

Attitudes are important in marketing decision making because of the assumed relationship between attitudes and behavior. Models that conceptualize the construct of attitude typically represent an attitude as a series of sequential components which lead to behavior. Research evidence indicates that the link between attitudes and behavior is not simplistic, and the decision maker and researcher should be cautious in assuming that such a relationship exists in a decision situation. The prediction of future behavior for an aggregate of buyers does appear to be higher than the prediction of behavior regarding an individual buyer. Since most decision situations are concerned with aggregate behavior rather than individual behavior, the attitude-behavior link does have some empirical support for many marketing decision situations. However, attitudes are only one influence on behavior, and in a particular decision situation other factors could be more influential than attitudes. An obvious example would be an individual who has a highly favorable attitude toward purchasing a new sports car but, because of economic constraints, has to purchase a less desirable used compact.

The marketing implications of this attitude-behavior link relate to measuring the cognitive and affective components of the buyer's attitude and being able to predict future purchase behavior. Alternatively, by influencing the cognitive and affective components, purchase behavior could be influenced.

Model of Behavioral Response

The purpose of marketing activity is to bring about some response from the targeted market segment. The response may be at the cognitive, affective, or behavioral level. Figure 8-2 shows these three basic levels of response plus a more detailed

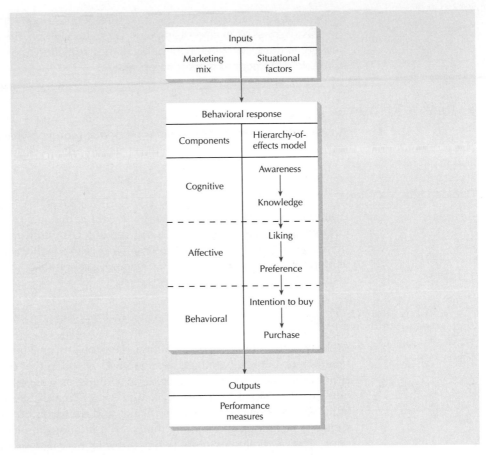

FIGURE 8-2   Model of behavioral response.

classification called the *hierarchy-of-effects model.* This model hypothesizes that the buyer passes through the stages of awareness, knowledge, liking, preference, intention to buy, and purchase in succession. Research suggests that these stages can occur in different sequences, depending on the degree of buyer involvement with the purchase and the degree of differentiation among the alternatives.

Cognitive Component   The *cognitive component* refers to the respondent's awareness of and knowledge about some object or phenomenon. This is some-times called the *belief component.* It is expressed by statements such as: "I believe product A does . . ." or "I know that product B will. . . ."

The cognitive component is of considerable importance for many types of information needs. Many decision situations require information regarding the market's awareness of or knowledge about product features, advertising cam-paigns, pricing, product availability, and so on.

Affective Component   The *affective component* refers to the respondent's liking and preference for an object or phenomenon. Sometimes called the *feeling component,* it is expressed by such statements as "I dislike product A," "Advertisement X is poor," and "I prefer product A to product B."

The affective component, like the cognitive component, is an important aspect of the information needs for many decision situations. Examples include determining buyers' positive and negative feelings and preferences regarding the organization's marketing program as well as those of competitors.

Behavior Component   The *behavioral component* refers to the respondent's intention to buy and actual purchase behavior. The *intention-to-buy stage* refers to the respondent's predisposition to action prior to the actual purchase decision. Marketers are interested in respondents' buying intentions as indicators of future purchase behavior. A well-known survey regarding purchase intentions is conducted by the Survey Research Center at the University of Michigan. The center asks consumers about their buying intentions for durable goods such as automobiles and appliances during the next few months. The assumption is that the decision process for durable goods involves extensive planning and that purchase intentions should correlate with actual purchase behavior. Despite this logic, the predictive ability of data regarding intentions appears to be lower than many would anticipate.

Behavior refers to what the respondents have done or are doing. In marketing, *behavior* refers to the buyer's purchase and use patterns for a product or service. Information needs typically focus on what is purchased, how much, where and when the purchase took place, the circumstances surrounding the purchase, and the characteristics of the buyer. The measurement of behavior involves the development of a comprehensive description of the purchase situation.

Difficulty of Measuring Attitude

As discussed in Chapter 7, the measurement task in marketing is typically more difficult and involves lower scales of measurement than are used in the physical sciences. A prime example of this difficulty is the measurement of the construct of attitude, which exists in the minds of individuals and is not directly observable. *Attitude scaling* refers to the various operational definitions developed for the measurement of this construct.

In measuring attitudes, one must be sensitive to the scale-level assumptions and the restrictions these assumptions impose on data analysis. Typically, attitudes are measured at the nominal or ordinal level, although several more complex scaling procedures allow measurement at the interval level. There is always the temptation to assume that the attitude measurements have the more powerful properties of an interval scale. The researcher must always be sensitive to these questions: (1) What are the characteristics of the construct being measured? (2) What properties of the number system properly relate to this construct?

ATTITUDE-SCALING PROCEDURES

"Attitude scaling" is the term commonly used to refer to the process of measuring attitudes. Attitude scaling in marketing tends to focus on the measurement of the respondent's beliefs about a product's attributes (cognitive component) and the respondent's feelings regarding the desirability of these attributes (affective component). Some combination of beliefs and feelings typically is assumed to determine intention to buy (behavioral component).

General Methods of Attitude Measurement

Attitude measurement procedures rely on data from respondents. The measuring techniques can be grouped into those based on communicating with respondents and those based on observing respondents.

Communication Techniques

1 *Self-reports.* Respondents are directly asked to report their beliefs or feelings by responding to one or more questions on a questionnaire. A number of scaling techniques have been developed to measure these beliefs and feelings.

2 *Responses to unstructured or partially structured stimuli.* The respondents are shown a picture of a product being purchased or used, or some other situation, and are asked to express their reaction. Other approaches include story telling, word-association tests, and sentence completion.

3 *Performance of objective tasks.* Respondents are asked to memorize and/or report factual information about products. These responses are analyzed, and inferences are drawn regarding the nature of the respondent's beliefs and feelings. The assumption is that respondents are more likely to remember the things that are consistent with their beliefs and feelings.

Observation Techniques

1 *Overt behavior.* Individuals are put in a situation that allows their behavior patterns to be exhibited. Inferences can thus be drawn regarding their beliefs and feelings. This technique is based on the assumption that people's behavior is dependent on their beliefs and feelings.

2 *Physiological reactions.* Respondents are exposed to products or advertisements, and their physiological reactions are measured. The measurement device typically is the galvanic skin response (GSR) technique, which measures sweating of the hand, or the eye dilation technique, which measures changes in the diameter of the pupil of the eye. A limitation of the physiological response approach is that it measures only the intensity of feelings and not their direction (positive or negative).

Of these general methods for measuring attitudes, the self-reporting technique is by far the most widely used, and the remainder of this chapter will focus on the various scaling procedures that use it. These procedures are most appropriate for conclusive research studies which require that attitudes be formally measured and quantified using a large sample of respondents. The remaining general methods for measuring attitudes are most appropriate for exploratory research designed to develop the nature of beliefs and feelings present in a decision situation. These remaining methods will be discussed in more detail in Chapters 10 and 11, which deal with data collection methods.

Self-Reporting Techniques

As stated above, the most common tool of attitude measurement is the self-reporting technique. Several self-reporting techniques will be discussed here, with emphasis on the development of unidimensional scales.

Nominal Scales   The simplest self-reporting scale is a *nominal scale,* where the respondent's beliefs are classified in two or more categories. For example, a nominal scale can be developed from responses to the question: "Does your automobile have radial tires—yes or no?" A third category of "don't know" might be included for those respondents who are not informed concerning this feature of their automobile. The result of this scaling is a three-category classification of respondents with respect to their responses—yes, no, and don't know. Here a nominal scale has been developed, and numbers can be assigned to the categories for data analysis purposes. Keep in mind that these numbers can be used only to identify the categories. Table 8-1 indicates that about 89 percent of businesses use nominal scales in their marketing research.

Rating Scales   *Rating scales* refer to measurement situations that involve ordinal, interval, and ratio scales. Typically, the focus of the measurement situation is on developing ordinal or interval scales of the affective component.

A rating scale requires the respondent to indicate the position on a continuum or among ordered categories that correspond to his or her attitude. Numerical values may be part of the scale or be assigned after the respondent completes the

TABLE 8-1   USE OF MEASUREMENT SCALES IN MARKETING RESEARCH BY BUSINESS

Type of scale	Percent usage		
	Frequent	Sometimes	Never
Nominal	63	26	12
Rating	77	20	3
Rank-order	53	35	12
Paired-comparison	31	35	34
Semantic differential	26	34	40
Staple	1	7	92
Likert	47	21	32

Source: Thomas C. Kinnear and Ann R. Root, *A Study of the Marketing Research Business,* unpublished study, 1994. Copyright 1994 Thomas C. Kinnear. Not to be reproduced.

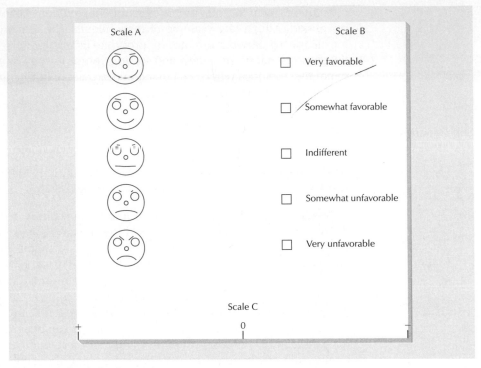

FIGURE 8-3   Graphic and verbal rating scales.

self-rating task. Table 8-1 indicates that about 96 percent of businesses use rating scales in their marketing research.

An ordinal scale is formed when respondents order themselves by responding to a question such as "Do you like or dislike radial tires, or are you indifferent to them?" The result of this scaling is a three-category ordinal scale that ranks the respondents according to their feeling about radial tires, that is, like—indifferent—dislike. Numbers can be assigned to these ordered categories for purposes of data analysis.

Graphic Rating Scales   A *graphic rating scale* requires the respondents to indicate their position on a continuum that ranges from one extreme of the attitude in question to the other extreme. The format of this graphic continuum is as varied as the imaginations of the researchers who devise such a scale.

Figure 8-3 presents two different examples of graphic scales (scales A and C). Let's assume that several respondents have sampled a new formulation of cake mix, and we want to measure their feelings about the sweetness of the cake mix. Scale A relies on a series of facial expressions to represent the varying degrees of like and dislike. The respondents are asked to indicate which of the facial expressions best represents their reaction to the sweetness level. A most favorable response means the sweetness level is "just right" (extreme smile) while a least favorable response (extreme frown) means the cake is either "too sweet" or "not sweet enough." Such an unfavorable response would require additional questioning of the respondent to determine what was wrong with the sweetness level. Graphic scales of this nature are especially useful when the researcher and the respondents speak different languages or when the respondents are children.

Scale C presents a positive-negative continuum. The respondents are asked to indicate their position by checking a location on this continuum. Once the judgments are recorded, the researcher can subdivide the continuum into an appropriate set of categories and assign numerals to the judgments. It is argued that the advantage of this continuous scale is that the respondent is not confronted with a predetermined set of response categories. Rather, the categorization of the scale is left to the respondent, who implicitly determines the number of categories during the judgment process. A disadvantage of this graphic scale is that it requires the respondent to deal with an abstract judgment situation. In addition, since the researcher does not know how the respondents subdivided the continuum, the comparison and grouping of responses across respondents are difficult to justify.

Verbal Rating Scales   *Verbal rating scales* are probably the most frequently used scales in marketing research. These require the respondents to indicate their position by selecting among verbally identified categories. Scale B in Figure 8-3 is an example; here, the respondents are asked to check the box adjacent to the phrase that best corresponds to their reaction given the question at hand.

It is important to understand the issues surrounding the construction of verbal rating scales. The major issues are: (1) number of categories, (2) odd or even number of categories, (3) balanced versus unbalanced scale, (4) extent of verbal description, (5) category numbering, (6) forced versus nonforced scales, and (7) comparative versus noncomparative scales.

While there is no established *number of categories* which is deemed optimal for a scale, in practice scales of five or six categories are typical. Some researchers argue that more than five or six are needed in situations where small changes in attitude are to be measured. Others argue that it is doubtful that the majority of respondents can distinguish between more than six to eight categories. Beyond this point, additional categories do not increase the precision with which the attitude is being measured. Most researchers find that it is as easy to administer and analyze a scale with five or seven categories as it is to use one with, say, three categories. Consequently, researchers typically utilize at least a five-category scale unless special circumstances dictate fewer or more categories.

Should the scale have an *odd or even number* of scale categories? The answer to this is unclear. If an odd number of categories is selected, the middle category is typically identified as a neutral position. If an even number is selected, the scale does not have a neutral category, and the respondent is forced to take a position expressing some degree of feeling. The results of a research study comparing an odd (seven-category) scale with an even (six-category) scale concluded that there was no significant difference in the results between scales.

Should the number of favorable and unfavorable categories be *balanced or unbalanced?* A balanced scale has the same number of favorable categories as unfavorable categories. The argument for an unbalanced scale relates to the nature of the attitude distribution to be measured. If the distribution is predominantly favorable, an unbalanced scale with more favorable categories than unfavorable categories will be appropriate. The argument for balanced scales emphasizes the potential biasing of responses which can result from limiting the response categories on the favorable or unfavorable side of the scale.

How extensive should the *verbal description* of a category be? Some researchers believe that clearly defined response categories increase the reliability of the measurements. It is argued that each category should have a verbal description and that these verbal descriptions should have a clear and precise wording such that each response category is differentiated.

In many situations the researcher believes that the respondent's judgments can be treated as interval data. Implicit in this decision is the assumption that the respondent views the differences between verbal descriptions to be equally spaced. When using the phrases "very good," and "neutral" as verbal descriptions for an interval scale, the researcher assumes that the distance between "very good" and "neutral" is twice the distance of that between "fairly good" and "neutral." A research study that measured the relative size of "very" and "fairly" found a respective weight of $+3.74$ and $+1.22$ rather than the assumed weight of $+2$ and $+1$, respectively. In this situation, the assignment of the weights $+2$ and $+1$ for purposes of data analysis would obviously introduce measurement error into the research results. It is common practice to treat rating scales as interval scales and to compute means and standard deviations on such measurements. The researcher should be sensitive to this practice and remember the potential for measurement error in the research findings.

Should *numbers* be assigned to the response categories? The argument is that they should be used when the researcher believes the respondent's judgments can be treated as interval data. The numbers 5, 4, 3, 2, and 1 could be used on a five-category scale to communicate to the respondent that the intervals between response categories are intended to be of equal distance.

Another issue in constructing a rating scale concerns the use of a *forced scale* versus a *nonforced scale.* A forced scale requires all respondents to indicate a position on the attitude scale. The argument for a forced scale is that those who are reluctant to reveal their attitude are encouraged to do so with the forced scale. Respondents who have no opinion or no knowledge typically mark the "neutral" category on the scale. In case a significant proportion of the respondents may have no opinion rather than a reluctance to reveal their feelings, it is best to include a category such as "no opinion" or "no knowledge" rather than forcing the respondents to choose the neutral category.

A final issue concerns the use of *comparative scales* versus *noncomparative scales.* A comparative scale requires the respondents to express their attitudes by making a direct comparison with a standard or reference point. This reference point could be the current brand used, an ideal product, or a competitive product. A comparative scale allows the researcher to report the respondents' attitudes relative to a standard that may be of importance in a decision situation. The argument for noncomparative scales is that they allow each respondent to choose his or her own reference point, and that consequently a more accurate measurement of the respondent's attitude is achieved. In practice, the selection of comparative and noncomparative scales is dependent on the specific information needs of the decision situation.

Rank-Order Scales   The *rank-order technique* involves having the respondent rank various objects with regard to the attitude in question. Thus, the respondent may be required to rank five print advertisements on the basis of awareness of, liking for, preference for, or intention to buy the product advertised.

The rank-order technique is widely used in marketing research. It is comparative in nature and forms an ordinal scale of the objects evaluated. Table 8-1 indicates that about 88 percent of businesses use rank-order scales in their marketing research.

This technique has important advantages. It is simple in concept, easy to administer, and less time-consuming to administer than other comparative techniques, such as paired comparison. The instructions for ranking objects are easy to comprehend; consequently, the technique can be used on self-administered questionnaires. In addition, it is argued that the technique is similar to the purchase decision process and forces respondents to discriminate among products in a realistic manner.

The limitations of rank-order techniques are important also. The forced-choice and comparative nature of the technique results in a ranking of objects regardless of the attitudinal position of the respondent to the objects as a group. It could be that the respondent "dislikes" all the objects in the set. In this case, the object ranked first is the least "disliked" of the objects in the set. Obviously the researcher must be sensitive to the attitudinal position of the respondent and be confident that a realistic set of objects is being evaluated.

Another limitation of the rank-order technique is the fact that it produces only ordinal data. While there are scaling technique that form higher-order scales based on ranked input data, these techniques bring a degree of complexity to the data collection and analysis phase which may be undesirable. Finally, several research studies have found that the ranking and rating-scale techniques yield similar results. Other things being equal, in selecting between these two techniques researchers must weigh the pros and cons of each technique against the specific needs of the research project.

Paired-Comparison Scales   On a *paired-comparison scale,* respondents are presented with two objects from a set and required to pick one with regard to the attitude in question. Thus, the respondent is required to make a series of paired judgments between objects regarding preference, amount of some attribute present, and so on. This sort of scale is used by 66 percent of businesses.

The data collection procedure typically requires the respondent to compare all possible pairs of the objects. If there are 5 objects ($n = 5$) to be evaluated, there will be 10 paired comparisons [$n(n - 1)/2$] required in the judgment task. The evaluation of 10 objects requires 45 paired comparisons. The geometric expansion in the number of paired comparisons limits the usefulness of this technique for the evaluation of large object sets.

In Table 8-2, matrix I presents paired-comparison data for five brands of cake mix, A, B, C, D, and E. The judgment task was to pick the cake mix sample that had the lightest and fluffiest texture. Each cell entry in matrix I represents the proportion of respondents who believed that the "column" brand has more of the attributes in question than the "row" brand. For example, in the brand A versus brand B comparison 90 percent of the respondents believed that brand B was lighter and fluffier than A. An inspection of the column proportions reveals that brand B dominates the other brands on this attribute.

How can an ordinal scale be developed, given these paired-comparison data? The first step is to convert matrix I to 0–1 scores, which indicate whether the column brand dominates the row brand and vice versa (see matrix II in Table 8-2). Here, "1" is assigned to a cell if the column brand dominates the row brand (if the proportion $>.5$), and "0" is assigned to a cell if the column brand does not dominate the row brand (if the proportion $\leq.5$). The ordinal relationship among brands is determined by totaling the columns. Here, the ordinal scaling of the brands is $B > C > A > E > D$. Thus, brand B has the lightest and fluffiest texture, followed by C, A, E, and D.

The arguments in favor of the paired-comparison technique relate to the simplicity of the judgment task, the comparative nature of the task, and the availability of scaling methods that produce interval data. This interval-scaling feature can be important in assessing differences among competitive products and advertisements.

TABLE 8-2   PAIRED-COMPARISON DATA

	Matrix I				
	A	B	C	D	E
A	—	.90	.64	.14	.27
B	.10	—	.32	.02	.21
C	.36	.68	—	.15	.36
D	.86	.98	.85	—	.52
E	.73	.79	.64	.48	—

	Matrix II				
	A	B	C	D	E
A	—	1	1	0	0
B	0	—	0	0	0
C	0	1	—	0	0
D	1	1	1	—	1
E	1	1	1	0	—
Total	2	4	3	0	1

The paired-comparison technique has important limitations. As the number of objects to be evaluated increases arithmetically, the number of paired comparisons increases geometrically. Consequently, the technique is limited to a small number of objects in order to control respondent fatigue during the judgment process. In addition, research indicates that the order in which the objects are presented can bias the results, that the paired-comparison task is not typical of the actual choice process present in the marketplace, and that simpler noncomparative rating scales provide results similar to those obtained from paired comparisons.

Semantic Differential Scales   Use of the *semantic differential scale* is a popular attitude measurement technique in marketing research. The main application of the semantic differential has been in connection with company and brand image studies. Table 8-1 indicates that about 60 percent of businesses use the semantic differential scale in their marketing research.

An image can be defined as an average of many separate attitudes toward a company, a brand, or a concept. As discussed previously, each separate attitude has three components—cognitive, affective, and behavioral. Consequently, image measurement requires the respondents to express their position on many attitudes using a multiscale questionnaire.

The semantic differential typically requires the respondents to evaluate an object on a 7-point rating scale bounded at each end by bipolar adjectives. For example:

Retail store X

Reliable	__:	__:	_X_:	__:	__:	__:	__:	**Unreliable**
Friendly	_X_:	__:	__:	__:	__:	__:	__:	**Unfriendly**
Modern	__:	__:	__:	__:	_X_:	__:	__:	**Old-fashioned**
Inexpensive	__:	__:	__:	__:	__:	_X_:	__:	**Expensive**
Progressive	__:	__:	__:	_X_:	__:	__:	__:	**Not progressive**

Respondents are instructed to check the blank location that most accurately reflects their position regarding the object in connection with each of the bipolar adjectives. The technique is typically adapted to fit the specific needs to the research project at hand, as the following examples demonstrate.

1 The single-word adjectives are sometimes replaced with descriptive phrases tailored to a particular company, product, or concept. The following could be used, for example, to measure the brand image of a cola soft drink:

Very special drink—Just another drink
Fun type of drink—Kind of serious drink
Regular people drink it—Snobs drink it

2 The polar opposites have been replaced with phrases that may not include extremes and may eliminate the negative portion of the scale. The reason is that some respondents are unwilling to check the extremes of a scale, and some either are unwilling to express a negative view or do not have negative views toward the objects under investigation. The following phrases represent this adaptation:

High-quality product—So-so product
Modern company—Somewhat old-fashioned company

3 Many researchers have the respondent evaluate an "ideal product" or an "ideal company" in addition to the objects under investigation. This approach allows the objects under investigation to be compared to a norm or standard.

4 Each position on the scale can be assigned a numerical value, such as 7, 6, 5, 4, 3, 2, 1 or +3, +2, +1, 0, −1, −2, −3. The assumption is that the respondents' judgments can be treated as interval data, which makes possible the calculation of the arithmetic mean for an object on each scale. This approach is widely accepted by researchers who use the semantic differential. However, there is a controversy as to whether these measurements can be treated as interval data. Critics argue that the median is the appropriate summary measure.

FIGURE 8-4   Profile analysis of beer brand images.

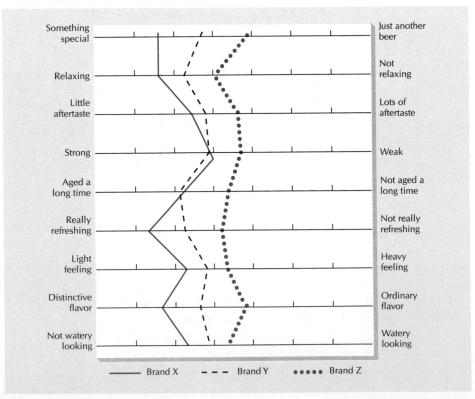

Semantic differential data are typically analyzed using the profile analysis approach. This involves calculating the arithmetic mean or median for each set of verbal phrases or polar opposites for each object evaluated. These summary measures are usually plotted on the scales such that the profiles of the objects can be compared. Figure 8-4 provides an illustration of the profiles for three brands of beer. Brand X has the most favorable brand image, while brand Z has the least favorable image. All three brand images are on the positive side of the scales.

The popularity of the semantic differential is attributed to its versatility and simplicity. The technique is easy to develop and administer, and the results can be readily communicated to management. In addition, it has been found to be a discriminating and reliable research tool.

The limitation of the schematic differential relates to the requirement that the scales be composed of true bipolar adjectives or phrases. It is argued that the pilot testing necessary to meet this requirement can be expensive and time-consuming. In practice, formal pilot testing is rarely done, and the bipolar adjectives or phrases are developed using the researcher's judgment.

Stapel Scales The *Stapel scale* is a modification of the semantic differential scale. Table 8-1 indicates that about 8 percent of businesses use the Stapel scale in their marketing research. It is a unipolar 10-point nonverbal rating scale with values ranging from $+5$ to -5. The scaling technique is designed to measure the direction and intensity of attitudes simultaneously. If differs from the semantic differential in that the scale values indicate how closely the descriptor or adjective fits the object evaluated.

Table 8-3 presents the format of a Stapel scale. Respondents are instructed to evaluate how accurately the adjective or phrase describes the object to be evaluated. The following instructions are given to the respondent:

You would select a *plus* number for words that you think describe (Bank A) accurately. The more accurately you think the word describes it, the larger the *plus* number you would choose. You would select a *minus* number for words you think do not describe

TABLE 8-3   STAPEL SCALE FORMAT

	Bank	
	$+5$	$+5$
	$+4$	$+4$
	$+3$	$+3$
	$+2$	$+2$
	$+1$	$+1$
Fast service	Friendly	
	-1	-1
	-2	-2
	-3	-3
	-4	-4
	-5	-5

it accurately. The less accurately you think a word describes it, the larger the *minus* number you would choose. Therefore, you can select any number from +5, for words that you think are very accurate, all the way to −5, for words that you think are very inaccurate.

Unipolar judgments can be analyzed the same way that semantic differential data are treated. Figure 8-5 presents hypothetical results of a profile analysis of two banks based on Stapel-scale data.

The arguments in favor of the Stapel scale relate to its convenience of administration and the absence of the requirement that the scales be composed of truly bipolar adjectives or phrases. Research indicates that the Stapel scale can produce results similar to those of the semantic differential. In addition, the scale has produced satisfactory results when administered over the telephone. Despite these advantages, the Stapel scale has experienced limited use in marketing research in comparison to the semantic differential. It appears to be a useful technique that is growing in popularity with researchers.

INTERNATIONAL ATTITUDE RESEARCH

The attitude measurement procedures described in this chapter are equally applicable to both domestic and international marketing research. As noted in Chapter 7, great care must be taken to assure the reliability and validity of the attitude measures used internationally. The Global Marketing Research Dynamics describes the use of life-style scales by international marketing research suppliers.

FIGURE 8-5   Stapel scale comparative profiles.

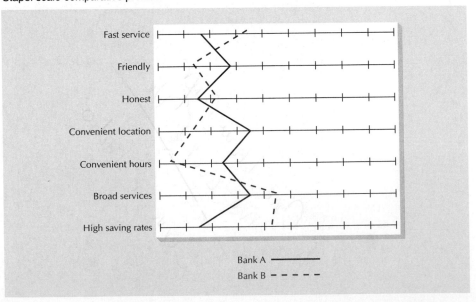

GLOBAL MARKETING RESEARCH DYNAMICS

INTERNATIONAL ATTITUDE MEASURES HELP IDENTIFY SEGMENTS

There are several attitude-based segmentation systems available to international marketers.

One such service is Global Scan. Developed by Backer Spielvogel & Bates Worldwide in 1985, this program includes 18 countries and uses a 250-question survey in which half the questions are specific to the respondents' country and half are "global" questions that measure values such as self-esteem and self-sufficiency. Six segments are consistently identified, as follows: (1) *Strivers*. Young people living hectic lives. (2) *Achievers*. People who have the success strivers want. (3) *Pressureds*. Mainly women who face constant financial and family pressures. (4) *Adapters*. Older people who are content with their lives. (5) *Traditionals*. People who resist change. (6) *Unassigneds*. People who defy the above classifications.

In the 1990s, SRI International established the Japan VALS program to determine the consumer effects of changing values and social attitudes in Japan. Ten segments were identified, as follows: (1) *Integrators*. Well-educated, modern people who enjoy the new and risky. (2) *Sustainers*. People who resist change. (3) *Self-innovators*.

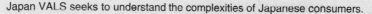

Japan VALS seeks to understand the complexities of Japanese consumers.

Young, active people who spend a lot of money on themselves. (4) *Self-adapters.* Shy people who pattern their buying after that of self-innovators. (5) *Ryoshiki ("social intelligence") innovators.* Career-oriented, highly educated middle-aged people. (6) *Ryoshiki adapters.* Shy people who pattern their behavior after that of ryoshiki innovators. (7) *Tradition innovators.* Middle-aged homeowners with middle management jobs who are active in community affairs. (8) *Tradition adapters.* Affluent, young, well-educated managers who travel frequently. (9) *High pragmatics.* The people least likely to agree with any attitude statement, unconcerned about self-improvement or preserving customs. (10) *Low pragmatics.* Attitudinally negative people with no identifiable psychological tendency who prefer inexpensive goods and established brands. SRI does not feel that any one segmentation system can be applied cross-culturally. The company is currently developing a Germany VALS and a Norway VALS.

Young & Rubicam, believing that people's goals, motivations, attitudes, and values determine consumers' choices, developed the Cross Cultural Consumer Characterization (4Cs) system of psychographic segmentation. The 4Cs system groups people into three major groups composed of seven segments. The *constraineds* include: (1) *Resigned poor.* People whose main goal is survival and subsistence. (2) *Struggling poor.* People whose goal is improvement and escape from hardship. The *middle majority* include: (3) *Mainstreamers.* People whose goal is security and conformity. (4) *Aspirers.* People, motivated by envy, whose goal is to appear successful. (5) *Succeeders.* People whose goals are control and "material success." *Innovators* include: (6) *Traditionals.* People whose goal is self-identity; they are motivated by rebellion and self-confidence, and they value self-satisfaction. (7) *Reformers.* People whose goal is social betterment. They value self-esteem and social altruism.

In these attitude-based segmentation systems, the percentage of people in each segment varies by country, and many researchers believe that no single segmentation system can be applied cross-culturally. As long as users realize the systems' limitations and are sensitive to cultural differences, these segmentation tools provide valuable starting points for international market development decisions.

Source: Adapted from Lewis C. Winters, "International Psychographics," *Marketing Research,* pp. 48–49, September 1992.

SUMMARY

1 Attitude measurement is important in marketing because of the central role it plays in developing a segmentation/positioning strategy, evaluating the effectiveness of advertising, predicting product acceptance, and facilitating the development of marketing programs.

2 An attitude represents an individual's enduring perceptual, knowledge-based, evaluative, and action-oriented processes with respect to an object or phenomenon. The three components of an attitude are (a) cognitive—relating to beliefs, (b) affective—relating to feelings, and (c) behavioral—relating to action tendency.

3 Marketing activities are designed to bring about some response from the targeted market segment. This response can be at the cognitive, the affective, or the behavioral level. The hierarchy of effects model hypothesizes a cognitive-affective-behavioral sequence resulting from the marketing effort. While the order of this sequence may vary, depending on the specifics of the marketing situation, the measurement of an attitude component early in the sequence may allow predictions regarding the character of subsequent components.

4 An attitude is a construct that exists in the minds of individuals. Attitude scaling refers to operational definitions for the measurement of this construct. This is a difficult measurement task, and typically it results in a nominal or ordinal scale.

5 The general methods for measuring attitudes rely on communicating with respondents and on observing respondents. Communication techniques include (a) self-reports, (b) responses to unstructured or partially structured stimuli, and (c) performance of objective tasks. Observation techniques include (a) overt behavior and (b) physiological reactions.

6 The self-reporting technique, the most widely used method of attitude measurement in marketing, is composed of many specific scaling approaches. Of these approaches, graphic and verbal rating scales are among the most frequently used. The major issues surrounding the construction of rating scales are (a) number of categories, (b) odd or even number of categories, (c) balanced versus unbalanced scale, (d) extent of verbal description, (e) category numbering, (f) forced versus nonforced scales, and (g) comparative versus noncomparative scales.

7 The rank-order scaling approach involves a ranking of objects with regard to the attitude in question. This popular approach results in an ordinal scaling of the objects.

8 The paired-comparison scaling approach involves a series of pairwise judgments among objects in a set. The more complex scaling approach results in an ordinal scale.

9 The semantic differential scaling approach is a popular way to measure "image," which can be defined as an average of many separate attitudes toward a company, a brand, or a concept. With this method, an object is evaluated on several rating scales bounded at each end by bipolar adjectives or phrases. The data are analyzed using the profile analysis approach.

10 The Stapel scale is a modification of the semantic differential scale. It uses a unipolar 10-point nonverbal rating scale to measure how closely the descriptor fits the object evaluated.

DISCUSSION QUESTIONS

1 What is an attitude?
2 What are the three main components of attitudes?

3 Describe the stages of the hierarchy-of-effects model.
4 What questions must the researcher always be concerned with when measuring attitudes?
5 What general methods of attitude measurement exist?
6 What self-reporting techniques are used in marketing research?
7 Discuss some of the issues involved in constructing a verbal rating scale.
8 What are the advantages and disadvantages of rank-order scales?
9 Describe the methods by which ordinal and interval scales can be derived from paired-comparison data.
10 What are the advantages and limitations of the paired-comparison technique?
11 Explain the profile analysis method of evaluating data from semantic differential scales.
12 How does the Stapel scale differ from the semantic differential scale?
13 Follow the instructions in each of the following scaling problems.

    a *Verbal rating scale construction.* Construct a verbal rating scale to measure high school students' attitudes toward attending your college. Briefly discuss the issues involved in constructing the verbal scale, and identify the appropriate level of measurement (ordinal, interval, or ratio).

    b *Image measurement.* Construct a scale to measure the image high school students have of your college and your top three competitors. Design the scale and briefly discuss the issues involved in constructing the scale.

    c *Measuring the hierarchy of effects.* Develop questions to measure each level of the hierarchy of effects (awareness, knowledge, liking, preference, intention-to-buy, and purchase) for *National Geographic* magazine. Obtain responses to your questions from two respondents. What do you conclude about *National Geographic* from your results?

    d *Paired-comparison data.* In matrix II, develop an ordinal scale of the five brands using the paired-comparison data in matrix I.

Matrix I				
	A	B	C	D	E
A	—	.60	.44	.59	.25
B	.40	—	.42	.52	.37
C	.56	.58	—	.52	.13
D	.41	.48	.48	—	.43
E	.75	.63	.87	.57	—

Matrix II				
	A	B	C	D	E
A	—				
B		—			
C			—		
D				—	
E					—
Total					

Ordinal scaling: >   >   >   >

14 MINICASE

Prepare a set of attitude measurement questions that Wal-Mart could have used in its attitude research in Hong Kong. (See the Marketing Research in Action at the beginning of the chapter.) Be sure to include an example of each of the following types of scales: a nominal scale, a verbal rating scale, a numeric rating scale, a graphic rating scale, a rank-order scale, a paired-comparison scale, a semantic differential scale, and a Staple scale.

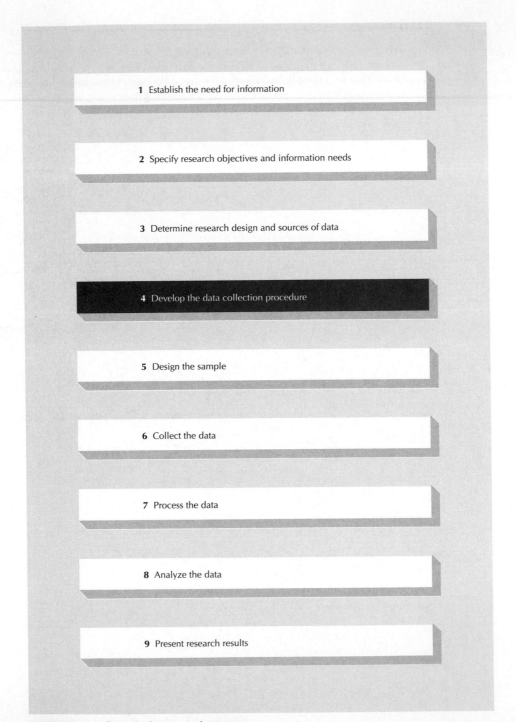

FIGURE 9-1   Steps in the research process.

CHAPTER 9

CAUSAL DESIGNS

MARKETING RESEARCH IN ACTION

EXPERIMENTAL FIELD STUDY REVEALS MEDIA AND CREATIVE IMPACTS ON V-8 COCKTAIL JUICE SALES

V-8 cocktail vegetable juice is a well-established, tomato-based canned beverage marketed by the Campbell Soup Company. V-8 had shown substantial growth over the years and was a price leader in the tomato-based juices category. Management attributed this strong sales growth to the brand's advertising campaign, which focused on V-8's superior taste relative to tomato juice.

When sales declined in 1973, advertising on the brand was discontinued in most markets. Management believed slackening sales trends were a sign of "advertising wearout." On two previous occasions, the institution of a new campaign had revived declining sales trends. Based on these past results, a new creative approach was developed and ready to roll by May 1975. In order to evaluate this new approach, the Campbell Soup Company conducted a series of studies for V-8 over a 5-year period. The first of these studies was a controlled experiment to evaluate the effectiveness of the new "I coulda had a V-8" campaign and media mix.

The new campaign differed from V-8's previous campaign on two important factors. The new campaign was primarily based on television, while the previous campaign has been primarily based on radio. Because of this, the new campaign required a significantly larger budget to achieve similar exposure goals. The controlled experiment was designed to evaluate the advantages, if any, of the new campaign.

The study was designed to evaluate both the new and old campaigns at the proposed higher budget using three different media mixes: a TV/radio mix, prime-time television only, and fringe television only. The old campaign was also tested using only radio. (The new campaign's design precluded a radio-only test.) A control component was also created using the old campaign, the old budget level, and the old media mix. The purpose of this control was to discern any start-up effects related to the mere act of advertising after a 6- to 9-month hiatus. Based on the assumption that the start-up effect was independent of the actual campaign, the study allowed marketers to estimate campaign and budget effects by comparing a test cell with the control cell. The structure of the study is presented in the diagram below.

Budget level	Media mix	New creative	Old creative
New budget	TV/radio	118.8* (2 markets)	111.2 (2 markets)
	Television, prime time	121.8 (2 markets)	116.6 (2 markets)
	Television, fringe	113.6 (2 markets)	116.2 (2 markets)
	Radio	Not tested	107.2 (4 markets)
Old budget	Primarily radio (old mix)	Not tested	110.0 15 markets (control)

*Entries are the ratios of cumulative actual sales to cumulative forecast sales in each market after 3 months, averaged over the markets in each cell and multiplied by 100. Under a null hypothesis of no treatment effect, the expected value of these entries is 100, assuming unbiased forecasts.

Selling Areas Marketing, Inc. (SAMI), defines experimental "markets" within geographical areas that receive their television signals from a central town or city. Because of this, a new media mix or advertising budget change can easily be implemented in a SAMI "market." SAMI also measures warehouse withdrawals on a monthly basis, by market, for each size and brand in a particular product category. This allowed marketers to track V-8 sales for each market. Thirty-one SAMI markets were used in the experiment, 15 as control cells, and 16 as various test cells.

With the same media mix, response to the new campaign was 4 percent higher than response to the old campaign. The new campaign, combined with the TV/radio and prime-time television media mixes, corresponded to a 10 percent increase in sales relative to the control group. The study identified a definite relationship between strong consumer response and the new creative approach, the media mix, and the budget level. The power of causal designs in marketing research is evident.

Source: Joseph O. Eastlack and Ambar G. Rao, "Modelling Response to Advertising and Pricing Changes for V-8 Cocktail Vegetable Juice," *Marketing Science,* pp. 245–259, Summer 1986.

In Chapter 3, improper causal inferences were identified as one type of nonsampling error. In this chapter, we shall discuss this problem in the context of different types of research designs and their ability to distinguish causality. The chapter first describes the necessary conditions for causality to be inferred, then the principles of experimental and quasi-experimental design, the managerial aspects of these designs, and finally the basics of designed experiments.

THE SEARCH FOR CAUSALITY

Introduction

Marketing managers want to be able to make *causal statements* about the effects of their actions: "The new advertising campaign we developed has resulted in a 10 percent increase in sales." In similar fashion, a sales manager might boast, "The new sales training program has resulted in lower sales-force turnover." In both of these examples the managers are making causal statements. Are these statements valid, however? We cannot answer, because we do not have enough information about the situations. The brand manager has observed that sales increased after the change in the advertising campaign. Similarly, the sales manager has observed lower sales-force turnover after the change in the sales training program. However, the fundamental question that should be asked in the presence of all causal statements has been neither asked nor answered. This question is, *Are there some other possible factors that could have caused the changes you observed?*

Our brand manager's increase in sales could have been caused by the increased product penetration in the distribution channel, a strike at a competitor's plant, a new package design, a decrease in price, or other causes. The decrease in sales-force turnover that the sales manager boasted about could have been caused by a new quota payment system, a change in the type of people hired by the company, or the fact that poor economic conditions have made job opportunities at other companies scarce, among other things. Clearly, marketing managers and researchers must be able to know the conditions under which proper causal statements may be applied. Also, it is in the nature of marketing decision making that not all the conditions allowing the most accurate causal statements are usually present. In these circumstances, causal inference will still be made by marketing managers. In doing so, they should clearly understand the risk of error they are taking. This error possibility should be explicitly considered and not just ignored. The information in this chapter provides the framework for understanding the conditions necessary for making causal inferences.

The Necessary Conditions for Causality

Before outlining the conditions that allow causal statements to be made, we must first develop a more formal understanding of the concept of causality. The scientific concept of causality is complex and differs substantially from the one held by the average "person on the street." Selltiz[1] and her colleagues identify some differences between the scientific and the so-called commonsense concepts of causality. The commonsense view holds that a single event (the "cause") always results in another event (the "effect") occurring. In science, we recognize that an event has a number of determining conditions or causes that act together to make the effect probable. Note that in the commonsense notion of causality, the effect always follows the cause. We refer to this as *deterministic causation.* In contrast, the scientific notion specifies the effect only as being probable. This is called *probabilistic causation.* The commonsense notion talks of proving that X causes Y; the scientific notion holds that we can only infer causality and never really prove it. This inference comes from analyzing data that we have generated. The chance of an incorrect inference is always thought to exist.

The world of marketing fits the scientific view of causality. Marketing effects are probabilistically caused by multiple factors, and we can only *infer* a causal relationship; we can never really prove it definitively. We must always live with the possibility that we have not identified the true causal relationship.

We now examine the conditions under which we can make causal inferences. These are (1) concomitant variation, (2) time order of occurrence of variables, and (3) elimination of other possible causal factors.

Concomitant Variation   Concomitant variation is the extent to which a cause X, and an effect, Y, occur together or vary together in the way predicted by the hypothesis under consideration. Consider the example of a marketer of small foreign cars. This company has undertaken a new advertising campaign "to improve the attitudes people have toward our cars and therefore to increase sales." Suppose that in testing the results of this campaign the company finds that both aims have been achieved: attitudes have become more positive, and sales have increased. We can then say that there is concomitant variation between attitudes and sales. Note that the implied hypothesis here is that improved attitudes cause sales to increase.

We can now conclude that the hypothesis of a causal relationship between attitudes and sales is tenable. However, it has not yet been proved. There are other possible explanations of the observed relationship that are equally tenable. Two examples follow: (1) The increase in sales has resulted in more people becoming more experienced with these cars, which may have resulted in the observed improvement in attitudes. That is, the increase in sales has caused the attitude change. (2) Some other variables may have caused the observed relationship. For example, the company may have improved the quality of its cars during the period in question. Clearly, we must go beyond concomitant variation before making valid causal inferences.

Time Occurrence of Variables   The hypothesis that improved attitudes cause increases in sales can be examined further by collecting data about attitudes from

---

[1]This section follows an excellent discussion in Claire Selltiz, Marie Jahoda, Morton Deutsch, and Stuart W. Cook, *Research Methods in Social Relations,* rev. ed. (New York: Holt, 1959), pp. 80–88.

people at various times in their purchase process, specifically (1) before exposure to the advertising campaign, (2) after exposure but before car purchase, and (3) after both exposure and car purchase. If attitudes improved only after exposure to the campaign but prior to car purchase, we would have more evidence that the hypothesis was tenable. If, however, attitudes improved only after car purchase, the hypothesis would be untenable. That sales increases caused improved attitudes would be a more tenable hypothesis in this situation.

The general statement of this very intuitive concept is that one event cannot cause another if it occurs after the other event. *The causing event must occur either before or simultaneously with the effect.*

There is one complication in this seemingly straightforward concept, namely, that it is possible for each of two events to be both a cause and an effect of the other. In our example, improved attitudes may cause increases in sales, *and* increased sales may cause improved attitudes. Thus, the relationship between attitudes and sales could be that they alternately "feed" on each other. This type of relationship would be demonstrated in a purchase decision study if attitudes improved both before and after an increase in sales occurred.

If we now had demonstrated concomitant variation and proper time occurrence of variables, we would still be left with the fundamental question of causality noted earlier: "Are there some other factors that could have caused the observed relationship between X and Y?"

Elimination of Other Possible Causal Factors Consider the case of a slightly mixed-up scientist who formulated the hypothesis that soda water causes intoxication. To test this hypothesis, the scientist gave a randomly selected group of animals soda water mixed with scotch, rye, bourbon, and vodka. Intoxication was observed in each case. The scientist then reasoned: "I have observed concomitant variation between soda consumption and intoxication. Also, the proper time order of events to infer causality is present. My hypothesis is, therefore, correct." Well, we all know that another factor, the presence of alcohol, was the true cause of what the scientist observed. He had not searched for other possible causes. Also, the research design used did not allow for the identification of the true causal relationship.

This ability of research design to assist in making proper causal inferences is the subject of the next section of this chapter. First, however, we should note that the brand manager and the sales manager who made the causal statements we examined early in this chapter were making exactly the same type of causal statement as our mixed-up scientist; they were no less mixed up than the scientist.

EXPERIMENTATION

The Use of Experiments in Marketing

The fundamental research tool used to help identify causal relationships is the experiment. The objective of an experiment is to measure the effect of explanatory variables or independent variables on a dependent variable while controlling for other variables that might confuse one's ability to make causal inferences. Experimentation has been used successfully to reach conclusive answers to such questions as the following.

1 Can we increase profits by servicing small accounts by mail rather than from branch stores?

2 Can we increase supermarket sales of our product by obtaining additional shelf space?

3 Will addition of stannous fluoride to our toothpaste reduce users' cavities?

4 Does the number of times that a salesperson calls on a particular account in a given time period affect the size of the order obtained from that account?

5 Is a given newspaper advertisement more effective in color than in black and white?

6 Which of several promotional techniques is most effective in selling a particular product?

7 Is it necessary for an advertisement to change the attitude of subjects in order to cause them to use more of the product?

This list could be extended indefinitely, for experimental procedures are useful across the whole domain of marketing decision making. This usefulness is noted in the V-8 Marketing Research in Action at the beginning of this chapter. In this example, the experimental approach served to reduce the risk of marketing decisions by measuring the effects of alternative courses of action.

Some Definitions and Concepts

To understand experimentation properly, we must first learn some basic definitions and concepts. These are discussed below.

Experiments   An *experiment* is executed when one or more independent variables are consciously manipulated or controlled by the person running the experiment, and their effect on the dependent variable or variables is measured.

In surveys and observational studies there is no manipulation of independent variables by the researchers. This is the fundamental difference between experimental and nonexperimental research. In searching for causal relationships in nonexperimental situations, the researcher must proceed ex post facto—that is, observe the effect and then search for a cause. In these circumstances, we can never be completely sure of the proper time order of occurrence of variables and the effects of other possible independent variables that have been excluded from consideration. The superiority of experiments in this regard is absolute.

Treatments   *Treatments* are the alternatives or independent variables that are manipulated and the effects of which are measured. Examples in marketing include product composition, advertising executions, and price levels. In a measurement sense, treatments need only form a nominal scale.

Test Units   The *test units* are the entities to whom (or to which) the treatments are presented and whose response to the treatments is measured. It is common in marketing for both people and physical entities, such as stores or geographic areas, to be used as test units. For example, people may be asked to try a product and then have their attitudes toward it measured. Here people are the test units. Alternatively, different end-aisle displays may be set up in supermarkets and sales levels measured. Here, supermarkets are the test units.

Dependent Variables   The *dependent variables* are the measures taken on the test units. Typical marketing examples include sales, preference, and awareness. In a measurement sense, the dependent variable must form an interval scale.

Extraneous Variables   The *extraneous variables* are all the variables other than the treatments that affect the response of the test units to the treatments. These variables can distort the dependent variable measures in such a way as to weaken or invalidate a researcher's ability to make causal inferences. For example, a book publisher attempting to measure the responses of buyers to two different cover designs would want to keep other aspects of the book the same for each buyer group. If the publisher allowed the extraneous variable "price" to vary between buyer groups, she could not be sure that she was measuring the effect of the cover. The price change would thus "confound" the experiment.

The researcher has three possible courses of action with respect to extraneous variables. First, an extraneous variable may be physically controlled. In our book example, the price of the book could be held constant. Second, if physical control is not possible, the assignment of treatments to tests units may be randomized. Our book publisher could randomly assign different prices to all buyers. In experiments with human test units, this usually takes the form of randomly assigning the test units to the different treatments. In this way, it is hoped that an extraneous factor (such as IQ or age) is equally represented in each treatment group. Obviously, we would prefer physical control, but, unfortunately, in marketing applications we must often rely on randomization.

The third way to control the effects of extraneous variables is through the use of specific experimental designs that accomplish this purpose. Much of the rest of this chapter discusses how specific designs can accomplish this task.

If physical control, randomization, and design features do not eliminate the differential effects of extraneous variables among treatment groups, the experiment has been confounded, and no causal statements are possible. We call such an extraneous variable a *confounding variable*. For example, suppose we are using two cities as our test units, and it rains in one city but not in the other. If rain affects the dependent variable (say, the number of car washes), our experiment has been confounded, and rain was the confounding variable.

Actually, we still have one line of defense against the confounding variable. We may statistically control the effects of this variable on the dependent variable with a technique called *analysis of covariance* (ANCOVA), which is discussed in Chapter 21. To make use of ANCOVA we must be aware of the confounding variable and be able to measure it. Therefore, the kind of extraneous variable that we are most worried about in experimentation is the one that operates differentially among treatment groups and is unknown to the experimenter.

Experimental Design   An *experimental design* involves the specification of (1) treatments to be manipulated, (2) test units to be used, (3) dependent variables to be measured, and (4) procedures for dealing with extraneous variables.

Validity In Experimentation

Two concepts of validity are relevant in experimentation: internal validity and external validity. These are described below.

Internal Validity   *Internal validity* is the basic minimum validity that must be present in an experiment before any conclusion about treatment effects can be made. It is concerned with the question of whether the observed effects on the test units could have been caused by variables other than the treatment. Without internal validity, the experiment is confounded.

External Validity   *External validity* is concerned with the "generalizability" of experimental results. To what populations, geographic areas, treatment variables, and measurement variables can the measured effect be projected?

The researcher, obviously, would like an experimental design to be strong in both kinds of validity. Unfortunately, it is sometimes necessary to trade off one type of validity for another. For example, in order to remove the effects of an extraneous variable, we may create a very artificial environment for an experiment. In doing this, we may decrease the generalizability of the results to more realistic environments. For example, an advertiser may ask respondents to view advertisements in a trailer. Can the effects that are measured in this environment be generalized to a home viewing environment?

Symbols Defined

To facilitate our discussion of specific experimental designs, we will make use of a set of symbols that are now almost universally used in marketing research, as follows:

X represents the exposure of a test group to an experimental treatment, the effects of which are to be determined.

O refers to processes of observation or measurement of the dependent variable on the test units.

R indicates that individuals have been assigned at random to separate treatment groups or that groups themselves have been allocated at random to separate treatments.

In addition, the following conventions are widely observed:

- Movement from left to right indicates movement through time.
- All symbols in any one row refer to a specific treatment group.
- Symbols that are vertical to one another refer to activities or events that occur simultaneously.

A few examples should make this symbolic scheme clear. The symbols

$$O_1 \quad X_1 \quad O_2$$

indicate that one group received a measurement of the dependent variable both prior to (O_1) and after (O_2) the presentation of the treatment (X_1). Further, the symbols

$$R \quad X_1 O_1$$
$$R \quad X_2 O_2$$

indicate that two groups of subjects were randomly assigned to two different treatment groups at the same time. In addition, the groups received different experimental treatments at the same time, and the dependent variables were measured in the two groups at the same time.

Types of Extraneous Variables

Previously, we discussed the need for controlling extraneous variables in order to ensure that the experiment has not been confounded. That is, we want to be assured that the experiment is internally valid.

History   *History* refers to the occurrence of specific events that are external to the experiment but that take place at the same time as the experiment. These events may affect the dependent variable. For example, consider the design

$$O_1 \quad X_1 \quad O_2$$

where O_1 and O_2 are measures of the dollar sales of sales personnel and X_1 represents a new sales training program. The difference $O_2 - O_1$ is the measurement of the treatment effect. However, the new sales training program is not the only possible explanation of a positive difference $O_2 - O_1$; an improvement in general business conditions between O_1 and O_2 is as plausible a hypothesis for explaining the observed increase in sales as is the new training program. The greater the length of time between observations, the greater the chance of history's confounding an experiment of this type. What we need is a procedure for controlling the effects of history.

Maturation   *Maturation* is similar to history except that it is concerned with changes in the experimental units themselves that occur with the passage of time. Examples would include getting older, growing hungrier, and growing more tired. In our sales training design, sales may have increased because the sales force has become somewhat older and more experienced. Clearly, people change over time. However, so do stores, geographic regions, and organizations. The longer the time between O_1 and O_2, the greater the chance that maturation effects will occur.

Testing   *Testing* is concerned with the possible effects on the experiment of taking a measure on the dependent variable before presentation of the treatment. There are two kinds of testing effects. The first could be called the *direct* or *main testing effect,* and it occurs when the first observation affects the second observation. For example, consider the case of respondents who have completed a pretreatment questionnaire. If they are asked to complete the same questionnaire after exposure to the treatment, they may respond differently just because they are now "experts" with that questionnaire. The internal validity of the experiment is then compromised.

The second testing effect affects external validity but is important enough to mention here. It is called the *reactive* or *interactive testing effect.* This is the situation where the test unit's pretreatment measurement affects the reaction to the treatment. For example, a pretreatment questionnaire that asks questions about shampoo brands may sensitize the respondent to the shampoo market and distort the awareness levels of a new introduction (the treatment). The measured effects are then not really generalizable to nonsensitized persons.

Instrumentation   *Instrumentation* refers to changes in the calibration of the measuring instrument used or changes in the observers or scorers used. In the sales training study mentioned previously, the dependent variable, sales, was measured in dollars. If there had been a price increase in the company's products between O_1 and O_2, the difference $O_2 - O_1$ could be explained by this change in instrumentation.

An interviewer presenting the pre- and posttreatment questionnaires in different fashions could also cause an instrumentation effect. Similarly, a difference in the presentation of the treatment itself to different test units could cause this effect.

Statistical Regression   *Statistical-regression* effects occur where test units have been selected for exposure to the treatment on the basis of an extreme pretreatment score. The effect is that such "outliers" tend to move toward a more average position with the passage of time. Suppose that in the sales training example above only poorly performing salespersons had been given the new training program. Subsequent sales increases might be attributed to the regression effect. This is because random occurrences such as weather, family problems, or luck helped define good and poor performance of salespersons in the pretreatment measurement. These same random occurrences will make some of the poor performers better performers in the next year, thus confounding the experiment.

Selection Bias   *Selection bias* refers to the assigning of test units to treatment groups in such a way that the groups differ on the dependent variable prior to the presentation of the treatments. If test units self-select their own groups or are assigned to groups on the basis of researcher judgment, the possibility of selection bias exists. Test units should be randomly assigned to treatment groups.

Test Unit Mortality   *Test unit mortality* refers to test units withdrawing from the experiment while it is in progress. What can we conclude if a number of salespersons quit the company between X_1 and O_2? It is possible that those who were not improving quit, or that just the opposite happened.

All these types of extraneous variables constitute alternative explanations of what is observed in an experiment. They are the rivals of the hypothesis that the researcher is testing. One objective of our research designs should be to eliminate the possibility that these effects will confound our results.

Three Preexperimental Designs

What follows is an examination of three preexperimental designs. They are considered preexperimental because inherent weaknesses in the designs make internal validity very questionable. This will highlight the sources of invalidity that may arise in non-true experiments.

One-Shot Case Study   The *one-shot case study design* is presented symbolically as

$$X \qquad O$$

In words, a single group of test units is first exposed to a treatment X, and then a measurement is taken on the dependent variables. Note that the symbol R does not appear in the design, so there was no random assignment of test units to the treatment group. The test units were self-selected or arbitrarily selected by the experimenter.

An example of this design might be as follows. A sales manager requests volunteers to take part in a new sales training program, and a measure of their sales performance is taken some time after the training program is completed. The impossibility of drawing meaningful conclusions from such a design should be apparent. The level of O is the result of many uncontrolled factors, and it cannot be deemed to be good or bad in the absence of a pretreatment observation of sales performance. Thus history, maturation, selection, and mortality problems all serve to render this design internally invalid.

One-Group Pretest-Posttest Design The *one-group pretest-posttest design* is presented symbolically as

$$O_1 \quad X \quad O_2$$

Here, for example, we have added a pretest measurement of sales performance to the one-shot case study design. If we then took the difference between O_2 and O_1 as our measure of experimental effect, would we have a valid measure of the effect of the sales training program? Clearly, a number of extraneous variables could explain the difference $O_2 - O_1$, rendering this design useless for reaching conclusive answers.

Specifically, (1) the economic situation could have changed (history); (2) the salespersons could have matured (maturation); (3) the premeasure could have affected performance (testing); (4) prices of goods sold could have changed (instrumentation); (5) the test units could have been self-selected (selection); (6) some test units could have dropped out, with an unknown result of O_2 (mortality); and (7) test units could have selected themselves on the basis of the bad year they had just experienced, and they could have a better subsequent year just because of luck (regression). Even if this design had been

$$R \quad O_1 \quad X \quad O_2$$

all sources of invalidity except selection would still apply.

This design is the one used by the mixed-up scientist doing the experiment with soda water. He had not controlled for the extraneous variable, intake of alcohol (history).

Static-Group Comparison The *static-group comparison design* uses two treatment groups, one that has been exposed to the treatment and one that has not. Both groups are observed only after the treatment has been presented, and test units are not randomly assigned to the groups. Symbolically, this design is

$$
\begin{array}{lll}
\text{Group 1:} & X & O_1 \\
\text{Group 2:} & & O_2
\end{array}
$$

Group 2 is called a control group because it has not received the treatment and so may serve as the baseline for comparison. In marketing we often define the control group treatment as the current level of marketing activity. This design is presented symbolically as

$$
\begin{array}{lll}
\text{Experimental group:} & X_1 & O_1 \\
\text{Control group:} & X_2 & O_2
\end{array}
$$

where X_2 is the baseline marketing program with which we wish to compare X_1. For example, in trying out the new sales training program on some salespersons, the sales manager would not be likely to drop all sales training for the other salespersons. The manager is interested in comparing one program with another, so the old program is the control group treatment.

The overwhelming source of invalidity in this design is selection. Test units have not been randomly assigned to treatment groups; therefore, the groups may differ on the dependent variable prior to the presentation of the treatment. The experimental result $O_1 - O_2$ could clearly be attributed to this pretest difference, caused by selection procedures. Differential test unit mortality is also possible because of the nature of the treatment. More experimental-group test units may have withdrawn because of the offensive nature of the new sales training program, for example.

Three True Experimental Designs

A true experimental design is one where the researcher is able to eliminate all extraneous variables as competitive hypotheses to the treatment. Three true experimental designs follow.

Pretest-Posttest Control Group Design   The *pretest-posttest control group design* is presented symbolically as

Experimental group: $\quad R \quad O_1 \quad X_1 \quad O_2$
Control group: $\quad\quad\quad R \quad O_3 \quad\quad\quad O_4$

where X_1 is the treatment of interest. Again the control group could have a baseline treatment applied to it. The random assignment of test units to the treatment groups eliminates selection bias as a potential confounding variable.

The premise here is that all extraneous variables operate equally on both the experimental group and the control group. The only difference between the groups is the presentation of the treatment to the experimental group. Therefore, the difference $O_2 - O_1$ is the sum of the treatment effect plus the effects of the extraneous variables, whereas the difference $O_4 - O_3$ is the sum of the extraneous variables only. In symbols:

$$O_2 - O_1 = TE + H + M + T + I + R + TM \tag{9-1}$$
$$O_4 - O_3 = \quad\quad H + M + T + I + R + TM \tag{9-2}$$

where TE = treatment effect
$\quad\quad H$ = history
$\quad\quad M$ = maturation
$\quad\quad T$ = testing
$\quad\quad I$ = instrumentation
$\quad\quad R$ = regression
$\quad\quad TM$ = test unit mortality

If we subtract Equation 9-2 from 9-1, we find that

$$(O_2 - O_1) - (O_4 - O_3) = TE$$

the true treatment effect we sought. So we have found a way to identify the effect of an independent variable. All potential destroyers of internal validity are controlled by this design. Note the fundamental principle of experimental design that is operative here: the experimenter does not care what extraneous variables are operative *so long as they operate equally on all treatment and control groups.* Even with a control group design, the experiment is confounded if an extraneous variable operates differentially among treatment and control groups. The assumption must be that they operate equally. Note in the V-8 Marketing Research in Action the use of control markets and the availability of premeasures based on the SAMI shipment data for the markets utilized.

A major difficulty with this design is the effect of the pretest measurement on the test units' reaction to the treatment (the interactive testing effect). Since this is a potential confounder of external validity, in the experimental group we must add another variable to the equation explaining the difference $O_2 - O_1$. This variable is IT, the interactive testing effect. If we also define EXT as the symbol indicating the sum of all other extraneous variables, then

$$O_2 - O_1 = TE + EXT + IT$$
$$O_4 - O_3 = \quad\quad EXT$$

Therefore

$$(O_2 - O_1) - (O_4 - O_3) = TE + IT$$

That is, we cannot separate the interactive testing effect from the treatment effect. We must always have some doubt about the generalizability of our treatment.

If the scientist doing the experiment with soda water had used this design, he would not have concluded that soda water causes intoxication, because the control group would have consumed the alcohol without the soda water. Clearly, the level of intoxication of the control group would have equaled that of the experimental groups. The possibility that the interactive testing effect will occur here is quite small. We should be able to measure pretest levels of intoxication in animals without sensitizing them to the coming treatment. Other researchers may not be quite so fortunate, however. A shampoo marketer using this design to measure the effect of a new advertising campaign may generate an interactive testing effect. Specifically, the pretest may sensitize test units in the experimental group to advertisements in the shampoo product category, and the resultant posttest levels of advertising awareness would not be generalizable to a nonsensitized population. In this case, the researcher would look to other designs to control for this effect.

Solomon Four-Group Design   The *Solomon four-group design* controls for all extraneous variable effects on internal validity, plus the interactive testing effect. Symbolically:

Experimental group 1:	R	O_1	X	O_2
Control group 1:	R	O_3		O_4
Experimental group 2:	R		X	O_5
Control group 2:	R			O_6

What we have done here is add another experimental group and another control group to the previous design. This second experimental group receives no pretest but otherwise is identical to the first experimental group. The second control group receives only a posttest measurement. What effects do the differences between the various pre- and postmeasures give us?

Experimental group 1:	$O_2 - O_1 = \text{TE} + \text{EXT} + \text{IT}$	(9-3)
Control group 1:	$O_4 - O_3 = \quad\quad\quad \text{EXT}$	(9-4)
Experimental group 2:	$O_5 - O_1 = \text{TE} + \text{EXT}$	(9-5)
	$O_5 - O_3 = \text{TE} + \text{EXT}$	(9-6)
Control group 2:	$O_6 - O_1 = \quad\quad\quad \text{EXT}$	(9-7)
	$O_6 - O_3 = \quad\quad\quad \text{EXT}$	(9-8)

Equations 9-5 and 9-6 are usually averaged to give

$$O_5 - \frac{O_1 + O_3}{2} = \text{TE} + \text{EXT} \qquad (9\text{-}9)$$

Also, Equations 9-7 and 9-8 are averaged to give

$$O_6 - \frac{O_1 + O_3}{2} = \text{EXT} \qquad (9\text{-}10)$$

The experimental treatment effect is then obtained by subtracting Equation 9-10 from 9-9. Thus,

$$\left(O_5 - \frac{O_1 + O_3}{2}\right) - \left(O_6 - \frac{O_1 + O_3}{2}\right) = \text{TE} + \text{EXT} - \text{EXT} = \text{TE}$$

which is the desired result.

This design also gives us a direct measure of the effect of extraneous variables, EXT, and allows us to calculate the interactive testing effect, IT. This effect is obtained by subtracting Equation 9-9 from Equation 9-3, as follows:

$$(O_2 - O_1) - \left(O_5 - \frac{O_1 + O_3}{2}\right) = \text{TE} + \text{EXT} + \text{IT} - \text{TE} - \text{EXT} = \text{IT}$$

that is, the interactive testing effect.

Now we have not only controlled all extraneous variables and the interactive testing effect, but we have also succeeded in measuring their effects. Unfortunately, these benefits come at the expense of increases in the time, cost, and effort needed to conduct the experiment, and consequently this design is little used in marketing practice. However, it does serve as a standard against which to compare other designs. What we would like is a smaller design that controls extraneous variables and the interactive testing effect. Such a design is the posttest-only control group design.

Posttest Only Control Group Design   The *posttest-only control group design* is written as follows:

$$\text{Experimental group:} \quad R \quad X \quad O_1$$
$$\text{Control group:} \quad R \qquad\quad O_2$$

It is essentially the last two groups of the Solomon four-group design. Here the O_1 and O_2 measurements are composed of the following parts:

$$O_1 = TE + EXT$$
$$O_2 = \quad\quad EXT$$

Therefore

$$O_1 - O_2 = TE + EXT - EXT = TE$$

that is, the treatment effect.

Since there is no pretest in this design, the interactive testing effect cannot occur. Also, the extraneous variables have been controlled, and we have a non-confounded measure of the treatment effect. But wait: suppose the pretreatment measures on the dependent variable were different between the experimental group and the control group? Would not this confound the experiment? Indeed, it would. What we must assume is that the random assignment of test units to the groups has resulted in the groups being approximately equal on the dependent variable prior to the presentation of the treatment to the experimental group. We also must assume that test unit mortality affects each group in the same way. With large enough samples and proper randomization, these assumptions are not unreasonable, a fact which, when combined with the reactive nature of a great deal of marketing research, helps explain why this design is probably the one used most often in marketing practice. The soda-testing scientist, the sales manager, and the shampoo manufacturer could all use this design to obtain a nonconfounded measure of their treatment effect.

QUASI EXPERIMENTATION

In designing a true experiment, the researcher often creates artificial environments in order to have control over independent and extraneous variables. As a result, serious questions are raised about the external validity of the experimental find-ings. One response to this problem has been the development and use of quasi-experimental designs.

A *quasi-experimental design* is one where the researcher has control over data collection procedures (i.e., the "when" and "to whom" of measurement) but lacks complete control over the scheduling of the treatments (i.e., the "when" and "to whom" of exposure) and also lacks the ability to randomize test units' exposure to treatments.

With loss of control of test unit assignments and treatment manipulations, the possibility of obtaining confounded results is great. The researcher must then be aware of what specific variables are not controlled. An attempt must be made to incorporate the possible effects of these uncontrolled variables into the interpre-tation of the findings. We now turn to an examination of selected quasi-experi-mental designs.

Specific Designs

Time-Series Experiment   A *time-series experiment* may be presented sym-bolically as

$$O_1 \quad O_2 \quad O_3 \quad O_4 \quad X \quad O_5 \quad O_6 \quad O_7 \quad O_8$$

The essence of this design is the undertaking of a periodic measurement on the dependent variables for some test units. The treatment is then introduced, or occurs naturally, and the periodic measurements are continued on the same test units in order to monitor the effects of the treatment.

Note how this design conforms to our definition of a quasi experiment. The researcher does have control over *when* measurements are taken and *on whom* they are taken. However, there is no randomization of test units to treatments, and the timing of treatment presentation, as well as exactly which test units are exposed to the treatment, may not be within the researcher's control. A common example of this type of design in marketing involves the use of consumer purchase panels. These panels provide periodic measures on their purchase activity (the O's). A marketer may undertake a new advertising campaign (the X) and examine the panel data to look for the effect. Here, the marketer has control over the timing of the advertising campaign but cannot be sure when the panel members were exposed to the campaign, or even whether they were exposed at all. Also, other consumers outside the panel would be exposed to the campaign. Attempting to make causal inferences from this type of situation is common in marketing.

This design is, of course, very similar to the preexperimental one-group pretest-posttest design, $O_1 \quad X \quad O_2$. Does not the time-series design suffer from all the same problems? The answer is no; the fact that we have taken many pretest and posttest measurements provides more control over extraneous variables. To illus-trate this increase in control, let's examine some possible results of this type of design (see Figure 9-2). Assume that X represents a change in advertising cam-

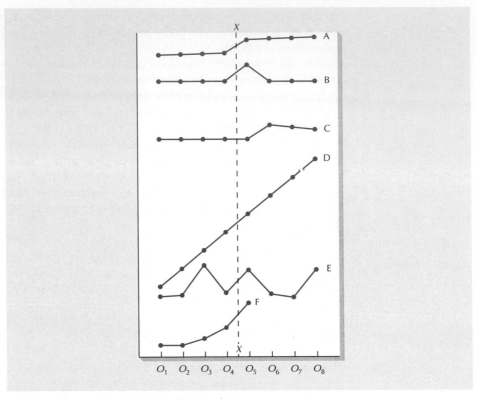

FIGURE 9-2 Some possible results of a time-series experiment.

paign, and the O's represent the market share of the product in question. The following conclusions about the advertising campaign seem reasonable.

1 In situation A, the campaign has had both a short-run and a long-run positive effect.

2 In situation B, the campaign has had a short-run positive effect.

3 In situation C, the campaign may have had a longer-term effect. Since the reaction was delayed for a period, we cannot be as sure as we were in A and B.

4 In situations D, E, and F, the changes that occur after X are consistent with the pattern prior to X. Therefore, we cannot infer that the advertising campaign had an effect.

Note that the one-group pretest-posttest design would have measured only O_4 and O_5. With these measures only, we could easily infer an effect of the campaign, $O_5 - O_4$, in situations D, E, and F; we could also miss the effect in C and the nature of the effects in A and B.

The multiple observations in this design also provide additional control of extraneous variables. For example, the maturation effect on $O_5 - O_4$ can be ruled out as a cause, because this effect would also show up in other observations. It would not affect the O_4 to O_5 period alone. By similar reasoning, main testing, instrumentation, and statistical regression effects can be ruled out. If we then randomly or with good judgment select our test units and take strong measures to prevent test unit mortality (i.e., panel members dropping out), we can at least partially rule out the effects of selection bias and test unit mortality.

The fundamental weakness of this design is the experimenter's inability to control history. But all is not lost; the experimenter can maintain a careful log of all possible relevant external happenings that could have an effect. If this process fails to turn up any unusual competitive activity, economic changes, and so on, the experimenter may reasonably conclude that the treatment has had an effect.

The other weakness of this design is the possibility of an interactive testing effect from the repeated measurements being made on test units. For example, panel members may become "expert" shoppers, thus making generalizations to other populations more difficult. This design is used a great deal, and it can provide meaningful information if used carefully.

Multiple Time-Series Design   In some studies utilizing the time-series design, it may be possible to find another group of test units to act as a control group, thus creating a *multiple time-series design*. For example, an advertiser may try out a new campaign in a few cities only. Panel members in these cities would constitute the experimental group, while members from other cities would constitute a control group. In symbols, this design is

Experimental group: O O O X O O O
Control group: O O O O O O

If the reseacher is very careful in selecting the control group, this design can add more certainty to the interpretation of the treatment effect than is obtainable with the straight time-series experiment. This is so because the treatment effect is tested both in its own group and against the control group. The main problem with this design lies in the possibility of an interactive effect in the experimental group.

Equivalent Time-Sample Design   An alternative to finding a control group is to use the experimental group itself as its own control, in what is called an *equivalent time-sample design*. In symbols, this design might be

$$O \quad X_1 \quad O \quad X_0 \quad OOO \quad X_1 \quad OO \quad X_0 \quad O$$

where X_1 is the experimental treatment and X_0 is the absence of the treatment. Here the treatment is repeatedly presented, measurements are repeatedly taken, and periods of treatment absence are spaced between. This design is best utilized when the effect of the treatment is transient or reversible.

An example of its use would be the testing of the effect of in-store conditions, such as music, on total purchases per customer. Here we could use a single store, whose customers make up the test units, and utilize equivalent sets of days with and without music over a period of many months.

The biggest problem with this design is the possibility of the interactive testing effect's occurring. It is basically a reactive design because of all the measurements taken, and therefore it is best used where the repeated measurements are non-reactive. In situations like the store example, we are able to measure per-customer sales without sensitizing customers to the treatment. If we did repeated interviewing of customers about in-store music, sensitization would no doubt be a problem.

Nonequivalent Control Group Design   In *nonequivalent control group design,* the last quasi-experimental design to be examined in this chapter, both the experimental group and the control group are given pretest and posttest measurements, but the two groups do not have preexperimental test unit selection equivalence. Symbolically, this design is as follows:

$$\text{Experimental group:} \quad O_1 \quad X \quad O_2$$
$$\text{Control group:} \quad \quad O_3 \quad \quad O_4$$

This is a quasi-experimental design because the groups were not created by the random assignment of test units from a single population. However, the existence of even a nonequivalent control group improves the ability of the researcher to interpret results in comparison to the one-group pretest-posttest design discussed previously. In this design the researcher has control over who is exposed to the treatment. Clearly, the more similar the experimental and control groups are in composition, and the closer the pretest measurements, the more useful the control group becomes. If these criteria are met, this design can effectively control the effects of history, maturation, main testing, instrumentation, selection, and test unit mortality. Regression may provide one major source of problems in this design, that is, if either group has been selected on the basis of extreme scores. In such cases some of the differences in pretest and posttest measures may result from regression effects. Care must be taken to avoid this problem. The possibility of an interactive testing effect is also present in this design.

MANAGERIAL ASPECTS OF EXPERIMENTATION AND QUASI EXPERIMENTATION

In this section, we shall discuss the types of issues that are important to managers in the use of experimental and quasi-experimental designs.

Comparison with Other Procedures

There are many procedures for collecting data in marketing research—for example, the use of secondary data, observation, survey, and simulation. They can all provide useful information for marketing decision making. However, since they are basically descriptive techniques, none of these procedures allows for the identification of causal relationships. Only experimental and quasi-experimental designs can identify such relationships; the other procedures can only find correlation. The cause and the effect cannot be separated. Yet all too often descriptive studies are used to argue causal relationships. For example, the National Tourism Council does a survey. In this survey, the respondents are measured on what is assumed to be an effect variable—say, the amount of money spent on vacations in Georgia. Then, in the same survey, the respondents are measured on a series of hypothesized causal variables. If one of these "causal" variables—say, awareness of Georgia tourism advertisements—is found to be correlated with the effect, the advertising is assumed to have caused dollars to be spent on tourism in Georgia. Clearly, this is ex post facto reasoning. What is observed is concomitant variation only. The time order of the two variables is not established, nor have other possible variables been eliminated. Only experimentation and quasi experimentation can do this.

This does not mean that a correct causal relationship cannot be established in descriptive studies, for the researcher may be absolutely correct with a causal guess. The point is that we can never be sure. Descriptive studies are the most frequently used type of study in marketing research practice, and they will continue to be used to state causal relationships. Constraints of time, money, and so on may make this the only type of study available to a manager. In using descriptive studies for causal purposes, the manager should be aware of the risk of error that is being taken.

Laboratory versus Field Environments

There are two types of environments in which an experiment may be conducted. The first is a laboratory environment, that is, one where the experimenter conducts the experiment in an artificial environment constructed expressly for the purpose of the experiment. The field environment is the alternative. Here, the experiment is conducted in actual market situations, and no attempts are made to change the real-life nature of the environment. An example of a laboratory experiment would be the showing of test commercials to test units in a theater. This same experiment could be conducted in the field by having test commercials run on actual televison programs.

Validity   Laboratory environments provide the researcher with maximum control over possible confounding variables. They have higher internal validity. A consequence of the artificial nature of a laboratory, however, is the loss of generalizability to more realistic situations. Thus, laboratory experiments have lower external validity. Experiments conducted in the field have lower internal validity and higher external validity. Often a field experiment provides so little control over extraneous variables that we must be content to conduct a quasi experiment.

Cost   Laboratory experiments are generally less expensive than field experiments. They tend to be smaller in size (i.e., with a smaller number of test units), shorter in duration, more tightly defined geographically, and therefore much easier to administer.

Time   The simpler nature of laboratory experiments also means that they require less time to execute.

The researcher must trade off these factors—validity, cost, and time—in selecting an environment for an experiment. Table 9-1 presents a summary of these factors.

Control of Invalidity

In presenting alternative experimental and quasi-experimental designs, we discussed possible sources of invalidity in detail; this section contains a managerial summary of these points. Table 9-2 presents the sources of invalidity of preexperimental and experimental designs, and Table 9-3 presents the same information for quasi-experimental designs. In these tables, a minus sign indicates a definite weakness in that design in controlling the relevant sources of invalidity; a plus sign indicates that the factor is controlled; a question mark indicates a possible source of concern; and a blank indicates that the factor is not relevant. Use these tables only when you are sure that you understand why each design is classified as it is.

Limitations of Experimentation

The manager should recognize the following limitations of experimentation:

1 It is not always possible to control the effects of extraneous variables. Differential effects among treatment groups can easily occur in field experiments.

2 In field experiments, lack of cooperation from wholesalers and retailers can limit experimental activity.

3 Lack of knowledge about experimental procedures on the part of marketing personnel may limit the use of experimentation, and in addition, it may lead to experimental conclusions being discarded as not meaningful.

4 Experiments can be costly and time-consuming.

5 In using people as test units, care must be taken that the experimenter does not say and do things that bias test unit responses.

TABLE 9-1   LABORATORY VERSUS FIELD
EXPERIMENTATION

Factor	Laboratory	Field
Internal validity	High	Low
External validity	Low	High
Cost	Low	High
Time	Low	High

TABLE 9-2   SOURCES OF INVALIDITY OF PREEXPERIMENTAL AND EXPERIMENTAL DESIGNS

Design	Internal — History	Maturation	Testing	Instrumentation	Regression	Selection	Mortality	External — Interaction of testing and X
Preexperimental designs:								
One-shot case study X O	−	−				−	−	
One-group pretest-posttest design O X O	−	−	−	−	?			−
Static-group comparison X O O	+	?	+	+	+	−	−	
True experimental designs:								
Pretest-posttest control group design R O X O R O O	+	+	+	+	+	+	+	−
Solomon four-group design R O X O R O O R X O R O	+	+	+	+	+	+	+	+
Posttest-only control group design R X O R O	+	+	+	+	+	+	+	+

Stages in Executing an Experiment

Once the researcher has acquired a firm understanding of procedures alternative to experimentation, has considered what environment might be used, has developed a good understanding of how to control sources of invalidity, and has recognized the limitations of experimental procedures, he or she is ready to begin the necessary steps for the proper execution of an experiment. These steps are

1 State the problem.
2 Formulate a hypothesis.

TABLE 9-3   SOURCES OF INVALIDITY OF QUASI-EXPERIMENTAL DESIGNS

| | Source of invalidity | | | | | | | |
| | Internal | | | | | | | External |
Design	History	Maturation	Testing	Instrument decay	Regression	Selection	Mortality	Interaction of testing and X
Times series O O O X O O O	−	+	+	?	+	+	+	−
Multiple time series O O O X O O O O O O O O O	+	+	+	+	+	+	+	−
Equivalent time sample O X_1O X_0O X_1O	+	+	+	+	+	+	+	−
Nonequivalent control group O X O O O	+	+	+	+	−?	+	+	−

3 Construct an experimental design.

4 Formulate made-up results and check to see that these results are the type required by the problem statement. In other words, be sure that the design answers the question at hand.

5 Check that the types of results that are possible can be analyzed by available statistical procedures. (See Chapter 21.)

6 Perform the experiment.

7 Apply statistical-analysis procedures to the results to see whether effects are real or just error or noise in the experiment.

8 Draw conclusions with concern for both internal and external validity.

Once again the emphasis is on a meaningful statement of a problem and the provision of information relevant to this problem. If these conditions are met, and only if they are met, the technical aspects of design and analysis are useful to the marketer.

The Future of Experimentation and Quasi Experimentation

Marketing research textbooks written 25 years ago contained little or no mention of the use of experimental and quasi-experimental procedures in marketing research. This accurately reflected the practices of the day. Since then, these procedures have gained substantially in use and are now considered viable alternatives to other types of studies. There are four reasons why this trend continues, as follows:

1 Experimentation works. Meaningful marketing results are generated by the procedures.

2 The costs of making wrong causal inferences in marketing are increasing.

3 Educational levels are rising, with an associated increase in the understanding of these procedures.

4 The capabilities of computerized analysis procedures have eliminated the tedium of hand analysis of results.

The modern marketing manager should understand what can be accomplished by experimental and quasi-experimental designs.

FOUR DESIGN PROCEDURES: AN OVERVIEW

We have just examined the design procedures that allow us to make proper causal inferences. Now we address the issue of statistical significance in experimentation. Specifically, we shall describe procedures that allow us to determine when a measured effect is greater than that due to sampling error. We shall do this in the context of some specific design procedures. This section presents only an overview of four experimental design procedures: (1) completely randomized design, (2) randomized block design, (3) Latin square design, and (4) factorial design. The detailed statistical calculations for these procedures are presented in the appendix to Chapter 21 dealing with analysis of variance (ANOVA).

Completely Randomized Design

A *completely randomized design* (CRD) is the simplest type of designed experiment. It is useful when the researcher is investigating *the effect of one independent variable.* This independent variable need only be a nominal scale, so that it may have many categories. Each category of the nominal independent variable is a treatment. As an example, suppose that the independent variable of interest is "type of sales training program," and it has the following three categories.

1 No sales training
2 Head office lectures for sales training
3 On-the-job sales training

So we have one independent variable, type of sales training program, with three categories. Each category represents a treatment, with category 1 representing the control group treatment.

In a CRD the experimental treatments are assigned to test units on a completely random basis. In our sales training example, salespersons would randomly receive the three treatments without any regard for external factors such as their previous experience, their ages, or the sizes of the sales territories to which they will be assigned. If sales were our dependent variable, we would then compare the average sales level of each of the three treatment groups to see which treatment was best.

Figure 9-3 indicates that about 52 percent of businesses use CRDs in their marketing research.

Randomized Block Design

In the CRD, all extraneous variables were assumed to be constant over all treatment groups. But what if this were not true? What if salespersons receiving on-the-job training tended to be assigned to larger territories than those in other treatment groups? Would not the results obtained be misleading? Indeed they would. The size-of-territory effect would be obscuring the measurement of the treatment effect. What we would like to do is "block out" this extraneous effect. One procedure for doing this is the *randomized block design* (RBD).

This design is built upon the principle of combining test units into blocks based on an external criterion variable. For example, size of sales territory could be such a criterion variable. These blocks are formed with the anticipation that the test units' scores on the dependent variable within each block will be more homogeneous, in the absence of treatment, than those of test units selected at random from all test units.

For example, let's divide our sales territories into three blocks, based upon sales potential, as follows:

Block number	Sales potential per year
1	$200,000–$999,999
2	$1,000,000–$1,999,999
3	$2,000,000–$2,999,999

The sales levels we would expect test units to have within these blocks would be more homogeneous than sales levels we would expect if we ignored the blocking and selected test units at random. Note that the assumption here is that the blocking factor, sales potential per year, is correlated with the dependent variable, salesperson sales level. Note also that the blocking is done prior to the presentation of the treatment.

Once the blocks have been established and test units identified by block, we are ready to assign treatments. In this design, each treatment must appear at least once in each block. Thus, each block must have, at a minimum, a number of test units equal to the number of treatments. In our example, we would need at least three salespersons in each sales potential block, each receiving a different sales training treatment.

The fundamental reason for doing blocking is to allow the researcher to obtain a measure of sampling error smaller than that which would result from a CRD. This occurs because some of the variation in the dependent variable is assigned to the blocking factor, leaving a smaller sampling error.

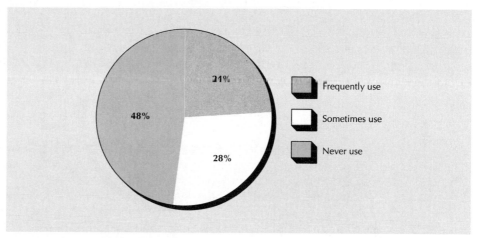

48%

24%

28%

Frequently use

Sometimes use

Never use

FIGURE 9-3 Use in practice of causal–completely randomized experimental design. (*Source:* Thomas C. Kinnear and Ann R. Root, *A Study of the Marketing Research Business,* unpublished study, 1994. Copyright 1994 Thomas C. Kinnear. Not to be reproduced.)

The parallel between blocking in experimentation and stratification in sampling should be apparent. In both situations, we form subgroups so that *the variable of interest is more homogeneous within the groups than it would be across all groups.* The result of this process is a smaller measure of sampling error.

In the RBD the researcher can make use of only one blocking factor. However, we can define the blocking factor by using more than one external variable. For example, in our sales training situation we could have defined our blocking factor using both sales potential in territories and age of salespersons. Assume that the sales potential categories were defined as before, and age was categorized as follows:

Category 1   18–30
Category 2   Over 30

Then, with three sales potential categories and two age categories, we would have a blocking factor composed of $3 \times 2 = 6$ blocks, as follows:

Block number	Description
1	$200,000–$999,999 potential and age 18–30
2	$1,000,000–$1,999,999 potential and age 18–30
3	$2,000,000–$2,999,999 potential and age 18–30
4	$200,000–$999,999 potential and age over 30
5	$1,000,000–$1,999,999 potential and age over 30
6	$2,000,000–$2,999,999 potential and age over 30

Note that blocks, like independent variables in experimentation, are nominally scaled. Figure 9-4 indicates that about 39 percent of businesses use RBD in their marketing research.

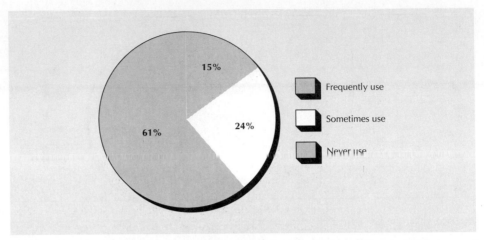

15%

24%

61%

☐ Frequently use

☐ Sometimes use

☐ Never use

FIGURE 9-4   Use in practice of causal randomized block experimental design. (*Source:* Thomas C. Kinnear and Ann R. Root, *A Study of the Marketing Research Business,* unpublished study, 1994. Copyright 1994 Thomas C. Kinnear. Not to be reproduced.)

The number of variables used to create a blocking factor can be extended beyond two. The problem is that the number of blocks required in the blocking factor increases as a multiplicative function of the number of categories in the external variables used. The other problem with blocking by using more than one external variable is that the researcher can measure only the overall effect of the blocking factor. The separate effects of the variables defining the blocking factor cannot be isolated. A possible partial solution to this problem is the Latin square design.

Latin Square Design

In situations where the researcher wishes to control and measure the effects of two extraneous variables, the *Latin square (LS) design* may be used. Table 9-4 illustrates the layout of an LS design applied to our sales training example. The rows and columns of Table 9-4 designate the extraneous variables that are to be controlled and measured. In our example, we have identified three categories for the row variable, age of salesperson, and three categories for the column variable, sales potential per year. The three treatments are identified by the letters *A, B,* and *C,* where *A* = no sales training, *B* = head office lectures for sales training, and *C* = on-the-job sales training. The number of categories of each variable to be controlled exactly equals the number of treatments. This is a necessary condition for using the LS design, and it is the reason we have three age categories in this situation while there were only two in the RBD, discussed previously. Without this condition we would not have a square design. Our example yields a 3 × 3 LS. If we had four treatments, we would have to designate four categories for the row and column variables. This would be a 4 × 4 LS.

TABLE 9-4 LS DESIGN FOR SALES TRAINING EXPERIMENT

| | Sales potential per year (in thousands) | | |
Ages of salespersons	$200–$999	$1000–$1999	$2000–$2999
18–25	A	D	C
26–30	B	C	A
Over 30	C	A	B

A = no sales training, B = head office lectures, for sales training, C = on-the-job sales training.

Another necessary condition for the use of the LS design relates to the way in which the treatments are assigned to cells of the square; they are assigned to cells randomly, subject to the restriction that each treatment occurs once with each blocking situation. Since each row and column category defines a blocking situation, each treatment must appear once in each row and once in each column. The treatments in Table 9-4 conform to this restriction.

Figure 9-5 indicates that about 22 percent of businesses use LS design in their marketing research.

Factorial Design

In marketing we are often interested in the *simultaneous effects* of two or more *independent variables*. The three design procedures discussed so far allow for the use of only one independent variable. If we wish to examine two or more independent variables in an experimental situation, we must use a factorial design. Suppose that, in our sales training example, the interest was in measuring the

FIGURE 9-5 Use in practice of causal Latin square experimental design. (*Source:* Thomas C. Kinnear and Ann R. Root, *A Study of the Marketing Research Business*, unpublished study, 1994. Copyright 1994 Thomas C. Kinnear. Not to be reproduced.)

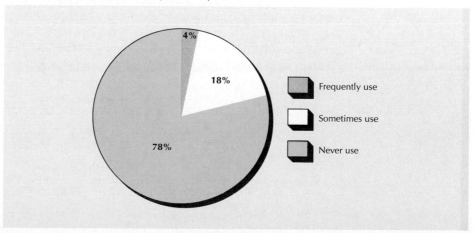

4%

18%

78%

Frequently use

Sometimes use

Never use

effects of the sales training procedure and the compensation scheme used. Suppose that there were two categories of compensation schemes to be tested, as follows:

Category number	Compensation type
1	Straight salary
2	Straight commission

So we have two independent variables; (1) type of sales training and (2) compensation scheme. Both form a nominal scale. The first has three categories, the second two. In a factorial design the categories of the independent variables are called *levels.* In the design, each level of each independent variable appears with each level of all other independent variables. In our example, we would say that we have a 3 × 2 factorial design. This design would yield 3 × 2 = 6 cells in a design matrix. Table 9-5 shows the layout of our 3 × 2 factorial experiment. If we were running an experiment with four independent variables, with 2, 3, 3, and 4 levels, respectively, we would have 2 × 3 × 3 × 4 = 72 cells in our design matrix. Obviously, one adds independent variables and levels with great care.

Note that we no longer call the individual independent variable categories "treatments." They are now called *levels.* The treatments are now the various combinations of levels that occur. In Table 9-5 we have six treatments defined by the combinations of training and compensation, $A_1B_1, \ldots, A_3B_2$.

A factorial design allows us to measure the separate effects of each variable working alone. Thus, the sales training effect calculated from a factorial design would be exactly the same as that calculated from a CRD, but the factorial design would also give us the individual effect of the compensation schemes. These individual effects of each independent variable are called the *main effects.*

There is one other type of effect that is important in factorial designs. This effect is used to recognize that a number of independent variables working together often have a total effect greater than the straight sum of their main effects. This extra effect is called an *interaction effect.* More formally, interaction occurs when the relationship between an independent variable and the dependent variable is different for different categories of another independent variable. In our example,

TABLE 9-5   3 × 2 FACTORIAL DESIGN FOR SALES TRAINING AND COMPENSATION EXPERIMENT

			B	
			B_1 Straight salary	B_2 Straight commission
	A_1	No sales training	A_1B_1	A_1B_2
A	A_2	Head office lectures	A_2B_1	A_2B_1
	A_3	On-the-job training	A_3B_1	A_3B_2

TABLE 9-6   AN ILLUSTRATION OF MAIN EFFECTS

		Compensation scheme	
		B_1	B_2
Training program	A_1	$200,000	$150,000
	A_2	$190,000	$140,000

the relationship between sales level (the dependent variable) and type of sales training program (the first independent variable) may vary, depending upon which compensation scheme was used (the second independent variable). If this were so, we would say that the two independent variables, type of training and compensation scheme, interacted.

Tables 9-6 and 9-7 illustrate the meaning of main and interaction effects. Table 9-6 presents a simplified version of our sales experiment. Here we have just two training programs, A_1 and A_2, and two compensation schemes, B_1 and B_2. The entries in the cells represent average salesperson sales in thousands of dollars during the experiment. We note that, regardless of the compensation scheme used, training program A_1 yields $10,000 more sales on average than A_2. The main effect of A_1 is then $10,000. Note also that, regardless of the sales training program used, compensation scheme B_1 yields $50,000 more sales than B_2 on average. The main effect of B_1 is then $50,000. The total effect of treatment $A_1 B_2$ is $10,000 + $50,000 = $60,000.[2] There is no interaction between sales training and compensation.

Table 9-7 presents the same design matrix with different results. Here, the effect of the training program depends on the compensation scheme used. Specifically, A_1 is $10,000 better than A_2 when B_1 is used and $40,000 better when B_2 is used. Similarly, B_1 is $20,000 better than B_2 when A_1 is used and $50,000 better when A_2 is used. Here, the effect of one independent variable on the dependent variable is different for different levels of the other independent variable. We have interaction. Statistical analysis procedures for factorial experiments can separate both the main effects and the interaction effect.

We should note that the number of interactions rises as the number of inde-

---

[2]"Main effect" and "total effect" are used here to illustrate these concepts and are not technically correct in a statistical sense. More formal definitions are presented in Chapter 21.

TABLE 9-7   AN ILLUSTRATION OF INTERACTION EFFECTS

		Compensation scheme	
		B_1	B_2
Training program	A_1	$200,000	$180,000
	A_2	$190,000	$140,000

pendent variables increases. For example, a listing of main and interaction effects for two and three independent variables follows:

Number of independent variables and description	Main effects	Interaction effects
2: *A* and *B*	*A, B*	*AB*
3: *A, B*, and *C*	*A, B, C*	*AB*
		AC
		BC
		ABC

In marketing, interaction among marketing variables is likely to be the rule rather than the exception. The factorial design is thus a very important one given its ability to identify and measure interaction. It may be used in a (CRD), with randomized blocks, or with a LS design. These two refinements are beyond the scope of this book.[3] We will examine the statistical analysis of a completely randomized factorial design later, in Chapter 21.

A final noteworthy aspect about interaction: The RBD assumes that there is no interaction between the blocking factor and the independent variable, and the LS design assumes that there is no interaction between the two blocking factors.

Figure 9-6 indicates that about 26 percent of businesses use factorial designs in their marketing research. The power of a factorial field experiment to provide insight to marketing managers is shown in the Marketing Research in Action on the Navy enlistment experiment. This example also shows the use of demographic and geographic blocking factors to provide statistical control in the experiment.

[3]If interested, consult a book on experimental design.

FIGURE 9-6   Use in practice of factorial experimental design. (*Source:* Thomas C. Kinnear and Ann R. Root, *A Study of the Marketing Research Business*, unpublished study, 1994. Copyright 1994 Thomas C. Kinnear. Not to be reproduced.)

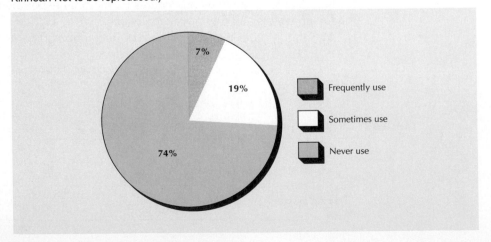

Usage in Practice

Almost all real marketing problems involve the need for the control of extraneous variables or the simultaneous application of more than one marketing variable. Thus RBDs, LS designs, and factorial designs are the most used in practice.

MARKETING RESEARCH IN ACTION

A FACTORIAL FIELD EXPERIMENT DETERMINES MARKETING EFFECTS ON NAVY ENLISTMENT

Marketing researchers conducted a study to evaluate the marketing effectiveness of the U.S. Navy recruiting program and to quantify the relationship between marketing efforts and enlistment achievements. This was done by estimating the impact of changes in the advertising budget and the size of the Navy recruiting force on Navy enlistment contracts for various categories of recruits. The study was based on a 1-year controlled experiment in which levels of Navy recruiters and advertising were systematically varied.

Researchers chose the Area of Dominant Influence (ADI) as their analysis unit for the experiment. ADIs are geographic areas that receive their television signals from a central city or town. Electronic media-rating services assign individual counties to ADIs based on media-use patterns of sampled households. ADIs allow researchers to execute and measure changes in electronic advertising throughout the experiment. Twenty-six of the more than 200 ADIs in the United States were chosen as experimental markets because of their relative insulation. An additional 17 markets were chosen as control cells.

The Wharton Applied Research Center team assigned various treatment conditions to each of the 26 treatment markets. A number of characteristics differed across these markets: demographic, socioeconomic, levels of total military enlistments per capita, and the Navy's share of total military enlistment. Since the Navy Recruiting Command believed the last two variables were major factors in the effectiveness of marketing efforts, the marketing research team ensured that markets exposed to treatment conditions covered a wide variety of "total enlistment" and "the Navy's share of total enlistment" levels. Markets were classified in terms of these variables and randomly assigned to treatment conditions. Treatment conditions included combinations of increasing or decreasing advertising by 50 percent or 100 percent, increasing or decreasing the number of recruiters by 20 percent, leaving advertising at prestudy levels, and leaving the number of recruiters at prestudy levels. Control conditions were created in the markets that maintained prestudy levels of both advertising and recruiters.

Detailed data were collected on the 42 chosen markets and divided into four broad categories: enlistment contracts, recruiters, advertising, and environmental variables. Monthly data were compiled for both Navy contracts and total Department of Defense contracts. This information was further sorted into the following categories: high school and non-high school, females, blacks, and two different mental groups. Navy recruiter data was collected on the basis of both applied worker-months and total recruiters present during each month. This information was divided into two groups: recruiters who were established in the recruiting function, and recruiters who were in the first 4 months or last 6 months of their tour (when researchers hypothesize they are less effective). Advertising deliveries, measured by both gross impressions and dollars, were collected for each ADI and broken down by national print (further divided into magazines, newspapers, and direct mail), national electronic (broken down into TV and radio), local, and joint campaigns for all the armed services. Four environmental variables were also taken into account: percentage of unemployment, median family income, percentage of black population, and urbanization (the percentage of 17- to 21-year-old males who reside in countries with populations of over 150,000). These variables served as blocking factors in the field experiment.

The experimental markets used, the structure of the assignment of treatment conditions, and the control markets used are noted in Figure 9-7.

Analysis of the data collected led to a number of conclusions. The number of recruiters did have a significant impact on enlistments. A recruiter's effectiveness was dependent on the recruiter's tenure. Only certain types of advertising expenditures were effective, with a wide variation in the degree of media impact. Socioeconomic factors also had major impacts on enlistment. And in addition to increasing Navy enlistments, the Navy's marketing efforts expanded the total market for military enlistments.

Source: Vincent P. Carroll, Ambar G. Rao, Hau L. Lee, Arthur Shapiro, and Barry L. Bayus (1985), ''The Navy Enlistment Marketing Experiment,'' *Marketing Science,* pp. 352–374, Fall 1985.

Commonly used blocking factors in marketing include store size, days of the week, time of the year, and geographical regions, all of which often contribute extraneous variation in the dependent variables that interest marketers. For example, you might be interested in measuring the effects of different prices on coffee sales. Suppose that these sales are measured in food stores on each day of the week and in different regions of the country. The actual sales of coffee that we observe might be affected by the different prices plus the different sizes of stores, the day of the week, and the region of the country. What we do is control the effects of these extraneous variables to get a clear measure of the price effect.

Even with great care to properly design a field experiment, and even with the provision of blocking for statistical control, it is difficult to have a completely controlled field experiment. There are too many things that can happen in the field to impact treatments differentially. Thus, it is common in marketing research to think of these experimental settings as being somewhat quasi-experimental.

INTERNATIONAL MARKETING EXPERIMENTS

The principles of causality, the structure of experimental design, and the nature of quasi experiments in the marketplace all hold equally well for both domestic and international marketing research. The Global Marketing Research Dynamics provides examples of international causal studies in marketing.

	Recruiters −20%	Recruiters same	Recruiters +20%
ADV +100%		Davenport–Rock Island	
ADV +50%	Tulsa Roanoke Syracuse	Washington Indianapolis Richmond	Boston St. Louis Charleston–Huntington
ADV same	Baltimore Cheyenne, WY Laurel, MS	Providence Terre Haute Springfield, IL*	Harrisburg South Bend Grand Junction, CO
ADV − 50%	Wilkes Barre Phoenix Odessa–Midland	Chicago Pittsburgh Columbus, OH	Dallas Louisville Lansing
ADV − 100%		Johnstown–Altoona	

* Additional control markets:

Nashville	Des Moines	Waco
Los Angeles	Youngstown	Sioux City
Charlotte	West Palm Beach	McAllen
Greenville	Chattanooga	Anniston
Knoxville	Huntsville	

FIGURE 9-7   Navy experimental design.

GLOBAL MARKETING RESEARCH DYNAMICS

CAUSAL STUDIES IN INTERNATIONAL MARKETING RESEARCH

• Procter & Gamble (P&G) in Europe ran a market test (a quasi experiment) in Berlin, prior to launching its Vizir brand of liquid laundry detergent in several European countries. The market test allowed P&G to better set sales objectives, product positioning against competition, and price point.

• Swatch Watch ran pricing quasi experiments in the United States, Germany, France, Italy, the United Kingdom (UK), Japan, and other countries prior to setting a world price for its basic watch. These tests allowed Swatch to reject the price that its management had originally desired.

• Unilever UK ran a full factorial experiment with consumers to test the taste and texture preferences for several different formulations of a new baking product. This experiment allowed Unilever to esablish the optimal ingredient mix of the product.

• An Italian advertising agency tested the effectiveness of alternative advertisements for its car company client in movie theaters in different cities in Italy and Spain. Three different advertising approaches in the ads were tested in different theaters in a total of ten cities. Only one ad was seen in any one theater on any given day. These theater tests allowed the agency to recommend to the client the ad that best created brand awareness and preference for the client's car.

Swatch's success required creativity and competent quasi-experimental research.

SUMMARY

1 Causality may be inferred when concomitant variation, the proper time order of occurrence of variables, and the elimination of other possible causal factors have all occurred.

2 An experiment is executed when one or more independent variables are consciously manipulated and controlled by the person running the experiment, and their effect on the dependent variable is measured.

3 Treatments are the alternatives that are manipulated and the effects of which are measured.

4 Test units are the entities to whom the treatments are presented and whose response to the treatments is measured.

5 Dependent variables are the measures taken on the test units.

6 Extraneous variables are all the variables other than the treatments that affect the response of the test units to the treatments. They may be physically controlled, or randomization may be used to obtain control of them.

7 Internal validity is concerned with the question of whether the observed effects could have been caused by variables other than the treatments.

8 External validity is concerned with the generalizability of experimental results.

9 Categories of extraneous variables are history, maturation, testing, instrumentation, statistical regression, selection bias, and test unit mortality.

10 Specific designs differ in their ability to control extraneous variables. (These specifics are summarized in Tables 9-2 and 9-3.)

11 Experimental and quasi-experimental procedures are the only ones that allow proper causal inferences to be made. All other study types proceed ex post facto.

12 In a completely randomized design (CRD), treatments are assigned to test units on a completely random basis.

13 In a randomized block design (RBD), test units are combined into blocks based on some external criterion variable. Treatments are then randomly assigned within blocks of test units.

14 RBD allows the measurement and control of one blocking factor.

15 In a Latin square (LS) design, test units are combined into blocks based on two external criterion variables. Treatments are then randomly assigned to blocks subject to the restriction that each treatment occurs once within each blocking situation.

16 LS design allows the measurement and control of two blocking factors.

17 A factorial design allows for the analysis of the main effects of more than one independent variable, plus the effect of the interaction among those independent variables.

18 Interaction occurs when the relationship between an independent variable and the dependent variable is different for different categories of another independent variable.

DISCUSSION QUESTIONS

1 What is the fundamental question that should be asked in searching for causality?

2 What are the necessary conditions to infer causality?

3 What is an experiment?

4 How does an experiment differ from a survey or an observational study?

5 What scale of measurement must the independent and dependent variables form in an experiment?

6 How may you control the effects of extraneous variables?

7 What are internal and external validity?

8 Describe seven different types of extraneous variables.

9 What is the interactive testing effect?

10 How can a design described as $R \quad O_1 \quad X \quad O_2$ be confounded?

11 What design could control the confounding variables in Question 10?

12 Under what circumstances is it impossible for even the best design to control an extraneous variable?

13 What is a quasi experiment?

14 How does a time-series experiment allow for the control of extraneous variables?

15 Compare laboratory and field experiments.

16 How do you choose between laboratory and field environments?

17 Outline the limitations of experimentation in marketing.

18 What steps should be taken in executing an experiment?

19 What is a CRD?

20 How does an RBD aid the experiment?

21 Why are LS designs so often utilized in marketing field experiments?

22 What is a factorial design?

23 For the V-8 and Navy experiments:

   a Describe the experiments in terms of the R, O, and X symbols.

   b How is control of extraneous variables handled in each experiment?

   c What factor could confound these experiments?

   d Could a LS design be used for these experiments? If so, present your design for each.

24 Find an organization's new marketing program or activity described in a newspaper or magazine—*Business Week* or *Advertising Age,* for example. The program might be a new advertising theme, distribution plan, or pricing strategy, for example. Your assignment is to design an experiment or a quasi experiment to measure the effectiveness of this new program or activity. Be sure to address the following six items.

   a Describe the new marketing program or activity.

   b Describe the treatments.

   c Describe the dependent variable (or variables) and how it (or they) will be measured.

   d What or who are the test units?

   e How will extraneous variables be controlled?

   f Using the symbols R, O, and X, describe the experiment.

25 **MINICASE**

Design an experiment to test the hypothesis "Attitudes toward foreign cars are influenced by price of the foreign cars." Record the required experimental components.

   a Describe the treatments.

   b Describe the dependent variable (or variables) and how it (or they) will be measured.

   c What are the test units?

   d Determine how extraneous variables will be controlled.

   e Using the symbols R, O, and X, describe the experiment.

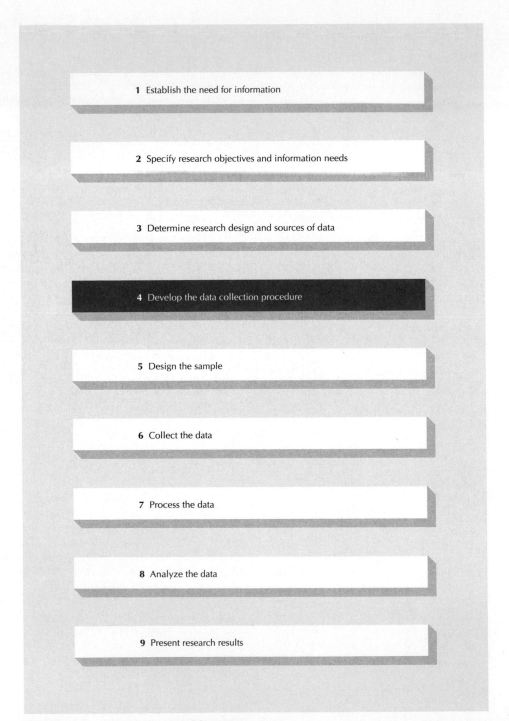

FIGURE 10-1 Steps in the research process.

CHAPTER 10

DATA COLLECTION: EXPLORATORY RESEARCH

MARKETING RESEARCH IN ACTION

CYBERSPACE FOCUS GROUPS

Many marketing researchers are getting wired on computer networks and finding that focus groups in cyberspace are faster and cheaper than the old-fashioned kind. A New York research firm specializing in children and teenagers will be conducting electronic research with 5- to 12-year-olds. The company will collect data using in-depth electronic chat sessions, and will sell the findings to corporations and advertising agencies.

Other companies are doing consumer research online. Prodigy Services markets a focus group package to companies and counts the three major television networks among its users. Viacom's Nickelodeon network established its own forum of 8- to 12-year-olds on the CompuServe network. Electronic participants get $35 to $50 per session—the same amount as is paid to members of traditional focus groups.

Electronic research can be cheaper than data gathering in the traditional focus group setting. A typical face-to-face focus group session costs $4000. Electronically, the same sort of session can be done for $1500. However, electronic research does not allow visual observation.

Marketing research experts are intrigued by the idea of electronic focus groups but caution that they won't replace traditonal focus groups yet. The number of potential respondents who are online is very small and consists mainly of upscale, highly educated males.

EXPLORATORY RESEARCH

Exploratory research is an initial or preliminary stage in the research process. In exploratory research, information is collected from either primary or secondary sources in order to provide insight into the management problem and identify courses of action.

As explained in earlier chapters, secondary sources such as library and syndicated information (e.g., census reports and industry surveys) can provide very useful background information on a management problem and can also bring a broad historical perspective to the nature of a problem situation. In addition, primary sources of information such as observation and qualitative techniques (e.g., focus group and in-depth interviews) provide current data on customer buying behavior, perceptions, attitudes, and motivations.

Our discussion of types of research assumes that the decision-making unit requires accurate information about the decision situation. Consequently, the decision-making unit will proceed through the steps in the decision-making process using research approaches (exploratory, conclusive, and performance monitoring) to increase the accuracy of the information to be used in the decision. The amount of accurate information needed in a decision situation is a matter of the uncertainty present and the risk levels acceptable to the decision-making unit. As a result, some steps in the research process may be skipped or eliminated depending on the specific context of the management problem.

For example, if the decision-making unit has previous accurate information about a decision situation, exploratory research may be all that is needed. The exploratory research may be used to explore whether the problem environment has changed or whether new alternatives exist. The decision-making unit may find that adequate information currently exists, given the findings of the exploratory phase, and may proceed to make a decision without conclusive research. In another situation, exploratory research may be used to identify decision options that are low-risk and do not require the conclusive research phase. In still another decision situation, the exploratory research phase may be skipped and conclusive research conducted. Here, the decision-making unit may be confronted with clear decision alternatives posing a high risk level and requiring extensive conclusive research.

QUALITATIVE TECHNIQUES

Qualitative techniques such as focus groups and in-depth interviews are often touted as the only types of research that allow the decision maker and the researcher to see respondents in the flesh and hear them talk about marketing issues in their own words. Qualitative techniques have the following characteristics.

1 Small convenience or quota samples are used.

2 The information sought relates to the respondents' motivations, beliefs, feelings, and attitudes.

3 An intuitive, subjective approach is used in gathering the data.

4 The data collection format is open-ended.

5 The approach is not intended to provide statistically or scientifically accurate data.

Quantitative data, on the other hand, are intended to quantify or precisely measure a problem, often using sophisticated statistical procedures and scientifically drawn samples. Quantitative data are usually associated with conclusive research.

A study by a committee of the Advertising Research Foundation—the Committee on Qualitative Research—asked research users (companies and advertising agencies), research suppliers (moderators and consultants), and the managers of field facilities about the size and composition of the qualitative research market, and about their attitudes and behaviors toward the use of qualitative research. Some of the findings of the study, which used 1989 data, are summarized in Figures 10-2, 10-3, and 10-4.

According to corporate respondents, the most prevalent reasons for using qualitative research are "actionability" of results, the chance to hear consumers' thoughts in their own words, and the speed of results.

In this chapter we shall focus on two qualitative methodologies: focus groups and in-depth interviews. These methods are unstructured—direct techniques in

FIGURE 10-2   Current usage of qualitative techniques by corporations and ad agencies. [*Source: Qualitative Research: An Industry Study* (New York: Advertising Research Foundation, 1989.)]

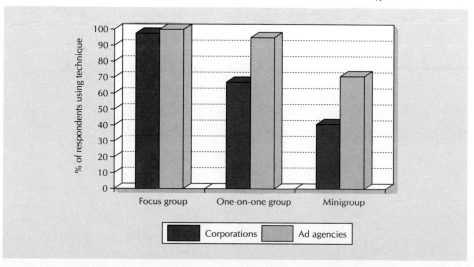

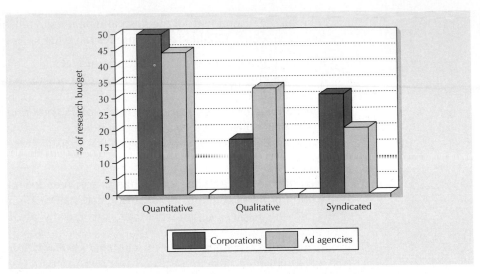

FIGURE 10-3   Percentage of research budget spent on type of research. [*Source: Qualitative Research: An Industry Study* (New York: Advertising Research Foundation, 1989.)]

which no rigid format is followed but the respondent is queried directly about the issue at hand.

Focus Groups

The focus group (see Figure 10-5 for a sample session) is one of the most frequently used techniques in marketing research. Figure 10-6 indicates that about 92 percent of businesses use focus groups in their marketing research. A *focus group* can be

FIGURE 10-4   Qualitative research techniques used by corporate respondents. [*Source: Qualitative Research: An Industry Study* (New York: Advertising Research Foundation, 1989.)]

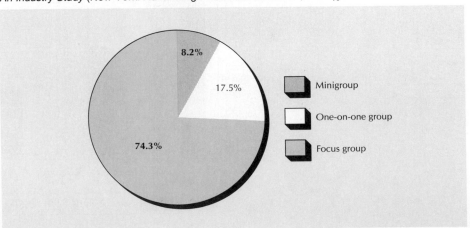

In this focus group session, 10 people are being asked questions about what they think about a new cereal, Kellogg's Raisin Squares. The participants are white, male, fortyish, and in the lower-middle to upper-middle income classes. Here are sample segments of that session.

Introduction
Moderator: Why don't you go ahead and introduce yourselves....

Ray:

My name is Ray. I am a business consultant with three children.

Jim:

My name is Jim. I own a trucking company in Chicago. I have three kids.

Kyle:

I'm Kyle. I am a paramedic and a fireman.

Probe on what is important in a cereal
Moderator: What kind of cereal do you like?

Ray:

I like the bran stuff because of the low cholesterol.

Kyle:

I don't like sugar cereals, only healthy cereals.

Jim:

I mainly eat Raisin Bran because it is good-tasting and good for you.

Introduction of Kellogg's Raisin Squares
Moderator: How many of you have heard of Kellogg's Raisin Squares?

Jim:

Yeah, I have heard of them before and tried them before.

Kyle:

Someone mentioned their name once and said they were overpriced.

Ray:

I have never heard of them before.

Moderator gives each participant a sample of Kellogg's Raisin Squares to taste-test.

Getting feedback
Moderator: What do you think of it now?

Jim:

You can taste the raisins a lot.

Kyle:

It doesn't have a lot of sugar— that's good.

Ray:

It's different. I thought it would taste blah.

Probing
Moderator: Ray, what do you mean by saying it tastes blah?

Ray:

I mean I expected it would be without any taste since it looked like a health cereal.

End
Moderator: I want to thank all of you for your time.

FIGURE 10-5   Sample focus group session.

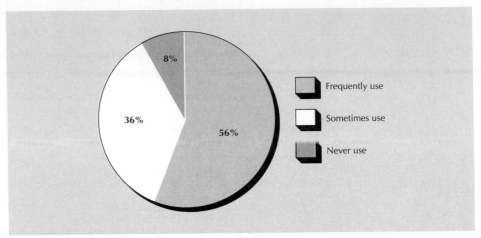

FIGURE 10-6   Use in practice of focus group interview. (*Source:* Thomas C. Kinnear and Ann R. Root, *A Study of the Marketing Research Business,* unpublished study. 1994. Copyright 1994 Thomas C. Kinnear. Not to be reproduced.)

defined as a loosely structured interactive discussion conducted by a trained moderator among a small group of respondents simultaneously. This technique has its origins in the group therapy methods used in the mental health field. While the interview does require a preinterview organization of topics or an interviewer guide, the setting emphasizes flexibility. The value of the technique lies in discovering the unexpected, which results from a free-flowing group discussion.

Figure 10-7 presents a brief practical guide to setting up and completing a focus group.

Focus groups can be used for a number of different purposes. Interviews with researchers suggest the following uses:

1 To generate hypotheses that can be further tested quantitatively
2 To generate information helpful in structuring consumer questionnaires
3 To provide overall background information on a product category
4 To get impressions on new-product concepts for which there is little information available
5 To stimulate new ideas about older products
6 To generate ideas for new creative concepts
7 To interpret previously obtained quantitative results
8 To understand emotional reactions to brands

Group Design Issues   In designing effective focus groups, the researcher must be very sensitive to management objectives and to the role of qualitative and quantitative research in meeting these objectives. Often managers believe they can use qualitative research as a substitute for quantitative research. The researcher must not allow the misuse of research methodology and must clearly

1 Establish objectives.
   - *Definition of management problem.* What does management want to achieve?
   - *Definition of marketing research objectives.* What information is needed to meet the needs of management?

2 Determine the research design.
   - *Target market segments.* What areas need exploring?
   - *Size of groups.* How many people are needed for the focus group?
   - *Number of groups.* Is more than one session required?
   - *Length of sessions and timing.* How long should the sessions last? What time of day should they be held?
   - *Location of group sessions.* Where should the sessions be held? If they are to meet in another city, state, or country, where should they be held?

3 Develop a screening profile for the focus group members—a way to select the type of people you need to look at.
   - *Demographic characteristics.* Look at sex, age, and so forth.
   - *Product or service experience.* Is the session going to be dealing with professionals or experienced people in this area?

4 Establish your budget.
   - *Expected costs:* Moderator costs, facilities costs, participant costs, incidentals, equipment rentals, travel expenses. If the session is to be held off-site, then all these items are factors in the budget.
   - *Incentive level for participants.* What will motivate people to participate in a focus group?
   - *Costs of analyzing the focus group results.* Once the session is done, how long will it take to review the data? How much will it cost?

5 Find and rent a location for the focus group. The environment may affect participants' answers, and the client may want to observe the sessions. The following are important criteria.
   - *Relaxed, comfortable atmosphere.*
   - *Availability of video/audio equipment as needed.*
   - *Client observation facilities, via mirrors or electronics.*
   - *Accessibility for focus group members.*

6 Screen and select focus group members. Now that the type of person needed is known, eliminate poor choices from the focus group candidate pool.
   - *Disqualify anyone who works in the marketing research business, for a competitor, and so forth.*
   - *Consider homogeneity of group members.*
   - *Work with the recruiting field service to assure choice of appropriate participants.*
   - *Check the completed screening questionnaires to be sure appropriate people were recruited.*

7 Select a moderator. Since a moderator is very important in a focus group, there are many factors to consider.
   - *Previous experience.*
   - *Familiarity with the product and/or the industry.*
   - *Cost.*
   - *Availability.*
   - *Sex of the moderator.*
   - *Use of one or more moderators, alternating.*

8 Develop a moderator's guide or agenda to be used to help the moderator achieve the goals of the marketing research.
   - *Research objectives.*
   - *Topics to be covered.*
   - *Time to be allocated.*

9 Meet with the moderator, to further prepare him or her for the session.
   - *Review the discussion guide and the research objectives.*
   - *Educate the moderator on the client's business and products.*

10 Conduct the focus groups.

11 Analyze the results. Compile all the data into meaningful information.

12 Write and present a report to management, explaining the findings and their consequences.

FIGURE 10-7   Guide for implementing a focus group.

communicate to management the role of qualitative research in the decision process. The following guidelines can be helpful in the design of an effective focus group study.

Homogeneity   The respondent group should be composed of people with fairly homogenous characteristics. One organization, which conducts approximately 600 focus groups per year, avoids combining married women who have children and who work full-time in the home and unmarried women who work outside the home, because their life-styles and objectives are substantially different. They also avoid grouping men and women together, as well as teenagers and younger children. It is important to maintain as much homogeneity or commonality among group members as possible, to avoid interactions and conflicts among group members on issues not relevant to the study objectives.

Size   The size of the group can be as large as 10 or 12 people for consumer goods research. Experience suggests that in a group with fewer than 8 people, the discussion will be dominated by a few respondents, and that having more than 12 people tends to diminish the opportunity for some respondents to participate. It is argued that for non-consumer goods research (pertaining to architects, doctors, industrial purchasers, engineers, investors, contractors, etc.), a group of 6 or 7 people may be best for maximum interaction among participants.

Screening   Most researchers believe that careful screening of respondents is essential to the success of the focus group. First, the group members must have had adequate experience with the object or issue being discussed. Second, respondents who have previously participated in a group session generally should not be included,[1] though some research organizations do accept respondents who have not participated in a session within the last year. The reason for this rule is that former participants often play the role of "expert" by dominating the discussion and trying to "show off" for first-time participants.

As part of the screening process, the researcher must be sensitive to potential participants' motivations for taking part in the focus group. The motivation is important not only for the ability to draw a large pool of respondents but also to understand whether the participant will be fully interested and involved in the group discussion. One study found that the top three reasons for participation (a respondent could have more than one reason) were "money" (54.4 percent), "focus groups are interesting/the topic was interesting" (34.5 percent), and "met qualifications/time was convenient" (25.0 percent).[2]

Another issue in respondent selection relates to allowing people to participate in a group that contains a relative, neighbor, or friend. Since friends sometimes tend to talk to each other and not to the whole group, many researchers will not select respondents from church groups or other organizations where participants have established relationships.

---

[1]Wendy Hayward and John Rose, " 'We'll meet again' . . .: Repeat Attendance at Group Discussions—Does It Matter?" *Journal of the Market Research Society*, vol. 32, no. 3, pp. 377–407, July 1990.

[2]Peter Tuckel, Elaine Leppo, and Barbara Kaplan, "Focus Groups under Scrutiny," *Marketing Research: A Magazine of Management & Applications™*, vol. 4, no. 2, pp. 12–17, June 1992.

A manager observes a focus group through a one-way mirror.

Length   The typical focus group lasts 1½ to 2 hours. This period of time is needed to establish rapport with the respondents and explore in depth their beliefs, feelings, ideas, and insights regarding the discussion topic.

The number of group sessions to be conducted depends on the nature of the issue at hand, the number of market segments involved, and the time and cost constraints of the project. Typically, the researcher must concentrate the group session on those segments most critical to the topic being considered. It is very desirable to replicate the focus group session for each market segment being studied. At least two focus group sessions can be held on an average day. Participants are generally available after work hours, and successive sessions can be arranged from 6 to 8 P.M. and from 8 to 10 P.M.

Environment   Most researchers believe the physical setting is very important to the effectiveness of the group session. The atmosphere should induce a relaxed feeling, so that informal and spontaneous comments will be encouraged. It is best to establish a coffee klatch or bull-session atmosphere in this regard.

A living room environment is considered more appropriate than a conference room setting, since the latter may inhibit many respondents and encourage others to play the role of expert. While a living room in a private home is ideal, most research organizations have participants come to a central facility—often a specially designed laboratory furnished like a comfortable, but not elaborate, living room. The advantage of holding sessions in a laboratory lies in the availability of facilities for recording the session and for indirect observation by the client, while the group session is in process.

Clients frequently observe the focus group session, and it is better to have them behind a two-way mirror rather than present in the room with the participants. This detached location avoids the danger of disrupting the group session by having the participants observe the client's reactions or note taking. If certain areas need more exploration, the client can let the moderator know during short breaks in the session.

Costs Generally, focus groups are faster and less expensive than quantitative research efforts. Focus groups can be administered in a matter of a few weeks. While costs will vary depending on the type of participant sought, the sophistication of the moderator, and other factors, a focus group report could end up costing between $5000 and $10,000. Figure 10-8 provides a breakdown of the expected costs of running a focus group.

Moderator The moderator's role is of prime importance to the success of the focus group technique.[3] Highly skilled moderators can ensure that proper respondent rapport is established, that the discussion is directed along relevant dimensions, that bias is not introduced into the findings,[4] and that the degree of probing and the depth of insight are sufficient to accomplish the research objectives. In addition, the moderator is central to the analysis and interpretation of the data. Great skill, experience, knowledge of the discussion topic, and intuitive insights into the nature of group dynamics are required to accomplish this

---

[3]William J. McDonald, "Focus Group Research Dynamics and Reporting: An Examination of Research Objectives and Moderator Influences," *Journal of the Academy of Marketing Science,* vol. 21, no. 2, pp. 161–168, May 1994.

[4]Deborah Potts, "Bias Lurks in All Phases of Qualitative Research," *Marketing News,* pp. 12–13, September 3, 1990.

FIGURE 10-8 Average focus group cost. (Assumes that two groups are held at one location, with 10 participants and two researchers per session.)

Room rental	$500
Respondent incentives	$1,000–2,000
Travel Expenses	$1,000–2,000
Moderator fee	$2,000
Data analysis and report production	$2,000
Total	$6,500–$8,500

task.[5] Consequently, the moderator is often a trained psychologist who has developed special moderator skills through intensive study and practice.

The moderator's skill is clearly demonstrated by the ability to maintain a high degree of interaction among group members. Unskilled moderators typically find themselves conducting individual interviews with each of the participants rather than stimulating interaction within the group. Only with interaction can the group interview (1) provide the desired spontaneity of response by participants, (2) produce the degree of emotional involvement essential to produce in-depth responses, and (3) produce the kind and degree of rapport which facilitates a give-and-take exchange of attitudinal and behavioral information.

The key qualities that a moderator should have are as follows:

1 *A combination of kindness and firmness.* In order to elicit necessary interaction, the moderator must combine disciplined detachment with understanding empathy.

2 *Permissiveness.* An atmosphere of permissiveness is desirable to encourage open communication. Yet the moderator must be at all times alert for any indications that the group atmosphere of cordiality is disintegrating.

3 *Ability to encourage involvement.* Since a principal reason for the group interview is to expose feelings and to obtain reactions indicative of deeper feelings, the moderator must encourage and stimulate intensive personal involvement.

4 *Ability to convey incomplete understanding.* An extremely useful skill for a group moderator is the ability to convey lack of complete understanding of the information being presented.

5 *Ability to provide encouragement.* Although the dynamics of the group situation facilitate the participation of all members in the interaction, there may be individuals who resist contributing. It is the moderator's job to draw these people into the discussion.

6 *Flexibility.* The moderator should be equipped prior to the session with a topic outline (see the discussion below) of the subject matter to be covered. He or she should commit the topics to memory before the interview, and should use the outline during the session only as a reminder of content areas omitted or covered incompletely. This allows the moderator to be flexible in terms of the flow of the discussion.

7 *Sensitivity.* The moderator must be able to identify, as the group discussion progresses, the informational level on which it is being conducted, and to determine whether this level is appropriate for the subject under review. Sensitive areas will frequently produce superficial rather than deep responses. Depth is achieved where there is a substantial amount of emotional response, as opposed to intellectual information. Indications of depth are provided when participants begin to show how they feel about the subject, rather than simply telling what they think about it.

---

[5]Naomi R. Henderson, ''Trained Moderators,'' *Marketing Research: A Magazine of Management & Applications*™, vol. 4, no. 2, pp. 20–23, June 1992.

Does the sex of the moderator influence the effectiveness of the group session? There are two views about this. The first holds that the sex of the moderator should be the same as that of the group members, to ensure proper rapport. The second view is that the sex of the moderator should be different from that of the group members. The argument here is that the participants will not assume that the moderator knows what they are talking about and will be more explanatory in their responses.

What special techniques can the moderator use in running a group session? When one person tries to dominate the discussion, the moderator can stop the proceedings and poll each participant regarding the issue at hand.[6] This technique is also useful to encourage the shy person to express a viewpoint and participate in the discussion. At the close of the session, each person can be asked to summarize what the group has resolved. Another useful technique is to call each of the participants a day or so after the completed session and have them express their viewpoints again. Many times, their viewpoints change with the passage of time or because they have done more reflective thinking on the issue.

Should the same moderator be involved in all group sessions on the topic? Most researchers believe so. With each session the moderator becomes more effective and gains additional insight into the analysis and interpretation of the sessions.

Moderator's Guide The moderator's guide, a key document in focus group situations, is a discussion agenda to be used by the moderator during the focus group session. It serves two purposes, as follows:

1 It provides a detailed outline of the issues to be addressed in the discussion, including the approach, the types of questions to be raised, the sequence of issues, and any stimuli to be introduced.

2 It serves as a memory aid for the moderator. The moderator's guide requires a thorough understanding of the objectives of the study. It is generally prepared using question or topic areas rather than specific questions. It is often used to begin with the most general topics and then move to specific topics. In using this approach, the researcher must anticipate whether the participants may take positions on a general topic that will prejudice their perception of new ideas, products, or concepts. The moderator will be more effective and insightful if he or she has been involved in drafting the guide. The process of drafting the guide will enable the moderator to gain a better understanding of the research objectives and how the findings will be used. The researcher can reduce reliability problems by introducing the guidelines for discussion, especially when multiple focus groups are scheduled. Figure 10-9 is an example of a moderator's guide.

Analyzing Focus Groups Suppose your boss approaches you with a new assignment—to prepare a report on the results of six recently conducted focus groups with business managers regarding the use and purchase of personal com-

---

[6]Judith Langer, ''How to Keep Respondents from Taking Over Focus Groups,'' *Quirk's Marketing Research Review,* pp. 34–38, December 1991.

1 Ask, "Do you have insurance on your automobile now?"

  a Ask those who do have it, "Why?" Also ask the following questions.

- "What are your most important reasons for having automobile insurance?"
- "What are some other reasons?"
- "What reasons have you heard—for instance, through advertising—that you think are not important?"
- "Have you ever driven without insurance?"
- "How did that happen?"
- "Would you do it again?"

Ask the others in the group, "What do you think? Would you drive without insurance?"

  b Ask those who are not carrying insurance the following questions.

- "Why do you not have automobile insurance?"
- "Have you ever had it?"
- "Why did you drop it?"
- "Do you expect to get some? When?"

2 Turn the discussion to types of auto insurance coverage.

  a Ask, "What is collision insurance?" Try to get the group to define it, but make sure they know that it means insurance that pays for damage to the owner's car as a result of an accident, no matter whose fault. Also ask these questions:

- "Do you have collision insurance?"
- "Why?"

    (Probe.) "Have you ever had it?"

    (If yes.) "Why did you drop it?"

- "Do you expect to get it again?"

Encourage discussion on the merits of this type of insurance between group members who do have it and those who don't.

  b Repeat the same questions for the following topics.

- *Liability insurance (bodily injury and property damage).* Insurance that pays for damage done by a driver to other cars or property or to other people.
- *Comprehensive insurance (fire, theft, etc.).* Insurance that pays for loss or damage to a car as a result of fire, theft, natural hazards, vandalism, and so forth.
- *Medical payments insurance.* Insurance that pays medical expenses of guests in the car.

FIGURE 10-9   Guide for focus group sessions on automobile insurance.

puters (PCs) for their businesses. The six tapes consist of two focus groups of small businesses (with 1 to 50 employees), two focus groups of medium businesses (with 51 to 500 employees) and two focus groups of large businesses (with over 500 employees). Each tape contains over 2 hours of comments, from a total of 48 people. You sit back in your chair and wonder, "How can I analyze over 12 hours of focus group tapes?" You should follow the steps outlined below.

   Step 1. Review the Research Purpose   While the purpose of focus groups can vary, the primary purpose is to build a foundation for the conclusive research phase of the project. Focus groups provide a wealth of insights regarding how and why buyers purchase products. This information can be used to formulate structured questions and to determine the sequence of these questions in the questionnaire.

Number	1	2	3	4	//	48
Respondent	Eric	Regine	Ashley	Bill	//	Samir
Firm size	14	20	993	180	//	330
Number of PCs owned	2	10	48	56	//	125
Type of business	Wholesale	Insurance	Manufacturing	Retail	//	Insurance

FIGURE 10-10 Demographic profile.

Step 2. Thoroughly Study the Group Discussions The raw data of focus groups are the tones, emotions, body movements, and verbatim comments involved in the group interaction. Consequently, the researcher must first thoroughly study the focus group videotapes to become familiar with the issues explored in the group sessions. A verbatim transcript of each videotape is a useful reference source for the researcher in this process. If verbatim transcripts are not available, repeated viewing of the tapes is required. At this stage, the researcher should be concerned about developing an understanding of the group dynamics and begin to form general impressions about the topics discussed. These general impressions will become more formalized in the next area of the analysis.

Step 3. Create Categories The first task in categorization is to develop a demographic profile of the respondent base. Figure 10-10 presents such a profile for the PC focus groups. The demographic information can come from the screening questionnaire used to select the focus group participants or from facts collected on a questionnaire administered before the start of the focus group session.

The second task in categorization is to develop a respondent profile based on what is observed in the focus group sessions. The moderator's guide serves as a useful starting point for developing categories. For example, the following issues were covered on the moderator's guide and discussed actively by the participants in all six groups.

1 Compatibility
2 Service and support
3 Price
4 Networking

Figure 10-11 presents selected comments by respondents on the important issues explored in the group sessions. Each respondent's comments on particular issues were categorized by the researcher as (1) very important, (2) somewhat important, or (3) not very important. Eric's comments on the "service and support"

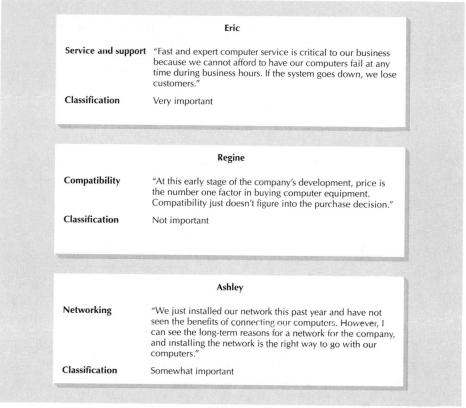

FIGURE 10-11   Selected comments by respondents.

issue were classified as "very important" (see Figure 10-11). Each of the 48 respondents was classified on all the issues discussed in the focus groups. Respondents who did not have opinions, or whose opinions were not observable on the tapes, were categorized as such.

Step 4. Identify Potential Relationships   Relationships in the qualitative data matrix can be explored with simple cross tabulations of variables. Figure 10-12 presents two such relationships between (1) firm size and compatibility and (2) firm size and service and support. While it is possible to use sophisticated computer programs to analyze this data set, remember the limitations of the data collected and the purpose of the analysis. This is not a quantitative data set on which inferences about a larger population can be drawn. Remember, the purpose of exploratory research is to develop insights and hypotheses that can be tested for validity in the conclusive research phase of the research project.

Step 5. Finishing Touches   The focus group report combines the work from the previous stages into a deliverable document. The report should cover the following areas.

Compatibility, frequency (%)

	High	Medium	Low	Total
Large	8 (50)	6 (38)	2 (12)	16 (100)
Medium	6 (38)	6 (38)	4 (24)	16 (100)
Small	3 (19)	5 (32)	8 (50)	16 (100)
Total	17	17	14	48

Hypothesis: Large businesses are more concerned with compatibility than are small and medium businesses

Service, frequency (%)

	High	Medium	Low	Total
Large	5 (32)	4 (25)	7 (44)	16 (100)
Medium	4 (25)	8 (50)	4 (25)	16 (100)
Small	9 (56)	4 (25)	3 (19)	16 (100)
Total	18	16	14	48

Hypothesis: Small businesses are more concerned with service and support than are large and medium businesses

FIGURE 10-12 Cross-tabulation analysis.

- Executive summary
- Research purpose
- Methodology
- Results and hypothesis identified
- Implications for further study

Variations on Focus Groups   There are a number of variations on the standard focus group.[7] These include:

1 *Minigroups.* The group consists of a moderator and 4 to 5 participants, rather than the usual 8 to 10 participants. The minigroup may be especially effective for private or sensitive issues or where greater depth of probing is sought.

2 *Two-way focus groups.* One target group listens in on a related group to gain an understanding or greater appreciation of an issue. The target group then holds its own discussion.

3 *Dual-moderator group.* Two moderators share or split the responsibilities of moderating the group, with the intention of allowing both to give more attention to the actual group discussion and to probing the selected issues.

[7]Hy Mariampolski, "Beyond Conventional Focus Groups: Emerging Options for Qualitative Research," *Quirk's Marketing Research Review,* pp. 16–43, December 1991.

4 *Client-participant groups.* Clients attend the focus group itself and are identified to the participants. The clients take part in the discussion and can answer questions or provide clarification.

The major *advantage* of the focus group interview rests on the premise that if you want to understand your consumers, you have to listen to them. There is much to be gained from listening to consumers describe a product in their own vernacular, and from having them portray how they buy products and how they perceive product benefits and limitations, using highly personalized terms. Data such as these can bring insight to potential problems and opportunities and can identify possible marketing program strategies that have not occurred to the manager.

In comparison to other data collection techniques, the focus group interview has these specific advantages:

1 *Synergism.* The combined effect of the group will produce a wider range of information, insight, and ideas than will an accumulation of the responses of a number of individuals when these replies are secured privately.

2 *Snowballing.* A bandwagon effect can operate in a group interview situation, in that a comment by one individual often triggers a chain of responses from the other participants.

3 *Stimulation.* Usually after a brief introductory period the respondents get "turned on." They want to express their ideas and expose their feelings as the general level of excitement over the topic increases in the group.

4 *Security.* The participants can usually find comfort in the group, as they discover that their feelings are not greatly different from those of other participants. With this encouragement, they become more willing to express their ideas and feelings.

5 *Spontaneity.* Since individuals aren't required to answer questions in a group interview, their responses can be more spontaneous and less conventional. This should provide a more accurate picture of their positions on some issues.

6 *Serendipity.* It is more often the case in a group rather than in an individual interview that some idea will "drop out of the blue."

7 *Specialization.* The group interview allows the use of a more highly trained, but more expensive, interviewer, since a number of individuals are being "interviewed" simultaneously.

8 *Scientific scrutiny.* The group interview allows closer scrutiny of the data collection process, in two ways: (1) several observers can witness the session, and (2) it can be recorded for later playback and analysis.

9 *Structure.* The group interview affords more flexibility than the individual interview with regard to the topics covered and the depth with which they are treated.

10 *Speed.* Since a number of individuals are being interviewed at the same time, the group interview speeds up the data collection and analysis process.

A major *disadvantage* of the focus group interview is that the decision maker cannot use the evidence in a conclusive research manner. The evidence is not

projectable to a target segment for two reasons. First, the sample is not representative of the target segment, in the sense that quantitative statements cannot be
made regarding the significance of the research findings. Second, the evidence
itself is highly dependent upon the experience and perception of the moderator
and other observers. The danger is that the decision maker may use the exploratory
findings as conclusive evidence to support preconceived notions about the decision situation.

As in any area of human endeavor, there are individuals who will compromise
proper research procedures for personal gain. With the focus group interview,
these improper procedures involve poor recruitment of participants, provision of
a poor physical environment, and use of an unskilled moderator.

The focus group is an exploratory research technique that can be extremely
valuable in developing hypotheses regarding problems and opportunities, facilitating the development of a clear statement of the decision problem, and stimulating the creative process so as to formulate alternative courses of action. Conclusive research is the next logical step in the testing of these hypotheses and the
evaluation of the courses of action. In special circumstances, the decision maker's
experience and judgment may be sufficient to enable selection of a course of
action without conclusive research evidence. Typically, however, such evidence
is required, and the decision maker would be making a serious error by assuming
that the focus group interview could provide evidence of a conclusive nature.
Conclusive research is the subject of the next chapter.

Depth Interview

The *depth interview* may be defined as an unstructured personal interview which
uses extensive probing to get a single respondent to talk freely and to express
detailed beliefs and feelings on a topic. The purpose of this technique is to get
below the respondent's surface reactions and to discover the more fundamental
reasons underlying the respondent's attitudes and behavior.[8]

The depth interview can last an hour or more, and the interviewer typically has
committed to memory the outline of topics to be covered. The actual wording
and sequencing of questions are left to the discretion of the interviewer, who tries
to identify general areas for discussion and then encourages the respondent to
discuss the topic of interest freely and in depth. The interviewer probes responses
that are of interest by asking such questions as "That's interesting; can you tell me
more?" and "Why do you say that?"

The interviewer plays a critical role in the success of the depth interview
technique. It is the interviewer's responsibility to create an environment where
the respondent feels relaxed and free to present beliefs and feelings without fear
of being criticized or misunderstood. As in the focus group interview, the interviewer's role is central. The interviewer must probe into attitudes, beliefs, and

[8]Hazel Kahan, "One-on-Ones Should Sparkle Like the Gems They Are," *Marketing News*, pp.
8–9, September 3, 1990.

feelings behind simple responses. The interviewer must avoid the appearance of superiority, while remaining objective and encouraging responses.

The depth interview, like the focus group interview, is used primarily for exploratory research. The technique is useful in developing hypotheses, defining decision problems, and formulating courses of action. The individual interview can be useful when the marketing problem relates to particularly confidential, sensitive, or potentially embarrassing issues, or when group pressure or norms would affect the responses.

The *experience survey* is a type of individual interview. In an experience survey, the researcher is interested in the views of a selective cross-section of people associated with the research problem. Interviewees are sought for their ability to articulate responses as well as their familiarity with the problem. For example, executives and distributors on different levels in a retail industry may be questioned on the effectiveness of a channel distribution. The research is looking for insights into the problem. The survey is usually informal, and the questions are open-ended.

One advantage of the depth interview over the focus-group interview relates to the greater depth of insight that can be uncovered and the ability to associate the response directly with the respondent. In the focus group interview, it can be difficult to determine which respondent made a particular response. Another advantage of the depth interview is that the interviewer can develop a high level of rapport with the respondent, which results in responses that are given more freely than may be possible in a focus group.[9]

The depth interview is seldom used in marketing research. The disadvantages of the technique contribute to its limited use.[10] Its success rests entirely upon the skills and experience of the interviewer. Since there are few adequately qualified interviewers and those who are qualified are highly paid, the technique has not gained wide acceptance as a regular research tool. The length of the interview combined with the high interviewer cost means that the number of persons interviewed in a project is small. The small sample size and the complete reliance on the interviewer for analysis and interpretation are important limitations that restrict use of this technique to special problem situations.

EXPLORATORY RESEARCH WORLDWIDE

As with conclusive research, what constitutes exploratory research is greatly similar in the United States and in the rest of the world. However, there are clear differences in the implementation of research methodologies such as focus groups and in-depth interviews. These differences result from variations in cultural and infrastructures characteristics among countries.

[9]Pamela Rogers, "One-on-Ones Don't Get the Credit They Deserve," *Marketing News,* pp. 9–10, January 2, 1989.
[10]Thomas L. Greenbaum, "Focus Groups vs. One-on-Ones: The Controversy Continues," *Marketing News,* p. 16, September 2, 1991.

In the United Kingdom, the majority of focus groups are held in interviewers' homes rather than in specially designed laboratory facilities. Consequently, clients rarely attend group sessions. The typical group size is smaller (six to eight people) in the UK. The smaller group size reflects the far greater variety of focus group formats used. The different types of groups used include peer groups, conflict groups, recall groups, delphi groups, and brainstorming groups. This diversity reflects a greater interest in the UK in understanding consumers' subconscious minds and motivations than is prevalent among U.S. clients.

In Asia, focus groups are a popular form of exploratory research, reflecting Asian marketers' belief that the focus group offers the best approach to understanding consumers. The implementation of focus groups in Asia is very similar to that in the United States.

SUMMARY

1 Exploratory research is used in the preliminary stage of a research project to define management problems and to explore alternative courses of action.

2 Qualitative techniques are important tools used in implementing the exploratory research phase of the research project. The techniques involve a high degree of flexibility in how the questions are asked and in the degree of probing used.

3 The primary qualitative techniques are (a) the focus group interview and (b) the in-depth interview. The former is the more popular of the two techniques.

4 The primary purpose of exploratory research is to build a foundation for the conclusive research phase of the project. It is important that the qualitative data be thoroughly analyzed to identify potential quantitative relationships and insights that can be validated in the conclusive research phase.

DISCUSSION QUESTIONS

1 What is the role of exploratory research in a research project?

2 Why are online focus groups, which were discussed in the Marketing Research in Action at the beginning of the chapter, a good medium for gathering qualitative data?

3 What are the characteristics of qualitative data?

4 Why are focus groups important in marketing?

5 Discuss some of the problems that may arise in designing or conducting a focus group.

6 What are some of the desirable characteristics of focus group moderators?

7 Discuss the advantages and disadvantages of focus groups.

8 When would an in-depth interview be more useful than a focus group? Give an example.

9 What are the issues and steps in the analysis of qualitative data?

10 MINICASE

Discuss the issues involved in determining when and where an automobile tire manufacturer should conduct focus groups to get feedback from customers on its line of winter tires. Give a brief description of customers who would be good candidates for this type of focus group.

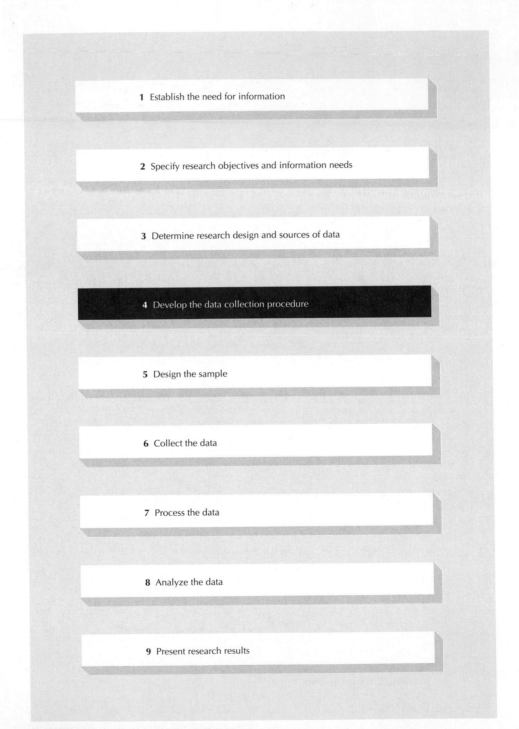

FIGURE 11-1   Steps in the research process.

CHAPTER 11

DATA COLLECTION: CONCLUSIVE RESEARCH

MARKETING RESEARCH IN ACTION

NORTHWEST AIRLINES USES IN-FLIGHT QUESTIONNAIRE TO TAP PASSENGERS' ATTITUDES AND BEHAVIOR

In an attempt to be more responsive to the needs of international travelers, the marketing research department of Northwest Airlines arranged for flight attendants to hand out questionnaires on its international flights. In a preamble to the questionnaire, Susan Goode, Northwest's director of marketing research, noted, "Because we value your business, our goal is to make your travel as enjoyable as possible. . . . You can assist us in our effort by taking a few moments to complete this survey." The questionnaire consisted of 28 questions, some of which are presented below. The major sections of the questionnaire were: (1) "About Today's Flight," (2) How We Are Doing," (3) "Your Travel Experiences," and (4) "About You."

Northwest Airlines' management had concluded that a self-administered questionnaire was an appropriate way to measure the flying public's attitudes toward and reactions to the airlines' service, food, and competitive position. This is but one of the methods that were available to Northwest Airlines for measuring the attitudes and behavior of air travelers; for example, focus groups or in-depth interviews could have been used to tap attitudes in a less structured way. In addition, indirect questionnaire approaches, such as inclusion of sentence completion items, could have tapped more deeply held attitudes about Northwest. All these approaches to obtaining information from respondents form the focus of this chapter and Chapter 10.

The Questionnaire

About Today's Flight

Please fill in the following information about your flight today.

_____   _____
         Flight number   Boarding city

_____   _____
         Destination   Date

1 How many days before the start of this trip was your . . .

	Same day	1–3 days	4–6 days	7–14 days	15–29 days	30 days or more
Trip first planned?	◯	◯	◯	◯	◯	◯
Airline reservation made?	◯	◯	◯	◯	◯	◯
Ticket purchased?	◯	◯	◯	◯	◯	◯
Boarding pass obtained?	◯	◯	◯	◯	◯	◯

4 Who chose Northwest for this flight? (Mark only one.)

◯ Travel agent
◯ Company travel office
◯ Secretary/business associate
◯ Government/military travel office
◯ I did personally
◯ Other family member/friend
◯ Part of a tour package
◯ Other

10 Why was Northwest chosen for this flight? (Mark all that apply.)

◯ Convenience of departure/arrival schedule
◯ Ticket price
◯ Direct/nonstop service to destination
◯ Part of tour package
◯ Only airline option to my destination
◯ To get Worldperks mileage
◯ Using Worldperks free travel award
◯ Prefer to fly Northwest over other airlines
◯ Company travel department selected
◯ Travel agent suggestion
◯ Don't know

How We Are Doing

11 Compared to other airlines, how would you rate Northwest's ground service personnel (ticket and gate agents) on the following:

	Other airlines much better						Northwest much better
Courtesy/friendliness	①	②	③	④	⑤	⑥	⑦
Responsiveness/ability to solve problems and answer questions	①	②	③	④	⑤	⑥	⑦
Keeping you informed about problems/delays	①	②	③	④	⑤	⑥	⑦
Efficiency of service	①	②	③	④	⑤	⑥	⑦
Professional appearance	①	②	③	④	⑤	⑥	⑦

13 Compared to other airlines, how would you rate this Northwest flight on the following:

	Other airlines much better						Northwest much better
Quantity of food served	①	②	③	④	⑤	⑥	⑦
Quality of food served	①	②	③	④	⑤	⑥	⑦
Type, variety of food offered	①	②	③	④	⑤	⑥	⑦
Timeliness of beverage service	①	②	③	④	⑤	⑥	⑦
Cabin cleanliness	①	②	③	④	⑤	⑥	⑦
Cabin temperature	①	②	③	④	⑤	⑥	⑦
Cabin ventilation	①	②	③	④	⑤	⑥	⑦
Cabin noise level	①	②	③	④	⑤	⑥	⑦
Seat comfort	①	②	③	④	⑤	⑥	⑦
Carry-on storage space	①	②	③	④	⑤	⑥	⑦
On-time performance	①	②	③	④	⑤	⑥	⑦
Cleanliness of gate area	①	②	③	④	⑤	⑥	⑦

14 Please indicate your level of agreement with the following statements, based upon your overall experience(s) with Northwest. (First-time fliers use today's experience.)

	Strongly disagree						Strongly agree
Northwest provides products/services that meet passenger needs.	①	②	③	④	⑤	⑥	⑦
Northwest performs to my expectations.	①	②	③	④	⑤	⑥	⑦
Northwest provides high-quality service.	①	②	③	④	⑤	⑥	⑦
Northwest provides consistent service.	①	②	③	④	⑤	⑥	⑦
Northwest introduces new and improved products/services in a timely manner.	①	②	③	④	⑤	⑥	⑦
I receive good value on Northwest for the price paid.	①	②	③	④	⑤	⑥	⑦
Northwest makes passengers feel they are important to the success of the airline.	①	②	③	④	⑤	⑥	⑦
I would fly Northwest in the future.	①	②	③	④	⑤	⑥	⑦
I would recommend Northwest to others.	①	②	③	④	⑤	⑥	⑦

About You

22 What is your occupation?
- ☐ Executive/managerial
- ☐ Professional/technical
- ☐ Sales representative/agent
- ☐ Teacher/professor
- ☐ Government/military
- ☐ Office worker/clerical/sales clerk/secretarial
- ☐ Craftsperson/mechanic/service worker
- ☐ Homemaker
- ☐ Student
- ☐ Retired
- ☐ Airline employee/travel agent
- ☐ Other

27 Where do you currently reside?

☐ United States	☐ Germany	☐ Japan
☐ Canada	☐ Great Britain	☐ Korea
☐ Mexico	☐ Holland	☐ Philippines
☐ Caribbean	☐ Scotland	☐ Taiwan
☐ Central America	☐ Other Europe	☐ Other Asia
☐ South America	☐ China	☐ Middle East
☐ Denmark	☐ Hong Kong	☐ Other (not listed)
☐ France		

28 If you live in the United States, what is your home zip code?

Zip code

```
(0) (0) (0) (0) (0)
(1) (1) (1) (1) (1)
(2) (2) (2) (2) (2)
(3) (3) (3) (3) (3)
(4) (4) (4) (4) (4)
(5) (5) (5) (5) (5)
(6) (6) (6) (6) (6)
(7) (7) (7) (7) (7)
(8) (8) (8) (8) (8)
(9) (9) (9) (9) (9)
```

Source: Northwest Airlines, Minneapolis, MN.

Chapter 10 emphasized the role of exploratory research in the early phase of the decision-making process. Typically, qualitative data are used in formulating problems and in stimulating the creative process involved in identifying alternative courses of action. The qualitative data provide an intuitive understanding of the problem. Once the decision problem has been clearly stated and the alternative courses of action specified, the conclusive research phase of the research project can be initiated.

Conclusive research involves a systematic and objective process through which a target market is sampled and responses are measured using a structured data collection technique. Sampling issues are discussed in later chapters. The focus of this chapter is on conclusive research data collection techniques—that is, what types of information we are looking for and how we go about getting it.

With this chapter, we begin to discuss the research design stage, where the market researcher begins the quantitative evaluation process for the alternative courses of action. The conclusive research results of this evaluation will be statistically and scientifically valid and can be used to forecast the success or failure of the different management alternatives.

Once the need for conclusive research has been established, the researcher must clearly state the objectives of the proposed research and develop a list of information needs. Assuming that secondary data sources do not completely meet the needs of the study, primary data must be obtained. Primary data sources can include (1) respondents, (2) analogous situations, and (3) experiments. Previous chapters have discussed the data sources of analogous situations and experimentation. This chapter focuses on gathering primary data from respondents.

TYPES OF RESPONDENT DATA ~ Start

In a fundamental sense, all marketing decision making is concerned with taking action today so that future objectives can be accomplished. In this context, marketing research can be viewed as a forecasting technique designed to facilitate the process of predicting market behavior. The types of data that can be obtained from respondents for use in forecasting market behavior are (1) past behavior, (2) attitudes, and (3) respondent characteristics.

Past Behavior

Evidence regarding the respondent's past behavior has wide usage as a predictor of future behavior. In our personal activities we all use evidence of past behavior to predict the future behavior of our friends and relatives. In similar fashion, a marketing research study can gather evidence on a respondent's behavior regarding purchase and use of a product or brand, for the purpose of predicting future behavior. The specific evidence gathered about this past behavior can include the following: (1) What was purchased and/or used? (2) How much was purchased and/or used? (3) How was it purchased and/or used? (4) Where was it purchased and/or used? (5) When was it purchased and/or used? (6) Who purchased and/or used it? There are many dimensions involved in understanding past behavior. The researcher must be sensitive to the key behavioral dimensions relevant to predicting future behavior when specifying the data required to meet the information needs of a study.

Attitudes

Attitudes are important in marketing because of the assumed relationship between attitudes and behavior. Attitudinal data are used to identify market segments, to develop a "positioning" strategy, and to evaluate advertising programs.

An attitude is generally considered to have three main components: (1) a *cog-*

nitive component—a person's knowledge about the object of concern, such as its speed or durability; (2) an *affective* component—a person's feelings about the object, such as "good" or "bad"; and (3) a *behavioral* component—a person's readiness to respond behaviorally to the object.

This measurement of attitudes was discussed extensively in Chapter 8. The emphasis was on the qualification of attitudes, using self-reporting scaling techniques. This chapter will discuss additional techniques for identifying the nature of attitudes and for measuring them.

Respondent Characteristics

The phrase *respondent characteristics* means descriptions of respondents on particular variables of interest, including demographic, socioeconomic, and psychological characteristics. For many products, variables of this nature have been found to be correlates of purchase behavior. In addition, variables such as age, sex, marital status, family size, income, occupation, and education level have been found useful in sample stratification and validation.

A popular way of describing a respondent is in terms of *life-style,* defined as a distinctive mode of living of a society, or of a segment of a society. Life-style research focuses on respondent *activities, interests, and opinions (A-I-O items),* and on demographic characteristics. Examples of A-I-O items are listed in Table 11-1.

The term "psychographics" is closely related to the concept of life-style. It is a broader term which includes the life-style concept. One definition is as follows:

> Psychographics is a quantitative research procedure which seeks to explain why people behave as they do and why they hold their current attitudes. It seeks to take quantitative research beyond demographic, socioeconomic, and user/nonuser analysis, but also employs three variables, of which life-style is one. The others are psychological and product benefits.[1]

[1]Emanuel Demby, "Psychographics and From Whence It Came," in William D. Wells (ed.), *Life Style and Psychographics* (Chicago: American Marketing Association, 1974), p. 24.

TABLE 11-1   LIFE-STYLE CHARACTERISTICS

Activities	Interests	Opinions
Work	Family	Themselves
Hobbies	Home	Social issues
Social events	Job	Politics
Vacations	Community	Business
Entertainment	Recreation	Economics
Club membership	Fashion	Education
Community	Food	Products
Shopping	Media	Future
Sports	Achievements	Culture

METHODS OF COLLECTING RESPONDENT DATA

The two basic methods of collecting data from respondents are communication and observation. We will first examine the communication method and then the observation method.

Communication Method

The communication method of data collection is based on the questioning of respondents. It is logical to ask respondents questions if you want to know what brand of soup they buy, which television programs they view, or why they shop at a particular store. Such questions may be asked verbally or in writing, and the responses may be in either form. The data collection instrument typically used in this process, as we have previously discussed, is a *questionnaire*. The questionnaire has come to be the predominant data collection instrument in marketing research. It is estimated that over half of the United States public has participated in one or more research studies of this nature.

Advantages of the Communication Method The main advantage of the communication method is its versatility. *Versatility* refers to the ability of the method to collect data on a wide range of information needs. The vast majority of marketing decision problems involve people. Consequently, the information needs focus on people's past behavior, attitudes, and characteristics. The communication method can gather data in all three of these areas.

Additional advantages relate to the speed and cost of the communication method as compared to the observation method. The speed and cost advantages are highly interdependent. The communication method is a faster means of data collection than observation in that it provides more control over the data collection process. The researcher does not have to predict when and where the behavior will occur, nor to wait for it to occur. For example, it would be much faster and cheaper to ask a respondent about the purchase of a dishwasher than to try to anticipate and observe the purchase.

Disadvantages of the Communication Method There are three important limitations to the communication method. The first relates to the respondent's *unwillingness to provide the desired data*. The respondent may refuse to take the time to be interviewed or refuse to respond to particular questions. The second limitation concerns the respondent's *inability to provide the data*. The respondent may not recall the facts in question or may never have known them.

The third limitation involves the *influence of the questioning process* on the responses. The respondents may bias their responses in order to give a socially acceptable answer or to please the interviewer. While these limitations can seriously reduce the validity of the communication method, they can also be controlled by properly designing the data collection instrument. More will be said about this in Chapter 12, where the design of data collection forms is discussed.

Communicating with Respondents

The four types of communication approaches available for obtaining data from respondents are (1) the personal interview, (2) the telephone interview, (3) the mail interview, and (4) the computer disk interview.

The first three of these communication approaches have traditionally been widely used in marketing research. Table 11-2 indicates that the telephone interview is used by about 97 percent of businesses, the personal interview by about 91 percent of businesses, and the mail interview by about 92 percent of businesses in their marketing research studies. The use of computer disks is growing as computer availability increases at home and in the office.

Personal Interview   In the *personal interview,* an interviewer asks questions of one or more respondents in a face-to-face situation. The interviewer's task is to contact the respondent or respondents, ask the questions, and record the responses. The questions must be asked in a clear manner and recorded accurately. The recording of responses can take place either during or after the interview.

The face-to-face interviewing process may cause respondents to bias their responses (for example, because of a desire to please or impress the interviewer). The potential for introduction of bias into personal interview data because of social motivations will be discussed in more detail in the section on criteria for selecting a communication medium.

Telephone Interview   In the *telephone interview,* an interviewer asks questions of one or more respondents via the telephone. Telephone interviewing is the most widely used of the three traditional communication media. The reasons for its popularity are its efficient and economical procedures and its application to a wide range of information needs.

With the telephone interview, the lower degree of social interaction between the interviewer and the respondent reduces the potential for bias in comparison to the personal interview. The basic limitations of the telephone interview relate to the limited amount of data that can be obtained and the potential bias that can result from an incomplete listing of the target population, as discussed later in this chapter.

TABLE 11-2   USE OF COMMUNICATION APPROACHES IN MARKETING
RESEARCH BY BUSINESS

Communication approach	Percent usage		
	Frequent	Sometimes	Never
Personal interview	48	43	9
Telephone interview	74	23	3
Mail interview	54	38	8

Source: Thomas C. Kinnear and Ann R. Root, *A Study of the Marketing Research Business,* unpublished study, 1994. Copyright 1994 Thomas C. Kinnear. Not to be reproduced.

Mail Interview   In the *mail interview,* a questionnaire is mailed to the respondent, and the completed questionnaire is returned by mail to the research organization. The mail interview is as popular as the personal interview but less popular than the telephone interview.

Mail interviews are flexible in their application and relatively low in cost, and they lack the potential for bias resulting from the interviewer-respondent interaction. Their major disadvantage relates to the problem of nonresponse error.

Many approaches to distributing and collecting the questionnaire can be used. The questionnaire can be left and/or retrieved by an individual rather than being sent by mail. It can be distributed in magazines and newspapers. Warranty cards packaged with products provide an opportunity to collect data regarding the characteristics of the purchaser and the purchase decision process.

The increasing use and popularity of the facsimile machine in the office environment has created an opportunity for a "hybrid" mail interview. Business respondents can now be reached quickly and easily with the latest fax technology. One study found quicker response times, increased response rates, and similar response content findings for fax questionnaires as compared to mail questionnaires.[2]

Computer Disk Interview   Because of the growing access to personal computers at the office and at home, computer disk interviews are an increasingly popular option. This is especially true in efforts to reach business professionals. Disk-based interviews can be used to ask for open-ended responses and to assess qualitative issues. The respondent can take his or her time in responding to the questions, resulting in better-quality comments. An advantage of disk-based interviews is their ability to branch and skip questions automatically. The respondent is not exposed to questions that have no relevance, based on earlier answers. With the right technology, compiling the responses can be relatively easy. Keypunch errors are avoided. The necessity for access to a computer limits the available respondent pool and may result in sampling error. Another major limitation is the need for compatibility between computer systems.

Criteria for Selecting the Communication Approach

In evaluating which communication approach best meets the needs of a research project, several criteria are relevant, namely: (1) versatility, (2) cost, (3) time, (4) sample control, (5) quantity of data, (6) quality of data, and (7) response rate. The importance assigned to these criteria, all of which are discussed below, will vary with the specific needs of the research project.

Versatility   *Versatility* refers to the ability of the approach to adapt the data collection process to the special needs of the study or the respondent. The personal

[2]John P. Dickson and Douglas L. MacLachlan, "Fax Surveys?", *Marketing Research: A Magazine of Management & Applications™*, vol. 4, no. 3, pp. 26–30, September 1992.

interview is the most versatile of the four communication approaches. Telephone interviews and computer disks are less versatile than personal interviews, while the mail interview is the least versatile.

The personal interview has high versatility in that the interviewing process involves a face-to-face relationship between the respondent and the interviewer. The latter can explain and clarify complex questions, administer complex questionnaires, utilize unstructured techniques, and present visual cues such as advertisements and product concepts to the respondent—all as part of the questioning process. The telephone interview is not as versatile as the personal interview in that the interviewer is not in a face-to-face relationship with the respondent. Consequently, it is more difficult to use unstructured techniques, to include complex questions, and to elicit in-depth answers to open-ended questions. Computer disks can allow for complex questions as well as in-depth answers. When the research design involves structured questions with simple instructions that can be answered easily by the respondent, the interviewer's role can often be eliminated, and the mail interview may be the more appropriate medium for the study.

With the advance of technology, personal and phone interviews are now usually conducted with the aid of computers. Computer-aided telephone interviewing (CATI) and computer-aided personal interviewing (CAPI) are conducted with computer software that enables the researcher to include complex questions, while allowing the computer to skip over or add questions depending on the respondent's answers. These types of computer-aided research increase the versatility of personal and phone interviews tremendously.

The researcher must determine the degree of versatility required in a research project and must select the communication approach that best meets the needs of the study. In practice, most research projects do not require the high versatility that the personal interview provides.

Cost   The number of hours of labor involved tends to determine the relative *costs* of the four communication approaches. Labor costs include the salaries of the interviewers and the supervisory costs associated with controlling the quality of the data collection process.

The personal interview is typically the most expensive approach per completed interview. Telephone interviews are usually more expensive than those conducted by mail. When the questionnaire is short, the cost of a telephone interview is usually comparable to that of a mail interview. Computer disks will cost marginally more up-front, but will save interviewer time.

While the cost of a communication approach is highly dependent upon the specific details of the research design, a general estimate of data collection cost per completed interview would be as follows: (1) personal interview, $20 to $40; (2) telephone and computer disk interviews, $10 to $25; and (3) mail interview, $10 to $20.[3]

---

[3]The total estimated cost per interview, including data collection, analysis, and report, would be: (1) personal interview, $50 to $100; (2) telephone or computer disk interview, $25 to $40; and (3) mail interview, $20 to $30.

Time   Of the four communication approaches, the telephone interview is the fastest way to obtain data. With a short questionnaire, an interviewer can complete perhaps 10 or more interviews per hour. Using the same questionnaire, a personal interviewer would be fortunate to complete two or three interviews per hour. Obviously, the travel time between interviews represents a serious time constraint on the personal interviewer's completion rate. Consequently, personal interview studies are typically larger in elapsed time from the beginning of field work to project completion than telephone, computer disk, or mail interview studies.

The total project completion time can be shortened by increasing the number of interviewers working on the study when the personal or telephone interview is used. With the telephone interview, it is reasonably easy to train, coordinate, and control the staff of interviewers. Since the interviewing staff can phone from a central location, the project supervisor can easily monitor the interviews and control the quality of the interviewing. Consequently, a large interviewing force can be efficiently used with telephone interviewing to meet the time constraint placed on a research project.

While the number of personal interviewers can also be increased to meet the time constraints placed on a project, the problems associated with training, coordinating, and controlling a large interviewing staff are compounded very quickly, to a point where it is neither feasible nor economical to increase the number of interviewers on the project. Consequently, personal interview studies typically consume longer elapsed time than mail or telephone studies.

It is very difficult to shorten the elapsed time for completing a computer disk or mail study. Once the questionnaires are mailed, there is little the researcher can do to speed the replies. A series of follow-up mailings may be required to stimulate the return of the remaining questionnaires. It may be necessary to wait 2 or more weeks after each follow-up mailing to determine whether an acceptable response rate is going to be achieved. While it could take several months to complete a mail or computer disk study, if the number of interviews to be completed is large, the elapsed time may not be as great as that required to conduct a similar study using personal interviews.

Sample Control   *Sample control* refers to the ability of the communication approach to reach the designated units in the sampling plan effectively and efficiently. The four communication approaches differ significantly in this regard.

The personal interview offers the best degree of sample control. As we will discuss in Chapter 15, area sampling procedures can overcome the problems created by the absence of a complete listing of the *sampling frame*—the list of population units from which the sample will be drawn. Sampling procedures that do not require a list of the sampling units rely heavily upon the personal interviewer in the process of selecting the sample. Working through the personal interviewer, the researcher can control which sampling units are interviewed, who is interviewed, the degree of participation of other members of the unit in the interview, and many other aspects of the data collection process.

The telephone interview is highly dependent upon a sampling frame. One or more telephone directories usually serve as the sampling frame, with respondents being selected from directories serving the population of interest through probabilistic selection procedures.

Telephone directories are often poor sampling frames in that they offer incomplete listings of persons in a given area, for the following reasons: (1) not everyone has a phone, (2) new phones that have been placed in service since the directory was published are not listed, and (3) some people have unlisted phones.

Telephone ownership in the United States is very high. In 1987 it was estimated that 93 percent of households in the nation had telephones,[4] and telephone ownership is nearer 100 percent in most areas. Consequently, phone ownership is typically not a serious problem for most telephone studies.

In some areas, estimates of the percentage of unlisted numbers run as high as 30 percent. This can be a serious source of bias, since research indicates that persons with voluntarily unlisted numbers differ from persons with listed numbers on a number of important demographic characteristics.

As a telephone directory grows older, an increasing proportion of persons who have moved to the area covered by the directory are not listed. Since persons who move frequently differ from less mobile persons on a number of demographic characteristics, aging phone directories become less and less representative of the population of phone owners.

Because of unrepresentative phone directories, the telephone interview permits only limited control over the sample. The procedure designed to overcome this problem is *random-digit dialing.* As discussed in Chapter 15, this procedure involves the random generation of at least some of the digits used in the sampling plan. A central interviewing facility can be used to place calls, using the Wide Area Telecommunications Service (WATS). This allows a geographically wide sampling plan. However, even with these improvements, telephone surveys still rely on simple random sampling or systematic sampling. As discussed in the sampling chapters, alternative sampling procedures exist which are more efficient than either of these.

The mail interview, like the telephone interview, requires a listing of the population elements. Ideally, this frame is composed of both names and addresses. Typically, telephone street directories are used for a listing of the general population. The problems in the use of this type of list have already been discussed.

Several commercial research firms maintain panels of respondents who have agreed to answer mail questionnaires sent to them. One such organization is National Family Opinion (NFO). This firm maintains a panel of over 150,000 U.S. families who have agreed to cooperate without compensation in completing questionnaires mailed to them on a variety of subjects. A current demographic profile is maintained for each family. Other organizations that maintain mail panels are the Home Testing Institute and Market Facts, Inc.

Mailing lists for specialized groups of respondents can be purchased from firms that specialize in the area. Catalogs are available which contain thousands of lists,

---

[4]*Statistical Abstract of the United States,* 108th ed. (Washington, D.C.: U.S. Bureau of the Census, 1988), p. 523.

many of which can be segmented in various ways.[5] Even with a mailing list that contains the target population, the researcher still has the problem of limited control over the person or persons at the mailing address who complete the questionnaire, as well as whether the questionnaire will be returned.

Sampling error is a concern with computer disk interviews. Computer disk interviews are more effective when qualitative data are sought, rather than quantitative data for which statistical validity is important. Computer disk interviews assume access to a compatible computer system, limiting the pool of respondents to certain socioeconomic and employment categories. Computer disk interviews share several of the disadvantages of telephones and mailing lists, including unrepresentative population lists and lack of control over who actually completes the interview questionnaire.

Quantity of Data   An established rule is that the largest amount of data can be collected using the personal interview, followed by the mail interview, and then by the telephone interview. There is growing evidence that the mail and telephone interview can collect more data than previously assumed. Computer disks are relatively new and do not have a history built up yet. In situations where the respondents are emotionally involved in the topic, all four approaches can provide substantial amounts of data. At normal involvement levels, however, the personal interview can collect substantially more data than the other three.

The main advantage of the personal interview stems from the social relationship between the interviewer and the respondent. This social setting typically motivates the respondent to spend more time in the interview setting. The University of Michigan Survey Research Center finds that a 75-minute interview is feasible with the personal interview, while the telephone interview must be limited to 30 to 40 minutes. It is much easier for the respondent to terminate the telephone or mail interview, because of its impersonal nature, than to terminate the personal interview.

An advantage that both the personal interview and the telephone interview have over the mail or computer disk interview is that less effort is required of the respondent in the data collection process. Here, the interviewer asks the questions, probes the responses, and records the answers. The personal interview has the added advantage of allowing the visual presentation of rating scale categories and other support material that can facilitate the respondent's comprehension of the questions asked. These advantages all contribute to the respondent's willingness to provide a greater quality of data.

Quality of Data   *Quality of data* refers to the degree to which the data are free from potential bias resulting from the use of a particular communication approach. When the subject matter is unemotional and the questionnaire is properly designed and administered, quality data will generally result regardless of which approach is used.

[5]*1994–95 Catalog of Mailing Lists* (New York: Fritz S. Hofheimer, Inc., 1994).

Researchers have found substantial differences among the three traditional approaches—personal, telephone, and mail interviews—when sensitive or embarrassing questions are involved—for example, questions about bank loans, income, and sexual behavior. There is evidence that mail surveys collect better-quality data on such sensitive topics than do personal interviews. Telephone interviews most likely would lie between these two approaches.

Another source of bias can result from confusion by respondents regarding the question asked. Since the respondent cannot seek clarification from the interviewer with the mail or computer disk interview, these methods offer the greatest chance for inaccurate results resulting from confusion. The telephone interview offers more potential for bias caused by confusion than does the personal interview, because of the lack of an interviewer's physical presence.

The mail interview has another potential for bias, in that the respondents may read through all the questions before answering them, or may change answers in the early parts of the questionnaire as a result of responses given later in the questionnaire. Both the personal and the telephone interview are free from this type of bias. The computer disk can be designed to prevent the respondent from either looking ahead or going back and changing responses.

The quality of data obtained in telephone interviews tends to be better than that in personal interviews because the data collection process can be better supervised and controlled. Fewer interviewers are needed for the telephone survey, and they can be trained and supervised at a central location.

Both the telephone interview and the personal interview have an important advantage over mail and computer disk interviews, in that they can be used to collect data near the time the behavior occurs. This reduces the bias associated with failure to recall events accurately.

A final consideration regarding the quality of data obtained concerns cheating by the interviewer. Cheating is easier with the personal interview than with the phone interview, since the latter can be directly monitored whereas the former cannot. Properly designed personal interview studies have procedures for controlling cheating which can be effective in minimizing the source of bias. Neither the mail nor the computer disk interview has an interviewer, and thus they are not subject to bias resulting from cheating.

Response Rate   The *response rate* is the percentage of the original sample that is actually interviewed. The *nonresponse error* is the difference between those who respond and those who do not respond. A low response rate can result in a high nonresponse error, which can invalidate the research findings.

Nonresponse error is one of the most serious sources of error confronting the researcher. Table 11-3 illustrates the type of difference that can exist between those who respond and those who do not respond. The median income of respondents for each of a series of callback interviews is shown. A policy of no callbacks (for which the median income would be $23,032) would have produced an estimate of income 44 percent below that found after extensive callbacks (median income of $40,932). This finding represents a clear example of nonresponse error.

TABLE 11-3   MEDIAN INCOME VARIATION BY NUMBER
OF CALLBACKS

Number of calls during which interviewed	Median income	Number of interviews
1	$23,032	427
2	32,337	391
3	33,052	232
4	34,097	123
5	33,052	77
6+	40,932	59
All	$30,786	1,309

Source: J. B. Lansing and J. N. Morgan, *Economic Survey Methods* (Ann Arbor: University of Michigan Press, 1971), p. 161. Used with the permission of the University of Michigan Press. Median income figures are adjusted for inflation for 1992.

The probability of nonresponse error increases as the survey response rate decreases. However, it is important to recognize that a low response rate does not in itself imply that a high nonresponse error is present in the data. It is only when there is a difference between respondents and nonrespondents on the variables of interest that nonresponse error occurs. If the reason for nonresponse is independent of the key variables of interest, there should be little difference between respondent and nonrespondent groups.

Nonresponse can result from two sources: (1) not-at-homes and (2) refusals. Nonresponse caused by the respondent not being at home can seriously affect telephone and personal interviews, but it has limited influence on mail surveys. Since respondents are more likely to answer a phone than to answer the door when a stranger is present, the telephone interview has traditionally had less of a not-at-home problem than the personal interview. Access to consumers through the telephone, however, is becoming increasingly difficult. The increasing use of telephone answering machines creates a stumbling block for the telephone interviewer.[6] New phone services allowing the blocking of calls from unfamiliar numbers may introduce additional potential for bias. Consumer reaction to telemarketing is affecting the marketing researcher's ability to gain cooperation.[7] As Figure 11-2 indicates, 65 percent of respondents in a recent survey believed that research surveys and telemarketing are the same thing, or else could not distinguish between the two. Telemarketing contact rises as respondents' ages, education levels, and incomes rise. Hostility toward telemarketing has increased the refusal rate on telephone research surveys, potentially leading to a less representative pool of cooperative respondents.

Once a potential respondent has informed the interviewer of an unwillingness

[6]Peter S. Tuckel and Barry M. Feinberg, "The Answering Machine Poses Many Questions for Telephone Survey Researchers," *Public Opinion Quarterly*, pp. 200–217, Summer 1991.
[7]Todd Remington, "Rising Refusal Rates: The Impact of Telemarketing," *Quirk's Marketing Research Review*, pp. 8–15, May 1992.

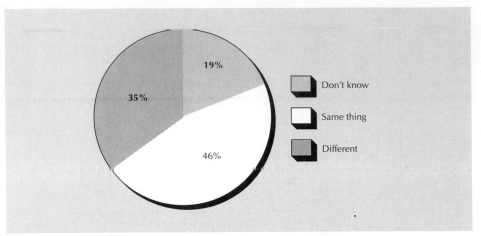

FIGURE 11-2 Telephone surveys and telemarketing: same or different. (*Source: Quirk's Marketing Research Review*, p. 12, May 1992.)

to be interviewed, there is little that can be done to reverse the respondent's position. While the offer to call at another time may be favorably received by some respondents, the majority still refuse the interview.

While the mail or computer disk interview avoids the nonresponse caused by not-at-homes, it is seriously influenced by the refusal to respond. However, the failure to complete and return the questionnaire on time does not imply a strong unwillingness to respond. Many respondents may be influenced to respond if reminded. In a computer disk interview, a compatible computer must be available to the respondent. Otherwise the respondent cannot even view the questions.

The major emphasis on reducing nonresponse in personal and telephone interviews centers on establishing contact with the potential respondent. A series of callbacks is required to reduce the proportion of not-at-homes. Most situations require a minimum of three callbacks. The callback schedule should be varied by time of day and by day of the week. An excellent guide for the scheduling of telephone and personal interviews is provided by *Who's Home When,* a publication of the Bureau of the Census.[8] This study provides estimates of the proportion of people at home between 8 A.M. and 9 P.M. on an hourly basis.

The reduction of nonresponse in mail and computer disk surveys focuses on motivating the respondent to answer the questionnaire and return it.[9] The response rate of the mail or computer disk interview is directly related to the respondent's interest in the survey topic. If the target population's interest in the survey topic varies, a serious source of nonresponse error can be introduced into the results.

[8]Bureau of the Census, *Who's Home When* (Washington, D.C.: U.S. Government Printing Office, 1973).

[9]Richard J. Fox, Melvin R. Crask, and Jonghoon Kim, ''Mail Survey Response Rate: A Meta-Analysis of Selected Techniques for Inducing Response,'' *Public Opinion Quarterly,* pp. 467–491, Winter 1988.

Some of the more successful ways to increase the response rate of mail and computer disk surveys are as follows:

1 Use an advance letter or a telephone call to notify the respondent of the study and to request cooperation.[10]

2 Use first-class postage in mailings to respondents, and provide hand-stamped return envelopes.

3 Consider the use of a monetary incentive in situations where motivation needs to be stimulated.[11]

4 Use a postcard or letter in follow-up contacts requesting completion and return of the questionnaire. Other follow-ups include making phone contact, sending a telegraph, mailing a new questionnaire, and making personal contact.

A five-step procedure for securing returns to mail surveys was proposed by Robin,[12] as follows: (1) Send a prequestionnaire letter. (2) Mail the questionnaire with a cover letter. (3) Send a follow-up letter. (4) Mail a second questionnaire. (5) Send a second follow-up letter. A 7-day interval between mailings is recommended. A 77.8 percent response rate was achieved using this five-step procedure in a mail survey of dentists.

Mail surveys conducted by experienced researchers should achieve response rates of over 50 percent, and some surveys achieve rates as high as 80 percent. A mail survey that achieves an 80 percent return rate is comparable to many personal and telephone interview studies, in terms of the proportion of completed interviews. An 80 percent response rate is suggested as the standard for mail surveys by the Advertising Research Foundation. In practice, most fall substantially below this rate.

For all four communication approaches, the decision regarding the number of callbacks involves weighing the benefits of reduced nonresponse error against the additional cost of the callback campaign. The central issue is: how different is the nonrespondent group from the respondent group? Several methods for estimating the degree of nonresponse error have been proposed and will be briefly discussed below.

---

[10]Robert Sutton and Linda L. Zeits, "Multiple Prior Notifications, Personalization, and Reminder Surveys," *Marketing Research: A Magazine of Management & Applications*™, vol 4, no. 4, pp. 14–21, December 1992.

[11]Paul M. Diner and Deborah L. Barton, "Justifying the Enclosure of Monetary Incentives in Mail Survey Cover Letters," *Psychology and Marketing,* pp. 153–162, Fall 1990; Mike Brennan, Janet Hoek, and Craig Astridge, "The Effects of Monetary Incentives on the Response Rate and Cost-Effectiveness of a Mail Survey," *Journal of the Market Research Society,* vol 33, no. 3, pp. 229–241, July 1991.

[12]S. S. Robin, "A Procedure for Securing Returns to Mail Questionnaires," *Sociology and Social Research,* vol. 50, pp. 24–35, October 1965. See also Paul R. Murphy, Douglas R. Dalenberg, and James M. Daley, "Improving Survey Responses with Postcards," *Industrial Marketing Management,* vol. 19, pp. 349–355, 1990; Dale F. Duhan and R. Dale Wilson, "Prenotification and Industrial Survey Responses," *Industrial Marketing Management,* vol. 19, pp. 95–105, 1990; Sandra J. London and Curt J. Dommeyer, "Increasing Responses to Industrial Mail Surveys," *Industrial Marketing Management,* vol. 19, pp. 235–241, 1990; Robert A Peterson, Gerald Albaum, and Roger A. Kerin, "A Note on Alternative Contact Strategies in Mail Surveys," *Journal of the Market Research Society,* vol. 31, no. 3, pp. 409–418, July 1989.

TABLE 11-4   SUMMARY OF COMMUNICATION APPROACHES

| Criteria | Communication approach | | | |
	Personal interview	Phone interview	Mail	Computer disk
Versatility	High[1]	Fair[1]	Very little	Fair
Cost	$50–100/interview	$25–40/interview	$20–30/interview	$10–25/interview
Time	Months	Days	Weeks to months	Weeks to months
Sample control	Highest	High	High	Fair
Quantity of data	Highest	High	High	N/A (no history)
Quality of data	High	High	Fair	High
Response rate[2]	Fair	Fair	Fair	Fair

[1]Varies greatly depending on whether computer-assisted software packages are being used; with the use of these software tools, the versatility increases tremendously.

[2]Varies greatly based on length of interview, callbacks (or number of mailings), and selection of respondents; the typical business interview is about 20 minutes, with two callbacks and a random selection of respondents.

1 *Sensitivity analysis.* Determine how different each successive callback group is from the previous respondent group. If the management decision is insensitive to this difference, cease further callbacks.

2 *Trend projection.* On the basis of the results of successive waves of callbacks, if a trend develops on the variables of interest, it can be used to estimate the characteristics of the nonrespondent group.

3 *Subsample measurement.* A specially designed telephone or personal interview is used to estimate the results of the nonrespondent group. This estimate is then incorporated into the data set of those who responded to the survey.

4 *Subjective estimate.* The researcher, given the nature of the survey topic, uses experience and judgment to estimate the degree of nonresponse error.

Observation Method

Observation involves the recording of the respondent's behavior; it is the process of recognizing and recording the behavior of people, objects, and events. This chapter presents the techniques used in formal observation. These techniques are designed to control sampling and nonsampling errors and to provide valid data for decision making.

It is rare for a research design to rely entirely on the observation method. Figure 11-3 indicates that about 33 percent of businesses use the observation method in their marketing research projects. In practice, observational techniques are used in conjunction with other data collection techniques. It is important to understand the advantages and disadvantages of the observation method so as to understand its role in the array of data collection tools available to the researcher.

Observational Techniques Classified

Observational techniques fall into five different classifications: (1) natural or contrived observation, (2) disguised or undisguised observation, (3) structured or un-

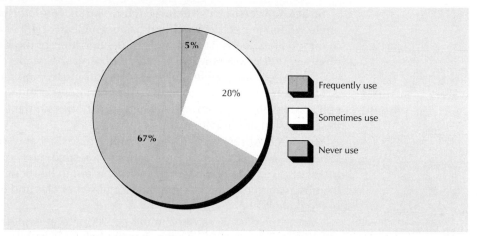

FIGURE 11-3   Use in practice of consumer observation. (*Source:* Thomas C. Kinnear and Ann R. Root, *A Study of the Marketing Research Business*, unpublished study, 1994. Copyright 1994 Thomas C. Kinnear. Not to be reproduced.)

structured observation, (4) direct or indirect observation, and (5) human or mechanical observation. Any given observational technique will typically possess degrees of two or more of these classifications, rather than representing any one dichotomous classification.

Natural versus Contrived Observation   *Natural observation* involves observing behavior as it takes place normally in the environment, for example, while people are shopping in a grocery store. *Contrived observation* involves creating an artificial environment and observing the behavior patterns exhibited by persons put in this environment, for example, having people shop in a simulated grocery store.

The advantage of a natural environmental setting is an increased probability that the exhibited behavior will accurately reflect true behavior patterns. Against this must be weighted the added costs of waiting for the behavior to occur and the difficulty of measuring behavior in a natural setting.

Disguised versus Undisguised Observation   *Disguised versus undisguised observation* refers to whether or not the respondents are aware they are being observed. The role of the observer should be disguised in situations in which people would behave differently if they knew they were being observed. Various approaches, such as two-way mirrors, hidden cameras, and observers dressed as salesclerks, can be used to disguise the observation.

Researchers disagree about how much the presence of the observer will affect people's behavior patterns. One position is that the observer effect is small and short-term, and the other is that the observer can introduce serious bias into observed behavior patterns.

Structured versus Unstructured Observation   *Structured observation* is appropriate when the decision problem has been clearly defined and the specification of information needs permits a clear identification of the behavior patterns to be observed and measured. *Unstructured observation* is appropriate in situations in which the decision problem has yet to be formulated and a great deal of flexibility is needed in the observation to develop hypotheses useful in defining the problem and in identifying opportunities. This distinction is similar to that drawn above, in the discussion of communication methods.

Structured observation is more appropriate in conclusive research studies. When using the structured approach, the research must specify in detail what is to be observed and how the measurements are to be recorded. The structuring of the observation reduces the potential for observer bias and increases the reliability of the data.

Unstructured observation is more appropriate in exploratory research studies. Here, the observer is free to monitor the behavior patterns that seem relevant to the decision situation. Since there is great opportunity for observer bias, the research findings should be treated as hypotheses to be tested with a conclusive research design.

Direct versus Indirect Observation   *Direct observation* refers to observing behavior as it actually occurs. *Indirect observation* refers to observing some record of past behavior. Here, the effects of behavior are observed rather than the behavior itself. This involves the examination of *physical traces,* a process which may include, for example, counting the number of empty liquor containers in trash cans to estimate the liquor consumption of households. A *pantry audit* is another example of the use of physical traces. Here, the observer asks respondents for permission to inspect their pantries for certain types of products. Success with the indirect observation approach rests upon the ability of the researcher to creatively identify the physical traces that can provide useful data for the problem at hand.

Human versus Mechanical Observation   In some situations it is appropriate to supplement or replace the human observer with some form of *mechanical observer.* The reason could be increased accuracy, lower costs, or special measurement requirements. The major mechanical devices used in observation include (1) the video camera, (2) the Audimeter, (3) the psychogalvanometer, (4) the eye-camera, and (5) the pupilometer.

The *video camera* can be used to record shopping behavior in supermarkets, drugstores, and the like. Here, the observer evaluates the film and measures the desired behavior. The use of several observers plus repeated viewing allows more accurate measurement of behavior.

The *Audimeter* is a device developed by the A. C. Nielsen Company to record when radio and television sets are turned on and the station to which they are tuned. The observations made from a sample of households are important in determining which programs are aired and which are canceled.

The *psychogalvanometer* measures changes in perspiration rate. Inferences are drawn from these measurements regarding the person's emotional reaction to stimuli present at the time of the measurement. The stimuli presented might include brand names, copy slogans, or advertisements. It is assumed that the stronger the reaction, the more favorable the person's attitude.

The *eye-camera* measures the movement of the eye. It is used to determine how a person reads a magazine, a newspaper, an advertisement, a package, or other printed material. Both the sequence of what is observed and the time spent looking at various sections are measured.

The *pupilometer* measures changes in the diameter of the pupil of the eye. An increase in pupil diameter is assumed to reflect the person's favorable reaction to the stimuli being observed.

Advantages of the Observation Method   The observation method has several advantages in comparison to the communication method. First, it does not rely on the respondent's willingness to provide the desired data. Second, the potential bias caused by the interviewer and the interviewing process is reduced or eliminated. Therefore, observational data should be more accurate. Third, certain types of data can be collected only by observation. An example is responses to humor.[13] In addition, it is obvious that behavior patterns of which the respondent is not aware can be recorded only by observation.

Disadvantages of the Observation Method   The observation method has two major weaknesses, which significantly limit its use. First is the inability to observe such things as awareness, beliefs, feelings, and preferences. In addition, it is difficult to observe a host of personal and intimate activities such as applying makeup and deodorant, eating, playing family games with the children, and watching television late in the evening. Second, the behavior patterns to be observed must be of short duration, must occur frequently, and/or must be reasonably predictable if the data collection costs and time requirements are to be competitive with other data collection techniques. This requirement limits the observation method to a unique set of circumstances.

Collecting Data from Children

With children today spending more than $2 billion a year on personal purchases, it's no wonder that marketers are anxious to understand their wants and needs. This is no simple task, though. Some children are reluctant to respond to any type of questioning; others do their best to resist giving accurate responses to the interviewer; and still others give what they feel is the "right answer," rather than divulging their true feelings. Researchers have come up with several techniques to help overcome these problems.

---

[13]Cliff Scott, David M. Klein, and Jennings Bryant, "Consumer Response to Humor in Advertising: A Series of Field Studies Using Behavioral Observation," *Journal of Consumer Research*, vol. 16, pp. 498–501, March 1990.

First, marketing information can be collected by observing children's play. Small groups are placed in structured lab settings, where products of possible interest to the kids are scattered throughout the lab. The manufacturer or advertisers can then observe the children's reactions to the various products. Other methods of analyzing play include having a researcher play games with the children while a psychologist observes and analyzes their reactions. "Games" can include charades, word associations, pretending to be mom or dad, and acting out favorite commercials.

Structured questions have been used successfully with children. The questionnaires are typically short (capable of being administered in 5 to 10 minutes) and are specifically designed for children in a particular age category. Research studies have found children's questionnaires to be reliable, having both statistically high internal consistency and test-retest reliability.

In using depth interviews with children, it often behooves an interviewer to ask for nonverbal, rather than verbal, responses, especially from younger children. Children are more likely to point to a picture or a smiling face to indicate the degree to which they like or dislike a product than they are to talk about their feelings. To ask young children to verbalize their responses is more to test their verbal capabilities than to elicit their opinions on the question posed.

The techniques described here are among the many employed by marketing researchers to discover the wants and needs of children. Children's increasing importance in the family decision-making process has made them a valuable source of marketing information.

CONCLUSIVE RESEARCH WORLDWIDE

International and national marketing research programs are undertaken for the same management reasons: to forecast market behavior based on respondents' (1) past behavior, (2) attitudes, and (3) characteristics. What is different in international marketing research is the implementation issues designed to overcome cultural and infrastructure differences across nations.

Personal Interview

Personal interviews are used extensively in international research. In many countries, cultural and infrastructure constraints eliminate telephone and mail interviews as research options. Interviews in the home are typical in most of the world. In addition, intercept interviews are common in places where the target market gathers, such as shopping areas, sporting events, and parks.

Telephone Interview

The use of the telephone interview depends on whether the respondents in the sample have telephones and are willing to be interviewed over the phone. The availability of phones varies widely across countries. In addition, cultures differ in terms of willingness to grant phone interviews. Attempting a phone interview in Brazil, for instance, would be considered inappropriate because use of the telephone is restricted to conversations between family members and close friends.

Mail Interview

Mail interviews are used widely in European countries, and in Canada and Japan. These countries have high literacy rates, well-developed postal systems, and address listings for target markets. This is not a good method in parts of the world that have poor infrastructures and low literacy rates. An example of poor infrastructure is that, in South America, the postal system may fail to deliver a proportion of domestic mail.

GLOBAL MARKETING RESEARCH DYNAMICS

CULTURAL DIFFERENCES IN INTERNATIONAL RESEARCH

Asia and the Pacific Rim

Surveys may be conducted with great success in Asia as long as the researchers are very careful about language and cultural differences. In Malaysia, there are Malays and Chinese who sometimes talk to each other and sometimes don't. The solution is to have Malaysian interviewers interview Malaysian bankers and Chinese interviewers interview Chinese bankers. Since both Malaysian and Chinese bankers are typically proficient in English, language is not an important consideration in this example. The language situation can be very different when dealing with small shop owners, for example.

Culture can affect many aspects of the research design. For example, when you offer a financial incentive for participating in a focus group or a survey, you must present the incentive in the proper context. In Japan, offering a cash payment is an insult, but a cash incentive, presented as a gift, is very acceptable. In Singapore, a $30 contribution to a charitable organization is acceptable.

Middle East

In many countries of the Middle East, questionnaires must be reviewed and approved by a government agency. In Saudi Arabia, the review process for one questionnaire took 3 weeks before the government agency approved its use.

Interviewing business executives in the Middle East can be very different from dealing with executives at similar levels in the West. In a banking survey, the interviews took between 1 and 4 hours because the bankers did more than one thing at a time. For example, one banker had the interviewer, a loan applicant, someone wanting to arrange a correspondent relationship in Turkey, someone else trying to get approval for a water project, and other people all in the same room. The banker took turns talking to all of them over a 4-hour period.

Source: Interviews with practitioners from leading worldwide marketing research organizations.

Observation Method

The observation method is less dependent upon infrastructure and cultural constraints than are the interview methods. Consequently, observation is used in worldwide research similarly to the ways it is used in the U.S. domestic market.

SUMMARY

1 Respondents are a primary source of marketing data. Data can be collected from respondents by means of communication and observation. Communication requires the respondent to provide data actively through verbal or written responses, while observation involves the recording of the respondent's behavior. There are three types of respondent data: (a) past behavior, (b) attitudes, and (c) respondent characteristics.

2 The advantages of the communication method are (a) versatility, (b) speed, and (c) cost. The possible disadvantages are (a) the respondent's unwillingness to provide data, (b) the respondent's inability to provide data, and (c) the influence of the questioning process.

3 The questionnaire is the most common data collection technique. Here, the questions asked and the possible responses are predetermined. In addition, the objective of the study is obvious to the respondent from the questions asked. This technique is used for conclusive research purposes.

4 Four communication approaches are available, as follows: (a) personal interviews, (b) telephone interviews, (c) mail interviews, and (d) computer disk interviews. The criteria for selecting among these approaches are (a) versatility, (b) cost, (c) time, (d) sample control, (e) quantity of data, (f) quality of data, and (g) response rate.

5 The advantages of the observation method are that (a) it does not rely on the respondent's willingness to provide data, (b) the potential for bias from the interviewer and interviewing process is reduced, and (c) certain types of data can be collected only with this method. The disadvantages are that (a) mental reactions and certain behavior patterns cannot be observed; and (b) cost and time constraints limit observation to behavior patterns that are short in duration, occur frequently, or are predictable. These disadvantages seriously limit the use of the observation method.

6 Observational techniques can be classified as (a) natural or contrived, (b) disguised or undisguised, (c) structured or unstructured, (d) direct or indirect, or (e) human or mechanical.

7 Children are a special case in which both communication and observational techniques are used. Children spend more than $2 billion on personal purchases, making them an important segment of the population.

DISCUSSION QUESTIONS

1 What is the objective of conclusive research? What approaches are used?

2 What types of data can be collected from respondents? Give examples of questions that would provide this type of data.

3 List the most common communication media used in respondent data collection. What criteria are used in selecting the medium to be used?

4 Identify and explain the techniques used for estimating nonresponse error when communication approaches are used.

5 What are the advantages and disadvantages of observation methods?

6 Discuss the classification of observational techniques. For each technique, give an example for which it would be suited.

7 What major mechanical devices are employed in observational techniques in marketing research? How are these devices used in marketing research? Give examples of particular types of marketing research for which each device would be best suited.

8 Give an example of a situation in which communication techniques would be more efficient than observational techniques. Give an example of another situation in which observational techniques would be more efficient than communication techniques.

9 MINICASE

What conclusive issues might Northwest Airlines be researching with the questionnaire that began this chapter? Be specific. Imagine a set of responses to this questionnaire, and indicate the associated conclusive actions implied for management.

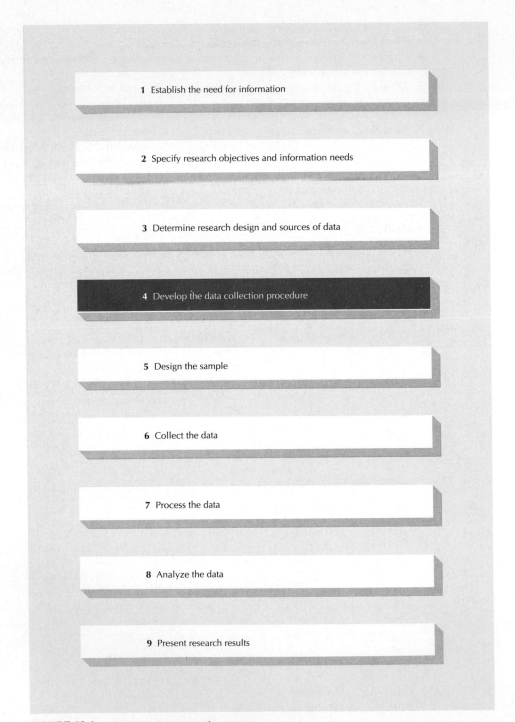

1 Establish the need for information

2 Specify research objectives and information needs

3 Determine research design and sources of data

4 Develop the data collection procedure

5 Design the sample

6 Collect the data

7 Process the data

8 Analyze the data

9 Present research results

FIGURE 12-1   Steps in the research process.

CHAPTER 12

DESIGNING DATA
COLLECTION FORMS

MARKETING RESEARCH IN ACTION

RELIABILITY OF QUESTIONNAIRES QUESTIONED

In recent years, research studies have proliferated in America. The business of study-ing consumer opinions and habits has vastly increased in the last 20 years. Sometimes such studies degenerate into corporate public relations efforts or product pitches.

In fact, a growth area of research is the "promotional" study. This is a study conducted solely for its public relations value. For example, Simplesse, maker of Simple Pleasures Ice Cream, conducted a study indicating that 44 percent of people who eat large amounts of ice cream are likely to take baths in a tub. "It was interesting to a lot of people. We timed the study for when the media wants to write about ice cream, and we have gotten a number of clips back," concludes Russ Klettke, Sim-plesse spokesperson.

A more serious problem occurs when a survey purporting to contain unbiased and useful information is approached in a way that biases the result. Bias can be introduced by deliberately skewing the construction of questions, or by using poor methodology.

An increasing number of studies quoted as "independent" are actually sponsored by groups with a significant interest in the results of the study. Such sponsorship can mean that questions are designed in such a way as to elicit the desired response. These errors may not be discoverable, since the text of these surveys is frequently not made available. For example:

• In 1991, Levi Strauss & Co. questioned students about which fashions would be most popular. Ninety percent of those surveyed said that Levi's 501 jeans would be most popular. The 501s were the only jeans listed on the questionnaire.

Although a researcher is never explicitly told by a sponsor what results are desired, an implicit message is often sent. The message is that favorable conclusions will result in further funding and additional work. In lean times, such as the present, these arguments carry more weight.

Budget constraints, combined with shorter timelines, also lead researchers to use smaller sample sizes. These samples cause problems when researchers attempt to project results onto a larger population. For example, most of the national polls taken during the time of the Clarence Thomas Supreme Court nomination hearings, when Anita Hill testified that Mr. Thomas had sexually harassed her, included only 500 to 700 people. When broken into segments, the margin for error could be as high as 12 percent. Therefore, when an ABC–*Washington Post* poll (in which 500 people were polled, of whom 50 percent were women) concluded that more women believed Thomas (38 percent) than Hill (28 percent), the opposite could equally have been true.

Other factors can affect a survey's credibility. The sample participants may not be representative of the general population, data analysis may not be correct, and the conclusions may be selected so that only the most favorable results are reported.

Here is an example of the consequences of unrepresentative samples.

• The most famous sampling error in history occurred in the early years of public opinion polling. In 1936, *Literary Digest* magazine declared Republican Alf Landon a landslide victor over Franklin D. Roosevelt. The sample contained only people who had telephones or owned an automobile, in the midst of the Great Depression— in other words, extremely affluent respondents.

The news media have often exacerbated the problems discussed above by seizing on biased studies and passing their conclusions on to consumers. Often, journalists make no attempt to see whether the study's methodology was properly carried out. (Sometimes this information is not easily obtainable; technical details are often considered proprietary.) Statistics are extensively cited, even when inappropriate sampling makes them meaningless.

Recently, the Council of American Survey Research Organizations, a trade group, published a code of standards covering methodology and sponsorship to increase researcher's responsibility to the public. A dual standard of information has been proposed, whereby "entertainment" and "informative" studies would be clearly separated. Until such standards are implemented, survey readers should be on their guard.

Source: Adapted from Cynthia Crossen, "Margin of Error: Studies and Surveys Proliferate, but Poor Methodology Makes Many Unreliable," *The Wall Street Journal,* p. A1, November 14, 1991.

In previous chapters we have discussed the types of primary and secondary marketing data, and now we consider the issues involved in designing data collection forms for primary data collection. The emphasis is on constructing forms appropriate for conclusive research, where the research design requires a structured data collection method capable of providing valid and relevant data for decision making.

Data collection forms are a central component of most research studies. All four communication media—personal, telephone, computer disk, and mail interviews—rely on questionnaires. Since questionnaire studies are far more prevalent than observational studies, the bulk of this chapter will be devoted to issues involved in questionnaire construction. Much of this discussion will be relevant to the issues involved in developing data collection forms for observation, and the final section will be specifically devoted to observational forms.

IMPORTANCE OF QUESTIONNAIRES — Start.

A *questionnaire* is a formalized schedule for collecting data from respondents. The function of the questionnaire is measurement. Questionnaires can be used to measure (1) past behavior, (2) attitudes, and (3) respondent characteristics.

The measurement of attitudes has grown in importance, and so has the number of attitude measurement techniques, several of which are discussed in Chapters 8 and 25. These techniques are typically incorporated into a questionnaire. The issue involved in questionnaire design directly relate to developing and administering these attitude measurement techniques.

Measurement error is a serious problem in questionnaire construction. For example, the Survey Research Center at the University of Michigan asked half of the sample in their May 1977 consumer survey the following question on attitudes toward a gasoline price increase: "Are you in favor of the proposed standby gasoline tax, starting with 5 cents and rising to 50 cents, which will be imposed if we do not meet conservation goals?" The results were that 27 percent favored the additonal taxes while 65 percent opposed them. The other half of the sample were asked, "If the United States had to choose between becoming dependent on uncertain foreign oil supplies or curbing gasoline use with rising taxes, which would you favor?" In contrast to the previous finding, 71 percent favored the higher tax alternative, with only 13 percent opting for uncertain oil sources. What could cause such a marked difference in responses? The answer lies in the question wording. The first question does not pose an explicit alternative to the consumer. Rather, the consumer is offered the implicit alternative of higher gasoline prices versus lower gasoline prices. It is not hard to see that consumers would prefer lower prices. The second question poses the alternative of higher prices now versus more dependence on foreign oil supplies in the future. The lesson to be learned from this example is that when a preference question is asked without posing realistic alternatives, the results can be meaningless.

Let's consider another example. Two rather similar ways of posing a question to a sample of nonworking women have been developed. The first way is "Would you like to have a job, if this were possible?" The second way is "Would you prefer to have a job, or do you prefer just to do your housework?" The second question makes explicit the implied choice in the first question. Each question was put to half of a sample of nonworking women. The first question resulted in 19 percent stating they would not like to have a job, while the second question resulted in 68 percent who would not like to have a job. This dramatic difference again emphasizes the importance of questionnaire wording. The researcher must ask, "Do the questions measure what they are supposed to measure?" If the answer is no, measurement error is present.

Both of the previous examples illustrate the importance of controlling measurement error in questionnaire construction. Rarely will sampling error result in outcomes of the magnitude observed in these examples. This point is expressed by one of the leading researchers in marketing research, as follows:

> Error or bias attributable to sampling and to methods of questionnaire administration were relatively small as compared with other types of variation—especially variation attributable to different ways of wording questions.[1]

Obviously, it takes skill to design a questionnaire so that the questions will measure what they are supposed to measure.

important.

QUESTIONNAIRE COMPONENTS

A questionnaire typically has five sections: (1) identification data, (2) request for cooperation, (3) instructions, (4) information sought, and (5) classification data.

Identification data, the first section of the questionnaire, asks for the respondent's name, address, and phone number. Part of all of this information is typically obtained prior to the interview from sources such as respondent lists or preinterview screening contacts. Any incomplete identification data can be determined at the end of the request for cooperation section or at the end of the questionnaire when more detailed classification data is collected. Additional data would include items such as the time and date of the interview plus the interviewer's name or code number.

The *request for cooperation* is an opening statement designed to enlist the respondent's help regarding the interview. This statement typically first identifies the interviewer and/or the interviewing organization. Next, the purpose of the study is explained, and the time required to complete the interview is given.

The *instructions* are comments to the interviewer or the respondent about how to use the questionnaire. The comments appear directly on the questionnaire in a mail or computer survey. With the personal or telephone survey, a separate sheet titled "Interviewer Instructions" explains the purpose of the study, the sampling plan, and other aspects of the data collection process. In addition, the question-

[1]Samuel A. Stouffer et al., *Measurement and Prediction,* vol. 4 of *Studies in Social Psychology in World War II* (Princeton, NJ: Princeton University Press, 1950), p. 709.

naire may contain special instructions on how to use specific questions—for example, an attitude scaling technique.

The *information sought* forms the major portion of the questionnaire. The remainder of this chapter deals with designing this aspect of the questionnaire.

The *classification data* section concerns the characteristics of the respondent. These data are provided directly by the respondent in the case of a mail or computer disk survey. In a personal or telephone interview survey the data are usually collected from the respondent by the interviewer. In some cases the personal interviewer may estimate sensitive types of data (for example, income) based on observation. Classification data are typically collected at the end of the interview, since some respondents may be reluctant to disclose personal data (income, age, and occupation) until rapport with the interviewing situation has been established through the question-and-answer process. However, some sampling procedures require that classification data be collected at the beginning of the interview, to determine whether the person qualifies as part of the sampling plan.

QUESTIONNAIRE DESIGN — *important*

Questionnaire design is more an art form than a scientific undertaking. No steps, principles, or guidelines can guarantee an effective and efficient questionnaire. Questionnaire design is a skill that the researcher learns through experience rather than by reading a series of guidelines. The only way to begin to develop this skill is to write a questionnaire, use it in a series of interviews, analyze its weaknesses, and revise it.

What we do know about questionnaire design comes from the experience of reseachers who have specialized in this area. From this accumulated experience have emerged a series of rules or guidelines that can be useful to the beginning researcher confronted with the task of designing a questionnaire. While these rules are useful in avoiding serious errors, the fine-tuning stage of questionnaire design requires the creative inspiration of the skilled researcher. While the guidelines discussed in this section lay the foundation for questionnaire design, ultimately the quality of the questionnaire depends on the skill and judgment of the researcher, a clear understanding of the information needed, a sensitivity to the role of the respondent, and extensive pretesting.

The discussion of questionnaire design will be organized as a series of seven steps. In each of these steps, various guidelines for questionnaire construction will be presented. While these rules are presented as part of a step-by-step approach to questionnaire development, in practice the steps are highly interrelated. Decisions made early in the sequence will often influence choices later in the sequence, and vice versa. The seven steps, as presented in Figure 12-2, are (1) review preliminary considerations; (2) decide on question content; (3) decide on response format; (4) decide on question wording; (5) decide on question sequence; (6) decide on physical characteristics; and (7) carry out pretesting and revision, and make the final draft.

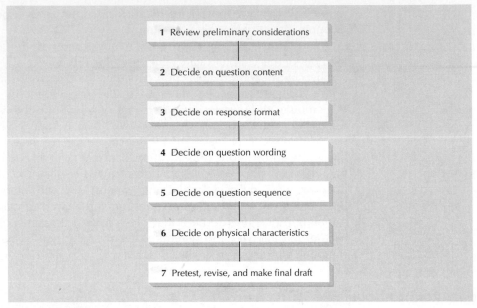

FIGURE 12-2   Steps in questionnaire design.

Preliminary Considerations

The preliminary considerations for conducting conclusive research were discussed in Chapter 4, which focused on methods of establishing an effective link between the decision-making process and the research process. Central to this process is the development of research objectives and the listing of information needs. The research design must be formulated and the steps in the research process visualized and planned. Many decisions must be made before the questionnaire can be designed.

Previous Decisions   The questionnaire design stage presumes that the research project is well under way and that many decisions have already been made. Decisions regarding questionnaire design must build upon and be consistent with decisions relating to other aspects of the research project.

Previous decisions regarding the type of research design and the sources of data directly influence the character and the role of the questionnaire in the research project (see Chapters 5 and 6). It is essential to have a clear picture of the target population and to know the details of the sampling plan (see Chapters 13, 14, and 15). Questionnaire design is highly influenced by the characteristics of the respondent group. The more heterogeneous the respondent group, the more difficult it is to design a single questionnaire that is appropriate for everyone. Typically, the questionnaire must be designed to be comprehensible to the least able respondent. The measurement scales and communication media that will be

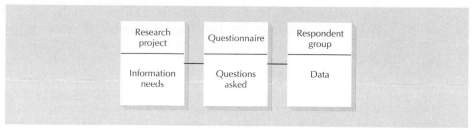

FIGURE 12-3   Information needs—data linkage.

used must be specified (Chapters 8 and 11). The data processing and analysis stages must be visualized, as well as the nature of the research findings. The tactical aspects of questionnaire design are closely related to these final stages of the research process. A review of Chapter 3 will refresh your memory about the nature of these decisions in the context of an actual research project.

Link between Information Needs and Data to Be Collected   Before designing the questionnaire, the researcher must have a detailed listing of the information needs as well as a clear definition of the respondent group. The questionnaire is the link between the information needed and the data to be collected. Figure 12-3 illustrates the nature of this linkage.

The questions on the questionnaire should flow logically from the list of information needs. It would seem obvious that no question should be included on the questionnaire unless it relates to a specific information need.[2] In practice, however, there is a strong tendency to include questions that seem "interesting" but have no specific link to the information needs. Unnecessary questions add expense to the survey and increase the demands placed on the respondent.

Decide on Question Content

The content of the questions is influenced by the respondent's ability and/or willingness to respond accurately.

Ability to Answer Accurately   Assuming the desired data are relevant to the decision problem, the reseacher must be sensitive to the respondent's ability to provide the data. Many types of data cannot be accurately collected from respondents. Inaccurate data can result from two sources: (1) the respondent is uninformed, and (2) the respondent is forgetful.

Respondent Is Uninformed   We are frequently asked questions to which we do not have the answers. As students, we confront this situation far more often

[2]Unnecessary questions can be justified if they facilitate gaining the respondent's cooperation or add continuity to the questioning process.

than we would like. Respondents may confront the same situation when they try to fill out a questionnaire. They may be asked to provide data about their spouses' monthly gross incomes or about credit card purchases, for example, for which they do not possess accurate data. They may be asked questions about advertisements, products, brands, or retail outlets of which they are unaware.

Researchers have discovered that respondents will often answer questions even though they have no knowledge of the topic, perhaps because they are unwilling to admit their lack of knowledge. This situation represents a serious source of measurement error.

Often the phrasing of a question will encourage the respondent to answer it by implying that the answer should be known. The question "What is the current interest rate you receive on your savings account?" implies that the respondent should know the answer. An alternative would be "Do you know the current interest rate on your savings account?" This question implies that some people do not know the interest rate, which makes it easier for the respondent to admit a lack of knowledge. If the respondent answers this quesiton affirmatively, the first question can then be asked.

Respondent Is Forgetful   People are frequently asked questions the answers to which they once knew but which have now forgotten. As students, we are continually confronted with this situation.

Research studies have shown that we forget most events fairly rapidly after we learn about them. The rate of forgetting is very rapid over the first few days and continues with the passage of time. The farther in the past the learning took place, the higher the chance of forgetting.

The probability of forgetting is influenced by the importance of the event and the repetition of the event. It is easier to remember important events such as the first person on the moon and the first car we purchased. In contrast, how many of us remember the second person on the moon and the second car we purchased? It is also easier to remember events that are repeated frequently, for example, frequently purchased products or frequently viewed advertisements.

When the information needs of a study require questions asking the respondent to recall events that are unimportant to the respondent or that occur infrequently, the researcher has a potentially serious problem in designing the questionnaire. He or she must not overestimate the ability of the respondent to recall the event and the surrounding circumstances accurately. This is an easy mistake to make when the topic of the questionnaire is an important one in the eyes of the researcher or decision maker.

In collecting data about "unimportant" or infrequently occurring events, there are several options available. First, the researcher can try to interview the respondents who are most likely to remember—for example, recent purchasers. Second, the questionnaire can include techniques that stimulate the respondent's recall of the event.

Several studies suggest that questions that rely on unaided recall—questions that do not give cues about the event—can underestimate the actual occurrence of the event. The aided-recall approach is an attempt to overcome the memory problem; it provides the respondent with cues regarding the event of interest. Students are familiar with the distinction between aided and unaided recall: an essay question is an example of unaided recall, while a multiple-choice question is an example of aided recall.

An unaided-recall question designed to measure the respondent's awareness of a commercial could be "What products do you recall were advertised last night on television?" The aided-recall approach would list a number of products for the respondent and then ask, "Which of these products were advertised on television last night?"

The advantage of aided recall comes from the cues used to stimulate the respondent's memory. The degree of stimulation can vary from limited hints to the presentation of the actual event. This approach to aided recall is called the *recognition method.* With increased attempts to stimulate the respondent's memory comes the possibility of suggestion bias resulting from the presentation of the cues. In the aided-recall approach, use of several levels of successive stimulation is often recommended. This allows the researcher to analyze the influence of the question sequence and to select the level of stimulation most appropriate for the study.

Willingness to Respond Accurately   Assuming that respondents can accurately answer the question, the next issue is to determine their willingness to do so. Unwillingness to respond accurately can be reflected in (1) refusal to respond to a question or a series of questions, that is, item nonresponse error; or (2) deliberate provision of an incorrect or distorted response to a question, that is, measurement error.

Respondents may be unwilling to respond accurately for any of the following three reasons: (1) They may consider the situation inappropriate for disclosing the data. (2) Disclosure of the data would be embarrassing. (3) Disclosure would be a potential threat to the respondents' prestige or normative views.

It is important to remember that the respondent has limited motivation to respond accurately to the questions. In a personal or telephone interview, the interviewer's presence can cause the respondent to be more concerned about how the interviewer may react to the responses than about the accuracy of responses. This is especially the situation if the questions are embarrassing or offer a threat to respondents' prestige or their normative viewpoints. The results can be item nonresponse or, worse yet, inaccurate responses.

The respondent's willingness to answer questions is conditioned by the interviewing context. A question regarding personal hygiene habits may be considered appropriate when asked by a nurse or doctor as part of a physical examination but inappropriate when asked by an interviewer conducting a study for a pharmaceutical manufacturer.

Respondents' willingness to answer a question is also a function of their understanding of whether the data are needed for a legitimate purpose. The collection of classification data can present a serious problem in this regard. A respondent may be hesitant to provide accurate data when abruptly faced with personal questions regarding age, occupation, and income. Here is an example of a request for personal data that does not explain to the respondent how the data are to be used: "Next, I would like to ask some questions about yourself. What is your . . . ?" Even a brief explanation such as the following can make such a request legitimate for most respondents, as in a statement like this: "To better understand how the reactions to this new product differ among people with different age, income, and occupational characteristics, we need to know your. . . ."

Questions that embarrass respondents or have an effect on their prestige or their adherence to social norms can result in biased responses. This is especially true in a personal or telephone interview. Researchers have found that questions on topics such as sexual behavior and attitudes, number of automobile accidents, or purchase of personal hygiene products and alcoholic beverages can embarrass the respondent and result in either a refusal to answer or a distortion of the response.

Questions that have a bearing on prestige or adherence to social norms include level of education, income earned, and amount of time spent reading or watching educational television. The answers to these types of questions typically result in an upward response bias.

Listed below are some approaches that have been developed to deal with the bias resulting from respondents' unwillingness to respond accurately.

1 *Counterbiasing statement.* Begin the question with a statement that suggests that the behavior in question is rather common and then ask the respondent the question.

2 *Indirect statement.* Phrase the sensitive question so that it refers to "other people." It is assumed that the respondent's own behavior or attitude will be reflected in the response.

3 *Labeled response categories.* Present the respondent with a card that lists the sensitive response alternatives and that has the responses identified by letters or numbers. The respondent uses the letter or number to indicate a response to the sensitive question.

4 *Randomized response technique.* Present the respondent with two questions, either of which can be answered yes or no. One question is the sensitive issue (e.g., "Have you shoplifted in the last month?"), while the other question is the insensitive issue (e.g., "Were you born in January?"). A random procedure (e.g., flipping a coin) performed by the respondent (with the outcome not known to the researcher) is used to determine which of the two questions will be answered. Since the response format of the two questions is identical (i.e., yes or no), the interviewer does not know which question the respondent has answered. The proportion of respondents who answer yes to the insensitive question is determined through secondary sources or through another research survey. The proportion of people who answer yes to the sensitive issue can be determined through use of the following formula:

P(yes to sensitive question)

$$= \frac{P(\text{yes}) - P(\text{insensitive question})P(\text{yes to insensitive question})}{P(\text{sensitive question})}$$

In the shoplifting study, if the proportion of respondents who answered yes is .10, the proportion born in January is .05 (found through a secondary source, the *Census of Population*), and the probability of answering each question is .5, the estimate of the proportion of respondents answering yes to the shoplifting question is as follows:

$$P(\text{yes to shoplifting}) = \frac{.10 - (.5)(.05)}{.5} = .15$$

The randomized response technique shows that 15 percent of the respondents have shoplifted.

Decide on Response Format

Once the problems related to the content of the questions have been analyzed, the next issue is the type of questions to use. The concern here is the degree of structure imposed on the person's responses. The three types of questions, which range from unstructured to structured response formats, are (1) open ended questions, (2) multiple-choice questions, and (3) dichotomous questions.

Open-Ended Questions   An *open-ended question,* also often referred to as a *free-response,* or *free-answer, question,* requires the respondents to provide their own answers to the question. In a mail or computer disk interview, space is provided in which the respondent can write or key in the answer. In the personal or telephone interview, the respondent verbally reports the answer to the interviewer, who records it on the questionnaire.

Here are some examples of open-ended questions.

What brand of laundry detergent did you last purchase?
What is the mission statement of your company?

Advantages of Open-Ended Questions   An open-ended question can serve as an excellent first question on a topic. These questions allow general attitudes to be expressed, which can aid in interpreting the more structured questions. In addition, they establish rapport and gain the respondent's cooperation in answering more specific and more structured questions. Introductory open-ended questions are especially important in mail or computer disk surveys.

Open-ended questions influence responses less than multiple-choice or dichotomous questions. Respondents are not influenced by a predetermined set of response alternatives and can freely express views divergent from the researcher's expectations. This characteristic makes open-ended questions useful for exploratory research purposes.

Finally, open-ended questions can provide the researcher with insights, side comments, and explanations that are useful in developing a "feel" for the research findings. The final report may include quotations from open-ended questions to add a sense of realism and life to the more structured research findings.

Disadvantages of Open-Ended Questions A major disadvantage of open-ended questions is the high potential for interviewer bias. Interviewers rarely record respondents' answers verbatim. This results in the interviewer summarizing the respondents' answers or deleting the aspects of an answer that he or she deems unimportant. In addition, interviewers who write slowly or do not take shorthand typically fail to record parts of answers due to time constraints. The more the interviewer summarizes and edits the respondent's answers, the more the recorded responses will vary from the actual responses. A tape recorder should be used if verbatim responses are required.

A second major disadvantage of open-ended questions lies in the time and cost associated with coding the responses. For a large survey, extensive coding procedures are required to summarize the divergent responses in a format useful for data analysis and presentation. The coding process can contribute significantly to the total cost of the research project.

Sometimes, in order to gain the advantages of open-ended questions yet avoid some of the time and cost associated with the editing and coding process, precoded questions are used. A precoded question is a multiple-choice question that is presented to the respondent as open-ended. The response alternatives are not read to the respondent. Rather, the interviewer selects the appropriate response alternative based on the respondent's reply to the open-ended question.

This approach works well when the response is easily formulated in the respondent's mind and the possible answers are limited in variety—for example, when the question concerns the number of household members, the age of the refrigerator, or monthly grocery expenditures. However, questions that are not well formulated in the respondent's mind and that result in a variety of answers have a high probability of interviewer bias.

Other disadvantages include the implicit extra weight given to respondents who are more articulate and tend to raise more points in their answers. Also, open-ended questions are less suited for self-administered questionnaires. The reason is that respondents tend to write more briefly than they speak, and there is also the problem of illegible handwriting. Finally, compared to questions that have structured response formats, open-ended questions are three to five times more costly because of the complexity associated with the data processing.

In general, open-ended questions are most appropriate for exploratory research purposes and for research designed to develop more structured questions. While the cost of developing effective structured questions can be high, it must be weighed against the disadvantages of open-ended questions.

Multiple-Choice Questions A *multiple-choice question* requires the respondent to choose an answer from a list provided either in the question proper or following the question. The respondent may be asked to choose one or more of the alternatives presented.

Here are some examples of multiple-choice questions:

Members of the U.S. Congress should be limited to two terms in office.

Strongly disagree		Neutral	Strongly agree	
1	2	3	4	5

What is your age?

_____ Under 18
_____ 18–25
_____ 26–35
_____ 36–45
_____ 46–55
_____ 56–65
_____ Over 65

Advantages of Multiple-Choice Questions Multiple-choice questions overcome many of the disadvantages associated with open-ended questions. Most important, they reduce interviewer bias and the cost and time associated with data processing. Typically, the interviewer will find multiple-choice questionnaires comparatively easy and fast to administer. Finally, with self-administered questionnaires, cooperation by respondents is difficult to maintain unless the bulk of the questions have a structured-response format.

Disadvantages of Multiple-Choice Questions Against these advantages must be weighed several disadvantages. First, the design of effective multiple-choice questions requires considerable time and cost. Typically, an exploratory study using open-ended questions is required to formulate the response alternatives. If the latter do not include one or more of the predominant responses, substantial bias can be introduced into the results. Even with an alternative of "other (specify)," there is a tendency for the respondent to choose from among the alternatives specified rather than to use the "other" alternative. Second, multiple-choice questions tend to bias the data by the order in which the response alternatives are listed.

Issues in Multiple-Choice Question Design The two issues in the design of multiple-choice questions are (1) the number of alternatives and (2) position bias.

The *number of alternatives* to include in a question is typically influenced by the following two guidelines. First, the response alternatives should be *collectively exhaustive,* that is, they should include all the possible response alternatives. The inclusion of the alternative labeled "other (specify)," accompanied by a space for recording the answer, is an attempt to comply with this guideline. It is hoped that major response alternatives that were excluded will be identified under "other." Second, the response alternatives should be *mutually exclusive,* that is, the respondents should be able to identify one alternative that clearly represents their response. In some situations the researcher may desire to have the respondent make two or more choices, but multiple responses create special data processing problems.

If the set of response alternatives is reasonably short, the alternatives may be included in the question proper. In most cases, there are too many alternatives to be included here, and they are listed at the end of the question. In a personal interview, if there is a long list of alternatives, the choices should be listed on a card and given to the respondent for inspection.

Another important issue concerns *position bias.* With a list of numbers, such as prices or how many times per week a respondent visits a store, there is a bias toward the central position of the number array. When ideas are involved, the first alternative on the list has a greater chance of being chosen. To control position bias, the researcher should alternate the order in which alternatives are listed, to average out the response bias. Unfortunately, it is not easy to rotate most numbers, since they logically should appear as a sequence (e.g., 5, 6, 7, 8, 9). Even if the numbers are presented out of order, the respondent may mentally sort them into sequence before making a choice.

Dichotomous Questions   A *dichotomous question* is an extreme form of the multiple-choice question which allows the respondent a choice of only two responses: "yes or no," "did or did not," "agree or disagree." Typically, the two alternatives of interest are combined with a neutral alternative, such as "no opinion" or "don't know."

Here are some examples of dichotomous questions:

Should children in the United States attend school year-round?

_____ Yes
_____ No
_____ No opinion

Have you purchased a new car within the last year?

_____ Did
_____ Did not

Advantages of Dichotomous Questions   The advantages of dichotomous questions are essentially the same as those mentioned for multiple-choice questions. The interviewers find the questions quick and easy to administer. There is little chance of interviewer bias, and the responses are easy to code, process, and analyze.

Disadvantages of Dichotomous Questions   There is a risk of assuming that the respondent group approaches the topic of interest in dichotomous terms when, in reality, many grades of feeling may be present or indecision may predominate. Forcing respondents to express their views in a dichotomous manner when they are not thus polarized can produce results that contain substantial measurement error. Dichotomous questions are especially susceptible to error resulting from how they are worded. For example, error in the examples presented early in this chapter resulted from implied versus explicit alternatives. In addition, the positive or negative posture of the question can have a strong effect on the nature of the response.

Issues in Dichotomous Question Design The central issue is whether to include a neutral response alternative in the question. If such an alternative is not included, the respondent is forced to select between the two positions presented. If a neutral alternative is available, and especially if it is shown to the respondent, the latter can avoid taking a position on the topic by selecting the neutral alternative. When the neutral alternative is included, the number of nonresponses should decline and the number of neutral responses should increase. If a significant number of respondents are truly neutral, the inclusion of the neutral alternative should increase the accuracy of the results. However, a source of bias can enter when respondents who are not neutral select the neutral alternative for reasons of convenience, embarrassment, or the like. If the proportion of respondents who are truly neutral is large, it is best to include the neutral alternative. If it is believed that the proportion of neutral respondents is small, it is best to force the respondents to select between the two positions of interest.

Decide on Question Wording

The heart of the questionnaire consists of the questions—the link between the data and the information needs of the study. It is critical that the researcher and the respondent assign the same meaning to the questions asked. Otherwise, serious measurement error will be present in the research results.

You should never be misled into believing that there are "right" and "wrong" ways of asking questions. In a real sense, survey data are created rather than unobtrusively collected. The manner in which data are collected determines to a large degree the character of the data. Consequently, researchers must be very sensitive to the effect of the question wording on the character of the results to be obtained.

Since no single wording of a question is correct, it is important to understand clearly what effect a particular wording can have on the results. The split-ballot technique, which divides the sample into groups and assigns alternative questions to each group, can be used for this purpose. The comparison of the answers to alternative questions determines how question wording affects the results. This technique allows a better interpretation of the survey results than is possible when a single version of the question is used.

Following are nine general guidelines that you should consider in designing the wording of a question.

1 Use simple words.
2 Use clear words.
3 Avoid leading questions.
4 Avoid biasing questions.
5 Avoid implicit alternatives.

6 Avoid implicit assumptions.
7 Avoid estimates.
8 Avoid double-barreled questions.
9 Consider the frame of reference.

These guidelines are discussed in detail below.

Use Simple Words   The words used in the questionnaire should be consistent with the vocabulary level of the respondents. If in doubt, it is best to err on the side of simplicity.

Questions designed for children obviously must have a simpler vocabulary than those designed for, say, medical doctors. When designing a questionnaire for the general public, however, keep in mind the surprising fact that the vocabulary skills of most seventh graders (children about 12 years of age) are greater than those of many adults. For example, a significant proportion of the general population do not understand the word "Caucasian," whereas most seventh graders are familiar with this term. Consequently, when designing a questionnaire, be certain that it is comprehensible to persons with minimal vocabulary skills.

Use Clear Words   Words that are "clear" have a single meaning which is known to all the respondents. Unfortunately, identifying words that are clear or unambiguous is more difficult than one might expect. Many words that might seem to be clear to everyone can have different meanings among population groups and geographic locations.

Consider the words "dinner" and "lunch." Studies indicate that middle- and upper-class families use "dinner" to refer to the evening meal and "lunch" to refer to the noon meal. In contrast, many working-class families refer to the evening meal as "supper" and the noon meal as "dinner." In designing a question that refers to mealtime, it would be better to use "noon meal" and "evening meal" rather than "lunch" and "dinner." Since comparable responses cannot be expected from respondents who assign different meanings to a word, serious measurement error would be introduced if the words "lunch" and "dinner" were used in the question.

In a study of soup usage in the home, the question "How often do you serve soup at home?" resulted in responses that suggested that soup usage was lower than believed by the management. Additional research indicated that to many respondents the word "served" meant used at a special occasion, such as when entertaining. Soup eaten by the family alone was not considered to be "served." A revised question with better wording was: "How often do you use soup at home?"

Researchers have found that words such as "usually," "regularly," "kind," "normally," and "frequently" are ambiguous. It is difficult to be sensitive to all the commonly used words that some respondents interpret one way, others another way. In this regard, Payne advises that the researcher consult a standard dictionary and a thesaurus, and also ask the following six questions about each word in the question.

1 Does this word mean what we intended?

2 Does it have any other meaning?

3 If so, does the context make the intended meaning clear?

4 Does the word have more than one pronunciation?

5 Is there any word with similar pronunciation that might be confused with this word?

6 Is there a simpler word or phrase that might be used?[3]

Avoid Leading Questions   A leading question is one in which the respondent is given a cue as to what the answer should be to the question. Leading questions often reflect the researcher's or the decision maker's viewpoint regarding the question's answer. A leading question causes a constant measurement error in the research findings.

In a question to measure the claim service of automobile insurance companies, the following statement preceded the question on claim service: "It has been alleged that some low-rate companies are much tougher in adjusting claims than standard-rate companies, and that you are more likely to have to go to court to collect the sum due you." This statement would probably influence responses to the questions on the companies' claim service. Be aware that statements designed to clarify a question can have an influence on the responses. Be sensitive to this source of measurement error.

Consider the question "Do you own a Zenith television set?" The researcher would find out that this was a leading question if the reported ownership of Zenith television sets were higher in response to this question than to the simpler question "What brand of television set do you own?" The use of a brand or company name in a question can cause the respondent to believe that this company is the sponsor of the survey. There is a tendency for the respondent to express positive feelings toward the survey sponsor, which can result in measurement error.

Avoid Biasing Questions   A biasing question includes words or phrases that are emotionally colored and that suggest a feeling of approval or disapproval. Most researchers would recognize the biasing effect of a question that began, "Don't you agree with Ralph Nader in the belief that . . . ?" or "Do you believe that the oil monopolies should be . . . ?" No reputable researcher would phrase questions in this manner. Unfortunately, the biasing effect of words and phrases is often far more subtle than these examples suggest.

The mere suggestion that an attitude or a position is associated with a prestigious or nonprestigious person or organization can seriously bias the respondent's reply. The question "Do you agree or disagree with the American Dental Association's position that advertising presweetened cereal to children is . . . ?" would have such an effect. The nature of the bias would be increased support reported for the position held by the prestigious person or organization over that reported when the person or organization was not included in the question.

[3]S. L. Payne, *The Art of Asking Questions* (Princeton, NJ: Princeton University Press, 1951), p. 41.

It is difficult to avoid leading questions because words or phrases that bias one respondent group can seem neutral to another group. Pretesting the questionnaire is one way to identify which respondent groups find the question biased.

Avoid Implicit Alternatives   Examples presented in the first section of this chapter ("Importance of Questionnaires") indicated marked differences in the answers to questions that pose implicit alternatives. Other research has demonstrated equally dramatic results. As a rule, it is best to state clearly all relevant alternatives to a question unless there is a special reason for not doing so.

Research indicates that the order in which explicit alternatives are presented can affect the response. When the number of alternatives is long and complex or close in preference, the alternatives presented at the end of the list have a higher chance of being selected. The split-ballot technique should be used to ensure that each alternative is tested at each location.

Avoid Implicit Assumptions   It is all too easy to design a question for which the answer is dependent upon a number of implicit assumptions. Consider the question "Are you in favor of curtailing the amount of sugar allowed in children's cereals?" Implicit in this question is the idea that this action will result in some favorable outcome, for example, a lower rate of tooth decay. An improved wording would be "Are you in favor of curtailing the amount of sugar allowed in children's cereal if it will result in . . . ?" The failure to make explicit the assumption in a question often results in overestimation of respondents' support for the issue at hand.

Avoid Estimates   The questions should be designed in such a way that the respondent does not have to answer by giving an estimate or making a generalization. Consider the question "How many boxes of powdered soap do you purchase in a year?" This question requires the respondent to determine the number of boxes of powdered soap purchased in a month and multiply by 12. The survey results would be more accurate if the question were phrased "How many boxes of powdered soap do you purchase in a month?" The yearly figure can be determined by multiplying by 12.

Avoid Double-Barreled Questions   A *double-barreled question* is one in which the wording calls for two responses. Consider the question "What is your evaluation of the snowmobile's ride and acceleration?" Here, two questions have been asked in the guise of a single question. As a rule, when the question includes "and," review it to see whether two responses are required.

Consider the Frame of Reference   *Frame of reference* refers to the respondent's viewpoint in responding to the question. Consider these two questions: "Are automobile manufacturers making satisfactory progress in controlling automobile emissions?" and "Are you satisfied with the progress automobile manufacturers are making in controlling automobile emissions?'' The viewpoint of the first question is that of an objective evaluation based on how people in general would react to this question. The second question is oriented toward the respondent's personal feelings regarding the issue of automobile emissions and thus is more subjective. The objectives of the research study will determine which frame of reference is more appropriate. The point is that you must be aware that the respondent's viewpoint can seriously influence the study results.

Following is an example of how a question evolves through a series of rewrites and clarifications.

Metamorphosis of a Question

Stage 1   Shouldn't there be changes in the existing gun control laws?

_____ Yes
_____ No

(*Problem:* This question begs for an affirmative answer.)

Stage 2   Should there be changes in the existing gun control laws?

_____ Yes
_____ No

(*Problem:* What kind of changes?)

Stage 3   Should there be more gun control laws?

_____ Yes
_____ No

(*Problem:* "More" does not make clear intent of laws.)

Stage 4   Should there be stricter gun control laws?

_____ Yes
_____ No

(*Problem:* Where are the laws?)

Stage 5   Should Minnesota have stricter gun control laws?

_____ Yes
_____ No

(*Problem:* Only one alternative given; what if existing laws are adequate?)

Stage 6   Should Minnesota have stricter gun control laws, or are existing laws adequate?

_____ Should have stricter laws
_____ Existing laws are adequate

(*Problem:* All alternatives still not stated; suppose less strict laws are desired.)

Stage 7   Should Minnesota have stricter gun control laws, less strict gun control laws, or are existing laws adequate?

_____ Should have stricter laws
_____ Should have less strict laws
_____ Existing laws are adequate

(*Problem:* Which guns and which laws?)

Stage 8   Should Minnesota have stricter laws regulating the sale and purchase of long guns and handguns, less strict laws, or are existing laws concerning these matters adequate?

_____ Should have stricter laws
_____ Should have less strict laws
_____ Existing laws are adequate

(*Problem:* This is a double-barreled question!)

Stage 9   Should Minnesota have stricter laws regulating the sale of handguns, less strict laws, or are the existing laws concerning these sales adequate?

_____ Should have stricter laws
_____ Should have less strict laws
_____ Existing laws are adequate

(*Problem:* This is excessively wordy.)

Stage 10   Minnesota laws that regulate the sale of handguns should:

_____ Be made more strict
_____ Be made less strict
_____ Remain the same
_____ Be eliminated[4]

Decide on Question Sequence

Once the wording of the questions has been determined, the next step is to establish their sequence, that is, the order or flow of the questions in the questionnaire. The sequencing of questions can influence the nature of the respondents' answers and be the cause of serious error in the survey findings. While this aspect of questionnaire design draws heavily on the skills of an experienced researcher, several guidelines are presented below which the beginning researcher should find useful.

Use a Simple and Interesting Opening Question   The opening question must capture the respondent's interest and curiosity immediately, or the respondent

[4]Taken from "Questionnaire Design and Use Workshop," a workshop presented by Anderson, Niebuhr & Associates, Inc., St. Paul, MN, in 1988.

may terminate the interview. Often, the opening question does not relate to the information needs of the study; its sole purpose is to gain the respondent's cooperation and establish rapport. In this regard, a simple question that asks the respondent to express an attitude is a good starter, since most people like to express their feelings and can do so easily. This approach gives respondents confidence that they can answer the remaining questions in the interview. For example, one company conducting a telephone survey on cookbooks opened with "Do you like to cook?"

Ask General Questions First   Within a topic, general questions should precede specific questions. Consider the following two questions: (1) "What considerations are important to you in buying cereal?" and (2) "When you are buying cereal, is the sugar content important to you?" If these questions were asked in reverse order, sugar content would be listed more frequently as a consideration in response to Question 1 than if the questions were asked in the order given here. Asking general questions first and specific questions second reduces the chance of sequence bias.

Place Uninteresting and Difficult Questions Late in the Sequence   Sequence any questions that are embarrassing, sensitive, complex, or dull well down in the questionnaire. After rapport has been established through familiarity with the interviewer and the questioning process, the respondent is less apt to object to more demanding questions, as well as to personal questions about income, age, or other sensitive issues.

Arrange Questions in Logical Order   The flow of the questioning process must be logical from the respondent's perspective. A question sequence designed to facilitate data processing or established from the perspective of the researcher can create confusion, frustration, and indecision among respondents, with serious adverse effects on cooperation and rapport. The question order that is most likely to get good response is (1) interest, (2) information, and (3) classification. First capture the respondent's attention, next elicit the necessary information, and then approach potentially sensitive demographic or classification questions.

When the information needs of a study are extensive and different groups within the sample need to be asked different questions, it is helpful to "flowchart" the question sequence. Figure 12-4 presents a flowchart plan for a questionnaire. Flowcharting can help researchers to visualize the structure of the questionnaire and to ensure that the questions flow logically.

Decide on Physical Characteristics

The physical appearance of the questionnaire can be influential in securing the cooperation of the respondent. This is particularly the case with mail surveys. The quality of the paper and printing often determines the respondent's first reaction

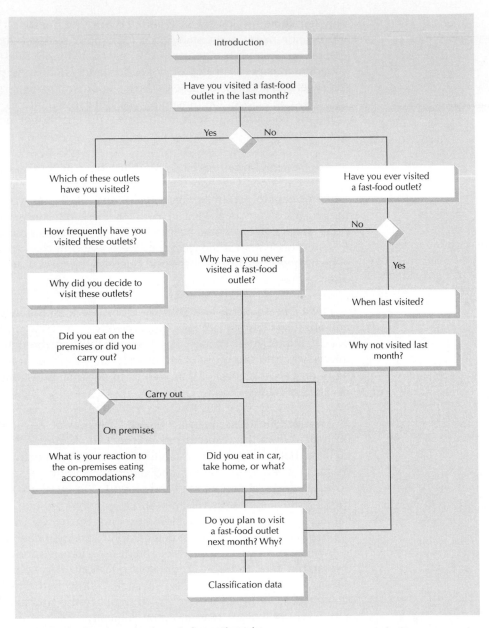

FIGURE 12-4   Example of a flowchart plan for a draft questionnaire.

to the questionnaire. It is important that the name of the organization sponsoring the survey (even though the name is often fictitious, to avoid introducing bias) and the project name appear clearly on the first page.

With personal and telephone interviews, the questionnaires should be numbered serially. This facilitates control of the questionnaires in field operations and during data processing. Mail questionnaires may not be identified numerically when respondent anonymity is important.

Because of the variety and quality of computer graphics now available, the potential for visual effects in designing the physical appearance of the computer disk presentation is nearly limitless. As with mail surveys, the quality of the presentation determines the respondent's first reaction.

Finally, the format of a question can influence the response. With both self-administered and interviewer-administered questionnaires, researchers have discovered that the more lines or space left for recording the response to open-ended questions, the more extensive the replies.

Carry Out Pretesting and Revision, and Make the Final Draft

Before the questionnaire is ready for field operations, it needs to be pretested and revised. *Pretesting* refers to the initial testing of one or more aspects of the research design. Regardless of the researcher's skill in questionnaire design, a pretest is needed to search out areas for improvement. Most questionnaires require at least one pretest and revision before they are ready for field operations.[5]

Consider the following issues as you prepare for the pretest:
In terms of physical appearance:

1 Will your questionnaire appeal to respondents and motivate them to cooperate? Is your questionnaire "sensuous"?

2 Does your questionnaire include brief and precise instructions?

3 Is your format conducive to your chosen method of data entry (e.g., keying, scanning, hand tabulation)?

In terms of content:

1 Does each question ask for only one bit of information?

2 Does the question presuppose a certain state of affairs? If so, is this supposition justified?

3 Does the question wording bias response?

4 Are any of the question's words emotionally loaded, vaguely defined, or overly general?

5 Do any of the question's words have a double meaning which may confuse respondents?

6 Does the question use abbreviations or jargon which may be unfamiliar?

7 Are the question's responses mutually exclusive and sufficient to cover each conceivable answer?[6]

---

[5]Nina Reynolds, Adamantios Diamantopoulos, and Bodo Schlegelmilch, "Pretesting in Questionnaire Design: A Review of the Literature and Suggestions for Further Research," *Journal of the Market Research Society,* vol. 35, no. 2, pp. 171–182, April 1993.

[6]Taken from "Questionnaire Design and Use Workshop," a workshop presented by Anderson, Niebuhr & Associates, Inc., St. Paul, MN, 1988.

In general, the questionnaire should be pretested in the manner intended for the final study, but it is best to pretest an early draft of the questionnaire using personal interviewers, even when the survey is to be administered by mail or telephone. It is important that only the best interviewers be used for pretest work. A skilled interviewer can respond to requests for explanation, detect areas of confusion, and probe the nature of this confusion. The interviewer should be sensitive to words that are not understood by all respondents, should test question sequence, and should note mechanical difficulties and the like. Ultimately, the revised questionnaire should be pretested in the manner intended for the final survey.

The open-ended response format can be used in the pretest to determine appropriate response categories for what will become a multiple-choice question in the final questionnaire. A new pretest should be conducted to uncover any problems with the standardized response categories created.

The number of people interviewed in a pretest can range from 15 to 30. The pretest sample should be similar to the sample that will be tested in the main study.

Whenever significant changes are made in the questionnaire, another pretest should be conducted. If the pretest results suggest minor changes, the questionnaire is ready for the final draft and distribution to field operators.

COMPUTER-AIDED QUESTIONNAIRE DESIGN

Personal computer-based questionnaire design programs have come into substantial use in marketing research over the last decade. (For example, Sawtooth Software has had great commercial success with its Ci3 system.) These programs have predefined question formats for attitude scales of all kinds, for paired comparisons, for demographics, and for virtually all other commonly used questions. They allow the designer to specify question switching and skip patterns based on previous answers, to randomize the order of presentation of brand names or other questions, to reverse positive and negative scale directions, and to custom-tailor standard question formats using a full-screen editor.

The resulting questionnaire may be generated in a paper-based form or stored electronically for use on the personal computer. Computer-based interviewing will be discussed in Chapter 16.

OBSERVATIONAL FORMS

Observational forms are easier to design than questionnaires, since the question-asking process is eliminated and design problems related to controlling nonsampling error are reduced. Even so, there are important issues in the construction of observational forms. The researcher needs to be very explicit about the types of observations to be made and how they are to be measured. The measurement process can involve an observer with observational forms, a mechanical recording device, or a combination of both.

The design of observational forms should flow logically from the listing of information needs, which must clearly specify the aspects of behavior that are to be observed. It is often useful to characterize the information needs as the "who, what, when, and where" of behavior. Consider the information needs for a study designed to observe shoppers purchasing cereal. The following items should be specified in detail.

1 *Who is to be observed?* Purchasers, lookers, males, females, couples, couples with children, children alone.

2 *What is to be observed?* Brands purchased, size, brands considered, influence of children and adults, price of product package inspected.

3 *When is observation to be made?* Days of week, hours, date, and time of purchase.

4 *Where should observations be made?* Type of store, location, how selected.

Observational forms should be simple to use. They should be designed so that they logically follow the behavior observed. They should permit the observer to record the behavior in detail, rather than requiring a summary regarding a number of behavior patterns. The physical layout of the form should follow the guidelines given above for questionnaires. Finally, observational forms need the same degree of pretesting and revision as questionnaires.

WORLDWIDE QUESTIONNAIRE DESIGN

This chapter has discussed the complexity of issues involved in the construction of an effective and efficient questionnaire given the U.S. language and culture. The difficulty of this task is increased significantly when the questionnaire is to be used in a foreign country. The issues that must be addressed are as follows:

1 The questionnaire format may have to be changed to reflect the different interviewing modes of personal, telephone, and mail.

2 The questionnaire will have to be translated from English to one or more foreign languages. The accuracy of the translation needs to be tested extensively in the countries where they will be administered. Typically this is done by having the questionnaire translated into the other language and then translated back into English, and then comparing the two English language versions.

3 In some parts of the world, special attention must be given to how answer categories are structured. In parts of Asia and the Middle East, people are reluctant to say no. Questions may have to be asked in several different ways in order to get accurate answers.

4 This type of complexity means that marketing research projects will take longer to complete in other countries than in the United States. The additional time involved can be from 3 to 4 months in most countries and up to 5 or 6 months in the Middle East.

5 Marketing research costs more internationally than in the United States. The cost for an in-person interview in the United States is from $40 to $60 (not including designing the questionnaire and analyzing the results). In Europe and Asia, the cost is nearly $400; in the Middle East and Latin America, nearly $250.

SUMMARY

1 A questionnaire is a formalized schedule for collecting data from respondents. It can collect data on past behavior, attitudes, and respondent characteristics. The questionnaire is a critical component of the research project in that a poorly designed questionnaire can be a major source of error in the research results.

2 The five sections of a questionnaire are (a) identification data, (b) request for cooperation, (c) instructions, (d) information sought, and (e) classification data.

3 While a number of guidelines are useful in designing a questionnaire, its final quality will depend on the skill and judgment of the researcher. The steps in questionnaire design are: (a) Review preliminary considerations. (b) Decide on question content. (c) Decide on response format. (d) Decide on question wording. (e) Decide on question sequence. (f) Decide on physical characteristics. (g) Carry out pretesting and revision, and make the final draft.

4 The design of the questionnaire is dependent upon previous decisions regarding the nature of the research design, the sources of data, the target population, the sampling plan, the communication media, the measurement techniques, and the data processing and analysis plan. The questionnaire is the link between the information needed and the data to be collected.

5 The question content is influenced by the respondent's ability and willingness to respond accurately. The response format can be open-ended, multiple-choice, or dichotomous.

6 The guidelines for designing the wording of a question are: (a) Use simple words. (b) Use clear words. (c) Avoid leading questions. (d) Avoid biasing questions. (e) Avoid implicit alternatives. (f) Avoid implicit assumptions. (g) Avoid estimates. (h) Avoid double-barreled questions. (i) Consider the frame of reference.

7 The guidelines for determining the question sequences are: (a) Use a simple and interesting opening question. (b) Ask general questions first. (c) Place uninteresting and difficult questions late in the sequence. (d) Arrange questions in logical order.

8 The physical characteristics of the questionnaire can influence the degree of respondent cooperation and the character of the responses.

9 A questionnaire needs to be pretested and revised before it is ready for use in the field.

10 Observational forms are easier to design than questionnaires, since some of the design problems associated with the questionnaire are reduced or eliminated in the observational form. Design of the data collection forms should flow logically from a clear specification of the types of observations to be made and how they are to be measured.

DISCUSSION QUESTIONS

1 What role does the questionnaire play in a research project?
2 What are the typical components of a questionnaire?
3 What decisions precede the questionnaire design stage?

4 What criterion governs the inclusion of questions in the questionnaire?

5 How does the respondent affect the content of the questions?

6 How can a researcher overcome the problems associated with collecting data about events that are unimportant to respondents or that occur infrequently?

7 Why may a respondent be unwilling to respond accurately to a given question?

8 What approaches are available for dealing with the bias resulting from a respondent's unwillingness to respond accurately?

9 What are the advantages and disadvantages of open-ended questions?

10 What are the advantages and disadvantages of multiple-choice questions?

11 What guidelines govern the design of responses to multiple-choice questions?

12 Under what conditions would dichotomous questions be inappropriate?

13 What general guidelines should be utilized in designing the wording of a question?

14 MINICASE

Develop a short questionnaire to measure your classmates' knowledge of and attitudes about laptop computers.

CASES FOR PART THREE

CASE 3-1   New England Soup Company

On January 11, 1995, William Kolander, president of the New England Soup Company of Boston, Massachusetts, was reviewing a research report he had received from a Boston-based research house. The report presented the findings of a study on the firm's new formulation of Kolander's Chowder brand canned soup. The study had also been sent to the firm's sales manager, Kirk George, and the production manager, Edward Corey. A meeting was scheduled for January 12 with the research firm and the New England Soup Company management. The purpose of the meeting was to discuss the research findings and to make decisions concerning Kolander's product offerings.

THE COMPANY

The New England Soup Company was a small firm that produced and distributed a line of specialty canned soup products to both the institutional and retail markets. Approximately 62 percent of their 1994 sales volume went to the institutional market ($68,526), and 38 percent went to the retail market ($42,102).

The company was founded by William Kolander in 1957. Kolander's father was a successful owner of several restaurants in the Boston area that were famous for their chowder. The young Kolander convinced his father in 1956 that there was a market to sell the chowder to local institutions (restaurants, hospitals, etc.) in the New England area, and he developed a canned chowder under his father's supervision. Production facilities were acquired in the same year.

After losses in the first few years, the business turned profitable in 1960. At this time, Kolander

decided to enter the retail market with Kolander's Chowder brand. Both the institutional and retail business grew rapidly during the 1960s, as did the firm's profitability. Expanded production facilities were built in 1968, and two additional specialty soup lines were introduced in 1970. These lines experienced limited success at retail but were reasonably profitable in the institutional market.

CURRENT SITUATION

The last four years had been a period of level and then declining sales for Kolander's Chowder (6943 cases in 1991, 5676 cases in 1992, 5105 cases in 1993, and 4900 cases in 1994[1]). Kolander attributed this decline in sales to the market entry of two new canned chowders in 1990 and 1991 (see Appendix A). The new competitors were Fisherman's Delight Chowder and Cape Cod Chowder. Both brands were produced locally and appeared very similar in formulation to Kolander's Chowder.

Both of the new competitors had entered the market with a somewhat lower selling price than the Kolander's brand. Distributors were also attracted by the slightly higher margins plus the desire to carry a competitive alternative to Kolander's Chowder. Several large retailers had advertised the Fisherman's Delight brand as a "weekly special" at 43 cents per can.

MANAGEMENT OBJECTIVE

Kolander recognized that the firm faced a serious competitive threat from the two new brand entries.

---

[1]Estimated from 1994 company records.

378

While there were several long-term issues he was considering, his immediate concern was one of developing a competitive strategy to counter the sales decline of Kolander's Chowder. Specifically, he wanted to recover the lost distribution of the brand and switch customers from competitive brands back to the Kolander's brand. This was to be accomplished within the next 12 months. While increased distribution outside the current market area was a possibility, Kolander's immediate objective was to improve the market position of Kolander's Chowder at retail within the New England area.

THE RESEARCH PROJECT

In October 1994, Kolander contacted a local research firm. After a number of meetings, the research firm recommended that a series of group interviews be conducted with current users of the two competitive chowder brands in order to explore reasons for product usage, reaction to the brands, and perceived product differences. Through group sessions of this nature, the research firm believed that the cause of declining sales of Kolander's Chowder could be established and potential solutions identified.

The results of the group sessions suggested that an important proportion of the competitive canned chowder users preferred a chowder that was thicker and creamier than the current Kolander's Chowder brand formulation. Of the former Kolander's Chowder users, the desire for a creamier formulation was the predominant reason for switching. Many of these chowder users had switched to either Fisherman's Delight or Cape Cod Chowder.

Based on these findings, the research firm recommended that further research be conducted to evaluate changing Kolander's Chowder to a creamier formulation. For purposes of the test, it was recommended that two creamier formulations be developed, a "creamy" version and an "extra creamy" version. These two new formulations would be evaluated in a taste test along with Kolander's current chowder plus the two competitive brands.

After several meetings on specific aspects of the proposed research design, Kolander decided to approve the project. Appendix B presents the results of this study.

CASE QUESTION

1 What action should Kolander take based on the research findings?

APPENDIX A   New England Soup Company, Audit of Retail Food Outlets

Fifty retail food outlets in the New England market area have been audited annually since 1975. These are deemed representative of the potential distribution out-lets of canned soups for the New England Soup Company.

SELECTED TABLES FROM THE REPORT

PERCENTAGE OF STORES STOCKING
CANNED CHOWDER BRANDS

Brand	1992	1993	1994
Kolander	94	86	82
Cape Cod	20	36	42
Fisherman's Delight	4	18	24

NUMBER OF BRANDS OF CANNED
CHOWDER STOCKED

Brand	1992	1993	1994
None	3	1	0
One	34	25	23
Two	10	20	24
Three	2	3	2
Four or more	1	1	1
Total stores	50	50	50

RANGE OF RETAIL PRICES OF CANNED
CHOWDER SOUP
(in Cents)

Brand	1992	1993	1994
Kolander	49–53	48–55	47–54
Cape Cod	48–51	49–53	48–51
Fisherman's Delight	46–50	47–51	47–49

APPENDIX B   Research Report: Evaluation of Two New Formulations of Kolander's Canned Chowder

Research Objectives   To evaluate the preference for two new chowder formulations among users of Kolander's Chowder, Cape Cod Chowder, and Fisherman's Delight Chowder.

Research Design and Procedure   Two hundred male ($n = 100$) and female ($n = 100$) canned chowder users were selected from four geographic locations representative of the New England market area. The subjects were selected using a probability sampling procedure involving a telephone-administered qualifying questionnaire. Each subject was paid $5 for participating in the test.

The subjects came to one of four test locations (local churches). They were tested individually in 30-minute sessions. Subjects were brought into the testing room and seated at stalls. An instruction sheet explained that the subject was to evaluate several samples of chowder, that the test would consist of three parts, and that they would be required to taste a total of 15 cups of chowder. Normal taste-testing procedures were followed.

The first part involved five samples of chowder and ranking them from "most preferred" to "least preferred." The five chowders were Kolander's regular chowder, Fisherman's Delight, Kolander's creamy (version 1), Cape Cod, and Kolander's extra creamy (version 2).

The second and third parts of the test involved tasting five samples again. The samples had different code letters and the subjects were not told the samples were identical to the previous five. After tasting the five samples, the subjects were again asked to rank-order the five samples.

For each subject, the test procedures resulted in three

TABLE 1   PREFERENCE ORDERINGS OF FIVE CANNED CHOWDERS

Subject	Kolander's regular	Fisherman's Delight	Kolander's creamy	Cape Cod	Kolander's extra creamy
1	1	2	3	4	5
2	2	1	3	4	5
3	1	2	3	4	5
4	5	4	3	2	1
5	5	4	3	2	1
6	5	4	1	2	3
7	1	2	3	4	5
8	5	4	3	2	1
9	1	2	3	4	5
10	5	4	3	2	1
11	3	1	2	4	5
12	5	2	1	3	4
13	5	4	3	1	2
14	5	3	1	2	4
15	1	2	3	4	5
16	1	2	3	4	5
17	5	4	2	1	3
18	3	2	1	4	5
19	5	4	3	2	1
20*	4	2	1	3	5
.	.	.	.	.	.
.	.	.	.	.	.
.	.	.	.	.	.
200	.	.	.	.	.
Total =	685	550	482	588	712
n =	200	200	200	200	200
Mean =	3.4	2.8	2.4	2.9	3.6

*The first 20 preference orderings are representative of the total sample of 200 subjects.

TABLE 2   PREFERENCE SCALE (*n* = 200)

Most preferred	1.00	
	1.25	
	1.50	
	1.75	
	2.00	
	2.25	
	2.50	← Kolander's creamy (2.4)
	2.75	← Fisherman's Delight (2.8)
	3.00	← Cape Cod (2.9)
	3.25	
	3.50	← Kolander's regular (3.4)
	3.75	← Kolander's extra creamy (3.6)
	4.00	
	4.25	
	4.50	
	4.75	
Least preferred	5.00	

preference orderings of the five chowder samples. The preference orderings were combined to form a composite ordering for each subject, a procedure that resulted in a more reliable measure of each subject's true preference ordering.

Results The data set consisted of 200 preference orderings of the five chowders. Table 1 presents 20 preference orderings which are representative of the entire data set. The difference between male and female preference orderings was not statistically significant.

The data set was analyzed by calculating the average rank order of each chowder and scaling the chowders on a five-point scale ranging from most preferred (1) to least preferred (5). Table 2 presents the results of this analysis.

Recommendation and Discussion Recommendation: Change the current Kolander's Chowder formulation to the version 1—"creamy"—formulation, and develop a new label which makes this change conspicuous at point of purchase.

The Table 2 results clearly indicate that the current Kolander's Chowder formulation and the "extra creamy" formulation ranked significantly (.05 level of significance) lower than the two competitors' brands and the "creamy" formulation. These findings suggest that the market position of Kolander's Chowder can be improved by a formulation change to the "creamy" version, which ranks higher than the two competitors and should recapture a significant share of sales lost to the Cape Cod and Fisherman's Delight brands.

CASE 3-2 Chrysler Car Leasing Satisfaction Study

One senior automobile executive noted that "the 1990s are the era of the lease in new car marketing." Indeed, there has been a dramatic increase in the percentage of new car "purchases," with leases in each successive year post 1990. Thus, automobile marketers have become concerned about customer satisfaction not only with the cars themselves, but also about customer satisfaction about the leasing arrangements.

The management of the Dodge division of Chrysler Corporation wanted to undertake periodic studies (every 6 months) of car satisfaction and lease satisfaction among recent leasees of their cars. They had approached a number of marketing research companies about possibly designing a measurement of customer satisfaction for this purpose.

One marketing research company proposed the following approach:

1 Rate 50 attributes of the car, such as fit of doors, quietness at high speed, and cargo capacity, on the following verbal scale: excellent, very good, good, fair, and poor. Also rate 10 attributes of the lease, such as down payment, monthly payment, and allowable mileage per year, on the same scale.

2 Rate the overall opinion about the car on the following satisfaction scale: completely satisfied, very satisfied, somewhat satisfied, somewhat dissatisfied, and very dissatisfied.

3 Rate both the information provided about the lease terms and conditions, and the leasing plan on the same satisfaction scale as in number 2 above.

4 Also collect data describing the car leased and the demographic characteristics of the lease.

There was concern among some of the Dodge marketing researchers about the measurement characteristics of the proposed approach. Others thought that any measure of satisfaction should consider the difference between (1) customer expectations of attributes and overall satisfaction and (2) the actual customer experience with these attributes and perception of satisfaction. Still others thought that any measure of satisfaction must allow customers to make trade-offs among car and lease attributes to determine which attributes were the most important to them.

CASE QUESTIONS

1 How is customer satisfaction for the car and for the lease being measured?

2 What are the measurement scale characteristics of these customer satisfaction measures?

3 What attitude measurement approach is being taken to the measurement of customer satisfaction?

4 How should the reliability and validity of these customer satisfaction measures be measured?

5 What alternative measures of customer satisfaction could be utilized? Be specific, and be sure to consider the expectation-based approach described above.

6 What use should be made of the demographic and car description data that are also proposed to be collected?

7 How might trade-off data on attributes, which yield the importance of each attribute in forming overall satisfaction, be useful to Dodge managers?

CASE 3-3 Mainline Package Goods*

Ken Gibbs was the recently promoted product manager for Ice-Away, a windshield de-icer marketed by Mainline Package Goods. Windshield de-icers are sprayed on car windows to instantly melt ice and frost. As brand manager, Gibbs was responsible for all marketing decisions related to Ice-Away. He was currently preparing Ice-Away's marketing plan for the next fiscal year and had to submit the finalized version to his boss in 2 weeks. Two major changes in package design had been test-marketed by Research Design, Inc. (RDI), and

*Source: Coauthored by Sheryl Petras.

Gibbs was in the process of reviewing the results. The field experiment was designed to measure the effects of different packaging on consumer attitudes and on sales of Ice-Away.

Mainline was one of the largest American package goods companies, marketing everything from floor wax to over-the-counter drugs. Ice-Away was the leader in its product category, windshield de-icers, with annual sales of $10 million and profits of $1.25 million. Ice-Away first entered the market in 1970, and by 1975 it was the number one brand, mostly due to intensive advertising and retail promotion. Ice-Away's main competition came from the other major brands on the market—Snowflake, No-Frost, and Melt It! All these brands were about the same price as Ice-Away and had equivalent distribution at retail. For the last 3 years, Ice-Away had been losing market share to the competition, and Gibbs was convinced that poor packaging was the reason.

Ice-Away's package, a metal aerosol can, had not materially changed since 1970. When the competition changed to nonaerosol containers, Ice-Away retained the same packaging, and it was then that Ice-Away's market share began to decline. Mainline's R&D department had come up with two alternatives to the metal aerosol can: first, a non-aerosol plastic container that utilized a pump mechanism to expel the de-icer, and second, a nonaerosol metal can that had an aerosol-like spray. On the front of the metal version, the words "NEW NONAEROSOL FORMULA" were printed in large letters to ensure that consumers would note the difference between new and old packages. The $25,000 RDI study examined the effects of the two new package designs on sales and consumer attitudes. The research report submitted by RDI appears below.

THE RESEARCH REPORT

Objectives

1 To test the relative effectiveness of alternative package designs for Ice-Away
2 To recommend the best design

Packaging Tested

1 Metal aerosol can (control market)
2 Plastic nonaerosol pump
3 Metal nonaerosol can

The price was the same for all three alternatives.

Test Markets Used   The three cities used were selected to be as similar as possible with respect to (1) the distribution penetration of Ice-Away and its three major competitors, and (2) the following economic characteristics:

	Newark	Cleveland	Denver
Population	1,870,000	1,840,000	1,580,000
Households	661,000	704,000	619,000
Effective buying income per household	$30,000	$25,000	$28,000
Retail sales index*	105	99	106

* National base of 100.

The metal aerosol can was tested in Newark, the metal nonaerosol can in Denver, and the plastic pump in Cleveland.

Data Collection Method   The data were collected by means of telephone interviews. Samples were chosen randomly from phone books in each of the three cities. To qualify for the questionnaire, a respondent had to be a user of windshield de-icer. The realized sample sizes were: Newark, 300; Cleveland, 297; and Denver 501. The following purchase measures were taken:

1 Brand of de-icer usually purchased
2 Brand of de-icer last purchased
3 Brand of de-icer the respondent intended to purchase next

Attitude measures were taken on (1) convenience (versus scraping the windows), (2) effectiveness in melting ice, (3) speed in de-icing, (4) aesthetic appeal of the package, (5) ease in using the package, and (6) frequency of use. Respondents were asked to rate each attribute on a 7-point scale, with a 1 indicating the lowest attitude measure and a 7 the highest.

Timing   The new package designs were introduced in December, and interviewing was done in March.

Results   Selected tables from the report appear below.

BRAND USUALLY PURCHASED

	Newark %	Cleveland %	Denver %
Ice-Away	12	10	17*
Snowflake	11	9	10
No-Frost	14	11	9
Melt It!	9	8	12*

*Significant difference from control at $p < .05$.

BRAND LAST PURCHASED

	Newark %	Cleveland %	Denver %
Ice-Away	11	11	15*
Snowflake	11	9	9
No-Frost	12	10	10
Melt It!	7	10*	13*

*Significant difference from control at $p < .05$.

ATTITUDE MEASURES

Attributes	Ice-Away			Snowflake			No-Frost			Melt It!		
	N	C	D	N	C	D	N	C	D	N	C	D
Convenience	5.4	5.6	5.5	5.5	5.8	5.6	5.8	5.1	5.4	5.5	4.9	4.6
Effectiveness melting ice	6.0	6.5*	6.0	5.9	6.0	5.8	5.7	5.8	5.6	5.2	5.0	5.7*
Speed in de-icing	5.9	6.1	5.8	6.0	5.8	6.1	5.4	5.8	5.1	5.7	5.9	6.0
Package appeal	6.2	6.1	6.4	6.0	6.0	6.0	5.2	5.0	4.9	5.1	5.2	5.0
Ease in using package	4.2	5.1	4.6	4.1	4.4	4.2	4.0	3.9	4.1	3.7	3.6	4.1
Frequency of use	4.5	4.0*	5.1*	4.9	4.9	4.8	4.7	4.9	4.7	4.9	4.5	4.6

Note: N — Newark (metal aerosol)
   C = Cleveland (plastic pump)
   D = Denver (metal nonaerosol)
*Significant difference from control at $p < .05$.

Recommendations   Ken Gibbs wanted to analyze the data himself before initiating a packaging change. If his analysis of the data did not lead to the same conclusions as the RDI analysis, Gibbs planned to adopt the package he felt was best, and to this end he began to review the data.

CASE QUESTIONS

1 Evaluate the experimental design used by Mainline Package Goods. Be sure to discuss the validity of the experiment.
2 Do you feel the design can be improved? If yes, indicate how you would do so. Be specific!
3 What conclusions can be drawn from the study? What action would you recommend if you were in Ken Gibbs's position?

CASE 3-4   Unilever's Persil Detergent

In 1994 Unilever launched its new Pan-European power detergent, Persil Power. After some early sales success, Persil Power came under fire from archrival Procter & Gamble, and from some government consumer affairs agencies. The charge was that Persil damaged clothes. There was also the possibility that the Good Housekeeping Institute would withdraw its seal of approval from Persil Power.

The product management team was under intense pressure to determine a course of action to save Persil Power. They asked marketing research at Unilever to help with this task. As a first step the brand group asked for a test "to demonstrate that Persil Power is safe for clothes." The management wanted to use the results of this test to help quiet the brands critics, and to help relaunch the brand in Europe.

CASE QUESTIONS

1 Prepare an experimental design that would allow management to determine the damage impact of Persil Power on clothes. Be sure to clearly identify test units, dependent variables, treatments, methods for control of extraneous variables, timing of measurements taken, selection of test units, and assignment of test units to treatments.
2 Display your design using the R, O, X symbols of experimental design.
3 Given brand management's statement of purpose for the research, how should Unilever's marketing researchers state the objective for the research?

CASE 3-5   European Alcohol Research Foundation

The European Alcohol Research Foundation (EARF) was a nonprofit public service group located in Brussels. EARF was dedicated to reducing the abuse of alcohol and to promoting moderate rates of consumption of alcohol among non-abusers. Its primary functions were the delivery of educational programs to schools and the promotion of proper use of alcohol through the broadcast media. It also had a staff who conducted both primary and secondary research on the consumption of alcohol.

Michelle Lafontaine, EARF's director of consumer research, often surveyed the published literature for relevant articles on the consumption of

alcohol. She had recently quickly read one such article. It was by Jim Williams, senior vice president and European director of planning and research for Young & Rubicam (Y&R), a large global advertising agency. He was located in the London office. The article seemed to offer fresh insights on the cross-cultural dynamics of alcohol consumption. Lafontaine wondered whether the approach outlined in the article could be used as the basis for a pan-European campaign against alcohol abuse. However, she was concerned about measurement issues and about the reliability and validity of the approach taken in the article. Selected excerpts from the article are shown in Exhibit 1.

EXHIBIT 1

EXCERPTS FROM THE WILLIAMS 4C'S ARTICLE*

At its most fundamental level, international marketing seeks to establish similar patterns of consumer behavior (i.e., the purchase and use of common products and brands) in culturally dissimilar markets.

Consider the pattern of beer and wine drinking in

**Source:* Edited from Jim Williams, "Constant Questions or Constant Meanings? Assessing Intercultural Motivations in Alcoholic Drinks," *Marketing and Research Today,* pp. 169–177, August 1991.

Europe (Figure 1). European countries can be divided into two clusters according to whether they drink most of their alcohol in the form of beer or in the form of wine. Generally speaking, the colder, northern countries are beer-drinking countries, and the warmer, southern countries are wine-drinking countries. Moreover, if we look at trends in beer and wine drinking in these countries, another clear pattern exists. Beer-drinking countries are gradually drinking less beer and more wine, whereas the wine-drinking countries are moving in the opposite direction and drinking less wine and more beer. On the

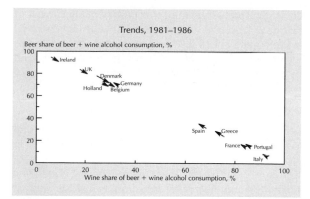

FIGURE 1   Consumption of alcoholic drinks in the EEC.

face of it, these appear to be opposite, and conflicting trends. Nevertheless, when you look at these trends, not in terms of what people are doing, but in terms of why they are doing it, they become just one trend: the trend toward drinking more modern, more unusual, "foreign" drinks. By drinking these "new" drinks, a consumer demonstrates his or her individuality and independence of the cultural norm.

People's behavior is determined not only by their attitudes or motivations but also by their surroundings and the context in which they make their behavioral decisions. As we all know, these contextual matters vary considerably from one country to another, and therefore so too does consumer behavior.

Motivations would therefore appear to be much more consistent from one culture to another, and thus the analysis of consumer motivations offers us an opportunity for getting behind the superficial behavioral differences between cultures, and for revealing underlying commonalties between them. This is the approach we have adopted at Y&R with our system of Cross Cultural Consumer Characterizations, which we normally refer to in its abbreviated form, the 4Cs.

Young & Rubicam's 4Cs

It would be inappropriate to give a full description of Y&R's 4Cs in this paper, and indeed time and space do not permit this. Nevertheless, for the rest of this paper to be meaningful, it is necessary first to summarize the essential features of the system.

From our own research, together with an analysis of available academic works on the subject, we have defined a base set of core consumer motivations, or values,

which seem to be important in determining people's purchasing behavior. These values are, in hierarchical order if Abraham Maslow is to be believed:

Survival
Escape
Security
Status
Control
Individuality
Self-fulfillment

Every individual is motivated by all these values to a greater or lesser degree, and our research aims to identify how important each of them is to each individual. We then classify each person as belonging to a particular 4Cs type according to which of the seven motivations is most important, and will therefore have the dominant shaping effect on the attitudes and behavior of that particular individual.

The classification into types runs as follows:

Dominant motivation	4Cs type
Survival	Resigned poor
Escape	Struggling poor
Security	Mainstreamer
Status	Aspirer
Control	Succeeder
Individuality	Transitional
Self-fulfillment	Reformer

Each group is defined by its dominant motivation, and the composition of the groups can vary considerably from culture to culture. However, certain key features do tend to remain fairly constant, and these are described below in order to give the reader a better feeling for each type.

1 *Resigned poor.* Generally speaking, the resigned poor are the old and the alone. Typically, they are widows and old-age pensioners who are living in reduced circumstances but who are tradition-minded people, accept that they cannot change things, and are resigned to their fate.

2 *Struggling poor.* The struggling poor are also poor but are younger and more active in their life-styles and attitudes. They do not accept that there is nothing they can do about their situations and are struggling against them, seeking to escape to a better life. Typically they might include disadvantaged racial minorities, the young unemployed, and drunken soccer fans who start fights at games.

Together with the resigned poor, the struggling poor are sometimes referred to as the "constrained," because their behavior is constrained by their physical needs and wants.

3 *Mainstreamer.* The mainstreamers are the biggest single group. They are the core of society, the silent, invisible majority—conventional, thrifty, patriotic, salt-of-the earth types who uphold traditional moral and family values.

4 *Aspirers.* Aspirers are people making their way up in the world. They are very concerned about extrinsics (the way things look) and are out to impress other people. They want to be admired, and they surround themselves with status symbols such as fast cars, cigars, designer labels, Gucci shoes, Rolex watches, and flashy jewelry.

5 *Succeeders.* Succeeders are materially the most successful. They are typically the managers and businesspeople who control most commercial enterprises. They are fairly conservative and traditional in their moral values, and they believe in standing on their own feet.

Together with the mainstreamers and the aspirers, the succeeders are sometimes referred to as the "middle majority." For all these three groups, what other people think is very important, and they live their lives in relation to the accepted norms of society.

6 *Transitional.* Transitionals, as the name implies, are people in a state of flux. They are young people who are breaking away from their parents' ways and from the traditional values of society. They are looking for their own ways of doing things. However, as yet, they have not found what they are looking for. They are constantly experimenting, trying new experiences in a voyage of self-discovery. An optimistic, creative group, they are the leaders of pop culture, music, and fashion.

7 *Reformers.* Finally, we come to reformers. Reformers are the most highly educated people in society, but they are people who have to a large extent traded off standard of living for quality of life. Like transitionals, they have rejected the traditional values and ways as being inadequate for their needs, and have developed their own, alternative, better ways. Furthermore, they are not simply content to run their own lives according to their new, better ways but want to reform society and convert it to their ways of thinking. They therefore tend toward positions where they can influence the thoughts of others. They are the lawyers, the teachers, the politi-

cians, the journalists, the broadcasters, and, in most of Europe at least, the marketing and advertising fraternity.

Reformers and transitionals together are sometimes referred to as "innovators," because, not feeling bound by convention, they are the groups most likely to try new products and start new trends.

Using 4Cs in the Alcoholic Drinks Market

Because of the enormous care we have taken to ensure that the groups we have defined in each country are in fact culturally equivalent, we believe that Young & Rubicam's 4Cs is uniquely powerful in exposing underlying similarities and differences in culturally diverse markets.

In doing so, the most important thing to recognize is that we do not necessarily expect 4Cs, which are in effect an analog of consumer motivations, to correlate directly with differences of consumer behavior in different countries. Consumer behavior is determined not only by consumer attitudes but also by the context in which the behavioral decision is made. Thus, in order to discriminate meaningfully in terms of consumer behavior, we need to add onto 4Cs the appropriate contextual variables. These may relate to national cultures, the product field, or both.

This can be demonstrated by considering the following analysis of the alcoholic drinks market in Europe.

Behavioral Mapping
In Figures 2 to 5 we have used correspondence analysis to map the usage of different types of alcoholic drinks in four different European markets. The input data are the penetration of heavy usership of each product among each of the seven 4Cs groups. These maps reveal interesting structural similarities and differences between the various national markets for alcoholic drinks.

Market Similarities
Examination of the maps for the four markets reveals a remarkable consistency in their basic structure. The predominant axes of discrimination seem to be traditional–modern and personal–social in every case. Furthermore, the positions of the seven different 4Cs groups are remarkably similar. The major difference would appear to be that the drinks markets in France and the United Kingdom (UK) are driven by transitional values, whereas those in the southern European countries of Spain and Italy are driven more by aspirer values.

4Cs can therefore provide a relatively stable framework for examining the relative positions of different products and brands in different markets.

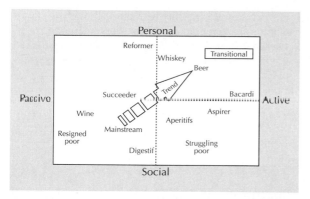

FIGURE 2   4Cs map of French alcoholic drinks market.

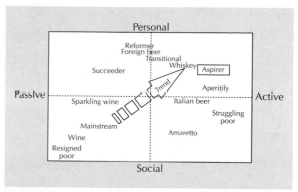

FIGURE 4   4Cs map of Italian alcoholic drinks market.

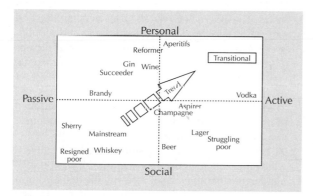

FIGURE 3   4Cs map of UK alcoholic drinks market.

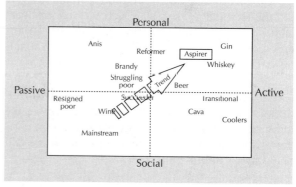

FIGURE 5   4Cs map of Spanish alcoholic drinks market.

Cultural Differences

The main differences between the maps in different countries can be found in the positions of individual alcoholic products. In France wine is seen to be a traditional, mainstream product, whereas in the UK it is reformer/succeeder. Whiskey, however, exhibits a contrary pattern, being mainstream in the UK and aspirer/transitional in France. Similar cultural differences can be observed in the position of beer in France, Italy, and Spain as compared to the UK.

Brand Implications

The maps here presented deal with overall product categories alone. Similar maps could of course be produced

showing the relative positions of individual brands within their product categories in different countries. These maps highlight essential similarities and differences between the competitive situations of a particular brand in different markets, and can therefore provide a much-needed framework for coordinating international marketing activity.

It is possible to create a robust framework for analyzing cultural similarities and differences in a market, and thereby for coordinating the international marketing activities of a brand.

CASE QUESTIONS

1 What is the 4Cs approach to consumer behavior measurement?
2 What are the measurement scale characteristics, and the reliability and validity of the 4Cs approach?
3 What conclusion for EARF can be drawn from this paper?
4 How could Y&R use the 4Cs approach with its clients who desire to market across borders in Europe?
5 On what basis should Y&R's clients be prepared to utilize these types of results in an advertising campaign?

CASE 3-6   Kellogg's Heartwise Cereal

According to the American Heart Association, 50 percent of middle-aged Americans have cholesterol levels above 200 milligrams per deciliter of blood. This is the level at which the risk of heart attack begins to rise "sharply." Moreover, an average of three Americans will suffer a heart attack every minute of the day.

Dietary intake is thought to play a significant role in these conditions. Studies have shown that populations with high-fiber diets have a lower incidence of coronary heart disease and colon cancer. There are two types of fiber: water-insoluble and water-soluble. Both are found in cereals, fruits, vegetables, dried peas, and beans. While insoluble fiber may help reduce the risk of colon cancer, research suggests that eating 10 to 15 grams of soluble fiber per day in a low-fat diet can lower elevated blood cholesterol levels. Research has identified the grain psyllium as one of the best sources of water-soluble fiber. Kellogg developed its psyllium-based Heartwise cereal in response to these claims.

A University of Kentucky study found that men on a high-fat diet lowered their elevated cholesterol levels by 15 percent after taking a psyllium formula three times a day for 2 months. The University of Minnesota decided to investigate the effect of using psyllium as an adjunct to a low-fat diet. This study formed the basis for the previous claims. In executing the psyllium study, scientists set up the following experiment:

The study involved 75 patients (38 male and 37 female) with mild to moderate levels of high cholesterol. All participants had to meet certain requirements. They were between the ages of 24 and 68 and had cholesterol levels (adjusted for age and sex) between the fiftieth and ninetieth percentile. Candidates were further screened on the basis of a list of medical conditions, their body weight as a percentage of ideal, and the absence of certain prescription drugs in their bloodstream. All participants were required to maintain constant body weights (plus or minus 5 percent) during the study.

The experiment was a study in which subjects were randomly assigned to test groups, it was double-blind in that neither the subjects nor the doctors knew which group the subjects had been assigned to, and it had a placebo control group. The study lasted 20 weeks and was conducted in three stages. The twelve weeks prior to the implementation of the experimental treatment are designated as minus $(-)$ weeks. After their initial visit, patients were given 6 weeks (weeks -12 to -7) to adapt to a step 1 diet (30 percent fat, 55 percent carbohydrates, 15 percent protein, and a maximum of 300 milligrams of dietary cholesterol). Participants were screened at the end of 6 weeks, and those who were likely to meet the entry criteria continued their diets for an additional 6 weeks (weeks -6 to 0). After 12 weeks of regulated dieting, they were screened again, and those who met the study's qualifications were randomized into two treatment groups and given their "medication."

One treatment group was given active medication, while the other group received a placebo. The active medication was orange-flavored sugar-free Metamucil, which contains psyllium. The placebo was an identical product, except that it contained an inert bulk fiber instead of psyllium. Identical doses of each product were given to each participant in matching foil packets. Participants were to take their medication in 8 ounces of water before each of their three meals each day. Adherence to instructions was monitored with patient interviews and by keeping track of unopened packets returned to the clinic at each visit.

Participants were evaluated at weeks 2, 4, 6, 7, and 8. Clinic visits were scheduled in the morning, after participants had not eaten for 12 hours. Various parameters were measured each time. Body weight, blood pressure, and pulse rate were measured at every visit. A complete lipid profile and a clinical chemistry screening were conducted on predetermined visits. Patients kept food records, which were analyzed by the Nutrition Coordinating Center every 8 weeks. To further monitor dietary adherence, a registered dietician also evaluated food frequency records at five different points throughout the study.

Various analytical methods were used to determine the effects of the active medication containing psyllium. Blood samples were collected and several medical tests were run to measure the levels of various lipids and proteins, as well as the participants' cholesterol levels. Researchers used several statistical methods to further analyze the results. They calculated baseline values as the average body weight, blood pressure, and lipid values for weeks -4, -2, and 0. Posttreatment baseline values were calculated as the average for weeks 6, 7, and 8. Scientists calculated the differences from the baseline at each eval-

uation, and the treatment groups were compared by analysis of variance and a rank sum test. They assessed the significance from baseline by paired t test and Wilcoxon signed rank tests.

Results for the two study groups were measured and analyzed. Both groups were well-matched according to sex, age, weight, and dietary intake at baseline. Both groups also had similar baseline cholesterol levels. After 8 weeks, the group receiving the psyllium product showed a 4.8 percent reduction in total cholesterol levels relative to placebo values, and 4.2 percent reduction relative to baseline values. The psyllium treatment had no significant effect on body weight, blood pressure, serum levels of glucose and iron, or the levels of several key proteins. Ninety-one percent of the psyllium participants and 95.4 percent of the placebo participants complied with the study's guidelines.[1]

CASE QUESTIONS

1 Identify the test units, dependent variable(s), independent variable(s), treatments, sources of extraneous variation, methods of obtaining control, timing of measurements, selection of test units, and assignment of test units to treatments.
2 Evaluate the internal and external validity of this study.
3 Is it a proper use of this research to make health claims for Heartwise cereal? Why or why not?

[1]"Cholesterol-Lowering Effects of Psyllium Hydrophilic Mucilloid," *Journal of the American Medical Association,* pp. 3419–3423, June 16, 1989.

CASE 3-7 Parkside Corporation

In early January 1995, Barbra Lott, vice president of marketing for Parkside Corporation, a leading manufacturer in the recreational vehicle (RV) market, was approached by Paul Ransom, Parkside's president and chief executive officer. Ransom, sensitive to continuing developments in the RV market, was concerned with whether Parkside's strat-

egy of concentrating on the motor home segment of the RV market was still sound.[1]

Given the company's strong cash position, Ran-

[1]The RV market is composed of motor homes (motor vehicle combined with living unit), travel trailers (living unit pulled by car or truck), campers (living unit sits in bed of truck), and accessories (sundry items purchased for RV vehicles).

som told Lott that she should analyze from a marketing perspective whether Parkside should expand into other RV markets and/or vertically integrate forward or backward in the RV supplier-manufacturer-distributor chain. If so, Ransom said, he knew of two companies that could be purchased. The first company, Travelall, was a respected, medium-sized manufacturer of travel trailers. The second company, Flushaway, was a small and expanding regional manufacturer of toilets for RVs, boats, and aircraft.

Lott recognized the need for marketing research as part of the process of addressing these strategic questions. She first talked with her assistant, Joel Christopherson, about the situation. Christopherson was a recent graduate of a leading business school and had specific training in the area of marketing research. After thoroughly discussing the decision situation, Lott and Christopherson formulated the following statement:

> Management objective: To expand Parkside's long-term profitability by entering new market segments within the RV market and/or by integrating forward or backward in the RV business.

The RV market segments were clearly defined as those of (1) travel trailers, (2) motor homes, (3) slide-in campers, and (4) RV accessories. Given the current alternatives of purchasing Travelall and/or Flushaway, it was decided to concentrate initial effort on the travel trailer segment (Travelall) and backward integration to a toilet supplier (Flushaway). Christopherson was directed to develop a written proposal for research directed at evaluating this issue within 3 days.

Returning to his office, Christopherson decided that his first steps were to formulate clear research objectives and to specify in detail the information needed. The more he investigated the situation, the more he recognized that very little was known about the travel trailer segment or the toilet aspect of the RV business in general.

Christopherson believed that a two-stage research program was needed. The first stage would be exploratory research designed to better understand the travel trailer owner and reactions to RV toilets. Is the reason for buying a travel trailer different from that for buying a motor home? What are the problems with travel trailers? What are the important considerations in purchasing a travel trailer? Is the toilet an important feature in buying an RV? Are there opportunities for product improvement? It seemed important to find out about questions of this nature before a more formal research program could be formulated. The second stage could involve large-scale telephone or personal interviews with RV owners.

Focus group interviews appeared to be the best choice for the exploratory research phase. Of immediate concern were the many details involved in designing a focus group study. How should the respondents be selected? Male or female? Age? Families or individuals? How experienced should the respondents be? Recent or lifetime owners? How many people should be in a session? How many sessions? Where should they be held? Who should conduct (moderate) the sessions? How long should the sessions run? Should the sessions be taped? What questions needed to be included on the interviewer's question guide?

CASE QUESTION

1 Design the focus group study and develop the interviewer's guide.

CASE 3-8 Midwest Marketing Research Associates (A)

Midwest Marketing Research Associates (MMRA) was awarded a contract to perform marketing research for National Markets, the largest supermarket chain in the Midwest. National's market share had been steadily declining for 18 months, and the marketing department was considering a promotional effort in which stores would provide shoppers with nutritional information for most of the packaged foods carried by National. National executives hoped that a goodwill measure such as this would stimulate sales, as well as create a loyal customer base. MMRA's job was to determine the extent to which nutritional information, if provided, would be used by consumers. José Martinez, president of MMRA, was meeting with National executives to outline the specifics of the research project. He opened the meeting as follows.

"Good afternoon, ladies and gentlemen. As you know, MMRA will soon be performing a major research project for National Foods. This meeting gives me the chance to clarify exactly what MMRA will be doing for National. In our research proposal, two key considerations were identified: (1) consumer attitudes toward nutritional information in general and (2) which of three presentation formats would be the most useful to shoppers.

"To uncover this information, MMRA has developed a list of interview questions which will be administered to shoppers sometime within the next couple of weeks. I have with me several copies of the questionnaire, which I will distribute to you for your approval."

CASE QUESTION

1 Read Case 1-1 (in Part One of this book) to develop an understanding of the decision situation related to the questionnaire in this case.

Read the questionnaire and determine how it should be modified based upon the rules of questionnaire construction presented in Chapter 12. Address the following areas:

a Proposed changes in question format, wording, content, and so forth

b Proposed changes in question sequence and general structure

c General comments and concerns regarding the design of the questionnaire

Questionnaire*

Location: _____

Date: _____

Time: _____

Interviewer: _____

Respondent's name: _____

Address: _____

Phone number: _____

"Hello, I'm [your name] from Midwest Marketing Research Associates. We're doing a survey to find out how shoppers go about getting nutritional information. Would you mind giving us a few minutes of your time to answer some questions? Are you the person who buys most of the groceries for the household?"

If respondent refuses an interview, or doesn't purchase most of the groceries for the household, thank the person for his or her time, and then call the next potential interviewee.

1 Where do you buy most of the food your family eats?

1 (   ) Large supermarket chain
2 (   ) Independent grocer
3 (   ) Farmer's market
4 (   ) Convenience store like 7–11 or Stop-N-Go
5 (   ) Other _____

2 Is this store helpful in providing nutrition information?

1 (   ) Yes
2 (   ) No

*Source: MMRA utilized formats developed by J. Edward Russo of Cornell University, Ithaca, NY.

3 Do you read the labels on packaged food?

1 (   ) Yes
2 (   ) No

4 Are you hesitant or uncertain about buying foods that don't have nutrition information provided on the label?

1 (   ) Yes
2 (   ) No

5 We're interested in finding out where you get information regarding nutrition, and what type of information you find. Do you get nutrition information from:

	Yes	No	What kind of information?
Food labels	( ) 1	( ) 2	_____
Friends or relatives	( ) 1	( ) 2	_____
Advertisements	( ) 1	( ) 2	_____
Books	( ) 1	( ) 2	_____
Magazines	( ) 1	( ) 2	_____
Doctor	( ) 1	( ) 2	_____
Store clerks	( ) 1	( ) 2	_____

6 Which of these sources do you use "Most often"? (Read list.) "Second most often"?

	Most often	Second most often
Advertisements	( ) 1	( ) 1
Books	( ) 2	( ) 2
Doctor	( ) 3	( ) 3
Food labels	( ) 4	( ) 4
Friends or relatives	( ) 5	( ) 5
Magazines	( ) 6	( ) 6
Store clerks	( ) 7	( ) 7

7 What problems do you have finding information about the nutritional content of your food?

8 In the past, the provision of nutritional information has been primarily for those on special diets. Do you have a special diet that requires you to restrict certain foods?

   1 (   ) Yes
   2 (   ) No (Skip to Question 10.)

9 Do you find that there is adequate information to meet your needs?

   1 (   ) Yes (Skip to Question 11.)
   2 (   ) No

10 What other types of information would you like to see?

11 Most people feel that, as consumers, we deserve detailed information about the nutritional content of all the foods we eat. Do you agree?

   1 (   ) Yes
   2 (   ) No

12 Would you like to have more nutrition information provided to you?

   1 (   ) Yes
   2 (   ) No

13 Which of these foods do you regularly purchase?

   1 (   ) Breakfast cereal
   2 (   ) Frozen vegetables
   3 (   ) Canned soup
   4 (   ) Canned or bottled fruit and vegetable juice
   5 (   ) Canned or bottled fruit
   6 (   ) TV (frozen) dinners

14 How often do you purchase _____?

	Don't	Every week	Every 2–3 weeks	Once a month or less
Breakfast cereal	( ) 1	( ) 2	( ) 3	( ) 4
Frozen vegetables	( ) 1	( ) 2	( ) 3	( ) 4
Canned soup	( ) 1	( ) 2	( ) 3	( ) 4
Canned or bottled fruit and vegetable juice	( ) 1	( ) 2	( ) 3	( ) 4
Canned or bottled fruit	( ) 1	( ) 2	( ) 3	( ) 4
TV (frozen) dinners	( ) 1	( ) 2	( ) 3	( ) 4

15 Do you look for nutritional information about _____? (Read list.)

	Yes	No
Breakfast cereal	( ) 1	( ) 2
Frozen vegetables	( ) 1	( ) 2
Canned soup	( ) 1	( ) 2
Canned or bottled fruit and vegetable juice	( ) 1	( ) 2
Canned or bottled fruit	( ) 1	( ) 2
TV (frozen) dinners	( ) 1	( ) 2

16 How easy do you find it to obtain nutritional information about _____? (Read name of specific item.) Is it "Very easy," "Somewhat easy," "Neutral," "Somewhat difficult," or "Very difficult"?

	Very easy	Somewhat easy	Neutral	Somewhat difficult	Very difficult
a Breakfast cereal	( ) 1	( ) 2	( ) 3	( ) 4	( ) 5

If "Difficult," ask: What makes it (somewhat/very) difficult? _____

_____

b Frozen vegetables	( ) 1	( ) 2	( ) 3	( ) 4	( ) 5

If "Difficult," ask: What makes it (somewhat/very) difficult? _____

_____

c Canned soup	( ) 1	( ) 2	( ) 3	( ) 4	( ) 5

If "Difficult," ask: What makes it (somewhat/very) difficult? _____

_____

d Canned or bottled fruit and vegetable juice	( ) 1	( ) 2	( ) 3	( ) 4	( ) 5

If "Difficult," ask: What makes it (somewhat/very) difficult? _____

_____

e Canned or bottled fruit	( ) 1	( ) 2	( ) 3	( ) 4	( ) 5

If "Difficult," ask: What makes it (somewhat/very) difficult? _____

_____

f TV dinners	( ) 1	( ) 2	( ) 3	( ) 4	( ) 5

If "Difficult," ask: What makes it (somewhat/very) difficult? _____

_____

17 Would readily available nutrition information influence your decision regarding which brand to buy?

1 (   ) Yes
2 (   ) No
3 (   ) Not sure

18 Would nutrition information influence you to try a new product?

1 (   ) Yes
2 (   ) No

19 Some people believe that grocery stores could help consumers by presenting nutrition information about the foods they sell in a format which is easy to read and understand. Do you think it would be helpful if, for example, a store posted the nutritional content of its products?

1 (   ) Yes
2 (   ) No (Skip to Question 21.)

20 What kinds of information would you like to see posted?

21 How would your opinion of a store that provided this type of information be affected? Would it be "Much higher," "Somewhat higher," "The same," "Somewhat lower," or "Much lower"?

1 (   ) Much higher
2 (   ) Somewhat higher
3 (   ) The same
4 (   ) Somewhat lower
5 (   ) Much lower

22 If a local grocer were to post these sheets for every type of food, would you be more likely to do your grocery shopping there?

    1 (   ) Yes
    2 (   ) No
    3 (   ) Don't know

23 In general, if more nutrition information were provided, would you use it in making purchase decisions?

    1 (   ) Yes
    2 (   ) No

24 I'm going to hand you three formats[1] which present some nutrition information for TV dinners. Take a few seconds to glance at these. Which do you find "Most helpful"? "Second most helpful"?

	Most helpful	Second most helpful
Matrix (format no. 1)	( ) 1	( ) 1
Summary (format no. 2)	( ) 2	( ) 2
Complete (format no. 3)	( ) 3	( ) 3

25 Why do you find format number _____ "Most helpful"?

26 Why do you find format number _____ "Second most helpful"?

27 Why do you find format number _____ "Least helpful"?

For the next part of the questionnaire, we're trying to find out what shoppers do and don't know about nutrition.

28 Do you think too much of some vitamins can be harmful?

    1 (   ) Yes
    2 (   ) No

29 Do you think that eating a variety of foods is ordinarily a sufficient intake of nutrients?

    1 (   ) Yes
    2 (   ) No

30 Do you think that fortification with seven vitamins and minerals provides all the essential nutrients?

    1 (   ) Yes
    2 (   ) No

31 Which of these foods do you feel is more nutritious:

    a Beef or turkey? ( ) 1 ( ) 2
    b Apple juice or tomato juice? ( ) 1 ( ) 2

Demographic Data

The following questions are for statistical purposes only. They are solely to help us analyze the data from the survey. In no way will you be identified with your answers.

32 What is your marital status?

    1 (   ) Single
    2 (   ) Married
    3 (   ) Widowed
    4 (   ) Divorced

33 Could you please tell us which age bracket you are in?

18–24 ( ) 1		45–54 ( ) 4	
25–34 ( ) 2		55–64 ( ) 5	
35–44 ( ) 3		65 or over ( ) 6	

34 What is your occupation? _____

35 What is the highest grade of school or college that you have completed?

    1 (   ) Grade school
    2 (   ) Some high school
    3 (   ) High school (graduate)
    4 (   ) Some college, trade, or technical school
    5 (   ) College (graduate)
    6 (   ) Postgraduate

[1]*Note:* MMRA utilized formats developed by J. Edward Russo of Cornell University, Ithaca, NY.

36 Do you have any children?

    1 (   ) Yes
    2 (   ) No (Skip to Question 39.)

37 What ages?

Age range	Number
1–5	_____
6–12	_____
13–19	_____
20 or over	_____

38 How many of the children are at home? _____

39 Including children and all others (relatives, boarders, etc.), how many persons live in your home? _____

40 Into which income category does your total family income fall?

    Under $7500   (   ) 1
    $7500–$12,000   (   ) 2
    $12,000–$18,000   (   ) 3
    $18,000–$27,000   (   ) 4
    $27,000–$45,000   (   ) 5
    $45,000–$60,000   (   ) 6
    Over $60,000   (   ) 7

41 Thank you for your participation in our study. If you would like a copy of the survey results sent to you, please tell us now.

    1 (   ) Yes
    2 (   ) No

STOP—the interview has concluded. Please use the coding manual to classify respondents based on their responses to previous questions.

1 = Bachelor
2 = Newly married
3 = Full nest
4 = Full nest II
5 = Full nest III
6 = Empty nest
7 = Empty nest II
8 = Solitary survivor in labor force
9 = Solitary survivor retired

EXAMPLE OF THE MATRIX FORMAT

TV dinners (serving size: 1 dinner)	Weight in ounces	Calories	Protein	Vitamin A	Vitamin C	Thiamine	Riboflavin	Niacin	Calcium	Iron
Beans and Franks, Banquet	10.75	591	25	40	15	20	10	15	15	20
Beef Chop Suey, Banquet	12.00	282	20	6	8	6	8	15	4	15
Beef Enchilada, Swanson	15.00	570	30	50	0	15	10	20	20	25
Beef Tenderloin, Steak House	9.50	920	70	2	30	20	20	45	4	35
Beef, Banquet	11.00	312	45	4	10	8	15	30	4	30
Beef, Chopped, Banquet	11.00	443	30	90	10	8	15	20	6	20
Beef, Chopped, Hungry-Man, Swanson	18.00	730	30	45	15	20	20	45	6	25
Beef, Hungry-Man, Swanson	17.00	540	60	2	4	20	30	30	4	20
Beef, Swanson	11.50	370	60	6	10	10	20	30	4	20
Chicken, BBQ, Hungry-Man, Swanson	16.50	760	60	110	6	30	35	60	8	30
Chicken, BBQ, Swanson	11.25	530	25	20	4	10	20	40	8	15
Chicken Crispy, Swanson	10.75	650	30	4	2	30	15	50	10	15
Chicken, Fried, Banquet	11.00	530	40	100	35	10	15	35	30	25
Chicken, Fried, Hungry-Man, Swanson	15.75	910	100	2	25	25	25	80	10	30
Chicken, Hungry-Man, Swanson	19.00	730	90	15	30	20	20	70	15	20
Chicken, Man-Pleaser, Banquet	17.00	1016	90	90	10	15	20	60	45	35
Chicken, Swanson	11.50	570	60	40	10	10	15	45	6	15
Chicken, 3-Course, Swanson	15.00	630	50	30	4	20	10	50	8	15
Chicken, Western Style, Hungry-Man, Swanson	17.75	890	70	10	0	25	35	40	10	15
Chicken, Western Style, Swanson	11.75	460	35	10	0	15	20	20	6	15
Chopped Sirloin, Steak House	9.50	760	90	2	35	20	20	50	4	35
Fish Dinner, Banquet	8.75	382	30	50	20	20	8	20	6	10
Fish N Chips, Swanson	10.25	450	50	6	10	15	8	25	4	10
.	.	.	.	.	.	.	.	.	.	.
.	.	.	.	.	.	.	.	.	.	.
.	.	.	.	.	.	.	.	.	.	.
Turkey, Banquet	11.00	293	35	80	35	10	10	35	8	15
Turkey, Hungry-Man, Swanson	19.00	740	100	20	40	20	15	60	10	25
Turkey, Man-Pleaser, Banquet	19.00	620	60	150	25	20	20	45	15	25
Turkey, Swanson	11.50	360	45	60	30	10	10	35	6	10
Turkey, 3-Course, Swanson	16.00	520	60	15	30	20	15	40	10	20
Veal Parmigian, Banquet	11.00	421	30	-40	20	15	15	20	20	15
Veal Parmigian, Hungry-Man, Swanson	20.50	910	60	10	6	20	30	30	25	30

EXAMPLE OF THE SUMMARY FORMAT

Nutrition quotient	TV dinners (serving size: 1 dinner)	Weight in ounces
2.2	Turkey, Banquet	11.00
1.9	Veal Parmigian, Banquet	11.00
1.7	Turkey, Man-Pleaser, Banquet	19.00
1.7	Turkey, Swanson	11.50
1.6	Chicken, Fried, Banquet	11.00
1.5	Italian, Banquet	11.00
1.4	Sirloin, Chopped, Swanson	10.00
1.4	Salisbury Steak, Banquet	11.00
1.4	Beef, Banquet	11.00
1.3	Macaroni & Cheese, Swanson	12.50
1.3	Beef, Chopped, Swanson	11.00
1.3	Chicken, BBQ, Hungry-Man, Swanson	16.50
1.2	Beef, Swanson	11.50
1.2	Fish Dinner, Banquet	8.50
1.2	Meat Loaf, Banquet	11.00
1.2	Meat Loaf, Man-Pleaser, Banquet	19.00
1.2	Turkey, 3-Course, Swanson	16.00
.	.	.
.	.	
.		.
.8	Chicken, BBQ, Swanson	11.25
.8	Spaghetti, Swanson	12.50
.8	Chicken, Western Style, Swanson	11.75
.7	Rib Eye, Steak House	9.00
.7	Meat Loaf, Swanson	10.75
.7	Salisbury Steak, Hungry-Man, Swanson	17.00
.7	Beef Tenderloin, Steak House	9.50
.7	Sirloin, Steak House	9.50
.7	Salisbury Steak, Swanson	11.50
.7	Veal Parmigiana, Hungry-Man, Swanson	20.50
.7	Chicken, Western Style, Hungry-Man, Swanson	17.75
.6	Noodles and Chicken, Swanson	10.50

EXAMPLE OF COMPLETE FORMAT

TV dinners (serving size: 1 dinner)	Weight in ounces	Calories	Protein	Vitamin A	Vitamin C	Thiamine	Riboflavin	Niacin	Calcium	Iron	Nutritional quotient
Beef Tenderloin, Steak House	9.50	920	70	2	30	20	20	45	4	35	.7
Beef, Banquet	11.00	312	45	4	10	8	15	30	4	30	1.4
Beef, Swanson	11.50	370	60	6	10	10	20	30	4	20	1.2
Chicken, BBQ, Hungry-Man, Swanson	16.50	760	60	110	6	30	35	60	8	30	1.3
Chicken, BBQ, Swanson	11.25	530	25	20	4	10	20	40	8	15	.8
Chicken, Fried, Banquet	11.00	530	40	100	35	10	15	35	30	25	1.6
Chicken, Western, Hungry-Man, Swanson	17.75	890	70	10	0	25	35	40	10	15	.7
Fish Dinner, Banquet	8.75	382	30	50	20	20	8	20	6	10	1.2
Turkey, Banquet	11.00	293	35	80	35	10	140	35	8	15	2.2
Turkey, Man-Pleaser, Banquet	19.00	620	60	150	25	20	20	45	15	25	1.7
Turkey, Swanson	11.50	360	45	60	30	10	10	35	6	10	1.7
Turkey, 3-Course, Swanson	16.00	520	60	15	30	20	15	40	10	20	1.2
Veal Parmigian, Banquet	11.00	421	30	140	20	15	15	20	20	15	1.9
Veal Parmigian, Hungry-Man, Swanson	20.50	910	60	10	6	20	30	30	25	30	.7

SAMPLING PLAN AND DATA COLLECTION

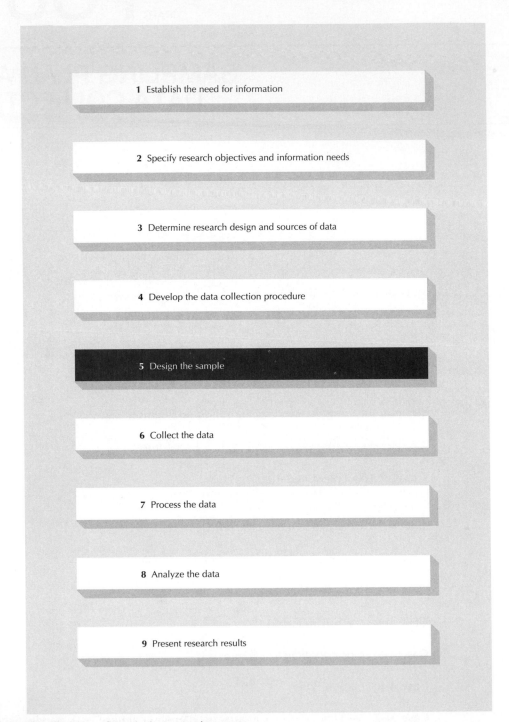

FIGURE 13-1 Steps in the research process.

CHAPTER 13

THE BASICS OF SAMPLING

MARKETING RESEARCH IN ACTION

BUREAU OF THE CENSUS USES SAMPLES TO CORRECT 1990 CENSUS

In a settlement of a lawsuit filed by major cities, the U.S. Bureau of the Census agreed to conduct a survey of 150,000 homes in order to correct for potential undercounting of racial, ethnic, and other groups. The Bureau of the Census agreed that its census fails to count some people, including those who do not answer the questionnaire because of distrust of the government, those who live in substandard housing, or those who are homeless.

The sampling will be of 150,000 housing units, including apartments, homes, and even sheds in 5000 blocks selected from urban and rural areas. In the selected blocks, interviewers will list every housing unit, every garage, and every shed that is inhabited. Residents of those housing units will be interviewed in person. The results of this sampling procedure will be compared to those in the census and adjustments will be made in all census results to reflect the sample results. The belief is that the sample provides a more accurate count than does the census itself.

This Marketing Research in Action illustrates the power of sampling to provide accurate and useful data for marketing research. This chapter and Chapters 14 and 15 discuss the theory and practical application of sampling to real marketing situations. We begin this chapter with an overview of sampling terminology and sampling procedures.

Without sampling, marketing research as we know it today would not exist. Virtually every marketing research study requires the selection of some kind of sample. When a new product is placed in households for trial, we must select the households to use; when we want to monitor the sales we are experiencing in a geographical area, we must select the stores in which we will record the sales; when we want to conduct a group interview about meat prices, we must select 8 to 10 people to take part in the group.

The alternative to sampling is taking a census. In a census, we execute our study using *all available elements of a defined population.* Thus, in the examples above, we would use all households for the product placement test, all stores in the area for the sales monitoring, etc.

In this chapter, we shall outline the basic terminology and concepts of sampling and then discuss three types of nonprobability sampling procedures. This chapter lays the basic groundwork necessary for an understanding of the probability sampling procedures that will be discussed in Chapters 14 and 15.

SAMPLING: AN INTRODUCTION

The Benefits of Sampling

Sampling is used very frequently in marketing research because it offers some major benefits over taking a census.

1 *A sample saves money.* The cost of an hour-long in-person interview may be about $40 to $85 per interview. Clearly, we would save money by interviewing, say, 1000 people rather than the 1 million who may make up the relevant population.

2 *A sample saves time.* In the above example, we would have 1000 hours of interviewing with a sample versus 1 million hours with a census. To this we must add the time for, say, printing questionnaires, training field interviewers, and preparing the completed questionnaires for data analysis. The problem that led to this study being undertaken is likely to be long forgotten before the census is complete.

3 *A sample may be more accurate.* Surprising as it may seem, this is indeed true. This results from several sources of inaccuracy, called *nonsampling errors,* that occur in the marketing research process. In a census study, we will need more interviewers, more supervisors of interviewers, more people to convert the raw questionnaires to computer input, etc. The smaller the study, the more likely we are to obtain more highly skilled people for each stage of the research process. As the staff gets bigger, the quality of people will fall, and the control and supervision of their activities will become more difficult. Also, a census may take so long that the marketing phenomenon of interest may have changed. For example, questions about the awareness of a new product have meaning only at one point in time. A census awareness level would be biased upward by the passage of time. All of this leads to more errors and less accurate results.

Like a census, a sample includes nonsampling errors too, but to a lesser degree. Unlike a census, a sample also gives us sampling error. This is a statistical concept that will be discussed in detail in Chapter 14. For now, we should just remember that a sample statistic provides an estimate of a population value. To the extent that the two values differ, sampling error has occurred.

Thus, a sample will be more accurate than a census if the total of sampling and nonsampling errors for the sample is less than nonsampling types of errors for the census.

4 *A sample is better in the event that the study results in the destruction or contamination of the element sampled.* Product usage tests result in the consumption of the product. Clearly, in a taste test, taking a census of Budweiser beer is not the way to run a profitable business. Similarly, interviewing people may sensitize them to the topic of the interview. We can say that they have been "contaminated" with respect to this topic. We may want to interview people again about the same topic to see whether, for example, our advertising campaign has had an impact. We would like to interview those who have not been contaminated by a previous interview. If a census were taken previously, all subjects of interest would have been contaminated.

Some Necessary Sampling Concepts

With the reasons for sampling established, we now turn to the question of how a sample is selected. First we must learn the definition of some basic sampling concepts, that is, the language of sampling.

Element   An *element* is the unit about which information is sought. It provides the basis of the analysis that we will undertake. The most common elements in marketing research sampling are individuals. In other instances, the elements could be products, stores, companies, families, etc. The elements in any specific sample would depend on the objectives of the study.

Population   A *population,* or *universe,* as it is also called, is the aggregate of all the elements defined prior to selection of the sample. A properly designated population must be defined in terms of (1) *elements,* (2) *sampling units,* (3) *extent,* and (4) *time.* For example, a survey of consumers might specify the relevant population as:

1	Element	Females 18–50
2	Sampling units	Females 18–50
3	Extent	Texas
4	Time	May 1–June 15, 1996

Alternatively, the population for a study designed to measure buyer reaction to a new industrial chemical might be:

1 Element   Chemical engineers
2 Sampling units   Companies purchasing over $300,000 of chemicals per year; then chemical engineers
3 Extent   The continental United States
4 Time   1996

Or, if we wished to monitor the sales of a new consumer product, the population might be:

1 Element   Our product
2 Sampling units   Supermarkets, drugstores, discount stores; then our product
3 Extent   Boston
4 Time   May 5–12, 1996

We cannot overstress how critical it is to define the population to this level of detail; nothing else constitutes proper sampling.

Sampling Unit Previously, we used the term "sampling unit" in defining a relevant population. It is now time to define this term more explicitly. A *sampling unit* is the element or elements available for selection at some stage of the sampling process. In the simplest type of sampling, single-stage sampling, the sampling units and the elements are the same. For example, in our first population illustration above, both the elements and the sampling units were "females 18–50." This indicates a direct, one-stage sampling process. We would select our sample of females 18–50 directly.

With more complex sampling procedures, different levels of sampling units may be utilized, and then the sampling units and elements differ in all but the last stage. Consider our second illustration above. Our elements of interest are chemical engineers. However, we are reaching these engineers indirectly, through a two-stage process. First, we will select a sample of "companies purchasing over $300,000 of chemicals per year." Then, within these selected companies we will select a sample of chemical engineers. This is a two-stage sampling process. Note that only at the final stage are elements and sampling units identical. Similarly, the third illustration above is also a two-stage process, with the stores constituting the first stage and "our product" the second.

A sampling process may have as many stages as the researcher desires. All he or she must do is specify the sampling unit at each stage. For example, a four-stage sample might be:

Stage 1 Cities over 500,000 population
Stage 2 City blocks
Stage 3 Households
Stage 4 Males 50 and over

The elements of interest in this study would, of course, be "males 50 and over." The terms "primary sampling units," "secondary sampling units," "tertiary sampling units," and "final sampling units" are often used to designate the successive stages of the process.

Sampling Frame A sampling frame is a list of all the sampling units available for selection at a stage of the sampling process. At the final stage, the actual sample is drawn from such a list. Some of the most creative thinking in a marketing research project may be related to the specification of a sampling frame. A frame may be a class list, a list of registered voters, a telephone book, an employee list, or even a map. In the case of a map we would be sampling pieces of geography. A city block would be an example. The frame list may be printed or stored in a computer file, on tape or disk. Once a population is specified, you then search for a good sampling frame. Often the availability of a sampling frame defines the population, as no perfect fit is available between population and frame. Each stage of a sampling process requires its own sampling frame. Thus, the four-stage sampling process listed above would require four sampling frames as follows: (1) a list of cities of over 500,000 population, (2) a list of city blocks within the selected cities, (3) a list of households within the selected city blocks, and (4) a list of males 50 and over within the selected households. A direct, one-stage sampling selection procedure would require only one sampling frame, which would contain all the elements in the population.

It should be noted that in marketing research an accurate, up-to-date sampling frame may not exist or may be very difficult to obtain. For example, lists of certain targeted consumer groups or targeted companies for marketing research are problematic. Consider, as an illustration, the fact that no list of allergy sufferers or of innovative production companies exists. Thus, the marketing researcher must attempt to create a sampling approach to find these types of targeted groups. Chapter 15 discusses some of the sampling approaches that the marketing researchers may use to address this problem.

Study Population A study population is the aggregate of elements from which the sample is drawn. Previously, we defined a *population* as the aggregate of the elements defined prior to the selection of the sample. Unfortunately, practical difficulties arise that cause the actual sample to be drawn from a somewhat different population from the one we defined a priori. What happens is that elements of the population are omitted from the sampling frame. For example, a club membership list may be incomplete, some people have unlisted phone numbers, a map may not include a new street.

The study population, then, is the aggregation of elements from which the sample is actually selected. It is with regard to this study population that we can make proper inferences, even though our real interest is the original population.

The Sampling Process: An Overview

Armed with the sampling concepts we just defined, we can describe in overview the steps in selecting a sample. Figure 13-2 presents this overview.

Step 1 Define the population. This would, of course, include (a) the elements, (b) the sampling units, (c) the extent, and (d) the time.

Step 2 Identify the sampling frame from which the sample will be selected.

Step 3 Decide on a sample size. Here we determine how many elements to include in the sample. Deciding when a sample is too big or too small is a difficult problem. We will discuss this in Chapter 14.

Step 4 Select a specific procedure by which the sample will be determined. Exactly how will the decision be made on which population elements to include in the sample? This issue is examined in this and the next two chapters. (In actuality, steps 3 and 4 are often done at the same time.)

FIGURE 13-2 Steps in selecting a sample.

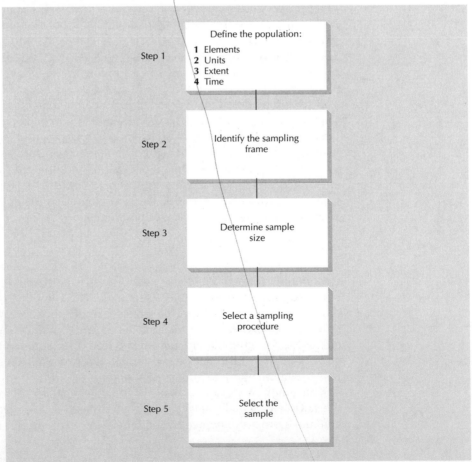

Step 5 Physically select the sample based upon the procedure previously described in step 4.

SAMPLING PROCEDURES

There are many different procedures by which researchers may select their samples, but one fundamental concept must be established at the outset—the distinction between (1) a probability sample and (2) a nonprobability sample.

In *probability sampling,* each element of the population has a known chance of being selected for the sample. The sampling is done by mathematical decision rules that leave no discretion to the researcher or field interviewer. Note that we said a "known chance" and not an "equal chance" of being selected. Equal-chance probability sampling is only a very special case of probability sampling, called *simple random sampling.* What probability sampling allows us to do is calculate the likely extent to which the sample value differs from the population value of interest. This difference is called *sampling error.* We will discuss sampling error in more detail in Chapter 14.

In *nonprobability sampling,* the selection of a population element to be part of the sample is based in some part on the judgment of the researcher or field interviewer. There is no known chance of any particular element in the population being selected. We are therefore unable to calculate the sampling error that has occurred. We have absolutely no idea whether or not the sample estimates calculated from a nonprobability sample are accurate or not. We are in the realm of a wish and a prayer.

There are a number of different sampling procedures that fall into the category of nonprobability methods and a number that are probability methods. Figure 13-3 lists them. In the rest of this chapter we will discuss the three kinds of nonprobability samples: convenience, judgment, and quota. Chapter 14 presents a discussion of both the most elementary type of probability sampling—simple random sampling—and the determination of sample size. Chapter 15 discusses the more complex probability sampling procedures, stratified and cluster sampling.

Nonprobability Sampling Procedures

Convenience Sampling Convenience samples are selected, as the name implies, on the basis of the convenience of the researcher. Examples here include (1) asking for people to volunteer to test products and then using these people, (2) stopping people in a shopping mall to get their opinion, (3) using students or church groups for conducting an experiment, (4) having "people-in-the-street interviews" conducted by a television station, and so on. In each instance, the sampling unit or element either is self-selected or has been selected because it was easily available. In all cases it is unclear what population the actual sample is drawn from. The television interviewer may state that her sample represents the community. Clearly, she is wrong. Most members of the community had no chance of being selected. It is only those who happened to be where the inter-

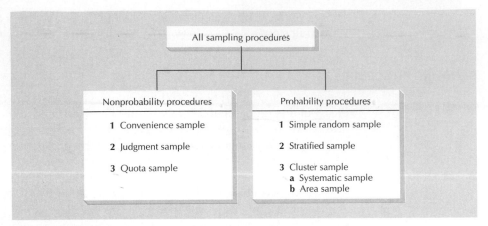

FIGURE 13-3 Sampling procedures.

viewer was at the time of the show who had a chance of being selected. Even the exact chance of these people's being selected is unknown.

In such cases, the difference between the population value of interest and the sample value is unknown, in terms of both size and direction. We cannot measure sampling error, and clearly we cannot make any definite or conclusive statements about the results from such a sample. However, convenience samples can be most easily justified at the exploratory stage of research, as a basis for generating hypotheses, and for conclusive studies where the manager is willing to accept the risk that the study results might have great inaccuracies. Convenience sampling is used in business practice by about 53 percent of businesses, as shown by Figure 13-4. Some of these uses are described in the Marketing Research in Action entitled "Business Uses Nonprobability Sampling" in this section.

Judgment Sampling Judgment samples (or purposive samples, as they are also called) are selected on the basis of what *some expert thinks* those particular sampling units or elements will contribute to answering the particular research question at hand. For example, in test marketing, a judgment is made as to which cities would constitute the best ones for testing the marketability of a new product. In industrial marketing research, the decision to interview a purchasing agent about a given product constitutes a judgment sample. The purchasing agent must be regarded as a representative of the company by the person who draws the sample. Other examples could include an instructor's choice of someone to start a class discussion; expert witnesses presenting their views in court; and the selection of stores in an area to try out a new display.

Again, the degree and direction of error are unknown, and definite statements are not meaningful. However, if the expert's judgment is valid, the sample will be a better one than if a convenience sample were used. Judgment sampling is used in business practice by about 49 percent of businesses, as shown by Figure 13-5. Some of these uses are described in the Marketing Research in Action entitled "Business Uses Nonprobability Sampling."

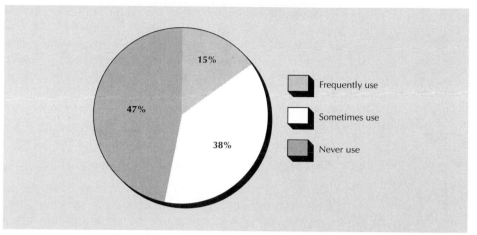

FIGURE 13-4 Use in practice of convenience sampling. (*Source:* Thomas C. Kinnear and Ann R. Root, *A Study of the Marketing Research Business*, unpublished study, 1994. Copyright 1994 Thomas C. Kinnear. Not to be reproduced.)

Quota Sampling Quota samples are a special type of purposive sample. Here the researcher takes explicit steps to obtain a sample that is similar to the population on some prespecified "control" characteristics. For example, an interviewer may be instructed to conduct half the interviews with people 30 years old and over, and half with people under 30. Here, the control characteristic is the age of respondents. Specifying this particular control statement implies, of course, that the researcher knows the population of interest is equally divided between persons

FIGURE 13-5 Use in practice of judgment sampling. (*Source:* Thomas C. Kinnear and Ann R. Root, *A Study of the Marketing Research Business*, unpublished study, 1994. Copyright 1994 Thomas C. Kinnear. Not to be reproduced.)

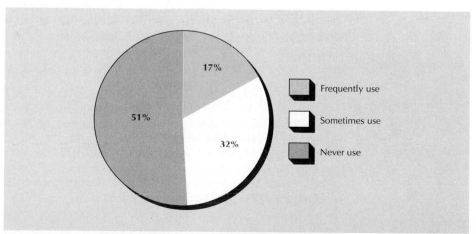

30 years old and over and persons under 30. Obviously this is a simple example, as only one control characteristic has been used.

More realistically, in order to be more representative of a population, we would have to "control" on a number of characteristics. Therefore, to properly select a quota sample we must (1) specify a list of relevant control characteristics and (2) know the distribution of these characteristics across our population. Let's look at an example. Suppose we have two control characteristics of interest, age and race, as follows:

1 Age   two categories—under 30, and 30 and over
2 Race   two categories—white and nonwhite

There are then four sampling cells of interest. They are (a) under 30 and white, (b) 30 and over and white, (c) under 30 nonwhite, and (d) 30 and over and nonwhite. What we must know is the proportion of the population in each of these cells. This is a much more complex question than just knowing the proportion of the population in a single control characteristic. Note what happens to the number of sampling cells as the number of control characteristics and associated categories increase. Suppose we had four characteristics for control, as follows:

MARKETING RESEARCH IN ACTION

BUSINESS USES NONPROBABILITY SAMPLING

A. Convenience Samples

• In a study of the predictors of effectiveness of salespersons, a sales consulting firm selected 80 full-time sales agents from a large insurance company that had agreed to cooperate with the study. Respondents were selected from training seminars held at the company based upon their willingness to participate.
• In a study of taste preferences for brands of soft drinks, a large marketing research firm selected a sample of 200 people from a large New Jersey mall over one weekend. Respondents were those who were asked and agreed to participate.

B. Judgment Samples

• For its relaunch of Irish Spring (see Chapter 1), Colgate Palmolive utilized the test cities of Marion, Indiana, and Visalia, California, to do extensive testing of its advertising and promotion. The judgment was that, on the important dimensions, these cities were representative of the country.
• In a study of consumers who overextended themselves on credit purchases, a sample was selected from consumers who had written or called a California self-help group. The judgment was made that these consumers would be representative of all consumers with similar credit problems.

C. Quota Samples

- In a study of purchase intentions conducted by the M/A/R/C research firm, a sample of 800 respondents was selected who were female heads of households and who maintained primary influence on buying decisions for the household.
- In a study of air travelers' use of credit cards, rental car companies, and hotel accommodations, the marketing research firm selected a sample based on the control characteristics of miles flown per year, nationality, and sex. One of the cells designated was "those who fly more than 100,000 miles per year, are Japanese, and are male."

1 Age	four categories—(a) under 18, (b) 18–30, (c) 31–50, (d) over 50	
2 Race	three categories—(a) white, (b) black, (c) other	
3 Education	four categories—(a) elementary school, (b) high school, (c) college, (d) graduate school	
4 Incomes	five categories—(a) under $5000 (b) $5000–$7499, (c) $7500–$9999, (d) $10,000–$14,999, (e) $15,000 and over	

This would result in $4 \times 3 \times 4 \times 5 = 240$ sampling cells. We would have to have information on the proportion of the population in each of these 240 cells. Such a description of the particular population that interests us may be extremely difficult or impossible to find. As a matter of fact, often our intent is to measure the population on these types of characteristics.

However, if up-to-date knowledge of the distribution of the control characteristics is available, we may determine the size of sample to select in each cell. Cell sample size is simply:

$$\text{Total sample size} \times \text{proportion desired in the cell}$$

For example, if our total sample is 1200 and the proportion in cell 1 is .05 (5 percent), the number of people with those characteristics in our sample for cell 1 would be:

$$1200 \times .05 = 60$$

We would then direct our interviewer to interview 60 people with these characteristics. The same procedure would be repeated for all cells. The actual selection of specific sample elements would be left to the judgment of the interviewer.

There are some problems with quota samples.

1 The proportion of respondents assigned to each cell must be accurate and up to date. This is often difficult or impossible.

2 The "proper" control characteristics must be selected; that is, all characteristics that are related to the measures of interest must be included. For example, if we want to learn people's attitudes toward males having long hair, it would be a mistake not to use age as a control factor, since age is probably related to the attitude toward long hair for males. In any particular study, we may omit a relevant control characteristic and not be aware of it. Consequently, our results can be misleading.

3 The third problem concerns the practical difficulties associated with including more and more control characteristics. As noted before, we end up with too many cells for the interviewers to work with; finding the desired respondents will not be easy.

4 A fourth difficulty concerns the interviewer's selection of the actual respondents to interview. In looking for people who fit the desired description, he or she may avoid people who look unfriendly, live in poorly painted houses, live in apartment buildings, and so on. An unknown bias is thus introduced into the study. Therefore, a quota sample and population may be exactly the same on measures for which we know the characteristics of both, but differ substantially on measures for which we have only the sample value. Indeed, it is these "sample only" measures that are the ones that really interest us to begin with. They are the reason for taking the sample. The sample provides estimates of the unknown population value. If we knew the population value, there would be no reason for sampling. The validity of a quota sample is often presented in terms of the match between known population and sample characteristics. Beware of this. The error in other sample measures is again of unknown size and direction.

Quota samples are useful in preliminary stages of research, and if done with great care, they can provide more definitive answers. However, they are likely to be less valid than a probability sample. Quota sampling is used in business practice by about 86 percent of businesses, as shown by Figure 13-6. Some of these uses

FIGURE 13-6 Use in practice of quota sampling. (*Source:* Thomas C. Kinnear and Ann R. Root, *A Study of the Marketing Research Business,* unpublished study, 1994. Copyright 1994 Thomas C. Kinnear. Not to be reproduced.)

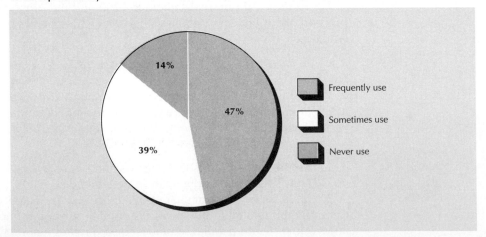

are described in the Marketing Research in Action entitled "Business Uses Non-probability Sampling."

Probability Sampling Procedures

Probability sampling is relatively new in terms of its actual application in marketing research. Before 1950, the nonprobability sample was almost the only kind used in real field studies. Advances in sampling theory and field sampling techniques since then have allowed probability sampling to become a real alternative for marketing researchers.

In probability sampling, the chance that a population element will be included in the sample is known, and the sample elements are selected by means of mechanical decision rules. No discretion is left to the researcher or field interviewer in selecting sample elements. There is no guarantee that the results obtained with a probability sample will be more accurate than those obtained with a nonprobability sample; what the former allows the researcher to do is to measure the amount of sampling error likely to occur in his or her sample. This provides a measure of the accuracy of the sample result. With nonprobability sampling no such error measure exists.

We will develop probability sampling concepts in more detail in the next two chapters.

INTERNATIONAL SAMPLING BASICS

The fundamental choices that relate to the type of sampling utilized in marketing research apply universally to both domestic and international marketing research. Indeed, the fundamentals of probability sampling that will be discussed in the next two chapters are based on mathematics and thus apply in all contexts.

There are some major difficulties in implementing probability sampling procedures in countries with underdeveloped marketing research institutions and poor telecommunications systems. If the marketing companies are not well developed, then the necessary population lists are less likely to be available, the expertise to draw samples will be reduced, and access to the smaller urban areas may be limited. These difficulties were clearly demonstrated in the Russian parliamentary election of December 1993, as noted in the Global Marketing Research Dynamics.

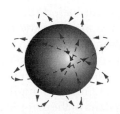

GLOBAL MARKETING RESEARCH DYNAMICS

ZHIRINOVSKY SUCCESS SURPRISES POLLSTERS

In the December 1993 Russian parliamentary elections, Vladimir V. Zhirinovsky's ultranationalistic, right-wing Liberal Democratic Party received something approaching 25 percent of the votes cast, which was more votes than any other party. This

Poor sampling gave misleading poll results to Boris Yeltsin and Vladimir Zhirinovsky.

came as a great surprise to Russian President Boris N. Yeltsin and the pollsters his party had hired to monitor the electorate. The Liberal Democrats had been predicted to receive less than 5 percent of the vote. How could such a poor prediction have been made? Here are some possible explanations.

• The pollsters tended to select their samples from the major urban areas where lists of households were more generally available. The rural areas voted much more heavily for the Liberal Democrats.
• In some parts of the country, quota samples were used. Those who agreed to participate in the poll tended to be more supportive of the Yeltsin government. The interviewers did not seek out or did not find a proportionate number of voters who were not Yeltsin supporters.
• Some of the polling was done by telephone. Voters who had phones were richer than those who did not, and the rich were more likely to support the Yeltsin reforms. Thus, a disproportionately large percentage of Yeltsin supporters appeared in the sample.
• There was a tendency for voters in Russia not to respond to polls in a way that ran counter to the sitting government. Thus, the Yeltsin support was overstated, and the Liberal Democratic support was understated.

SUMMARY

1 Sampling is an activity carried on in almost all marketing research.
2 The advantages of sampling rather than conducting a census include saving money, saving time, obtaining more accurate information, and avoiding the destruction or contamination of all the elements in the population.
3 An element is the unit about which information is sought. A population is the aggregate of the elements defined prior to selection of the sample. It is defined in terms of (a) elements, (b) sampling units, (c) extent, and (d) time. A sampling unit is the element or elements available for selection at some stage of the sampling process. A sampling frame is a list of all the sampling units available for selection at a stage of the sampling process.

4 The steps in the sampling process are: (a) define the population, (b) identify the sampling frame, (c) decide on the sample size, (d) select a specific procedure by which the sample will be determined, and (e) physically draw the sample.

5 In probability sampling, each element of the population has a known chance of being selected. In simple random sampling, each element has an equal chance of being selected. In nonprobability sampling, the selection of elements is based in some part on the judgment of the researcher.

6 Nonprobability sampling procedures include the use of convenience, judgment, and quota samples. Convenience samples are selected at the convenience of the researcher, judgment samples on the basis of the expert opinion of the researcher, and quota samples on the basis of the distribution of the defined population across control characteristics.

DISCUSSION QUESTIONS

1 Why is sampling so often used in marketing research?

2 Distinguish among the following sampling concepts: element, population, sampling unit, sampling frame, and study population.

3 Distinguish between probability and nonprobability sampling.

4 What is the nature of the error generated by a nonprobability sampling procedure?

5 Distinguish among three types of nonprobability sampling procedures?

6 Why are nonprobability sampling procedures so often used in practice?

7 Evaluate each of the samples listed in the Marketing Research in Action entitled "Business Uses Nonprobability Samples." What potential errors could occur in results from these samples?

8 Is it appropriate for the Bureau of the Census to agree to adjust the census count on the basis of sample results? What are the pros and cons?

9 General Motors does some evaluations of car designs and advertising themes using focus groups. These groups consist of from 8 to 10 potential customers who match the target segment profile for the car being evaluated. The focus group interviewees are selected by a research firm for General Motors by a telephone solicitation of people who are qualified as matching the required target profile. This qualification of participants is done by a series of questions asked over the phone. The phone directories used to identify which individuals to call are from geographic areas where cars like the one being evaluated have historically sold well.

  a What sampling procedure is being used?

  b Evaluate the sampling procedure used.

  c What inferences to the whole target segment population can be drawn from this sampling approach?

  d What biases may exist due to the sample selection method?

10 Kraft Foods does some mall-intercept interviewing to evaluate new food product offerings. These samples are typically done in only a few malls for any one test. Subjects who pass by particular locations in the mall are recruited on the basis of appearing to match certain demographic characteristics: sex, age, and so on.

  a What sampling procedure is being used?

  b Evaluate the sampling procedure used.

  c What inferences to the broader population can be drawn?

  d Why has mall-intercept sampling become so widely used in practice?

  e What biases may exist due to the sample selection method?

11 MINICASE

Xyco Semiconductor supplies computer chips to the aerospace, automobile, major appliance (stoves, refrigerators, etc.), and consumer electronics industries. Xyco sells to different-sized companies in each of these industries and to companies in all regions of the world. Historically, Xyco's management has noted sales differences by industry type, size, and geographic region. Xyco desires to select a quota sample to predict the sales level of a new product offering.

a What control characteristics should be used for this quota sample?

b What would one need to know about these control characteristics for them to be useful in this study?

c Explain how many respondents would be specified for each cell.

d What inferences could be drawn about Xyco's entire customer base from such a sample?

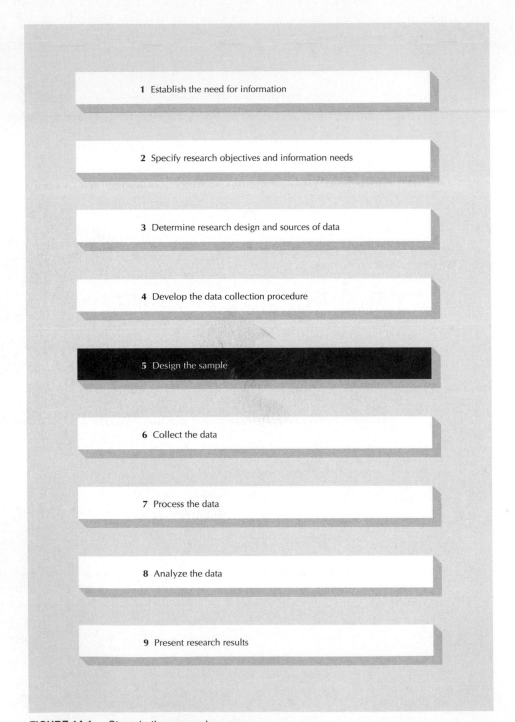

FIGURE 14-1   Steps in the research process.

SIMPLE RANDOM
SAMPLING
AND SAMPLE SIZE

MARKETING RESEARCH IN ACTION

GETTING IT RIGHT WITH PROBABILITY SAMPLES

The capacity of probability samples to provide accurate measures of marketing for both profit and nonprofit organizations is well documented. The following profiles illustrate this point.

 • A major oil company was able to select sites for combination gasoline stations–grocery stores and to very accurately forecast sales at these locations. To do this, marketing researchers selected a probability sample comprising about 1 percent of target customers in the regions in which the company operated. Sample members' attitudes, driving patterns, and shopping behavior accurately represented the whole population.

 • Levi Strauss conducted a segmentation study of the U.S. men's wear market using a probability sample of about 1200 men. The study provided extremely useful insights for product development and advertising decisions.

 • A large Japanese financial institution conducted a life-style study of rich Japanese households (those with incomes over $80,000), using a probability sample of

1000 households. From this study, the researchers were able to accurately describe five different life-style segments of the rich, the uses that the rich made of their money, their consumption of foreign goods, and their attitudes toward changes in the Japanese society. They were also able to identify areas where there were great opportunities for providing new products to these segments.

The previous chapter presented concepts essential for understanding sampling in marketing research and also drew the fundamental distinction between probability and nonprobability sampling procedures. This chapter presents a detailed description of the most elementary type of probability sampling: simple random sampling. Care is taken to present a step-by-step approach, because the principles developed here have direct application to the more frequently used and more complex sampling procedures discussed in Chapter 15. We will also look here at the issue of the accuracy of sample results.

Integral to the question of sample result accuracy is the issue of how to determine the sample size to use. This is discussed later in this chapter.

SIMPLE RANDOM SAMPLING

It is our assumption in writing this chapter that you have had one course in statistics. However, experience tells us that most students have found statistics difficult and welcome a review of basic concepts. Its usefulness to real problems may also have been obscure until now. Our discussion will therefore start with basics, stay at an elementary level, and sacrifice technical elegance for communication purposes. We hope to demonstrate that basic probability sampling concepts are fundamental to the practice of marketing research. Indeed, simple random sampling, the simplest of the probability sampling procedures, is utilized by 90 percent of businesses, as noted in Figure 14-2. This is greater utilization than any nonprobability sampling procedure. The reason for this is simply that probability procedures provide more accurate results.

We have placed some of the material of this chapter in a technical appendix at the end of the chapter. This material presents the fundamental statistical theory that is necessary for the marketing researcher to know. However, some readers will not want this depth of presentation and others will have already mastered it. At appropriate points in the chapter, we will refer you to the technical appendix in case, given your background and interest, you need to read it.

Some Terms and Symbols Defined

To begin our discussion of simple random sampling, we must again define a few terms.

Parameter   A *parameter* is a summary description of a measure in the defined population. This is the true value we would obtain if we undertook a census that

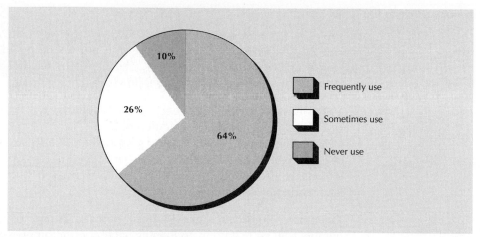

FIGURE 14-2 Use in practice of simple random sampling. (*Source:* Thomas C. Kinnear and Ann R. Root, *A Study of the Marketing Research Business,* unpublished study, 1994. Copyright 1994 Thomas C. Kinnear. Not to be reproduced.)

did not contain any nonsampling errors. The average age of a class in marketing research and the average income of new business school graduates are parameters.

Statistic   A *statistic* is a summary description of a measure in the selected sample. The sample statistic is used to estimate the population parameter. Thus, the average age of a class in marketing research and the average income of new business school graduates would also be statistics if measured by means of a sample.

Some Symbols to Get Straight   There are certain conventions that are used in sampling and statistics. The following symbols and associated meanings will be used in this book. Basically, Greek letters are used for population parameters and English letters for sample statistics. (See Table A-7 in the end-of-book Appendix for a complete listing of the Greek alphabet.) We also distinguish between the symbols for population size, N, and sample size, n.

	Concept	Population symbol	Sample symbol
A. Continuous measures	Mean or average of continuous variable	μ	$\bar{X}$
	Variance of continuous variable	σ^2	s^2
B. Dichotomous or two-answer measures or binomial measures (e.g., "Are you female—yes or no?")	Proportion answering yes	π	p
	Proportion answering no	$(1 - \pi)$	$(1 - p)$ or q
	Variance of proportion	σ^2	s^2

A Population to Examine

Table 14-1 presents a population that we will use to illustrate sampling concepts. This population consists of students who are taking an introductory marketing course from a particular professor. The professor has collected three pieces of information from the students, as follows:

1 The student number of each student (column 1)
2 The age of each student (column 2)
3 A statement as to whether the student intends to take the course in marketing research before graduation, with answers coded as follows: 1 = yes, the student intends to take marketing research; and 0 = no, the student does not intend to take marketing research (column 3)

The other columns in Table 14-1 will be used in later calculations. The student number will be used only to identify each population element. It is the other two items that interest us from a measurement point of view. We note that age is a continuous variable, and election of marketing research is a dichotomous variable. Let's identify them as follows:

$$Age = X_1$$
$$Election\ of\ marketing\ research = X_2$$

The population average and the standard deviation for age and election of marketing research for the data in Table 14-1 are:

	Average	Standard deviation
Age	23.7	4.1
Election of marketing research	.34	.473

The calculation of these population values is presented in Part A of the appendix to this chapter.

Calculation of Sample Statistics for Continuous Variables

What we have done in Part A of the appendix is calculate parameters that describe a known population. Let us now proceed to sample from this population. Our interest in the samples we draw will be to calculate statistics that describe the sample, and to make inferences about how well these statistics estimate the parameters of the population. In the terms of a statistics course, we are interested in descriptive and inferential statistics, respectively. Let us now draw a sample from that population and calculate the mean, variance, and standard deviation of the sample. Our method of sampling will be simple random sampling.

There are two conditions that define the existence of simple random sampling. They are: (1) each element has an equal chance of being selected and (2) each combination of the *n* sample elements has an equal chance of being selected.

TABLE 14-1 CENSUS OF AGE AND ELECTION OF MARKETING RESEARCH COURSE AS OPTION OF STUDENTS

Student number (1)	Age (X_1) (2)	Election of marketing research course 1 = yes 0 = no (X_2) (3)	$x = X_1 - \mu$ (4)	$x^2 = (X_1 - \mu)^2$ (5)
1	25	1	1.3	1.69
2	27	0	3.3	10.89
3	29	1	5.3	28.09
4	31	1	7.3	53.29
5	25	0	1.3	1.69
6	29	0	5.3	28.09
7	27	0	3.3	10.89
8	24	0	.3	.09
9	27	1	3.3	10.89
10	28	1	4.3	18.49
11	33	0	9.3	86.49
12	29	1	5.3	28.09
13	26	0	2.3	5.29
14	28	0	4.3	18.49
15	28	1	4.3	18.49
16	26	0	2.3	5.29
17	26	1	2.3	5.29
18	36	1	12.3	151.29
19	29	0	4.3	18.49
20	26	0	2.3	5.29
21	21	0	−2.7	7.29
22	19	0	−4.7	22.09
23	24	0	.3	.09
24	22	0	−1.7	2.89
25	20	1	−3.7	13.69
26	22	0	−1.7	2.89
27	19	1	−4.7	22.09
28	20	0	−3.7	13.69
29	19	0	−4.7	22.09
30	24	0	.3	.09
31	25	0	1.3	1.69
32	22	1	−1.7	2.89
33	20	0	−3.7	13.69
34	21	1	−2.7	7.29
35	21	0	−2.7	7.29
36	23	1	−.7	.49
37	21	0	−2.7	7.29
38	23	0	−.7	.49
39	18	0	−5.7	32.49
40	21	1	−2.7	7.29
41	19	0	−4.7	22.09
42	23	0	−.7	.49
43	22	1	−1.7	2.89
44	19	0	−4.7	22.09
45	20	0	−3.7	13.69
46	20	0	−3.7	13.69
47	21	0	−2.7	7.29
48	20	1	−3.7	13.69
49	19	0	−4.7	22.09
50	18	0	−5.7	32.49
	$\Sigma X_1 = 1184$	$\Sigma X_2 = 17$	$\Sigma(X_1 - \mu) = 0$	$\Sigma(X_1 - \mu)^2 = 844.90$

Previously we noted only the first condition as defining simple random sampling; this was done to keep the discussion simple. Now we must note that there are other probability sampling procedures in which the elements have an equal chance of selection. However, in all other sampling procedures, constraints are put on the possible combinations of sampling elements such that all combinations of elements are not equally likely. Mechanically, we use a set of random numbers to make the selection. The list of random numbers in Appendix Table A-1 (at the end of this book), as the name implies, is composed of numbers that have no pattern of occurrence. Any number is as likely to appear in any spot on the table as any other. Each student is identified by a two-digit student number ranging from 01 to 50. Thus, we could use the table to give us a two-digit number between 01 to 50 to select an element for the sample. We would use as many of these two-digit numbers as we wanted elements in the sample.

An example will help make this clear. Suppose we wished to select a sample with $n = 5$. If we started on Appendix Table A-1 at an arbitrary point in the 36th row, first column, and moved horizontally, we would select a sample consisting of elements numbered 32, 17, 05, 37, and 41. These are the first five two-digit numbers between 01 and 50 that we would meet. Our sample values for age and election of marketing research would be:

Element	Age	Elective
32	22	1
17	26	1
05	25	0
37	21	0
41	19	0

We have selected a sample of size 5 from a population of size 50. Thus we have selected n/N, or 5/50, or 1/10, or .1 of the population elements. We say that the *sampling fraction* is .1.

The sampling fraction can be used to estimate total population usage of a product or service from the total sample usage. Suppose that our sample of 5 students used a total of 35 gallons of gasoline a week. Then the estimated total population usage of gasoline would be

$$\frac{\text{Total sample usage}}{\text{Sampling fraction}} = \frac{35}{.1}$$

$$= 350 \text{ gallons}$$

The *mean* or *average* of the sample is simply the sum of the values divided by the sample size. Thus,

$$\bar{X} = \frac{\sum_{i=1}^{n} X_i}{n}$$

$$= \frac{22 + 26 + 25 + 21 + 19}{5}$$

$$= \frac{113}{5}$$

$$= 22.6$$

Our mean sample statistics value for age is 22.6. We note that this is slightly lower than our true population mean age of 23.7. In most real problems we would not know the true mean age and so would use the sample mean as our best estimate of the true value.

The *sample variance* is the sum of squared deviations about the mean divided by the degrees of freedom we have available.

$$s^2 = \frac{\sum_{i=1}^{n} (X_i - \bar{X})^2}{\text{degrees of freedom } (df)}$$

A sample is capable of allowing us to calculate a number of statistics. The first statistic limits the values that other statistics may take.[1] We say that one degree of freedom was used in calculating the first statistic. More generally, *degrees of freedom* equal the number of independent observations on the variables of interest minus the number of statistics calculated. Or

$$df = \text{sample size} - \text{number of statistics calculated}$$

In calculating the mean for our sample we used up one degree of freedom, and we must take this into consideration in calculating the variance. Thus, the degrees of freedom for our sample variance are $n - 1$. So

$$s^2 = \frac{\sum_{i=1}^{n} (X_i - \bar{X})^2}{n - 1}$$

---

[1]An example might help. If we have two numbers, 2 and 3, we calculate the mean as 2.5. If someone is told that we have two numbers, that one number is 2, and that the mean of the numbers is 2.5, he or she knows the other number must be 3; it has no freedom to take any value except 3. Thus this sample of $n = 2$ has one degree of freedom $(n - 1)$.

$$= \frac{(22 - 22.6)^2 + (26 - 22.6)^2 + (25 - 22.6)^2 + (21 - 22.6)^2 + (19 - 22.6)^2}{5 - 1}$$

$$= \frac{(-.6)^2 + (3.4)^2 + (2.4)^2 + (-1.6)^2 + (-3.6)^2}{4}$$

$$= \frac{.36 + 11.56 + 5.76 + 2.56 + 12.96}{4}$$

$$= \frac{33.20}{4}$$

$$= 8.3$$

Our population variance was 16.9, so our sample has understated it somewhat. Note that if we had divided by n instead of $n - 1$, the variance would have been even smaller. This is generally what happens. Division by n leads to an understatement of the variance.

The standard deviation would be

$$s = \sqrt{8.3}$$

$$= 2.88$$

We have now calculated descriptive statistics for our continuous variable. Let's look at the numerator of our variance equation. It is

$$\sum_{i=1}^{n}(X_i - \bar{X})^2$$

In words, it is the sum of squared deviations about the mean. Or, more simply, we will refer to it as *the sum of squares,* or SS. We will use this terminology throughout the book. We note, then, that the variance is simply

$$\frac{SS}{df}$$

Remember this!

We now introduce a simplification of our formula for calculating variance and standard deviation for a continuous variable. This new formula is called the *computational formula* for calculating variance. It is

$$s^2 = \frac{\sum X^2 - [(\sum X)^2/n]}{n - 1}$$

and

$$s = \sqrt{\frac{\Sigma X^2 - [(\Sigma X)^2/n]}{n - 1}}$$

In our sample of 5,

$$\Sigma X^2 = (22)^2 + (26)^2 + (25)^2 + (21)^2 + (19)^2 = 2587$$

$$(\Sigma X)^2 = (22 + 26 + 25 + 21 + 19)^2 = (113)^2 = 12{,}769$$

Thus,

$$s^2 = \frac{2587 - (12{,}769/5)}{4}$$

$$= \frac{2587 - 2553.8}{4}$$

$$= \frac{33.2}{4}$$

$$= 8.3$$

and

$$s = \sqrt{8.3} = 2.88$$

We note that these values for s^2 and s are exactly the same as previously calculated. In all future calculations of s^2 and s we will use the computational formula, as it saves a great deal of work.

Calculation of Sample Statistics for Dichotomous Variables

Now let's calculate the mean, variance, and standard deviation of our dichotomous variable, election of marketing research.

$$p = \frac{\sum_{i=1}^{n} X_i}{n}$$

$$= \frac{1 + 1 + 0 + 0 + 0}{5}$$

$$= \frac{2}{5}$$

$$= .4$$

We note that $q = (1 - p) = (1 - .4) = .6$.
The variance is

$$
\begin{aligned}
s^2 &= \frac{\displaystyle\sum_{i=1}^{n}(X_i - p)^2}{df} \\[2mm]
&= \frac{(1 - .4)^2 + (1 - .4)^2 + (0 - .4)^2 + (0 - .4)^2 + (0 - .4)^2}{5 - 1} \\[2mm]
&= \frac{(.6)^2 + (.6)^2 + (-.4)^2 + (-.4)^2 + (-.4)^2}{4} \\[2mm]
&= \frac{1.2}{4} \\[2mm]
&= .3
\end{aligned}
$$

The standard deviation is

$$
\begin{aligned}
s &= \sqrt{.3} \\
&= .548
\end{aligned}
$$

We note that the general formula for the variance is

$$
s^2 = pq\left(\frac{n}{n-1}\right) \quad \text{or} \quad \frac{npq}{n-1}
$$

$$
= (.4)(.6)\left(\frac{5}{4}\right) = .3 \quad \text{or} \quad \frac{(5)(.4)(.6)}{4} = .3
$$

The standard deviation formula is

$$
s = \sqrt{\frac{npq}{n-1}}
$$

We have now calculated statistics for our dichotomous variable. These are estimates of the population parameters. The usefulness of these statistical estimates is based on the concept of the sampling distribution of the mean and the theory of statistical inference. An overview of this theory is presented in Part B of the appendix to this chapter. The following sections of this chapter presume that this theory is understood.

Drawing Inferences about Population Parameters from Sample Statistics for Continuous Variables

Using the Theory   Our sample of the ages of five students was selected from a population distribution that was close to normal, so we know that the mean we calculated is from a normal distribution of means. We estimate

1 The mean of the sampling distribution as $\overline{X}$
2 The standard deviation of the sampling distribution[2] (standard error) as

$$s_{\overline{X}} = \frac{s}{\sqrt{n}} = \frac{\sqrt{n \sum_{i=1}^{n} (X_i - \overline{X})^2/(n-1)}}{\sqrt{n}}$$

In our example, $\overline{X} = 22.6$ and $s = 2.88$; thus

$$s_{\overline{X}} = \frac{2.88}{\sqrt{5}} = \frac{2.88}{2.24} = 1.3$$

Now let's calculate the size of the intervals at ± 1 standard deviation from the mean, then ± 2, then ± 3 standard deviations from the mean. At ± 1 standard deviation, the interval is

$$22.6 \pm 1.3 = 21.3 - 23.9$$

We know that 68 percent of the means from our sampling distribution are contained in this interval if our calculated sample mean $\overline{X}$ is truly the mean of the sampling distribution. (Remember $\mu = 23.7$.) At ± 2 standard deviations, the interval is

$$22.6 \pm 2(1.3) = 22.6 \pm 2.6 = 20.0 - 25.2$$

We know that 95 percent of the means from our sampling distribution are contained in this interval if our calculated sample mean $\overline{X}$ is truly the mean of the sampling distribution. At ± 3 standard deviations, the interval is

$$22.6 \pm 3(1.3) = 22.6 \pm 3.9 = 18.7 - 26.5$$

---

[2]Technical purists will note that with a population as small as this one, we should apply a correction factor to the formula. However, in practice most populations are quite large, and the correction factor is not needed. So, to aid in student understanding, we are ignoring the point for now. We will address it later in the chapter.

We know that 99.7 percent (virtually all) of the means from our sampling distribution are contained in this interval if our calculated mean $\bar{X}$ is truly the mean of the sampling distribution.

We refer to these intervals that we have calculated as *confidence intervals.* The first interval was a 68 percent confidence interval, the second was a 95 percent confidence level, and the last one was a 99.7 percent confidence level. Note that we must designate the level of confidence before we can calculate an interval; it is our knowledge that the mean comes from a normal distribution of means that allows us to calculate an interval.

Exactly what does a confidence interval mean? Let's use the 95 percent confidence level as an illustration. We noted previously that the mean of the sampling distribution is the population mean, and that we use one sample mean, $\bar{X}$, an estimator of the mean of the sampling distribution. But we have selected only one sample, and thus we do not know what the true mean of the sampling distribution is. It is therefore possible to select a sample such that the true population mean is not contained within the 95 percent (or other level) confidence interval calculated from the sample. The population mean either is or is not contained within the 95 percent confidence interval calculated from a sample. A 95 percent confidence interval does not mean that there are 95 chances in 100 that the population mean is contained within the interval; it means that if we selected 100 different random samples and calculated 100 different 95 percent confidence intervals, we could expect the true mean to be contained within the 95 percent confidence interval in 95 out of the 100 samples. So again we note that concepts of classical statistics have meaning in terms of repeated sampling.

The 95 percent confidence interval we calculated was 22.6 ± 2.6, or 20.0 to 25.2. Under repeated sampling, we would expect the true population mean to fall within such intervals in 95 samples out of 100. In our example we note that the population mean of 23.7 does fall within the 95 percent confidence interval we calculated from our sample of 5. Also, we can say that our estimate has a *precision* of ±2.6 years at a 95 percent level of confidence. Note that the size of the precision has meaning only at a designated level of confidence. At 99.7 percent the precision of our estimate is ±3.9 years. Precision then is the width of the confidence interval.

The calculation of a confidence interval provides us with the measure of *sampling error* and sample accuracy we were in search of earlier. Again it is only the use of probability-based selection procedures that allows us to properly calculate the confidence interval. We know nothing about the sampling distribution of means for nonprobability sampling and thus cannot calculate a meaningful confidence interval. We should note that it is common practice for confidence intervals to be calculated from nonprobability samples; the manager who uses these intervals, however, is implicitly assuming that the nonprobability sampling procedure has yielded a simple random sample.

Confidence intervals are used in practice (one hopes, used properly) by about 83 percent of businesses, as noted in Figure 14-3.

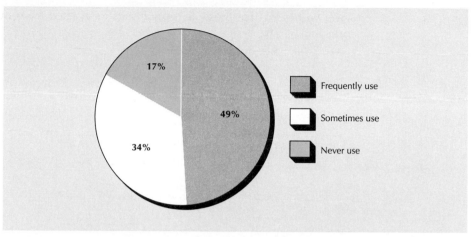

FIGURE 14-3   Use in practice of confidence intervals. (*Source:* Thomas C. Kinnear and Ann R. Root, *A Study of the Marketing Research Business,* unpublished study, 1994. Copyright 1994 Thomas C. Kinnear. Not to be reproduced.)

The Effect of Sample Size on Precision   As stated previously, the formula for the standard deviation of the sampling distribution of the mean is

$$s_{\bar{X}} = \frac{\sqrt{\sum_{i=1}^{n} (X_i - \bar{X})^2/(n - 1)}}{\sqrt{n}}$$

or more simply it is

$$s_{\bar{X}} = \frac{s}{\sqrt{n}}$$

where s is the standard deviation of the distribution of the variable of interest. We note that $s_{\bar{X}}$ will vary inversely with the square root of the sample size we select. That is, $s_{\bar{X}}$ will get smaller by the square root of the sample size as the sample size increases. Notice that the confidence interval around $\bar{X}$ will get smaller as $s_{\bar{X}}$ gets smaller, and we will be more certain of the accuracy of our estimate.

We can illustrate this by again using our student population, but this time assume that the population really has 500,000 elements and not 50 and that the population mean and variance are as before. Now let's assume we selected a number of simple random samples from this population, and in each case the mean and variance we calculated from these samples were identical, as follows:

$$\bar{X} = 22.6 \qquad s^2 = 8.3 \qquad s = 2.88$$

You will recognize these as the statistics calculated from our sample of 5 taken previously. The different sample sizes are

(1) $n = 5$ (4) $n = 1000$

(2) $n = 30$ (5) $n = 2000$

(3) $n = 100$

For each sample size we calculate $s_{\bar{x}}$, as follows:

$$(1)\ \ s_{\bar{x}} = \frac{2.88}{\sqrt{5}} = 1.3$$

$$(2)\ \ s_{\bar{x}} = \frac{2.88}{\sqrt{30}} = \frac{2.88}{5.48} = .53$$

$$(3)\ \ s_{\bar{x}} = \frac{2.88}{\sqrt{100}} = \frac{2.88}{10} = .29$$

$$(4)\ \ s_{\bar{x}} = \frac{2.88}{\sqrt{1000}} = \frac{2.88}{31.7} = .09$$

$$(5)\ \ s_{\bar{x}} = \frac{2.88}{\sqrt{2000}} = \frac{2.88}{44.8} = .06$$

The associated 95 percent confidence intervals are

(1) $22.6 \pm 2(1.3) = 22.6 \pm 2.6 = 20.0 - 25.2$

(2) $22.6 \pm 2(.53) = 22.6 \pm 1.06 = 21.5 - 23.7$

(3) $22.6 \pm 2(.29) = 22.6 \pm .58 = 22.0 - 23.2$

(4) $22.6 \pm 2(.09) = 22.6 \pm .18 = 22.4 - 22.8$

(5) $22.6 \pm 2(.06) = 22.6 \pm .12 = 22.5 - 22.7$

As n has increased from 5 to 2000, the width of confidence interval has decreased from 5.2 to .2, which shows how much more confident in our estimate we can be as the sample size increases. That is, for $n = 2000$, we would expect that the true mean would fall in an interval only .2 wide in 95 samples out of 100.

In this example, the true mean, 23.7, does not fall in the interval from 22.5 to 22.7. This has happened because we forced all the sample means to be the same, no matter what the sample size. We did this just to illustrate the effect of sample size on the size of a calculated confidence interval. In truth, as we increase the sample size, the sample mean would approach the population mean in value. A statistic that approaches the population parameter in value as the sample size

increases is called a *consistent estimator*. Obviously we want consistent estimators, so our sample mean for $n = 2000$ would be much closer to 23.7 than
the $n = 5$ mean we used above. This should make intuitive sense. The more
elements we include, the more representative our sample should be.

The other component of the calculation that affects the size of $s_{\bar{x}}$, and thus our
confidence interval, is the standard deviation of the distribution of the variable, s.
It is the numerator of $s_{\bar{x}}$. Thus, we would like our estimate of $\bar{X}$ to have as small
a variance and therefore as small a standard deviation as possible. An estimator
that provides this minimum variance and thus the minimum standard error for any
given sample size is called the *most efficient estimator*. We want efficient estimators.

Drawing Inferences about Population Parameters from Sample Statistics for Dichotomous Variables

All the theory and procedures we applied to continuous variables also apply to
dichotomous variables. The sample mean of the proportion of students electing
marketing research in our sample of 5 was .4. This is but one sample mean from
a distribution of means of the proportion that would result from repeated samplings
of size 5. Again, the central-limit theorem applies. In this case the mean of the
sampling distribution of means is π, and the standard deviation of the sampling
distribution is $\sqrt{\pi(1 - \pi)/n}$. We do not know these population values, so we
estimate them as follows:

$$\text{Mean} = p$$

$$\text{Standard error} = s_p = \sqrt{\frac{p(1 - p)}{n}} \quad \text{or} \quad \sqrt{\frac{pq}{n}}$$

We now calculate the 95 percent confidence interval for our sample of 5. The
formula would be

$$p \pm 2 \sqrt{\frac{pq}{n}}$$

In our example, $p = .4$ and $n = 5$. The 95 percent interval is

$$.4 \pm 2 \sqrt{\frac{(.4)(.6)}{5}} = .4 \pm 2\sqrt{.048}$$

$$= .4 \pm 2(.22) = .4 \pm .44$$

$$= 0 - .84$$

This is a very wide interval because the sample size is small and the value pq of
the variable is large. What we can say is that in 95 samples out of 100, we would

expect the true proportion mean to be contained in this type of interval. The true mean, .27, is contained in this interval.

Again, let us note the effect on the confidence interval of an increase in the sample size to 2000. If $p = .4$ again, the 95 percent confidence interval would be

$$.4 \pm 2 \sqrt{\frac{(.4)(.6)}{2000}} = .4 \pm 2\sqrt{.00012}$$

$$= .4 \pm 2(.011) = .4 \pm .022$$

$$= .38 - .42$$

Again because we constrained p to equal .4, a result obtained from a sample of 5, the true mean falls outside this tight interval. If the sample size were 2000, the sample mean would move closer to the population value. That is, p is a consistent estimator of π. We would then expect the true mean to fall in this type of small interval in 95 samples out of 100.

Note that for any given sample size the value of s_p is maximum when $p = .5$. This is because $pq = .25$. For no other value of p is pq this large. If $p = .6$, $pq = .24$; if $p = .7$, $pq = .21$; if $p = 8$, $pq = .16$; if $p = 9$, $pq = .09$; if $p = .99$, $pq = .0099$. What this indicates is that the more undefinitive the results (the closer p is to .5), the larger the amount of error. This is because the variance of a proportion depends on the actual proportion measured, p. Note that the variance and standard deviation formulas depend on the value of p. This is a significant result for dichotomous measures where the true population variance is unknown. Due to the variance formula, the variance of a proportion will be maximum when $p = .5$. The practical implication of this conclusion is that marketing researchers can plan sample size for the maximum variance they may encounter when the true variance is unknown.

We have now calculated a measure of sampling error for both a continuous and a dichotomous variable.

The Question of Population Size

The discussion to date had made no mention of the size of the population as being important in our calculations. Technically this is not correct, but most marketing-related populations are large enough so that the concern about population size is not important, and this extra level of complexity would have made the previous discussion harder to follow.

The problem of population size is simply that for finite populations we must change the formula we use in calculating the standard error of the sampling distribution of the mean. What we do is apply the *finite population correction* or "finite correction factor" to our previous formula, so that

$$\sigma_{\bar{x}} = \frac{\sigma_x}{\sqrt{n}} \sqrt{\frac{N - n}{N - 1}} \quad \text{and} \quad s_{\bar{x}} = \frac{s}{\sqrt{n}} \sqrt{\frac{N - n}{N - 1}}$$

$$\sigma_p = \sqrt{\frac{\pi(1 - \pi)}{n}} \sqrt{\frac{N - n}{N - 1}} \quad \text{and} \quad s_p = \sqrt{\frac{pq}{n}} \sqrt{\frac{N - n}{N - 1}}$$

The value $\sqrt{(N - n)/(N - 1)}$ is the finite correction factor. For large values of N relative to n, the value of $\sqrt{(N - n)/(N - 1)}$ is approximately equal to 1. Thus we can just use the basic formula for $\sigma_{\bar{x}}$ and $s_{\bar{x}}$ and for σ_p and s_p.

The value of the correction factor is always between 0 and 1. It is zero when $N = n$. That is, when we take a complete census we cannot calculate a standard error. This is as we should expect. Standard error has meaning only for samples, not for a census. The value of the correction factor approaches 1 as N gets bigger relative to n. So we see that multiplying by the correction factor will always lower the size of the standard error (except when it equals 1). Thus, if we choose to ignore the correction factor, we overstate the standard error and increase the size of our confidence interval. We err on the side of conservatism.

In most marketing applications it is safe to ignore the correction factor. As a rule of thumb, some suggest applying the correction factor when the sample includes more than 5 percent of the population (when the sampling fraction exceeds .05). Like all rules of thumb, 5 percent is not a definite guide; others have suggested 10 percent as the magic number. Simply be sensitive to this issue when dealing with small populations.

In our example we selected 10 percent ($\frac{5}{50}$) of the population. We should have applied the correction factor.

A Warning about Nonsampling Errors

The calculation of confidence intervals about an estimator gives us the feeling that we know just how much error we are dealing with. For most marketing research studies this can be very misleading. Our measurement of error was that of sampling error only. A confidence interval does not take nonsampling errors into account at all. If nonsampling errors occur, a bias is introduced into our estimate of unknown degree and magnitude. Control of nonsampling errors is therefore critical. (Nonsampling errors were discussed in detail in Chapter 3.)

The Accuracy of Probability Samples

Probability samples can be extremely accurate. In fact, the Gallup and Harris polls have successfully predicted the outcome of every presidential election in which they have applied probability sampling procedures. What about 1948, you say. Didn't the polls predict that Dewey would defeat Truman? They did, but the samples were quota samples, as probability sampling was new at that time.

Let's discuss two presidential elections. In 1936 the *Literary Digest* conducted a poll by mail. Their sample size was over 2 million. They predicted a victory for Landon over Roosevelt by about 15 percent; in fact, Roosevelt won easily. In 1992, using a probability sample of less than 2000 out of over 90 million voters, Gallup predicted that Bill Clinton would get 43 percent of the vote. He got 42.9 percent. The sampling frame used by the *Literary Digest* was more well-to-do than the true population of voters. The poor people who supported Roosevelt did not get a chance to respond to the poll.

The sampling procedures outlined in this chapter provide tools that enable the researcher to give accurate estimates of the parameters of interest. The major problem area lies in the nonsampling errors that arise.

In Chapter 15, we shall continue our discussion of probability sampling. Specifically, we shall discuss two types of sampling procedures—stratified sampling and cluster sampling. These procedures are more complex than simple random sampling but are used more often in practice. But before turning to these procedures, we must first address the issue of sample size.

THE DETERMINATION OF SAMPLE SIZE

Armed with an understanding of sampling error and nonsampling error, we turn our attention to the question of sample size determination. Both types of error bear on this question. First, let's examine sample size in statistical theory.

The Question of Sample Size in Statistical Theory

In simple random sampling for a known sample size, we calculated the confidence interval of our estimate at a given level of confidence. To do this for a continuous measure we had the following information, which sums up what we have covered in this chapter:

1 An estimate of the mean, $\bar{X}$.
2 An estimate of the standard deviation, s.
3 A sample size.
4 A level of confidence.
5 Using items 2 and 3, we calculated the standard error, $s_{\bar{x}}$. We then calculated the relevant confidence interval. The equation to do this at the 95 percent confidence level was

$$\text{Confidence interval} = \bar{X} \pm 2\frac{s}{\sqrt{n}}$$

We have calculated $\bar{X}$ and s, and know n, so we can solve this equation for the confidence interval. Or, we could calculate the precision we obtained using part of the above equation as follows:

$$\text{Precision} = \pm 2\,\frac{s}{\sqrt{n}}$$

Now suppose we want to reach a given level of precision. If we have a value for s, we can solve this equation for the required sample size.[3]

Let's illustrate this conclusion. Suppose that at the 99.7 percent level of confidence we wish to obtain an estimate of the mean age of a target segment for a new magazine that is within ± 1.5 years of the true mean age. In addition, we will assume that we have an estimate of $s = 6.0$. The required sample size is obtained by solving the following equation for n:

$$\text{Precision} = \pm 3\,\frac{s}{\sqrt{n}}$$

$$\pm 1.5 \text{ years} = \pm 3\,\frac{6.0}{\sqrt{n}}$$

$$1.5 = \frac{18}{\sqrt{n}}$$

$$1.5\sqrt{n} = 18$$

$$\sqrt{n} = \frac{18}{1.5}$$

$$\sqrt{n} = 12$$

$$n = 144$$

A sample size of 144 will assure us a precision of ± 1.5 years, if $s = 6.0$.

In this example we expressed the precision in units (years). When we use units to do this, it is called *absolute precision*. We might also have expressed precision as a percentage of the mean value we calculate. Here the precision in units varies depending on the size of the mean.

Precision expressed in percentages is called *relative precision*. Let's do an example to calculate sample size to assure a specified relative position. Assume that $\bar{X} = 25$, $s = 6.0$, the required precision is ± 10 percent (.1), and a 95 percent level of confidence is desired. The required equation is

[3]If we know the true standard deviation, σ, we can also calculate the required sample size. Here,

$$\text{Precision} = +2\,\frac{\sigma}{\sqrt{n}}$$

Our presumption is that it is unrealistic to think that we would know σ. In all likelihood this is one parameter we are trying to estimate. We will use statistical values in this section ($\bar{X}, s, p$), although parameters (μ, σ, π) are technically more correct.

$$\pm .b\bar{X} = \pm 2 \frac{s}{\sqrt{n}}$$

where $.b$ is the precision percentage expressed as a decimal. In our example the equation becomes

$$\pm .1(25) = \pm 2 \frac{6.0}{\sqrt{n}}$$

$$2.5 = \frac{12}{\sqrt{n}}$$

$$2.5\sqrt{n} = 12$$

$$\sqrt{n} = \frac{12}{2.5}$$

$$\sqrt{n} = 4.8$$

$$n = 23$$

The required sample size is 23 if $\bar{X} = 25$ and $s = 6.0$.

We need to note one statistical theory issue here. We know that, due to the central-limit theorem, a sample size of 23 would be appropriate only if the original distribution from which the sample was selected were a normally distributed one. For any other type of distribution, the sampling distribution of the mean will be normal only if the sample size is 30 or more. Thus, in this example, we must know that the original distribution is normal to be satisfied with a sample size of 23. (Remember your statistics course or see the appendix to this chapter for a discussion of the central-limit theorem.)

We could rearrange our relative precision equation as follows (we can ignore the $\pm$ signs, as they drop out in the calculation):

$$.b\bar{X} = 3 \frac{s}{\sqrt{n}}$$

$$.b\bar{X} \sqrt{n} = 3s$$

$$.b \sqrt{n} = 3 \frac{s}{\bar{X}}$$

Rearranging the equation in this fashion demonstrates that we really do not need to know both $\bar{X}$ and s but only the ratio of the standard deviation to the mean, $s/\bar{X}$. This ratio is called the *coefficient of variation*.

Another term related to precision that is used in practice and is relevant for our sample size discussion is *relative allowable error*.

$$\text{Relative allowable error} = \frac{.5[\text{precision}]}{\text{mean}}$$

This defines the size of the error acceptable to the manager relative to the size of the mean. For example, in the last example above, the precision was defined as $+10$ percent of the mean of 25, that is, $\pm.1[25] = \pm2.5$. This yields a total precision of 5. Managers are more likely to express the error they will accept as a percentage of the mean, and to express it in terms related to half of the precision. For example, a manager might say here: "I will accept an error of 2.5 years if the average age is 25." Thus the relative allowable error is $2.5/25 = .1$.

It is not necessary to make this calculation every time you wish to approximate optimal sample size. Most marketing research firms have developed graphic solutions to the relevant equation. This graph is called a *nomograph.* The nomograph developed by Audits and Surveys, Inc., for determining sample size for problems related to estimating the mean for infinite (large) populations is presented in Figure 14-4. Audits and Surveys's approach utilizes the coefficient of variation, and relative allowable error, to determine sample size. In the sample size calculation we just made:

$$\text{Coefficient of variation} = \frac{s}{\bar{X}} - \frac{6}{25} - .24$$

$$\text{Relative allowable error} = \frac{.5[\text{precision}]}{\bar{X}} = \frac{.5[\pm.1(25)]}{25} = \frac{2.5}{25} = .1$$

Now place your ruler on values $R = .1$ and $C = .24$ in Figure 14-4. Note that the line formed by these two points intersects the sample size line for the 95 percent confidence level at approximately $n = 23$. Nomographs can be developed for any level of confidence of interest to the researcher.

Difficulties with the Optimal Sample Size Calculation

The troublesome thing about our calculations of required sample size is that we need a value of s for absolute precision and a value for $s/\bar{X}$ for relative precision.

If we do have these values, in all likelihood we already know what we want to know about a particular variable. Also, for absolute precision the required sample size varies (1) inversely with the size of the precision desired, (2) directly with s, and (3) directly with the size of the confidence level desired. In most studies we want to measure many variables. To the extent that they differ in terms of precision desired, s, or confidence level, the required sample sizes will differ. There is no one sample size that is statistically optimal for any study. The only way to assure the required precision would be to select the largest sample. In this way the variable requiring the largest sample size would reach its specified precision, and all the others would have tighter precision than specified.

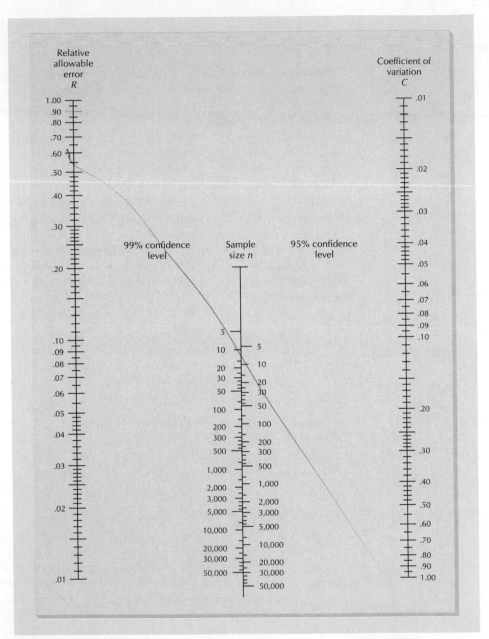

FIGURE 14-4 Nomograph to determine sample size in simple random sampling for estimation problems of the mean for an infinite population. (*Source:* Audits and Surveys, Inc. Used with permission.)

All is not lost, however, in the search for optimal sample size. If a researcher has experience with the problem at hand, then very accurate estimates of s are likely to be available at the time the sample size is being planned. For example, suppliers of store audit data have a great deal of knowledge in this area because of their experience. Additionally, the scale on which the variable of interest is measured sets limits on the size of s. For example, a 7-point attitude rating scale is likely to have an s in the 2–3 range, and it is impossible for it to be as large as 7. In contrast, a 100-point rating scale could easily have an s of 20–30. Thus, if the experienced researcher understands the effects that the measurement scale being used will have on s, then a very good estimate can be made of optimal sample size.

Optimal Sample Size for a Proportion

To be sure that you understand how to calculate the required sample size and the limitations of such a calculation, let's now calculate n for a dichotomous variable. The confidence interval for a dichotomous variable at the 95 percent level of confidence is

$$p \pm 2 \sqrt{\frac{pq}{n}}$$

Thus,

$$\text{Absolute precision} = \pm 2 \sqrt{\frac{pq}{n}}$$

Assume we have an estimate of $p = .3$ and that we want $\pm .04$ as the absolute precision at the 95 percent level of confidence. Then

$$.04 = 2 \sqrt{\frac{(.3)(.7)}{n}}$$

is the required equation. Solving for n, we get

$$.04 = 2 \sqrt{\frac{.21}{n}}$$

Dividing through by 2, we get

$$.02 = \sqrt{\frac{.21}{n}}$$

$$.02\sqrt{n} = \sqrt{.21}$$

$$\sqrt{n} = \frac{\sqrt{.21}}{.02}$$

$$\sqrt{n} = \frac{.46}{.02}$$

$$\sqrt{n} = 23$$

$$n = 529$$

The required sample size is 529.

It is also possible to utilize a nomograph with sample size problems dealing with proportions. Figure 14-5 presents Audits and Surveys's nomograph for this purpose when dealing with infinite population, for the 95 percent confidence level. To use this nomograph, we need to know the proportion p expressed as a percentage, and the allowable error expressed as a percentage. The allowable error here is simply half of the precision without reference to the mean.

In our example above, $p = .3$, or 30 percent, and the allowable error $= .04$, or 4 percent. Now place your ruler on values $p = 30$ and allowable error $= 4$. Note that the line formed by these two points intersects the sample size line at approximately $n = 529$.

To calculate relative precision at the 99.7 percent level of confidence, the equation is

$$.bp = 3\sqrt{\frac{pq}{n}}$$

where $.b$ is the precision percentage expressed as a decimal. If the required precision is ± 5 percent (.05), the equation becomes

$$.05\,(.3) = 3\sqrt{\frac{(.3)(.7)}{n}}$$

$$.015 = 3\sqrt{\frac{.21}{n}}$$

Dividing through by 3, we get

$$.005 = \sqrt{\frac{.21}{n}}$$

$$.005\sqrt{n} = \sqrt{.21}$$

$$\sqrt{n} = \frac{.46}{.005}$$

$$\sqrt{n} = 92$$

$$n = 8464$$

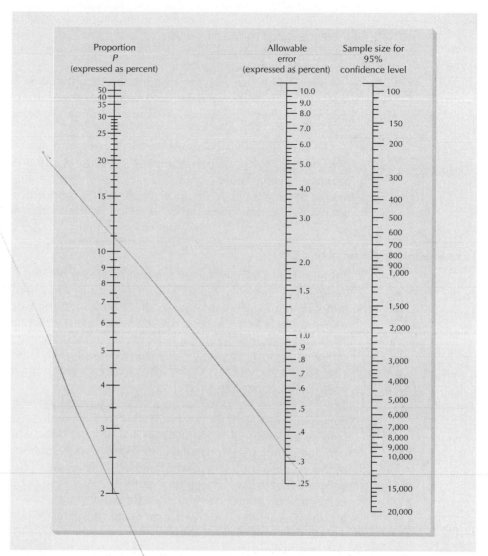

FIGURE 14-5   Nomograph to determine sample size in simple random sampling for estimation problems of the mean for an infinite population. (*Source:* Audits and Surveys, Inc. Used with permission.)

The required sample size is 8464, reflecting our use of the 99.7 percent level of confidence and a very tight precision specification.

We note that in order to determine required sample size for a dichotomous variable we need to know the mean value *p*. Regrettably, *p* is probably the value we are trying to determine in the first place. So be wary of people who claim that they have determined the statistically optimal sample size for a study, for such a statement is nonsense—unless they are experienced in the problem being researched and know the effect of the measurement scales they are using. This does not mean that the calculation of required sample size is of no value. It can provide a general guide to the researcher as to the required sample size under differing types of findings. That is, assume different values for $\bar{X}$, s, p, and so on and see what sample sizes are required.

This would be one factor affecting the determination of sample size for the study. Other factors in the decision would be the study objectives, the cost involved, the time requirements, the type of data analysis planned, and the existence of nonsampling errors.

The sample size calculations we made here were for simple random samples only. In the more complex sampling procedures discussed in Chapter 15 the formulas become more complicated. However, the principle is exactly the same; that is, we must specify the level of confidence and precision, and then we use the relevant formula for standard error to find the sample size.

Sample Size and Nonsampling Error

No one should blindly accept the sample size generated by a statistical formula. One reason for not doing so is the existence of nonsampling errors. Some nonsampling errors will get larger as the sample size increases—for example, nonresponse errors, interviewer errors, data processing errors, and data analysis errors. Thus, a decrease in sampling error occurs at the expense of an increase in nonsampling error. A carefully done study with $n = 200$ may have a smaller total error than a study of $n = 2000$. The problem is that many researchers, managers, and media people like to refer to the statistical precision of estimates. Rarely do they mention other possible errors. Look beyond the statistical formulas to the details of how the study was done. The general public also seems to believe that larger samples are necessarily better than smaller ones, which is incorrect, but the company doing research that will be exposed in the public domain must be aware of this perception. It just seems more credible to say, "Based on a study of 3000 people" than to say, "Based on a study of 250." Researchers must respond to this perception for outside use, but they should never be fooled with the same reasoning for internal use reports. Larger is not necessarily better. Also, a very small sample may yield a statistical precision at a level suitable to the needs of marketing decision makers.

Sample Size and Other Factors

A marketing research study is always a compromise between technical elegance and practical constraints faced by researchers and managers. These constraints affect sample size decisions, and several are discussed below.

Study Objectives   The use that management intends to make of the information provided by a study affects the sample size. A decision that does not need precise informational inputs can make do with a very small sample size. A company may be happy to measure interest in its new product within 15 to 20 percent.

In contrast, a political pollster can be off by less than 1 percent and fail to predict the election outcome in the study objective. The latter obviously needs a larger sample than the former.

Time Constraints   Often research results are needed "yesterday." Of course, some time for presenting results is agreed upon. The time period may be too short for anything but a small sample to be used. The larger the study, the more time needed.

Cost Constraints   A limit on the amount of money available for a study obviously could limit the sample size. Alternatively, the existence of a lot of money for a study should not be the sole motivation for a large sample size. Available dollars can be a downward constraint on sample size. It should never be the reason for increasing the sample size beyond that needed to meet the study objectives.

Audience Acceptability and Politics   The results of marketing research are subject to judgments by the audience to whom the findings are communicated. The politics surrounding a marketing decision may not allow a study with a small, but statistically optimal, sample size to have the influence of a larger sample size. Consider the example of a sample size of 23 that we calculated as optimal earlier. This small sample size would likely be attacked by members of the executive team who opposed the study's conclusions. All too often the results of a marketing research study must be sold to management, and sample size is often an issue.

Data Analysis Procedures   Data analysis procedures have an effect on the sample size for a study. The most basic type of analysis that can be performed deals with only one variable at a time. This is called *univariate analysis* (see Chapter 18). The relationship between sample size and precision of estimates on one variable is exactly what we have been discussing in this chapter.

When we examine the relationship of two variables at a time, the sample size issue becomes more complex. This is called *bivariate analysis* (see Chapter 19). Suppose we wanted to examine the relationship between usage of a product and income. Suppose also that each variable is composed of five categories. Therefore, the cross tabulation of usage by income results in a table of 25 cells. Suppose we had a sample of 250 people. If these people were spread evenly across the crosstab table, there would be only 10 respondents per cell. An even distribution across cells is not likely. However, the point is that some cell sizes will be quite small, and the precision of estimates within cells obviously will be less than those obtained in a univariate analysis. Thus, the types of bivariate analysis planned and the precision required within cells will affect the choice of sample size. A study doing only univariate analysis may require only 200 respondents, whereas a similar study doing bivariate analysis may require over 1000 respondents.

We might want to examine the relationships among more than two variables at a time. This is called *multivariate analysis* (see Chapters 20 and 21). Different multivariate techniques require different sample sizes to allow the researcher to make valid estimates of population parameters. In general, the more parameters we are estimating, the larger the sample size must be. Beyond this statement it is difficult to make simple generalizations. Some multivariate techniques can be used legitimately with small sample sizes. These include factor analysis, cluster analysis, multidimensional scaling, and small regression and analysis of variance models. At the other extreme, some techniques were designed for very large samples. The AID (automatic interaction detector) model is one example of this situation. The details of these analysis models and their sample size requirements are left to Chapters 20 and 21. In summary, the researcher must think ahead to the plan of data analysis in determining sample size.

It should now be clear that the choice of a sample size is situation-specific. It depends on statistical precision requirements, concern for nonsampling error, study objectives, time available, cost, and the data analysis plan. There is no one correct answer for the choice of sample size for a study.

SUMMARY

1 A parameter is a summary description of a measure in the defined population. A statistic is a summary description of a measure in the selected sample.

2 The ratio of sample size n to population size N is called the sampling fraction.

3 We are able to calculate the mean and the standard deviation for a population and for a simple random sample. We can do this for both continuous and dichotomous variables. Variance is simply SS/df.

4 Any simple random sample that we draw is just one of the $C(N, n)$ samples that could have been drawn.

5 In simple random sampling, each element has an equal chance of being selected, and each combination of n sample elements has an equal chance of being selected.

6 The central-limit theorem tells us that the mean of the sample that we did select comes from a distribution of sample means that form a normal curve if $n \geq 30$, no matter what the shape of the underlying variable distribution. Also, if the variable distribution is normal, then the sampling distribution of the mean is always normal, no matter what the sample size is.

7 Using our knowledge of the area under a normal curve, we can calculate confidence intervals about our sample mean. Specifically, the 95 percent interval will be $\overline{X} \pm 2s_{\overline{x}}$, and the 99.7 percent interval will be $\overline{X} \pm 3s_{\overline{x}}$, where $s_{\overline{x}} = s/\sqrt{n}$.

8 Precision is the absolute size of the confidence interval about the mean; e.g., at the 95 percent level of confidence, absolute precision $= \pm 2s/\sqrt{n}$.

9 A sample statistic whose expected value equals the population parameter is called an unbiased statistic. A sample statistic that has the minimum variance is the most efficient estimator.

10 The confidence interval provides a measure of accuracy of an estimator.

11 Beware of nonsampling errors.

12 Probability samples can provide very accurate estimates if they are properly executed.

13 Sample size should not be determined by the use of statistical formulas alone.

14 The choice of sample size is made involving trade-offs among sampling error, nonsampling error, study objectives, time constraints, cost constraints, and data analysis plans.

DISCUSSION QUESTIONS

1 What is the difference (if any) between a parameter and a statistic?

2 Identify the symbols that denote common parameters and statistics of both continuous and dichotomous variables.

3 Define the mean and variance in words and in mathematical notation for both a population and a sample, treating the variable first as continuous and then as dichotomous.

4 Why is the central-limit theorem critical to measuring sampling error?

5 What is a confidence interval?

6 What affects the size of a confidence interval?

7 What are the desirable properties of estimators?

8 To what extent do confidence intervals increase our certainty with regard to making inferences?

9 Most political pollsters judged the 1980 presidential election to be too close to call. Explain how this could happen.

10 What problems are likely to occur in implementing a field study using simple random sampling?

11 Why do some researchers calculate confidence intervals from data generated from nonprobability samples?

12 Since nonprobability samples do not yield a measure of sampling error, why are these procedures so extensively used in commercial and academic practice?

13 What is absolute precision? What is relative precision?

14 What information is necessary in order to calculate a statistically optimal sample size for (a) a continuous variable and (b) a dichotomous variable?

15 What factors should you consider in determining the sample size for a study?

16 The membership director of a national fraternity wanted to do an attitude study of the fraternity's 2500 currently active members and the 12,000 alumni.

a What sampling frame or frames would likely be available for this purpose?

b Explain how you would select a simple random sample of current members and alumni.

c Most of the questions were to be on a 7-point rating scale. For a sample size of 200 current members, what is the 95 percent confidence interval for a rating scale result where the mean answer is 2.4 and the standard deviation is 1.1?

d One question dealt with the proportion of alumni members who attend meetings of the local chapter. Historically, this proportion has been about 20 percent. The membership director reasoned that an error of ± 5 percent was acceptable for making this estimate. What is the sample size that will yield this quality of estimate at the 95 percent confidence level?

17 MINICASE

The coffee institute wanted to estimate the number of cups of coffee consumed per day by residents of California. The coefficient of variation on previous studies of this type had been .31. Management wanted a precision of ±5 percent of the mean, and was willing to use the 95 percent level of confidence.

a What is an appropriate sample size?

b If management changed the required precision to ±2 percent of the mean, and if a better estimate of the coefficient of variation was deemed to be .4, what would the appropriate sample size be?

APPENDIX   Statistical Concepts for Marketing Research

PART A. CALCULATION OF POPULATION PARAMETERS FOR TABLE 14-1

Calculation of Population Parameters for Continuous Variables

As a way of clarifying the nature of sample statistics, we will calculate the parameters from a census. Table 14-1 presents a census of the age and the election of marketing research course as an option of students in an introductory marketing course.

The measure in column 2, age, is a continuous variable. Let's calculate a measure of central tendency and a measure of dispersion for age as follows:

Central tendency. The mean or average = μ.
Dispersion. The variance and the standard deviation = σ^2 and σ, respectively.

For population, the *mean* is simply the sum of the values divided by the number in the population. Thus,

$$\mu = \frac{\sum_{i=1}^{N} X_i}{N}$$

$$= \frac{25 + 27 + \cdots + 18}{50} = \frac{1184}{50}$$

$$= 23.7$$

So the average age in the class is 23.7.

The *variance* of a population measure is the sum of the squared deviations about the mean divided by the number in the population. Thus

$$\sigma^2 = \frac{\sum_{i=1}^{N}(X_i - \mu)^2}{N}$$

Column 4 of Table 14-1 lists the deviations from the mean, and column 5 lists the squares of these deviations. Here,

$$\sigma^2 = \frac{(25 - 23.7)^2 + (27 - 23.7)^2 + \cdots + (18 - 23.7)^2}{50}$$

$$= \frac{(1.3)^2 + (3.3)^2 + \cdots + (-5.7)^2}{50}$$

$$= \frac{1.69 + 10.89 + \cdots + 32.49}{50}$$

$$= \frac{844.90}{50}$$

$$= 16.9$$

The *standard deviation* is the square root of the variance, as follows:

$$\sigma = \sqrt{16.9}$$

$$= 4.1$$

Calculation of Population Parameters for Dichotomous Variables

Column 3 of Table 14-1 presents the values associated with the dichotomous variable, the election of marketing research as an option. It is dichotomous because only the answers yes and no are allowed. Yes is coded 1, and no is coded 0 (zero).

In the same way that we calculated the mean, the variance, and the standard deviation of age, let us now turn to the election of marketing research.

$$\pi = \frac{\sum_{i=1}^{N} X_i}{N}$$

$$= \frac{(1 + 0 + \cdots + 0)}{50}$$

$$= \frac{17}{50}$$

$$= .34, \text{ and } (1 - \pi) = .66$$

The proportion of the population electing marketing research is .34. The variance, as before, is

$$\sigma^2 = \frac{\sum_{i=1}^{N}(X_i - \pi)^2}{N}$$

$$= \frac{(1 - .34)^2 + (0 - .34)^2 + \cdots + (0 - .34)^2}{50}$$

We note that $(1 - .34)^2$ occurs every time $X_2 = 1$. Thus it occurs .34 of the time. Also we note that $(0 - .34)^2$ occurs every time $X_2 = 0$, or .66 of the time. Thus

$$\sigma^2 = (1 - .34)^2(.34) + (0 - .34)^2(.66)$$

$$= (.66)^2(.34) + (- .34)^2(.66)$$

$$= .2244$$

Then

$$\sigma = \sqrt{.2244}$$

$$= .473$$

The general formula for σ^2 is

$$\sigma^2 = \pi(1 - \pi)$$

$$= (.34)(.66)$$

$$= .2244$$

and

$$\sigma = \sqrt{\pi(1 - \pi)} = \sqrt{.2244} = .473$$

PART B. THE SAMPLING DISTRIBUTION OF THE MEAN AND STATISTICAL INFERENCE

The Basic Theory

In the text we calculated the mean age of a sample we randomly selected from our student population. In order to tell how good an estimate of the population parameter this sample statistic really is, we must understand the theory of statistical inference.

First we assume a second student population that consists of five elements. In this case, the students are identified by the letters A, B, C, D, and E. Suppose we wish to select a single random sample of size $n = 2$ from this population. There are a number of combinations of elements that could form the sample—that is, there are a number of possible samples. They are:

Sample number	Elements in sample
1	AB
2	AC
3	AD
4	AE
5	BC
6	BD
7	BE
8	CD
9	CE
10	DE

There are 10 possible combinations of two elements from a population of five. Mathematically, this is simply the calculation of the number of all possible combinations without replacement. The general formula for this is

$$C_n^N = \binom{N}{n} = C(N,n)$$

$$= \frac{N!}{n!(N-n)!}$$

In our example, $N = 5$ and $n = 2$; therefore

$$C(5,2) = \frac{5!}{2! \; 3!} = \frac{5 \cdot 4 \cdot 3 \cdot 2 \cdot 1}{2 \cdot 1 \cdot 3 \cdot 2 \cdot 1}$$

$$= \frac{20}{2}$$

$$= 10$$

Each of the 10 possible samples would yield an estimate of the mean of the population.

We now turn our attention back to the population of 50 students in Table 14-1. Previously we selected one sample of five from this population. The number of possible samples of size 5 from this population is

$$C(50,5) = \frac{50!}{5! \; 45!} = \frac{50 \cdot 49 \cdot 48 \cdot 47 \cdot 46}{5 \cdot 4 \cdot 3 \cdot 2 \cdot 1}$$

$$= \frac{254,251,200}{120}$$

$$= 2,118,760 \text{ possible samples}$$

So we selected one of the 2,118,760 possible samples of size $n = 5$. Just consider the number of possible samples from a realistic population of interest. For example, if there are 70 million voters in a presidential election and we select a sample of 1000, this sample is only one of C (70 million, 1000) possible samples.

$$C(70 \text{ million}, 1000) = \frac{70 \text{ million}}{1000!(70 \text{ million} - 1000)!}$$

The important point is that in any population there are many possible samples. We must also understand that classical statistical inference is based on what happens when we repeatedly select different samples from a population.

Previously we did select one sample of $n = 5$ from

our population, and this sample yielded a mean age of 22.6. Now suppose we select another sample of $n = 5$ and calculate the mean. In this sample the mean might be 23.4 years. If we again repeat the process, we may get a third sample mean of 24.2 years. Seemingly, we have confused ourselves in that we now have three estimates of the population parameter. However, in statistical theory we would not stop at three samples; we could sample again and again, and in repeating this process we would note that certain mean values repeated themselves. Specifically, we would note that sample means closer in value to the population mean tended to repeat themselves more often than those farther removed from the population mean. This should make intuitive sense. We could plot these means values, and they would seem to be forming the familiar bell-shaped (or normal) curve. This distribution of sample means is called the *sampling distribution of the mean,* or simply the *sampling distribution.* The sampling distribution is important for two reasons: (1) the sample means in this distribution are distributed around the population mean in a known way; (2) using this distribution, we can determine how closely the sample statistics are distributed around the population parameter.

In order to derive these benefits from the sampling distribution, we must formalize the nature of the sampling distribution of the mean. To do this we turn to the *central-limit theorem* of statistics, which states that:

1 If a population distribution for a measure is normal, the sampling distribution of the mean will be normal for all sample sizes.

2 If a population is non-normal for a measure, the sampling distribution of the mean approaches normal as the sample size increases.

3 The mean of the sampling distribution of the mean is the population mean. In the type of situation in which the expected value of an estimator (the mean of the sampling distribution for the statistic) is the parameter or population value, the statistic is said to be *unbiased.*

4 The standard deviation of the sampling distribution of the mean is the population standard deviation divided by the square root of the sample size. Thus,

$$\sigma_{\bar{x}} = \frac{\sigma}{\sqrt{n}}$$

This value is often called the *standard error* of the mean.

In practice we do not know μ or σ, so we estimate

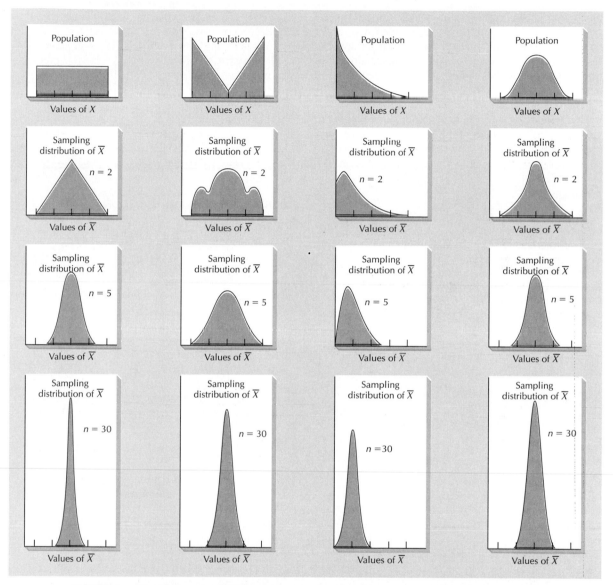

FIGURE 1   Distribution of sample means for samples of various sizes and different population distributions. (*Source:* Ernest Kurnow, Gerald J. Glasser, and Frederick R. Ottman, *Statistics for Business Decisions,* Homewood, IL: Irwin, 1959, pp. 182–183. Reproduced with permission.)

them with $\bar{X}$ and *s,* respectively, calculated from the one sample we do select; so,

$$s_{\bar{X}} = \frac{s}{\sqrt{n}}$$

Figure 1 demonstrates the central-limit theorem. Four different population distributions for a variable are presented. Only in the situation depicted at the right is this distribution normal. However, we note that for each population the sampling distribution of the mean is virtually normal when $n = 5$ (it is truly normal for the normal population) and truly normal when $n = 30$ or greater. So when we calculate the mean from any one sample of $n = 30$, we can be sure that this mean comes from a distribution that is normal, with a mean of μ and a standard error of $\sigma/\sqrt{n}$.

There is one other aspect about a normal curve that must be understood before we can put all this theory to work. This aspect relates to the area contained under a normal curve. Figure 2 shows a normal curve with an amount of area contained within different standard deviations from the mean. Specifically, we note that approximately

1 68 percent of cases will be within ± 1 standard deviation from the mean.

2 95 percent of cases will be within ± 2 standard deviations from the mean.

3 99.7 percent (almost all) cases will be within ± 3 standard deviations from the mean.

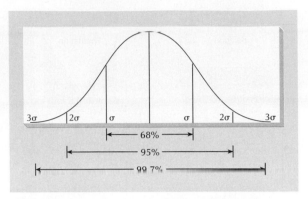

FIGURE 2   Area under the normal curve.

We now have all the pieces of theory in place that are needed to determine how good an estimate our sample mean is.

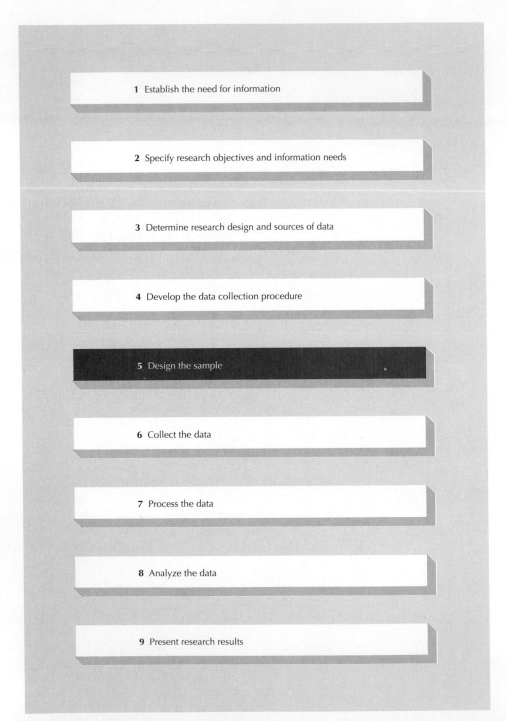

FIGURE 15-1 Steps in the research process.

CHAPTER 15

MORE COMPLEX
SAMPLING PROCEDURES

MARKETING RESEARCH IN ACTION

AT&T SELECTS A SAMPLE TO TEST SERVICE ALTERNATIVES

For proposed new pricing systems for one of its services, American Telephone & Telegraph (AT&T) needed to forecast consumer sales of this product under the alternatives proposed. In addition, AT&T was testing the impact of different promotions and distribution approaches. To do this, a purchase intention questionnaire was developed that asked consumers to rate the likelihood that they would buy the service at a specified price. In this context there was a need to select a sample that could represent AT&T's customer population of many millions of customers. This sample also needed to represent the different prices, promotions, and distribution alternatives being examined.

AT&T selected a sample of over 2600 respondents. The selection process involved stratification of the population into 16 groups to control for any impact on sales forecasts of effects due to market segment, product price, promotion, and distribution on the relationship between purchase intention and purchase behavior. Thus, the sample was selected from within two segments that had been exposed to one of two product prices, one of two promotions, and one of two distribution systems (2 × 2

$\times$ 2 $\times$ 2 = 16 groups). Within the identified 16 groups a probability sample was selected from the AT&T customer list in two states.

With this approach AT&T was able to make quite accurate forecasts of the actual sales in the whole marketplace of the service package of price, promotion, and distribution. Key to this success in forecasting is the selection of a sample using a type of probability sampling that will be discussed in this chapter: stratified sampling.

Source: William J. Infosino, "Forecasting New Product Sales from Likelihood of Purchase Ratings," *Marketing Science,* vol. 5, no. 4, pp. 372–384, Fall 1986.

We now continue our discussion of probability sampling procedures. The first part of this chapter deals with stratified sampling, and the remainder describes two types of cluster sampling: systematic sampling and area sampling. These three sampling procedures are more complex than simple random sampling, but they are also much more frequently used in practice.

STRATIFIED SAMPLING

Purpose

One property that we want in our estimators is efficiency—that is, we want to have as small a standard error as possible. Stratified sampling may result in a *decrease in the standard error of the estimator.* Thus the confidence interval we calculate will be smaller.

Method of Selection

A stratified sample is selected as follows:

1 Divide the defined population into mutually exclusive and collectively exhaustive subgroups or strata. Strata are mutually exclusive if membership in one stratum precludes membership in any other stratum. For example, a population may be divided into two strata on the basis of sex; that is, there will be a male stratum and a female stratum. An individual person cannot belong to both strata, and thus these strata are mutually exclusive. Strata are collectively exhaustive if all possible categories of a variable are used to define the strata. That is, the categories "male and female" define the complete domain of the variable "sex." No other category is possible, and thus the defined strata are collectively exhaustive of the variable "sex."

2 Select an independent simple random sample in each stratum.

An Illustration

How does such a two-stage procedure decrease the standard error of an estimator? It does so only if the designated strata are *more homogeneous* on the variable on which we are calculating our statistics. If the strata are as heterogeneous on this variable as the unstratified whole population, no decrease in the standard error will occur.

Let's illustrate the standard error-reducing property of stratified sampling. Again we use part of the data presented in Table 14-1. The student number and age of students are presented in Table 15-1. We will use the age data to illustrate the standard error reducing property.

Perhaps you noted in reading Table 14-1 that the ages of students numbered 1–20 seemed higher than the ages of students numbered 21–50. This is indeed true. A piece of information that was missing in Table 14-1 was that students 1–20 are graduate students and students 21–50 are undergraduate students. We would expect graduate students to be older than undergraduates, and they are. Note that the group of students numbered 1–20 has a more homogeneous age profile than the population as a whole, and so does the group of students num-

TABLE 15-1   CENSUS OF AGE OF STUDENTS

	Student number	Age (X_1)		Student number	Age (X_1)
Graduate students	1	25	**Undergraduate students**	21	21
	2	27		22	19
	3	29		23	24
	4	31		24	22
	5	25		25	20
	6	29		26	22
	7	27		27	19
	8	24		28	20
	9	27		29	19
	10	28		30	24
	11	33		31	25
	12	29		32	22
	13	26		33	20
	14	28		34	21
	15	28		35	21
	16	26		36	23
	17	26		37	21
	18	36		38	23
	19	28		39	18
	20	26		40	21
				41	19
				42	23
				43	22
				44	19
				45	20
				46	20
				47	21
				48	20
				49	19
				50	18

bered 21–50. By using a *stratification variable,* "graduate versus undergraduate," we have identified two strata that are more homogeneous than the population on the variable of interest, age. We have presented the necessary condition to take advantage of stratification.

The Sample

Now let us draw a simple random sample of $n = 2$ from the graduate stratum and a simple random sample of $n = 3$ from the undergraduate stratum. Note that the ratio of our sample sizes by strata is in proportion to the ratio of the number of population elements by strata. Here the sample ratio $\frac{2}{3}$ is proportionate to the population ratio 20/30. This is called *proportionate stratified sampling,* and it occurs when the total sample elements are allocated to strata *in proportion to the number of population elements in the strata.* The researcher also has the option of allocating the total sample to strata on a basis disproportionate with the population distribution among strata. We shall discuss disproportionate stratified sampling later in this chapter. Also note that all possible combinations of elements are not equally likely, as we are selecting some elements from each stratum. Thus, combinations of elements drawn completely within one stratum are impossible.

As a basis for facilitating the discussion that follows, we identify the following notation:

$N_{st.1}$ = population size in stratum 1 $\qquad$ $\bar{X}_{st.1}$ = sample mean of stratum 1
$N_{st.2}$ = population size in stratum 2 $\qquad$ $\bar{X}_{st.2}$ = sample mean of stratum 2
$n_{st.1}$ = sample size in stratum 1 $\qquad$ $s^2_{st.1}$ = sample variance of stratum 1
$n_{st.2}$ = sample size in stratum 1 $\qquad$ $s^2_{st.2}$ = sample variance of stratum 2

Now let's draw a simple random sample of $n = 2$ from stratum 1 and $n = 3$ from stratum 2. Conveniently, the sample of $n = 5$ we drew in Chapter 14 was just this kind of sample, so we do not have to select a new sample. Specifically, the sample by strata is as follows:

Student number	Age
Stratum 1	
05	25
17	26
Stratum 2	
32	22
37	21
41	19

Calculation of Statistics within Strata

When we calculate the mean, the variance, and the standard deviation within each stratum and compare these results to the results to the sample as a whole, we get interesting results. The details of these within-strata calculations are presented in the appendix to this chapter.

Table 15-2 summarizes these results. We note that the variance and the standard deviation within each stratum are much lower than the variance and standard deviation of the total sample. This points out one advantage of stratified sampling—that is, we can do analysis within strata with a smaller standard error than that available for the whole sample. Our within-strata confidence interval would thus be smaller than that generated by the use of the standard error of the whole sample.

Calculation of the Mean and Standard Error for the Whole Sample

We next consider how to calculate the mean and the standard error for the whole sample on the basis of within-strata results. The overall sample mean, $\bar{X}_{st.}$, is simply a *weighted average of the within-strata means*. The weight for a stratum is the ratio of the population size of that stratum to the total population size,

$$\frac{N_{st.j}}{N}$$

where $N_{st.j}$ is the population size within stratum j. Therefore,

$$\bar{X}_{st.} = \sum_{j=1}^{A} \left(\frac{N_{st.j}}{N}\right) X_{st.j}$$

where $A =$ the number of strata.

In our example we have two strata; thus $A = 2$, and so,

$$\bar{X}_{st.} = \sum_{j=1}^{2} \left(\frac{N_{st.j}}{N}\right) \bar{X}_{st.j} - \left(\frac{N_{st.1}}{N}\right) X_{st.1} + \left(\frac{N_{st.2}}{N}\right) \bar{X}_{st.2}$$

$$= \left(\frac{20}{50}\right) 25.5 + \left(\frac{30}{50}\right) 20.7$$

$$= .4(25.5) + .6(20.7)$$

$$= 10.2 + 12.4$$

$$= 22.6$$

TABLE 15-2   TOTAL SAMPLE AND WITHIN-STRATUM MEAN, AND VARIANCE OF SAMPLE

	Mean	Variance	Standard deviation
Without stratification	22.6	8.3	2.88
Within stratum 1	25.5	.5	.71
Within stratum 2	20.7	2.35	1.53

This is exactly the same mean we calculated without stratification.

The ratio $N_{st.j}/N$ is the relative weight attached to each stratum. For future reference, let's call this ratio W_j.

In our example,

$$W_1 = .4 \quad \text{and} \quad W_2 = .6$$

The calculation of the *standard error* of the mean from within-strata information is more complex. It is *the square root of the weighted combination of the square of the standard error within each stratum*. The weighting factor in this case is the square of the relative weight of each stratum.

The formula[1] is

$$s_{\bar{X}} = \sqrt{s_{\bar{X}}^2}$$

where

$$s_{\bar{X}}^2 = \sum_{j=1}^{A} \left(\frac{N_{st.j}}{N}\right)^2 s_{\bar{X} \, st.j}^2$$

$$= \sum_{j=1}^{A} W_j^2 s_{\bar{X} \, st.j}^2$$

In our example (using the values in Table 15-2), we have for stratum 1:

$$s_{\bar{X}_{st.1}} = \frac{.71}{\sqrt{2}} = \frac{.71}{1.41}$$

$$= .50$$

$$s_{\bar{X} \, st.1}^2 = .25$$

and for stratum 2:

$$s_{\bar{X}_{st.2}} = \frac{1.53}{\sqrt{3}} = \frac{1.53}{1.73}$$

$$= .88$$

$$s_{\bar{X} \, st.2}^2 = .78$$

[1]Again we will ignore the finite-population correction factor.

Therefore,

$$s_{\bar{X}}^2 = (.4)^2(.25) + (.6)^2(.78)$$

$$= (.16)(.25) + (.36)(.78)$$

$$= .04 + .28$$

$$= .32$$

$$s_{\bar{X}} = \sqrt{.32}$$

$$= .57$$

Note that we took the square of the weighting factor for each stratum and the square of the standard error. We cannot take a simple weighting of the strata weight and the associated standard errors.

Alternatively, we may calculate $s_{\bar{X}}^2$ directly without first calculating the standard errors within each stratum. The formula for doing this is

$$s_{\bar{X}}^2 = \sum_{j=1}^{A} \frac{\left(\dfrac{N_{st.j}}{N}\right)^2 s_{st.j}^2}{n_{st.j}}$$

$$= \sum_{j=1}^{A} \frac{(W_j)^2 s_{st.j}^2}{n_{st.j}}$$

In our example, with $A = 2$,

$$s_{\bar{X}}^2 = \frac{(W_1)^2 s_{st.1}^2}{n_{st.1}} + \frac{(W_2)^2 s_{st.2}^2}{n_{st.2}}$$

$$= \frac{(.4)^2(.5)}{2} + \frac{(.6)^2(2.35)}{3}$$

$$= (.16)(.25) + (.36)(.78)$$

$$= .04 + .28$$

$$= .32$$

$$s_{\bar{X}} = \sqrt{.32} = .57$$

The value of $s_{\bar{X}}$ is identical to that previously calculated.

In Chapter 14 we calculated the standard error of the mean, using the unstratified sample, to be 1.3. Now that we have stratified the sample, the standard error has been reduced to .57.

Calculation of Associated Confidence Interval

The 95 percent confidence interval for the stratified sample is 22.6 ± 2(.57) = 22.6 ± 1.1 = 21.5–23.7. The unstratified 95 percent interval was 20.0–25.2. Thus the size of the interval has been reduced from 5.2 to 2.2 and the absolute precision from ±2.6 to ±1.1. Note that the population mean, 23.7, does fall in this new interval. Note also that the stratified 99.7 percent confidence interval would be smaller than the unstratified 95 percent interval. The 99.7 percent interval is 22.6 ± 3(.57) = 22.6 ± 1.7 = 20.9–24.3. Clearly a stratified sampling procedure is more efficient than an unstratified one. This fact helps account for the moderately high use of stratified sampling in practice.

Why do we get such a reduction in standard error and associated precision using a stratified sampling procedure? It is because we use only within-stratum variability in calculating the overall standard error. Across-strata variability becomes irrelevant. The statistical theory that supports the observed reduction in standard error, and that allows us to apply the concept of a confidence interval for stratified samples, is presented in Part B of the appendix to this chapter. Review this material if it is needed for your understanding.

The effect with stratified sampling is that we can increase the precision of our estimates with the same sample size we used in an unstratified fashion. Alternatively, we could obtain the same precision as with an unstratified sample with a smaller sample and thus a lower cost.

Usefulness in Marketing Research

This improvement in precision for any given sample size has resulted in about 85 percent of businesses utilizing stratified sampling in practice as noted in Figure 15-2. The types of variables often measured in marketing research show high variability that can be reduced by stratification. As an example, suppose that we are asked to monitor the retail sales of Folger's coffee. To do this we want to measure the unit sales level of Folger's in a sample of stores. What stratification variables should we use? First we must answer another question: "What factors contribute to the variability in the variable we intended to measure?" In the Folger's example, contributing factors to variability would include:

1 *Size of store.* Big stores would have higher sales than small stores.
2 *Day of the week.* Stores sell more coffee on weekends than early in the week.
3 *Region of the country.* Folger's is a more established brand in the western states, so we would find higher sales there than in other regions.

Other factors may also contribute to the variability in sales. If we thought they were important contributors, we would also include them as stratification variables. If we distinguished three sizes of stores, two types of days of the week, and four regions of the country, we would have 3 × 2 × 4 = 24 different cells or strata. The similarity to quota sampling in the way the number of cells expands is obvious. However, in quota sampling we have no error measure.

In the stratum composed of "large stores—weekends—western regions," we

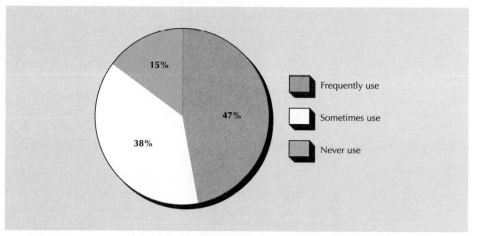

FIGURE 15-2   Use in practice of stratified sampling. (*Source:* Thomas C. Kinnear and Ann R. Root, *A Study of the Marketing Research Business*, unpublished study, 1994. Copyright 1994 Thomas C. Kinnear. Not to be reproduced.)

might find case sale numbers like 150, 170, and 205. In the stratum composed of "small stores—weekdays—eastern region," however, we might find case sale numbers like 10, 6, and 7. The across-strata variability is much greater than that within each stratum. We would thus obtain more efficient estimates using stratification.

The stratification variables worked because they are all *correlated* with the sales of Folger's. In general, we add stratification variables as long as they contribute meaningfully to the variability of the variable we are measuring. Of course, we also consider the *cost* of stratification is deciding on the number of stratification variables.

Most studies are designed to measure many variables. A good stratification variable for some of these may not be as good for others. In selecting stratification variables, we want those that will contribute most meaningfully across all variables of interest.

Disproportionate Stratified Sampling

The overall sample size *n* can also be allocated to strata on a basis *disproportionate* with the population sizes of the strata. Proportionate allocation is straightforward, so why should we complicate things by allocating on some other basis? The answer lies in the differences in variability within strata. Generally, for a fixed sample size we can reduce the overall standard error of the estimate by sampling more heavily in strata with higher variability. Suppose that we had added another stratification variable to our age example and that by doing so we obtained a population stratum with the elements 21, 21, 21 in it. There is no variability in this stratum, and a sample of one is all that is needed to measure perfectly the mean of this stratum. Alternatively, a stratum with much variability will require a large sample size to produce an efficient estimate of the mean. This is true because, in order to calculate the standard error within a stratum, we divide the standard deviation within the stratum by the square root of the stratum sample size, $n_{st.j}$.

An optimal allocation of a fixed sample size among strata is one that generates the minimum standard error of the overall estimate. To find this optimal allocation we must know something about the variability within strata before sampling. Experience and past studies may provide such knowledge. Companies doing retail store audits often sample the larger stores at a disproportionately high level because these larger stores exhibit more variability in sales than small stores. The result is a smaller standard error and a more reliable estimate. Figure 15-3 illustrates this approach as applied in retail store audits of sales by the marketing research company, A. C. Nielsen, in its Nielsen Distribution Index (NDI). Note that the sampling fraction is 1 out of 49 for the chain stores, while it is only 1 out of 133 for the small independents.

There are mathematical formulas for determining the optimal allocation of a sample to strata, but they are complex and beyond the scope of this book. In general, these formulas indicate that (1) the larger the stratum, the larger the sample, and (2) the greater the variability within a stratum, the larger the sample.

How are the overall mean and standard error calculated with a disproportionate stratified sample? Exactly the same formulas are used as before in proportionate stratified sampling. This is the case because

$$W_j = \frac{N_{st.j}}{N}$$

FIGURE 15-3   Disproportionate stratified sampling in retail store audits. (*Source:* Nielsen Retail Index Services, A. C. Nielsen Company, Northbrook, IL, 1983. Reprinted with permission.)

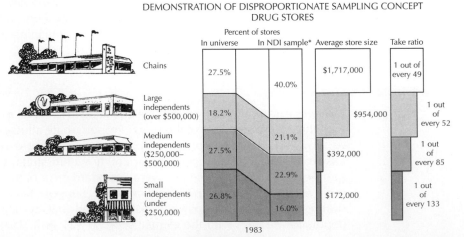

DEMONSTRATION OF DISPROPORTIONATE SAMPLING CONCEPT
DRUG STORES

*NDI = Nielsen Distribution Index

That is, it is the size of the population within strata and the total population that determine the weighting factors. The sample sizes within strata are used only to calculate within-strata means and standard errors.

CLUSTER SAMPLING

Overview

In all the probability sampling methods we have discussed so far, the elements that form the sample are selected individually. In cluster sampling, *a cluster or group of elements is randomly selected at one time.* Thus, before we can select a cluster sample, the population must be divided into mutually exclusive and collectively exhaustive groups. We then select a random sample of these groups.

Suppose we had a population of 20 elements divided into 4 equal-sized groups, as follows:

Group	Population element number
1	1, 2, 3, 4, 5
2	6, 7, 8, 9, 10
3	11, 12, 13, 14, 15
4	16, 17, 18, 19, 20

If we wanted to select a probability sample of 10 elements, we could select elements individually using simple random sampling, or we could randomly select two of the four groups and use all the elements in those two groups. The situation where we directly select groups and then use *all* the elements in these groups is called *one-stage cluster sampling.* If we had selected a random sample of elements from within the selected groups, we would call this a *two-stage cluster sample.* In both cluster and simple random sampling the sampling fraction would be the same, .5. However, not all possible combinations of elements are equally likely in cluster sampling. Most combinations are impossible.

What if the clusters we select have elements that are not representative of the population? Wouldn't our estimates be biased? The answer is yes. This points out the criterion we should use in forming groups. We want them to be as close in heterogeneity on the variables of interest as the population as a whole. If the groups are exactly as heterogeneous as the population, any one group we select will accurately represent the population; in practice, however, this ideal is never reached. Note that in cluster sampling the criterion used in forming groups is exactly the opposite of that used in stratified sampling. In stratified sampling we want homogeneous groups, whereas in cluster sampling we want heterogeneous groups.

How does the size of the standard error generated from a cluster sample compare to the size of the standard error generated from a simple random sample? The answer depends on the similarity of the heterogeneity in the formed groups compared with the population, as follows:

1 If the groups are exactly as heterogeneous as the population, both methods will yield the same standard error.

2 If the groups are less heterogeneous than the population, the standard error will be greater with cluster sampling than with simple random sampling.

We refer to this comparison of the standard errors generated by various sampling procedures as an assessment of the *statistical efficiency* of the procedures.

In practice, sample clusters are often much less heterogeneous than the population, which means that in most cases they are less statistically efficient than simple random samples. For reasons of cost, however, cluster samples are very extensively used in practice. They are often much cheaper than other procedures for a given sample size. Alternatively, for a given dollar budget we can generate a larger sample using cluster sampling. When we combine the statistical efficiency of a procedure with its cost, we refer to this as the *overall efficiency,* or *total efficiency,* of the procedure. Cluster sampling is often the most overall efficient procedure. That is, we get a smaller standard error per dollar spent. The next section discusses the most straightforward type of cluster sampling, systematic sampling.

SYSTEMATIC SAMPLING

The Method

In systematic sampling, the researcher selects *every kth element in the frame, after a random start somewhere within the first k elements.* Suppose we wanted to select a systematic sample of $n = 5$ from our student population in Tables 14-1 and 15-1. Here

$$k = \frac{50}{5} = 10$$

In general,

$$k = \frac{N}{n}$$

which is the reciprocal of the sampling fraction we desire and is called the *sampling interval.* Thus, to select our systematic sample of $n = 5$, we do the following:

1 Obtain a random number between 1 and 10. This element will be our starting point and the first element of the sample.

2 Add 10 to this random number. This element will be the second element of the sample. Add another 10 to get the third element, and so on.

If the random number were 2, our sample would include the elements

2, 12, 22, 32, 42

Once the sampling interval and random starting point have been specified, the elements that are included in the sample become automatic. They form a cluster of elements. In our population of 50, there are only 10 possible systematic samples of size $n = 5$ that can be drawn, because each cluster includes $\frac{1}{10}$ of the population. In general, the number of possible samples is equal to k, the sampling interval. With populations that are large relative to the sample size, the value of k, and therefore the number of possible samples, increases substantially.

Because we use all the elements in the cluster generated by systematic sampling, the procedure is called a *one-stage cluster sampling procedure*. Also, it is clear that all possible combinations of elements are not equally likely. We have reduced the number of possible samples from over 2 million with simple random sampling to 10 with systematic sampling.

Fortunately, it can be shown that the mean of the sampling distribution of means generated by repeated systematic sampling is equal to the population mean. That is, the mean from any one systematic sample is an unbiased estimator of the population mean. We may then calculate meaningful confidence intervals as we did with simple random sampling.[2] In fact, if the frame from which we are sampling is truly random, a systematic sample may be thought of as being identical to simple random sampling. In most applications the results are almost identical.

The mean age for the systematic sample we drew is (reading the ages associated with the selected elements from Table 15-1)

$$\bar{X} = \frac{27 + 29 + 19 + 22 + 23}{5}$$

$$= \frac{120}{5}$$

$$= 24.0$$

and

$$\Sigma X^2 = (27)^2 + (29)^2 + (19)^2 + (22)^2 + (23)^2$$

$$= 729 + 841 + 361 + 484 + 529$$

$$= 2944$$

$$\frac{(\Sigma X)^2}{n} = \frac{(120)^2}{5}$$

$$= \frac{14400}{5}$$

$$= 2880$$

[2]There are some very technical aspects related to the calculation of standard error that apply here. They are well beyond the scope of this book and have been ignored. In most situations these refinements add little to real managerial understanding of sampling results. We proceed here as if the formulas related to simple random sampling apply.

Therefore,

$$s^2 = \frac{2944 - 2880}{4}$$

$$= \frac{64}{4}$$

$$= 16$$

Then

$$s = 4$$

The standard error is

$$\frac{4}{\sqrt{5}} = \frac{4}{2.24}$$

$$= 1.79$$

The 95 percent confidence interval is then

$$24.0 \pm 2(1.79) = 24.0 \pm 3.58$$

$$= 20.4 - 27.6$$

The true mean is again contained within the 95 percent interval. Because of the particular elements that formed the cluster we selected, the standard error is larger than in the simple random sample we selected earlier; thus, so is the confidence interval.

Systematic sampling is often used in practice because it is easy and cheap to select a systematic sample. With systematic sampling we do not jump back and forth all over our sampling frame wherever our random number leads us, nor do we have to worry about checking for duplication of elements. In simple random sampling both of these problems occur. Because systematic sampling is a close substitute for simple random sampling, we may use it to select elements within strata in stratified sampling.

There is one other benefit of systematic sampling over simple random sampling: we do not need a complete sampling frame to draw a systematic sample. An interviewer instructed to interview every twentieth customer can do so without a list of all customers. Similarly, he or she could select a sample of every third house without a full list of the houses available. About 49 percent of businesses indicate use in practice of systematic sampling, as noted in Figure 15-4.

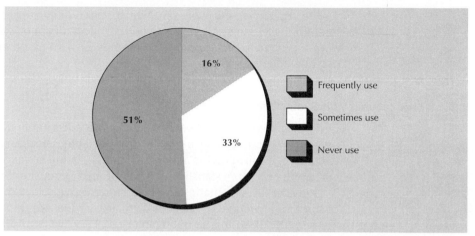

FIGURE 15-4 Use in practice of systematic sampling. (*Source:* Thomas C. Kinnear and Ann R. Root, *A Study of the Marketing Research Business,* unpublished study, 1994. Copyright 1994 Thomas C. Kinnear. Not to be reproduced.)

The Problem of Periodicity

There is one major problem with systematic sampling, namely that we will obtain biased estimates if the list of elements forming the frame forms a cyclical pattern that coincides with a multiple of the size of the sampling interval. This type of frame is said to have *periodicity.* We may illustrate this problem with two examples. Suppose we wanted to interview residents of a student housing complex and selected housing units from a list of all units arranged in numerical order: 1, 2, ..., 599, 600. Suppose our sampling interval was 10 and our random starting number 5. Our sample would contain the 60 housing units numbered 5, 15, 25, ..., 585, 595. Now suppose that the complex was built such that the units ending in 5, 25, 45, 65, and 85 were corner units. These corner units had one more bedroom than the other units and had higher rent. They also were allocated to students on the basis of seniority (number of years in the complex) and on the basis of having at least three children. So half of our sample would consist of people with at least three children who had been in the complex a number of years and were willing to pay the higher rent. Our sample would not be representative of the complex. Note here that the cyclical pattern is twice the size of the sampling interval. The pattern could be any multiple of the sampling interval and cause bias in our estimates.

As a second example, consider the problem of a movie theater manager who wants to estimate total popcorn sales by using a sample of certain days' sales. Suppose it is decided to select one day from each week of the year—that is, $n = 52$. The sampling interval is then $365/52 = 7$. The sample would then allow the recording of popcorn sales only on the same day of the week for all 52 weeks. A sample of Saturdays would obviously overstate sales, whereas a sample of Tuesdays would understate sales.

The researcher must be sensitive to periodicity in a sampling frame if the intention is to use systematic sampling. If periodicity exists, it must be removed from the frame by rearranging the elements, or some other sampling procedure must be adopted.

Implicit Stratification with Systematic Sampling

Ordered frames are not always bad for systematic sampling. If the frame is ordered on what might be used as a stratification variable, selection of a systematic sample will automatically provide a stratified sample. In this situation, a systematic sample will produce a more statistically efficient result than simple random sampling.

Consider the systematic sample of students we selected. We know that the list of students is ordered by whether they are graduate or undergraduate students, in the ratio 20/30. With a sampling interval of 10, we know that the first two sample elements must come from the graduate stratum and the last three from the undergraduate stratum. Thus we automatically selected a proportionate stratified sample of students with our systematic sample.

If the researcher is aware of the implicit stratification that has occurred, it is possible to use stratified formulas to calculate the sample mean and standard error. The result is a smaller confidence interval. In our student age sample, the ages of the students within strata would be

Stratum 1   27, 29
Stratum 2   19, 22, 23

We encourage you to do the necessary calculations to show the reduction in standard error. It should now be intuitively obvious by just looking at the numbers arranged in strata.

In summary, systematic sampling offers potential advantages in (1) ease of sample selection, (2) cost, (3) removal of the need for a complete frame, and (4) implicit stratification of properly ordered frames. Difficulties are related to (1) the problem of possible periodicity and (2) possible technical problems in calculating standard error.

AREA SAMPLING

The Basics

With simple random sampling, stratified sampling, and most applications of systematic sampling discussed so far, a complete and accurate listing of the elements of the population is required. Unfortunately, for a great many marketing research applications such lists are impossible to generate at a reasonable cost. Lists are not available for such populations as all the adults in the United States, all the inhabitants of a state or city, all users of a particular product, or all university students or church members. It may be possible to obtain such lists, but the cost would be extremely high, and the lists would probably contain many inaccuracies.

A properly selected respondent can provide information on the broader population.

Sampling practitioners have developed an ingenious solution to this problem. They reasoned that people reside on a specific piece of land, so why not sample pieces of land and interview the persons who reside there? So the word "area" in "area sample" originally referred to a piece of land. *An area sample is actually a sampling of areas.*

Many real marketing research problems do not have a list of sampling elements available to select from. As a result, as noted in Figure 15-5, about 52 percent of businesses utilize area sampling.

We shall illustrate this concept by outlining what a one-stage area sample might look like. Suppose we want to run an in-home usage test of a new formulation of a shampoo. We have decided to run this test in Atlanta. An accurate listing of all

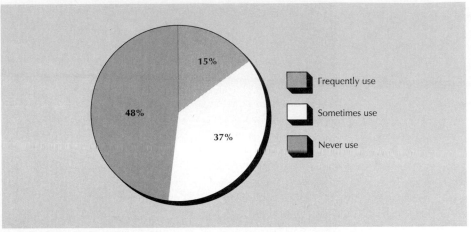

FIGURE 15-5   Use in practice of area sampling. (*Source:* Thomas C. Kinnear and Ann R. Root, *A Study of the Marketing Research Business*, unpublished study, 1994. Copyright 1994 Thomas C. Kinnear. Not to be reproduced.)

households in Atlanta is unavailable, since the city directory and telephone book are both very out of date even as they are published. So we select an area sample using the following method:

1 List all city blocks in Atlanta, N_B.
2 Choose a simple random or systematic sample of n_B city blocks from the population of N_B city blocks.
3 Attempt to place the product in all households in the chosen blocks, n_B.

This is a probability sampling procedure because the probability of any household's being selected is equal to the sampling fraction n_B/N_B. If Atlanta had 10,000 blocks and we selected a sample of 20 blocks, the probability of any household's being selected would be 20/10,000 = .002. The reason this probability equals the sampling fraction for the blocks is that we are using all households in the selected blocks as part of the sample.

Multistage Area Samples

An area sample can have as many stages as the researcher desires. Most area samples have more than one stage. What would a two-stage area sample designed for our product usage look like? The steps would be:

1 List all city blocks in Atlanta, N_B.
2 Choose a simple random sample or systematic sample of n_B city blocks.
3 List the households located in the selected city blocks, N_H.
4 Select a simple random or systematic sample of n_H households from the selected n_B city blocks.

Note that the first two steps in two-stage area sampling are the same as in one-stage area sampling. With the latter, however, we were required to make one list (of blocks), and we used probability sampling procedures only once (to select the blocks. In two-stage area sampling we were required to make two lists (blocks and then households), and we used probability sampling procedures twice (to select blocks and then households). In a two-stage area sample we twice repeated the sequence "list population sampling units, and then sample." Thus, in a k-stage area sample we would go through this sequence k times.

A multistage area sample may be illustrated by describing the five-stage area sampling process used by the Survey Research Center of the Institute for Social Research of the University of Michigan for its many national studies.[3] Figure 15-6 gives a graphic view of the five stages of this process. The five stages are:

Stage 1   The continental United States is divided into 74 "primary areas." These areas are usually counties, groups of counties, or metropolitan areas. A probability sample of primary areas is then made. That is, the researchers list the areas and then sample from this list. The top row of Figure 15-6 depicts the primary areas on the map of the continental United States and shows the selection of one primary area. It is common for the researchers to stratify the primary-area population to assure themselves that their sample will include the proper proportion of primary areas of different types. For example, a geographic stratification would ensure that each region of the country was represented. Multiple stratification variables are often used.

Stage 2   A listing is made of the large cities, medium-sized towns, and remaining areas in the selected primary areas. In the example of Figure 15-6, the selected area consists of one large city, four medium-sized towns, and open space. This area would probably be stratified into three groups: (1) large cities, (2) smaller cities and towns, and (3) open space. Then one or more of what are called "sample locations" would be selected by probability methods from each stratum. Again the researchers list the population sampling units and select a probability sample.

We should also note that they have again been stratified to ensure a representative sample. The connected circles running from "primary area" to "sample location" in Figure 15-6 illustrate stage 2 for the selection of one sample location from one primary area previously selected.

Stage 3   A listing is made of the geographic areas within the sample location. These geographic areas must have identifiable boundaries—for example, city blocks, rural roads, rivers, or county lines. These geographic areas are referred to as "chunks." On the average, chunks are designed to contain from 16 to 40 dwellings, but they may contain more in large cities. A probability sample of chunks is then selected from each selected sample location obtained in stage 2.

[3]This section is based on the *Interviewer's Manual,* rev. ed. (Ann Arbor: Survey Research Center, Institute for Social Research, University of Michigan, 1976).

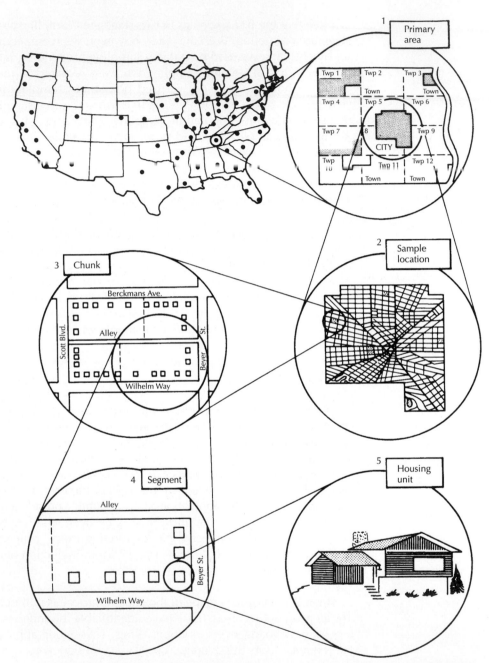

FIGURE 15-6   An illustration of area sampling. [*Source:* Adapted from *Interviewer's Manual,* rev. ed. (Ann Arbor: Survey Research Center, Institute for Social Research, University of Michigan, 1976), p. 36.]

The theme of "list sampling units and select a probability sample" should be very obvious. The connected circles running from "sample location" to "chunk" on Figure 15-6 illustrate stage 3 for the selection of one chunk from one sample location previously selected.

Stage 4   A listing is made of all the housing units in the selected chunk, which is then divided into smaller units called "segments," containing from 4 to 16 housing units. A probability sample of segments is then selected. The connected circles running from "chunk" to "segment" on Figure 15-6 illustrate the selection of one segment from a chunk that was previously selected.

Stage 5   From the listing of housing units in segments, a probability sample of housing units is selected. The connected circles running from "segment" to "housing units" on Figure 15-6 illustrate the selection of one housing unit from one segment that was previously selected. If this process continued to include the listing of persons within housing units and then selected a probability sample of persons, it would be a six-stage area sample. Note that a housing unit does not have to be a single-family dwelling. A full 70-unit apartment building would count as 70 housing units.

The Properties of Multistage Area Samples

Multistage area sampling is much less statistically efficient than simple random sampling. In a simple random sample a single sampling error is calculated. A two-stage area sample is subject to two sampling errors. The selection of the clusters at the first stage is only an estimate of the population of clusters; that is, sampling error occurs. In this way, the selection of elements from within a cluster is only an estimate of the population of elements within that cluster. Thus, a five-stage area sample would contain five sampling errors. The formulas for calculating the standard error from a multistage area sample are too complex to be discussed here. Researchers should be sensitive to this issue and prepared to consult a technical expert for the proper calculation. In practice, the results obtained from the final stage are often treated as if they came from a direct probability sampling of a list of final elements. That is, the formulas used are those for simple random sampling and stratified sampling. The net effect of doing this is to understate the sampling error that has occurred. However, for decisions where the risk of such an understatement is explicitly tolerated, we cannot be too critical of such a shortcut procedure.

The technical aspects may seem complex enough at this point, but there are still some basics concerning the sampling error generated in multistage area sampling that should be understood. Sampling error is decreased by an increase in (1) sample size and (2) the homogeneity of the elements being sampled. Sample size and homogeneity affect sampling error at each stage of a multistage sample design. Thus, to have a small sampling error at the time of selecting clusters, we would like to select a large number from a group of very similar clusters. Similarly, to have a small sampling error at the time of selecting elements from a given cluster, we would like to select a large number from a group of very similar elements. For any given sample size, we cannot increase the number of clusters without decreasing the number of elements within each cluster. Therefore, cluster-level error would seem to be decreased at the expense of element-level error. This is true, but the effect is limited by the fact that elements within area sample clusters tend to be more homogeneous than the population as a whole. For example, the residents of a city block are more similar than those in the country or even city as a whole. Therefore, the sample size within clusters of this type can be quite small and still yield a reasonable sampling error. Clusters, on the other hand, tend to be more heterogeneous. Thus, a large number of clusters may be necessary to reduce the sampling error to a reasonable size at the cluster selection level. This discussion leads to the conclusion that we should select a large number of clusters and a small number of elements within each cluster in order to have the best statistical efficiency.

But what about total efficiency? It does have a role to play. The more clusters we select, the more lists of elements we have to prepare, the more geographic areas we have to send interviewers to, the more administrative complications we will have to deal with. All these factors increase the cost of the study, so the final sample design involves a trade-off between statistical efficiency and cost. There is no optimal choice available. The researcher must make this trade-off based on the objectives of the study, the amount of money available, and the amount of error that is acceptable. The accuracy of this type of sampling is clearly noted in the accuracy of presidential election polling. Every election using this approach has been correctly predicted. Its usefulness to marketers is illustrated by the Marketing Research in Action entitled "Lou Harris Selects a Sample for STP."

Equal-Probability Area Sampling

Earlier we defined probability sampling as a technique in which each element has a known chance of being selected. In all the types of sampling discussed so far, except disproportionate statistical sampling, each element has had an equal chance of being selected. This is the easiest way to ensure that the sample selected represents the population. In this section we shall discuss how we obtain equal probabilities for each element. Later in the chapter we shall discuss sampling with unequal probabilities for the elements.

There are two ways to assure equal-chance selection of elements in an area sample.

1 Equal-Chance Selection of Clusters—Equal-Proportion Selection of Elements within Clusters   In this method each cluster is given an equal chance of selection regardless of size; then the same proportion of the elements is selected from within each cluster. Thus, each element has an equal chance of being selected. To illustrate, suppose we have 1000 elements divided into 50 clusters of different sizes. If we select a sample of 5 clusters, each cluster has a $\frac{5}{50}$ chance of being selected. If we then select one-fifth of the elements within each cluster, the total probability of an element being selected is

$$\frac{5}{50} \times \frac{1}{5} = .1 \times ? = .02$$

In this way bigger clusters have more elements selected. This balances the fact that these clusters had only as high a chance of being selected as smaller clusters. This process would require a sample size of .02 × 1000 = 20 elements. Note that for equal-probability sampling, the probability of an element being selected is equal to the sampling fraction. In this case $^{20}/_{1000}$ = .02.

More typically we would have a specified sample size and would be asked to select the number of clusters and proportion of elements within each cluster. A number of combinations of numbers of clusters and within-cluster proportions could accomplish this task. For example, the following combinations yield a probability of selection of .02:

$$10 \text{ clusters and } \frac{1}{10} \text{ of the elements} = \frac{10}{50} \times \frac{1}{10}$$

$$= .2 \times .1 = .02$$

$$20 \text{ clusters and } \frac{5}{100} \text{ of the elements } = \frac{20}{50} \times \frac{5}{100}$$

$$= .4 \times .05 = .02$$

We can apply this procedure to multistage designs as long as we continue to select the elements at each stage with equal proportion. Let's use the Institute for Social Research design to illustrate this. Suppose that at stage 1 we selected 10 of the 74 "primary areas." These primary areas vary in size, so at stage 2 we select $\frac{2}{5}$ of the "sample location sections" in each primary area; each sample location section therefore has an equal probability of being selected equal to

$$\frac{10}{74} \times \frac{2}{5} = .14 \times .4 = .056$$

Now for stage 3, if we select a sample of "chunks" from each sample location section at the rate of $\frac{7}{400}$, each chunk will have an equal chance of being selected even if the sample location sections are of different sizes. If the stage 4 proportion to select "segments" is $\frac{1}{4}$ and the stage 5 proportion to select "housing units" is $\frac{1}{5}$, the probability of selecting any housing unit is

$$
\begin{array}{ccccccccccc}
\begin{array}{c}\text{House-}\\\text{hold unit}\\\text{probability}\end{array} & = & \begin{array}{c}\text{stage 1}\\\text{proportion}\end{array} & \times & \begin{array}{c}\text{stage 2}\\\text{proportion}\end{array} & \times & \begin{array}{c}\text{stage 3}\\\text{proportion}\end{array} & \times & \begin{array}{c}\text{stage 4}\\\text{proportion}\end{array} & \times & \begin{array}{c}\text{stage 5}\\\text{proportion}\end{array}
\end{array}
$$

$$= \frac{10}{74} \times \frac{2}{5} \times \frac{7}{400} \times \frac{1}{4} \times \frac{1}{5}$$

$$= .14 \times .4 \times .018 \times .25 \times .2$$

$$= .00005$$

In a household population of 70 million this design would require a sample size of $.00005 \times 70$ million $= 3500$. Of course, given a sample size of 3500 and a sampling fraction objective of .00005, we can adjust the proportions of sampling units selected at various stages as long as their product continues to equal .00005.

What makes this yield equal probability for each household is that we select an equal proportion within each cluster at each stage. Thus different-size clusters are automatically taken care of. Clearly, if we had selected the same number of sampling units at each stage, the household unit elements would have different probabilities—those from big clusters would have much less chance of being selected than those from small clusters. This process would yield equal probabilities for elements only if all clusters were the same size.

2 Probability Proportionate to Size   There is another method of obtaining equal element probabilities that is more statistically efficient than the equal-proportion method discussed above. In the equal-proportion method, a relatively small number of large clusters are selected, and thus the elements selected to represent all large clusters are selected from a few clusters. In response to this problem, the more recommended method of selecting first-stage clusters is the *probability proportionate to size (PPS)* method.

A two-stage PPS procedure would be done as follows: In the first stage of the method, each cluster would be assigned a chance of selection proportionate to the number of second-stage elements it contained, with the result that larger clusters would have a better chance of selection than small ones. Then in the second stage the same number of sampling units would be selected from each selected cluster. Thus a smaller proportion of elements would be selected from larger clusters than from small ones, with the result that the probability of all elements being selected at the second stage would be the same. As an illustration, suppose we have 10 city blocks as follows:

Block number	Number of households
1	10
2	20
3	30
4	10
5	100
6	30
7	70
8	30
9	50
10	50
Total households	400

The relevant probability proportionate to size for block B is

$$PPS_B = \frac{\text{number of households in block } B}{\text{total number of households}}$$

For block 1,

$$PPS_1 = \frac{10}{400} = .025$$

For block 9,

$$PPS_9 = \frac{50}{400} = .125$$

We mechanically select a PPS block sample by calculating the cumulative number of households and assigning random numbers in proportion to this cumulative distribution.

Block number	Number of households	Cumulative number of households	Associated random numbers
1	10	10	001–010
2	20	30	011–030
3	30	60	031–060
4	10	70	061–070
5	100	170	071–170
6	30	200	171–200
7	70	270	201–270
8	30	300	271–300
9	50	350	301–350
10	50	400	351–400
Total	400		

If we wanted a sample of three blocks, we would obtain three 3-digit random numbers between 001 and 400. Suppose we obtained the numbers 124, 302, and 027; our sample would be blocks 5, 9, and 2. We would then select five households from blocks 2, 5, and 9. The probabilities of selecting elements are:

Probability of element in block B
$$= \text{block probability} \times \text{within-block element probability}$$

$$\text{For elements in block 2} = \frac{20}{400} \times \frac{5}{20}$$

$$= .05 \times .25$$

$$= .0125$$

$$\text{For elements in block 5} = \frac{100}{400} \times \frac{5}{100}$$

$$= .25 \times .05$$

$$= .0125$$

$$\text{For elements in block 9} = \frac{50}{400} \times \frac{5}{50}$$

$$= .125 \times .1$$

$$= .0125$$

The stage 1 and stage 2 probabilities balance each other to give equal probability of selection for all elements. The same result also holds for the unselected blocks.

In a multistage area sample we can use the PPS method for the first two stages to ensure equal probabilities to that point. Then we can select equal proportions from that point on to yield equal probabilities of all elements at the final stage. For example, if we really had a five-stage area sample and used PPS as in the example above, the element probability at the final stage might be:

Element probability = probability after 2 stages × probability at other stages

$$= .0125 \times .018 \times .50 \times .3$$

$$= .00003$$

PPS is used to help ensure that large clusters are represented in the sample. Alternatively, this may be done by stratifying the first-stage cluster by size and sampling within clusters. PPS and stratification on size would not be used together.

The STP/Lou Harris Marketing Research in Action notes the selection of geographic areas with probability proportionate to size. This is an often-used approach in practice.

Unequal-Probability Area Sampling

In all the probability sampling methods discussed so far, except disproportionate stratified sampling each population element had an equal chance of selection. Recall that in our original definition of probability sampling each element only needed a known chance of being selected to be a probability procedure. Often in area sampling, elements are selected disproportionately; that is, elements have different probabilities of being selected. The research may yield unequal probabilities for a number of reasons, including:

1 Wanting to do detailed subgroup analysis, the researcher purposely oversamples a small subgroup to have a large enough sample to do meaningful analysis for that group. Such a subgroup might be a specific ethnic group.

2 The researcher is doing disproportionate stratified sampling to reduce within-stratum and overall sampling error.

3 A sample yields a smaller proportion of a particular subgroup than the population proportion.

4 A PPS design requires knowledge of cluster sizes. If these sizes turn out to be incorrect, the result is that the cluster will be given a disproportionately high or low probability of being selected.

Thus, we may obtain unequal probabilities for element selection from a number of deliberate or accidental happenings. They present no problems as long as the researcher is interested in doing only within-subgroup analysis. Suppose, for example, we were estimating the weekly gasoline consumption among undergraduate and graduate students in our population of 50 students. If we took a sample of 10 from each subgroup, the graduate students would have a probability of selection of $^{10}/_{20} = .5$, and the undergraduates $^{10}/_{30} = .33$. Note that the overall sampling fraction $^{20}/_{50} = .4$ does not equal the probability of each element being selected. This relationship now holds only within the subgroups. Suppose we estimated the average gasoline consumption of graduate students as $^{100}/_{10} = 10$ gallons per week, and of undergraduates as $^{50}/_{10} = 5$ gallons per week. Those estimates are valid, and we can compare them with each other. However, if we combine the subgroups to make an overall estimate, the higher consumption of graduate students would be overrepresented, thus biasing the estimate upward. This average is

$$\bar{X}_{gasoline} = .5(10) + .5(5)$$
$$= 5 + 2.5$$
$$= 7.5$$

What we want is to have the weights reflect the subpopulation sizes. So the unbiased estimate is

$$\bar{X}_{gasoline} = .4(10) + .6(5)$$
$$= 4 + 3$$
$$= 7$$

You will recognize these weights as the population proportions from the stratified sampling section. This example was easy because we knew all about the subpopulation sizes. More realistically, we are likely to know the probability of selecting an element from subgroups. Can we use element probabilities directly to obtain proper weights? The answer is yes.

The rule is that an element should be assigned a weighting factor *in proportion to the inverse of its probability of being selected.*

In our gasoline example,

1 For graduate students:

Probability of selection $= .5$

Inverse $= \dfrac{1}{.5} = 2.0$

2 For undergraduate students:

Probability of selection $= .33$

Inverse $= \dfrac{1}{.33} = 3.0$

With this information there are two ways to obtain our overall average of 7 gallons. The first is to multiply the total gallons in each subgroup and the number in the sample in each subgroup by their respective inverses, and then take the average. Here we get the results shown below.

Graduates:

$$100 \text{ gallons} \times 2 = 200$$

$$10 \text{ students} \times 2 = 20$$

Undergraduates:

$$50 \text{ gallons} \times 3 = 150$$

$$10 \text{ students} \times 3 = 30$$

$$\text{Total gallons} = 200 + 150 = 350$$

$$\text{Total students} = 20 + 30 = 50$$

$$\text{Average gallons} = \frac{350}{50} = 7$$

The 50 is called the *weighted sample size.* The alternative is to convert the inverses to proportions with respect to each other, and then take a weighted average, as follows:

$$\text{Graduate inverse} = 2$$

$$\text{Undergraduate inverse} = 3$$

$$\text{Total of inverses} = 5$$

$$\text{Proportion graduate} = \frac{2}{5} = .4$$

$$\text{Proportion undergraduate} = \frac{3}{5} = .6$$

You will recognize these as our population weighting factors.

The latter method is much preferred for large studies with small subgroup sampling fractions. For example, if three subgroups had probabilities of element selection of .00005, .000047, and .000052, the respective inverses would be 20,000, 21,277, and 19,231. Multiplying by these weights is certainly more complicated than taking their proportions, which are .33, .35, and .31. Note that in equal-probability sampling each element would be assigned the same weight, as the inverses would be equal. This, of course, is as it should be.

Weighting can be handled in a number of ways. If we have our data on computer cards, we can simply duplicate cards for various subgroups to bring them up to the proper proportions. In our gasoline example, we would reproduce the graduate cards twice and the undergraduate ones three times. This method will do for small jobs but is impossible for large ones. Fortunately, most good computer data analysis packages have procedures in which the researcher can specify weighting factors. The analysis program then automatically includes them as part of the analysis.

Statistical Inference and Complex Sampling Procedures

Statistical inference was developed on the basis of simple random sampling. Can it be meaningfully applied to samples of the complexity we have seen in this chapter? The evidence leads us to believe that it can. Frankel's significant study in this area concluded that (1) the sample estimates were approximately unbiased, (2) the sample variances of these estimates were approximately unbiased, and (3) the calculated standard error allowed for the calculation of valid confidence intervals.[4]

You should now be able to outline the design of a sampling plan to meet your objectives. For the complexities of statistical inference in these complex designs, consult a technical specialist.

RANDOM-DIGIT DIALING

Within the context of all the probability sampling procedures discussed in Chapters 14 and 15, there is a very important procedure for actually selecting a sample element that needs to be understood. This procedure is *random-digit dialing.* It has become increasingly important with the growing dominance of telephone interviewing as a means of contacting respondents. An advantage of this procedure is that it allows contact with people who have unlisted numbers, who have moved since the directory was printed, or whose number is in error in the telephone directory. One possible drawback is that it can overcount homes with multiple phone lines, a now rare but growing phenomenon.

In a pure form, all seven digits of a telephone number can be generated randomly. However, this is both costly and inefficient, as many unused numbers are generated. What is more common in practice is that numbers are selected from a telephone directory using a systematic sampling procedure, and then the last one or two digits of these numbers are replaced with random numbers. This procedure gives a much higher percentage of used telephone numbers and has the properties of a true probability sample.

This procedure can be used with any of the probability sampling methods discussed so far. Let's use an area sampling context as an example. Looking back at Figure 15-2, we could use random-digit dialing in the context of a multistage area sample as follows: (1) proceed exactly as described in Figure 15-6 down as far as the sample location level which gives you a city or town, (2) obtain the telephone directories for the selected cities or towns and systematically select a sample of telephone numbers from the directories, (3) replace the last one or two

---

[4]Martin R. Frankel, *Inference from Survey Samples: An Empirical Investigation* (Ann Arbor: Survey Research Center, Institute for Social Research, University of Michigan, 1971), pp. 104–116.

digits of these selected numbers with random numbers, and (4) call the resultant numbers.

The STP/Lou Harris Marketing Research in Action notes the utilization of this random-digit-dialing approach. About 60 percent of businesses use random-digit dialing, as noted in Figure 15-7.

SAMPLE SIZE

The selection of a sample size in the more complex sampling procedures discussed in this chapter involves a trade-off among the same factors discussed in Chapter 14. If we use the concept of statistically optimal sample size as part of this decision process, there is one modification that must be made. While we must make a precision and confidence level designation and apply the formula for size of standard error, the formula for standard error differs in stratified and area sampling from that of simple random sampling. Be careful to use the right formula.

INTERNATIONAL SAMPLE SELECTION

There are special difficulties in selecting samples in some counties, as was mentioned in Chapter 13. This is especially true in the selection of the types of complex probability samples discussed in this chapter.

The more difficult problems arise from the lack of the needed census demographic data and the lack of adequate lists from which to draw samples. In all but the most developed nations, census track and census block data, along with telephone directories, street housing guides, and detailed demographic data, are often not available to the marketing researcher. For example, in almost all of the

FIGURE 15-7   Use in practice of random-digit dialing. (*Source:* Thomas C. Kinnear and Ann R. Root, *A Study of the Marketing Research Business*, unpublished study, 1994. Copyright 1994 Thomas C. Kinnear. Not to be reproduced.)

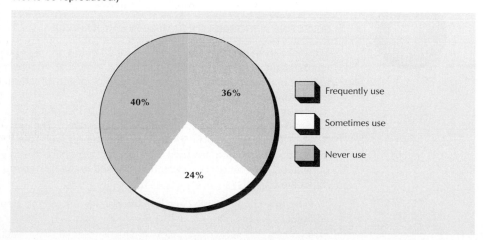

Middle East, in South America, and in Mexico, accurate street maps are unavailable. In some Asian cities, maps do not identify street names or house numbers. In contrast, such data are readily available in Japan and in Nationalist China.

The absence of these types of data makes the selection of probability-based area samples virtually impossible. In addition, the absence of the required knowledge about characteristics of the population prevents both the use of stratified samples and the selection of samples with probability proportionate to size.

Proper sample selection is also hampered in some countries by a poor telephone system, the lack of penetration of phones to households, and a poor transportation system that prevents interviewers from reaching areas of the country easily. A probability sample of the population in such circumstances is impossible. Thus, marketing researchers in these types of countries rely on a combination of probability samples, where they are possible, and quota and judgment samples.

As an example, the difficulties of sample selection in the Middle East are illustrated in the Global Marketing Research Dynamics.

MANAGERIAL SUMMARY OF SAMPLING

To end this section on sampling, we shall present a brief summary of some of the dimensions of various sampling procedures. Table 15-3 is the heart of this summary. It presents comparisons among a census and various sampling procedures on a number of dimensions. The first is the ability of the procedure to generate a measure of sampling error, and the second is the related concept of statistical efficiency. The third dimension is the need for a list of population elements in order to draw the sample, the fourth is the cost of the procedure, and the fifth is the frequency of use in practice. A manager should consider all these aspects when choosing a sampling procedure.

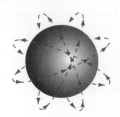

GLOBAL MARKETING RESEARCH DYNAMICS

SELECTING A PROBABILITY SAMPLE IN SAUDI ARABIA

The management of Saudi Aramco—a joint venture in oil exploration, refining, and retail distribution—was interested in doing a tracking study of Saudi consumer attitudes about the image of the company, and of customer satisfaction levels in regard to the company's retail service.

The managers contracted with the Cairo-based office of a major international marketing research firm to undertake this research. The research firm and Saudi Aramco agreed that, insofar as possible, the samples selected should reflect the total Saudi adult population. In attempting to select a probability sample of the adult Saudi population, the marketing researcher assigned to the task encountered the following difficulties:

• No official or reliable census of the population and the associated census tracks and blocks existed.

TABLE 15-3 MANAGERIAL SUMMARY OF SAMPLING

Dimensions	Nonprobability samples					Probability samples				
	Census	Convenience	Judgment	Quota	Simple random	Stratified	Systematic	Area
1 Generation of sampling error	No	No	No	No	Yes	Yes	Yes	Yes
2 Statistical efficiency	Very high	—No measurement—			The level compared to	High when stratification variables work	Somewhat low	Low
3 Need for population list	Yes	No	No	No	Yes	Yes	Not necessary in all applications	Only for selected clusters
4 Cost	Very high	Very low	Low	Moderate	High	High	Moderate	Moderate to high
5 Frequency of use in practice	Low	53%	49%	86%	90%	85%	49%	52%

- No private listings of households existed.
- Maps of cities and towns were notoriously inaccurate, and often were years out of date.
- Telephone directories were incomplete, inaccurate, and out of date.
- Voter registration lists were nonexistent.

Source: Based upon Cecil Tuncalp, "The Marketing Research Scene in Saudi Arabia," *European Journal of Marketing,* vol. 22, no. 5, pp. 15–22, 1988.

SUMMARY

1 Stratified sampling allows for the reduction of the standard error over simple random sampling.

2 To select a stratified sample, divide the population into mutually exclusive and collectively exhaustive strata, and then select a probability sample from each stratum. The strata are designed to be more homogeneous than the total population.

3 A proportionate stratified sample is one in which the sample size is allocated to strata in proportion to the number of population elements in the strata.

4 Sample elements may also be allocated on a basis disproportionate with the population size of strata. The objective here is to oversample the strata with the higher variability in order to reduce the standard error within the strata.

5 The overall mean in stratified sampling is the weighted average of the within-strata means. The weighting factor is the ratio of the stratum population size to total population size, $N_{st.j}/N$ or W_j.

6 The overall standard error is the square root of the weighted combination of the square of the standard error within each stratum. The weighting factor is the square of the W_j. The standard error is smaller than with simple random sampling because we use only within-stratum variation to calculate the overall standard error.

7 The number of possible stratified samples is the product of the number of all possible samples within each stratum.

8 For a stratification variable to be useful, it must be correlated with the variable we are measuring.

9 In cluster sampling we randomly select a cluster or group of sampling units at one time. To do this the population is divided into mutually exclusive and collectively exhaustive groups.

10 These groups are designed to be as heterogeneous as the population.

11 Statistical efficiency involves the comparison of the standard errors of different sampling procedures.

12 Overall efficiency involves the comparison of the standard error per dollar spent.

13 In systematic sampling, we select every kth element in the frame, after a random start somewhere within the first k elements.

14 The sampling interval equals N/n and is equal to the number of possible samples in a systematic procedure.

15 A frame with a cyclical pattern that coincides with a multiple of the size of the sampling interval will yield biased results in systematic sampling.

16 A systematic sample of a frame ordered on a stratification variable yields a proportionate stratified sample.

17 Area sampling involves selecting pieces of geography.

18 A multistage area sample involves the repeated process of listing sampling units and selecting a probability sample from this list.

19 A multistage sample will have equal probability of the selection of each element if the selection at each stage involves a given proportion of sampling units. The probability of element selection equals the product of the individual proportions.

20 Alternatively, equal element probability can be obtained by selecting the first-stage sampling units with probabilities proportionate to size, and then selecting the same number of second-stage sampling units in each selected first-stage unit.

21 Elements may be selected with unequal probabilities.

22 With disproportionate sampling, the elements must be weighted before meaningful total-sample analysis can be done.

23 An element should be assigned a weighting factor in proportion to the inverse of its probability of being selected.

24 Random-digit dialing is a method of drawing a probability sample for telephone interviewing. In practice, it usually involves drawing a systematic sample of telephone numbers from phone directories and then replacing the last one or two digits of these selected numbers with random numbers.

DISCUSSION QUESTIONS

1 How is a stratified sample selected?
2 What is the objective of stratified sampling?
3 What is proportionate stratified sampling?
4 What is disproportionate stratified sampling?
5 How are the whole-sample mean and the standard error calculated from a stratified sample?
6 Under what circumstances does stratified sampling reduce the standard error?
7 Why does stratified sampling reduce the standard error?
8 What is cluster sampling?
9 What are statistical efficiency and overall efficiency?
10 How is a systematic sample selected?
11 What is periodicity? How is it caused and cured?
12 How does implicit stratification occur?
13 What is area sampling?
14 What is multistage area sampling?
15 How do you get equal probability of element selection using a multistage area sampling procedure?

16 Why do you sometimes get unequal probabilities of element selection?

17 How are whole-sample estimates made when elements have unequal selection probabilities?

18 Outline the steps in random-digit dialing.

For questions 19 through 21 prepare a sampling design. Be sure to have your design include a description of each of the following items, and a statement of your reasoning.

  a The population

  b The sampling frame

  c The sample size

  d The sampling procedure (be sure to include a step-by-step description of how the sample will actually be drawn)

  e A method for determining the accuracy of sample results.

19 Frank Jackson was the director of student services in the business school of a major university. He wanted to conduct a survey of both B.B.A. and M.B.A. students to determine their attitudes toward course offerings, counseling services available, and job opportunities. There were a total of 3000 B.B.A. students and 700 M.B.A. students in the business school. Since a census was not possible, Frank needed to develop a sampling design.

20 Sara Ranski is a consultant to the World Church Council. One information need of the council is to develop a demographic profile of church members in the United States. Ranski has been asked to develop a sampling design to facilitate the collection of this information.

21 Roy Lena was the product manager for a new brand of cereal, named Multi-Vit, that was currently under development by a major packaged goods company located in New York City. The product offered vitamins and other nutrients not available in other cereals. Lena was in the process of designing an in-home usage test for the product. The object of the test was to measure the reaction of adults to the product's taste. Results of this test would be used to further refine the product before it was submitted to additional in-home and market tests. The problem facing Lena was to design the sample for the in-home placement test.

22 For the STP/Lou Harris Marketing Research in Action, answer the following questions:

  a What sampling units were defined by this procedure? What were the sampling frames?

  b Why was stratification used?

  c What purpose was there in selecting cities or towns with probability proportionate to census estimates of their respective household populations? How could this be accomplished?

  d What alternative sampling procedures could be used here?

23 For the AT&T Marketing Research in Action at the beginning of this chapter:

  a Why was the sample selected from a stratified population?

  b Why was the sample size over 2600? Is this the appropriate sample size for this study?

24 MINICASE

For Case 4-1, the Milan Food Cooperative (A) case, the population mean for weekly food expenditures is $43.20. Select the samples listed below from these data, and estimate the mean weekly food expenditures and the associated confidence interval.

Use Table A-1 in the Appendix at the end of the book to obtain random numbers.
a Simple random sample, $n = 10$
b Simple random sample, $n = 30$
c Stratified sample, $n = 10$
d Systematic sample, $n - 10$
e Convenience sample, $n = 10$
f Quota sample, $n = 10$
What conclusions can you draw about each of these sampling methods?

APPENDIX   Statistical Concepts for More Complex Sampling Procedures

PART A. CALCULATION OF SAMPLE STATISTICS WITHIN STRATA

In Chapter 14 we calculated the mean, the variance, and the standard deviation of the total sample without stratification. There,

$$\bar{X} = 22.6 \qquad s^2 = 8.3 \qquad \text{and} \qquad s = 2.88$$

Now we calculate the mean, the variance, and the standard deviation within each stratum. For stratum 1,

$$\bar{X}_{st.1} = \frac{\sum\limits_{i=1}^{n_{st.1}} X_i}{n_{st.1}}$$

$$= \frac{25 + 26}{2}$$

$$= \frac{51}{2}$$

$$= 25.5$$

To find $s^2_{st.1}$ using our computational formula, we calculate

$$\sum X^2_{st.1} = (25)^2 + (26)^2 = 625 + 676 = 1301$$

and

$$\frac{(\sum X_{st.1})^2}{n} = \frac{(51)^2}{2} = \frac{2601}{2} = 1300.5$$

$$s^2_{st.1} = \frac{1301 - 1300.5}{1}$$

$$= .5$$

$$s_{st.1} = .71$$

For stratum 2,

$$\bar{X}_{st.2} = \frac{22 + 21 + 19}{3}$$

$$= \frac{62}{3}$$

$$= 20.7$$

$$\sum X^2_{st.2} = (22)^2 + (21)^2 + (19)^2$$

$$= 484 + 441 + 361$$

$$= 1286$$

$$\frac{(\sum X_{st.2})^2}{n} = \frac{(62)^2}{3}$$

$$= \frac{3844}{3}$$

$$= 1281.3$$

$$s^2_{st.2} = \frac{1286 - 1281.3}{2}$$

$$= \frac{4.7}{2}$$

$$= 2.35$$

$$s_{st.2} = 1.53$$

PART B. STATISTICAL ASPECTS OF STRATIFIED SAMPLES

The Number of Possible Samples

The sampling fraction in stratum 1 was $\frac{2}{20} = .1$, and in stratum 2 it was $\frac{3}{30} = .1$. Both of these sampling fractions are identical to the sample we selected in Chapter 14, $\frac{5}{50} = .1$. Under both stratified and unstratified procedures each population element had an equal chance, .1, of being selected. However, with stratified sampling *not all possible combinations of elements are equally likely.* To illustrate, we shall use a population of elements identified as A, B, C, D, and E. This, of course, is the population that yielded 10 possible simple random samples of size 2. Now assume that elements A and B are from one stratum, while C, D, and E are from another. Again we wish to draw a sample of $n = 2$, but this time we restrict the sample to one element from each stratum. The possible sample element from stratum 1 is either A or B, and within stratum 2 it is C, D, or E. Combining possible elements from each stratum, we get the possible samples:

Sample number	Elements in sample
1	AC
2	AD
3	AE
4	BC
5	BD
6	BE

There are 6 possible samples with stratification, and 10 without. The possible samples that have been eliminated are those that could occur within one stratum before; for example, AB and CD are no longer possible as samples. Note that it is these within-strata means that are the outliers of our distribution of means in simple random sampling. To illustrate this result, we may assign scores to these population elements as follows:

Element	Score
Stratum 1	
A	1
B	2
Stratum 2	
C	3
D	4
E	5

The mean of this distribution of scores is $15/5 = 3.0$. The possible stratified samples of $n = 2$ are

Sample elements	Sample mean
AC	$(1 + 3)/2 = 2.0$
AD	$(1 + 4)/2 = 2.5$
AE	$(1 + 5)/2 = 3.0$
BC	$(2 + 3)/2 = 2.5$
BD	$(2 + 4)/2 = 3.0$
BE	$(2 + 5)/2 = 3.5$

These sample means cluster reasonably tightly about the true mean of 3.0.

Now we examine the mean values generated by samples that are not allowed to occur in this example of stratified sampling, that is, the within-stratum sample means. These means are

Sample elements	Sample mean
Stratum 1	
AB	$(1 + 2)/2 = 1.5$
Stratum 2	
CD	$(3 + 4)/2 = 3.5$
CE	$(3 + 5)/2 = 4.0$
DE	$(4 + 5)/2 = 4.5$

These means are less well clustered about the mean of 3.0, that is, they are the outliers on the distribution of means. In our age example, we get means like 26, 27, and so on, in stratum 1, or like 20 or 21 in stratum 2. These types of means are not as likely when we combine elements from different strata, as we do when we estimate the means with a stratified procedure. Removal of some outliers in stratified sampling would thus decrease the variability of the distribution of sample means. That is, the standard error becomes smaller. Not all combinations of elements are equally likely. This is one aspect that distinguishes stratified sampling from simple random sampling. Note that the number of possible samples with stratification is the product of the number of all possible samples within each stratum. In our example the formula with two strata is

$$\text{Number of possible samples} = C\,(N, n)_{st.1} \cdot C\,(N, n)_{st.2}$$

$$= C(2, 1) \cdot C(3, 1)$$

$$= \frac{2!}{1!\,1!} \cdot \frac{3!}{1!\,2!}$$

$$= 2 \cdot 3 = 6$$

In our student age example, the number of possible samples with stratification is

$$C(20,2) \quad C(30,3) - \frac{20!}{2! \, 18!} \cdot \frac{30!}{3! \, 27!}$$

$$= \frac{20 \cdot 19}{2 \cdot 1} \cdot \frac{30 \cdot 29 \cdot 28}{3 \cdot 2 \cdot 1}$$

$$= 190 \cdot 4{,}060$$

$$= 771{,}400 \text{ possible samples}$$

In Chapter 14 we noted that there were over 2 million possible simple random samples of size 5 in a population of 50. The number of possible samples has decreased substantially, although it is still very large. Further, once again the sampling distribution of the means of these samples will form a normal curve. The standard error will be smaller than with simple random sampling, as we previously noted in our calculations. Thus, we can again calculate a legitimate confidence interval.

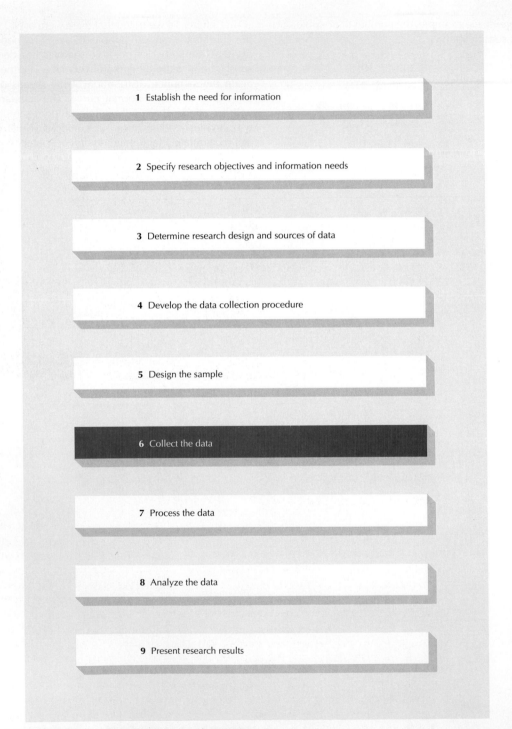

1 Establish the need for information

2 Specify research objectives and information needs

3 Determine research design and sources of data

4 Develop the data collection procedure

5 Design the sample

6 Collect the data

7 Process the data

8 Analyze the data

9 Present research results

FIGURE 16-1   Steps in the research process.

CHAPTER 16

FIELD OPERATIONS

MARKETING RESEARCH IN ACTION

BAD DAY AT TWELVE PINES MALL

Darlene O'Hara was a field interviewer for Field Interviewing Services, Inc., of Denver, Colorado. She was an experienced telephone interviewer. However, her current assignment to do in-person interviews in the Twelve Pines Mall was her first real "field" interviewing experience. The client for the interviewing assignment was a large regional discount department store. The target quota sample included a broad range of age and income groups, both sexes, and different geographic distances from the mall. Her target was to complete 50 interviews for the day.

Upon arrival at the mall at 10 A.M. on Saturday, Darlene was surprised to find the local high school band setting up for a concert in the center courtyard of the mall. Once the concert began at 10:30, Darlene had difficulty obtaining high school-age people to participate in the study. Most were attending the band concert.

At 12:30 P.M. a group of 20 animal rights picketers set up in front of the main department store in the mall to protest the sale of furs by this store. The media were also present to tape the protest, which drew a large crowd. Unfortunately, this was the location that Darlene had found to be most effective for obtaining respondents for her survey. After a while, the police arrived in force to disperse the crowd. During this period, Darlene completed few interviews.

At 3 P.M., the forecasted heavy snowstorm for the Denver area began. The mall began to empty a great deal, except for the groups of teenagers that called the mall their gathering place. Darlene had difficulty getting those shoppers who were in a hurry to get home to stop and be interviewed; even those who did stop were reluctant to complete the interviews once they were started. She resisted the temptation to finish these partially completed questionnaires herself. It was a new feeling for her.

At 5 P.M. the snow had let up and the crowd at the mall had picked up again. In order to get at least some of her respondents quota cells filled, Darlene actively sought out people who appeared to her to be "happy" in their shopping, and for whom she thought she would have empathy. Thus her "women" cells began to fill up fast. She enjoyed talking to these women and relished the freedom to chat with them that was not allowed in the telephone interview. The men she tried to interview seemed uncooperative, and she "forced" them to complete the questionnaire by taking "short forms" of some of the questions. At 7 P.M. Darline called it a day, having completed 31 interviews.

The opening Marketing Research in Action illustrates some of the problems that arise in the real world of field work. This chapter is concerned with the proper approach to this all-important area. If the data are not obtained properly, all else is not of much consequence.

The methods of collecting data and the design of data collection forms have been discussed in the previous two chapters. This chapter completes the section on collecting data from respondents by discussing field operations.

The field operation is that phase of the project during which researchers make contact with the respondents, administer the data collection instruments, record the data, and return the data to a central location for processing. The wisdom behind the research design and the skill involved in developing the data collection instrument will be wasted if the field operation is poorly administered. An important source of error in the research process can be identified with the field operation.

The planning of the field operation is highly influenced by the data collection method employed; for example, the field operation for a personal interview study is substantially different from that for a mail interview study. However, given these differences, there are some basic issues that are common to all field operations.

This chapter will first discuss the common issues in planning and controlling field operations. Next, the more specific aspects of field operations associated with alternative data collection methods will be introduced. The last part of the chapter will be devoted to the sources of error in field operations and the presentation of various guidelines for controlling these errors.

PLANNING FIELD OPERATIONS

Four aspects of planning are common to all field operations: (1) time schedule, (2) budget, (3) personnel, and (4) performance measurement.

Start

Time Schedule

Every project must have a time schedule specifying (1) when the project is to begin and end and (2) the sequencing of activities within this time frame. The number of days needed to complete various activities must be estimated and the degree of overlap among activities determined. It is very important that realistic time periods be established so that the project can be completed in a reasonable amount of time. Often target completion dates are set which do not realistically reflect the time required to carry out field operations properly. Attempts to cut corners to reach unreasonable completion dates can be costly and decrease the accuracy of the results.

Figure 16-2 presents a detailed time schedule for a personal interview study. Experience suggests that those activities for which time requirements are most likely to be underestimated are the final approval and printing of the questionnaire, the selection of interviewers, the evaluation of the pretest, and the cleanup in the field. It is best to leave room in the schedule for inaccurate time estimates and unforeseen events.

Budget

The budget involves the assignment of costs to specific activities identified in the field time schedule. The budget and the time schedule are closely interrelated. In

FIGURE 16-2   Field time schedule flow diagram.

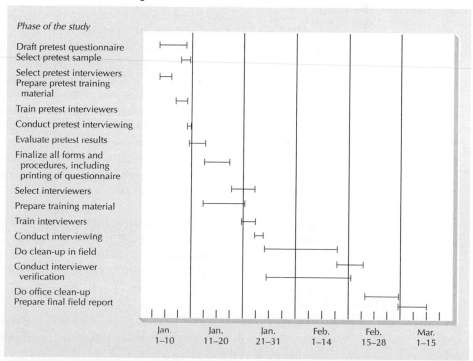

most cases they are prepared together, since changes in one can result in changes in the other.

The main cost categories for a personal interview study are (1) office wages and salaries, (2) materials and supplies, (3) telephone, (4) field supervisors or interviewing services, (5) interviewers' compensation, and (6) reproduction of questionnaires and other field forms. These cost categories can be further segmented and assigned to the stages of the data collection process: (1) pretest, (2) selection and hiring of interviewers, (3) interviewer training, (4) final field reports, and (5) data collection.

Effective budgeting and cost control requires a detailed breakdown of the major cost categories into their smallest components. Specific categories need to be reviewed to see whether the costs have been underestimated, and a reserve fund is needed for unforeseen contingencies. Finally, the budget should be reviewed and possibly approved by those individuals responsible for carrying out the activities associated with the cost category.

Personnel

The success of the field operation depends on the quality of the personnel used to execute the plans. Skilled personnel are required, along with the clear assignment of responsibility for all aspects of the plan, if completion dates are to be met and costs controlled. Finally, the personnel must clearly understand what is expected of them and how this performance will be measured.

Performance Measurement

To control activities and accomplish objectives, clear performance measures are required. Too often, the number of interviews to be completed is the only measure clearly specified for a study, yet it is just as important to specify the number of expected refusals, noncontacts, and other noninterviewing situations. Table 16-1 presents these performance measures in a format in which expected results can be compared to actual results. The ratios presented at the bottom of the table are used to derive the figures in the body of the table. These ratios can be determined by pretest results and/or the past experience of the researcher.

The totals in Table 16-1 should be broken down by region, interviewing agency, supervisor, and other categories useful for control purposes. The personnel responsible for accomplishing the expected results should participate in determining whether they are reasonable.

Most research projects exceed their initial research budgets. The causes are changes in the research design, poor time scheduling, and inaccurate budget estimates. Upon the completion of a study, the final costs should be compared to the budget so that future budget estimates can be more accurate.

DATA COLLECTION METHODS

This section presents those aspects of field operations which differ according to whether personal interview, telephone interview, mail interview, or observation is used to collect the data.

TABLE 16-1   STUDY PERFORMANCE MEASURES: EXPECTED AND ACTUAL

Performance measure	Expected	Actual
1 Total eligible respondents	___	___
1.1 Interviews	___	___
1.2 Refusals	___	___
1.3 Noncontacts (assumed eligible)	___	___
1.4 Other (specify)		
2 Total ineligible respondents	___	___
2.1 Moved	___	___
2.2 Other (specify)	___	___
3 Total sample	___	___
Response rate (1.1 ÷ 1)	___	___
Refusal rate (1.2) ÷ (1.1 + 1.2)	___	___
Contact rate [(1 − 1.3) ÷ 1]	___%	___%
Eligibility rate (1 ÷ 3)	___%	

Personal Interview

The use of interviewers in a face-to-face setting presents special problems relating to their selection, training, and supervision. Researchers have three options in this regard—they can use their own research organization, contract with an outside field work agency, or do both. No matter which option is chosen, sufficient time and money must be assigned to this very expensive and complicated aspect of the field operation.

Finding qualified interviewers is a difficult task. First, the researcher must specify the job qualifications needed for the project. Next, applicants must be located, screened, and hired in those geographic locations required by the sampling plan. Typically, outside field work organizations are hired to conduct the interviewing. These organizations maintain contact with interviewers and have files on their qualifications.

Once the interviewers are selected, they must be trained. The objective of training is to establish a high degree of commonality in the data collection process among interviewers. Because of time constraints and geographic dispersion in the sampling plan, most training programs consist of written instructions to the interviewer covering areas such as the purpose of the study, how to carry out the sampling plan, and how to approach the respondent, establish rapport, ask the questions, and the like. For complex studies, the training may be conducted by supervisors in person at one or more central locations.

The pretest results should provide valuable insights into the nature and extent of the training required. It is important to allot enough time in the schedule for adequate training.

Following the training program, the interviewer begins the interviewing process. During this process there should be constant monitoring to determine whether the interviewer is adhering to plans. Completed interviews need to be inspected for completeness, accuracy, neatness, and so on. If the work of an interviewer is unsatisfactory, retraining or dismissal may be required.

How should the interviewer be compensated—hourly or by the interview? The common answer is to pay by the hour, since an incentive pay scheme may cause the interviewer to rush through the interview and seriously reduce the quality of the data gathered. This could be reflected in cheating or falsification of interviews, failure to ask all the questions, and failure to probe answers adequately.

The argument for an incentive pay scheme, where personnel are paid per interview, is that the interviewers can earn more money by planning their activities more efficiently. It is argued that target completion dates are reached more often and that the quality of data collected can be higher if only those interviews which meet specified standards are acceptable for payment. The important element in the successful use of the incentive pay scheme appears to be the extensive use of controls.

Finally, the success of the field work is dependent on the skill and experience of the field supervisor. The competence of a new supervisor should be checked by contacting previous clients, and only the highest-quality supervisors should be used in field work.

Telephone Interview

Most of the issues involved in the selection, training, and supervision of personal interviewers apply equally well to telephone interviewers. This is particularly the case if the telephone interviews are to be conducted from several geographic locations. However, if they are to be conducted from a central location, the ability to control the field work closely becomes an important distinguishing factor. The entire interviewing process can be directly monitored and the quality of the interview evaluated. Poor-quality interviewing can be detected early and corrected. In addition, problems resulting in a delay in the interviewing time schedule can be detected immediately and, one hopes, corrected.

Delays in the interviewing time schedule usually are attributed to (1) an inadequate population list, (2) a higher rate of callbacks required than planned, and (3) interviews taking longer than expected because of questionnaire length and/or complexity. Problems of this nature typically result from inadequate pretesting of the questionnaire and the data collection process.

A major budget item is the phone calls, especially if WATS lines are not available.

Mail Interview

The mail interview is distinguished from other data collection methods in that more aspects of the data collection process are under the central control of the researcher. This is because of the elimination of the interviewer from the field operation. Consequently, mail surveys are more likely to meet time schedules and stay within budgets than other data collection methods.

The time schedule should classify activities into phases, such as (1) drafting the questionnaire, (2) pretesting, (3) questionnaire finalization and production, (4) first mailing, (5) second or third mailing if used, (6) check of nonrespondents, and (7) data collection from a subsample of nonrespondents. The experience of the researcher is the key to developing realistic time schedules for mail surveys.

Computer-Based Interviewing

Computer-based interviewing is primarily used in computer-aided telephone interviewing (CATI). However, it is increasingly being used also in personal interviews and in mail surveys. (For example, Sawtooth Software's Ci3 system is an excellent commercial package for computer-based interviewing.) For personal interviews, a laptop computer is utilized by the interviewer at the site of the interview. For mall-intercept interviews this is easy, as the computer does not need to be transported. However, with very lightweight computers, it is possible to do in-person interviews at the respondents' location without great difficulty. Computer-based mail surveys are possible now due to the large number of personal computers available to certain target samples. Here, a computer disk is mailed to the respondent, who answers the questionnaires using his or her own personal computer. The answers are automatically stored on the disk as the respondent answers the questions. The disk is then returned to the sender. This is a technique that has attained some use, especially for samples of executives and industrial personnel.

There are interviewing advantages, plus data processing and data analysis advantages, of computer-based interviewing. We will discuss the latter two in Chapter 17. The interviewing advantages are: (1) quicker interviews; (2) higher-quality interviews, as certain human errors such as wrong skipping patterns are eliminated; (3) the ability to rotate or randomize brand or attribute lists; (4) control over the numbers in the cells of a quota sample, as the computer will not accept a response if the quota cell is full; (5) the ability to generate random-digit phone numbers; (6) the ability to personalize questions for respondent characteristics; (7) control of proper skip patterns; (8) the ability to refer to or insert a previous answer; (9) the provision of consistency checks among answers, which yields more truthful responses; (10) the ability to instantly identify responses that are out of the allowable range, either by the respondent's answer or by the interviewer's recording, as the computer will not accept these responses; and (11) the capacity to apply a computer security system to the answers.

There are also some disadvantages to computer-based interviewing. These are: (1) open-ended questions are not easily usable, as responses are difficult to record quickly; (2) response mistakes by interviewers are still possible for answers within the range allowed by the question; (3) there is an up-front investment required to prepare the questionnaire for the computer; (4) there is significant cost for computers and interviewer training; (5) there is risk of computer failure, thus requiring the repeating of interviews; and (6) when disks are mailed to respondents, there is a need for compatible equipment (the disk-drive size and density, for example, are elements that must be compatible).

Computer-based interviewing in action.

The Marketing Research in Action describes the benefits derived by Hallmark Cards in the use of computer-based interviewing.

MARKETING RESEARCH IN ACTION

HALLMARK CARDS DERIVES BENEFITS FROM COMPUTER-BASED INTERVIEWING

Hallmark Cards engages in extensive research to make certain that its cards remain up to date. Until 1988, the company's researchers performed studies via personal interviews using pencil and paper. These studies, with sample sizes of 200, took 35 days to perform and analyze. In 1988, Hallmark executives requested that the research department perform 23,000 interviews. This was five times as many interviews

Results of surveys aid Hallmark in highly competitive greeting card market.

as the department had completed in 1985. Hallmark decided to switch to computer-assisted interviewing in order to save time (and money).

In order to assess the differences between the two methods, Hallmark conducted three studies by both the traditional method and the computer method. Computer interviews required only 18 minutes to complete when respondents were answering an interviewer's questions; the interviews took 28 minutes if the respondents answered the computer questionnaire on their own. The computer automatically tracked responses to make sure that the respondent had evaluated each card and warned the interviewer if an invalid number was entered as a response.

At Hallmark, computer-based interviewing decreased the amount of time needed to complete a study and improved the quality of the data. It also provided consumers with a quick and painless research experience. All of these benefits improved marketing manager's decisions.

Source: Adapted from Diane L. Pyle, "How to Interview Your Customers," *American Demographics,* pp. 44–45, December 1990.

Observation

The nature of the plans for observation field operations depends on the complexity of the research design and whether personal or mechanical recording is to be used. When field personnel are to be used, the previous discussion regarding personal interviews applies here. When mechanical recording is to be used, special problems are presented. The budget and time schedule must consider the equipment costs, setup time, maintenance, breakdown, and the like.

ERRORS IN FIELD OPERATIONS

The validity of research results is directly related to the number and size of sampling and nonsampling errors. This section describes sources of error connected with field operations. Previous sections of the book have discussed sampling and nonsampling errors as they relate to other aspects of the research process.

The main sources of error to be discussed here are (1) sample selection errors, (2) nonresponse errors, and (3) interviewing errors.

Sample Selection Errors

The chapters on sampling have discussed the quota sampling procedure. It was noted that this nonprobability sampling procedure is very common in marketing research and requires the interviewer to select the individuals to be included in the study, subject to various quotas specified in the sampling plan. This interviewer control of the sample selection process is likely to result in respondent selection error.

Despite formal quotas and procedures for sample selection, interviewers will sometimes try to bend or falsify rules and select respondents who are most convenient or who offer the least resistance. For quotas on economic levels, interviewers tend to focus on the middle-income levels and to avoid high- and low-income respondents.

Probability sampling procedures that appear to eliminate interviewer sample selection errors still contain the potential for error. The interviewer usually participates in the probability procedure used to identify the list of dwelling units, to select the dwelling unit, and to select the individual to be interviewed in the unit. In listing dwelling units, interviewers tend to underlist low-income blocks. Random selection procedures for selecting from the list are typically biased by the interviewer in favor of middle-income dwellings. Within the dwelling unit, interviewers tend to select the more accessible persons in the unit.

Nonresponse Errors

Nonresponse error, described in detail in Chapter 11, refers to the difference between those who respond to a survey and those who do not respond. It can be one of the most serious sources of error confronting the researcher. We will briefly build on the earlier discussion of the topic and emphasize its importance to field operations.

Nonresponse can result from two sources: (1) not-at-homes and (2) refusals. The nonresponse problem appears to be increasing. In the 1960s, researchers obtained response rates of 80 to 85 percent using three or four callbacks, but in the 1990s response rates dropped to 60 to 65 percent. The nonresponse is equally divided between not-at-homes and refusals.

The most common procedure for increasing the response rate is to make callbacks. The cost of a callback program can be reduced by the use of the telephone and/or the self-administered questionnaire. The telephone can be used to contact respondents and make appointments for the personal interview. When appropriate, self-administered questionnaires with stamped, self-addressed envelopes can be left at the dwellings of all not-at-homes.

Interviewing Errors

With the personal and telephone interview, the interviewer can be a serious source of errors. These errors are related to (1) interviewer-respondent rapport, (2) asking the questions, (3) recording responses, and (4) cheating.

Interviewer-Respondent Rapport   An interview involves a social interaction between two people. During this interaction, the respondent's perception of the interviewer can directly affect the latter's ability to establish proper rapport. Interviewers who can establish effective relationships with respondents are able to collect more complete and accurate data.

With the personal interview, the interviewer's style of dress should resemble that of the respondent. The interviewer's dress and grooming are important in establishing rapport in that they are regarded by most people as indications of a person's attitudes and orientation. The demeanor of the interviewer should be pleasant, if nothing else.

As a general rule, the more the interviewer and respondent have in common, the greater the opportunity for rapport. Basically, the respondent should see the interviewer as capable of understanding his or her viewpoint.

Asking the Questions   Guidelines appropriate for most interviewing situations have been developed and are briefly outlined in this section.

1 Be thoroughly familiar with the questionnaire   The interviewer must study the questionnaire carefully, question by question, and practice reading it aloud. Each question must be read without error or stumbling over words and phrases. The interviewer's role resembles that of an actor reading lines in a play or motion picture. The questions must be read naturally and conversationally.

2 Ask the questions exactly as they are worded in the questionnaire   Researchers have found that even a slight change in wording can distort results. The interviewer must be sensitive to inadvertent changes in a question, such as leaving out part of a question, changing a word, or adding a few words at the end of the question for conversational purposes.

3 Ask the questions in the order in which they are presented in the questionnaire   In the design of the questionnaire, the question sequence was established to ensure that questions early in the sequence will not bias the answers to questions later in the sequence. In addition, the question sequence was designed from the respondent's perspective to create a sense of continuity in the topic covered.

4   Ask every question specified in the questionnaire   The respondent's answer to one question may answer another question later in the questionnaire. In this situation, the interviewer should never skip the question which appears to have been answered earlier. It is the interviewer's responsibility to ask every question, even when it has clearly been answered previously. This can be done by letting the respondent know that the interviewer is aware of the earlier response and is asking the respondent's cooperation in answering again. The interviewer might say, for example: "We have already touched on this, but let me ask you. . . ."

5   Use probing techniques to get the respondent to answer the question   The questions have been designed to be understood by all respondents in the sampling plan. However, at times the interviewer may find respondents who misunderstand or misinterpret what is asked, who are reluctant to give a complete answer, or who get sidetracked onto another topic in answering the question. The quality of the data collected depends upon the interviewer's skill in overcoming these problems through the use of *neutral* probing techniques.

Probing techniques are intended to perform the following two functions without introducing bias: (a) to motivate the respondents to communicate more fully so that they can enlarge on, clarify, or explain the reasons behind what is said; and (b) to help the respondent focus on the specific content of the interview so that irrelevant or unnecessary data can be avoided.

There are several kinds of neutral probing techniques that may be used to stimulate a fuller, clearer response:

a *Repeating the question.* A very effective approach is to repeat the question just as it is written in the questionnaire. Typically, further probes are unnecessary.

b *Pausing expectantly.* The interviewer's silence or pause is an effective cue to the respondent that a more complete response is expected. This is often difficult for new interviewers to do.

c *Repeating the respondent's reply.* Respondents often are stimulated to make further comments if they hear their thoughts repeated. This can be done while the interviewer is recording the comments on the questionnaire.

d *Reassuring the respondent.* If the respondent appears hesitant to respond, it may be helpful to use a comment such as "We're just trying to get people's ideas on this" or "There are no right or wrong answers, just your ideas on it." If the respondent needs an explanation of a word or phrase, the interviewer should not offer a definition; rather, the responsibility for the definition should be returned to the respondent. This might be done as follows: "Just whatever it means to you— anything you would call. . . ."

e *Asking neutral questions or making neutral comments.* Several examples of the most commonly used probes and their "key word" phrases or abbreviations are presented in Table 16-2. The standard abbreviations are to be recorded on the questionnaire in parentheses next to the question asked. The new interviewer will

TABLE 16-2   COMMONLY USED PROBES

Interviewer's probe	Standard abbreviation
Repeat question	RQ.
Anything else?	AE or Else?
Any other reason?	AO?
How do you mean?	How mean?
Could you tell me more about your thinking on that?	Tell more.
Would you tell me what you have in mind?	What in mind?
What do you mean?	What mean?
Why do you feel that way?	Why?
Which would be closer to the way you feel?	Which closer?

find it useful to have a copy of Table 16-2 available for easy reference during the interview.

f *Asking for further clarification.* Asking the question "I'm not quite sure I know what you mean by that; could you tell me a little more?" can arouse the respondent's desire to cooperate with the interviewer who appears to be trying to do a good job. It is often effective to appear somewhat bewildered by the respondent's answer when asking this question.*

In summary, effective probing requires that the interviewer recognize immediately just how the respondent's answer has failed to meet the objectives of the specific question. Next, the interviewer must be able to select an appropriate probing technique to elicit the data required by the question. Each question should have instructions indicating how forcefully the interviewer should probe.

6 Keep track of changes made in the questionnaire   If the interviewer makes any changes—even inadvertent ones—in the wording, phrasing, or order of questions, they should be clearly noted on the questionnaire. This allows the researcher to analyze the potential bias and decide how the data should be coded.

7 Provide a logical reason for collecting personal data   If the respondent asks why the interviewer needs to know age, religion, income, and the like, the following explanation could be used:

Well, as I was saying earlier, we are talking with people of different ages and various occupations in all parts of the country. We put all of the interviews together, and then count them up to see whether men feel differently from women, whether young people feel differently from older people, and so on. To do this we need to know a few things about the people we talk to. So I have just a few questions on that type of thing.

Recording Responses   Even though an error-free job of asking questions has been accomplished, the next concern is recording the data in an unbiased form that can be interpreted accurately by the coders. Each interviewer must use the

*Interviewer's Manual, rev. ed. (Ann Arbor: Survey Research Center, Institute for Social Research, University of Michigan, 1976), pp. 15–16.

same format and conventions in recording the interviews and in editing each completed interview.

Rules for Recording Responses   The interviewer should record not only what was said but also how it was said. The recording method should transmit a picture of the respondent's personality and the interview situation. The following six rules are designed to aid in accomplishing this type of recording:

1 Record responses during the interview.
2 Use the respondent's own words.
3 Do not summarize or paraphrase the respondent's answers.
4 Include everything that pertains to the question objectives
5 Include all probes and comments by entering them next to the questions in parentheses.
6 Hold the respondent's interest by repeating the response as it is written down.

Tips on Note Taking   The skill of note taking is developed with practice. Practice by recording the comments of friends or by recording news broadcasts. Keep in mind the following:

1 When you start the interview, try to find a place where you will be able to write comfortably.
2 When the respondent starts to talk, begin to write immediately.
3 Abbreviate words and sentences. During the editing process, put these in along with punctuation.

Mechanics of Recording and Editing Interviews   These procedures are suggested to facilitate the recording and editing process.

1 Use a pencil to record.
2 Write legibly.
3 Use parentheses to indicate the interviewer's words or observations.
4 Do not put anything the respondent says in parentheses.
5 During editing, cross-reference the responses to one question that also apply to other questions.
6 For each question, record either an answer or an explanation of why it was not answered.
7 Make sure the identification data are complete—name, date, interviewer number, project number, and the like.

Cheating   What is cheating? In practice, it is hard to define. Obviously, the personal interviewer who sits at home and fills out the questionnaire is cheating. More frequently, cheating is defined as the falsification of a question or questions within the questionnaire. This type of cheating is extremely difficult to detect. Phone calls to respondents to determine whether personal interviews took place will not detect partial falsifications of questionnaires. The monitoring of phone interviews is an effective way to control cheating with the telephone interview.

INTERNATIONAL FIELD OPERATIONS

In Chapter 15 we outlined some of the difficulties of selecting samples in certain parts of the world. There are similar problems in implementing field operations in various parts of the world. These problems include the lack of efficient phone systems; the lack of penetration of phones in the population; the need for more supervision of interviewers, in countries where lack of experienced interviewers is the norm; the difficulties of interviewing in regions of a country that are not very accessible; the desire to give answers that will please the interviewer, in certain cultures; the unwillingness to reveal true attitudes in cultures where this has been historically dangerous; and the absence of computer and scanning types of technology. The Global Marketing Research Dynamics insert gives examples of these types of issues.

GLOBAL MARKETING RESEARCH DYNAMICS

THIS FIELD WORK IS NOT LIKE OMAHA!

Listed below are examples of difficulties in field operations that have arisen in the implementation of marketing research by various firms:

- A multinational study of consumer attitudes toward "green" marketing practices was designed to be implemented in the field by phone. The study countries included Australia, Canada, the UK, Israel, Norway, France, Germany, Italy, Japan, and Singapore. In Norway the penetration of phones in households was about 35 percent. Thus, the attempt to implement phone field work in Norway resulted in nonrepresentative results.
- A study of laundry product usage was implemented in Europe and in North Africa. In certain Muslim countries of North Africa, it was considered inappropriate and a religious affront to speak to women as they were shopping.
- A major U.S.-based interviewing company expanded its mall intercept interviewing approach into Europe. In France, with the exception of a few major cities, there were very few malls in which to implement the firm's standard approach.
- In Singapore all interviewing of its citizens must be approved by a government agency. This hurt the timeliness of survey results and limited the amount of data that could be collected.
- A marketing research firm in Pakistan implemented a telephone survey. The absence of computer hardware and advanced computer-assisted software in Pakistan slowed down the process and reduced the accuracy of the results.

SUMMARY

1 Four areas are common to planning all field operations: (a) time schedules, (b) budgets, (c) personnel, and (d) performance measurement. The time schedule specifies when the project is to begin and end, and also the sequencing of activities within this time period. The budget involves the assignment of costs to the specific activities identified in the time schedule. Skilled personnel are required, along with the clear assignment of responsibility for activities, if completion dates are to be met and costs controlled. Finally, clear performance measures are required if activities are to be controlled and objectives met.

2 Field operations differ according to whether personal interview, telephone interview, mail interview, or observation is used to collect data. When interviewers are used to collect the data, they must be selected, trained, and supervised, which involves time-consuming and expensive activities. When telephone interviews are conducted from a central location, the ability to control the interviewing activity closely is an important distinction from personal interviewing. With the mail interview, the elimination of the interviewer from the data collection process allows the centralization of the field operation directly under the researcher's control. When observers are used in observational studies, the nature of the field operation is similar to that of the personal interview study. If mechanical recording is to be used, special problems are presented for field operations.

3 The main sources of error in field operations relate to (a) sample selection errors, (b) nonresponse errors, and (c) interviewing errors. The more control the interviewer has over who will be interviewed, the greater the opportunity for sample selection error. Nonresponse error refers to the difference between those who respond and those who do not. Nonresponse can result from (a) not-at-homes and (b) refusals. The callback procedure is most commonly used to increase the response rate.

4 The major sources of interviewing error occur in the areas of (a) interviewer-respondent rapport, (b) asking the questions, (c) recording errors, and (d) cheating.

5 For the new interviewer, guidelines are available regarding the process of asking questions and recording answers. These guidelines, combined with practice sessions, will be useful in improving the new interviewer's skills and reducing interviewing errors.

DISCUSSION QUESTIONS

1 What four areas are important in the planning of field operations?
2 What are the problems peculiar to the use of the personal interview in field operations?
3 Evaluate the use of the telephone interview in field operations.
4 What are the main sources of error in field operations?
5 What is nonresponse error?
6 How can the interviewer contribute to measurement error?
7 What guidelines should an interviewer be given regarding the asking of questions?

8 **MINICASE**

For each of the examples in the Global Marketing Research Dynamics, outline an approach to field work that will address the problems.

CASES FOR PART FOUR

CASE 4-1 Milan Food Cooperative (A)

Joyce Lauchner was the general manager of the Milan Food Cooperative (MFC). She had become concerned of late that she had lost touch with the buying patterns of the cooperative members. MFC just seemed so big now compared to the early days. She wondered whether she could make use of some data that were already available to her to increase her understanding of the members' purchasing habits. She hoped that she could use this knowledge to better plan the mix and quantity of goods that MFC carried.

BACKGROUND OF MFC

The MFC was founded in 1974 by Lauchner and a small group of volunteers. It had grown from 10 original members in January 1974 to 500 members in September 1994. It was located in an old warehouse on the northwest side of Milan, Michigan. Milan was a community of 7500 people located in southeast Michigan, about 40 miles southwest of Detroit. MFC drew membership from a number of communities around Milan, including Ann Arbor and Monroe.

The objective of MFC was to provide high-quality food products at prices below those available at local supermarkets. To accomplish this, MFC used shipping cartons as shelves, required shoppers to mark their own prices on goods, carried only the best-selling brands, and generally did not offer the "luxuries" associated with traditional supermarkets. To shop at MFC one had to be a member. The membership fee was $25 per year. Any profits earned by MFC in a year were returned to the members as credits against purchases. Lauchner thought that the members bought most of their food at MFC.

Lauchner's Concerns

In the early days of MFC Lauchner had prided herself on knowing all its members. She had spent a great deal of time in the store and felt she knew what people were buying and how much they were spending. As the membership grew, her administrative duties kept her in her office much more. She no longer knew all the members, nor did she have a good feel for their expenditure patterns. She wanted to develop a better understanding of these aspects of her business and thought perhaps some of the data that had already been collected on the membership might provide answers.

The Available Data

In June 1994 a questionnaire was used to collect data on the membership. During the month all members came into the cooperative at least once. Thus, data were available on all members. The data consisted of demographic characteristics of the members plus their weekly food expenditures.

The data were available on the cards that were filled out by the members at the time of the interview. Lauchner had these cards in a filing cabinet in her office. A description of the contents of the cards is presented in the next section. Actual card values are tabulated in Table 1.

As a first step in understanding the membership, Lauchner wanted to know members' average weekly expenditure on food. Since time was short, she wanted to do this without having to look at all 500 cards. However, she also wanted the average she calculated to be an accurate one. She wondered how she could make an accurate calculation.

MFC DATA

Explanation of Items A–K in Table 1 (the Variables)

A = household identification number (1–500)

B = weekly food expenditure, actual (e.g., $37.50)

C = number of persons in household, actual (1–9)

D = annual income of household, actual (e.g., $17,500)

E = education of head of household coded into five categories (1–5)

F = age of head of household, actual (e.g., 38)

G = weekly food expenditure, coded into seven categories (1–7)

H = any children under 6 years old in household, actual (1–2)

I = any children 6–18 years old in household, actual (1–2)

J = annual income of household, coded into six categories (1–6)

K = age of head of household, coded into seven categories (1–7)

Category Definitions for Variables

Variable C   Number of persons in household.

1 = one person

2 = two persons

3 = three persons

4 = four persons

5 = five persons

6 = six persons

7 = seven persons

8 = eight persons

9 = nine or more persons

Variable E   Education of head of household.

1 = less than grade 8

2 = grades 9–11

3 = high school graduate

4 = some college

5 = college graduate

Variable G   Weekly food expenditures.

1 = less than $15

2 = $15–29.99

3 = $30–44.99

4 = $45–59.99

5 = $60–74.99

6 = $75–89.99

7 = $90 or over

Variable H   Any children under 6 years old in household.

1 = no

2 = yes

Variable I   Any children 6–18 years old in household.

1 = no

2 = yes

Variable *J* Annual income of household.

1 = less than $3,000

2 = $3,000–5,999

3 = $6,000–9,999

4 = $10,000–14,999

5 = $15,000–24,999

6 = $25,000 or over

Variable *K* Age of head of household.

1 = less than 25

2 = 25–34

3 = 35–44

4 = 45–54

5 = 55–64

6 = 65–74

7 = 75 or older

TABLE 1

A	B	C	D	E	F	G	H	I	J	K
1	12.00	1	2500	1	56	1	1	1	1	5
2	16.50	1	2800	1	70	2	1	1	1	6
3	18.00	1	2000	1	20	2	1	1	1	1
4	17.00	1	4500	1	60	2	1	1	2	5
5	46.50	1	8000	1	40	4	1	1	3	3
6	45.00	1	7000	1	51	4	1	1	3	4
7	15.00	1	3500	1	76	2	1	1	2	7
8	60.00	2	2800	1	20	5	1	1	1	1
9	15.00	2	2500	1	51	2	1	1	1	4
10	18.00	2	4000	1	32	2	1	1	2	2
11	22.50	2	5000	1	47	2	1	1	2	4
12	20.00	2	8000	1	35	2	1	1	3	3
13	97.00	2	5500	1	58	7	1	1	2	5
14	57.00	2	6000	1	27	4	1	1	3	2
15	39.00	2	3000	1	38	3	1	1	2	3
16	30.00	2	4000	1	40	3	1	1	2	3
17	42.00	2	3000	1	19	3	1	1	2	1
18	30.00	2	3000	1	50	3	1	1	2	4
19	30.00	2	6000	1	41	3	1	1	3	3
20	32.00	2	6500	1	34	3	1	1	3	2
21	33.00	2	13000	1	23	3	1	1	4	1
22	30.00	2	15000	1	34	3	1	1	5	2
23	37.50	2	22000	1	42	3	1	1	5	3
24	110.00	3	11000	1	43	7	1	2	4	3
25	53.00	3	6500	1	51	4	1	2	3	4
26	34.00	3	28000	1	50	3	1	2	6	4
27	27.00	4	4000	1	46	2	1	2	2	4
28	39.00	5	12000	1	56	3	1	2	4	5
29	67.50	7	11000	1	48	5	1	2	4	4
30	22.50	2	1900	1	40	2	2	1	1	3
31	7.50	3	2800	1	20	1	2	1	1	1
32	19.00	3	3200	1	24	2	2	1	2	1
33	22.50	4	5000	1	30	2	2	2	2	2
34	28.50	5	7000	1	33	2	2	2	3	2
35	34.50	5	10000	1	38	3	2	2	4	3
36	52.50	6	2500	1	37	4	2	2	1	3
37	58.00	8	10000	1	42	4	2	2	4	3
38	7.00	1	2500	1	19	1	1	1	1	1
39	26.00	1	500	1	68	2	1	1	1	6
40	15.00	1	2500	1	20	2	1	1	1	1
41	30.00	1	6000	1	34	3	1	1	3	2
42	25.50	1	6000	1	66	2	1	1	3	6
43	7.50	1	1500	1	67	1	1	1	1	6
44	12.00	1	1500	1	72	1	1	1	1	6
45	13.50	2	4000	1	28	1	1	1	2	2
46	18.00	2	2500	1	20	2	1	1	1	1
47	30.00	2	2500	1	21	3	1	1	1	1
48	12.00	2	500	1	26	1	1	1	1	2
49	15.00	2	1500	1	19	2	1	1	1	1
50	7.50	2	500	1	19	1	1	1	1	1
51	10.50	2	1500	1	33	1	1	1	1	2

TABLE 1 *Continued*

A	B	C	D	E	F	G	H	I	J	K
52	12.00	2	1500	1	36	1	1	1	1	3
53	15.00	2	500	1	30	2	1	1	1	2
54	20.00	2	2500	1	45	2	1	1	1	4
55	16.00	2	500	1	54	2	1	1	1	4
56	15.00	2	500	1	56	2	1	1	1	5
57	26.00	2	6200	1	26	2	1	1	3	2
58	15.00	2	1500	1	39	2	1	1	1	3
59	30.00	2	2500	1	21	3	1	1	1	1
60	22.00	2	2500	1	40	2	1	1	1	3
61	22.50	2	2500	1	48	2	1	1	1	4
62	24.00	2	2500	1	60	2	1	1	1	5
63	20.00	2	3500	1	23	2	1	1	2	1
64	11.00	2	500	1	26	1	1	1	1	2
65	16.50	2	2500	1	64	2	1	1	1	5
66	15.00	2	500	1	70	2	1	1	1	6
67	15.00	2	2500	1	31	2	1	1	1	2
68	30.00	2	6300	1	32	3	1	1	3	2
69	28.00	2	4500	1	44	2	1	1	2	3
70	30.00	2	6000	1	49	3	1	1	3	4
71	37.50	2	3500	1	35	3	1	1	2	3
72	60.00	2	3500	1	22	5	1	1	2	1
73	24.00	2	2500	1	28	2	1	1	1	2
74	7.50	2	2500	1	51	1	1	1	1	4
75	87.00	3	11000	1	69	6	1	1	4	6
76	30.00	3	6300	1	43	3	1	1	3	3
77	21.00	3	2500	1	33	2	1	1	1	2
78	120.00	3	8000	1	39	7	1	1	3	3
79	20.00	3	8500	1	58	2	1	1	3	5
80	22.50	3	2500	1	19	2	1	1	1	1
81	30.00	3	10000	1	33	3	1	1	4	2
82	40.00	3	6000	1	41	3	1	1	3	3
83	37.50	3	6000	1	47	3	1	1	3	4
84	30.00	4	4500	1	48	3	1	2	2	4
85	38.00	4	2500	1	55	3	1	2	1	5
86	60.00	4	6400	1	36	5	1	2	3	3
87	37.50	5	6000	1	57	3	1	2	3	5
88	75.00	6	4500	1	49	6	1	2	2	4
89	37.50	6	3500	1	32	3	1	2	2	2
90	75.00	4	5000	1	32	6	2	1	2	2
91	51.00	4	6000	1	44	4	2	2	3	3
92	75.00	4	4500	1	40	6	2	2	2	3
93	50.00	5	2500	1	29	4	2	2	1	2
94	39.00	5	6000	1	47	3	2	2	3	4
95	60.00	5	9200	1	58	5	2	2	3	5
96	37.50	5	8000	1	51	3	2	2	3	4
97	80.00	6	12000	1	43	6	2	2	4	3
98	30.00	6	3500	1	39	3	2	2	2	3
99	40.00	6	14000	1	39	3	2	2	4	3
100	75.00	6	4500	1	33	6	2	2	2	2
101	15.00	7	1500	1	49	2	2	2	1	4
102	100.00	7	6000	1	53	7	2	2	3	4

TABLE 1 *Continued*

A	B	C	D	E	F	G	H	I	J	K
103	30.00	9	2500	1	43	3	2	2	1	3
104	34.50	9	3500	1	60	3	2	2	2	5
105	60.00	1	8500	2	45	5	1	1	3	4
106	45.00	1	11000	2	45	4	1	1	4	4
107	51.00	1	15000	2	53	4	1	1	5	4
108	36.00	1	4000	2	42	3	1	1	2	3
109	37.50	1	4500	2	33	3	1	1	2	2
110	30.00	1	4200	2	59	3	1	1	2	5
111	15.00	1	2500	2	21	2	1	1	1	1
112	20.00	1	6000	2	64	2	1	1	3	5
113	7.50	1	500	2	69	1	1	1	1	6
114	10.00	1	1500	2	39	1	1	1	1	3
115	6.00	1	6000	2	26	1	1	1	3	2
116	15.00	2	2000	2	39	2	1	1	1	3
117	66.00	2	18000	2	62	5	1	1	5	5
118	20.00	2	10000	2	58	2	1	1	4	5
119	50.00	2	11000	2	38	4	1	1	4	3
120	57.00	2	13000	2	29	4	1	1	4	2
121	47.00	2	13000	2	60	4	1	1	4	5
122	48.00	2	12000	2	50	4	1	1	4	4
123	45.00	2	27000	2	40	4	1	1	6	3
124	15.00	2	4500	2	26	2	1	1	2	2
125	22.50	2	1500	2	24	2	1	1	1	1
126	52.50	2	2500	2	29	4	1	1	1	2
127	15.00	2	2500	2	31	2	1	1	1	2
128	20.00	2	8600	2	46	2	1	1	3	4
129	22.50	2	3500	2	30	2	1	1	2	2
130	30.00	2	6000	2	48	3	1	1	3	4
131	30.00	2	4500	2	36	3	1	1	2	3
132	37.50	2	6000	2	30	3	1	1	3	2
133	30.00	2	6000	2	70	3	1	1	3	6
134	30.00	2	3500	2	39	3	1	1	2	3
135	60.00	2	6200	2	44	5	1	1	3	3
136	50.00	2	6000	2	56	4	1	1	3	5
137	52.00	3	25000	2	59	4	1	1	6	5
138	15.00	3	4500	2	29	2	1	1	2	2
139	40.00	3	3500	2	46	3	1	1	2	4
140	50.00	3	17000	2	32	4	1	1	5	2
141	36.00	4	9000	2	73	3	1	1	3	6
142	30.00	4	6000	2	40	3	1	1	3	3
143	16.50	2	2800	2	59	2	1	2	1	5
144	40.00	2	3500	2	49	3	1	2	2	4
145	33.00	3	2500	2	47	3	1	2	1	4
146	40.00	3	3500	2	52	3	1	2	2	4
147	43.00	3	5000	2	48	3	1	2	2	4
148	44.00	3	6000	2	56	3	1	2	3	5
149	30.00	3	10000	2	24	3	1	2	4	1
150	68.00	4	9000	2	51	5	1	2	3	4
151	36.00	4	8000	2	38	3	1	2	3	3
152	45.00	4	6000	2	47	4	1	2	3	4
153	52.50	4	9900	2	58	4	1	2	3	5

TABLE 1   *Continued*

A	B	C	D	E	F	G	H	I	J	K
154	75.00	5	12000	2	50	6	1	2	4	4
155	28.00	5	6500	2	49	2	1	2	3	4
156	39.00	5	6000	2	61	3	1	2	3	5
157	37.50	5	6000	2	53	3	1	2	3	4
158	50.00	5	6000	2	42	4	1	2	3	3
159	54.00	5	8500	2	39	4	1	2	3	3
160	21.00	6	12500	2	48	2	1	2	4	4
161	37.50	6	11500	2	47	3	1	2	4	4
162	39.00	6	16000	2	50	3	1	2	5	4
163	90.00	6	6000	2	46	7	1	2	3	4
164	11.00	3	5000	2	46	1	2	1	2	4
165	36.00	3	2800	2	31	3	2	1	1	2
166	35.00	3	3900	2	20	3	2	1	2	1
167	37.50	3	8000	2	29	3	2	1	3	2
168	24.00	3	2500	2	23	2	2	1	1	1
169	30.00	3	17000	2	41	3	2	1	5	3
170	30.00	3	4500	2	37	3	2	1	2	3
171	55.00	4	13000	2	30	4	2	1	4	2
172	23.00	4	2500	2	53	2	2	1	1	4
173	27.00	4	2500	2	31	2	2	1	1	2
174	45.00	6	2500	2	33	4	2	1	1	2
175	45.00	7	2500	2	35	4	2	1	1	3
176	52.00	3	9000	2	38	4	2	2	3	3
177	30.00	3	3500	2	37	3	2	2	2	3
178	45.00	4	12000	2	30	4	2	2	4	2
179	45.00	4	8000	2	41	4	2	2	3	3
180	37.50	4	6000	2	45	3	2	2	3	4
181	45.00	4	4500	2	30	4	2	2	2	2
182	55.00	4	17000	2	34	4	2	2	5	2
183	25.00	4	4500	2	29	2	2	2	2	2
184	80.00	5	13000	2	36	6	2	2	4	3
185	100.00	5	12500	2	30	7	2	2	4	2
186	60.00	5	8700	2	37	5	2	2	3	3
187	37.50	5	3500	2	36	3	2	2	2	3
188	65.00	5	21000	2	40	5	2	2	5	3
189	35.00	5	4500	2	39	3	2	2	2	3
190	37.50	5	7500	2	28	3	2	2	3	2
191	27.00	6	13000	2	38	2	2	2	4	3
192	58.00	6	11000	2	39	4	2	2	4	3
193	42.00	6	7000	2	33	3	2	2	3	2
194	37.50	6	4500	2	40	3	2	2	2	3
195	40.00	6	6000	2	48	3	2	2	3	4
196	45.00	6	6000	2	32	4	2	2	3	2
197	73.00	7	12000	2	30	5	2	2	4	2
198	39.00	7	12500	2	42	3	2	2	4	3
199	53.50	7	8500	2	36	4	2	2	3	3
200	57.00	8	20000	2	39	4	2	2	5	3
201	42.00	8	22000	2	39	3	2	2	5	3
202	38.00	8	9000	2	38	3	2	2	3	3
203	45.00	8	6000	2	41	4	2	2	3	3

TABLE 1   *Continued*

A	B	C	D	E	F	G	H	I	J	K
204	52.50	9	6500	2	40	4	2	2	3	3
205	67.50	9	9500	2	45	5	2	2	3	4
206	75.00	9	500	2	05	6	2	2	1	3
207	63.00	1	4000	3	56	5	1	1	2	5
208	65.00	1	10000	3	59	5	1	1	4	5
209	45.00	1	2800	3	22	4	1	1	1	1
210	48.00	1	4500	3	24	4	1	1	2	1
211	57.00	1	5000	3	58	4	1	1	2	5
212	45.00	1	9000	3	36	4	1	1	3	3
213	45.00	1	25000	3	61	4	1	1	6	5
214	30.00	1	10000	3	36	3	1	1	4	3
215	37.50	1	14000	3	58	3	1	1	4	5
216	30.00	1	12000	3	29	3	1	1	4	2
217	30.00	1	12000	3	47	3	1	1	4	4
218	30.00	1	24000	3	32	3	1	1	5	2
219	60.00	1	3500	3	22	5	1	1	2	1
220	18.00	1	3500	3	29	2	1	1	2	2
221	20.00	1	4500	3	74	2	1	1	2	6
222	22.50	1	2500	3	20	2	1	1	1	1
223	30.00	1	6800	3	53	3	1	1	3	4
224	72.00	2	7000	3	30	5	1	1	3	2
225	67.50	2	10000	3	24	5	1	1	4	1
226	65.00	2	12000	3	54	5	1	1	4	4
227	60.00	2	17000	3	37	5	1	1	5	3
228	60.00	2	26000	3	66	5	1	1	6	6
229	45.00	2	18000	3	44	4	1	1	5	3
230	54.00	2	22000	3	42	4	1	1	5	3
231	48.00	2	18000	3	63	4	1	1	5	5
232	46.50	2	26000	3	50	4	1	1	6	4
233	42.00	2	13000	3	38	3	1	1	4	3
234	35.00	2	14000	3	59	3	1	1	4	5
235	37.50	2	10000	3	61	3	1	1	4	5
236	30.00	2	11500	3	44	3	1	1	4	3
237	45.00	2	30000	3	40	4	1	1	6	3
238	30.00	2	9000	3	29	3	1	1	3	2
239	38.00	2	4500	3	23	3	1	1	2	1
240	40.00	2	18000	3	57	3	1	1	5	5
241	20.00	2	6000	3	21	2	1	1	3	1
242	22.50	2	7000	3	27	2	1	1	3	2
243	25.00	2	18000	3	41	2	1	1	5	3
244	20.00	2	9000	3	34	2	1	1	3	2
245	30.00	2	24000	3	60	3	1	1	5	5
246	37.50	2	11000	3	23	3	1	1	4	1
247	60.00	2	9000	3	59	5	1	1	3	5
248	22.50	2	27000	3	46	2	1	1	6	4
249	15.00	2	3500	3	22	2	1	1	2	1
250	30.00	2	4500	3	63	3	1	1	2	5
251	37.50	2	7000	3	25	3	1	1	3	2
252	40.00	2	3500	3	68	3	1	1	2	6
253	45.00	2	15000	3	54	4	1	1	5	4

TABLE 1 *Continued*

A	B	C	D	E	F	G	H	I	J	K
254	37.50	2	26000	3	34	3	1	1	6	2
255	45.00	2	17000	3	26	4	1	1	5	2
256	30.00	3	10000	3	50	3	1	1	4	4
257	45.00	3	14000	3	49	4	1	1	4	4
258	37.50	3	4500	3	62	3	1	1	2	5
259	18.00	3	7000	3	58	2	1	1	3	5
260	60.00	3	8000	3	31	5	1	1	3	2
261	45.00	3	8000	3	43	4	1	1	3	3
262	37.50	3	4500	0	27	3	1	1	2	2
263	37.00	3	6000	3	27	3	1	1	3	2
264	40.00	4	28000	3	39	3	1	1	6	3
265	45.00	4	19000	3	67	4	1	1	5	6
266	60.00	4	11000	3	59	5	1	1	4	5
267	30.00	4	6500	3	33	3	1	1	3	2
268	45.00	4	10000	3	68	4	1	1	4	6
269	50.00	4	6000	3	76	4	1	1	3	7
270	60.00	3	16000	3	40	5	1	2	5	3
271	20.00	3	2600	3	38	2	1	2	1	3
272	55.00	3	10000	3	45	4	1	2	4	4
273	50.00	3	10000	3	50	4	1	2	4	4
274	33.00	3	9000	3	40	3	1	2	3	3
275	33.00	3	11000	3	48	3	1	2	4	4
276	45.00	3	19000	3	49	4	1	2	5	4
277	18.00	3	6000	3	32	2	1	2	3	2
278	37.50	3	15000	3	50	3	1	2	5	4
279	45.00	3	8000	3	43	4	1	2	3	3
280	70.00	3	8800	3	58	5	1	2	3	5
281	67.50	4	10000	3	47	5	1	2	4	4
282	69.00	4	15000	3	34	5	1	2	5	2
283	120.00	4	13500	3	48	7	1	2	4	4
284	45.00	4	12000	3	33	4	1	2	4	2
285	42.00	4	10000	3	40	3	1	2	4	3
286	30.00	4	14000	3	49	3	1	2	4	4
287	39.00	4	10000	3	46	3	1	2	4	4
288	36.00	4	12000	3	57	3	1	2	4	5
289	39.00	4	12000	3	43	3	1	2	4	3
290	37.50	4	6000	3	28	3	1	2	3	2
291	45.00	4	18000	3	49	4	1	2	5	4
292	37.50	4	6000	3	31	3	1	2	3	2
293	45.00	4	6000	3	54	4	1	2	3	4
294	25.00	4	6000	3	29	2	1	2	3	2
295	50.00	4	8000	3	34	4	1	2	3	2
296	40.00	4	17000	3	38	3	1	2	5	3
297	54.00	4	20000	3	45	4	1	2	5	4
298	45.00	4	6000	3	39	4	1	2	3	3
299	60.00	4	8000	3	56	5	1	2	3	5
300	45.00	4	8000	3	49	4	1	2	3	4
301	45.00	4	15000	3	41	4	1	2	5	3
302	35.00	4	8000	3	33	3	1	2	3	2
303	80.00	5	11000	3	49	6	1	2	4	4

TABLE 1 *Continued*

A	B	C	D	E	F	G	H	I	J	K
304	55.00	5	13000	3	48	4	1	2	4	4
305	37.50	5	10000	3	48	3	1	2	4	4
306	55.00	5	20000	3	42	4	1	2	5	3
007	35.00	5	2500	3	49	3	1	2	1	4
308	52.50	5	15500	3	34	4	1	2	5	2
309	80.00	6	14000	3	49	6	1	2	4	4
310	86.00	6	10000	3	56	6	1	2	4	5
311	110.00	6	13000	3	52	7	1	2	4	4
312	95.00	7	19000	3	39	7	1	2	5	3
313	45.00	7	6000	3	49	4	1	2	3	4
314	60.00	8	21000	3	44	5	1	2	5	3
315	67.50	9	15000	3	47	5	1	2	5	4
316	18.00	3	2500	3	27	2	2	1	1	2
317	47.00	3	11000	3	32	4	2	1	4	2
318	50.00	3	14000	3	29	4	2	1	4	2
319	45.00	3	16000	3	28	4	2	1	5	2
320	36.00	3	12000	3	28	3	2	1	4	2
321	30.00	3	6000	3	22	3	2	1	3	1
322	67.50	3	12000	3	24	5	2	1	4	1
323	22.50	3	6000	3	23	2	2	1	3	1
324	26.00	3	2500	3	32	2	2	1	1	2
325	27.00	3	3500	3	25	2	2	1	2	2
326	45.00	3	6000	3	35	4	2	1	3	3
327	30.00	3	10000	3	19	3	2	1	4	1
328	35.00	3	8000	3	30	3	2	1	3	2
329	52.50	3	8000	3	27	4	2	1	3	2
330	55.00	3	6000	3	20	4	2	1	3	1
331	35.00	3	20000	3	32	3	2	1	5	2
332	51.00	4	4000	3	24	4	2	1	2	1
333	37.50	4	12000	3	32	3	2	1	4	2
334	30.00	4	13000	3	30	3	2	1	4	2
335	75.00	4	8000	3	26	6	2	1	3	2
336	40.00	4	6000	3	22	3	2	1	3	1
337	37.50	4	4500	3	27	3	2	1	2	2
338	21.00	4	7000	3	30	2	2	1	3	2
339	30.00	4	6000	3	29	3	2	1	3	2
340	22.50	4	9500	3	28	2	2	1	3	2
341	67.50	4	14000	3	25	5	2	1	4	2
342	60.00	4	8000	3	33	5	2	1	3	2
343	87.00	5	14000	3	33	6	2	1	4	2
344	45.00	5	14000	3	29	4	2	1	4	2
345	50.00	5	9000	3	31	4	2	1	3	2
346	48.00	6	6000	3	38	4	2	1	3	3
347	60.00	7	4500	3	29	5	2	1	2	2
348	90.00	4	14000	3	34	7	2	2	4	2
349	45.00	4	14000	3	35	4	2	2	4	3
350	54.00	4	12500	3	30	4	2	2	4	2
351	37.50	4	17500	3	30	3	2	2	5	2
352	33.00	4	4500	3	29	3	2	2	2	2
353	72.00	5	14000	3	36	5	2	2	4	3

TABLE 1   *Continued*

A	B	C	D	E	F	G	H	I	J	K
354	51.00	5	11000	3	35	4	2	2	4	3
355	36.00	5	14500	3	36	3	2	2	4	3
356	65.00	5	8000	3	32	5	2	2	3	2
357	60.00	5	16000	3	34	5	2	2	5	2
358	45.00	5	21000	3	40	4	2	2	5	3
359	45.00	5	7500	3	29	4	2	2	3	2
360	37.50	5	6000	3	31	3	2	2	3	2
061	67.50	5	6000	3	36	5	2	2	3	3
362	39.00	5	8000	3	40	3	2	2	3	3
363	45.00	5	3500	3	37	4	2	2	2	3
364	37.50	5	4500	3	46	3	2	2	2	4
365	24.00	6	8500	3	38	2	2	2	3	3
366	42.00	6	13000	3	39	3	2	2	4	3
367	60.00	6	6000	3	35	5	2	2	3	3
368	40.00	6	6000	3	41	3	2	2	3	3
369	37.50	6	6000	3	33	3	2	2	3	2
370	60.00	6	6000	3	38	5	2	2	3	3
371	73.50	7	12000	3	38	5	2	2	4	3
372	105.00	7	20000	3	38	7	2	2	5	3
373	52.50	7	6000	3	36	4	2	2	3	3
374	35.00	7	3500	3	37	3	2	2	2	3
375	37.50	7	6000	3	31	3	2	2	3	2
376	50.00	7	7000	3	47	4	2	2	3	4
377	49.00	7	8000	3	44	4	2	2	3	3
378	60.00	8	6000	3	41	5	2	2	3	3
379	67.50	8	6000	3	47	5	2	2	3	4
380	45.00	8	4500	3	51	4	2	2	2	4
381	75.00	8	18000	3	36	6	2	2	5	3
382	52.50	8	9000	3	46	4	2	2	3	4
383	54.00	9	20000	3	45	4	2	2	5	4
384	50.00	9	2500	3	50	4	2	2	1	4
385	75.00	9	18000	3	49	6	2	2	5	4
386	52.50	9	8000	3	44	4	2	2	3	3
387	35.00	1	4000	4	71	3	1	1	2	6
388	30.00	1	5000	4	28	3	1	1	2	2
389	36.00	1	5000	4	36	3	1	1	2	3
390	18.00	2	13000	4	56	2	1	1	4	5
391	52.00	2	5000	4	35	4	1	1	2	3
392	53.00	2	11000	4	40	4	1	1	4	3
393	45.00	2	10000	4	45	4	1	1	4	4
394	25.00	2	15000	4	24	2	1	1	5	1
395	27.00	2	18000	4	34	2	1	1	5	2
396	15.00	2	4500	4	26	2	1	1	2	2
397	75.00	2	22000	4	41	6	1	1	5	3
398	25.00	2	2500	4	69	2	1	1	1	6
399	22.00	2	17500	4	58	2	1	1	5	5
400	58.00	3	14000	4	40	4	1	1	4	3
401	40.00	3	30000	4	47	3	1	1	6	4
402	37.00	3	8000	4	45	3	1	1	3	4
403	27.00	3	20000	4	60	2	1	1	5	5

TABLE 1 *Continued*

A	B	C	D	E	F	G	H	I	J	K
404	30.00	3	3500	4	59	3	1	1	2	5
405	50.00	3	4500	4	39	4	1	1	2	3
406	30.00	3	24000	4	62	3	1	1	5	5
407	75.00	3	6000	4	77	6	1	1	3	7
408	45.00	4	30000	4	52	4	1	1	6	4
409	55.00	3	28000	4	48	4	1	2	6	4
410	40.00	3	8000	4	23	3	1	2	3	1
411	60.00	3	22000	4	42	5	1	2	5	3
412	45.00	3	35000	4	44	4	1	2	6	3
413	60.00	4	14500	4	56	5	1	2	4	5
414	26.70	4	18000	4	54	2	1	2	5	4
415	51.00	4	11000	4	51	4	1	2	4	4
416	45.00	4	14500	4	56	4	1	2	4	5
417	57.00	4	10000	4	34	4	1	2	4	2
418	65.00	4	19000	4	47	5	1	2	5	4
419	115.00	4	3500	4	31	7	1	2	2	2
420	45.00	4	4500	4	55	4	1	2	2	5
421	60.00	4	9000	4	49	5	1	2	3	4
422	55.00	4	20000	4	41	4	1	2	5	3
423	75.00	4	22000	4	51	6	1	2	5	4
424	75.00	4	18000	4	33	6	1	2	5	2
425	48.00	4	17000	4	29	4	1	2	5	2
426	45.00	5	6000	4	31	4	1	2	3	2
427	52.50	5	8000	4	43	4	1	2	3	3
428	35.00	5	500	4	28	3	1	2	1	2
429	45.00	5	28000	4	36	4	1	2	6	3
430	52.50	5	4500	4	55	4	1	2	2	5
431	45.00	5	8000	4	48	4	1	2	3	4
432	135.00	6	22000	4	44	7	1	2	5	3
433	70.00	6	24000	4	44	5	1	2	5	3
434	60.00	6	24000	4	39	5	1	2	5	3
435	60.00	3	13000	4	33	5	2	1	4	2
436	51.00	3	10000	4	28	4	2	1	4	2
437	30.00	3	4000	4	32	3	2	1	2	2
438	53.00	3	8000	4	27	4	2	1	3	2
439	30.00	3	6000	4	23	3	2	1	3	1
440	70.00	4	14000	4	29	5	2	1	4	2
441	30.00	4	8000	4	28	3	2	1	3	2
442	37.50	4	4500	4	30	3	2	1	2	2
443	30.00	5	6000	4	32	3	2	1	3	2
444	48.00	4	13500	4	40	4	2	2	4	3
445	35.00	4	5500	4	29	3	2	2	2	2
446	55.00	4	20000	4	36	4	2	2	5	3
447	40.00	4	25000	4	41	3	2	2	6	3
448	27.00	5	12000	4	43	2	2	2	4	3
449	100.00	5	14000	4	36	7	2	2	4	3
450	57.00	5	9500	4	36	4	2	2	3	3
451	75.00	6	13000	4	40	6	2	2	4	3
452	45.00	6	8000	4	39	4	2	2	3	3
453	85.00	7	18000	4	38	6	2	2	5	3

TABLE 1 *Continued*

A	B	C	D	E	F	G	H	I	J	K
454	100.00	7	20000	4	48	7	2	2	5	4
455	45.00	7	36000	4	43	4	2	2	6	3
456	50.00	7	4500	4	32	4	2	2	2	2
457	48.00	1	14000	5	24	4	1	1	4	1
458	52.50	1	12500	5	60	4	1	1	4	5
459	34.50	1	14000	5	28	3	1	1	4	2
460	9.00	1	2500	5	25	1	1	1	1	2
461	15.00	1	6000	5	28	2	1	1	3	2
462	13.00	2	13000	5	25	1	1	1	4	2
463	54.00	2	14500	5	47	4	1	1	4	4
464	25.00	2	8000	5	78	2	1	1	3	7
465	30.00	2	28000	5	64	3	1	1	6	5
466	35.00	2	3500	5	76	3	1	1	2	7
467	12.00	2	2500	5	23	1	1	1	1	1
468	39.00	3	13000	5	39	3	1	1	4	3
469	45.00	3	42000	5	54	4	1	1	6	4
470	37.50	3	17000	5	52	3	1	2	5	4
471	40.00	3	24000	5	40	3	1	2	5	3
472	52.50	3	17000	5	40	4	1	2	5	3
473	60.00	3	32000	5	48	5	1	2	6	4
474	37.50	4	17000	5	56	3	1	2	5	5
475	55.00	4	24000	5	44	4	1	2	5	3
476	56.00	4	16000	5	36	4	1	2	5	3
477	75.00	5	23000	5	48	6	1	2	5	4
478	45.00	5	6000	5	37	4	1	2	3	3
479	100.00	5	39000	5	44	7	1	2	6	3
480	72.00	2	14000	5	30	5	2	1	4	2
481	33.00	3	20000	5	36	3	2	1	5	3
482	30.00	3	22000	5	33	3	2	1	5	2
483	37.50	3	8000	5	28	3	2	1	3	2
484	30.00	3	9000	5	32	3	2	1	3	2
485	22.00	3	7000	5	30	2	2	1	3	2
486	60.00	4	5000	5	28	5	2	1	2	2
487	20.00	4	9000	5	30	2	2	1	3	2
488	25.50	4	4500	5	26	2	2	1	2	2
489	33.00	4	6000	5	32	3	2	1	3	2
490	51.00	4	9000	5	34	4	2	1	3	2
491	45.00	7	26000	5	39	4	2	1	6	3
492	75.00	4	14500	5	34	6	2	2	4	2
493	18.00	4	14000	5	36	2	2	2	4	3
494	40.00	4	15500	5	40	3	2	2	5	3
495	75.00	5	28000	5	42	6	2	2	6	3
496	24.00	5	24000	5	33	2	2	2	5	2
497	115.00	6	24000	5	36	7	2	2	5	3
498	75.00	7	28000	5	37	6	2	2	6	3
499	105.00	7	20000	5	39	7	2	2	5	3
500	75.00	8	33000	5	42	6	2	2	6	3

CASE QUESTIONS

1 What are the available alternative sampling procedures for estimating average weekly food expenditures?
2 Explain how each of these sampling procedures would be carried out.
3 Discuss the pros and cons of each alternative sampling procedure.

CASE 4-2 Cynthia Lu, Student Council Candidate

Cynthia Lu is a business major at Arizona State University, Tempe. She has entered the race for president of the undergraduate business school council. This council represents approximately 9000 undergraduate business students in their dealings with the dean and other university officials, plus arranges social events. A week prior to the election, Cynthia asks you to determine her chances of winning the coming election against the other two candidates.

CASE QUESTION

1 Prepare a sampling plan. Be sure to designate a population definition, a sampling frame, a sampling procedure, and a method for determining the accuracy of the results.

CASE 4-3 United Airlines

The marketing manager for United Airlines is trying to develop a marketing plan designed to increase the use of United Airlines by college students. As part of this process, he wants to obtain information on college students' attitudes toward commercial flying in general and United Airlines in particular. You have been retained by the marketing manager to design the sample for this study.

CASE QUESTION

1 Prepare a sampling plan. Be sure to designate a population definition, a sampling frame, a sampling procedure, and a method for determining the accuracy of the results.

CASE 4-4 Ice Cream Castle*

Lynne Adams is the manager of Ice Cream Castle, an ice cream parlor located in Castle City, Arizona. She plans to place an advertisement in Sunday's *Castle City Chronicle,* the local newspaper, announcing "Silver Anniversary Savings Days" on the upcoming Monday and Tuesday. You have been retained to develop a

*Source: Coauthored by Sheryl Petras.

plan for sampling the customers who come into the store on those two days. A questionnaire will be administered to the sample to determine what influence the Sunday advertisement had on their coming to the store.

CASE QUESTION

1 Prepare a sampling plan. Be sure to designate a population definition, a sampling frame, a sampling procedure, and a method for determining the accuracy of the results.

CASE 4-5   *Cosmopolitan* Magazine*

Cosmopolitan magazine (which has a circulation of over 3 million) ran a 79-question survey concerning the social habits and attitudes of American females. Over 106,000 questionnaires were returned to *Cosmopolitan*. Linda Wolfe, the author of an article and a book based upon the returned questionnaires, indicated great enthusiasm for the research based on the sample size generated. She noted that a previous, more academic study had had "only 6000 women" and another had had "at best, a few hundred" in their respective samples.

After noting that sample size isn't everything, she emphasized the great dispersion of the respondents in variables such as age, marital status, size of city or town lived in, and income. This diversity was part of her argument that this sample represented American females.

Relevant results for respondents by age were: 18–24, 47 percent; 25–34, 40 percent; and 35 and over, 11 percent, with 2 percent being under 18. Results by marital status were: single, 44 percent; married, 40 percent; divorced/separated, 15 percent; and widowed, 1 percent.

Because not all *Cosmopolitan* readers responded to the questionnaire, there was concern that the results did not represent all *Cosmopolitan* readers and also did not represent American families in general. The research report indicated that while not all *Cosmopolitan* readers might have exactly the same attitudes, the results "can probably be descriptive of most *Cosmopolitan* readers." As for American women as a whole, the author noted that she was reasonably certain that results for American females in general wouldn't be much different.

CASE QUESTIONS

1 What is the population definition in this study? Does it differ from the study population?
2 What is the sampling frame used?
3 What sampling procedure was used?
4 Is the study superior to previous academic studies based upon the larger sample size? How was *Cosmopolitan*'s sample size determined?

Source: This case was written with the assistance of Michele M. Schira.

CASE 4-6   Gallup Polls

In the final days before a presidential election in the United States the results of the Gallup political poll are reported extensively by the media and used by the political campaigners to plot final strategy. Because of the potential importance of the Gallup poll, the method used to perform it is critical.

During the Gallup poll selection process a sample is chosen from 360 primary sampling units (PSUs). The PSUs are selected with probabilities proportional to available census data. The sampling units are stratified by size-of-place and by region. Within each PSU one precinct is selected using probabilities proportional to the number of voters from each precinct in the previous election. Each precinct is then divided into 10 approximately equal parts. Interviewers are then instructed to complete one interview in each of the 10 parts.

CASE QUESTIONS

1 What is the study population? What sampling units were defined by this procedure? What were the sampling frames?
2 Are there any problems presented by the method used to define the study population, the sampling unit, or the sampling frame?
3 Why was the stratification used? Are there additional strata that should be considered?
4 What purpose was there in selecting PSUs and precincts with probability proportionate to census estimates of their respective household populations? How could this be accomplished?
5 What problems could result from sampling individuals who are not likely to actually vote in the election?

CASE 4-7   A Day in the Careers of Pamela Palmers and Sandy Sanders—Professional Interviewers

Pamela Palmers and Sandy Sanders, professional interviewers for Tri-State Interviewing, were working on a project involving in-store interviews with female supermarket shoppers. The study was to determine homemakers' reactions to two brownie mix formulations. One version (sample R) was the formula used in the client's current brownie mix, which had achieved a substantial market share. The second version (sample G) was a new R&D formulation. The client was concerned about homemakers' preferences for the two formulations and wanted to get their comments or reactions in depth.

Palmers and Sanders had spent the previous afternoon in a briefing session with the client concerning the study procedure and questionnaire execution. Both women were to interview as many female shoppers as possible in the period from 9 A.M. to 9 P.M. The two brownie samples would be prepared locally by a home economist from the client's R&D facilities.

The questionnaire and "contact sheets" are reprinted at the end of the case.

The following interviews are representative of those conducted by Palmers and Sanders during the 1-day brownie taste test.

TYPICAL INTERVIEWS: PAMELA PALMERS (PP)

Kroger Supermarket, Saturday, July 14th
Contact No. 1 (9:08 A.M.)

A middle-aged woman approaches the test area with a few items in her cart from the entry displays.

PP: Good morning! I am Pamela Palmers, and wo are having a brownie taste test this morning. I would like to have you try our two brownie samples and give us your reaction.

Resp.: Why yes, I love brownies.

PP: Please sit down at our test table and try the brownies. (The respondent sits down and proceeds to taste the brownies marked "G" and "R.")

PP: After you have had time to try each brownie, I'd like to ask you a few questions. It will only take a few minutes. Can I get you a cup of coffee?

Resp.: Yes—black, please.

PP: Which of the two brownie samples did you prefer?

Resp.: Sample G.

PP: What did you particularly like about the brownies?

Resp.: I liked the taste of G.

PP: What was there about the taste of G that you liked?

Resp.: The chocolate taste was good.

PP: In what way was the chocolate taste good?

Resp.: It wasn't too bitter and it wasn't too sweet-tasting; it was just the right taste.

PP: Sorry for the delay—I am writing this down, and I want to be sure I am writing it just as you are telling it to me. What else did you like about sample G?

Resp.: Well, I like the color; it's a nice light brown, just a perfect chocolate color for a brownie.

PP: What else did you like?

Resp.: I guess I've told you everything I like about sample G.

PP: What did you like about sample R?

Resp.: There wasn't anything I liked about it.

PP: What did you particularly dislike about the brownies?

Resp.: Well, sample R was sweet, and the texture was terrible.

PP: In what ways was the texture terrible?

Resp.: It's too fluffy: I hate cake brownies.

PP: What else didn't you like about sample R?

Resp.: That's about it.

PP: What did you dislike about sample G?

Resp.: It's a little crumbly.

PP: What else didn't you like?

Resp.: Nothing, it is really an excellent brownie.

Recorded Answer—Question 2

(Sample G.) I liked the taste (taste); the chocolate taste was good (good). It wasn't too bitter and it wasn't too sweet-tasting; it was just the right taste. (P.) Well, I liked the color, it's a nice light brown, just a perfect chocolate color for a brownie. (P.) I guess I've told you everything I liked about sample G. (Sample R.) There wasn't anything I liked about it.

Recorded Answer—Question 3

(Sample R.) Well, sample R was sweet, and the texture was terrible (texture). It's too fluffy; I hate cake brownies! (P.) That is about it. (Sample G.) It is a little crumbly. (P.) Nothing, it is really an excellent brownie!

Contact No. 4 (10:43 A.M.)

A family with two children, aged approximately 4 and 7, enters the test area. The woman is pushing the cart, with the 4-year-old riding.

PP: Good morning, sir. I'm Pamela Palmers, and we are having a brownie taste test. Won't you try one? Coffee is available on the table. (The man picks up the brownie and proceeds to the table for a cup of coffee.)

PP: I would like to have your wife try two samples of our brownies and answer a few brief questions. Do you mind watching the children while she tries the brownies? It will just take a minute. (The man smiles at Ms. Palmers and suggests to his wife that she try brownies. The interview is then completed.)

Contact No. 7 (11:32 A.M.)

A middle-aged woman enters the test area pushing the cart at a brisk pace.

PP: Good morning! I'm Pamela Palmers, and we are conducting a brownie taste test this morning. I would like to have you try our brownies and answer a few questions.

Resp.: Sorry, honey, I'm in a hurry. (She proceeds down the aisle, stopping briefly to grab a loaf of bread. Interview was not completed.)

Contact No. 18 (3:32 P.M.)

A young woman enters the test area and smiles as she sees Pamela.

PP: Mary, how good to see you. I didn't know you shopped at Kroger.
Resp.: Sometimes they have good specials. What are you doing here, running one of those surveys?
PP: How about helping me out and trying our brownies?
Resp.: Love to. (Mary sits down and tastes the two samples.)
PP: Which of the two brownie samples did you prefer?
Resp.: G.
PP: What did you particularly like about the brownies?
Resp.: They taste homemade, especially G.
PP: In what way does sample G taste like homemade?
Resp.: It's very chewy and not too sweet.
PP: What else did you like about sample G?
Resp.: Nothing.
PP: What did you particularly like about sample R?
Resp.: It's very light.
PP: What do you mean by light?
Resp.: The weight of the sample, it is more like a cake in its texture.
PP: What else did you like about sample R?
Resp.: That's about it.
PP: What did you particularly dislike about the brownies?
Resp.: Sample R had a strong chocolate flavor.
PP: What do you mean by strong chocolate flavor?
Resp.: Rather sweet chocolate taste.
PP: What else didn't you like about sample R?

Resp.: Nothing else, I guess.

PP: What did you particularly dislike about sample G?

Resp.: Could be somewhat more chewy.

PP: What else didn't you like?

Resp.: That's it; it is really a good brownie, like I make at home. (The rest of the interview is completed, and Pamela and Mary discuss personal matters for a few minutes.)

Contact No. 24 (8:03 P.M.)

A middle-aged couple enter the test area. Pamela approaches their cart, smiles at both, and addresses the woman:

PP: Good evening. I am Pamela Palmers, and we are conducting a brownie taste test this evening. I would like to have you try our brownies and answer a few brief questions. It will only take a minute or so. (Turning to the man, and smiling.)

PP: We have coffee available on the table, and you are free to try brownies yourself while I talk with your wife. (The woman looks at her husband. He nods his head in approval. The woman sits down and tries the brownies. The interview is completed.)

TYPICAL INTERVIEWS: SANDY SANDERS (SS)

A&P Supermarket, Saturday, July 14
Contact No. 1 (9:22 A.M.)

A young woman and a 1-year-old child approach the test area. The young child is riding quietly in the cart.

SS: Hi, we are testing brownies this morning—please try some.

Resp.: Okay.

SS: Please sit down at the table and taste the two samples I have labeled "R" and "G." Would you like some coffee?

Resp.: Yes, cream and sugar. (The woman tries each of the brownies.)

SS: How did you like the brownies?

Resp.: They were good.

SS: Which of the two brownie samples did you prefer?

Resp.: Sample G.

SS: What did you like about sample G?

Resp.: The nice flavor. The texture of G was good; I like a moist brownie.

SS: By moist, do you mean chewy?

Resp.: Yes, I like a chewy brownie.

SS: How about sample R? You said they were both good.

Resp.: I like R, but it didn't have the flavor of G.

SS: Is there anything else?

Resp.: No.
SS: What didn't you like about the brownies?
Resp.: I like my brownies warm.
SS: Anything about sample G you didn't like?
Resp.: It was a little heavy.
SS: Anything else?
Resp.: No.
SS: How about sample R?
Resp.: Rather sweet.
SS: Anything else?
Resp.: No.

Recorded Answer—Question 2

Both good. (G.) Nice flavor, texture good, moist (moist), chewy. (R.) OK, flavor not as good. (R.) No.

Recorded Answer—Question 3

Not warm enough. (G.) Heavy. (P.) No. (R.) Sweet. (P.) No.

Contact No. 3 (10:24 A.M.)

An elderly couple slowly push their cart to the test area.

> *SS:* Hello, would you like to try some brownies this morning?
> *Resp.:* (Male) No, can't eat that stuff—dentures. (The couple passes through the test area. Interview not completed.)

Contact No. 4 (10:27 A.M.)

A middle-aged couple enters the test area. They have with them two girls aged 5 and 8. The 8-year-old is pushing the cart, while the husband and wife are talking about the grocery list.

> *SS:* How are you this morning? We are testing brownies; would you be interested?
> *Resp.:* (Female) No, not today. (Interview not completed.)

Contact No. 14 (2:13 P.M.)

A middle-aged woman briskly pushes her cart toward the test area.

SS: Hi, we are testing brownies this morning. Would you care to try our two versions and answer some questions?

Resp.: How long will it take?

SS: Just 2 or 3 minutes. We have coffee also.

Resp.: I don't drink coffee—do you have tea?

SS: No.

Resp.: How about milk?

SS: No.

Resp.: Well, I'll try them quickly.

SS: Please sit down at the table. Here are the two samples. I think you will like them. (The woman quickly tastes each sample.)

SS: Which did you prefer?

Resp.: Sample R.

SS: What did you like about R?

Resp.: It was tasty, more like homemade.

SS: Anything else?

Resp.: It was light; the other one was too chewy.

SS: Anything else?

Resp.: No.

SS: How about G, what did you like about it?

Resp.: Nothing.

SS: What did you particularly dislike about the brownies?

Resp.: G was too chewy, and the flavor was poor.

SS: What do you mean—poor?

Resp.: It was flat.

SS: Anything else?

Resp.: No.

SS: How about R?

Resp.: It was great.

(The rest of the interview is completed.)

Contact No. 21 (4:30 P.M.)

A young teenage couple enters the test area. The male is pushing the cart.

SS: Hi, we are having women try brownies this afternoon. Do you have time to try them and answer some questions?

Resp.: (Female) No.

Resp.: (Male) They look good—you don't mind if I try one? (He picks up three brownies, and the couple proceeds. Interview not completed.)

Contact No. 27 (7:42 P.M.)

A young couple enters the test area. A boy, about 5, is trying to push the cart while his father guides it from the front.

SS: Hello, we are having women taste two versions of brownies this evening. Would you please try them for us? We have coffee if you would like some.

Resp.: (Male) Go ahead, honey, I'll grab a cup of coffee and meet you in the cereal section.

SS: Please be seated at our test table and try the two samples marked "R" and "G." (The woman tastes each sample.)

SS: Which sample did you like best?

Resp.: They were both good.

SS: You must have liked one better than the other.

Resp.: Well, G was a little better, but not much.

SS: What did you like about G?

Resp.: It was light and mild.

SS: Do you mean its weight?

Resp.: No, its color.

SS: Anything else?

Resp.: Not really.

SS: What did you like about R?

Resp.: It had a rich flavor.

SS: What do you mean by rich?

Resp.: The texture was light and delicate.

SS: Anything else?

Resp.: No, that's it.

SS: What did you particularly dislike about the brownies?

Resp.: As I said before, I liked them equally well. They're both excellent.

SS: There must be something you didn't like. Was the color too dark on R?

Resp.: No, it was fine. (The interview is completed.)

At 9:32, Sandy meets Pamela at a nearby cocktail lounge. They both order drinks and proceed to check their completed questionnaires for completeness and legibility. By 11:03 they have completed their work and proceed to the local post office to mail the questionnaires to the client's home office.

CASE QUESTION

1 How would you evaluate the interviewing skills of Pamela Palmers and Sandy Sanders? What specific suggestions would improve their effectiveness?

Questionnaire

Store _____

Interviewer _____

Date _____

Time _____

Brownie Study

1 Which of the two brownie samples did you prefer?
   Sample R ( )   Sample G ( )   No preference ( )
2 What did you particularly like about the brownies? (Probe and clarify fully.)
   _____
   _____
   _____
   _____

3 What did you particularly dislike about the brownies? (Probe and clarify fully.)
   _____
   _____
   _____
   _____

4 How frequently do you serve brownies to your family?
   Once a week ( )   Every two weeks ( )
   Once a month ( )   Less frequently ( )
5 Do you make your brownies from a mix or from scratch?
   Mix ( )   Scratch ( )   Both ( )
6 If mix, or both, what brand of mix do you usually buy? Brand name(s):
   _____ , _____

Questions 7 through 11 contained demographic information.

Contact Sheet

Interviewer *Pamela Palmer*

Firm *Tri-State*

Place *Kroger*

Address *1436 Maple*

City/State *St. Louis, Mo.*

Date *Sat. July 14th*

	Contact Time	Couple	Female	Completed Yes	Completed No
1	9:08 A.M.		✓	✓	
2	9:20 A.M.		✓		✓
3	9:31 A.M.	✓		✓	
4	10:43 A.M.	✓		✓	
5	11:14 A.M.		✓		✓
Total	28	15	13	16	12

Contact Sheet

Interviewer *Sandy Sanders*

Firm *Tri-State*

Place *A + P*

Address *1592 Maple*

City/State *St. Louis, Mo*

Date *Sat. July 14th*

	Contact Time	Couple	Female	Completed Yes	No
1	9:22 am		✓	✓	
2	9:50 am	✓		✓	
3	10:24 am	✓			✓
4					
.					
.					
.					
Total	39	18	21	12	27

PART **FIVE**

DATA ANALYSIS
AND REPORTING
RESEARCH FINDINGS

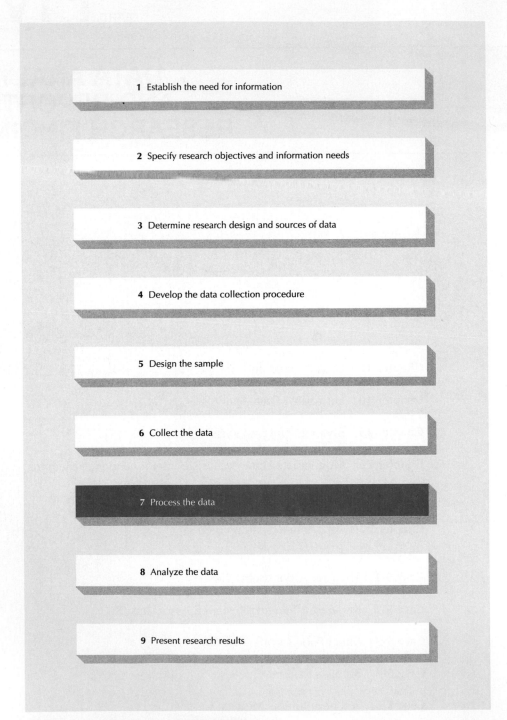

FIGURE 17-1   Steps in the research process.

CHAPTER 17

DATA PROCESSING

MARKETING RESEARCH IN ACTION

XEROX CUSTOMER SATISFACTION DATA NEEDS ANALYSIS

Xerox Corporation is highly committed to a program of measuring and responding to the level of satisfaction in its customers. This involves a series of different surveys, including a periodic survey of Xerox customers and a survey of Xerox competitors' customers to determine Xerox's competitive positioning. The marketing research department at Xerox receives about 10,000 completed surveys a month, each with about 35 responses. This means that about 350,000 pieces of data arrive at Xerox every month. Obviously, there is a need to plan to handle all this data in such a way that it can be easily analyzed by computer.

Many types of questions are asked in the customer satisfaction surveys, including 5-point attitude scales, product usage questions, paired comparison of brands, demographic and industry descriptors, and open-ended questions. The task of the marketing researchers assigned to analyze these data requires the use of commercially available data analysis packages such as SPSS-PC (which stands for Statistical Package for the Social Sciences, for personal computers) and SAS. Prior to sending the customer satisfaction questionnaires to the respondents, there is a need to have a complete scheme for representing the data for computer analysis.

The analyst assigned to these studies clearly has a need to understand the proper approach to assigning numeric values to respondent's answers to a questionnaire.

A description of the functions necessary to prepare raw data collection forms, called *instruments,* for data analysis constitutes the topic of this chapter. We begin with a description of some of the basic terms and concepts of data processing as applied to marketing research. Next we discuss the decision concerning whether a particular respondent's instrument should be prepared for data analysis. It may not be filled out properly, and thus we may not want to use it. Other sections will cover the editing of data collection instruments, coding, data cleaning, creation of new variables, and data weighting.

SOME BASIC CONCEPTS

Our basic task in data processing is to *convert the raw data in the data collection instrument into a computer-readable form.* We can then make use of computerized data analysis procedures to extract information from the data. Before we see how this is done, there are some concepts and terms that we need to understand.

Case   A *case* is a specific unit of analysis for the study. Quite often the unit of analysis is the respondent to a questionnaire, so each respondent is considered a case, and the total number of cases equals the sample size.

Computer Representation of Data   The data provided by a research instrument must be converted into a computer-readable form. Historically the computer card was the basic device used for this purpose. Almost always now the data are either entered directly into the computer at the time they are collected in telephone interviews (see Chapter 16) or typed directly into the computer from the data collection instrument without using a computer card as an intermediate step. The latter approach is common with mail and personal interviews. However, no matter what approach is used, the basic logic is the same. The data are typed into a numeric-only file, called an ASCII file (ASCII stands for American Standard Code for Information Interchange) that is structured like a spreadsheet or matrix. We will use a spreadsheet analogy to explain this data structure.

A spreadsheet or matrix is divided into cells by horizontal rows and vertical columns. Each row of the spreadsheet represents a unit of analysis or a case, often a respondent to a questionnaire. One or more of the vertical columns of the spreadsheet are assigned to represent the available responses for a unique variable in the study, such as age or income. Then, a unique number or numbers is placed in the cell defined by the case row and variable column or columns. This number or numbers may represent one particular respondent's answer to a question, or it may be a descriptor of the size of a particular firm, for instance. If it represents a respondent's answer, the person's year in college might be assigned to column 1 in the spreadsheet. If the respondent is a senior, a 1 could be entered in column 1; if the respondent is a junior, a 2 could be entered in column 1; and so on.

If a straight ASCII format is being used, and if a variable contains more than 10 categories or requires two or more digits to represent the data, the specific variable in question must be assigned as many columns as necessary to represent the data. In a commercial spreadsheet such as Lotus 123 or Excel, the data may be entered into one column, if the column has previously been defined as wide enough to hold the number or numbers required to represent the data. For example, a respondent's score on each part of the Scholastic Aptitude Test (SAT) would require three digits, as the highest possible score is 800. In a straight ASCII format, this would require three columns in the spreadsheet. Columns 2 to 4 might be assigned to this variable, and the exact score would be entered in the columns. If the score were 625, the 6 would be entered in column 2, the 2 in column 3, and the 5 in column 4. If Lotus 123 or Excel were being used, then column 2 could be set as three digits wide and used for all three digits.

Figure 17-2 illustrates both the straight ASCII and the commercial spreadsheet structures for representing numeric data. The ASCII representation in part A of Figure 17-2 contains only the numbers 0 through 9 in each column, but represents exactly the same data as presented in the spreadsheet representation in part B. Note that column 1, representing the year in college, is identical in the two formats. This is because only one column is needed to represent the relevant answers to the question. The SAT score requires three columns in ASCII format, but only one in the commercial spreadsheet structure. The data in part A need five columns but represent only three variables. The three variables of data in part B require only three proper-width spreadsheet columns.

Data Matrix The standard marketing research database is formed into an $n \times m$ (n by m) *data matrix for data analysis.* The spreadsheet or data matrix can be as large as required by the number of respondents (the rows) and the number of variables (the columns). The number of cases and variables in a data matrix is limited by the capacity of the computer data analysis software package being utilized. It is not uncommon in practice to have a data matrix that is 2500×200 or even larger. All that is required is that a specific row within the data matrix be assigned to a specific case, and that a specific column be assigned to a specific variable. The computer can then make use of the numeric representation of the data.

Data Storage Once the data have been read into the computer, the researcher may use the computer capabilities to store the data either in a disk or a tape. Data stored on a disk or tape are easy to access for later data analysis.

With direct computer entry systems, the answer to any specific question is identified as being in a particular location in the computer data file, in the same way that it is given a specific location in the computer spreadsheet.

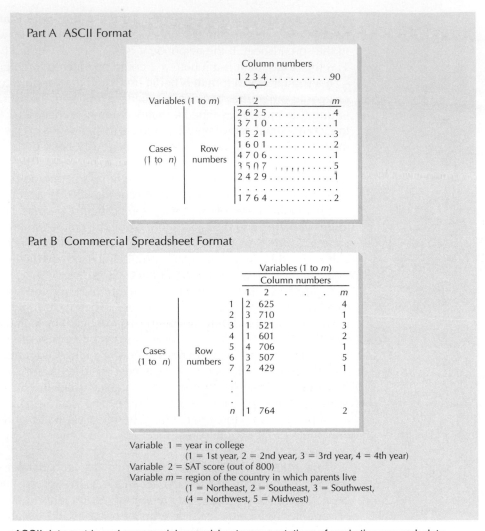

FIGURE 17-2   ASCII data matrix and commercial spreadsheet representations of marketing research data.

Keeping these basic concepts in mind, we will now examine the individual steps in the flow of data processing.

DATA PROCESSING FLOW

Figure 17-3 presents an overview of the traditional sequence of functions to be performed in data processing. These include (1) deciding whether to use the data collection instrument for analysis, (2) editing the data, (3) coding the data, (4) entering the data on the computer, and verifying them, (5) converting the datafile

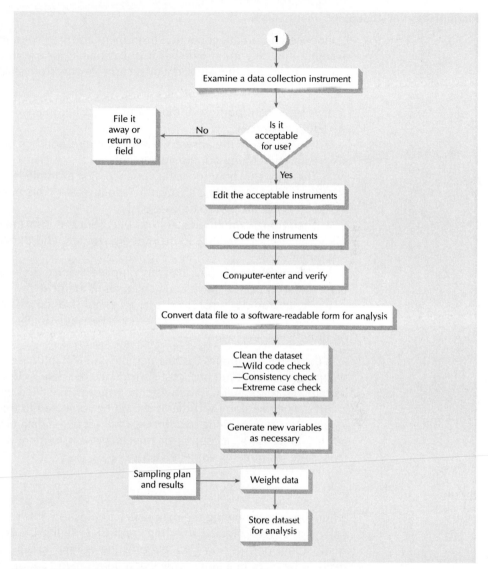

FIGURE 17-3   Classic data processing flow.

to a computer software-readable form for analysis, (6) cleaning the dataset, (7) generating new variables as necessary, (8) weighting the data in accordance with the sampling plan and the results, and (9) storing the dataset on disk or tape. The following section presents a discussion of each of these functions.

With direct computer entry systems, some of these steps are unnecessary or may be done simultaneously with entry. However, the function performed by each step is necessary in the computer-based systems, and needs to be understood.

Identification of Acceptable Instruments

Upon receiving a data collection instrument from the field, the researcher should examine it to determine whether it is acceptable for use in the study. The exact criteria for judging an instrument unacceptable vary from study to study, but those listed below are typical.

1 A significant portion of the instrument is left unanswered, or key elements are left unanswered.

2 It is clear from the answers given that the respondent did not understand the task required in filling out the instrument.

3 The answers show too little variance. For example, the answers to a series of attitude questions are all 3s on a 7-point scale. This is evidence that the respondent is not taking the task seriously.

4 The wrong sample element has filled out the instrument. For example, the study calls for respondents to be working women, and a man has completed the instrument.

5 The instrument is physically incomplete. For example, a page may not have been included or may have been taken off in the field.

6 The instrument is received after an established cutoff date. If you wait for all instruments to be returned from the field, the study likely will not be completed on time.

If the researcher thinks that the particular defect in question could be corrected within reasonable time and cost constraints, the data collection instrument may be returned to the field. Otherwise, the instrument is filed away.

All data collection instruments should be subjected to this type of preliminary examination before being sent through the rest of the data processing flow. Above all, the criteria for accepting or rejecting an instrument should be established before the instruments are received.

Editing

Editing means reviewing the data collection instruments to ensure maximum accuracy and unambiguity. It is important that editing be done consistently. In a small study, one person may perform the editing function, and consistency is likely to be high. In a large study that requires many editors, an editing supervisor is necessary to ensure that consistency is maintained among editors. This person will have to sample-check different editors on different sections of the instrument. Alternatively, each editor could be made responsible for a different section of the instrument and edit all instruments for this section.

In performing the editing function, the editor should be concerned with the areas described below.

1 Legibility   To be properly coded later, the data must be legible. Sometimes an illegible response can be corrected by contacting the person who recorded it, and sometimes the correct response can be inferred from other parts of the instrument. If no definitive answer is available, the response should be designated as missing data. To sum up, the editor takes the ambiguity out of the recorded data, so that the coder will know exactly what to do.

2 Completeness Questions that are not answered may be treated in one of three ways. First, the editor may contact the interviewer to try to determine whether the respondent did not answer the question or whether the interviewer just failed to record the response. In doing this, there is a risk that the interviewer will not remember this particular interview correctly. Alternatively, the respondent may be contacted again for a response to a specific question. The second approach is to designate this particular piece of data as missing. Finally, if the editor deems that too many data items are missing, the whole instrument may be sent back to the field or removed from the study.

3 Consistency At this point, a preliminary check is made on the consistency of the data. (A more detailed check will be performed later by the computer.) For example, the editor might verify that respondents who claim to buy gasoline by credit card do hold credit cards. The editor may ask the interviewer to resolve any inconsistencies, designate the responses to these questions as missing data, or remove the instrument from the study.

4 Accuracy The editor needs to be attentive to evidence of inaccuracy in the data. The most important area here relates to possible interviewer bias or cheating. Such activities may be spotted by looking for a common pattern of responses in the instruments of a particular interviewer or recorder.

5 Response Clarification Sometimes the responses to open-ended questions are difficult to interpret clearly. The recorder's words may have abbreviated the answer too much, or some words may be ambiguous. The editor may designate a meaning for the response or ask the interviewer what was meant. The risk of error is high in both instances. Obviously, good field work in the first place can prevent many problems from arising.

Difficulties also occur when questions are not answered in the way the instructions to the instrument required. This is especially a problem in mail surveys. For example, a respondent may be asked to underline a number on a 7-point rating scale. Suppose he or she underlines the numbers 4 and 5. Does this mean that 4.5 is intended as the response? The editor must decide whether to designate the response as a 4 or as a 5, or to record it as missing data.

Coding

Coding involves the assignment of a designated numeric symbol into a designated spreadsheet column, or into ASCII file columns, to represent a specific response on a data collection instrument. We saw examples of this earlier in the chapter.

The coding examples that follow all use the ASCII format. (Also see the Global Marketing Research Dynamics later in this chapter.)

Closed- and Open-Ended Questions   For structured or closed-end questions, the coding scheme is usually designated prior to the undertaking of field work. This may go as far as having the actual codes printed on the data collection instruments. For example, a designation of gender may appear on the instrument as:

31	What is your gender?
1	Female
2	Male

The numbers on the left side of the question indicate the coding scheme. Here 31 indicates that the response to this question will appear in the 31st column of the ASCII file for this respondent. A 1 in this column designates a female and a 2 designates a male. This same approach can be used for coding numeric data that either are not to be coded into categories or have had their relevant categories specified. A respondent's age may be requested and coded as:

6–7	What is your age? _____

or as:

6	What is your age?
1	0–18
2	19–35
3	36–50
4	over 50

In both cases the codes can be specified prior to the field work. If the codes are written on all questions, the questionnaire is said to be wholly precoded. The former representation requires two ASCII columns, the latter only one.

Open-ended questions present a more complex problem for coding. Here the verbatim responses of respondents are recorded by the interviewer. How do you convert data like these into a numeric representation? There are two general approaches to the problem. The first is the preparation of a relatively well-developed coding scheme prior to the completion of the field work. To be able to do this, the researcher must be guided by the results of previous studies or by some overriding theoretical considerations. The major task of the researcher is then to train coders so that they will convert the verbatim responses into the correct code categories.

The second approach involves waiting until the instruments return from the field before developing the coding scheme. Here the researcher lists, say, 50 to

100 of the responses to the specific question. He or she then examines this list and decides what categories are appropriate for summarizing the data. The researcher then trains the coders in this scheme and also alerts them to watch for other responses that occur with some frequency. If this happens, it may be necessary to go back and revise the coding scheme and thus to recode all instruments on this question.

Rules and Conventions for Code Construction   There are a number of rules or conventions that make the coding function work well. They are:

1 *Establish mutually exclusive and collectively exhaustive code categories.* It is easy to make categories collectively exhaustive by adding, for example, the code category "other," "no information," or "none" to the major categories for the variable in question. *Mutually exclusive* means that every response must fit into one and only one code category. Categories must not overlap; this is the one hard-and-fast rule of all coding. The other items in this selection are best described as useful conventions, not rules.
2 If uncertainty exists about possible uses for a particular variable in analysis, the data should be coded so as to *retain a great deal of detail.* It is possible to combine code categories at the time of analysis if such detail is not required. However, it is impossible to "expand" codes for analysis if they have been recorded with too little detail. We may therefore want to code in more detail than we intend to use in analysis. An example would be to code the respondent's exact age, and then to combine ages into categories at the time of analysis.
3 Follow these layout conventions:
   a Use only one ASCII number per column.
   b Use only numeric codes, not special characters or blanks.
   c The ASCII file position for a variable may consist of as many columns as are necessary, but no more than one variable may be assigned to a single column.
   d Use standard codes for missing data, if at all possible. For example, some researchers always use 9 to designate a missing one-column variable, 99 for a missing two-column variable, and so on. The researcher may have a number of different types of missing data, such as "don't know," "does not apply," and "refused to answer." If this detail is to be preserved, a standard code should be set for each one. This facilitates coding and later interpretation of data analysis.
4 In choosing breakpoints for continuous variables, consider the following questions.
   a Into how many categories should the variable be cast, given the plan of analysis that has been developed?
   b Should the categories be equal-interval (0–9, 10–19, 20–29, etc.), or should they be constructed so that each category has about the same number of cases?

c Should the extreme categories be open (under $9000; $60,000 and over) to take in a wide range of extreme scores, or should the intervals be fixed?

In making these decisions the researcher must recognize that the use of equal intervals allows for easier statistical analysis later and that the number of categories selected affects the detail of the information retained from the instruments. The more categories you have, the greater the detail. In the end, the number and definition of categories selected must satisfy the user of the research. The researcher must consult with the manager on this issue.

5 Put a respondent identification number on each row in the data matrix. With the rows identified in this manner, you can instruct the computer to check on whether the required number of cases is in the data matrix. Identification numbers also facilitate data cleaning later.

Multiple Responses   The problem of multiple responses arises in two contexts. The first is where the researcher expects to receive a single answer. In this case the decision may be to select one of the answers on some established priority basis—for example, the answer written down first. Alternatively, you may develop code categories to represent combinations of responses. For example, a 7 may represent those respondents who said that flavor and baking time are important cake mix attributes. Finally, you may designate this response as missing data.

In situations where the researcher expects more than one answer, two procedures are available. The first is to treat each possible response as a separate variable, with a separate column. For example, a question may ask what sports a respondent plays. Each sport would be answered yes or no and assigned to a unique column. The second option is available where the researcher has a specific number of responses expected. The researcher could assign a separate column for "first responses," another for "second responses," and so on. The codes within each column would be the same, representing the available options. For example, a 1 in the first response column could indicate that flavor was the first response for this respondent as an important attribute for cake mix. A 1 in the second response column would indicate that flavor was the second response as an important attribute for cake mix. In analysis, the researcher could either examine each response column separately or combine the columns to get total responses. Care should be taken in combining data of this type; it is possible that an attribute placed second or third, and so on, by a great many respondents could have more total mentions than another attribute that had more first mentions. A simple sum of mentions across the columns could confuse managers. They should be consulted as to the importance they place on second- or third-mention levels, and so on, before a combining scheme is developed.

It should be recognized that coding is a potentially boring task. After working hard and creatively to develop the coding scheme, the actual coding process may seem very tedious. In addition, this function is often not a highly paid job, which results in problems with quality of personnel. Coding errors often occur unless the researcher maintains close supervision over the coding. You can keep the coders on their toes by asking to see how a sample of instruments was coded. This sort of check will also give you a sense of the report that is going to emerge later.

The detail of the coding scheme needs to be documented, and this documentation is placed in what is called a codebook.

Codebook   A *codebook* is the place where all the needed information about variables in the data set is documented. The codebook has three functions. First, it serves as a guide to the coders; second, it helps researchers locate the variables they desire to use in a particular data analysis run; and third, it allows for the proper identification of variable categories as computer output is interpreted. The researcher would literally be lost without a good codebook.

The contents of the codebook vary. For a very simple study, you may just write the relevant column number and response number on the instrument itself. A completely precoded questionnaire could serve as its own codebook.

In more complex studies, it is useful to have a codebook that contains more information. The researcher often wants the details of open-ended questions documented, or wishes to refer to variables by number for designation in a computer run. So a codebook might contain (1) the question number, (2) the variable number, (3) the relevant ASCII columns, (4) the format (any implied decimal places), (5) the variable name, and (6) the category definitions. Table 17-1 presents a portion of an illustrative codebook. A quick look at the codebook informs us exactly how the variables (gender, age, and grade point average, or GPA) appear in the ASCII data matrix and how we will refer to them in later analysis. For example, GPA is called variable 121, is in ASCII columns 91 to 93, and has an

TABLE 17-1   AN ILLUSTRATIVE CODEBOOK

Question number	Variable number	ASCII file column	Format*	Variable name	Category definitions
35	46	52	I1	Sex	1 = female 2 = male 9 = missing data
36	47	53–54	I2	Age	Two-digit number 00–98 99 = missing data
.	.	.	.	.	
.	.	.	.	.	
.	.	.	.	.	
74	121	91–93	F3.2	GPA	Three-digit number 000–400 with decimal place two places to left in field given

*The use of "I" refers to an integer value in card column(s). The number after the I indicates the number of digits in the variable. For example, I1 indicates a one-digit integer variable and I6 indicates a six-digit integer variable.

The use of "F" indicates that other variables in the card column or columns can take on real values. That is, the variable with an F can have a decimal place. The position of the decimal is given by the number after the decimal place, and the number of digits is given by the number before the decimal. For example, F3.2 indicates a real variable containing three digits with the decimal place position before the second digit. That is, the decimal is two places from the end of the field.

implied decimal place two places to the left of the end of the field, that is, between columns 91 and 92. We never insert the decimal place; we need only tell the computer with the format statement. The GPA was obtained in question 74 on the instrument. For a complex open-ended question, the description of the code categories may be quite lengthy.

One of the advantages of computer-based systems is that once the coding structure has been set in the computer the system can automatically create and print out a codebook.

Actual Coding   Once the code categories are established, the actual coding can take place. Here, the coders write the proper codes in the designated location on column paper or on a special "code sheet." The code sheet may be thought of as a paper version of an ASCII data matrix. Once this is done, the coding is completed.

Computer Entry and Verification

The completed coding sheets are delivered to computer entry personnel, who enter the exact numbers on the sheets into an ASCII file in the computer. The file is then ready to be converted into a spreadsheet or a data matrix. It is of course possible to enter the data directly into a spreadsheet from the coding sheets, but care must be taken with this approach, because it is easy to make a mistake in data entry. It is therefore wise to have the data verified after they have been entered but before the file is converted. The result of this process should be an accurate database.

Conversion of the Datafile to a Software-Readable Form for Analysis

The datafile must now be presented to the computer in such a way that data analysis computer programs can make use of it. Most programs that a researcher is likely to use are contained within a package of programs. Data from spreadsheets can be output to ASCII files readable by most statistical packages. In addition, many statistical packages now read common spreadsheet formats. Moreover, spreadsheet and database software programs are now enhancing their statistical analysis capabilities.

One such package of programs, as mentioned previously, is called SPSS-PC. There are many others, but we shall use SPSS-PC to illustrate the structure of these packages. Figure 17-4 gives an overview of what is done to make an SPSS-PC datafile out of the raw datafile. The datafile is read into the computer along with a number of descriptions, including (1) variable numbers and names, (2) variable format, (3) missing-data codes, and (4) variable-category descriptors (if the user desires to have them on computer printouts). The result of this is an SPSS-PC datafile ready for analysis. It has in essence made an SPSS-PC-readable data matrix out of the datafile, and all SPSS-PC analysis programs can make use of this one datafile. We can do an analysis run without worrying about properly locating and

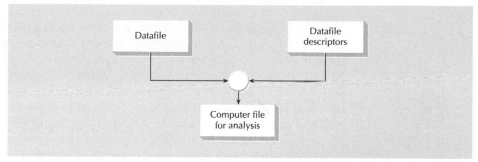

FIGURE 17-4   Creation of a computer file for analysis.

defining missing-data codes for the variables of interest in our data check. All we need to do is refer to the desired variable numbers in the SPSS-PC datafile. This leads to great efficiencies in data analysis.

An item that *must* be included as a variable in the datafile is the case identification number. This will help expedite the data cleaning that is to follow.

Cleaning the Dataset

We now have a dataset structured as a computer datafile, but we must still attempt to clean possible errors out of the dataset. Three types of checks are run on the dataset, namely, (1) a wild code check, (2) a consistency check, and (3) an extreme-case check.

Wild Code Check   The first items we want to get out of our dataset are so-called wild codes, that is, codes that are not defined in the codebook for a particular variable. For example, the variable "gender" may have three legitimate codes (the third being for missing data). A number 4 or greater for this variable would be a wild code, probably the result of an error in coding or data computer entry. This check can be done by having the computer list the numbers of responses in each category of each variable, which will tell us whether a wild code exists. But in which case does it occur? This represents no problem if we have made case number a variable. All we do is command the computer to print out the case numbers for those cases that have a wild code, examine the data collection instruments for these cases, and make the appropriate corrections in the datafile. Most computer analysis packages allow us to do this easily.

Consistency Check   The next step is to check the consistency of responses within each case. During the editing task we did a preliminary consistency check, but the one performed by the computer can be much more complete. For example, we might check on whether respondents who have a mortgage also own a house. There are two types of consistency checks: one-way and two-way. In a one-way consistency situation, A is true if B is true, but the reverse need not hold. In a two-way consistency situation, A is true if and only if B is true, and vice versa. The house and mortgage example above would be an example of a one-way consistency check. That is, a respondent who has a mortgage must own a house, but some homeowners may not have mortgages. A two-way consistency check could be done in a study of university students. A check could be made between credit hours obtained and year of standing in school (senior, junior, etc.). If a junior is someone with between 60 and 90 credit hours, a two-way check could be made between credit hours and year of standing. That is, people with between 60 and 90 credit hours would be checked to see that they were classified as juniors, and junior classified people would be checked to see that they have the proper number of credit hours. A good data analysis package should have the commands necessary to do this type of checking. Again, once an error is found, the case number is printed out, the data collection instrument is examined, and the correction is made.

Extreme-Case Check   An extreme case is defined as a response on a variable that is well out of the ordinary. For example, an SAT score recorded as 796 in the datafile may be substantially higher than all other scores. We could command the computer to print out the case numbers of all cases with SAT scores above 775. We would then check to see whether these scores were correct. This is another way of identifying possible coding or computer entry errors.

Generating New Variables

Once the originally coded dataset is cleansed, we can proceed to add new variables to this dataset that will be used later in analysis. Again, the computer's capabilities make this task simple. There are a number of circumstances where we might generate new variables:

1 We may want to add data not collected in the interview. For example, we may want to add census information about the area in which a respondent lives.

2 We may want to collapse an interval variable, such as income, into categories, or we may want to combine the categories of some variables to give a variable with fewer categories.

3 We may want to form a variable to be defined by combinations of other variables. For example, the variable "stage of family life cycle" is formed using age, marital status, presence of children, and so on.

4 We may want to create an index to represent a number of variables. For example, we may simply add a set of scaled measures about a product to form an index related to interest in the product. More complex indexes are also possible.

These new variables are placed in the dataset for each case and assigned a variable number. They must also be entered in the codebook with a detailed description of how they were formed.

Weighting

There is one task that may need to be performed on the datafile, namely, weighting the data in accordance with the sampling plan or because of unexpected sampling results. (Weighting was discussed in detail in Chapter 15.) Basically, we need to weight if the probability of element selection varies across subgroups, and if we wish to do analysis with the whole sample. We command the computer to assign the appropriate weights to cases. If we desire to do subgroup analysis, we simply command the analysis program to ignore the weighting.

Storing

We now have a dataset completely ready for analysis. It is generally stored on disk or tape, with a copy made on another disk or tape to be put away for safekeeping. We are ready to do data analysis.

CHALLENGES OF INTERNATIONAL CODING

Even an activity as seemingly straightforward as coding has special dynamics associated with it when international marketing research is undertaken. Coding plays a major part in the quality of international surveys. It is especially complicated with open-ended questions. Despite the difficulties involved in coding these responses, open-ended questions play a valuable part in these surveys, since there is usually insufficient time to conduct qualitative research in all the countries involved. The combined experience of the agency researcher, the client, and the product manager may not be enough to enable them to draw up a comprehensive list of precoded responses. Use of open-ended questions also allows the researcher to interpret the responses on the basis of the respondent's exact words, instead of having to rely on the respondent's or the interviewer's interpretation. This creates more control and more consistency. The Global Marketing Research Dynamics discusses five basic approaches to the coding of international studies.

GLOBAL MARKETING RESEARCH DYNAMICS

COMPLEXITIES OF INTERNATIONAL CODING

Five basic methods of international coding can be defined, and each has its relative advantages and disadvantages. These five methods can be explained in the context of a medical survey of doctors concerning drugs and diagnoses. The home country for this survey is the United Kingdom (UK), and the other countries surveyed are France, Germany, and Italy.

The first method assumes that the whole world thinks the way the English think (or the way the Germans, the French, or the Italians think). The field work is conducted simultaneously in all the countries, but the field work of the home country, the UK, will probably be completed first. The local researcher receives the questionnaires from the home country, lists the responses, produces the code frames, and sends them back to the home country, where they will be translated back into the home-country language and coded. While this is the quickest method, and as such probably the cheapest, it lacks control and quality. The project leader has little control over the coding of the responses if the code frames are sent out from the head office and only coded questionnaires are received in return. Quality is poor, since this approach assumes that a German doctor thinks like an English doctor, and classifies the German's responses on the basis of the code work generated in the UK, instead of in the language actually used by the respondent.

The second method assumes that the world thinks in English. All responses in every country are translated into English. The translated responses are returned to the head office and compiled, and a code frame is developed from them by English-speaking coders. Translation of the responses makes this method slower and more expensive, but the control and quality are better, since more of the process is done at the home office where the project leader can better control the coding of the responses. Some quality is still sacrificed, since this method incorrectly assumes that nothing is lost or altered in translating responses from German, French, or Italian into English and then, after processing, from English back into German, French, or Italian. This is not usually the case.

The third method allows the local agencies to list their responses, draw up their own code frames, and code the open-ended questions locally. The home office then pulls the results together in the analysis stage. This method offers speed and cost effectiveness. With high-quality local coders, valid results can be obtained for each individual country. Adding together and comparing the results of surveys conducted by four different agencies is difficult at best, making comparability a major problem. There is also no control from the head office, so that the quality of the results is called into question as well.

The fourth method solicits responses from the first 50 to 100 doctors in each country. The head office uses these responses to develop code frames which are valid in all the countries, but which are expressed in the language of each individual country, rather than using translations from English. Coding is then done either centrally at the home office by French, German, and Italian coders or in the local agencies by experienced medical coders. While this method is slower and more expensive than the previous methods, the elimination of translation plus the high degree of central processing gives it superior quality and control.

The fifth method, computerized coding, is effective for quantitative surveys, such as coding symptoms and simple product characteristics. While computerized analysis of open-ended responses can be valuable in identifying keywords for content analysis purposes, such as the sorting and retrieval of a doctor's exact words, great care must be taken not to stretch these applications to include the interpretation of verbal responses. For example, when asked to translate the phrase "out of sight, out of mind" one computerized program translated it as "blind idiot," and another translated "hydraulic ram" as "wet sheep." While the surface-level interpretation of the words was correct in each instance, the deeper and contextual interpretation was completely wrong.

Though the "ideal" coding approach for a given situation may vary depending on the time available, the budget, and the detail needed from open-ended responses, three main criteria must be considered. The project leader must have control over all stages of the coding process and must involve the clients wherever possible. The quality of the results must be defined by accurately expressing the words and feelings of the respondents, in this case the doctors. The responses must not be diluted or distorted through translation. As in all multicountry studies, comparability must be achieved. The research should be accurate at the local level, allowing Italians to see what the Italian doctor said, but also allowing the results to be compared across various countries in order to show similarities and differences.

Source: B. Owen, "Approaches to Coding International Research," *Journal of Marketing Research Society,* vol. 33, no. 1, pp. 323–333, 1990.

ALTERNATIVE PROCESSING FLOWS

Although the data processing flow presented in the previous section represents the classic approach, there are alternative ways of transferring the data from acceptable data collection instruments into the computer.

Type One Processing: Traditional   This is the method that we have just presented. In review, its steps are (1) coding of instruments, (2) transferring of codes to coding sheets, and (3) computer entry and verification.

This type receives substantial usage, especially in mail surveys.

Type Two Processing: Edge Coding   It is possible to eliminate the step requiring the transferring of codes to coding sheets by doing what is called *edge coding.* The outside margin of each page of the data collection instrument is marked with spaces representing the columns of a computer card. The coder writes the relevant codes in these spaces instead of on the coding sheets. The edge-coded instruments are then delivered to data entry personnel to be entered and verified.

Type Three Processing: Mark-Sensed Entry   It is possible to eliminate the manual entry and verifying of the data by having coders use special mark-sensed coding sheets to record the data codes. These sheets can then be read into the computer by an optical scanner. The computer can store the data in a disk file. Here the coder fills in appropriate spaces on the mark-sensed sheets with a special pencil. Most coders find this a difficult task. The marks must be made with care, as the optical scanner has tight tolerances and errors can easily result. Also, if the mark-sensed sheets are damaged, the scanner may be unable to read them.

Type Four Processing: Respondent Mark-Sensed Entry   In order to get around the coding problems inherent in type four processing, the respondents can be asked to indicate their responses by filling out the mark-sensed sheet themselves. Students completing a multiple-choice examination are often asked to do this. Both coding and manual entry are thus eliminated in the flow. For this technique to work properly, the respondents must have the proper type of pencil and must understand exactly how to record their responses on the sheets. Close supervision by the researcher is a necessity. Thus, mail instruments are not compatible with this approach. Also, only closed-ended questions can be used here.

Type Five Processing: Direct Computer Entry It may be possible to eliminate both the coding step and the transferring of codes to coding sheets. That is, we may be able to have data entry personnel directly enter and verify the data from the edited data collection instrument itself. To do this, we need an instrument that is made up of closed-ended questions that are wholly precoded. Also, the instrument must be laid out in such a way that the data entry person can easily follow the flow of responses.

This type of processing is most often used in telephone interviewing, but it is becoming increasingly used in personal and disk-based mail interviews, as noted in Chapter 15. The interviewer sits in front of the computer monitor and commands the computer to display the questions one at a time. Precoded answers are also displayed on the computer monitor. The respondent indicates a response, and the interviewer types this response directly into a computer file. Thus editing, coding, and verifying of written questionnaires are eliminated. The data are ready for instant cleaning and analysis. Also, the computer will remember phone numbers that need to be called back; take the correct branching and skip patterns in the questionnaire based upon a respondent's answers; rotate alternative parts of questions (for example, use random order of brand names in a question); and inform the interviewer if an illegal code is entered. The consistency of answers can also be checked instantly, and tabulations of responses to questions are available immediately (see Chapter 18). Results may even be tabulated prior to the completion of the interviewing to allow for response monitoring and preliminary conclusions to be noted. The advent of inexpensive PC-based systems such as Sawtooth Software's Ci3 system have helped to greatly expand the use of this type of processing.

Selection of a Type Choice of a data processing type depends on the availability of computer hardware, optical scanners, and so on. It also depends on the time and cost constraints imposed on the study and the degree of complexity in the data collection instrument. Generally, the more complex the instrument, the more a researcher would tend to do traditional type one processing. Other types can be used as the instrument becomes more structured and as time and cost constraints put pressure on the researcher. If we can get the respondents to fill out a mark-sensed card, we obviously save time and money. The computer entry type saves time but costs more money. The researcher must pick a data processing track that fits the type of study being undertaken and the constraints imposed upon its execution.

We now know exactly what the research analyst at Xerox described earlier in this chapter must do to get data collection instruments ready for analysis. Data processing is not the most exciting area of marketing research, but it is very important. Since a significant proportion of nonsampling errors occur in data processing, the researcher and manager must be attentive to this area.

SUMMARY

1 Data processing is the conversion of raw data in a data collection instrument into computer-readable form.

2 A traditional approach to data processing includes the functions of (a) deciding whether to use the data collection instrument, (b) editing, (c) coding to coding sheets, (d) computer entry and verifying, (e) putting the resultant data deck into computer-readable form, (f) cleaning the data, (g) generating new variables, (h) weighting, and (i) storing the dataset on disk or tape.

3 It is possible to eliminate some of these functions by using edge coding, by entering data directly from the data collection instruments, by using mark-sensed coding sheets, or by recording respondent answers directly into the computer.

DISCUSSION QUESTIONS

1 How are responses to a questionnaire represented in an ASCII file? On a spreadsheet?

2 How do you identify data collection instruments that are unacceptable for data processing?

3 What should an editor do in examining an instrument?

4 What are the fundamental rules of code construction?

5 How should multiple responses be handled?

6 What is a codebook? What should it contain?

7 How is a dataset cleaned?

8 Why would you want to create new variables?

9 What are the alternative data processing types?

10 How do you select a type?

11 You have been assigned the task of preparing a coding manual for a study of personal computer users in 15 countries: the United States, Canada, Mexico, Brazil, Japan, China, the UK, France, Italy, Germany, Spain, Austria, Hungary, New Zealand, and Australia.

Outline your approach to this task.

12 MINICASE

Presented below are selected questions that were developed for the survey conducted in relation to the nutritional labeling case presented in Part One of this book. For each question, give an appropriate coding scheme.

1 Where do you buy most of the food your family eats?
(   ) Large supermarket chain
(   ) Independent grocer
(   ) Farmer's market
(   ) Convenience store like 7–Eleven or Stop-N-Go
(   ) Other _____

2 Is this store helpful in providing nutrition information?
(   ) Yes
(   ) No

6 Which of the following sources do you use "Most often"? (Read list.) "Second most often"?

	Most often	Second most often
Advertisements	( )	( )
Books	( )	( )
Doctor	( )	( )
Food labels	( )	( )
Friends or relatives	( )	( )
Magazines	( )	( )
Store clerks	( )	( )

7 What problems do you have in finding information about the nutritional content of your food?

38 How many children live at home? _____

39 List all the brands of cereal purchased in the last month.

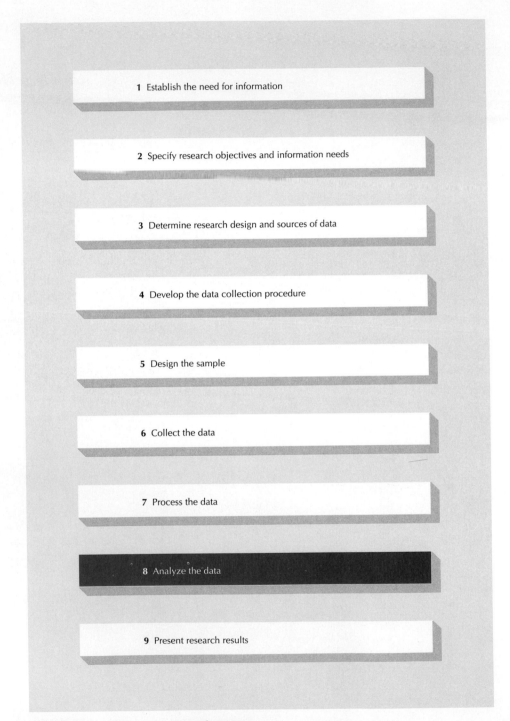

1 Establish the need for information

2 Specify research objectives and information needs

3 Determine research design and sources of data

4 Develop the data collection procedure

5 Design the sample

6 Collect the data

7 Process the data

8 Analyze the data

9 Present research results

FIGURE 18-1   Steps in the research process.

CHAPTER 18

UNIVARIATE DATA ANALYSIS

MARKETING RESEARCH IN ACTION

A ONE-WAY TABULATION OF SURVEY OF MARKET FACTS PANEL REVEALS APPLIANCE BUYER PROFILE

A national sample implemented for companies in the major appliance industry and for federal regulators was drawn from a Market Facts (a marketing research supply firm) mail panel. This study was designed to profile the needs of purchasers and their use of energy and other information in their choice of appliance brands. Simple one-way tabulations formed part of the data analysis plan for the study. Some of these results are presented in the following tables.

REPORTED AWARENESS OF APPLIANCE YEARLY
ENERGY COST

Refrigerator respondents	Percent
Aware	15.9
Unaware (no, no answer, DK)*	84.1
Base	(n = 301)

* DK = don't know

REFRIGERATOR BUYERS' (UNAIDED) MENTIONS
OF FACTORS IMPORTANT IN PURCHASE DECISIONS

Attribute	Percent
Size	61.1
Color, appearance	30.2
Price	19.9
Doors—number/position	30.6
Energy efficiency (net)	21.7
Separate meat compartment	13.3
Separate temperature controls	7.6
Brand name	15.6
It was on sale	4.3
Self-defrosting/frost-free	28.2
Ice maker/water dispenser	18.6
	$(n = 301)$

REFRIGERATOR BUYERS' REPORTED USE OF
ENERGY LABEL INFORMATION
(Base = Respondents Recalling Label and Content)

Question	Percent
Did the label affect buying decision in any way? (Q14c)	47.1
How was decision to buy affected? (Q14f)	
_____ Saved money/energy	62.5
_____ Used to compare appliances	12.5
_____ Other	25.0
Total percent of sample affected	100.0

Even this simple tabulation of these three questions revealed useful information to the researchers. We easily see the position of various attributes in the refrigerator purchase, and the relatively midrange position that energy concerns hold. In addition, the great unawareness of yearly energy costs is noted, as is the impact energy label information had on the buying decision. Clearly those in the industry and government who desire that consumers use energy information extensively have their work cut out for them. This Marketing Research in Action illustrates the power and usefulness of one-way tabulations.

Source: Adapted from Robert F. Dyer and Thomas J. Maronick, "An Evaluation of Consumer Awareness and Use of Energy Labels in the Purchase of Major Appliances—A Longitudinal Analysis," *Journal of Public Policy and Marketing,* vol. 7, pp. 83–97, 1988. Copyright 1988, University of Michigan. Used with permission.

Once the collected data have been properly converted to a computer file, as described in the previous chapter, we are ready to turn our attention to data analysis. Improper data analysis can be a significant source of nonsampling error.

The primary objective of the data analysis chapters in this book is to provide an overview of when specific analysis techniques may properly be used. In order to reach this objective we shall identify a number of data analysis techniques, list the circumstances in which they may be used, and give examples of their use. We shall not attempt to list all techniques or to explain their computational aspects in any detail, because we believe that the purpose of data analysis is to provide meaningful information for decision making and that much valuable information can be provided by means of relatively simple data analysis procedures.

Some marketers and others mistakenly think that data analysis is the most important aspect of marketing research. Our premise is that the most sophisticated data analysis available cannot make up for poor problem definition, bad study design, improper sampling, poor measurement, bad field work, or sloppy data processing. Data analysis is just one of many activities that must be done correctly to yield relevant information for decision making. However, it too must be done properly.

We shall begin this first chapter on data analysis by distinguishing among univariate, bivariate, and multivariate data analysis procedures. Then we shall distinguish between procedures with the objective of describing the sample-based dataset at hand and procedures with the objective of making inferences about the population from which the dataset was selected. Finally, we shall discuss a number of descriptive and inferential techniques appropriate for univariate analysis.

OVERVIEW OF DATA ANALYSIS PROCEDURES

The fundamental data analysis question facing a marketing manager or researcher is: "What data analysis technique should be used?" The answer is provided by outlining specifics about the situation faced by the marketer. Here are three overview questions that help the marketer begin to identify the appropriate technique: (1) How many variables are to be analyzed at the same time? (2) Do we want description or inference questions answered? (3) What level of measurement (nominal, ordinal, interval) is available in the variable or variables of interest?

Number of Variables to Analyze

The first specific aspect of the situation that must be clarified relates to the *objectives of the analysis.* This is the number of variables the marketer wishes to have analyzed at the same time. Figure 18-2 shows this decision question, the possible outcomes to the question, and where in this book the relevant techniques are discussed.

If you wish to examine the analysis of one variable at a time, this is called *univariate data analysis,* and it constitutes the topic of this chapter. The relationship of two variables at a time is examined by means of *bivariate data analysis,* the subject of Chapter 19. The relationships of more than two variables at a time call for *multivariate data analysis,* to be covered in Chapters 20 and 21.

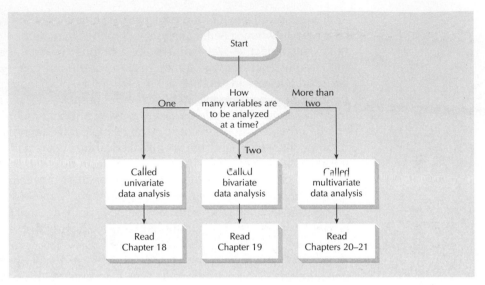

FIGURE 18-2   Overview of data analysis techniques.

Description versus Inference

The second question that must be answered is whether you are interested in the *description of the sample* or in making *inferences about the population* from which the sample was drawn. Descriptive statistics is a branch of statistics that provides researchers with summary measures for the data in their samples. It provides answers to such questions as: (1) What is the average age in the sample? (2) What is the dispersion of ages in the sample? and (3) What is the level of association between age and income in the sample? Inferential statistics is a branch of statistics that allows researchers to make judgments about the whole population based upon the results generated by samples. It is based upon probability theory. It provides answers to such questions as: (1) Is the average age of the population 25? (2) Is the level of association between age and income in the population greater than zero? (3) Are the population treatment means in an experiment equal to each other? Both descriptive and inferential statistics have important applications in marketing research. Marketers must know which type of analysis they are interested in.

Level of Measurement

The third question that must be answered is whether the variable or variables to be analyzed have been measured at a *nominal-, ordinal-, or interval-scale level.*[1]

---

[1]There are procedures available for ratio data only. However, they have little relevance to real marketing research problems. Any ratio data in marketing research are usually analyzed by procedures relevant to interval data.

Both descriptive and inferential techniques vary by the scale level inherent in the variable or variables being analyzed.

If marketers know the number of variables to be analyzed at a time, whether the interest is in description or inference, and the scale level of the variable or variables, they are then in a position to select the appropriate statistical procedure. The rest of this chapter identifies and describes the relevant techniques for the analysis of one variable at a time. In presenting this material we recognize that a computer will be doing the calculations. This does not negate the need for us to know when to use what procedure, because the computer will calculate any statistic we ask it to, even if that statistic is not appropriate for the data.

OVERVIEW OF UNIVARIATE DATA ANALYSIS PROCEDURES

Figure 18-3 presents an overview of statistical techniques available for univariate data analysis. It is often important in studies to do a univariate analysis on some variables. For example, the manager might want a description of the sample's demographic characteristics, of the usage of the company's product, or of respondent attitudes toward a competitive activity. In each situation, the researcher can gain useful information by examining statistics related to one variable at a time. To make sure we are looking for the right procedure, we begin the process described in Figure 18-3 by asking whether we want to analyze one variable at a time. Only if this question is answered positively does Figure 18-3 provide us with a guide to the correct procedure. Our next question concerns the scale level of

FIGURE 18-3   Overview of univariate data analysis procedures.

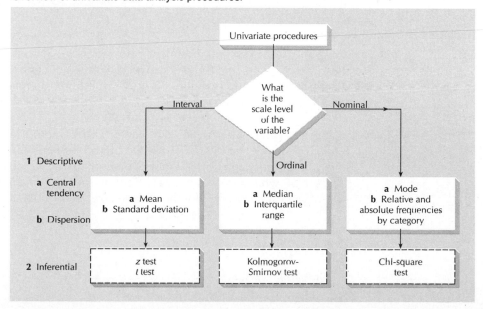

the variable to be analyzed. It may be nominal, ordinal, or interval. Below each of these possible answers to the scale-level question on Figure 18-3, two sets of boxes are shown. The first set presents the relevant descriptive statistics. The top part of these boxes presents the appropriate measure of central tendency, while the bottom part presents the appropriate measure of dispersion. The boxes defined by dashed lines, positioned below the descriptive statistics boxes, show the appropriate tests of statistical inference for each data type. Note that statistics appropriate for lower scales can be applied to higher scales. For example, a mode and a median can properly be calculated for interval data. However, the opposite is not true, the mean is not an appropriate statistic for ordinal or nominal data.

It is not our purpose here to give details of every descriptive statistic and every test of inference for every measurement level. This task would take too long. The discussion presented in these chapters will deal with only those techniques that are most relevant to marketing research practice. Thus in this chapter we will not discuss the interquartile range statistic or the Kolmogorov-Smirnov test, for these are not in the mainstream of marketing research practice. What follows, then, is a discussion of those statistical procedures with which we feel a practicing marketing researcher should be familiar.

DESCRIPTIVE STATISTICS

The objective of descriptive statistics is to provide summary measures of the data contained in all the elements of a sample. In doing so the marketing researcher is usually concerned with measures of central tendency and measures of dispersion. We now turn our attention to identifying these measures by measurement scale level.

Measures of Central Tendency

Three measures of central tendency are often used in marketing research: the mean, the median, and the mode. The usefulness of central tendency measure to practitioners is noted in Figure 18-4, with about 91 percent of businesses using them in their marketing research.

Interval Data—The Mean   The mean is the appropriate measure of central tendency for interval data. The reader should be familiar with the concept of a mean, since we made use of it for both a continuous variable and a proportion in Chapter 14, when discussing simple random sampling. To review, the *mean* is the sum of the values divided by the sample size. In formula,

$$\bar{X} = \frac{\sum_{i=1}^{n} X_i}{n}$$

Thus, if our sample yielded the values 22, 26, 25, 21, and 19, the mean would be 113/5 = 22.6.

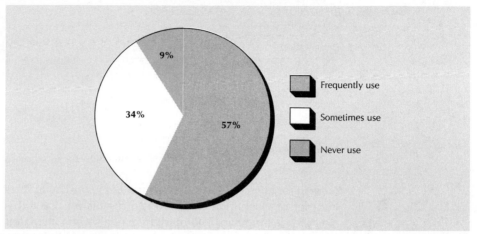

FIGURE 18-4 Use in practice of measures of central tendency. (*Source:* Thomas C. Kinnear and Ann R. Root, *A Study of the Marketing Research Business,* unpublished study, 1994. Copyright 1994 Thomas C. Kinnear. Not to be reproduced.)

It is also possible to calculate a mean when interval data are grouped into categories or classes. Here the formula for the mean is

$$\bar{X} = \frac{\sum_{i=1}^{k} f_i X_i}{n}$$

where f_i = frequency of the ith class
$\quad\quad X_i$ = midpoint of the ith class
$\quad\quad k$ = number of classes

Table 18-1 illustrates such a calculation.

Ordinal Data—The Median   If our data form an ordinal or interval scale, we may legitimately make use of the median as a measure of central tendency. The

TABLE 18-1   CALCULATION OF THE MEAN USING GROUPED INTERVAL DATA

Age classes	Number in class, f_i	Midpoint, X_i	$f_i X_i$
15 to under 20	10	17.5	175
20 to under 25	20	22.5	450
25 to under 30	30	27.5	825
30 to under 35	20	32.5	650
$k = 4$	$\Sigma f_i = 80 = n$		$\Sigma f_i X_i = 2100$
$\bar{X} = 2100/80 = 26.25$			

TABLE 18-2   IDENTIFICATION OF THE MEDIAN FOR
UNGROUPED DATA

Observation	Score or value of X_i
X_1	10
X_2	20
X_3	70 ← median
X_4	140
X_5	500

median for ungrouped data is defined as the midvalue when the data are arranged in order of magnitude. Table 18-2 presents an ordered set of observations and identifies the median. The median may also be calculated for grouped data. The formula for doing so is complex and would add little to our understanding of the concept here. What is important is that the median can be applied to either ordinal or interval data.

Nominal Data—The Mode   The *mode* is a measure of central tendency appropriate for nominal or higher-order scales. It is the category of a nominal variable that occurs with greatest frequency. It should not be applied to ordinal or interval data unless these data have been grouped first. For example, in Table 18-1 the modal class is formed by the ages 25 to under 30.

Sometimes a variable is bimodal. That is, two classes have relatively similar frequencies. This should be a tip-off to the researcher to look for some other variable in the situation that may be causing this situation. For example, coffee sales recorded at both large and small stores could yield a bimodal distribution. The researcher should have been aware of this. Also, if the distribution is bimodal, the mean and median do not describe the variable well. They are simply some "midpoints" between the modes. It is therefore a good idea to look at measures of dispersion. Note in the Marketing Research in Action on appliance purchases at the beginning of this chapter that "size" is the modal category for attribute importance for refrigerator purchases.

Measures of Dispersion

Measures of central tendency do not provide enough information for researchers to fully understand the distribution they are examining. For example, the numbers 10, 15, 20 and 5, 10, 30 both have a mean of 15. Clearly, we need a measure of the spread of the distribution of the variable, that is, a measure of dispersion. The usefulness of measures of dispersion to practitioners is shown in Figure 18-5, with about 84 percent of businesses using them in their marketing research.

Interval Data—The Standard Deviation   The appropriate measure of dispersion for interval data is the standard deviation, the measure we calculated for a

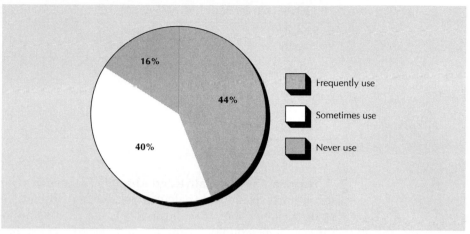

FIGURE 18-5 Use in practice of measures of dispersion. (*Source:* Thomas C. Kinnear and Ann R. Root, *A Study of the Marketing Research Business,* unpublished study, 1994. Copyright 1994 Thomas C. Kinnear. Not to be reproduced.)

continuous variable and a proportion in Chapter 14. In formula, the standard deviation of a sample is

$$s = \sqrt{\frac{\sum_{i=1}^{n}(X_i - \bar{X})^2}{n - 1}}$$

We calculated this value in detail in Chapter 14 and will therefore not repeat the calculation here.

Whether or not a particular size of standard deviation constitutes a large or small dispersion depends on the size of the mean with which it is associated. For example, to be told that a standard deviation is 100 does not help us much. However, if we are told that in this case the mean is 200, we can conclude that the variable has a large dispersion. If the mean were instead 2000, we could conclude that the variable had a small dispersion. We formalize this type of conclusion by calculating what is called the coefficient of variation. In formula:

$$CV = \frac{s}{\bar{X}}$$

where CV is the coefficient of variation. Thus CV is the standard deviation expressed as a percentage of the mean. In our example above,

$$CV_1 = \frac{100}{200} = .5 \quad \text{and} \quad CV_2 = \frac{100}{2000} = .05$$

TABLE 18-3   PRESENTATION OF RELATIVE AND ABSOLUTE FREQUENCIES FOR NOMINAL VARIABLE

Region of the country	Absolute frequency (number)	Relative frequencies (percentage)
East	210	20.2
West	405	38.9
North	109	10.5
South	316	30.4
Total	1040	100.0

Nominal Data—Relative and Absolute Frequencies   For nominal data or better, we may legitimately calculate relative and absolute frequencies as measures of dispersion. Table 18-3 illustrates such a calculation for the nominal variable "region of the country." Absolute frequencies are just the numbers in the sample that appear in each category of the nominal variable. Thus, in our example in Table 18-3, 210 elements were found to have come from the east. Relative frequencies are the percentages of the total elements that appear in each category; thus 20.2 percent (210/1040) of the elements are from the east.

Often, just describing what is in the sample is not enough. We may also want to make inferences from the sample to the population from which it was drawn. It is to this issue that we now turn our attention. In order to understand properly the following discussion on inference, you must understand the basics of hypothesis testing, which we present first.

HYPOTHESIS TESTING

Hypothesis testing is a procedure that is familiar to those who have had a basic statistics course. We assume that you have had such a course but would benefit from the review which follows.

The Concept of a Null Hypothesis

Hypothesis testing begins with the statement of a hypothesis in a *null form,* that is, a form that supposes that a population parameter takes on a particular value or set of values. For example, we might wish to test to see whether the mean age of a class was 25 years. The null hypothesis (H_0) is

$$H_0: \mu = 25$$

It is the null hypothesis that we evaluate in hypothesis testing. A null hypothesis may be rejected and some alternative hypothesis accepted. Alternatively, the null hypothesis may not be rejected in the test. In this situation, we do not conclude that the null hypothesis is valid. We do not accept a null hypothesis. All we can say is that we do not have the evidence to reject it. It may later be proved incorrect with the collection of new sample data. Note that we test the value of a population parameter with data generated by a sample; thus, the sample value might differ from the population value simply because of sampling error. By examining the sampling distribution of a statistic we can determine whether the sample value is different enough from the proposed null hypothesis value to have occurred just by sampling error. If this difference were greater than that due to sampling error, we would reject the null hypothesis. Stating the null hypothesis as we did above implies a number of *alternative hypotheses*. One such hypothesis is that the mean age is not 25. We can write the null and alternative hypotheses as

$$H_0: \mu = 25$$

$$H_1: \mu \neq 25$$

In testing this null hypothesis, we would reject it if the mean age were either greater or less than 25. We are thus interested in the sampling distribution of mean ages on both sides of 25. This type of test is called a "two-tailed" test since we will examine both ends of the sampling distribution to see at what level of chance the mean value of our sample generated could have occurred just because of sampling error.

Another alternative hypothesis in this situation is that the mean age is greater than 25. We write

$$H_0: \mu = 25$$

$$H_1: \mu > 25$$

Here, our interest is only in the upper part of the sampling distribution of means. A hypothesis test applied here is called a "one-tailed" test since we have a specific direction in mind for the alternative hypothesis. The final alternative hypothesis here is that the mean age is less than 25. Again this would be a one-tailed test.

It is possible to phrase the null hypothesis to cover a range of values. For example,

$$H_0: \mu \leq 25$$

implies an alternative hypothesis:

$$H_1: \mu > 25$$

With a direction given to the alternative hypothesis, a one-tailed test applies. Take care to phrase the null hypothesis in such a way as to accept the alternative hypothesis that is really of interest if the null hypothesis is rejected.

Possible Errors

In hypothesis testing the decision maker either rejects or does not reject H_0. The decision may or may not be correct. If H_0 is true and is not rejected, the decision is correct. Also, if H_0 is false and is rejected, the decision is correct. Alternatively, the rejection of a true H_0 or the nonrejection of a false H_0 would indicate that an error had been made. These errors are named *type I* and *type II* errors, respectively. They are also referred to as α error and β error, respectively. Table 18-4 presents a summary of sample conclusions and their possible outcomes.

Also summarized in Table 18-4 are the probabilities of being correct and of making each type of error. The usual beginning point in testing a null hypothesis is to specify the level of type I error the researcher is willing to tolerate. You know that a null hypothesis is tested with sample data, so you expect some sampling error to be in the data. The further the sample result is from the null hypothesis, the more likely that H_0 is not true. However, you recognize that the sample estimate you have generated may have come from the tail of the sampling distribution of the statistic about the true value H_0. It may be an outlier. In specifying an α error level, the researcher indicates that an α proportion of the outlying part of the sampling distribution of the statistic will be assumed to be too far from H_0 not to reject H_0. In doing so, you recognize the probability equal to α of making a type I error. This designation of α is referred to as the *significance level* of the hypothesis test. For example, a researcher may specify $\alpha = .05$, indicating that there is a probability of .05 that a type I error has been made. We say *the test is performed at the .05 significance level.*

Instead of looking at the probability of making an α error, we could also consider the probability of not rejecting H_0 when it is true. This probability is $1 - \alpha$ and is referred to as the *confidence level* of the test. The more confidence we want in the test, the smaller we make α. A test performed at the .05 significance level is thus performed at the $1 - .05 = .95$ confidence level. The confidence level discussed here is exactly the same concept as the confidence level we discussed in connection with calculating confidence intervals in Chapter 14 (which dealt with simple random sampling). It relates to the proportion of the sampling distribution of a statistic that is within a certain distance from the true population value.

Now we examine the possible outcomes when H_0 is false. If we do not reject H_0 when it is false, we have made a type II or β error. This occurs when we observe what we think is an outlier of the sampling distribution of the statistic

TABLE 18-4   SUMMARY OF HYPOTHESIS TESTING ERRORS

	True condition	
Sample conclusion	H_0 is true	H_0 is false
Do not reject H_0	1 Correct decision 2 Confidence level 3 Probability = $1 - \alpha$	1 Type II error 2 Probability = β
Reject H_0	1 Type I error 2 Significance level 3 Probability = α	1 Correct decision 2 Power of the test 3 Probability = $1 - \beta$

about H_0, when we really are looking at a value drawn from a sampling distribution about a value other than H_0. The farther an observed value of a statistic is from H_0, the more likely it is that it comes from another sampling distribution. Thus, the smaller we set α, the larger the probability of a type II error. We call this probability of a type II error β.

If H_0 is false and we reject it, we have made a correct decision. We describe the probability of rejecting a false null hypothesis as the power of the test. The measure of this probability is $1 - \beta$. β and therefore $1 - \beta$ take on a specific value only when a specific alternative hypothesis value for a statistic is given. For now, it is enough to recognize that β increases as α decreases for a given sample size. In practice β is often determined only after the sample has been selected, or it is just ignored. The problem with this approach in marketing is that the cost of a type II error to an organization may be much greater than the cost of a type I error. Consider this example:

> In the case of making a type I error in the choice of the best promotional strategy for a new product introduction, suppose that we reject the true hypothesis (conclude that one promotional strategy was better than the others) even though all were, in fact, equally effective. Since we have to select one of the equally effective alternatives, there is actually little risk associated with our choice of strategies.
>
> On the other hand, we might accept the hypothesis (conclude that there is no difference in the effectiveness of the three promotional strategies) when one promotional strategy is, in fact, more effective than the others. This type II error could be very expensive, in terms of opportunity costs, if we select one of the less effective strategies.[2]

Obviously, then, there are compelling managerial reasons for choosing a level of significance (α) in the .10 to .25 range instead of the traditional .01 or .05 levels used in social science research.

Steps in Hypothesis Testing

The steps we will use in hypothesis testing are:

1 Formulate a null and an alternative hypothesis.

2 Select the appropriate statistical test given the type of data the researcher has.

3 Specify the significance level, α.

4 Look up the value of the test statistic in a set of tables (see the Appendix at the end of this book) for the given α; these tables give points on the sampling distribution of the statistic in question that occur with different α probabilities.

5 Perform the statistical test chosen in step 2 on the data available; this yields a value of the relevant statistic.

6 Compare the value of the statistic calculated in item 5 with the value looked up in step 4. If step 5 value is greater than step 4 value, we reject the null

---

[2]Keith K. Cox and Ben M. Enis, *Experimentation for Marketing Decisions* (Scranton, PA: International Textbook Company, 1969), p. 11.

hypothesis, because the value of step 5 has come too far out on the sampling distribution to be considered by us a part of the sampling distribution about H_0.

As Figure 18-6 indicates, this formal use of statistical significance in hypothesis testing is used in practice by about 89 percent of businesses in their marketing research.

In the next sections of this chapter, we will apply these steps.

INFERENTIAL STATISTICS

The appropriate test of statistical inferences also varies by the scale level of the data available.

Interval Data

Two different tests, the z test and the t test, are appropriate for interval data. The choice between the two depends on the researcher's knowledge of the population standard deviation and the sample size used. These tests are tests about the size of the population mean.

z Test The z test allows researchers to compare the mean generated from a sample with a mean hypothesized to exist in the population, and to decide whether the sample mean allows them to conclude that the hypothesized population mean is true. The z test is appropriate for interval data in situations where (1) the sample size is any size and the population standard deviation σ is known or (2) the sample size is greater than 30 and the population standard deviation σ is unknown. In situations where $n < 30$ and σ is unknown, the t test should be used. It will be discussed shortly.

FIGURE 18-6 Use in practice of statistical significance. (*Source:* Thomas C. Kinnear and Ann R. Root, *A Study of the Marketing Research Business,* unpublished study, 1994. Copyright 1994 Thomas C. Kinnear. Not to be reproduced.)

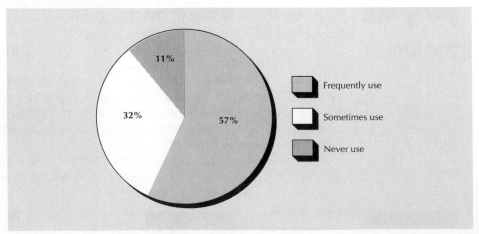

Let us illustrate the z test for the continuous variable "age," using the following steps in hypothesis testing. Also, let us assume that a sample of university students taking marketing research has yielded the following information: $\bar{X} = 24$, $s = 5$, and $n = 100$.

Step 1. Formulate null and alternative hypotheses   In this situation the null and alternative hypotheses are

$$H_0: \mu = 23$$

$$H_1: \mu \neq 23$$

So the researcher wants to know whether the sample mean age of 24 will allow the conclusion that the population mean age is 23. The alternative hypothesis, H_1, is phrased so that we know that a sample value too far above or below 23 will allow us to reject H_0. Thus, we will be using a two-tailed test. If $H_1: \mu < 23$ were the alternative hypothesis, we would reject H_0 only if the mean age were far below H_0. This would be a one-tailed test. It is important to know which test you are doing, because the number of tails affects the position in a statistical table that you consult to find the critical value of the statistic involved.

Step 2. Select the appropriate statistical tests   The appropriate test here is the z test because $n > 30$ and we are testing a hypothesis about means. This test is based on the nature of the sampling distribution of the mean as discussed in Chapter 14. We know by the central-limit theorem that the mean value we generated from our sample comes from a sampling distribution of means that forms a normal curve. Also, we know the area under a normal curve and thus the number of sampling means located within a certain number of standard errors of the mean of this distribution. Because of this we can determine the probability that any sample mean could have come from a sampling distribution of means that lies about the hypothesized population mean. This was essentially what we were doing in Chapter 14 when we calculated confidence intervals.

The critical values of the z statistic are given in Table A-2 in the Appendix at the end of the book for a two-tailed test and in Table A-3 for a one-tailed test. The values in these tables are given for a mean of zero and a standard deviation of 1. Thus to use these tables we will have to convert data from a sample to remove the effects of the unit of measurement. The values in the first column and first row of the table are combined to give the z values (i.e., the number of standard deviations about the mean that interest the researcher). The values in the body of the table give the area contained in the tail or tails of the distribution. This provides a measure of the probability of rejecting a true null hypothesis. In other words, these values are α, the probability of making a type I error.

For example, in Table A-2 for $\alpha = .05$, we find that this is 1.96 (1.9 from column 1 + .06 from row 1) standard deviations from the mean. We note that this represents the 95 percent confidence level. In Chapter 14, it was stated that the 95 percent confidence interval was $\bar{X} \pm 2$ times the standard error; in truth it is $\bar{X} \pm 1.96$ times the standard error, but we simply rounded it off to facilitate the discussion in that chapter. What the 1.96 tells us is that the probability of getting a value of z greater than 1.96 is less than .05. In Table A-3 we note that the probability of getting a value of z greater than 1.96 is less than .025. Thus, here we would be using a test with α = .025. For α = .05 in a one-tailed test, we note that z = 1.64. Thus the probability of getting a z value greater than 1.64 in a one-tailed test is less than .05.

Step 3. Specify the significance level   The researcher must specify a significance level, α. In doing so you must recognize that the smaller you set α, the bigger β will be for any given sample size. In our example we shall use α = .1.

Step 4. Look up the z value for α = .1   We note in Table A-2 that z = 1.64 for α = .1. This is our critical value of z. If the z calculated from the data exceeds 1.64, we will reject the null hypothesis.

Step 5. Perform the statistical test   If the population standard deviation is known,

$$z = \frac{\bar{X} - \mu}{\sigma_{\bar{X}}} = \frac{\bar{X} - \mu}{\sigma/\sqrt{n}}$$

If σ is not known,

$$z = \frac{\bar{X} - \mu}{s_{\bar{X}}} = \frac{\bar{X} - \mu}{s/\sqrt{n}}$$

In our example, σ is not known, so we use the latter formula. What the formula does is express the difference between the observed mean $\bar{X}$ and the hypothesized mean μ as a measure expressed as a number of standard errors. The question is: Is the difference $\bar{X} - \mu$ expressed in standard error (the calculated z value) large enough to be likely to occur by sampling error less than .1 of the time?

In our example,

$$z = \frac{24 - 23}{5/\sqrt{100}} = \frac{1}{.5}$$

$$= 2.0$$

Thus the difference $24 - 23$ is equal to 2 standard errors.

Step 6. Compare z values   The calculated z value exceeds the z value for α = .1 (2.0 > 1.64), and thus we reject the null hypothesis. We may not conclude that the average age in the population is 23.

The z test may also be applied to a proportion. Here, for a situation where $n > 30$ and σ_p is unknown,[3]

---

[3]For small n the binomial distribution must be used. This is so atypical of real marketing research problems that it is not discussed here.

$$z = \frac{p - \pi}{s_p} = \frac{p - \pi}{\sqrt{pq/n}}$$

where p = sample proportion

π = hypothesized proportion

s_p = standard error of the proportion

In a situation designed to measure market share, a sample might generate an estimate of market share p. We might wish to compare this with a target market share of over π. If $p = .3$, $n = 30$, $H_0: \pi \leq .25$, $H_1: \pi > .25$,

$$z = \frac{.3 - .25}{\sqrt{(.3)(.7)/30}} = \frac{.05}{.084} = .60$$

The difference between the observed and hypothesized proportions is .60 standard error. At $\alpha = .01$ in the one-tailed test, $z = 2.32$. Therefore, because the calculated z is less than the critical z from the table, we cannot reject the null hypothesis that $\pi \leq .25$. Therefore, we cannot conclude in a managerial sense that we have reached our target market share of over 25 percent. Note that this is true even though the sample market share was 30 percent.[4]

t Test The t test is appropriately used in hypothesis testing about means for all sample sizes when σ is unknown. The reason we use z when $n > 30$ is that the t distribution and the z distribution are virtually identical when $n > 30$, and the values of the t distribution have not been calculated for large sample sizes. In a t test we estimate σ by using s. The critical values of the t statistics are presented in Table A-4 in the Appendix at the end of the book. The critical value of t varies by the α level selected, the number of degrees of freedom in the sample, and whether a one- or two-tailed test is needed. For example, we note that for $\alpha = .05$ in a one-tailed test with 10 degrees of freedom, $t = 1.812$. There are always $n - 1$ degrees of freedom in a t test of the mean, because we are using s as an estimate of σ, and s has $n - 1$ degrees of freedom. The t table gives values of t that can occur simply as a result of sampling error.

Let us quickly illustrate a t test. Suppose that in attempting to estimate yearly rates of cola consumption per capita,

$$H_0: \mu = 100 \text{ gallons}$$

$$H_1: \mu > 100 \text{ gallons}$$

and a sample has yielded the following:

$$\bar{X} = 120 \qquad s = 15 \qquad n = 7$$

[4]For any given α, n, and related sample results, it is possible to calculate the probability of making a type II error, β, and the resultant power of the test, $1 - \beta$. However, these are complex statistical topics which are almost never calculated in real marketing research problems. Thus, we have omitted their calculation from the current discussion. If you are interested, you should consult any good basic statistics book.

Here

$$t = \frac{\bar{X} - \mu}{s_{\bar{X}}} = \frac{\bar{X} - \mu}{s/\sqrt{n}}$$

$$= \frac{120 - 100}{15/\sqrt{7}} = \frac{20}{5.67}$$

$$= 3.53$$

The critical value of t at $\alpha = .1$ for a one-tailed test at 6 df is 1.44. Since our calculated t exceeds the critical t we reject the null hypothesis and accept the alternative that per capita cola consumption in the population exceeds 100 gallons.

Nominal Data

Researchers are interested in more than just hypotheses about the mean. Often they wish to make inferences about how respondents are distributed across the possible categories of a nominal variable. For example, in a sample of families who purchase returnable bottles, the researcher might want to know whether these respondents are distributed equally in all occupational categories. The chi-square test is a procedure for comparing a hypothesized population distribution across categories against an observed distribution.

Chi-Square Test   In a chi-square test, a hypothesized population distribution is compared with a distribution generated by a sample. The formula for chi square is

$$\chi^2 = \sum_{i=1}^{k} \frac{(O_i - E_i)^2}{E_i}$$

where k = number of categories of the variable
O_i = observed number of respondents in category i
E_i = hypothesized number of respondents in category i

Table A-6 in the Appendix at the end of the book gives the critical values of the chi-square distribution. These are the values of chi square that can occur by chance (due to sampling error) for various degrees of freedom and various α levels. The number of degrees of freedom is given in the left-hand column of Table A-6. It is referred to as n on the table. In a univariate chi-square test, the degrees of freedom equal $k - 1$, since for a given sample size, once the number of respondents in $k - 1$ categories is known, the number in the k category is automatically

TABLE 18-5 CALCULATION OF CHI SQUARE FOR OCCUPATIONAL CATEGORIES

Occupational category	O_i	E_i	$O_i - E_i$	$(O_i - E_i)^2$	$(O_i - E_i)^2/E_i$
Labor	15	25	−10	100	4
Clerical	20	25	−5	25	1
Managerial	00	25	5	25	1
Student	35	25	10	100	4
Total	100	100			10

$df = k - 1 = 3$; calculated $\chi^2 = 10$; critical χ^2 at 3 df and $\alpha = .1 = 6.25$.

determined. The top row in Table A-6 gives the value of $1 - \alpha$. So if we want $\alpha = .05$, we look in the column for $1 - \alpha = .95$. Let's see how to find a critical value of chi square. Suppose that we have a variable with 7 df and have specified that $\alpha = .05$. Then we look down the $1 - \alpha = .95$ column until it intersects with the row representing 7 df. The critical chi square would be 14.1.

Column 1 of Table 18-5 gives the observed distribution of returnable-bottle users across occupational categories. The null hypothesis here is that there is no difference in the population of returnable-bottle users across occupational categories. Thus we would expect an equal number of respondents in each occupational category. These expected numbers are given in column 2 of Table 18-5. The remaining columns of the table present the steps necessary to calculate chi square in this situation. We see that the calculated chi square equals 10. If we set $\alpha = .1$, the critical chi square from Table A-6 at 3 df is 6.25. Since the calculated chi square exceeds the critical chi square, we reject the null hypothesis and conclude that users of returnable bottles differ in occupational category. Note that the chi-square test merely tells us that there is a significant relationship. We must then go back and look at the distribution itself to see the nature of the relationship. Here we see that students form the modal category.

It is not necessary to have the null hypothesis that all categories have an equal number of respondents; the chi-square test may be used to compare observed results with any hypothesized distribution.

Of course, a good computer data analysis package would provide all the procedures presented in this chapter. The purpose of this chapter has been to let you know which statistics to ask the computer to generate in a univariate context.

SUMMARY

1 The choice of data analysis procedure depends upon the number of variables to be analyzed at the same time, whether the interest is in description or inference, and the level of measurement of the variable or variables.

2 Descriptive statistics provide summary measures of the data contained in the sample.

3 Inferential statistics allow the researchers to make judgments about the population based upon the sample results.

4 The mean and the standard deviation are the relevant descriptive measures of central tendency and dispersion, respectively, for interval data.

5 The median is the relevant descriptive measure of central tendency for ordinal data.

6 The mode and relative and absolute frequencies are the relevant descriptive measures of central tendency and dispersion, respectively, for nominal data.

7 A null hypothesis is a statement that a population parameter takes on a particular value or set of values.

8 A null hypothesis may be rejected or not rejected. If it is rejected, the alternative hypothesis is accepted. A null hypothesis is never accepted.

9 Type I error occurs when you reject a true null hypothesis. It occurs with a probability of α, where α is called the significance level of the hypothesis test.

10 $1 - \alpha$ is the probability of not rejecting a true null hypothesis. It is called the level of confidence.

11 Type II error occurs when we do not reject a false null hypothesis. It occurs with a probability of β.

12 $1 - \beta$ is the probability of rejecting a false null hypothesis. It is called the power of the test.

13 From a management point of view, the cost of a type II error may be greater than that of a type I error.

14 The steps in hypothesis testing are: (a) Formulate null and alternative hypotheses. (b) Select the appropriate statistical test. (c) Specify the significance level. (d) Find the critical value of the test statistic in tables. (e) Calculate the statistic using the sample data. (f) Compare the statistic values. If (e) is greater than (d), reject the null hypothesis.

15 The z test is the appropriate inferential test about means for interval data when σ is known for any sample size, or for situations where σ is unknown and $n > 30$.

16 The t test is the appropriate inferential test about means for interval data when σ is unknown.

17 The chi-square test is the appropriate inferential test for the distribution of subjects across a nominal variable.

DISCUSSION QUESTIONS

1 What is univariate data analysis?
2 Distinguish between descriptive and inferential statistics.
3 Why are both measures of central tendency and measures of dispersion necessary to describe a variable?
4 Describe the steps in hypothesis testing in general.
5 Distinguish between significance level and confidence level.
6 What are type I and type II errors?
7 What is the power of the test?

8 From a sample of Sega game users, the following frequency count was generated for the categories of the variable age.

Age	Frequency
55 and over	110
40–54	115
25–39	205
18–24	315
	$n = 745$

Is Sega usage spread evenly across the population in terms of age?

9 The manager of a movie theater hypothesized that twice as many of the theater's patrons were under 30 as were 30 and over. A sample of patrons yielded the following results:

Age	Frequency
Under 30	450
30 and over	240
	$n = 690$

Is the theater manager's hypothesis about the population of patrons correct?

10 A sales manager had promised the entire sales force a special trip if average daily sales per salesperson were $8000 or more. A sample of 10 salespersons yielded the following results: average daily sales per salesperson = $7800; standard deviation = $400. Can the sales manager conclude that the entire sales force has reached the goal?

11 A political research firm undertook a sample of registered voters in a small community to see whether a particular candidate would win the election. The sample size was 50, and the result was that 51 percent of the sample favored this candidate. If people vote as they say they will, do the results indicate that this candidate will win the election?

12 A company had adopted the following decision rule with respect to introducing a new product: If average monthly consumption is 300 ounces or more, we will enter into test market. An in-home placement test of $n = 80$ yielded the following results: average monthly consumption = 290 ounces; standard deviation = 45. Given their decision rule, what decision should they make?

13 MINICASE

The Lake City chief of police wanted to discover how fast the average car traveled on a particular stretch of highway. To get this information, he placed a hidden radar device beside the highway and clocked speeds for an hour. The following data were recorded by the device:

73	49	70	63	83	61
55	61	60	68	62	64
52	56	69	60	55	71
65	66	59	62	59	58

Questions:

a Calculate the appropriate statistics for central tendency and dispersion.

b What are the problems with this design?

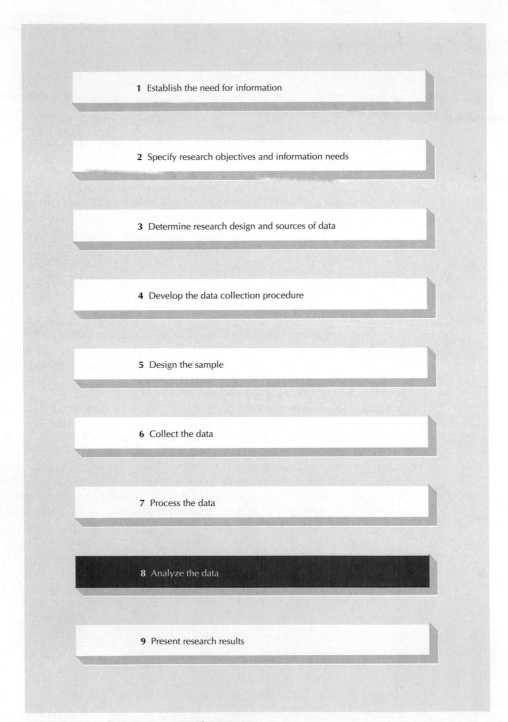

FIGURE 19-1 Steps in the research process.

CHAPTER 19

BIVARIATE DATA ANALYSIS

MARKETING RESEARCH IN ACTION

A TWO-WAY TABULATION OF SURVEY DATA REVEALS PROFILE OF FINANCIAL SERVICES SEGMENTS

Greenwood Federal Savings and Loan (GF) is a profitable institution located in the upper midwest. As part of its marketing plan to improve its customer service, GF did an extensive survey of its customers and potential customers. The data were collected from the upper midwest regional part of National Family Opinion's consumer panel, and from GF's customer list. A total of 712 people responded to the mail questionnaire. This study was used to identify segments that exist in the financial marketplace. A profile was then developed of the financial holdings, attitudes, and preferences for services of each of these segments. Two-way tabulations or cross tabulations were used to develop these segment profiles. One of these cross tabulations was as follows:

Attribute	Segment 1	Segment 2	Segment 3	Segment 4	Segment 5
Percent of total study	13%	11%	22%	33%	19%
Liquid cash	$8,078	$4,707	$5,034	$2,556	$3,007
Stocks and bonds	$27,401	$8,360	$14,362	$7,019	$5,285
Total cash, stocks, and bonds savings	$71,677	$35,312	$38,097	$20,945	$16,498

Even this simple cross-tabular table provides useful information related to the differences in the financial holding of the five segments. This information is then useful in developing different services for each of the segments. For example, segment 1 could have more need for brokerage services than segments 4 and 5, while the latter two segments might be better targets for loan-based products. When this information was combined with that from other cross tabulations related to segment attitudes, demographics, and product preferences, GF was able to develop an effective marketing plan to compete in the marketplace.

Source: Kenneth L. Bernhardt and Thomas C. Kinnear, "Greenwood Federal Savings and Loan," *Cases in Marketing Management,* 6th ed. (Homewood, IL: Business Publications, Inc., 1994). Used with permission.

In most marketing research studies the interests of the researcher and the manager go beyond the univariate data analysis discussed in Chapter 18. They are often interested in the relationship between variables taken two at a time. Typical questions for which bivariate analysis can provide answers include: (1) What is the relationship between use of our brand and media viewing habits? (2) What is the relationship between sales force turnover and sales manager age? (3) Is there a difference between attitudes toward our brand and toward other brands?

This chapter presents those data analysis procedures that are appropriate for bivariate relationships. Again, the appropriate technique depends upon the scale level of the variables involved and whether the researcher wants a descriptive statistic or an inferential test. We shall also discuss some issues related to the interpretation of cross-tabulation tables.

OVERVIEW OF BIVARIATE PROCEDURES

Figure 19-2 presents an overview of some bivariate descriptive statistics and inferential tests. Here we must be sure that we want to analyze two variables at a time. If this is the case, the scale level of the variables involved then guides us to the appropriate statistic. Not all possible combinations of bivariate relationships are presented in Figure 19-2. For example, it is possible to analyze an interval and an ordinal variable together, or a nominal and an ordinal variable, and so on. These types of bivariate relationships are not discussed here, as they have little application in marketing research. Further, some of the procedures presented in Figure 19-2 do not as yet have wide application in marketing research and will not be discussed here. Instead, this chapter will be devoted to the bivariate procedures that are most relevant to real marketing research problems. Specifically, from descriptive statistics for interval variables we shall discuss (1) the linear correlation coefficient, r, and (2) simple regression. Also, from inferential statistics for interval variables we shall discuss (1) the *t* test on the regression coefficient, (2) the *z* test on the difference between means, and (3) the *t* test on the difference between means. Finally, from inferential statistics for nominal variables, we shall discuss the chi-square test.

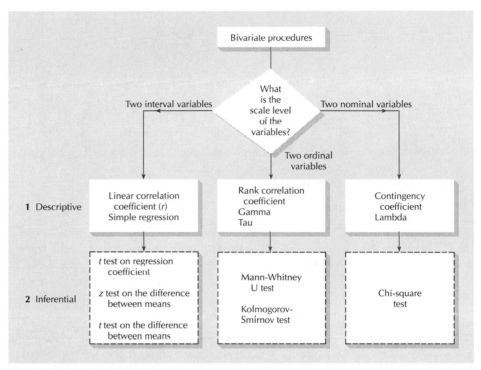

FIGURE 19-2   Bivariate data analysis procedures.

DESCRIPTIVE STATISTICS

Often the interest of the research is in describing the nature of bivariate relationships generated from a sample. This section presents a description of two relevant descriptive statistical procedures appropriate for use with two interval variables. They are (1) the linear correlation coefficient and (2) simple regression.

Linear Correlation Coefficient

Linear correlation is a measure of the degree to which two interval variables are associated. For example, suppose we have data on grades on a marketing management course, X, and data on grades in a marketing research course, Y. Our interest is in determining the level and direction of a relationship between these two variables—for example, are high grades on X associated with high grades on Y, or vice versa, or is there no relationship between the two? The linear correlation coefficient, r_{XY}, is a measure of the linear relationship between X and Y. The importance of these relationship questions to marketing researchers is noted in Figure 19-3, which indicates that about 83 percent of businesses utilize correlation in their marketing research.

In examining the relationship between two interval variables, a useful beginning is to plot the data on a scatter diagram. Figure 19-4 is an example of a plot for

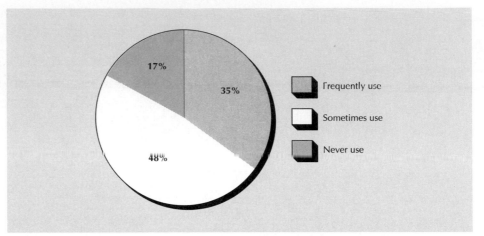

FIGURE 19-3   Use in practice of correlation. (*Source:* Thomas C. Kinnear and Ann R. Root, *A Study of the Marketing Research Business*, unpublished study, 1994. Copyright 1994 Thomas C. Kinnear. Not to be reproduced.)

two variables, X and Y. If we draw the means of the two variables, $\bar{X}$ and $\bar{Y}$, on the scatter diagram, a first impression of possible relationships can be obtained. Drawing in the mean values divides the scatter diagram into four quadrants, labeled 1, 2, 3, and 4 in Figure 19-4. For data points in quadrant 1, both the X and the Y values are above their respective means; that is, they have positive deviations from their means. For quadrant 2, X values have negative deviations and Y values have positive deviations; for quadrant 3, both have negative deviations; and for quadrant 4, X values have positive deviations and Y values have negative deviations. If the data points tend to be in diagonal quadrants, this would be evidence of a relationship between the two variables. For example, if most points were in quadrants 1 and 3, positive deviations on X would be associated with positive deviations in Y (quadrant 1), and negative deviations in X would be associated with negative deviations in Y (quadrant 3); that is, as X increases, Y increases. X and Y would be positively related.

On the other hand, if data points tend to be in quadrants 2 and 4, negative deviations in X are associated with positive deviations in Y (quadrant 2), and vice versa (quadrant 4). This situation would indicate a negative relationship between X and Y. The intent of the correlation coefficient, r_{XY}, is to quantify the relationship between the variables.

We begin this process by developing a distance measure between each point's X and Y values and the means of X and Y. We define:

$$x = (X_i - \bar{X})$$

and

$$y = (Y_i - \bar{Y})$$

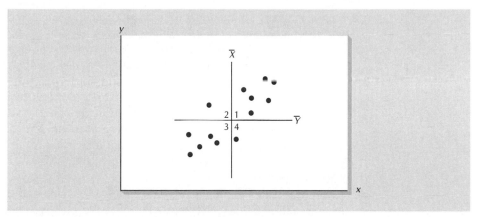

FIGURE 19-4   An example of a scatter diagram and associated quadrants.

These measures are deviations from their respective means, as discussed above. Each deviation calculated in the equations above has a sign attached. If the value of X_i or Y_i is greater than the mean, the sign is positive. If the value X_i or Y_i is less than the mean, the sign is negative. By multiplying the two deviations together we get a signed value. The sign of this number tells us something about the quadrant a data point falls into. We define:

$$xy = (X_i - \bar{X})(Y_i - \bar{Y})$$

Thus:

1 If x is positive and y is positive, xy is positive, and the data point falls in quadrant 1.

2 If x is negative and y is positive, xy is negative, and the data point falls in quadrant 2.

3 If x is negative and y is negative, xy is positive, and the data point falls in quadrant 3.

4 If x is positive and y is negative, xy is negative, and the data point falls in quadrant 4.

We see that xy is positive in quadrants 1 and 3 and negative in 2 and 4. Data points in quadrants 1 and 3 indicate a positive relationship between X and Y, as noted previously, and data points in quadrants 2 and 4 indicate a negative relationship between X and Y. Therefore, the sign of xy indicates the direction of relationship.

If we add up all the xy's for each data point, to get $\Sigma_{i=1}^{n} xy$, the sign of this number will indicate the overall direction of relationship. For example, if the data come mostly from quadrants 1 and 3, positive values of xy will outweigh negative values, and $\Sigma_{i=1}^{n} xy$ will be positive, indicating a positive relationship between X and Y. The opposite is true if the data come mostly from quadrants 2 and 4. If the data are evenly split among all four quadrants, positive and negative values of xy will tend to cancel, and $\Sigma_{i=1}^{n}$ will be zero.

The value of $\Sigma_{i=1}^{n}xy$ is an improvement over visual examination of the scatter diagram. However, it has two significant weaknesses. First, the value of $\Sigma_{i=1}^{n}xy$ is partially dependent on the number of data points, n. As n increases, the value of $\Sigma_{i=1}^{n}xy$ also increases. Comparison of relationships involving different numbers of observations would then not be meaningful. Second, the value of $\Sigma_{i=1}^{n}xy$ depends in part on the unit of measurement being used on X and Y. For example, if an exam is marked out of 25 we would get a smaller value for $\Sigma_{i=1}^{n}xy$ than if the exam was marked out of 50, and a smaller value if it was out of 50 than if out of 100, and so forth.

We must then eliminate the effects of sample size and units from our measure of association $\Sigma_{i=1}^{n}xy$. We may eliminate the effects of sample size by dividing through $\Sigma_{i=1}^{n}xy$ by the degrees of freedom in the sample size, $n - 1$. This gives us a measure of the covariance of X and Y, as follows:

$$Cov\,(X,\ Y) = \frac{\Sigma(X_i - \bar{X})(Y_i - \bar{Y})}{n - 1}$$

Note that we will use Σ by itself to indicate addition across all n cases.

Covariance is positive if the values of X_i and Y_i tend to deviate from their respective means in the same direction. It is negative if they tend to deviate in the opposite direction. If X and Y are statistically independent, $Cov\,(X,\ Y) = 0$. We eliminate the effect of units by dividing $Cov\,(X,\ Y)$ through by the standard deviations of X and Y. We define this value as the correlation coefficient, r_{XY}. Thus,

$$r_{XY} = \frac{\Sigma(X_i - \bar{X})(Y_i - \bar{Y})}{(n - 1)s_X s_Y}$$

This formula may be simplified to yield

$$r_{XY} = \frac{\Sigma(X_i - \bar{X})(Y_i - \bar{Y})}{\sqrt{\Sigma(X_i - \bar{X})^2\Sigma(Y_i - \bar{Y})^2}}$$

or, alternatively,

$$r_{XY} = \frac{\Sigma xy}{\sqrt{\Sigma x^2\Sigma y^2}} \qquad (19\text{-}1)$$

We see then that correlation is just a standardized measure of covariation. This standardization allows two correlations to be compared independently of the units in which observations are measured. The correlation coefficient may take on any value between -1.00 and $+1.00$. When $r = 1.00$, this indicates a perfect positive correlation. When $r = -1.00$, this indicates a perfect negative correlation. If $r =$

0, there is no relationship between the variables. Thus correlation provides a measure of the direction and strength of the relationship between two variables.

Correlation is a measure of the extent to which two variables share variation between them. The exact percentage of variation shared by two variables is calculated by squaring r. This r^2 is called the *coefficient of determination.*

In general, if r is bigger than 0.8 (sign of relationship ignored), the relationship between the variables is very strong; if r is between 0.4 and 0.8, the relationship is a moderate to strong one; and if r is less than 0.4, the relationship is a weak one.

A Numerical Example   The first two columns of Table 19-1 present the grades of 10 students in a course in marketing management, X, and in marketing research, Y. Figure 19-5 shows a scatter plot of the grades in the two courses. What we want to know is the correlation coefficient between the grades in the two courses. We have calculated the necessary values for Equation 19-1 on Table 19-1. Thus,

$$r_{XY} = \frac{1200}{\sqrt{1290 \times 1450}}$$

$$= \frac{1200}{1368}$$

$$= .88$$

The percentage of variation shared by these two variables is given by the coefficient of determination:

$$r^2 = (.88)^2 = .77$$

This represents the amount of variation in one of the variables we can explain by knowledge of the other variable.

TABLE 19-1   MARKETING MANAGEMENT (X) AND MARKETING RESEARCH (Y) GRADES FOR 10 STUDENTS

X	Y	$x = (X - \bar{X})$	$y = (Y - \bar{Y})$	xy	x^2	y^2
75	85	1	10	10	1	100
80	85	6	10	60	36	100
60	65	−14	−10	140	196	100
55	60	−19	−15	285	361	225
85	80	11	5	55	121	25
95	95	21	20	420	441	400
70	60	−4	−15	60	16	225
75	80	1	5	5	1	25
80	80	6	5	30	36	25
65	60	−9	−15	135	81	225
$\Sigma X = 740$	$\Sigma Y = 750$	$\Sigma x = 0$	$\Sigma y = 0$	$\Sigma xy = 1200$	$\Sigma x^2 = 1290$	$\Sigma y^2 = 1450$
$\bar{X} = 74.0$	$\bar{Y} = 75.0$					

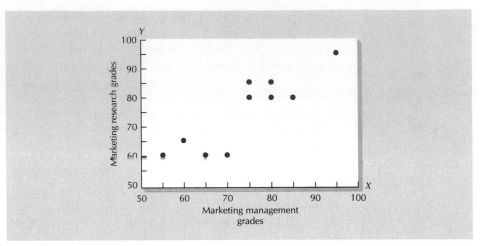

FIGURE 19-5   Scatter diagram of course grades.

Often the interests of the research go beyond the direction and strength of association between two variables. In this circumstance, simple regression is often useful.

Simple Regression

Regression is a method of analysis that applies when the research is dealing with one intervally scaled dependent variable and a number of intervally scaled independent variables. The purposes of regression are to show *how* the independent variables in the analysis are related to the dependent variable, and to make *predictions* about scores on the dependent variable based upon knowledge of independent variable scores. We begin our study of regression by examining the special case in which we have one dependent variable and only one independent variable. Regression used in this context is called *simple regression.* The data on course grades presented in Table 19-1 will again be used. The marketing management grade, X, will be designated as the independent variable, and the marketing research grade, Y, will be designated as the dependent variable. We could fit a linear relationship to these data by drawing an eye-fitted line through the middle of the scatter plot in Figure 19-5. However, we want to be more precise than this, so we look for a mathematical procedure to define the required straight line.

Partitioning the Sum of Squares   We begin this process by defining:

$Y_i =$ the ith observation on the dependent variable

$\bar{Y} =$ the mean of all the Y's

$\hat{Y}_i =$ the predicted value of the ith observation of the dependent variable

We can write any observation as a deviation from the mean value, Y.

$$\text{Total deviation for } i\text{th observation} = (Y_i - \bar{Y})$$

This represents the total deviation of Y_i, because if we know nothing about X values, we can still guess $\bar{Y}$ as our estimate of Y. Total deviation must then be expressed as deviation from $\bar{Y}$. We can partition this deviation into components:

Total deviation = deviation due to X's + deviation due to error

$$\underset{\downarrow}{(Y_i - \bar{Y})} \quad = \quad \underset{\downarrow}{(\hat{Y}_i - \bar{Y})} \quad + \quad \underset{\downarrow}{(Y_i - \hat{Y}_i)} \qquad (19\text{-}2)$$

$$\text{Total variation} = \underset{\text{by regression}}{\text{variation explained}} + \underset{\text{by regression}}{\text{variation unexplained}}$$

Figure 19-6 graphically shows this partitioning of total deviation. Note that the explained deviation is the amount the total deviation is reduced by our knowledge of the regression line from the level of deviation present by knowledge of $\bar{Y}$. If we add the deviation in Equation 19-2 across all observations and square this equation, we can partition the sums of squares into the part explained by the regression equation and the part that is unexplained, as follows:

$$\Sigma(Y_i - \bar{Y})^2 = \Sigma(\hat{Y}_i - \bar{Y})^2 + \Sigma(Y_i - \hat{Y}_i)^2$$

$$SS_{\text{total}} \quad = SS_{\underset{\text{by regression}}{\text{explained}}} + SS_{\underset{\text{by regression}}{\text{unexplained}}}$$

$$\underset{\text{variation}}{\text{Total}} = \underset{\text{variation}}{\text{explained}} + \underset{\text{variation}}{\text{unexplained}}$$

Presenting the deviations in this fashion provides a conceptual understanding of how a regression aids our understanding of the dependent variable. However, we still have not developed a procedure to fit a line to the data.

Fitting the Regression Line   We want to be able to predict a Y value based on knowledge of an X value and to note the direction of relationship (positive or negative) and rate of change (slope level) between X and Y. These tasks require us to fit a mathematical linear equation to the data. Of course, we want an equation that fits the data well. A good fit could be one that minimizes the error or unexplained deviation. The criterion usually used is to minimize the sum of the squares of the errors. The "least squares" solution has desirable statistical properties that are well dealt with in texts on regression. Intuitively, we can see that large errors

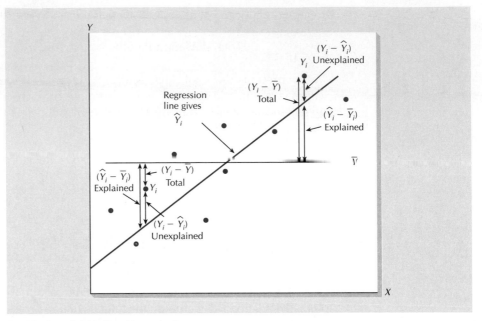

FIGURE 19-6   Partitioning of deviations in regression.

are avoided as much as possible, thereby providing a good fit; thus, we want to fit a line of the form

$$Y = a + bX$$

where a = the value of the intercept on the Y axis
     b = the slope of the line

Using our knowledge of the X and Y values, we solve for a and b. One way to do this is to first cast the X values as deviations from their mean: $x_i = X_i - \bar{X}$. Now we are solving for an equation of the form $Y = a + bx$. We want to find the values of a and b that minimize the sum of squared errors $\Sigma(Y_i - \hat{Y}_i)^2$.

The mathematical knowledge necessary to develop the formulas for the a and b values is beyond the scope of this book. The resultant formulas are

$$a = \bar{Y}$$

$$b = \frac{\sum_{i=1}^{n} Y_i x_i}{\sum_{i=1}^{n} x_i^2}$$

A Numerical Example   Let us do a regression with the data on grades that we used to calculate the correlation coefficient. The basic data and calculations are presented in Table 19-2. The resultant equation is

$$\hat{Y}_i = 75.0 + .93x_i \qquad\qquad (19\text{-}3)$$

In making predictions it is sometimes easier to deal with X_i values and not the deviations x_i. Thus Equation 19-3 becomes

$$\hat{Y}_i = 75.0 + .93(X_i - \bar{X})$$

$$= 75.0 + .93(X_i - 74.0)$$

$$= (75.0 - 68.8) + .93X_i$$

$$= 6.2 + .93X_i \qquad\qquad (19\text{-}4)$$

We note in Equation 19-4 that the *b* value or slope remains the same. Only the intercept has shifted.

The Meaning of the Coefficients   What exactly do the coefficients we calculated mean? The *a* tells us the predicted value of *Y* when *X* is zero. In our example we would predict a score of 6.2 in the marketing research course even if the grade in marketing management were zero. Obviously, such a person should not even be allowed to take marketing research. This points up a general comment, namely, that the *a* coefficient is generally of less interest to us than the *b* coefficient.

The b represents the amount of change we would predict in Y for a one-unit change in X. Thus, in our example we would predict a .93 increase in the grade in marketing research for each increase of one grade point obtained in marketing management. A negative sign on a *b* coefficient would indicate that as *X* increases, *Y* decreases. Graphically, *b* is the slope of the regression line.

We may use the regression equation to generate predicted values of *Y*. These $\hat{Y}_i$'s are presented for the given X_i's in Table 19-2. We can then calculate the difference between the observed and predicted values, $Y_i - \hat{Y}_i$. If we square these values and add them across all observations, we get the sum of squares error, $\Sigma(Y_i - \hat{Y}_i)^2$. These values are calculated in Table 19-2. The sum of squares error here is 334.17. No other values of *a* and *b* would give this small an SS_{error}. This is the meaning of a "least squares" solution.

Explained Variation   The question naturally arises as to how much of the variation in *Y* was explained by our knowledge of *X*. This question is answered by calculating the ratio of explained variation to total variation. Previously we defined the coefficient of determination, r^2, as the amount of variation explained in a correlation context. The same concept applies here, except that in simple regression

TABLE 19-2 REGRESSION CALCULATIONS FOR DATA IN TABLE 19-1

X_i	Y_i	$x_i = (X_i - \bar{X})$	$Y_i x_i$	x_i^2	$\hat{Y}_i = 75 + .93X_i$	$(Y_i - \hat{Y}_i)$	$(Y_i - \hat{Y}_i)^2$
75	85	1	85	1	75.9	9.1	82.81
80	85	6	510	36	80.6	4.4	19.36
60	65	-14	-910	196	62.0	3.0	9.00
55	60	-19	-1140	361	57.3	2.7	7.29
85	80	11	880	121	85.2	-5.2	27.04
95	95	21	1995	441	94.5	0.5	0.25
70	60	-4	-240	16	71.3	-11.3	127.69
75	80	1	80	1	75.9	4.1	16.81
80	80	6	480	36	80.6	-.6	0.36
65	60	-9	-540	81	66.6	-6.6	43.56
$\Sigma X_i = 740$ $\bar{X} = 74.0$	$\Sigma Y_i = 750$ $\bar{Y} = 75.0$	$\Sigma x_i = 0$	$\Sigma Y_i x_i = 1200$	$\Sigma x_i^2 = 1290$		$\Sigma(Y_i - \hat{Y}_i) = 0$	$\Sigma(Y_i - \hat{Y}_i)^2 = 334.17$

$$a = \bar{Y} = 75.0$$

$$b = \frac{\Sigma Y_i x_i}{\Sigma x_i^2} = \frac{1200}{1290} = .93$$

$$\hat{Y}_i = 75.0 + .93 x_i$$

$$r^2_{XY} = \frac{\text{explained variation}}{\text{total variation}}$$

$$= \frac{\Sigma(\hat{Y}_i - \bar{Y})^2}{\Sigma(Y_I - \bar{Y})^2}$$

$$= \frac{SS_{\text{explained}}}{SS_{\text{total}}}$$

r^2_{XY} is again called the coefficient of determination, and it represents the proportion of the total variation in Y explained by fitting the regression line.

From Table 19-1, we note that for our grades example

$$SS_{\text{total}} = \Sigma(Y_i - \bar{Y})^2 = \Sigma y^2 = 1450$$

Also from Table 19-2, we note that

$$SS_{\text{error}} = \Sigma(\hat{Y}_i - Y_i)^2 = 334.17$$

Thus,

$$SS_{\text{explained}} = \Sigma(\hat{Y}_i - \bar{Y})^2$$
$$= SS_{\text{total}} - SS_{\text{error}}$$
$$= 1450 - 334.17$$
$$= 1115.83$$

Therefore,

$$r^2_{XY} = \frac{1115.83}{1450} = .77$$

This is exactly the value of r^2 we obtained by squaring the correlation coefficient, as we would expect.

In practice, the size of r^2's obtained from regression vary greatly. In forecasting applications where the environment is quite stable, r^2's may be as high as .8 or .9. In situations in which the environment changes a great deal, or in which we are trying to predict individual attitudes or behavior, r^2's may be in the .15 to .3 range. These latter small r^2's indicate the lack of ability of marketers to fully understand the world in which they are working. However, all is not lost. Individual coefficients may still provide useful information even though the total r^2 is small.

Correlation and simple regression allow the researcher to describe the relationship between two individual variables. For example, we could describe the relationship between (1) age and amount of credit card usage, (2) income and wine consumption per year, (3) advertising expenditures and attitudes toward a brand, (4) years of education and expenditures on housing per year, or (5) number of advertising insertions and brand awareness. These are but a few examples of possible situations in which correlation and simple regression could be useful. The usefulness of simple regression and related more complex regression procedures (see Chapter 21) is indicated in Figure 19-7. About 81 percent of businesses use regression in their marketing research.

It should be recognized that correlation and regression provide measures of association, not causation. However, marketing managers may use these procedures to help them better understand the nature of the implicit or explicit causal model they are using.

INFERENTIAL STATISTICS

As with univariate analysis, the interest of the researcher often goes beyond describing sample relationships to making judgments about population parameters. In theory it is possible to test a hypothesis about any descriptive statistic. Thus, for example, we could test hypotheses about the size of the population correlation coefficient. However, in this chapter we will restrict our attention to a few bivariate inferential tests. Specifically, for interval data we shall discuss (1) the t test on the regression coefficient, (2) the z test on the difference between means, and (3) the t test on the difference between means. These tests are somewhat mathematically detailed, and for some readers they will constitute a restatement of material already covered in a basic statistics course. Thus, the discussion of these tests is continued in the appendix at the end of this chapter.

FIGURE 19-7   Use in practice of regression. (*Source:* Thomas C. Kinnear and Ann R. Root, *A Study of the Marketing Research Business*, unpublished study, 1994. Copyright 1994 Thomas C. Kinnear. Not to be reproduced.)

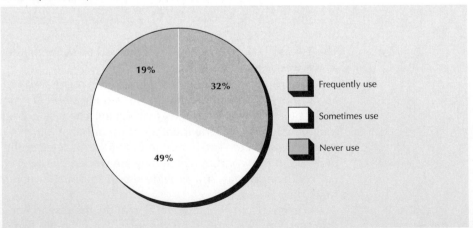

One bivariate inference test will be discussed here, namely, the chi-square test, which is appropriate for examining the relationship between two nominal variables. It is discussed here because of its usefulness in analyzing cross-tabulation tables, and because it is often not covered in basic statistics courses.

The Chi-Square Test

Perhaps the most common type of bivariate analysis in practice is the cross tabulation of two nominal variables. In truth we need not have nominal variables to do this; interval or ordinal variables can be analyzed in this fashion if we first group them into classes or categories. Typical questions addressed by cross tabulation might be: (1) Is there a relationship between age and media habits? (2) Is there a relationship between region of the country and brand preference? (3) Is there a relationship between life-style types and car ownership?

As we see from the examples, the objective of cross tabulation is to identify a relationship between variables. In data from a sample we might observe what appears to be a relationship between two nominal variables. A question naturally arises as to whether this observed relationship is simply the result of sampling error, and the chi-square test is designed to answer this question. The null hypothesis for a chi-square test is that the two variables are *independent* of each other. The alternative hypothesis is that they are not independent, that is, that there is a relationship between the two variables.

Let's illustrate the chi-square test. Table 19-3 presents the cross tabulation of an income measure and a measure of brand purchased last. The cell entries indicate the numbers in the sample that form the various combinations of income and brand categories. For example, we note that there were 50 people earning less than $20,000 who purchased brand 1 last. The expected number in each cell is not the same, as it was with the univariate chi square. This is so because the totals for each category of each variable are not the same. For example, with 650 people earning between $20,000 and $40,000, we should certainly not expect the cells to be equal. What then should be the expected cell values? To answer this question we turn to one of the elementary rules of probability theory.

TABLE 19-3   CROSS TABULATION OF INCOME AND BRAND PURCHASED LAST

		B Brand purchased last			
	Income	B_1 Brand 1	B_2 Brand 2	B_3 Brand 3	Total
A	A_1 Less than $20,000	50	200	125	375
	A_2 $20,000–$40,000	200	100	350	650
	A_3 Over $40,000	100	25	50	175
	Total	350	325	525	1200

Note in Table 19-3 that we have defined income as variable A_i and the categories of income as A_1, A_2, and A_3. "Brand purchased last" is defined as variable B_j, and the categories as B_1, B_2, and B_3. The various combinations of A_iB_j's are the occurrences of various events. Let us use A_1B_1 to illustrate the required theory.

If A and B are independent, the probability of A_1 and B_1 occurring is the product of the probability of A_1 times the probability of B_1. This is the multiplication theorem of statistics. In symbols,

$$P(A_1 \text{ and } B_1) = P(A_1)P(B_1)$$

Also we note that

$$P(A_1) = \text{relative frequency of } A_1 \text{ over all } A's$$

$$= \frac{A_1}{A} = \frac{375}{1200}$$

$$P(B_1) = \text{relative frequency of } B_1 \text{ over all } B's$$

$$= \frac{B_1}{B} = \frac{350}{1200}$$

$$P(A_1 \text{ and } B_1) = \frac{375}{1200} \times \frac{350}{1200} = .091$$

The expected number in cell A_1B_1 is then

$$n[P(A_1 \text{ and } B_1)] = 1200\left(\frac{375}{1200} \times \frac{350}{1200}\right)$$

$$= 109.38$$

In general, the formula for expected value is

$$E_{ij} = \frac{n_{A_i}n_{B_j}}{n}$$

where E_{ij} = expected number
n_{A_i} = number of elements in category A_i
n_{B_j} = number of elements in category B_j

For A_1B_1 the expected number is

$$E_{11} = \frac{(375)(350)}{1200} = 109.38$$

We can repeat this process for all cells.

Table 19-4 presents the observed and expected numbers for each cell and the calculation of the associated chi square. The relevant formula is

$$\chi^2 = \sum_{i=1}^{R} \sum_{j=1}^{C} \frac{(O_{ij} - E_{ij})^2}{E_{ij}}$$

where R = number of categories of the row variable
 C = number of categories of the column variable
 O_{ij} = observed number in cell ij
 E_{ij} = expected number in cell ij

The calculated chi square is 252.2. The number of degrees of freedom is $(R - 1)(C - 1)$, since once the number of elements in $R - 1$ row categories and the total are known, the number in the last category is determined. A similar argument holds for column degrees of freedom. In our example there are $(3 - 1)(3 - 1) = 4$ degrees of freedom. If $\alpha = .01$, the critical value of chi square at 4 df is 13.3 (see Table A-6 of the Appendix at the end of the book). Since the calculated chi square exceeds the critical value, we reject the null hypothesis that income and brand purchased last are independent.

In using the chi square, we should have all the expected cell sizes equal to at least 5. If this is not the case, it is generally recommended that cells be combined to give an expected frequency of at least 5. It is also important to have the two measurements independent of each other. That is, we should not use the chi square to compare repeated measures on the same variable.

The chi-square test may tell us that two variables are not independent. However, it does not tell anything about the nature of the relationship. To determine this, we must look back into the table of interest. In Table 19-3, we see that as income increases, "brand purchased last" shifts from brand 2 to brand 3 and then to brand 1. A researcher often confronts many cross-tabulation tables. A good strategy to use in evaluating these tables is first to examine the chi square for

TABLE 19-4   CALCULATION OF BIVARIATE CHI SQUARE

Cell number	O_{ij}	E_{ij}	$O_{ij} - E_{ij}$	$(O_{ij} - E_{ij})^2$	$(O_{ij} - E_{ij})^2 / E_{ij}$
1,1	50	109.38	−59.38	3526.0	32.2
1,2	200	101.56	98.44	9690.4	95.4
1,3	125	164.06	−39.06	1525.7	9.3
2,1	200	189.58	10.42	108.6	0.6
2,2	100	176.04	−76.04	5782.1	32.8
2,3	350	284.38	65.62	4306.0	15.1
3,1	100	51.04	48.96	2397.1	47.0
3,2	25	47.40	−22.40	501.8	10.6
3,3	50	76.56	−26.56	705.4	9.2
Total	1200	1200.00			252.2

$\chi^2 = 252.2$

significance, then examine closely those tables with significant chi squares. For-tunately, all good data analysis programs offer the chi-square test as part of a cross-tabulation output. There are a number of other issues related to interpreting cross-tabulation tables that will be addressed.

INTERPRETATION OF CROSS-TABULAR TABLES

The position of cross-tabular tables in marketing research practice is so important that we must go beyond the mere concern about significance discussed previously in our examination of the chi square test. Certain fundamental issues related to the interpretation of these tables must be clarified: (1) the use of percentages and (2) the elaborations of discovered relationships with the introduction of additional variables.

Use of Percentages

In doing the chi-square test we use the raw frequency counts in each cell. This is fine for this test, but raw frequencies are often difficult to interpret. To aid in the interpretation of significant relationships it usually helps to cast the data in the cross-tabular table in percentage form. The problem is that the researcher has three alternative ways to calculate percentage: (1) row percentages, such that the percentages in each row add to 100 percent; (2) column percentages, such that the percentages in each column add to 100 percent; or (3) cell percentages, such that the percentages added across all cells equal 100 percent. Table 19-5 presents four alternatives. The first is a set of raw frequencies in a cross tabulation between income and consumption of types of wines. The other three show the raw fre-quencies in row, column, and cell percentage form.

Which of these percentages is most useful to the researcher? We may try to determine a general rule by examining Table 19-5. Clearly, cell percentages tell us little about the relationship between income and type of wine consumed. They are generally useful only in identifying the size of particular segments, not for assisting one in understanding relationships. If we looked at the column percent-ages, we would make conclusions such as the following: 65.2 percent of those consuming cheap wine earn less than $25,000, while only 34.8 percent of those consuming cheap wine earn $25,000 and over. This sort of conclusion seems to imply that type of wine consumed is having an effect on income earned. This is obviously not what we mean in this case. Clearly, we expect that income is having the effect on type of wine consumed and not the other way around. Examination of the row percentages shows us the type of relationship we were looking for. Here we could make conclusions such as: 88.2 percent of those earning less than $25,000 consume cheap wine, while only 11.8 percent of these people consume premium wine. This conclusion implies that income is affecting the type of wine consumed.

The rule, then, is to *cast percentages in the direction of the causal factor.* Thus, if the causal factor is the row factor, calculate (by computer) row percentages and vice versa.

TABLE 19-5   ALTERNATIVE WAYS OF PRESENTING CROSS-TABULAR RESULTS

A Raw frequencies

Income	Type of wine consumed		Total
	Cheap	Premium	
Less than $25,000	75	10	85
$25,000 and over	40	80	120
Total	115	90	205

B Row percentages

Income	Type of wine consumed		Total
	Cheap	Premium	
Less than $25,000	88.2%	11.8%	100.0
$25,000 and over	33.3	66.7	100.0

C Column percentages

Income	Type of wine consumed	
	Cheap	Premium
Less than $25,000	65.2%	11.1%
$25,000 and over	34.8	88.9
Total	100.0%	100.0%

D Cell percentages

Income	Type of wine consumed	
	Cheap	Premium
Less than $25,000	36.6%	4.9%
$25,000 and over	19.5	39.0
	Total 100.0%	

Elaboration of Relationships

Care must be taken in the use of cross-tabular tables. It is possible that the true relationship is more complex than one that can be properly identified by looking at the cross tabulation of two variables. This is especially true if the user believes that there is a causal relationship between the variables. You might ask: Does this relationship hold when other variables are considered? For example, how are type of wine consumed and income related for different age groups, or different regions of the country, or different genders, and so on? What we need to do is elaborate on the relationship that was discovered in two-way tables. We do this by obtaining the cross tabulation of the same variables as before, except that now we get one cross tabulation of these variables for each category of some other variable or variables. Thus, we could see whether there was a different relationship for males and females, and so on.

The original association between the two variables is called the *total* or *zero-order association*. The tables showing the association between the two variables within categories of other variables are called *conditional tables* and reveal *conditional associations*. The variables on which the cross tabulation is conditional are called *control variables*. Therefore, we might ask for the cross tabulation of income and type of wine consumed, controlling on age. When conditional tables are developed on the basis of one control variable, they are called *first-order conditional tables*. It is also possible to control on more than one variable. Here conditional tables are developed for elements within the various combinations of control categories. For example, one control combination might be "females from California" in the use of the two control variables, sex and region of the country. We would then obtain a table for each combination of sex and region. When two controls are present, the tables are called *second-order conditional tables;* if three control variables are present, they are called third-order conditional tables, and so on. The more control variables we add, the more tables we will obtain, and the harder will be the interpretation of the results. For example, if we had three control variables with 2, 3, and 4 categories, respectively, we would then get 2 $\times$ 3 $\times$ 4 = 24 conditional tables. Thus, we add control variables with care, usually being guided by some theory of the underlying relationship in doing so. Our discussion of this elaboration process will be limited to first-order conditional tables.

The possible outcomes of elaboration depend on the original conclusion. Suppose the original zero-order table leads to the conclusion of a relationship between the variables. Then from the conditional tables we might (1) retain the original conclusion that a relationship exists, (2) specify a different relationship by control categories, or (3) identify the original relationship as spurious. On the other hand, the original table may have led to the conclusion of no relationship. Then from the conditional tables we might (1) retain the original conclusion that there was no relationship or (2) identify a relationship. The next two sections of this chapter illustrate these outcomes.

Zero-Order Relationship Found

This section presents illustrations of the various possible outcomes of conditional table analysis when a zero-order relationship is found.

Retain Original Conclusion of a Relationship Existing   Table 19-6 illustrates a situation in which the original conclusion that a relationship exists is retained. The numbers in parentheses in the table indicate the frequency counts for the cells. Part A of the table shows the relationship between income and credit card usage, obtained using the whole sample. Clearly, higher income is associated with greater use of credit cards. Part B of the table shows this same cross tabulation presented for two age categories. Note that the conclusion about income and credit card usage is retained.

Specification of Original Relationship A good question to ask about a cross-tabular relationship is: Under what conditions does this relationship hold? For example, it is possible that the relationship between credit card usage and income could have been different for the different age categories. If the relationship between the dependent variable (credit card usage) and the independent variable (income) is different for different categories of the control variable (age), we say that the independent variable and control variables are interacting. The search for this type of statistical interaction is called *specification of the relationship.* Table 19-7 illustrates a situation in which interaction is present. Again we present the whole sample and conditional tables. In this instance, the same initial relationship between income and credit usage is present, except that it is not as strong as before. The conditional tables reveal two different relationships between income and credit card usage. Conditional table B-1 (of Table 19-7) gives one picture. Here, lower income is slightly more associated with credit card usage. B-2 shows

TABLE 19-6 RETAIN ORIGINAL CONCLUSION THAT A RELATIONSHIP EXISTS

A Total sample ($n = 1000$)

Use credit cards	Income			
	Under $25,000		$25,000 and over	
Yes	(100)	25.0%	(500)	83.3%
No	(300)	75.0	(100)	16.7
Total	(400)	100.0%	(600)	100.0%

B Conditional on age

B-1 For ages 18–35 ($n = 350$)

Use credit cards	Income			
	Under $25,000		$25,000 and over	
Yes	(34)	29.6%	(199)	84.7%
No	(81)	70.4	(36)	15.3
Total	(115)	100.0%	(235)	100.0%

B-2 For ages over 35 ($n = 650$)

Use credit cards	Income			
	Under $25,000		$25,000 and over	
Yes	(66)	23.2%	(301)	82.5%
No	(219)	76.8	(64)	17.5
Total	(285)	100.0%	(365)	100.0%

TABLE 19-7　SPECIFICATION OF RELATIONSHIP

A Total sample ($n = 1000$)

	Income			
Use credit cards	Under $25,000		$25,000 and over	
Yes	(175)	43.8%	(350)	58.3%
No	(225)	56.2	(250)	41.7
Total	(400)	100.0%	(600)	100.0%

B Conditional on age

B-1 For ages 18–35 ($n = 350$)

	Income			
Use credit cards	Under $25,000		$25,000 and over	
Yes	(100)	76.9%	(150)	68.2%
No	(30)	23.1	(70)	31.8
Total	(130)	100.0%	(220)	100.0%

B-2 For ages over 35 ($n = 650$)

	Income			
Use credit cards	Under $25,000		$25,000 and over	
Yes	(75)	27.8%	(230)	60.5%
No	(195)	72.2	(150)	39.5
Total	(270)	100.0%	(380)	100.0%

a different pattern. It shows a stronger positive relationship between income and credit card usage than that found in the whole sample table. It appears that younger people earning less than $25,000 are more likely to use credit cards than older people of the same income. Age and income are interacting to affect credit card usage.

Identification of a Spurious Relationship　Table 19-8 illustrates the situation in which the zero-order table reveals a relationship between two variables, while the conditional tables reveal that the relationship was spurious. That is, the original relationship *disappears* when a control variable is present. In this example, the cross tabulation is between attendance at theater movies and ownership of a television set. The whole-sample table reveals that people who own television sets are more likely to attend theater movies.

Graphically, this hypothesis can be represented as:

$X \longrightarrow Y$

Ownership of a	Attendance at
television set	theater movies
(cause)	(effect)

TABLE 19-8 IDENTIFICATION OF A SPURIOUS RELATIONSHIP

A Total sample (n = 1430)

| Attendance at theater movies | Television ownership | | | |
	No		Yes	
Yes	(240)	36.4%	(610)	79.2%
No	(420)	63.6	(160)	20.8
Total	(660)	100.0%	(770)	100.0%

B Conditional on income

B-1 For income under $25,000 (n = 550)

| Attendance at theater movies | Television ownership | | | |
	No		Yes	
Yes	(40)	9.1%	(10)	9.1%
No	(400)	90.9	(100)	90.9
Total	(440)	100.0%	(110)	100.0%

B-2 For income $25,000 and over (n = 880)

| Attendance at theater movies | Television ownership | | | |
	No		Yes	
Yes	(200)	90.9%	(600)	90.9%
No	(20)	9.1	(60)	9.1
Total	(220)	100.0%	(660)	100.0%

Source: Adapted from Herman J. Loether and Donald G. McTavish, *Descriptive Statistics for Sociologists* (Boston: Allyn and Bacon, 1974), pp. 276–287.

This result seems somewhat illogical, since it is not clear how television ownership is causing attendance at theater movies. We might hypothesize that a third variable is operative that is causing both television ownership and attendance at movie theaters. This variable might be income. Graphically, this hypothesis can be represented as:

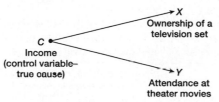

Here income is hypothesized to be causing both *X* and *Y*. If the original relationship between *X* and *Y* is indeed a causal one, we would expect it to be maintained within categories of the control variable. Part B of Table 19-8 reveals that this is not true. For those earning less than $25,000, the pattern of attendance at theater movies is the same whether the individual owns a television set or not. Specifically, both television ownership and attendance are low. For those earning $25,000 and over, the pattern of attendance is the same for both categories of television ownership. Here, both television ownership and attendance are high. Thus, the original relationship was spurious.

No Zero-Order Relationship Found

This section presents illustrations of the various possible outcomes of conditional-table analysis when no zero order relationship is found.

Retain Original Conclusion of No Relationship   Table 19-9 illustrates the situation in which the whole-sample table revealed no relationship between two variables and the conditional tables show no relationship. The cross tabulation is between home ownership and region of the country. The control variable is income.

TABLE 19-9   RETAIN ORIGINAL CONCLUSION OF NO RELATIONSHIP

A Total sample ($n = 1000$)				
	Region of the country			
Home ownership	East		West	
Yes	(205)	41.0%	(201)	40.2%
No	(295)	59.0	(299)	59.8
Total	(500)	100.0%	(500)	100.0%

B Conditional on income				
B-1 For income under $25,000 ($n = 300$)				
	Region of the country			
Home ownership	East		West	
Yes	(60)	40.0%	(63)	42.0%
No	(90)	60.0	(87)	58.0
Total	(150)	100.0%	(150)	100.0%
B-2 For income $25,000 and over ($n = 700$)				
	Region of the country			
Home ownership	East		West	
Yes	(145)	41.4%	(138)	39.4%
No	(205)	58.6	(212)	60.6
Total	(350)	100.0%	(350)	100.0%

Identify a Relationship Table 19-10 illustrates the possibility of a control variable assisting the researcher in identifying a relationship where none seems to exist on the basis of examining zero-order results. In this context the control variable is acting to suppress the observed relationship between two variables, and it is called a *suppressor variable*. This can happen when a relationship in one conditional table is equal in size but in the opposite direction to the relationship in the other conditional table. The result is that the relationships cancel each other when presented in the zero-order situation.

Table 19-10 presents the cross tabulation of income and credit card usage, controlling for gender. The total-sample table shows no relationship between income and credit card usage. On the other hand, the conditional tables for male and female show strong but opposite relationships. Males earning $25,000 and over are much more likely to use credit cards than those males earning under $25,000. Exactly the opposite is true for females. Note that this is a special case of interaction. Here gender and income are interacting to hide the effect on credit card usage.

TABLE 19-10   IDENTIFICATION OF A RELATIONSHIP

A Total sample (n = 1000)

Use credit cards	Income			
	Under $25,000		$25,000 and over	
Yes	(160)	40.0%	(240)	40.0%
No	(240)	60.0	(360)	60.0
Total	(400)	100.0%	(600)	100.0%

B Conditional on Sex

B-1 For males (n = 500)

Use credit cards	Income			
	Under $25,000		$25,000 and over	
Yes	(30)	15.0%	(200)	66.7%
No	(170)	85.0	(100)	33.3
Total	(200)	100.0%	(300)	100.0%

B-2 For females (n = 500)

Use credit cards	Income			
	Under $25,000		$25,000 and over	
Yes	(130)	65.0%	(40)	13.3%
No	(70)	35.0	(260)	86.7
Total	(200)	100.0%	(300)	100.0%

Concluding Comment on Cross Tabulation

In any dataset containing even a small number of variables, there are a great many possible cross-tabular tables. If one attempts to elaborate on these, the number of possible tables becomes huge. Obviously, researchers cannot just go on a "shopping trip" to find relationships, for they would be overwhelmed with computer output. They must have a model of the problem that focuses on the interrelationships among relevant variables to do proper cross-tabulation analysis. A good definition of the problem at hand combined with the specification of information needs can go a long way in guiding the data analysis process.

BANNER FORMAT

In the past few years, the presentation of data in banner form has gained in popularity as an alternative to the cross tabulation format. In a banner format typically one row variable is cross tabulated with a series of column variables. Table 19-11 presents an example of a banner. Here the row variable, income, is simultaneously cross-tabulated with the variables: persons in the household, head of household occupation, and rooms in the house. In standard cross tabulations, percentages can be cast in either direction. In banner format, percentages are cast in one direction only, limiting the information generated. Also, the direction of the percentages must be by column even when the causal direction is really by row. This is true in the data given in Table 19-11. Income is the causal variable, yet banner format requires percentages cast the other way.

Cross-tabular tables are probably the most popular method of presenting in-house data, while banners are favored among marketing research vendors due to their ability to simplify data presentation. The popularity of cross tabulations can be attributed to many factors: (1) They are easily presented and understood by management; (2) they allow for statistical hypothesis tests on nominal data (generally chi-square tests); (3) the categories are flexible and can be easily redefined; and (4) they are helpful in exposing hidden and spurious relationships that may otherwise go unnoticed.

Cross tabulations and banners are not a marketing research panacea, though. Cross tabulations have several disadvantages. First, each cell must have at least five pieces of data in order to have reliable chi-square estimates. Second, cross tabulations can result in a deluge of worthless data in the hands of an inexperienced researcher. For example, 40 pieces of data would yield 780 two-way cross tabulations. Third, the commonly used chi-square test indicates only the existence, not the strength, of cross-tabular relationships. Fourth, and perhaps the biggest disadvantage, is the difficulty they present in discovering covariation in a hidden variable.

Banners are basically a variation of the two-way cross tabulation with the percentages cast in only one direction. Thus, many of the advantages and disadvantages are the same for banners as for cross tabulations. Banners, though, unlike cross tabulations, allow many variables to be presented at once. But because the

TABLE 19-11   EXAMPLE OF BANNER FORMAT: FAMILY INCOME FOR 1995

Income group	Sample	Total persons in household				Head of household occupation								Rooms	
		Children		Teenagers		Prof., tech.	Man-agers	Sales clerical	Craft operators, lab tech.	Service workers	Students, home-makers	Retired	Unem-ployed	5 or fewer	6 or more
		None	1+	None	1+										
$15,999 or less	243	81	38	93	20	4	3	11	11	14	45	83	33	136	98
	9%	9	5	9	4	1	1	5	2	10	38	18	35	16	6
$16,000–$19,999	280	112	44	116	39	8	8	21	28	24	29	116	25	129	144
	11%	13	6	11	8	2	2	10	4	18	25	25	27	15	8
$20,000–$24,999	328	115	72	134	33	16	22	55	69	25	15	98	13	150	170
	12%	13	9	13	7	3	6	25	11	18	13	21	14	18	10
$25,000–$29,999	340	121	102	147	58	47	24	42	127	17	9	58	7	117	218
	13%	14	13	14	11	10	7	19	20	12	8	12	8	14	13
$30,000–$34,999	351	110	126	155	73	65	46	29	138	22	6	35	4	104	243
	13%	13	17	15	14	14	13	13	22	16	5	7	4	12	14
$35,000–$39,999	269	80	109	115	59	62	49	9	117	12	1	15	1	60	205
	10%	9	14	11	12	14	14	4	18	9	1	3	1	7	12
$40,000–$44,999	218	71	88	94	49	62	45	19	64	9	1	13	1	32	184
	8%	8	12	9	10	14	13	9	10	7	1	3	1	4	11
$45,000 or more	434	144	146	151	146	176	141	23	51	9	4	21		52	375
	16%	16	19	14	29	38	39	11	8	7	3	4		6	22
Refused/no answer	172	39	34	42	30	19	20	8	36	5	8	28	9	63	77
	.7%	4	4	4	6	4	6	4	6	4	7	6	10	7	4
Total	2635	873	759	1047	507	459	358	217	641	137	118	467	93	843	1714
	100%	100	100	100	100	100	100	100	100	100	100	100	100	100	100

Source: Updated from "Banner Format Aids Understanding," Marketing News, vol. 13, pp. 11, May 13, 1983.

percentages are cast in only one direction, banners do not allow the reader of the tables to look for alternative conclusions. Oftentimes banners collapse several categories, making it difficult to infer accurate results from the data. The probability of obtaining a spurious relationship increases. Also, the chance of discovering hidden variables decreases, as does the possibility of detecting covariation.

Because banners prevent the researcher from discovering misleading relationships and inhibit the exploration of alternative conditions in which a relationship may or may not exist, banners should not be used as a substitute for cross tabulations. They can be used, however, to complement cross tabulations as a way of simplifying the presentation of results.

SUMMARY

1 Bivariate analysis involves analyzing two variables at a time.

2 The choice of which statistical procedure to use depends on the scale level of the variables and on whether the researcher wants a descriptive statistic or an inferential test.

3 Linear correlation, (r) is a measure of the degree to which two interval variables are linearly associated.

4 The coefficient of determination (r^2) is the amount of variation in one variable that can be explained by knowledge of the other.

5 Simple regression is appropriate for one intervally scaled dependent variable and one intervally scaled independent variable.

6 Simple regression shows how the independent variable is related to the dependent variable.

7 The simple regression model can be presented as

$$SS_{total} = SS_{explained} + SS_{unexplained}$$

8 The simple regression equation is

$$\hat{Y}_i = a + bX_i$$

where a is the intercept and b is the slope or the amount of increase in $\hat{Y}$ predicted to occur with a one-unit increase in X.

9 A t test on the b coefficient provides a measure of the null hypothesis that the population regression coefficient is zero. (See the appendix to this chapter.)

10 The coefficient of determination in regression (r^2) equals

$$\frac{\text{Explained variation}}{\text{Total variation}} = \frac{SS_{explained}}{SS_{total}}$$

11 The difference between two sample means may be tested to see whether the population means are really different. This may be done with a z or t test, depending on the circumstances. (See the appendix to this chapter.)

12 The chi-square test evaluates the null hypothesis that two nominal variables are independent.

13 Cast percentages in cross-tabular tables in the direction of causation.

14 Total-sample cross-tabular tables may be elaborated by using control variables.

15 If a total-sample relationship is found, this elaboration may find the same relationship, interaction, or spuriousness.

16 If no total-sample relationship is found, this elaboration may find no relationship again or identify a relationship.

17 Banners provide benefits in data presentation but have limitations related to complex causal structures in data.

DISCUSSION QUESTIONS

1 What questions must you answer in order to select the appropriate bivariate statistical procedure?

2 What is linear correlation?

3 What is the coefficient of determination?

4 When can simple regression be used?

5 How do you test to see whether a simple regression has explained a significant portion of the variation in the dependent variable?

6 When should the z and t tests on the difference between means be used?

7 What is the chi-square test a test for?

8 In what alternative ways may percentages be calculated in a cross-tabular table? Which way is the best?

9 What is elaboration?

10 What may be found in elaboration?

11 A marketing manager was given the following table of frequency counts to show the nature of the relationship between age and attendance at NFL games. What conclusion should be drawn?

Attend NFL games	Age		Total
	Under 40	40 and over	
Yes	466	231	697
No	224	323	547
Total	690	554	1244

12 The same marketing manager also had a table of frequency counts between age and attendance at college football games. What conclusion should be drawn?

Attend college football games	Age		Total
	Under 40	40 and over	
Yes	242	271	513
No	251	265	516
Total	493	536	1029

13 In a study of advertising effects, two waves of consumers were interviewed. Wave 1 took place before a new campaign was introduced, and wave 2 a few months after the new campaign had started. As part of the analysis of the data, a comparison was made between the demographic characteristics of the consumers in wave 1 and wave 2. The hope was that the demographics would be the same. Typical of the reported results is the following:

	Sex	
	Male	Female
Wave 1	52%	47%
Wave 2	48	53
(Chi square = 4.16)		

What conclusion can be drawn from this result?

14 The same study used in questions 11 and 12 yielded the following data concerning the number of NFL home games attended in a year and the number of years the person has lived in the city:

Case	Number of home games attended	Years lived in city
1	8	28
2	2	6
3	1	3
4	3	12
5	8	20
6	4	23

What is the relationship between the two variables?

15 Mark Schwinn and Jennifer Grier were resident advisors (RAs) assigned to the first coed hall at Montana College. A welcome party was scheduled to take place the weekend after classes started, and the RAs had the responsibility of ordering the soft drinks. They couldn't, however, agree on kinds of soft drinks they should order (diet cola versus regular cola versus other assorted flavors). A total of 30 to 40 cases was to be ordered, and any unopened cans could be returned. Mark wanted 16 cases of regular cola, 6 diet cola, 6 regular noncola, and 2 diet noncola. Jennifer wanted to order, respectively, 11, 6, 9, and 4 cases. To avoid running out of anything, they decided to get the highest estimate of each kind, making a 35-case order (16 cases regular cola, 6 diet cola, 9 regular noncola, and 4 diet noncola). The actual consumption at the party was 12 cases of regular cola, 4 diet cola, 8 regular noncola, and 1 diet noncola.

Question:

a Is there a difference in preferences between regular versus diet pop? Cola versus noncolas? Are the two variables independent?

16 MINICASE

In a recent study on American travel habits, the following data were obtained:

Case	Gender	Children at home?	Respondent's age	Vacations per year
1	M	Y	25	1
2	M	N	52	16
3	F	N	34	8
4	F	Y	33	1
5	F	Y	51	5
6	F	Y	29	0
7	M	Y	35	2
8	F	N	27	8
9	M	Y	46	4
10	M	N	30	10
11	F	N	45	14
12	M	Y	38	3

Questions:

a Is there a relationship between the presence of children at home and the gender of the respondent?

b What is the relationship between age and the presence of children at home? (*Hint:* Create nominal age categories.)

c What is the relationship between age and number of vacations taken per year? Calculate *r* squared. (*Hint:* Plot the data points before doing a regression analysis. Look for the interaction of an extraneous variable, and calculate your least-squares regression line or lines accordingly. Is one equation appropriate? Would two explain the data better?)

d Is your answer to question c significant (i.e., was a significant proportion of the variance in the dependent variable explained by the regression)? (See the chapter appendix.)

e Using the equation or equations you computed in the previous problem, complete the following dataset:

Case	Gender	Children at home?	Respondent's age	Vacations per year
a	M	Y	40	_____
b	F	N	40	_____
c	M	Y	65	_____
d	F	N	18	_____

APPENDIX   Bivariate Inference Tests

This appendix contains a description of a number of bivariate inference tests, specifically (1) the t test on the simple regression coefficient, (2) the F test on the explained sum of squares in regression, (3) the z test on the difference between means, and (4) the t test on the difference between means. All tests presented here assume that the variables of interest are intervally scaled.

THE t TEST ON THE REGRESSION COEFFICIENT

The null hypothesis that interests the researcher with respect to simple regression is that the slope is zero. In formula, the null and alternative hypotheses are:

$$H_0: \beta = 0$$

$$H_1: \beta \neq 0$$

where β is the population regression coefficient. In essence, we are testing to see whether the X values make a significant contribution to the explanation of the Y values. We begin the t test by first calculating the standard error of the estimate.

Standard Error of the Estimate

The measure of the scatter of the actual Y_i values about the regression line, $\hat{Y}_i$, is called the standard error of the estimate. It is the standard deviation of Y_i about $\hat{Y}_i$.

$$\text{Standard error of the estimate} = s_{YX} = \sqrt{\frac{\Sigma(Y_i - \hat{Y}_i)^2}{n - 2}}$$

We divide by $n - 2$ to adjust for sample bias effect on this estimator because one degree of freedom is used up in fitting the regression line, and there are $n - 1$ degrees of freedom in the sample. The slope of the regression line requires 1 degree of freedom. A small standard error of the estimate indicates a tight scatter of observations about the regression line, and vice versa. We could use this value to calculate a confidence interval about the regression line. However, this is not our interest here. For our purposes the standard error of the estimate will be used as an intermediate step in testing the null hypothesis that $\beta = 0$.

From the data in Table 19-2,

$$\Sigma(Y_i - \hat{Y}_i)^2 = 334.17$$

thus

$$s_{YX} = \sqrt{\frac{334.17}{10 - 2}}$$

$$= \sqrt{41.77125}$$

$$= 6.5$$

Standard Error to the Regression Coefficient

We may also calculate the standard error or standard deviation of the sampling distribution of the regression coefficient. It is a measure of the amount of sampling error present in the determination of b, as follows:

$$s_b = \frac{s_{YX}}{\sqrt{\Sigma x^2}}$$

or, since $x = X_i - \bar{X}$,

$$s_b = \frac{s_{YX}}{\sqrt{\Sigma(X_i - \bar{X})^2}}$$

In our example,

$$s_b = \frac{6.5}{\sqrt{1290}}$$

$$= \frac{6.5}{35.9}$$

$$= .18$$

The t Test

The standard error of the regression coefficient can be used to test the statistical significance of the b coefficient. We do this by use of the knowledge that

$$t = \frac{b}{s_b}$$

We then compare this computed t value with the value in the t distribution given in Table A-4 of the Appendix at the end of the book, at $n - 2$ degrees of freedom.

In our example,

$$b = .93 \quad \text{and} \quad s_b = .18$$

then

$$t = \frac{.93}{.18}$$

$$= 5.17$$

At 8 degrees of freedom and $\alpha = .05$, for a two-tailed test, the critical value of t is 2.306. Therefore our b coefficient is statistically significant. We conclude that the population regression coefficient is not zero. Thus, knowledge of grades in marketing management is significantly helping us explain grades in marketing research. For $n > 30$, the value of t calculated is compared with z values of the normal distribution given in Table A-2 of the Appendix at the end of the book.

THE F TEST ON THE EXPLAINED SUM OF SQUARES

Since we have calculated SS associated with the regression and SS error, we are in a position to convert these SS to variances (or mean squares, as they are called) by dividing by the relevant number of degrees of freedom. We could then compare the regression-associated variance with the error variance and determine whether the regression has explained a statistically significant portion of the variance in Y. Here the F statistic is the appropriate test. Specifically,

$$F = \frac{\text{variance explained by regression}}{\text{variance unexplained}}$$

$$= \frac{SS_{\text{explained}}/df}{SS_{\text{unexplained}}/df}$$

Table 1 presents the calculation of the F value for our grades data. As always, there are $n - 1$ degrees of freedom in the sample. The b coefficient requires 1 degree of freedom, thus leaving $n - 2$ for the error term. The calculated F is 26.71. The critical F (given in Table A-5 of the Appendix at the end of the book) at $\alpha = .05$, and at 1 and 8 degrees of freedom, is 5.32. Thus we conclude that the regression has explained a significant proportion of the variance in Y.

TABLE 1   SIGNIFICANCE TABLE FOR GRADES DATA

Source of variation	SS	df	Mean square (MS)	F
$SS_{\text{explained}}$ $\Sigma(\hat{Y}_i - \bar{Y})^2$	1115.83	1	1115.83	26.71
$SS_{\text{unexplained (error)}}$ $\Sigma(Y_i - \hat{Y}_i)^2$	334.17	$n - 2 = 8$	41.77	
SS_{total} $\Sigma(Y_i - \bar{Y})^2$	1450.00	$n - 1 = 9$		

Previously, we calculated $t = 5.17$ for the b coefficient. This value is the square root of the F value we just calculated. We then note the fundamental relationship between the F and t distributions:

$$F = t^2$$

A t test on the b coefficient or an F test on the variance will lead to similar conclusions with regard to statistical significance in simple regression. In regression with more than one independent variable, the difference between the t and F tests will become important. This will be discussed in Chapter 21; for now, we merely note the two procedures.

THE z TEST ON THE DIFFERENCE BETWEEN MEANS

A question that often arises in marketing research is whether or not an observed difference between two means generated by a sample is large enough to be a significant difference. That is, are the population means really different from each other? For example, we might want to know whether the mean consumption levels of two brands of cola are the same, or whether the mean attitude scores of male and female salespersons about their jobs are the same, or whether the mean sales levels generated by two coupon plans are equal. To do this we may use either the z or the t test on the difference between the mean values. The choice between a z and a t test is made on essentially the same basis as in univariate analysis. Specifically, we use z when the population standard deviation, σ, is known for both measures under consideration, or if $n > 30$ for both measures. We use t when the population standard deviation is unknown for either measure when $n \leq 30$.

The null hypothesis is usually that the two population means are equal. However, it is possible to test that the difference between two means is some specific value. The relevant formula if σ is known is

$$z = \frac{(\bar{X}_1 - \bar{X}_2) - (\mu_1 - \mu_2)}{\sigma_{\bar{x}_1 - \bar{x}_2}}$$

where $\bar{X}_1$ = sample mean for the first variable
$\bar{X}_2$ = sample mean for the second variable
μ_1 and μ_2 = hypothesized population means for the two variables
$\sigma_{\bar{x}_1 - \bar{x}_2}$ = standard error of the difference between the means (standard deviation of the sampling distribution of the difference between means)

The central-limit theorem applies to this sampling distribution of the difference between means, except that the formula for the standard error is different. Specifically,

$$\sigma_{\bar{x}_1 - \bar{x}_2} = \sqrt{\sigma_{\bar{x}_1}^2 + \sigma_{\bar{x}_2}^2} = \sqrt{\frac{\sigma_1^2}{n_1} + \frac{\sigma_2^2}{n_2}}$$

where σ_1^2 and σ_2^2 are the population variances for the two variables of interest and n_1 and n_2 are the respective sample sizes.

Suppose that we knew the following related to the average weekly consumption of two cola brands.

Brand A: $\bar{X}_1$ = 50 ounces per week; σ_1 = 12; n_1 = 40

Brand B: $\bar{X}_2$ = 60 ounces per week; σ_2 = 16; n_2 = 40

Here the null and alternative hypotheses are

$H_0: \mu_1 = \mu_2$ or $(\mu_1 - \mu_2) = 0$
$H_1: \mu_1 \neq \mu_2$ or $(\mu_1 - \mu_2) \neq 0$

The standard error is

$$\sigma_{\bar{x}_1 - \bar{x}_2} = \sqrt{\frac{(12)^2}{40} + \frac{(16)^2}{40}} = \sqrt{10} = 3.16$$

and so the calculated z value is

$$z = \frac{(50 - 60) - (\mu_1 - \mu_2)}{3.16} = \frac{-10 - 0}{3.16}$$

$$= -3.16$$

The calculated z value exceeds the critical z value of -1.96 at $\alpha = .05$ for a two-tailed test. Therefore, we reject the null hypothesis and conclude that brand B has significantly more consumption than brand A.

If σ_1 and σ_2 are unknown and not assumed to be equal, we use s_1 and s_2 to estimate $S_{\bar{x}_1 - \bar{x}_2}$ as follows:

$$s_{\bar{x}_1 - \bar{x}_2} = \sqrt{s_{\bar{x}_1}^2 + s_{\bar{x}_2}^2} = \sqrt{\frac{s_1^2}{n_1} + \frac{s_2^2}{n_2}} \quad \text{(A19-1)}$$

If σ_1 and σ_2 are unknown but assumed to be equal, we can pool our sample results to estimate $s_{\bar{x}_1 - \bar{x}_2}$ using this formula:

$$s_{\bar{x}_1 - \bar{x}_2} = \sqrt{\left(\frac{n_1 s_1^2 + n_2 s_2^2}{n_1 + n_2 - 2}\right)\left(\frac{n_1 + n_2}{n_1 n_2}\right)} \quad \text{(A19-2)}$$

It is just a matter of plugging the value of n_1, s_1, and so on, into the relevant formula and getting $s_{\bar{x}_1 - \bar{x}_2}$. If n_1 and $n_2 > 30$, we can calculate z as follows:

$$z = \frac{(\bar{X}_1 - \bar{X}_2) - (\mu_1 - \mu_2)}{s_{\bar{x}_1 - \bar{x}_2}}$$

THE t TEST ON THE DIFFERENCE BETWEEN MEANS

The t statistic can be calculated when σ_1 and σ_2 are unknown in a manner parallel to the calculation for z, as follows:

$$t = \frac{(\bar{X}_1 - \bar{X}_2) - (\mu_1 - \mu_2)}{s_{\bar{x}_1 - \bar{x}_2}}$$

where t has $n_1 + n_2 - 2$ degrees of freedom. The values of $S_{\bar{x}_1 - \bar{x}_2}$ can be calculated using either Equation A19-1 or Equation A19-2, depending on whether the researcher assumes that the population variances are equal or not. Suppose a sample yielded the following results:

Coupon plan A:
$\bar{X}_1$ = 20 sales per day; s_1 = 3; n_1 = 10

Coupon plan B:
$\bar{X}_2$ = 16 sales per day; s_2 = 2; n_2 = 5

and the researcher assumes that $\sigma_1^2 = \sigma_2^2$. Thus, the formula in Equation A19-2 should be used, and

$$s_{\bar{x}_1 - \bar{x}_2} = \sqrt{\left(\frac{(10)(3)^2 + (5)(2)^2}{10 + 5 - 2}\right)\left(\frac{10 + 5}{(10)(5)}\right)}$$

$$= \sqrt{(8.46)(.3)} = \sqrt{2.54} = 1.59$$

then

$$t = \frac{(20 - 16) - (\mu_1 - \mu_2)}{1.59} = \frac{4 - 0}{1.59} = 2.52$$

At $\alpha = .1$ and 13 df, the critical t value from Table A-4 of the Appendix at the end of the book for a two-tailed test is 1.77. Since the calculated t is greater than the critical t, we reject the null hypothesis that the means are equal.

DIFFERENCE BETWEEN PROPORTIONS

We may apply the same type of hypothesis-testing procedures to the difference between two proportions when $n > 30$.[1] If σ_1 and σ_2 are known (i.e., if π_1 and π_2 are known), we use the formula

$$z = \frac{(p_1 - p_2) - (\pi_1 - \pi_2)}{\sigma_{p_1 - p_2}}$$

where p_1 and p_2 are the two observed sample proportions, and

$$\sigma_{p_1 - p_2} = \sqrt{\sigma_{p_1}^2 + \sigma_{p_2}^2} = \sqrt{\frac{\pi_1(1 - \pi_1)}{n_1} + \frac{\pi_2(1 - \pi_2)}{n_2}}$$

When π_1 and π_2 are not known (and therefore σ_1 and σ_2 are not known), we use the formula

$$z = \frac{(p_1 - p_2) - (\pi_1 - \pi_2)}{s_{p_1 - p_2}}$$

Since the null hypothesis is that $\pi_1 = \pi_2$, we are assuming that $\sigma_1 = \sigma_2$, and so we can pool our sample results to estimate $S_{p_1 \ p_2}$ using the formula

$$s_{p_1 - p_2} = \sqrt{(p^*q^*)\left(\frac{n_1 + n_2}{n_1 n_2}\right)}$$

[1] When $n < 30$, the binomial distribution should be used. This situation will not be discussed in this book.

where

$$p^* = \frac{n_1 p_1 + n_2 p_2}{n_1 + n_2}$$

$$= \frac{\text{total number of yes answers in the two samples}}{\text{total number of answers in the two samples}}$$

and

$$q^* = 1 - p^*$$

That is, p^* is a pooled estimate of p.

Let us illustrate the latter situation where π_1 and π_2 are not known. Suppose that the two different product concepts are tested with the following results:

$$\text{Concept A: } p_1 = .20; \, n_1 = 40$$

$$\text{Concept B: } p_2 = .24; \, n_2 = 60$$

where p_i = the number of people who indicated they would buy the ith product concept. Here:

$$H_0: \pi_1 = \pi_2$$

$$H_1: \pi_1 \neq \pi_2$$

$$p^* = \frac{(40)(.20) + (60)(.24)}{40 + 60} = .224$$

and

$$s_{p_1 - p_2} = \sqrt{(.224)(.776)\left(\frac{40 + 60}{(40)(60)}\right)}$$

$$= .085$$

then

$$z = \frac{(.20 - .24) - (\pi_1 - \pi_2)}{.085} = \frac{.04 - 0}{.085}$$

$$= -.47$$

That is, the difference between the two proportions is equal to .47 of a standard error. For $\alpha = .05$ and a two-tailed test, the critical $z = 1.96$. Since the calculated z is less than the critical z, we cannot reject the null hypothesis that the two population proportions are equal.

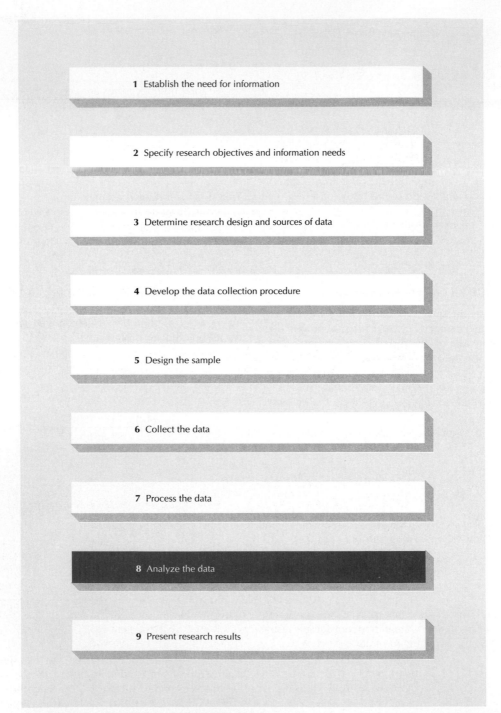

FIGURE 20-1   Steps in the research process.

CHAPTER 20

MULTIVARIATE DATA ANALYSIS I:
INTERDEPENDENCE METHODS

WESTERN FEDERAL SAVINGS

MANUFACTURERS HANOVER

Member FDIC

MARKETING RESEARCH IN ACTION

FACTOR ANALYSIS OF BANKING COMPETITION REVEALS UNDERLYING DIMENSIONS OF COMPETITIVE SUCCESS

A study of the factors that contribute to the marketing strategy success of banks was conducted in 50 standard metropolitan statistical areas (MSAs) in seven states. The study collected data on 27 attributes that were believed to define the domain of competitive activity among banks. Of interest to the marketing researchers was determining the underlying strategic thrusts that defined the competition among these banks. To do this, the researchers analyzed the responses on the 27 attributes for all banks in the sample. The technique they used to determine these underlying competitive dimensions was factor analysis. The 27 attributes in the study are listed on the left side of the table on the next page. The relationship between the attributes and the underlying competitive factors that were found is shown in the numeric values in the table. The higher the numeric value, the higher the relationship. The attributes have been grouped to show those attributes that are highly related to the same factor. The results are shown in the table.

FACTOR ANALYSIS OF COMPETITIVE BANKING ATTRIBUTES

Marketing activities	Factor*					
	1	2	3	4	5	6
TV advertising expenditures	.06	−.02	.81	.01	.08	.16
Radio advertising expenditures	−.04	.01	.80	−.11	.14	−.09
Newspaper advertising expenditures	.09	.19	.75	.07	.06	.04
Expenditures on all ad media	.09	.09	.93	.06	.04	−.02
Contact with legislators	.14	.17	.10	.01	.81	.15
Contact with regulatory officials	.13	.03	.14	.07	.68	.17
Contact with city council members	.13	−11	.09	.03	.52	.23
Survey of current customers	.58	.01	.04	.15	.16	.25
Focus groups with current customers	.68	.10	−.01	.09	−.13	−.02
Shopping competing firms for information	.76	.11	.08	.06	−.13	−.02
Surveying competitors' customers	.60	.14	.17	.03	.25	.18
Collecting traffic counts at competitor or at other locations	.78	.03	.03	.01	−.09	−.01
Focus groups with competitors' customers	.73	.09	−.04	.02	.29	.03
Reevaluating service charges	.02	.15	.04	−.03	.01	.81
Reevaluating charges for extra services	.03	.05	−.03	.01	.17	.80
Gathering information on competitors' prices	.19	.21	.06	.04	.18	.50
Personality tests conducted on tellers	.10	.83	.01	.15	.01	.09
Aptitude tests conducted on tellers	−.04	.80	.09	.06	.01	.05
Personality tests conducted on officers	.11	.85	.06	.05	−.06	.14
Aptitude tests conducted on officers	.21	.82	.09	.06	.01	.05
Training, including product information	.09	.10	−.05	.56	−.15	.05
Training in communication techniques	.37	.09	−.04	.51	−.20	.21
Training in company mission	.18	.04	−.01	.50	−.25	.23
Training to handle complaints	.21	−.05	.07	.45	−.04	.31
Providing officers with customer deposit history	−.19	.09	.09	.59	.23	−.21
Providing officers with customer business profile	−.04	.10	−.04	.61	.10	−.04
Providing officers with customer services profile	.03	.08	.05	.58	.23	−.15
Percentage variance explained	19.4	10.2	9.2	7.4	6.3	5.1

* Underlying dimensions:
F1 = market scanning
F2 = screening of customer contact personnel
F3 = advertising

F4 = support of customer contact personnel
F5 = political activity
F6 = pricing analysis

The study revealed six underlying dimensions of competition: (1) market scanning—the use of marketing research to stay close to the customer; (2) screening of customer-contact employees for their fit with the job requirements; (3) advertising activity; (4) the provision of support for customer-contact personnel; (5) contact with political groups; and (6) activity related to pricing. This information would be very useful to a bank in planning its marketing strategy. To get this information, the researchers utilized factor analysis, one of the dependence methods described in this chapter.

Source: Adapted from Daryl O. McKee, P. Rajan Varadarajan, and William M. Pride, "Strategic Adaptability and Firm Performance: A Market-Contingent Perspective," *Journal of Marketing,* vol. 53, pp. 21–35, July 1989.

In Chapters 18 and 19 we examined data analysis as it relates to univariate and bivariate situations. These analysis types are the heart of current data analysis in marketing research practice. As a result, we presented the appropriate univariate and bivariate procedures in some detail.

The next two chapters are a brief overview of a number of *multivariate data analysis procedures,* which involve the simultaneous analysis of more than two variables. The objectives of our discussion of these techniques are (1) to make you aware of the existence of the techniques, (2) to position each technique in terms of the type of input data required, and (3) to discuss the type of output generated by each technique.

Great care should be taken in applying the techniques presented in this and the next chapter. There are a number of problems and statistical assumptions related to each technique that we do not discuss at all. You should recognize that these techniques are extremely dangerous *when used by unskilled people.* Unfortunately, a proper step-by-step description of how each procedure works, the assumptions made, and the problems in using them would at least double the size of this book. We leave it to a more advanced course in marketing research to cover this material in the required depth.

In utilizing multivariate data analysis methods, successful marketing researchers have some common approaches. First, they rarely do multivariate analysis until they have tested hypotheses through cross tabulation. This keeps researchers close to their data and allows for better interpretation of the multivariate results. Second, if the multivariate results disagree with the bivariate results, they tend to put more belief in the latter. Third, they ask a lot of basic questions of their statistical experts, so that they can communicate these complex results in plain managerial language to their nonstatistician management. Fourth, they take the time to educate themselves about the basics of these data analysis methodologies. This allows them to make better use of their statistical experts.

Despite this, there is a growing understanding in marketing research of the need for, and usefulness of, multivariate data analysis procedures. There are a number of reasons for this trend. First, marketing problems are usually not completely described by one or two variables. Many variables combine to yield marketing outcomes. Second, the advent of high-speed computers and associated analysis software has made the solution of multivariate statistical procedures relatively easy. Problems that were virtually impossible to solve by human calculation 20 years ago can now be solved in less than a second with a computer. The 1990s technology of the PC allows virtually all these multivariate techniques to be run at one's desk. Packages such as SPSS-PC and SYSTAT are powerful and readily available. Third, improved understanding of statistical concepts among marketing researchers and managers has increased the likelihood of multivariate procedures being used to make decisions.

This chapter begins by distinguishing multivariate procedures that do not specify a dependent variable from those that do specify a dependent variable. Then three procedures are discussed which do not require that a dependent variable be specified. These procedures are factor analysis, cluster analysis, and multidimensional scaling.

INTERDEPENDENCE VERSUS DEPENDENCE METHODS

The multivariate analysis chapters in this book are organized around a scheme that divides procedures into interdependence and dependence procedures. The fundamental differentiating aspect between the two is whether or not one or more variables have been designated as dependent on other variables. In *dependence methods,* one or more variables are designated as being predicted by (dependent on) a set of independent variables. Regression is an example of this type of analysis. In *interdependence methods,* no variable or variables are designated as being predicted by others. It is the interrelationship among all the variables taken together that interests the researcher. Factor analysis is an example of this type of procedure. Figure 20-2 illustrates this fundamental distinction and notes where in this book the various methods are presented.

This chapter discusses three interdependence methods: factor analysis, cluster analysis, and multidimensional scaling.

FACTOR ANALYSIS

Factor analysis is a procedure that takes a large number of variables or objects and searches to see whether they have a small number of factors in common which account for their intercorrelation. For example, we might attribute the high association between grades in business administration courses to the factor of intelligence, or the association between certain chemical attributes of coffee and the factor of acidity (pH level).

The Marketing Research in Action on bank marketing strategy at the beginning of this chapter illustrates the power of factor analysis in finding underlying dimensions.

Marketing Applications

Factor analysis has a number of possible applications in marketing research. These include data reduction, structure identification, scaling, and data transformation.

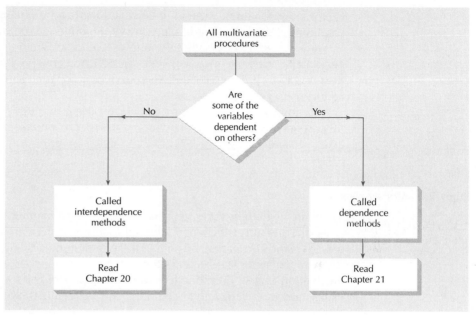

FIGURE 20-2   Interdependence versus dependence methods.

Data Reduction   Factor analysis can be used for reducing a mass of data to a manageable level. For example, the researcher may have collected data on 50 attributes of a product. The analysis and understanding of these data may be aided by reducing the attributes to a minimum number of factors that underlie the 50 attributes. These factors may then be used in further analysis in place of the original attributes.

Structure Identification   Factor analysis may be used to discover the basic structure underlying a set of measures. For example, the above 50 attributes may reduce to two factors identified by the researcher as (1) sweetness/bitterness and (2) degree of freshness. The assumption is that at least some of the measures taken are redundant. The factor analysis then finds the underlying structure of the redundancy by placing the measures on underlying factors or dimensions.

Scaling   A researcher may wish to develop a scale on which subjects can be compared. A problem in developing any scale is in weighting the variables being combined to form the scale. Factor analysis helps the process by dividing the variables into independent factors. Each factor represents a scale measure of some underlying dimension. Further, factor analysis gives the weights to use for each variable when combining them into a scale.

Data Transformation   A number of dependence analysis techniques require independent variables that are themselves uncorrelated (e.g., multiple regression).

Factor analysis can be used to identify factors that are uncorrelated. These factors can then be used as input in the relevant dependence method.

Thus, the following have all made use of factor analysis: the development of personality scales, market segments based upon psychographic data, the identification of key product attributes, similarities among magazines, and uncorrelated factors for regression analysis.

The ability of factor analysis to perform these functions has resulted in about 58 percent of businesses utilizing it in their marketing research, as noted in Figure 20-3.

Steps in Factor Analysis

There are essentially three steps in a factor analysis solution. The first is to develop a set of correlations between all combinations of the variables of interest. Since we are using correlations, we must then be assuming that the input variables are intervally scaled. The second step is to extract a set of initial factors from the correlation matrix developed in the first step. The third step is to "rotate" the initial factors to find a final solution. The concept of rotation will be discussed later in the chapter. There are a number of decisions that a researcher must make at each of these steps that determine the type of factor analysis that will take place.

Calculation of Correlations   With respect to the calculation of the correlation matrix, two broad classes of factor analysis may be distinguished. These are (1) *R*-factor analysis and (2) *Q*-factor analysis. In *R*-factor analysis, these correlations are calculated *between variables;* in *Q*-factor analysis, they are calculated *between cases.* Cases could be people, products, or whatever else the variables have

FIGURE 20-3   Use in practice of factor analysis. (*Source:* Thomas C. Kinnear and Ann R. Root, *A Study of the Marketing Research Business*, unpublished study, 1994. Copyright 1994 Thomas C. Kinnear. Not to be reproduced.)

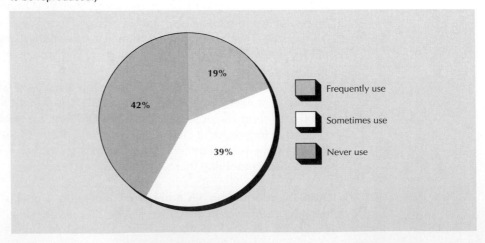

been measured on, so a *Q*-factor analysis would group cases on specific factors. Such a procedure could then be used to find similar products or people who belong to different segments. For example, Levi Strauss makes use of *Q*-analysis to identify and profile segments within the male and female clothing market.

Figure 20-4 shows how *R*- and *Q*-type correlations are developed from the basic data matrix. The solid arrow going down indicates that *R*-type correlations are calculated between variables by using data from all cases. With *m* variables in the data matrix, the result of this process is an *m*-by-*m* correlation matrix among variables. The dashed arrow going horizontally to the right indicates that *Q*-type correlations are calculated between cases by using data from all variables. With *n* cases in the data matrix, the result of this process is an *n*-by-*n* correlation matrix among cases. The calculation of correlation coefficients has been discussed in detail in Chapter 19, where the example given is of an *R*-type correlation coefficient, since it shows the relationship between two variables. To calculate a *Q*-type correlation coefficient, we simply treat the cases as if they were variables, and vice versa.

FIGURE 20-4   Development of *R*- and *Q*-type correlation matrices.

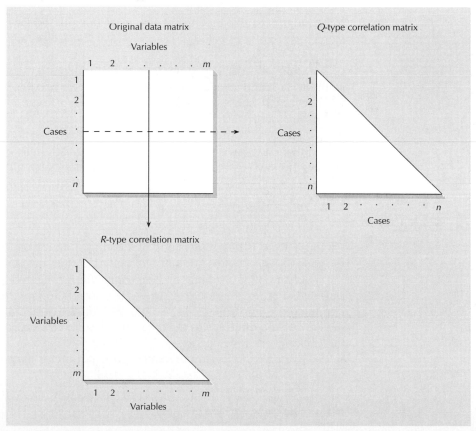

Extraction of Initial Factors   There are many methods for extracting the initial factors from the correlation matrix. In general, these methods are far too numerically complex to even begin to discuss here, but one of them is worthy of our consideration. It is used extensively in practice and will serve to illustrate the nature of factor extraction. It is called the *principal factors method.*

The object of factor extraction is to find a set of factors that are formed as a linear combination of the variables in the correlation matrix. Thus, if the variables X_1, X_2, and X_3 were highly correlated with one another, they would be combined together to form one factor. A linear combination could be defined as follows:

$$z = b_1 X_1 + b_2 X_2 + \cdots + b_m X_m$$

Here z is the linear combination, and it is called a *principal component* or a *principal factor.* The principal-factors methodology involves searching for the values of the b's above which form a linear combination that explains more variance in the correlation matrix than any other set of b's. This is called the first principal factor. This explained variance is then subtracted from the original input matrix to yield a residual matrix. Then a *second principal factor* is extracted from this residual matrix. This factor explains more of the variance in the residual matrix than any other. The procedure is then repeated until there is very little variance remaining to be explained. The nature of this procedure is such that the factors extracted are uncorrelated with each other. The factors are said to be *orthogonal.*

Rotation   The initial factors are often very difficult to interpret. Thus the initial solution is rotated to yield a solution that is more amenable to interpretation. There are two broad classes of rotation—(1) *orthogonal rotation,* which maintains the factors as uncorrelated with one another, and (2) *oblique rotation,* which allows the factors to be correlated with one another. The basic idea of rotation is to yield factors that each have some variables that correlate highly and some that correlate poorly. This avoids the problem of having factors with all variables having mid-range correlations, and thus it allows for easier interpretation.

An Example[1]

Factor analysis is best understood by looking at an example. This one is designed to reduce a set of coffee attributes to a set of underlying factors. Table 20-1 shows the set of 14 coffee attributes on which data were collected on a 10-point semantic differential scale. This table also gives the correlation matrix between the various combinations of attributes. Table 20-2 presents the principal factors extracted from the correlation matrix, plus the orthogonally rotated factors (varimax rotation) and the obliquely rotated factors.

Let us first examine the unrotated principal-factor matrix. Note that there are

[1]This example is adapted and updated to 1995 from Bishwa Nath Mukherjee, "A Factor Analysis of Some Qualitative Attributes of Coffee," *Journal of Advertising Research,* vol. 5, pp. 35–38, March 1965.

TABLE 20-1   COFFEE ATTRIBUTES AND INTERCORRELATIONS AMONG ATTRIBUTE RATINGS

14 coffee attributes investigated
Pleasant flavor—Unpleasant flavor
Stagnant, muggy taste   Sparkling, refreshing taste
Mellow taste—Bitter taste
Cheap taste—Expensive taste
Comforting, harmonious, smooth, friendly taste—Irritating, discordant, rough, hostile taste
Dead, lifeless, dull taste—Alive, lively, peppy taste
Tastes artificial—Tastes like real coffee
Deep, distinct flavor—Shallow, indistinct flavor
Tastes warmed over—Tastes just brewed
Hearty, full-bodied, full flavor—Watery, thin, empty flavor
Pure, clear taste—Muddy swampy taste
Raw taste—Roasted taste
Fresh taste—Stale taste
Overall preference: Excellent quality—Very poor quality

Note: Ten blank boxes separated each set of opposing statements. Subjects checked the position that came closest to describing how they felt toward the product.

Intercorrelations among attribute ratings													
	1	2	3	4	5	6	7	8	9	10	11	12	13	14
1 Pleasant flavor	1.00	.76	.81	.79	.83	.81	.74	.66	.65	.71	.76	.65	.71	.75
2 Sparkling taste		1.00	.78	.85	.77	.87	.83	.65	.70	.78	.85	.69	.74	.83
3 Mellow taste			1.00	.77	.85	.81	.77	.60	.65	.64	.75	.69	.69	.74
4 Expensive taste				1.00	.78	.87	.83	.76	.69	.81	.81	.64	.71	.87
5 Comforting taste					1.00	.82	.77	.66	.60	.69	.82	.69	.69	.74
6 Alive taste						1.00	.88	.70	.74	.80	.81	.65	.77	.87
7 Tastes like real coffee							1.00	.67	.76	.75	.79	.62	.76	.87
8 Deep distinct flavor								1.00	.51	.84	.70	.54	.59	.70
9 Tastes just brewed									1.00	.67	.65	.67	.80	.75
10 Hearty flavor										1.00	.83	.65	.72	.76
11 Pure clear taste											1.00	.66	.73	.76
12 Roasted taste												1.00	.78	.61
13 Fresh taste													1.00	.73
14 Overall preference														1.00
Mean rating*	4.5	4.3	4.4	4.6	4.4	4.2	4.2	4.3	4.3	4.2	4.3	4.4	4.6	6.9
Standard deviation	1.6	1.3	1.4	1.4	1.3	1.4	1.6	1.5	1.5	1.5	1.4	1.2	1.4	2.7

* The 10 scale categories were assigned successive integers, beginning with 1 at the favorable side of the scale. Thus ratings could vary from 1 (very "good") to 10 (very "bad") on an attribute.

Source: Updated to 1995 from Bishwa Nath Mukherjee, "A Factor Analysis of Some Qualitative Attributes of Coffee," *Journal of Advertising Research,* vol. 5, p. 36, March 1965. Used with permission.

four factors underlying the 14 attributes. The elements in this matrix listed under the factors are called *unrotated factor loadings.* The loadings measure which variables are involved in which factor pattern, to what degree, and in what direction. They can be interpreted like correlation coefficients. The square of the loading equals the proportion of the variation that a variable has in common with an unrotated factor.

Another way to conceptualize this relationship is to remember that a loading is a correlation coefficient between a variable and a factor. In essence, when we square a loading we are calculating a coefficient of determination, r^2, between a variable and a factor. Thus, the squared loading represents the amount of shared variation between a variable and a factor.

The h^2 measures are called *communalities*. Communality is the proportion of a variable's total variation that is involved in the factors. Mathematically, h^2 equals the sum of the squared loading of a variable on all factors. For example, for attribute 1:

$$h^2 = (.86)^2 + (-.01)^2 + (-.20)^2 + (.04)^2 = .78$$

Communality may be interpreted as a measure of uniqueness. By subtracting h^2 from 1.0, the degree to which a variable is unrelated to the others may be calculated. Here we note that 78 percent of the variation in scores on attribute 1 can be predicted from the other variables, leaving 22 percent uniquely related to this attribute.

To get the percentage of total variance in the data explained by the four factors, we simply calculate H, where

$$H = \frac{\text{sum of all } h^2\text{'s}}{\text{number of variables}} \times 100$$

$$= \frac{11.61}{14} \times 100$$

$$= 83\%$$

This value is called the *common variance* explained by the factors.

To calculate the amount of variation in the data accounted for by a factor, we square each loading for a factor, add, and then divide the result by the number of variables. For example, for factor 1 the value is

$$(.86)^2 + (.91)^2 + (.86)^2 + \cdots + (.90)^2 = 10.42$$

This value is called an *eigenvalue* in the vocabulary of factor analysis. Thus, the percentage of total variance explained by factor 1 is $10.42/14 = 74.4$ percent. The percentage of common variance explained by this factor is then $10.42/11.61 = 90$ percent. We note that the percentages of both common variance and total variance are presented in Table 20-2.

In order to obtain an interpretation of the results we examine the rotated factors. Table 20-3 presents one such interpretation. There the factors have been placed with high-loading variables and each given a "creative" name by the author of the study. Note that there is no unique definition of the meaning of any factor; it

TABLE 20-2   FACTOR LOADINGS

	Principal factor matrix					Rotated (varimax) matrix				Oblique factor matrix			
	I	II	III	IV	h^2	A	B	C	D	A	B	C	D
1	.86	-.01	-.20	.04	.78	.63	.38	.36	.34	.34	.01	.07	-.03
2	.91	-.01	-.01	-.09	.83	.48	.43	.53	.38	.14	.04	.23	.04
3	.86	.11	.28	.002	.83	.70	.26	.38	.36	.36	.13	-.003	-.01
4	.91	.15	-.001	-.10	.87	.46	.53	.54	.29	.16	-.05	.34	-.07
5	.87	-.002	-.31	.10	.87	.74	.38	.30	.32	.47	.01	-.004	-.08
6	.93	.03	-.02	-.16	.90	.49	.43	.59	.35	.12	.07	.30	-.01
7	.90	-.02	.04	-.21	.86	.42	.38	.64	.37	.03	.11	.33	.04
8	.77	.36	.11	.16	.77	.31	.74	.27	.22	.24	-.40	.32	-.10
9	.79	-.28	.24	-.09	.76	.23	.24	.52	.62	-.15	.11	.14	.37
10	.87	.25	.22	.17	.89	.28	.75	.33	.39	.14	.38	.31	.07
11	.89	.11	.05	.10	.82	.51	.55	.36	.36	.28	-.15	.7	-.01
12	.76	-.29	.04	.27	.74	.43	.28	.16	.67	.18	-.08	-.18	.38
13	.84	-.27	.19	.12	.83	.33	.32	.36	.70	.01	-.03	-.001	.41
14	.90	.04	.08	-.23	.86	.38	.43	.65	.34	.002	.08	.39	.01
Percent common variance	90.0	4.1	3.3	2.6									
Percent total variance	74.4	3.4	2.7	2.6									

Source: Adapted and updated to 1995 from Bishwa Nath Mukherjee, "A Factor Analysis of Some Qualitative Attributes of Coffee," *Journal of Advertising Research,* vol. 5, p. 37, March 1965. Used with permission.

TABLE 20-3   INTERPRETATION OF FACTORS

Variable	Attribute	Varimax	Oblique
Factor A (comforting quality)			
1	Pleasant flavor	.625	.340
3	Mellow taste	.698	.359
5	Comforting taste	.736	.465
11	Pure clear taste	.512	.283
Factor B (heartiness)			
8	Deep distinct flavor	.742	.396
10	Hearty flavor	.745	.380
Factor C (genuineness)			
2	Sparkling taste	.524	.232
4	Expensive taste	.541	.334
6	Alive taste	.594	.301
7	Tastes like real coffee	.636	.328
8	Deep distinct flavor	.268	.323
10	Hearty flavor	.332	.310
14	Overall preference	.653	.387
Factor D (freshness)			
9	Tastes just brewed	.621	.359
12	Roasted taste	.670	.465
13	Fresh taste	.698	.238

Source: Updated to 1995 from Bishwa Nath Mukherjee, "A Factor Analysis of Some Qualitative Attributes of Coffee," *Journal of Advertising Research,* vol. 5, p. 37, March 1965. Used with permission.

is up to the creativity of the researcher. Unfortunately, researchers can all too easily fool themselves with wonderful-sounding interpretations. Great care must be taken in this regard.

The presentation of factor analysis has concentrated on the nature of the input and output. There are many more issues on all aspects of factor analysis not covered here. You should consult a more advanced reference if interested.

CLUSTER ANALYSIS

Factor analysis allows the researcher to study the structure of a set of variables or objects in relation to how their variance is explained by a set of underlying factors. Cluster analysis allows the researcher to *place variables or objects into subgroups, or clusters.* These clusters *are not defined a priori* by the researcher but are formed by the cluster analysis procedure itself. In actuality, cluster analysis is a group of ad hoc computational procedures. The common dimensions of these procedures are:

1 They form subgroupings and assign variables or objects to these groups.

2 They take as input a matrix of associations between variables or objects; a correlation matrix is an example of one such matrix. There are clustering algo-

rithms available that take nominal, ordinal, interval, or ratio measures in this matrix of associations as input.

3 They assume that natural clusters exist within the data.

The number and diversity of these algorithms make a detailed presentation of cluster analysis procedures impossible in anything except a long book.

We noted that cluster analysis can be applied to either variables or objects (people, products, places, etc.). However, its major application is in the placement of objects into clusters, based upon the values these objects have for a set of variables. Thus, our input matrix will contain the measures of association between objects. This was basically the approach used in *Q*-type factor analysis. In fact, some researchers consider *Q*-factor analysis to be a form of cluster analysis.

In general, an object is assigned to a cluster in such a way that it is more associated (as measured by the appropriate measure of association in the input matrix) with the other objects in its cluster than with objects in any other cluster. At a minimum, the computer output of a cluster analysis run identifies the objects of interest by cluster. Sometimes a number of alternative groupings of objects into clusters are presented. These alternative clusters differ in the level of association within the cluster. The researcher then selects the solution for the level of association that seems appropriate. This type of solution is called *hierarchical* because solutions are presented at many different levels of within-cluster association. For example, you may want clusters that have $r = .5$ to .6 for the objects within the clusters. You would then be considering r's of less than .5 to be too weak, and r's over .6 to be too stringent a requirement. Of course, once clusters are formed it is up to the researcher to give them a marketing interpretation. This, like naming factors in factor analysis, is an art and must be done with great care.

Cluster analysis has been used in marketing to do such things as develop consumer segments based upon demographic and psychographic profiles, identify test market cities, determine similar markets in various countries, and find similar groups of magazine readers to aid in media selection. Figure 20-5 indicates that 63 percent of businesses use cluster analysis in their marketing research.

MULTIDIMENSIONAL SCALING

Overview

Multidimensional scaling encompasses a set of computational procedures that can summarize an input matrix of associations between variables or objects. Generally, its main thrust in marketing has been to examine relationships among objects—usually brands of a particular product group. These techniques take as input a matrix of relationships between objects that have an unknown underlying dimensionality. Then they determine *the minimum dimensionality of the relationships between the objects and the position of each object on each dimension.*

Although multidimensional scaling can be used to analyze virtually any matrix of associations, its fundamental applications in marketing have been to analyze (1) consumer perceptions of the similarity of brands and (2) consumer preferences for brands. In this context, multidimensional scaling is really an extension of the

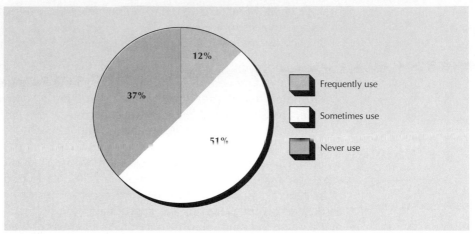

FIGURE 20-5   Use in practice of cluster analysis. (*Source:* Thomas C. Kinnear and Ann R. Root, *A Study of the Marketing Research Business*, unpublished study, 1994. Copyright 1994 Thomas C. Kinnear. Not to be reproduced.)

unidimensional attitude scales discussed in Chapter 8 (e.g., semantic differential). Instead of positioning attitudes about brands on unidimensional scales, we can use multidimensional scaling to position brands in an *n*-dimensional space, where *n* is the minimum underlying dimensionality of the relationship. Thus, we can speak of positioning brands and preferences related to brands in a perceptual space.

There are in general three types of multidimensional scaling. These types, which relate to the nature of the input and output data, are as follows:

1 *Fully metric.* These methods require intervally or ratio-scaled input measures and generate a set of relationships among objects that is also interval or ratio.

2 *Fully nonmetric.* These methods take ordinally scaled input measures and generate the rank order of each object on each dimension.

3 *Nonmetric.* These methods take ordinally scaled input measures and generate a set of relationships among the objects that is interval. That is, the distances between objects in the perceptual space have useful meaning. It is nonmetric multidimensional scaling that has obtained the most frequent marketing application.

The mathematics of nonmetric multidimensional scaling are far too complex to discuss here. What follows is an example of this technique in which the nature of the input and output will be discussed.

An Example

Suppose that we wanted to measure consumer perceptions of the similarity of, and their preference for, 11 car models: (1) Ford Taurus, (2) Mercury Sable, (3)

TABLE 20-4   RANK ORDER OF SIMILARITIES BETWEEN PAIRS OF CAR MODELS

Stimuli	1	2	3	4	5	6	7	8	9	10	11
1	—	8	50	31	12	48	36	2	5	39	10
2		—	38	9	33	37	22	6	4	14	32
3			—	11	55	1	23	46	41	17	52
4				—	44	13	16	19	25	18	42
5					—	54	53	30	28	45	7
6						—	26	47	40	24	51
7							—	29	35	34	49
8								—	3	27	15
9									—	20	21
10										—	43
11											—

The rank number "1" represents the most similar pair.

Lincoln Continental, (4) Ford Thunderbird, (5) Ford Escort, (6) Cadillac Eldorado, (7) Jaguar XJ Sedan, (8) Mazda 626, (9) Dodge Intrepid, (10) Buick Le Sabre, and (11) Chevrolet Cavalier.

For similarities we need to obtain from the consumers the rank order of the similarity of all 55 combinations of car models taken two at a time. In general, there are $n(n - 1)/2$ rank orders to obtain, where n is the number of objects of interest. One way to do this is to put each of the 55 combinations on a separate card. The respondents are then asked to rank-order the cards in terms of the most similar pair to the least similar pair.[2] One consumer's possible ranking of the pairs of models is given in Table 20-4. Here, for example, the consumer considered cars 1 and 2 (Taurus and Sable) to be the eighth most similar pair, and the Lincoln (car 3) and Cadillac (car 6) to be the most similar. Preference data could be collected by asking each consumer to simply rank-order the 11 cars from most preferred to least preferred.

Figure 20-6 illustrates the type of output generated by analyzing the similarities matrix given in Table 20-4. In this case a two-dimensional perceptual space was deemed appropriate to represent the data. We note that the positioning of the car models with respect to one another seems to give us competitive segments. For example, the Taurus, Sable, Mazda 626, and Dodge Intrepid are positioned close to one another.

The preference data can be analyzed so that they are positioned within the similarities space in Figure 20-6. Each consumer would be positioned within this space. These positions are referred to as "ideal points." For example, consumer A, who likes big luxury cars, may have an ideal point near Lincoln and Cadillac. When each consumer's ideal point is positioned in the space, we can determine the size of the ideal point locations. That is, we may get clusterings of

[2]This task can become difficult as the number of objects increases. A number of other procedures are available, but they are not discussed here.

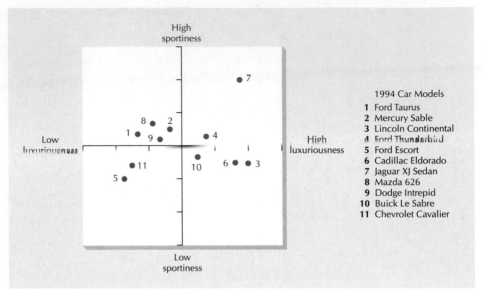

FIGURE 20-6   Perceptual space solution based on data in Table 20-4.

ideal points in particular locations, and this can be used to predict market shares. In Figure 20-6, the two dimensions are labeled "sportiness" and "luxuriousness." These labels, like factor labels in factor analysis, are based upon research judgment.

The questions naturally arise: (1) How do we get interval output from ordered input? (2) How do we determine the required dimensionality? We get interval output because the large number of rank-order pairs in the input matrix puts so many constraints on the positioning of objects that we find an underlying interval relationship. The dimensionality of the space is determined by calculating a goodness-of-fit measure between the input rank order and the output. This measure is called *stress*. Stress gets smaller as the number of dimensions increases. When a rule-of-thumb acceptable level is reached, the dimensionality is determined.

Marketing Applications

There are a number of possible applications of nonmetric multidimensional scaling in marketing. These include:

1 The identification of salient product attributes perceived by buyers in a market
2 The combination of attributes most preferred
3 The products that are viewed as substitutes and those that are differentiated from one another

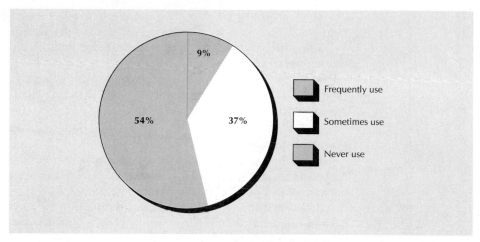

FIGURE 20-7   Use in practice of multidirectional scaling. (*Source:* Thomas C. Kinnear and Ann R. Root, *A Study of the Marketing Research Business,* unpublished study, 1994. Copyright 1994 Thomas C. Kinnear. Not to be reproduced.)

4 The viable segments that exist in a market
5 The "holes" in a market that can support a new product venture

The method also appears applicable to problems of product life-cycle analysis, market segmentation, vendor evaluation, advertising evaluation, test marketing, salesperson and store image, brand switching research, and attitude scaling.

This usefulness has resulted in about 46 percent of businesses utilizing multidimensional scaling in their marketing research, as noted in Figure 20-7.

Final Comment

This presentation of multidimensional scaling has ignored many computational issues, and it has not discussed the limitations of the technique; this is also true for our discussion of factor analysis and cluster analysis. If interested, you should consult a more advanced source. We must also leave you with a final word of warning. All three techniques discussed in this chapter leave the researcher with major interpretation difficulties after the output is generated, and different computer programs for a technique often yield different results. Great care and skill are required in their application.

SUMMARY

1 Dependence methods designate one or more variables as being predicted by a set of independent variables.
2 Interdependence methods do not designate any variables as being predicted

by others. The interest is in the interrelationship among all the variables taken together.

3 Interdependence methods include factor analysis, cluster analysis, and multidimensional scaling.

4 Factor analysis is a procedure that takes a large number of variables or objects and searches to see whether they have a small number of factors in common which account for their intercorrelations.

5 Applications of factor analysis include data reduction, structure identification, scaling, and data transformation.

6 Factor analysis takes a correlation matrix as input. In *R*-factor analysis these correlations are between variables, and in *Q*-factor analysis these correlations are between cases or objects.

7 The factor analysis output gives the loading of each variable on each underlying factor. This output may be rotated to give either uncorrelated or correlated factors.

8 Cluster analysis places variables or objects into subgroups or clusters that are defined by the procedure. It is generally used for objects.

9 The cluster analysis input is a matrix of associations between variables or objects. These measures can be for different scale levels, depending on the computer procedure.

10 The output of cluster analysis places objects in clusters or a set of alternative clusters at different levels of association.

11 Multidimensional scaling takes a matrix of relationships between objects as input, then determines the underlying dimensionality and places each object on each dimension.

12 Multidimensional scaling is generally used in marketing to measure the perception of brand similarities and preferences.

13 Nonmetric multidimensional scaling takes ordinal input measures and generates a set of relationships among the objects that is interval.

DISCUSSION QUESTIONS

1 Why is multivariate analysis becoming more used in marketing research?

2 Distinguish between dependence and interdependence methods.

3 What is the overall objective of factor analysis?

4 Describe the nature of the input and output of factor analysis.

5 What are *R*- and *Q*-type factor analyses?

6 What is the objective of cluster analysis?

7 Describe the nature of the input and output of cluster analysis.

8 What is the objective of multidimensional scaling?

9 What is nonmetric multidimensional scaling?

10 Describe the nature of the input and output of nonmetric multidimensional scaling.

11 How do you name factors, clusters, and dimensions for interdependence methods?

12 If you were marketing vice president of a major bank, how might you use the factor analysis results given in the Marketing Research in Action at the beginning of this chapter?

13 MINICASE

It is standard practice in the automobile industry to use multidimensional scaling representations of automobile brands in marketing planning. Why would this be so? How could an automobile marketing person use the scaling results given in Figure 20-6? What additional data would assist in the interpretation of these scaling results?

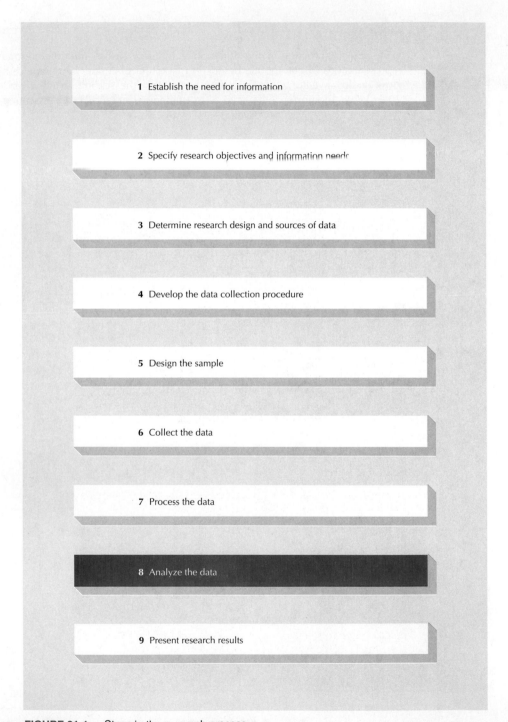

1 Establish the need for information

2 Specify research objectives and information needs

3 Determine research design and sources of data

4 Develop the data collection procedure

5 Design the sample

6 Collect the data

7 Process the data

8 Analyze the data

9 Present research results

FIGURE 21-1　Steps in the research process.

CHAPTER 21

MULTIVARIATE DATA ANALYSIS II: DEPENDENCE METHODS

MARKETING RESEARCH IN ACTION

MULTIPLE REGRESSION ANALYSIS REVEALS PREDICTORS OF GAPS IN EXPECTATION OF PHYSICIAN SERVICE QUALITY

One of the important marketing questions of the 1990s relates to the quality of service delivered by an organization. This is especially true in the highly competitive world of the marketing of medical services. In order to develop a better understanding of the gap between patients' expectations of service quality and that perceived to be actually delivered by medical organizations, marketing researchers did a study of the issue. A survey was completed on 1128 users of medical services.

In order to understand the relationship between the gap in expectations versus perceived performance, a multiple regression analysis was run. The dependent variable (the variable we wish to predict) was the size of the gap between expectations and performance and service quality. The independent variables (the variables used to predict the size of the gap) were a set of measures related to the interactions of the patient with the medical practitioners and support staff. The independent variables were: (1) the nature of the interaction with the actual physician, (2) the degree of interest the doctor showed in the patient, (3) the availability of the doctor in an emergency, (4) the professionalism of the doctor and other staff, (5) the reasonableness of fees, (6) the medical competence of the doctor, (7) the use of the latest technology, (8) the appropriate use of diagnostics, (9) the interactions with office staff and other administrative personnel, and (10) the availability of brochures and other materials related to medical issues.

The regression explained 60 percent of the variance in the expectation-performance gap. All but the last two independent variables were significantly related to the size of the gap. In addition, the most important independent variables were found to be interaction with the physician, professional competence of the doctor, interest by the doctor in the patient, and availability of the latest technology. These results are clearly useful to the health maintenance organization interested in focusing on the key activities that drive the perception of service quality.

Source: Adapted from Stephen W. Brown anad Teresa A. Swartz, "A Gap Analysis of Professional Service Quality," *Journal of Marketing,* vol. 53, pp. 92–98, April 1989.

This Marketing Research in Action illustrates the power of one of the multivariate methods discussed in this chapter to provide meaningful answers to marketing questions.

This chapter is a direct follow-up to Chapter 20. Here we present an elementary discussion of a number of dependence methods of multivariate analysis. Again the mathematical complexities are omitted, with the emphasis being on the nature of input and output of the procedures. Each of the techniques discussed in this chapter has a number of important statistical assumptions and limitations associated with it. These assumptions and limitations are not included here because of their complexity. Our approach is simply to present a brief overview of each technique. Again, if you are interested in using these techniques, you should consult a technical specialist or a more advanced book. *The techniques are extremely dangerous when used by unskilled people.* Don't just let SPSS-PC run wild.

The specific techniques we will touch on are multiple regression, analysis of variance, analysis of covariance, dummy-variable multiple regression, automatic interaction detector, discriminant analysis, conjoint measurement, canonical correlation, and multivariate analysis of variance.

CLASSIFICATION OF PROCEDURES

The selection of the appropriate dependence procedure depends on (1) the number of variables that have been designated as dependent and (2) the scale levels of the dependent and independent variables. Figure 21-2 presents a flowchart that will guide you to the appropriate procedure. It is based on decision points related to the number of dependent variables designated, and on the scale level of the dependent and independent variables. Find the appropriate technique by following the flow of questions in the figure. Table 21-1 summarizes the situations in

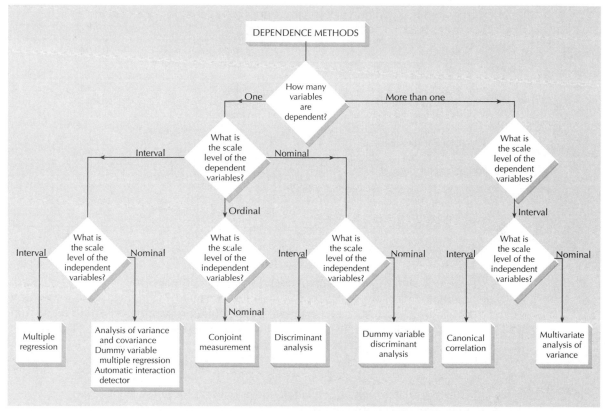

FIGURE 21-2   Classification of dependence methods. (*Source:* Adapted from a scheme presented in Thomas C. Kinnear and James R. Taylor, "Multivariate Methods in Marketing Research: A Further Attempt at Classification," *Journal of Marketing,* vol. 35, pp. 56–59, October 1971.)

which the specific techniques are appropriate. It should be recognized that each technique has some additional statistical assumptions.

The rest of the chapter discusses each of these procedures.

MULTIPLE REGRESSION

Multiple regression is a straightforward extension of simple regression as discussed in Chapter 19. The difference is that in multiple regression the analysis is done with *more than one independent variable.* The usefulness of multiple regression is seen in the Marketing Research in Action at the beginning of this chapter. In Chapter 19 we noted that regression procedures are utilized by 81 percent of businesses in their marketing research (see Figure 19-6).

The predictive equation for a two-independent-variable situation would be

$$\hat{Y}_i = a + b_1 X_1 + b_2 X_2$$

TABLE 21-1   SITUATIONS IN WHICH THE SPECIFIC DEPENDENCE METHODS ARE APPROPRIATE

Technique	Dependent variable scale level	Independent variable scale level
A One dependent variable		
1 Multiple regression	Interval	Interval
2 Analysis of variance and covariance	Interval	Nominal
3 Dummy-variable multiple regression	Interval	Nominal
4 Automatic interaction detector	Interval	Nominal
5 Discriminant analysis	Nominal	Interval
6 Dummy-variable discriminant analysis	Nominal	Nominal
7 Conjoint measurement	Ordinal	Nominal
B More than one dependent variable		
8 Canonical correlation	Interval	Interval
9 Multivariate analysis of variance	Interval	Nominal

where X_1 and X_2 are the independent variables and a, b_1, and b_2 are the regression coefficients generated from our sample data. Again, we recognize that these coefficients are statistics that estimate the population parameters of the regression. We can easily generalize the equation to m independent variables. Here

$$\hat{Y}_i = a + b_1 X_1 + b_2 X_2 + \cdots + b_m X_m$$

The formulas for the coefficients are too complex to present, even for a two-independent-variable situation.

Multiple regression requires that both the dependent and the independent variables be intervally scaled. Also, it assumes that the underlying relationship is linear, although data transformations can overcome this problem. Finally, the sample size must be large enough to give many observations per independent variable. The more independent variables, the larger the sample size should be.

The total variation in the dependent variable may be partitioned in exactly the same fashion as with simple regression. Specifically,

$$SS_{\text{total}} \quad = SS_{\text{explained}} + SS_{\text{unexplained}}$$
$$\downarrow \qquad\qquad \downarrow \qquad\qquad \downarrow$$
$$\Sigma(Y_i - \bar{Y})^2 = \Sigma(\hat{Y}_i - \bar{Y})^2 + \Sigma(Y_i - \hat{Y}_i)^2$$

We can convert these SS to variances by dividing them by the appropriate degrees of freedom. We could then compare the explained variance with the error variance to see whether the regression as a whole has explained a significant amount of the variance in Y. We would use an F test, a detailed description of which is presented in the appendix to this chapter. (The use of the F test for simple regression was discussed in the appendix to Chapter 19.)

The only difference in doing this in multiple regression as opposed to simple regression is that the degrees of freedom are different. Each independent variable requires one degree of freedom. Thus, with $n - 1$ degrees of freedom in the whole sample, the error degrees of freedom will be $n - 1 - m$, where m is the number of independent variables. The number of explained degrees of freedom is simply m. We may also calculate the standard error and thus the significance of each regression coefficient. Here we use a t test. In simple regression an F test on SS and a t test on the coefficient yielded identical results; in multiple regression the F test tells us whether the regression as a whole is significant, and the t tests tell us which coefficients are statistically significantly different from zero.

An Example

An example should help clarify the nature of results generated by a multiple regression program. Table 21-2 presents regression results for the following situation: (1) The dependent variable is the dollar amount of life insurance owned, (2) the independent variables are income and family size, and (3) the sample size is 15.

We see that with two independent variables the regression degrees of freedom equals 2, and within 15 cases the error degrees of freedom is $n - 1 - m = 15 - 1 - 2 = 12$. The calculated F is 162. The critical F at $\alpha = .01$ and 2 and 12 degrees of freedom is 6.93 (see Table A-5 in the Appendix at the end of the book). The regression clearly explains a significant amount of the variation in Y. Similarly, the critical t value for the coefficients at $\alpha = .01$ and 12 degrees of freedom is 3.055. Thus we can reject the null hypothesis that the income coefficient is zero, while we cannot do so for the family size coefficient. Note that if we had set $\alpha = .1$, the critical t would be 1.782, and we would have concluded that the family size coefficient was significant.

TABLE 21-2   REGRESSION RESULTS

Source	SS	Df	Mean square	F
Regression	15,552	2	7,776	162
Error	574	12	48	
Total	16,126	14		

Variable	Coefficient	Standard error	t statistic
Constant	−1305.2		
Income	2.3	.13	18.03
Family size	−2620.8	1320.6	−1.98

Multiple $R = .98205$ Multiple $R^2 = .96441$

Source: Adapted from an example prepared by Prof. William Wrobleski, the University of Michigan.

The *size* and *direction* of the coefficients also have meaning. In general, a positive coefficient indicates a direct relationship between that independent variable and the dependent variable. A negative coefficient indicates an inverse relationship. The size of the coefficient indicates the amount of change in the dependent variable associated with a one-unit increase in that independent variable, given that all other independent variables remain constant. In our example, the amount of life insurance will increase by $2.30 for every $1.00 increase in income, given that family size is held constant.

The computer is also likely to generate the *multiple correlation coefficient, R.* This is the correlation coefficient between the observed Y_i and the estimated Y_i''s. The closer the regression equation predictions are to the actual observations, the higher will be R. We may also calculate the *coefficient of multiple determination,* which is R^2. It is the proportion of the variation in Y explained by the regression. Alternatively, the coefficient of multiple determination may be obtained by taking the ratio $SS_{explained}$ over SS_{total}. In our example,

$$R^2 = \frac{15,552}{16,126} = .96441$$

The type of regression in our example is called *total regression;* with this type, all the independent variables are entered into the regression equation in one step. An alternative type is called *stepwise regression;* here the independent variables enter the regression equation one at a time. The variable selected to enter first is the one that explains the most variation in Y. The next variable to enter is the one that explains the greatest amount of the variation in Y after the effect of the first variable has been removed. This process continues until no significant variation remains or no variable is left that explains a significant amount of the variation.

Another point about the regression coefficients is important: The size of the coefficient does not provide a measure of its importance in the regression. In the case being studied, the smaller coefficient is the better one because the independent variables are measured in different units (people and dollars). It is possible to take the effects of units used out of the regression. We do this by means of the same principle with which we obtained unit-free measures in correlation calculations. That is, we divide the observed values' deviations from the mean by their standard deviation. We define x^0 and y^0 as measures of X and Y that have the units removed. In formula,

$$x^0 = \frac{X - \bar{X}}{s} \quad \text{and} \quad y^0 = \frac{Y - \bar{Y}}{s}$$

This expresses values of X and Y as a number of standard deviations. We can then directly compare regression coefficients to see their relative importance.

The applications of multiple regression in marketing are the same as for simple regression, except that the use of more independent variables allows one to specify the relationship more precisely.

ANALYSIS OF VARIANCE

Analysis of variance (ANOVA) is a statistical procedure most used in the analysis of experimental data. It requires an intervally scaled dependent variable and a nominally scaled independent variable or variables. The details of ANOVA are important but also complex. Thus it is discussed in the appendix at the end of this chapter.

ANALYSIS OF COVARIANCE

Analysis of covariance (ANCOVA) is appropriate in experimental situations in which it is discovered after the experiment that some extraneous source of variation is contributing to the values of the dependent variable. For example, we may discover that store size has contributed to sales in an experiment we ran to test the effect of alternative coupon plans; that is, large stores automatically sell more than small stores.

A detailed example of ANCOVA would take too much space. What follows here, then, is a conceptual overview of how ANCOVA works. To use ANCOVA we must have an intervally scaled dependent variable and nominally scaled independent variables, and the variables to be controlled must be measured at an interval level. These latter variables are called *covariates*. ANCOVA essentially undertakes the following:

1 A regression is run with the covariates as independent variables (e.g., store size) and the dependent variable from the experiment as the dependent variable (sales).

2 The regression estimates, the $\hat{Y}_i$'s, are calculated for each covariate observation.

3 The estimated $\hat{Y}_i$'s are subtracted from the observed experimental data Y_i; the result of this is a set of experimental data that has the effect of the covariates removed; we define $Y'_i = Y_i - \hat{Y}_i$, where Y'_i is a covariate-free observation.

4 ANOVA is then undertaken on the Y'_i's in a regular fashion.

In doing this, be careful to keep the degrees of freedom straight. Since we are using regression, each covariate uses one degree of freedom. Thus if we have k covariates, the total degrees of freedom left to do the ANOVA is $n - 1 - k$. From this adjusted number of degrees of freedom, the treatment and error degrees of freedom for ANOVA are calculated in the usual manner; if we had two covariates, one treatment with four categories, and 50 test units, the total degrees of freedom for ANOVA would be $50 - 1 - 2 = 47$. The treatment degrees of freedom would be $t - 1 = 4 - 1 = 3$, and the error would be $47 - 3 = 44$. (See the appendix to this chapter for details.)

Figure 21-3 shows that about 70 percent of businesses use either analysis of variance or analysis of covariance in their marketing research.

DUMMY-VARIABLE MULTIPLE REGRESSION

The use of regression in marketing research could be severely hampered by the fact that the independent variables must be intervally scaled. Fortunately there is a way to use nominal independent variables in a regression context. The procedure that we use is called *dummy-variable multiple regression (DVMR)*. Basically, DVMR converts nominal variables into a series of binary variables that are coded 0–1. For example, suppose we wish to use the nominal variable "gender" in a regression. We could code it as follows:

Category	Code
Male	0
Female	1

The interval 0 to 1 is equal and thus acceptable to regression. Note that we have converted a two-category nominal variable into one 0–1 variable. We may extend this approach to a multicategory nominal variable. The four-category nominal variable "region of the country" could be converted to three dummy variables, X_1, X_2, and X_3 as follows:

Category	X_1	X_2	X_3
East	1	0	0
West	0	1	0
North	0	0	1
South	0	0	0

This four-category nominal variable is now converted to three 0–1 variables. In general, a k-category nominal variable converts to $k - 1$ dummy variables, because once we know whether the first $k - 1$ categories are 0 or 1, the kth category is automatically determined as 0 or 1. To create a kth dummy variable would be redundant, and in fact it would invalidate the whole regression. The choice of the category that will have all zeros is arbitrary.

To illustrate DVMR, suppose that sales of Japanese cars represents the dependent variable. The regression equation might be:

$$\hat{Y}_i = 250,000 + 50,000X_1 + 80,000X_2 - 6,000X_3$$

Note that only one of either X_1, X_2, or X_3 will take on the value 1 for any one subject, and the other two X's will be zero. The coefficients provide a measure of the effect of being from a particular region. The equations by region are:

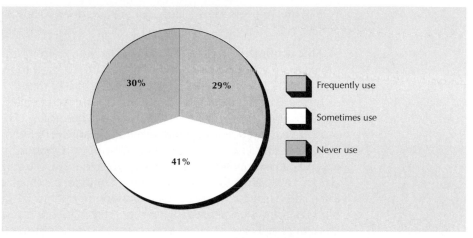

FIGURE 21-3   Use in practice of analysis of variance or covariance. (*Source:* Thomas C. Kinnear and Ann R. Root, *A Study of the Marketing Research Business,* unpublished study, 1994. Copyright 1994 Thomas C. Kinnear. Not to be reproduced.)

East: $\hat{Y}_i = 250{,}000 + 50{,}000(1) = 300{,}000$

West: $\hat{Y}_i = 250{,}000 + 80{,}000(1) = 330{,}000$

North: $\hat{Y}_i = 250{,}000 - 6{,}000(1) = 244{,}000$

South: $\hat{Y}_i = 250{,}000$

We can have as many dummy variables as we need in regression, subject to the constraint that each dummy variable uses a degree of freedom. Thus, we must have an adequate sample size.

A special computational version of DVMR, called *multiple classification analysis (MCA),* has attained significant marketing application. The specific nature of this procedure, however, lies beyond the scope of this book.

AUTOMATIC INTERACTION DETECTOR

The *automatic interaction detector (AID)* is another technique that is used with an interval dependent variable and a set of nominal independent variables. Its basic objective is to break down a total sample into a number of subgroups that are more homogeneous on the dependent variable than the sample as a whole. It does this by the repeated application of one-way ANOVA. Specifically, AID does the following:

1 It calculates the explained SS ($SS_{\text{between}}/SS_{\text{total}}$) on the dependent variable for each combination of categories for the independent variables.

2 It splits the sample into two groups based on the categories of that independent variable that explain the most SS.

3 It then repeats steps 1 and 2 for the two new groups, then splits these groups, and so on.

AID is primarily used in marketing to help identify market segments and to identify variables that seem to be importantly related to the dependent variable. These variables could then be used in a DVMR analysis.

Figure 21-4 illustrates AID output. This output is called an *AID tree.* The top number in each box is the sample size for that group. The lower number is the probability of a subject purchasing a nonphosphate detergent. Here the dependent variable is the likelihood of someone using a nonphosphate detergent, and the independent variables are a set of attitude measures. Group 1 is the whole sample size of 1499. Note that the overall probability of a subject drawn at random from the sample using a nonphosphate laundry product is .37 (group 1's mean probability). Group 5 has a probability of purchasing a nonphosphate detergent of .75. It is composed of consumers who state an extreme self-interest in pollution aspects of products, and who are willing to accept a "moderately or more less clean" wash. In contrast, group 12 has a probability of purchase of .06. It is composed of consumers who are less than extremely interested in the pollution aspects of products, who perceive consumers as less than highly effective to act against pollution, who do not wish to urge their friends to act against pollution, and who are not willing to accept less clean clothes. Clearly the AID analysis has found very distinct segments.

The major constraint for use of AID is that a large sample size (1000 plus) is

FIGURE 21-4   AID tree for use of nonphosphate laundry products.

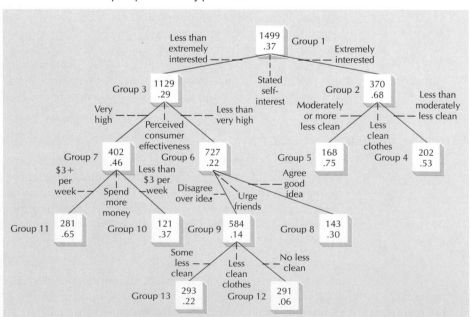

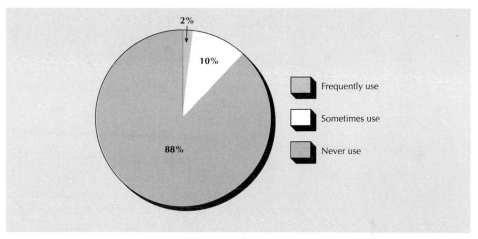

FIGURE 21-5   Use in practice of the AID technique. (*Source:* Thomas C. Kinnear and Ann R. Root, *A Study of the Marketing Research Business,* unpublished study, 1994. Copyright 1994 Thomas C. Kinnear. Not to be reproduced.)

needed; otherwise the subgroups become too small too soon. Figure 21-5 shows that about 12 percent of businesses use the automatic interaction detector procedure in their marketing research.

DISCRIMINANT ANALYSIS

Discriminant analysis (DA) is a technique that is appropriate with a nominal dependent variable and interval independent variables. Nominal dependent variables are very common in marketing; for example, good versus bad credit risks, brand-loyal versus nonloyal consumers, different brand users, and successful versus unsuccessful salespersons. As a result of this, DA has received extensive application in marketing research.

The basic idea of DA is to find a linear combination of the independent variables that makes the mean scores across categories of the dependent variable on this linear combination maximally different. This linear combination is called the *discriminant function (DF)*. In symbols,

$$DF = v_1 X_1 + v_2 X_2 + \cdots + v_m X_m$$

where X_m is the mth independent variable. The objective is to find the values for the v's that give us the required DF. The criterion used to decide when group means are maximally different is the familiar ANOVA F test for the differences among means. Thus, the v's are derived such that

$$F = \frac{SS_{\text{between}}}{SS_{\text{within}}}$$

is maximized.

TABLE 21-3   CONFUSION MATRIX FOR CREDIT RISKS

	Predicted category	
Actual category	Good	Bad
Good	800	40
Bad	60	100

The output of DA usually includes the values of the v's, plus what is called a *confusion matrix.* This matrix compares the category of the dependent variable that the discriminant function predicts a subject will be in with the category that the subject is actually in. Table 21-3 presents a confusion matrix for good and bad credit risks based upon a set of demographic independent variables (e.g., age, income, years in the same house, etc.). Note that it is the elements on the diagonal running from top left to bottom right that give those subjects that are correctly classified by the DA. Ninety percent of subjects in this example are correctly classified. This example is for a two-category dependent variable (often called two-group). It can easily be extended to a k-group dependent variable.

The constraint of having to have interval independent variables is really no problem. As we did with regression, we can convert nominal independent variables to dummy variables in order to yield, in this instance, *dummy-variable discriminant analysis (DVDA).* Figure 21-6 shows that about 50 percent of businesses use discriminant analysis in their marketing research.

CONJOINT MEASUREMENT

A set of procedures that has attracted much attention in marketing research is *conjoint measurement (CM),* or *conjoint analysis.* CM is concerned with the joint effects of two or more nominal independent variables on the ordering of a dependent variable. Thus, CM is appropriate for nominal independent variables and an ordinal dependent variable. It is in essence an analysis of variance of rank-order data. The benefit of CM is that it generates interval-level measures of the effects of the categories of the independent variables.

Its primary marketing application has been to measure the trade-offs that consumers make on product attributes, as the following example shows. Suppose we are concerned with the attributes of an airplane, and suppose that (for simplicity) only two attributes are noteworthy—price and cruising speed. Table 21-4 presents an input matrix to CM for the two attributes for one individual. Three different prices and cruising speeds are given. The entries in the matrix are the rank order of the preferences for the attribute combinations for one consumer. You can follow the trade-offs this consumer will make by following the rank order.

We shall illustrate the nature of CM by discussing how an additive version of CM could utilize the input data from Table 21-4. The basic idea is that CM develops measures of the effect of each level of each attribute such that the additive combination of these effects optimally maintains the rank order of the

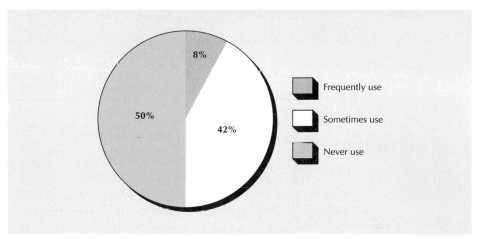

FIGURE 21-6   Use in practice of discriminant analysis. (*Source:* Thomas C. Kinnear and Ann R. Root, *A Study of the Marketing Research Business,* unpublished study, 1994. Copyright 1994 Thomas C. Kinnear. Not to be reproduced.)

input preferences. Table 21-5 gives a possible result of a CM analysis of Table 21-4. Here the interval-level effects are given in parentheses. The numbers in the matrix are the various sums of the effect combinations. For example, the combination of 300 mph and $400,000 is valued at $.20 + .52 = .72$. Note that the interval values in the matrix perfectly maintain the input rank order. This is not always possible, but CM finds the effect measures that achieve it best.

The effect measures may be interpreted as the utility the consumer places on a particular attribute. The number of independent variables can easily be extended to more than two. Thus we can realistically use this technique to measure the total utility a consumer places on various possible attribute combinations for a product. If we did this for a sample of consumers, we could use CM to predict market share, profitability, and so on, of a product offering various attribute combinations. The Marketing Research in Action shows AT&T's use of conjoint measurement in the data communications terminal market.

There are a number of commercially available conjoint analysis packages available for marketing research. Sawtooth Software's ACA (Adaptive Conjoint Analysis) is typical of these packages. It contains three modules: (1) a computer-driven

TABLE 21-4   RANK-ORDER JOINT-EFFECT INPUT MATRIX

Cruising speed, mph	Price levels		
	$400,000	$600,000	$800,000
300	7	8	9
400	3	4	6
500	1	2	5

TABLE 21-5   INTERVALLY SCALED EFFECT MEASURES FOR ATTRIBUTE LEVELS

Cruising speed, mph	Price levels		
	$400,000 (.52)	$600,000 (.45)	$800,000 (.30)
300 (.20)	.72	.65	.50
400 (.61)	1.13	1.06	.91
500 (.75)	1.27	1.20	1.05

interviewing structure for trade-off problems, (2) a routine to calculate the relevant utilities, and (3) a market simulator to make predictions of market behavior. Figure 21-7 shows that about 52 percent of businesses use conjoint analysis in their marketing research. Note that the AT&T example utilized all three of these types of modules. Marriott also used this approach to develop the very successful concept of the Courtyard by Marriott. In this latter example, consumers made trade-off judgments among many attributes, including size of room, nature of meal service, price, and nature of surroundings.

CANONICAL CORRELATION

Canonical correlation (CC) is a technique that is occasionally used in marketing research. It is appropriate when you have both a set of intervally scaled dependent and a set of independent variables. For example, an organization might want to know how a set of attitude measures relates to a set of behaviors. Basically, CC forms one linear combination of the dependent variables and one of the inde-

FIGURE 21-7   Use in practice of conjoint analysis. (*Source:* Thomas C. Kinnear and Ann R. Root, *A Study of the Marketing Research Business,* unpublished study, 1994. Copyright 1994 Thomas C. Kinnear. Not to be reproduced.)

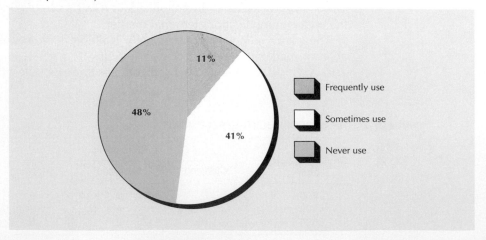

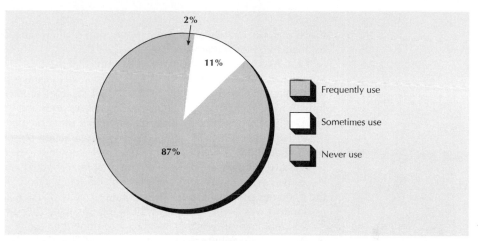

FIGURE 21-8   Use in practice of canonical analysis. (*Source:* Thomas C. Kinnear and Ann R. Root, *A Study of the Marketing Research Business,* unpublished study, 1994. Copyright 1994 Thomas C. Kinnear. Not to be reproduced.)

pendent variables. It finds the values of the coefficients of these combinations that yield the maximum correlation between the combinations. Figure 21-8 shows that about 13 percent of businesses use canonical correlation analysis in their marketing research.

MULTIVARIATE ANALYSIS OF VARIANCE

Multivariate analysis of variance (MANOVA) is appropriate when you have two or more intervally scaled dependent variables and one or more nominally scaled independent variables. A straightforward extension of ANOVA, it is used when the researcher wishes to test the effects of the independent variables on a series of dependent variables. For example, sales and attitude measures may be deemed appropriate dependent variables in an experiment. MANOVA allows you to judge whether the treatments were significant on the set of dependent variables as a group, and in addition it gives an ordinary ANOVA on each one individually.

MARKETING RESEARCH IN ACTION

AT&T USES CONJOINT ANALYSIS

Conjoint analysis, coupled with attitude research, was a major influence in AT&T's decision to enter the data communications terminal market. These techniques even allowed AT&T to predict what its market share would be 4 years down the road.

According to Rochelle L. Benbenisty, research manager at AT&T, Parsippany, New Jersey, the primary objectives of AT&T's data terminal research were to discover the key product attributes, determine the total market share, and come up with an estimate for AT&T's potential market.

First, AT&T did a virtual survey of all firms that used a significant number of data communication terminals. From these interviews, attribute performance and purchase intent were determined. Second, AT&T selected a probability sample of U.S. firms having 100 or more employees. Interviews were then conducted with those persons having influence over the data terminal purchase decision.

To facilitate data collection and analysis, marketing personnel reduced the 110 product attributes identified in the first survey down to 16. Respondents from the probability sample were presented with a table and asked which attribute pair corresponded to their first choice, their second choice, and so on. This would determine the trade-offs potential buyers were willing to make on each attribute. An individual respondent was asked to rate only 24 of the possible 120 pairs of attributes.

Conjoint analysis was then used to determine the relative utility scores of the 16 attributes. These utility scores were considered along with the total market demand, estimated from the first survey, to get an expected AT&T market share.

A simulation model designed to maximize share was used. Competitive products and AT&T's proposed product were entered into the model in terms of the 16 product attributes used in the interviews. The model compared the actual products' benefits with the consumers' wants in order to help determine future market shares.

The first result (4.7 percent market share, $114/month rental fee), proved too low to be profitable. So AT&T identified four possible product changes that might improve their projected share. When these modifications were run on the simulator, AT&T found that a $150/month rental price would be optimal, and that market share would be 8 percent in 4 years after introduction.

Benbenisty said, "We waited and waited and counted and counted to see how well our predictions had done. Believe it or not, the simulator's estimate of the [AT&T] share was achieved and demand reached a level just under 8 percent by the fourth year.

"This is but one way attitude research can be used in making marketing decisions. Through the conjoint analysis approach, you can identify how respondent attitudes on a myriad of variables interact and lead to buyer preferences and purchase decisions."

SUMMARY

1 The choice of dependence method depends on the number of variables that have been designated as dependent and on the scale level of the dependent and independent variables.

2 Multiple regression is used with one intervally scaled dependent variable and a set of intervally scaled independent variables.

3 Analysis of variance, dummy-variable multiple regression, and the automatic interaction detector are used with one intervally scaled dependent variable and a set of nominally scaled independent variables.

4 Discriminant analysis is used with one nominally scaled dependent variable and a set of intervally scaled independent variables.

5 Dummy-variable discriminant analysis is used with one nominally scaled dependent variable and a set of nominally scaled independent variables.

6 Conjoint measurement is used with one ordinally scaled dependent variable and a set of nominally scaled independent variables.

7 Canonical correlation is used with a set of intervally scaled dependent variables and a set of intervally scaled independent variables.

8 Multivariate analysis of variance is used with a set of intervally scaled dependent variables and a set of nominally scaled independent variables.

9 All the techniques discussed in this chapter are very complex, and in most cases a marketing research generalist would consult with a technical specialist when using them.

DISCUSSION QUESTIONS

1 How are dependence methods classified?

2 What is the coefficient of multiple determination? How is it calculated from a regression printout?

3 What does a coefficient mean in multiple regression?

4 How does ANCOVA work?

5 How are nominal independent variables handled in a regression?

6 How is AID related to ANOVA?

7 What is a discriminant function? What criterion is used to derive its coefficients?

8 How could conjoint measurements be used to predict market share?

9 The regression coefficients expressed in standardized form, and with the sign removed (the impact of units of measurement has been removed) for the service quality Marketing Research in Action at the beginning of this chapter are:

Predictor variable	Regression coefficient
Physician interaction	.6155
Doctor interest	.1616
Emergency availability	.1096
Professionalism	.1104
Reasonable fees	.1122
Medical competence	.2044
Latest technologies	.1443
Diagnostics available	.0866
Staff interactions	.0757
Brochures available	.0688

a What do these coefficients indicate?

b What other information would you like to have about the regression coefficients?

10 MINICASE

Prepare a set of trade-off matrices that Marriott could use in the development of the Courtyard by Marriott concept of motel. Be sure to consider the relevant attributes, the appropriate levels of each attribute, and the task required of respondents in the study.

APPENDIX   Analysis of Variance

STATISTICAL ANALYSIS OF EXPERIMENTS

We are now ready to develop an understanding of the ANOVA procedure. ANOVA is a method of analysis that applies when the researcher is dealing with *one intervally scaled dependent variable and one or more nominally scaled independent variables.* ANOVA is related to a number of other data analysis procedures that were discussed in this chapter. An understanding of the basics of ANOVA will add greatly to our understanding of these other techniques. The procedures discussed here can be applied to any of the designs presented in Chapter 9, what we are adding now is the flesh that goes with the bones given in Chapter 9. Again, all that the statistics allow us to do is to identify when an effect is greater than we could expect by chance.

There are actually three different ANOVA procedures. They are:

Model I. Fixed Effects   In this model the researcher makes inferences only about differences among the *j* treatments actually administered, and about no other treatment that might have been included. In other words, no interpolation between treatments is made. For example, if the treatments were high, medium, and low advertising expenditures, no inferences are drawn about advertising expenditures between these points.

Model II. Random Effects   In the second model, the researcher assumes that only a random sample of the treatments about which he or she wants to make inferences has been used. Here, the researcher would be prepared to interpolate results between treatments.

Model III. Mixed Effects   In the third model, the researcher has independent variables that are both fixed and random types.

The major differences among these models relate to the formulas used to calculate sampling error and to some data assumptions. We shall show the calculations only for the fixed-effects model, since the basic approach and the principles to be established are the same for the other models. Also, in marketing research most experiments fit the fixed-effects model, as the experiments usually include all treatments that are important in relation to the decision to be made.

In applying the fixed-effects model, the researcher makes assumptions about the data. Specifically:

1 For each treatment population, *j*, the experimental errors are independent and normally distributed about a mean of zero with an identical variance.

2 The sum of all treatment effects is zero.

3 In the calculations presented here, each treatment group has the same number of observations. This assumption is not generally necessary, but it makes the calculations easier.

In experimentation, the null hypothesis is that *the treatment effects, effects that might apply, equal zero.* If τ_j represents the effect of treatment *j*, we can write the null hypothesis as

$$\tau_1 = \tau_2 \cdots = \tau_j = 0$$

or

$$\tau_j = 0 \qquad (j = 1,2, \cdots ,j)$$

where j = a specific treatment. The alternative hypothesis is that

$$\tau_j > 0 \qquad (j = 1,2, \cdots ,j)$$

If the treatments have had no effect, we would expect the scores on the dependent variable to be the same in each group. Thus, the mean values would be the same in each group. So our null hypothesis is equivalent to the statement that

$$\mu_1 = \mu_2 \cdots = \mu_j = \mu$$

where 1, 2, . . . , j represent treatment groups, and μ represents the whole population mean without regard to groups. ANOVA is the hypothesis-testing procedure used in experimentation. It is essentially a procedure for simultaneously testing for the equality of two or more means.

Completely Randomized Design

ANOVA applied to a completely randomized design (CRD) is called "one-way" ANOVA because it is being applied to categories of one independent variable. Table 1 presents results generated by a CRD. The measures on the dependent variable, Y, are taken on the

TABLE 1   COMPLETELY RANDOMIZED DESIGN WITH THREE TREATMENTS
(Coupon Plans)

	Treatments (j)		
	Coupon plan 1	Coupon plan 2	Coupon plan 3
Test units (i)	20	17	14
	18	14	10
	15	13	7
	11	8	5
Treatment totals	$\Sigma Y_{.1} = 64$	$\Sigma Y_{.2} = 52$	$\Sigma Y_{.3} = 36$
Treatment means	$\bar{Y}_{.1} = M_1$ $= \Sigma Y_{.1}/n_1$ $= 64/4 = 16$	$\bar{Y}_{.2} = M_2$ $= \Sigma Y_{.2}/n_2$ $= 52/4 = 13$	$\bar{Y}_{.3} = M_3$ $= \Sigma Y_{.3}/n_3$ $= 36/4 = 9$
		Grand total	$\Sigma Y_{..} = 64 + 52 + 36 = 152$
		Grand mean	$\bar{Y}_{..} = M = \Sigma Y_{..}/(n_1 + n_2 + n_3)$ $= 152/12 = 12.7$

Note: $n_1 = n_2 = n_3 = n_j = 4$.

test units. Here there are four test units in each of three treatments. We have $4 \times 3 = 12$ test units. The units are stores in the relevant geographic region where each of three coupon plans was applied. The dependent variable is the number of cases of cola sold the day after the different coupons were run in the local papers. The treatments are the three categories of the independent variable, T.

T_1 Coupon plan 1
T_2 Coupon plan 2
T_3 Coupon plan 3

So we have 3 treatments, 12 test units, and an interval-dependent variable measure on each test unit.

In Table 1, we define the mean of each treatment group as

$$\bar{Y}_{.j} = M_{.j} = \frac{\Sigma Y_{.j}}{n}$$

The use of the period (.) in front of the j implies that we are calculating the mean by adding all i's in the jth treatment group. Note also that $\Sigma Y i.$ would indicate the sum of all j's for given i, and $\Sigma Y_{..}$ would indicate the sum of all i's and all j's. In our example,

$$\bar{Y}_{.1} = M_{.1} = \frac{64}{4} = 16$$

$$\bar{Y}_{.2} = M_{.2} = \frac{52}{4} = 13$$

$$\bar{Y}_{.3} = M_{.3} = \frac{36}{4} = 9$$

We also define the *grand mean* of all observations across all treatment groups as $\bar{Y}_{..}$ or M. Here

$$M = \frac{64 + 52 + 36}{12} = 12.7$$

These various means will be used in order to understand the meaning of ANOVA. In an experimental context, we want to determine whether the treatments have had an effect on the dependent variable. (By "effect" we mean a functional relationship between the treatment T_j and the dependent variable Y.) That is, do different treatments give systematically different scores on the dependent variable? For example, in our coupon plan situation, if the plans have had differing effects on sales, we would expect the amount of sales in the stores in treatment T_1 to differ systematically from T_2 and T_3. If in fact they did, the mean of each treatment group would also differ. In ANOVA an *effect* is defined as a difference in treatment means from the grand mean. What we are doing in ANOVA is determining whether differences in treatment means are large enough to have occurred other than just by chance.

Some Notation and Definitions   Let Y_{ij} be the score of the ith test unit on the jth treatment. For example, in Table 1,

$$Y_{11} = 20, \qquad Y_{42} = 8, \qquad \text{etc.}$$

We define any individual test unit's scores as equal to

$$Y_{ij} = \text{grand mean} + \text{treatment effect} + \text{error}$$

or

$$Y_{ij} = \mu + \tau_j + \epsilon_{ij}$$

This is a simple linear, additive model with values specified in terms of population parameters. Since we are going to be using sample results to make our inferences, we can rewrite this model as

$$Y_{ij} = M + T_j + E_{ij} \tag{1}$$

where M = the grand mean
 T_j = the effect of the jth treatment
 F_{ij} = the statistical error of the ith test unit in the jth treatment

In this model the treatment effect is defined as the difference between the treatment mean and the grand mean:

$$T_j = M_{\cdot j} - M$$

The reason we use M as the base from which to compare the various $M_{\cdot j}$'s is that even if we did not know from which treatment a test unit came, we could still guess the grand mean as their score on the dependent variable. Knowledge of treatment group memberships improves our ability to predict scores as an improvement over M.

The error for an individual unit, E_{ij}, is estimated by the difference between an individual score and the treatment group mean to which the score belongs.

$$E_{ij} = Y_{ij} - M_{\cdot j}$$

It is a measure of the difference in scores that occur which are not explained by treatments. This is the measure of sampling error in the experiment. It is also called *experimental error*. For example, if all scores within a treatment are close together, the individual scores will be close to the treatment mean and the error will be small, and vice versa. This deviation is a measure of the random variation within each treatment in an experiment.

We can rewrite Equation 1 as

$$Y_{ij} \quad = \quad M \quad + (M_{\cdot j} - M) + (Y_{ij} - M_{\cdot j})$$
$$\downarrow \qquad\qquad \downarrow \qquad\quad \downarrow \qquad\qquad \downarrow$$

$$\underset{\text{score}}{\text{Individual}} = \underset{\text{mean}}{\text{grand}} + \underset{\text{effect}}{\text{treatment}} + \text{error} \tag{2}$$

Alternatively, we can write any observation as a deviation from the grand mean. We do this by moving M to the left side of Equation 2:

$$(Y_{ij} - M) \quad = \quad (M_j - M) \quad + \quad (Y_{ij} - M_j)$$

↓	↓	↓
Individual score deviation from grand mean	deviation of group mean from grand mean (i.e., treatment effect)	individual score deviation from group mean (i.e., error)

$=$ between first and plus between, with (3) at right.

Individual score deviation from grand mean $=$ deviation of group mean from grand mean (i.e., treatment effect) $+$ individual score deviation from group mean (i.e., error)   (3)

Partitioning the Sum of Squares   The idea of ANOVA is built around the concept of the sum of squared deviations from the grand mean and from group means. We partition the total sum of squares into components. Begin by squaring the deviation from the grand mean, M, for each score in the sample and then sum these squared deviations across all test units, i, in all groups, j. Do this by squaring Equation 3 for all individuals in all groups, which becomes

$$\sum_{i=1}^{n} \sum_{j=1}^{t} (Y_{ij} - M)^2 = \sum_{i=1}^{n} \sum_{j=1}^{t} [(M_j - M) + (Y_{ij} - M_j)]^2 \tag{4}$$

All the $\sum_{i=1}^{n}\sum_{j=1}^{t}$ means is that we are doing this for all individuals in all treatments. Equation 4 expanded becomes

$$\sum_{i=1}^{n} \sum_{j=1}^{t} (Y_{ij} - M)^2 = \sum_{i=1}^{n} \sum_{j=1}^{t} (M_j - M)^2 + \sum_{i=1}^{n} \sum_{j=1}^{t} (Y_{ij} - M_j)^2$$
$$+ 2\sum_{i=1}^{n} \sum_{j=1}^{t} (M_j - M)(Y_{ij} - M_j) \tag{5}$$

This is simply squaring an equation of the form

$$A = B + C$$

to get

$$A^2 = B^2 + C^2 + 2BC$$

The sum of deviations about any mean equals zero.[1] Therefore the

$$2\sum_{i=1}^{n} \sum_{j=1}^{t} (M_j - M)(Y_{ij} - M_j)$$

part of Equation 5 is zero, as

$$\sum_{i=1}^{n} (Y_{ij} - M_j) = 0$$

[1]This basic finding of statistics is easily illustrated. $10 + 5 + 15 = 30$ and the mean is $30/3 = 10$. The sum of deviations $= (10 - 10) + (5 - 10) + (15 - 10) = 0 + (-5) + 5 = 0$.

and

$$\sum_{j=1}^{t} (M_j - M) = 0$$

Also note that

$$\sum_{i=1}^{n} \sum_{j=1}^{t} (M_j - M)^2 = \sum_{j=1}^{t} n_j(M_j - M)^2$$

where n_j is the number of subjects in group j. This is so because $M_j - M$ is a constant (as we are dealing with means only) for each individual i in a particular group j. We can then multiply this constant by the number in the group to yield an equivalent number. Equation 5 then becomes

$$\sum_{i=1}^{n} \sum_{j=1}^{t} (Y_{ij} - M)^2 = \sum_{j=1}^{t} n_j(M_j - M)^2 + \sum_{i=1}^{n} \sum_{j=1}^{t} (Y_{ij} - M_j)^2 \qquad (6)$$

Total sum of squared deviations from the grand mean	=	weighted sum of squared deviations of group means from grand mean	+	sum of squared deviations within groups
Total sum of squares (SS_T)	=	sum of squares between groups	+	sum of squares within groups
		treatment effect sum of squares (SS_{TR})	+	error sum of squares (SS_E)

What we have done is divide the total sum of squares into two components. These components are the sum of squares *within* groups and the sum of squares *between* groups. These are measures of variation. If the treatments have had no effect, the scores in all treatment groups should be similar. If this were so, the variance of the sample calculated using all test unit scores, without regard to treatment groups, would equal the variance calculated within treatment groups. That is, the *between*-group variance would equal the *within*-group variance. If the treatments *have* had an effect, however, the scores within groups would be more similar than scores selected from the whole sample at random. Thus, the variance taken within groups would be smaller than the variance between groups. Therefore, we could compare the variance between groups with the variance within groups as a way of measuring for the presence of an effect. This is exactly what is done.

But how do we get variance from the sum-of-squares terms we have in Equation 6? Since variance equals SS/df, all we need to do is divide each component of Equation 6 by its appropriate df, and we will have the necessary variance terms. To obtain the required degrees of freedom we apply the rule we learned in Chapter 14. For the sample as a whole we used up one degree of freedom to calculate the grand mean; therefore, the relevant number of degrees of freedom for the SS_T is the total number of test units minus one. For the SS_{TR} the number of degrees of freedom is always one less than the number of treatments, because once we have determined $t - 1$ group means and the grand mean, the last group mean can take on only one value. The degrees of freedom for the error term equals the number of test units minus the number of treatment groups, because we only use the t within-group means to calculate the error sum of squares. In summary:

	General formula	Our example
df for $SS_T =$	$tn - 1$	$(3 \times 4) - 1 = 11$
df for $SS_{TR} =$	$t - 1$	$3 - 1 = 2$
df for $SS_E =$	$tn - t$	$(3 \times 4) - 3 = 9$

Note: df for $SS_{TR} + SS_E = df$ for SS_T.

Knowledge of the SS_{TR} and SS_E, plus their relevant degrees of freedom, allows us to calculate an estimate of the associated treatment and error variances. These estimates of population variances are called *mean squares (MS)* in experimental situations. This term recognizes the fact that they are estimates of population variances.

One more piece of information is needed before we can determine the significance of an effect. Since our test of effect involves taking the ratio of MS_{TR} to MS_E, we need to know the sampling distribution of this ratio under the null hypothesis (that there is no effect). It can be shown that this ratio is distributed as the F statistic with $t - 1$ df for the numerator and $tn - t$ df for the denominator. (The critical values of the F distribution are given in Table A-5 in the Appendix at the end of the book.) If the treatments have had no effect, the scores in all treatments should be similar, and so the treatment and error mean squares should be almost identical. The calculated F would then equal 1, or nearly so. The larger the treatment effect, the larger the ratio MS_{TR} to MS_E will be. The calculated F value will then get larger. The F distribution in Table A-5 (in the end-of-book Appendix) gives the F values that can occur at various type I error levels given the null hypothesis of no effect. What we do is compare the calculated F against the table value for F at a designated α. If the calculated F exceeds the table F, we reject the null hypothesis. Table 2 presents the various components of the calculation of the experimental F value in formula form.

A Calculated Example We now apply what has been developed to see whether there is a significant treatment effect in the data presented in Table 1.

TABLE 2 ANOVA TABLE FOR COMPLETELY RANDOMIZED DESIGN

Source of variation	Sum of squares (SS)	Degrees of freedom (df)	Mean square (MS)	F ratio
Treatments between groups	SS_{TR}	$t - 1$	$MS_{TR} = \dfrac{SS_{TR}}{t - 1}$	$\dfrac{MS_{TR}}{MS_E}$
Error (within groups) Total	SS_E SS_T	$tn - t$ $tn - 1$	$MS_E = \dfrac{SS_E}{tn - t}$	

TABLE 3   ANOVA FOR COUPON EXPERIMENT WITH COMPLETELY RANDOMIZED DESIGN

Source of variation	Sum of squares (SS)	Degrees of freedom (df)	Mean square (MS)	F ratio
Treatments	98.7	2	49.4	3.3
Error	134.0	9	14.9	
Total	232.7	11		

Total Sum of Squares[2]

$$SS_T = \sum_{i=1}^{n} \sum_{j=1}^{t} (Y_{ij} - M)^2$$

$$= (20 - 12.7)^2 + (17 - 12.7)^2 + \cdots + (5 - 12.7)^2$$

$$= 232.7$$

Treatment Sum of Squares

$$SS_{TR} = n_j \sum_{j=1}^{t} (M_{.j} - M)^2$$

$$= 4[(16 - 12.7)^2 + (13 - 12.7)^2 + (9 - 12.7)^2]$$

$$= 98.7$$

Error Sum of Squares

$$SS_E = \sum_{i=1}^{n} \sum_{j=1}^{t} (Y_{ij} - M_{.j})^2$$

$$= (20 - 16)^2 + (17 - 13)^2 + \cdots + (5 - 9)^2$$

$$= 134$$

Note that once we have obtained SS_T and SS_{TR} we can calculate SS_E by subtracting SS_{TR} from SS_T. However, we can double-check our calculations by using the formula for SS_E.

By applying the appropriate df to these SS, we can obtain the mean squares necessary to calculate F. Table 3 presents the calculations of F for these data.

The calculated F value is

$$F = \frac{49.4}{14.9} = 3.3$$

at 2 and 9 df. Now look up the critical value of F in Table A-5 (in the end-of-book Appendix). In this table, degrees of freedom for the numerator are the column headings, and degrees of freedom for the denominator are the row headings. The table gives critical values at

---

[2]We could, of course, use the computational formula for SS that was presented in Chapter 14.

different levels of confidence $(1 - \alpha)$. The intersection of a given row and column at a given $1 - \alpha$ gives the critical values at the α level of significance. In our example, the critical F value at $\alpha = .1$ for 2 and 9 df is 3.01. Our calculated F was 3.3, so our F value could have occurred by chance less than 10 percent of the time, and we reject the null hypothesis of no treatment effect.

Our result would not be significant if we had to set $\alpha = .05$, as the critical value is 4.26. Given our choice of $\alpha = .1$, we conclude that the choice of coupon plan does make a difference in sales. We would then examine the data to see which plan was best. In this case, it is obviously plan 1. Note that all an F test does is tell us that there has been a significant effect. We must dig back into the data to see which treatment is causing the effect.

We have now established the procedure for determining the significance of an effect in a completely randomized design. The procedures for other designs apply exactly the same principles; the only difference relates to some extra computations.

RANDOMIZED BLOCK DESIGN

ANOVA for a *randomized block design (RBD)* involves only one more step than that for a CRD. Table 4 presents the data for our CRD coupon experiment as if the experiment had been blocked. Note that the table is the same as Table 1, except that the i's now represent blocks instead of test units, and we have calculated row totals and means in addition to column totals and means. Let's assume that the blocks represent different store sizes. In essence, we are saying that we expect some variation in cola sales just due to the differences in the size of the test unit stores. Block 1 represents the largest stores, block 2 the next largest, and so on. We must also assume that treatments were randomly assigned to test units within blocks to apply the RBD.

TABLE 4 RANDOMIZED BLOCK DESIGN WITH THREE TREATMENTS AND FOUR BLOCKS

Blocks (i) store sizes	Treatments (j)			Block totals	Block means
	Coupon plan 1	Coupon plan 2	Coupon plan 3		
1	20	17	14	$\Sigma Y_{1.} = 51$	$\bar{Y}_{1.} = M_{1.} = 51/3 = 17$
2	18	14	10	$\Sigma Y_{2.} = 42$	$\bar{Y}_{2.} = M_{3.} = 42/3 = 14$
3	15	13	7	$\Sigma Y_{3.} = 35$	$\bar{Y}_{3.} = M_{3.} = 35/3 = 11.7$
4	11	8	5	$\Sigma Y_{4.} = 24$	$\bar{Y}_{4.} = M_{4.} = 24/3 = 8$
Treatment totals	$\Sigma Y_{.1} = 64$	$\Sigma Y_{.2} = 52$	$\Sigma Y_{.3} = 36$		
Treatment means	$\bar{Y}_{.1} = M_{.1}$ $= \Sigma Y_{.1}/n_1$ $= 64/4$ $= 16$	$\bar{Y}_{.2} = M_{.2}$ $= \Sigma Y_{.2}/n_2$ $= 52/4$ $= 13$	$\bar{Y}_{.3} = M_{.3}$ $= \Sigma Y_{.3}/n_3$ $= 36/4$ $= 9$		

Grand total		$\Sigma Y_{..} = 64 + 52 + 36 = 152$
Grand mean		$\bar{Y}_{..} = M = \Sigma Y_{..}/(n_1 + n_2 + n_3)$ $= 152/12 = 12.7$

Partitioning the Sum of Squares   In the RBD we define an individual observation as

$$Y_{ij} = \text{grand mean} + \text{treatment effect} + \text{block effect} + \text{error}$$

or, In population parameter terms,

$$Y_{ij} = \mu + \tau_j + \beta_i + \epsilon_{ij}$$

Again, we will be estimating this model with sample results, so we state the model as

$$Y_{ij} = M + T_j + B_i + E_{ij} \tag{7}$$

where B_i is the effect of the ith block and the other terms are defined as in the CRD. We have previously defined the M and T_j items in this model. We must define the blocking effect and also redefine the error term. We define blocking effect in a parallel manner to the treatment effect, the only difference being that the blocking effect is stated in terms of row means instead of column means.

$$B_i = (M_{i.} - M)$$

Here knowledge of blocking group membership *improves our ability to predict scores as an improvement over the grand mean.* We assume that $\Sigma_{i=1}^{n} B_i = 0$. That is, the net block effect is zero. We can rewrite Equation 7 as

$$
\begin{array}{ccccccccc}
Y_{ij} & = & M & + (M_{.j} - M) & + (M_{i.} - M) & + & E_{ij} \\
\downarrow & & \downarrow & \downarrow & \downarrow & & \downarrow \\
\text{Individual} & = & \text{grand} & + \text{treatment} & + \text{blocking} & + & \text{error} \\
\text{score} & & \text{mean} & \text{effect} & \text{effect} & &
\end{array}
\tag{8}
$$

We can then solve this equation for E_{ij} to get the measurement of error effect.

$$
\begin{aligned}
E_{ij} &= Y_{ij} - M - (M_{.j} - M) - (M_{i.} - M) \\
&= Y_{ij} - M - M_{.j} + M - M_{i.} + M \\
&= Y_{ij} - M_{.j} - M_{i.} + M \quad \text{or} \quad Y_{ij} + (M - M_{.j} - M_{i.})
\end{aligned}
$$

The error terms thus represent the difference between an individual score, Y_{ij}, and the net difference between the grand mean and the sum of the treatment and block means. If the blocking effect is significant, this error will be smaller than an error defined without blocking. As an illustration, look at score Y_{21} in Table 4. This score is 18. The error without blocking is

$$Y_{ij} - M_{.j} = 18 - 16 = 2$$

Without blocking, the error is

$$Y_{ij} + M - M_{.j} - M_{i.} = 18 + 12.7 - 16 - 14 = .7$$

A similar pattern would be found with the other scores. Thus blocking reduces the size of experimental error. We may rewrite Equation 8 as

$$Y_{ij} = M + (M_{.j} - M) + (M_{i.} - M) + (Y_{ij} - M_{.j} - M_{i.} + M) \tag{9}$$

If we move M to the left side of Equation 9, sum the resultant deviations across all blocks and all treatments, and square both sides, we get

$$\sum_{i=1}^{n} \sum_{j=1}^{t} (Y_{ij} - M)^2 = n \sum_{j=1}^{t} (M_{.j} - M)^2 + t \sum_{i=1}^{n} (M_{i.} - M)^2 + \sum_{i=1}^{n} \sum_{j=1}^{t} (Y_{ij} + M - M_{.j} - M_{i.})^2$$

You should recognize this result as

$$SS_T = SS_{TR} + SS_B + SS_E$$

It follows from the fact that all the cross products again become zero because each involves a sum of individual deviations about a mean. Also, we may write

$$t \sum_{i=1}^{n} (M_{i.} - M)^2 \quad \text{instead of} \quad \sum_{i=1}^{n} \sum_{j=1}^{t} (M_{i.} - M)^2$$

because we are again adding constant means over the t treatments. It is just simpler to multiply by t than to add the same thing t times. Note that this result was obtained by exactly the same principle as that used in a CRD.

   The relevant df for the block is $n - 1$, because once this number of block means is determined, the other is automatically fixed given the grand mean value. If we subtract the treatment and block degrees of freedom from the total degrees of freedom, we get the error degrees of freedom as

$$\text{Error } df = \text{total } df - \text{treatment } df - \text{block } df$$
$$= (tn - 1) - (t - 1) - (n - 1)$$
$$= tn + 1 - t - n$$

TABLE 5   ANOVA TABLE FOR RANDOMIZED BLOCK DESIGN

Source of variation	Sum of squares (SS)	Degrees of freedom (df)	Mean square (MS)	F ratio
Treatments (between columns)	SS_{TR}	$t - 1$	$MS_{TR} = \dfrac{SS_{TR}}{t - 1}$	$\dfrac{MS_{TR}}{MS_E}$
Blocks (between rows)	SS_B	$n - 1$	$MS_B = \dfrac{SS_B}{n - 1}$	$\dfrac{MS_B}{MS_E}$
Error	SS_E	$(t - 1)(n - 1)$	$MS_E = \dfrac{SS_E}{(t - 1)(n - 1)}$	
Total	SS_T	$tn - 1$		

In our example, the error $df = (3 \times 4) + 1 - 3 - 4 = 6$. More generally, the same result may be obtained by applying the formula

$$\text{Error } df = (t - 1)(n - 1)$$

Table 5 presents the ANOVA table for an RBD.

A Calculated Example   We shall now apply the RBD ANOVA procedure to the data in Table 4.

Total Sum of Squares

$$SS_T = \sum_{i=1}^{n} \sum_{j=1}^{t} (Y_{ij} - M)^2$$
$$= (20 - 12.7)^2 + (17 - 12.7)^2 + \cdots + (5 - 12.7)^2$$
$$= 232.7$$

Thus SS_T is exactly the same here as with the CRD, as we would expect.

Treatment Sum of Squares

$$SS_{TR} = n \sum_{j=1}^{t} (M_j - M)^2$$
$$= 4[(16 - 12.7)^2 + (13 - 12.7)^2 + (9 - 12.7)^2]$$
$$= 98.7$$

Note that the SS_{TR} is exactly the same as with the CRD.

Block Sum of Squares

$$SS_B = t \sum_{i=1}^{n} (M_{i.} - M)^2$$
$$= 3[(17 - 12.7)^2 + (14 - 12.7)^2 + (11.7 - 12.7)^2 + (8 - 12.7)^2]$$
$$= 129.8$$

Error Sum of Squares

$$SS_E = SS_T - SS_{TR} - SS_B$$
$$= 232.7 - 98.7 - 129.8$$
$$= 4.2$$

Table 6 presents the calculated F values for the treatment and block effects.
For the treatment effect, the critical value of F for $\alpha = .1$ at 2 and 6 df is 3.46. For the blocking factor, the critical value of F for $\alpha = .1$ at 3 and 6 df is 3.29. Both the treatment and the block effects are statistically significant, but in this case even at $\alpha = .01$ the

TABLE 6   ANOVA TABLE FOR COUPON EXPERIMENT WITH BLOCKING FOR STORE SIZE

Source of variation	Sum of squares (SS)	Degrees of freedom (df)	Mean square (MS)	F ratio
Treatment	98.7	2	49.4	70.6
Block	129.8	3	43.3	61.9
Error	4.2	6	0.7	
Total	232.7	11		

treatment effect is now significant (critical $F = 10.9$). By blocking we have obtained a smaller measure of error and thus a more reliable measure of the treatment effect. All the SS_B comes out of the SS_E for the CRD; that is,

$$SS_E(\text{with blocking}) = SS_E(\text{without blocking}) - SS_B$$

In our example,

$$SS_E(\text{with blocking}) = 134.0 - 129.8 = 4.2$$

LATIN SQUARE DESIGN

If we wanted to block out and measure the effects of two extraneous variables, we could use the *Latin square (LS)* design. In an LS design the number of categories of each blocking variable must equal the number of treatment categories, and each treatment must appear once and only once in each row and column of the design. Table 7 shows selected LS designs of different sizes. The letters *A, B, C,* and so on represent treatments. To generate the treatment assignment pattern for a particular study, pick the appropriately sized layout from Table 7 and randomize the column order. For example, a 3×3 LS might yield the following treatment pattern when the columns are randomized with the random numbers 3, 1, 2:

$$C \quad A \quad B$$
$$A \quad B \quad C$$
$$B \quad C \quad A$$

Now randomize the row assignments within columns, subject to the constraint that each treatment may appear only once in each row. One such result of this process could be the following LS:

$$B \quad C \quad A$$
$$C \quad A \quad B$$
$$A \quad B \quad C$$

We can now illustrate the LS design with a numerical example. Suppose we ran our coupon experiment again to see whether the results could be replicated in other areas. The only difference is that this time we want to block out and measure the effect on sales of

TABLE 7   ILLUSTRATIVE LATIN SQUARE LAYOUT

3 × 3						4 × 4		
A	B	C			A	B	C	D
B	C	A			B	C	D	A
C	A	B			C	D	A	B
					D	A	B	C

5 × 5					6 × 6					
A	B	C	D	E	A	B	C	D	E	F
B	C	D	E	A	B	C	D	E	F	A
C	D	E	A	B	C	D	E	F	A	B
D	E	A	B	C	D	E	F	A	B	C
E	A	B	C	D	E	F	A	B	C	D
					F	A	B	C	D	E

both store size and day of the week. In doing so, we must expect significant variation in cola sales simply because of these factors. For one reason or another, we have been unable to measure sales on the same day of the week for each test unit. Since there are three treatments (coupon plans), we must have three categories of store size and three categories of days of the week to use the LS design. Table 8 presents the data generated from this LS design experiment. The pattern of treatment assignments is the one generated previously by randomization with these three plans, as follows:

A   Coupon plan 1

B   Coupon plan 2

C   Coupon plan 3

The treatment designation is noted next to the cola sales on Table 8.

Partitioning the Sum of Squares   In the LS design we define an individual observation as

$$Y_{ijk} = \text{grand mean} + \text{row effect} + \text{column effect} + \text{treatment effect} + \text{error}$$

where Y_{ijk} = the measured result when the kth treatment is applied to the ith row and the jth column. In population parameter terms, the model is

$$Y_{ijk} = \mu + \alpha_i + \beta_j + \tau_k + \epsilon_{ijk}$$

Again we will be estimating this model with sample results, so we state the model as

$$Y_{ijk} = M + R_i + C_j + T_k + E_{ijk} \tag{10}$$

where R_i = the effect of the ith row block (i.e., store size)
C_j = the effect of the jth column block (i.e., day of the week)
T_k = the effect of the kth treatment (i.e., coupon plan)
E_{ijk} = the experimental error of the ijk observation
$i,j,k = 1,2, \ldots , t$ where t = the number of treatments

TABLE 8   LATIN SQUARE DESIGN WITH THREE TREATMENTS

Rows (*i*)	Columns (*j*)			Row totals	Row means
	1 Mon.–Tues.	2 Wed.–Thurs.	3 Fri.–Sun.		
1 Large stores	25 (*B*)	15 (*C*)	50 (*A*)	$\Sigma Y_{1..} = 90$	$M_{1..} = 90/3 = 30.0$
2 Medium stores	5 (*C*)	25 (*A*)	25 (*B*)	$\Sigma Y_{2..} = 55$	$M_{2..} = 55/3 = 18.3$
3 Small stores	15 (*A*)	15 (*B*)	14 (*C*)	$\Sigma Y_{3..} = 44$	$M_{3..} = 44/3 = 14.7$
Column totals	$\Sigma Y_{.1.} = 45$	$\Sigma Y_{.2.} = 55$	$\Sigma Y_{.3.} = 89$	$\Sigma Y_{...} = 189$	
Column means	$M_{.1.} = 45/3$ $= 15.0$	$M_{.2.} = 55/3$ $= 18.3$	$M_{.3.} = 89/3$ $= 29.7$		$M = 189/9$ $= 21.0$

Treatments (*k*)	*A**	*B*	*C*
Treatment totals	$\Sigma Y_{..1} = 90$	$\Sigma Y_{..2} = 65$	$\Sigma Y_{..3} = 34$
Treatment means	$M_{..1} = 90/3$ $= 30.0$	$M_{..2} = 65/3$ $= 21.7$	$M_{..3} = 34/3$ $= 11.3$

* For example, $\Sigma Y_{..1} = 15 + 25 + 50 = 90$; i.e., we add the scores at all the places where *A* appears.

The three effects of interest are:

1 Row effect (i.e., effect of store size) = $(M_{i..} - M)$, the difference between the row mean and the grand mean, adding across all *j*'s and *k*'s.

2 Column effect (i.e., effect of the day of the week) = $(M_{.j.} - M)$, the difference between the column mean and the grand mean, adding across all *i*'s and *k*'s.

3 Treatment effect (i.e., effect of coupon plan) = $(M_{..k} - M)$, the difference between the treatment mean and the grand mean, adding across all *i*'s and *j*'s.

We assume that the net effect of each effect is zero. That is,

$$\sum_{i=1}^{t} R_i = 0 \qquad \sum_{j=1}^{t} C_j = 0 \quad \text{and} \quad \sum_{k=1}^{t} T_k = 0$$

We can then rewrite Equation 10 as

$$Y_{ijk} = M + (M_{i..} - M) + (M_{.j.} - M) + (M_{..k} - M) + E_{ijk}$$

$$\downarrow \qquad \downarrow \qquad \downarrow \qquad \downarrow \qquad \downarrow \qquad \downarrow$$

$$\begin{array}{c}\text{Individual}\\ \text{score}\end{array} = \begin{array}{c}\text{grand}\\ \text{mean}\end{array} + \begin{array}{c}\text{row}\\ \text{effect}\end{array} + \begin{array}{c}\text{column}\\ \text{effect}\end{array} + \begin{array}{c}\text{treatment}\\ \text{effect}\end{array} + \text{error}$$

We can solve this equation for E_{ijk} to get the measurement of error:

$$E_{ijk} = Y_{ijk} - M - (M_{i..} - M) - (M_{.j.} - M) - (M_{..k} - M)$$
$$= Y_{ijk} + 2M - M_{i..} - M_{.j.} - M_{..k}$$

If both blocking factors are correlated with the dependent variable, this error measure will be smaller than that obtained with a CRD or RBD that uses only one blocking factor.

If we moved M to the left side, added all these deviations across all rows and columns, and squared the equation, we would obtain the required SS. The model would then be

$$SS_T = SS_R + SS_C + SS_{TR} + SS_E$$

as again all the cross products fall out to zero. Table 9 shows the ANOVA layout for an LS design. SS_R, SS_C, and SS_{TR} each have $t - 1$ df. With $(t)(t) - 1$ or $t^2 - 1$ df in the whole sample, this leaves $(t - 1)(t - 2)$ df for the error term.

A Calculated Example   We shall now apply the LS design ANOVA to the data in Table 8.

Total Sum of Squares

$$SS_T = \sum_{i=1}^{t} \sum_{j=1}^{t} (Y_{ijk} - M)^2$$

$$= (25 - 21)^2 + (15 - 21)^2 + \cdots + (14 - 21)^2$$

$$= 1302$$

Row Sum of Squares

$$SS_R = t \sum_{i=1}^{t} (M_{i..} - M)^2$$

$$= 3[(30 - 21)^2 + (18.3 - 21)^2 + (14.7 - 21)^2]$$

$$= 383.9$$

Column Sum of Squares

$$SS_C = t \sum_{j=1}^{t} (M_{.j.} - M)^2$$

$$= 3[(15 - 21)^2 + (18.3 - 21)^2 + (29.7 - 21)^2]$$

$$= 356.9$$

Treatment Sum of Squares

$$SS_{TR} = t \sum_{k=1}^{t} (M_{..k} - M)^2$$

$$= 3[(30 - 21)^2 + (21.7 - 21)^2 + (11.3 - 21)^2]$$

$$= 526.7$$

Error Sum of Squares

$$SS_E = SS_T - SS_R - SS_C - SS_{TR}$$

$$= 1302 - 383.9 - 356.9 - 526.7$$

$$= 34.5$$

TABLE 9   ANOVA TABLE FOR LATIN SQUARE DESIGN

Source of variation	Sum of squares (SS)	Degrees of freedom (df)	Mean square (MS)	F ratio
Between rows	SS_R	$t - 1$	$MS_R = \dfrac{SS_R}{t - 1}$	$\dfrac{MS_R}{MS_E}$
Between columns	SS_C	$t - 1$	$MS_C = \dfrac{SS_C}{t - 1}$	$\dfrac{MS_C}{MS_E}$
Between treatments	SS_{TR}	$t - 1$	$MS_{TR} = \dfrac{SS_{TR}}{t - 1}$	$\dfrac{MS_{TR}}{MS_E}$
Error	SS_E	$(t - 1)(t - 2)$	$MS_E = \dfrac{SSE}{(t - 1)(t - 2)}$	
Total	SS_T	$t^2 - 1$		

Table 10 presents the calculated F values for the treatment and the two blocks. For the treatment and blocking factors, the critical value of F for $\alpha = .1$ at 2 and 2 df is 9.0. Therefore, both blocking factors and the treatment are significant. Note that none of these effects would have been significant at $\alpha = .05$, as the critical F is 19.0. If we had used a CRD or blocked with just one of our two blocking factors in an RBD, the treatment effect would not have been significant at $\alpha = .1$. This is so because the SS_R and SS_C would be added back into the LS design SS_E to give the SS_E for the CRD. As for the RBD, either SS_R or SS_C would be added back to the LS design SS_E to give the SS_E for the RBD. In either instance, the SS_R or SS_C is large enough to render the calculated F ratio nonsignificant at $\alpha = .1$. Here we needed two blocking factors to find a significant treatment effect. The value of blocking in marketing experiments should be clear. Again note that we must look into the data to see that treatment A is the best coupon plan.

FACTORIAL DESIGN

In a *factorial design (FD)* we measure the effects of two or more independent variables and their interactions. Suppose that in our coupon experiment we are interested not only in the effect of coupon plans, but also in the effect of the media plans that support the coupon plans. Table 11 presents data generated from such an experiment. You should recognize

TABLE 10   ANOVA TABLE FOR COUPON EXPERIMENT WITH 3 × 3 LATIN SQUARE DESIGN

Source of variation	Sum of squares (SS)	Degrees of freedom (df)	Mean square (MS)	F ratio
Row effect (store size)	383.9	2	192.0	11.1
Column effect (days of week)	356.9	2	178.5	10.3
Treatment	526.7	2	263.4	15.2
Error	34.5	8	17.3	
Total	1302.0			

TABLE 11   A 2 × 3 FACTORIAL DESIGN WITH MEDIA PLANS AND COUPON PLANS AS INDEPENDENT VARIABLES

		Coupon plans (j)			Media totals	Media means
		B_1	B_2	B_3		
Media plans (i)	A_1	20 18	17 14	14 10	$\Sigma Y_{1..} = 93$	$M_{1..} = 93/6 = 15.5$
	A_2	15 11	13 8	7 5	$\Sigma Y_{2..} = 59$	$M_{2..} = 59/6 = 9.8$
Coupon totals		$\Sigma Y_{.1.} = 64$	$\Sigma Y_{.2.} = 52$	$\Sigma Y_{.3.} = 36$	$\Sigma Y_{...} = 152$	
Coupon means		$M_{.1.} = 64/4 = 16$	$M_{.2.} = 52/4 = 13$	$M_{.3.} = 36/4 = 9$		$M = 12.7$

Treatment cell (ij)	A_1B_1	A_1B_2	A_1B_3	A_2B_1	A_2B_2	A_2B_3
Cell total Cell mean	$\Sigma Y_{11.} = 38$ $M_{11} = 38/2$ $= 19$	$\Sigma Y_{12.} = 31$ $M_{12.} = 31/2$ $= 15.5$	$\Sigma Y_{13.} = 24$ $M_{13.} = 24/2$ $= 12$	$\Sigma Y_{21.} = 26$ $M_{21.} = 26/2$ $= 13$	$\Sigma Y_{22.} = 21$ $M_{22.} = 21/2$ $= 10.5$	$\Sigma Y_{23.} = 12$ $M_{23.} = 12/2$ $= 6$

Note: $n_{ij} = 2$ for all i's and j's.

these as the data we used in Table 1 for our CRD. All we have done here is regroup the data and present them as if they came from an FD.

Partitioning the Sum of Squares   In the FD with two independent variables, we define an individual observation as

Y_{ijk} = grand mean + effect of treatment A
+ effect of treatment B + interaction effect AB + error

where Y_{ijk} = the kth observation on the ith level of A and the jth level of B.
For example, here

$$Y_{111} = 20 \quad \text{and} \quad Y_{231} = 7$$

In population parameter terms, the model is

$$Y_{ijk} = \mu + \alpha_i + \beta_j + (\alpha\beta)_{ij} + \epsilon_{ijk}$$

Again, we will be estimating this model with sample results, as we write

$$Y_{ijk} = M + A_i + B_j + (AB)_{ij} + E_{ijk} \tag{11}$$

where A_i = the effect of the ith level of A (media plan), $i = 1, \cdots, a$, where a is the number of levels in A

B_j = the effect of the ith level of B (coupon plan), $j = 1, \cdots, b$, where b is the number of levels in B

$(AB)_{ij}$ = the effect of the interaction of the ith level of A and the jth level of B

E_{ijk} = the error of the kth observation in the ith level of A and the jth level of B, that is, the ij cell

In our example $n_{ij} = 2$ for all ij cells.

The four effects of interest are:

1 A_i effect (i.e., media plan) = $(M_i - M)$, the difference between the row mean and the grand mean.

2 B_j effect (i.e., coupon plan) = $(M_{.j.} - M)$, the difference between the column mean and the grand mean.

3 Error = $(Y_{ijk} - M_{ij.})$, the difference between an individual observation and the cell mean to which it belongs. That is, the only difference within a cell should be random chance.

4 Interaction effect $(AB)_{ij}$ = any remaining variation in the data after main effects and error have been removed.

We can rewrite Equation 11 as

$$Y_{ijk} = M + (M_{i..} - M) + (M_{.j.} - M) + (AB)_{ij} + (Y_{ijk} - M_{ij.})$$

and solve for the interaction term, $(AB)_{ij}$:

$$\begin{aligned} (AB)_{ij} &= Y_{ijk} - M - (M_{i..} - M) - (M_{.j.} - M) - (Y_{ijk} - M_{ij.}) \\ &= Y_{ijk} - M - M_{i..} + M - M_{.j.} + M - Y_{ijk} + M_{ij.} \\ &= M + M_{ij.} - M_{i..} - M_{.j.} \end{aligned}$$

In our example,

$$(AB)_{11} = 12.7 + 19 - 15.5 - 16 = 0.2$$

and

$$(AB)_{23} = 12.7 + 6 - 9.8 - 9 = -0.1$$

Results like this suggest that there is little interaction in the data. We may now rewrite Equation 11 as

$$Y_{ijk} = M + (M_{i..} - M) + (M_{.j.} - M) + (M + M_{ij.} - M_{i..} - M_{.j.}) + (Y_{ijk} - M_{ij.})$$

If we moved M to the left side, added all the deviations across all scores k in all ij cells, and squared the equation, we would obtain the required SS. The model would then be

$$SS_T = SS_{TRA} + SS_{TRB} + SS_{INT(AB)} + SS_E$$

where SS_{TRA} = sum of squares of treatment A

SS_{TRB} = sum of squares of treatment B

$SS_{INT(AB)}$ = sum of squares for interaction of A and B

This result occurs because all the cross products fall out to zero, as we would now expect. Table 12 shows the ANOVA layout for a two-factor FD. Each factor has one degree of freedom less than its number of categories, and the interaction term has $(a - 1)(b - 1)$ df. With $abn - 1$ df in the whole sample, this leaves $ab(n - 1)$ for the error term.

A Calculated Example   Now let us apply the FD to the data in Table 11.

Total Sum of Squares

$$SS_T = \sum_{i=1}^{a} \sum_{j=1}^{b} \sum_{k=1}^{n} (Y_{ijk} - M)^2$$

$$= (20 - 12.7)^2 + (17 - 12.7)^2 + \cdots + (5 - 12.7)^2$$

$$= 232.7$$

Again note that the SS_T is the same as in the CRD and RBD, as it must be.

Treatment A Sum of Squares

$$SS_{TRA} = bn \sum_{i=1}^{a} (M_{i..} - M)^2$$

$$= (3)(2)[(15.5 - 12.7)^2 + (9.8 - 12.7)^2]$$

$$= 97.5$$

Treatment B Sum of Squares

$$SS_{TRB} = an \sum_{j=1}^{b} (M_{.j.} - M)^2$$

$$= (2)(2)[(16 - 12.7)^2 + (13 - 12.7)^2 + (9 - 12.7)^2]$$

$$= 98.7$$

TABLE 12   ANOVA TABLE FOR A TWO-FACTOR FACTORIAL DESIGN

Source of variation	Sum of squares (SS)	Degrees of freedom (df)	Mean square (MS)	F ratio
Treatment A	SS_{TRA}	$a - 1$	$MS_{TRA} = \dfrac{SS_{TRA}}{a - 1}$	$\dfrac{MS_{TRA}}{MS_E}$
Treatment B	SS_{TRB}	$b - 1$	$MS_{TRB} = \dfrac{SS_{TRB}}{b - 1}$	$\dfrac{MS_{TRB}}{MS_E}$
Interaction AB	$SS_{INT(AB)}$	$(a - 1)(b - 1)$	$MS_{INT(AB)} = \dfrac{SS_{INT(AB)}}{(a - 1)(b - 1)}$	$\dfrac{MS_{INT(AB)}}{MS_E}$
Error	SS_E	$ab(n - 1)$	$MS_E = \dfrac{SS_E}{ab(n - 1)}$	
Total	SS_T	$abn - 1$		

TABLE 13 ANOVA TABLE FOR MEDIA AND COUPON EXPERIMENT USING A TWO-FACTOR 2 × 3 FACTORIAL DESIGN

Source of variation	Sum of squares (SS)	Degrees of freedom (df)	Mean square (MS)	F ratio
Treatment A (media)	97.5	1	97.5	16.3
Treatment B (coupon)	98.7	2	49.4	8.2
Interaction (AB)	0.7	?	.4	.1
Error	35.8	6	6.0	
Total	232.7	11		

Note that this is the SS_{TR} we found for the CRD. In other words, the main effect of the coupon plan is identical under both analysis procedures, as we would expect.

Interaction Sum of Squares

$$SS_{INT(AB)} = n \sum_{i=1}^{a} \sum_{j=1}^{b} (M + M_{ij.} - M_{i..} - M_{.j.})^2$$

$$= 2[(12.7 + 19 - 15.5 - 16)^2]$$

$$+ (12.7 + 15.5 - 15.5 - 13)^2 + (12.7 + 12 - 15.5 - 9)^2$$

$$+ (12.7 + 13 - 9.8 - 16)^2 + (12.7 + 10.5 - 9.8 - 13)^2$$

$$+ (12.8 + 6 - 9.8 - 9)^2$$

$$= 0.7$$

Error Sum of Squares

$$SS_E = \sum_{i=1}^{a} \sum_{j=1}^{b} \sum_{k=1}^{n} (Y_{ijk} - M_{ij.})^2$$

$$= SS_T - SS_{TRA} - SS_{TRB} - SS_{INT(AB)}$$

$$= 232.7 - 97.5 - 98.7 - 0.7$$

$$= 35.8$$

Table 13 presents the calculated F values for the two treatments and the interaction. For treatment A, the critical F for $\alpha = .05$ at 1 and 6 df is 5.99. Therefore, the media effect is significant. For treatment B, for $\alpha = .05$ at 2 and 6 df the critical F is 5.14. Thus, the coupon effect is also significant. Since the calculated interaction F is less than 1, we know it is not significant without even using the F table. We can now go back to the data to see that it is media plan A_1 and coupon plan B_1 that yield the best results.

This two-factor ANOVA is called "two-way" ANOVA. The factorial procedure can be extended to N independent variables. This is called "N-way" ANOVA. The calculations for an ANOVA greater than two-way are too complex to present here. The analysis of such an experiment is, however, easily handled by computer programs. In any event, the principle of these more advanced calculations is exactly the same as you have just learned.

SUMMARY OF APPENDIX

1 ANOVA is simply the calculation of different variances, SS/df.

2 The fixed-effects model allows inferences only about the different treatments actually used. It is most relevant in marketing.

3 In ANOVA an effect is defined as a difference in treatment means from the grand mean.

4 Experimental error is the difference between an individual score and the treatment group mean to which the score belongs.

5 ANOVA is calculated by partitioning the SS_T into SS_{TR} and SS_E and dividing each of these by their relevant degrees of freedom to yield an estimate of treatment and error variances called the mean squares (MS_{TR} and MS_E). That is, the one-way ANOVA model is partitioned as follows: $SS_T = SS_{TR} + SS_E$.

6 The relevant statistic for a significance test is the F statistic, where $F = MS_{TR}/MS_E$.

7 The CRD measures the effect of one independent variable without statistical control of extraneous variation. Its basic composition is $SS_T = SS_{TR} + SS_E$.

8 The RBD design measures the effect of one independent variable with statistical control of one extraneous factor. Its basic composition is $SS_T = SS_{TR} + SS_B + SS_E$.

9 The LS design measures the effect of one independent variable with statistical control of two extraneous factors. Its basic composition is $SS_T = SS_R + SS_C + SS_{TR} + SS_E$.

10 The FD measures the main and interaction effects of two or more independent variables. Its basic composition for a two-way ANOVA is $SS_T = SS_{TRA} + SS_{TRB} + SS_{INT(AB)} + SS_E$.

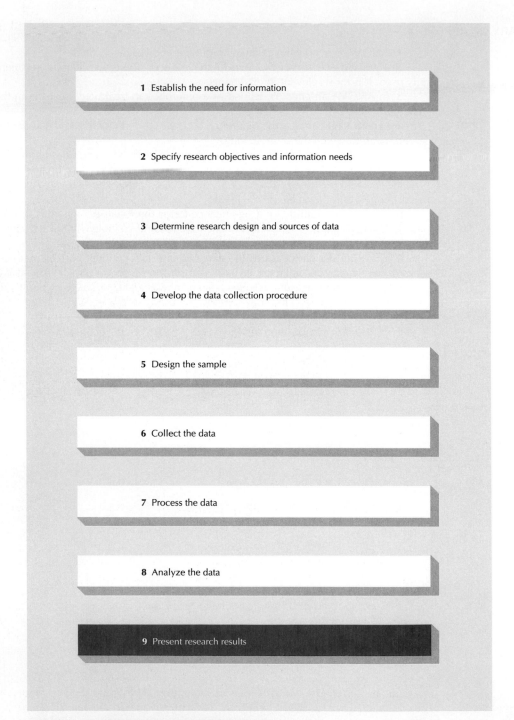

FIGURE 22-1   Steps in the research process.

CHAPTER 22

REPORTING RESEARCH FINDINGS

MARKETING RESEARCH IN ACTION

MARKETING RESEARCH PRESENTATION ENDS IN "COMBAT"—FILM AT 11:00

Lisa Barnes and Carver Thomas were the marketing research director and senior researcher of a major multidivision industrial corporation. They worked out of the head office of the corporation in Connecticut. Senior corporate management had become increasingly concerned about the decreasing market share and profitability of its industrial equipment division (which made road graders, cranes, etc.). The senior management of the industrial equipment division considered themselves to be quite independent of the head office, and they had basically been left alone on operations questions for years. However, they had reluctantly agreed with corporate management to undertake a marketing research study in the field to determine the causes of the declining situation.

The marketing research study consisted of field interviews with customers, distributors, and industry experts, plus the examination of a rich set of secondary data that was available. By all accepted marketing research standards, the study was competently done. During the study the research team had received reluctant cooperation from the division management. One division manager had indicated that, "We know what the problems are, and don't need a study to tell us the obvious."

Barnes and Thomas prepared long and hard for the presentation that they were going to make to the division management. Their primary findings were that customers perceived a lack of quality in the new product lines that had been introduced 2 years earlier, and that competition from new offshore entries was giving better service support to the distributors and end customers. Their presentation was spectacular in terms of the written report graphics, overheads, and even a videotape of represen tation interviews

About 10 minutes into the presentation the general manager of the division stood up and shouted, "You researchers don't understand our markets. I've been in this business for 25 years and know our customers too well to believe these results. We are the top-quality product and service company. I know we are." At that point the corporate executive vice president strongly supported the findings as being consistent with corporate management's beliefs. Then chaos occurred, with shouting between the division management and the corporate representative. Barnes and Thomas tried in vain to return the conversation to a discussion of the reasonableness of the finding by discussing the method used and asking to show some of the field interviews on videotape.

After 10 minutes of angry words, the general manager of the division walked out of the meeting, shouting, "Leave it to us who are close to the business to handle these problems."

Obviously not many presentations are as dramatic as this one. However, presentations are extremely important for the effective utilization of marketing research.

The final step in the research process is the preparation and presentation of the research report. This could very well be the most important part of the research process. If the report is confusing or poorly written, all the time and effort spent gathering and analyzing data will have been for naught. The purpose of this chapter is to give you guidance in preparing a research report—which is simply the presentation of research findings to a specific audience. We shall cover written and oral reports, since both are usually prepared at the completion of a research project.

For many executives, the only aspect of a research project they perceive is an oral or written report. Their evaluation of weeks (or months!) of research rests solely upon this presentation. The best research methodology in the world will be useless to managers and executives if they can't wade through the research report. This chapter will offer advice on how to present research findings in a clear, interesting manner.

WRITTEN REPORT GUIDELINES

Researchers who are effective in report writing agree that there are a series of guidelines that should be followed. These guidelines are listed below.

Consider the Audience   Make the report clear; use only words familiar to the readers, and define all technical terms. To make the comparison of figures easier, use percentages, rounded-off figures, ranks, or ratios; put the exact data in a table within the text or in the appendix. Use graphic aids (charts, graphs, pictures, etc.) whenever they help clarify the presentation of data.

Address the Information Needs   Remember—the research report is designed to communicate information to decision makers. Make sure it clearly relates the research findings to the objectives of management.

Be Concise, Yet Complete   Most managers will not want to read about the details of a research project. Knowing what to include and what to leave out is a difficult task. It is up to you, the researcher, to take into account the information needs of the decision maker when writing your report.

Be Objective   You will probably face at least one situation in which you know that the results will not be easily accepted by the client. The findings may conflict with the decision maker's experience and judgment, or they may reflect unfavorably on the wisdom of previous decisions. In these circumstances, there is a strong temptation to slant the report, making the results seem more acceptable to management. A professional researcher, however, will present the research findings in an objective manner (i.e., without bias) and will defend their validity if they are challenged by the client.

Style   Writing style is a topic for an English or communications course, but here are a few tips to help you write a report that is easy to read.

- Write in brisk, businesslike English.
- Use short words and sentences.
- Be concise.
- Consider appearance. White space (portions of the page that are blank) makes a long report easier to read. Graphs and charts, used primarily to visually illustrate statistical ideas, are also useful for creating white space.
- Avoid clichés.
- Write in the present tense.
- Use the active voice.
- Place short quotes from respondents throughout the report. This makes it more interesting and readable, and may provide insight or spark new ideas.

REPORT FORMAT

While there is no single format that is appropriate for all situations, the following outline is generally accepted as the basic format for most research projects.

1 Title page
2 Table of contents

3 Table of tables (or figures, graphs, etc.)
4 Management summary
   a Objectives
   b Results
   c Conclusions
   d Recommendations
5 Body
   a Introduction
   b Methodology
   c Results
   d Limitations
6 Conclusions and recommendations
7 Appendix
   a Sampling plan
   b Data collection forms
   c Supporting tables not included in the body

Title Page

The title page should contain a title that conveys the essence of the study, the date, the name of the organization submitting the report, and the name of the recipient organization. If the report is confidential, the individuals to receive the report should be named on the title page.

Table of Contents

The table of contents lists sequentially the topics covered in the report, along with their page references. Its purpose is to help readers find the particular sections of the report that are of most concern to them. See Exhibit 1 for an example of the table of contents used in reports written by the General Foods Corporation marketing research department.

Table of Tables (or Table of Figures, Illustrations, etc.)

This table lists the titles and page numbers of all visual aids. This table can be placed either on the same page with the table of contents or on a separate page.

Management Summary

The management summary is a condensed, accurate statement of what is important in the report. This one- to two-page synopsis is a must for most research reports. Since many executives read only the management summary, it is extremely important that this section be both accurate and well written.

   The management summary is not a miniature of the main report. Rather, it provides the decision maker with those research findings having the most impact

EXHIBIT 1

TABLE OF CONTENTS

on the decision to be made. The management summary is written specifically for decision makers and should enable them to take action.

Your management summary should include:

1 Objectives of the research project
2 Nature of the decision problem
3 Key results
4 Conclusions (opinions and interpretations based on the research)
5 Recommendations for action

Body of Report

The details of the research project are found in the body of the report. This section includes (1) introduction, (2) methodology, (3) results, and (4) limitations.

Introduction   The purpose of the introduction is to provide the reader with background information needed to understand the remainder of the report. The nature of the introduction is conditioned by the diversity of the audience and their familiarity with the research project. The more diverse the audience, the more extensive the introduction.

The introduction must clearly explain the nature of the decision problem and the research objective. Background information should be provided on the product or service involved and the circumstances surrounding the decision problem. The nature of any previous research on the problem should be reviewed.

Methodology   The purpose of the methodology section is to describe the nature of the research design, the sampling plan, and the data collection and analysis procedure. This is a very difficult section to write. Enough detail must be conveyed so that the reader can appreciate the nature of the methodology used, yet the presentation must not be boring or overpowering. The use of technical jargon must be avoided.

The methodology section should tell the reader whether the design was exploratory or conclusive. The sources of data—secondary or primary—should be explained. The nature of the data collection method—communication or observation—must be specified. The reader needs to know who was included in the sample, the size of the sample, and the nature of the sampling procedure.

The methodology section is designed (1) to summarize the technical aspects of the research project in a style that is comprehensible to the nontechnician and (2) to develop confidence in the quality of the procedures used. The technical details should be minimized in this section and placed in an appendix for those who desire a more detailed methodological discussion.

Results   The bulk of the report is composed of the research findings, which should be organized around the research objectives and information needs. This presentation should involve a logical unfolding of information—as if you were telling a story. The reporting of findings must have a definite point of view and fit together into a logical whole; it is not just the presentation of an endless series of tables. Rather, it requires the organization of the data into a logical flow of information for decision-making purposes.

Limitations   Every research project has weaknesses which need to be communicated in a clear and concise manner. In this process, the researcher should avoid belaboring minor study weaknesses. The purpose of this section is not to disparage the quality of the research project, but rather to enable the reader to judge the validity of the study results.

The limitations of a marketing research project generally involve sampling and nonresponse inadequacies and methodological weaknesses. The writing of the conclusions and recommendations section is naturally affected by the recognized and acknowledged study limitations. It is the researcher's professional responsibility to clearly inform the reader of these limitations.

Conclusions and Recommendations

The conclusions and recommendations must flow logically from the presentation of the results. The conclusions should clearly link the research findings with the information needs, and based on this linkage recommendations for action can be formulated.

Many executives and researchers feel that the researcher shouldn't make recommendations. They argue that the recommendations for action must reflect a blend of the decision maker's experience and judgment with the findings from the research study. Since few researchers possess this degree of experience and judgment, the researcher's recommendations may be weighed more heavily in favor of the research findings.

Alternatively, many others feel strongly that the research report should include recommendations. They argue that as long as the decision maker recognizes the context in which recommendations are made, there are clear benefits from having them in the research report. First, the researcher must focus on the decision problem and think in terms of action. Second, the researcher must appreciate the broader management issues and the role of research in the decision-making process. Finally, the researcher may identify recommendations not otherwise considered by the decision maker. In the final analysis, however, the action taken is the responsibility of the decision maker, and the recommendations put forth in the research report may or may not be followed.

Appendix

The purpose of the appendix is to provide a place for material that is not absolutely essential to the body of the report. This material is typically more specialized and complex than material presented in the main report, and it is designed to serve the needs of the technically oriented reader. The appendix will frequently contain copies of the data collection forms, details of the sampling plan, estimates of statistical error, interviewer instructions, and detailed statistical tables associated with the data analysis process.

PRESENTATION OF DATA

Whenever you must present numerous figures or describe a technical process or procedure, graphic aids can help communicate this information to your audience more quickly. The two graphic aids most used in research reports are tables and graphs. Besides making the report easier to read and understand, graphic aids improve its physical appearance. This section will illustrate the various ways to present quantitative data by using tables and graphs.

General Guidelines for Presenting Graphic Aids

Usually it is best to place an illustration within the text if the reader will need to refer to it while reading the report. It should be placed as close to the discussion as possible. If the information is supplemental or extremely lengthy, it can be placed in the appendix.

Always introduce the reader to the illustration before you present it; a couple of sentences will usually suffice. You can highlight the extremes, averages, or other aspects of the data that are significant to your report development. Don't, however, discuss minute details of the illustration—readers will find them redundant and boring.

All graphic aids should contain the following elements:

1 *Table or figure number.* This permits easy location in the report.
2 *Title.* The title should clearly indicate the contents of the table or figure.
3 *Boxhead and stub head.* The boxhead contains the captions or labels to the columns in a table, while the stub head contains the labels for the rows.

TABLE 22-1   WEEKLY TRAFFIC COUNT BY STORE LOCATION
(August 8–14, 1995)

Store	Number of persons entering	Percentage of total
West	4,731	25
North	4,821	26
East	3,514	19
South	3,534	19
Central	2,210	11
Total	18,810	100

4 *Footnotes.* Footnotes explain or qualify a particular section or item in the table or figure.

Data can be presented in tabular or graphic form. The tabular form (tables) consists of the numerical presentation of data. Table 22-1 presents an illustration.

The graphical form (figures) involves the presentation of data in terms of visually interpreted sizes. The key to good presentation of graphics is simplicity. Graphics can dress up a presentation by calling attention to important points that can't be explained clearly in tables or words. They are a quick and attractive means of conveying numbers, trends, and relationships.

Once your data are in hand, you must select the best graphic format for your situation. This sounds easy, but deciding which format is most appropriate can be an arduous task. Pie, bar, and line charts are the formats used most frequently in business communication because they provide direct visual representation of complex data.

Pie Chart   The pie chart, which really is shaped like a pie, is one of the simplest and most effective ways to dramatize proportional relationships. It is a circle divided into sections such that the size of each section corresponds to a portion of the total. Figure 22-2 presents the data shown in Table 22-1 in the form of a pie chart. Notice how clearly the figure depicts the relative differences in weekly traffic counts by retail store.

Be wary of the tendency to pack excessive information into a single pie. Too many divisions will make the resulting portions too small to label. Stick to five or six segments, and group segments representing very small percentages (usually less than 5 percent) into a collective "other" category.

One dressy technique that has become popular in business presentations is the practice of exploding, or separating, segments of the pie from the rest of the drawing (see Figure 22-3). This technique directs attention to the most important pieces of information, but it may make the chart more complicated for the viewer. Limit the number of segments you explode to one or two. An alternative to using the exploding pie chart is to highlight the important segments with bright, solid colors.

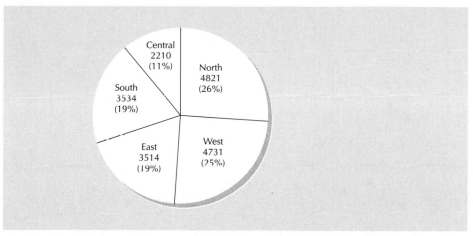

FIGURE 22-2 Pie chart of weekly traffic count by retail stores (August 8–14, 1995).

Pie charts do not lend themselves to illustrating the passage of time, nor do they allow you to compare more than one group of data within a single chart. Comparing multiple entities requires multiple pie charts. If you find yourself using more than four pies, you may want to consider a bar chart instead.

Bar Chart A bar chart depicts magnitudes of the data by the length of various bars that have been laid out with reference to a horizontal or vertical scale. When carefully designed, a bar (or column) chart is the easiest graphic image to under-

FIGURE 22-3 Exploding pie chart.

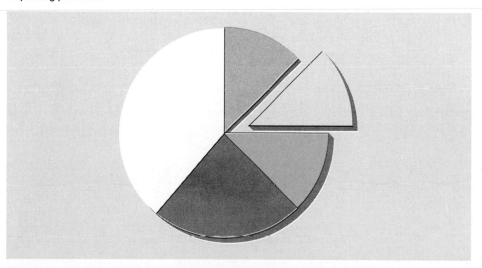

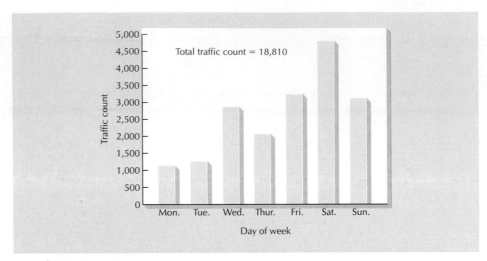

FIGURE 22-4   Bar chart of traffic count of retail stores by day of week (August 8–14, 1995).

stand. It is a tried-and-true business graphics standard. Figure 22-4 presents a bar chart depicting differences in retail store traffic count by day of the week.

Bar charts are best at illustrating multiple comparisons and complex relationships. To compare several distinct sets of data in one chart, use a clustered bar graph. Clustered bars are like an outline for a report: they group general subjects together and then divide the information into specific categories. They are used for comparing different but related types of data within a group and over a period of time.

For simplicity, cluster bar charts should be limited to four groups and four types of data within each group (see Figure 22-5). It is very important to label a clustered

FIGURE 22-5   Cluster bar chart.

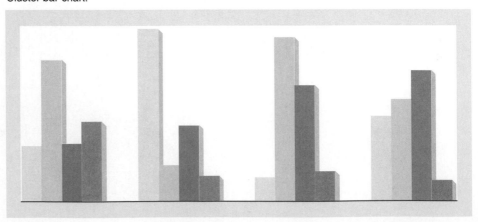

chart clearly. Each cluster should have a label, and each bar within a cluster should be identified. Since there is usually insufficient room for all those labels, draw each bar in a different pattern or color and describe the bars in a legend under the graph.

Line Chart   Line charts effectively illustrate trends over a period of time. Such charts use a continuous line to trace the relationship between data points. The data presented in Figure 22-4 (bar chart) can be presented in the form of a line chart. Figure 22-6 presents a line chart depicting differences in retail store traffic count by day of the week.

A line chart is preferred over a bar chart in the following situations: (1) when the data involve a long time period, (2) when several series are compared on the same chart, (3) when the emphasis is on the movement rather than the actual amount, (4) when trends of frequency distribution are presented, (5) when a multiple-amount scale is used, or (6) when estimates, forecasts, interpolation, or extrapolation are to be shown.

Computer graphics is a rapidly evolving method for conveniently displaying research data in the form of pie, bar, and line charts. Special computer graphics software packages have been developed that complement popular data analysis and spreadsheet software packages. These new software packages allow the researcher to operate directly from large amounts of data to produce an array of graphs, preview them on a graphics terminal, decide which to use, and have the graphs drawn on a hard copy device—all in short order.

As companies become more market-oriented, they are increasingly swamped with data on their markets, their competition, and their marketing programs' effectiveness. A computer has the ability to spew out more data than a researcher can examine, interpret, and present in a manageable format, and computer graph-

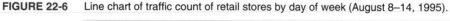

FIGURE 22-6   Line chart of traffic count of retail stores by day of week (August 8–14, 1995).

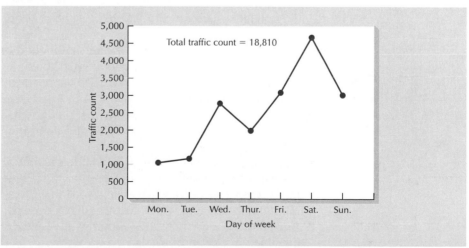

ics has the potential to redress this imbalance resulting from the overflow of market information and the overload on human resources charged with its analysis and reporting.

ORAL PRESENTATION

Many companies require oral presentations of research reports. Before the presentation:

1 Check all equipment (e.g., lights, microphones, projectors, and other visual aid equipment) thoroughly before the presentation.
2 Have a contingency plan for equipment failure.
3 Analyze your audience. How will they react to the research findings? Will they be in agreement? Hostile? Indifferent? Gauge your opening statements accordingly. It's usually wise to begin a presentation with ideas about which there is agreement.
4 Practice the presentation several times. If possible, have someone comment on how to improve its effectiveness.

During the presentation:

5 Start the presentation with an overview—tell the audience what you are going to tell them.
6 Face the audience at all times.
7 Talk to the audience or decision maker, rather than reading from a script or a projection screen. Use notes only to make sure you don't forget any important points and to keep the presentation flowing in an organized manner.
8 Use visual aids effectively. Charts and tables should be simple and easy to read.
9 Avoid distracting mannerisms while speaking. Constant or unnecessary motion is bothersome; make certain your movements have purpose. Also refrain from adding "fillers" such as "uh," "um," "y'know," and "OK" between words or sentences.
10 Remember to ask the audience if they have questions after your report is concluded. During the question period you should:
   a Concentrate on the question. Don't think about the answer until the speaker has completed the question.
   b Repeat the question. If it's a tough one, rephrase it. This assures that everyone in the audience has heard the question, and gives you the time to formulate an answer.
   c Don't fake an answer. Admit that you don't know the answer, then tell the speaker that you will try to find it. After the presentation, find out where that person can be reached when you do in fact get the answer to the question. (Make sure you follow through on your promise!)
   d Answer questions briefly and support your answers with evidence whenever possible.

SUMMARY

1 A research report is the presentation of the research findings to a specific audience for a specific purpose. The presentation can be written or given orally, or both.

2 Some guidelines for making written and oral reports are (a) consider the audience, (b) be concise yet complete, and (c) be objective yet effective.

3 The main elements of the written report are (a) the title page, (b) the table of contents, (c) the management summary, (d) the body of the report, (e) the conclusions and recommendations, and (f) the appendix.

4 The research data can be presented in tabular or graphic form. Three types of graphic forms are (a) the pie chart, (b) the bar chart, and (c) the line chart.

DISCUSSION QUESTIONS

1 Why is the research report important?

2 What general guidelines exist for the preparation of written research reports?

3 How might an oral presentation supplement a written research report?

4 What components are typically included in a research report?

5 What are the alternative means of displaying data graphically?

6 MINICASE

You are giving a presentation of a marketing research report related to which new advertising campaign your food product employer should run for its new low-fat snack cookies. There has been a great deal of debate among the marketing managers about whether the product should take a "health" position or a "taste" position. Your research has results related to this positioning issue, as well as the test results for the copy test of ads for each position. Discuss how you would handle the following events at the presentation.

a One manager keeps interrupting you to ask questions about issues that will be presented later in your report.

b A professional health positioning manager argues that your whole research seems to have too small a sample ($n = 300$), has a sample that was collected improperly (you used a syndicated ad testing service mall intercept), and that the statistical test (the z test) is suspect due to the lack of an underlying normal distribution in the population. These and other similar technical arguments arose when your early results seemed to question health positioning.

c A professional taste manager draws a conclusion about what the strategy and execution should be—a conclusion that uses your results improperly.

d One manager states, "I don't care what the copy testing results are. That ad will lack true impact in the market place. I've been in this business too long to accept that test result."

e The general manager asks what decision you would make based upon the marketing research.

CASES FOR PART FIVE

CASE 5-1 *The Ann Arbor Metro Times*

The Ann Arbor Metro Times (AAMT) is a weekly entertainment newspaper covering music, arts, and current events. It is distributed free throughout the Ann Arbor, Michigan, metropolitan area. Its revenue is generated largely through the sale of advertising space to local merchants. The *AAMT* was established in 1988 to specifically address the needs of the Ann Arbor area in much the same manner as its parent publication, the *Detroit Metro Times. AAMT* issues include articles on a variety of subjects, music reviews, arts and theater reviews, classified ads, and a detailed current events calendar.

The management of the *AAMT* decided to conduct a mail-in reader survey to identify and gauge its readership. Exhibit 1 presents the questionnaire used in the survey.

CASE QUESTION

1 Prepare a coding manual for the *AAMT*'s questionnaire.

EXHIBIT 1

THE ANN ARBOR METRO TIMES QUESTIONNAIRE

    1 *The Ann Arbor Metro Times* comes out every Wednesday. Not including this issue, how many of the last six issues have you read or looked into?

        (   ) Six
        (   ) Five
        (   ) Four
        (   ) Three
        (   ) Two
        (   ) One
        (   ) This is the first.

2 Under column A, please check the features you read regularly. Under column B, check the one you enjoy the most.

A   **B**

( )   ( ) "Ashes & Diamonds"
( )   ( ) "Toni Swanger"
( )   ( ) "Letters"
( )   ( ) "Rock & Roll Confidential"
( )   ( ) "What's Happening In and Around Ann Arbor"
( )   ( ) "What's Happening In and Around Detroit"
( )   ( ) "Hot Dates"
( )   ( ) "Pick of the Week"
( )   ( ) "Flicks"
( )   ( ) "Mondo Video"
( )   ( ) "Real Astrology"
( )   ( ) "The Comics Page"
( )   ( ) "Detroit Live"
( )   ( ) Classified ads
( )   ( ) Display ads

3 Under column A, check the following *Ann Arbor Metro Times* cover stories of which you read some or all. Under column B, also please check the one story you enjoyed the most.

A   **B**

( )   ( ) "U-M may Flunk"—a feature about the firing of three faculty members during the McCarthy era
( )   ( ) "Motor City Gothic"—an investigation into the Heinz architecture building in Detroit
( )   ( ) "EYF"—the fashion issue
( )   ( ) "The Greening of Valarie Ackerman"—a profile of a Green Party city council candidate
( )   ( ) "Rob Tyner's Grande Days"—a music feature on Tyner's new band and a look back at MC5
( )   ( ) "Aggressing the Retina"—a profile of Victor Vasaraly, optical artist
( )   ( ) "A Hard Rain's Gonna Fall"—an exposition on Earth Day, environmental efforts and regional events

4 Which of the following stories did you read?

( ) "Cyberpunk Packs Literary Punch—the fiction of Mark Leyner
( ) "Radical Makeover for Ms."—changes at *Ms.* magazine
( ) "Still Faithfull"—interview with Marianne Faithfull
( ) "Dance: Encounter with a Diary"—People Dancing show at Michigan Theater
( ) "Nicaraguan Election Surprises Ann Arbor"—Juigalpa, our sister city
( ) "Film Fest Warms Up"—the 28th annual 16mm Ann Arbor Film Festival
( ) "Are You Ready for 110 Decibels?"—a preview of the Chelsea band, The Holy Cows
( ) "Can't Play Without My Hair"—a preview of Ann Arbor band, Big Chief
( ) "Activist Professor in Residence"—the proposal to establish a visiting "activist" professorship at the University of Michigan

5 What type of music would you like to see more *Ann Arbor Metro Times* coverage of?

( ) Jazz
( ) Classical
( ) Blues
( ) R&B
( ) Hard rock
( ) Heavy metal
( ) Other _____

6 [Deleted]

7 What type of coverage do you like the best?

( ) Music
( ) Visual arts
( ) Investigative news
( ) Profiles
( ) Opinion/essay
( ) Interviews
( ) Photo stories
( ) Other _____

8 Which of the following publications have you looked into or read in the past 7 days?

( ) *The Ann Arbor News*
( ) *The Ann Arbor Observer*
( ) *The Michigan Daily*
( ) *Current*
( ) *The Detroit Free Press*
( ) *The Detroit News*
( ) *Prospect Magazine*
( ) *The University Record*
( ) *Agenda*
( ) *The Michigan Review*
( ) *The New York Times*
( ) *Spotlight*
( ) *Jam Rag*

9 If you could add anything to *The Ann Arbor Metro Times,* what would it be?

_____

_____

_____

10 Your gender.

( ) Female
( ) Male

11 Including yourself, please indicate where people in your household fall in the following age categories.

(   ) 5 years or younger
(   ) 6–11 years
(   ) 12–17 years
(   ) 18–29 years
(   ) 30–49 years
(   ) 50 or older

12 What is your age? _____

13 What is your marital status?

(   ) Single
(   ) Married
(   ) Separated or divorced
(   ) Widowed

14 Which best describes your current employment status?

(   ) Full-time—30+ hours per week
(   ) Part-time—1–29 hours per week
(   ) Retired
(   ) Homemaker
(   ) Volunteer
(   ) Full-time student—12+ credit hours
(   ) Part-time student—1–11 credit hours
(   ) Other _____

15 Please check the box that describes your employment income:

(   ) Under $10,000
(   ) $10,000–14,999
(   ) $15,000–19,999
(   ) $20,000–29,999
(   ) $30,000–39,999
(   ) $40,000–49,999
(   ) $50,000–59,999
(   ) $60,000–69,999
(   ) $70,000–79,999
(   ) $80,000–89,999
(   ) $90,000–99,999

16 In what kind of business, industry, or profession are you employed?

_____

17 What is your highest level of education?

(   ) High school   (   ) Advanced degree: (   ) Master's
(   ) College   (   ) Doctorate
(   ) Postgraduate

18 As your primary place of residence, do you:

(   ) Own a private home
(   ) Own a condo or co-op
(   ) Rent a house
(   ) Rent an apartment
(   ) Live in student housing
(   ) Live in cooperative housing

19 Do you plan to purchase a house, condo, or co-op in the next 12 months?

(   ) Yes
(   ) No

20 Do you plan to rent an apartment in the next 12 months?

(   ) Yes
(   ) No

21 Please indicate which of the following activities you have actively participated in, within the last 12 months.

(   ) Adult education courses
(   ) Antique shopping
(   ) Aerobics
(   ) Bicycling (outdoor)
(   ) Cooking for leisure
(   ) Golf
(   ) Hiking or camping
(   ) Jogging or distance running
(   ) Outdoor gardening
(   ) Photography
(   ) Racquet sports
(   ) Sailing
(   ) Canoeing or kayaking

22 How many times have you gone to the movies in the last 30 days? _____

23 How many times have you attended a lecture or seminar open to the public in the last 60 days? _____

24 How many times have you gone to the following in the last 30 days?

_____ Art gallery
_____ Dance performance
_____ Live theater
_____ Concert (pop, rock, other)
_____ Concert (classical)
_____ Bar in which you consumed an alcoholic beverage
_____ Restaurant in which you ate lunch
_____ Restaurant in which you ate dinner

25 Please indicate how many of the following items you have purchased in the past 12 months.

_____ Compact disk
_____ Hardcover book
_____ Paperback book
_____ Record album
_____ Prerecorded cassette
_____ Prerecorded videocassette

26 Please indicate which of the following items you or other members of your household have bought in the last 12 months.

( ) Car stereo
( ) Home stereo system
( ) CD player
( ) Videocassette recorder
( ) Video camcorder
( ) Camera
( ) Personal computer
( ) Car phone
( ) Small household appliance (toaster, blender, etc.)
( ) Lamp
( ) Blinds
( ) Couch, sofa, loveseat
( ) Health club membership
( ) Bicycle

27 How many passenger cars are currently owned by all the people in your household?

_____ Please indicate make/year for each car: _____

Purchased new ( ) or used ( )

Purchased new ( ) or used ( )

Purchased new ( ) or used ( )

Purchased new ( ) or used ( )

28 Do you or members of your household plan to purchase a new or used car for personal use only in the next 12 months?

( ) Yes
( ) No
If yes, check the type you will purchase:
( ) New car
( ) Used car

CASE 5-2 Midwest Marketing Research Associates (B)

This case presents the coding manual proposed for the draft questionnaire in the Midwest Marketing Research Associates (A) case (Case 3-8).

CASE QUESTIONS

1 Critically evaluate the coding manual. Make specific recommendations for changes.

2 Use the questionnaire in a personal interview, and use the coding manual to code it.

CODING MANUAL

File column	Question number	Variable number	Description	Format	Coding notes
1–3	—	1	Respondent number.	I3	3-digit number 001-999
4	—	2	Mode of interview.	I1	1 = personal 2 = telephone
5	1	3	Where buy food?	I1	0 = no response 1 = supermarket chain 2 = independent grocer 3 = farmer's market 4 = convenience store 5 = other
6	2	4	Store helpful?	I1	0 = no response 1 = yes 2 = no
7	3	5	Read label?	I1	0 = no response 1 = yes 2 = no
8	4	6	Hesitant to buy food without label information?	I1	0 = no response 1 = yes 2 = no
9	5a	7	Information from food labels?	I1	0 = no response 1 = yes 2 = no
10–11	5a	8	Kind of information from labels?	I2	00 = no response 01 = ingredients 02 = vitamins 03 = % of U.S. RDA 04 = additives 05 = warnings 06 = calorie content 07 = preservatives 09 = cholesterol levels 10 = sodium 11 = taste of "nutritious" foods 12 = manufacturer's claims and reputation

File column	Question number	Variable number	Description	Format	Coding notes
					13 = general information
					14 = 5 and 9
					15 = 1 and 3
					16 = 1, 4, and 11
					17 = 4 and 5
					18 = 1, 3, 4, and 9
					19 = 1 and 9
					20 = 7 and 10
					21 = 1, 8, and 10
					22 = 1, 4, and 9
					23 = 1, 8, and 9
					24 = 2, 8, and 9
					25 = 8 and 9
					26 = 4 and 12
					27 = 4, 9, and 12
					28 = 1, 3, and 4
					29 = 4 and 9
					30 = 3 and 8
					31 = 6 and 10
					32 = 4 and 8
					33 = 3 and 9
					99 = other
12	5b	9	Information from friends or relatives?	I1	0 = no response 1 = yes 2 = no
13–14	5b	10	Kind of information from friends or relatives.	I2	(Same code as variable 8)
15	5c	11	Information from advertisements?	I1	0 = no response 1 = yes 2 = no
16–17	5c	12	Kind of information from advertisements.	I2	(Same code as variable 8)
18	5d	13	Information from books?	I1	0 = no response 1 = yes 2 = no
19–20	5d	14	Kind of information from books.	I2	(Same code as variable 8)
21	5e	15	Information from magazines?	I1	0 = no response 1 = yes 2 = no
22–23	5e	16	Kind of information from magazines.	I2	(Same code as variable 8)
24	5f	17	Information from doctor?	I1	0 = no response 1 = yes 2 = no
25–26	5f	18	Kind of information from doctor.	I2	(Same code as variable 8)

File column	Question number	Variable number	Description	Format	Coding notes
27	5g	19	Information from store clerks?	I1	0 = no response 1 = yes 2 = no
28–29	5g	20	Kind of information from store clerks.	I2	(Same code as variable 8)
30	6a	21	Most useful information source.	I1	0 = no response 1 = advertisements 2 = books 3 = store clerks 4 = food labels 5 = friends or relatives 6 = magazines 7 = doctor
31	6b	22	Second most useful information source.	I1	0 = no response 1 = advertisements 2 = books 3 = doctor 4 = food labels 5 = friends or relatives 6 = store clerks 7 = magazines
32–33	7	23	Problems finding information.	I1	00 = no response 01 = no sales clerks to help 02 = information not on label 03 = information on label confusing 04 = information on label hard to find 05 = conflicting sources of information 06 = cannot read the label 07 = other problems
34	8	24	Special diet?	I1	00 = no response 01 = no 02 = yes
35	9	25	Adequate information?	I1	00 = no response 01 = no 02 = yes
36	10	26	Other types of information would like to see.	I1	0 = no response 1 = ingredients 2 = sodium 3 = vitamins and minerals 4 = calories 5 = sugar 6 = fat 7 = cholesterol 9 = other

File column	Question number	Variable number	Description	Format	Coding notes
37	11	27	Deserve nutrition information?	I1	0 = no response 1 = yes 2 = no
38	12	28	Like to see more information?	I1	0 = no response 1 = yes 2 = no
39	14a	29	Purchase cereal?	I1	For each variable, columns 39–44:
40	14b	30	Purchase frozen vegetables?	I1	0 = no response
41	14c	31	Purchase soup?	I1	1 = don't purchase
42	14d	32	Purchase juice?	I1	2 = every week
43	14e	33	Purchase fruit?	I1	3 = every 2 to 3 weeks
44	14f	34	Purchase TV dinners?	I1	4 = once a month or less 5 = don't know
45	15a	35	Look for breakfast cereal information?	I1	For each variable, columns 45–50: 1 = yes
46	15b	36	Look for frozen vegetable information?	I1	2 = no
47	15c	37	Look for soup information?	I1	
48	15d	38	Look for juice information?	I1	
49	15e	39	Look for fruit information?	I1	
50	15f	40	Look for TV dinner information?	I1	
51	16a	41	Ease in finding information about cereal.	I1	0 = no response 1 = very easy 2 = somewhat easy 3 = neutral 4 = somewhat difficult 5 = very difficult
52	16a	42	Reason for difficulty.	I1	0 = no response 1 = not on label 2 = no information books available 3 = information sources conflict 4 = too many cereals to compare
53	16b	43	Ease in finding information about vegetables.	I1	0 = no response 1 = very easy 2 = somewhat easy 3 = neutral 4 = somewhat difficult 5 = very difficult
54	16b	44	Reason for difficulty.	I1	0 = no response 1 = ice on label makes it hard to read 2 = information not on label 3 = no published information

File column	Question number	Variable number	Description	Format	Coding notes
55	16c	45	Ease in finding information about soup.	I1	0 = no response 1 = very easy 2 = somewhat easy 3 = neutral 4 = somewhat difficult 5 = very difficult
56	16c	46	Reason for difficulty.	I1	0 = no response 1 = ingredients not on label 2 = in-house brands not labeled 0 = sources conflict 4 = not published in books
57	16d	47	Ease in finding information about juice.	I1	0 = no response 1 = very easy 2 = somewhat easy 3 = neutral 4 = somewhat difficult 5 = very difficult
58	16d	48	Reason for difficulty.	I1	0 = no response 1 = conflicting information between brands so can't believe any of it 2 = books only have information on national brands 3 = no information on labels
59	16e	49	Ease in finding information about fruit.	I1	0 = no response 1 = very easy 2 = somewhat easy 3 = neutral 4 = somewhat difficult 5 = very difficult
60	16e	50	Reason for difficulty.	I1	0 = no response 1 = conflicting information between brands so can't believe any 2 = books only have information on national brands or fresh fruits 3 = no information on labels 4 = regional brands not in books 5 = regional brands rarely labeled
61	16f	51	Ease in finding information about TV dinners.	I1	0 = no response 1 = very easy 2 = somewhat easy 3 = neutral 4 = somewhat difficult 5 = very difficult

File column	Question number	Variable number	Description	Format	Coding notes
62	16g	52	Reason for difficulty.	I1	0 = no response 1 = so many brands makes it confusing 2 = packages are cold so don't bother to read labels 3 = hard to estimate portions of each food in the meal
63	17	53	Information influence on brand decision?	I1	0 = no response 1 = yes 2 = no
64	18	54	Information influence to try new products?	I1	0 = no response 1 = yes 2 = no
65	19	55	Helpful if store posted information?	I1	0 = no response 1 = yes 2 = no
66	20	56	Kinds of information would like to see.	I1	0 = no response 1 = ingredients 2 = sodium 3 = vitamins and minerals 4 = calories 5 = sugar 6 = fat 7 = cholesterol 99 = other
67	21	57	How would opinion of store be affected?	I1	0 = no response 1 = much lower 2 = somewhat lower 3 = same 4 = somewhat higher 5 = much higher
68	22	58	More likely to shop at store where nutrition information posted?	I1	0 = no response 1 = yes 2 = no
69	23	59	Would use posted information?	I1	0 = no response 1 = yes 2 = no
70	24a	60	Most useful format.	I1	0 = no response 1 = matrix 2 = summary 3 = complete
71	24b	61	Second most useful format.	I1	0 = no response 1 = matrix 2 = summary 3 = complete

File column	Question number	Variable number	Description	Format	Coding notes
72	24c	62	Least useful format.	I1	0 = no response 1 = matrix 2 = summary 3 = complete
73–74 75–76 77–78	25 26 27	63 64 65	Why most helpful? Why second most helpful? Why least helpful?	I1 I1 I1	Use for columns 73–78: 00 = no response 01 = gives all the desired information 02 = not confusing 03 = easy to understand 04 = summarizes everything 05 = quickest comparison 06 = too summarized 07 = not enough information 08 = nutrition quotient confusing 09 = 1 and 7 10 = 1 and 3 11 = 4 and 5 12 = 6 and 7 13 = 4 and 6 99 = other
79	28	66	Too many vitamins harmful?	I1	0 = no response 1 = yes 2 = no
80	29	67	Variety of foods sufficient nutrition?	I1	0 = no response 1 = yes 2 = no
81	30	68	Fortification sufficient?	I1	0 = no response 1 = yes 2 = no
82	31a	69	More nutritious food?	I1	0 = no response 1 = beef 2 = turkey
83	31b	70	More nutritious food?	I1	0 = no response 1 = apple juice 2 = tomato juice
84	32	71	Marital status.	I1	0 = no response 1 = single 2 = married 3 = widowed 4 = divorced
85	33	72	Age bracket.	I1	0 = no response 1 = 18–24 2 = 25–34 3 = 35–44 4 = 45–54

File column	Question number	Variable number	Description	Format	Coding notes
					5 = 55–64
					6 = 65+
86–87	34	73	Occupation.	I1	00 = no response
					01 = laid off or unemployed but seeking employment
					02 = student
					03 = unskilled labor
					04 = semiskilled labor
					05 = skilled labor
					06 = clerical or salesperson
					07 = self-employed in business
					08 = professional or technical person (lawyer, medical, etc.)
					09 = housewife or househusband
					10 = retired or disabled
					11 = "free spirit"
88	35	74	Education.	I1	0 = no response
					1 = grade school
					2 = some high school
					3 = high school graduate
					4 = some college, trade, or technical school
					5 = college graduate
					6 = postgraduate
89	36	75	Children.	I1	0 = no response
					1 = yes
					2 = no
90	37	76	Children 1–5.	I1	For each age group, columns 90–93:
91	37	77	Children 6–12.	I1	0 = no response
92	37	78	Children 13–19.	I1	1 = none
93	37	79	Children 20+.	I1	2 = one
					3 = two
					4 = three
					5 = four
					6 = five or more
					7 = other
94–95	38	80	No children home.	F2.0	2-digit number
96	39	81	Total residents.	I1	0 = no response
					1 = none
					2 = one
					3 = two
					4 = three
					5 = four
					6 = five
					7 = six
					8 = seven
					9 = eight or more

File column	Question number	Variable number	Description	Format	Coding notes
97	40	82	Income.	I1	0 = no response 1 = under $7500 2 = $7500–$12,000 3 = $12,000–$18,000 4 = $18,000–$27,000 5 = $27,000–$45,000 6 = $45,000–$60,000 7 = over $60,000
98	41	83	Send copy of results?	I1	0 = no response 1 = yes 2 = no
99	42 (37–38)	84	Stage in life cycle (see appendix).*	I1	0 = no response 1 = bachelor stage 2 = newly married couple 3 = full nest 4 = full nest II 5 = full nest III 6 = empty nest 7 = empty nest II 8 = solitary survivor in labor force 9 = solitary survivor retired

* In order to properly assign respondent to life-cycle categories: (1) read the appendix, "An Overview of the Life Cycle"; (2) determine from responses to questions 37 and 38 which life cycle your respondent belongs to; (3) record the appropriate response.

Appendix An Overview of the Life Cycle[1]

Bachelor Stage: Young Single People Not Living at Home

Few financial burdens
Fashion opinion leaders
Recreation-oriented
Buy: Basic kitchen equipment, basic furniture, cars, equipment for the mating game, vacations

Newly Married Couples: Young, No Children

Better off financially than they will be in near future
Highest purchase rate and highest average purchase of durables
Buy: Cars, refrigerators, stoves, sensible and durable furniture, vacations

Full Nest I: Youngest Child Under 6

Home purchasing at peak
Liquid assets low
Dissatisfied with financial position and amount of money saved

[1]William D. Wells and George Gubar, "The Life Cycle Concept in Marketing Research," *Journal of Marketing Research,* p. 362, November 1966.

Interested in new products
Like advertised products
Buy: Washers, dryers, TV sets, baby food, chest rubs and cough medicine, vitamins, dolls, wagons, sleds, skates

Full Nest II: Youngest Child 6 or Over

Financial position better
Some wives work
Less influenced by advertising
Buy larger sized packages, multiple-unit deals
Buy: Many foods, cleaning materials, bicycles, music lessons, pianos

Full Nest III: Older Married Couples with Dependent Children

Financial position still better
More wives work
Some children get jobs
Hard to influence with advertising
High average purchase of durables
Buy: New, more tasteful furniture; auto travel; unnecessary appliances; boats; dental services; magazines

Empty Nest I: Older Married Couples, No Children Living with Them, Head in Labor Force

Home ownership at peak
Most satisfied with financial position and money saved
Interested in travel, recreation, self-education
Make gifts and contributions
Not interested in new products
Buy: Vacations, luxuries, home improvements

Empty Nest II: Older Married Couples, No Children Living at Home, Head Retired

Drastic cut in income
Keep home
Buy: Medical appliances; medical care; products which aid health, sleep, and digestion

Solitary Survivor, in Labor Force

Income still good but likely to sell home

Solitary Survivor, Retired

Same medical and product needs as other retired group; drastic cut in income; special need for attention, affection, and security

CASE 5-3   Milan Food Cooperative (B)

The data presented in the Milan Food Cooperative (A) (Case 4-1) was subjected to correlation and regression analysis with the following three objectives in mind.

TABLE 1   CORRELATION RESULTS

	Expenditures	Persons	Income	Children 6–8	Children < 6	Education	Age
Expenditures	—						
Persons	.43	—					
Income	.38	.16	—				
Children 6–18	.40	.70	.19	—			
Children < 6	.16	.56	−.01	.25	—		
Education	.23	.11	.48	.11	.11	—	
Age	.07	.02	.14	.08	−.32	−.03	—

1 Determination of the strength of association between families' food spending and demographic characteristics (correlation and regression)

2 Determination of a function by which we can estimate a family's spending from its demographic data (regression)

3 Determination of the statistical "confidence" in the above tests

The variables included in this analysis were as follows:

1 Weekly food expenditures ($)

2 Number of persons in household

3 Total annual income of household ($)

4 Children, 6–18 years old (0 or 1)

5 Children, < 6 years old (0 or 1)

6 Education of head of household (5 levels)

7 Age of head of household (years)

Assume for the purposes of interpreting the results of this analysis, presented in Tables 1 and 2, that the 500 households used are randomly selected from a much larger population of households.

TABLE 2   REGRESSION RESULTS
Six-Variable Regression: Weekly Food Expenditures in Dollars

Variable	Coefficient	Standard error	t	Significance level
Constant	13.78	4.95	2.78	.0056
Persons	3.51	.71	4.94	.0000
Children < 6	−1.87	2.23	−.84	.3998
Children 6–18	5.30	2.30	2.31	.0215
Education	1.11	.76	1.47	.1431
Income	.768	.13	5.99	.0000
Age	.025	.069	.37	.7088
$R^2 = 0.296$	Error = 17.65			

CASE QUESTIONS

1 For the correlation results:
   a What interpretation can you give to the results shown?
   b What assumptions underlie your interpretations?
   c How could these assumptions be tested?
2 For the regression results:
   a What interpretation can you give to these results?
   b What assumptions underlie your interpretations?
   c How could these assumptions be tested?
   d Does the low R^2 imply that our independent variables are poor predictors of food expenditures?
   e Support your position.

CASE 5-4   Bernie's Student Cafeteria

James Burnett was head of Southwest University (SU) food services. SU had a student population of 25,000 and a faculty of 1800. In the fall of 1994, SU food service had opened a 24-hour cafeteria on central campus for SU students and faculty. "Bernie's" offered breakfast from 4:30 A.M. until noon, and complete hot meals between 10 A.M. and 10 P.M. It also served salads, deli sandwiches, pizza, burgers, desserts, and beverages around the clock. The food was high-quality (better than the typical dormitory fare), yet priced lower than comparable food at other restaurants. Students who had meal plans through their dormitories could get, as compensation for missed meals, deductions from their bills when they ate at Bernie's. In addition to food, Bernie's carried morning newspapers and the "essential" school supplies—pens, pencils, paper, and blue books.

One year after the opening of Bernie's, the president of Southwest commissioned Burnett to conduct a study to find out students' opinions about the new 24-hour cafeteria. The university was in dire need of office space, and if students weren't satisfied with Bernie's, the president was going to have it remodeled into offices. The president was most particularly interested in: (1) student awareness of Bernie's, (2) student use of the 24-hour cafeteria, and (3) overall student satisfaction with Bernie's. Since Burnett was fairly certain that the study results would favor keeping Bernie's, he decided to include questions in the survey that would help him to improve the existing services. Burnett wanted to know what specific things the students liked and disliked about Bernie's, and what they felt could be added or improved upon.

The questionnaire for the study was designed, pretested, and finalized by the University Research Center (URC). The version that was finally administered to students appears in Exhibit 1. A URC computer generated a simple random sample of 1300 students for the purposes of the study. In January 1996 these students were mailed copies of the questionnaire. Burnett purposely chose January because it was long enough after the initial opening and far enough into the school year for an optimal number of students to have been exposed to Bernie's. The ques-

(Continued on p. 716.)

EXHIBIT 1

QUESTIONNAIRE

1 How often do you eat out?
_____ Less than once a month
_____ One to three times a month
_____ Once a week
_____ Two to three times a week
_____ More than three times a week

2 Please rank the following characteristics in order of their importance to you when you dine out. (1 — most important)
_____ Food
_____ Service
_____ Atmosphere
_____ Price

3 What type of food do you usually eat when you dine out?
_____ Breakfast
_____ Deli sandwiches
_____ Salad bar
_____ Typical "fast food" (burgers, fries, hot dogs, etc.)
_____ Pizza
_____ Complete meals (hot entrees)
_____ Other (please specify) _____

4 Are you aware that the University Food Service has a 24-hour cafeteria, Bernie's, located on central campus?   Yes _____   No _____

5 Have you ever eaten at Bernie's?   Yes _____   No _____
If you have never been to Bernie's, please skip to question 9.

6 How many times since its opening in September 1984 have you eaten at Bernie's?
_____ 1
_____ 2–5
_____ 6–10
_____ 11–15
_____ More than 15

7 Based on your experience with Bernie's, we would like you to rank the following list of items as excellent (E), good (G), fair (F), or poor (P).

Item	E	G	F	P
Service				
Friendly	____	____	____	____
Courteous	____	____	____	____
Quick	____	____	____	____
Order taken correctly	____	____	____	____
Other _____	____	____	____	____
Overall service	____	____	____	____
Food				
Appearance	____	____	____	____
Taste	____	____	____	____

Variety	___	___	___	___
Portion size	___	___	___	___
Other _____	___	___	___	___
Overall service	___	___	___	___

Atmosphere

Cleanliness	___	___	___	___
Noise level	___	___	___	___
Adequate seating	___	___	___	___
Other _____	___	___	___	___
Overall atmosphere	___	___	___	___
Overall experience	___	___	___	___

8 How do Bernie's prices compare with the prices of similar foods at other restaurants?

	Bernie's price:					
	Not sure	Much higher	Somewhat higher	About the same	Somewhat lower	Much lower
Food item						
Breakfast	___	___	___	___	___	___
Burgers	___	___	___	___	___	___
Fries	___	___	___	___	___	___
Hot entries	___	___	___	___	___	___
Deli sandwiches	___	___	___	___	___	___
Pizza	___	___	___	___	___	___
Salad bar	___	___	___	___	___	___
Desserts	___	___	___	___	___	___
Beverages	___	___	___	___	___	___

Overall, Bernie's prices are:
_____ Much higher
_____ Somewhat higher
_____ About the same
_____ Somewhat lower
_____ Much lower
_____ I'm not sure

9 Do you plan to eat at Bernie's within the next month?
Yes _____ No _____ Don't know _____

10 Personal Information:
  a What is your age? _____
  b Male or female? _____
  c Married or single? _____
  d Are you a full-time or a part-time student? _____
  f If you do not live in university housing, about how many miles are you from central campus?
    _____ Less than ½ mile
    _____ ½ mile up to (but not including) 1 mile
    _____ 1 mile up to (but not including) 2 miles
    _____ 2 miles or more

g Do you have a meal contract through the university? _____

h Please indicate number of years you have attended Southwest (as of May 1986).

_____ Less than 1

_____ 1

_____ 2

_____ 3

_____ 4

_____ More than 4

i Please list the first three digits of your hometown zip code: _____

Additional comments: Please feel free to make any complaints or suggestions regarding Bernie's in the space provided below.

Thank you for your cooperation in responding to this survey. Please mail your completed questionnaire within 7 days. A postage-paid envelope has been provided for your convenience.

tionnaire was mailed with a cover letter and a return envelope. A copy of Bernie's menu and two coupons for $1 off any $5 purchase at Bernie's were included as incentives. The cover letter contained a request for cooperation and assured the students of anonymity. It requested that the students complete the questionnaire and return it within 7 days. Due to time constraints, questionnaires returned after 2 weeks were not included in the study.

Forty-nine percent (637) of the questionnaires were returned within 2 weeks after the mailing. Twenty of those were not usable, leaving 47 percent suitable for analysis. This was unusually high—the last university-conducted mail survey had had only a 28 percent return rate. Burnett was extremely pleased with the success of the study. He had to give a presentation to the president in 2 days, so he sat down to begin analyzing the results. Exhibit 2 is a copy of the results as presented to Burnett by URC.

EXHIBIT 2

RESULTS

TABLE 1   HOW OFTEN DO YOU EAT OUT?
($n = 617$)

Less than once a month	21.1%
One to three times a month	34.5
Once a week	27.5
Two to three times a week	10.5
More than three times a week	6.3

TABLE 2 IMPORTANCE OF RESTAURANT CHARACTERISTICS WHEN DINING OUT
[1 = Most important (n = 617)]

Characteristic	Rating			
	1	2	3	4
Food	47.2%	38.2%	14.4%	0.2%
Service	5.2	9.4	36.3	49.1
Atmosphere	15.9	21.2	24.1	38.7
Price	31.8	31.1	25.1	12.0

TABLE 3 ARE YOU AWARE OF BERNIE'S EXISTENCE?
(n = 617)

Yes	97.1%
No	2.9

TABLE 4 HAVE YOU EATEN AT BERNIE'S?
(n = 617)

Yes	82.2%
No	17.8

TABLE 5 HOW MANY TIMES HAVE YOU EATEN AT BERNIE'S?
(n = 488)

1	37.1%
2–5	24.2
6–10	19.3
11–15	15.6
More than 15	3.8

TABLE 6 RATINGS OF SERVICE, FOOD, ATMOSPHERE, AND OVERALL EXPERIENCE AT BERNIE'S
(n = 507)

Characteristic	Average score
Overall food	3.5
Overall service	3.7
Overall atmosphere	2.4
Overall experience	3.1

Respondents rated the items on an "excellent, good, fair, poor" scale. For data analysis, this has been converted into a 4-point numeric scale, with 4 being excellent and 1 being poor. This table presents the average of the respondents' scores.

TABLE 7 DO YOU PLAN TO EAT AT BERNIE'S WITHIN THE NEXT MONTH?
($n = 617$)

Yes	20.3%
No	23.7
Don't know	56.1

TABLE 8 KNOWLEDGE OF BERNIE'S BY YEAR ON CAMPUS
($n = 617$)

wrong

	Years on campus						
Knowledge	Less than 1	1	2	3	4	More	Total
Yes	0%	29.7%	24.4%	18.9%	17.4%	9.6%	100.0%
No	16.7	27.8	22.2	16.7	5.6	11.0	100.0

$p < .005.$ (All tests are chi square.)

TABLE 9 NUMBER OF TIMES HAVING EATEN AT BERNIE'S BY HOW OFTEN EATEN OUT
($n = 488$)

wrong

Number of times eaten at Bernie's	Eating-out frequency					
	Less than once a month	1–3 times a month	Once a week	2–3 times a week	More than 3 times a week	Total
Once	32.0%	33.1%	29.3%	3.3%	2.3%	100.0%
2–5	26.3	36.4	26.3	4.2	6.8	100.0
6–10	10.6	39.4	24.5	19.1	6.4	100.0
11–15	0	38.2	28.9	22.4	10.5	100.0
More	0	5.3	26.3	26.3	42.1	100.0

$p < .005.$

TABLE 10 UNIVERSITY MEAL CONTRACT BY NUMBER OF TIMES EATEN AT BERNIE'S
($n = 488$)

right

Meal contract?	Times eaten at Bernie's					
	1	2–5	6–10	11–15	More	Total
Yes	13.8%	32.4%	35.7%	10.0%	8.1%	100.0%
No	22.3	30.6	33.5	9.7	4.0	100.1

$p < .1.$

TABLE 11 DISTANCE FROM CENTRAL CAMPUS BY HAVING EATEN AT BERNIE'S
($n = 545$)

right

Eaten at Bernie's	Distance from campus				
	In dorm	Less than 1 mile	1 mile	1–2 miles	2+ miles
Yes	90.0%	84.5%	85.6	65.6%	15.0%
No	10.0	15.5	14.4	34.4	85.0
Total	100.0	100.0%	100.0%	100.0%	100.0%

$p < .005.$

718

TABLE 12 OVERALL EXPERIENCE BY INTENT TO EAT AT BERNIE'S IN THE NEXT MONTH
($n = 507$)

Rating of overall experience	Intend to eat at Bernie's in next month (% of those who gave yes/no responses)			
	Yes	No	Don't know	Total
Excellent	70.7%	29.3%	57	100%
Good	63.2	36.8	000	100
Fair	6.4	93.6	0	100
Poor	0	100.0	0	100

$p < .005.$

TABLE 13 HAVING EATEN AT BERNIE'S BY SEX
($n = 617$)

Eaten at Bernie's	Male	Female
Yes	42.0%	58.0%
No	26.4	73.6

$p < .005.$

TABLE 14 TYPE OF FOOD USUALLY EATEN WHEN DINING OUT BY SEX
($n = 617$)

Food Type	Male	Female
Breakfast	14.0%	4.0%
Deli sandwiches	12.0	10.1
Salad bar	7.9	18.9
Typical "fast food" (burgers, fries, hot dogs, etc.)	19.0	13.1
Pizza	26.0	29.9
Complete meals (hot entrees)	21.1	24.0
Other (please specify)	0	0
Total	100.0%	100.0%

$p < .005.$
Note: Totals may not add to 100% due to rounding error.

CASE QUESTIONS

1 What conclusions can be drawn on the basis of the univariate analysis?
2 What conclusions can be drawn on the basis of the bivariate analysis? Be sure to write down the relevant conclusion for each cross-tabular table. Are all the percentages cast in the correct direction to aid in your interpretation?
3 Indicate which bivariate tables should be elaborated. Be specific with respect to the control variables you would use and with respect to the effect the elaboration might have on the conclusions drawn from the bivariate table.
4 Write a management summary of the major findings of this study.

CASE 5-5 Southern Illinois Medical Center*

INTRODUCTION

The Southern Illinois Medical Center (SIMC) was a small hospital and clinic located in a small rural community in southern Illinois. Its focus was on primary health care, with a few specialties. Most patients in need of specialty care were referred to larger urban-based hospitals outside the SIMC area.

The advent of managed health care in the United States had raised major concerns for the management of SIMC. These managed health care businesses operated health maintenance organizations (HMOs) that attempted to tie the patient to its group of hospitals and clinics for both primary and specialty health care. Thus, there was concern that much of SIMC's patient base would join an urban-based HMO, and then by-pass SIMC for their primary medical care. This would have devastating financial consequences to SIMC and limit its capacity to serve its remaining rural patients.

MARKETING RESEARCH STUDY

A marketing research study of this issue was undertaken to determine the driving factors behind the choice of local rural versus urban hospital. A survey of 500 rural consumers of health care was conducted by mail. A total of 260 usable questionnaires were realized in this study. One key area of data in the survey was consumer perceptions of two potential hospitals: their local hospital (like SIMC) and a more distant urban hospital. The comparison was on a list of quality-related attributes believed to be related to the consumer's evaluation of overall quality. Attributes were rated on a 7-point scale with anchor points of "outstanding" and "poor."

In addition, the study collected data on the perceived out-of-pocket cost of utilizing out-of-area hospitals, as well as perceptions of travel time and distance to alternative hospitals. Consumers' current hospital utilization and future utilization intentions were also collected.

RESULTS

One part of the data analysis of the survey involved a factor analysis of the quality-related attributes. Table 1 presents the results of this factor analysis. An oblique rotation of factors was used to allow for the expected correlation of underlying dimensions. Four significant factors were found with the following correlation

*Source: Based on an article by Sandra K. Smith Gooding, "Hospital Outshopping and Perceptions of Quality: Implication for Public Policy," *Journal of Public Policy and Marketing*, vol. 13, no. 2, pp. 271–280, Fall 1994.

TABLE 1   FACTOR ANALYSIS RESULTS

	Factor 1	Factor 2	Factor 3	Factor 4
Staff courtesy (AH)	.790			
Staff compassion (AH)	.809			
Access (AH)	.771			
Building condition (AH)	.679			
Dependability (AH)	.648			
Quality of medical care (AH)	.669			−.273
Staff competency (AH)	.640			
Confidentiality (AH)	.649			
Hospital reputation (AH)	.495			−.373
Emergency care (AH)	.443			−.403
Staff compassion (LH)		.846		
Staff courtesy (LH)		.786		
Dependability (LH)		.796		
Staff competency (LH)		.733		
Hospital reputation (LH)		.666		
Emergency care (LH)		.645		
Quality of medical care (LH)		.659	.331	
Access (LH)		.682		
Building condition (LH)		.563		
Confidentiality (LH)		.494	.241	
Level of technology (LH)			.756	
Range of services (LH)			.702	
Size of hospital (LH)		.317	.333	
Level of technology (AH)				−.915
Range of services (AH)				−.888
Size of hospital (AH)				−.403
Percent of variance	32.10	24.40	3.30	3.10
Eigenvalue	8.34	6.35	.86	.82

LH = local hospital.
AH = alternative hospital.

among factors: between 1 and 2, .144; between 1 and 4, −.610; between 2 and 3, .479; between 2 and 4, .101; and between 3 and 4, .079.

CASE QUESTIONS

1 What overall managerial conclusions would you draw for the management of SIMC based upon the results of the factor analysis?
2 Which factors are the most important? Why do you conclude this?
3 How would you interpret the managerial relevance of the correlation among the factors?
4 How would you expect an orthogonal rotation of factors to change the results of the factor analysis?
5 How could these factor analysis results be utilized with the cost perceptions data, and hospital choice intentions data that were collected, to provide meaningful managerial conclusions?

CASE 5-6 The Sophisticated Research Group

As part of a major consumer study completed for one of the largest European candy companies, the Sophisticated Research Group prepared the multidimensional scaling map presented in Figure 1. The European candy company was considering introducing some candy bars into the extremely competitive U.S. market.

CASE QUESTIONS

1 What interpretation would you give to the axis of the map?
2 What market opportunities for a new candy bar can be seen in the map?
3 What market segments do you think exist in this map?
  Hint: You must speculate, as no preference data are present.

FIGURE 1 Multidimensional scaling map for candy bars.

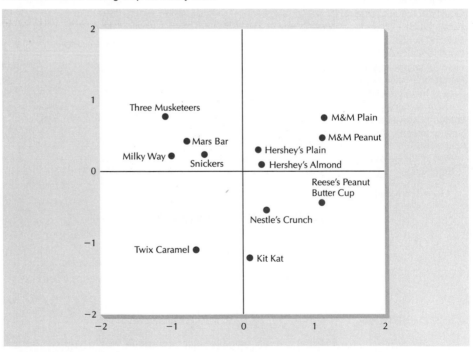

APPLICATIONS

CHAPTER 23

DEMAND MEASUREMENT AND FORECASTING

MARKETING RESEARCH IN ACTION

BET-THE-FIRM SALES FORECASTING

It was 8 P.M. and Debra Clipper was in her office, staying late for yet another night, working on the sales forecast for 1996 for Tele Turbo, Inc. (TTI). TTI was a 2-year-old high-technology start-up company that developed and marketed hardware and software products that allowed businesses to operate extremely efficiently on the so-called information superhighway.

TTI had 30 employees: 15 in product development engineering; 5 in production and logistical support; 5 in marketing and sales; and 5 in administration of finance, personnel, and so forth. Debra was vice president of marketing and sales. She had an extensive educational and employment background in computer networking and telecommunications. However, there seemed to be little in her previous experience at AT&T and IBM that had prepared her for the difficulty and risk associated with preparing a forecast for such a completely new product as TTI's Network Connect product.

Network Connect made use of advanced digital telecommunications lines to allow for the ultra-fast transfer of data and graphics over phone lines. Unlike its major established competitors, Network Connect did not require special dedicated phone lines and extensive phone routing equipment to provide this ultra-fast transfer of data and graphics. TTI's product only required that there be one of its "boxes" at each end of the phone connection, and that its special proprietary software be installed and operational in the boxes. The TTI concept was totally new to the marketplace. It did offer major cost savings but was virtually unknown to potential users. Sales for the first 2 years of TTI's operations had been $100,000 in year one, and $350,000 in year two. The firm needed at least $4 million in sales to break even.

Debra knew the consequences of an inaccurate sales forecast. If the forecast was too low, some potential venture capitalist investors would lose interest in investing in TTI. If the sales forecast was too high and not attained the next year, profitability and cash flow needs would likely mean that the company would need to raise additional cash to survive. With actual sales below forecast, raising additional capital would be almost impossible. Debra knew that the future of the firm as well as her stock options and even her job were at stake as she worked on the sales forecast. How should she approach preparing this forecast? It was late and she was tired, but the board of directors' meeting was next week. The sales forecast needed to be done.

The importance of sales forecasting is well illustrated in this Marketing Research in Action. Even for large firms, the consequences of production planning, service scheduling, materials ordering, sales-force hiring and allocation, profitability, and so forth are large. In this chapter, we present approaches to the measurement and forecasting of demand.

The measurement of demand is an essential activity for an organization. Based on the 1994 American Marketing Association (AMA) survey,[1] about 80 percent of the companies surveyed did research in at least one of the following areas:

1 Determining market characteristics
2 Measuring market potential
3 Short- and long-range forecasting

In this chapter we will define the major concepts and terms in demand measurement and present the methods for measuring demand potential as well as the methods for forecasting demand.

CONCEPTS AND TERMINOLOGY

Demand measurement involves developing a quantitative estimate of demand. Demand can be measured on four dimensions: (1) product, (2) geographic location, (3) time period, and (4) customer. Table 23-1 shows the many levels of measurement possible. Be aware that there are many combinations of these four

---

[1]Thomas C. Kinnear and Ann R. Root, 1994. *Survey of Marketing Research* (Chicago: American Marketing Association, 1994).

TABLE 23-1   FOUR DIMENSIONS OF DEMAND MEASUREMENT AND FORECASTING

Product	Geographic location	Time period	Customer
Industry	World	Current	Consumer
Company	United States	Short-range	Business
Product line	Region	Long-range	Government
Product class	Territory		
Product item			

dimensions (5 $\times$ 4 $\times$ 3 $\times$ 3 = 180), each representing a potential demand measurement and forecasting situation. Each can pose a different type of problem in which the purpose, data availability, and techniques for measurement differ substantially. Let's discuss in detail the concepts and terminology used in measuring these demand situations.

Market Demand

The market demand for a product is a concept that requires careful specification of several elements. For example, consider the following definition of market demand for automobiles: *The 1995 U.S. market demand for automobiles is the total unit volume that was sold by all manufacturers (domestic and foreign) in the United States to all buyers (consumer, business, and government).*

This definition stipulates that the market demand for a *product* is the total volume that *would* be purchased by a defined *customer group* in a defined *time period and geography,* given the 1995 *environment and marketing programs.* Here, market demand refers to a single number, say, 15 million automobiles. If the definition of market demand is expanded to include alternative environments and marketing programs, it becomes apparent that market demand could have been higher or lower than 15 million automobiles, depending on the nature of the marketing programs employed and the state of the environment. Consequently, given alternative environments and marketing programs, market demand can be expressed as a series of numbers or functions rather than a single number.

The importance of recognizing that market demand is a function becomes clear when it is related to the concepts of *market potential* and *market forecast.* Figure 23-1 illustrates the relationship between market potential, market forecast, and market demand function. Market demand is shown to be a function of the level of industry marketing effort plus a given environment. A market forecast is shown to be the level of market demand given an *expected* level of industry marketing effort and an *assumed* environment. Market potential then becomes the *limit* approached by market demand within an assumed environment as industry marketing effort approaches infinity. Market potential therefore establishes an upper limit to market demand, while a market forecast specifies the expected level of market demand for a particular time period.

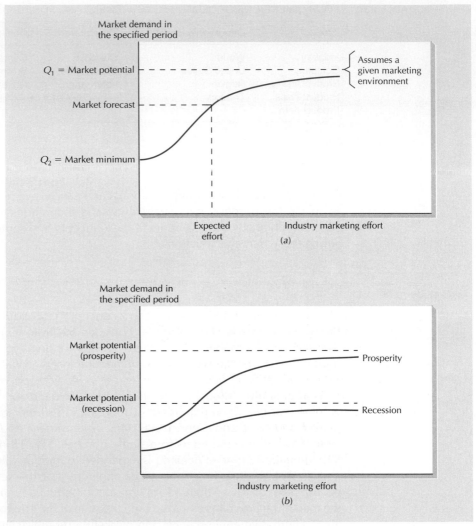

FIGURE 23-1   Market demand concepts and terminology. (*a*) Market demand as a function of industry marketing effort (assumes a particular marketing environment. (*b*) Market demand as a function of industry marketing effort (two different environments assumed). [*Source:* Philip Kotler, *Marketing Management,* 4th ed. (Englewood Cliffs, NJ: Prentice-Hall, 1990), p. 216.]

Company Demand

Company demand is the company's share of the market demand. For example, consider the following definition of company demand: *The 1995 company demand for General Motors is 30 percent of market demand, or 4.5 million automobiles.* Company demand, like market demand, is a function. This function is called the company demand function or sales response function. It describes estimated company sales at alternative levels of company marketing effort. *Com-*

pany sales potential is the limit approached by company demand as company marketing effort increases relative to competitors.

The *company sales forecast* is the expected level of company sales based on a chosen marketing plan and an assumed environment. It is important to recognize that this definition implies that the company sales forecast *does not* establish a basis for deciding on the amount and composition of marketing effort. Rather, this forecast is the *result* of a chosen marketing program and an assumed environment.

Two additional concepts are used in relation to the company forecast. A *sales quota* is the sales goal set for a product line, a company division, or a sales representative. A *sales budget* is a conservative estimate of the expected volume of sales. A sales budget is lower than the company forecast in order to avoid excessive investment in purchasing, production, and cash flow in case the forecast is not realized.

ESTIMATION OF CURRENT DEMAND

Marketing researchers are frequently asked to measure the current market and sales potential for a new product or existing product. Such information is essential for designing sales territories, determining sales quotas, allocating sales-force effort, allocating advertising and sales promotion budgets, determining sales compensation levels, finding prospect accounts, dropping products, and making new-product go, no-go decisions.

It should be recognized that different methods are required for new versus established products or services. The distinction between new and established products is based on whether the product is new to the industry rather than to the individual seller. The research methods for new products tend to be more subjective than those for established products.[2]

The focus of this section will be on methods for estimating potential for established products. These methods may be classified into two groups: breakdown method and buildup method.

Breakdown Method

The breakdown method begins with aggregate industry or market data and breaks down the data into units of interest to the firm. Two approaches are used with the breakdown method—the direct data method and the indirect data method.

Direct Data Method　The direct data method relies on total industry or market data (usually shipments or consumption) as the basis for estimating market and sales potentials. The typical approach is to establish a sales or consumption index based on total industry or market data. If these data are reasonably accurate and timely, potentials based on them are theoretically the most accurate.

Table 23-2 exemplifies the direct data method. A manufacturer of cutting tools

---

[2]For a discussion of methods for evaluating the market potential for new products, see Chapter 24.

needed a market potential index for each of its exclusive industrial distributors. Since trade associations are a primary source of total industry shipments data, the company contacted the American Supply and Machinery Manufacturers Association, which issues a yearly report on sales made through industry distributors by its members. Total shipments are classified by product categories, one of which is "cutting tools." This information is broken down by state and by metropolitan statistical area (MSA).

For example, in Table 23-2, territory number 3 includes the Chicago MSA plus 10 percent of the Illinois sales volume outside the Chicago MSA. The market potential index of .073 for territory number 3 would be determined as follows:

Total cutting tool sales $91,739,531
Illinois sales   12,741,237
Chicago MSA sales   6,025,402

$$\frac{\text{Market potential index}}{\text{for territory 3}} = \frac{(\$12,741,237 - \$6,025,402).1 + \$6,025,402}{\$91,739,531}$$

$$= .073$$

Company sales potential can be derived by estimating the share of market potential available to the firm. The usual approach is: (1) determine the market shares held by the firm in territories or segments where performance is judged to be superior under relevant business conditions, and (2) use these shares to establish sales potentials.

Using this approach, assume that the company has determined that it holds a 20 percent share of the cutting tool business with well-established and effective distributors. Applying the 20 percent share to the market potential of $91,739,531 yields a potential of $18,347,906. Multiplying this sales potential by the market potential index for each distributor yields a distributor sales potential estimate; that is, $18,347,906 × .073 = $1,339,397.

Comparison of potential sales with actual sales indicates that distributors 1 and 4 are close to potential while distributors 2 and 3 are weak. The weak distributors could be investigated to determine why they are not achieving a higher share of

TABLE 23-2   EXAMPLE OF DIRECT DATA METHOD

Exclusive distribution territories	Market potential index: cutting tools	Company sales potential	Actual company sales
1	.009	$ 165,131	$ 159,421
2	.004	73,392	10,734
3	.073	1,339,397	804,793
4	.031	568,785	501,732
⋮	—	—	—
Total		$18,347,906	$12,784,701

potential sales. The cost of exploiting additional sales or the local competitive environment could explain such a deficit.

There are several sources of industry sales data available for this type of analysis. Sales data are recorded by federal and state agencies because of licensing and taxation. Trade associations compile sales data for an array of business organizations. A useful guide to many such sources of market potential data is the federal government publication *Measuring Markets.*

The main advantage of using total industry sales to measure market potential is the validity of the data, given they are current and accurate. The direct data method is fairly simple and requires a few basic calculations to determine market and sales potentials.

The direct data method is not used frequently for two reasons. First, detailed industry and sales data are not available for many products and services. Second, when data is available, they may not reflect current market potential due to their historical nature.

Indirect Data Method   The indirect data method for determining market and sales potentials is based on the development of an index of potential from one or more statistical series related to the consumption or purchasing power of the product or service in question. The concept is to logically relate a series of data, such as number of employed persons, to industry sales for the product or service. This second series of data, being more detailed by market segments, may be used to indicate the distribution of industry sales in the market segments of concern. It is important to note that, in order to determine the market potential for an area or segment, it is necessary to have an estimate of total potential in dollars or units.

Table 23-3 illustrates this approach using a *single-factor index* to determine the market and sales potential for a drug item. It assumes that the market potential for drugs is directly related to a single factor, such as population. Since population data are available by states, a simple calculation determines drug market potential by state. Assuming that this drug should achieve a 5 percent share of market, the company sales potential can easily be determined by state.

The limitation of this example is that rarely will a single factor such as population correlate highly with the sales of a product or service. Obviously, drug sales

TABLE 23-3   EXAMPLE OF DIRECT DATA METHOD

States	Population (000)	Population percent	Drug market potential*	Company potential†
Michigan	8,073	.035	$ 350,000	$ 17,500
New York	15,529	.067	670,000	33,500
Florida	7,151	.031	310,000	15,500
⋮	—	—	—	—
Total	230,667	1.00	$10,000,000	$500,000

* Determined by multiplying the population percent by $10 million—total competitive product sales in 1982.
† Determined by multiplying market potential by 5 percent—company-estimated potential share of market.

by state can be influenced by additional factors such as age distribution, disposable income, and number of physicians per thousand people. This leads to developing a *multiple-factor index,* each factor given a specific weight in the index.

A widely used multiple-factor index of area demand is the *Annual Survey of Buying Power* published by *Sales and Marketing Management.* This index is designed to reflect relative buying power in the different regions, states, and metropolitan areas of the nation. It is constructed from three factors—income, retail sales, and population. Income is weighted 5, sales 3, and population 2. For each county in the United States, income, retail sales, and population are determined as a percent of the total. These percentages are weighted as indicated above, then summed, and the total is divided by the sum of weights, which is 10.

A major limitation of such a *general multiple-factor index* is that it assumes the relative market potential in a given area is the same for an array of products. This is a weak assumption for most products. The market potential for powdered soft drinks and hot chocolate mixes differs substantially in a market depending upon the season of the year. Thus, while general multiple-factor indexes may be useful for certain products or certain circumstances, more accurate market potentials may be found by developing special indexes.

The development of *special multiple-factor indexes* is not easy. In preparing such an index, factor selection and weighting can be very judgmental. Whether this judgment is sound or not is difficult to demonstrate since such judgments are based on how closely the indexes obtained correspond to actual sales results. But remember that actual sales results are not available for the purpose of comparison; if they were, there would be no need to develop an index.

For industrial goods, a widely used general single-factor index is *Sales and Marketing Management*'s "Survey of Industrial Purchasing Power." This annual survey provides data on the value of shipments of manufactured products by the Standard Industrial Classification (SIC) industry groups and geographic areas. When this index is used, it is assumed that the value of shipments of an industry is an accurate indicator of the purchasing power of the industry and thus suitable as a single-factor index of market potential.

Buildup Method

This approach to estimating market and sales potentials involves the aggregation, or buildup, of data from the customer or account level to the industry or market level. Data are collected on customers' past purchases or probable requirements for future purchases, and data are classified according to the principal products/services produced, the number of employees, and other relevant statistical series.

These data may be obtained from customers by mail, telephone, or personal interviews. Personal interviews are required for highly technical products or services. Telephone and mail surveys are appropriate when factual data on past purchases and classification data are sought. If a mail survey is to be used, the researcher should be sensitive to the many sources of error possible with this approach.

The buildup method, like the breakdown indirect method, seeks to establish a relationship between the purchase of a given product or service by firms within market groups (e.g., SIC classification) and one or more statistical series (e.g., number of employees). The following example will illustrate the steps in this approach.

Timken, the largest producer of tapered roller bearings, was interested in determining the market and sales potential for its products. Major users and potential users were identified using internal sales records and management expertise. A sample of firms was drawn from this prospect-user list, and members were personally interviewed. The buildup method was used to determine market and sales potentials.

Table 23-4 presents the results of the buildup method for four market segments. The firms surveyed produced both data on their total purchases of tapered roller bearings from all sources for the preceding calendar year and data on the average number of production employees in the firm during the year. The average purchases per employee was calculated from these data for each of the market segments or user industries. The latest data from the *Annual Survey of Manufacturers* were used to estimate the total employment for each user industry. (The employment data represent all firms in the population from which the sample survey is drawn.) In Table 23-4 the market potential for SIC code 3573 was determined by multiplying the average purchases per employee ($23.08) by total number of production employees (78,000) in all firms in the market segment or user industry. Market potentials for states, counties, and smaller geographic areas

TABLE 23-4   EXAMPLE OF THE BUILDUP METHOD

		Market survey data			U.S. total production employees	Estimated U.S. market potentials
SIC code	Industry	Product purchases	Number of production employees	Average purchases per employee	U.S. total production employees	Estimated U.S. market potentials
3573	Computers and related equipment	$201,627	8,736	$23.08	78,000	$1,800,240
3585	Refrigeration and heating equipment	851,552	15,270	54.17	120,000	6,500,400
3721	Aircraft industry	292,692	20,020	14.62	130,000	1,900,600
3811	Engineering and scientific institutions	178,200	4,950	36.00	25,000	900,000

Notes: "Market survey data" are based on personal interviews with known users of roller bearings. "Product purchases" are totals purchased from all suppliers in previous calendar year. "Number of production employees" is the average employment during previous calendar year in user sample firms. "Average purchases per employee" is obtained from product purchases by the number of production employees. "U.S. total production employees" data are estimated from the latest U.S. Bureau of the Census, *Annual Survey of Manufacturers—General Statistics for Industry Groups and Industries.* "Estimated U.S. market potentials" are derived by multiplying "U.S. total production employees" by "average purchases per employee."

were similarly derived by substituting the employment data for these areas in place of the U.S. figures. Each market segment's sales potential was determined by estimating Timken's market share in each sample account and calculating a weighted average market share for each segment. Timken's sales potential in each market segment was determined by multiplying this weighted market share by the market potential.

The buildup method relies on valid published market data through which the survey results can be projected. As we saw, the SIC provides the market data on industrial products for such projections of market and sales potential. It is important enough for us to examine the system a little more closely.

The Standard Industrial Classification   The SIC system was developed by the federal government and is by far the most widely used system of industrial classification. (See Chapter 6.) Most economic data published by U.S. government agencies are organized on the basis of the SIC system. In addition, a growing proportion of data from state and local governments, trade associations, publishing firms, and other private organizations uses the SIC system.

The SIC system covers all economic activities within our society and classifies them into agriculture; forestry and fisheries; mining; construction; manufacturing; transportation; communication; electricity, gas, and sanitary services; wholesale and retail trade; finance, insurance, and real estate; service; and public administration. Within each economic classification, there is a further breakdown into industries and products.

Each firm or business entity is classified within this scheme on the basis of its principal product or business activity, and is given a four-digit code. Related four-digit industries are combined into three-digit groups; in turn these are combined into two-digit major groups.

Products are classified on the basis of five or more digits: the first four digits are based on the industries in which the products are primarily produced. Based on the SIC system, the Commerce Bureau publishes the *Census of Manufacturers,* which contains key manufacturing and sales data.

While the SIC system is a valuable tool, it is not without its drawbacks, some of which are listed below.

1 *Multiproduct establishments.* If an establishment produces two or more products that are classified into more than one four-digit industry, the establishment will be assigned to a single industry, based on its primary activity. This practice leads to a tendency to overstate statistics for principal products and to understate statistics for secondary products.

2 *Captive plants.* An establishment may have a "captive" operation that produces components for its primary and secondary products, although the components are also produced by other firms as a final product.

3 *Varying production and purchasing methods.* This situation makes it difficult to identify potential customers and to estimate market size.

4 *Need for finer classification.* The four-digit classification system results in an aggregation of data that is sometimes dysfunctional for firms interested in specific product markets within the industry.

METHODS FOR FORECASTING DEMAND

In this section we examine forecasting the future demand for a product or service. The topics covered are (1) the importance of sales forecasting; (2) the accuracy of sales forecasting; (3) forecaster qualifications; (4) procedural guidelines for preparing a forecast; (5) management requirements for the forecasting report; and (6) forecasting techniques.

Importance of Forecasting

The forecasting of sales is a critical input to marketing decision making as well as that of other functional areas such as production, finance, and personnel. Poor forecasting can result in excessive inventory, inefficient sales-force expenditures, costly price reductions, lost sales, inefficient scheduling of production, and inadequate planning for cash flow and capital investments.

The importance of forecasting has increased because of the dynamic and hostile environment of the past decades. The shortages and high inflation of the early 1970s, followed by major recessions and high interest rates, plus the recession in the early 1990s, have focused renewed attention on forecasting and the benefits it can provide.

Accuracy of Sales Forecasts

Sales forecasts are numerical estimates of the future sales of products or services of a company or industry. You should realize that sales forecasting is always wrong; that is, the numerical estimates always differ from actual sales results. Consequently, the issue of accuracy is one of how close the forecast is to actual reported sales. But this measure of accuracy is always too late; that is, it comes after the sales have been recorded. Therefore, there is no direct measure of forecasting accuracy ahead of the forecasting period.

If the accuracy of a forecast cannot be determined until after the forecast time period has expired, how can the quality of a forecast be judged beforehand? The answer lies in evaluating the characteristics of the forecasting process. Accurate forecasting, like any marketing research project, should (1) utilize systematic and objective procedures that are sensitive to statistical and nonstatistical sources of error and (2) employ valid data sources that provide timely information of adequate detail to meet the needs of the decision maker.

Forecaster Qualifications

Forecasters should have the level of training and experience appropriate for the requirements of the forecasting task. They can range from persons with bachelor's and master's degrees to highly trained statisticians or econometricians with advanced graduate degrees. The last section of this chapter reviews an array of forecasting techniques. Several require that the forecaster have special knowledge and skills if the techniques are to be used properly. Sophisticated techniques in the hands of unqualified persons can result in inaccurate forecasting.

Another perspective on forecaster qualifications relates to who should be discouraged from sales forecasting despite having the appropriate credentials. There are three types: those who believe that the future is only a straight-line extrapolation of the past, those who substitute arithmetic for sense, and those who think they have the only magic formula.

Procedural Guidelines for Forecasting

The following guidelines are useful in starting a forecasting project:

1 *Define the purpose for which the forecast is intended.* Will the forecast be used to determine sales quotas, to set production levels, or to establish promotion budgets? How accurate must the forecast be for various purposes?

2 *Define the products and product segments.* Is a separate forecast needed for each product? How detailed or segmented should the forecast be?

3 *Prepare an initial forecast.* Recognize that there are various stages to developing a forecast. The first stage is relatively crude and simple but serves the purpose of defining data needs and the formation of hypotheses to be tested.

4 *Relate the forecast to company capabilities and objectives.* The final forecast should be consistent with corporate objectives as well as production, financial, and marketing capabilities.

5 *Review trends in the environment.* The forecast should reflect new variables or changes in the rates of historical variables. Areas such as competition, economic climate, and market trends should be analyzed carefully and incorporated into the forecasting model.

Management Requirements for Forecasting

There are several requirements that the forecaster should be sensitive to in preparing the forecast. From the manager's perspective, the forecast should meet the following requirements:

1 Management should be given an industry (or all-company) forecast as an essential element in the company forecast package.

2 Management should expect a clear, brief statement of the assumptions underlying the forecast.

3 Forecasts should not be unduly qualified.

4 Management should require a clear statement of the period covered.

5 Management is entitled to a forecast that is not changed too often.

6 Details and techniques should be omitted from the forecast unless specifically requested. Most managers prefer this.

7 Management has a right to expect that forecasts be checked against what actually took place.

Sales Forecasting Techniques

Table 23-5 groups eight forecasting techniques into three classifications:

1 *Qualitative methods.* These methods involve collecting judgments or opinions from knowledgeable individuals. These individuals may have access to quantitative or factual information about markets, products, and economic trends, but their judgments represent subjective conclusions on all the knowledge that they deem relevant to the forecasting situation. Such forecasts can use inputs from company management, sales-force personnel, and customers.

2 *Time-series methods.* These methods apply statistical techniques to historical sales data over time to make numerical sales forecasts.

3 *Causal methods.* These methods apply statistical models to historical sales data plus measures of the underlying causes of sales dynamics.

Qualitative Methods   Judgment- or opinion-based forecasting techniques are the most popular methods of forecasting. Table 23-6 shows the frequency of use of these methods (executive consensus, aggregate of sales force, and buyer or consumer surveys) compared to time-series analysis and causal models. Qualitative methods maintain their high usage levels across consumer, industrial, and service industries.

Executive Opinion   This qualitative method involves tapping the judgments of a group of managers regarding the forecast. The method is based on the assumption that several experts can arrive at a better forecast than one expert.

There are a number of ways of combining the judgments of a group of executives. The *group discussion method* involves meeting as a committee and coming up with a group consensus forecast. There is no secrecy among respondents, and communication is encouraged. However, the forecast may not reflect a true consensus in that individual judgments can be influenced by group pressure. A second approach is the *pooled individual estimates method.* Here, each executive separately submits estimates to a project leader who combines them into a single forecast. This procedure overcomes the potential group pressure bias of the open discussion approach. The third approach is called the *Delphi method,* which has become a popular market and technological forecasting approach. Group members are asked to make individual judgments about a forecast. The group judg-

TABLE 23-5   FORECASTING METHODS

Qualitative methods	Time-series methods	Causal methods
Executive opinion	Moving average	Leading indicators
Sales force—distributor estimates	Exponential smoothing	Regression models
Buyer or consumer surveys	Time-series decomposition	

TABLE 23-6   USAGE LEVEL OF MAJOR SALES FORECASTING METHODS
Percentage of Firms' Rating Techniques as First or Second Most Valued

	Category			
Method	All firms	Industrial product	Consumer product	Service
Executive consensus	54	50	64	72
Aggregate of sales force	56	62	40	42
Buyer or consumer surveys	29	35	13	7
Time-series analysis	30	35	46	34
Causal models	15	14	20	36
Number of firms	161	93	39	20

ments are recorded and resubmitted to each group member. After comparing the anonymous judgments with their own, the executives can revise their judgments. In so doing, each person can justify the logic of the forecast that will be communicated to other members. After several iterations, group members typically reach a consensus. The assumption underlying this method is that it yields a more accurate forecast than the previous two methods.

Sales-Force/Distributor Estimates   A common method of sales forecasting, especially among industrial firms (see Table 23-6), is to aggregate individual forecasts of salespeople or distributors. An advantage of this method is that a salesperson or distributor is close to the market and hence a fairly good judge of the peculiarities of demand in a sales region. Such forecasts are fairly accurate in the short run, that is, the next month, quarter, or perhaps year, but they are increasingly unreliable and even meaningless over longer time periods.

One problem with this method is of an administrative nature—getting a salesperson to make a conscientious forecast and turn it in on time. The other problem is one of reliability. Forecasts may be biased upward or downward depending on the motivations of the salesperson or distributor. For example, a sales representative paid on a commission basis may feel that a conservative forecast results in lower sales quotas. A distributor, fearful of potential out-of-stock problems, may project an optimistic forecast. An additional source of bias is the salesperson's or the distributor's ignorance of broad economic trends which would affect sales in that particular region.

Short-term forecasts based on this method can be very helpful if properly conducted using valid data collection procedures. Even when more sophisticated methods are adopted, a salesperson or distributor estimate could always be carried out to serve as a second forecast for comparison purposes.

Buyer or Consumer Surveys   Forecasts can be based on judgments of buyers as to their intended purchase of goods and services. It is most appropriate when there are a limited number of buyers who have clear purchase intentions and are willing to disclose their intentions. Consequently, this method is used more for industrial products than for consumer products or services. (See Table 23-6.)

For many companies, an alternative to going directly to consumers is to subscribe to publications of consumer surveys which reveal broad information of buyer intentions. One such service is the quarterly survey of consumer finances carried out by the Institute for Social Research at the University of Michigan. Other surveys of planned business plant and equipment expenditures are conducted and published by the Securities and Exchange Commission, McGraw-Hill, Inc. (in *Business Week*), the National Industrial Conference Board, and *Fortune* magazine. Information from these sources can be used as input for the executive opinion method.

Time-Series Methods   The time-series approach to forecasting involves the extrapolation of historical sales data forward as a linear or curvilinear trend. This can be done by visual examination or by using statistical techniques. For short-term forecasting, time-series extrapolation can be a very effective tool.

Several conditions are necessary for time-series forecasting to be appropriate. First, it is best suited to rather stable situations in which the future will be mainly an extension of the past. In other words, a time-series forecast is inappropriate for forecasting "turning points." Second, the historical sales data must have clear patterns or trends that are distinctive from the random-error component in the data.

Time-series forecasting raises a number of issues. First, how far back should the historical data go? Do older data represent conditions that have changed and therefore would more likely detract from the accuracy of the forecast? Second, given a time series, how should the data be weighted? Should each time period be given equal weight, or should the most recent observations be given more weight? Third, should the data be decomposed into trend, cycle, season, and error? The following time-series methods differ in how to deal with these issues.

Moving Average   This method uses the average of the last *n* data points as the basis for trend extrapolation. In developing a short-term forecast, the random element in the data set is of major concern. One way to minimize the impact of random error is to average several of the past data points. This consists of weighting *n* of the recently observed data points by $1/n$.

For example, if a marketing manager desired a monthly forecast of product shipments to key accounts, a 12-month moving average could be used. Next month's forecast would be based on data points for the past 12 months. Each month's product shipment data would be given a weight of $1/12$, and the summed weighted values would form the forecast.

This method becomes a "moving" average when new data points become available and they are incorporated in the calculation for the next forecasting period. In addition, when a moving average period is selected which corresponds to a complete seasonal pattern (e.g., 12 months of data cover an annual seasonal sales pattern), the effect of seasonality is removed from the forecast since data points for each period of the season are included in the moving average.

Exponential Smoothing   This approach differs from the moving average method in that it does not use a constant set of weights for the data points. Rather, an exponentially decreasing set of weights is used. Here, the more recent data points receive more weight than older data points. The logic of this approach is that the more recent data are given greater weight, which should result in a more accurate forecast.

There are several different variations of exponential smoothing which build on the application of decreasing weights to older data points. These higher forms of exponential smoothing make adjustments for such things as trend and seasonal patterns.

Time-Series Decomposition   This widely used method consists of measuring four temporal components of a time series: (1) trend, (2) cycle, (3) season, and (4) error.

The trend component results from basic drivers of sales, such as disposable income, population, and technology. It is typically found to be a straight line or a gradually curved line when fitted to the data points.

The cycle component results from fairly systematic changes in the amplitude and periodicity of general economic activity. It is found by fitting a wavelike curve to the sales data.

The seasonal component results from changes in sales levels due to weather, holidays, and so on. It is represented in the data by a consistent pattern of sales for periods within a year (quarters, months, or weeks).

The error component results from such erratic events as price wars, blizzards, and strikes. The analytical problem in time-series decomposition is to separate the error component from the underlying systematic components of trend, cycle, and season.

Causal Methods   Causal models involve statistical techniques relating historical sales data to the economic forces that cause sales to rise or fall. These methods represent the most sophisticated sales forecasting tools. They are most accurate when relevant historical data are available on the major variables causing changes in sales.

The attraction of causal methods lies in three areas. First, they can predict turning points more accurately than time-series methods. Second, causal models have the potential to explain more of the variation in sales data and thus reduce the random-error component to a greater degree than may be possible with time-series methods. Third, an understanding of causal relationships in a market has more relevance to marketing decision making than is possible with isolated sales projections.

Leading Indicators   This approach involves the identification of leading indicators whose movement up or down usually precedes the sales variation of a good or service. With monitoring of changes in indicators, it may be possible to forecast turning points in sales. The following are examples of leading indicators: (1) new housing starts lead major appliance sales, (2) number of births leads the sale of infant-related goods and services, and (3) disposable income leads demand for many durable goods. Frequently, leading indicators can be included in regression models.

Regression Models   Simple regression refers to two variables, where the explanatory or causal (independent) variable is considered to have a causal effect on the dependent variable of sales. As discussed in Chapter 19, the regression equation would be

$$\text{Sales forecast} = Y = a + bX$$

where Y = the dependent variable of sales
X = the independent variable
a = the value of the intercept on the Y axis
b = the slope of the line

As we saw in Chapter 21, multiple regression allows us to determine the causal relationship between several independent variables and the item being forecast, that is, sales. The multiple regression model extends the simple regression theory to a predicting equation like

$$Y = a + b_1 X_1 + b_2 X_2 + b_3 X_3$$

This equation is fitted by the least squares criterion and has three independent variables X_1, X_2, and X_3, which are the assumed causes for past sales variations, Y.

The regression model has a wide variety of applications to sales forecasting situations. The method is used extensively in practice and can be a very accurate sales forecasting technique. Of course, regression shows only the association among variables. The causal interpretation of these relationships is added by the marketer based upon a good understanding of the world from which it comes.

INTERNATIONAL DEMAND MEASUREMENT AND FORECASTING

Within the advanced nations of the world, it is often difficult to obtain the required quality of data necessary for useful demand measurement and forecasting. Even more difficult is the conducting of demand measurement and forecasting directed marketing research within less developed countries (LDCs). In estimating demand and forecasting within LDC markets, difficulties often arise in accessing quality information. Sophisticated data analysis methods are often rendered inappropriate or ineffective. These problems are especially apparent in countries where demand typically exceeds supply, creating little motivation for producers to either study the market or satisfy consumers.

Several problems should consistently be anticipated in conducting marketing research and market forecasting in LDCs. These include inaccessibility or absence of published data, lack of research resources (survey funds, agencies, data processing facilities, trained interviewers, etc.), hostility among local nationals toward survey and interview methods, and/or "halo" effects caused by respondents' efforts to please the interviewer. These problems lead to three types of suboptimization in research: (1) forced simplification of research methods, (2) improvisation in the use of proxy data, and (3) use of "guesstimates" to replace missing or unavailable data.

Alternative techniques for measuring demand in LDC markets can be categorized in the following groups: (1) method of analogy (including cross-section comparisons and time-series analyses), (2) macro surveys, (3) multiple-factor indexes, (4) chain ratio method, (5) use of proxy indicators, (6) trade audits, and (7) analysis of production and import trends. The first three of these methods are discussed earlier in this chapter. The last four methods are used in the two examples of demand estimation in Morocco in the Global Marketing Research Dynamics.

GLOBAL MARKETING RESEARCH DYNAMICS

CHALLENGES OF DEMAND MEASUREMENT AND FORECASTING IN DEVELOPING COUNTRIES: THE CASE OF MOROCCO

Morocco: The Environmental Context

Morocco is a Muslim Arab kingdom at the western end of the Mediterranean. Notable characteristics of Moroccan business customs include a relentless drive to preserve business and administrative secrecy at all levels, a general fascination with novelty and innovation, and widespread and rapid imitation of successful new ideas.

These cultural characteristics provide both barriers to and opportunities for the development of marketing research. Marketing research activities of any type meet with much resistance, being considered an invasion of privacy by businesspeople and consumers alike, but once successful inroads are made, "me-too" activities will soon follow. The following two examples illustrate the interaction of these cultural traits with the typical practical and conceptual problems of conducting market demand analysis in an LDC. Both concern consumer products—wallpaper and adhesive bandages—but different techniques are used to solve the respective demand estimation problems.

Estimation of Market Demand for Wallpaper

Unlike traditional Moroccan homes which use ceramic tiles to decorate floors and ceilings, "modern" homes were the target market for wallpaper. All wallpaper was supplied to the local market by nine importers. Seeing an opportunity, the leading local printer commissioned a market evaluation study. The objective was to track past demand patterns with a view to forecasting future demand. Initial data requirements included data by value and volume, domestic sales records, discretionary income by type of household, income distribution, home construction data, and general lifestyle information. Because of the large degree of uncertainty involved in researching LDC markets, it is typical to collect a wide range of general supporting

Marketers in Morocco must understand the uniqueness of the Moroccan consumer.

data in order to establish as coherent a picture as possible of these often chaotic markets.

This study revealed four potentially useful sources of secondary data, each with various advantages and deficiencies. The first source was *import statistics*. While this information was available for 10 years prior to the research, wallpaper imports were recorded by weight in kilograms and by value in dirhams. This information is of limited value since different qualities and different designs of wallpaper have different weights and values, and there is no clear method to determine the number of rolls sold during a period, let alone the number of rolls bought by modern households. The second source was the *domestic water-heater industry study* completed by the National Economic Development Bank.. The original purpose of this study was to determine the market for large, electric, domestic water heaters, modern conveniences indicating modern homes. These proxy data, collected for a market whose modern consumption patterns resembled those of the wallpaper market, allowed the indirect identification of the target market of modern homes, as well as providing population growth statistics and annual home construction figures. The third data source was a *study of the potential market for locally produced wallpaper*. While this study seemed to be the most relevant, it was actually the most useless, since it calculated future demand per inhabitant by weight, as well as defining the potential market as all consumers and making no distinction between traditional and modern or urban and rural—both invalid assumptions. The fourth data source was an *income distribution study*. While the study was seemingly relevant, its title, "Inequality for How Long?"—indicated that a careful researcher should interpret the statistics cautiously. The statistics compiled showed that 20 percent of the population owned 65.4 percent of the national income and purchased the most luxury and status items, allowing researchers to extrapolate that 20 percent of the national population was the maximum size of the target market for wallpaper. Using the national average of five persons per household, they could then estimate the number of households in the target market.

Researchers compiled several tables showing projected estimates of wallpaper consumption using the chain ratio method, proxy data, and import data. The three methods produced a wide range in the magnitude of the estimates. The import data, converted from weight to number of rolls, gave the most conservative figures. The use of proxy data, the data from the water-heater study, gave the highest figures. The chain ratio method combined income and population estimates to give a middle range of values. The results for the chain ratio method and import data analysis converged for years 10 and 11. The proxy data results were three times higher in these years, confirming the general principle that the further a researcher strays from "hard" data, the greater the margin for variation and error. While there was no way to confirm the accuracy of the estimates, researchers were able to confirm that a growth market existed and to establish a broad range for future demand, which served as a guideline for planning production capacity.

Estimation of Market Demand for Adhesive Bandages

The market for adhesive bandages was supplied wholly through imports, and the segment was growing rapidly, creating a market opportunity for the leading local pharmaceutical producer and marketing company. Entry into this market was impeded by the lack of accurate statistical data indicating the actual current market demand, which would then allow estimation of future market potential. Existing statistics did not isolate adhesive bandages as a specific product group, and an active black market added unknown quantities of imported adhesive bandages to the undefined number imported legally. In order to attain more complete data, exploratory interviews with the pharmaceutical company members researched consumer buying behavior, pricing practices, and distribution channels. The results of these interviews indicated that a trade audit would be the most appropriate research methodology, allowing researchers to collect statistical data on actual purchases at each stage of the distribution channels and thus to estimate the total current market for adhesive bandages, including the smuggled quantities.

Field surveys were carried out using standardized questionnaires administered during personal interviews. Census interviews were attempted among importers and wholesalers, but as anticipated, refusals made this research incomplete. Judgmental sampling was carried out in the public sector and focused on the largest customers. Pharmacies were surveyed according to a stratified random sampling plan. The strata were defined as distinct zones within cities such as old and new medinas, industrial areas, and city centers. Interpretation of the results had to take into account the incomplete survey results, inadequate sampling, guesstimates by respondents, exaggeration, and refusals. One major problem with the trade audit was the lack of supporting data with which to verify accuracy or reliability of results. Another was the questionable validity of the assumption that past economic conditions would continue into the future. Despite these ambiguities, several trends were identified, including a basic trend toward growth in the market and the importance of representation at each stage of the distribution channel.

These two examples of demand estimation in Morocco further emphasize the need for creativity and flexibility in conducting marketing research abroad, especially in developing countries. While relevant primary information is usually more reliable, it is often unavailable. Improvisation and local market knowledge are often critical and can develop a fairly accurate picture of past, present, and future market situations.

Source: Lyn S. Amine and S. Tamer Cavusgil, "Demand Estimation in a Developing Country Environment: Difficulties, Techniques and Examples," *Journal of the Market Research Society,* vol. 28, no. 1, pp. 43–65, 1985.

SUMMARY

1 The development of quantitative measures of demand, present and future, is an essential activity in every organization.

2 Demand can be measured on four dimensions: (a) degree of product aggregation, (b) geographic location, (c) time horizon, and (9) customer type.

3 Essential demand measurement concepts distinguish between market demand and company demand, both of which have corollary concepts of potential and forecast.

4 The approaches used to measure current demand are the breakdown and buildup methods. Breakdown methods can be classified as direct data and indirect data approaches.

5 In estimating future demand, a firm may use one method or a combination of methods. These methods can be classified as: (a) qualitative methods, (b) time-series extrapolation, and (c) causal methods.

6 Qualitative methods of forecasting include (a) executive opinion, (b) sales-force/distributor estimation, and (c) buyer or consumer surveys. These approaches are frequently used in consumer, industrial, and service organizations. Inexpensive and fast, they integrate the diverse information available to knowledgeable persons in the business. Qualitative methods are limited by the degree to which subjective judgments are biased and/or uninformed regarding key forecasting variables.

7 Time-series methods of forecasting include (a) moving average, (b) exponential smoothing, and (c) time-series decomposition. These methods are well suited to short-term forecasts when the historical data contain clear trend, seasonal, or cyclical patterns. They are ineffective in forecasting turning points.

8 Causal methods of forecasting include (a) use of leading indicators and (b) regression models. These approaches require a thorough understanding of market dynamics, specifically the factors that influence sales. Causal methods can be used to help predict turning points.

9 Cultural dynamics and data limitations often add difficulty to measuring demand and forecasting in LCDs. Flexibility and creativity are required in researching international markets.

DISCUSSION QUESTIONS

1 Develop four alternative definitions of market demand for television sets.

2 What is the difference between market potential and market forecast? Why is this difference important?

3 What is the difference between a market forecast and a company sales forecast?

4 Compare and contrast the breakdown and buildup methods of estimating current demand.

5 Why is accurate sales forecasting important to an organization?

6 How would you determine the accuracy of a proposed forecast?

7 Compare and contrast the three classifications of sales forecasting techniques: (a) qualitative methods, (b) time-series methods, and (c) causal methods. Why is this distinction important?

8 Evaluate the forecasting approach used for the wallpaper and adhesive bandages examples in Morocco in the Global Marketing Research Dynamics.

9 MINICASE

Outline an approach that Debra Clipper should use to prepare a sales forecast for the Network Connect product of TTI. (See the Marketing Research in Action at the beginning of this chapter.)

CHAPTER 24

PRODUCT RESEARCH AND TEST MARKETING

MARKETING RESEARCH IN ACTION

PRODUCT DEVELOPMENT RESEARCH HELPS BUILD WINNERS AT HITACHI IN JAPAN OVER THREE DECADES

Marketing research plays an important part in new-product planning at Hitachi. The evolution of its washing machine is a prime example. Though the agitator-type washing machine had been developed in North America, simulating the region's traditional "agitating" method of cleaning clothes, the pulsator-type washing machine had been developed in Japan to correspond to that region's traditional "rubbing" method of cleaning clothes. The pulsator system cleaned by using the force of a water current produced by rotary blades installed at the bottom of the washtub, and while it cleaned quickly, this system tended to tangle, twist, and damage clothes.

The washing machine was a mature product in Japan by the end of the 1970s. In an attempt to change and improve this situation, Hitachi conducted in-depth marketing research on consumers' changing needs. Several significant trends were discovered. People were acquiring both a larger number of clothes and more expensive clothes. Washing frequency increased from "washing because clothes are dirty" to "washing because clothes have been worn once." At the same time, consumers still valued stain removal. Hitachi concluded that a need existed for a new washing method that would clean clothes more gently without sacrificing traditional cleaning power. In response, Hitachi improved the pulsator system by adding an upright rod to the rotary vane, reducing tangling and damage to clothing while retaining cleaning capability. The machine was a success.

In the 1980s, Hitachi's continuous marketing research in Japan revealed a change in habitual washing times. As the number of women working in the cities began to outnumber those staying at home, more people began to wash clothes at night or early in the morning, instead of during the day. This created a potential problem with noise, especially for those living in small living quarters. Hitachi developed a machine with significantly reduced noise levels and used advertising that showed babies sleeping next to an operating washing machine to emphasize the advantages of this new product. By understanding the changing trend in consumers' life-styles, conducting tests to achieve the desired target (the low noise level), and creating and communicating a concept that appealed to consumers' needs, Hitachi developed another successful product.

In yet another successful product move, Hitachi conducted marketing research on why so few consumers bought clothes driers. Indifferent respondents said they did not need one. Interested respondents said they would like to buy a drier if they had space for it in their home. Hitachi used the interested respondents' input to develop a space-saving home laundry system which combined a washer and a drier into one unit. It was a great success.

Hitachi's experience with marketing research has led its managers to develop a firm belief in creative, marketing research-based action. They use marketing research to proactively forecast future needs and to propose new ideas to consumers. Marketing research has allowed Hitachi to focus its innovations on real consumer needs, with outstanding success.

Source: Toru Nishikawa, "New Product Planning at Hitachi," *Long Range Planning,* vol. 22, no. 4, pp. 20–24, August 1989.

One of the major applications areas of marketing research is in product research. A 1994 American Marketing Association study indicated that 90 percent of consumer goods firms and 79 percent of industrial goods firms undertake some form of product research. In addition, 83 percent of health services companies, 79 percent of financial services firms, 94 percent of advertising agencies, and 77 percent of publishers and broadcasters undertake such research[1] The high use of marketing research in product decisions is easily understood when we consider the importance of those decisions. For many organizations, product decisions are the single most important set of decisions made by managers, since they form the basis of the firm's marketing strategy. In addition, expenditures on product development can run into the millions of dollars for a single product. For example, the average consumer product costs over $7 million to develop, and the average

[1]Thomas C. Kinnear and Ann R. Root, *1994 Survey of Marketing Research* (Chicago: American Marketing Association, 1994), pp. 42–46.

industrial product costs almost $3 million to develop.[2] Many products cost much more than this. And new-product failure rates are estimated to be quite high— from about 30 percent to as high as 80 percent.[3] The power of marketing research to aid the product development process is clearly illustrated in the Hitachi Marketing Research in Action at the beginning of this chapter.

Procedures used in product research include concept generation and testing techniques, laboratory testing, and test marketing. All these procedures will be discussed in this chapter. Test marketing (or market testing, as others call it) in particular has major applications not only for product research but also for other elements of the marketing mix. It will be covered extensively in this chapter.

The stages in the development of new products are: (1) idea generation, (2) concept development and testing, (3) business analysis, and (4) commercialization. Marketing research techniques can be applied in all these stages, although the specific techniques used are different at each stage.

IDEA GENERATION

The first stage in the product development process is *idea generation.* Here the objective is to come up with completely new ideas for products, or new attributes for current products, or new uses for current products. At this stage of the product development process, a great deal of flexibility and creativity is needed in the research procedures used. Two exploratory research procedures can be useful: the repertory grid technique and various types of focus group interviews.

Repertory Grid

The repertory grid technique helps to generate a list of attributes that consumers can use to describe similarities and differences among products. The intention is to identify the attributes that will be important to consumers in their evaluation of new products in the product category or to identify an attribute that was previously not associated with a particular product.

The steps in the repertory grid technique are:

1 The products being tested are selected and printed on a set of cards; for example, if 10 snacks were being examined, one snack would appear on each card.

2 The respondent sorts through the cards and removes cards for products that are unfamiliar.

3 Three cards are selected as directed by a prespecified plan, and the respondent is asked to "think of a way in which any two of the three items are similar

[2]Glen L. Urban and John R. Hauser, *Design and Marketing of New Products* (Englewood Cliffs, NJ: Prentice-Hall, 1993), pp. 60–61.

[3]David S. Hopkins and Carl L. Bailey ("New Product Pressures," *The Conference Board Record,* pp. 16–24, June 1971) give the high estimate, whereas David Hopkins ("Survey Finds 60 Percent of New Products Succeed," *Marketing News,* vol. 13, p. 1, Feb. 8, 1980) gives the low estimate.

to each other and different from the third." This identifies one attribute used by consumers in their perceptions of this product group.

4 The process is repeated with another group of three cards, but this time the respondent is asked for some new way in which two products differ from the third. This identifies a second attribute.

5 The process is repeated until the respondent can no longer identify additional product attributes. The average consumer can identify between 15 and 20 attributes in this way.

If the products are established ones, the researcher seeks new dimensions of consumer perception. For example, a major motorcycle firm identified a previously unrecognized dimension, "power image at a standing-still position," using the repertory grid procedure; it has since been incorporated in the company's product design and advertising. This procedure can also be used with a product concept statement included with established products or even with a group of concept statements. For example, the concept of an "electric car" could be teamed in the repertory grid procedure with a car already established in the "second car of the family" category.

Focus Groups

Consumer focus groups, described in Chapter 10, are used extensively in idea generation for new products. In addition, a special type of focus group using experts as respondents, called a *synectic session,* or *brainstorming session,* may be used. Here the moderator carefully directs the discussion from general to increasingly specific issues. The idea is to generate as many ideas as possible without being critical, allowing the group activity to refine and improve them. Brainstorming is looser and less evaluative than a standard focus group.

CONCEPT DEVELOPMENT AND TESTING

Many new-product ideas are eliminated if they can't be undertaken by the company. This can be because of lack of fit with production or marketing skills, technical impossibility, and so on. Ideas that do survive this kind of screening are then taken to consumers for testing.

The major objectives of concept testing are (1) to get a first-cut reaction as to consumers' views of the product idea, (2) to give direction to future development of the project, (3) to select the most promising concepts for further development, and (4) to get an initial evaluation of potential commercialization prospects for the product. The research is exploratory in nature and thus tends to use small samples selected in nonprobability fashion—usually a judgment or quota sample.

The questions you want to answer with a concept test include: (1) Do consumers understand the concept? (2) Does the concept have a crucial flaw? (3) Does the product meet the needs of some segment? (4) What alternate concepts would be preferred?

Relevant marketing research techniques used in concept testing are focus group interviews, monadic ratings, paired-comparison ratings, conjoint analysis, and usage tests. Before examining these techniques, we will first address the issue of the nature of concept to be tested. Exhibit 24-1 presents more detailed guidelines for the preparation of concepts to be tested.

The Nature of the Concept Tested

The nature of the concept presented to consumers depends on the position in the product development process that has been reached. In the very early stages of the process, the concept description may be a few sentences or short paragraphs. For example, a major food marketer tested and refined its concept for a diet gravy product based solely on verbal descriptions. As the process advances, the concept may also include drawings or even roughed-out advertisements. Chatham Supermarkets, a large midwestern chain, tests advertising concepts using such ads. At a later stage, mock-ups or even prototypes of the product may be presented. Automobile companies test car designs with consumers by using full-scale clay models of their cars.

At some point it is important for the concept to include the essence of the marketing program that will support it. This is because consumers react to all marketing aspects of a product offering, including its price, its name, its advertising position, and even the type of store in which it is sold.

Focus Group Interviews

Given the exploratory nature of most concept testing, focus group interviews are frequently used.

The moderator directs the group discussion much more specifically than in an idea-generating session. The objective is to address the specific concepts being evaluated by the firm, always seeking insights for further refinements.

Monadic Ratings

In a monadic rating session, respondents are divided into as many groups as there are product concepts to test. Each respondent examines only one product concept and evaluates it on explicitly identified dimensions such as intention to purchase or level of liking. The scale used for recording the evaluations could be any of the attitude rating scales discussed in Chapter 8. It is common to use numeric rating scales.

The scores on the scale are averaged for each product concept, and comparisons are made across groups. The highest scoring concepts are subjected to further evaluation. Note that the comparison is an absolute one, as each respondent does the rating without reference to other concepts. Because this is so, it is important to control sample differences across the groups of concept evaluators. For example, if age profiles in the groups were quite different, and if the product concepts

EXHIBIT 24-1   BASIC GUIDELINES FOR CONCEPT WRITING

A Concept Is a Set of Promises

Normally, a concept consists of two major elements: (1) a concrete description of a product and (2) a selling argument that attempts to present the product in a persuasive manner. *unique selling proposition*

Concepts are especially useful in the development of new products. If we find through appropriate marketing research methods that the basic idea has appeal, we can justify the investment necessary to build a prototype. If we cannot excite any consumers with the idea, there is no point in spending money developing the hardware.

A Concept Should Never Be Objective

Some marketing research practitioners are horrified with the idea that a concept should actually try to "sell" the product in question. While this argument sounds logical, it is totally wrong. Its weakness stems from the fact that in real life, consumers are almost never exposed to an "objective" expression of the product. A product, like a person, usually attempts to put its best foot forward.

A concept must always take a very clear, definite stand with respect to the product. It should describe the product and its benefits clearly. Indeed, the more the concept simulates advertising (or the retail package), the closer we are to obtaining a realistic understanding of consumer attitudes and purchase intentions.

The Concept Should Present the Product as a Real Thing that People Are Buying

We never want to force respondents to answer hypothetical questions. If we make this mistake, the result will be hypothetical, artificial responses. Generally, we add realism to a concept by presenting the product idea in a context that is familiar to consumers. For example, if the idea is a new food product, it may be described in this manner:

Here is a new food product that was introduced recently in most supermarkets in the Dallas area. The product is called Lunch Pops; it is a line of frozen sandwiches that you prepare by heating them in the microwave oven.

Lunch Pops come in different varieties, including bacon and cheese, pizza style, and sloppy joe. Each Lunch Pop has an outer layer of French-style bread with a delicious filling inside.

A carton of three Lunch Pops sells for $2.95. Look for Lunch Pops in the frozen food section of your favorite supermarket.

Notice that this concept includes a number of elements to make Lunch Pops sound like a real product. It includes a name, a price, where it is now being sold, its varieties, and so on. All of this helps give it a believable context and at the same time creates a picture of the product in the consumer's mind.

A Concept Is a Highly Delicate Tool

Probably the best way to explain this point is to say that the entire impression created by the particular concept statement can sometimes be altered dramatically by the change of a single word or phrase. For example, an instant coffee that is described as "flavor granules" can create very different taste expectations from those produced by a coffee described as an "instant powder." Even though the physical product remains the same, the words we attach to it can have a tremendous influence on the way consumers perceive the product. Thus, any concept development work must be highly sensitive to both the positive and the negative feelings that can surround a specific word.

A Concept Should Be Short and Simple

Since a concept should be designed to simulate either an ad or a package, it must satisfy some of the very same communication requirements. The message should be dramatic and interesting but also very simple.

The Structure of the Concept Should Reflect the Ultimate Marketing Plan

Just how simple a concept must be is influenced partly by the company's marketing plan. For example, if a food company plans to do no advertising and to place the entire selling burden on point-of-sale display, obviously the concept statement must be designed to be no more complicated than the ultimate package.

On the other hand, if the company intends to support this new product with a massive advertising campaign, the concept statement can be more complicated and can consist of more ideas and elements. If the method of selling is a one-page letter, the concept statement should be a simulation of this letter. If a company expects to sell door-to-door, the concept statement should include this feature.

Concepts Come in Different Formats ⑧

For purposes of discussion, it is useful to envision concepts in four formats, as follows:

The simple concept statement. This is nothing more than a written description of a product and its benefits. It is rarely more than one page long, usually half a page, and double-spaced. This format is used most often because it is the least expensive to create and to revise.

Concept statement with visual. Sometimes a product idea can be effectively communicated only through use of a drawing, a photograph, or some other kind of illustration. This is especially true of products whose major benefit is an aesthetic one.

Concept statement with physical prototype. Sometimes a concept needs not only a picture but also a physical model of the product. This can be as crude as a miniature model made of cardboard.

Handmade packages of ads. Most companies do not go to the expense of creating a preliminary package or print ad unless earlier research indicates that the product idea has definite consumer appeal. Typically, the research process follows these lines: A concept statement is developed through a series of three or four focus group interviews. Then the concept is "tested" among a sample of 400 consumers. If it still seems to have appeal, it is translated into either a rough package or a print ad. These materials are then subjected to consumer review through focus groups to ensure that the package or ad is communicating as effectively as the final concept statement.

Concepts Usually Have to Go ⑨ (Many iterations) through a Refinement Process

Most concepts have weaknesses that can be identified only when the concepts are exposed to consumers. Concepts can easily go through four or five different versions before the expression that optimizes the selling strategy is developed. Since refinement is almost always necessary, it is important to use a small-sample research tool, like the focus group interview. Once the concept is fully developed, a more expensive test using a large sample of several hundred consumers can be conducted.

Source: David M. Stander, president, Stander Research Associates, Grosse Pointe, MI. Used with permission.

---

in question had age-related dynamics, then biased scores could result, depending on which age group received which concept.

Paired-Comparison Ratings

Sample group differences and a lack of other product concepts to compare against may make monadic ratings somewhat unreliable. An alternative is the paired-comparison test. Each respondent tests a set of product concepts two at a time and states which of the two is preferred. (The nature of paired-comparison tests was discussed in detail in Chapter 8.)

An alternative with some characteristics of both monadic and paired-comparison tests is a *sequential monadic,* or *nondirect comparison,* test. The subject is exposed to a product concept, waits some prescribed time period, and then is exposed to another concept. After a number of products have been shown to the respondents, ratings of the products on a scale are taken. The order of presentation of product concepts to respondents may bias results, so randomization of the order across subjects is necessary. Proponents of this method argue that the sequential order of presentation reflects the way consumers actually evaluate products in the marketplace, and also that it avoids the artificial forced-choice situation that paired-comparison tests make. In a paired-comparison test, respondents may select one product over another just because they have to and may do so using some trivial attribute.

Conjoint Analysis

Conjoint analysis, already introduced in Chapter 21, is another technique that can be used in concept testing. The researcher wants to measure the utility that respondents assign to each level of each explicitly defined attribute of a product concept. For example, the Canadian government in conjunction with Air Canada tested 13 attributes of a proposed new plane and associated services using verbal descriptions of such attributes as speed, food service, ticket prices, and seating arrangements. This procedure gives insight into the relative importance of product attributes and how they relate to each other, and allows researchers to determine the best combination of attributes.

Usage Tests

Once the marketer has developed a physical version of the product, it may be tested in various types of usage situations. The product may be tested in the "laboratory." The Betty Crocker kitchens at General Mills are continuously trying new formulations of their products, and automobile companies test-drive vehicles on their test tracks. Laboratory testers of products usually are more careful to follow instructions than actual consumers, who may evaluate the product on attributes not deemed important by research and development people. In the early development of Gaines burgers dog food, for example, General Foods management found that in the laboratory the product tested well, but in actual consumer use the product was misused: dog owners tended to overfeed their dogs, making the dogs become ill. Clearly, consumer tests are also necessary.

In a *consumer usage test,* the product is given to a small sample of end consumers who are instructed to use it in a normal fashion. Typically, it is placed in the user's home (or company, in the case of industrial products). For example, a small computer company placed its new desktop computer and software system in five east coast companies. The managers were then able to identify problems in the instruction manual and to pinpoint some mechanical malfunctions. Respondents for a use test may be recruited by phone, by mail, or even through personal contacts in shopping malls.

One variation on the consumer usage test is the *blind usage test.* It is most typically used immediately after laboratory testing has been completed. The product is given to the consumer without its brand name or any supporting advertising copy. The intention is to get a reaction to the physical product without the effect of other marketing program variables. Firms frequently test a new formulation of an established brand in this fashion. Often the consumer will test more than one product in a specified sequence.

In usage tests the researcher must try to make sure that respondents follow instructions, actually use the product, and do not give biased responses just because they were given a free product. Usage tests do not measure acceptance of the product over the long run, and they tend to furnish inflated estimates if respondents are asked to state whether they intend to purchase the product. However, the main objective of this method is to test the acceptance of the physical product, rather than to predict sales.

Simulated Purchase Testing

In this type of testing the participant is usually brought to a location where a display of the relevant product is set up in a storelike presentation. Some form of script (monopoly dollars, chips, etc.) is then given to the participant to use in a simulated purchase within the product category being tested. The brand "purchased" is then recorded. This approach lends itself to an experimental design where variations in the product design, packaging, price, and so forth can be tested. The Coca-Cola Marketing Research in Action illustrates the use of simulated purchase testing, and also demonstrates how conjoint analysis can serve as an alternative method.

MARKETING RESEARCH IN ACTION

COCA-COLA TESTS PACKAGING WITH SIMULATED PURCHASE TESTING AND CONJOINT ANALYSIS

Coca-Cola uses both simulated-purchase testing and conjoint (trade-off) analysis to measure consumer preferences. The simulated-purchase testing involves screening for eligible respondents in the target market and then taking them to an interview location with a product display setup. The soft-drink display includes all major brands involved in the study. Each "product" (a brand/package combination) is labeled with a price. Researchers give each respondent 10 poker chips to place in front of his or her next 10 soft-drink purchases, allowing the respondent to "buy" 10 of one brand/package combination or to divide them among different brand/package alternatives. This phase of the test measures the current market situation and serves as the control for the experiment.

Researchers then take the respondents to a second beverage display to which one new variable has been added, such as a new package for a particular brand. This is the test station. Because the only difference between the control situation and the test station is the new package, any change in a product's market share (chip allocation) is thought to be directly attributable to the new package.

Conjoint analysis also begins by screening for target market respondents. Qualified respondents are taken to a central location where they choice-rank pairs of priced products. Approximately 20 pairs of products are presented to each respondent, with each pair uniquely defined. Each product combines a relevant brand, a package, and a price point. The relative degree of importance or preference placed on each product reflects each respondent's value system and provides a basis for constructing a conjoint-based market simulation model that estimates market share under alternative scenarios.

Coca-Cola has run three sets of simulated purchase tests and trade-off studies in parallel, using independent but matched random samples of respondents. The subject was three new package configurations being considered for Coca-Cola. When the results of the corresponding studies were compared, there was no statistically significant difference in the respondents' preferences. This indicates that simulated-purchase testing and trade-off analysis give approximately the same results.

Despite the similarity in results between the two methods, certain situations favor one approach over the other. Simulated-purchase testing is usually preferred under the following conditions: (1) Only one or two tests are desired. (2) Variable pricing is not a major research issue. (3) Decision makers are more familiar with and/or prefer simpler, more traditional simulated-purchase testing. (4) Trade-off expertise and software are not available.

Conjoint analysis is preferred when: (1) Multiple market scenarios are of interest. (2) Sensitivity (including posterior) analyses of alternative product attributes are relevant. (3) Price is an important variable. (4) Trade-off expertise and computer programs are available.

Like many other companies, Coca-Cola has applications for both methods and uses these basic guidelines to determine which method will be more effective for a given situation.

Source: N. Carroll Mohn, "Simulated-Purchase 'Chip' Testing vs. Tradeoff (Conjoint) Analysis—Coca-Cola's Experience," *Marketing Research,* pp. 49–54, March 1990.

BUSINESS ANALYSIS AND COMMERCIALIZATION

Product ideas that survive the concept testing process are often then subjected to a more conclusive business analysis. If this analysis indicates that the product's sales level and profitability are good enough, the product is then commercialized—taken to the marketplace. The research objective of business analysis is to estimate the sales level and profitability of the product. Two important techniques used for this purpose are test marketing and simulated test marketing, usually conducted in a laboratory environment.

Both of these procedures involve the application of experimental and quasi-experimental designs.

The high use of these types of procedures was noted in Chapter 9 in our discussion of causal designs. The V-8 and Navy experiments described in Marketing Research in Actions in Chapter 9 illustrate experimentally structured approaches to test marketing. These types of experimental and quasi-experimental approaches are extensively used because they work.

TEST MARKETING

Test marketing is a field-oriented testing activity that may be either an experiment or a quasi experiment, depending on how it is structured. In most cases, it attains only quasi-experimental status. Our reason for dedicating a significant portion of

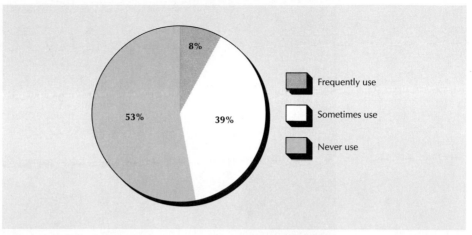

FIGURE 24-1   Use in practice of test marketing. (*Source:* Thomas C. Kinnear and Ann R. Root, *A Study of the Marketing Research Business*, unpublished study, 1994. Copyright 1994 Thomas C. Kinnear. Not to be reproduced.)

this chapter to test marketing relates to our underlying philosophy for this book, which is that we want you to get beyond technical concepts and into the flavor of the real world of marketing research. Test marketing is a very real activity that allows you to observe the use of experimental and quasi-experimental procedures, and it allows us to tie in some of the syndicated data services discussed in Chapter 5. Also, since test marketing is heavily used in marketing research, it merits presentation here. Figure 24-1 indicates that about 47 percent of businesses use test marketing in their marketing research.

This section first describes the possible uses of test marketing, then discusses when test marketing should be undertaken as well as what its limitations are. A number of implementation decisions in test marketing will be covered, specifically the choice of the number of cities to use, the criteria for selecting test cities, the distinction between standard test cities and control test cities, and the length of time a test should run.

Test Marketing Defined

Before proceeding further, we need a formal definition of test marketing. Achenbaum defines test marketing from the research-oriented person's point of view as follows:

> It is a controlled experiment, done in a limited but carefully selected part of the marketplace, whose aim is to predict the sales or profit consequences, either in absolute or relative terms, of one or more proposed marketing actions.[4]

[4]Alvin R. Achenbaum, "Market Testing: Using the Marketplace as a Laboratory," in Robert Ferber (ed.), *Handbook of Marketing Research* (New York: McGraw-Hill, 1974), pp. 4–31 to 4–54.

Thousands of new consumer package goods products are test marketed in the United States each year.

Achenbaum goes on to explain that, at the other extreme, some people define test marketing loosely as "trying something out in the marketplace."[5] He recognizes that most test marketing activity falls between these two extremes. Cost and time pressures are the main reasons the research-oriented extreme is not often used. But Achenbaum notes that "no matter what choice is made, one thing is common to all such tests: the results are used as if they were predictive"[6] of the whole marketplace. It should not be surprising that, with so much test marketing activity positioned toward the loose end of the definitional spectrum, it is easy to find examples of test marketing failures.

In our definition of test marketing, we shall take account of the practice of this activity. Specifically we define *test marketing* as the implementation and monitoring of a marketing program in a small subset of the target market areas for the product in question. This definition takes in designs that are not even good quasi experiments, let alone experiments, but this is the nature of this activity.

THE SELECTION OF ALTERNATIVES TO TEST

A product manager was overheard to say to a researcher, in discussing the introduction of a new product, "I want to test at least two price levels, three different

---

[5]Ibid.
[6]Ibid.

advertising executions, two coupon alternatives, two package designs, three point-of-purchase presentations, and two product formulas." This test could be designed as a controlled experiment, using a factorial design; but look how many test cities we would need to conduct this experiment! At a minimum it would require:

2 (prices) $\times$ 3 (advertising executions) $\times$ 2 (coupons) $\times$ 2 (packages)
$\times$ 3 (point-of-purchase presentations) $\times$ 2 (product formulas) = 144 cities

Obviously, the cost of such a test would be unreasonably high. This points out that true field experiments can test only a few levels of a few variables.

What the product manager must do in this situation is eliminate some combinations of variables prior to undertaking the test market. Basically, all the possible combinations of marketing variables must be reduced to a few alternative strategies. For example, two strategies might be:

1 Price $1.15, advertising which depicts a hidden-camera interview, a 10-cents-off coupon, a plastic package, an end-aisle display, and a strong product formula.
2 Price $0.98, advertising using "slice-of-life" execution, a 15-cents-off coupon, cardboard packages, a middle-aisle display, and a medium-strength product formula.

This test could be conducted in two cities (at a minimum). However, it does not allow the measurement of separate main effects or interaction effects. We can only grossly measure the effect of the two strategies. Hence, most test marketing would be best described as a quasi experiment.

How do researchers reduce to a few strategies the number of possible combinations they are interested in? They use personal judgment, based on the experience of both the manager and the company, and they also undertake research on each aspect of the strategy prior to the test market. For example, a researcher could (1) test the product formula in a home placement test, (2) do copy testing on the advertising executions, and (3) consult previous company experience with similar products to compare end-aisle displays with middle-aisle displays and to study the results of various coupon plans. A great many judgments must be made, and a great deal of research undertaken, prior to the test market.

THE USES OF TEST MARKETING

No matter how formal or informal the design of a test market, there are two fundamental uses for it[7]:

1 Test marketing can serve a *managerial control function*. That is, it can allow an organization to gain needed information or experience before undertaking a project on a grand scale.

[7]This section follows an excellent discussion in ibid., pp. 4–33 to 4–38.

2 Test marketing can serve a *predictive research function.* That is, it can predict the outcome of alternative courses of action. This input can be used to decide whether or not to undertake a course of action.

Test Marketing as a Managerial Control Tool

In undertaking any new marketing activity there is risk that something will go wrong. This is especially true in the marketing of new products or brands, but it is also true in established product categories where some innovation is being introduced. A test market here would be designed as a pilot operation for later larger-scale national introduction. It would give us needed experience in many areas, including the following:

1 We could gain experience in physically handling the product—shelf life, breakage, storage, shipping, and so on. We could identify costly mistakes and thereby avoid them on a national basis. In the case of Nabisco's Legendary Pastries, a few months after the product was introduced in a test market, the cans of cherry topping began exploding. It seems that an apparently innocuous ingredient in the mix was fermenting the cherries. Consider the problem if Nabisco had put this product into national distribution.

2 It could give us experience in simply learning how things get done in marketing this product. We could learn the difficulties of gaining distribution, of producing a new commercial, of making our price hold at retail, and so on. This experience would be used later in our national rollout.

In designing test marketing programs for managerial control purposes we need not worry about having a correct experimental design. We are simply gaining experience, not making sales or profit projections, and therefore are not making go, no-go decisions.

Test Marketing as a Predictive Research Tool

Of more interest to marketing researchers is test marketing as a predictive device. In fact, most test markets are used in this manner, no matter how badly designed. There are two situations in which test marketing is used as a predictive device: (1) in new-product or new-brand introductions, and (2) in the evaluation of alternative marketing programs for existing brands—that is, evaluating either individual marketing variables or programs. These two uses require reasonably tight experimental or quasi-experimental executions in order to generate reasonable predictions. Their only real difference from each other, from a methodological point of view, is that the testing of alternative marketing programs requires a control group (i.e., the present program).

In new-product or new-brand tests management wants to know how its new product or brand will do in terms of sales and profits in a national introduction. You may well wonder how one projects from test marketing results to a national performance, and indeed this is a very difficult problem. Projections are often made with what turns out to be a very large error when the national results are compared with the projection. Gold has suggested an approach to this problem,[8] offering three different methods for making this prediction.

1 Buying Income Method   Here sales of the test brands are expanded by the ratio of the test area's buying income to the buying income of the country. In formula:

$$\text{National sales estimate} = \frac{\text{total U.S. income}}{\text{test area income}} \times \text{test area sales}$$

2 Sales Ratio Method   Here sales of the test brand are compared with the sales of another brand where a logical sales relationship may be expected. That is:

$$\text{National sales estimate} = \frac{\text{national sales of other product}}{\text{test area sales of this other product}}$$
$$\times \text{test area sales of test product}$$

The firm may have related experience with other brands that they assume to be similar to the new brand.

3 The Share-of-Market Method   Here sales of a test brand are related to sales of the product category as a whole in the area where the new brand is being tested. In formula:

$$\text{National sales estimate} = \frac{\text{test area sales of new brand}}{\text{test area sales of this whole product category}}$$
$$\times \text{national sales of this whole product category}$$

In Gold's study, the share-of-the-market method was found to be the most accurate, but it also is the most expensive, as it requires the auditing of all the competitive brands in the product category. It also assumes that the test product will not expand sales of the product category.

A number of other procedures for projecting test marketing results have been proposed which are more sophisticated mathematically than Gold's approach. Our intention here is not to present the details of the mathematics of these approaches, but rather to give a brief overview of the similarities among them. Basically, these approaches have the following steps:

[8]Jack A. Gold, "Testing Test Marketing Predictions," *Journal of Marketing Research,* vol. 1, p. 10, August 1964.

1 In undertaking a test market, collect purchase data from a panel in the test market area.

2 Obtain measures from the panel on the cumulative growth in the number of new buyers of the brand under study and the rate of repurchase activity for this brand over a number of purchase cycles.

3 Formulate a mathematical model to describe the demand for this brand. The model is expressed in terms of the measures taken in step 2, that is, cumulative growth rate and repurchase rate, plus the size of the panel relative to the national population.

4 Use this model, and the growth and repurchase rates obtained from the consumer panel in the test market, to project national sales levels.

Proponents of this type of method have reported very accurate projections from panel results to national outcomes.[9] Note that the Gold approach takes only gross measures of test marketing results, whereas the other approaches measure purchase activity on an individual household basis by using a panel. An individual firm should develop projection formulas of its own to fit its own circumstances. The advent of scanner panels (see Chapter 5) enhanced the ability of panels to be useful to marketers in test marketing situations. Of course, the test must then be run in cities where scanner services are available. As yet, the cities available for scanner test markets are limited and are somewhat atypical.

Some of the specific types of information a test market might provide for a company are:

1 Sales in units and dollars.

2 Market share.

3 Profitability and return on investment.

4 Consumer behavior and attitudes with respect to the product—who does and doesn't buy, who makes the buying decision, how the product is used, repurchase patterns, perceptions of the product, and so on.

5 Effectiveness of alternative marketing strategies, and possibly of the various components such as coupon plans, advertising executions, and so on.

6 Reaction of the trade to the product and its marketing program—willingness to stock it, location on shelf, use of point-of-purchase materials, assessment of the sales force's presentation, and so on.

In obtaining this information the company can make use of any of a number of syndicated test marketing services, some of which are discussed later in this chapter. Also, the firm is likely to need customized studies to measure some of

---

[9]Those who are interested in the details of these newer approaches should consult a number of excellent references, including J. H. Parfitt and B. J. K. Collins, "Use of Consumer Panels for Brand-Share Prediction," *Journal of Marketing Research,* vol. 5, pp. 131–145, May 1968; David H. Ahl, "New Product Forecasting Using Consumer Panels," *Journal of Marketing Research,* vol. 7, pp. 160–167, May 1970; Gerald J. Eskin, "Dynamic Forecasts of New Product Demand Using a Depth of Repeat Model," *Journal of Marketing Research,* vol. 10, pp. 115–129, May 1973; Benjamin Lipstein, "Modelling and New Product Birth," *Journal of Advertising Research,* vol. 10, pp. 3–11, October 1970.

the variables of interest. The power of test marketing to aid in decision making is illustrated in the Marketing Research in Action on Cyanamid.

THE DECISION TO UNDERTAKE TEST MARKETING

The decision to undertake test marketing involves the examination of the costs of the test market against the expected benefit. This section examines some of the specific areas of costs that are related to test marketing, the potential benefits having been discussed in the previous section. The problems associated with test marketing will also be discussed here. One example of the successful use of test marketing is illustrated in the Combat Marketing Research in Action.

MARKETING RESEARCH IN ACTION

CYANAMID TESTS COMBAT

"It looked like a pretty good opportunity for us," says Dr. Ted Shapas, group leader for insecticide research at the Shulton Research Division, who explains that Americans spend about $400 million a year on household insecticides targeted for controlling roaches. Yet most people are unhappy with the products they use, for three reasons: (1) sprays and foggers are smelly and messy; (2) they're toxic to humans and pets; and (3) one application is effective for only a few days. Sticky traps, although easy to use, have the highest consumer dissatisfaction rate (70 percent), says Shapas, because they make no appreciable dent in the roach population of a house or apartment.

Shulton expected Combat to test well because, enthuses Shapas, "it addresses the frustrations people have been having. It's childsafe, and there's no odor or mess. Efficacy results are so positive we're able to offer a money-back guarantee for 3 months of roach control."

Although Cyanamid researchers were convinced of the superiority of Combat, they braced themselves for skepticism on the part of test market consumers who had learned to mistrust glowing claims for household insecticides. "Combat is different from sprays and foggers," explains Jim Janis, Shulton's strategic business unit manager for new ventures. "We knew we had to educate consumers about the high-tech nature of the product, tell them why it was so revolutionary." As a result, he says, "Our whole test marketing campaign took an educational approach to the cockroach problem."

The three-pronged attack included: (1) public relations, relying heavily on radio and TV talk-show interviews with leading entomologists who talked about cockroach behavior and control; (2) advertising, which, unlike most entrants in the field, is neither flippant nor cartoonlike; and (3) use of an 800 number on package inserts and advertising, to position the company as an authority on cockroach control.

The test was conducted in Kansas City and New Orleans, and ran for 2 years. "As you might expect," explains Shapas, "sales of insecticides are really skewed depending on the part of the country you're in. We wanted to test Combat in an average area, but also in a city where things are about as bad as they can get roachwise. The 100 line on the category development index for ant and roach insecticide goes right through Kansas City; south of that it gets increasingly higher: New Orleans is in the 300s, making it serious roach country."

Combat was sold primarily in food stores, but also in some drug chains, explains product manager Maria Miller. The test was heavily supported with advertising and consumer promotion dollars "approximately equal to what we are getting ready to introduce nationally," she says. (Combat's national rollout in the spring was backed by a first-year $16 million advertising and promotion budget.) "It was a full plan both years," reports Miller, "including TV and print advertising; consumer promotion events like Sunday inserts, as well as on package promotional coupons, prepacked display shippers, and discounts to dealers."

Results were tracked through Nielsen and SAMI reports of warehouse withdrawals. However, says product manager Miller, "We want to do our own research with consumers, not just rely on share data, so we conducted consumer tracking studies and attitude and usage studies."

One result of the research, says Miller, was a change in emphasis for the ad campaign during the test market that was carried through in the national rollout. "The initial advertising focused on three-month kill," she says, "but we found out from consumers that a real attribute of the brand from their point of view was that it didn't have any mess or odor and was child-safe. All the benefits were being played back in the attitude and usage studies. That was a hot button we could definitely push, so we broadened the ads to say that Combat provided a superior combination of efficacy, aesthetic benefits, and safety versus the competition."

Shulton keeps all its test marketing data secret, but Miller claims that the product met or exceeded all its objectives. "Test marketing success," she says, "gives a margin of comfort for the national plan."

Source: Sales and Marketing Management, pp. 92–96, Mar. 11, 1985.

Costs of Test Marketing

There are both direct and indirect costs of test marketing. The direct costs include:

1 A pilot plant to make the product (if the test is for a new product)
2 Commercials
3 Payments to an advertising agency for services
4 Media time at a higher rate because of low volume
5 Syndicated research information
6 Customized research information and associated data analysis costs
7 Point-of-purchase materials
8 Couponing and sampling
9 Higher trade allowances to obtain distribution

The typical two-city test market in 1995 had direct costs of $650,000, and a four-city test cost of $1 million. Long-running, complex tests can have direct costs of over $1.5 million.

To these costs we must also add the indirect costs of the test to the company, which include:

1 Opportunity cost of lost sales that would have occurred in a successful national introduction

2 Cost of management time spent on the test market

3 Diversion of sales-force activity from money-making products

4 Possible negative impact on other products carrying the same family brand

5 Possible negative trade reactions to your products if you develop a reputation for "bombing"

6 Cost of letting your competitors know what you are doing, allowing them to develop a better strategy or beat you to the national market with a new product like yours

These costs are indeed high. In deciding whether or not to undertake a test market, marketers must also consider some of the problems associated with test marketing.

Problems of Test Marketing

A number of problems occur with test marketing, and they will be listed later in this section. All of them, however, give rise to one overriding negative consequence—the lack of projectivity of the test market results to the national rollout of the product.

There are a number of reasons for this poor projectivity in test marketing, including the following:

1 The salespersons in the selected area are stimulated beyond normal activity levels by the mere awareness that a test is being conducted in their market.

2 The trade is made aware of the test and gives artificially high distribution and retailer support.

3 Special introductory offers and promotions are often made to the trade and to consumers because it is so important to get and maintain distribution during the test to measure repurchase activity. Their offers are then not available at the scale of the test for a national rollout.

4 Competitive efforts, both deliberate and coincidental, have profound effects on the test marketing results. These efforts are then different on a national basis. At an extreme, competitors can attempt to destroy your ability to make judgments from a test by increasing their efforts in your test cities out of proportion with their national efforts. Purex began a test of a liquid bleach in Erie, Pennsylvania. In response, Procter & Gamble increased its advertising efforts in Erie and also went into a heavy cents-off campaign for its Clorox brand. Purex had to cancel the test, as no meaningful results were possible.

5 Measurement accuracy can yield ambiguous data. Auditing store sales can often give inaccurate data because of poor store records or incomplete knowledge of the store's billing and handling systems. Also, only a sample of stores is used, with a resultant sampling error occurring. These sample results must also be weighted properly to take account of large versus small stores in the population of stores. This is especially a problem when the measurements are made on a temporary basis for this one test.

6 Competitors may use your test market to learn of your activities and monitor your results. They may then beat you to the national market with the same type of product. Having this competitor in the national market would obviously make the test results less projectable. This happened to Lever Brothers in testing their Mrs. Butterworth syrup, and also to Procter & Gamble in testing Bounce fabric softener. Calgon used P&G's test to beat P&G to the national market with its Cling Free brand. P&G rushed its Crest pump to market without test when it lost significant market share to the Colgate pump.

When to Test Market

With a firm understanding of the costs and limitations of test marketing in mind, we are ready to turn to a checklist of points to consider in deciding when to test market:

1 Consider the cost and risk of failure versus the profit and probability of success. A product with low costs and low risk of failure may not need testing.

2 Consider the plant investment needed to go national versus that required for the test. Lean toward a direct national rollout if little extra plant investment is necessary, and vice versa.

3 Consider the likelihood and speed with which the competition will copy and/or preempt your product or campaign. The faster they will respond, and the more likely they are to do so, the more reason there is for skipping the test.

4 Consider the effects of a national failure on the trade and on consumers. Will the company's reputation and other products suffer?

Thus, if the costs and risk are low, little incremental plant investment is needed for a national rollout, competitors are likely to be able to copy your program quickly, and a failure is not likely to have major long-term consequences on the company's reputation, you would probably not do test marketing before a national launch. A company may consider one of these factors important and decisive enough on its own. For example, Pillsbury developed a powdered soft drink to compete with Kool-Aid (General Foods), Wyler's (Borden), and Hawaiian Punch (R.J.R. Foods), all well-established competitors. Pillsbury's product, called Squoze, had half the sugar and half the calories of the other mixes. Pillsbury reasoned that they would lose out if they gave their product a test market, because the competitors would easily match them and preempt the national market; so they skipped the test market. The product was a market failure.

DESIGNING TEST MARKETS

Three design issues will be covered in this section: (1) the choice of how many cities to use in the test, (2) the criteria to be used for selecting cities, and (3) the length of time the test should run.

The Number of Cities

Some suggested guidelines for the number of cities are:

1 Select at least two cities for each program variation to be tested.
2 Where projectivity is important, at least four geographic areas should be used.

We would of course consider the cost of adding more cities against the expected benefits. In general, the greater the risk of loss on a national basis, the more alternative programs should be considered; and the greater the regional differences in relation to your product, the more cities should be used.

Criteria for City Selection

No one city or group of cities can represent the whole United States. However, we should try to select cities that have the following characteristics:

1 The markets should not be overtested.
2 The markets should have normal historical development in the product class.
3 The markets should represent a typical competitive advertising situation.
4 The markets should not be dominated by one industry.
5 Special resident profile markets should be avoided (for example, college towns and retirement areas).
6 If sales are different by region, each region should be tested.
7 The markets should have little media spillover into other markets and should receive little outside media impact.
8 The markets should have a media usage pattern similar to the national pattern.
9 The markets should not be too small to provide meaningful results or so large that testing becomes too expensive.

To this list we might add:

10 The markets should have representative distribution channels.
11 The competitive situation should be similar to the national situation.
12 Sales auditing and other research services should be available.
13 The company must be able to ship the product to the test areas at a reasonable cost.
14 The demographic profile of the cities should be "representative."

Obviously, not all these criteria are met by one city. This list is just the standard to shoot for.

In test marketing we distinguish between the two types of test cities: (1) control markets and (2) standard markets. *Control markets* (or minimarkets, as they are called) are cities where a research supply house has paid retailers to guarantee that they will carry products that it designates. The research company (1) handles the placing of products on shelves in retail stores, (2) services these products regularly to ensure that the required in-stock condition is maintained, (3) audits product class sales, and (4) observes competitive action that would affect the test. In other words, the environment is controlled to allow for tight designs. Control markets offer the advantages of (1) speedier access to distribution and readings on results, (2) reduced cost per market, (3) no distraction of sales-force attention from other lines, and (4) greater secrecy, as most control markets are small and are not automatically audited by A. C. Nielsen or SAMI, and so on. Thus, competitors must expend more time and effort to monitor your results.

The major drawbacks to control markets is the fact that true trade reaction to your product cannot be obtained, and this is often important to the marketer. These markets tend to be smaller, making national projections more difficult. Also, they generally do not have isolated media. This results in spillover of advertising into other areas where the product is not available. This wastes money, and in addition it can cause ill will among consumers and retailers who cannot buy the advertised product. Control markets are a fairly recent development in test marketing. The research companies that run these control markets have reported extensive use of this service. They also report success in having control market tests reasonably accurately predict national sales levels.

The alternative to control markets is the use of what are called *standard markets,* where the company must fight for trade support in the same fashion as in a national rollout. There is no guarantee of getting retail distribution at all, let alone getting particular shelf facing and special stocking. This type of test provides a more realistic picture of the likely trade reaction to your product. It is, however, more expensive, slower, more distracting to the sales force, and more easily monitored by the competition. This type of test is still the dominant one in practice.

The reasons Marion, Indiana, is used as a standard test marketing city and as a controlled scanner market for Information Resources, Inc., are presented in the Marketing Research in Action.

Exhibit 24-2 lists both standard and some control markets for selected research firms that are frequently used for test marketing in practice.

The Length of a Test

The average market test runs from 6 to 12 months. How do you decide how long a test should run for a particular situation? The following factors are relevant:

1 The test must run long enough for repurchase activity to be observed. This gives a measure of the "staying power" of a new product or program. The shorter the average repurchase period, the shorter the test can be. Cigarettes, soft drinks, and perishable foods are purchased every few days, whereas shaving cream, toothpaste, and so on are purchased only every few months. The latter type of product would require a longer test than the former. The product should be allowed to go through a number of repurchase cycles.

2 How soon will competitors react? The faster this reaction, the shorter the test.

3 The cost of the test must also be considered. At some point the value of additional information is outweighed by its costs.

EXHIBIT 24-2

FREQUENTLY USED TEST MARKETS

Standard Markets	Denver, CO	Lynchburg, VA	Reno, NV
	Des Moines, IA	Macon, GA	Richmond, VA
Akron, OH	Detroit, MI	Madison, WI	Roanoke, VA
Albany, NY	Dubuque, IA	Manchester, NH	Rochester, NY
Albuquerque, NM	Duluth, MN	Marion, IN	Rockford, IL
Ann Arbor, MI	Durham, NC	Melbourne, FL	Rome, GA
Anniston, AL	Eau Claire, WI	Memphis, TN	Sacramento, CA
Appleton, WI	El Paso, TX	Miami, FL	St. Louis, MO
Asheville, NC	Elkhart, IN	Midland, TX	St. Paul, MN
Atlanta, GA	Erie, PA	Milwaukee, WI	St. Petersburg, FL
Augusta, GA	Eugene, OR	Minneapolis, MN	Salem, NC
Austin, TX	Evansville, IN	Mobile, AL	Salem, OR
Bakersfield, CA	Fargo, ND	Modesto, CA	Salinas, CA
Baltimore, MD	Flint, MI	Monterey, CA	Salt Lake City, UT
Bangor, ME	Fort Collins, CO	Montgomery, AL	San Antonio, TX
Baton Rouge, LA	Fort Lauderdale, FL	Nashville, TN	San Diego, CA
Battle Creek, MI	Fort Smith, AR	New Haven, CT	San Francisco, CA
Beaumont, TX	Fort Wayne, IN	New Orleans, LA	Savannah, GA
Binghamton, NY	Fort Worth, TX	New York, NY	Schenectady, NY
Birmingham, AL	Fresno, CA	Newport News, VA	Scranton, PA
Boise, ID	Grand Junction, CO	Oklahoma City, OK	Seattle, WA
Boston, MA	Grand Rapids, MI	Omaha, NE	Shreveport, LA
Boulder, CO	Green Bay, WI	Orange, TX	Sioux Falls, SD
Buffalo, NY	Greensboro, NC	Orlando, FL	South Bend, IN
Canton, OH	Greenville, NC	Pensacola, FL	Spartanburg, NC
Carson City, NV	Harrisburg, PA	Peoria, IL	Spokane, WA
Cedar Rapids, IA	Hartford, CT	Philadelphia, PA	Springfield, MA
Champaign, IL	High Point, NC	Phoenix, AZ	Springfield, MO
Charleston, SC	Houston, TX	Pittsburgh, PA	Springfield, IL
Charleston, WV	Huntsville, AL	Pittsfield, MA	Stockton, CA
Charlotte, NC	Hutchinson, KS	Poland Spring, ME	Superior, MN
Chattanooga, TN	Indianapolis, IN	Port Arthur, TX	Syracuse, NY
Chicago, IL	Jacksonville, FL	Portland, ME	Tacoma, WA
Cincinnati, OH	Kalamazoo, MI	Portland, OR	Tallahassee, FL
Cleveland, OH	Kansas City, KS	Poughkeepsie, NY	Tampa, FL
Colorado Springs, CO	Kansas City, MO	Providence, RI	Toledo, OH
Columbia, SC	Knoxville, TN	Pueblo, CO	Topeka, KS
Columbus, GA	Lansing, MI	Quad Cities: Rock Island	Troy, NY
Columbus, OH	Las Vegas, NV	and Moline, IL; Dav-	Tucson, AZ
Corpus Christi, TX	Lexington, KY	enport and Bettendorf,	Tulsa, OK
Council Bluffs, NE	Lincoln, NE	IA (Davenport–Rock	Washington, DC
Dallas, TX	Little Rock, AK	Island–Moline	Waterloo, IA
Dayton, OH	Los Angeles, CA	metropolitan market)	West Palm Beach, FL
Daytona Beach, FL	Louisville, KY	Raleigh, NC	Wichita, KS
Decatur, IL	Lubbock, TX	Reading, PA	Wilkes-Barre, PA

Winston, NC
Yakima, WA
York, PA
Youngstown, OH

Controlled Markets

AUDITS & SURVEYS
*Based on Metropolitan
    and TV Markets*
Akron
Albany–Schenectady
Albuquerque
Ann Arbor
Atlanta
Austin
Bakersfield
Baton Rouge
Binghamton
Birmingham
Buffalo
Charleston, SC
Charleston, WV
Cincinnati
Colorado Springs
Columbus, GA
Columbus, OH
Corpus Christi
Dayton
Daytona Beach
Denver–Boulder
Des Moines
Duluth
Erie
Evansville
Flint
Fort Lauderdale
Fort Wayne
Grand Rapids
Greensboro
Harrisburg
Huntsville
Jacksonville
Kalamazoo
Kansas City
Knoxville
Las Vegas
Lexington
Little Rock

Louisville
Lubbock
Macon
Manchester
Memphis
Miami
Milwaukee
Mobile
Modesto
Montgomery
New Orleans
Newport News
Oklahoma City
Omaha
Orlando
Pensacola
Phoenix
Portland, ME
Portland, OR
Providence
Raleigh–Durham
Reading
Roanoke
Rockford
Sacramento
Salem, OR
Salt Lake City
San Antonio
San Diego
Savannah
Seattle
Shreveport
South Bend
Spokane
Springfield, IL
Syracuse
Tacoma
Tampa
Toledo
Tucson
Tulsa
West Palm Beach
Wichita

SPAR/BURGOYNE
*Based on Metropolitan
    Markets*
Albuquerque
Bangor
Binghamton

Boise
Charleston, SC
Erie
Evansville
Flint
Fort Wayne
Fresno
Grand Rapids–
    Kalamazoo
Green Bay
Harrisburg
Lansing
Lubbock
Madison
Peoria
Portland, ME
Portland, OR
Quad Cities, IL/IA
Rockford
South Bend
Spokane
Springfield, IL
Tucson

**EHRHART-BABIC
ASSOCIATES**
*Based on Metropolitan
    and TV Markets*
Albuquerque
Austin
Bangor
Binghamton
Boise
Charleston, SC
Charlotte
Chattanooga
Corpus Christi
Des Moines
Erie
Fort Wayne
Fresno
Grand Rapids–
    Kalamazoo
Green Bay
Harrisburg
Lansing
Lexington
Lubbock
Madison
Peoria

Portland, ME
Quad Cities, IL-IA
Rochester
Rockford
San Antonio
South Bend
Spokane
Syracuse
Tucson

**INFORMATION
RESOURCES**
*BehaviorScan Electronic
    Markets*
Cedar Rapids
Eau Claire
Grand Junction
Marion
Midland
Pittsfield
Rome
Salem, OR
InfoScan Selected Markets
Albany
Albuquerque
Atlanta
Baltimore, MD–Wash-
    ington, DC
Birmingham
Boise
Boston
Buffalo–Rochester
Charleston, SC–Savannah,
    GA
Charlotte
Chicago
Cincinnati
Cleveland
Columbus, OH
Dallas–Fort Worth
Denver
Des Moines
Detroit
El Paso
Grand Rapids
Green Bay
Harrisburg–York
Hartford
Houston
Indianapolis

Jacksonville	Tulsa	Salinas–Monterey	Detroit
Kansas City, KS–MO	Wichita	San Antonio	Grand Rapids
Knoxville		Savannah	Hartford–New Haven
Little Rock	**MARKETFEST**	South Bend	Houston
Los Angeles	**(Div. of Market Facts)**	Spokane	Indianapolis
Louisville	Albuquerque	Springfield, MA	Jacksonville
Memphis	Austin	Springfield, MO	Kansas City
Miami	Bangor	Syracuse	Little Rock
Milwaukee	Beaumont–Port Arthur	Tucson	Los Angeles
Minneapolis	Binghamton	Wichita	Louisville
Nashville	Boise	Yakima	Memphis
New Orleans	Charleston, SC		Miami
New York	Chattanooga	**NIELSEN MARKETING**	Milwaukee
Oklahoma City	Columbia	**RESEARCH (Div. of**	Minneapolis
Omaha	Columbus, GA	**Dun & Bradstreet Corp.)**	Nashville
Orlando	Erie	*Data Markets*	New Orleans, LA–Mobile,
Peoria	Eugene	Boise	AL
Philadelphia	Evansville	Charleston, SC	New York
Phoenix–Tucson	Flint	Green Bay	Oklahoma City–Tulsa
Pittsburgh	Fort Wayne	Peoria	Omaha
Portland, ME	Fresno	Portland, ME	Orlando
Portland, OR	Grand Rapids	Savannah	Philadelphia
Providence	Green Bay	Tucson	Phoenix
Raleigh–Durham	Harrisburg		Pittsburgh
Richmond	Lansing	**SCANTRACK**	Portland, OR
Roanoke	Las Vegas	*Major Markets*	Raleigh–Durham
Sacramento	Lexington	Albany	Richmond
St. Louis	Lincoln	Atlanta	Sacramento
Salt Lake City	Little Rock	Baltimore	St. Louis
San Antonio	Lubbock	Birmingham	Salt Lake City, UT–Boise, ID
San Diego	Madison	Boston	San Antonio
San Francisco	Modesto	Buffalo–Rochester	San Diego
Scranton–Wilkes-Barre	Nashville	Charlotte	San Francisco
Seattle–Tacoma	Omaha	Chicago	Seattle
Shreveport	Peoria	Cincinnati	Syracuse
Spokane	Portland, ME	Cleveland	Tampa
Syracuse	Poughkeepsie	Columbus, OH	Washington, DC
Tampa–St. Petersburg	Rockford	Dallas	
Toledo	Salem, OR	Denver	
		Des Moines	

Source: Sales and Marketing Management, various years.

MARKETING RESEARCH IN ACTION

MARION FITS THE TEST MARKET BILL

Marion, Indiana, is one of nine cities regularly used by Information Resources, Inc. (IRI), to test-market new products and marketing techniques. According to John Johnson, vice president of marketing operations for IRI, "When we first looked at Marion it was the demographics . . . it's not a mirror image of the United States, but it had enough people in certain categories to satisfy us." The desired categories included: There was an average of 2.73 people per household; 31 percent of the households were headed by someone under 35; 37 percent of the families earned more than $25,000 per year; and 12 percent of the households were composed of more than five people.

Manufacturers think Marion has more to offer than desirable statistics. For one thing, the town of 36,000 is fairly isolated. As Johnson points out, "You would rarely drive to Indianapolis to get your groceries, so we've captured the universe of grocery buyers there." The young families in Marion use a wide variety of consumer products. A Procter & Gamble spokesperson noted that the company would not test a new brand of peanut butter in an area like Florida, which is mainly populated by older people, because children are the main consumers of peanut butter.

Marion's profile incites the makers of many products to spend hundreds of thousands of dollars testing the town's consumers to see how the companies' display, advertisement, color, scent, and price of products affect what consumers buy. Procter & Gamble representative Linda Ulrey noted that while test marketing is not a cheap process, it is a lot less expensive than taking a product national and then discovering that it is a flop.

IRI carefully selects towns that fit its consumer profile and then equips the groceries and drugstores in these towns with scanners that record purchases. The company then conducts two different kinds of test marketing. The first is InfoScan, which uses cash register scanners to track the sales and volume of every product sold in about 2400 stores nationwide. This number includes all the grocery and drugstores in Marion.

The second type of test marketing is BehaviorScan. This program involves about 4000 Marion residents who carry Shoppers Hotline cards. These consumers present their cards whenever they buy merchandise. Cashiers punch in consumers' individual codes and then ring up their purchases. The code numbers provide a wide range of information for the product's manufacturer. It tells what was bought, the shoppers' ages, how many children they have in their families, their incomes, and numerous other pieces of data. Monetary prizes are randomly offered to encourage people to use their cards.

IRI also monitors the effect that certain television ads have on shoppers' behavior. The 4000 Marion residents involved in the BehaviorScan program must have cable TV to participate. By attaching a small box to these people's televisions, IRI can monitor the commercials the shoppers see and determine which ones may have motivated them to buy. The research company can also insert their own ads into the BehaviorScan homes to monitor the effects of these specific ads.

Source: "Indiana City Is Test-Market Hotspot," *Marketing News,* p. 46, Aug. 29, 1988.

The Use of Research Suppliers

Marketing research suppliers are very active in the business of test marketing. Their primary activities include (1) providing retail store and warehouse sales or shipment information through audits, (2) selling consumer panel data on purchases and attitudes, and (3) providing control market tests. They are also able to design and execute customized research for a company doing test marketing. Exhibit 24-2 presents a listing of some of the major companies providing test marketing services. (A more detailed description of these companies was presented in Chapter 5.) The major trend in test marketing services in the 1990s has been the use of scanner services. IRI's BehaviorScan and Nielsen's ERIM services are two examples. (See Exhibit 24-2 and the appendix to Chapter 5.)

Test marketing can be a very useful activity if executed with great care and with no illusions about the precision of estimates that it will produce. It provides the most realistic test of alternatives under consideration.

SIMULATED TEST MARKETS

The problems and high costs of test marketing noted earlier have led to the development and increasing use of simulated test markets for frequently purchased consumer goods. Simulated test markets take place in a laboratory environment and involve shopping in a simulated retail store. The objective is to predict actual market sales of a product based upon the trial and repeat purchase patterns of consumers in the simulation. This is done in much the same way that trial and repurchase patterns of panel members are used to predict sales in an actual test market, as discussed earlier.

There are many research suppliers who now offer simulated test marketing services. Yankelovich, Skelly, and White have run such an operation for more than 15 years and have tested over 500 products. Elrick and Lavidge's COMP procedure completed over 200 studies in its first 10 years of operation. Other well-known procedures include Management Decision Systems, Inc.'s ASSESSOR and Robinson Associates' SPEEDMARK. Although these systems differ somewhat from each other, they are basically very similar. Since ASSESSOR is a well-documented approach we will use it to describe the nature of simulated test markets.[10]

ASSESSOR costs about $35,000–$60,000 per study and takes about 3 months to complete. This is substantially cheaper and of shorter duration than test marketing. The steps in evaluating a product with ASSESSOR are:

1 A group of respondents, usually about 300 people, is recruited at shopping malls to match the target segment of the test product.

2 Respondents are taken to a nearby laboratory facility to complete a questionnaire. They are asked about whether or not they purchase any brand in the

---

[10]Alvin J. Silk and Glen L. Urban, "Pre-Test Market Evaluation of New Package Goods: A Model and Measurement Methodology," *Journal of Marketing Research,* 15, pp. 171–191, May 1978. Other models include BBDO's NEWS model. See "NEWS: A Decision-Oriented Model for New Product Analysis and Forecasting," *Marketing Science,* vol. 1, no. 1, pp. 1–29, Winter, 1982.

product category, and then about unaided brand awareness, advertising awareness, brand preference, importance ratings of product attributes, and ratings of brands on these attributes.

3 Respondents are then exposed to advertisements for the new brand and the leading competitive brands in the category.

4 After the advertising presentation, respondents are taken to a simulated retail store where the test product is on a shelf display with a complete set of competing products. They are given $2 to use to buy a brand from the category if they wish. Those who do not want to buy any brand are given free samples of the new brand as a way of simulating free samples in the marketplace.

5 After the simulated shopping trip, respondents are interviewed about what brand they purchased, if any, and about their reactions to the product and its advertising.

6 The respondents then return home with the test product and with instructions to use it. Follow-up interviews are conducted by telephone several weeks later. The measures taken are similar to the preexposure to advertising measures (preference, importance of attributes, and brand ratings), except that the new brand is now included in the brand set. In addition, usage of the test product is determined, and the respondents are offered a chance to repurchase the new brand (using their own money) and to have it delivered by mail. Those who do not want to repurchase in this way are asked to indicate their intention to purchase the new brand on a 5-point scale if the brand were available in a store in the future.

These data are then used to predict market share for the new brand in one of two ways. First, preference judgments predict the proportion of respondents who will purchase the new brand. Market sales are estimated by adjusting this proportion to reflect the proportion of all target consumers who will have the new brand available to them for selection and who will be exposed to its advertising.

The second method predicts market share utilizing estimates of trial levels and repurchase rates that are based upon respondents' purchase levels and intention-to-purchase statements. Purchase levels are based upon the proportion of respondents who purchase the brand in the simulated retail store, plus the marketing actions that management intends to take with respect to distribution penetration, advertising, and free samples. The repurchase rate is estimated based upon the proportion of respondents who purchase the brand during the follow-up telephone interview and the intention levels of those who do not repurchase at that time. The purchase level and repurchase rates are then used by the ASSESSOR model to predict market share. (The mathematical details of this are beyond the scope of this book.) Figure 24-2 presents a graphic summary of the flow of a simulated test market.

The reported accuracy of ASSESSOR is very high as compared to results generated by actual test markets.[11] To work effectively, simulated test marketing methods must have a well-established product category in terms of substitutes and usage, purchase rates must be the same for established brands and the new brand,

---

[11]Ibid.

A consumer provides valuable feedback on product-use experiences.

and consumption and attitude formation about the brand must occur quickly enough that preference structure can stabilize in a short period of time.[12]

The 1990s find the success of packaged goods simulated test marketing methods being adapted and applied to consumer durables. Urban, Hauser, and Roberts

[12]Ibid.

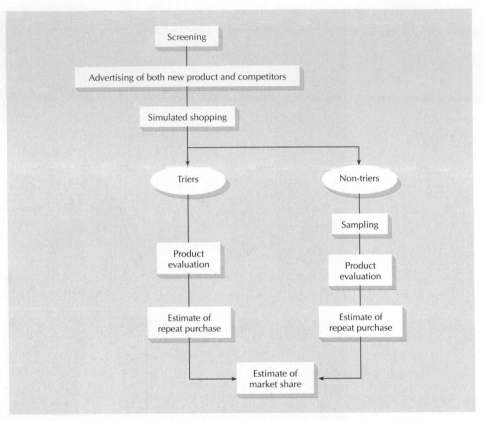

FIGURE 24-2   Most simulation models operate in the same general framework. (*Source: Advertising Age*, p. M-11, Feb. 22, 1982. Reprinted with permission of Crain Publications, Inc.)

reported very accurate forecasts of actual sales of new automobiles based upon simulated test markets.[13] The consumers in these simulated test markets were exposed to product concepts, videotapes of products, and test drives. Preference measures were taken from the consumers tested, and sales were forecasted based upon these preferences and other factors such as life cycle.

The great success of simulated test markets has led some people to conclude that they will replace test marketing. To date this has not occurred, and both test marketing and simulated test markets are growing in use.

[13]Glen L. Urban, John R. Hauser, and John H. Roberts, *Prelaunch Forecasting of New Automobiles: Models and Implications* (Cambridge, MA: Marketing Science Institute, 1989). See also Glen L. Urban, John S. Hulland, and Bruce D. Wenberg, "Premarket Forecasting for New Consumer Durable Goods: Modeling Categorization, Elimination, and Consideration Phenomena," *Journal of Marketing*, vol. 57, no. 2, pp. 47–63, April 1993.

SUMMARY

1 Research procedures used in new-product idea generation are repertory grid and focus group interviews.

2 Research procedures used in concept development and testing are focus group interviews, monadic ratings, paired-comparison ratings, conjoint analysis, and usage tests.

3 Research procedures used in business analysis are test marketing and simulated test marketing.

4 Test marketing is frequently used but is a controversial subject in marketing research.

5 Definitions of test marketing range all the way from "controlled experiments" to "trying something out." We define test marketing as the implementation and monitoring of a marketing program in a small subset of the target market areas for the product in question.

6 Selection of alternatives to test must involve other research and judgment prior to the test marketing.

7 Most test marketing procedures are quasi experiments at best.

8 Test marketing may be used as a managerial control function or as a predictive research function. The latter use may involve either new-product or new-brand introductions, or the evaluation of alternative marketing programs for existing brands.

9 In projecting test marketing results to a national product, the researcher may use the buying income method, the sales ratio method, the share-of-market method, or panel methods.

10 Direct costs of test marketing run at about $450,000 for a two-city test. Indirect costs are also high.

11 Test marketing often yields estimates of national outcomes that are inaccurate.

12 Reasons for unsatisfactory results include abnormal behavior by salespersons and the trade, special campaigns by the company doing the test, competitive actions, and measurement accuracy problems.

13 Consider test marketing when the costs and risk of failure are high, and/or the plant investment of a national rollout is high relative to the test, and/or the competition is not likely to respond quickly, and/or the effects of a national failure on your company's reputation would be high.

14 In designing a test market, the researcher must make decisions with respect to what information to collect, the number of cities to use, the specific cities to use, and the length of time the test should run. You must also decide what marketing research supplier services to use.

15 Simulated test markets take place in a laboratory environment where respondents shop in a simulated retail store after being exposed to advertisements for the new brand and competing brands. In-home usage of the test product follows, and purchase levels and repurchase rates are estimated and used to predict market share.

DISCUSSION QUESTIONS

1 Why are focus groups used for both idea generation and concept testing?

2 What are monadic ratings?

3 Describe the structure of a usage test for a new cake mix.

4 What is test marketing?

5 On what basis would you select alternative courses of action for use in test marketing?

6 What are the two fundamental uses of test marketing?

7 How can test marketing results be projected to national results?

8 What information can test marketing provide?

9 What are the costs of test marketing?

10 Why do test marketing results often give poor projections?

11 Under what circumstances should a company undertake test marketing?

12 What type of cities should be used in test marketing?

13 What is a control market?

14 What are the pros and cons of control markets?

15 How long should a test marketing procedure run?

16 Outline the steps in a simulated test marketing procedure?

17 How could simulated test marketing procedures be applied to consumer durables, such as dishwashers or personal computers? Be specific.

18 MINICASE

Kenner Toys uses the following procedure to test new toys. Evaluate this approach:

Ouija Boards, the Magic 8 Ball, and dart boards are three popular toys that have enjoyed long-lived success. These toys, however, are not used to try to predict the next big winner in the very fast moving and unpredictable toy industry, even though such predictions may prove more accurate than marketing research performed with 5-year-olds!

Kenner has developed a method for testing toys. Mock stores are set up in several locations around the country with a wide variety of toys, including the new test concepts, the company's existing products, and current competing products. Two hundred children, the sample, are individually shown videotapes depicting the concepts and product demonstrations for each of the toys under research. After viewing the videotape, each child is escorted into the mock store and given tokens to use in making purchases.

The simulated purchase situation is believed to be necessary because observation is a much more reliable measurement of the behavior of young children than are focus groups, interviewing, or other more conventional and less expensive marketing research methods.

19 MINICASE

Coca-Cola is considering entering the bottled, fruit-based drink market in direct competition with Snapple. Outline a complete program of marketing research for the development and commercialization of this new drink product at Coca-Cola. Describe specific marketing research activities and studies.

20 MINICASE

The concept presented below was evaluated negatively by consumers in a focus group. Using concepts presented in the chapter, revise the original concept statement; then test the concept with individuals (depth interviews) or groups (focus groups). Also: (a) explain and justify the changes from the original concept statement; (b) explain the method used to evaluate the revised concept statement and the nature of the findings; and (c) based on your research findings, explain what changes you would now make, if any.

DIET GRAVY—"The Healthiest Gravy You Can Eat"

Here's a product that a lot of families have been waiting for—a new diet gravy that contains only 4.8 calories per tablespoon and also has reduced cholesterol.

People have been complaining for years that whenever they have to go on a diet, one of the first things they are told to give up is gravy (it's no wonder, because natural home-made gravy contains 55 to 60 calories per tablespoon). But now you won't have to give up gravy any more, because this new diet gravy is just perfect for people who are really sincere about losing weight and staying healthy.

And it's so convenient to prepare—just mix with 1 cup of water, bring to a boil, and heat for just 1 minute. Available in four gravy flavors: brown, chicken, onion, and mushroom.

Sells for just 19 cents for each packet. Makes a 1-cup serving of gravy.

Consumer reaction

Reaction to this concept in the first focus group interview was totally negative. People almost gagged at the thought of serving this to their families. Their main complaint centered on taste. Several said flatly, "This sounds like medicine, and I'm sure it will taste like it!" The concept must obviously be changed, but what revisions should be made?

CHAPTER 25

ADVERTISING RESEARCH

MARKETING RESEARCH IN ACTION

PASSIVE PEOPLE METER TO REVOLUTIONIZE MEDIA ADVERTISING RESEARCH?

A. C. Nielsen Co., in conjunction with the David Sarnoff Research Center, has developed a "passive" people meter for measuring TV viewership. While this device is designed primarily to measure programming viewership, its technology will enable Nielsen to measure commercial viewership much more effectively than Nielsen's current people meters.

Nielsen's new system uses a device resembling a VCR. It combines a computer with a small camera and can identify the individuals who are actually watching TV. It is intended to record both a person's presence in the room and his or her TV viewership at any given second, making it possible to record accurate TV ratings specifically for commercials.

The computer is initially "introduced" to members of the family. Using a form of artificial intelligence, it then matches characteristics to those it "sees" watching TV. One drawback is that the system is unable to identify visitors watching TV.

Nielsen is committed to developing accurate commercial viewing measurements. While the current people meters compile minute-by-minute viewing data, the new system compiles second-by-second viewing data. This precision is crucial in determining true ratings for TV spots. The company will tie this commercial viewing information to its "single-source" panel. By deriving TV viewing and purchasing information from single-source families, advertisers and agencies will be able to study the correlation between advertising and purchasing decisions. The passive people meter approach is as yet not well accepted by the media as a measurement tool that they are willing to pay for. Its long-term acceptance is still in doubt.

According to Michael Drexler, executive vice president of media at Bozell Advertising, New York, "There's no doubt advertisers want this type of information. We've been trying to get audience measures for relevant exposure versus program ratings. We want it and we hope it is coming." Yet the ramifications of such a system are infinite. Both agencies and networks are already developing software capable of analyzing second-by-second data and tentatively pricing commercial inventory according to position within a commercial break. Networks will undoubtedly negotiate higher prices for certain key positions if the new data show a correlation between commercial viewing and the time a spot airs within a break. The current media pricing structure and buying process could be rendered obsolete.

Source: "Nielsen's New Meter May Give Ratings for Ads," *Advertising Age,* p. 1, June 5, 1989. Cheryl Heuton, "Nielsen, Nets Spar on Ratings, *Media Week,* p. 8, July 4, 1994.

This attempt to develop an advanced people meter is but one example of marketing research applied to advertising issues. In this case we see marketing research applied to media audience measurement problems. This chapter presents many other uses of marketing research applied to the advertising areas of media, copy testing, campaign pretesting, and campaign posttesting.

One of the major application areas of marketing research is in advertising. There is good reason for this, since 1993 advertising expenditures in the United States were $182 billion.[1] The 1994 American Marketing Association (AMA) survey on the use of marketing research reported that 70 percent of all companies do some form of advertising research. In the consumer products area, 78 percent of companies do advertising research.[2] Marketing research is used in a number of aspects of advertising, including measuring media audiences and testing the effectiveness of advertising messages. The use of marketing research in these two areas constitutes the topic of this chapter.

MEDIA RESEARCH

One of the major decisions that marketers have to make involves the selection of media vehicles to use in an advertising plan. Thus, they must make choices

---

[1]*Advertising Age,* April 13, p. 1, 1994.
[2]Thomas C. Kinnear and Ann R. Root, *1994 Survey of Marketing Research* (Chicago: American Marketing Association, 1994).

between media types—television versus radio versus newspapers and so forth—and choices of specific inserts within a selected media type. For example, choices must be made concerning which specific television time or magazine to use. Both of these decisions require the availability of data about media.

The Advertising Research Foundation (ARF) suggested that six different types of data ideally would be available about media vehicles and that these data would distinguish between the prospects and nonprospects of the product being advertised. These data are:

1 *Media vehicle distribution.* The circulation number for a magazine or newspaper or the number of television or radio sets available to carry the advertising.

2 *Media vehicle audience.* The number of people exposed to the media vehicle. Here we measure the number of readers of a given issue of a magazine or newspaper or the number of viewers of a specific television show. Media audience is typically larger than media distribution, because more than one person reads the same magazine or watches on the same television set, as Figure 25-1 illustrates.

FIGURE 25-1   A model for evaluation advertising.

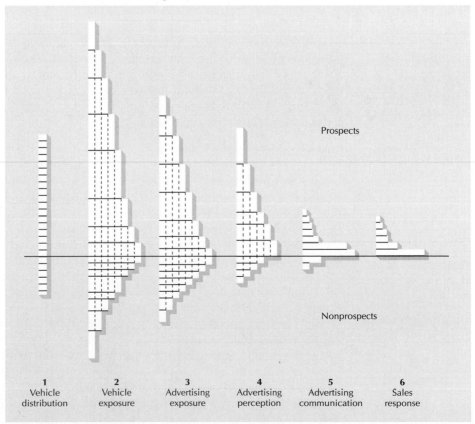

3 *Advertising exposure.* The number of people exposed to a specific advertisement in the media vehicle. People may be exposed to a media vehicle but not notice a specific advertisement because of the creative aspects of the ad or the nature of the environment of exposure. This number is typically much less than vehicle audience. At this point, the data we desire start to mix both questions of media and of the creative "copy" in the advertisements. (This is also true of data types 4, 5, and 6 listed below.)

4 *Advertising perception.* The number of people who perceived the advertising in question. This could, of course, be influenced by the color and size of the ad, positioning in the vehicle, and type of product involved. The number of people actively perceiving an ad is typically less than the number of those exposed to it, as Figure 25-1 illustrates.

5 *Advertising communication.* The number of people who comprehend specific things about the advertising, which is typically less than those perceiving the ad.

6 *Sales response.* The number of people who take buying action as a result of the placement of the specific advertising. Fewer people respond to an ad by purchasing the product than have actually received its communication, yielding the pattern of numbers for people in Figure 25-1.

In the last four categories of data (types 3 to 6), media and message interact. It thus becomes very difficult to assign numbers related to the media alone in these cases. Because of this difficulty, media vehicle data are typically obtained for only two of the above categories: media vehicle distribution and media vehicle audience. In this section, we will follow advertising research practice by examining the first two levels in the context of media research, and leave the last four levels for our discussion of message research.

Media Vehicle Distribution

Data about media vehicle distribution are the most readily attainable and are relatively free of controversy in terms of their accuracy. In the print media the most important agency is the Audit Bureau of Circulation (ABC), a group sponsored by advertisers, advertising agencies, and publishers. ABC audits and reports on the circulation levels of its members, publications that have at least 70 percent of their circulation paid for at a price of not less than half the established price. For special audience publications distributed to the business community sometimes on a free basis, such as *Production* magazine, the circulation is audited by the Business Publications Audit of Circulation. In addition, the Verified Audit Circulation, an independent organization, audits both the paid and nonpaid circulation of newspapers and magazines.

For the broadcast media the measurement of vehicle distribution is much less important. Over 99 percent of all U.S. households have at least one television set, while about 99 percent have radios.[3] For television and radio, the more important research questions relate to vehicle audiences.

[3]*Broadcasting Yearbook,* 1994.

For outdoor media, the Traffic Audit Bureau takes measurements and reports on the number of persons passing specific locations to give a "circulation" measure for this medium.

Media Vehicle Audience

The media vehicle audience is the number of people actually exposed to the vehicle at least once. The methods of measurement at this level vary greatly by medium.

Magazine Audiences   The sizes of these audiences are measured by so-called pass-along studies. The intent is to measure the total circulation of the magazine, plus all the people who read it when it is passed along to them. Two major organizations are active in this area, each using a different measure of readership. The first is the Simmons Market Research Bureau (SMRB). SMRB samples about 15,000 individuals annually using a cluster sampling procedure. The readership measurement taken uses the *through-the-book editorial interest method.* Here respondents, shown logos of magazine titles, are told, "Pick out those you might have read or looked into during the last 6 months, either at home or someplace else." This is verified later in the interview, after the respondent goes through a stripped-down version of each magazine. The total size of the audience is estimated by dividing the audience size in the sample by the sampling fraction (see Chapter 14).

While SMRB is the dominant supplier, a major competitor has established itself: Mediamark Research, Inc. (MRI). MRI draws a cluster sample of about 30,000 individuals (15,000 in the spring and fall) and measures audience size with the *modified recent reading method.* Respondents are given a list of about 160 magazines and asked to note the ones they have read during the most recent publication interval. They do this in two steps. First, the respondent sorts a deck of cards containing magazine logos to indicate those read in the last 6 months. The cards for these magazines are sorted again to indicate those read in the last publication interval. With differences in the methods of audience measurement, and some differences in sampling procedures, it is little wonder that SMRB and MRI report different audience sizes. The result is a great controversy as to which has the correct estimate.

In one reporting period MRI's audience estimates were as high as 162 percent and as low as 34 percent of those reported by SMRB among the 104 magazines reported in common. To the magazines in question, these differences can affect advertising rates. The MRI and SMRB numbers are usually greeted with great emotion. The ARF investigated this and found that the differences resulted from the methodological differences in the studies and not from execution problems. Ways to make the results of MRI and SMRB more in line with each other are being investigated.

Newspaper Audiences   A newspaper reader is typically defined as someone who claims to have read part of the newspaper in question on a given day. The survey method is again used. The ABC's Newspaper Audience Research Data Bank (NARDB) provides such data. The NARDB combines data that are self-collected by cooperating newspapers in the top 100 markets. To be part of NARDB, however, the information given must meet both methodological and format specifications. In general, advertisers must rely on newspaper-collected audience data.

Another source of newspaper audience data is Three Sigma, founded in 1974, which conducts surveys on 180 newspapers to measure audience size and demographic profile. These studies are done every few years. Three Sigma is subscribed to by all major dailies and about 40 advertising agencies. It is now part of the SMRB.

Television Audiences   The audience size affects television more than any other medium. Charges for commercial time and even decisions on what shows remain on the air are greatly influenced by audience size. The two companies dominating the television ratings business are A. C. Nielsen and Arbitron. Nielsen is dominant for national ratings, and Arbitron for local.

Television audience data are collected by four methods: (1) diary, (2) meters, (3) coincidental telephone recall, and (4) personal interview recall.

In the *diary method* viewers record the name of the shows that they watch and mail the diary back to the research firm. The major advantage of a diary is that it is relatively inexpensive. It is the dominant mode in the measurement of local television audiences. Arbitron contacts over 2 million households annually to place its diaries. Local audiences are usually measured in November, February, and May, and local television rates are set from these results. These are called "sweeps" months. A major problem with sweeps ratings is that networks and stations try to hype their ratings with great movies, specials, and so on. The major disadvantages of the diary method are that respondents fail to record shows watched, or forget what they watched, or even untruthfully record what shows they watched.

These problems have led to the use of *meters* to record what channel the set is tuned to and when it is on. A. C. Nielsen uses a device called an *Audimeter* for network ratings, the Nielsen Television Index (NTI). This device is connected electronically to a computer and records what the television is tuned to, if anything. NTI gives two major measures: (1) the share of households for a show (the percentage of television homes tuned to a network program for at least 6 minutes) and (2) the share of audience (the number of homes watching a specific show over the total number of homes watching any program at that time). Since meters are expensive, they are used mostly for national ratings, although Arbitron uses meters in its local ratings in Chicago, New York City, and Los Angeles. Also, meters do not record whether anyone is watching the TV set while it is on, a problem that affects up to 25 percent of an audience measurement. Controversy about the accuracy of NTI has raged for years, but almost all advertisers and agencies use it. In measuring local markets with its Nielsen Station Index (NSI), Nielsen uses both diaries and meters. The metered cities are the same as those used by Arbitron, except Nielsen also uses San Francisco. Recently, both Nielsen and Arbitron have begun to measure the size of cable television audiences using meters and diaries.

The key problem with the Audimeter is that it does not indicate the number of people watching a given television set or the demographic characteristics of the audience. The response to these problems has been the *people meter.* This is a device that is attached to the television. It allows each member of a family to separately "log on" and "log off" her or his television viewing time. The demographic characteristics of each family member are collected, and viewing habits are correlated with these demographic data. A. C. Nielsen is the leader in the development of people meters, and it maintains a people meter panel of 4000 households.

People meters do not measure visitors to the household as part of an audience, nor are they attached to television sets smaller than 5 inches. In addition, they do not measure actual commercial viewership. The Marketing Research in Action at the beginning of this chapter illustrates one attempt to address some of these problems. It is clear at this time that people meters in some form are the wave of the future in television audience measurement.

In the *coincident telephone recall method,* a sample of households is telephoned and asked what show is being watched at that time, if any, and also asked to identify the sponsor or product being advertised. The latter question is a validity check on the response given. Ratings are calculated on the percentage of homes watching a particular program. This method is quick and inexpensive but has some limitations. Nontelephone homes are excluded, and rural homes are underrepresented owing to the cost of sampling them. Thus, the total size of the audience is hard to estimate accurately. Also, only certain hours (8 A.M. to 10 P.M.) can be measured this way, and respondents often try to indicate that they are watching socially acceptable programs.

The *personal interview recall method* involves in-home interviews with a sample of respondents shortly after the time period of interest. A list of the shows by quarter hours (8 A.M. to 10 P.M.) can be measured this way, and respondents often try to dictate which shows were watched. Respondents' poor memory and untruthfulness, plus the expense of personal interviews, are the biggest problems here.

Radio Audiences   Measurement of radio audience presents some unique problems, as radios are used almost everywhere. Thus, meters have not been useful. The only major supplier of local radio audience data is Arbitron. In recent years, a number of major suppliers have failed to crack Arbitron's position. These include the Pulse, Inc.; Audits & Survey's TRAC-7; and Burke's Broadcast Research, Inc. Arbitron uses the mail diary method to gather data. During the selected 7-day period in which ratings are taken, the sample members are called twice to make sure they understand the required task and are reminded to complete and return the diary. Demographic data are also collected. The hyping of ratings by stations running contests or specials is again a problem, as it was for television.

Network radio audiences are measured by two primary services: Arbitron (using diaries) and RADAR (Radio's All Dimension Audience Research). RADAR uses the telephone coincidental method in the form of panels. Two telephone panels are set up, one in the spring and one in the fall. Each panel household is phoned eight times on consecutive days and is asked about radio listening for each quarter hour for the preceding 24 hours. In this way weekly cumulative audiences can be measured. Both Arbitron and RADAR also collect demographic data in order to allow audience profiles to be presented.

As the above discussion indicates, even measuring audience size is difficult and expensive. To date, little progress has been made in measuring advertising exposure at a general level in a given vehicle. No syndicated sources are available, and the advertisers usually must rely on information supplied by the media itself. Moreover, most advertisers want to know how their own ad did and not what the general exposure in the vehicle was. Thus, they are frequently more interested in copy testing for this purpose.

COPY TESTING

Copy testing addresses issues related to the effectiveness of each advertisement. A better term would probably be "message research," as copy testing suggests written parts of print ads. However, the term "copy testing" is used in practice to refer to all aspects (color, graphics, pictures, action, and so on) of ads appearing in all media. Many marketing research suppliers provide copy-testing services. Reliability and validity as well as the procedures used by these services are of great concern to advertisers. Twenty-one of the largest U.S. advertising agencies endorsed a set of principles aimed at improving copy testing. These principles are called PACT (Positioning Advertising Copy Testing) and they state that a "good" copy-testing system has the following characteristics:[4]

1 It provides measurements that are relevant to the objectives of the advertising.

2 It requires agreement about how the results will be used in advance of each specific test.

3 It provides multiple measurements, because single measurements are generally inadequate to assess the performance of an ad.

4 It is based on a model of human response to communication—the reception of a stimulus, the comprehension of the stimulus, and the response to the stimulus.

5 It allows for consideration of whether the advertising stimulus should be exposed more than once.

6 It recognizes that the more finished a piece of copy is, the more soundly it can be evaluated, and it requires, as a minimum, that alternative executions be tested in the same degree of finish.

7 It provides controls to avoid the biasing effects of the exposure context.

8 It takes into account basic considerations of sample definition.

9 It demonstrates reliability and validity.

[4] "21 Ad Agencies Endorse Copy Testing Principles," *Marketing News*, pp. 1 and 9, Feb. 19, 1982.

Most advertisers put a great deal of time and money into copy testing. An ad may be tested at a number of different phases of its development: as a written concept, a set of storyboards or drawings, a rough animated version, or a finished ad. In addition, it may be tested before or after media dollars are spent on it at the level they are planned for in the campaign. The former are called *pretests* and the latter *posttests.*

The Marketing Research in Action on Royal Crown Cola illustrates the power of advertising research to guide managers in the selection of a copy approach.

Idealized Procedure

Pomerance[5] outlined one view of an *idealized* copy-testing procedure by raising four questions:

1 *What measure should be taken?* The concern here is with what level or levels in the hierarchy-of-effects model (see Chapter 8) should be measured. Ideally, we would like to know the profit implications of our advertising. Figure 25-2 summarizes what we need to measure, and the arrow notes the direction of the ideal situation.

2 *What degree of finished form should the ad be in?* Should we test a rough sketch of the ad or a cheap film or a videotape version or the final version? Ideally we would like to test the final version since this is what people will be reacting to. However, cost and time may require the use of less finished versions. Figure 25-2 relates the measure to be taken to the form the ads should be in; the arrows again indicate the ideal direction.

[5]Eugene C. Pomerance, "How Agencies Evaluate Advertising," *Reflections on Progress in Marketing* (AMA), pp. 167–172, December 1964.

FIGURE 25-2 What to measure. (*Source:* Eugene C. Pomerance, "How Agencies Evaluate Advertising," in *Reflections on Progress in Marketing,* American Marketing Association, pp. 167–172, December 1964.)

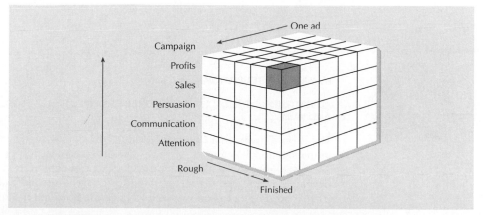

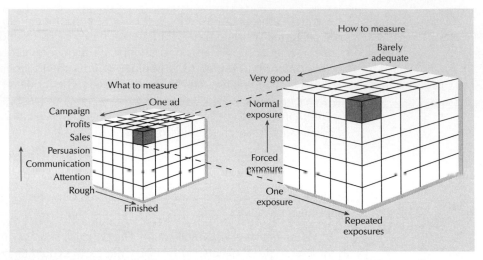

FIGURE 25-3 What and how to measure. (*Source:* Eugene C. Pomerance, "How Agencies Evaluate Advertising," in *Reflections on Progress in Marketing,* American Marketing Association, pp. 167–172, December 1964.)

3 *Should we measure the effect of one ad or of a whole campaign?* Clearly, we would like to know the effect of our campaign as opposed to that of an isolated ad. Figure 25-2 shows the shaded cube as the ideal situation. We would like to measure the profits generated by a whole campaign of finished ads.

4 *How should the measurements be made?* Here the subquestions are: Should the ad be exposed in a normal advertising vehicle or in a less normal fashion? How many times should it be exposed? Should the sampling and measurement techniques be technically optimal or something less? We would, of course, prefer the ideal: repeated exposures in a normal fashion, with a truly representative sample, and so on. Figure 25-3 shows the choices available, all leading to the ideal, represented by the shaded cube.

MARKETING RESEARCH IN ACTION

ADVERTISING RESEARCH HELPS ROYAL CROWN COLA IN THE UNITED STATES AND IN BRAZIL

The Royal Crown Cola Company (RC) utilizes extensive advertising research in all its markets to develop more effective advertising themes and actual advertising copy. The first illustration below shows how RC management used in-depth interviews to develop a U.S.-based theme for Diet RC Cola. The second example illustrates the use of copy testing to find workable copy in the Brazilian market.

1 Diet RC Cola in the United States

RC had tried a number of different marketing approaches with its low-calorie cola, Diet Rite. Ad campaigns were developed pushing themes such as taste, lower price, and calorie content, but nothing had worked: Diet Rite was mired in a dismal third place behind market leaders, Diet Pepsi and Diet Coke. The beverage had not differentiated itself from the competition, and it owned a measly .8 percent of market share.

Frustrated by its inability to increase sales, Royal Crown asked its advertising agency, DFS Dorland, to develop an emotional hook for its product that would distinguish it from major competitors.

Dorland began performing extensive marketing research to find out some of the attitudes people had toward Diet Rite and other low-calorie beverages. Researchers knew that people bought diet drinks because they wanted to control their weight, but they wanted to learn more about the psychological motivations behind consumer buying patterns.

Using clinical psychologists as interviewers, Dorland conducted interviews with dozens of women dieters. The psychologists identified several traits among the women: they considered their bodies unattractive, or they used food as a substitute for a balanced family life, or they were raised in homes where food was used as a punishment or reward. In addition, all the women said dieting was difficult and made them feel more vulnerable.

Based on the information obtained from these interviews, Dorland's research and planning division decided the Diet Rite campaign should not feature beautiful women in tiny bathing suits, because women with poor self-images could not relate to them. Instead, the agency felt the audience would empathize more with dieters who appeared to be vulnerable and hard-working.

The resulting campaign that was developed featured actors such as Lee Majors and Tony Danza in situations that emphasized humor and vulnerability. In one ad a slightly overweight Danza is coaching a girls' softball team. With his team losing 24 to 0, the girls ask Danza to play, and soon he is struggling around the bases. "His mind is alert, his body is shot," says one girl to a teammate. Throughout the ad Danza is drinking Diet Rite.

All the ads accent such warmth, stressing humor over perfection. RC is counting on this novel approach, based on marketing research, to appeal to a wide audience and to help its diet cola catch up with the leaders.

2 Finding Great Advertising Copy for Brazil

RC's market entry into Brazil was a challenge because the brand was unknown to Brazilians and most of the Portuguese-speaking population needed to be taught how to pronounce "RC Cola." In addition, both Coke and Pepsi were mounting extensive campaigns: Coke had budgeted $40 million for advertising, Pepsi about $50 million.

RC set up a field-based test of its advertising copy in three Brazilian states. This test was backed with $750,000 in media expenditures. The winner of the test was the copy slogan "Shake things up." Consumer surveys indicated that this copy generated the best attention, awareness, interest, and trial for RC cola.

Source: Adapted from *Forbes,* vol. 139, iss. 6, pp. 134–138, Mar. 23, 1987; and from Claudia Penteado, "Pepsi's Brazil Blitz," *Advertising Age,* p. 12, Jan. 16, 1995.

Robinson, Dalbey, Gross, and Wind[6] extended this type of reasoning to formulate an *idealized measurement procedure (IMP)*. They designated a number of basic attributes of all measurement techniques and came up with the ideal situation; namely, many ads in all relevant media would measure natural purchase or profits; the exposure would occur in a natural environment and a natural advertising context, with the measurement taken by means of an audit unobserved by the purchaser; the sample should be a probability sample with no geographic, media, or participation biases, and should be large enough that similar results would occur if the test were replicated. Table 25-1 summarizes this ideal situation.

Of course, such considerations as time and money force all advertising measurement procedures, syndicated or internal, to compromise this ideal. However, the IMP is a good benchmark to work from. Deviation from it should be backed up with reasoning. For example, we might decide to measure awareness instead of sales because we believe awareness is a more meaningful measure in our particular situation. Or we may not use a national probability sample because we cannot afford it. Let's now move on to commonly used pretesting procedures.

PRETESTING PROCEDURES

There are many different procedures used to pretest advertising. The ones we will touch on here are (1) consumer jury, (2) portfolio tests, (3) physiological methods, (4) dummy advertising vehicles, (5) inquiry tests, (6) on-the-air tests, (7) theater tests, (8) trailer tests, and (9) laboratory stores.

Consumer Jury

In the *consumer jury* procedure, 50 to 100 consumers from the target audience are interviewed either individually or in small groups. The jury members are asked to rank a set of ads that are typically in rough, unfinished form, often displayed on storyboards. Questions relate to such matters as: Which ad would you most likely read? Which headline is most interesting? Which interests you in buying the product the most? The respondent rank-orders the ads on each of these dimensions. Alternatively, a paired-comparison procedure to rank the ads may be used.

It is also common to have jury members use a numeric rating scale to rate the ads on explicitly identified dimensions. This procedure can be standardized and is thus susceptible to comparisons over time. Norms give average past ratings by product class or even the previous ads for the same brand. The McCollum/Spielman procedure for pretesting television ads in a laboratory setting is an example of a service that uses rating scales with a consumer jury and gives norms. Almost all major copy testing services report some form of norms.

Rating scales allow the degree of intensity of response to ads to be measured,

[6]Patrick J. Robinson, Homer M. Dalbey, Irwin Gross, and Yoram Wind, *Advertising Measurement and Decision Making* (Boston: Allyn & Bacon, Inc., 1968), p. 37a.

TABLE 25-1   THE SEVEN BASIC ATTRIBUTES OF A MEASUREMENT TECHNIQUE

Attribute	IMP
1 Scope of the advertising being measured	
a Insertions	Many
b Media	All relevant media for planned campaign
2 Responses measured	Natural purchase (overtime)
3 Conditions of exposure	
a Exposure environment	Natural
b Advertising context	Natural
4 Condition of measurements	
a Method of data collection	Unobserved audit
b Measurement environment	Natural
5 Sampling procedure	
a Sample element	Individual purchase unit
b Restrictions	None
c Method	Probability
d Size	Optional*
6 Type of comparison	Alternative advertisement or campaign
7 Data handling	Unweighted

* Large enough so that similar results would be obtained if test were repeated.
Source: Patrick J. Robinson, Homer M. Dalbey, Irwin Gross, and Yoram Wind, *Advertising Measurement and Decision Making* (Boston: Allyn & Bacon, Inc., 1968), p. 37a.

which is an advantage over ranking procedures. An extension of this type of rating is the Leo Burnett advertising agency's Viewer Response Profile (VRP) system for testing television ads. It attempts to tap viewers' experience with the advertisement on seven dimensions: entertainment, confusion, relevancy, brand reinforcement, empathy with characters and situation in the ad, familiarity, and alienation. Thus, the ratings go beyond the ad itself to the emotions associated with it.

The reliability and validity of virtually all jury systems is a serious question, given the artificiality of the exposure to the ads and the questioning procedure. Unfortunately, most services do not provide the data for a critical appraisal of these issues. For the most part, it is up to the individual advertiser to press for these measures.

Portfolio Tests

The *portfolio test* procedure involves the forced exposure of a group of target consumers to a package of both test and control ads, called a portfolio. Respondents are asked to look through the portfolio, reading whatever interests them. The effectiveness of the test ad is measured by the respondent's ability to recall the ad and then recall specifics about the ad, with the portfolio closed. Recall measures are generally unaided by any interviewer prompting, except on occasion.

Portfolio tests have been widely used in practice but have some problems. Fundamentally, there is concern that differences in recall of a set of test ads may result from differences in consumers' interest in the products involved in the test ads. To the degree that this is true, the portfolio method does not differentiate between ads on the basis of creative presentation.

Physiological Methods

A number of laboratory procedures have been developed that measure various physiological responses to ads. These procedures are not the mainstream of copy testing practice but continue to attract both practitioner and academic interest.

One procedure uses an *eye camera* to track the movement of the eye as it examines an ad. The layout of the ad is then examined in the context of this movement to determine which sections receive and hold attention, which parts seem interesting, and what level of confusion can be related to sections of the ad. Unfortunately, interpreting eye movements is difficult; does lingering at a given location indicate interest or confusion? Researchers continue to work on the eye movement approach. Applied Science Laboratories developed a computer-based eye position tracking system called the EVM Series 1998EHT. In this system the eye point of gaze, pattern of movement, blink rate, and pupil diameter are recorded 60 times a second.

Galvanic skin response (GSR) is another physiological response to ads that has received some attention. GSR is measured by attaching electrodes from a recording device to respondents, who are then exposed to test and control ads. GSR measures changes in the electrical resistance of the skin. When GSR increases, it is considered to be a measure of the *arousal* that the ad causes in subjects. The major problem here is that arousal is not necessarily related to a positive reaction to the ad.

The *tachistoscope* is another physiologically related testing device. It is a slide projector with special capabilities that allow for the presentation of ads under different levels of speed and illumination. Researchers can measure the rate at which an ad conveys information or recognition. This can be especially important in magazine and outdoor presentations.

Brain-wave analysis is another physiological method receiving experimental attention from advertising researchers. The human brain emits electrical waves that can be measured. The approach taken is to measure these waves as the subject is exposed to the advertisement. In this way the attention, interest, or emotional reaction to the advertisement can be assessed. The higher the wave amplitude, the more brain activity at that point in the advertisement. In addition, the differences in left hemisphere and right hemisphere brain activity can be measured. The left hemisphere is dominant in verbal and rational thinking, while the right side of the brain is dominant in pictorial and emotional thinking. The measurement of activity in these hemispheres can be tied to verbal and argumentative parts of an advertisement versus pictorial and emotional aspects of ads. The measurement of brain waves must take place in a laboratory setting, and must be considered very experimental in the context of providing useful information for advertisers.

Dummy Advertising Vehicles

In this procedure, test and control ads are inserted into a magazine format with editorial features of lasting interest. Thus, the only variation in the dummy magazine in a given year is the test ads. The dummy magazine is then distributed to a random sample of households in various regions of the country. The respondents are told that the publisher is interested in their evaluation of the editorial content and are instructed to read the magazine in a normal fashion. A follow-up interview covers both editorial and advertising content. Measures taken include awareness, recall, copy readership level, and product interest induced by the ad. This procedure can be questioned on the same basis as portfolio tests except that it takes place under natural readership conditions, and thus recall scores are likely to be more realistic.

Inquiry Tests

Inquiry tests measure the effectiveness of an ad on the basis of either measured sales or consumer inquiries that result directly from the ad. This may be measured by levels of coupon returns for a contest or orders received for a direct-action ad, such as a Book of the Month Club ad. The consumer response is a directly measurable sale.

Different creative approaches can be compared in three ways: (1) by placing the ads in successive issues of the same magazine or newspaper, (2) by placing them simultaneously in different vehicles, and (3) by placing different versions in "split runs" of the publication—half the copies of the vehicle contain one ad and the other half another ad.

Inquiry tests provide a direct measure of response with no interview being required, reducing costs and artificial reactions due to the interviewing process. On the other hand, limitations include the following: The presence of a coupon itself may attract attention and obscure creative differences among ads; some people may perceive and be attitudinally influenced by the ad but not return the coupon; and the inquiry does not necessarily translate into long-term action. The latter point is especially true in industrial marketing advertising; consumers may inquire about a new computer system featured in an ad but may not buy even after a later sales presentation. The inquiry test is most appropriate when a coupon return or direct sale is the objective of the advertisement.

On-the-Air Tests

Research services are available that measure responses to ads that are placed on actual television or radio programs in test areas. These procedures offer the same advantages and disadvantages as dummy vehicles. In television some of the best-known services used are Burke Marketing Services' Day-After Recall (DAR), Gallup and Robinson's Total Prime Time (TPT), Burke's AdTel cable system, IRI's BehaviorScan, and Nielsen's ERIM.

DAR tests typically involve about 200 respondents who are contacted by telephone in any of 34 cities and who claim that they watched a particular television show the night before. Measures are taken in both unaided and aided recall fashion. To begin with, respondents are asked whether they remember seeing a commercial for a product in the product class of interest. If they do not, then they are asked if they remember a commercial for the specific test brand. Those who recall the ad in either fashion are asked what they remember about the specific copy points of the ad.

DAR tests dominate the television pretesting business but do have some critics. Foote Cone & Belding, Inc., the advertising agency, released a study comparing DAR tests and their own method for creative executions that are "thinking"-based and "feeling"-based.[7] They proposed a *masked recognition test (MRT)* that involves deleting all audio and video reference to the brand name in a commercial that respondents saw in its entirety the previous day. The respondent is then asked to identify the brand in the masked commercial. The reason for this approach is that DAR tests ask consumers to verbalize the advertising message, and it is believed that this is especially difficult when the appeal is emotional. All the MRTs so far have involved on-air cable audiences who have agreed in advance to watch the program in which the ad appeared. Scores for "feeling" ads are significantly higher for MRT than for DAR.

In addition, a study conducted by J. Walter Thompson and supported by six major advertisers, indicated that show environment was an important influence on the effects of commercials on audiences, and the DAR scores should consider this. In one instance a brand recall was 41 percent on one show and 53 percent on another. This raises serious questions about reported DAR norm scores, and about comparison scores of different executions that are tested on different shows. Burke has indicated that their methods of measurement differ from J. Walter Thompson's and that their research on this issue indicates "that program has no effect on a commercial's related test score when [our] standard procedures are followed. [We are] aware, however, of some broadcast situations which can affect a commercial score, and we advise our clients not to test in these situations."[8]

Total Prime Time (TPT) is a service of Gallup and Robinson (G&R) that can test, either on a pre- or a posttesting basis, commercials that appear in prime time. They survey about 700 men and 700 women in the Philadelphia area. Qualified respondents are those who have watched at least 30 minutes of network prime time the previous night. Another service that is used strictly for pretesting is G&R's In-View. Respondents are called in advance and invited to watch the show in which the test ad will appear. About 150 men and 150 women are used in In-View, again all from the Philadelphia area.

Measures taken for both TPT and In-View include:

1 *Proven commercial registration (PCR).* Percentage who can recall (from company or brand cues) and accurately describe the ad

---

[7]"FCB Says Masked-Recognition Test Yields Truer Remembering Measures than Day-After-Recall Test," *Marketing News,* pp. 1–2, June 12, 1981.

[8]"On-Air Ad Testing Misses Show Differences: Yuspeh," *Marketing News,* p. 4, Apr. 6, 1979.

2 *Idea communication.* Percentage of those who can recall specific sales points in the ad

3 *Favorable attitude.* Percentage of favorable comments about the brand offered by the respondent

AdTel, a division of SAMI Burke, offers testing of alternative ads at the same time in the same show environment through cable television. By using special dual-cable systems in selected test cities, AdTel can direct an A ad and a B ad to different cable subscribers. Purchase diaries are kept by a panel of people who are in the A and B groups. Thus, the measure of effectiveness is actual purchase. Recently AdTel has expanded its services by offering results based on a scanner panel (see Chapter 5).

The early 1990s found a major technological battle being waged between IRI's BehaviorScan and Nielsen's ERIM system for on-the-air testing dollars.

Theater Tests

Television commercials are also tested in theater environments. Advertising Research System (ARS) and ASI Market Research, Inc., offer such services. Samples involve 250 to 600 recruited respondents in selected major cities. Ads are shown in the context of a standard television show. Typical measures taken are for brand preference shift based upon before and after exposure to test and control ads and recall of the copy points in the commercial. The artificial nature of the test environment is a major concern.

Trailer Tests

An alternative to a theater test is to recruit respondents from shopping malls and take them to a trailer near the mall or even a room in the mall itself. There they are shown several ads with or without surrounding programming, and recall, recognition, and product preference measures are taken. Again, artificiality is a problem.

Laboratory Stores

Commercials may be tested for sales and attitude input in a simulated shopping environment, like the new-product simulated test markets described in Chapter 24.

POSTTESTING PROCEDURES

The three major posttesting procedures described here are recognition tests, recall tests, and sales tests.

Recognition Tests

The readership of print ads is primarily measured with *recognition* procedures. The leading supplier in this area is Starch Readership Service. In the recognition method, personal interviews are conducted with a sample of 100 to 150 adults of each sex for each issue of a magazine. (If the magazine or newspaper has a youthful audience, a younger sample is recruited.) The respondent is asked whether or not the specific periodical has been read. For those who answer positively, the issue is opened at a page specified in advance to prevent order bias and then three measures of recognition are taken:

1 *Noted.* Percentage of readers who remember seeing the ad

2 *Seen-associated.* Percentage of readers who saw or read a part of the ad that indicates the brand or advertiser

3 *Read most.* Percentage of readers who read half or more of the written material in the ad

In addition, these scores are ranked for all the ads in the periodical, and cost ratios are given which relate readers to the money spent on the ad. Norm scores for types of product classes and periodicals are also available.

Recognition procedures are limited by the possibility of respondents confusing ads with other similar ones, forgetting, and false claiming. Also, product interest may distort memory of ads.

Recall Tests

Gallup and Robinson (G&R) offer a posttesting readership service called Magazine Impact Research Services (MIRS). Copies of test magazines are delivered to a sample of 150 to 300 respondents, and telephone interviews are arranged for the next day. Respondents, who are in 10 major geographic areas, are asked to read the magazines in a normal fashion. In the follow-up interview, readership is verified, and then a list of ads appearing in the magazine is read. Respondents identify those they remember. Result scores are similar to G&R's television service: proven name recognition, idea communication, and favorable attitude. Measurement goes beyond recognition to recall of specifics of the ad and its impact.

A twist on MIRS is G&R's Tip-In, which is really a pretesting service that uses a regular magazine into which test ads have been inserted to look like normal ads in the publication. Methods and measures are the same as MIRS.

Other similar recall-based readership services available are READEX, Starch Reader Impression Studies, Chilton Ad-Chart Readership Service, AD-Q, and the Advertising Index. Commonly used measures include unaided and aided recall scores.

Recall tests may understate the ad's impact, as the cues given to stimulate respondent memory are not strong. This is why some prefer recognition tests, especially for nondistinctive appeals and for low-involvement products. Also, despite G&R's use of the term "impact" for its service, recall does not necessarily relate to the respondent's undertaking the desired buying behavior or the advertising's reaching its objectives.

Sales Tests

Sales tests measure the impact of the ad on the sales of the product. Since sales are influenced by so many factors, great care must be taken in evaluating advertisements in this manner. Thus, these tests often involve the application of the experimental and quasi-experimental procedures discussed in Chapter 9, plus the mechanics of test marketing discussed in Chapter 24. AdTel and other panel procedures can also be used.

Recently, a number of significant new services that attempt to tie advertising activity to sales have been developed by major marketing research suppliers. The basis approach of these services is an extension of the standard advertising tracking of advertising awareness (aided and unaided) and brand awareness over time. In standard advertising tracking, respondents fitting the target market profile are interviewed, usually by telephone, to measure their levels of awareness, attitudes about the advertising and the brand, and recent purchases. The tracking survey is repeated periodically with other samples of respondents, selected in the same fashion, to allow the tracking of awareness levels, and other factors over time. The recent advances that tie advertising to sales combine the standard tracking approach with additional sales data from panels or scanner sales information with sophisticated multivariate analysis models (see Chapter 22). The Marketing Research in Action describes the approach used by some of these new service providers.

MARKETING RESEARCH IN ACTION

NEW TRACKING APPROACHES TIE ADVERTISING TO SALES

1 ASI Monitor

ASI utilizes three sets of data: (1) traditional advertising tracking by telephone and mail; (2) Nielsen household panel purchase data for market share and other behavioral shopping data; and (3) Nielsen Monitor Plus data for advertising campaign gross rating points (GRP) related measure. All three types of data have the same sampling time frame, sample population, competitive dynamics affecting them, and so forth. Thus simultaneous tracking of all these measures is possible.

Multiple regression–based sales response modeling is then used to relate the advertising awareness and brand attitudes to sales. Effects of a specific campaign can be isolated in this fashion.

2 The Consumer Affinity Company

The Consumer Affinity Company is a joint venture of the BASES Group and Media Market Assessment, Inc. The approach used extends standard advertising tracking to

People meter from A. C. Nielsen monitors audience viewing.

include information about competitive marketing programs whose effects are perceived by the respondents to the tracking.

The measurement of incremental advertising awareness is derived from the advertising awareness tracking. The drivers of this incremental awareness are then determined by examining the company's and competitors' marketing programs. An "efficiency index" is assigned to each element of the marketing program, not just advertising. These indexes are then used in a multiple regression–based sales volume model that relates the marketing programs, consumer perceptions, and attitudes to sales measured by retail scanner data. Thus, the impact of specific advertising awareness and attitude measures on sales can be identified.

3   Market Facts, Inc.: BrandVision

The BrandVision approach utilizes a proprietary nonlinear model (advanced regression type) to separate advertising into base and incremental components. The incremental component is characterized as the effect of a specific advertising campaign. Inputs to the model include advertising awareness, GRPs for the advertising program, an awareness decay function over time, and an advertising diminishing returns function. Competitive GRP diagnostics data come from Nielsen Monitor Plus or from Arbitron's Mediawatch.

These data are then used as input to another proprietary model, called the Conversion Model. This model segments consumers into four groups based upon their "commitment" to a brand: entrenched, average, shallow, and convertible. Factors used to place consumers in these groups include involvement in a product category and satisfaction with a brand. Each segment varies in its importance to a brand. The model estimates the impact of a brand's advertising awareness on the size of each segment. The brand shares are then estimated in each segment separately and summed across the segments to give total brand share and thus sales. Thus the advertising awareness is tied to the predicted sales of a brand.

4 Millward Brown, Inc.'s, SALES LINK and AHF's LoMACAST

The SALES LINK service of Millward Brown, Inc., and the LoMACAST service of AHF Marketing Research, Inc. are other competitors in the effort to track the relationship of advertising to sales. It is a new area and one that is likely to evolve quickly over the next few years.

Source: Lawrence N. Gold, "Advertising Tracking: New Tricks of the Trade," *Marketing Research,* vol 5, no 3, pp 42–44, 1993.

SUMMARY

1 Media vehicle and message research constitute the major application areas of marketing research within advertising.

2 Media research focuses its attention on media vehicle distribution and media vehicle audience.

3 Measurements related to advertising exposure, advertising perception, advertising communication, and sales response—although media-related—are usually dealt with more in message or copy research.

4 Media vehicle distribution research measures the circulation of print media and the penetration level of broadcast media in households.

5 Media vehicle audience research measures the size of the audience exposed to a given vehicle. Periodical pass-along or readership studies and radio and television ratings are the modes here.

6 Survey methods dominate print media audience measurement, while diary, meter, coincident telephone, and personal interview recall methods are important in television. Radio uses diary and telephone panels.

7 Copy testing measures the effectiveness of the ad itself. Ads may be tested in a number of developmental or finished stages as well as in natural or artificial environments. The more finished and more natural the exposure, especially repeated exposures, the more ideal the procedure.

8 Pretesting of ads occurs prior to commitments of media dollars at the level planned in the campaign. Pretesting procedures include consumer jury, portfolio

tests, physiological methods, dummy advertising vehicles, inquiry tests, on-the-air tests, theater tests, trailer tests, and laboratory stores.

9 Posttesting of ads occurs after the ads have been run at the planned level in the media. Posttesting procedures include recognition tests, recall tests, and sales tests.

10 Good copy-testing procedures should follow certain principles, including: use relevant measures, provide multiple measures, consider models of human response to communication, allow for number of exposures, compare the same degree of finished ads, provide controls against bias in the exposure environment, and demonstrate reliability and validity

DISCUSSION QUESTIONS

1 Why is advertising research so much used in practice? Why is this true, given the great experience base among marketing managers in advertising?

2 What different types of data would advertisers like to have about media vehicles?

3 Why are some of these data so difficult to obtain? Be specific.

4 Why do the SMRB and Mediamark Research, Inc., obtain estimates of magazine audience sizes that differ? Which method of measurement is better?

5 What methods may be used to measure the sizes of television audiences? Evaluate each.

6 What are the characteristics of an ideal copy-testing procedure? Why does practice not follow the ideal?

7 How can you measure the reliability and validity of a copy-testing procedure? Why is this important?

8 How are ads pretested? Evaluate each method.

9 In posttesting recognition and recall, two different measures are taken. Give an example of each and evaluate the two.

10 Why aren't sales tests the most common form of posttesting?

11 Sometimes marketing research can reveal feelings about products that might easily have been overlooked. When the Timberland company wanted a new print campaign for its shoes, the rugged footware was riding a new wave of popularity as a fashion item. Research showed, however, that consumers actually bought the shoes because they were durable, and that the consumers also thought the shoes improved with age. As a result, Timberland's agency resisted a campaign that presented the shoes as fashion accessories and instead developed one that emphasized how long the shoes lasted.

a What research design could be used to determine these conclusions?

b How should a researcher measure the level of success of the advertising campaign that was actually implemented?

12 What are the research limitations of the passive people meter described in the Marketing Research in Action at the beginning of this chapter? How might the passive people meter change the pricing and buying of advertising space on television?

13 MINICASE

Advertising Testing Services, Inc. (ATSI), is a small marketing research supplier specializing in the copy testing of television commercials. ATSI is located in Princeton, New Jersey, and numbers among its clients some of the nation's largest advertisers. ATSI tests both animated and finished versions of commercials.

ATSI's typical testing procedure is as follows:

a Approximately 150 respondents in total are recruited from five to seven different shopping centers around the country. Typical locations would be St. Louis, Missouri; Hartford, Connecticut; Tampa, Florida; Denver, Colorado; and Charlotte, North Carolina. Potential respondents are screened to make sure they are in the target audience of the commercial being tested and are users of the product category being tested. This is done by asking potential respondents whether or not they have bought or used products in many product categories, including the one of interest.

b Respondents are taken to a viewing area where they are shown the test commercial along with six other commercials for noncompetitive products.

c After viewing all the commercials once, each respondent is given a personal interview.

The response measures recorded in the postexposure interview include the following:

a The respondent is asked to name three brands from the advertising he or she has just seen. This serves as an unaided awareness measure. The order in which the three brands are mentioned is also recorded.

b If the test brand is not mentioned, the respondent is asked whether he or she remembers the commercial for the test brand. This is a measure of aided awareness.

c The main points from the test commercials are then asked for, to measure unaided recall of the content of the ad.

d The test commercial is then shown again to the respondent, and the main points are asked for, to measure aided recall. In addition, the thoughts and feelings generated by the ad are probed, along with any confusion or lack of understanding that is generated; the respondent's ideas on believability; and his or her likes and dislikes about the ad.

e Finally, questions are asked about the brand itself, including an indication of liking for the brand compared to how it was viewed before the test commercial, and a series of rating scales on brand descriptions were seen. Demographic data on respondents are also recorded.

Results are reported on all the measures taken and compared to norm scores. These norms may be for other similar product commercials that have been tested in the same way. If the user has employed the service enough, the norm may be the scores from a set of the user's own commercials. Both the norm and test scores are indexed for ease of interpretation.

In comparing test results against the norm, the following guide is offered for noting significant differences at the 80 percent confidence level.

Proportion observed, percent	Differences in reported percentages necessary for significance
50	8
30–40 or 60–70	7
20 or 80	6
10 or 90	4

An example of part of a typical report of test results for a new car is presented below.

RESULTS FOR CAR ADVERTISEMENT

	Norm*		Test advertisement	
	Percent	Index	Percent	Index relative to norm
Overall reaction				
Liked the commercial very much	00	100	66	111
Brand image				
Made me feel that this car is:				
Of the highest quality	42	100	71	169
Better-driving than most other cars	52	100	59	113
For people who love to drive	60	100	81	135
My kind of car	26	100	34	130
Clarity and drawing power				
Not confusing	79	100	68	86
Convincing	26	100	28	108
Unaided awareness				
Percent of time test ad is named among first three	64	100	59	92

* Based upon six commercials for same car brand.

a Evaluate the procedure used by ATSI.
b Evaluate the measures taken by ATSI.
c In comparing test results against the norm, is the stated significant difference level in scores appropriate? From a statistical testing point of view, is type I or type II error more important here?
d How should the reliability and validity of ATSI's results be determined?
e What conclusions for the advertiser would you draw from the results reported?

CHAPTER 26

DISTRIBUTION AND PRICING RESEARCH

MARKETING RESEARCH IN ACTION

SCANNER DATA + DEMOGRAPHICS HELP MANUFACTURERS AND RETAILERS DEFINE MARKETS

Local marketing activity is becoming increasingly more important to both manufacturers and retailers. This approach takes into account the differences that exist among a retail customer's store choices, as well as variances among those stores' clientele.

SAMI Information Services recently conducted distribution research based on the integration of UPC scanner data and a database of store trading-area demographics from Market Metrics, Inc. The database covered about 500 demographic variables for about 30,000 grocery stores nationwide, plus 70 other descriptive facts about each store's physical layout.

Market Metrics then constructed trading areas for each individual store from models that took into account the individual census tracts plus an array of factors such as store size and reach, natural and human-made boundaries and barriers, the proximity of competitive stores, and transportation access routes to each store. Combining this information with a store's scanner data allowed SAMI to identify specific ways in which demographic factors affected the occurrence of store sales for different brands and categories.

For example, SAMI conducted a regression analysis of a major eastern market to determine the impact of household income on store sales levels for two different brands in the frozen entree category. The results confirmed information derived from purchase-panel data which indicated that each brand appealed to a different end of the income range and could support different price points.

Another important use for this combination of scanner and demographic information is the evaluation of minorities' effect on category sales. For example, a 10 percent increase in the density of the Mexican-Hispanic population was found to increase a store's sale of meat and fish by 4 percent while decreasing its sale of potatoes by 6 percent and of juice by 5 percent. This type of information is extremely valuable to manufacturers and retailers interested in adjusting their product offerings and promotional activities to specific local preferences.

A combination of clustering and data reduction techniques allows researchers to "filter" desired information from large databases of merged data. This procedure allows manufacturers to identify major patterns of sales activity, along with their potential causes. Major store segments can be defined that cover a broad range of demographic groupings.

For example, a recent SAMI study of ready to eat (RTE) Cereal used this technique to identify two distinct and different store segments for a large west coast retailer. One store segment was dominated by young families with a high percentage of children in the 6- to 17-year age range. The other type of store was dominated by older, retired, "empty-nest" households. The segmentation study discovered that the young-family stores had very high sales levels for presweetened cereals and low velocities for bran and nutritional cereals. The opposite pattern was found in the empty-nest stores: there were low sales figures for presweetened cereals and high sales figures for bran and nutritional cereals.

Retailers and manufacturers, especially those interested in local marketing, can derive many benefits from linking UPC scanner data with store demographic and descriptive data. Manufacturers can identify the demographic factors that affect their brands' sales in designated markets. Specific stores can be pinpointed that have a high concentration of target demographic groups, allowing local marketers to improve marketing and selling efficiencies by targeting efforts to these specific stores. Manufacturers and retailers both benefit from the ability to segment stores and to define the impact of demographic factors across many brands and categories at the same time. This also facilitates the improvement of product mix and space allocation at the store and local market level.

Source: "New Way to Use Scanner Data and Demographics Aids Local Marketers," Marketing News, p. 8, Sept 11, 1989.

The Marketing Research in Action illustrates the power of marketing research to aid marketing decision making related to distribution strategy decisions for both manufacturers and retailers. It also hints at the usefulness of marketing research in making pricing decisions. Both distribution and pricing marketing research form the topics of this chapter. We will begin our discussion with distribution research, and deal with pricing research later in this chapter.

DISTRIBUTION RESEARCH

A 1994 American Marketing Association (AMA) study indicated that about 40 percent of businesses undertake some form of distribution research.[1] For consumer product companies this utilization is 73 percent, and for industrial firms it is about 65 percent. The importance of marketing research in the distribution area is heightened by the fact that for many products the cost of distribution is greater than manufacturing costs or other marketing costs. Our discussion of distribution will be divided into two parts: (1) research undertaken about activities and performance in the channel of distribution, and (2) research undertaken by members of the channel of distribution about their own marketing activities.

Marketing Research on Channel Activities and Performance

There are four areas of marketing research on channel activities and performance that will be discussed here. They are (1) the use of syndicated services to monitor product flow at the wholesale and retail levels; (2) the use of attitude studies of channel members; (3) the use of experimental and quasi-experimental test markets to measure responses to marketing activity; and (4) the use of internal records, surveys, and observation to monitor the performance of channel members. Other types of studies are also possible, but they are not discussed here.

Syndicated Services to Monitor Product Flow Syndicated data are mainly used to measure the flow of goods within the channel of distribution at both the wholesale and retail levels. These services are used mostly to monitor the flow of competitors' products and to determine market share in the channel and at retail. At the wholesale level, Nielsen, Pipeline Research, SAMI/Burke, and other services provide sample-based audit data on packaged goods in the drug and food trade. (See Chapter 5 and its appendix for a detailed outline of these services.) Trade associations also provide this type of data for industrial products; for example, the Pulp and Paper Association provides production and shipment data to its members.

At the retail level, Nielsen; IRI; Audits and Surveys, Inc.; Burgoyne, Inc.; and many other services provide sample-based store audit data of products sales. (See Chapter 5 for a detailed description of these services.) In addition, trade associations grouped by store type, such as the retail drug trade group, provide data on product sales to its members.

---

[1]Thomas C. Kinnear and Ann R. Root, *1994 Survey of Marketing Research* (Chicago: American Marketing Association, 1994).

Attitude Studies of Channel Members   It is also possible to apply the principles of attitude measurement discussed earlier in this book to both wholesale and retail trade members. Examples here would include the measurement of quality perceptions of a firm's product, a firm's perceived service quality to the channel, evaluations of promotions directed at the channel, and the preferences and purchase intentions of channel members for different product types and brands. The use of questionnaires administered by independent marketing research firms to keep the client unknown to the respondent is common in this type of research.

Experimental/Quasi Experimental Test Markets   In controlled test market cities the acceptance of the channel of distribution to the product offerings of the marketer is assured by agreement between the research supply house and the members of the trade in that area. In many instances, the reaction of the trade in a free-choice situation is as important to the success of the product and marketing program as final consumer acceptance. Thus, the use of standard test market cities is common so that the trade reaction can be measured and reacted to by the marketer. The V-8 test market experiment described at the beginning of Chapter 9 is an example of this approach. The full power of experimental and quasi-experimental approaches for all types of firms can be applied to trade-directed marketing programs.

Internal Records, Surveys, and Observation of Performance   Marketers also undertake their own primary research to measure performance of the channel members against objectives. Performance measures utilized include sales levels by product type, customer service levels, inventory levels maintained, in-store display usage, proper use of cooperative advertising dollars, and quality of sales personnel and their customer interactions.

These measurements can be taken using many of the approaches discussed earlier in the book. A firm's product sales to various trade members can be measured by internal company sales records. The key here is that these records must be detailed enough so that product characteristics such as size, color, design pattern, and so on can be matched with the individual trade member to whom the product is shipped. It is common in Japanese firms to rely heavily on this type of shipment data in marketing decisions.

It is also possible to make use of survey methodology to measure customer responses to sales personnel, service quality, and so on. In addition, the observational method is very appropriate for measuring in-store customer-salesperson interactions, stores' compliance with point-of-purchase display agreements, and even cooperative advertising activity among newspapers and catalogs. Observation of channel members by senior marketing personnel is common among Japanese firms. Their belief is that this approach keeps the firms closer to the customer than does the survey approach. For example, U.S. Pioneer Electronics (a U.S. subsidiary of Pioneer of Japan) used observers in stores to determine that retail sales personnel were attempting to switch customers from the Pioneer brand of stereo equipment to other brands.

Marketing research is also very useful to members of the channel for their own marketing decisions. We now turn our attention to this type of research.

Marketing Research by Channel Members

There are three areas of marketing research by channel members that we will discuss here. They are (1) attitude studies, especially image studies, (2) location studies, and (3) conjoint studies to develop product configurations. Other types of studies are also possible, but they are not discussed here.

Attitude/Image Studies   Both wholesalers and retailers can utilize attitude measurement procedures to determine the perception that current and potential customers and suppliers have of them on a battery of attributes. Retailers commonly use the semantic-differential scale to measure the "image" that their stores hold in the marketplace. See Chapter 8 for an example of this approach applied to a retail situation.

Location Studies   One of the key activities of marketing researchers in the retail setting is performing location studies. The best location for a retail outlet is a critical success factor for a retailer. This section describes a commonly used approach to finding the best location. The five steps in this marketing research approach are: (1) define the relevant market trading area or areas, (2) identify population characteristics within the trading area, (3) determine the competitors' locations, (4) determine shopping patterns within the trading area, and (5) develop a store patronage forecasting model based on the above factors. The Marketing Research in Action on the location of bank branches in Hong Kong illustrates this approach. We now examine each of these steps.

MARKETING RESEARCH IN ACTION

HONG KONG BANK USES MARKETING RESEARCH TO LOCATE BRANCHES

A marketing research study was undertaken to systematically evaluate retail locations for a major commercial bank in Hong Kong. Past experience indicated that "good" sites had 20 times the potential of "poor" sites, and the considerable investment involved made the selection of branch location sites one of the single most important decisions in retail banking.

The first step in this process was to develop customer profiles and analyze trading areas. The Hong Kong bank used as the subject in this study had 20 branches in different areas of Hong Kong. This bank was widely known for its strong ties to the community, and top management wanted to use this image to attract additional business of the same nature. The process here was to identify and understand the "typical" customer for each product offered by the bank. This was done by sampling

Location-potential marketing research helps Hong Kong banks find the right place.

the existing customers and analyzing their backgrounds. Sampling was conducted by individual branches and for the individual products offered at each branch.

The study then analyzed each branch's trading area for each product offered by the branch. If the branch drew most of its business from its immediate neighborhood, it was classified as a low-level service branch. If it drew customers from everywhere, it was classified as a high-level service branch. The researchers were mainly interested in low-level service branches, since they better fit the bank's desired "neighborhood bank" image, and since their demand potential could be estimated on the simple basis of residential population.

The bank's existing branches were divided into low-level and high-level service branches. Customers in the study's sample were asked to provide their addresses. Researchers then constructed customer-spotting maps for each product of each branch by drawing a circle, using the branch office as its center point and a designated distance (in this case 1750 meters) as its radius. The addresses of all the customers in the sample were then recorded on the map. This allowed researchers to determine the percentage of customers residing within the circle. Branches with over 60 percent of their customers within the circle were classified as low-level service branches because most of their business came from the immediate neighborhood. Branches with less than 60 percent of their customers within the circle were classified as high level service branches and eliminated as potential new branch locations.

Primary trading areas for each product offered by the bank were identified by further evaluation of the low-level service branches. Customer-spotting maps were combined with relevant population data from census and statistics reports, allowing researchers to calculate the probabilities of patronage for each street block on the map. This was done by dividing the customer distribution for each block (as shown by the customer-spotting maps) by the population distribution for that same block. Researchers used these probabilities to zone the trading areas by street blocks, from highest to lowest probability of patronage. This was done in order to define the primary trading area for each banking product offered at a low-level service branch. A primary trading area was defined as the area closest to the branch where the branch had at least a 60 percent chance of neighborhood patronage.

The next step in evaluating retail locations was to draw a combined primary trading area for each branch by examining the primary trading areas of various products for that branch to identify the median primary trading area for each branch. Researchers then used the median of these branch-level primary trading areas to define the pattern of the primary trading area for a "typical" branch of the bank. Competition in each trading area was also accounted for by using a market-share adjustment model. This model calculated the distance from customers' addresses in the defined primary trading area to competitive bank branches, and assigned customer usage patterns in inverse proportion to the distance from the customers' addresses to the available competitive branches.

Potential new sites were then analyzed using (1) the "typical" pattern of the current branches, (2) the size of the population in the defined primary trading areas, and (3) the expected customer travel patterns. This process provided a fairly dependable system for using limited market data and research facilities to estimate demand and evaluate retail location sites for bank branches in Hong Kong.

Source: Kam-Hon Lee, "A Research Design for Exploring Retail Locations for Commercial Banks in Hong Kong," *International Journal of Bank Marketing,* vol. 4, no. 3, pp. 19–30, 1986.

1 Defining the Trading Area   The first step in location analysis is to define the relevant trading area for a current or proposed site. This typically involves identifying the purchase patterns for the relevant product or service related to that location. Purchase pattern identification can be accomplished with a survey of current customers, as we see in the Marketing Research in Action about a Hong Kong bank, or with a survey of users of the product or service, independently of whether or not they are current customers. The survey is used to define a spatial zone or zone around the relevant locations. These geographic zones contain customers with different probabilities of using a particular location. For example, the Hong Kong bank used a 60 percent probability to define its relevant trading area. It is possible to define more than one zone for any location. For example, there could be a 90 percent zone, a 70 percent zone, and so on. The expectation is that the farther away the customer is from the location of interest, the lower the probability of that particular retail location being used. The marketing research survey defines the geographic spread of these probability zones. Typical examples of findings are: the 60 percent probability zone for a bank is only a few miles or so, while that for an automobile dealer is over 10 miles.

2 *Determining Population Characteristics in the Trading Area* The second step in location analysis involves defining the demographic characteristics of customers or potential customers within the defined trade zones. This can be done using the same survey that defined the zones. More typically, it is done by matching the defined zones to census tract information. The demographic data used are often supplied by companies that supply census-type estimates for the years between the census. The National Planning Data Corporation (NPDC) is a major U.S. supplier of such data. Figure 26-1 shows an NPDC analysis of Dallas County in terms of the percentage of families in a tract that have a household income of over $35,000 per year, and the locations of bank branches. This information would be combined with the defined zones to profile the demographics of these zones.

One problem that arises in this regard is that the defined zones do not match the shape of the census tract. This problem is handled by the use of *centroids*. A centroid is the geographic point that marks the center of each of the 260,000 block groups and enumeration districts in the U.S. Census.[2] Centroids can be used to redefine census tracts in other shapes. The relevant zone around a retail location may be in the form of a circle, a rectangle, a polygon, or some other shape. Having decided upon a shape in step 1 above, the marketing research proceeds as follows to use centroids to match the tract data to the desired shape.

a The latitude and longitude of the centroid of each block group are located, and the address or street intersection is identified on a map such as that produced by the U.S. Geological Survey.

b The trading area's population is assessed by adding up the demographic characteristics of the trade area's component pieces of geography.

c When a standard census area such as a tract or minor civil division (MCD) falls entirely within a trading area, all the characteristics of the component piece are assigned to that area. For the tracts or MCDs that are divided by the trade area boundary, only some of the original data are assigned.

d Along the boundary where tracts or MCDs are split by the trading area, some block group centroids are inside the trading area and some are outside. If, for example, the block group centroids that fall within the trading area represent 20 percent of the tract's population, then 20 percent of the tract's demographics is allocated to the trade area. For example, if a tract has 1000 households with an income of $70,000 and above, this approach would allocate 20 percent, or 200 households of this income, to the trade area. Figure 26-2 illustrates this approach in the context of a circular trading area.

The assumption of the centroid method is that households are the same across block groups of a tract. The more variance that exists within a block group, the

---

[2]This section is based on Stephen J. Tordella, "How to Relate to Centroids," *American Demographics,* vol. 9, no. 5, pp. 46 and 50, May 1987.

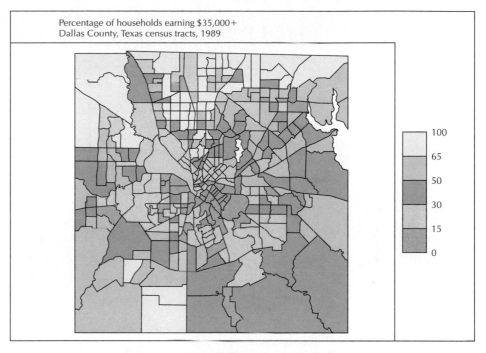

Percentage of households earning $35,000+
Dallas County, Texas census tracts, 1989

	100
	65
	50
	30
	15
	0

Base map of Dallas County, Texas, showing income by Census tracts

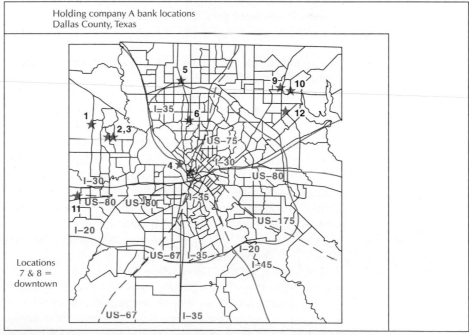

Holding company A bank locations
Dallas County, Texas

Locations
7 & 8 =
downtown

FIGURE 26-1   NPDC data on income and locations for Dallas County. (*Source:* P. K. Skipper, "Prospecting for Deposits with MAX and Map Analysis," *Demometrics,* vol. 6, no. 4, p. 4, Autumn 1989.)

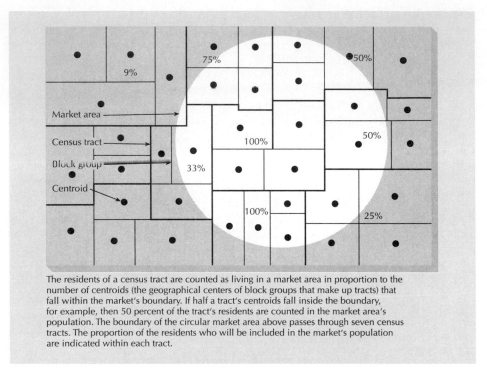

The residents of a census tract are counted as living in a market area in proportion to the number of centroids (the geographical centers of block groups that make up tracts) that fall within the market's boundary. If half a tract's centroids fall inside the boundary, for example, then 50 percent of the tract's residents are counted in the market area's population. The boundary of the circular market area above passes through seven census tracts. The proportion of the residents who will be included in the market's population are indicated within each tract.

FIGURE 26-2   Illustration of the centroid method. (*Source:* Stephen J. Tordella, "How to Relate to Centroids," *American Demographics,* vol. 9, iss. 5, p. 50, May 1987.)

less valid will be the results of the trading area analysis. For many applications this is a reasonable assumption.

3 Determine the Competitors' Locations   The locations of relevant competitors are placed in the map, and the distances from the zones to each competitor within the defined trading area are determined.

4 Determine the Shopping Patterns within the Trading Area   Survey, diary panel, or scanner panel methodology, or even an actual purchase record for the product class, can then be used to determine the target group's shopping patterns related to all competitors within the trade area. For example, automobile companies, through records of vehicle identification numbers, have access to addresses of purchasers and the purchase locations for all car brands. The purpose of determining shopping patterns is to tie together the location of the target purchaser with retail location behavior.

5 Develop a Store Forecasting Patronage Model   All the data collected and organized in steps 1 to 4 are then used to forecast patronage based upon a model of how target consumers shop in the marketplace. These models usually include the distance factor as the prime driver, as the Hong Kong Marketing Research in Action notes. The closer the distance, the more patronage is expected. However, other factors such as time in transit, and store or mall characteristics (including size, advertising, and product offerings) also play a role. The marketing research works to define the relative importance of these factors by the use of surveys, trade-off analysis, and so on.

Conjoint Studies to Develop Product Configurations   The last area of marketing research used by channel members that we will discuss here is conjoint studies to help determine product configurations. This trade-off analysis approach was discussed in Chapters 21 and 24. The same approach discussed there can be used to measure consumer utility attached to different store layouts, product lines carried, store sizes, hours open, price points, and so on. As we noted in Chapter 24, Marriott used this approach to develop the Courtyard by Marriott concept. The use of conjoint analysis for pricing research is noted later in this chapter. Now we turn our attention to the important topic of marketing research on pricing.

PRICING RESEARCH

Pricing decisions directly impact revenue (unit price $\times$ units sold = revenue). Consequently, the quality of information available to a manager regarding the determinants of price directly impact revenue levels and profitability. These determinants are: (1) demand sensitivity to price changes, (2) costs, (3) competitive price levels, and (4) organizational objectives.

A study of marketing research practices indicates that about 57 percent of businesses do cost analysis research, 71 percent do competitive price analysis research, and only 56 percent conduct price elasticity research.[3] The purpose of this section is to present the research procedures for measuring price sensitivity. Each procedure offers particular advantages over the others, so the selection process involves matching the appropriate procedure to the decision situation confronting the manager.

Measurement Procedures

There are numerous procedures involved in measuring price sensitivity. These procedures can be evaluated on the dimensions of (1) degree of research control and (2) nature of variables measured. Table 26-1 presents these procedures classified on these two dimensions.

The degree of research control varies from a highly controlled research setting to an uncontrolled setting where the researcher is an observer of real marketplace events. In the uncontrolled setting, the researcher records how people behave and what they say about this behavior. For example, the researcher may use a survey of retail shoppers to record people's reactions to a product's price relative to

[3]Thomas C. Kinnear and Ann R. Root, *1994 Survey of Marketing Research* (Chicago: American Marketing Association, 1994), p. 42.

TABLE 26-1   CLASSIFICATION OF PROCEDURES FOR MEASURING PRICE SENSITIVITY

Nature of variables measured	Degree of control	
	High	Low
Indirect — Preference, Intention to buy	Simulated purchase survey Conjoint measurement	Survey research
Direct ——→ Purchase	Field experiment Laboratory experiment	Company sales records Panel store data Retail store audit data

competitors' prices. Questions could be asked about how buyers would react to higher or lower prices. In contrast, a highly controlled research environment could be created where price levels and other marketing variables could be manipulated by the researcher. This experimentally controlled research design would expose buyers of a product to various levels of price and to variations in product features. Such an experiment could be conducted in a simulated store environment where prices and product features could be manipulated for randomly selected groups of buyers and where price sensitivities could be measured.

The advantage of experimentally controlled procedures is that the interval validity of the measurements can be accurately determined. However, the cost of gaining this information must be balanced against the potential loss of external validity caused by the controlled environmental setting. If the controlled environment significantly biases the price sensitivity measurements, the researcher should use less controlled survey procedures in which the degree of internal validity may be more difficult to determine but the external validity is not in question. Typically, experimentally controlled measurement of price sensitivity is more accurate and more useful than uncontrolled procedures. However, this research procedure can be expensive and time-consuming.

When price sensitivity is estimated, the variables measured can be direct or indirect indicators of purchase behavior. Direct or actual purchase studies measure real-market purchases. Indirect indicators are preference and purchase intention studies that measure the judgments or choices of people in a hypothetical purchase environment. Indirect indicators are assumed to predict actual purchase behavior. The questionable accuracy of the prediction is the main limitation of indirect research studies. Consequently, research studies that measure purchase behavior directly are more desirable. However, such studies are costly and time-consuming.

The selection of an appropriate research design involves many issues specific to the managerial problem situation; the following overview of research procedures is intended to be relevant to the choice of a research design for measuring price sensitivity.

Low Control: Prepurchase Measures

Survey Research   The use of survey research to measure preferences and purchase intentions is the most popular technique for estimating price sensitivity. The advantages of this procedure are: (1) The cost of data collection is often less than direct measures of purchase. (2) The procedure is flexible to product/market requirements. (3) It can be used in product development. (4) The procedure allows for fast data collection.

The main disadvantage of survey research in the measurement of price sensitivity is the lack of external validity. The problem is that customer preferences and intention-to-buy judgments may not predict actual purchase behavior.

Survey questions that directly ask customers how much they would pay for a product rarely elicit valid judgments of price sensitivity. Customers often respond to such questions in a context of bargaining and will answer with a lower price than they would pay in a real purchase situation. Other times, customers may state a higher price in order to impress the interviewer. Consequently, the external validity of direct questions about price is typically low and potentially very misleading. Although with the direct questioning approach to measuring price sensitivity, the potential for bias is high, it can be a valuable predictive tool when past experience has identified the nature and direction of biases. Here, the research findings can be modified for the biases, and predictions can be made more accurately.

An example of this approach would involve measuring customers' intentions to buy a new product by having them indicate which one of the following statements best describes their likelihood of purchase at a given price.

If this product were priced at $1.40, which of the following statements would best describe your intention to buy?

(Check one)

Definitely would buy	( )
Probably would buy	( )
Might/might not buy	( )
Probably should not buy	( )
Definitely would not buy	( )

A price elasticity curve could be developed by randomly dividing the sample into, say, five respondent groups and asking each group about a different level of price. Figure 26-3 depicts how the price elasticity curve appears when the proportion of responses for "Definitely would buy" and "Probably would buy" are tabulated for each of five different price levels. Note that demand becomes more elastic above the $1.20 price point than below it. An experienced researcher who understands the potential biases with this prepurchase measurement procedure may develop valid predictive measures of actual purchase elasticities of demand.

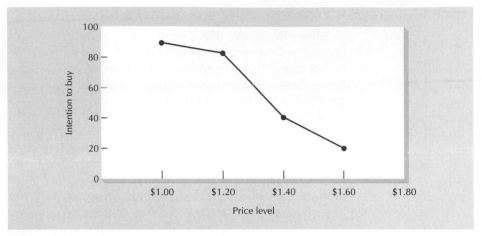

FIGURE 26-3   Intention-to-buy elasticity of demand curve for a new product.

High Control: Prepurchase Measures

The external validity of prepurchase measures can be improved by better control over the biases influencing customers' judgments. The goal is to create a research environment very similar to the actual purchase setting. Two approaches to this problem are (1) a simulated purchase survey and (2) conjoint measurement.

Simulated Purchase Survey   The simulated purchase survey attempts to get customers to visualize the actual purchase environment. The researcher may show the customer a visual representation of the purchase situation, present actual products or concepts, and then ask for preferences or intentions to buy where price levels are varied for different groups of customers.

The goal is to increase the external validity of the survey technique by having the respondent imagine a purchase situation and then think about the survey question in the context of that situation. It is hoped that if the survey question requires a choice among alternative products, the consumer's decision process will closely follow the actual purchase process. If so, the survey result may predict price sensitivity reasonably well. The validity of this assumption needs to be judged by a researcher experienced in the product category under study.

Conjoint Measurement   An important survey technique called trade-off measurement, or conjoint measurement, has become a popular way to measure price sensitivity. The conjoint measurement procedure can disaggregate a product's price into the values consumers attach to each attribute or benefit being offered to them. The term "conjoint" is used to emphasize that if the relative values of attributes are considered jointly they can be measured more accurately than if they are considered one at a time. Consequently, the basic data for conjoint measurement are not consumers' answers to questions about purchase intentions, but their answers to questions designed to measure their preferences for combinations of price and nonprice attributes important in the selection of a product. Since the procedure typically requires a respondent to complete a series of detailed paired-comparison or ranking judgments, the preference data must be collected under controlled conditions in which the respondent will take the time to understand the instructions and complete the series of preference judgments.

After the consumers' preferences have been measured, the trade-off judgments are analyzed to determine the relative value or utility each consumer places on the attributes studied. Given this information, the researcher can predict the price sensitivity of a change in the product benefit package. An example of the use of conjoint measurement in pricing research is given in the Marketing Research in Action on a new financial service.

Low Control: Purchase Measures

Historical sales data may be useful in estimating price sensitivity of customers. The three types of sales data are (1) company sales records, (2) panel sales data, and (3) retail store audit data.

Company Sales Records   Company sales records are data from a company's accounting system, such as shipments data. These data represent a company's sales transaction with the buyer of a product or line of products, since companies typically sell to members of the distribution channel rather than directly to the final customer. These data sources do not contain information on the prices retailers are offering customers. Consequently, company sales records are rarely useful in measuring price sensitivity of buyers to the diversity of retailer prices offered to customers over time.

Panel Sales Data   Panel sales data are collected from a panel of customers; these data include purchases and prices measured over time. Several marketing research companies maintain panels of households which can number in the thousands. Weekly or biweekly records are available for each household. These records also contain information on conditions of sales, such as coupon usage, price specials, and so on. Information on competitive prices and type of retail outlet is available. Various demographic information on the customer makes it possible to correlate price sensitivity with customer profiles.

Retail scanner technology has eliminated the requirement that panel members record their purchases on a questionnaire and return them weekly. Instead, purchases are recorded automatically by in-store scanners whenever panel members identify themselves at the checkout counter. This technology has simplified the requirements of panel membership, making it easier to have a representative sample of households and eliminating the biases in customer-reported sales transaction information.

Retail Store Audit   A popular source of purchase data comes from auditing sales and prices at retail outlets. Scanner technology has made sales and price data available in many retail outlets at reasonable cost. As scanner technology spreads to more types of retailers, a new source of information on the price sensitivity of products will be available to more types of manufacturers.

MARKETING RESEARCH IN ACTION

USE OF CONJOINT MEASUREMENT TO DETERMINE THE OPTIMAL PRICE-ATTRIBUTE COMBINATION FOR A NEW FINANCIAL SERVICE

A major U.S. brokerage firm was interested in launching a new service that would permit customers to deal with the firm via their personal computers. Although management felt that brokerage customers would pay a fee to have computer access to their accounts, the company was not exactly sure what features the service should have or how to price it. The basic problem for the firm was to identify the optimal service combination of features and price. The more features the system included, the more it would cost to set up and maintain. Thus management wanted to include only the features that customers were willing to pay for.

The firm contacted Clancy, Shulman & Associates to undertake a trade-off analysis of the proposed service. Clancy, Shulman interviewed 500 prospective users randomly selected from a master list of all the firm's customers with current account balances of a respectable size. Interviews were conducted in the customers' homes and averaged approximately 45 minutes.

During the interview, respondents were shown 18 different combinations of features and prices. These 18 services represented a carefully selected mix of six different factors: hours of operation, the types of information that could be requested, the ability to move funds between accounts, the ability to place orders, access to a personal line of credit, and the monthly charge for the service.

Respondents were asked to rate each configuration. Later, respondents rated individual factors and levels using simple ratings of purchase interest. These data were then used by Clancy, Shulman to develop a "micromodel" of the potential market, which enabled the firm to estimate the number of consumers who—once they became aware of the product—would sign up for each of the more than 500,000 possible combinations of features.

The trade-off analysis showed that price was a critical determinant of interest in this new home banking service. Averaging across different combinations of features, the effects of price were as follows:

Monthly service charge ($)	Predicted percentage of customers who would sign up (assuming awareness and opportunity)
5*	49
10	37
15*	23
20	15
25*	9
30	4

* These three levels were included in the trade-off experiment. The other levels were estimated.

Given the importance of price, management wanted to ensure that only those features were included in the service that were justified by their value to potential users. Consequently, management paid particular attention to the utilities attached to various attributes. For example, the utilities associated with hours of operation and with price were as follows:

Hours of operation	Utility*	Monthly service charge ($)	Utility*
8 hours, weekdays (9 A.M.–5 P.M., Mon.–Fri.)	−67	5	+48
12 hours, weekdays (8 A.M.–8 P.M., Mon.–Fri.)	+ 6	15	−15
24 hours, weekdays	+24	25	−33
24 hours, every day	+37		

* In this case, the utility values were scaled to represent increases or decreases from the predicted share of customers who would sign up for this service (given awareness and opportunity) if the product configuration was a particular one favored by the client's management. More commonly, conjoint studies present only unadjusted utility values on a scale from −1 to +1.

Thus management learned that customers would find a service that was available 12 hours daily and cost $15 slightly more attractive than one that was available only 8 hours daily and cost only $5. They could conclude this from the fact that the utility difference between the 8- and 12-hour availability was 73 units, 10 units more than the utility difference between the $5 and $15 prices. The smaller utility increases for 24-hour and every-day service (18 and 13 units, respectively) indicate that customers would be unwilling to pay an additional $10 for those features.

Using a proprietary procedure, this research company was able to estimate utilities for more features and price levels than were actually included in the trade-off questionnaire. The company could then forecast the gain (or loss) in sales for any price increase (or decrease) that might accompany a change in the features offered. By evaluating the sales gains and losses associated with various combinations of features, the brokerage management was able to select an optimal combination of just those features whose cost was justified by the increased value they offered potential customers.

Source: Provided by Yankelovich, Partners, a marketing research, modeling, and consulting firm in Westport, CT.

High Control: Purchase Measures

An experimental design for estimating price sensitivity with purchase data is starting to be used more frequently. Such price elasticity data can come from pricing experiments conducted in actual retail stores or simulated retail stores without telling customers that prices are being changed. Since the researcher controls the experimental setting, price variations can be controlled while other marketing variables, such as point-of-purchase promotions and competitive price variations, can be held constant. These latter variables can bias price sensitivity results when less controlled procedures are used. Consequently, experimental research of this

Conjoint analysis can aid financial services companies to find appropriate product attribute-price mixes.

nature provides very valid estimates of price sensitivity. The two most popular procedures are (1) field or in-store purchase experiments and (2) laboratory or simulated store-purchase experiments.

Field Experiments   A field experiment relies on actual purchase data collected when buyers are not aware of the experimentation. The data can be collected in a natural purchase environment such as a supermarket. In the case of mail-order purchases, the researcher randomly selects a subset of the mailing list to receive prices different from the prices in the regular catalog mailing. Price sensitivity can be measured by comparing the level of purchases using the "normal" price to the level of purchases resulting from a higher or lower price.

A popular design for field pricing experiments involves measuring sales volume at the "normal" level to obtain a baseline of sales and then raising or lowering the price to determine the sensitivity of the new price level. Since this "before-and-after" design fails to have a control condition, the researcher must assume that the change in sales volume resulted from the price change, not from other factors that could impact sales. Such factors could be competitive promotions or even the weather.

An improved design would involve the use of a control store similar to the experimental store. Both would have the sales volume monitored to obtain a baseline of sales. The price change would be made in the experimental store, and sales volume would be monitored in both stores. The change in sales volume in the experimental store would be compared to the change in sales volume in the control store, to determine the impact of the price change on sales volume.

Laboratory Experiments   In a laboratory experiment, consumers make real purchases in an artificial store environment. Frequently, a research facility at a shopping mall will be used. Potential buyers are recruited and screened from shoppers in the mall. The buyers' purchasing patterns and demographic profile can be determined to ensure that the experimental sample is representative of the target population under study.

The advantage of the laboratory experiment is administrative control of the participants and the easy manipulation of prices and other aspects of the purchase environment. Also, the researcher can eliminate external factors such as competitive price changes that can contaminate the validity of an in-store field experiment. Consequently, the high degree of control possible in the laboratory setting enables the researcher to draw inferences about price sensitivity from a smaller number of purchases in much less time than is possible in the field.

The weakness of the laboratory experiment is the artificiality of the setting. A simple purchase environment may consist of an interviewing room with a display of products from a single product category. The prices are clearly marked and the customer is asked to purchase from the category. This simple setting could encourage the buyer to give more attention to prices than would be typical in a field shopping situation. In addition, buyers know that they are being observed, which could make their behavior different from what it would be in a field study.

While problems of this nature may be overcome to some degree by larger and more sophisticated laboratory facilities, the buyer still knows that observation is occurring. Still, researchers who use laboratory experiments argue effectively that the problem of bias is small in a realistic and well-designed laboratory experiment. As a result, leading firms rely extensively on this type of research to measure price sensitivity.

SUMMARY

1 Marketing research procedures used in channel activities and performance are syndicated services to monitor product flow at the wholesale and retail level; attitude studies of channel members; test marketing activity; and the use of internal records, surveys, and observation to monitor the performance of channel members.

2 Marketing research performed by channel members includes attitude studies, location studies, and conjoint studies to define product configurations.

3 Location studies involve defining the trade area, identifying population characteristics in the trading area, determining competitors' locations, determining consumers' shopping patterns, and developing a store patronage model.

4 The quality of information available to management regarding the price elasticity of demand directly impacts revenue and profit performance. The procedures for measuring demand sensitivity to price changes can be evaluated on the dimensions of (a) the degree of research control and (b) the nature of the variables measured.

5 The use of survey research procedures typically involves a low degree of control when respondents are interviewed about their preferences or their intentions of buying a product. A high degree of control can be achieved when a simulated purchase survey or a conjoint measurement study is used. Here, a research environment can be created where price levels and other marketing variables are manipulated. The advantage of increased control can be achieved by using research design procedures in which the internal validity of the measurements is more accurately determined.

6 Field and laboratory experiments, company sales records, and panel and retail store data involve direct indicators of purchase behavior. Although these studies are typically more accurate than studies using indirect measures, they can be costly and time-consuming.

DISCUSSION QUESTIONS

1 A marketer of industrial electronic components such as switches and wire sells these items through electrical distributors to hardware stores. How could marketing research be used to determine the channel members' support of the marketing effort?

2 How may scanner data and demographic data be combined to provide useful information to the local retailer and to the packaged goods marketer?

3 Design an "image" study for your favorite local restaurant.

4 Ford Motor Company is trying to determine the location for a new dealership in the Santa Clara area of California. Describe what marketing research you would do to help pick the appropriate location.

5 Design a conjoint study to determine an appropriate set of attributes for the student lounge at your school.

6 A food manufacturer has developed a new frozen dessert. Design a research study that would determine the price sensitivity of this product to prices of $0.99, $1.09, and $1.19.

7 A manufacturer of consumer light bulbs has historical sales and price data on its line of soft white light bulbs. The company would like you to determine the price elasticity of this product line based on historical changes in manufacturers' selling prices and shipment data. Can you do this? Why or why not?

8 MINICASE

The owner of a new apartment building is interested in pricing the apartments based on market demand. The apartments have one and two bedrooms, and are located from the basement through the eighth floor. Half have river views, and half have parking lot views. Design a conjoint study to measure price elasticity.

CASES FOR PART SIX

CASE 6-1   Techno Forecasts, Inc.

Techno Forecasts, Inc., is a Phoenix-based marketing research firm specializing in providing forecasts of economic trends, social trends, and sales levels for its clients. Described below are three forecasting problems they confronted for separate clients. For each situation, the student is provided with:

1 *A statement of objective.* This statement explains in very general terms what students are expected to do as their assignment for the case.

2 *A statement of the kind of business the decision maker or researcher is in.*

3 *A statement of the problem.* This statement provides a detailed description of the problem that the researcher must solve using the data and assumptions provided.

4 *A list of the published statistical data sources from which case information has been taken.* In essence, the case writers have made the problem somewhat simpler than it would be in a real-life company, as they have looked up the necessary data for us.

5 *A list of assumptions.* Almost all situations require assumptions that go beyond available data to allow the researcher to answer the specific questions at hand. This section provides a set of assumptions for the student to work with.

6 *A data table or tables.* Here the student is given the necessary data from the actual data sources mentioned previously.

CASE ASSIGNMENT

The student assignment for each situation is to solve the problem given, using the data and assumptions presented.

This is the nature of the use of most statistical data. That is, for any one specific problem to be solved, the data available must be manipulated using specific assumptions. Thus, the student must think of a way to use the data available to answer the problem. In none of the cases is it just a simple matter of looking up the right number in a table.

The student should ask himself or herself, "How can I manipulate the given data using the given assumptions to answer the questions?" The real thinking in the exercise is to develop a logical approach for using the data.

A Ready Made Containers, Inc.

Objective To estimate the total market potential for corrugated and solid fiber boxes in a given area.

Kind of Business Manufacturer of corrugated and solid fiber boxes.

Problem The sales manager for a manufacturer of corrugated and solid fiber boxes in one of the mountain states decided that he wanted to intensify the company's efforts in Arizona, one of the states which the firm served. In the Phoenix standard MSA (coextensive with Maricopa County), for example, the firm's sales totaled $850,000 in 1995—$680,000, or 80 percent, to firms within the food and kindred products industry, and the remaining $170,000, or 20 percent, to firms manufacturing electrical equipment and supplies. The sales manager felt this was a very poor sales record, considering the diversity of industry in the Phoenix area.

In view of this preliminary analysis, he decided to determine the market potential for fiber boxes in the Phoenix area, as the first step in establishing the firm's sales potential (or market share) and setting a realistic sales quota for the area.

Source of Data

1 *County Business Patterns*
2 *U.S. Industrial Outlook*
3 Fiber box statistics

B The XYZ Company

Objective To establish national, state, and county sales quotas and a method for estimating potential market in 1996 for battery replacements for automobiles.

Kind of Business Manufacturer of automobile batteries.

Problem The XYZ Company, which for many years had been estimating sales potential and quotas for battery replacements for automobiles based on past performance, decided to develop a mathematical procedure for projecting sales of replacement batteries by territory, since many of the company's sales managers felt their assigned quotas did not reflect the potential of their territory.

Source of Data

1 *Highway Statistics*
2 *Pennsylvania Statistical Abstract*

Assumptions

1 The normal life cycle of an automobile battery is 3 years. Therefore, almost one in three automobiles will need a new battery in any given year. Since there

DATA ON THE VALUE OF BOX SHIPMENTS FOR THE UNITED STATES BY SIC MAJOR
GROUP CODE, PLUS EMPLOYMENT BY INDUSTRY GROUP FOR THE UNITED STATES
AND MARICOPA COUNTY

SIC major group code	Consuming industries	Value of box shipments by end use* ($1000) (1)	Employment by industry group† (2)	Maricopa County employment by industry group† (3)
20	Food and kindred products	1,171,800	1,536,307	4,971
21	Tobacco manufacturers	29,400	63,919	—
22	Textile mill products	121,800	935,925	—
23	Apparel and other textile products	54,600	1,349,000	3,158
24	Lumber and wood products	42,000	579,037	1,736
25	Furniture and fixtures	147,000	468,311	1,383
26	Paper and allied products	567,000	631,588	284
27	Printing and publishing	58,800	1,056,336	4,346
28	Chemicals and allied products	260,400	849,969	1,133
29	Petroleum and coal products	33,600	139,228	—
30	Rubber and miscellaneous plastic products	163,800	555,539	779
31	Leather and leather products	21,000	277,371	—
32	Stone, clay, and glass products	365,400	588,897	2,270
33	Primary metal industries	42,000	1,144,327	2,036
34	Fabricated metal products	184,800	1,312,595	3,271
35	Machinery, except electrical	105,000	1,769,738	14,691
36	Electrical equipment and supplies	256,200	1,698,725	23,788
37	Transportation equipment	109,200	1,700,723	2,484
38	Instruments and related products	29,400	383,585	D
39	Miscellaneous manufacturing industries	403,200	411,967	868
90	Government	33,600	—	—
	Total‡	4,200,000	—	—

Data in columns 1 and 2 are for the entire United States.
D = data withheld to avoid diisclosure of individual reporting units.
* Based on data reported in *Fibre Box Industry Annual Report*, Fibre Box Association.
† *County Business Patterns*, U.S. Department of Commerce, Bureau of the Census.
‡ *U.S. Industrial Outlook*, Bureau of Domestic Commerce, U.S. Department of Commerce.

are more cars manufactured than scrapped during the year, a percentage of less
than one-third was decided upon, namely 31 percent.

2 Replacement automobile batteries average $12 each, FOB plant.

3 The XYZ Company has maintained approximately an 11 percent share of
total market for replacement automobile batteries over the past 4 years. However,
management feels that a more realistic figure would be a 14 percent share of
market.

4 Total automobile registration will continue to increase at an average annual
rate of 3.8 percent as in the past 10 years, 1984 to 1994.

Note: Not all the data are presented here, since the procedure should be easily generalizable to the states (and counties) not included here.

AUTOMOBILE REGISTRATION FOR SELECTED STATES, AND BY COUNTIES FOR PENNSYLVANIA

States and counties	Automobile registrations* (1000)
Alabama	1,650
Arizona	885
Arkansas	747
California	10,166
Colorado	1,170
Illinois	4,686
Missouri	1,944
New Jersey	3,337
North Carolina	2,345
Ohio	5,328
Pennsylvania†	5,260
Allegheny	716
Berks	132
Erie	118
Jefferson	19
Montgomery	279
Philadelphia	896
Somerset	34
Westmoreland	168
All other counties	2,898
Total United States	92,301

* *Highway Statistics*, U.S. Bureau of Public Roads.
† *Pennsylvania Statistical Abstract*, Pennsylvania Department of Commerce.

C Ward Manufacturing Company

Objective   To disperse advertising budget for 1995 in proportion to the potential markets, by states, in the South Atlantic region.

Kind of Business   Manufacturer of highly crafted household furniture.

Problem   Ward was introducing a new line of furniture and desired to construct a simplified model for allocating total introductory advertising budget, by state, so as to reach the customers who were most likely to be the prime buyers for their products.

Source of Data   *Statistics of Income: Individual Income Tax Returns.*

Assumptions

1 The company decided to direct its advertising to families or individuals with an adjusted gross income of $65,000 or more, based on studies of other companies marketing similar furniture.

2 An introductory advertising budget of $150,000 was established.

NUMBER OF INDIVIDUAL INCOME TAX RETURNS WITH AN
ADJUSTED GROSS INCOME OF $65,000 OR MORE IN 1994

South Atlantic census region	Number of returns
Delaware	39,406
District of Columbia	44,123
Florida	337,954
Georgia	195,907
Maryland	323,217
North Carolina	176,698
South Carolina	79,038
Virginia	276,550
West Virginia	54,446
Total	1,527,339

Source: Statistics of Income: Individual Income Tax Returns, Internal Revenue Service, U.S. Department of the Treasury.

CASE 6-2 "No Sweat"*

San Francisco Package Goods (SFPG) was one of the largest companies in the United States. In the previous decade, it had had many new-product successes. Its newest venture was an antiperspirant/deodorant, based on a new formulation, tentatively called "No Sweat." After a favorable employee reaction to the product, SFPG decided to conduct a concept test. Production of the new product would require considerable investment in plant and equipment, so SFPG managers planned to base much of their go, no-go decision on the results of this test. A concept test, rather than an actual product test, was undertaken because production costs were so great, and also the R&D crew was still trying to make minor improvements in the product.

The SFPG marketing department was considered to be one of the best in the industry. Unlike many other companies, SFPG conducted its own marketing research. Bill Freeland, a recent B.B.A. graduate, was asked to prepare the concept statement and to design the testing procedure for No Sweat. His concept statement and portions of his design are presented in Exhibit 1.

*Source: Coauthored by Sheryl Petras.

EXHIBIT 1

STUDY PROPOSAL

Concept Statement for a New Antiperspirant/Deodorant

A major producer of soaps, shampoos, and other personal hygiene goods has developed a new antiperspirant/deodorant stick. The company has combined ingredients which have, in the past, been difficult to stabilize in stick form. The product has a unique appearance. Its white antiperspirant center is surrounded by an outer ring of green gel deodorant. This antiperspirant/deodorant combination provides both males and females with the highest degree of protection available against odor and wetness. This new product will be available in a 2.5-ounce size for $3.50 and a 1.5-ounce size for $2.20.

Objective

Our objective is to identify the potential market for No Sweat, the new antiperspirant/deodorant created by SFPG. Given its unique appearance and its dual-action formula, we hope No Sweat will find a niche in an already flooded market. Consumer attitudes regarding specific characteristics of the product will be investigated, as well as their overall reaction to the product concept. At the request of the new-product manager, we will dif-ferentiate between spray, stick, and roll-on users in the presentation of our data.

Method

Personal interviews will be used due to the length of the survey and the quality of data that must be procured. A random sample of 50 men and 50 women will be selected from the Los Angeles phone book. Because the sample will be random, we can be assured of proportional representation of roll-on, stick, and spray antiperspirant and deodorant users. Soliciting for personal interviews will be conducted over the phone between 12 noon and 9 P.M. This will ensure that all members of the population have an equal chance of being contacted.

The Interview

Interviews will be conducted without any reference to SFPG, thus eliminating a potential source of respondent bias. All subjects will be shown the concept statement. They will then be asked to give opinions regarding specific attributes of the product. Finally, intent to purchase will be measured. The respondents will also be shown the proposed package design for No Sweat. Their feedback will be recorded and used to suggest possible changes in the design.

The study was undertaken using the methodology proposed by Freeland. Approximately 400 phone calls were made to set up the 100 interview appointments. Two of the scheduled subjects (both male) canceled their appointments before being interviewed, making the actual sample size 98. Selected results from the experiment appear in Exhibit 2.

EXHIBIT 2

STUDY RESULTS

Primary Type of Antiperspirant/Deodorant Used ($n = 98$)

	Percent	Number
Roll-on	47	46
Stick	39	38
Spray	11	11
Other	3	3

Respondents were given a list of several product characteristics, then asked to use the 7-point scale appearing below to record what influence each characteristic had on purchase intent. Subjects were divided into four classes: roll-on, stick, spray, and "other" users. The table following the scale presents the average score each characteristic received within those divisions.

Influence on purchase intent						
Definitely would not influence purchase decision					Definitely would influence purchase decision	
1	2	3	4	5	6	7

Characteristic	Most common type of antiperspirant or deodorant used			
	Roll-on	Stick	Spray	Other
Can be used by both sexes	4.2	4.0	3.9	4.4
Effective at stopping wetness	6.2	5.9	6.1	5.8
Effective at stopping odor	6.4	6.0	6.0	6.7
Product appearance	2.5	3.1	3.6	3.0
Product (roll-on, stick, spray, other)	2.8	6.3	2.6	2.2
New formula	4.1	4.5	4.2	3.9
Package design	3.1	3.0	2.7	2.9
Package size	4.0	4.1	4.1	4.6
Package shape	3.9	3.8	3.9	3.6
Price	4.7	6.1	3.2	5.4

The following table summarizes the results into two categories: the data from respondents who said they would try the product and the data from those who said they wouldn't. Within each group (triers and nontriers), the table presents the percentage of people who rated the characteristic: (a) 1 or 2; (b) 3, 4, or 5; and (c) 6 or 7.

Characteristic	Rating	Triers	Nontriers
Effectiveness at stopping wetness	1–2	0%	1%
	3–4–5	32	39
	6–7	68	60
Effectiveness at stopping odor	1–2	0	0
	3–4–5	30	32
	6–7	70	68
Price	1–2	20	67‡
	3–4–5	74	32‡
	6–7	6	1
Product appearance	1–2	52	74†
	3–4–5	36	18*
	6–7	12	8
New formula	1–2	2	11
	3–4–5	64	76
	6–7	34	13†
Total number		25	73

* Significant difference at 90% confidence level.
† Significant difference at 95% confidence level.
‡ Significant difference at 99% confidence level.

Reasons for trial: Those who said they would try the product (*n* = 25):

Dissatisfaction with current brand	14%
Curiosity	58
Other	28

Reasons for no trial: Those who said they would not try the product (*n* = 73):

Price	25%
Satisfaction with current brand	64
Other	11

The product package results are shown in the following table.

	Yes	No	Indifferent
Do you like the package shape?	47%	21%	31%
Do you like the package colors?	29	58	13
Do you like the lettering?	62	26	12
Do you like the package overall?	45	47	8

CASE QUESTIONS

1 Evaluate the concept statement.
2 Critique the methodology of the study.
3 What conclusions can be drawn from this study?
4 What further research needs to be done before this product is introduced? Be specific.

CASE 6-3 Executive Express*

Heather Clayton is president of Express Air, a small commuter airline company based in St. Andrew. Express Air currently provides air taxi and corporate flight services to local businesses. To boost company profits, Clayton is considering offering a regular service between St. Andrew and Bayville, a major city about 340 miles from St. Andrew. There are presently no regular flights between St. Andrew and Bayville. St. Andrew–Bayville fliers must either charter a plane or leave from Eastport City Airport, which is about 50 miles from St. Andrew. Before establishing this Executive Express service, however, Clayton wants to see what kind of demand there is for it. She begins by evaluating the current service and the type of travelers who currently use it. Brief descriptions of the current service, the cities involved, and the potential customers follow.

*Source: Coauthored by Sheryl Petras.

Bayville   Bayville is a major metropolitan area of more than 6 million people. It hosts the main offices of several Fortune 500 companies, so it is frequently visited by executives from Eastport and St. Andrew. Most of these business travelers arrive in the morning and leave at the end of the day. Bayville is also a cultural center; it has fine restaurants, museums, playhouses, and a world-class symphony orchestra—making it a popular weekend vacation spot.

Bayville has two airports: Central and Lake. Central Airport is extremely busy because all major airlines land there. It is also located 25 miles from the downtown business district. Lake Airport is smaller, less busy, and closer to downtown, so business travelers generally prefer to arrive there. Both Central and Lake airports offer regular service to Eastport.

Eastport   Eastport, also highly populated, has about 4 million inhabitants. Eastport City Airport offers hourly jet service to Bayville's Lake Airport. Flights to Central are less frequent.

St. Andrew   St. Andrew is much smaller than either Bayville or Eastport, claiming slightly fewer than 100,000 residents. It is the home of St. Andrew College, which has an enrollment of 20,000 students. More than 800 businesses are located in the area, including several banks and consulting firms. Travelers flying from St. Andrew to Bayville must go via Eastport City Airport, and thus the trip takes about 2 hours; a 1-hour drive to Eastport (this includes parking and check-in) and a 1-hour flight to St. Andrew.

The proposed St. Andrew-Bayville service would cut travel time in half, to 1 hour (including the drive to the airport). There is a major drawback to this service, however. The St. Andrew Airport cannot accommodate jets because its runway is too short.

Since jets cannot be used, Express Air is considering two types of prop planes for the service. The first type, CASA, is unpressurized. This means it cannot attain the same altitudes that pressurized planes do. Because of this, CASA might not be able to fly above bad weather conditions to escape turbulence. CASA has 24 seats, and passengers are able to stand up inside the plane. Metroliner, the other aircraft being considered, does have a pressurized cabin. Thus, it can fly higher than the CASA and probably escape bad weather conditions. But the 18-seat Metroliner is not large enough to allow passengers to stand upright inside the plane. The Metroliner and the CASA have virtually identical cruising speeds.

CASE QUESTIONS

1 Assume that Clayton has come to you for advice. What information will she need before deciding whether or not this service is feasible?
2 How would you obtain this information?
3 Assuming that part of this information would be collected by a conjoint measurement study, identify the appropriate attributes, attribute levels, and data instrument structure.

CASE 6-4   The Cupertino Group*

Express Air is a small commuter airline based in St. Andrew. It presently provides charter service to local companies. Heather Clayton, president of Express Air, is considering the feasibility of a regular service between St. Andrew and Bayville, a major business center located 340 miles northeast of St. Andrew. Currently, travelers must drive 50 miles to Eastport City Airport before catching a flight to Bayville. Clayton's proposed service would eliminate the 50-mile drive by flying directly from St. Andrew Airport to Lake Airport in Bayville. Express Air could offer three flights per day from St. Andrew, which is not many when compared to the 7:00 A.M. to 7:00 P.M. hourly service available from Eastport. Because jets are unable to land at St. Andrew Airport (the runway is too short), Express Air would employ prop planes.

Clayton had hired the Cupertino Group, a small specialty marketing research company, to research the demand for the new service. She has just received the data and is ready to interpret the findings. The survey and questionnaire results appear below. Additional cost data are presented in the appendix.

SURVEY

Findings from a preliminary telephone survey of local travel agencies and businesses:

1 At least 50 persons per business day travel to Bayville.

2 Sixty percent of the businesses get their St. Andrew–Bayville tickets through travel agencies.

3 Travel agents believe that a St. Andrew–Bayville service would be popular.

4 The majority of businesses said that they would take advantage of such a service.

5 According to the Chamber of Commerce, "the proposed service would be substantially used by St. Andrew businesses as a more efficient and economical means of transportation to and from the Bayville area."

QUESTIONNAIRE

The half-hour mail survey shown in Exhibit 1 was given to 50 local business-persons who had traveled to Bayville within the last 6 months. Travel agents provided the names of potential respondents. Results follow each question. (All questions were open-ended, so the response categories were created by the researchers in order to analyze the data.)

For the next set of questions, respondents were asked to fill in several matrices similar to the one shown in Table 1. They were told to place a 1 in the cell they liked most, and to place the highest ranking of 9 in the cell they liked least.

*Source: Coauthored by Sheryl Petras.

EXHIBIT 1

QUESTIONNAIRE

1 When was your last trip to Bayville?

64%	Within the last month
12	More than 1, but less than 2 months ago
8	More than 2, but less than 3 months ago
16	More than 3, but less than 6 months ago

2 How did you get there?

92%	Plane	8	Car

3 What was the purpose of the trip?

74%	Business
20	Pleasure
4	Business/pleasure
2	Transfer planes

4 How often do you go to Bayville per year by plane? By car or train?

Average number of plane trips per year   7.3
Average number of car or train trips per year   2.8

5 At what time of day do you usually leave for Bayville?

96%	Before 10:00 A.M.	4	Noon

6 When do you like to leave Bayville?

68%	Between 5:00 P.M. and 6:00 P.M.
14	Between 6:01 P.M. and 7:00 P.M.
10	Between 7:01 P.M. and 8:00 P.M.
4	Between 8:01 P.M. and 9:00 P.M.
4	The following morning at 8:30 A.M.

7 How do you feel about the existing service from Eastport to Bayville?

Q: How is the airport?
A: Many respondents said they disliked the parking facilities.
Q: The schedule?
A: 98% were completely satisfied.
Q: The price?
A: For most people the price was unimportant, although 11 respondents thought it was too high for such a short distance.
Q: The service aboard?
A: Not important.

8 A small aircraft leaves from St. Andrew airport and flies to Bayville Lake Airport in 1 hour. It departs from St. Andrew at 8:30 A.M. and the return flight leaves from Bayville at 5:30 P.M. that same evening. The price is $110 one way. Would you consider taking such a flight when you go to Bayville?

70%	Yes	30	No

TABLE 1

	Time of traveling (one way)		
Price (one way)	2 hours	1½ hours	1 hour
$170			
120			
70			

Assume that all combinations are possible.
Note: The time of traveling includes the time it takes to
get to the airport.

Data obtained from several of these matrices were analyzed using a conjoint measurement computer program. For each individual matrix, the program calculated utility values between 0 and 1 (with 1 being highest utility) for every category of every variable in the matrix. For the above example the following utilities occurred.

Price (one way)	Utility value	Travel time, hours	Utility value
$170	.16	2	.17
120	.56	1½	.58
70	.78	1	.75

Add these utility values to get utilities of the various combinations of variables. The program assigns utility values so that the utilities for the cells in the matrix are in the same order as the rank order (1, 2, 3, etc.) given by the respondents. For example, a 2-hour trip costing $170 has a utility of .17 + .16 = .33, the lowest value in the price–travel time matrix (see Table 2). This combination was also ranked last by the respondents. The ordering of calculated utilities does not always coincide with the respondent rankings, but this program generates the values that come closest to accomplishing that task.

TABLE 2

	Time of traveling (one way)		
Price (one way)	2 hours (.17)	1½ hours (.58)	1 hour (.75)
$170 (.16)	9 (.33)	7 (.74)	6 (.91)
120 (.56)	8 (.73)	4 (1.14)	3 (1.31)
70 (.78)	5 (.95)	2 (1.36)	1 (1.53)

The relative importance of the variables has also been calculated for each matrix. Relative importance = (range of the utility values of variable a)/(range of values of variable a + range of values of variable b).

TABLE 3   PRICE AND SORT OF
PLANE

Price (one way)	Utility
$170	.23
120	.51
70	.78

Sort of plane	Utility
DC-9	.87
Metroliner	.60
CASA	.23

Relative importance	
Price	.46
Plane	.54

Relative importance of price and travel time:

Price: .52 (.52 = .62/1.20),

where .62 = .78 − .16, the range of the price utility values

Travel time: .48 (.48 = .58/1.20)

This means that the importance of two variables in the decision-making process is almost the same, with price having slightly more influence. In other words, a higher price is rejected slightly more than a longer travel time. The utility values and relative importance for other pairs of variables are as shown in Tables 3 to 10.

TABLE 4   PRICE AND AIRPORT OF
DEPARTURE

Price (one way)	Utility
$170	.17
120	.51
70	.82

Airport	Utility
St. Andrew	.72
Eastport	.28

Relative importance	
Price	.60
Airport	.40

TABLE 5   PRICE AND COMFORT OF THE PLANE

Price (one way)	Utility
$170	.21
120	.55
70	.74

Comfort	Utility
Possible to stand upright; bathroom	.86
Not possible to stand upright; bathroom	.54
Possible to stand upright; no bathroom	.50
Not possible to stand upright; no bathroom	.10

Relative importance	
Price	.42
Comfort	.59

CASE QUESTIONS

1 What do these findings mean? What characteristics do potential customers find important? Unimportant?

2 Should Clayton go ahead with the service?

TABLE 6   TRAVEL TIME AND SORT OF PLANE

Travel time, hours	Utility
1	.74
1½	.61
2	.15

Plane	Utility
DC-9 commercial jet	.79
Metroliner pressurized prop jet (18 seats)	.51
CASA unpressurized prop jet (24 seats)	.20

Relative importance	
Time	.50
Plane	.50

TABLE 7   TRAVEL TIME AND SCHEDULE

Travel time, hours	Utility
1	.70
1½	.62
2	.18

Schedule	Utility
Leave St. Andrew or Eastport: 8:00 A.M. and 5:00 P.M. Leave Bayville: 9:30 A.M. and 6:30 P.M.	.17
Leave St. Andrew or Eastport: 8:00 A.M., 1:00 P.M., 7:00 P.M. Leave Bayville: 9:30 A.M., 2:30 P.M., 8:30 P.M.	.42
Leave St. Andrew or Eastport: 8:00 A.M., 1:00 P.M., 5:00 P.M. Leave Bayville: 9:30 A.M., 2:30 P.M., 6:30 P.M.	.51
Leave St. Andrew or Eastport: hourly from 7:00 A.M. to 7:00 P.M. Leave Bayville: hourly from 8:30 A.M. to 8:30 P.M.	.90

Relative importance	
Time	.42
Schedule	.58

APPENDIX

Cost Data   The price for Eastport–Bayville flights varies with the time of day, the flight date, and the date of reservation. Clayton plans to have a flat rate for the proposed St. Andrew–Bayville service. The fares used in the questionnaire represent the highest ($170) and lowest ($70) fares charged in the last year for the Eastport–Bayville flight, and the fare at the time the questionnaire was printed ($120). The typical fare (for weekday flights) ranges from $110 to $130.

TABLE 8   SORT OF PLANE AND AIRPORT OF DEPARTURE

Sort of plane	Utility
DC-9	.84
Metroliner	.46
CASA	.21

Airport	Utility
St. Andrew	.74
Eastport	.26

Relative importance	
Plane	.57
Airport	.43

TABLE 9   SORT OF PLANE AND COMFORT

Sort of plane	Utility
DC-9	.76
Metroliner	.44
CASA	.30

Comfort*	Utility
Stand; bathroom	.93
Can't stand; bathroom	.54
Stand; no bathroom	.40
Can't stand; no bathroom	.14

Relative importance	
Plane	.37
Comfort	.63

* See Table C for complete descriptions.

Projected Quarterly Cash Flows for Express Air
Outflows

Fixed costs	$ 85,000
Direct operating costs	275,000

TABLE 10   AIRPORT OF DEPARTURE AND SCHEDULE

Airport of departure	Utility
St. Andrew	.66
Eastport	.34

Schedule	
Leave St. Andrew or Eastport: 8:00 A.M. and 5:00 P.M. Leave Bayville: 9:30 A.M. and 6:30 P.M.	.16
Leave St. Andrew or Eastport: 8:00 A.M., 1:00 P.M., 7:00 P.M. Leave Bayville: 9:30 A.M., 2:30 P.M., 8:30 P.M.	.40
Leave St. Andrew or Eastport: 8:00 A.M., 1:00 P.M., 5:00 P.M. Leave Bayville: 9:30 A.M., 2:30 P.M., 6:30 P.M.	.49
Leave St. Andrew or Eastport: hourly from 7:00 A.M. to 7:00 P.M. Leave Bayville: hourly from 8:30 A.M. to 8:30 P.M.	.95

Relative importance	
Airport	.29
Schedule	.71

Inflows   Depends on fare charged and the number of passengers per flight.

Breakeven   Assume that each passenger buys one round-trip fare. At $240 round trip, breakeven occurs at 1500 passengers per quarter (23 per day).

$$\frac{\$360,000 \text{ cash outflow per quarter}}{\$240 \text{ per flight}} = 1500 \text{ passengers per quarter}$$

CASE 6-5   Paradise Foods*

Paradise Foods was a large, successful manufacturer of packaged foods and household products whose markets were becoming increasingly competitive. In 1983, Paradise Foods launched La Treat, the first "super-premium" frozen dessert to enter national distribution. It consisted of 3.5 ounces of vanilla ice cream dipped in penuche fudge and covered with almonds. Individual bars were served on a stick and sold for just under $2, while a package of four was $7.

Barbara Mayer had been the product manager who launched La Treat. Under Barbara, annual sales of La Treat reached $40 million, and the dessert began making a significant contribution to dessert group profits. It accounted for almost 5 percent of the market despite a price about 50 percent higher than standard frozen specialties. After 2 years of burgeoning sales, tough challenges emerged from three direct competitors, as well as several parallel concepts at various stages of test marketing. The total frozen specialties market had grown fast enough to absorb these new entrants without reducing La Treat sales, but revenues had been essentially flat through 1986 and 1987. Barbara was currently the group manager responsible for all established dessert products.

Paradise had a new product in test markets that it hoped would complement the established La Treat brand frozen dessert. This new product, Sweet Dream, consisted of sweet cream ice cream between two oversized chocolate cookies and coated with dark Belgian chocolate. Its price was comparable to La Treat's.

Bill Horton, group manager responsible for all new dessert products, was the product manager for Sweet Dream. Bill believed that Paradise Foods was vulnerable to increasing competition in its markets because of its failure to keep pace with technological change—especially the increasing sophistication of marketing research based on computer modeling, supermarket scanner data, and targetable cable television. Though Paradise used these tools, Bill felt that top management did not embrace them with the same enthusiasm as other companies did.

When Bill became product manager for Sweet Dream, he promised himself he would do a state-of-the-art research job. The plan was to compare the performance of Sweet Dream in two test markets in order to expose different advertising and promotion strategies. One campaign was conducted in Midland, Texas, and Pitts-

*Source: Steven H. Star and Glen L. Urban, "The Case of the Test Market Toss-up," *Harvard Business Review,* pp. 4–7, September-October 1988.

field, Massachusetts, and struck an overtly self-indulgent tone: "Go Ahead, You Deserve It." It used limited price promotion to induce trial. The other campaign was conducted in Marion, Indiana, and Corvallis, Oregon, and emphasized superior quality: "Taste the Goodness." This campaign also used promotion aggressively. Sunday newspapers in the latter two cities frequently carried 50-cents-off coupons, and Sweet Dream boxes included a 75-cent rebate voucher.

Bill used two computer-based research services—InfoScan and BehaviorScan—to evaluate Sweet Dream's performance and long-term potential. InfoScan tracked product purchases on a national and local basis for the packaged goods industry. It collected point-of-sale information on all bar-coded products sold in a representative sample of supermarkets and drugstores. It generated weekly data on volume, price, market share, the relationship between sales and promotional offers, and merchandising conditions. Bill subscribed to InfoScan in order to monitor competitive trends in the frozen specialties segment.

BehaviorScan was used in marketing tests to measure the effect of marketing strategies on product purchases. In a typical BehaviorScan test, one group of consumer panelists was exposed to certain variables (i.e., print or television advertisements, coupons, free samples, in-store displays), while other participating consumers served as a control group. Company analysts used supermarket scanner data on both groups of consumers (who presented identification cards to store checkout clerks) to evaluate purchasing responses to marketing campaigns. A typical BehaviorScan test lasted about 1 year.

Bill Horton's marketing research program had generated a stack of computer printouts several feet high. He had spent much of the spring trying to unravel the complex interactions between different advertising and promotion strategies for Sweet Dream, the various promotion deals Paradise was running on La Treat, and the proliferation of other frozen specialties.

After 18 months of product development and test markets, the marketing committee at Paradise Foods met to decide whether it should authorize a national rollout of Sweet Dream. After the meeting, Bob Murphy, Bill Horton's boss, informed Bill that the committee had reached a no-launch decision, and that, based on the test results, the returns were not there. Bill disagreed.

"Not there? All they had to look at was Appendix B in my report—the data from Midland and Pittsfield. Sweet Dream got a 3 percent share after 26 weeks. A trial rate of 15 percent. A repurchase rate of 45 percent. If national performance were anything close to that, we'd have our launch costs back in 14 months. Who can argue with that?"

"I'm on your side here, but I had only one vote," Bob said defensively. "We both knew what Barbara's position was going to be—and you know how much weight she carries around here these days. And to be honest, it was tough to take issue with her. What's the point of introducing Sweet Dream if you end up stealing share from La Treat? In fact, Barbara used some of your data against us. She kept waving around Appendix C, griping that 75 percent of the people who tried Sweet Dream had bought La Treat in the previous 4 weeks. In addition, repurchase rates were highest among La Treat heavy users. You know how the fourteenth floor feels about La Treat. Barbara claimed that adjusting for lost La Treat sales meant Sweet Dream wouldn't recover its up-front costs for 3 years."

Bill again disagreed. "You and I both know that things are more complicated than Barbara would have people believe. There wasn't the same cannibalization effect in Marion and Corvallis. And we never did a test in Midland and Pittsfield where Barbara's people were free to defend La Treat. We might be able to have it both ways. . . ."

Bob interrupted. "The committee has made its decision. You know how this company works. We don't hold withdrawal of a new product against the manager if withdrawal is the right decision. The fact is, the committee was impressed as hell with the research you did—although to be honest, you may have overwhelmed them. A 40-page report with 30 pages of appendixes. I had trouble wading through it all. But that doesn't matter. You did a great job, and the people who count know that."

Instead of playing golf over the weekend as Bob had recommended, Bill ran more numbers on the marketing research. Barbara was waiting for him in his office Monday morning. She commended his market tests, expressed her disappointment with the no-launch decision, but said the data were pretty clear and left no choice. Bill said he thought the data were clear in the opposite direction.

"Come on, Bill, you can understand the logic of the decision. The Midland and Pittsfield numbers were fine, but they were coming at the expense of La Treat. There wasn't so much cannibalization in Marion and Corvallis, but the Sweet Dream numbers weren't as good either. Trial was acceptable, but repurchase was low. We might make money, but we'd never meet the hurdle rate. Every so often a product just falls between two stools."

Bill suggested doing more tests. Barbara said 18 months was long enough for tests and it was time to try new concepts. Bill expressed fear of (1) losing the valuable freezer space they had been maintaining at stores and (2) having their competitors monitor Sweet Dream's tests and launch a clone. One such competitor, Weston & Williams, had recently rushed a new product to market on the basis of very preliminary tests and data from another competitor's test markets.

"Bob made that argument Friday," Barbara said. "But you can guess how far he got. The guys upstairs have a tough enough time taking our own computer data seriously. They don't buy the idea that someone else is going to jump into the market based on our tests. Plus, that would be a huge risk."

"From what I can tell, Barbara, the only issue that counted was cannibalization. I understand you want to protect La Treat, and I understand that the company wants to protect La Treat. But it seems to me we're protecting a product that's getting tired." Bill further asserted that La Treat was maintaining market share only through heavy promotion. He called up a series of graphs on his computer. The first showed the growing percentage of La Treat sales connected with promotional offers. The second graph disaggregated La Treat's promotion-related sales by four buyer categories Bill had created from BehaviorScan data. "Loyalists" were longtime customers who increased their purchases in response to a deal. "Trial users" bought La Treat for the first time because of the promotion and seemed to be turning into loyal customers. "Accelerators" were longtime customers who used coupons or rebates to stock up on a product they would have bought anyway. "Switch-on-deal" customers were nonusers who bought La Treat when there were promotions but demonstrated little long-term loyalty. Bill's graph showed an increasing majority of La Treat's coupon redeemers fell into the last two categories. His ultimate evidence was a graph that adjusted La Treat sales to eliminate the effect of promotions and showed that without promotions, sales of La Treat had been essentially flat since April 1987.

"I'm amazed you spent your weekend doing this," Barbara said, "but I'm glad you did. It'll help us think through future marketing strategies for La Treat. But it doesn't change what the committee decided. It's time to move on."

"I'm not sure," Bill replied. "I hope you don't mind, but I think I should show these data to Bob. Maybe he can convince the committee to reconsider. After all, if La Treat is weakening, it's going to show up in your profit figures sooner or later."

"Data don't make decisions, Bill, people do. And the people on the marketing committee have been in the industry a lot longer than you. Their gut tells them things your computer can't. Besides, you and I both know when you collect this much data, you can make it show just about anything. Go ahead and talk to Bob, but I'm sure he'll see things the same way I do."

CASE QUESTIONS

1 Should management at Paradise Foods reevaluate the no-launch decision for Sweet Dream? Why or why not?
2 Assuming that the decision was to reevaluate the no-launch decision, which would you recommend—more test marketing or a national launch? Support your position.
3 Evaluate the performance of Bill Horton, Barbara Mayer, and Paradise Food's senior management.

GLOSSARY

absolute frequency A measure of dispersion for nominal data, defined as the number of total elements appearing in a given category.

absolute precision Precision expressed in units.

acquired source A source that has procured data from an original or primary source.

affective component One of three main components of attitudes, concerned with a person's feelings regarding an object or phenomenon (in a marketing model, includes liking and preference stages).

aided recall An approach to questioning that provides a respondent with cues regarding the event of interest.

alternative forms reliability Estimating reliability by giving a respondent two forms that are judged equivalent but not identical and comparing the two measurements for degree of discrepancy in scores, as in the test-retest approach.

alternative hypothesis A hypothesis that states a population parameter, taking on a different value from that stated in the null hypothesis.

analysis of covariance (ANCOVA) A dependence method of multivariate data analysis appropriate for use with an intervally scaled dependent variable, nominally scaled independent variables, and one or more intervally scaled covariates; useful in assessing the effects of extraneous sources of variation in an experiment ex post facto.

analysis of variance (ANOVA) A method of analysis used when dealing with one intervally scaled dependent variable and one or more nominally scaled independent variables; used primarily in the analysis of experiments to determine whether treatment population means are equal.

applied research An investigation the aim of which is to assist managers in decision making.

area sampling A form of sequential cluster sampling which samples areas in the first $n - 1$ stages and elements in the nth stage.

attitude An individual's enduring perceptual, knowledge-based, evaluative, and action-oriented processes with respect to an object or a phenomenon.

attitude scaling The various operational definitions developed for the measurement of the construct "attitude."

Audimeter A mechanical device used to record the channel that a television set is tuned to, if any.

automatic interaction detector (AID) A dependence method of multivariate data analysis appropriate for use with an intervally scaled dependent variable and nominally scaled independent variables; a technique that involves the repeated application of one-way ANOVA to reduce the total sample to a number of subgroups which are more homogeneous on the dependent variable than the sample as a whole.

balanced scale A rating scale providing the same number of favorable and unfavorable categories.

bar chart A graphic representation of magnitude in the dataset depicted by the lengths of various bars that have been laid out with reference to a horizontal or vertical scale.

basic research Investigation whose aim is to extend the boundaries of knowledge regarding some aspects of the marketing system.

Bayes' rule

$$P(A|B) = \frac{P(A \cap B)}{P(B)} = \frac{P(A) \cdot P(B|A)}{[P(A) \cdot P(B|A)] + [P(A') \cdot P(B|A')]}$$

The conditional probability of A given B equals the joint probability of A and B divided by the unconditional probability of B.

behavioral component One of three main components of attitudes, concerned with a person's readiness to respond behaviorally to an object or a phenomenon (in a marketing model, includes intention-to-buy and purchase stages).

bipolar adjectives A pair of adjectives defining opposite ends of a continuum regarding some attitude or belief; used in the semantic differential scale.

bivariate analysis The analysis of two variables at a time.

blocking A method for attempting to control external effects from experiments.

breakdown method An approach to estimating current demand that begins with aggregate industry or market data and breaks down the data into units of interest to the firm.

buildup method An approach to estimating current demand that involves the aggregation of data from the customer or account level to the industry or market level.

buying income method One method of projecting the results of a test marketing program to national performance, based on income and estimated as:

$$\text{National sales estimate} = \frac{\text{total U.S. income}}{\text{test area income}} \times \text{test area sales}$$

canonical correlation A dependence method of multivariate data analysis appropriate for use with a set of intervally scaled dependent variables and a set of intervally scaled independent variables.

cartoon completion A technique in which a respondent is presented with a cartoon drawing depicting people in a situation and is asked to complete a cartoon in response to the comment of a cartoon character.

case A specific unit of analysis for a study; typically a respondent.

case history The intensive study of situations that are relevant to a particular decision problem in order to gain insight into the variables operating in the situation.

causal model forecasting methods Methods that apply statistical models to historical sales data and measure the underlying causes of sales dynamics.

causal research A mode of conclusive research designed to gather evidence on cause-and-effect relationships.

census A study using all available elements of a defined population.

central-limit theorem The fundamental theorem of probability sampling. It allows us to measure sampling error, and it shows that the sampling distribution of the mean is normal when (1) the population distribution is normal for all sample sizes and (2) the sample size increases ($n \geq 30$) for nonnormal population distributions.

central tendency measures One type of descriptive statistics, including such measures as the mean, the median, and the mode.

chi-square test A test designed for comparing a hypothesized population distribution with a distribution obtained by sampling; used with nominal variables in either univariate or bivariate analysis.

closed-ended question A question on a data collection instrument with structured answers.

cluster analysis An interdependence multivariate data analysis technique which uses as input a matrix of associations between variables or objects; the technique forms subgroupings and assigns variables or objects to these groups.

cluster sampling Sampling in which clusters or groups of elements are randomly selected. It is composed of two steps: (1) the population is divided into mutually exclusive and collectively exhaustive groups, and (2) a probability sample of the groups is selected.

codebook A listing of the documentation of the coding scheme and other information regarding the variables in a dataset.

coding In the research process, establishing categories for responses or groups of responses such that numerals can be used to represent the categories.

coefficient of determination, r^2 The exact percentage of variation shared by two variables, obtained by squaring the correlation coefficient.

coefficient of multiple determination In multiple regression, the proportion of the variation in Y explained by the regression, which can be calculated as $SS_{explained}/SS_{total}$.

coefficient of variation An expression for the standard deviation as a percentage of the mean, formally defined as $CV = S/\bar{X}$.

cognitive component One of three main components of attitudes, concerned with a person's beliefs about some object or phenomenon (in the marketing behavioral response model, includes the awareness and knowledge stages).

communality In factor analysis, the proportion of a variable's total variation that is involved in the factors; defined mathematically as the sum of the squared loading of a variable on all factors (h^2).

communication method A general method of collecting data involving the questioning of respondents, either verbally or by means of written questionnaires.

communication techniques One type of attitude measurement procedure, including such techniques as self-reports, responses to unstructured or partially structured stimuli, and performance of objective tasks, in which the measurement process is based on some sort of communicated response by the subject.

company demand The company's share of market demand.

company sales forecast The expected level of company sales based on a chosen marketing plan and an assumed environment.

company sales potential   The limit approached by company demand as company marketing effort increases relative to competitors.

completely randomized design (CRD)   The simplest type of designed experiment; it involves only one independent variable, and the treatments are assigned to test units at random.

computer graphics   Computer software packages that display research data in the form of pie, bar, and line charts.

conclusive research   Research designed to help a decision maker evaluate courses of action and select the best one.

concomitant variation   The extent to which a cause, X, and an effect, Y, occur together or vary together as hypothesized.

concurrent validity   A method of assessing validity that involves correlating two different measurements of the same marketing phenomena that have been administered at the same point in time.

conditional association   The association between two variables conditional on one or more control variables.

conditional probability   The probability assigned to an event when another event has occurred or is assumed to have occurred; in symbols, $P(A|B)$, the probability of A given B.

confounding variable   An uncontrolled extraneous variable, the effect of which is to invalidate conclusions from an experiment.

conjoint measurement   A dependence method of multivariate data analysis appropriate for use with an ordinally scaled dependent variable and nominally scaled independent variables; essentially an analysis of variance of rank-order data that generates intervally scaled measures of the effects of the categories of the independent variables.

consistent estimator   A statistic that approaches the population as sample size increases.

construct validity   A means of estimating validity that relies on an understanding of the theoretical rationale underlying the obtained measurements.

consumer jury   A pretesting method of copy testing using consumer ratings of ads in a forced exposure setting.

content validity   Assessing validity by the subjective judgment of an expert as to the appropriateness of the measurements.

contingency planning   Specification of alternative courses of action by an organization to meet invalid planning assumptions or unanticipated changes in the situational factors.

contrived observation   An observation technique in which an artificial environment is created and the behavior of persons put in the environment is observed.

control markets   Test market cities in which a research supply house has paid retailers for a guarantee that they will carry products designated by the supply house; also known as minimarkets.

convenience sample   A sample that is selected on the basis of the convenience of the researcher.

correlation coefficient, r   A bivariate descriptive statistic, appropriate in dealing with two intervally scaled variables, which provides a measure of the linear direction and strength of the relationship between these variables.

cross-sectional design   A research design (typically associated with descriptive research) that involves taking a sample of population elements at one point in time.

cross-tabulation table   A matrix display of the categories of two nominally scaled variables, containing frequency counts of the number of subjects in each bivariate category.

data   Observations and evidence regarding some aspect of the marketing system.

data deck   The complete set of computer cards containing all the data from a given study.

data matrix   A rectangular array of data storage with n rows and m columns, where the number of rows equals the number of cases and the number of columns equals the number of variables.

decision criteria   The rules for selecting among courses of action given various data outcomes.

decision problem   A situation in which management has an objective to accomplish, two or more alternative courses of action exist which may reach the objective, and uncertainty is present regarding the best course of action.

degrees of freedom   The number of independent observations on the variable of interest minus the number of statistics calculated.

dependence methods   Multivariate data analysis procedures that specify a dependent variable.

dependent variable   The presumed effect in a cause-and-effect relationship.

depth interview   An unstructured personal interview using extensive probing in such a way that the respondent talks freely and expresses detailed beliefs and feelings on a topic.

descriptive research   Marketing research aimed at characterizing marketing phenomena and identifying association among selected variables.

descriptive statistics   The branch of statistics that provides researchers with summary measures for the data in samples.

deterministic causation   The "commonsense" concept of causality, in which a single event (a cause) always results in another event (an effect).

diary method   A procedure for collecting consumer purchase data or media habits that requires respondents to complete a written report of their behavior.

dichotomous question   A form of multiple-choice question that provides only two response alternatives.

discriminant analysis   A dependence method of multivariate data analysis appropriate for use with a nominally scaled dependent variable and intervally scaled independent variables; a technique that derives a linear combination of the independent variables such that the mean scores across categories of the dependent variable in this linear combination are maximally different.

disguised observation   Observation techniques in which the respondents are not aware that they are being observed.

disproportionate stratified sampling   Sampling in which the overall sample size is allocated to strata on a basis disproportionate with the population sizes of the strata.

division   A geographic unit of the Bureau of the Census, third highest in level of aggregation; the regions are divided into nine divisions.

dummy advertising vehicle   An advertising pretesting procedure in which test and control ads are inserted into a magazine format with editorial features of lasting interest. Respondents are asked to read the magazine normally. Response measures include awareness, recall, copy readership level, and product interest.

dummy-variable multiple regression   A dependence method of multivariate data analysis appropriate for use with an intervally scaled dependent variable and nominally scaled independent variables; an extension of multiple regression to less than interval data through the creation of a series of binary variables coded as 0–1.

editing   The process of reviewing data collection instruments to ensure maximum accuracy and unambiguity; checks for legibility, consistency, and completeness.

effect   In ANOVA, a difference in treatment means from the grand mean.

efficient estimator   An estimator that has the minimum variance.

eigenvalue   In factor analysis, the amount of variation in the data accounted for by a factor.

element   The unit in a sample about which information is sought.

ex post facto   Searching for a cause following the observation of an effect.

expected monetary gain of imperfect information (EMGII)   The value of a research study net of its cost. Used in decision theory; calculated as EMGII = EMVII − cost of information.

expected monetary value (EMV) criterion   Selection of the alternative with the highest expected monetary value.

expected monetary value of imperfect information (EMVII)   In marketing research terms, the measure of the value of a study; calculated as EMVII = EMV (with study) − EMV (without study).

expected monetary value of perfect information (EMVPI)   Equal to EMV(C) − EMV(UC); this represents the gain over expected outcomes under uncertainty and represents the absolute theoretical limit of the amount one would be willing to pay for perfect information. EMV(C) and EMV(UC) are EMVs under certainty and uncertainty, respectively.

expected utility value (EUV) criterion   Selection of the alternative with the highest expected utility value; this takes into account the attitude toward risk as well as monetary payouts.

experiment   A process in which a person consciously manipulates or controls one or more independent variables to measure their effect on the dependent variable or variables.

experimental design   The specification of treatments, test units, dependent variables, and extraneous variables to be considered in an experiment.

exploratory research   Research designed to formulate hypotheses regarding potential problems and/or opportunities present in the decision situation.

external data   Data obtained from a source other than the organization for which the research is being conducted.

external validity   The generalizability of experimental results to test units other than those used.

extraneous variable   Any variable other than the treatments that affects the response of the test unit to the treatments.

extreme case   A response on a variable that is so far out of the ordinary that it might represent a coding or punching error.

factor analysis   An interdependence multivariate analysis method that takes a large number of variables or objects and attempts to find a small number of factors in common which account for their intercorrelation.

factorial design   An experimental design useful for measuring simultaneously the effects of two or more independent variables.

field operation   That phase of a research project which makes contact with respondents, administers the data collection instrument, records the data, and returns the data to a central location for processing.

fixed effects model   An ANOVA procedure in which inferences about differences among treatment administered are made, but no interpolation between treatments is made.

focus group interview   A loosely structured interview conducted by a trained moderator simultaneously among a small number of respondents; also known as a group depth interview.

forced scale   A rating scale which does not include a "no opinion" or "no-knowledge" category and thus requires respondents to indicate a position on the attitude scale.

grand mean   In ANOVA, the mean of all observations across all treatment groups.

hierarchy-of-effects model   A marketing behavioral response model consisting of stages which a buyer is hypothesized to pass through, including awareness, knowledge, liking, preference, intention to buy, and purchase.

history   An extraneous variable referring to the occurrence of specific events that are external but concurrent to the experiment.

hypothesis   A conjectural statement about the value of a variable or the relationship between two or more variables.

independent variable   The presumed cause in a cause-and-effect relationship.

indirect observation   An observation technique in which some record of past behavior is used, rather than observation of behavior as it occurs.

indirect scale   A self-reporting technique in which a respondent's judgments on several questions are combined in order to develop a measure of his or her position on the attitude in question.

inferential statistics   The branch of statistics that allows researchers to make judgments concerning the population based on the results generated by samples.

information   Data that reduce the uncertainty in a decision situation.

inquiry tests   An advertising pretesting procedure in which the response measure is either measured sales or consumer inquiries that result directly from the ad.

instrumentation   An extraneous variable referring to changes in the calibration of the measuring instrument used or changes in the observers or scorers used.

item nonresponse error   Refusal by a respondent to answer a question or a series of questions.

interaction effect   An effect (that the total effect is greater than the sum of their main effects) that occurs when the relationship between an independent variable and the dependent variable is different for different categories of another independent variable.

interdependence methods   Multivariate data analysis methods in which no variable or variables are designated as dependent on others.

internal data   Data that originate within the organization for which research is being conducted.

internal validity   The extent to which experimental results are caused by the treatment variables as opposed to extraneous variables.

interval scale   A scale of measurement in which the distances among the numbers correspond to the distances among the objects or events on the characteristic being measured; intervals between numbers are assumed to be equal.

joint probability   The probability that two or more events will occur; in symbols, $P(A \cap B)$, the probability of A and B.

judgment sample   A sample that is selected on the basis of what some expert thinks particular sampling units or elements will contribute to answering the research question at hand.

Laplace criterion   Selection of the alternative with the highest average value.

Latin square design   An experimental design useful for controlling and measuring the effects of two extraneous variables.

level of confidence   The probability of not rejecting the null hypothesis when it is true, equal to $1 - x$.

levels   The categories of the independent variables in a factorial design experiment.

Likert scale   An indirect scale in which a respondent indicates his or her degree of agreement or disagreement with each of a series of statements; each response is subsequently numerically scored by the researcher, and a summary score for each respondent is obtained.

line chart A graphic presentation of magnitude in the dataset depicted by the slope of a line (or lines) which has been laid out with reference to a horizontal or vertical scale.

longitudinal design A research design in which a fixed sample of population elements is measured over time.

market demand The total volume of a product that would be purchased by a defined customer group in a defined time period and geography, given an environment and marketing program.

market forecast The level of market demand, given an expected level of industry marketing effort and an assumed environment.

market potential The limit approached by market demand within an assumed environment, as industry marketing effort approaches infinity.

marketing information system (MIS) The systematic and continuous gathering, analysis, and reporting data for decision-making purposes.

marketing mix The independent variables over which an organization exerts some degree of control (product, price, place, and promotion).

marketing research A systematic and objective approach to the development and provision of information for the marketing management decision-making process.

marketing research system An information center for decision making.

maturation An extraneous variable concerned with changes in experimental units that occur over time.

maximax criterion Selection of the alternative that maximizes the maximum payoff.

maximin criterion Selection of the alternative that maximizes the minimum payoff.

mean A measure of central tendency for interval data; the average value.

measurement The assignment of numbers to characteristics of objects or events according to rules.

measures of dispersion A type of descriptive statistic, including such measures as the standard deviation, the coefficient of variation, the interquartile range, and relative and absolute frequencies.

mechanical observation Observation techniques involving mechanical observers in conjunction with or in place of human observers. Examples are the motion picture camera, the Audimeter, the psychogalvanometer, the eye-camera, and the pupilometer.

median A measure of central tendency for ordinal data, defined for ungrouped data as the middle value when the data are arranged in order of magnitude.

metropolitan statistical area (MSA) A geographic unit of the Bureau of the Census consisting of (1) a city with 50,000 or more inhabitants or (2) an urbanized area of at least 50,000 inhabitants and a total MSA population of at least 100,000 (75,000 in New England).

minimax regret criterion The alternative selected with the minimum opportunity loss.

mixed effects model An ANOVA procedure including independent variables of both the fixed and the random types.

mode A measure of central tendency for nominal data, defined as the category that occurs with the greatest frequency.

monadic rating An evaluating procedure whereby respondents rate items on a rating scale without reference to other comparison items.

multidimensional scaling An interdependence multivariate data analysis method that uses as input a matrix of relationships between objects with unknown underlying dimensionality, determines the minimum dimensionality of the relationships between the objects, and positions each object on each dimension.

multiple-choice question   A question which requires a respondent to select or answer from among a list provided in the question proper or following the question.

multiple correlation coefficient   In multiple regression, the correlation coefficient between the observed Y_i and the estimated $\hat{Y}_i$'s.

multiple regression   A dependence method of multivariate data analysis appropriate for use with an intervally scaled dependent variable and intervally scaled independent variables; an extension of the simple regression technique to more than one independent variable.

multivariate analysis   The analysis of more than two variables at a time.

multivariate analysis of variance   A dependence method of multivariate data analysis appropriate for use with two or more intervally scaled dependent variables and one or more intervally scaled independent variables; the multivariate extension of ANOVA to more than one dependent variable.

nominal scale   A measurement scale in which numbers serve only as labels to identify or categorize objects or events.

nonprobability sampling   A sampling procedure in which the selection of population elements is based in part on the judgment of the researcher or field interviewer.

nonresponse errors   The differences in measures between test units who respond to a survey and those who do not respond.

nonsampling errors   All the errors that may occur in the marketing research process, except the sampling error.

null hypothesis   The hypothesis that states that a population parameter takes on a particular value or set of values.

O   An experimental design symbol, referring to processes of observation or measurement of the dependent variable on the test units.

observation method   A general method of collecting data from respondents in which the respondent's behavior is recorded.

observation techniques   Attitude measurement procedures, including such techniques as overt behavior and physiological reaction measurement, in which the procedures are based on observing the behavior of the subject.

omnibus panel   A fixed sample of respondents measured on different variables over a period of time.

on-the-air tests   Advertising pretesting procedures that measure responses to ads that are placed on actual television or radio programs in test areas.

one-tailed test   A test in which the alternative hypothesis is stated such that one specific direction (one tail of the possible distribution of values) is considered.

one-way ANOVA   ANOVA applied to a CRD; that is, ANOVA applied to categories of one independent variable.

open-ended question   A question that requires respondents to provide their own answers.

opportunity   The presence of a situation where performance can be improved by undertaking new activities.

ordinal scale   A scale of measurement which defines the ordered relationships among objects or events.

original source   The source which generated the data.

overall efficiency   A relative assessment of a sampling procedure based on its statistical efficiency and cost; defined as the cost per standard error.

paired comparison scale   A self-reporting technique presenting the respondent with two objects from a set and requiring the respondent to pick one with regard to the attitude in question.

parameter   A summary description of a measure in the defined population.

performance-monitoring research   Research designed to provide information about the outcomes of marketing activities.

periodicity   In systematic sampling, a cyclical pattern within a list of elements forming the sampling frame that coincides with a multiple of the size of the sampling interval.

pie chart   A circle divided into sections such that the size of each section corresponds to a portion of the total.

population   The aggregate of the elements defined prior to the selection of the sample.

portfolio tests   A pretesting procedure using a package of control and test ads: consumers are asked to read whatever interests them; recall measures are then taken.

posterior analysis   The combination of prior information with additional information to provide revised (posterior) probability estimates, which are then used to calculate a posterior EMV.

posttesting   The evaluation of advertising after it has run in the media.

power of test   The probability of rejecting a false null hypothesis, equal to $1 - \beta$.

precision   The width of a confidence interval expressed either absolutely in units or relative to the size of the mean.

predictive validity   A means of assessing validity that involves the ability of a measure of marketing phenomena to predict other marketing phenomena.

preexperimental design   Experimental designs with inherent weaknesses with the consequence that questionable internal validity results.

preposterior analysis   A method of analysis allowing the researcher to measure the value of alternative research studies prior to undertaking research.

pretesting   The initial testing of one or more aspects of a research design, or the evaluation of advertising prior to a fully funded run in the media.

prior analysis   The application of the decision theory approach when the probabilities of outcomes are assessed on the basis of present judgment, without benefit of additional information.

probabilistic causation   The scientific concept of causality, in which one event or a series of events results in the probable occurrence of another event.

probability sampling   A sampling procedure in which each element of the population has a known chance of being selected for the sample.

problem   The independent variables that cause an organization's performance measures to be below objectives.

profile analysis   A method of analyzing semantic differential data, in which an arithmetic mean or median is calculated for each set of polar opposites for each object evaluated.

programmed decisions   Decisions of a repetitive nature for which a manager's experience and judgment provide the key input.

proportionate stratified sampling   Stratified sampling in which the number of elements drawn from each stratum is proportionate to the relative number of elements in each stratum of the population.

q-type analysis   A casewise factor analysis.

qualitative forecasting methods   Methods that involve collecting judgments or opinions from knowledgeable individuals.

qualitative research Questioning knowledgeable respondents individually or in small groups regarding the "why" of behavior.

quantitative research Questioning large groups of respondents regarding the "what, when, where, and how" of behavior.

quasi experimentation An experimental design in which the researcher has control over data collection procedures but lacks complete control over the scheduling or randomization of the treatments.

questionnaire A formalized schedule for collecting data from respondents.

quota sample A sample selected so as to match the population on prespecified "control" characteristics.

r An experimental design symbol, indicating that a randomizing process has been used in assigning test units and treatments.

r-type analysis A factor analysis calculated by variables.

random-digit dialing A method of identifying households in a telephone interview whereby either all seven digits are randomly generated, or numbers are randomly selected from a directory and the last one or two digits are replaced with random numbers.

random effects model An ANOVA procedure in which interpolation of results between treatments is allowed.

random error Bias in the measurements caused by the transient aspects of the respondent or measurement setting.

random number list A list of numbers that have no pattern of occurrence.

randomized block design (RBD) An experimental design in which test units are blocked on the basis of some external criterion variable, in such a way that scores within the blocks on the dependent variable are likely to be more homogeneous than in the absence of blocking.

rank-order scale A self-reporting technique in which the respondent ranks various objects with regard to the attitude in question.

rating scale A self-reporting scale involving ordinal, interval, or ratio scales in which the respondent indicates the position on a continuum or among ordered categories corresponding to his or her attitude; includes both graphic rating scales and verbal rating scales.

ratio scale A scale of measurement that has all the properties of an interval scale plus an absolute zero point.

recall tests Advertising posttesting procedures that emphasize respondents' ability to recall, unaided and aided, ads they have previously been exposed to.

recognition method Aided recall in which an actual event is presented to a respondent.

recognition tests Advertising posttesting procedures that emphasize respondents' ability to recognize ads they were previously exposed to in an interview.

region A geographic unit of the Bureau of the Census, second highest in level of aggregation; the United States is divided into four regions.

relative frequency A measure of dispersion for nominal data, defined as the percentage of the total elements appearing in a given category.

relative precision Precision expressed as a percentage of the mean.

reliability The extent to which the measurement process is free from random errors.

repertory grid A method of identifying attributes which consumers can use to describe their perceptions of products; respondents repeatedly think of ways in which any two of three items are similar to each other and different from a third.

research design   The basic plan that guides the data collection and analysis phases of a research project.

research report   Presentation of research findings to a specific audience to accomplish a specific purpose.

respondent characteristics   One of three types of data that can be obtained from respondents to forecast market behavior; this type describes respondents in terms of demographic, socioeconomic, and psychological characteristics.

response bias   An inaccurate response, resulting from such factors as respondent fatigue, boredom, or desire to please.

role playing   A technique in which a respondent is presented with a verbal situation and asked how the beliefs and feelings of another person relate to the situation; also known as the third-person technique.

sales budget   A conservative estimate of the expected volume of sales.

sales ratio method   A method of projecting the results of a test marketing program to national performance, based on sales of another brand and estimated as:

$$\text{National sales estimate} = \frac{\text{national sales of other product}}{\text{test area sales of this other product}} \times \text{test area sales of test product}$$

sampling distribution   The distribution formed by a statistic that is calculated for each of all possible samples of a certain size from a given population.

sampling error   The difference between the observed probability sample statistic and the population parameter.

sampling fraction   The proportion of the number of sample elements to the number of population elements.

sampling frame   A list of all the sampling units in the population.

sampling interval   The size of the step between selected elements in systematic sampling; the reciprocal of the sampling fraction, that is, N/n.

sampling unit   The element or elements available for selection at some stage of the sampling process.

scanner data   Data recorded by passing merchandise over a laser scanner that optically reads the bar-coded description printed on the merchandise.

secondary data   Published data that have been compiled for a purpose other than the present study.

selection bias   The assignment of test units of treatment groups such that the groups differ on the dependent variable prior to the presentation of the treatments.

semantic differential scale   A self-reporting scale requiring the respondent to evaluate an object on a 7-point rating scale bounded on each end by bipolar adjectives.

sentence completion   A technique in which an incomplete sentence is presented to the respondent, who is asked to complete the sentence.

share-of-market method   A method of projecting the results of a test marketing program to national performance, based on sales in the test area of the product category as a whole, and estimated as:

$$\text{National sales estimate} = \frac{\text{test area sales of new brand}}{\text{test area sales of this whole product category}} \times \text{national sales of this whole product category}$$

significance level   The specified level of x indicating the probability of making a type I error.

simple random sampling   A probability sampling procedure in which each element has an equal chance of being selected and each combination of elements is equally likely.

simple regression   A bivariate statistical procedure, applicable to intervally scaled variables, used to demonstrate how an independent variable is related to a dependent variable and to make predictions about scores on the dependent variable, given knowledge of the scores on the independent variable.

simulated test market   A laboratory-based method of forecasting product sales based upon pretest interviews, forced advertising exposures, simulated store shopping, product trials, and follow-up interviews to measure repurchase rate.

simulation   An incomplete representation of the marketing system designed to explicate the dynamics of the variables operating within that system.

situational analysis   The process of analyzing the past and future situations facing an organization in order to identify problems and opportunities.

situational factors   Independent variables that are not under the control of the organization.

Solomon four-group design   A true experimental design which controls for both extraneous variable effects and interactive testing effects.

split-half reliability   Estimating reliability by dividing a multi-item measurement device into equivalent groups and correlating the item responses to estimate reliability.

spurious relationship   An observed relationship between variables when no relationship really exists; the relationship disappears with elaboration.

SS_B   In a randomized block design ANOVA, the blocking effect sum of squared deviations.

SS_C   In a Latin square design ANOVA, the column effect sum of squared deviations.

SS_E   In ANOVA, the sum of squared deviations related to error.

$SS_{INT(AB)}$ In a factorial design ANOVA, the interaction effect sum of squared deviations.

SS_R   In a Latin square design ANOVA, the row effect sum of squared deviations.

SS_T   In ANOVA, the total sum of squared deviations from the grand mean.

SS_{TR}   In ANOVA, the sum of squared deviations resulting from the treatments.

SS_{TRA}   In a factorial design ANOVA, the treatment A effect sum of squared deviations.

standard deviation, s   A measure of dispersion for interval data.

standard error of the coefficient, s_b   A measure of the amount of sampling error present in the determination of b in a regression equation; more precisely, the standard deviation of the sampling distribution of the regression coefficient.

standard error of the estimate, s_{YX}   The measure of the scatter of the actual Y_i values about a regression line $\hat{Y}_i$; more precisely, the standard deviation of Y_i about $\hat{Y}_i$.

standard error of the mean   The standard deviation of the sampling distribution of the mean.

Standard Industrial Classification (SIC) code   A system of classification based on the products produced or the operations performed. The federal government uses SIC codes in its Census of Manufacturers.

standard markets   Test market cities in which no guarantees of retail distribution support are made; the traditional alternative to control markets.

Stapel scale   A modification of the semantic differential scale, using a unipolar 10-point ($+5$ to -5) nonverbal rating scale, designed to measure the direction and intensity of attitudes simultaneously.

statistic   A summary description of a measure in the selected sample.

statistical efficiency   Comparison of the standard errors generated by various sampling procedures.

statistical regression   The phenomenon that outliers tend to move toward a more average position over time.

strategy   Board principles as to how the marketing program is to operate in achieving objectives.

stratified sampling   A two-stage probability sampling procedure in which the population is divided into mutually exclusive and collectively exhaustive strata, and a random sample is drawn from each stratum.

study population   The aggregate of elements from which the sample is drawn.

symptom   A condition that signals the presence of a problem or an opportunity.

syndicated source   A profit-making organization that provides standardized data to an array of clients.

systematic error   An error that causes a constant bias in measurements.

systematic sampling   A type of cluster sampling in which every kth element is selected from the frame, after a random start somewhere within the first k elements, where $k =$ sampling interval.

t test   A test designed for comparing the sample mean with a hypothesized mean of a population, appropriate for all sample sizes when σ is unknown; also, a test designed for comparing the difference between two means.

test marketing   The implementation and monitoring of a marketing program in a small subset of the target market area for the product in question.

test-retest reliability   Estimating reliability by repeating the measurement using the same scaling device under conditions that are judged to be very similar.

test units   The entities in an experiment to whom the treatments are presented and whose response to the treatments is measured.

test unit mortality   Test units' withdrawal from the experiment before completion.

testing effect   An extraneous variable consisting of the effect on the experiment of taking a measure on the dependent variable before presenting the treatment. The *main testing effect* refers to the effect of the first measurement on the second measurement, while the *interactive testing effect* refers to the effect of the first measurement on the test unit's response to the treatment.

theater test   An advertising pretesting procedure that exposes respondents to control and test ads in the context of a theater-shown television program.

Thematic Apperception Test (TAT)   A projective technique using one or more pictures or cartoons. A situation is depicted and the respondent is asked to describe what has happened or will happen as a result of the situation.

time-series experiment   A quasi-experimental design involving a periodic measurement on the dependent variables for some test units.

time-series forecasting methods   Methods that apply statistical techniques to historical sales data over time to make numerical sales forecasts.

tracks   Alternative ways of processing the data from collection instruments to the computer.

tracts   Small areas into which large cities and their adjacent areas have been divided for statistical purposes by the Bureau of the Census.

traditional panel   A fixed sample measured over a period on the same variables.

trailer tests   An advertising pretesting procedure that recruits respondents from shopping malls for forced exposure to ads in a trailer near the mall or in a room in the mall itself.

treatment   The alternatives which are manipulated and the effects of which are measured in an experiment.

true experimental design   An experimental design in which all extraneous variables are eliminated or controlled.

two-tailed test   The situation in which an alternative hypothesis is stated in such a way that both ends of the sampling distribution are considered (no specified directionality).

type *I* error (α error)   The rejection of a true null hypothesis.

type *II* error (β error)   The nonrejection of a false null hypothesis.

unaided recall   A questioning approach that does not provide the respondent with cues about the event.

unbiased estimator   An estimator the expected value of which is the parameter or population value.

uncertainty   A lack of complete knowledge about the possible outcomes of actions, with the probabilities of the possible outcomes not known.

unconditional probability   The probability assigned to an event that is independent of other events; also known as marginal probability.

univariate analysis   The analysis of one variable at a time.

unprogrammed decision   A decision involving a somewhat new, atypical situation in which a manager's experience and judgment are of limited usefulness.

validity   The extent to which a measurement process is free from both systematic and random error.

variable   A property that takes on different values at different times.

variance   A measure of the dispersion of the distribution of an interval variable.

wild codes   Codes that are not defined in a codebook for a particular variable.

word association   A technique in which a series of words is presented to a respondent, who is to respond to each one with the first word that comes to mind.

X   An experimental design symbol, representing the exposure of a test group to an experimental treatment.

***z* test**   A test designed for comparing the sample mean with a hypothesized mean of a population; it is appropriate for interval data when σ is known for any sample size, or for situations of sufficiently large sample size ($n > 30$) and σ unknown.

zero-order association   Also known as total association, this is the original association between two variables, without controlling for any other variables (as contrasted with conditional association).

APPENDIX

TABLE A-1   ABRIDGED LIST OF RANDOM NUMBERS

```
10 09 73 25 33    76 52 01 35 35    34 67 35 48 76    80 95 90 91 17    39 29 27 49 45
37 54 20 48 05    64 89 47 42 96    24 80 52 40 37    20 63 61 04 02    00 82 29 16 65
08 42 26 89 53    19 64 50 93 03    23 20 90 25 60    15 95 33 47 64    35 08 03 36 06
90 01 90 25 29    09 37 67 07 15    38 31 13 11 65    88 67 67 43 97    04 43 62 76 59
12 80 79 99 70    80 15 73 61 47    64 03 23 66 53    98 95 11 68 77    12 17 17 68 33

66 06 57 47 17    34 07 27 08 50    36 69 73 61 70    65 81 33 98 85    11 19 92 91 70
31 06 01 08 05    45 57 18 24 06    35 30 34 26 14    86 79 90 74 39    23 40 30 97 32
85 26 97 76 02    02 05 16 56 92    68 66 57 48 18    73 05 38 52 47    18 62 38 85 79
63 57 33 21 35    05 32 54 70 48    90 55 35 75 48    28 46 82 87 09    83 49 12 55 24
73 79 64 57 53    03 52 96 47 78    35 80 83 42 82    60 93 52 03 44    35 27 38 84 35

98 52 01 77 67    14 90 56 86 07    22 10 94 05 50    00 07 00 01 00    60 60 07 30 09
11 80 50 54 31    39 80 82 77 32    50 72 56 82 48    29 40 52 42 01    52 77 56 78 51
83 45 29 96 34    06 28 89 80 83    13 74 67 00 78    18 47 54 06 10    68 71 17 78 17
88 68 54 02 00    86 50 75 84 01    36 76 66 79 51    90 36 47 64 93    29 60 91 10 62
99 59 46 73 48    87 51 76 49 69    91 82 60 89 28    93 78 56 13 68    23 47 83 41 13

65 48 11 76 74    17 46 85 09 50    58 04 77 69 74    73 03 95 71 86    40 21 81 65 44
80 12 43 56 35    17 72 70 80 15    45 31 82 23 74    21 11 57 82 53    14 38 55 37 63
74 35 09 98 17    77 40 27 72 14    43 23 60 02 10    45 52 16 42 37    96 28 60 26 55
69 91 62 68 03    66 25 22 91 48    36 93 68 72 03    76 62 11 39 90    94 40 05 64 18
09 90 32 05 05    14 22 56 85 14    46 42 75 67 88    96 29 77 88 22    54 38 21 45 98

91 49 91 45 23    68 47 92 76 86    46 16 28 35 54    94 75 08 99 23    37 08 92 00 48
80 33 69 45 98    26 94 03 08 58    70 29 73 41 35    53 14 03 33 40    42 05 08 23 41
44 10 48 19 49    85 15 74 79 54    32 97 92 65 75    57 60 04 08 81    22 22 20 64 13
12 55 07 37 42    11 10 00 20 40    12 86 07 46 97    96 64 48 94 39    28 70 72 58 15
63 60 64 93 29    16 50 53 44 84    40 21 95 25 63    43 65 17 70 82    07 20 73 17 90

61 19 69 04 46    26 45 74 77 74    51 92 43 37 29    65 39 45 95 93    42 58 26 05 27
15 47 44 52 66    95 27 07 99 53    59 36 78 38 48    82 39 61 01 18    33 21 15 94 66
94 55 72 85 73    67 89 75 43 87    54 62 24 44 31    91 19 04 25 92    92 92 74 59 73
42 48 11 62 13    97 34 40 87 21    16 86 84 87 67    03 07 11 20 59    25 70 14 66 70
23 52 37 83 17    73 20 88 98 37    68 93 59 14 16    26 25 22 96 63    05 52 28 25 62

04 49 35 24 94    75 24 63 38 24    45 86 25 10 25    61 96 27 93 35    65 33 71 24 72
00 54 99 76 54    84 05 18 81 59    96 11 96 38 96    54 69 28 23 91    23 28 72 95 29
35 96 31 53 07    26 89 80 93 54    33 35 13 54 62    77 97 45 00 24    90 10 33 93 33
59 80 80 83 91    45 42 72 68 42    83 60 94 97 00    13 02 12 48 92    78 56 52 01 06
46 05 88 52 36    01 39 09 22 86    77 28 14 40 77    93 91 08 36 47    70 61 74 29 41

32 17 90 05 97    87 37 92 52 41    05 56 70 70 07    86 74 31 71 57    85 39 41 18 38
69 23 48 14 06    20 11 74 52 04    15 95 66 00 00    18 74 39 24 23    97 11 89 63 38
19 56 54 14 30    01 75 87 53 79    40 41 92 15 85    66 67 43 68 06    84 96 28 52 07
45 15 51 49 38    19 47 60 72 46    43 66 79 45 43    59 04 79 00 33    20 82 66 95 41
94 86 43 19 94    36 16 81 08 51    34 88 88 15 53    01 54 03 54 56    05 01 45 11 76

93 08 62 48 26    45 24 02 84 04    44 99 90 88 96    39 09 47 34 07    35 44 13 18 80
33 18 51 62 32    41 94 15 09 49    89 43 54 85 81    88 69 54 19 94    37 54 87 30 43
80 95 10 04 06    96 38 27 07 74    20 15 12 33 87    25 01 62 52 98    94 62 46 11 71
79 75 24 91 40    71 96 12 82 96    69 86 10 25 91    74 85 22 05 39    00 38 75 95 79
18 63 33 25 37    98 14 50 65 71    31 01 02 46 74    05 45 56 14 27    77 93 89 19 36

74 02 94 39 02    77 55 73 22 70    97 79 01 71 19    52 52 75 80 21    80 81 45 17 48
54 17 84 56 11    80 99 33 71 43    05 33 51 29 69    56 12 71 92 55    36 04 09 03 24
11 66 44 98 83    52 07 98 48 27    59 38 17 15 39    09 97 33 34 40    88 46 12 33 56
48 32 47 79 28    81 24 96 47 10    02 29 53 68 70    32 30 75 75 46    15 02 00 99 94
69 07 49 41 38    87 63 79 19 76    35 58 40 44 01    10 51 82 16 15    01 84 87 69 38
```

Source: Reproduced with permission from the RAND Corporation, *A Million Random Digits with 100,000 Normal Deviates* (New York: The Free Press, 1955).

HOW TO USE A RANDOM NUMBER TABLE*

Random samples are often used in marketing research. One easy way to obtain a random sample is through the use of a random number table. Random number tables are constructed so that each digit occurs with approximately equal probability. To explain how to use such a table, consider the following example.

Suppose you have a list of 100,000 households that recently purchased a certain product. You wish to obtain a random sample of three households from this population. First you number the population (list) from 1 to 100,000.

Then you open a random number table to any page. Let us assume the first page is used. Select your first number from anywhere on the page. Let us say the number in the third row, second column, is selected as the first number. Proceed down the column or across the row; either path will suffice. Select your other four numbers. If any repetitions occur, discard the duplicate and select a replacement at the end of the group of numbers chosen.

For example, if this process were followed with the table below, the three numbers chosen would be 06907; 48360; and 93093. Allowing household numbers 1 through 99999 to be represented by those numbers in the table and 00000 to represent household number 100000, you would interview household #6097, #48360 and #93093 on your list of households.

If you had a much smaller population, such as a list of 100 households, you could use as few digits as necessary to identify your element. For example, using the same three numbers, you would interview households 6, 48, and 93. (00 would be household number 100.)

Column	1	2	3	4
Row				
1	02011	10480	15011	01536
2	85393	22368	**06907**	25595
3	97265	24130	**48360**	22527
4	61680	42167	**93093**	06243

*Adapted from James T. McClave and P. George Benson, *Statistics for Business and Economics,* 4th ed. (San Francisco, CA: Dellen Publishing Company, 1988).

TABLE A-2   AREAS IN TWO TAILS OF THE NORMAL CURVE AT SELECTED VALUES OF x/σ FROM THE ARITHMETIC MEAN

This table shows:

x/σ	.00	.01	.02	.03	.04	.05	.06	.07	.08	.09
0.0	1.0000	.9920	.9840	.9761	.9681	.9601	.9522	.9442	.9362	.9283
0.1	.9203	.9124	.9045	.8966	.8887	.8808	.8729	.8650	.8572	.8493
0.2	.8415	.8337	.8259	.8181	.8103	.8026	.7949	.7872	.7795	.7718
0.3	.7642	.7566	.7490	.7414	.7339	.7263	.7188	.7114	.7039	.6965
0.4	.6892	.6818	.6745	.6672	.6599	.6527	.6455	.6384	.6312	.6241
0.5	.6171	.6101	.6031	.5961	.5892	.5823	.5755	.5687	.5619	.5552
0.6	.5485	.5419	.5353	.5287	.5222	.5157	.5093	.5029	.4965	.4902
0.7	.4839	.4777	.4715	.4654	.4593	.4533	.4473	.4413	.4354	.4295
0.8	.4237	.4179	.4122	.4065	.4009	.3953	.3898	.3843	.3789	.3735
0.9	.3681	.3628	.3576	.3524	.3472	.3421	.3371	.3320	.3271	.3222
1.0	.3173	.3125	.3077	.3030	.2983	.2937	.2891	.2846	.2801	.2757
1.1	.2713	.2670	.2627	.2585	.2543	.2501	.2460	.2420	.2380	.2340
1.2	.2301	.2263	.2225	.2187	.2150	.2113	.2077	.2041	.2005	.1971
1.3	.1936	.1902	.1868	.1835	.1802	.1770	.1738	.1707	.1676	.1645
1.4	.1615	.1585	.1556	.1527	.1499	.1471	.1443	.1416	.1389	.1362
1.5	.1336	.1310	.1285	.1260	.1236	.1211	.1188	.1164	.1141	.1118
1.6	.1096	.1074	.1052	.1031	.1010	.0989	.0969	.0949	.0930	.0910
1.7	.0891	.0873	.0854	.0836	.0819	.0801	.0784	.0767	.0751	.0735
1.8	.0719	.0703	.0688	.0672	.0658	.0643	.0629	.0615	.0601	.0588
1.9	.0574	.0561	.0549	.0536	.0524	.0512	.0500	.0488	.0477	.0466
2.0	.0455	.0444	.0434	.0424	.0414	.0404	.0394	.0385	.0375	.0366
2.1	.0357	.0349	.0340	.0332	.0324	.0316	.0308	.0300	.0293	.0285
2.2	.0278	.0271	.0264	.0257	.0251	.0244	.0238	.0232	.0226	.0220
2.3	.0214	.0209	.0203	.0198	.0193	.0188	.0183	.0178	.0173	.0168
2.4	.0164	.0160	.0155	.0151	.0147	.0143	.0139	.0135	.0131	.0128
2.5	.0124	.0121	.0117	.0114	.0111	.0108	.0105	.0102	.00988	.00960
2.6	.00932	.00905	.00879	.00854	.00829	.00805	.00781	.00759	.00736	.00715
2.7	.00693	.00673	.00653	.00633	.00614	.00596	.00578	.00561	.00544	.00527
2.8	.00511	.00495	.00480	.00465	.00541	.00437	.00424	.00410	.00398	.00385
2.9	.00373	.00361	.00350	.00339	.00328	.00318	.00308	.00298	.00288	.00279

x/σ	.0	.1	.2	.3	.4	.5	.6	.7	.8	.9
3	.00270	.00194	.00137	$.0^3967$	$.0^3674$	$.0^3465$	$.0^3318$	$.0^3216$	$.0^3145$	$.0^4962$
4	$.0^4633$	$.0^4413$	$.0^4267$	$.0^4171$	$.0^4108$	$.0^5680$	$.0^5422$	$.0^5260$	$.0^5159$	$.0^6958$
5	$.0^6573$	$.0^6340$	$.0^6199$	$.0^6116$	$.0^7666$	$.0^7380$	$.0^7214$	$.0^7120$	$.0^8663$	$.0^8364$
6	$.0^8197$	$.0^8106$	$.0^9565$	$.0^9298$	$.0^9155$	$.0^{10}803$	$.0^{10}411$	$.0^{10}208$	$.0^{10}105$	$.0^{11}520$

TABLE A-3   AREAS IN ONE TAIL OF THE NORMAL CURVE AT SELECTED VALUES OF x/σ FROM THE ARITHMETIC MEAN

This table shows:

x/σ	.00	.01	.02	.03	.04	.05	.06	.07	.08	.09
0.0	.5000	.4960	.4920	.4880	.4840	.4801	.4761	.4721	.4681	.4641
0.1	.4602	.4562	.4522	.4483	.4443	.4404	.4364	.4325	.4286	.4247
0.2	.4207	.4168	.4129	.4090	.4052	.4013	.3974	.3936	.3897	.3859
0.3	.3821	.3783	.3745	.3707	.3669	.3632	.3594	.3557	.3520	.3483
0.4	.3446	.3409	.3372	.3336	.3300	.3264	.3228	.3192	.3156	.3121
0.5	.3085	.3050	.3015	.2981	.2946	.2912	.2877	.2843	.2810	.2776
0.6	.2743	.2709	.2676	.2643	.2611	.2578	.2546	.2514	.2483	.2451
0.7	.2420	.2389	.2358	.2327	.2296	.2266	.2236	.2206	.2177	.2148
0.8	.2119	.2090	.2061	.2033	.2005	.1977	.1949	.1922	.1894	.1867
0.9	.1841	.1814	.1788	.1762	.1736	.1711	.1685	.1660	.1635	.1611
1.0	.1587	.1562	.1539	.1515	.1492	.1469	.1446	.1423	.1401	.1379
1.1	.1357	.1335	.1314	.1292	.1271	.1251	.1230	.1210	.1190	.1170
1.2	.1151	.1131	.1112	.1093	.1075	.1056	.1038	.1020	.1003	.0985
1.3	.0968	.0951	.0934	.0918	.0901	.0885	.0869	.0853	.0838	.0823
1.4	.0808	.0793	.0778	.0764	.0749	.0735	.0721	.0708	.0694	.0681
1.5	.0668	.0655	.0643	.0630	.0618	.0606	.0594	.0582	.0571	.0559
1.6	.0548	.0537	.0526	.0516	.0505	.0495	.0485	.0475	.0465	.0455
1.7	.0446	.0436	.0427	.0418	.0409	.0401	.0392	.0384	.0375	.0367
1.8	.0359	.0351	.0344	.0336	.0329	.0322	.0314	.0307	.0301	.0294
1.9	.0287	.0281	.0274	.0268	.0262	.0256	.0250	.0244	.0239	.0233
2.0	.0228	.0222	.0217	.0212	.0207	.0202	.0197	.0192	.0188	.0183
2.1	.0179	.0174	.0170	.0166	.0162	.0158	.0154	.0150	.0146	.0143
2.2	.0139	.0136	.0132	.0129	.0125	.0122	.0119	.0116	.0113	.0110
2.3	.0107	.0104	.0102	.00990	.00964	.00939	.00914	.00889	.00866	.00842
2.4	.00820	.00798	.00776	.00755	.00734	.00714	.00695	.00676	.00657	.00639
2.5	.00621	.00604	.00587	.00570	.00554	.00539	.00523	.00508	.00494	.00480
2.6	.00466	.00453	.00440	.00427	.00415	.00402	.00391	.00379	.00368	.00357
2.7	.00347	.00336	.00326	.00317	.00307	.00298	.00289	.00280	.00272	.00264
2.8	.00256	.00248	.00240	.00233	.00226	.00219	.00212	.00205	.00199	.00193
2.9	.00187	.00181	.00175	.00169	.00164	.00159	.00154	.00149	.00144	.00139

x/σ	.0	.1	.2	.3	.4	.5	.6	.7	.8	.9
3	.00135	$.0^3968$	$.0^3687$	$.0^3483$	$.0^3337$	$.0^3233$	$.0^3159$	$.0^3108$	$.0^4723$	$.0^4481$
4	$.0^4317$	$.0^4207$	$.0^4133$	$.0^5854$	$.0^5541$	$.0^5340$	$.0^5211$	$.0^5130$	$.0^6793$	$.0^6479$
5	$.0^6287$	$.0^6170$	$.0^7996$	$.0^7579$	$.0^7333$	$.0^7190$	$.0^7107$	$.0^8599$	$.0^8332$	$.0^8182$
6	$.0^9987$	$.0^9430$	$.0^9282$	$.0^9149$	$.0^{10}777$	$.0^{10}402$	$.0^{10}206$	$.0^{10}104$	$.0^{11}523$	$.0^{11}260$

Source: This table is copyrighted by Prentice-Hall, Inc. It is reproduced by permission of Frederick E. Croxton.

TABLE A-4   TABLE OF CRITICAL VALUES OF t

Df	\begin{tabular}{c}Level of significance for two-tailed test\end{tabular}								Df
	0.5	0.4	0.3	0.2	0.1	0.05	0.02	0.01	
	Level of significance for one-tailed test								
	0.25	0.20	0.15	0.10	0.05	0.025	0.01	0.005	
1	1.000	1.376	1.963	3.078	6.314	12.706	31.821	63.657	1
2	.816	1.061	1.386	1.886	2.920	4.303	6.965	9.925	2
3	.765	.978	1.250	1.638	2.353	3.182	4.541	5.841	3
4	.741	.941	1.190	1.533	2.132	2.776	3.747	4.604	4
5	.727	.920	1.156	1.476	2.105	2.571	3.365	4.032	5
6	.718	.906	1.134	1.440	1.943	2.447	3.143	3.707	6
7	.711	.896	1.119	1.415	1.895	2.365	2.998	3.499	7
8	.706	.889	1.108	1.397	1.860	2.306	2.896	3.355	8
9	.703	.883	1.100	1.383	1.833	2.262	2.821	3.250	9
10	.700	.879	1.093	1.372	1.812	2.228	2.764	3.169	10
11	.697	.876	1.088	1.363	1.796	2.201	2.718	3.106	11
12	.695	.873	1.083	1.356	1.782	2.179	2.681	3.055	12
13	.694	.870	1.079	1.350	1.771	2.160	2.650	3.012	13
14	.692	.868	1.076	1.345	1.761	2.145	2.624	2.977	14
15	.691	.866	1.074	1.341	1.753	2.131	2.602	2.947	15
16	.690	.865	1.071	1.337	1.746	2.120	2.583	2.921	16
17	.689	.863	1.069	1.333	1.740	2.110	2.567	2.898	17
18	.688	.862	1.067	1.330	1.734	2.101	2.552	2.878	18
19	.688	.861	1.066	1.328	1.729	2.093	2.539	2.861	19
20	.687	.860	1.064	1.325	1.725	2.086	2.528	2.845	20
21	.686	.859	1.063	1.323	1.721	2.080	2.518	2.831	21
22	.686	.858	1.061	1.321	1.717	2.074	2.508	2.819	22
23	.685	.858	1.060	1.319	1.714	2.069	2.500	2.807	23
24	.685	.857	1.059	1.318	1.711	2.064	2.492	2.797	24
25	.684	.856	1.058	1.316	1.708	2.060	2.485	2.787	25
26	.684	.856	1.058	1.315	1.706	2.056	2.479	2.779	26
27	.684	.855	1.057	1.314	1.703	2.052	2.473	2.771	27
28	.683	.855	1.056	1.313	1.701	2.048	2.467	2.763	28
29	.683	.854	1.055	1.311	1.699	2.045	2.462	2.756	29
30	.683	.854	1.055	1.310	1.697	2.042	2.457	2.750	30
35						2.030		2.724	35
40						2.021		2.704	40
45						2.014		2.690	45
50						2.008		2.678	50
60						2.000		2.663	60
70						1.994		2.648	70
80						1.990		2.638	80
90						1.987		2.632	90
100						1.984		2.626	100
125						1.979		2.616	125
150						1.976		2.609	150
200						1.972		2.601	200
300						1.968		2.592	300
400						1.966		2.588	400
500						1.965		2.568	500
1000						1.962		2.561	1000
∞	.67449	.84162	1.03643	1.28155	1.64485	1.95996	2.32634	2.57582	∞

Source: Table is abridged from table III of Fisher and Yates, *Statistical Tables for Biological, Agricultural and Medical Research* (Edinburgh and London: Oliver & Boyd Ltd.). Reprinted by permission of the authors and publishers.

TABLE A-5 UPPER PERCENTAGE POINTS OF THE F DISTRIBUTION

n	1 − α	m=1	2	3	4	5	6	7	8	9	10	12	15	20	30	60	120	∞
1	0.90	39.9	49.5	53.6	55.8	57.2	58.2	58.9	59.4	59.9	60.2	60.7	61.2	61.7	62.3	62.8	63.1	63.3
	0.95	161	200	216	225	230	234	237	239	241	242	244	246	248	250	252	253	254
	0.975	648	800	864	900	922	937	948	957	963	969	977	985	993	1,000	1,010	1,010	1,020
	0.99	4,050	5,000	5,400	5,620	5,760	5,860	5,930	5,980	6,020	6,060	6,110	6,160	6,210	6,260	6,310	6,340	6,370
	0.995	16,200	20,000	21,600	22,500	23,100	23,400	23,700	23,900	24,100	24,200	24,400	24,600	24,800	25,000	25,200	25,400	25,500
2	0.90	8.53	9.00	9.16	9.24	9.29	9.33	9.35	9.37	9.38	9.39	9.41	9.42	9.44	9.46	9.47	9.48	9.49
	0.95	18.5	19.0	19.2	19.2	19.3	19.3	19.4	19.4	19.4	19.4	19.4	19.4	19.5	19.5	19.5	19.5	19.5
	0.975	38.5	39.0	39.2	39.2	39.3	39.3	39.4	39.4	39.4	39.4	39.4	39.4	39.4	39.5	39.5	39.5	39.5
	0.99	98.5	99.0	99.2	99.2	99.3	99.3	99.4	99.4	99.4	99.4	99.4	99.4	99.4	99.5	99.5	99.5	99.5
	0.995	199	199	199	199	199	199	199	199	199	199	199	199	199	199	199	199	199
3	0.90	5.54	5.46	5.39	5.34	5.31	5.28	5.27	5.25	5.24	5.23	5.22	5.20	5.18	5.17	5.15	5.14	5.13
	0.95	10.1	9.55	9.28	9.12	9.01	8.94	8.89	8.85	8.81	8.79	8.74	8.70	8.66	8.62	8.57	8.55	8.53
	0.975	17.4	16.0	15.4	15.1	14.9	14.7	14.6	14.5	14.5	14.4	14.3	14.3	14.2	14.1	14.0	13.9	13.9
	0.99	34.1	30.8	29.5	28.7	28.2	27.9	27.7	27.5	27.3	27.2	27.1	26.9	26.7	26.5	26.3	26.2	26.1
	0.995	55.6	49.8	47.5	46.2	45.4	44.8	44.4	44.1	43.9	43.7	43.4	43.1	42.8	42.5	42.1	42.0	41.8
4	0.90	4.54	4.32	4.19	4.11	4.05	4.01	3.98	3.95	3.93	3.92	3.90	3.87	3.84	3.82	3.79	3.78	3.76
	0.95	7.71	6.94	6.59	6.39	6.26	6.16	6.09	6.04	6.00	5.96	5.91	5.86	5.80	5.75	5.69	5.66	5.63
	0.975	12.2	10.6	9.98	9.60	9.36	9.20	9.07	8.98	8.90	8.84	8.75	8.66	8.56	8.46	8.36	8.31	8.26
	0.99	21.2	18.0	16.7	16.0	15.5	15.2	15.0	14.8	14.7	14.5	14.4	14.2	14.0	13.8	13.7	13.6	13.5
	0.995	31.3	26.3	24.3	23.2	22.5	22.0	21.6	21.4	21.1	21.0	20.7	20.4	20.2	19.9	19.6	19.5	19.3
5	0.90	4.06	3.78	3.62	3.52	3.45	3.40	3.37	3.34	3.32	3.30	3.27	3.24	3.21	3.17	3.14	3.12	3.11
	0.95	6.61	5.79	5.41	5.19	5.05	4.95	4.88	4.82	4.77	4.74	4.68	4.62	4.56	4.50	4.43	4.40	4.37
	0.975	10.0	8.43	7.76	7.39	7.15	6.98	6.85	6.76	6.68	6.62	6.52	6.43	6.33	6.23	6.12	6.07	6.02
	0.99	16.3	13.3	12.1	11.4	11.0	10.7	10.5	10.3	10.2	10.1	9.89	9.72	9.55	9.38	9.20	9.11	9.02
	0.995	22.8	18.3	16.5	15.6	14.9	14.5	14.2	14.0	13.8	13.6	13.4	13.1	12.9	12.7	12.4	12.3	12.1
6	0.90	3.78	3.46	3.29	3.18	3.11	3.05	3.01	2.98	2.96	2.94	2.90	2.87	2.84	2.80	2.76	2.74	2.72
	0.95	5.99	5.14	4.76	4.53	4.39	4.28	4.21	4.15	4.10	4.06	4.00	3.94	3.87	3.81	3.74	3.70	3.67
	0.975	8.81	7.26	6.60	6.23	5.99	5.82	5.70	5.60	5.52	5.46	5.37	5.27	5.17	5.07	4.96	4.90	4.85
	0.99	13.7	10.9	9.78	9.15	8.75	8.47	8.26	8.10	7.98	7.87	7.72	7.56	7.40	7.23	7.06	6.97	6.88
	0.995	18.6	14.5	12.9	12.0	11.5	11.1	10.8	10.6	10.4	10.2	10.0	9.81	9.59	9.36	9.12	9.00	8.88
7	0.90	3.59	3.26	3.07	2.96	2.88	2.83	2.78	2.75	2.72	2.70	2.67	2.63	2.59	2.56	2.51	2.49	2.47
	0.95	5.59	4.74	4.35	4.12	3.97	3.87	3.79	3.73	3.68	3.64	3.57	3.51	3.44	3.38	3.30	3.27	3.23
	0.975	8.07	6.54	5.89	5.52	5.29	5.12	4.99	4.90	4.82	4.76	4.67	4.57	4.47	4.36	4.25	4.20	4.14
	0.99	12.2	9.55	8.45	7.85	7.46	7.19	6.99	6.84	6.72	6.62	6.47	6.31	6.16	5.99	5.82	5.74	5.65
	0.995	16.2	12.4	10.9	10.1	9.52	9.16	8.89	8.68	8.51	8.38	8.18	7.97	7.75	7.53	7.31	7.19	7.08
8	0.90	3.46	3.11	2.92	2.81	2.73	2.67	2.62	2.59	2.56	2.54	2.50	2.46	2.42	2.38	2.34	2.31	2.29
	0.95	5.32	4.46	4.07	3.84	3.69	3.58	3.50	3.44	3.39	3.35	3.28	3.22	3.15	3.08	3.01	2.97	2.93
	0.975	7.57	6.06	5.42	5.05	4.82	4.65	4.53	4.43	4.36	4.30	4.20	4.10	4.00	3.89	3.78	3.73	3.67
	0.99	11.3	8.65	7.59	7.01	6.63	6.37	6.18	6.03	5.91	5.81	5.67	5.52	5.36	5.20	5.03	4.95	4.86
	0.995	14.7	11.0	9.60	8.81	8.30	7.95	7.69	7.50	7.34	7.21	7.01	6.81	6.61	6.40	6.18	6.06	5.95

TABLE A-5 Continued

$1-\alpha$	n \ m	1	2	3	4	5	6	7	8	9	10	12	15	20	30	60	120	∞
0.90	9	3.36	3.01	2.81	2.69	2.61	2.55	2.51	2.47	2.44	2.42	2.38	2.34	2.30	2.25	2.21	2.18	2.16
0.95		5.12	4.26	3.86	3.63	3.48	3.37	3.29	3.23	3.18	3.14	3.07	3.01	2.94	2.86	2.79	2.75	2.71
0.975		7.21	5.71	5.08	4.72	4.48	4.32	4.20	4.10	4.03	3.96	3.87	3.77	3.67	3.56	3.45	3.39	3.33
0.99		10.6	8.02	6.99	6.42	6.06	5.80	5.61	5.47	5.35	5.26	5.11	4.96	4.81	4.65	4.48	4.40	4.31
0.995		13.6	10.1	8.72	7.96	7.47	7.13	6.88	6.69	6.54	6.42	6.23	6.03	5.83	5.62	5.41	5.30	5.19
0.90	10	3.29	2.92	2.73	2.61	2.52	2.46	2.41	2.38	2.35	2.32	2.28	2.24	2.20	2.15	2.11	2.08	2.06
0.95		4.96	4.10	3.71	3.48	3.33	3.22	3.14	3.07	3.02	2.98	2.91	2.84	2.77	2.70	2.62	2.58	2.54
0.975		6.94	5.46	4.83	4.47	4.24	4.07	3.95	3.85	3.78	3.72	3.62	3.52	3.42	3.31	3.20	3.14	3.08
0.99		10.0	7.56	6.55	5.99	5.64	5.39	5.20	5.06	4.94	4.85	4.71	4.56	4.41	4.25	4.08	4.00	3.91
0.995		12.8	9.43	8.08	7.34	6.87	6.54	6.30	6.12	5.97	5.85	5.66	5.47	5.27	5.07	4.86	4.75	4.64
0.90	12	3.18	2.81	2.61	2.48	2.39	2.33	2.28	2.24	2.21	2.19	2.15	2.10	2.06	2.01	1.96	1.93	1.90
0.95		4.75	3.89	3.49	3.26	3.11	3.00	2.91	2.85	2.80	2.75	2.69	2.62	2.54	2.47	2.38	2.34	2.30
0.975		6.55	5.10	4.47	4.12	3.89	3.73	3.61	3.51	3.44	3.37	3.28	3.18	3.07	2.96	2.85	2.79	2.72
0.99		9.33	6.93	5.95	5.41	5.06	4.82	4.64	4.50	4.39	4.30	4.16	4.01	3.86	3.70	3.54	3.45	3.36
0.995		11.8	8.51	7.23	6.52	6.07	5.76	5.52	5.35	5.20	5.09	4.91	4.72	4.53	4.33	4.12	4.01	3.90
0.90	15	3.07	2.70	2.49	2.36	2.27	2.21	2.16	2.12	2.09	2.06	2.02	1.97	1.92	1.87	1.82	1.79	1.76
0.95		4.54	3.68	3.29	3.06	2.90	2.79	2.71	2.64	2.59	2.54	2.48	2.40	2.33	2.25	2.16	2.11	2.07
0.975		6.20	4.77	4.15	3.80	3.58	3.41	3.29	3.20	3.12	3.06	2.96	2.86	2.76	2.64	2.52	2.46	2.40
0.99		8.68	6.36	5.42	4.89	4.56	4.32	4.14	4.00	3.89	3.80	3.67	3.52	3.37	3.21	3.05	2.96	2.87
0.995		10.8	7.70	6.48	5.80	5.37	5.07	4.85	4.67	4.54	4.42	4.25	4.07	3.88	3.69	3.48	3.37	3.26
0.90	20	2.97	2.59	2.38	2.25	2.16	2.09	2.04	2.00	1.96	1.94	1.89	1.84	1.79	1.74	1.68	1.64	1.61
0.95		4.35	3.49	3.10	2.87	2.71	2.60	2.51	2.45	2.39	2.35	2.28	2.20	2.12	2.04	1.95	1.90	1.84
0.975		5.87	4.46	3.86	3.51	3.29	3.13	3.01	2.91	2.84	2.77	2.68	2.57	2.46	2.35	2.22	2.16	2.09
0.99		8.10	5.85	4.94	4.43	4.10	3.87	3.70	3.56	3.46	3.37	3.23	3.09	2.94	2.78	2.61	2.52	2.42
0.995		9.94	6.99	5.82	5.17	4.76	4.47	4.26	4.09	3.96	3.85	3.68	3.50	3.32	3.12	2.92	2.81	2.69
0.90	30	2.88	2.49	2.28	2.14	2.05	1.98	1.93	1.88	1.85	1.82	1.77	1.72	1.67	1.61	1.54	1.50	1.46
0.95		4.17	3.32	2.92	2.69	2.53	2.42	2.33	2.27	2.21	2.16	2.09	2.01	1.93	1.84	1.74	1.68	1.62
0.975		5.57	4.18	3.59	3.25	3.03	2.87	2.75	2.65	2.57	2.51	2.41	2.31	2.20	2.07	1.94	1.87	1.79
0.99		7.56	5.39	4.51	4.02	3.70	3.47	3.30	3.17	3.07	2.98	2.84	2.70	2.55	2.39	2.21	2.11	2.01
0.995		9.18	6.35	5.24	4.62	4.23	3.95	3.74	3.58	3.45	3.34	3.18	3.01	2.82	2.63	2.42	2.30	2.18
0.90	60	2.79	2.39	2.18	2.04	1.95	1.87	1.82	1.77	1.74	1.71	1.66	1.60	1.54	1.48	1.40	1.35	1.29
0.95		4.00	3.15	2.76	2.53	2.37	2.25	2.17	2.10	2.04	1.99	1.92	1.84	1.75	1.65	1.53	1.47	1.39
0.975		5.29	3.93	3.34	3.01	2.79	2.63	2.51	2.41	2.33	2.27	2.17	2.06	1.94	1.82	1.67	1.58	1.48
0.99		7.08	4.98	4.13	3.65	3.34	3.12	2.95	2.82	2.72	2.63	2.50	2.35	2.20	2.03	1.84	1.73	1.60
0.995		8.49	5.80	4.73	4.14	3.76	3.49	3.29	3.13	3.01	2.90	2.74	2.57	2.39	2.19	1.96	1.83	1.69
0.90	120	2.75	2.35	2.13	1.99	1.90	1.82	1.77	1.72	1.68	1.65	1.60	1.54	1.48	1.41	1.32	1.26	1.19
0.95		3.92	3.07	2.68	2.45	2.29	2.18	2.09	2.02	1.96	1.91	1.83	1.75	1.66	1.55	1.43	1.35	1.25
0.975		5.15	3.80	3.23	2.89	2.67	2.52	2.39	2.30	2.22	2.16	2.05	1.94	1.82	1.69	1.53	1.43	1.31
0.99		6.85	4.79	3.95	3.48	3.17	2.96	2.79	2.66	2.56	2.47	2.34	2.19	2.03	1.86	1.66	1.53	1.38
0.995		8.18	5.54	4.50	3.92	3.55	3.28	3.09	2.93	2.81	2.71	2.54	2.37	2.19	1.98	1.75	1.61	1.43
0.90	∞	2.71	2.30	2.08	1.94	1.85	1.77	1.72	1.67	1.63	1.60	1.55	1.49	1.42	1.34	1.24	1.17	1.00
0.95		3.84	3.00	2.60	2.37	2.21	2.10	2.01	1.94	1.88	1.83	1.75	1.67	1.57	1.46	1.32	1.22	1.00
0.975		5.02	3.69	3.12	2.79	2.57	2.41	2.29	2.19	2.11	2.05	1.94	1.83	1.71	1.57	1.39	1.27	1.00
0.99		6.63	4.61	3.78	3.32	3.02	2.80	2.64	2.51	2.41	2.32	2.18	2.04	1.88	1.70	1.47	1.32	1.00
0.995		7.88	5.30	4.28	3.72	3.35	3.09	2.90	2.74	2.62	2.52	2.36	2.19	2.00	1.79	1.53	1.36	1.00

Source: Abridged from Maxine Merrington and Catherine M. Thompson: Tables of percentage points of the inverted beta distribution, *Biometrika*, vol. 33, pp. 73–88, 1943. Published here with the kind permission of the editor of *Biometrika*.

TABLE A-6　PERCENTAGE POINTS OF THE CHI-SQUARE DISTRIBUTION

$1-\alpha$ / n	0.005	0.010	0.025	0.050	0.100	0.250	0.500	0.750	0.900	0.950	0.975	0.990	0.995
1	0.0^4393	0.0^3157	0.0^3982	0.0^2393	0.0158	0.102	0.455	1.32	2.71	3.84	5.02	6.63	7.88
2	0.0100	0.0201	0.0506	0.103	0.211	0.575	1.39	2.77	4.61	5.99	7.38	9.21	10.6
3	0.0717	0.115	0.216	0.352	0.584	1.21	2.37	4.11	6.25	7.81	9.35	11.3	12.8
4	0.207	0.297	0.484	0.711	1.06	1.92	3.36	5.39	7.78	9.49	11.1	13.3	14.9
5	0.412	0.554	0.831	1.15	1.61	2.67	4.35	6.63	9.24	11.1	12.8	15.1	16.7
6	0.676	0.872	1.24	1.64	2.20	3.45	5.35	7.84	10.6	12.6	14.4	16.8	18.5
7	0.989	1.24	1.69	2.17	2.83	4.25	6.35	9.04	12.0	14.1	16.0	18.5	20.3
8	1.34	1.65	2.18	2.73	3.49	5.07	7.34	10.2	13.4	15.5	17.5	20.1	22.0
9	1.73	2.09	2.70	3.33	4.17	5.90	8.34	11.4	14.7	16.9	19.0	21.7	23.6
10	2.16	2.56	3.25	3.94	4.87	6.74	9.34	12.5	16.0	18.3	20.5	23.2	25.2
11	2.60	3.05	3.82	4.57	5.58	7.53	10.3	13.7	17.3	19.7	21.9	24.7	26.8
12	3.07	3.57	4.40	5.23	6.30	8.44	11.3	14.8	18.5	21.0	23.3	26.2	28.3
13	3.57	4.11	5.01	5.89	7.04	9.30	12.3	16.0	19.8	22.4	24.7	27.7	29.8
14	4.07	4.66	5.63	6.57	7.79	10.2	13.3	17.1	21.1	23.7	26.1	29.1	31.3
15	4.60	5.23	6.26	7.26	8.55	11.0	14.3	18.2	22.3	25.0	27.5	30.6	32.8
16	5.14	5.81	6.91	7.96	9.31	11.9	15.3	19.4	23.5	26.3	28.8	32.0	34.3
17	5.70	6.41	7.56	8.67	10.1	12.8	16.3	20.5	24.8	27.6	30.2	33.4	35.7
18	6.26	7.01	8.23	9.39	10.9	13.7	17.3	21.6	26.0	28.9	31.5	34.8	37.2
19	6.84	7.63	8.91	10.1	11.7	14.6	18.3	22.7	27.2	30.1	32.9	36.2	38.6
20	7.43	8.26	9.59	10.9	12.4	15.5	19.3	23.8	28.4	31.4	34.2	37.6	40.0
21	8.03	8.90	10.3	11.6	13.2	16.3	20.3	24.9	29.6	32.7	35.5	38.9	41.4
22	8.64	9.54	11.0	12.3	14.0	17.2	21.3	26.0	30.8	33.9	36.8	40.3	42.8
23	9.26	10.2	11.7	13.1	14.8	18.1	22.3	27.1	32.0	35.2	38.1	41.6	44.2
24	9.89	10.9	12.4	13.8	15.7	19.0	23.3	28.2	33.2	36.4	39.4	43.0	45.6
25	10.5	11.5	13.1	14.6	16.5	19.9	24.3	29.3	34.4	37.7	40.6	44.3	46.9
26	11.2	12.2	13.8	15.4	17.3	20.8	25.3	30.4	35.6	38.9	41.9	45.6	48.3
27	11.8	12.9	14.6	16.2	18.1	21.7	26.3	31.5	36.7	40.1	43.2	47.0	49.6
28	12.5	13.6	15.3	16.9	18.9	22.7	27.3	32.6	37.9	41.3	44.5	48.3	51.0
29	13.1	14.3	16.0	17.7	19.8	23.6	28.3	33.7	39.1	42.6	45.7	49.6	52.3
30	13.8	15.0	16.8	18.5	20.6	24.5	29.3	34.8	40.3	43.8	47.0	50.9	53.7

Source: Abridged from Catherine M. Thompson: Tables of percentage points of the incomplete beta function a nd of the chi-square distribution, *Biometrika*, vol. 32, pp. 187–191, 1941. Published here with the k nd permission of the editor of *Biometrika*.

TABLE A-7 THE GREEK ALPHABET

Letters	Name	English equivalent	Letters	Name	English equivalent
A α	Alpha	a	N ν	Nu	n
B β	Beta	b	Ξ ξ	Xi	x
Γ γ	Gamma	g	O o	Omicron	o
Δ δ	Delta	d	Π π	Pi	p
E ε	Epsilon	e	P ρ	Rho	r
Z ζ	Zeta	z	Σ σ	Sigma	s
H η	Eta	—	T τ	Tau	t
Θ θ	Theta	—	Υ υ	Upsilon	u or y
I ι	Iota	i	Φ φ	Phi	—
K κ	Kappa	k	X χ	Chi	—
Λ λ	Lambda	l	Ψ ψ	Psi	—
M μ	Mu	m	Ω ω	Omega	—

NAME INDEX

SUBJECT INDEX

First iteration due Oct. 10th TR:

Office hours   MW - 10 - 1
                TTRE 9³⁰ - 11³⁰

ps. 761 3 formulas